Mexican Political Biographies

Mexican
Political
Biographies

1935–1981

SECOND EDITION
Revised and Expanded

Roderic A. Camp

THE UNIVERSITY OF ARIZONA PRESS
TUCSON, ARIZONA

About the Author

Roderic A. Camp became Director of Latin American Studies at Central College, Pella, Iowa, in 1976. He holds a Ph.D. in Comparative Government from the University of Arizona and has carried out research on Mexico under fellowships from the American Philosophical Society, National Endowment for the Humanities, and Fulbright-Hays. He has written more than 30 articles on Mexico, published in American and Mexican journals, and continues his research interests in the area. In 1982 he was appointed the ongoing contributing editor of the politics section of the *Handbook of Latin-American Studies,* which is published biennially by the University of Texas under the auspices of the Hispanic Division of the Library of Congress. He is the author of *Mexican Political Biographies, 1935–1975; The Role of Economists in Policy Making: Mexico and the United States;* and *Mexico's Leaders: Their Education and Recruitment.*

Second Edition, Revised and Expanded

THE UNIVERSITY OF ARIZONA PRESS

This book was set in 9/10 V-I-P Times Roman from a computerized word-processor file without Spanish diacritical marks.
Manufactured in the U.S.A.

Library of Congress Cataloging in Publication Data

Camp, Roderic Ai.
   Mexican political biographies, 1935–1981.

   Rev. ed. of: Mexican political biographies, 1935–
1975. c1976.
    Bibliography: p.
    1. Statesmen—Mexico—Biography. 2. Mexico—
Biography. I. Title.
F1235.5.A2C35 1982   972'.08'0922 [B]   82-2768

ISBN 0-8165-0743-0   AACR2

Contents

A Note to the Reader

Designed to carry out a more specific function than a general *Who's Who,* this volume contains the biographies of public men, living or deceased, who have been prominent in Mexican political life from 1935 to mid 1980. Since 1968 when he began research on the career patterns of Mexican public figures, the author has found both a lack of available information and when biographical data were available, contradictory information. Errors ranged from six different birth dates for a single person to the crediting of individuals with positions they did not hold. Not only did errors appear rather frequently in Mexican sources, they were repeated in many of the major English-language reference works and scholarly studies of Mexico by North Americans. And they in turn were repeated by other scholars. In addition to the most accurate information available about the career patterns of numerous public men, this volume contains appendices of the most important elective, appointive, and party positions in Mexico, with the names of the persons who have held them and their tenure in office. By having lists of positions as well as biographies of persons who have held them, the reader who does not have a person in mind will be able to find information about someone who has held a specific position in Mexican government without knowing his name. Thus, the book will also provide scholars with a selective version of a government organizational manual for Mexico from 1935 to 1980.

This book was compiled with the purpose of alleviating a dearth which has existed since 1946, when Ronald Hilton edited the last volume of *Who's Who in Mexico.* Even though the 1946 edition and the two editions which preceded it were typical of the standard *Who's Who,* they were scholarly and accurate and provided researchers with the only English language source for biographical information on living Mexicans who had distinguished themselves in all fields. Unfortunately, that series was terminated with the third edition, and no single comprehensive and detailed biographical reference work on Mexico has been published in English in the last three decades. The biographical essay following the appendices will make clear the limitations of available works in Spanish which have been published in Mexico.

This revised and enlarged edition contains significant changes. The information in the first edition, current through January, 1974, has been completely updated, both in the appendices and the biographies themselves. Of the original 900 biographies, more than half have undergone significant additions or changes to one or more categories, while many others have had minor changes. Furthermore, 450 new biographies have been added, increasing the coverage of political leaders prominent in the period covered by the first edition, in addition to biographies of prominent office- holders during the last two years of the Echeverria administration and the first three-and-a-half years of the Lopez Portillo regime.

In response to several suggestions made by colleagues and critics, I have added information about family ties, especially the names of wives, where available. Also, I have added several new categories to the appendices, most notably the names of *oficiales mayores,* the third-ranked cabinet position; as well as the names of other important party presidents, several new ambassadorial positions, and union leaders. Biographies of these persons, where possible, were included in the biographical section, as were additional biographies of leftist political activists who may not have held formal government posts.

The designation of Miguel de la Madrid Hurtado as the official party pre-candidate for President of Mexico, tantamount to his election as President for the 1982–88 term, provides further evidence of recent trends in the career patterns of those who rise to the top of the Mexican political system. Sr. de la Madrid, whose biography appears in both editions, follows the pattern of his predecessor, Jose Lopez Portillo, representing the Mexican public figure who has made his career in the federal bureaucracy, never having held an elective post or having been an active militant of the official party. Furthermore, although de la Madrid is from a long line of ancestors from the coastal state of Colima, making him the first president in the twentieth century from the west, he is truly a product of Mexico City, like Luis Echeverria and Lopez Portillo. Regionalism, which long has played a significant role in Mexican politics, is fast disappearing from the scene. Moreover, the continued dominance of the National University, especially the National School of Law, on the professional education, socialization, teaching experience, and early political recruitment of political leaders is reinforced in the next president's educational background. The new president will be the first in Mexican history to have an advanced degree, in public administration from Harvard, from the United States. And finally, the next president, like most public figures, is from a middle class family; his father and uncle were public employees. The majority of those who will be designated as the closest collaborators of the next president, and will have had similar career experiences, are also likely to be included in this volume. Thus, the incremental changes in Mexican public careers and political recruitment patterns are fully documented, from generation to generation, in the biographies in this book.

Acknowledgments

A book of this sort relies upon the good will and assistance of many people, but especially those whose biographies it contains. The author owes a debt to librarians, government officials, scholars, and relatives of the biographees. Among the first group, the author would like to express his thanks to Nettie Lee Benson and Lutie L. Higley of the University of Texas and University of Arizona libraries respectively, for their invaluable assistance. Further, he would like to thank the staffs of the Hispanic Section, Library of Congress, the Columbus Memorial Library of the Pan American Union, the University of Iowa Library, the Carlos Menendez Library, Merida, Yucatan, the United States Department of State Library, and the Library of the Supreme Court of Justice of Mexico. A special thanks goes to Alice Lammers, Central College Library, for arranging many difficult loans of reference works.

The number of Mexican government officials, both at the state and national levels, who have helped with this work are too numerous to mention. The author would like to single out Ambassador Jose Juan de Olloqui, who has taken more than a passing interest in this research project and has made sources of information far more accessible.

For helpful suggestions along the way, the author thanks Ronald Hilton, Stanley R. Ross, and James Wilkie, all pioneers in Mexican written and oral biography and bibliography, and Clifton E. Wilson, for early editorial suggestions. Without the assistance of several other colleagues, this work would be far less complete. In particular, Peter H. Smith provided supporting data for both the appendices and numerous biographies from his own vast biographical study of Mexico, and helpful source suggestions and encouragement along the way. Paul Kelso supplied the author with critical biographical data from a personal note file extending back many years. Rudy de la Garza provided the majority of data for the appendices on federal deputies, especially data on committee assignments. And last, Donald Mabry shared information on opposition party leaders.

The Central College Research Council provided some funds for the completion of this book. A special note of thanks to Evelyn Loynachan for graciously offered and efficient clerical assistance; to my editor, Stephanie Chase, who took more than a professional interest in editing and reading the first edition of this work; to the University of Arizona Press for making publication possible; and to my wife Emily, who sacrificed many hours in libraries in Mexico and the United States to help make this work possible.

Additions to the second edition benefitted greatly from Peter H. Smith's data bank, which made possible the cross-checking and completion of approximately fifty important biographies not included in the first edition. Furthermore, Ambassador Jose Juan de Olloqui again assisted the author's research efforts in Mexico. Additionally, the author would like to thank Fernando Zertuche Munoz for his assistance in obtaining additional information to complete the appendices; and to Luis Medina and Lorenzo Meyer, for easy access to library materials in the Colegio de Mexico. Lastly, the second edition would not have been possible without the efforts of John Riegsecker and Evelyn Loynachan, who created the computer file from which the manuscript was typeset. This file lacked Spanish diacritical marks, but made production of the present volume economically feasible.

R. A. C.

How to Use This Book

The author has adhered to the Mexican custom of using the father's surname followed by the mother's maiden name for biographees' names. When the biographee's second surname is not commonly used in other printed sources, it appears in parentheses. The date of death, when known, follows the name. Because no obituary index for Mexican newspapers is available, and therefore correct information was not always accessible, all persons for whom no death date is given are not necessarily alive although it can be presumed that the majority of them are. Further information is usually available in the issues of the major Mexican newspapers and *El Tiempo* near date of death. The biographical information in the entries is divided into twelve categories, each denoted by a bold-faced letter. Where no code letter appears, no substantiated information was available. The word *none* indicates that the biographee has no representation in that category, such as no major political position, no military career, or no pursuit of formal education. When an office is underlined in a biography, the individual and his position are also listed in the appendices. When the name of a supervisor, teacher, relative, or mentor is underlined within a biography, that individual has his or her own biographical entry or is listed in the appendices. The categories are:

a) Date of Birth.

b) Geographical location of birthplace: city or municipality, state, region, and rural-urban. The regional classifications, based on the divisions used by Howard F. Cline, are: *West*, Aguascalientes, Baja California del Sur, Colima, Durango, Jalisco, Nayarit, and Sinaloa; *North,* Baja California del Norte, Chihuahua, Coahuila, Nuevo Leon, Sonora, Tamaulipas; *Gulf*, Campeche Quintana Roo, Tabasco, Vera Cruz, Yucatan; *South*, Chiapas, Guerrero, Oaxaca; *West Central*, Guanajuato, Mexico, Michoacan; *East Central*, Hidalgo, Puebla, Queretaro, San Luis Potosi, Tlaxcala, and Zacatecas. The Rural-Urban classification is based on a cutoff figure of 5,000 persons and was determined using the 1900, 1910, 1920, 1930, and 1940 census figures closest to the date of birth. All municipal names and spellings follow the 1970 edition of the *Diccionario Porrua*.

c) Education: primary, secondary, and preparatory education, and professional and college education with the dates of attendance and graduation, if possible. The most complete biographies will give thesis titles as well. Also included at the end of the educational category are teaching positions, whether they are on the primary, secondary, or college-level, and other educational positions.

d) Elective positions: any positions which at least nominally are attained through the electoral process, from Councilman to President. (Legislatively appointed Governors are not included in this category, but rather under the governmental positions category.)

e) Party positions: both formal and informal positions which persons have held for any political party or campaign in Mexico. Party candidates for public office are also included. The word *None* indicates that the person has not held any position on the National Executive Committee of PRI, or the equivalent of that position for other political parties, from June 18, 1935 to June 1, 1980.

f) Governmental positions: the most important appointive governmental positions on the local, state, and national level. They generally follow in chronological order, and it is not unusual for a person to hold more than one of these positions simultaneously, especially advisory positions in the federal bureaucracy.

g) Interest group activity: rather broadly, union positions, and positions in numerous professional and student organizations which have politically oriented activities in Mexico, such as the National Student Federation.

h) Other positions: lesser governmental positions, private positions which the person may have held, or self-employment, such as his own medical or legal practice. This category also includes authorship, significant professional offices, and unusual awards.

i) Parents, spouses, and friends: relevant personal data, including the father's occupation, as well as information about relatives and friends who may have held governmental positions. Readers should note that any person serving as a private secretary or a secretary general of government has been appointed by a person who has considerable confidence in him/her and therefore, the mentor should be a significant career contact. These persons, however, appear in the government positions category and their names are not repeated here.

j) Military experience: career information, with the exception of high-level appointive positions normally thought of as bureaucratic positions in the Secretariat of National Defense (these offices appear in the governmental positions category). An attempt has been made to give the highest rank achieved by the person and the date when he received promotion. This category also includes information about the person's Revolutionary activities, if any.

k) Miscellaneous information: specifics about the biographee's career from various sources, whether they are strictly informative, complimentary, or critical. The author does not necessarily agree with all statements, favorable or unfavorable, presented in this section, but the sources for these statements will be indicated or will be cited in the source section. The purpose of this category is to give the reader more insight into the career of each individual than can be obtained through a perusal of biographical facts, and to repeat evaluations made by official government publications such as *Polemica* and such highly critical publications as *Por Que?* Also included in this section are statements about any unusual aspects of the biographee's political career.

l) Additional sources: books, reference works, data banks, government directories, newspapers, and magazines in which additional information about the individual can be found. Most biographical monographs about an individual are not cited, since these are more commonly known and readily available to the reader. Newspaper dates are included because they may indicate that additional information about that person might be found in other newspapers of a corresponding date. The word *letter* indicates that some or all information in the biography was confirmed by the biographee himself, a government agency, or a friend or relative of the biographee, which is true of more than 250 biographies.

How Persons Were Selected For Inclusion

The two criteria for inclusion were Frank Brandenburg's top six levels of political prestige, with some modifications, as outlined in *The Making of Modern Mexico,** and cross-referencing of biographical data in a minimum of two sources, preferably an official government source as well as a private source. Using Brandenburg's categories, the author has concentrated on those positions which are stepping stones to even more influential positions in Mexico.

As Brandenburg makes quite clear in his work, his prestige ladder includes only those persons with *political* prestige; it does not include, for example, businessmen and religious leaders, although some prominent businessmen who have become involved in politics are included. Brandenburg includes the following in his list:

1. The Head of the Revolutionary Family. While this person, by Brandenburg's own analysis, may or may not be the President of Mexico, since 1935 every person who has held this position has been President before, during, or after his tenure as Head of the Family.

2. The President of Mexico.

3. Members of the Inner Circle and factional leaders of the Revolution. Persons in this high prestige category have at one time or another held one of the formal governmental positions making up the following three categories. All persons whom Brandenburg classifies as Inner Circle leaders are labeled as such in the biographies, and all of them are included in this directory.

4. Cabinet members, including the Governor of the Federal District, the Military Chief of Staff, the Private Secretary to the President, managers of major state industries, and directors of large semiautonomous agencies, commissions, banks, and boards.

5. Governors of the larger states and the federal territories, ambassadors in prestigious posts, regional strongmen not in the Inner Circle, the two presidential legislative spokesmen in the respective Houses of Congress, Military Zone Commanders, and the official-party president.

6. Supreme Court Justices, Senators, Undersecretaries of cabinet ministries and Assistant Directors of large state industries, commissions, boards, and dependencies; the Secretary General and sector heads of the official party; leaders of major opposition parties; and the Secretaries General of the major unions.

The author has broadened his coverage to include other influentials not falling within Brandenburg's categories. Included in both the biographical section and the appendices are two positions which Brandenburg omits entirely, the rectors of the two major universities in Mexico, D.F., the National Autonomous University (UNAM) and the National Polytechnic Institute (IPN). A number of cabinet-level individuals have held these positions, as well as the directorships of the major schools at UNAM (Law, Economics, and Medicine), either on the way up, between other positions, or after service in the cabinet.

A majority of the individuals who have served as *oficial mayor*, usually the third-ranked position in cabinet agencies, have been included. Many of the biographees have held an *oficial mayor* position immediately before moving up to a Subsecretaryship, as in the case of President Luis Echeverria Alvarez, who was *oficial mayor* both of Public Education and of the official party PRI, before becoming Subsecretary of Government in 1958. *Oficiales mayores* may well be filling some of the cabinet positions in later administrations, and therefore, a concentrated effort has been made to include most of them.

---

*Frank Brandenburg, *The Making of Modern Mexico* (Englewood Cliffs, New Jersey: Prentice-Hall, 1964), pp. 158–59.

In addition to the broad coverage given to the official party PRI, and despite a critical lack of information, an attempt was made to include candidates from other parties for higher elective offices. The only opposition parties listed in the appendices are the National Action Party (PAN), the Authentic Party of the Mexican Revolution (PARM), and the Popular Socialist Party (PPS). However, presidential candidates and party leaders who have provided opposition to the official party since 1934; and precandidates for president within PRI have been included. All official party presidents have been included in the biographical section.

The appendices include a large section on Federal Deputies, which Brandenburg relegates to category 9. Because of the rubber stamp function which most Mexicanists attribute to Congress, there has been a tendency to underrate the position of Federal Deputy, even though it provides an important training ground for persons moving up the prestige ladder through elective positions. The author has concentrated on persons who have held a Deputyship more than once, or who have held positions of considerably higher prestige after holding the Deputyship. An examination of the biographies included will show that recruitment to Brandenburg's levels 4 and 5 often occurs because of contacts made in the Chamber of Deputies. Deputies definitely rank higher than Ambassadors, Ministers, and Consuls General, which Brandenburg has placed in a lower category, equated with Governors of small and medium-sized states.

Other positions included in the appendices are those which appear most often in the career paths of persons reaching the top four categories, positions which themselves serve as stepping stones to the highest offices in Mexico. For example, with the exception of the Ambassador to the United States (a stepping stone to Secretary of Foreign Relations or Secretary of the Treasury) and the Ambassador to the United Kingdom, no specific ambassadorship has consistently had any significance in the career paths of public figures. Instead they have been interim positions for influentials who are on the out or sinecures for persons leaving more influential positions. However, because they have been held repeatedly by high-level government officeholders, ambassadors to France, Cuba and the Soviet Union have been added to the second edition. Regional strongmen and Military Zone Commanders who have become Governors, Senators, Deputies, or Cabinent Secretaries have been included. Governors of all states, large and small, have been included in the appendices, and an attempt has been made to include as many of them as possible in the biographical section, even though Brandenburg places Governors of small and medium-sized states in category 7.

The second criterion, the cross-referencing of factual data, dictated that no person was included in the biographical section unless the major positions held were cross-referenced in a minimum of two sources, preferably an official government source, as well as a private source. This does not mean that the information contained in the biographies and the appendices is infallible, since even government sources proved to be inaccurate on occasion, but that no biographical data or listings of positions were included unless the information could be substantiated from other sources. As a result of this and the simple lack of information on some people and positions, over 100 persons who fitted the political criteria for inclusion in this directory were rejected because of incomplete or unsubstantiated biographies. No biography is included if information was missing for three or more of the career categories. For approximately half of the people in this directory, conflicting information exists about their careers, and the author has had to judge to the best of his ability which facts are the most valid ones.

Source Abbreviations

Aguirre	Celso Aguirre Bernal, *Compendio historico-biografico de Mexicali, 1539–1966* (Mexicali, 1966)
Alonso	Jorge Alonso, *La Dialectica clases-elites en Mexico* (Mexico: Centro de Investigaciones Superiores del INAH, 1976)
Analisis Politico	*Analisis Politico*
Anderson	Roger C. Anderson, ''The Functional role of the Governors and Their States in the Political Development of Mexico,'' Unpublished Ph.D. dissertation, University of Wisconsin, 1971
Annals	*Annals of the American Academy of Political and Social Sciences*
Baker	Richard D. Baker, *Judicial Review in Mexico* (Austin: University of Texas Press, 1971)
BdM	Banco de Mexico, *Programa de becas y datos de los becarios* (Mexico, 1961)
Beltran	Enrique Beltran, *Medio siglo de recuerdos de un biologo mexicano* (Mexico: Sociedad Mexicana de Historia Natural, 1977)
Bermudez	Antonio J. Bermudez and Octavio Vejar Vazquez, *No dejes crecer la hierba* (Mexico: Costa Amic, 1969)
Bezdek	Robert R. Bezdek, ''Electoral Opposition in Mexico: Emergence, Suppression, and Impact on Political Processes,'' Unpublished Ph.D. dissertation, Ohio State University, 1973.
Brandenberg	Frank Brandenburg, *The Making of Modern Mexico* (Englewood Cliffs: Prentice-Hall, 1964)
Bremauntz	Alberto Bremauntz, *Setenta anos de mi vida* (Mexico: Ediciones Juridico Sociales, 1968)
Cadena Z.	Daniel Cadena Z., *El Candidato presidencial, 1976* (Mexico, 1975)
Campa	Valentin Campa, *Mi testimonio* (Mexico: Ediciones de Cultura Popular, 1978)
Casasola V	Gustavo Casasola, *Seis siglos de historia grafica de Mexico*, Vol. 6 (Mexico: Editorial Gustavo Casasola, 1971)
CB	*Current Biography*
C de D	*Directorio de la Camara de Diputados* (Mexico: Imprenta de la Camara de Diputados, various years)
C de S	*Directorio* (Mexico: Camara de Senadores, various years)
CH	*Current History*
Cline	Howard F. Cline, *The United States and Mexico* (New York: Atheneum, 1965)

Colin	Mario Colin, *Semblanzas de personajes del estado de Mexico* (Mexico, 1972)
Correa	Eduardo J. Correa, *El Balance de Avila Camacho* (Mexico, 1946)
Correa 41	Eduardo J. Correa, *El Balance de Cardenismo* (Mexico, 1941)
Covarrubias	Ricardo Covarrubias, *Los 67 gobernantes del Mexico independiente* (Mexico: PRI, 1968)
Crowson	Benjamin Franklin Crowson, *Biographical Sketches of the Governors in Mexico* (Washington: Crowson International Publishers, 1951)
CyT	Enrique Cordero y Torres, *Diccionario biografico de Puebla*, 2 Vols. (Mexico, 1972)
DAPC	Presidencia de la Republica, *Directorio de la Administracion Publica Centralizada, 1977* (Mexico, 1977)
DBC	Octavio Gordillo y Ortiz, *Diccionario biografico de Chiapas* (Mexico: Costa Amic, 1977)
DBM68	*Diccionario Biografico de Mexico (1966–68)* (Monterrey: Editorial Revesa, 1968)
DBM70	*Diccionario Biografico de Mexico (1968–70)* (Monterrey: Editorial Revesa, 1970)
D del S	*Diario del Sureste* (Merida, Yucatan)
D de Y	*Diario de Yucatan* (Merida, Yucatan)
DEM	Aurora M. Ocampo, *Diccionario de escritores mexicanos* (Mexico: UNAM, 1967)
DGF47	Mexico, Direccion tecnica de organizacion, *Directorio del gobierno federal,* 1947
DGF50	Mexico, Direccion tecnica de organizacion, *Directorio del gobierno federal*, 1950
DGF51	Mexico, Direccion tecnica de organizacion, *Directorio del gobierno federal*, 1951
DGF56	Mexico, Direccion tecnica de organizacion, *Directorio del gobierno federal*, 1956
DJBM	*Directorio Juridico Biografico Mexicano, 1972* (Mexico: Sociedad Mexicana de Informacion Biografica Profesional, 1972)
DNED	*Directorio Nacional de Economistas* (Mexico, 1959)
DP64	*Diccionario Porrua* (Mexico: Editorial Porrua, 1964)
DP70	*Diccionario Porrua* (Mexico: Editorial Porrua, 1970)
DPE61	*Directorio del poder ejecutivo, 1961* (Mexico, 1961)
DPE65	*Directorio del poder ejecutivo, 1965* (Mexico, 1965)
DPE71	*Directorio del poder ejecutivo federal, 1971* (Mexico: Secretaria de la Presidencia, 1971)
Daniels	Josephus Daniels, *Shirt-Sleeve Diplomat* (Chapel Hill: University of North Carolina Press, 1947)
Directorio, 1970–72	*Directorio general de presuntos diputados al xlviii congreso de la union* (unpublished)
Dulles	John W. F. Dulles, *Yesterday in Mexico* (Austin: University of Texas Press, 1961)
EBW46	*Biographical Encyclopedia of the World* (New York: Institute for Research in Biography, 1946)
ELD	Mexico City, *Escuela Libre de Derecho aniversario de su fundacion, 1912–22* (Mexico, 1922)
El Dia	*El Dia* (Mexico City)
El Universal	*El Universal* (Mexico City)

Enc Mex	*Enciclopedia de Mexico* (Mexico: various years)
Encinas Johnson	Luis Encinas Johnson, *La alternativa de mexico* (Mexico: Ediciones Sonot, 1969)
EN de E	Mexico City, UNAM, Escuela Nacional de Economia, *Anuario, 1959* (Mexico: UNAM, 1959)
Excelsior	*Excelsior* (Mexico City)
Fuentes Diaz	Vicente Fuentes Diaz, *Los Partidos politicos en Mexico* (Mexico, Editorial Altiplano, 1969)
Func.	Sergio Serra Dominguez and Robert Martinez Barreda, *Mexico y sus funcionarios* (Mexico: Litografico Cardenas, 1959)
Garrido	Luis Garrido, *El tiempo de mi vida* (Mexico: Porrua, 1974)
GofM	Marvin Alisky, *The Governors of Mexico*, Southwestern Studies, Monograph 12, 1965
G of NL	Marvin Alisky, *Government of the Mexican State of Nuevo Leon* (Tempe: Arizona State University, 1971)
G of S	*Guide to the Government of the Mexican State of Sonora* (Tempe: Arizona State University, 1971)
Gaxiola	Francisco Javier Gaxiola, Jr., *El Presidente Rodriguez* (Mexico: Cultura, 1938)
Gaxiola 2	Francisco Javier Gaxiola, *Memorias* (Mexico: Editorial Porrua, 1975)
Glade	William P. Glade, Jr. and Charles W. Anderson, *The Political Economy of Mexico* (Madison: University of Wisconsin Press, 1963)
Glade & Ross	William P. Glade and Stanley R. Ross, eds. *Criticas constructivas del sistema politico mexicano* (Austin: Institute of Latin American Studies, 1973)
Gomez Maganda	Alejandro Gomez Maganda, *Bocetos presidenciales* (Mexico: Editorial Joma, 1970)
Gonzalez Navarro	Moises Gonzalez Navarro, *La Confederacion Nacional Campesina* (Mexico: Costa Amic, 1968)
Greenberg	Martin H. Greenburg, *Bureaucracy and Development: A Mexican Case Study* (Lexington: D.C. Heath, 1970)
Gruening	Ernest Gruening, *Mexico and Its Heritage* (New York: D. Appleton-Century, 1928)
HA	*Hispano Americano* or *Tiempo*
Haddox	John H. Haddox, *Antonio Caso, Philosopher of Mexico* (Austin: University of Texas Press, 1971)
HAHR	*Hispanic American Historical Review*
HAR	*Hispanic American Report*
Hayner	Norman S. Hayner, *New Patterns in Old Mexico* (New Haven: College and University Press, 1966) Heroic *Mexico* William Weber Johnson, *Heroic Mexico* (New York: Doubleday, 1968)
Heroic Mexico	William Weber Johnson, *Heroic Mexico* (New York: Doubleday, 1968)
Hoy	*Hoy*
Ind Biog.	Arturo R. Blancas and Tomas L. Vidrio, *Indice biografico de la XLIII Legislatura Federal* (Mexico, 1956)
Inf. Please	*Information Please?* (New York: Macmillan, various years)
Informe	State of the Union addresses by governors published by the state government for each year in office

IWW	*International Who's Who* (London: Europa Publications, various years)
Johnson	Kenneth F. Johnson, *Mexican Democracy: A Critical View* (Boston: Allyn and Bacon, 1971)
Johnson, 1978	Kenneth F. Johnson, *Mexican Democracy, A Critical View,* 2nd Edit. (New York: Praeger, 1978)
Justicia	*Justicia* (legal review) (Mexico City) 1967–1968
Kirk	Betty Kirk, *Covering the Mexican Front* (Norman: University of Oklahoma Press, 1942)
La Nacion	*La Nacion* (National Action Party publication)
Latin America	*Latin America* (London)
Lemus	George Lemus, ''Partido Accion Nacional: A Mexican Opposition Party,'' Unpublished MA thesis, University of Texas, 1956.
letters	Indicates correspondence concerning the biographee from a friend, relative, state or federal agency, or the biographee himself
LAD	*Latin American Digest*
Libro de Oro	H. Ruiz Sandoval, Jr. *El Libro de oro de Mexico* (Mexico: 1967–68)
Lieuwen	Edwin Lieuwen, *Mexican Militarism: The Political Rise and Fall of the Revolutionary Army* (Albuquerque: The University of New Mexico Press, 1968)
Lopez	Jose Lopez Escalera, *Diccionario biografico y de historia de Mexico* (Mexico: Editorial del Magistrado, 1964)
Loret de Mola	*Confesiones de un gobernador* (Mexico: Editorial Grijalbo, 1978)
Loret de Mola, *91*	Carlos Loret de Mola, *Los ultimos 91 dias* (Mexico: Editorial Grijalbo, 1978)
Mabry	Donald J. Mabry, *Mexico's Accion Nacional* (Syracuse: Syracuse University Press, 1973)
McAlister	Lyle N. McAlister, *The Military in Latin American Socio-political Evolution: Four Case Studies* (Washington, D.C.: Center for Research in Social Systems, 1970)
Medina, 20	Luis Medina, *Historia de la revolucion mexicana, periodo 1940–1952,* Vol. 20 (Mexico: El Colegio de Mexico, 1979)
Meyer, No. 12	Lorenzo Meyer, et. al, *Historia de la revolucion mexicana periodo 1928–1934* Vol. 12 (Mexico: El Colegio de Mexico, 1978)
MGF69	Mexico, Secretaria de la Presidencia, *Manual de organizacion del gobierno federal, 1969–70* (Mexico, 1970)
MGF	Mexico, Secretaria de la Presidencia, *Manual de organizacion del gobierno federal, 1973* (Mexico, 1973)
Michaels	Albert L. Michaels, *The Mexican Election of 1940* (Buffalo: Council on International Studies, State University of New York, 1971)
Millon	Robert P. Millon, *Mexican Marxist, Vicente Lombardo Toledano* (Chapel Hill: University of North Carolina Press, 1966)
Moncada	Carlos Moncada, *Anos de violencia en Sonora, 1955–1976* (Mexico: Editorial V Siglos, 1977)
Morton	Ward Morton, *Women Suffrage in Mexico* (Gainesville: University of Florida Press, 1962)
Nicholson	Irene Nicholson, *The X in Mexico: Growth within Traditionalism* (London: Faber and Faber, 1965)

Nov de Yuc	*Novedades de Yucatan* (Merida, Yucatan)
Novo	Salvador Novo, *La Vida en Mexico en el periodo presidencial de Miguel Aleman* (Mexico: Empresas Editoriales, 1967)
Novo35	Salvador Novo, *La Vida en Mexico en el periodo presidencial de Lazaro Cardenas* (Mexico: Empresas Editoriales, 1964)
NYT	*New York Times (The)*
PdM	*Personalidades de Monterrey* (Nuevo Leon: Vega y Asociados, 1967)
Padgett	L. Vincent Padgett, *The Mexican Political System* (Boston: Houghton Mifflin Co., 1966)
Peral	Miguel Angel Peral, *Diccionario biografico mexicano* (Mexico: Editorial PAC, 1945?)
Peral47	Miguel Angel Peral, *Diccionario biografico mexicano-suplemento* (Mexico: Editorial PAC, 1947)
Peral60	Miguel Angel Peral, *Diccionario historico, biographico, geografico e industrial de la republica* (Mexico: Editorial PAC, 1960)
Polemica	*Polemica* (April, 1969)
Politica	*Politica*
Proceso	*Proceso*
Por Que?	*Por Que?*
Q es Q	Carlos Morales Diaz, *Quien es Quien en la nomenclatura de la ciudad de Mexico* (Mexico: Costa Amic, 1971)
Q es QY	*Quien es Quien: Diccionario biografico peninsular* (Merida: Editorial Marina, 1971)
Quien Sera	Arturo Gomez Castro, *Quien sera el fururo presidente de Mexico?* (Mexico, 1963)
Raby	David L. Raby, *Educacion y revolucion social en Mexico* (Mexico: Secretaria de Educacion Publica, 1974)
Romero Flores	Jesus Romero Flores, *Maestros y Amigos* (Mexico: Costa Amic, 1971)
Ronfeldt	David Ronfeldt, *Antencingo, The Politics of Agrarian Struggle in a Mexican Ejido* (Stanford: Stanford University Press, 1973)
Scott	Robert E. Scott, *Mexican Government in Transition* (Urbana: University of Illinois Press, 1964)
STYRBIWW	*International Yearbook and Statemen's Who's Who* (by year)
Semblanzas	Antonio Armendariz, *Semblanzas* (Mexico, 1968)
Siempre	*Siempre*
Simpson	Lesley Byrd Simpson, *Many Mexicos* (Berkeley: University of California Press, 1964)
Smith	Peter H. Smith, biographical data file, personal collection
Strode	Hudson Strode, *Timeless Mexico* (New York: Harcourt, Brace, 1944)
Tiempo	*Hispano Americano* (Mexican version)
Tiempo Mexicano	Carlos Fuentes, *Tiempo Mexicano* (Mexico: Joaquin Mortiz, 1972)
Tucker	William P. Tucker, *The Mexican Government Today* (Minneapolis: University of Minnesota Press, 1957)
Uriostegui	Pindaro Uriostegui Miranda, *Testimonios del proceso revolucionario de Mexico* (Mexico: Argrin, 1970)

UTEHA   *Diccionario Enciclopedia UTEHA* (Mexico: UTEHA, 1950)

Vazquez de Knauth   Josefina Vazquez de Knauth, *Nacionalismo y educacion en Mexico* (Mexico: El Colegio de Mexico, 1970)

Villasenor, E.   Eduardo Villasenor, *Memorias-Testimonio* (Mexico: Fondo de Cultura Economica, 1974)

Villasenor   Victor Manuel Villasenor, *Memorias de un hombre de izquierda*, 2 Vols. (Mexico: Editorial Grijalbo, 1976)

WB48   *World Biography* (New York: Institute for Research in Biography, 1948)

WB54   *World Biography* (New York: Institute for Research in Biography, 1954)

Wences Reza   Rosalio Wences Reza, *El Movimiento estudiantil* (Mexico: Editorial Nuestro Tiempo, 1971)

Weyl   Nathanial Weyl and Sylvia Weyl, *The Reconquest of Mexico* (New York: Oxford University Press, 1939)

Wilkie   James Wilkie and Edna Wilkie, *Mexico Visto en el siglo xx* (Mexico: Instituto Mexicano de Investigaciones Economicos, 1969)

WNM   Lucien F. Lajoie, *Who's Notable in Mexico* (Mexico, 1972)

Womack   John Womack, Jr., *Zapata and the Mexican Revolution* (New York: Knopf, 1968)

WWLA35   *Who's Who in Latin America* (Stanford: Stanford University Press, 1935)

WWLA40   *Who's Who in Latin America* (Stanford: Stanford University Press, 1940)

WWM45   *Who' Who in Latin America: Mexico* (Stanford: Stanford University Press, 1946)

WWMG   Marvin Alisky, *Who's Who in Mexican government* (Tempe: Arizona State University, 1969)

WWW70-71   *Who's Who in the World*, 1970–71

Abbreviations Used in the Text

ACJM	Catholic Association of Mexican Youth
CEMLA	Center for Monetary Studies of Latin America
CEN	National Executive Committee
CEPES	Center of Economic, Political, and Social Studies (local and regional version of IEPES)
CNC	National Farmers' Confederation
CNOP	National Federation of Popular Organizations
CONASUPO	National Company of Public Commodities
CONCAMIN	Federation of Chambers of Industry of Mexico
CONDUMEX	Conduit of Mexico
CORDEMEX	(government enterprise which produces henequen)
CROC	Revolutionary Federation of Workers and Farmers
CROM	Regional Federation of Mexican Workers
CTM	Mexican Federation of Laborers
DTyTF	Federal District and Federal Territories
FSTSE	Federation of Government Employees' Union
IEPES	Institute of Economic, Political and Social Studies
IMSS	Mexican Institute of Social Security
IPN	National Polytechnical Institute
ISSSTE	Institute of Security and Social Studies for Federal Employees
NAFIN	Nacional Financiera
NOTIMEX	Mexican News and Information Agency
PCM	Mexican Communist Party
PEMEX	Petroleos Mexicanos
PIPSA	Producer and Importer of Paper
PNR	National Revolutionary Party (1929–1938)
PPS	Popular Socialist Party
PRM	Party of the Mexican Revolution (1938–1946)
PRI	Institutional Revolutionary Party
PST	Socialist Workers Party
SITMMRM	Independent Union of Metalurgical Mining Workers
STFRM	Mexican Railroad Workers Union
STPRM	Mexican Petroleum Workers Union
SNTE	National Union of Educational Workers
SUTDDF	Union of the Workers of the Federal District
UNAM	National Autonomous University or National University of Mexico

The Biographies

Abarca Alarcon, Raimundo

a-Mar. 4, 1906. b-Chilpancingo, Guerrero, *South, Urban*. c-Medical degree, Military Medical School, Mexico, D.F.; Professor of Physics, Chemistry, and Psychology. d-Mayor of Iguala, Guerrero, 1949–50; *Governor of Guerrero, 1963–69*. e-President of PRI in Iguala, Guerrero; Secretary General of CNOP of PRI in Guerrero. f-Director of the Hospital of Iguala. g-Secretary General of the National Medical Federation. h-Physician for the National Railroads of Mexico; surgeon for the ISSSTE; Chief of Medical Services for the 27th Military Zone, Acapulco, Guerrero; President of the Iguala Red Cross. j-None. k-None. l-WWMG, 5; DBM68, 1; HA, 10 Jun. 1974, 13.

Abundez (Chavez), Benigno

(Deceased 1958)

a-Feb. 13, 1880. b-Xochipala, Jojutla, Morelos, *West Central, Rural*. c-Early education unknown; no degree. d-*Senator* from the State of Morelos, 1934–40; *Federal Deputy* from the State of Morelos, Dist. 2, 1955–58, member of the Committee on Natural Resources, the Committee on Social Welfare, and the Committee on National Lands. e-Founding member of the PNR, 1929; President of the PNR in Morelos; President of the Zapatista Front. f-None. g-Founder of the League of Agrarian Communities in Morelos. h-Farmer for many years. j-Joined Emiliano Zapata's forces under General Francisco Mendoza Palma, 1911; fought with Zapata in Morelos until 1918; reached rank of general under the Zapatistas; joined the federal army in 1920; rank of brigadier general, 1920; incorporated in the First Division under the command of General *Genovevo de la O;* commander of the 48th, 51st and 53rd battalions; commander of the Legionnaire Division of Morelos. k-Precandidate for governor of Morelos, 1938. l-Peral, 11; DP70, 4; IndBiog., 7.

Aceves Alcocer, Gilberto

a-June 10, 1921. b-Tototlan, Jalisco, *West, Rural*. c-Completed primary, secondary and preparatory studies; took some commercial courses, no degree; never taught. d-*Federal Deputy* from the Federal District, Dist. 5, 1967–70, member of the public works and the rules committees; *Federal Deputy* from the state of Jalisco, Dist. 7, 1973–76. e-None. f-Head of the second shift of the guard house, Department of the Federal District, Mexico City. g-Secretary General of the Union of Workers of the Federal District; Secretary of Bureaucratic Action, National Federation of Popular Organizations in the Federal District; Secretary of Social Action of the FSTSE; Secretary of Bureaucratic Action, National Executive Committee, CNOP, 1974–75; *Secretary General of the FSTSE*, 1970–75. i-Married Consuelo Velasco Lara. j-None. k-None. l-HA, 27 Dec. 1971, 24; MGF69, 90; *Excelsior,* 13 Mar. 1973, 13; C de D, 1973–76, 12.

Aceves de Romero, Graciela

a-Sept. 6, 1931. b-Guadalajara, Jalisco, *West, Urban*. c-Teaching certificate; completed preparatory studies in pre-medicine; no degree. d-*Federal Deputy* (Party Deputy from PAN) from the Federal District, Dist. 12, 1967–70. e-Member of PAN. f-None. g-None. i-Married Humberto Romero C. j-None. k-None. l-C de D, 1967–70.

Aceves Parra, Salvador

a-Apr. 4, 1904. b-La Piedad, Michoacan, *West Central, Urban*. c-Primary studies in Guadalajara, Jalisco; secondary studies, Mexico, D.F.; preparatory studies at the National Preparatory School in Mexico, D.F., 1920–24; medical degree, National School of Medicine, UNAM; graduate fellow in cardiology, United States (many times); Professor of Medical Pathology, National School of Medicine, UNAM, 1933–69; adviser to many state universities; member of the Governing Council of UNAM, 1964. d-None. e-Active supporter of Jose Vasconcelos in 1929 presidential campaign. f-Chief of Medical Services, General Hospital, Mexico, D.F., 1938–44; Chief of Medical Services, National Institute of Cardiology, 1944–61; Director of the National Institute of Cardiology, 1961–65; *Subsecretary of Health*, 1964–67; *Secretary of Health*, 1968–70. **g-** None. **h-**Assistant at the Medical Clinic, UNAM, 1934; Director of the Medical Clinic, UNAM, 1934; intern, General Hospital, Mexico, D.F., 1933–36; medical adviser for Internal Medicine, General Hospital, Mexico, D.F., 1936–38. **i-**Professor of Medicine with *Rafael Moreno Valle* at UNAM; attended UNAM with a number of members of the *Aleman* Generation, including *Manuel Gual Vidal*, Salvador Azuela, *Rogerio de la Selva*, and *Antonio Dovali Jaime;* close friend of *Antonio Armendariz* at UNAM; married Garcia. **j-**None. **k-**None. **l-**DBM68, 3–4; *Hoy*, 25 Oct. 1969, 17; HA, 7 Aug. 1944, 7; letters.

Acosta Garcia, Isauro

a-June 11, 1899. **b-**Ursulo Galvan, Municipio de San Carlos, Veracruz, *Gulf, Rural*. **c-**Completed primary studies; no degree. **d-**Local deputy to the 32nd State Legislature of Veracruz; *Senator* from the State of Veracruz, 1952–58, member of the Committee on Industries and the Committee on Small Agricultural Properties; alternate member of the Economy and Statistics Committee. **e-**None. **f-**None. **g-**Began agrarian activities as an organizer in Chixicastle, Municipio de Puente Nacional, Veracruz, 1918; organizer for agrarian unions, 1918–20; co-founder with Ursulo Galvan of the League of Agrarian Communities, 1923; co-founder of the National Peasant League with Ursulo Galvan and leader of that organization, 1926–30; President of the League of Agrarian Communities of Veracruz, 1928–30, 1943–44; representative of the League of Agrarian Communities of Veracruz before the Mixed Agrarian Commission. **h-**Campesino at the age of 16. **j-**Soldier in the 86th Line Battalion in opposition to the Adolfo de la Huerta rebellion, 1923. **k-**Elected as the Alternate Senator but replaced *Roberto Amoros* who resigned his senate seat to become Director General of the National Railroads, 1952. **l-**DGF56, 8, 10, 11, 14; IndBiog., 8.

Acosta Romo, Fausto

a-Oct. 20, 1915. **b-**Sonora, *North*. **c-**Primary studies in Hermosillo; normal degree; law degree National School of Law, UNAM, 1937; with a thesis on "The Strike Law and Obligatory Arbitration in Our Social Law." **d-***Senator* from the State of Sonora, 1952–58, member of the Committee on Immigration, the Health Committee, the Third Labor Committee, the Second Balloting Committee; substitute member of the Tax Committee, the National Waters and Irrigation Committee, and the Livestock Committee. **e-**PRI campaigner; President of PNR in Sonora; general delegate of PRI to Jalisco and Queretaro; directed *Juan C. Gorraez's* gubernatorial campaign,

1955. **f-***Assistant Attorney General of Mexico* (2), 1964–66; Secretary General of Government of the State of Sonora under Governor *Ignacio Soto*, 1949–52; Acting Governor of Sonora, August-September, 1951; Gerente of Comisiones and Servicios, S.A., an agency of CONASUPO. **g-**None. **h-**Practicing lawyer, El Aguila Petroleum Company; Director of the Legal Department, Director of the Trust Department, National Bank of Ejido Credit, Cuidad Obregon, Sonora; lawyer for PEMEX, 1938. **i-**Co-student with *Antonio Rocha Cordero*. **j-**None. **k-**Precandidate for Governor of Sonora on the PRI ticket, 1961 and 1967; according to Roger Anderson he was the choice of national PRI leaders for governor in 1961, but was unpopular among state leaders. **l-**WWMG, 5; DPE65, 209; HA, 21 Dec. 1964, 10; DGF51, I,92; Anderson, 112–3; IndBiog., 9–10; Moncada, 56.

Acosta Velasco, Ricardo

(Deceased Jan. 13, 1978)
a-May 11, 1908. **b-**Molango, Hidalgo, *East Central, Rural*. **c-**Engineering agronomy degree, National School of Agriculture, San Jacinto, Federal District, 1927; studied at the TVA, United States, 1947–51; advanced studies in irrigation at the National School of Agriculture, Chapingo, Mexico. **d-***Federal Deputy* from the State of Guanajuato, Dist. 3, 1940–43; member of the Great Committee of the Justice Committee. **e-**Technical adviser to *Octaviano Campos Salas* for the IEPES of PRI and author of special projects for PRI; in charge of developing an agricultural program for presidential candidate *Adolfo Ruiz Cortines;* collaborated in developing an agricultural program for presidential candidate *Gustavo Diaz Ordaz*. **f-**Member of the Technical Board, National Irrigation Commission, 1929; Director of the Technical Board of the CNI for the State of Morelos, 1929–33; Director of the National Office of Agrarian Organizations of the Federal District, 1933–34; Director General of the Mexican Agrarian Organizations, Department of Agrarian Affairs, 1934; delegate of the Department of Agrarian Affairs, 1938; delegate of the Department of Agrarian Affairs in San Luis Potosi, 1939; organizer and Technical Director of the National Maiz Commission, 1946–47; technical adviser, National Sugar Cane Commission, 1951–52; Director General of Agriculture, Secretariat of Agriculture and Livestock, 1952–59; technical adviser to Psytonsyo del Maguey, 1961; *Subsecretary of Agriculture, 1964*–70. **g-**None. **h-**Author of several articles on agrarian subjects. **i-**Father-in-law of Joaquin Pria Olavarrieta, President of CANACINTRA, 1978; married to Emma Brambila. **j-**None. **k-**None. **l-**WWMG,5; DGF56, 224; DBM68,5–6; HA, 4 Jan. 1965, 28; DGF50, 160; DGF51,II,231.

Agramont Cota, Felix

a-1917. b-La Paz, Baja California del Sur, *West, Urban.* c-Primary studies at the Escuela Emiliano Zapata; secondary and normal studies at the Escuela Normal Rural de Todos Santos, 1933–37; agricultural engineering degree, August, 1945, National School of Agriculture, 1939–45; received recognition as one of the outstanding students in the field of agricultural research. d-*Governor of Baja California del Sur,* 1970–75. e-None. f-Technical Subdirector of the Productora Nacional de Semillas, 1961–70; General Agent for the Secretary of Agriculture and Livestock in Jalisco, 1958–60; Administrator of the National Commission of Maiz. g-None. h-Worked on the ejido El Pescador as a child; recipient of a Rockefeller Foundation Study Grant for research on seed production, 1947. j-None. k-President *Echeverria* was present at Governor Agramont Cota's first State of the Union message in 1972. l-*Hoy, 26 Dec. 1970, 5;* HA, 13 Dec. 1971, 35; HA, 7 Dec. 1970, 20; letter.

Aguilar Alvarez, Ernesto

a-Jan. 25, 1910. b-Tacubaya, *Federal District, Urban.* c-Primary studies at the Colegio Luz Savinon; secondary studies at the Colegio Frances Morelos; preparatory at the National Preparatory School, Mexico, D.F.; law degree, National School of Law, UNAM, August 10, 1933; Professor of Civic Education, National Preparatory School, June 1, 1938–66; Professor of Mercantile Law, School of Commerce and Administration, UNAM, 1938–66; Professor of Amparo, UNAM, 1938–66. d-None. f-Executor Judge, Ninth District, December 1, 1933; Judge of the Superior Tribunal of Justice, State of Veracruz; Judge of the First Instance; Magistrate of the Superior Tribunal of Justice of the Federal District; President of the Superior Tribunal of Justice of the Federal District; Magistrate of the Collegiate Tribunal, First Circuit; *Justice of the Supreme Court,* 1966–77. g-None. h-Member of the Mexican delegation to the United Nations Meeting, San Francisco, 1945. i-Knew *Antonio Luna Arroyo* at the National School of Law; attended secondary school with President *Lopez Mateos.* j-None. k-None. l-*Justicia.*

Aguilar (Castillo), Magdaleno

a-July 22, 1900. b-Rancho de la Reforma, Municipio de Juamave, Tamaulipas, *North, Rural.* c-Early education unknown; none; none. d-Local Deputy to the State Legislature of Tamaulipas, 1938; *Senator* from Tamaulipas, 1946–52; member of the Gran Comision, member of the Committees on the Agrarian Department and Agricultural Development, member of the First Balloting Committee and substitute member of the Committee on Foreign and Domestic Commerce; *Governor of Tamaulipas,* 1940–45;

Senator from Tamaulipas, 1964–70. e-Member of the 1929 delegation from Tamaulipas to select a presiential candidate; *Secretary of Agrarian Action of the CEN of PRI,* 1953–59, 1959–64; chief of *Aleman's* campaign for President in the state of Tamaulipas, 1945. f-None. g-President of the Executive Agrarian Committee responsible for receiving presidential resolutions for the ejidos of La Libertad and La Mision, 1925; First Secretary of the League of Agrarian Communities and Farmer Unions of Tamaulipas, 1926; president of that union, 1927–28, 1934; Secretary of Organization of the CNC. h-Adviser to the National Bank of Agricultural Credit, 1928–29. i-Political supporter of *Emilio Portes Gil* early in his career. j-None. k-Considered for secretary general of the CNC, 1962. l-HA, 26 Nov. 1943, 15; HA, 18 Aug. 1942, 14; HA, 15 Dec. 1944, IV; DBM68, 9; DGF51, I, 89, 10–12; Enc. Mex. I, 214; WWMG, 5; Peral, 18; letter; Lopez 23; Navarro, 232.

Aguilar Chavez, Salvador

b-Zacatecas, Zacatecas, *East Central, Urban.* c-Engineering degree, National School of Engineering, UNAM, 1936. d-None. e-None. f-Subdirector of Construction, Director of Construction, National Irrigation Commission; Director of Fincas in the Secretariat of Public Works; Director of Railroads in the Secretariat of Public Works; Comptroller General of the Secretariat of Hydraulic Resources, 1952–58; *Subsecretary of Hydraulic Resources, 1964–70.* g-None. h-Construction engineer, public works projects; Assistant to the Superintendent of Construction, Marte R. Gomez Dam; President of the Mexican Association of Engineers and Architects, 1973–74. i-Married Elvira Leal. j-None. k-None. l-HA, 21 Dec. 1964, 4; DGF56, 413; HA, 26 Mar. 1973, 25.

Aguilar Hernandez, Francisco

a-July 10, 1924. b-Pachuca, Hidalgo, *East Central, Urban.* c-Primary studies in the Melchor Ocampo School, Hidalgo; secondary studies at the University of Guanajuato; preparatory studies at the National Preparatory School; medical degree from the National School of Medicine, UNAM. d-*Senator* from the State of Morelos, 1970–76, President of the Small Agricultural Property Committee and the Third Labor Committee, Second Secretary of the Insurance Committee, First Secretary of the Health Committee. e-Secretary of Popular Action of PRI in Morelos; Delegate of PRI. f-Representative of the IMSS in Morelos; President of the IMSS, Cuernavaca, Morelos. g-Secretary General of the CNOP in Morelos; delegate of the SNTE; leader of CNOP in the State of Hidalgo. h-Employee of the Green Cross, 1949–50; practicing physician. j-None. k-None. l-C de S, 1970–76, 71.

Aguilar Pico, Rigoberto
(Deceased June 27, 1974)
a-June 2, 1906. b-Mazatlan, Sinaloa, *West, Urban*. c-Primary studies in Mazatlan; medical degree, National School of Medicine, UNAM, 1930, with a specialty in pediatrics; specialized studies in pediatrics, Paris, Bordeaux, Hamburg and Berlin; Professor of Clinical Pediatrics, National School of Medicine, UNAM. d-None. e-None. f-*Substitute Governor of Sinaloa,* February 28, 1953 to December 31, 1956. g-None, h-Founding director, Dolores Sainz Infant Hospital; chief of services, Infant Hospital of Mexico, 1937-57. i-Son of General Jose Aguilar B.; brother of Saul Aguilar Pico, law graduate of the National School of Law, 1932, and Superior Court Justice of Sinaloa, 1950s to 1970s; married Clotilde Bernal. j-None. k-He was not a militant party member when selected as governor to replace *Enrique Perez Arce.* l-DGF56, 100; HA, 2 Sept. 1953, 18; HA, 26 Sept. 1952; HA, 6 Mar. 1953, 12-13; Peral60, 149; *Excelsior,* 29 June 1974, 2; WNM, 3.

Aguilar (Vargas), Candido
(Deceased Mar. 19, 1960)
a-Feb. 12, 1888. b-Congregacion de Palma y Monteros, Veracruz, *Gulf, Rural.* d-Governor of Veracruz, June 20, 1914, to June 24, 1917; Deputy to the Constitutional Convention of 1917; First Vice President of the Convention; *Senator* from Veracruz, 1934-40; *Federal Deputy,* Dist. 8 from Veracruz, 1943-46. e-President of the Party of the Revolution, 1951. f-Secretary of Foreign Relations from February 4, to November 9, 1918; Confidential Ambassador to the United States and Europe, 1919. g-Founder of the League of Agrarian Communities in Veracruz. h-Milkman before the Revolution. i-Son-in-law of President Carranza; married Virginia Carranza; brother of *Silvestre Aguilar*; uncle of *Hesiquio Aguilar,* federal deputy from Veracruz, 1967-70. j-Joined the anti-Reelectionist movement under Francisco Madero in 1910, served under General Gavira, and became a Constitutionalist in 1913; served as a chief of operations, but left the army after President Carranza was killed; rank of division general, 1944; Commander of the Legion of Honor, 1950. k-Remained loyal to Carranza; joined the De la Huerta rebellion in 1923 and was exiled; lived in San Antonio, Texas, 1920-25; publicized the corruption in the PRM and was thrown out of the official party on June 10, 1944; went into self exile in Cuba and El Salvador, 1952-54; imprisoned for political reasons in Veracruz, 1952. l-Peral 47, 5-6, DP70, 35, letter, Gruening, 584, UTEHA, 284; Correa, 238; Lopez, 21.

Aguilar, Jr. (Vargas), Silvestre
(Deceased 1955)
b-Cordoba, Veracruz, *Gulf, Urban.* c-Primary studies in Cordoba; no degree. d-Deputy to the Constitutional Convention of 1917; *Federal Deputy* from the State of Veracruz, Dist. 9, 1937-40; *Federal Deputy* from the State of Veracruz, Dist. 6, 1943-46; *Federal Deputy* from the State of Veracruz, Dist. 9, 1949-51, member of the Committee on Forest Affairs, the Library Committee, the First Balloting Committee, and Executive Secretary of the First Instructive Committee for the Grand Jury. e-None. f-Oficial Mayor of the State of Veracruz under Governor *Jorge Cerdan, 1940-*43; Treasurer of Veracruz, 1946. i-Brother of *Candido Aguilar,* son-in-law of Venustiano Carranza and Senator from Veracruz, 1934-40; son, Hesiquio Aguilar, was a federal deputy from Veracruz, 1967-70. k-In exile in the United States and Cuba, 1920. l-Peral, 20; C de D, 1937-40, 5; C de D, 1943-46, 5; C de D, 1949-51, 61; DGF51, 26,30,34.

Aguilar y Maya, Guillermo
b-Guanajuato, *West Central.* c-Law degree, National School of Law, UNAM, November, 1935, with a thesis on a critique on crimes pursued in guerilla warfare. d-*Federal Deputy,* State of Guanajuato, Dist. 7, 1943-44. e-None. f-Justice of the Superior Tribunal of Justice of the Federal District, 1946-52; *Attorney General of the Federal District and Federal Territories,* 1952-56; President of the National Council of Unrenewable Resources, 1956-58. g-None. i-Brother of *Jose Aguilar y Maya.* j-None. k-None. l-DGF56, 502; D de Y, 2 Dec. 1952, 1; DGF51, I, 487; HA, 10 Dec. 1956, 5; HA, 5 Nov. 1956.

Aguilar y Maya, Jose
(Deceased Nov. 30, 1966)
a-July 28, 1897. b-Jerecuaro, Guanajuato, *West Central, Rural.* c-Primary, secondary, and preparatory; Seminario de Morelia, Michoacan, and Colegio de Guanajuato; law degree, National School of Law, UNAM; Professor of Spanish and Literature, Preparatory School, Guanajuato; Professor of General Theory and of Public Law, UNAM, for ten years, during which he gained national recognition; Head, Department of Justice and Public Instruction, Guanajuato. d-Federal Deputy, State of Guanajuato, 1924-16, 1926-28, 1928-30; *Federal Deputy,* State of Guanajuato, Dist. 7, 1937-40; *Governor of Guanajuato,* 1949-55. e-None. f-Attorney General of DFyTF, 1928; Attorney General of DFyTF, 1930-32; *Attorney General of Mexico, 1940-46; Attorney General of Mexico,* 1955-58. g-None. h-Director General of Seguros de Mexico, SA, 1948;

author of many works and emergency war legislation for President *Avila Camacho*. **i-**Brother of *Guillermo Aguilar y Maya;* friend of Senator Enrique Colunga, who was Governor of Guanajuato, 1923–27, and Minister of Government under President Obregon; married Maria Tinajero. **j-**None. **k-**Attributes his nomination as Governor of Guanajuato to teaching students who later became pivotal men in the Mexican political system; leader of political faction in Guanajuato known as the Reds; supported candidacy of *Ernesto Hidalgo as* governor, 1943. **l-**WWM45, 1; HA, 18 Feb. 1957, 6; HA, 28 Sept. 1953; DP, 38; Gruening, 429; DGF51, I, 89, 487; Peral, 18–19; STYRBIWW54, 573; Enc. Mex. I, 214–15; UTEHA, 286; WWLA35, 16; Lopez, 25; Anderson, 85–86.

Aguilar y Salazar, Manuel
(Deceased 1959)
a-1892. **b-**Sitacoyoapan, Oaxaca, *South, Rural.* **c-**Primary at Sitacoyoapan; secondary studies in Puebla; law degree, Institute of Arts and Sciences in Oaxaca, Oaxaca; Professor of Law at the Institute of Arts and Sciences; director of various private schools. **d-**Deputy to the Constitutional Convention, 1917; *Federal Deputy* from Oaxaca, Dist. 3, 1952–55, member of congressional committees on livestock and the Second Committee on Justice. **f-**Agent of the Ministerio Publico for the Federal Attorney General in Oaxaca; Chief of the Department of Justice of the State of Oaxaca; consulting lawyer to the state government of Oaxaca. **g-**None. **h-**Practicing lawyer. **j-**None. **k-**Member of the National Action Party. **l-**C de D, 1952–54; Morton, 67; DP70, 2360.

Aguilera Dorantes, Mario
a-Aug. 15, 1907. **b-**Oaxaca, Oaxaca, *South, Urban.* **c-**Teaching credential, Escuela Nacional de Maestros, 1927; graduate studies in primary education in the United States; professor of secondary and normal schools in the Federal District, including Progreso No. 6, San Lucas and Coyoacan, **d-**None. **e-**None. **f-**Normal school director, Federal District; Director of Federal Education, Secretariat of Public Education; Director General of Pilot Project for the Secretariat of Public Education, 1951; Director General of Agricultural and Rural Normal Instruction, Secretariat of Public Education; Director General of Agricultural Education; Coordinator of Indigenous Affairs, Secretariat of Public Education; *Oficial Mayor,* Secretariat of Public Education, 1961–64; *Oficial Mayor,* Secretariat of Public Education, 1964–70; President, National Technical Council of Education, 1970–73; Coordinator General of Literacy and Extracurricular Education, Secretariat of Public Education, 1977. **g-**None. **h-**Author of several works on

education. **i-**Married Teodosia Martinez. **j-**None. **l-**DBM70, 8–9; DGF51, I, 294; DPE61, 97; DBM68, 12; Enc. Mex., I, 161–162; HA, 25 Apr., 1977, F; DAPC, 1977, 1.

Aguirre Andrade, Patricio
a-May 27, 1907. **b-**Federal District, *Federal District, Urban.* **c-**Primary, secondary and preparatory studies at the Colegio de Estado of Aguascalientes; medical degree, National School of Medicine, UNAM, with a thesis on blood transfusions from cadavers to living persons; specialty in the field of the conservation of tissues. **d-***Alternate Federal Deputy* from the Federal District, Dist. 3, 1952–55; *Federal Deputy* from the Federal District, Dist. 3, 1955–58; member of the Sugar Industry and the First Section of the General Means of Communications Committees. **e-**Founding member of PAN, 1939; official of the PAN Regional Committee of the Federal District; Member of the National Council of PAN, 1952–56. **f-**None. **g-**None. **h-**Practicing physician, 1947; surgeon, Streetcar Company of Mexico; laboratorist, Hospital Ingles, 1940–46; owner, textile industry, 1947–55. **i-**Son of Gustavo Aguirre Ortiz, revolutionary major and veterinarian. **j-**None. **k-**None. **l-**DGF66, 22,34,37; IndBiog., 12–13.

Aguirre Beltran, Gonzalo
a-Jan. 20, 1908. **b-**Tlacotalpan, Veracruz, *Gulf, Rural.* **c-**Preparatory studies at the National Preparatory School, Mexico, D.F.; Bachelor of Science degree from the UNAM, 1927; Doctor of Medicine degree, National School of Medicine, UNAM, 1931; Rockefeller Fellow, Northwestern University; Rector of the University of Veracruz, 1956–63. **d-***Federal Deputy* from the State of Veracruz, Dist. 12, 1961–64, member of the Committee on Bellas Artes and the Second Committee on Public Education; member of the Gran Comision; member of the Interparliamentary Delegation to the United States. **e-**None. **f-**Head of the Sanitary Unit for Huatusco, Veracruz, 1939–40; Head, Department of Demography, Secretariat of Government, 1942–51; Director General of Indigenous Affairs, Secretariat of Public Education, 1946–52; Director of the Coordinating Indigenous Center for the Tzeltal-Tsotzil Region, 1951–53; *Subsecretary of Cultural Affairs, Secretariat of Public Education,* 1970–76; Director General of the National Indigenous Institute, 1971–72. **g-**None. **h-**Intern, General Hospital, Mexico, D.F., 1931–32; biologist, Department of Demography, Secretariat of Government, 1942; practicing physician, Veracruz, 1938–41; Secretary General of the Mexican Society of Anthropology; Director of the Inter-American Indigenous Institute, 1966–70; author of many scholarly works on history, agriculture, and Indians; recog-

nized scholar in the field of anthropology. i-Married Judith Avendano. j-None. k-None. l-WWM45, 2; DGF47, 172; HA 20 Sept. 1971,22; HA 14 Dec. 1970, 22; DGF50, II, 465; DGF51, I, 68; II, 636; WB48, 60; WWW70–71.

Aguirre (de Castillo), Vicente

a-1907. b-Ixmiquilpan, Hidalgo, *East Central, Rural.* c-Primary studies in Ixmiquilpan; preparatory studies in Mexico City; law studies at the National School of Law, UNAM, 1928–32, law degree, 1933. d-*Federal Deputy from the State of Hidalgo, Dist. 4, 1937–40; Senator from the State of Hidalgo, 1940–46; Governor of Hidalgo, 1946–51.* e-President of the PRM in Hidalgo. f-Chief of Political Control, State of Hidalgo; Private Secretary to *Javier Rojo Gomez* as Governor of Hidalgo, 1937. g-None. i-Brother of *Victor M. Aguirre,* federal deputy from Hidalgo, 1943–46 and 1949–52; relative of *Javier Rojo Gomez;* law school classmate of *Carlos Ramirez Guerrero.* j-None. k-Supported *Javier Rojo Gomez's* precandidacy for president of Mexico, 1946. l-Peral60, 166–67; HA 13 Dec. 1946, 6; Correa, 7; letter; Gaxiola, 318.

Aguirre (del Castillo), Victor M.

a-Mar. 24, 1914. b-Ixmiquilpan, Hidalgo, *East Central, Rural.* c-Primary studies in Ixmiquilpan; secondary studies in Mexico City; studies in agricultural engineering, National School of Agriculture, Chapingo, no degree. d-Mayor of Tula, Hidalgo; Mayor of Pachuca, Hidalgo; *Federal Deputy* from the State of Hidalgo, Dist. 3, 1943–46; *Federal Deputy* from the State of Hidalgo, Dist. 3, 1949–52, member of the Gran Comision, the 4th Ejido Committee and an alternate to the War Materiels Committee. g-None. i-Brother of *Vicente Aguirre,* Governor of Hidalgo, 1946–51. j-None. k-None. l-DGF51, 22,29,32,35; Peral60, 167; C de D, 1943–46; C de D, 1949–52.

Aguirre (Palancares), Norberto

a-1906. b-Pinotepa Nacional, Oaxaca, *South, Rural.* c-Agricultural engineering degree, National School of Agriculture, Chapingo; Professor of Economy at the National School of Economics, UNAM. d-*Federal Deputy,* State of Oaxaca, Dist. 7, 1943–46; *Federal Deputy,* State of Oaxaca, Dist. 7, 1949–52, member of the Agriculture and Development Committee and the Second Treasury Committee; *Federal Deputy,* State of Oaxaca, 1961–64; member of the Small Agricultural Properties Committee, the Committee of Legislative Studies (Agricultural Section), the Administration Committee, and the Gran Comision; Federal Deputy from State of Oaxaca, Dist. 8, 1979–82. f-Director of Agrarian Laws, 1943–46, Department of Agrarian Affairs; Director of the National Commission of Maiz, 1949–53; Rector of the University of Sonora, 1953–56; Secretary General of Government, State of Oaxaca, 1956–61; *Head of the Department of Agrarian Affairs and Colonization, 1964–70.* g-Secretary General of the League of Agrarian Communities and Farmers Union, State of Oaxaca. h-Agricultural engineer in charge of agrarian reform projects, 1929–43; founding member of the National Commission of Maiz (Vocal); adviser to the Mexican delegation at the Inter-American Conferences at Chapultepec in 1945 and Caracas in 1942; adviser to the Mexican Delegation to the United Nations, 1946. i-Married Pilar Salazar; son Amando was a precandidate of PARM for federal deputy from Oaxaca. j-None. k-Expelled from the League of Agrarian Communities in Oaxaca for supporting General *Henriquez Guzman,* 1952. l-DBM70, 12–13; HA, 13 May 1968, 7; DBM68, 14; DGF50, II, 159; C de D, 1949–51; C de D, 1961–63; DGF51, I, 24, 30, 32–33; II, 231; HA, 10 Jul. 1972, 10; WWW70–71; WB48; Correa, 366; HA, 4 Oct. 1976, 15.

Aguirre (Samaniego), Manuel Bernardo

a-Aug. 20, 1903. b-Parral, Chihuahua, *North, Urban.* c-Primary studies at the Colegio Palmore, Parral, and in Ciudad Juarez, Chihuahua; secondary studies in the Federal District; engineering degree from the National School of Engineering, UNAM. d-Mayor of Chihuahua, Chihuahua, 1947–49; *Federal Deputy* from the State of Chihuahua, Dist. 4, 1940–43; Secretary to the President of the Chamber of Deputies, 1940; President of the Gran Comision, 1940–43; member of the Committee on National Waters and Irrigation and the Committee on Highways; *Federal Deputy* from the State of Chihuahua, Dist. 1, 1961–64, President of the Chamber of Deputies, November, 1961; member of the Gran Comision; member of the Committee on Public Works, the Indigenous Affairs Committee, the Committee on Forest Affairs and the Library Committee; *Senator* from Chihuahua, 1964–70, President of the Senate, November, 1966; President of the Gran Comision, 1967; *Governor of Chihuahua, 1974–80.* e-Founding member of the PNR, 1929; director of the presidential campaign for Plutarco E. Calles, Parral and Ciudad Juarez, Chihuahua, 1924; Director of PRI in Chihuahua, 1944–45; first Oficial Mayor of the CNOP of PRI, 1945–46; delegate of the CEN of PRI to nineteen different entities; *Secretary of Political Action of the CEN of PRI,* 1964. f-Head of the Federal Office of the Secretariat of the Treasury for the First District, Mexico, D.F., 1957–60; *Secretary of Agriculture and Livestock, 1971–74.* g-None. h-Legal representative for American Smelting and Refining and for West Mexico Mines. i-Brother, Salvador Aguirre, was an engineer; married Paula

Aun. **j**-None. **k**-None. **l**-WWMG, 5; HA, 25 Jan. 1971, 28; EBW46, 42; DGF61, 46; WWW70–71; WB48, 61; HA, 24 Dec. 1973, 24–25; *Excelsior,* 8 Jan. 1974; HA, 8 July 1974, 32; *Excelsior,* 16 Dec. 1973, 1; Enc. Mex., 1977, Annual, 542–43.

Ainslie (Rivera), Ricardo

a-1897. **b**-Guerrero, Coahuila, *North, Rural.* **c**-Primary education at public schools in Guerrero and Piedras Negras; no degree. **d**-Local deputy to the state legislature of Coahuila, 1924; Federal Deputy from Coahuila, 1930–32, member of the Gran Comision; Federal Deputy from Coahuila, 1932–34, member of the Gran Comision; *Alternate Senator* from the State of Coahuila, 1946–52. **e**-President of the Railroad Union's Party in Coahuila, 1919. **f**-Provisional Governor of Coahuila, October 25, 1925 to November 30, 1925; *Interim Governor of Coahuila,* 1947–48; Treasurer General of Coahuila (eight years). **g**-None. **i**-Father a British immigrant. **j**-Joined the Revolutionary Army in 1913; reached the rank of major. **k**-Forced to resign as Governor of Coahuila in March, 1948, as a result of a dispute over his successor with leaders of the PNR. **l**-Anderson; HA 6 Feb. 1948, 8; letter; DGF47, 19; DGF51, 5; Enc. Mex., 1977, II, 530.

Alamillo Flores, Luis

a-Dec. 27, 1904. **b**-Fortin de la Flores, Veracruz, *Gulf, Rural.* **c**-Early education unknown; military studies at the University of Puebla, the National Military College, the Sorbonne, the Military Engineering School of Versailles, the Superior War College, Paris, and George Washington University. **d**-None. **e**-None. **f**-Military attache, Mexican Embassy, Washington, D.C., 1943–45; military adviser, Mexican delegation to the United Nations, San Francisco, 1945; military attache, Mexican Embassy, Paris; Assistant Chief of Staff, Pacific Military Region; Director, Superior War College; Director, National Military College, 1945; Chief of Staff, Pacific Military Region; Chief of Staff, Secretariat of National Defense. **g**-None. **h**-None. **i**-Married Herlinda Landin. **j**-Commander of the 4th Military Zone, Hermosillo, Sonora, 1966–68. **k**-None. **l**-NYT, 7 Sept. 1945, 5; WWM45, 2; DBM68, 15.

Alanis Fuentes, Agustin

a-Feb. 19, 1930. **b**-Federal District, *Federal District, Urban.* **c**-Primary studies at Jose Enrique Rodo and El Pensador Mexicano schools; secondary studies at Secondary School No. 4; preparatory studies at the National Preparatory School; legal studies at the National School of Law, UNAM, 1948–52, degree, 1953, with a thesis on criminal confessions, for which he received an honorable mention; professor at the National Preparatory School, Mexico, D.F.,

1950, subjects included civics; professor at the National School of Law, 1964- ; professor of history at UNAM, 1966, member of the University Council of UNAM, 1952; professor of Labor Law, UNAM, 1968. **d**-None. **e**-Auxiliary general delegate of the CEN of PRI to Guanajuato, 1969–70. **f**-Administrative official of the Superior Tribunal of Justice of the Federal District and Federal Territories, 1947–50; administrative official of the Secretariat of National Patrimony, 1947; Agent of the Ministerio Publico of the Attorney General of the Federal District and Federal Territories, 1951–53; head of the Evaluation Section of the Department of Social Welfare of the Secretariat of Labor, 1958–63; Subdirector of the Department of Social Welfare of the Secretariat of Labor, 1963–65; Director of the Department of Social Welfare of the Secretariat of Labor, 1965–70; *Subsecretary B of the Secretariat of Labor,* 1970–76; *Attorney General of the Federal District,* 1976- . **g**-Student leader at the National Preparatory School and the National Law School. **h**-Technical adviser to the Mexican Institute of Social Security, 1967–70. **j**-None. **k**-None. **l**-DPE65, 156; HA, 14 Dec. 1970, 23; *El Dia,* 1 Dec. 1976, 10; HA, 7 Mar. 1977, 24–25.

Alarcon, Alfonso G.

(Deceased 1953)
a-June 25, 1884. **b**-Chilpancingo, Guerrero, *South, Urban.* **c**-Primary and secondary studies at the Colegio de Puebla; medical degree, University of Puebla, 1910; Rector, University of Puebla; Director, Department of Pediatrics and Infant Hygiene, National School of Medicine, UNAM. **d**-*Federal Deputy* from the State of Guerrero, Dist. 1, 1914–16; *Senator* from the State of Guerrero, 1952. **e**-None. **f**-Delegate of the Department of Health; Director of the Office of Infant Hygiene, Department of Health, 1935; Secretary General of the Department of Health; Director of the Office of Infant Hygiene, Puebla; Governor of Guerrero (appointed by the Local Legislature), 1933. **g**-None. **h**-Practicing pediatrician in Tampico (twenty-five years); Director of *Labor Medica* and the *Gaceta Medica* of Tampico; author of many works. **j**-Precursor, 1910 Revolution; participant, 1910 Revolution. **k**-None. **l**-DGF56, 6; PS; WWM45, 2; Enc. Mex., I, 194.

Alatriste (Abrego) Jr., Sealtiel

a-1904. **b**-Libres, Puebla, *East Central, Urban.* **c**-Primary studies in Mexico City; preparatory studies at the National Preparatory School; accounting degree (certified public accountant), UNAM, 1925; economics degree, National School of Economics, UNAM, Dec. 20, 1938, with a thesis on Mexican Banks; professor at the National School of Commerce and Administration, UNAM; professor at the

National School of Law; administrator of the National Polytechnic Institute. d-None. e-None. f-Treasurer of the Federal District, 1947–52; member of the Administrative Council of the Small Business Bank of the Federal District, 1951; *Subsecretary of Government Properties*, 1959–64; *Director General of the Mexican Institute of Social Security*, 1964–66. g-Vice President of the National College of Economists; President of the National Institute of Accountants. h-Worked as a private accountant in the firm of Roberto Casas Alatriste; accountant in the National Workers Bank; translator of many economic works; author of three technical books and many articles on economics and accounting; practicing accountant, 1967–78. i-Son of Sealtiel L. Alatriste, member of the pre-Revolutionary Liberal Clubs in Mexico; grandson of General Miguel Castulo de Alatriste, an important Liberal in the 1850s and Governor of Puebla. j-None. k-Forced to resign in the midst of an anti-corruption campaign he was conducting at IMSS in 1966. l-*El Univ.* 1 Dec. 1964; DGF4, 97; IWW66, 16; DP70, 54; DGF51; II, 507, 577, 679; Johnson; letter.

Alavez Flores, Rodolfo

a-Apr. 18, 1915. b-Oaxaca, Oaxaca, *South, Urban.* c-Primary studies at the public school in Oaxaca; secondary studies at the Institute of Arts and Sciences of Oaxaca; preparatory studies at the Institute of Arts and Sciences; law degree from the Institute of Arts and Sciences and from the National School of Law, UNAM. d-Local deputy to the State Legislature of Oaxaca, 1944–47; *Alternate Federal Deputy* from Oaxaca, Dist. 8, 1949–51; *Federal Deputy* from the State of Oaxaca, Dist. 7, 1964–67; Vice President of the Chamber, November, 1966, member of the Second Eijdo Committee and the Pharmaceutical-Chemical Industry Committee; *Federal Deputy* from the State of Oaxaca, Dist. 2, 1970–73, member of the Arid Zones Committee, the Indigenous Affairs Committee, the Legislative Studies Committee, Sixth Section on Agrarian Affairs, and the Gran Comision; *Alternate Senator* from the State of Oaxaca, 1976–82, but replaced Senator *Eliseo Jimenez Ruiz,* 1977. e-President of the State Committee of PRI, Oaxaca. f-Counselor, Federal Board of Conciliation and Arbitration; assistant to the Federal Board of Conciliation and Arbitration of the Federal District; agent of the Ministerio Publico of the Attorney General's Office; Subsecretary of Government of the State of Oaxaca; Oficial Mayor of Oaxaca, 1951. g-Secretary of Press and Publicity of the National Committee of the CNC; Secretary of the League of Agrarian Communities of Oaxaca. h-None. j-None. l-*Directorio,* 70–72; C de D, 1964–66, 82, 87; C de D, 1970–72, 99; C de D, 1949–51, DGF51, 91.

Alayola Barrera, Cesar

(Deceased)

a-June 30, 1892. b-Campeche, Campeche, *Gulf, Urban.* c-Primary studies in Merida, Yucatan; secondary studies at the Instituto Literario; law degree, School of Law, University of Yucatan, June 12, 1920; Professor of Spanish Etymology, 1916–23, Mixed Normal School of Yucatan; Professor of Private International Law, School of Law, University of Yucatan; Professor of First Year Philosophy, Instituto Literario, Merida, Yucatan, 1927–30. d-Federal Deputy from the State of Yucatan, 1928–30; Senator from the State of Yucatan, 1930–34; *Governor of Yucatan,* 1934–36. e-Member of Southeast Socialist Party; joined the PNR. f-Agent of the Ministerio Publico attached to the Second Criminal Judicial Division, Yucatan; First Justice of the Peace, Merida, Yucatan; Third Criminal Judge; Assistant Attorney General of Yucatan; Secretary General of Government of the State of Yucatan; Interim Governor of Yucatan. g-None. h-Practicing lawyer; consulting lawyer to the United Railroads of Yucatan, S.A., 1924. i-Son of Professor Jose Alayola Preve. j-None. k-Took a leave of absence from the Governorship, then resigned for reasons of health, February, 1936. l-HA, 12 Jun. 1942, 30; Peral, 30; letter.

Alba Leyva, Samuel

a-1929. b-Durango, Durango, *West, Urban.* c-Primary studies at the Florencio M. del Castillo public school; secondary studies at Secondary School No. 4, Mexico City; preparatory studies at the National Preparatory School, Mexico City; studies in law at the National School of Law, UNAM, 1947–51, law degree, November 28, 1952, with a thesis on family patrimony, received the Justo Sierra medal for the second highest grade point average of his law generation. d-None. e-None. f-Supervisory judge, Department of the Federal District, 1955–58; Agent of the federal Ministerio Publico; Agent of the Ministerio Publico of the Assistant Attorney General's Office, 1962; Advisory lawyer to the federal tax attorney, 1968; Director, Department of Plea Control, Attorney General's Office; Subdirector and director of the Central Office of Investigatory Preparations, Attorney General's Office; Private Secretary to *Julio Sanchez Vargas,* Attorney General of Mexico, 1969–71; Director of the Docket Office, Attorney General's Office, 1971–72; Inspector General of the Attorney General of Mexico, 1972–73; Coordinator General of the Anti-Narcotics Campaign, 1976; *Assistant Attorney General (2) of Mexico,* 1974–76, 1976- . g-None. h-None. i-Married to Esther Martinez. j-None. k-None. l-HA, 14 Jan. 1974; HA, 13 Dec. 1976, 10; letter.

Alcala (Anaya), Manuel

a-1915. b-Federal District, *Federal District, Urban.*
c-Early education unknown; Master of Arts, UNAM,
1944; Ph.D. in letters, School of Philosophy and Letters, UNAM, 1948; Professor at UNAM, 1940–64.
d-None. e-None. f-Member of the Technical Council
of the Humanities, UNAM, 1956–65; Director of the
National Library, 1956–65; Member of the National
Consultative Council of Mexico to UNESCO,
1965–70; Ambassador to Paraguay, 1971–74; Director General of Archives, Library and Publications,
Secretariat of Foreign Relations, 1974- . g-None.
h-Author of many works. j-None. k-None. l-Enc.
Mex., 1977, I, 205; MGF69, 184; DAPC, 1.

Alcala de Lira, Alberto

a-Apr. 23, 1917. b-La Reforma, Municipio of
Aguascalientes, Aguascalientes, *West, Rural.*
c-Primary studies in Aguascalientes; teaching certificate, Matias Ramos Colony School, Zacatecas;
school teacher. d-Member of the City Council of
Aguascalientes, 1954–55; Local Deputy to the State
Legislature of Aguascalientes; *Federal Deputy* from
the State of Aguascalientes, Dist. 1, 1955–58,
member of the Sugar Industry Committee and the
Agrarian Department Committee; *Senator* from the
State of Aguascalientes, 1964–70. e-Representative
of the Agrarian Sector to the National PRI Assemblies. f-None. g-Secretary General of the League
of Agrarian Communities, 1954–56. h-Farmer.
j-None. k-None. l-Ind. Biog., 13–14; DGF56, 21,
32, 34; C de D, 1955–58; C de S, 1964–70; MGF69.

Alcala Ferrera, Ramon

a-Jan. 17, 1912. b-Champoton, Campeche, *Gulf,
Rural.* c-Primary, secondary and preparatory studies
in Campeche; graduated from the Naval Academy at
Veracruz, Veracruz. d-*Federal Deputy* from the
State of Campeche, Dist. 1, 1967–70; *Senator* from
the State of Campeche, 1970–76, member of the
Gran Comision, President of the First Naval Commit-
tee, first secretary of the War Materiels Committee,
second secretary of the National Defense and the
Military Health Committee. e-Founding member of
PRI, 1946. f-Director of Social Security, Secretariat
of the Navy, 1965. g-None. h-None. i-Married Es-
peranza Guadarrama. j-Career Naval officer; rank of
Vice Admiral; Chief of Aides to the Commanding
General of the Fleet, *Antonio Vazquez del Mercado,*
1956. k-None. l-C de S, 1970–76, 69; DPE65, 53;
DGF56, 386; C de D, 1967–70.

Alcala Quintero, Francisco

b-Federal District, *Federal District, Urban.*
c-Accounting degree (certified public accountant),
School of Business and Administration, UNAM; degree from the Graduate School of Business and Administration, UNAM, post-graduate studies abroad;
professor at UNAM and IPN. d-None. e-None.
f-Joined the Bank of Mexico, 1927; Subgerente of
the National Bank of Foreign Commerce, 1946–52;
*Subdirector General of the National Bank of Foreign
Commerce*, 1953–58; *Subdirector General of the National Bank of Foreign Commerce*, 1958–65; *Subsecretary of Revenues of the Secretariat of the Treasury*, 1965–70; *Director General of the National
Bank of Foreign Commerce*, 1970–76, 1976–79;
Ambassador to Spain, 1979- . g-None. h-Member of
the Administrative Council of the National Bonded
Warehouses. j-None. k-None. l-DGF56, 4222; D de
Y, 2 Dec. 1970; DGF51, II, 571, 586; HA, 7 May,
1979, 19; *Excelsior,* 1 Dec. 1976, 1; HA, 9 Apr.
1979, 9.

Alcerreca Garcia Pena, Luis Gonzaga

a-Feb. 9, 1899. c-Primary and secondary studies at
public schools in Mexico, D.F.; studies at the National School of Agriculture on a scholarship from
the State of Veracruz, 1915; engineering degree, National School of Agriculture, 1919–24; Director,
School of Engineering, University of Michoacan,
1928–35. d-None. e-None. f-Engineer, Local Agrarian Commission of Michoacan, official of the state
government of Michoacan, 1928–32, under General
Cardenas; Director, Technical Department, Secretariat of Agriculture, 1935; delegate of the Department of the Federal District, 1936; senior member of
the Agricultural Advisor Office, Secretariat of Agriculture, 1943–64; Director of Advisory Section
No. 2, Secretariat of Agriculture, 1951–64; *Secretary General of the Department of Agrarian Affairs
and Colonization,* 1964–70. g-None. h-Author of
various books. i-Parents from the lower-middle class;
nephew of General Angel Garcia Pena, Secretary of
War under Madero; married Josefina Ramirez.
j-Joined the Constitutional Army, Nov. 15, 1915,
under General Pablo Gonzalez. k-None. l-DPE61,
127; DGF51, 466; *Justicia,* Feb. 1972; MGF69, 355.

Aldrete, Alberto V.

(Deceased 1959)
a-Mar. 6, 1892. b-Ensenada, Baja California del
Norte, *North, Rural.* c-Primary and secondary in Ensenada; preparatory studies in Los Angeles; none.
d-Mayor of Ensenada, 1926–27; *Governor of Baja
California del Norte,* 1946–47, resigned from office.
e-None. f-Administrator of the *Periodico Oficial;*
Treasurer General of Baja California del Norte,
1920–24. g-None. h-Wheat rancher, installed the
first flour mill in Mexicali Valley, founder of the
Cia. Mexicana de Malta, S.A.; founder and owner of
the Cerveceria Tecate, S.A. i-Personal friend of Pres-

ident *Miguel Aleman*. **j-**None. **k-**Anderson says he resigned because of reaction to his imposing municipal officials; declared bankruptcy, 1948; fled to Spain, 1951, after a warrant was issued for his arrest. **l-**DP70, 63; HA, 27 Dec. 1946; letter; Anderson; Aquirre, 491.

Aldrett Cuellar, Pablo

a-1903. **b-**Matehuala, San Luis Potosi, *East Central, Urban.* **c-**Early education unknown; none. **d-**Councilman for Matehuala, San Luis Potosi, 1930; Mayor of Matehuala, 1932; Local Deputy to the State Legislature of San Luis Potosi, 1939; *Federal Deputy* from the State of San Luis Potosi, Dist. 2, 1943–46; Local Deputy to the State Legislature of San Luis Potosi, 1946; *Alternate Senator* from the State of San Luis Potosi, 1946–52; *Federal Deputy* from the State of San Luis Potosi, 1952–55; *Senator* from the State of San Luis Potosi, 1958–64, member of the committees on administration, colonization, and the Agrarian Department, and also a member of the First Ejido Committee and the Second Balloting Group. **e-**Founding member of the PNR, 1929; campaigned for *Lazaro Cardenas*, 1934. **f-**None. **g-**Secretary General of the Agrarian Communities and Agrarian Unions of San Luis Potosi (twice); Secretary of Interior of the CNC. **h-**None. **i-**Parents were peasants. **k-**None. **l-**Func. 340; C de D, 1952–54; C de D, 1943–45; C de S, 1958–64, 30,33,35–36,46,49,51.

Alegria (Escamilla), Rosa Luz

b-Federal District, *Federal District, Urban.* **c-**Primary and secondary studies in Mexico City; MS in sciences, UNAM; Ph.D. in science from the National University; post-graduate studies in science, French Petroleum Institute; post-graduate studies in econometrics, Colegio de Francia and UNAM; professor of science, National School of Architecture and National School of Economics, UNAM; researcher in basic elementary and higher education; researcher for the Mexican Institute of Petroleum. **d-**None. **e-**None. **f-**Researcher for Pemex; coordinator of expression and communication section, Free Textbook Commission, primary education level; scientific adviser, National Population Council; scientific adviser, Secretariat of Public Education; member of the Executive Committee of the National Technical Council of Education; *Subsecretary of Evaluation,* Secretariat of Programming and Planning, 1976–80; *Secretary of Tourism,* 1980- . **g-**None. **i-**Former daughter-in-law of Luis Echeverria. **j-**None. **k-**None. **l-**HA, 31 Oct. 1977, 6; letter; HA, 3 Mar. 1980, 8.

Alejo, Francisco Javier

a-Dec. 30, 1941. **b-**Federal District, *Federal District, Urban.* **c-**Primary and secondary studies in Mexico City; economics degree from the National School of Economics, UNAM, 1969, with a thesis on "The Strategy of Economic Development in Mexico From 1920–1970;" advanced courses in developmental economic planning, United Nations Institute of Latin American Planning, Santiago, Chile; work towards a Ph.D. in economics, Oxford University; professor of economic development, Mexican economic policy, and lineal programming, National School of Economics, UNAM, 1962–71; full-time researcher, Colegio de Mexico, 1969–71. **d-**None. **e-**None. **f-**Economist for Nacional Financiera; economist for the National Bank of Foreign Commerce; economist for the Secretariat of Industry and Commerce; economist for the Secretariat of the Presidency; Director General of the Fondo de Cultura Economica, 1971–74; *Subsecretary of Income,* 1974–75; *Secretary of National Properties,* 1975–76; Director General of the Ciudad Sahagun Industrial Complex, 1976–78; Ambassador to Japan, 1979–. **g-**None. **i-**Student of *Horacio Flores de la Pena,* whom he replaced as Secretary of National Properties. **j-**None. **k-**Resigned as Director General of the Ciudad Sahagun Industrial Complex, June 29, 1978, after the government announced an administrative reorganization of the major industries. **l-**HA, 21 Oct. 1974, 21; HA, 13 Jan. 1975, 8; *Excelsior,* 29 June 1978, 4.

Aleman (Valdes), Miguel

a-Sept. 29, 1900. **b-**Sayula, Veracruz, *Gulf, Rural.* **c-**Not permitted to study in the Sayula schools because of father's political beliefs; primary and secondary studies in Acayucan, Coatzacoalcos, and Orizaba; preparatory studies at the National Preparatory School, Mexico, D.F., where he founded the newspaper *Eureka,* 1920–25; law degree from the National School of Law, 1925–28, with a thesis on occupational diseases and accidents among workers. **d-***Senator* from the State of Veracruz, 1934–36; *Governor of Veracruz,* 1936–39; *President of Mexico,* 1946–52. **e-**President of the Unifying Committee of Plutarco Elias Calles in Veracruz, 1933; national head of the presidential campaign for *Avila Camacho,* 1939–40. **f-**Justice of the Superior Tribunal of Justice of the Federal District, 1930–35, member of the Federal Board of Conciliation and Arbitration, 1930; legal adviser to the Secretary of Agriculture and Livestock, 1928–30; *Secretary of Government,* 1940–45; Director General of the National Tourism Commission, 1958- . **g-**None. **h-**Fluent in English; practiced law in Mexico, D.F., 1928–30, specialized in cases involving compensation for miners and railroad employees; worked as an assistant to a geologist during the summers, 1925–28. **i-**As a law student at UNAM, knew *Angel Carvajal, Manuel Sanchez Cuen, Hector Perez Martinez,*

Andres Serra Rojas, Manuel Ramirez Vazquez, Luis Garrido Diaz, Antonio Carrillo Flores, Alfonso Noriega, Antonio Dovali Jaime, and *Jose Castro Estrada;* father, Miguel Aleman, was originally a storekeeper and then a Revolutionary General, later serving as a Federal Deputy, 1927–28; he was killed in 1929 opposing the reelection of Obregon; son, Miguel Aleman, Jr., served as Director of News for Telesistema de Mexico, 1970s; married Beatriz Velasco. **j-**None. **k-**Leader of the right wing of PRI after his presidency; major investor in several industries, owns the Continental Hotel. **l-**DP70; 64–65; Covarrubias, 96; DBM68, 23–24; WWMG, 6; WWM45, 3; letters; DGF50, II, 149; DGF47; DGF51, I, 47; DP70, 64; CB, Sept. 1946, 3–5; CN Sept. 1946, 3–5; UTEHA, 421; Q es Q, 13; Wise, 58; Scott, 218.

Alonzo Sandoval, Jose Luis

a-Feb. 24, 1937. **b-**San Pedro, Coahuila, *North, Urban.* **c-**Primary studies in the Francisco Sarabia Public Rural School, El Compas, Durango; secondary studies in the Rural Normal School of Tamatan, Tamaulipas; normal certificate from the Normal School, Saltillo, Coahuila; preparatory studies at the Night Preparatory School of the State of Coahuila; law degree, National School of Law, UNAM. **d-**Federal Deputy from the Federal District, Dist. 3, 1970–73, member of the Department of the Federal District Committee, the Desert Zones Committee and the Forest Affairs Committee. **e-**Secretary of Organization of the PRI in the Federal District, 1973–75; President of the Third District Committee of PRI for the Federal District; President of PRI in the Federal District, 1979- . **f-**Auxiliary Secretary to the Secretary General of Olympic Games Organizing Committee; Private Secretary to the Director General of Higher Education, Secretariat of Public Education. **g-**Secretary of Organization of the CEN of CNOP, 1972–73; President of the Society of Students of the School of Law, UNAM, 1962. **h-**None. **i-**Married Maria Elena Valencia Chavez. **j-**None. **k-**Opposed *Jesus Reyes Heroles* and *Agustin Alanis Fuentes* for Dean of the Law School as a student leader, 1961; expelled from the National University, 1962. **l-***Excelsior,* 10 Feb. 1979, 14; *Directorio, 1970–72;* C de D, 1970–73, 100.

Altamirano, Manlio Fabio

(Deceased Jan. 25, 1936)
a-Oct. 12, 1892. **b-**Jalapa, Veracruz, *Gulf, Urban.* **c-**Primary studies in Misantla, Veracruz; preparatory studies at the National Preparatory School, law degree from the National Law School, UNAM. **d-**Federal Deputy from the State of Veracruz (five times), 1916–25; *Senator* from Veracruz, 1934–35; *Governor-elect* of Veracruz, 1936. **e-**Member of the

Obregonista Party; signer of the Declaration by General Calles setting forth the formation of the National Revolutionary Party, December 1, 1928. **f-**Director of Talleres Graficos de la Nacion; Gerente of the government daily newspaper *El Nacional.* **g-**Member of the radical groups supporting the Casa del Obrero Mundial. **j-**None. **k-**Assassinated as Governor-elect before he could take office, an event which opened up the governorship to *Miguel Aleman,* launching his national career. **l-**DP70, 78; Peral, 43; Gruening, 480; Gaxiola, 303, 23; Enc. Mex. I, 168; Gonzalez Navarro, 128–19; Q es Q, 17–18; Lopez, 45.

Altamirano Herrera, Rafael

(Deceased)
a-July 25, 1908. **b-**Queretaro, Queretaro, *East Central, Urban.* **c-**Primary studies in Queretaro, Queretaro; secondary studies in Mexico City; preparatory studies in Mexico City; law degree from the National School of Law, UNAM, 1932, with a specialization in penal law; professor by opposition of Roman Law, National School of Law, UNAM, 1944–53. **d-***Senator* from the State of Queretaro, 1958–. **e-**None. **f-**Penal Judge in Aguascalientes, Aguascalientes, 1932–34; Judge of Civil and Treasury Matters, Aguascalientes, 1934–35; Juvenile court judge, 1935–41; Judge of the Eleventh Civil Judicial District, 1941; Auxiliary Secretary to the 5th Division of the Superior Tribunal of Justice of the Federal District; Justice of the Superior Tribunal of Justice of Queretaro; Private Secretary to the Director General of Pensions, 1953. **g-**None. **j-**None. **k-**None. **l-**Func., 330; C de S, 1958–64, 10.

Alvarado, Jose

(Deceased Sept. 23, 1974)
a-Sept. 21, 1911. **b-**Lampazos, Nuevo Leon, *North, Rural.* **c-**Secondary studies in Monterrey; preparatory studies at the Colegio Civil, Monterrey; completed studies in law, National School of Law, UNAM, but never completed his thesis for a degree; professor of literature and philosophy, National Preparatory School; professor at the University of Nuevo Leon; Rector of the University of Nuevo Leon, 1961–63. **d-**Candidate for Federal Deputy from the Popular Party, 1952. **e-**Supporter of Jose Vasconcelos for president, 1929; member of the CEN of the Popular Party, 1948. **f-**None. **g-**Secretary of the National Student Federation, 1933. **h-**Writer for *Barandal;* collaborator with the Spanish exiles on *Romance* and *Futuro;* wrote for *El Popular* in the 1940s; journalist for *El Nacional* until 1948; wrote for *Combate* and since the 1950s until 1974, was a writer for *Excelsior.* **i-**Friend of *Eduardo Livas* since primary school days, recommended him for rector as Governor of Nuevo Leon; friend of *Alejandro Gomez Arias* since 1929 in Monterrey; companion of *Enrique*

Ramirez y Ramirez as a writer for *Claridad,* 1930; his father was a professor and secretary of the University of Nuevo Leon; married Candida Perez. **j-**None. **k-**Resigned from the rectorship of the University of Nuevo Leon after being attacked as a communist by certain interest groups. **l-***Excelsior,* 26 Sept. 1974; *Excelsior,* 24 Sept. 1974; HA, 7 Oct. 1974; letter.

Alvarado (Alvarado), Silverio Ricardo

a-Feb. 7, 1917. **b-**Ozuloama, Veracruz, *Gulf, Rural.* **c-**Primary studies in Veracruz; completed rural normal certificate; no degree. **d-***Alternate Federal Deputy* from the State of Veracruz, Dist. 2, 1943–46, under *Rafael Murillo Vidal;* member of the City Council of Tuxpan, Veracruz, 1943–46; Local Deputy to the State Legislature of Veracruz, 1950–53; Local Deputy to the State Legislature of Veracruz, 1962–65; *Federal Deputy* from the State of Veracruz, Dist. 2, 1967–70; *Federal Deputy* from the State of Veracruz, Dist. 1, 1973–76; *Senator* from the State of Veracruz, 1976–82. **e-**President of the PRM in Tuxpan, Veracruz, 1940. **f-**None. **g-**Secretary of Organization of the Federation of Workers and Peasants of Northern Veracruz, 1941; Secretary of Organization of the Only Union of Workers of Veracruz, 1947; Secretary General of the Only Union of Workers of Veracruz, 1950; Secretary of Organization of the Revolutionary Federation of Workers and Peasants (CROC) of Veracruz, 1952–55; Secretary General of CROC in the State of Veracruz, 1958–61, 1964–67; Secretary of Technical and Economic Affairs of CROC, 1968–70; President of CROC, 1970–71. **h-**None. **i-**Married Celestina Roldan Casados. **j-**None. **k-**None. **l-**C de D, 1943–46; C de D, 1967–70; C de D, 1973–76; C de S, 1976–82.

Alvarado Aramburo, Alberto

a-Feb. 4, 1925. **b-**La Paz, Baja California del Sur, *West, Urban.* **c-**Primary and secondary studies in Baja California del Sur; preparatory studies in biological sciences, National Preparatory School; completed two years of medical studies, National School of Medicine, UNAM. **d-***Alternate Federal Deputy* from the State of Baja California del Sur, Dist. 1, 1961–64, under *Antonio Navarro Encinas; Federal Deputy* from the State of Baja California del Sur, Dist. 1, 1964–67; *Senator* from Baja California del Sur, 1976– . **e-***Secretary of Organization of the CEN of PRI,* 1976. **f-**Director of the Office of the Federal Electric Commission in Baja California del Sur; Director of the Office of Population, State of Baja California del Sur; Director of Property Control, State of Baja California del Sur; Delegate of the City of La Paz, 1954–56. **g-**None. **h-**None. **j-**None. **k-**None. **l-**C de D, 1961–64, 6; C de D, 1964–67, 45; PS.

Alvarado Gonzalez, Agustin

a-June 2, 1912. **b-**Martinez de la Torre, Veracruz, *Gulf, Rural.* **c-**Primary studies at the Benito Juarez School; no secondary or college studies. **d-**Local Deputy, State Legislature of Veracruz; *Alternate Federal Deputy,* State of Veracruz, Dist. 4, 1952–55; *Federal Deputy,* State of Veracruz, Dist. 5, 1970–73, member of the Committees on National Lands, Agricultural Development, and the Ejido (Third Accounts). **e-**None. **f-**Director of the Department of Indigenous Affairs, Director of Agriculture, State of Veracruz. **g-**Secretary General of the League of Agrarian Communities of the State of Veracruz. **h-**None. **j-**None. **k-**None. **l-**C de D, 1952–54; *Directorio,* C de D, 1970–72, 100.

Alvarez, Luis Hector

a-Oct. 25, 1919. **b-**Camargo, Chihuahua, *North, Rural.* **c-**Primary studies in Camargo; secondary studies in Ciudad Juarez and at El Paso High School, El Paso, Texas; studied at University of Texas; engineering degree from the Massachusetts Institute of Technology; Master of Science degree. **d-**None. **e-**Candidate for Governor of Chihuahua, National Action Party, 1956; joined PAN about 1953; member of the CEN of PAN; presidential candidate of PAN, 1958. **f-**None. **g-**None. **h-**Involved in agricultural enterprises, 1942–46; textile manufacturer in Chihuahua, 1946–57; Director General of the Compania Industrial Rio Bravo, 1957; President of the Educational Center for Ciudad Juarez. **j-**None. **k-**None. **l-**Scott, 184, 240; HAR, 12 Dec. 1957, 645–46; HA, 2 Dec. 1957; Morton, 105–06; Johnson, 33; Mabry, 155, 215, 55.

Alvarez Acosta, Miguel

a-Sept. 29, 1907. **b-**San Luis Potosi, San Luis Potosi, *East Central, Urban.* **c-**Primary studies in San Luis Potosi, teaching certificate, Normal School of San Luis Potosi, 1925; law degree, University of San Luis Potosi, 1931; Professor of Sociology, Civics, History, and Political Economy, Normal School of San Luis Potosi; Director of Primary School, San Luis Potosi; Director of the Superior School of Xilitla. **d-**None. **e-**None. **f-**Technical adviser to the Secretariat of Foreign Relations; Consul to the United States and to Central America; Career Consul, 1939; Agent of the Ministerio Publico of the Office of the Attorney General; Judge of the First Instance, Matehuala, San Luis Potosi; Magistrate of the Superior Tribunal of Justice of the State of San Luis Potosi; Substitute Governor of San Luis Potosi, 1938; representative to the Food and Agriculture Organization; Judge of the Federal Tax Court, 1942–54; Director General of the National Institute of Bellas Artes, July 29, 1954–58; Director General of Organizations for the International Promotion of Culture; rank of ambassador in the Mexican Foreign Service; *Subsecretary of Broadcasting; Secretariat of Communications and Transportation,* 1972–76. **g-**Secretary General of the National Teachers Union, 1958. **h-**Author of many novels and articles; legal adviser to the National Mixed Agrarian Commission. **j-**None. **k-**None. **l-**DEM,. 15; HA, 23 Oct. 1972, 18; HA, 9 Aug. 1954, 5; MGF69, 179.

Alvarez Amezquita (Chimalpopoca), Jose

a-Aug. 4, 1911. **b-**Federal District, *Federal District, Urban.* **c-**Primary and secondary studies at the Colegio Frances de Morelos; preparatory studies at the National Preparatory School (evening sessions) in Mexico, D.F.; medical degree, National School of Medicine, UNAM, 1935; Professor of Medicine and of specialized courses, National School of Medicine, UNAM, 1938–58. **d-**None. **e-**None. **f-**Chief of Surgical Services, Juarez Hospital, Mexico, D.F., 1948; Director General of Medical Services, Secretariat of Labor, 1956–58; *Secretary of Health and Public Welfare,* 1958–64. **g-**President of the National Association of Surgeons, 1952. **h-**Intern, Juarez Hospital, Mexico, D.F., 1933–34, 1935–39; Director General of Medical Assistance, Secretariat of Health and Public Welfare, 1949–52; founder of the Mexican Hospital Society. **i-**Attended secondary school with *Adolfo Lopez Mateos;* son of a doctor. **j-**None. **k-**None. **i-**HA, 9 Nov. 1964, 15–16; WWMG, 6; IWW66, HA, 8 Dec. 19558, 28; DBM68, 28–29; DGF51, 340; *Quien Sera,* 128; Func, 183; WWW70–71, 24.

Alvarez Borboa, Teofilo

(Deceased 1962)
a-Jann. 8, 1891. **b-**Villa de Higueras de los Monzones, Badirahuato, Sinaloa, *West, Rural.* **c-**Primary studies in Villa de Higueras; secondary studies in the Federal District; teaching certificate from the Normal School, 1910. **d-***Senator* from the State of Sinaloa, 1958–64, President of the Committee on Military Justice; member of the Second Naval Committee. **e-**None. **f-**Oficial Mayor of Government under *Juan de Dios Bojorquez,* 1934–35. **g-**None. **h-**None. **i-**School companion with *Jose Angel Ceniceros.* **j-**Joined the Revolution under General Obregon, April 9, 1914, with the rank of 2nd Lieutenant; Commander of the 51st Battalion, 1925–26; Commander of the 42nd Battalion; Director of Justice for the 1st Military Zone; Brigade General, November, 1934; Supreme Chief of the Military Tribunal; Director of Infantry, Secretary of National Defense; Commander of the 7th Military Zone, Sonora and Sinaloa, 1951–57; rank of Divisionary General, 1958. **k-**None. **l-**Func, 350; C de S, 1961–64, 51; DGF56, 201; DGF51, 103; DP70, 88–89.

Alvarez del Castillo (Labastida), Enrique

b-Guadalajara, Jasisco, *West, Urban.* **c-**Early education unknown; law degree from the National School of Law, UNAM, 1947; LLD from the National School of Law, UNAM; Professor of Labor Law, National School of Law, UNAM. **d-***Federal Deputy* from the State of Jalisco, Dist. 25, 1976–79, member of the Section on Higher Education of the Educational Development Committee, the Section on Amparo of the Legislative Studies Committee, the Third Labor Committee and the Public Budget Committee. **e-***Subsecretary General of the CEN of PRI,* 1978. **f-**Department head, Division of Labor Relations, IMSS; *Secretary General of the Mexican Institute of Social Security,* 1965–66; Oficial Mayor of the Organizing Committee for the Olympic Games. **g-**None. **h-**Author of many articles and books on labor law. **i-**Married Virginia Baeza. **j-**None. **k-**None. **l-**DBM68, 29–30; D de C, 1976–79, 21,53,78; C de D, 1976–79.

Alvarez Guerrero, Alejandro

a-Dec. 24, 1925. **b-**Federal District, *Federal District, Urban.* **c-**Chemical engineering degree, National School of Chemical Sciences, UNAM. **d-**None. **e-**None. **f-**Subgerente of CONDUMEX, 1953; Director General of CONDUMEX, 1970–72. **g-**President of CONCAMIN, 1972–73. **h-**Vice President and President of the Board for fourteen private companies; President of the Mexican Institute of Chemical Engineers; author of two books. **j-**None. **k-**Responsible for the Secretary of Industry and Commerce's creation of a Department of Rural Industrialization; founder of the Association of Electrical Engineers. **l-**HA, 2 Aug. 1971, 18.

Alvarez Lopez, Manuel

(Deceased June 27, 1960)
a-Sept. 15, 1885. **b-**Colima, Colima, *West, Urban.* **c-**Primary and secondary studies at the Seminario Conciliar of Colima; no degree. **d-***Federal Senator* from the State of San Luis Potosi, 1946–52, member of the Health Committee and alternate member of the Second Ejido Committee; *Governor* of San Luis Potosi, 1955–59. **e-**None. **f-**Consul General in Buenos Aires; Consul General in Brasil. **g-**None. **h-**Industrialist. **i-**Part of *Gonzalo N. Santos* clique. **j-**Joined the Revolution, 1911, supported Francisco Madero. **k-**Anderson reports that he was forced out of the governorship of San Luis Potosi in January, 1959, because of close ties with *Gonzalo Santos* and his attempts to control state politics. **l-**DGF56, 99; NYT, 26 Oct. 1958, 19; HA, 3 Oct. 1955, 20–21; Anderson; DGF51, 7, 11, 14; PS.

Alvarez Nolasco, Ernesto

a-Mar. 20, 1920. **b-**Ahome, Sinaloa, *West, Rural.*

c-Completed primary, secondary and preparatory studies; no degree. d-*Federal Deputy* from the State of Sinaloa, Dist. 1, 1961–64, member of the Waters and National Irrigation Committee and the National Properties Committee; *Federal Deputy* from the State of Sinaloa, Dist. 4, 1967–70. e-*Subsecretary of Press and Publicity of the CEN of PRI,* 1974–76. f-Director of the Federal Treasury Office, Los Mochis, Sinaloa; Director General of Information, Secretariat of the Government, 1976–79; Director General of Public Relations for the President of Mexico, June 6, 1979–. g-Secretary General of CNOP for Sinaloa. h-Journalist. i-Married Felisa Valdes. j-None. k-None. l-C de D, 1961–64; 70; C de D, 1967–70; PS.

Alvarez Ponce de Leon, Griselda

a-Apr. 5, 1913. b-Guadalajara, Jalisco, *West, Urban.* c-Normal teaching certificate; advanced studies at the Specialization Normal School, Secretariat of Public Education; degree in Spanish letters, UNAM; professor at the Specialization Normal School, 1951; primary school teacher. d-*Senator* from Chiapas, 1976–79; *Governor* of Chiapas, 1979–. e-None. f-Director of the Division of Social Action, Secretariat of Public Education, 1961–64; Subdirector of the Division of Social Action, 1959–61; Director of the Division of Social Work, Secretariat of Health; Head of the Department of Social Work and Inspection, INDECO; Chief of Archives, Secretariat of Health; Director of Social Welfare Services, IMSS, 1976. g-None. h-Author and poet. i-Daughter of Miguel Alvarez Garcia, governor of Colima; great-grand daughter of Manuel Alvarez, the first governor of Colima; niece of Higinio Alvarez, senator, deputy and acting governor of Colima. j-None. k-First woman governor in Mexican history. l-HA, 10 May 1976, 12–13; DPE61, 103; Latin America, 26 Jan. 1979, 20; *Excelsior,* 7 Jan. 1979, 12; Enc. Mex., I, 1977, 163.

Alzalde Arellano, Ricardo

a-Apr. 3, 1907. b-Torreon, Coahuila, *North, Urban.* c-Early education unknown; no degree. d-*Federal Deputy* from the State of Baja California del Norte, 1949–52, Dist. 1, member of the Library Committee, the Hunting and Fishing Committee, the Second Ejido Committee, the Social Welfare Committee and the Gran Comision; *Federal Deputy* from the State of Baja California del Norte, 1958–61 Dist. 1, member of the Hunting and Fishing Committee, the National Lands Committee and the Budget and Accounts Committee. e-None. f-Director of Agrarian Affairs, Baja California del Norte, 1965. g-Peasant leader in Baja California del Norte, 1937; Secretary General of the League of Agrarian Communities of Baja California del Norte, 1948–49. h-Ejidatario.

j-None. k-Moved to Baja California del Norte in 1937 as a peasant. l-DGF51, 19,29,30,31,32,35; C de D, 1958–61, 69; C de D, 1949–52, 6, 63; Aguirre, 492; Func., 124.

Amaro, Joaquin
(Deceased 1952)
a-Aug. 16, 1889. bb-Corrales de Abrego, Sombrerete, Zacatecas, *East Central, Rural.* c-Early education unknown; no degree. d-None. e-None. f-Subsecretary of the Secretariat of National Defense, 1924; Secretary of National Defense, December 30, 1924 to November 30, 1928; Secretary of National Defense, November 30, 1928 to March 2, 1929; Secretary of National Defense, May 20, 1930 to October 15, 1931; Director of the National Military College, 1931–35; Director of Military Education, 1935–36. g-None. h-None. i-Married Elisa Izaguirre. j-Joined the Revolution in 1910, serving under Gertrudis Sanchez; fought against the forces of Bernardo Reyes, 1911; fought against the forces of Emiliano Zapata, 1913; participated in the battle of Celaya, 1915; joined Plutarco Calles and Alvaro Obregon in support of the Plan of Agua Prieta against Venustiano Carranza, 1919; rank of divisionary general, 1920; Commander of the 5th Division of the North, 1920; fought against the forces of Adolfo de la Huerta in the Bajio region, 1923; Director of the military prison camps, 1924; commander of the military zones of Chihuahua, Durango, Nuevo Leon, Coahuila and San Luis Potosi; commander of the 28th Military Zone, Oaxaca, Oaxaca, 1947. k-Precandidate for president of Mexico, 1939. l-Libro de Oro, 1935–36, 21; Enc. Mex., I, 1977, 277–78; DP70, 94–95; Lopez, 52; NYT, 18 Feb. 1940, 23; WWM45, 4.

Amaya Brondo, Abelardo

a-Apr. 19, 1918. b-Ciudad Juarez, Chihuahua, *North, Urban.* c-Agricultural engineering degree, National School of Agriculture, 1941. d-None. e-None. f-Gerente General of Hydraulic Resources in the State of Nuevo Leon, 1959–61; Subdirector General of Irrigation Districts of the Secretariat of Hydraulic Resources, 1961–64; Director General of Irrigation Districts of the Secretariat of Hydraulic Resources, 1964–70; *Subsecretary B of Hydraulic Resources,* 1970–76. g-None. i-Brother Mario was director of public works in Baja California del Norte for many years; married Alicia Enderle. j-None. k-None. l-D de Y, 2 Dec. 1970; DGF69, 302; DPE65, 130; HA, 14 Dec. 1970, 22; BCN, 492.

Amilpa (y Rivera), Fernando
(Deceased 1952)
a-May 30, 1898. b-Jojutla de Juarez, Morelos, *West Central, Rural.* c-Primary and secondary studies in

public schools in Morelos; no degree. **d-***Federal Deputy* from the State of Morelos, Dist. 6, 1937–40; Vice President of the Gran Comision, 1939; Secretary of the Gran Comision, September, 1937. *Senator* from Morelos, 1940–46; *Federal Deputy* from the Federal District, Dist. 8, 1946–49, member of the Committee on Labor, the Committee on General Communication Lines; President of the Chamber of Deputies, November, 1948. **e-**None. **f-**None. **g-**Member of the Confederation of Mexican Workers; worked with labor movement under General Obregon; represented the labor unions when the government established the first Board of Conciliation and Arbitration; member of the Secretariat of the Union of Bus Drivers of the Federal District; labor representative on the municipal council of the Federal District; member of the Secretariat of the Transportation Union Workers of the Department of Transportation of the Federal District; Secretary General of the General Federation of Workers and Peasants, 1935–36; *Secretary General of the Confederation of Mexican Workers*, 1946–50. **h-**None. **i-**Three of his daughters became active as leaders in the CTM; helped *Vicente Lombardo Toledano* and *Fidel Velazquez* organize the CTM. **j-**Fought with Emiliano Zapata in Morelos, 1915. **k-**None, **l-**EBW46, 48; DP70, 100; Novo35, 130; C de D, 1946–49, 64; *Excelsior*, 31 Mar. 1947; WB48, 167; Gonzalez Navarro, 141.

Amoros (Guiot), Roberto

(Deceased Aug. 14, 1973)
a-June 8, 1914. **b-**Coatepec, Veracruz, *Gulf, Rural*. **c-**Primary studies in Jalapa; secondary studies in Veracruz; law degree, National School of Law, UNAM, April 17, 1935; fellowship in economics, University of Rome. **d-***Senator* from Veracruz, 1952. **e-**Active in *Avila Camacho's* presidential campaign, 1940; Director of the Office of Policy Coordination and Technical Affairs, *Ruiz Cortines'* campaign, 1952. **f-**Oficial Mayor of the Presidency, June 9, 1943, to July, 1946; *Secretary of the Presidency*, July, 1946, to November 30, 1946; *Oficial Mayor of the Presidency*, December 1, 1946, to January 1, 1948; *Subsecretary of the Presidency*, January 1, 1948, to November 13, 1951; *Director General of the National Railroads of Mexico*, 1952–58; *Director General of CONASUPO*, 1958–64; Auxiliary Secretary to the President of Mexico, 1964–70. **g-**Secretary General of the National Union of Educational Workers, 1939. **h-**Director of the Department of Conventions, Secretariat of Labor, 1940; President of the Board of Directors of PIPSA; legal consultant to the Secretariat of the Presidency; Director of Editoral Ruto; President of the National Council of Sugar, Secretariat of Labor; government representative to the National Printing Office, 1970–73;

author of several books on law and articles on decentralized government agencies. **i-**Collaborated professionally with *Benjamin Mendez Aguilar* and *Carlos Hank Gonzalez*; married Karin Riekfol. **j-**None. **k-**None. **l-***Hoy*, 2999 Apr. 1967, 60; DGF56, 8; DGF47; D del S, 5 Dec. 1946, l; DGF50, II, 189, 355, 361; DGF51, I, 55; II. 510; Enc. Mex. I, 390; Func. 107; *Quien Sera*, 152; HA, 2 July 1956, 42; Novo, 657; *Excelsior*, 15 Aug. 1973, 2B; HA, 20 Aug. 1973.

Anderson Nevarez, Hilda

a-Oct. 10, 1938. **b-**Mazatlan, Sinaloa, *West, Urban*. **c-**Primary studies at the Escuela Josefa Ortiz de Dominguez, Mazatlan; secondary studies at the Secondary School No. 4, Federal District; Teacher's Normal School (2 years); female literacy course, International Labor Organization, Geneva, Switzerland; studied at St. John's College, Maryland; intensive course on female labor, Ebert Foundation; Bonn, Germany. **d-***Federal Deputy* from the Federal District, Dist. 13, 1964–67, Secretary, 1965; member of the Social Action Committee, the Radio Industry Committee, and the Mexican-United States InterParliamentary Congress; *Federal Deputy* from the Federal District, Dist. 19, 1970–73, member of the Department of the Federal District Committee, and the Foreign Relations Committee; *Senator* from Sinaloa, 1976–, president of the Chamber, December, 1976. **e-***Secretary of Feminine Action of the CEN of PRI*, 1972. **f-**None. **g-**President of the Women's Subcommittee for the Labor Congress; Secretary General of the Workers Federation of Women's Organizations of the Mexican Revolution of the CTM; Secretary of the Institute of Worker's Education, CTM; Secretary of Relations for the Radio Industry Workers Union. **h-**None. **i-**Father an engineer; mother a school teacher. **j-**None. **k-**None. **l-***Directorio*, 70–72; C de D, 1964–66, 77, 87; C de D, 1970–722, 100; HA, 20 Dec. 1976, 43.

Andrade de (del Rosal), Marta

b-Hidalgo, *East Central*. **c-**Secondary studies at the Rural Normal School in Actopan, Hidalgo; education studies at the National School of Teachers in Mexico, D.F.; studies in social science at the Superior Normal School in Mexico, D.F.; teaching certificate for secondary schools; studied social policy at Claremont College, California, 1941; rural school teacher at age 12 in Actopan, Hidalgo; teacher of civics, Spanish literature, history, and other subjects in the secondary schools of the Federal District. **d-***Federal Deputy* from the Federal District, Dist. 6, member of the Social Welfare Committee (1st year), member of the Second Government Committee, 1958-61; *Federal Deputy* from the Federal District, Dist. 12,

1964-67, member of the Committee on the Diplomatic and Consular Service, the Second Public Education Committee, and the Library Committee (1st year); *Federal Deputy* from the Federal District, Dist. 21, 1976-79, member of the Social Action Committee, the Middle Education Section of Educational Development, Development of Tourism Committee, Housing Development Committee, Federal District Committee. e-Member of the Confederation of Mexican Youth, Mexican Revolutionary Party, 1937; head of Policy Inspection for the Confederation of Mexican Youth; member of the National Directive Committee for *Avila Camacho,* 1934-40; head of the Department of Feminine Action of the Youth Activities Section, 1939; organized the first Women's Committee, 1939; Secretary of the Organization of the Mexican Revolutionary Party, 1939; organized the National Women's Committee in favor of *Ruiz Cortines* for President, 1951; Secretary of the National Women's Committee of Political Action of the National Executive Committee of PRI, 1952; Secretary of the Organization of the Women's Council of the Executive Regional Committee of the Federal District, 1952; Director of Women's Action of the Regional Committee of PRI in the Federal District, 1953; official orator of PRI, 1953; official orator in the *Diaz Ordaz* campaign, 1964; state delegate of PRI to Mexico, Veracruz, Hidalgo, and the Federal District; member of the National Women's Council of the CNOP of PRI; Oficial Mayor of PRI in the Federal District, 1976. f-Head of the Nursery Department, Secretariat of Public Education, 1946-47. g-Organized the first nursery for the children of employees of the Secretariat of Public Education in the Federal District. h-Author of articles on women in Mexico. j-None. k-Members of the feminine sector of PRI opposed her candidacy in 1957-58 as a federal deputy from the Federal District because of her campaign trip through the state of Puebla which caused considerable dissension; candidate for Federal Deputy from the ninth district of the Federal District, 1955. l-C de D, 1958-60; C de D, 1964-66; DBM68, 188-90; DGF 47, 171; Morton, 87, 100-01, 107-08; Func., 181; D de C, 1976-79, 4, 20, 41, 44, 47.

Andrade Ibarra, Jose Luis

a-May 27, 1939. b-Amatlan, Jalisco, *West, Rural.* c-Primary studies begun at the age of eight and completed at age fourteen; secondary studies in La Paz, Baja California del Sur and in Mexicali; normal certificate, Mexicali; special studies in civics and pedagogy, Superior Normal School of Jalisco; three years of studies in mathematics; secondary school teacher, Mexicali. d-None. e-None. f-None. g-Secretary of Labor and Conflicts, Section 37 of the SNTE, Mexicali; Secretary General of various sec-

tions of the SNTE; Secretary General of Section 37 of the SNTE; Secretary General of the SNTE, 1977-80; President of the Congress of Labor, 1980. h-As a child worked in the fields. j-None. k-None. l-HA, 3 Apr. 1978, 8; *Excelsior,* 3 Feb. 1980, 6.

Andreu Almazan, Juan
(Deceased Oct. 9, 1965)
a-May 12, 1891. cb-Olinala, Guerrero, *South, Rural.* c-Primary studies in Olinala; preparatory studies at the Colegio del Estado de Puebla, 1903-08; medical studies, Colegio del Estado de Puebla, 1908-10, no degree. d-None. e-None. f-Secretary of Communications and Public Works, 1930-32. g-None. h-Director of the Anahuac Construction Company. i-Parents were wealthy landowners; friend of Revolutionary precursor, Aquiles Serdan; brother of *Leonides Andreu Almazan.* j-Joined the Revolution in 1910 under Madero; fought under Emiliano Zapata, 1911; rank of brigadier general, May 3, 1911; joined General Huerta, 1913; opposed Madero, 1912-13; fought against Romulo Figueroa; opposed Carranza, 1915-20; one of the youngest Revolutionary generals; joined Obregon, 1920; rank of Divisionary General, January 1, 1921; Commander of the 5th Military Zone, Monterrey, Nuevo Leon, 1924-34; appointed Chief of Staff to Carranza, but never served in that position; commander of a military column against General Escobar, 1929; Commander of the 6th Military Zone, Torreon, Coahuila; fought against De la Huerta, 1923. k-Went into exile after General Huerta was defeated; resigned from the Army in 1939 to become a presidential candidate of the Revolutionary Party of National Unification; after defeat went into exile in Panama, Cuba, and the United States, 1940-47, but later returned to Mexico; Brandenburg considers him in the Inner Circle from 1935-40; was one of the wealthiest men in Mexico. l-DP70, 107; Kirk, 233ff; Enc. Mex. I, 407; Brandenburg, 80; CB, 27 July 1940, 14-16; NYT, 1 Aug. 1938; CH, Apr. 1940, 36; Michaels, 25-30; WB54, 136; Daniels, 80-81; Peral, 55; Bermudez, 141; NYT, 11 Oct. 1965, 39.

Andreu Almazan, Leonides
(Deceased Jan. 18, 1963)
a-Aug. 8, 1896. b-Olinala, Guerrero, *South, Rural.* c-Preparatory studies in Puebla; medical degree from the National School of Medicine, UNAM, 1923; hygienist at the University of Paris; Professor of Medicine at the Military Medical School. d-Governor of Puebla, 1929-33, resigned shortly before completion of term. e-None. f-Ambassador to Great Britain, 1935; Minister to Germany, October 27, 1935, to 1938; *Head of the Department of Health,* 1938-39. g-None. h-Chief of the Clinic of the Necker Institute in Mexico, D.F.; Chief of

Urological Services of the Military Hospital in Mexico, D.F.; Chief of the Pharmacy Department of the Mexican Institute of Social Security; advisor to the Mexican Institute of Social Security. **i-**Brother of *Juan Andreu Almazan*, resigned as Head of the Health Department to direct brother's campaign for president, 1939; related to *Miguel Andreu Almazan*, Federal Deputy from Guerrero, Dist. 4, 1937–39. **j-**Fought with Emiliano Zapata during the Revolution. **l-**Peral, 55; D del S, 17 Jan. 1938; DP70, 106–07.

Anguiano (Equihua), Victoriano
(Deceased, 1958)
a-1908. **b-**Michoacan, *West Central*. **c-**Early education unknown; law degree, University of Michoacan; professor of law, University of Michoacan; Rector, University of Michoacan, 1940; professor of law and history, UNAM. **d-**Federal Deputy from the State of Michoacan, Dist. 7, 1935–37; *Federal Deputy* from the State of Michoacan, Dist. 5, 1946–49, member of the Immigration Committee and the Library Committee. **e-**Supporter of Jose Vasconcelos, 1929; Secretary General of the National Independent Democratic Party, 1946, which supported *Ezequiel Padilla* for president of Mexico; Assistant Secretary General of the Popular Party, 1947; Secretary General of the Popular Party, 1948–49; Member of the National Coordinating Committee of the Popular Party, 1947. **f-**Agent of the Ministerio Publico of the Attorney General's Office; Secretary General of Government of the State of Michoacan; Justice of the Superior Tribunal of Justice of the State of Michoacan, 1951–58. **g-**None. **i-**Mother a Tarascan Indian. **j-**None. **k-**Resigned as Secretary General of the Popular Party after he was criticized for his denunciation of *Lazaro Cardenas* as a cacique in Michoacan; political enemy of *Lazaro Cardenas*. **l-***Excelsior*, 14 Nov. 1949; Villasenor, II, 120; DGF47, 9; C de D, 1946–49; Enc. Mex., 1977, I, 309–10.

Angulo, Mauro
(Deceased 1948)
a-1894. **b-**Santa Ana Chiautempan, Tlaxcala, *East Central, Rural*. **c-**Law degree from the Colegio del Estado de Puebla, 1915. **d-**Local deputy to the State Legislature of Tlaxcala (twice); Federal Deputy from the State of Tlaxcala, Dist. 3, 1920–22; Federal Deputy from the State of Tlaxcala, Dist. 1, 1928–30; Provisional Governor of Tlaxcala, 1933; *Senator* from Tlaxcala, 1934–40; *Federal Deputy* from the State of Tlaxcala, Dist. 1, 1943–44; *Interim Governor of Tlaxcala,* 1944–45; *Senator* from Tlaxcala, Tlaxcala, 1946–48. **f-**Legal adviser to the State of Tlaxcala, 1920; Attorney General of Justice of the State of Puebla; Secretary General of Government of

the State of San Luis Potosi. **g-**None. **h-**None. **j-**None. **k-**Assassinated in Mexico, D.F. in 1948. **l-**DP70, 111; letter; Peral, 56; DGF47, 22.

Angulo, Melquiades
(Deceased 1966)
a-July 26, 1889. **b-**Hacienda de San Jose de Porras, Municipio de Allende, Chihuahua, *North, Rural*. **c-**Degree in engineering from the College of Mining, 1917. **d-**None. **e-**None. **f-**Oficial Mayor and Secretary of Government of the State of Chihuahua, 1918–20; Provisional Governor of Chihuahua, 1919–20; *Subsecretary of Public Works*, 1938–39; *Secretary of Public Works, 1939–40*; Chief of the Department of Railroads of the Secretariat of Public Works, 1934–38. **g-**None. **h-**Employed for many years by the Secretariat of Public Works; became a rancher in Jalisco, 1940. **j-**None. **k-**Participated in the planning at the Convention of Queretaro 1916–17. **l-**DP70, 111; D de Y, 6 Apr. 1938, 1.

Apodaca Osuna, Francisco
a-Apr. 2, 1910. **b-**Rosario, Sinaloa, *West, Rural*. **c-**Law degree, National School of Law, UNAM, 1940–45; advanced studies in law, University of Paris, 1947–48; advanced studies in economics, London School of Economics, 1950–53; Professor of Law at the National Law School, UNAM, 1946–47. **d-**None. **e-**None. **f-**Subdirector General of Credit, Secretariat of the Treasury, 1954–58; scientific investigator for the Department of Credit, Secretariat of the Treasury, 1957–58; executive adviser to the council on foreign commerce attached to the Secretariat of Foreign Relations; head of the council 1961–64; *Ambassador to France*, 1965–70, **g-**None. **h-**First job as a lawyer for the Secretariat of the Treasury, 1945; scientific investigator for the Secretariat of the Treasury, 1946; Subdirector General for the Secretariat of National Patrimony, 1947; subdelegate to Europe for the Secretariat of National Patrimony, 1948; investigator for the Institute of Comparative Law, 1949; scientific investigator for the Secretariat of the Treasury, 1950. **i-**Married Beatriz Najera. **j-**None. **k-**None. **l-**DGF56, 163; BdM, 60–61; DPE61, 19; MGF69, 181.

Aragon Rebolledo, Eliseo
a-1917. **b-**Morelos, *West Central*. **c-**Primary studies in Morelos; secondary and preparatory studies in Mexico City; law degree from the National School of Law, UNAM. **d-**City councilman; Local Deputy to the 36th State Legislature of Morelos; *Federal Deputy* from the State of Morelos, Dist. 2, 1943–46; *Senator* from the State of Morelos, 1958–64, President of the Special Tourist Affairs and the Special Legislative Studies Committees; member of the Gran Comision; and the Protocol, Migration, Rules and First Foreign Relations Committees.

e-Founding member of the PNR, PRM and the PRI. f-Appeals court judge. g-None. j-None. k-None. l-Func., 280; C de S, 1958–64, 9, 51.

Aranda del Toro, Luis

a-1901. b-Tepic, Nayarit, *West, Urban.* c-Secondary and Preparatory Studies at the University of Guadalajara; medical degree, School of Medicine, University of Guadalajara. d-*Federal Deputy* from the State of Nayarit, Dist. 1, 1937–40; *Senator* from the State of Nayarit, 1940–46, President of the Economy and Statistics Committee, First Secretary of the Colonization Committee and Prosecretary of the Senate, 1946. e-None. f-Chief of Medical Services, Department of Pensions. g-None. h-Practicing physician. i-His friendship with *Miguel Aleman* launched his public career in 1937. j-None. k-None. l-C de S, 1940–46; Libro de Oro, 1946, 5; PS; C de D, 1937–40.

Aranda Osorio, Efrain

a-Nov. 17, 1905. b-Motozintla de Mendoza, Chiapas, *South, Rural.* c-Primary studies in Motozintla; secondary in Mexico City; preparatory studies at the National Preparatory School, Mexico, D.F.; law degree, National School of Law, UNAM, 1932. d-*Federal Deputy* from the State of Chiapas, Dist. 4, 1937–40, President of the Chamber of Deputies, President of the Political Control Committee; *Governor of Chiapas* 1952–57; *Senator* from the State of Chiapas, 1946–52. e-Chief of *Miguel Aleman's* presidential campaign in the State of Chiapas, 1945–46. f-Judge of Soconusco, Veracruz; Civil Judge, Tapachula, Chiapas; Civil Judge of the Federal District; lawyer attached to the Office of the Attorney General of Mexico; Judge of the Superior Tribunal of the Federal District, 1943; private secretary to the Governor of Chiapas; Secretary General of Government of the State of Chiapas; Ambassador to Guatemala, 1958–61. g-None. h-Working own cattle ranch, 1958. i-Nephew *Antonio Aranda Osorio* was a federal deputy, 1970–73; brother-in-law of *Octavio Cal y Mayor.* j-None. k-Candidate for Governor of Chiapas, 1943. l-HA, 6 Feb. 1948, 9; HA 29 Oct. 1943, 14; *Siempre*, 28 Jan. 1959, 6; DGF47, 19; DGF56, 91; letter, DGF51, 5; WB48, 233; DPE61, 22; HA, 4 Nov. 1955, 18; DBC, 10.

Araujo (y Araujo), Emilio

(Deceased Oct. 18, 1953)
a-Aug. 9, 1892. b- Tuxtla Gutierrez, Chiapas, *South, Urban.* c-Law degree, National School of Law, UNAM, 1913–17. d-Represented the State of Chiapas at the Constitutional Congress, 1916–17; Mayor of Tuxtla Gutierrez; Federal Deputy and President of the Chamber of Deputies, 1917–20; *Federal*

Deputy from State of Chiapas, Dist. 3, 1937–40; *Interim Governor of Chiapas,* 1938; *Senator* from Chiapas, 1940–46; President of the Senate, 1942; president of the First Justice Committee, secretary of the Constitutional Affairs, Foreign Relations, and Consular and Diplomatic Service Committees, and member of the First Balloting Group. f-Judge of the lower court in Chiapas; legal adviser to the Department of the Federal District; legal adviser to the Mexican delegation at the United Nations Conference in San Francisco, 1945; Secretary General of Government of the State of Chiapas (twice). g-None. h-Member of various commercial and scientific commissions in Europe, 1920–37. i-Close to President Carranza during constitutionalist movement, fled with Carranza in 1920. j-None. k-President of the Mexican Democratic Party which ran *Ezequiel Padilla* for president in 1945–46. l-WWM45, 5; DP70, 129; Peral, 61; letter.

Arellano Belloc, Francisco

(Deceased Mar. 9, 1972)
a-Feb. 9, 1900. b-Rioverde, San Luis Potosi, *East Central, Urban.* c-Law degree, founder of the Michoacan Academy of Science, Letters, and Poetry. d-*Federal Deputy* from the State of San Luis Potosi, Dist. 3, 1937–40. f-Oficial Mayor of Government of the State of Michoacan, 1924; Judge of the First Instance in the State of Veracruz; Secretary General of Government under *Lazaro Cardenas*; Secretary of Resolutions of the Supreme Court of Justice; Acting Governor of the State of Sonora; Judge of the Superior Tribunal of Justice of the Federal District and Federal Territories; chief of the legal department of Petroleos Mexicanos; legal advisor to Petroleos Mexicanos, 1972. g-None. h-Founder of the magazine *Mastiles*, published poetry with *Jaime Torres Bodet*, 1918; member of United Nations' missions to Latin America to establish petroleum legislation. j-None. k-None. l-HA, 20 Mar. 1972, 24; Peral, 62; Novo35, 235.

Arellano Tapia, Alicia

b-Magdalena, Sonora, *North, Rural.* c-Primary and secondary studies in Magdalena; preparatory studies at the University of Guadalajara; medical degree as a dental surgeon, School of Medicine, University of Guadalajara, 1952; Professor of Oral Pathology, School of Medicine, IPN; Chief of Dental Services, IPN. d-*Alternate Federal Deputy* from the State of Sonora, 1958–61; *Federal Deputy* from the State of Sonora, Dist. 2, 1961–63, member of the Public Health and Library Committees; *Senator* from the State of Sonora, 1964–70; Mayor of Magdalena, Sonora, 1974–77; Mayor of Hermosillo, Sonora, 1979- . e-Director of Women's Action of PRI in Sonora; Director of a Free Dental Clinic for the poor for PRI; Auxiliary Secretary of the CEN of PRI, 1966. **f-**None. **g-**National Coordinator of the CEN of CNOP. **h-**Practicing Dentist. **i-**Married Dr. Pavolich. **j-**None. **k-**First female senator from Sonora; first woman senator along with *Maria Lavalle Urbina* in Mexico. **l-***Excelsior,* 8 July 1979, 18; WWMG, 7; PS; G of S, 34; *Excelsior,* 9 Apr. 1979, 14; HA, 7 Mar. 1966, 17.

Argil Camacho, Gustavo

a-Nov. 6, 1901. **b-**Federal District, *Federal District, Urban.* **c-**Primary and secondary studies in Mexico, D.F.; medical degree, National School of Medicine, UNAM, March 22, 1923, with a thesis on renal insufficiencies; Professor of Clinical Medicine and Pathology, National School of Medicine, UNAM, 1933–70; Professor of Pathology, 1927. **d-**None. **e-**None. **f-**Laboratory doctor, General Hospital, Mexico, D.F., 1926–40; Director of the General Laboratories, General Hospital, Mexico, D.F., 1941–52; President of the Technical-Sanitation Council, Papaloapan Commission, 1948–52; Director of the Department of Clinical Investigations, National School of Medicine, UNAM, 1934–46; Director of the National School of Medicine, UNAM, 1942–44; *Oficial Mayor* of the Secretariat of Health, 1946–48; *Subsecretary of Health,* 1948–52. **g-**None. **h-**Founder and Director of the *Revista Medica,* 1920–70, when he was a fourth-year medical student; author of two basic medical texts with *Fernando Ocaranza* as well as other medical works. **i-**Graduated from UNAM with *Rafael P. Gamboa.* **j-**None. **k-**None. **l-**Letter, DGF51; DGF47, 197; Peral, 47, 31; DGF50, II, 445; DGF51, I, 335.

Armendariz (Cardenas), Antonio

a-Sept. 29, 1905. **b-**Palo Blanco, Coahuila, *North, Rural.* **c-**Primary in Mexico, D.F.; secondary at the Superior School of Commerce, 1920–22, Mexico, D.F.; preparatory at the National Preparatory School in Mexico, D.F., 1923–27; law degree, National School of Law, UNAM, 1928–33; Professor of Sociology and Economy at UNAM, 1930–60. **d-**None. **e-**None. **f-**Secretary for the National Commission of Economic Studies, 1933; lawyer for the National Banking Commission, 1933–34; Director of Securities for the Bank of Mexico, 1933; Secretary General of UNAM, 1933–34; Director General of Secondary Education of the Secretariat of Public Education, 1941–45; *Subsecretary of the Treasury,* 1952–58; *Ambassador to Great Britain,* Sept., 1960, to Feb., 1965; *Director General of the Bank of Foreign Commerce,* 1965–70; Director General of the National Bonded Warehouses, 1970–75. **g-**None. **h-**Legal adviser to the Bank of London, National Ejido Bank, and many other banks; President of the National Commission of Securities, 1949–52;

private law practice, 1943–53; editorialist for the two Mexican newspapers, *Excelsior* and *Novedades,* 1940–70; Editor of *Comercio Exterior,* official publication of the National Bank of Foreign Commerce. **i-**Knew *Antonio Carrillo Flores, Andres Serra Rojas, Alfonso Guzman Neyra, Manuel Gual Vidal, Agustin Garcia Lopez, Antonio Ortiz Mena, Angel Carvajal* and others as students at the National School of Law. **j-**None. **k-**None. **l-**WWM45, 6; DBM68, 40–41; DBM70, 46; letter; *Semblanzas*; DGF50, II, 57, 211, 273; DGF51, 65; Enc. Mex., I, 263.

Arrayales de Morales, Aurora

a-June 28, 1918. **b-**Mazatlan, Sinaloa, *West, Urban.* **c-**Early education unknown; teaching certificate; specialist in abnormal children; teacher. **d-***Federal Deputy* from Sinaloa, Dist. 4, 1958–61, member of the Social Action Committee, the Second Public Education Committee and the Second Instructive Committee for the Grand Jury; Councilwoman of Mazatlan, Sinaloa. **e-**President of Feminine Social Action of PRI in Mazatlan. **f-**Delegate of the Department of the Federal District to Xochimilco, 1977. **g-**None. **h-**None. **j-**None. **k-**None. **l-**C de D, 1958–61, 70; Func., 355.

Arreguin (Velez) Jr., Enrique

a-Aug. 6, 1907. **b-**Morelia, Michoacan, *West Central, Urban.* **c-**Primary and secondary at the Escuela Oficial Miguel Hidalgo, Morelia; preparatory at the Colegio San Nicolas, Morelia, 1917; medical degree from the University of Michoacan, June 8, 1928; Professor of Hygiene, Secondary School of Coyoacan, Mexico, D.F.; Professor of Geology, Paleontology, and Zoology at the Colegio de San Nicolas; Professor of Medicine, History, General Biology, General Pathology, and Medical Pathology at the University of Michoacan; Rector of the University of Michoacan, 1934–35. **d-**None. **e-**None. **f-**Member of the Council of Superior Education and Scientific Investigation, 1936–37; Secretary of the Presidential Studies Commission, 1937; President of the Presidential Studies Commission, 1938; *Subsecretary of Public Education,* 1940–41. **g-**None. **h-**Director of the Central Office of Professional Liabilities of the Mexican Institute of Social Security, 1950–64; Director of the Department of Professional Liabilities of the Mexican Institute of Social Security, 1964–70; Chief of the Bacteriology Section and the Clinical Laboratory Analysis of the General Hospital, Mexico, D.F. **i-**Son of Enrique Arreguin, Sr., who was local deputy to the State Legislature of Michoacan in 1912, Director of the State of Michoacan Pawnshop, and professor for twenty years at the Colegio de San Nicolas. **j-**None. **k-**Head of the Vanguardias Nicolaitas; resigned from the

Secretariat of Public Education because of adverse political pressures against the implementation of a socialist education program. l-D del S, 2 Dec. 1940, 1, 6; DGF69, 6633; DGF50, 109.

Arriaga Rivera, Agustin

a-1925. b-Michoacan, *West Central*. c-Preparatory studies from the Colegio de San Nicolas, Morelia; economics degree from the National School of Economics, UNAM, December 14, 1951, with a thesis on Social Security in Mexico; graduated with a perfect grade point average; Professor at the University of Michoacan, 1952–54; professor at the University of Tamaulipas, 1955–58; professor at the National School of Economics, UNAM, 1949–51. d-*Federal Deputy* from the State of Michoacan, 1952–55, member of the Social Welfare Committee, the First Balloting Committee, the Legislative Studies Committee (2nd year), and the Permanent Commission; *Governor of Michoacan*, 1962–68. e-Member of the National Committee of PRI, 1949–51; Secretary of Youth Action of PRI, 1950–51; General Delegate of the CEN of PRI to Oaxaca, 1978. f-Adviser to the Mexican delegation to the United Nations, 1945; Subdirector of Social Action of the Secretariat of Public Education, 1949–53; Chairman of the Board for Material and Moral Improvement, Nuevo Leon, 1955–59; Director General of the National Bank of Cinematography, 1959–62. g-President of the National Federation of University Students of Mexico, 1949; president of the 1946 student generation at the National School of Economics; Director of the National Institute of Mexican Youth, 1959–62. h-None. i-Initially served with *Luis Echeverria* and *Hugo Cervantes del Rio* as a youth member of the National Committee of PRI under the tutelage of *Rodolfo Sanchez Taboada*; student at UNAM with *Luis Echeverria*. j-None. k-Confronted with a major student riot as Governor of Michoacan in 1966; considered to be the first governor of Michoacan after 1940 not hand-picked by *Lazaro Cardenas*. l-WWMG, 7; DBM68, 44; DGF56, 437; Diaz Fuentes, 265; DGF51, I, 291; C de D, 1952–54, 52, 57; HA, 12 Jan. 1959, 14; DPE61, 108; *Excelsior*, 17 Dec. 1974, 4; NYT, 20 May 1962, 30; NYT, 30 June 1962, 17; Enc. Mex., 1977, I, 428–29.

Arrieta Garcia, Atanasio

b-Durango, *West*. c-Primary studies only; no degree. d-*Senator* from the State of Durango, 1946–52, member of the National Properties Committee, the Indigenous Affairs Committee, the Second Ejido Committee and the First Mining Committee. e-None. f-None. g-None. h-Businessman. i-Son of General *Domingo Arrieta*, senator from Durango, 1934–40. j-None. k-Precandidate for governor of Durango,

1949, but lost to *Enrique Torres Sanchez*. l-DGF51, I, 6, 10, 11, 13; C de S, 1946–52.

Arrieta, Domingo

(Deceased Nov. 18, 1962)
a-Aug. 4, 1874. b-Municipio de Candelas, Durango, *West*, *Rural*. c-Early education unknown; none. d-Constitutional Governor of Durango, August 1, 1917 to May 24, 1920; *Senator* from Durango, 1936–40. e-None. f-Governor and military commander of Durango, 1914–16. g-None. h-Before joining the Revolution was a miner and a muleteer in Durango. i-Brother of Mariano Arrieta, who was an early Revolutionary leader in the State of Durango, became Governor of Durango for several months in 1915, and continued career as a military officer; father of *Atanasio Arrieta Garcia*, senator from Durango, 1946–52. j-Joined the Revolution under Madero, 1910; commander of the garrison of Durango, 1911–13; fought against Huerta in 1913; general of the Revolutionary forces which took Durango, 1913; became military commander of Durango, 1913–14; fought against Francisco Villa, 1914–16; constitutionalist, 1916–20; fought against General Obregon, 1920–24; became a division general on November 16, 1940; retired from the army August 1, 1944. k-Remained faithful to Carranza when he fled the presidency; pardoned by Obregon, May 7, 1924; rejoined the army September 11, 1927. l-DP70, 149–50; Peral, 72; Q es Q, 43–45; Enc. Mex., Annual, 1977, 478–79.

Arrieta M., Dario L.

a-Dec. 26, 1901. b-Iguala, Guerrero, *South, Urban*. c-Engineering degree, National School of Agriculture, 1934; Professor, National School of Agriculture. d-None. e-None. f-Director General of Agriculture, Secretariat of Agriculture, 1943–49; Executive Coordinator of Agricultural Investigation, 1949; Director of Agricultural Defense, 1954; *Substitute Governor of Guerrero*, 1954–57; Director General of Agricultural Defense, 1958–61. g-None. h-Technical advisor to the Secretariat of Agriculture, 1954, j-None. k-None. l-DPE61, 72; HA, 31 May 1954, 5; DGF56, 93; *Siempre*, 14 Jan. 1959, 6.

Arroyo Ch., Agustin

(Deceased Apr. 24, 1969)
a-Aug. 28, 1891. b-Irapuato, Guanajuato, *West Central, Rural*. c-Primary studies at Pueblo Nuevo, secondary at private schools in Guanajuato; no degree. d-Local deputy, State of Guanajuato, Federal Deputy from Guanajuato, 1919–24; Governor of Guanajuato, 1927–31. f-*Subsecretary of Government*, 1935–36; first Director of the Department of Press and Publicity (which became PIPSA), 1936–40; *Secretary of Labor and Social Welfare*,

1940; President of the Administrative Council of PIPSA, 1958–62; publisher of the official government newspaper *El Nacional*, 1962–68; member of the Board of PIPSA, 1967–69. **g-**None. **h-**Post office employee, Celaya, Guanajuato, 1915; worked in the department of General Provisions, under *Francisco Mugica*. **i-**Close personal friend of Governor Enrique Colunga of Guanajuato 1923–27, who imposed *Arroyo Ch.* as Governor; also a friend of Governor Antonio Madrazo, 1920–23; early supporter of *Francisco Mugica* as president, 1939–40; political advisor of *Lazaro Cardenas*; married Carolina Damian; son *Agustin* was a federal deputy from Guanajuato, 1955–58 and 1964–67. **j-**Joined the Revolution while quite young. **k-**He and Colunga controlled state politics in Guanajuato. **l-**Dulles; WWMG, 7; *Hoy*, 10 May 1969, 8; HA, 29 Dec. 1958, 8; Peral, 73; Gruening, 427, 487–88; Kirk, 3; Enc. Mex. I, 303; NYT, 21 Jan. 1940, 21; Michaels, 21.

Arroyo Damian, Agustin

a-Mar. 12, 1919. **b-**Celaya, Guanajuato, *West Central, Urban*. **c-**Early education unknown; medical degree, National School of Medicine, UNAM, with a specialty as a surgeon in opthamology; post-graduate work at various universities in the United States; Professor of Chemistry, National School of Medicine, UNAM. **d-***Federal Deputy* from the State of Guanajuato, Dist. 8, 1955–58, member of the Mail and Telegraph Committee, the Sugar Industry Committee and the Committee on Health; *Federal Deputy* from the State of Guanajuato, Dist. 8, 1964–67, member of the Public Health Committee and the Military Health Committee. **e-**None. **f-**None. **g-**None. **h-**Practicing surgeon; founder of the Beatriz Velasco de Aleman Opthamology Clinic, Celaya, Guanajuato; Chief of Opthamological Services, French Hospital. **i-**Son of *Agustin Arroyo Ch.*, Secretary of Labor, 1940. **j-**None. **k-**None. **l-**DGF56, 24,32,34,37; C de D, 1955–58; C de D, 1964–67, 45; IndBiog., 17.

Arteaga y Santoyo, Armando

a-Oct. 26, 1906. **b-**Monterrey, Nuevo Leon, *North, Urban*. **c-**Law degree, National School of Law, UNAM, 1925–32. **d-***Federal Deputy* from the State of Nuevo Leon, Dist. 2, 1946–49, member of the Gran Comision and the Committee on Administration; *Federal Deputy* from the State of Nuevo Leon, Dist. 4, 1961–64, member of the Gran Comision, the Domestic and Foreign Commerce Committee, the Legislative Studies Committee (Labor), and the Permanent Commission, 1963; Vice President of the Chamber, September, 1962; Secretary of the Preparatory Council, 1961–63; *Senator* from Nuevo Leon, 1964–70. **e-***Director of the IEPES of the CEN of PRI*, 1946–52; *Director of the IEPES of the CEN of PRI*, 1953; *Secretary of Political Action of the CEN of PRI*, 1965; representative of the New Advisory Council of the IEPES of PRI in charge of structural reforms, June 28, 1972; general delegate of the CEN of PRI more than twenty-five times. **f-**Agent of the Ministerio Publico of the Attorney General of Mexico in the Federal District, 1935–41; Oficial Mayor of the State of Nuevo Leon, 1941–43; Secretary General of the Government of the State of Nuevo Leon, 1943–44; Private Secretary to the Governor of the State of Nuevo Leon, *Arturo B. de la Garza*, 1944–45; Administrator of CEIMSA, 1958. **g-**None. **h-**Practicing lawyer in Mexico, D.F., 1970–73. **i-***Santiago Roel* was his political disciple. **j-**None. **k-**None. **l-**WWM45, 6; *Siempre*, 4 Feb. 1959, 6; letter; HA, 10 July 1972, 10.

Asiain, Rodolfo

(Deceased 1963)
a-1907. **b-**Tula, Hidalgo, *East Central, Rural*. **c-**Primary and secondary in Hidalgo, preparatory at the Literary Institute of Hidalgo, law degree from the National School of Law, UNAM, 1917–22. **d-**None. **e-**None. **f-**Secretary General of Government of the State of Hidalgo under Governor Amado Azuara, 1921–23; Correctional Judge of the Federal District, 1925; Penal Judge of the Federal District, President of Disputes and Magistrate of the Tribunal Superior of Justice; *Justice of the Supreme Court*, 1936–40; consulting lawyer to the Tariff Commission of Electricity and Gas, chief of the Legal Department of the Tariff Commission of Electricity and Gas. **g-**None. **h-**None. **k-**Played a prominent role in the Supreme Court decision on the expropriation of the oil companies in 1938. **l-**DP70, 158; letter; DGF50, II, 239; DGF51, II, 338.

Aubanel Vallejo, Gustavo

a-July 23, 1904. **c-**Early education unknown; medical degree. **d-***Federal Deputy* from the State of Baja California del Norte, Dist. 2, 1961–64, member of the Indigenous Affairs Committee and the First Balloting Committee; *Federal Deputy* from the State of Baja California del Norte, Dist. 2, 1967–70, member of the Gran Comision, the Pharmaceutical and Chemical Industry Committee, and the Social Welfare Committee; *Senator* from the State of Baja California del Norte, 1970–76, member of the Gran Comision and the First Balloting Committee; second secretary of the Second Foreign Relations Committee, the National Properties Committee and the Tax Committee; first secretary of the Social Welfare Committee and president of the Public Assistance Committee, member of the Interparliamentary Committee, 1973; Mayor of Tijuana, 1954–56. **e-**None. **f-***Substitute Governor* of Baja California del Norte, December

19, 1964, to November 30, 1965. **h-**Coauthor of the constitution for Baja California del Norte; operated a medical clinic in Tijuana, 1931- . **j-**None. **k-**Appointed by the state legislature as Governor of Baja California del Norte. **l-**C de D, 1967–69, 76; C de D, 1961–63, 71; MGF69, 89; HA, 28 Dec. 1964, 14; C de S, 1970–76, 7, 70.

Avila Breton, Rafael

a-Feb. 15, 1893. **b-**Tlaxcala, Tlaxcala, *East Central, Urban*. **c-**Preparatory and legal studies at the Colegio del Estado de Puebla; law degree, National School of Law, UNAM; Professor of Industrial Law and Civil Procedure, National School of Law, UNAM. **d-***Senator* from the State of Tlaxcala, 1940–46; *Governor of Tlaxcala*, 1946–51. **e-**None. **f-**Public Defender, 1917; Penal Judge, Pachuca, Hidalgo, 1918–20; Auxiliary Agent, Ministerio Publico of the Federal District; Judge of the Civil Division, Federal District; Justice, Superior Tribunal of Justice of the State of Tlaxcala. **g-**None. **h-**Public welfare attorney. **i-**Married Herlinda Hoyos. **j-**None. **k-**Reportedly being investigated for illicit land dealings, 1971. **l-**STYBIWW544, 593; LAD, 14 Oct. 1971; HA, 15 Nov. 1946, 11; letter; WB54, 323.

Avila Camacho, Manuel
(Deceased Oct. 13, 1955)

a-Apr. 24, 1897. **b-**Teziutlan, Puebla, *East Central, Rural*. **c-**Primary educaton in Teziutlan, secondary studies in accounting at Liceo Teziuteco, 1912; studied at the National Preparatory School; no degree. **d-***President of Mexico*, 1940–46. **e-**Secretary and stenographer to Jose I. Novelo, president of the Cooperativist Labor Party, 1919. **f-**Oficial Mayor of the Secretariat of National Defense, 1933–34; *Oficial Mayor* of the Secretariat of National Defense, 1934–36; *Subsecretary of National Defense* in charge of the Secretariat, 1936–37; *Secretary of National Defense,* 1937–39. **g-**Secretary of local agrarian committee of Sierra, Puebla. **h-**None. **i-**Close friend of *Lazaro Cardenas* since 1920; childhood friend of *Vicente Lombardo Toledano*; brother *Maximino Avila Camacho* was Governor of Puebla; and brother *Rafael Avila Camacho* was an Army general and Governor of Puebla, 1951–57; parents were middle class ranchers. **j-**Joined the Army in 1914 at the age of seventeen with the rank of 2nd lieutenant; Major in 1918; Colonel, 1920; Chief of Staff of the State of Michoacan under *Lazaro Cardenas*, 1920; commander of the military zone in Colima, 1929; fought against the Cristeros; fought Yaquis in Sonora, 1920; Chief of Military Operations, Isthmus, 1920; fought against the De la Huerta Rebellion in Michoacan, 1924; Commander of the 38th Cavalry Regiment, 1924; fought under General *Cardenas* against the Escobar Rebellion, 1929; Brigadier General in 1924, Brigade General, 1929,

in charge of the Military Zone of Tabasco, 1932–33. **k-**None. **l-**WWM45, 6; DP70, 179–80; Peral, 76; *Hoy*, Dec. 1940, 19–21; NYT, November 3, 1939; Kirk; UTEHA, 1222; WB48, 323; Enc. Mex. I, 410–11; Q es Q, 48; Gaxiola, 2, 254.

Avila Camacho, Maximino
(Deceased Feb. 17, 1945)

a-Aug. 23, 1891. **b-**Teziutlan, Puebla, *East Central, Urban*. **c-**Primary studies in Teziutlan; cadet at the National Military College; no degree. **d-**Governor of Puebla, 1937–41. **e-**None. **f-**Chief of Political Police, Secretariat of Government, 1925; *Secretary of Public Works*, 1941–45. **g-**None. **h-**Post office employee; farmer; sales agent for the Singer Sewing Machine Company; cowboy; professional bullfighter; horse breeder; cattleman; owned several ranches by 1940; his wealth was estimated at 2 to 3 million pesos. **i-**Brother of President *Manuel Avila Camacho* and *Rafael Avila Camacho,* Governor of Puebla, 1951–57; parents were middle-class landowners. **j-**Joined the Revolution in 1914; Brigadier General, 1929; military caudillo of Puebla during the late 1920s and early 1930s, Chief of the 51st Cavalry, in charge of prison where Vasconcelistas were murdered; Assistant Inspector General of the Army; Acting Inspector General of the Army; Divisionary General, 1940. **k-**Leader of the right wing of the National Revolutionary Party. **l-**DP70, 180; HA, 28 May 1943, 9; DGF56, 98; Scott, 122; Kirk, 93, 245; UTEHA, I, 1222; Morton, 49; Peral, 77; Q es Q, 48; Wilkie; Skirius, 188; NYT, 5 May 1941, 8; CyT, 64.

Avila Camacho, Rafael
(Deceased March 20, 1975)

a-Dec. 14, 1905. **b-**Teziutlan, Puebla, *East Central, Urban*. **c-**Primary studies in Teziutlan; graduated from the National Military College, 1925, as a 2nd lieutenant; enrolled in the Applied Military College, 1934; Director of the National Military College, 1948–50. **d-**Federal Deputy from the State of Puebla, 1935–37; Mayor of Puebla, Puebla; *Governor of Puebla*, 1951–57. **e-**President of the State Committee of the PRM, Puebla. **f-***Oficial Mayor of Industry and Commerce*, 1942–45; *Subsecretary of Public Works*, 1945–46. **g-**None. **h-**Retired to private life as a rancher, 1958–75. **i-**Brother of *Maximino* and *Manuel Avila Camacho*; longtime friend of *Alejandro Gomez Maganda*; nephew of *Andres Figueroa*. **j-**Career army officer; aide to Commander of the 13th Military Zone; aide to the Oficial Mayor and the Subsecretary of War; rank of Lt. Colonel, 1940; rank of Colonel, 1943; rank of Brigadier General, 1946; rank of Divisionary General, 1961. **k-**None. **l-**DGF56, 98; DGF51, II, 679; Peral, 77; Gomez Maganda, 105; CyT, 64–65; *Excelsior*, 21 Mar. 1975, 4; HA, 31 Mar. 1975, 21.

Aznar Zetina, Antonio J.
a-June 12, 1904. **b**-Campeche, Campeche, *Gulf, Rural.* **c**-Primary and secondary studies in Campeche; preparatory studies at the Campeche Normal School; degree from the Naval College in Veracruz; advanced studies at the Superior War College, Mexico, D.F. **d**-None. **e**-None. **f**-Naval Attache to the Mexican Embassy, Paris; Naval Attache to the Mexican Embassy, Washington, D.C..; *Subsecretary of the Navy,* 1965–70. **g**-None. **h**-None. **i**-Son of a lawyer; uncle *Tomas Aznar Cano* served as a Senator. **j**-Commander of the coastguard ship 24; Director of the Naval College; Chief of Staff of the Navy, 1958–61; Commander of the Transport Progreso; Commander of the Destroyer Guanajuato; Commander of the 2nd Naval Zone; Vice Admiral, 1965; rank of Admiral. **k**-None. **l**-DBM68; 50; DBM70; 56; DPE65, 48; DE61, 39; Q es Q, 30.

Azuara, Juan Enrique
(Deceased 1958)
a-1895. **b**-Tampacan, San Luis Potosi, *East Central, Rural.* **ca**-Primary studies in Tampacan; secondary and preparatory studies at the Scientific and Literary Institute of San Luis Potosi; law degree, Scientific and Literary Institute of San Luis Potosi, 1922. **d**-Federal Deputy from the State of San Luis Potosi, 1926–18; *Senator* from the State of San Luis Potosi, 1958, died in office. **e**-None. **f**-Public defender; Judge of the First Instance in Ciudad Valles; District Judge of Toluca, Mexico; Magistrate of the Collegiate Circuit Tribunal of the Federal District; President of the Collegiate Circuit Tribunal, 1952–58. **g**-None. **h**-None. **j**-Civilian employee in the Revolution. **k**-None. **l**-DP70, 192; C de S, 1958–64; Func., 341.

Azuela (Rivera), Mariano
a-Mar. 15, 1904. **b**-Lagos de Moreno, Jalisco, *West, Urban.* **c**-Primary studies in Lagos de Moreno and Guadalajara; preparatory studies at the National Preparatory School, Mexico, D.F.; law degree, National School of Law, UNAM, 1928; LLD, UNAM; professor at the University of San Luis Potosi and the University of Monterrey; senior professor, course in amparo, National School of Law; Professor of Public Law, Graduate School, National School of Law, UNAM; Professor of Guarantees and Amparo, National School of Law, UNAM, 1930–58. **d**-*Senator* from the State of Jalisco, 1958–60. **e**-None. **f**-Judge of the Federal Tax Court of Mexico, 1937–51; President of the Federal Tax Court of Mexico, 1949–51; *Justice of the Supreme Court*, 1951–57, 1960–64, 1964–70, 1970–71. **g**-None. **h**-Worked for a Federal District Judge as a student, 1927, practiced law with *Manuel Gomez Morin*, 1930–35, member of the Commission for Legal Studies, Office of the Attorney General; author of various articles on amparo.

i-Son of author Mariano Azuela; friend of *Antonio Luna Arroyo*; married Dolores Guitron. **j**-None. **k**-Was not a member of PRI while serving on the Supreme Court. **l**-Lib de Oro, 1967, xlvi; Func, 238; *Excelsior*, 6 April, 1971, 1, 14; DGF51, 468; C de S, 1961–64, 13.

Badillo (Garcia), Roman
a-Feb. 24, 1895. **b**-Otumba, Mexico, *West Central, Rural.* **c**-Primary studies in Mexico City; preparatory studies at the National Preparatory School; law degree from the National School of Law, UNAM. **d**-None. **e**-Leader at the Anti-Reelectionist Party Convention, 1934, considered a supporter of Antonio Diaz Soto y Gama as a presidential candidate of that party. **f**-Agent of the Ministerio Publico; 1926–27; criminal judge in Veracruz; Judge of the Superior Tribunal of Justice of Veracruz, 1927; Secretary General of Government of the State of Queretaro; adviser to the President of Mexico, 1940–46; *Oficial Mayor* of the Department of Agrarian Affairs, 1958–62. **g**-None. **h**-Practicing lawyer. **i**-Practiced law with Antonio Diaz Soto y Gama. **j**-None. **k**-None. **l**-Lopez, 75; Balboa, 95; DPE61, 126.

Baeza Somellera, Guillermo
a-June 20, 1937. **b**-Guadalajara, Jalisco, *West, Urban.* **c**-Primary studies at the Institute of Sciences, Guadalajara, 1945–51; secondary studies at the Institute of Sciences, 1951–53; preparatory studies at the Institute of Sciences, 1952–54; law degree, University of Guadalajara, 1954–59. **d**-Candidate for Federal Deputy from Jalisco, 1967; candidate for Councilman of Guadalajara, 1964; *Federal Deputy* from the State of Jalisco, Dist. 4, 1970–73, member of the Legislative Studies Committee (1st year) on General Affairs; *Federal Deputy* (party deputy), 1973–76. **e**-Joined PAN, 1951; Secretary General of the Regional Committtee of National Action for Jalisco; President of PAN for Jalisco, 1970; member of the National Council of PAN, 1971. **f**-None. **g**-None. **i**-Married Villanueva. **j**-None. **k**-None. **l**-*Directorio*, 70–72; C de D, 70–72, 102; Mabry.

Balboa Gojon, Praxedes
b-Ciudad Victoria, Tamaulipas, *North, Urban.* **c**-Primary studies at the Normal School Anex, Ciudad Victoria, 1907–12; secondary and preparatory studies at the Colegio Civil of Monterrey, Nuevo Leon, 1914–1919; law degree from the National School of Law, UNAM, 1925. **d**-Federal Deputy from the State of Tamaulipas, 1928–30; Federal Deputy from the State of Tamaulipas, Dist. 4, 1930–32; Federal Deputy from the State of Tamaulipas, Dist. 4, 1934–37; *Governor of Tamaulipas,* 1963–69; **e**-member of the Constitutional Convention of the PNR, 1929; president of the PNR in Tamaulipas; campaign

manager for Antonio Villarreal as governor. **f**-Chief, Department of Labor, Secretariat of Industry and Commerce, 1929–30; Federal Conciliator, Mixed Commission of the National Railroads of Mexico, 1929; Director of the Legal Department of Petroleos Mexicanos, 1938; Head of Legal Department, PEMEX in Mata Redonda, 1938–40; lawyer for Legal Department, PEMEX, 1940–52; *Administrative Subdirector of Petroleos Mexicanos*, 1952–58; *Administrative Subdirector of Petroleos Mexicanos*, 1958–62. **g**-Student leader at UNAM, organized a group in support of Plutarco Calles as president, 1923. **h**-Had an active role in the formulation of the Federal Labor Law and the Agrarian Reform Law which modified the original 1915 legislation. **i**-Attended the National Law School with *Eduardo Bustamante* and *Agustin Garcia Lopez*; grandson of General Juan Gojon, governor of Tamaulipas; father a doctor. **j**-None. **k**-Removed as a federal deputy by *Lazaro Cardenas*, September 12, 1935; became a political enemy of *Emilio Portes Gil*. **l**-WWMG, 7–8; letters, Ex*celsior*, 24 Jan. 1973, 19.

Ballesteros Prieto, Mario

a-Nov., 1912. **b**-Oaxaca, Oaxaca, *South, Urban*. **c**-Early education unknown; graduated from the National Military Academy; advanced studies Higher War College, 1939–42; instructor, Higher War College; advanced studies, Command and Staff School, Ft. Leavenworth, Kansas. **d**-None. **e**-None. **f**-Chief of Staff of the Secretariat of National Defense, 1964–67. **g**-None. **h**-None. **j**-Career army officer; 2nd Lieutenant, Tenth Cavalry Regiment; various staff positions, Chief of Staff, Secretariat of National Defense; Chief of Staff of the 15th Military Zone, 1964; rank of brigadier general. **k**-None. **l**-HA, 21 Dec. 1964, 10; DPE65, 33.

Bandala, Bernardo

a-Aug. 20, 1893. **b**-Teziutlan, Puebla, *East Central, Urban*. **c**-Early education unknown; no degree. **d**-Federal Deputy from the State of Puebla, Dist. 2, 1932–34, Secretary of the National Revolutionary Bloc in the Chamber of Deputies; *Senator* from the State of Puebla, 1934–40. **e**-President of the PNR in the state of Puebla. **f**-None. **g**-None. **i**-Brother Homero Bandala was a federal deputy from Puebla; grew up in Teziutlan at the same time as the *Avila Camacho* family. **j**-Officer in the Constitutional Army; member of the Chief of Staff under President Carranza. **k**-None. **l**-C de D, 1932–34; C de S, 1934–40; PS, 0539.

Banuelos, Felix

a-Oct. 1, 1878. **b**-Jalisco, *West*. **c**-Early education unknown; no degree. **d**-*Governor of Zacatecas*, 1937–40. **f**-Governor of Quintana Roo. **g**-None. **h**-None. **j**-Joined the Revolution and was a supporter of Francisco Villa until 1920; supported the government against De la Huerta in 1923; Brigadier General on May 30, 1923; retired from the army on Jan. 1, 1944. **k**-In June of 1939, while Governor of Zacatecas, the press alleged that he was trying to leave the Party of the Mexican Revolution (PRM), but two days later he claimed to have made no such statement. **l**-Peral, 86; D de Y, 20 June 1939, 1.

Barba Gonzalez, Silvano

(Deceased August, 1967)

a-Nov. 29, 1895. **b**-Valle de Guadalupe, Jalisco, *West, Rural*. **c**-Primary studies in Tepatitlan, Jalisco, and San Juan de Los Lagos, Jalisco; secondary studies in San Juan de Los Lagos; preparatory studies in Guadalajara; law degree from the University of Guadalajara, Jalisco, Oct. 2, 1920; Rector of the University of Guadalajara, 1927–28. **d**-Local deputy to the legislature of Jalisco, 1920 (for two successive terms); *Governor of Jalisco*, 1939–43; *Senator* from Jalisco, 1952–58; member of the Foreign Relations Committee, the Mail and Telegraph Committee and President of the Migration Committee. **e**-Private Secretary to *Lazaro Cardenas* during 1934 presidential campaign; *President of the CEN of PRI*, Aug. 20, 1936, to Apr. 2, 1938. **f**-Attorney General of the State of Jalisco, 1922–24; Secretary General of the Government of Jalisco, 1925; Provisional Governor of Jalisco, 1926–27; District Court Judge of Guadalajara, Tepic and Monterrey, 1928–34; Oficial Mayor of the Secretariat of Government; *Secretary of Labor*, 1934–35; *Secretary of Government*, June 18, 1935, to Aug. 20, 1936; *Head of the Department of Agrarian Affairs and Colonization*, 1944–46; political adviser to the President of Mexico, 1965–67. **g**-None. **h**-Author of the Labor Law of Jalisco; author of a biography on the Mexican caudillo Manuel Luzada. **i**-Friend of Jose Guadalupe Zuno, Governor of Jalisco, 1923–26; relative of Marcelino Barba Gonzalez, Federal Deputy from Jalisco, Dist. 3, 1937–39; longtime supporter of *Lazaro Cardenas*; married Esther Padilla. **j**-Fought against the Cristeros, 1926–28 and against the military uprising in Sonora, 1929. **k**-None. **l**-DBM68, 87; DGF56, 6; DP70, 219; *Polemica*, 68; Gruening, 444, 448; Wilkie, 192; Kirk, 126–27; Ind Biog., 20–21.

Barberena (Vega), Miguel Angel

a-Aug. 4, 1928. **b**-Jesus Maria, Aguascalientes, *West, Rural*. **c**-Primary, secondary and preparatory at the Autonomous Institute of Sciences, Aguascalientes; professional studies at the University of Sinaloa, degree in geological engineering; special studies in the United States in mechanical and nuclear engineering; Ph.D. in science; Director, School of Science, University of Veracruz, 1961–62; Director, National Calculating Center, IPN,

1964; Director of Workshops, IPN, 1963–64; Member of the University Council of the University of Veracruz, Jalapa, Veracruz, 1958–63. **d-**Alternate Senator from Aguascalientes, 1970, but replaced *Gomez Villanueva*, 1971–76, member of the Second Section of the Legislative Studies Committee, First Secretary of the Second Consular and Diplomatic Service Committee, Second Secretary of the Railroad Committee. **e-**Secretary of Organization of the CEN of PRI, 1973–74; *Secretary General of the CEN of PRI*, 1974–75; General Delegate of the CEN and of the IEPES of PRI. **f-**Member of the delegation from Mexico to UNESCO in Italy; President of the Coordinating Committee on Transportation, Secretariat of Communication and Transportation, 1969; Director General of Railroads, Secretariat of Communication and Transportation, 1964–71; *Subsecretary of Communication and Transportation*, 1976– . **g-**None. **i-**Collaborator of *Jose Antonio Padilla Segura* at IPN and the Secretariat of Communication and Transportation. **j-**None. **k-**None. **l-**C de S, 1970–76, 70; DAPC,6; MGF69, 277.

Barbosa Heldt, Antonio
(Deceased Sept. 18, 1973)
a-1909. **b-**Colima, *West, Urban*. **c-**Primary and secondary studies in Colima; teaching certificate in rural education from the Normal School of Colima; graduate work in normal and technical training, Graduate Teachers College; rural teacher in Colima and Baja California del Sur. **d-**Governor-elect of Colima, 1973. **e-**None. **f-**Director General of Education in the Cuenca de Papaloapan, 1953; Subdirector General of Primary Education, Calendar B, Secretariat of Public Education, 1961–65; Director General of Education for the Cuenca del Grijalva and the Cuenca del Fuerte; Federal Inspector, Mexicali Valley, Sonora; Administrator, Plan Chontalpa; Director General of Primary Education, Dist. 4, Federal District, Secretariat of Public Education, 1965–70; *Oficial Mayor of Public Education*, 1970–73. **g-**None. **h-**Director General of the Scholastic and Physical Education Department of the Secretariat of Hydraulic Resources. **i-**Married to Francisca Stevens. **j-**None. **k-**Considered to be an apostle of rural education in Mexico; committed suicide because he contracted a fatal disease. **l-**HA, 26 Mar. 1973, 38; *Excelsior*, 12 Mar. 1973, 12; HA, 14 Dec. 1970, 23; DPE61, 99; *Excelsior*, 8 Mar. 1973, 14; HA, 26, Mar. 1973, 38.

Barocio Barrios, Alberto
(Deceased 1966)
a-1890. **b-**Montemorelos, Nuevo Leon, *North, Urban*. **c-**Preparatory in Mexico, D.F.; engineering degree from the National School of Engineering, UNAM, 1914; graduate studies at Columbia University, New York; professor at the Higher School of Mechanical and Electrical Engineering (18 years); Professor of Hydraulics, National School of Engineering, UNAM, 1941; Director of the National School of Engineering, UNAM; professor at the Constructors School. **d-**None. **e-**None. **f-**Subinspector of Ports, Secretariat of Communication; Chief of the Photo-Topographical Department of the National Irrigation Commission; Chief of the Water Section, Secretariat of Public Health; Director of the Department of Bridges, Secretariat of Communication; *Subsecretary of Government Properties*, 1953–58. **g-**None. **h-**Chief of the Laboratory, National School of Engineering, UNAM; engineering specialist, Department of the Federal District; specialist in material costs for Petroleos Mexicanos; held many positions in Petroleos Mexicanos until 1966. **j-**Engineer for the Division of the North, 1915; Captain of the Engineers for General Benjamin Hill, 1916. **k-**Important member of Masonry in Mexico. **l-**DGF56, 431; DP70, 224; DGF47, 271.

Barra Garcia, Felix
a-Sept. 26, 1934. **b-**Castillo de Teayo, Veracruz, *Gulf, Rural*. **c-**Primary studies in the Maria Enriqueta Article 123 School, Poza Rica de Hidalgo, Veracruz; secondary at the Salvador Diaz Miron School, Poza Rica de Hidalgo, 1948–50; preparatory at the National Preparatory School, 1951–52; began studies at the National School of Political Science, UNAM, graduated with a thesis on "The Traditional and Newer Forms of Intervention;" professor of social, economic and political problems of Mexico, National School of Political Science, UNAM, until 1974; instructor in literacy classes, IMSS. **d-**None. **e-**None. **f-**Director of the Institute of Socio-Economic Research, UNAM, 1958–70; Director General of Orientation and Social Services, UNAM, 1970–72; *Secretary of Agrarian Reform*, 1975–76. **g-**None. **i-**Co-student with *Augusto Gomez Villanueva* at UNAM. **j-**None. **k-**Arrested and charged with criminal fraud in 1977. **l-**HA, 6 Oct. 1975, 8; *Excelsior*, 27 Sept. 1977, 1; *Proceso,* 18 Dec. 1976, 9–10.

Barragan (Rodriguez), Juan
(Deceased Sept. 28, 1974)
a-Aug. 30, 1890. **b-**Rioverde, San Luis Potosi, *East Central, Urban*. **c-**Primary and secondary studies in San Luis Potosi; preparatory studies at the Scientific and Literary Institute of San Luis Potosi; completed fourth year of law school. **d-**Deputy to the Constitutional Convention, 1916–17; Senator, 1918–20; *Federal Deputy* from the State of San Luis Potosi, 1964–67, Dist. 1, member of the Military Industry Committee, the Military Justice Committee; *Federal Deputy* from the State of San Luis Potosi,

Dist. 10, Party Deputy for PARM, 1970–73, member of the Department of the Federal District Committee, the Legislative Studies Committee, General Means of Communication and Transportation, and the Public Security Committee. e-*President of the Authentic Party of the Mexican Revolution*, 1965–74. f-None. g-None. i-Great grandfather Miguel Francisco Barragan was Interim President of Mexico in 1836; grandfather was a senator under Benito Juarez; father, a rancher, served as mayor of Ciudad del Maiz; sister, Maria, married to *Mariano Moctezuma*, Subsecretary of Industry and Commerce, 1936–38; intimate collaborator of *Jacinto B. Trevino*, co-founder of PARM; married to Teresa Alvarez. j-Joined the Revolution in 1913, served under *Jesus Agustin Castro*; Lt. Col. in 1920; Chief of staff for President Carranza, 1920; career army officer, rank of General; incorporated back into the army by President *Cardenas*. k-Organized a strike at the Scientific and Literary Institute of San Luis Potosi in support of Madero; imprisoned after the murder of Venustiano Carranza, 1920; escaped into exile in the United States and Cuba; supported the Serrano-Gomez Rebellion in 1927. l-HA, 28 May 1973, 9; C de D, 1970–72, 102; C de D, 1964–66, 87; letter.

Barraza Allande, Luciano

a-1940. b-Gomez Palacio, Durango, *West, Urban*. c-Agricultural engineering degree, National School of Agriculture, Chapingo; Master of Science in Economics, University of Wisconsin, Madison; Ph.D. in Economics, University of Wisconsin, Madison; Professor of Econometrics, Graduate College, National School of Agriculture; Professor of Economic Development and Theory, Colegio de Mexico. e-None. f-Analyst, Department of Economic Studies, Bank of Mexico; advisor to the Second United Nations Seminar on Developmental Problems, Amsterdam; Director General, Agricultural Economy, Secretariat of Agriculture; *Oficial Mayor of the Secretariat of Agriculture and Livestock*, Aug. 3, 1972, to Aug. 25, 1972; Director General of Guanos and Fertilizers, Aug. 25, 1972–76. g-None. h-Author of ten books. j-None. k-None. l-*Excelsior*, 26 Aug. 1972, 1, 9; *Excelsior,* 4 Aug. 1972, 19; HA, 4 Sept. 1972, 30.

Barrera Fuentes, Florencio

a-Aug. 23, 1920. b-Saltillo, Coahuila, *North, Urban*. c-Primary studies at the Colegio Roberts, Saltillo; first year of secondary at the Ateneo Fuente, Saltillo; completed secondary at the National Preparatory Night School, Mexico City; preparatory studies at the National Preparatory School, Mexico City; law degree from the National School of Law, UNAM, Mar. 25, 1950. d-*Alternate Federal Deputy* from the State of Coahuila, Dist.1, 1949–52; *Federal Deputy* from the State of Coahuila, Dist.1, 1958–61, member of the Gran Comision, President of the Chamber of Deputies, October, 1960, and member of the Legislative Studies Committee, Library Committee and President of the Second Constitutional Affairs Committee; member of the Mexican delegation to the First InterParliamentary Conference of Mexico and the United States, 1961; *Senator* from the State of Coahuila, 1964–70, President of the Senate, 1967, President of the Legislative Studies Committee, the Second Treasury Committee and the Electrical Industry Committee, representative of the Senate to the Federal Electoral Commission, 1970. e-joined PRM, Oct. 15, 1940, as a member of the labor sector; Auxiliary Secretary of the CEN of PRI, 1961–63; general delegate of the CEN of PRI to municipal elections in the states of Mexico, Oaxaca, Nayarit, Morelos, Coahuila, Nuevo Leon, Guanajuato, Hidalgo and Durango; general delegate of the CEN of PRI to federal deputy elections in Colima and Chihuahua. f-Typist, Section Head, National Lottery, 1936–44; Private Secretary to *Nazario Ortiz Garza*, Director General of CONASUPO, 1944–46; Private Secretary to *Nazario Ortiz Garza*, Secretary of Agriculture, 1946–49; Director General of Administration and Accounting, Secretariat of Agriculture, 1949–51; *Oficial Mayor of Agriculture*, 1951–52; Assistant to the Director of the Federal Electric Commission, Manuel Moreno Torres, 1961–64. g-None. h-Writer for many newspapers, including *El Universal*. i-Father a physician. j-None. k-None. l-Func., 140; C de D, 1949–52; C de D, 1958–61; DGF51, 19; C de S, 1964; PS, 0580.

Barrios (Castro), Roberto

a-Mar. 19, 1910. b-Atlacomulco, Mexico, *West Central, Rural*. c-Primary studies in Atlacomulco; teaching certificate, Normal School of Toluca, Mexico; educator and secondary school teacher. d-Local deputy to the State Legislature of Mexico during the governorship of *Isidro Fabela*, 1942–45; *Federal Deputy* from the State of Mexico, Dist. 1, 1952–55, member of the Credentials Committee and the Library Committee. e-General delegate of PRI for various states during the campaign of *Adolfo Ruiz Cortines*, 1951–52; general delegate of the CEN of PRI to the States of Tabasco and Chiapas; chief of the campaign of *Alfredo del Mazo Velez* for Governor of Mexico, 1945; director of *Miguel Aleman's* campaign for President in the State of Mexico, 1946. f-Representative of the federal government on the Advisory Council of the National Bank of Ejido Credit, 1950; Subdirector of the Department of Literacy, Secretariat of Public Education; Director of Colonization, Cuenca de Papaloapan; *Head of the*

Department of Agrarian Affairs and Colonization, 1958–64. **g-**Founding member of the National Confederation of Campesinos (CNC), 1938; Secretary General of the League of Agrarian Communities and Agricultural Unions of the State of Mexico; *Secretary General of the CNC*, 1947–50; founder of the National Association of Teachers, member of the Valle de Bravo Teacher's Association. **h-**None. **i-**Disciple of *Graciano Sanchez*, longtime labor leader; active in union movement with *Adolfo Lopez Mateos*; married Luz Maria del Valle. **j-**None. **k-**Involved in a scandal over ejido lots which was accomplished with the forged signature of *Adolfo Lopez Mateos*. **l-**El *Universal*, 2 Dec. 1958; HA, 8 Dec. 1958, 30, 32; C de D, 1955, 6; DGF50, II, 139; *Quien Sera*, 132–33; *Excelsior*, 13 May 1963; *Por Que,* 11 Sept. 1969, 35; Gonzalez Navarro, 256–57; Func., 93.

Barros Sierra, Javier
(Deceased Aug. 15, 1971)
a-Feb. 25, 1915. **b-**Federal District, *Federal District, Urban*. **c-**Primary studies, Colegio Frances Alvardo, Mexico, D.F., 1928; secondary studies, Public School No. 3, 1931; preparatory studies, National Preparatory School, Mexico, D.F., 1934; civil engineering degree, National School of Engineering, UNAM, 1940; Master of Science in Mathematics, School of Science, UNAM, 1947; Professor of Mathematics, UNAM, 1938–58; Director of the National School of Engineering, UNAM, 1955–58. **d-**None. **e-**None. **f-**President of the Permanent Commission of UNAM; Director of the Mexican Institute of Petroleum; *Secretary of Public Works*, 1958–64; *Rector of UNAM*, 1966–70. **g-**None. **h-**Investigator for the Institute of Mathematics, UNAM, 1943–57; Secretary of the Mexican Society of Mathematics, 1943–57; adviser in mathematics to the National Preparatory School; adviser, School of Science, UNAM; adviser to the National Chamber of Industries; Gerente of Estructuras y Construcciones, S.A. **i-**Brother of *Manuel Barros Sierra*; grandson of Justo Sierra; student at UNAM of *Antonio Dovali Jaime*; nephew, Carlos J. Sierra Bravota, was private secretary to *Carlos Sansores Perez* as Governor of Campeche; son Javier Barros Valero was private secretary to *Fernando Solana* as Secretary of Public Education; close friend of *Fernando Espinosa Gutierrez*; married Maria Cristina Valero. **j-**None. **k-**Submitted his resignation as Rector of UNAM in 1968 but more than 1000 students asked him to remain; one of the few rectors in recent years to complete his term at UNAM. **l-**HA, 8 Dec. 1958, 28, 30; *Hoy*, 4 April, 1970; HA, 23 Aug. 1971, 15; WWMG, 8 Func. 75; El *Universal*, 2 Dec. 1958, 8; Enc. Mex. I, 530; letter.

Barros Sierra, Manuel
(Deceased 1967)
a-1916. **b-**Federal Distrcict, *Federal District, Urban*. **c-**Primary and secondary studies, Mexico, D.F.; preparatory, National Preparatory School, Mexico, D.F.; law degree, National School of Law, UNAM, 1940; with a thesis on the "Problems of Expert Testimony and Its Value in Civil Law." **d-**None. **e-**None. **f-**Assistant to the Director of the Banco Nacional Hipotecario Urbano y de Obras Publicas, 1953–54; Gerente of the Trust Department of the Banco Nacional Hipotecario Urbano, 1954–61; *Subdirector of Finances of Petroleos Mexicanos*, 1964–67; Executive Director of the Inter-American Development Bank, 1963–66. **g-**General Subdirector of the National Union of Sugar Producers, 1962–64. **h-**Member of the administrative councils of the Industrial Complex of Sahagun City, the Mexican Institute of Petroleum, and others, member of the Mexican delegation to the Regional Conference of the International Organization of Labor in Buenos Aires, 1958, The World Conference on Trade and Development, 1964. **i-**Brother of Javier Barros Sierra, Secretary of Public Works, 1958–64. **j-**None. **k-**None. **l-**HA, 4 Jan. 1965, 27; DP70, 2365, letter.

Bartlett (Bautista), Manuel
(Deceased 1963)
a-Dec. 23, 1893. **b-**Tenosique, Tabasco, *Gulf, Rural*. **c-**Primary studies, Tenosique; secondary studies, Colegio de Tenosique and the Mexican Methodist Institute of Puebla; preparatory studies, the Juarez Institute of Villahermosa, Tabasco, 1909–15; law degree, UNAM, 1920; editor of student paper *El Estudiante*. **d-**Local deputy to the Legislature of the State of Tabasco, 1921–22; *Governor of Tabasco*, 1953–55, did not complete constitutional term. **f-**Consulting lawyer for the Council of Mexico, D.F., 1920; public defender for the military, 1922; consulting lawyer for the Secretariat of the Treasury, 1924–28; chief of the legal department of the Secretariat of the Treasury, 1929; Judge of the District Court in the States of Veracruz, Puebla, and Mexico; Judge of the First District Court (Administrative Affairs); *Justice of the Supreme Court*, 1941–52. **g-**None. **h-**Practicing attorney, 1920; lawyer for the Office of Common Jurisdiction, Federal District, 1923. **i-**Son Manuel was Auxiliary Secretary to the President of Mexico, 1964–70, and Director General of the Department of Government, Secretariat of Government, 1970–72. **j-**None. **k-**Active in revolutionary movements in 1914–15; led a student protest strike on the death of Madero and was expelled from school; asked state legislature for a leave of absence after the federal government pressured him to resign following numerous riots against his administration as

governor. l-DP70, 232; DGF47, 29; WWM45, 9; WB48, 459; Scott, 276; EBW46, 421; NYT, 18 Mar. 1955, 15; NYT, 24 Mar. 1955, 11.

Bassols, Narciso

(Deceased July 24, 1959)
a-1897. b-Tenango del Valle, Mexico, *West Central, Urban.* c-Preparatory studies, National Preparatory School, Mexico, D.F., 1911–15; law degree, National School of Law, UNAM, May 29, 1920; Professor of Ethics, Logic, and Constitutional Law at the National School of Law, UNAM, 1920–31; Director of the National School of Law, UNAM, 1928–29. d-None. e-Founder of the League of Political Action with *Vicente Lombardo Toledano*; founder and Vice President of the Popular Party, 1947–49. f-Secretary General of Government of the State of Mexico under Governor Carlos Riva Palacio, 1925–26; Secretary of Public Education, 1931–34; Secretary of Government, 1934; Secretary of the Treasury, 1934–35; *Ambassador to Great Britain*, 1935–37; delegate to the League of Nations, 1937; *Ambassador to France,* 1938–39; *Ambassador to Russia,* 1944–46; adviser to *Adolfo Ruiz Cortines,* 1952–54. g-None. h-Founder of the National School of Economics, UNAM; author of the Agrarian Law of 1927; author of many articles. i-Longtime friend of *Vicente Lombardo Toledano*; student with *Gilberto Loyo* and *Rafael de la Colina* at the National Preparatory School and at UNAM; studied sociology under *Antonio Caso* at UNAM; father, Narciso Bassols was a judge; great nephew of Sebastian Lerdo de Tejada; mentor to *Ricardo J. Zevada* and *Victor Manuel Villasenor*; married Clementina Batalla. j-None. k-Participated in the gubernatorial campaign in Aguascalientes, 1919, writing campaign speeches; Calles considered him as a successor to Ortiz Rubio as president of Mexico, 1932; ran for Federal Deputy from the State of Mexico and lost; resigned as Director of the Law School after a student rebellion against the introduction of a tri-semester system; considered one of the most brilliant law professors at UNAM. l-WWM45, 9; DP70, 235; letters, EBW46, 212, Kirk, 222, 269–70; Peral, 96; Enc. Mex., II, 533; *Excelsior*, 14 Nov. 1949; NYT, 17 Oct. 1954, 16.

Batiz Vazquez, Bernardo

a-Sept. 14, 1936. b-Federal District, *Federal District, Urban.* c-Primary studies in the state of Chiapas and the Federal District; secondary studies at Diurna No. 1, Mexico, D.F.; preparatory studies at the National Preparatory School, Mexico, D.F.; law degree from the National School of Law, UNAM; teacher at the Benito Juarez Night Preparatory School and the Hispano-American Institute; Professor of

Sociology at the Ibero-American University, Mexico, D.F. d-*Alternate Federal Deputy*, Party Deputy, 1967–70, Federal District; *Federal Deputy* from the Federal District, Dist. 16, 1970–73; member of the Department of the Federal District Committee, the Ejidal No. 1 Committee, and the Money and Credit Institutions Committee. e-Joined PAN, 1955; President of the Regional Committee of PAN for the Federal District, member of the Regional Committee of PAN for the Federal District; *Secretary General of PAN*, 1972–75. f-None. g-None. h-Practicing lawyer, 1975. i-Married to Dolce Maria Zavala. j-None. k-None. l-*Directorio*, 1970–72; letter; C de D, 1970–72, 103; HA, 19 Feb. 1979, vii.

Bautista (Castillo), Gonzalo

(Deceased October 7, 1952)
a-Jan. 1, 1896. b-Puebla, Puebla, *East Central, Urban.* c-Primary at the Escuela Ventanas in Puebla; secondary studies in Puebla; preparatory and beginning of professional studies in Puebla; medical degree from the National School of Medicine; UNAM. d-Local deputy to the Legislature of the State of Puebla; Federal Deputy from the State of Puebo, 1922–28, 1930–34; *Senator* from the State of Puebla, 1934–40; Mayor of Puebla, 1940–41; *Governor of Puebla*, 1941–46. e-Member of the League of Professionals and Intellectuals of the Mexican Revolutionary Party. f-None. g-Student delegate to the 2nd National Student Congress with *Leonides Andreu Almazan*, 1921. h-Author. i-Father of *Gonzalo Bautista O'Farrill; Gustavo Diaz Ordaz* served under him as Secretary General of Government. j-Joined the Revolution in 1910. k-President *Avila Camacho* personally attended the inauguration ceremonies of *Gonzalo Bautista* as Governor of Puebla. l-Correa47, 20; DP70, 238; letter, Peral, 98.

Bautista O'Farrill, Gonzalo

a-Apr. 16, 1922. b-Puebla, Puebla, *East Central, Urban.* c-Primary, secondary and preparatory studies in Puebla; biology degree from the University of Puebla, 1947; Professor of Bacteriology, School of Medicine, University of Puebla, 1950–53; Rector of the University of Puebla, 1953–54; Professor of Virology of the School of Medicine at the University of Puebla, 1957–60. d-*Federal Deputy* from the State of Puebla, Dist. 5, 1961–64; President of the Editorial Committee, President of the Committee on Health and Welfare, member of the Child Assistance and Social Security Committee, President of the Interparliamentary Committee, President of the Complaints Committee; *Senator* from the State of Puebla, 1964–70; Oficial Mayor of the Gran

Comision, President of the Administrative Committee, President of the Committee on Social Security; Secretary of the First Committee on Tariffs and Foreign Trade; Secretary of the First Committee on Public Education; *Interim Governor of Puebla*, Apr., 1972 to Mar. 8, 1973; Mayor of Puebla, 1970– 72. e-Director of Economic and Social Planning for the presidential campaign of *Adolfo Lopez Mateos* in Puebla, 1958; general delegate of PRI to Veracruz, Sonora, Jalisco, Baja California del Norte, Sinaloa and Nayarit. f-None. g-None. h-Resident in the Hospital of Nutritional Illnesses, 1948; investigator at Columbia University, New York, on scholarship, 1954; worked in the Laboratory of Viral Investigations, Columbia University, 1955– 56. i-Son of *Gonzalo Bautista (Castillo)*. k-Resigned governorship under pressure. l-HA, 24 April 1972; DBM68, 62– 63; *Hoy*, 6 May 1972, 60– 61.

Baz (de Prada), Gustavo

a-May 1, 1894. b-Tlalnepantla, Mexico, *West Central, Rural*. c-Primary and secondary studies, Guadalajara; preparatory studies, Scientific and Literary Institute of Toluca, Mexico; began professional studies at the Military Medical School, 1913, on a scholarship; medical degree from the National School of Medicine, UNAM, Mar. 1, 1920; graduate studies in the United States at Harvard University, Boston University, and the Agustana Hospital in Chicago; studies in Europe on a private scholarship; Director, National School of Medicine, UNAM, 1935– 36; Professor of Medicine at the National School of Medicine, UNAM, 1920– 46; *Rector of UNAM*, 1939– 40. d-*Governor of Mexico*, 1957– 63; *Senator* from the State of Mexico, 1976- . e-Member of the League of Professionals and Intellectuals of the Party of the Mexican Revolution, 1939, member of the Advisory Committee of the IEPES of PRI, 1972. f-Chief of Medical Services, Hospital Juarez, Mexico, D.F., 1925; *Secretary of Health and Public Welfare*, 1940– 46; Director of the Juarez Hospital, Mexico, D.F., 1925; *Secretary of Fund of the Hospital of Jesus*, 1964– 70. g-President of the Student Society at the National School of Medicine. h-Director of the Military Medical School, 1936– 39; created the Social Service for Medical Students in Mexico, 1938; initiated the standard method of medical documentation in Mexico, 1925; practicing physician. i-Personal friend of *Manuel Gual Vidal*; married Elena Diaz Lombardo; son Gustavo is married to the daughter of *Pasqual Gutierrez Roldan*; was the personal physician of *Manuel Avila Camacho* before he became president. j-Joined the Revolution, 1914– 15; served as a Colonel under Emiliano Zapata; rank of

General; Military Governor of the State of Mexico, 1918. k-Donated salary to maternal and child welfare centers when he served as Secretary of Health. l-HA, 2 Nov. 1959, 19; WWMG, 8; WWM45, 10; Hayner, 24546; Peral, 98– 99; HA, 4 Aug. 1944, 7; HA, 22 Sept. 1944, 6; WB48, 492; *Excelsior*, 13 Jul. 19722, 19; DGF51, II, 687; letter; *Excelsior*, 8 June 1978, 12.

Becker Arreola, Juan Guillermo

a-Aug. 30, 1931. b-Canatlan, Durango, *West, Rural*. c-Early education unknown; studies at the National School of Economics and the National School of Law, UNAM; law degree, National School of Law, UNAM. d-None. e-None. f-Joined the Secretariat of Industry and Commerce, 1952; Director General of Industries, Secretariat of Industry and Commerce, 1961– 64; Director General of Standards, Secretariat of Industry and Commerce, 1965– 67; Director General of Industries, 1967– 74; *Subsecretary of Industry and Commerce*, 1974– 76; Financial Subdirector of INFONAVIT, 1976- . g-None. i-Studied under *Agustin Lopez Munguia*. j-None. k-None. l-HA, 28 Jan. 1974, 18; DPE65, 96.

Bellizzia Castaneda, Pascual

a-1933. b-Frontera, Tabasco, *Gulf, Rural*. c-Primary studies at the Tomas Garrido School, Tabasco; secondary studies at the Palavicini School, Tabasco; studies in law, Sorbonne, Paris, France; law degree, National School of Law, UNAM. d-Local Deputy to the State Legislature of Tabasco, 1961– 64; *Senator* from the State of Tabasco, 1970– 76, First Secretary of the First Committee on Mines, President of the Livestock Committee; Mayor of Villahermosa, Tabasco, 1980- . e-Joined PRI, 1955; member of the Technical Advisory Council of PRI. f-None. g-Leader of the Farmer and Rancher's Association, Tabasco; Secretary of Labor for the CEN of CNOP; adviser to the CEN of CNOP. i-From a peasant background. j-None. k-None. l-C de S, 1970– 76, 70; PS, 0630.

Beltran Beltran, Amando

b-Tantoyuca, Veracruz, *Gulf, Rural*. c-Primary studies at the Gabino Barreda School, Tampico; preparatory at the National Preparatory School; law studies from 1928– 32 at the National School of Law, UNAM, degree, April 13, 1934; professor of world history at the National Preparatory School No. 2, 1936– 72; Director of the National Preparatory School No. 2. d-None. e-None. f-Secretary of Group Five, Federal Board of Conciliation and Arbitration, 1933; President of Group Five, Federal Board of Conciliation and Arbitration, 1936; Director of the

Strike Department, Secretariat of Labor; Director of Labor and Social Welfare, Secretariat of Labor; Alternate President of the Federal Conciliation and Arbitration Board; President of the Federal Conciliation and Arbitration Board; Head of the Labor Office for Auxiliary Agents, Office of the Attorney General, 1951; Secretary of the Board of Directors of the National Railroads of Mexico, 1948; Oficial Mayor of the National Railroads of Mexico, 1960; Director of Personnel, National Railroads of Mexico, 1969; Subdirector of Administration, National Railroads of Mexico, 1973. **g**-None. **h**-Practicing lawyer. **i**-Collaborator of *Francisco Trujillo Gurria*, Secretary of Labor, 1943–46. **j**-None. **k**-None. **l**-letter; MGF69, 588; DGF51, I, 536.

Beltran (Castillo), Enrique

a-Apr. 26, 1903. **b**-Federal District, *Federal District, Urban*. **c**-Secondary studies at the Pablo Moreno Secondary School, Federal District, 1916; preparatory studies at the National Preparatory School; Bachelor of Science in Zoology, UNAM; Sc.D. from UNAM, 1926; Ph.D. in Zoology, Columbia University, 1931–33; Professor of Natural Sciences, UNAM, 1922–26; Professor of Zoology, National School of Agriculture, 1934–38; Professor of Biology and Zoology, National Preparatory School, 1931–58; Professor of Protozoology, Graduate School, UNAM, 1946–50; Assistant in Botany, UNAM, 1922–26; Professor of Zoology, Higher Normal School, 1936–58; Professor of Protozoology, National School of Biological Sciences, 1940–58; Professor of Biological Education, National Teachers School, 1935–47; Professor of Parasitology, School of Health and Hygiene, Secretariat of Agriculture, 1945–46. **d**-None. **e**-Founder of the Revolutionary Anti-Clerical Group, 1929; member of the Communist Party, 1930–31. **f**-Assistant, Museum of Natural History, Secretariat of Agriculture, 1923; Microbiologist, Division of Biological Studies, Secretariat of Agriculture, 1924–25; Founder and Director, Marine Biological Station of the Gulf, 1926–28; member of the Reorganization Committee for the Secretariat of Agriculture, 1933; Founder and Director, Biotechnical Institute, Secretariat of Agriculture; Chief, Department of Secondary Instruction, Secretariat of Public Education, 1937–38; Director, Department of Protozoology, Institute of Health and Tropical Diseases, Secretariat of Health, 1939–51; *Subsecretary of Forest Resources and Fauna, Secretariat of Agriculture*, 1958–64. **g**-None. **h**-Director, Mexican Institute of Renewable Natural Resources, 1952–79; author of hundreds of articles and books on conservation and biology. **i**-Professor of *Luis Echeverria, Emilio Martinez*

Manautou, Renaldo Guzman Orozco and *Guillermo Soberon*. **j**-None. **k**-None. **l**-Enc. Mex. I. 552; HA, 22 Dec. 1958; DPE61, 69; WWW70–71, 80–81; letter.

Benitez Claveli, Vicente L.

b-Federal District, *Federal District, Urban*. **c**-Primary and secondary studies, Mexico, D.F.; college degree, Mexico, D.F. **d**-Federal Deputy from the State of Aguascalientes (twice); *Senator* from Aguascalientes, 1934–40; precandidate for the Governorship of Aguascalientes, 1941. **e**-None. **f**-Ambassador to Nicaragua, 1941–43; special post in the Secretariat of Foreign Relations, 1943; Ambassador to Venezuela, December, 1943, to February, 1945; Ambassador to Guatemala, July, 1945, to 1948; Ambassador to Argentina, 1954; Ambassador to Yugoslavia, 1958–61. **g**-None. **h**-Journalist. **j**-Participated in the Revolution. **k**-None. **l**-EBW46, 23; DPE61, 25; WB54, 547; IYBSTWW54, lxxviii, 609.

Berber, Alberto F.

a-June 12, 1885. **b**-Chilpancingo, Guerrero, *South, Urban*. **c**-Primary studies, Chilpancingo; None, None. **d**-Mayor of Acapulco, 1934; Federal deputy from the State of Guerrero, Dist. 5, 1935–37; *Governor of Guerrero*, 1937–41. **e**-None. **g**-None. **j**-Career army officer; Commander of the Garrison, Acapulco, 1932–33; rank of Brigadier General, June 1, 1941. **k**-Removed as Governor February 19, 1941 because he tried to continue his political power by imposing his half-brother, Francisco Carreto. **l**-letter; D de Y, 2 Nov. 1940, 1; Peral, 105; Anderson, 79–80.

Bermudez (Jaquez), Antonio J.

(Deceased Feb. 10, 1977)
a-June 13, 1892. **b**-Chihuahua, Chihuahua, *North, Urban*. **c**-Secondary studies from the Los Angeles Business College; no degree. **d**-Mayor of Ciudad Juarez, Chihuahua, 1942–45; *Senator* from Chihuahua (never served in the position), 1946. **f**-Treasurer of Ciudad Juarez, Chihuahua, 1945–46; *Director General of Petroleos Mexicanos*, 1946–58; Ambassador to Arab countries, 1958–61; Director of the National Frontier Program, 1961–65. **g**-None. **h**-Founded his own business in Chihuahua while very young, later became a very wealthy businessman after founding a whiskey factory in Ciudad Juarez; his career in local politics was noted for increasing revenues as treasurer, and fighting vice in Ciudad Juarez. **i**-Parents, well-to-do landowners; married to Hilda Mascarena. **j**-None. **k**-Pre-candidate for president of Mexico, 1951–52; did not accept a salary as director of Pemex, **l**-HA, 18 Mar. 1949, 26;

DGF47, 20; DGF50, II, 279, 80; DGF51, II, 383–84, I, 6; HA, 21 Feb. 1977, 13; *Proceso*, 19 Feb. 1977, 29; NYT, 28 July 1957, 2; NYT, 30 July 1951, 5; NYT, 17 Aug. 1950, 6.

Bermudez Limon, Carlos

a-1936. b-Tampico, Tamaulipas, *North, Urban*. c-Economics degree, National School of Economics, UNAM, 1954–58; thesis, 1960, on ''Public Works and Economic Development in Mexico''; graduate studies at Yale University on a United Nations and Secretariat of the Treasury Fellowship; graduate studies at the U.S. Department of the Treasury, Washington, D.C.; Professor of Mexican Economic Problems, School of Economics, National Polytechnic Institute, and the Technological Institute of Mexico, 1962–68. d-None. e-Adviser to the CEPES for the Valley of Mexico. f-Adviser and Analyst, Department of Treasury Studies, Secretariat of the Treasury; Subdirector, Department of Economic Studies, Secretariat of the Treasury; Director of the Center for Development Studies; Director General of PIPSA, 1970–74. g-President of the League of Revolutionary Economists of Mexico; President of the National College of Economists; Vice President of the 1954 Generation, National School of Economics. h-Author of various articles; Director of the Center for Economic Studies of the Private Sector; economic consultant. i-Attended college with *Jesus Silva Herzog F.*, *Agustin Olachea Borbon, Eliseo Mendoza Berrueto*. j-None. k-None. l-Hoy, 10 Jun. 1972, 13; letter; *Latin America*, 12 Mar. 1976, 83.

Bernal de Pina de Badillo, Zorayda

a-Feb. 25, 1934. b-Oaxaca, *South*. c-Early education unknown; graduate of the Latin American Hospital, Puebla, in nursing; advanced studies in social work in Rumania and Peru; courses on labor law, Academy of Law and Social Welfare. d-*Federal Deputy* from the State of Oaxaca, Dist. 7, 1976–79, member of Railroad Section of the General Means of Communication Committee, the Economic, Cultural and Social Development of Peasant Women Section of the Agrarian Affairs Committee, the Artisan and Small Industries Development Committee, the Mail and Telegraph Section of the Development of Means of Communication, the Isthmus Section of the Regional Development Committee, the Infant and Maternal Welfare Section of the Social Security and Public Health Committee and the National Properties Committee. e-None. f-None. g-Secretary General of the Political Committee of the National Railroad Workers Union; Vice-president of the Congress of Female Workers. i-Married Dr. Jesus Badillo Chavez. j-None. k-None. l-C de D, 1976–79, 5; D

de C, 1976–79, 8, 14, 22, 28, 34, 40, 63; *Excelsior*, 27 Aug. 1976, 1C.

Bernal Miranda, Benito

(Deceased October 21, 1974)
a-1892. b-Alamos, Sonora, *North, Urban*. c-Early education unknown. d-Mayor of Navajoa, Sonora; *Senator* from Sonora, 1970–74, member of the Gran Comision, president of the Third National Defense Committee, first secretary of the Military Health and the Pensions and Military Retirement Committees, second secretary of the Livestock Committee and member of the Fishing Committee. e-Activist in the Anti-Reelectionist Party, 1910. f-None. g-None. h-None. i-Married Carlota Dominguez; son *Benito Bernal Dominguez* was a federal deputy from Sonora, 1958–61. j-Joined the Revolution, 1910; fought in various battles under Captain Lucas Giron, 1910; 2nd lieutenant in the 5th Sonoran Irregulars under Lt. Col. Jesus Chavez Camacho, 1912; served under Alvaro Obregon, 1913; Chief of Staff for General Obregon; career officer, reached the rank of Divisionary General, March 1, 1962. k-None. l-*Excelsior*, 22 Oct. 1974; HA, 28 Oct. 1974, 14; C de S, 1970–76, 15.

Bernal (Tenorio), Antonio

a-1911. b-Toluca, Mexico, *West Central, Urban*. c-Law degree, National School of Law, UNAM; professor at the Worker's University; teacher in various secondary schools; professor at the National Preparatory School, Mexico, D.F. d-*Federal Deputy* from the State of Mexico, Dist. 8, 1967–70, member of Committee on Motor Transportation, First Committee on National Defense, and the Third Section on Criminal Law of Legislative Studies. e-First Secretary of the Political Commission of the Federation of the Union of Workers of the Federal Government (FSTSE), assisting in the campaign of *Miguel Aleman*, 1946; Secretary General of Disputes of the National Confederation of Popular Organizations of PRI, 1965–66. f-Adviser to the President of Mexico, 1946–52; adviser to the President of Mexico, 1952–58; *Director General of Federal Highways and Bridges and Adjacent Entrances and Exits*, 1970–76. g-Member of the Judicial Workers Union; Secretary General of the Mexican Chauffeurs Union; candidate for Secretary General of the FSTSE, 1946; *Secretary General of the FSTSE*, 1965–67; President of the Congress of Labor, 1966; Secretary General of the Union of Federal Judicial Workers, 1977- . h-Employee of the Fourth Division of the Supreme Court; one of the founders of the magazine *Futura*. j-None. k-Ran for Alternate Federal Deputy with *Victor Manuel Villasenor*, 1943, as a militant leftist. l-HA, 15 Nov. 1946, 4; HA, 7 Dec. 1970, 27; Villasenor, II, 33.

Bernard, Miguel

(Deceased Oct. 25, 1939)
a-1873. **b-**Brownsville, Texas, *Foreign, Urban*.
c-Engineering degree, National Military College, Mexico, D.F., February 5, 1889; Professor of Math, Physics and Mechanics, National Military College; Professor of the School of Artillery, National Military College; Organizer and Director of the School of Mechanical and Electrical Engineering. **d-**None. **e-**None. **f-**Chief of the Department of Technical, Industrial, and Commercial Instruction, Secretariat of Public Education; *Oficial Mayor of the Secretariat of Industry and Commerce*, 1937–38; *Director General of the National Poytechnic Institute*, 1939. **g-**None. **h-**Chairman, technical military commissions in the United States, Europe, and Japan. **j-**Joined the Revolution; Technical Artillery Lieutenant, 1893; rank of Colonel, February 14, 1913; Brigadier General, 1914. **k-**None. **l-**DP70, 257; Enc. Mex. I, 561; Q es Q, 71.

Berrueto Ramon, Federico

(Deceased Jan. 15, 1980)
a-Oct. 2, 1900. **b-**Sabinas, Coahuila, *North, Rural*.
c-Teaching credential from the Normal School in Coahuila, 1921; teaching credential from the Normal School of Mexico, November 18, 1937, with a thesis on adolescent problems; professor at Texas State College for Women; professor at the Higher School of Agriculture; Professor at Normal School in Mexico, D.F., and Secondary School in Coahuila. **d-***Federal Deputy* from the State of Coahuila, Dist. 1, 1946–49, member of the Gran Comision, the Second Committee on Public Education, and the Budget Committee; *Senator* from Coahuila, 1958–64; member of the Gran Comision, President of the Committee on Indigenous Affairs, First Vocal of the Second Committee on Public Education, and the Committee on Electrical Industry. **e-**Representative on the National Advisory Council of PRI from the National Confederation of Popular Organizations, 1946; state committeeman for PRI from Coahuila; President of PRI in Coahuila. **f-**Director of the Department of Public Education for Coahuila, 1953; Director of the Normal Schools for Coahuila; Subdirector of Primary Schools in Saltillo, Coahuila; *Subsecretary of Public Education*, 1964–70. **g-**Founding member of the Federation of Teachers' Unions in Coahuila, Secretary General of the Federation of Teachers' Unions in Coahuila, 1933. **h-**Educational consultant to the Secretariat of Public Education. **i-**Brother, Professor *Mauro Berrueto Ramon*, served as a Federal Deputy, 1964–67. **j-**None. **k-**Precandidate for governor of Coahuila, 1963 and in 1969. **l-**WWMG, 9; DBM68, 72; DBM70, 82; D del S, 22 Jan. 1946, 1; Func., 138; Enc. Mex., II, 106; *Excelsior*, 16 Jan. 1980, 12.

Betancourt Perez, Antonio

a-June 13, 1907. **b-**Merida, Yucatan, *Gulf, Urban*.
c-Primary studies at the Escuela Modelo, Merida; preparatory at the Literary Institute of Yucatan; normal studies at the Escuela Rodolfo Menendez de la Pena; studied social science at the Lenin Institute, Moscow. **d-***Federal Deputy* from the State of Yucatan, Dist. 3, 1940–43, member of the Second Balloting Committee, the First Public Education Committee, and the Protocol Committee; Vice President of the Chamber of Deputies, Nov. 1942; member of the Permanent Commission, 1941. **e-**None. **f-**Director of the Department of Public Education, State of Yucatan; Director of Federal Education, State of Yucatan; Director General of *Diario del Sureste*, Merida, Yucatan, 1972–73. **g-**None. **h-**Employee of the Department of the Federal District; employee of the Secretariat of Public Education; author of numerous articles on history and education. **j-**None. **k-**None. **l-**C de D, 1940–42, 6, 47, 49.

Beteta (Monsalve), Mario Ramon

a-July 7, 1925. **b-**Federal District, *Federal District, Urban*. **c-**Primary and secondary studies in Mexico, D.F., law degree from the National School of Law, UNAM, Dec. 4, 1948, with a thesis on the responsibility for illegal acts; Professor at Secondary Schools No. 8 and 10, Mexico, D.F., 1945–48; Professor of Introductory Economics, National School of Economics, 1954–56; Professor of Monetary Theory, National School of Economics, UNAM, 1951–59; Master of Arts in Economics, University of Wisconsin, June 16, 1950, with a thesis on the institutional focus of economic planning. **d-**None. **e-**Member of the New Advisory Council of the IEPES of PRI, in charge of structural reforms of the party June 28, 1972. **f-**Advisor to the Office of the Director General of the Bank of Mexico; assistant to the Gerente of the Bank of Mexico; Subgerente of the Bank of Mexico, 1957; Gerente of the Bank of Mexico, 1960–63; Director General of Credit of the Secretariat of the Treasury, 1964–70; *Subsecretary of the Treasury*, 1970–75; *Secretary of the Treasury*, 1975–76; President of the SOMEX Group, 1977- . **g-**None. **h-**Investigator of the Department of Economic Studies of the Bank of Mexico, 1948; Mexican delegate to major international monetary conferences. **i-**Nephew of *Ramon Beteta*, former Secretary of the Treasury, 1946–52; son of General Ignacio Beteta Quintana, Chief of Staff during the presidency of *Lazaro Cardenas* and well-known Mexican artist; married Gloria Leal Kuri. **j-**None. **k-**None. **l-**BdeM, 72–73; *Hoy*, 24 June 1967, 26; HA, 14 Dec. 1970, 20–21; HA, 29 Mar. 1976; LAD, 5 Dec. 1975, 379; HA, 6 Oct. 1975, 9; *Excelsior*, 27 Sept. 1975, 22.

Beteta, Ramon

(Deceased Oct. 5, 1965)
a-Oct. 7, 1901. **b-**Federal District, *Federal District, Urban.* **c-**Primary and secondary studies in Mexico, D.F.; preparatory studies at the National Preparatory School; attended UNAM, 1919–20; degree in economics from the University of Texas, 1920–23; law degree from the National School of Law, 1925–26; Ph.D. in Social Sciences from UNAM, 1934 (first Ph.D. in this field); Professor of Economics at the National School of Economics, UNAM, 1924–42; Professor of Law at the National Law School, UNAM; Professor at the National Preparatory School in Mexico, D.F., 1925–28; Professor at secondary schools in Mexico, D.F. **d-**None. **e-**Member of the League of Professionals and Intellectuals of the Mexican Revolutionary Party, 1939; director of *Miguel Aleman*'s campaign for president, 1945–46. **f-**Legal consultant to the Agricultural Bank, 1926–28; private secretary to the Secretary of Public Education *(Ezequiel Padilla),* 1928–29; legal adviser to the Secretary of Public Education, 1929–30; head of the Department of Education and Social Services, Department of the Federal District, 1930–31; head of the Department of Securities, Secretariat of Industry and Commerce, 1931–32; Oficial Mayor of the Secretariat of Industry and Commerce, 1932–33; Director General of the Department of National Statistics, Secretariat of Industry and Commerce, 1933–35; technical adviser to President *Lazaro Cardenas,* 1935; *Subsecretary of Foreign Relations;* 1936–40; *Subsecretary of the Treasury,* 1940–45; *Secretary of the Treasury,* 1946–52; Ambassador to Italy, 1952–55; Ambassador to Greece, 1955–58. **g-**None. **h-**Minor administrator of the Secretariat of the Treasury, 1924; member of the Mexican delegation to the Inter-American Peace Conference in Buenos Aires, 1936; editor of the *News* and *Novedades,* 1958–64. **i-**Personal advisor to *Lazaro Cardenas;* professor of *Antonio Armendariz* and *Hugo B. Margain* at UNAM; close friend of Moises Saenz; brother of General Ignacio Beteta Quintana, Director of Military Industry and Chief of Staff under President *Cardenas;* uncle of *Mario Ramon Beteta;* father, a lawyer; his mother came from a wealthy landowning family. **j-**None. **k-**Precandidate for President of Mexico, 1951, but too strongly identified with the right wing of PRI; actually born in Hermosillo, Sonora, but registered his birth in the Federal District. **l-***Hoy,* 4 Nov. 1939, 18; DBM68, 72–73; IWW66, 111; EBW46, 125; WWM45, 13; DGF56, 126–27; Scott, 214; letters.

Biebrich Torres, Carlos Armando

a-Nov. 19, 1939. **b-**Sahuaripa, Sonora, *North, Rural.* **c-**Preparatory studies in humanities, University of Sonora; law degree, University of Sonora,

1963 (fifth person to graduate in law); thesis on labor law; Professor of Labor Law, School of Business and Administration, University of Sonora, 1964–66. **d-***Federal Deputy* from the State of Sonora, Dist. 4, 1967–70, member of the Gran Comision, the Committee on Taxes, the Committee on Constitutional Affairs, the Committee on the Budget, and the Seventh Section on Commerce and Credit of the Legislative Studies Committee; *Governor of Sonora,* 1973 to October 25, 1975. **e-**State Director of PRI in Sonora; Auxiliary Secretary to *Luis Echeverria* during his presidential campaign, 1970; gave two hundred speeches during the Echeverria campaign. **f-**Secretary of the City Council of Ciudad Obregon, 1961–63; under Mayor *Faustino Felix Serna;* Secretary of the City Council of Cajeme, Sonora; Auxiliary Secretary to the Governor of Sonora, 1964–67; *Subsecretary of Government,* 1970–73. **g-**President of the Federation of University Students of the University of Sonora, 1958; active journalist for student newspapers; winner of the National Oratory Contest of PRI, 1963; organized the Assembly for the Political Orientation of Youth for PRI, 1958. **h-**None. **i-**From modest middle-class background; friend of *Luis Encinas Johnson,* whom he supported for governor in 1961; supporter of *Mario Moya Palencia* for president, 1975; married Socorro Gandara, related to one of the wealthiest families in Sonora. **k-**Resigned from the governorship after internal political struggle with collaborators of *Luis Echeverria.* **l-***Hoy,* 19 Dec. 1970, 60; HA, 14 Dec. 1970, 19–20; HA, 1 Jan. 1973, 29; HA, 10 Sept. 1973, 40; *Excelsior,* 26 Oct. 1975, 1; *Excelsior,* 13 Nov. 1975.

Blanco Caceres, Othon P.

(Deceased)
a-March 7, 1868. **b-**Ciudad Victoria, Tamaulipas, *North, Rural.* **c-**National Military College, 1885–89, graduating as a 1st lieutenant. **d-**None. **e-**None. **f-**Head of the Department of the Navy in the Secretariat of War, 1918–20; Inspector General of the Fleet and Head of the Department of the Navy, 1930s; *Subsecretary of the Navy,* 1940–46. **g-**None. **h-**None. **j-**2nd lieutenant in 1893; participated in the campaign against the Mayan uprising, 1907; captain of a frigate, 1909; Full Captain of the Navy, 1913, and in 1912, Commander of the *Guerrero;* Commodore and then Vice Admiral in 1914; Chief of Naval Forces in the East of the Yucatan Peninsula; Commander of the *Bravo;* Commanding General of the Gulf Fleet. **k-**None. **l-**D de Y, 5 Dec. 1940, 1; DP70, 268; letter; Peral, 110–111.

Blas Briseno (Rodriguez), Jose

a-Aug. 28, 1938. **b-**Zitacuaro, Michoacan, *West Central, Rural.* **c-**Primary, secondary and preparatory in the Federal District; teaching certificate from the Higher Normal School, Mexico City, with a specialty in pedagogy; accounting degree from the Autonomous Technological Institute of Mexico; master of arts in business and administration. **d**-*Alternate Federal Deputy* from the Federal District, Dist. 9, 1964–67; *Federal Deputy* from the National Action Party (Party Deputy). **e**-Joined PAN in 1955. **f**-None. **g**-None. **h**-Operates consulting firm specializing in the administration of construction firms. **j**-None. **k**-None. **l**-C de D, 1970–73, 145; C de D, 1964–67.

Bobadilla Pena, Julio

a-1918. **b**-Progreso, Yucatan, *Gulf, Urban*. **c**-Primary studies in Yucatan; secondary and preparatory studies in Merida, Yucatan; no degree. **d**-Local Deputy to the State Legislature of Yucatan, 1963; *Federal Deputy* from the State of Yucatan, Dist. 2, 1967–70, member of the Gran Comision. **e**-General Delegate of the CEN of PRI in Colima, Campeche and Yucatan; member of the State Committee of the PRM, Yucatan; Secretary of Popular Action of PRI in Yucatan, 1963; *Secretary of Popular Action of the CEN of PRI*, 1971. **f**-Agent of the National Lottery in Yucatan; Director, Department of Cooperatives, Division of Agriculture, State of Yucatan; Secretary General of Government of the State of Yucatan, 1964; Oficial Mayor of the State of Yucatan; *Oficial Mayor of the Secretariat of Communications*, 1973–76; Delegate of the Department of the Federal District, 1976–78. **g**-Student leader in the Federation of University Students and the Unified Socialist Youth of Mexico; Secretary General of CNOP in Yucatan, 1963; member of the CEN of CNOP, 1971; *Secretary General of CNOP*, 1971–72. **h**-None. **i**-Father a modest employee of Yucatan Railroads and founder of the Socialist Party of the Southeast; later Mayor and President of the Federal of Labor Leagues of Progreso; son, Julian Bobadilla Novelo was a precandidate for federal deputy, 1979. **j**-None. **k**-Schers says he was chosen as Secretary General of CNOP because of close relation to *Luis Escheverria*; lost as a pre-candidate for governor of Yucatan, 1975. **l**-Schers, 27; C de D, 1967–70; PS, 695.

Bobadilla Romero, Manuel
(Deceased July 16, 1978)
a-Sept. 23, 1909. **b**-Bacubirito, Sonora, *North, Rural*. **c**-Primary studies in Los Mochis, Sinaloa; no degree. **d**-Local Deputy to the State Legislature of Sonora; *Federal deputy* from the State of Sonora, Dist. 3, 1964–67, member of the Desert Zones Committee and the Military Justice Committee; *Federal Deputy* from the State of Sonora, Dist. 3, 1970–73, member of the First Railroads Committee, the First Balloting Committee and the Small Agricul-

tural Property Committee. **e**-None. **f**-None. **g**-Secretary General of the Union of Workers (CTM) of Sonora, 1937–78; Secretary of Agriculture of the CTM, 1978. **h**-None. **i**-Married Carlota Icedo. **j**-None. **k**-Assumed the directorship of the Sonora CTM while in jail as a labor agitator in Ciudad Obregon. **l**-Directorio, 1970–72, 22; *Excelsior,* 18 July 1978, 12; C de D, 1964–67, 89, 96; C de D, 1970–73, 103.

Bojorquez, Juan de Dios
(Deceased 1967)
a-March 8, 1892. **b**-San Miguel Horcasitas, Sonora, *North, Rural*. **c**-Agricultural engineering degree, National School of Agriculture, San Jacinto, Federal District, 1912; Professor of Mexican History, Normal School, Hermosillo, Sonora, 1918. **d**-Deputy to the Constitutional Convention at Queretaro, 1916–17; Federal Deputy from the State of Sonora, 1918–20; *Senator* from Sonora, 1964–67. **f**-Governor of Baja California del Sur; Subsecretary of Agriculture, 1914; Minister to Honduras; Minister to Guatemala, 1922; Minister to Cuba, 1926; head of the Department of Statistics, 1926–32; head of the Department of Labor, 1932–34; Secretary of Government, 1934–35; Director General of the Small Business Bank of the Federal District, 1950–52; Director General of Maiz Industrializado. **g**-Organized the Local Agrarian Commission of Sonora, 1916; Secretary of the Local Agrarian Commission of Sonora; founder and President of the Intellectual Workers' Block. **h**-Author of many biographies; agricultural engineer in Sonora, 1913; Administrator of the Secretariat of Industry and Commerce, 1914; Director of the government newspaper, *El Nacional*. **j**-Participated in the Revolution as a Constitutionalist, 1913. **k**-None. **l**-DP70, 273; WWM45, 13–14; DGF50, II, 414; Gaxiola, 92ff; Peral, 115; Morton, 7; Enc. Mex., II, 128.

Bolanos Cacho (Guendulain), Raul
a-1916. **b**-Oaxaca, Oaxaca, *South, Rural*. **c**-Early education unknown; law degree, School of Law, Institute of Arts and Sciences of Oaxaca, 1940; Professor of General Theory of the State and of Mexican History, Benito Juarez University, Oaxaca. **d**-*Federal Deputy* from the State of Oaxaca, Dist. 3, 1955–58; *Senator* from the State of Oaxaca, 1964–70; President of the Chamber of Deputies, 1955. **e**-President of PRI in Oaxaca. **f**-Director of the Cultural Department of Youth Affairs, State of Oaxaca; Syndic of the City Council of Oaxaca, Oaxaca. **g**-Secretary General of CNOP of Oaxaca. **i**-Son *Raul Bolanos Cacho Guzman* was a federal deputy from Oaxaca, 1976–79; cousin *Demetrio Bolanos Espinosa* was a federal deputy from Oaxaca, 1934–37, 1940–43; son of Miguel Bolanos Cacho, lawyer and

governor of Oaxaca. **j-**None. **k-**None. **l-**C de S, 1964; C de D, 1955–58; DGF56; Peral, 115.

Bolanos Espinosa, Demetrio

b-Oaxaca, Oaxaca, *South, Urban*. **c-**Primary studies at the Institute of Arts and Sciences, Oaxaca; engineering degree from the National School of Agriculture. **d-**Federal Deputy from the State of Oaxaca, 1934–36; *Federal Deputy* from the State of Oaxaca, Dist. 4, 1940–43, member of the Securities Committee; member of the city council of Mixcoac, 1926. **e-**Director of the PRM radio station, Mexico, D.F., 1937. **f-**Founder and Director of the Office of Economic Information for States and Federal Territories, 1938–46; founder and first director of *Proa,* first newspaper of the Mexican congress, 1934; editor of *El Universal*, 1946. **g-**None. **h-**Journalist since 1920; editor of *El Universal Ilustrado*; author and translator under the name of Oscar Leblanc. **i-**Nephew of Miguel Bolanos Cacho, lawyer and governor of Oaxaca; cousin *Raul*, served as a Federal Deputy from Oaxaca, 1955–57. **j-**None. **k-**None. **l-**EBW46, 60; Peral, 115; C de D, 1940–42, 48.

Bonfil, Ramon G.

a-Feb. 10, 1905. **b-**Tetepango, Hidalgo, *East Central, Rural*. **c-**Teaching certificate in elementary level education; elementary teacher in the Normal School for Men; started legal studies at UNAM but left to continue rural teaching; higher studies in Geneva, 1956, and in Paris, 1958, 1960; director of various primary and normal schools. **d-***Federal Deputy* from the State of Hidalgo, Dist. 2, 1943–46. **e-**Founding member with *Carlos Madrazo* and *Lauro Ortega* of the National Confederation of Popular Organizations of PRI (CNOP), January 18, 1942. **f-**Director of Federal Education, Jalisco, 1932; Director General of Literacy of the Secretariat of Public Education, 1964–68; Director General of Teacher's Education of the Secretariat of Public Education, 1969–70; *Subsecretary General of Public Education*, 1970–76. **g-**First Secretary General of the Mexican Federation of Teachers, 1932–33. **h-**Worked for the Regional Center of Fundamental Education of UNESCO in Patzcuaro. **i-**Married Guadalupe Castro; father of *Alfredo V. Bonfil*; friend of *Adolfo Lopez Mateos* since 1933. **j-**None. **k-**Precandidate for governor of Hidalgo, 1974. **l-**DPE65, 140; HA, 14 Dec. 1970; *Excelsior*, 20 Oct. 1974, 9; Raby, 70; Enc. Mex., II, 140–41.

Bonfil (Pinto), Alfredo V.

(Deceased Jan. 25, 1973)
a-Nov. 28, 1936. **b-**Queretaro, Queretaro, *East Central, Urban*. **c-**Primary and secondary studies at the Escuela Anexa a la Normal, Saltillo, Coahuila; preparatory studies at the Ateneo Fuente, Saltillo;

law degree, National School of Law, UNAM, 1954–58; Professor of World History, Mexican History and Social Studies, National Preparatory School, 1959–67. **d-***Federal Deputy* from the State of Queretaro, Dist. 2, 1970–73, member of the Gran Comision, the Agrarian Affairs Committee, the Second Government Committee, the Sugar Industry Committee, and the Second Constitutional Affairs Committee. **e-**Campaigned for *Francisco Lopez Serrano* as a precandidate for Governor of Coahuila; Director of Youth for PRI, Federal District; Secretary of Agrarian Action of PRI for the Federal District; Director of Citizen Education for the National Institute of Mexican Youth, 1964–70; campaign coordinator of the CNC for *Luis Echeverria*, 1970; *Secretary of Agrarian Action of the CEN of PRI*, 1970–73; member of the Program and Ideology Committee of the New Advisory Commission to PRI, 1972. **f-**Private Secretary to *Francisco Lopez Serrano*, Secretary General of the Department of Agrarian Affairs, 1959–64; Director General of the New Centers of Population, Department of Agrarian Affairs. **g-**Member of the Governing Board of the Student Association of the National Preparatory School No. 1, 1952–53; member of the Technical Board of the CNC, 1964; Oficial Mayor of the CNC, 1967–68; Secretary of Organization of the CNC, 1968–70; *Secretary General of the CNC*, 1970–73. **h-**None. **i-**Intimate friend of *Augusto Gomez Villanueva*; served with *Enrique Soto Izquierdo, Pedro Vazquez Colmenares*, and *Pindaro Uriostegui* as leaders of the Student Society of the National Preparatory School, 1952–53; close friend and collaborator with *Pindaro Uriostegui*; son of *Ramon G. Bonfil*, Subsecretary of Education, 1970–76; married Yolanda Ojeda. **j-**None. **k-**Lost as a precandidate for Governor of Queretaro, 1973; badly injured by a bus while leading a student strike against increased fares, 1958. **l-**HA, 26 Apr. 1971, 8; HA, 10 Jul. 1972, 10; *Directorio*, 1970–72; *Excelsior*, 6 Feb. 1973, 18; *Excelsior*, 29 Jan. 1973, 11; HA, 12 Nov. 1973, 10.

Bonilla, Adolfo

(Deceased)
a-June 24, 1880. **b-**Tlaxco, Tlaxcala, *East Central, Rural*. **c-**Primary education in Huamantla, Tlaxcala; no college degree. **d-***Governor of Tlaxcala*, 1933–37. **e-**None. **f-**President of the Military Tribunal in Puebla, 1927. **g-**None. **h-**None. **i-**Father of *Ignacio Bonilla Vazquez*, who served as his inspector of police and himself became governor; political enemy of *Luciano Huerta Sanchez*. **j-**Became active in the anti-reelectionist movement in 1910 and joined the Revolution in 1911; reached the rank of General in the Army, November 17, 1915; fought with Francisco Villa and Emiliano Zapata until 1920; Commander of the 98th Regiment against the De la

Huerta rebellion. **k**-Dissolved the Puebla State Legislature, November 15, 1935. **l**-Peral, 116; D de Y, 1 Jan. 1936, 4.

Bonilla Cortes, Roberto T.

a-May 28, 1893. **b**-Tetela de Ocampo, Puebla, *East Central, Rural*. **c**-Primary education in Puebla; secondary education at the Normal School in Puebla, 1908, and the Normal School in Mexico, D.F.; law degree, Escuela Libre de Derecho, May 2, 1925, with a thesis on the public jury in Mexico; teacher in the Normal School of Puebla; normal school teacher, 1915–26; professor at the Military College, 1924; professor at the National Polytechnic Institute, 1925–41; Professor of Law at the National School of Law, UNAM, 1937–39. **d**-None. **e**-None. **f**-Military Judge, 1927–35; Judge of the Supreme Tribunal of Military Justice, 1935–40; Attorney General of Military Justice, 1940–41; *Subsecretary of Public Education*, September 9, 1941, to 1943; Secretary General of Government of the State of Puebla, 1951–56. **g**-None. **h**-Military adviser, 1925–26. **i**-Friend of *Rafael Avila Camacho* and *Lauro Ortega*; brother of *Javier Bonilla Cortes*, federal deputy, 1955–58; joined the Revolution as a normal school student with *Jose A. Ceniceros* and *Jesus Gonzalez Lugo*. **j**-Served in the Revolution, 1914; rank of Brigadier General of the Army, 1941. **k**-None. **l**-WWM45, 14; *Hoy*, 20 Sept. 1941, 3; DHF56, 98; Correa, 46, 77; Kirk, 150; DGF51, 91.

Bonilla Vazquez, Ignacio

(Deceased Jan. 19, 1970)

a-1901. **b**-Apizaco, Tlaxcala, *East Central, Rural*. **c**-Early education unknown; no degree. **d**-*Senator* from the State of Tlaxcala, 1964–68; *Governor of Tlaxcala*, 1969–70. **e**-None. **f**-Inspector of Police for the State of Tlaxcala; Director General of Fishing and Related Industries, Secretariat of the Navy, 1952–58; Chief of Purchasing for the Secretariat of National Defense, 1959–63. **g**-None. **h**-None. **i**-Son of *Adolfo Bonilla;* collaborator of *Rodolfo Sanchez Taboada* as president of PRI where he met *Luis Echeverria*. **j**-Career army officer; rank of Brigadier General; retired from active duty. **k**-*Por que* claims he made a personal fortune as Chief of Purchasing for National Defense; fought a bitter campaign against *Luciano Huerta Sanchez* for governorship of Tlaxcala, 1968. **l**-WWMG, 9; DGF56, 383; DP70, 280; *Por que*, 4 July 1969, 15.

Borunda, Teofilo R.

a-1913. **b**-Chihuahua, *North*. **c**-Primary, secondary and preparatory studies in Chihuahua; no degree. **d**-Mayor of Chihuahua; *Federal Deputy* from the State of Chihuahua, Dist. 3, 1943–46; *Federal Deputy* from the State of Chihuahua, Dist. 3, 1949–52,

President of the Gran Comision; *Alternate Senator* from the State of Chihuahua, 1946–52; *Senator* from the State of Chihuahua, 1952–56, member of the Gran Comision, member of the Committee on Taxes, the First Committee on Government, and the Special Commission on Tourist Affairs; substitute member of the First Committee on Petroleum; *Governor of Chihuahua*. 1956–62. **e**-*Secretary General of the National Executive Committee of PRI*, 1946–50. **f**-None. **g**-First Secretary of Educational Action of the CNOP, 1943. **i**-Friend of *Rodolfo Sanchez Taboada*. **j**-None. **k**-Precandidate for the office of Senator from Chihuahua, 1970, but did not win the nomination. **l**-*Hoy*, 21 Mar. 1971, 4; DGF47, 22; DGF56, 6; D del S, 6 Dec. 1946, 1; HA, 9 May 1955, 3; DGF51, 6, 20, 27, 29; C de D, 1949–51.

Bosquez Saldivar, Gilberto

a-July 20, 1892. **b**-Villa de Chiahutla, Puebla, *East Central, Rural*. **c**-Primary studies in Chiahutla, completed his studies at the Normal Institute of the State of Puebla; continued his studies in 1911; teaching certificate; professor at the Normal Institute of Puebla; teacher at the primary and secondary level in Puebla; Professor of Spanish, Higher School of Construction, Secretariat of Industry and Commerce. **d**-Federal Deputy from the State of Puebla to the Constitutional Convention at Queretaro, 1917; Federal Deputy from the State of Puebla, 1922–24, 1934–37, President of the Chamber of Deputies. **e**-*Secretary of Press and Publicity for the CEN of the PRM*, 1937–39. **f**-Employee of the Department of Technical Education for Women, Secretariat of Public Education; employee of the Press Department, Secretariat of the Treasury, 1929; Director General of *El Nacional*, 1938; First Consul General, Paris, France, 1938–42; Charge d'Affaires, Vichy, France, 1939–42; Minister to Portugal, 1946–50; Minister to Finland, 1950–53; *Ambassador to Cuba*, 1953–64; retired from the Foreign Service, 1967. **g**-President of the Executive Committee of the Association of Normal Students, 1910; Director of the Maderista student movement of the State of Puebla, 1910. **h**-Journalist, Mexico, D.F., 1920. **i**-Participated in the Aquiles Serdan conspiracy; organized students and teachers against Victoriano Huerta, 1913; good friend of *Narciso Bassols*. **k**-Prisoner in Germany, 1942–44; precandidate for governor of Puebla, 1949. **l**-DBP, 721–22, letter; Casasola, V; CyT, 115.

Bracamontes, Luis Enrique

a-June 22, 1923. **b**-Talpalpa, Jalisco, *West, Rural*. **c**-Preparatory at the National Preparatory School, Mexico, D.F.; engineering degree from the National School of Engineering, UNAM, Aug. 22, 1946, with a thesis on "Planning Civil Engineering Works"; graduate studies for a Master's degree in physical science; professor at the National Preparatory School, Mexico, D.F., 1940–47; professor at the National School of Engineering, UNAM, 1944–52, in the field of topography. **d-**None. **e-**None. **f-**Head of the University City construction in Mexico, D.F., for the Secretariat of Public Works, 1950–55; *Subsecretary of Public Works*, 1952–58; *Subsecretary of Public Works*, 1958–64; Director General of the National Commission of Secondary Roads, 1952–64; *Secretary of Public Works*, 1970–76. **g-**None. **h-**Construction engineer on urban projects in the Federal District and other parts of Mexico, 1946–49; engineer for the University City project; adviser to the National Railroads, 1953–58, the National Urban Mortgage Bank, and the Secretariat of Public Works, 1953–64; Director General of the Mexican Company of Engineering Consultants, S.A., 1965–70; Director General of the Ciudad Industrial del Valle de Cuernavaca, 1966–70. **i-**Friend of *Carlos Lazo*, student of *Antonio Dovali Jaime* at the National School of Engineering, father was an engineer; married Beatriz del Valle. **j-**None. **k-**One of the youngest men to ever become a subsecretary in a Mexican Cabinet; precandidate for president of Mexico, 1975. **l-**HA, 7 Dec. 1970, 25; *Hoy*; DBM68, 78; DGF56, 251; letters; Cadena, 34; Enc. Mex., II, 153.

Brauer Herrera, Oscar

a-Dec. 14, 1922. **b-**Jalapa, Veracruz, *Gulf, Urban*. **c-**Primary and secondary studies in Jalapa; agricultural engineering degree with a speciality in parasitic plants, National School of Agriculture, 1952; Master of Science, University of California, Davis, 1954–55; Ph.D., Georg August University, Gottingen, Germany, 1960–62; Professor of Genetics, Graduate School, National School of Agriculture, 1959–60, 1962–69; Research Professor, 1959–65; Director of the Graduate School, National School of Agriculture, 1965–69. **d-**None. **e-**None. **f-**Investigator of horticulture, Office of Special Studies, Secretariat of Agriculture, 1952–58; Researcher on hybrid corn for the Rockefeller Foundation, 1954–63; Director of the Center for Agricultural Investigations, Central Plateau, Office of Special Studies, Chapingo, Mexico, 1958; Director of the Center of Agricultural Investigations, Sinaloa, 1969–70; Director, National Institute of Agricultural Research; *Subsecretary of Agriculture,* 1972–74; *Secretary of Agriculture,* 1974–76. **g-**None. **h-**Agronomist, Anderson Clayton Matamoros, 1951–52; author of many technical books and articles; speaks four languages and reads seven. **j-**None. **k-**None. **l-**letter; HA, 30 Oct. 1972, 30; HA, 14 Jan. 1974, 14.

Bravo Ahuja, Rodrigo

a-June 23, 1913. **b-**Tuxtepec, Oaxaca, *South, Rural*. **c-**Business administration studies; private accoun-

tancy degree. **d-***Federal Deputy* from the State of Oaxaca, Dist. 4, 1967–70; *Federal Deputy* from the State of Oaxaca, Dist. 4, 1976–79. **e-**Member of PRI. **f-**None. **g-**None. **i-**Brother of *Victor Bravo Ahuja*, Secretary of Public Education, 1971–76. **j-**None. **k-**PAN has accused him of being a cacique in Oaxaca. **l-***Excelsior*, 8 Dec. 1975, 17; C de D, 1967–70; C de D, 1976–79.

Bravo Ahuja, Victor

a-Feb. 20, 1918. **b-**Tuxtepec, Oaxaca, *South, Rural*. **c-**Degree in aeronautical engineering from the School of Engineering, National Polytechnic Institute, Aug. 20, 1940; postgraduate work in science at the National University, Cal Tech, 1943–44, and University of Michigan, 1944–45; Master of Science, University of Michigan, 1945; Professor at the Military School of Aviation, 1938–39; Professor of Physics of the School of Sciences, UNAM, 1941–42; Professor of Engineering, National Polytechnic Institute, 1941, 1945–68; Professor at the Graduate School of the Technical Institute of Monterrey; Professor at the Military College, 1942–43; member of many educational advisory boards in Mexico; President of the Center of Investigations and Advanced Studies, 1961–68; founder and Director of the Institute of Industrial Investigation of Monterrey, 1950–59; Director of Summer Sessions of the Technical Institute of Monterrey, 1951–55; Director of the Engineering School of the Technical Institute of Monterrey, 1955–58; Secretary General of the Technical Institute of Monterrey, 1958–59; Rector of the Technical Institute of Monterrey, 1959. **d-***Governor of Oaxaca*, 1968–70. **e-**None. **f-***Subsecretary of Technical and Vocational Education*, 1958–64; *Subsecretary of Technical and Graduate Education*, 1964–68; *Secretary of Public Education*, 1971–76. **g-**None. **h-**Consultant to UNESCO, 1958–68; author of many articles in his professional field. **i-**Brother of *Rodrigo Bravo Ahuja*, federal deputy from Oaxaca, 1967–70, 1976–79. **j-**None. **l-**HA, 7 Dec. 1970, 25; WWMG, 9; GdNL, 17; letter; HA, 21 Dec. 1964, 6; HA, 22 Feb. 1971, 17; *Excelsior*, 8 Dec. 1975, 17; Enc. Mex., II, 162.

Bravo Carrera, Luis

a-Nov. 1, 1902. **b-**Oaxaca, Oaxaca, *South, Urban*. **c-**Primary education in Oaxaca; preparatory at the Institute of Arts and Sciences in Oaxaca; graduated from the Naval College at Veracruz, November 16, 1924. **d-**None. **e-**None. **f-**Naval attache to the Mexican Embassy in Rome; *Secretary of the Navy*, 1970–76. **g-**None. **h-**None. **i-**Married Graciela Roman. **j-**Career naval officer; Subdirector of Naval Boat Construction, Spain; Commander of the Sixth Naval Zone; rank of Corvette Captain, June 1, 1941; Director, Naval School of the Pacific, Mazatlan,

Sinaloa, 1947; rank of Rear Admiral, 1952; Commander of the Third Naval Zone, Veracruz, 1956; Chief of Staff of the First and the Third Naval Zones; Director of the Naval College at Veracruz; Chief of Staff of the Navy; Director General of the Fleet, 1958–61; rank of Admiral, November 20, 1963; Oficial Mayor of the Navy. **k-**Was on the retired list when he was appointed Secretary of the Navy. **l-**DGF47, 234; D de Y, 6 Dec. 1970, 2; HA, 7 Dec. 1970, 24; DGF56, 386; DPE61, 39; *Excelsior*, 8 Dec. 1975, 17; HA, 21 June 1976, 11.

Bravo Hernandez, Mayo Arturo

a-May 14, 1938. **b-**Federal District, *Federal District, Urban*. **c-**Primary and secondary studies in the Federal District; accounting degree in the Federal District. **d-***Federal Deputy* from the Federal District for PAN (Party Deputy), 1970–73. **e-**Joined PAN, 1965; member of the Regional Committee of PAN for the Federal District; Chief of the Regional Committee of PAN for Dist. 20 of the Federal District. **f-**None. **g-**None. **i-**Married Maria Emma Hernandez. **j-**None. **k-**None. **l-**C de D, 1970–73, 145.

Bravo Izquierdo, Donato

(Deceased Aug. 21, 1971)

a-Dec. 6, 1890. **b-**Coxcatlan, Tehuacan, Puebla, *East Central, Rural*. **c-**Early education unknown; no degree. **d-**Deputy to the Constitutional Congress of Queretaro, 1916–17; Federal Deputy from the State of Puebla, 1918–20; Provisional Governor of Puebla, 1928; *Senator* from Puebla, 1958–64, President of the War Materiels Committee; member of the Railroad Committee; substitute member of the Military Justice Committee, the Second Petroleum Committee, and the First Balloting Committee. **f-**None. **g-**None. **h-**None. **j-**Career military officer; joined the Revolution in 1913 under the command of General Barbosa; Zone Commander of the First Military Zone; Inspector General of the Army of the Third Inspection Commission; rank of Brigadier General, 1942. **k-**None. **l-**WWM45, 15; McAlister, 224; Peral, 118; C de S, 1961–64, 52; Func., 316.

Bravo Silva, Jose

a-1926. **b-**Morelia, Michoacan, *West Central, Urban*. **c-**Early education unknown; studies in economics from the School of Economics, Technological Institute of Mexico, Mexico City, 1946–50; received economics degree in 1953 with a thesis on An Essay on the Administrative Control of Prices. **d-**None. **e-**None. **f-**Subdirector, Department of Prices, Division of Prices, Secretariat of Industry and Commerce, 1955; *Subdirector General of the National Bank of Foreign Commerce*, 1970–76. **g-**None. **i-**Supported *Carlos Torres Manzo* for Governor of Michoacan, 1974. **j-**None. **k-**None. **l-**letter; DNED, 46; *Excelsior*, 19 Jan. 1974, 8.

Bravo Valencia, Enrique

a-1909. **b-**Jiquilpan, Michoacan, *West Central, Urban*. **c-**Primary and secondary studies in Jiquilpan; completed second year of secondary; no degree. **d-**Mayor of Jiquilpan, Michoacan; *Federal Deputy* from the State of Michoacan, Dist. 4, 1946–49, member of the Mail and Telegraph, Indigenous Affairs and Social Action Committees; local deputy to the State Legislature of Michoacan; Mayor of Morelia, Michoacan; *Senator* from Michoacan, 1952–58, member of the National Properties and Resources Committee, the Second Ejido Committee, the First Mines Committee and the First Balloting Group. **e-**Secretary General of the Regional Committee of PRI in the Federal District; President of PRI in Michoacan, 1952; Secretary of Organization in the campaign of *Damaso Cardenas* for governor of Michoacan, 1950. **f-**President of the Federal Board of Moral and Civic Improvement, Morelia; Director of the Federal Treasury Office, No. 17, 1964–70; Director of the Federal Treasury Office, No. 4, 1971–76. **g-**None. **h-**None. **j-**None. **k-**Precandidate for governor of Michoacan in 1956, 1962, 1968 and 1974. **l-**Ind. Biog., 28; *Excelsior*, 20 Dec. 1973, 9; C de S, 1952–58; C de D, 1946–49, 6.

Bremauntz, Alberto

(Deceased Dec. 9, 1978)

a-Aug. 13, 1897. **b-**Morelia, Michoacan, *West Central, Urban*. **c-**Primary studies in Morelia, Uruapan and Ciudad Hidalgo; studies at the Colegio de San Nicolas, 1910; graduated from the Normal School of Michoacan, 1916; law degree from the University of Michoacan, 1929, with a thesis on participation in utilities and salaries in Mexico; professor of economics at the University of Michoacan; secondary teacher at various schools; professor and director, School of Business, University of Michoacan; Rector of the University of Michoacan, 1963–66. **d-**Mayor of Morelia, 1929; Federal Deputy from the State of Michoacan, 1932–34; *Alternate Senator* from Michoacan, 1934–40. **e-**Secretary General of the PNR for Michoacan; founding member of the Socialist Party of Michoacan; Secretary General of *Francisco J. Mujica's* campaign for governor of Michoacan, 1920. **f-**Stenographer for *Francisco Mujica*, Department of General Provisions, Federal District Department, 1918–20; Private Secretary to *Francisco Mujica*, 1920; Judge of the First Penal Court, Federal District, 1934; Justice of the Superior Tribunal of Justice of the Federal District, 1935–63. **g-**Founder of the Socialist Front of Mexican Lawyers, 1934. **h-**Founded several newspapers in Michoacan; agent of the Ministerio Publico in Michoacan; public defender; consulting lawyer to *Agustin Lenero*, Secretary General of Government, Michoacan, 1929–30; consulting lawyer to *Lazaro Cardenas* and *Damaso Cardenas*. **i-**Father a musician and pharmacist; uncle of *Ernesto Soto Reyes*, Senator from Michoacan, 1934–40; uncle of *Jose Maria Mendoza Pardo*, Governor of Michoacan, 1944–49. **j-**None. **k-**President of the education committee of the Chamber of Deputies which presented the revision of Article 3 to include socialist education, 1933. **l-**Garrido, 201; Bremauntz.

Bremer Martino, Juan Jose

a-1944. **b-**Federal District, *Federal District, Urban*. **c-**Law degree, National School of Law, UNAM, Oct. 2, 1967, honorable mention, with his thesis on international law; received a 9.6 grade average out of 10 for all courses at law school. **d-**None. **e-**Professor of Analysis of the Mexican Constitution, Institute of Political Education, PRI. **f-**Personal Secretary to the Private Secretary, *Ignacio Ovalle Fernandez*, of the President of Mexico, 1970–72; Private Secretary to President *Luis Echeverria*, 1972–75, *Subsecretary of the Presidency*, 1975–76; Director General of the Institute of Fine Arts, 1976- . **g-**Leader of 1966 student strike; president of the 1962 Generation of Law Students, 1963. **i-**Son of Juan Jose Bremer, well-known law professor at UNAM; married Ana Maria Villasenor. **j-**None. **k-**None. **l-**HA, 25 Sept. 1972, 1; DAPC, 77, 9.

Brena Torres, Rodolfo

a-May 16, 1911. **b-**Ejutla, Oaxaca, *South, Rural*. **c-**Secondary and preparatory studies at the Benito Juarez University of Oaxaca; preparatory studies continued at the National Preparatory School, UNAM; studied at the National School of Law, UNAM, but discontinued studies due to lack of money in 1931; law degree from the Scientific and Literary Institute of the State of Mexico, 1949. **d-***Senator* from the State of Oaxaca, 1958–62; President of the Gran Comision; head of the Committee on Foreign Affairs and Tariffs; head of the Committee on National Properties and Resources; member of the First Committee on Petroleum and the Second Committee on Labor; *Governor of Oaxaca*, 1962–68. **e-**None. **f-**Agent of the Ministerio Publico for the Federal Attorney General's Office in the State of Mexico, 1950; public defender in the State of Mexico, 1950; delegate of the Mexican Economic Commission to the Organization of American States, 1959. **g-**Attorney for the Mexican Petroleum Workers Union, 1940. **h-**Practicing attorney in Mexico, D.F., in the field of labor law. **j-**None. **k-**None. **l-**G o M, 10; DBM68, 80; letter; Func. 302.

Brito Foucher, Rodulfo

(Deceased May 15, 1970)
a-Nov. 8, 1899. **b-**Villahermosa, Tabasco, *Gulf, Urban*. **c-**Primary studies in private school, Villahermosa, 1907–12; preparatory education at the Institute of Tabasco, 1913–17, and at the National Pre-

paratory School, 1917–18; law degree from the National School of LAW, UNAM, December 28, 1923; attended New York University, Columbia University, and the University of Berlin; Professor of General Theory at the National School of Law, UNAM, 1927–35; Director of the National School of Law, UNAM, 1932–33. **d-**None. **e-**None. **f-**Subsecretary of Foreign Relations and Subsecretary of Government, de la Huerta Rebellion, 1923; later became secretary, 1923; served as governor of Campeche before his forces were defeated, 1923; *Rector of UNAM*, 1942–44. **g-**President of the Student Federation; delegate to the First National Student Congress, 1921. **h-**President of the White Cross in Mexico, D.F., 1942–68; practicing attorney in private law firm in Mexico, D.F., 1940–70, at time of death. **i-**Friend of *Agustin Garcia Lopez*, when both were students at the National School of Law; father a close collaborator of the governor of Tabasco; grandfather was governor of Tabasco. **j-**None. **k-**An active Mason; headed punitive expedition to Villahermosa during the reign of Garrido Canabal which cost the lives of his brother and several other followers on July 14, 1935. The killings caused an outcry in the press which eventually produced the fall of the Garrido Canabal regime. In exile, 1924–27, New York; in exile in Berlin, Washington, D.C. and New York, 1936–40. **l-**DBM68, 82; DBM70, 90; WWM45, 15; Simpson, 354; Kirk, 155; letter; HA, 4 Aug. 1944, 7; DP70, 295; Peral, 121.

Brito Rosado, Efrain

a-Sept. 2, 1912. **b-**Merida, Yucatan, *Gulf, Urban*. **c-**Primary studies in Merida; secondary studies in Mexico City; preparatory studies at the National Preparatory School; law degree from the National School of Law, UNAM, Dec. 17, 1936, with a thesis on "The Significance of Politics"; Professor of World History and the History of Art. **d-***Federal Deputy* from the State of Yucatan, Dist. 2, 1943–46; *Federal Deputy* from the State of Yucatan, Dist. 3, 1949–52, member of the Inspection Committee of the General Accounting Office; *Senator* from the State of Yucatan, 1952–58, member of the Foreign and Domestic Trade Committee, the First Government Committee, the Electrical Industry Committee, and the Legislative Studies Committee; substitute member of the Health Committee. **e-**Orator for the National Anti-reelectionist Party, 1927; supporter of Jose Vasconcelos in the 1929 campaign; orator and Secretary General of the Revolutionary Party of National Unification, 1940; orator for *Miguel Aleman*, 1946. **f-**President of the Legislative Studies Commission, Secretariat of Public Education; Founder and Director of the School for Citizenship Training, Secretariat of Public Education; Director of Social Action, Department of the Federal District; First Secretary, Legation to Spain, 1936; Charge d'Affaires,

Brazil. **g-**Student leader of the autonomy movement at UNAM, 1929; President of the Federation of University Students, 1930–31; National Oratory Champion, 1928. **h-**Columnist and editorialist for *Critica* (Buenos Aires). **i-**Friends with *Miguel Aleman* and *Adolfo Lopez Mateos* during student days. **j-**None. **k-**Fled Mexico with *Jose Castro Estrada* with the help of *Agustin Garcia Lopez* after supporting *Juan Andreu Almazan*, 1940; remained in exile several months; precandidate for governor of Yucatan, 1951. **l-**Letter; C de S, 1952–58; DGF56, 8, 10, 11, 12, 14; C de D, 1943–45, 7; C de D, 1949–51, 65; Casasola, V; Ind. Biog., 29–30.

Buchanan (Lopez), Walter Cross
(Deceased September 21, 1977)
a-Apr. 29, 1906. **b-**San Luis de la Paz, Guanajuato, *West Central, Rural*. **c-**Engineering degree from the Higher School of Mechanical and Electrical Engineering, National Polytechnic Institute, 1931; professor at the School of Engineering, UNAM, 1931–55; professor specializing in steam powered machinery and railroads at the National Polytechnic Institute, 1931–35; Director of the Higher School of Mechanical and Electrical Engineering at the National Polytechnic Institute, 1944; founder of the major in communication and electronics at the National Polytechnic Institute, 1937. **d-**None. **e-**None. **f-**Head of the Department of Control for Industrial Electricity, Secretariat of Public Works, 1951; *Subsecretary of Public Works*, 1952–55; *Secretary of Public Works*, 1955–58; *Secretary of Communications and Transportation*, 1958–64. **g-**None. **h-**President of the Board of Directors of Radio Aeronautica Mexicana, S.A., 1965–77. **i-**Father, an engineer. **j-**None. **k-**None. **l-**HA, 4 Aug. 1958, 11; HA, 8 Apr. 1957; DGF56, 251; Func. 77; NYT, 10 Nov. 1955, 2.

Bucio Alanis, Lauro
a-Aug. 18, 1928. **b-**Ciudad Hidalgo, Michoacan, *West Central, Urban*. **c-**Early education unknown; agricultural engineering degree, National School of Agriculture, July 25, 1954; Master of Science degree, Iowa State University, Sept., 1955; Bank of Mexico fellowship to Iowa State University, 1955. **d-**None. **e-**None. **f-**Agronomist, Office of Special Studies, Secretariat of Agriculture; Field Director, Agricultural Experiment Station, Jaloxtoc, Morelos; Director of the Maiz Germinating Plasma Bank; Director of Maiz Improvement Program, Tamaulipas and Bajio, National Maiz Commission; Director of the Basic Seeds Department, National Maiz Commission; *Oficial Mayor of Agriculture*, 1972–76. **g-**None. **j-**None. **k-**None. **l-**BdM, 77–78.

Bueno Amezcua, Jose de Jesus
(Deceased 1969)
a-Oct. 10, 1930. **b-**Guadalajara, Jalisco, *West, Urban*. **c-**Law degree, University of Guadalajara, 1955. **d-***Federal Deputy* from the State of Jalisco, Dist. 8, 1967–70, member of the Legislative Studies Committee. **e-**Student member of the Revolutionary Youth group of the PRI; participated in the founding of the Middle Class League, a basic sector of the National Confederation of Popular Organizations of PRI in Jalisco, 1952; headed different political commissions for PRI, 1953–59; member of the Economic Planning Council of PRI for the campaign of *Adolfo Lopez Mateos*, 1958; participated in the mayoralty campaign of *Francisco Medina Asencio*, 1962; participated in the gubernatorial campaigns of *Francisco Medina Asencio, Agustin Yanez,* and *Juan Gil Preciado* for Governor of Jalisco. **f-**Private secretary to the Mayor of Guadalajara, 1962–64; private secretary to the Governor of Jalisco, 1965–67. **g-**Held many positions in the Federation of University Students of the University of Guadalajara. **h-**Official of the Legal Department of CONASUPO; First Officer of the Administrative Section of CONASUPO. **i-**Friend of *Francisco Medina Asencio*, Governor of Jalisco, 1965–69. **j-**None. **k-**None. **l-**DBM68, 83–84; letter; C de D, 1967–69.

Buenrostro Ochoa, Efrain
(Deceased Mar. 11, 1973)
a-Oct. 28, 1896. **b-**Jiquilpan, Michoacan, *West Central, Rural*. **c-**Primary education in Jiquilpan; secondary in Guadalajara, Jalisco; three years of engineering school at the Liceo de Varones in Guadalajara; no degree. **d-**None. **e-**None. **f-**Vice consul in various cities of the United States, 1918–28; Secretary General of Government of the State of Michoacan, 1928–32; Assistant Treasurer General of Mexico, 1932–34; *Subsecretary of the Treasury, 1934–39; Secretary of Industry and Commerce, 1939–40; Director General of Petroleos Mexicanos,* 1940–46; Director General of Cia. Industrial de Atenquique, 1964–70. **g-**None. **i-**Intimate friend of *Lazaro Cardenas;* school friend of *Cardenas* during his first five years of primary education in Jiquilpan, Michoacan; married Carmen Araiza; son a physician in Mexico City. **j-**None. **k-**None. **l-**DBM68, 84; HA, 6 Oct. 1944, 28; Dulles 608; *Excelsior,* 13 Mar. 1973.

Burguete Farrera, Ezequiel
(Deceased Oct. 7, 1975)
a-Mar. 7, 1907. **b-**Tuxtla Gutierrez, Chiapas, *South, Urban*. **c-**Primary studies in Tuxtla Gutierrez; preparatory studies at the National Preparatory School, 1920–24; law degree, National School of Law,

UNAM, Mar. 8, 1929; Professor of Civics and Economics, University Preparatory School; Professor of Penal Law at the National School of Law, Jan. 1, 1939 to 1972. d-None. e-None. f-Representative of the Federal Treasury (estates) in Tuxtla Gutierrez, 1929–30; Court Clerk of the Chiapas District Court in charge of civil and penal sections, 1930–31; consulting lawyer to the Office of the Attorney General of Mexico, June, 1932, to Feb. 1933; Agent of the Ministerio Publico of the Consulting Department of the Attorney General, Jan., 1933, to Sept., 1933; special agent of the Ministerio Publico of the Attorney General in the investigation of the role of Father Jimenez in the death of President Obregon, 1933–34; agent of the Ministerio Publico in charge of preparatory investigations, 1934–35; head of the Department of Preparatory Investigations of the Office of the Attorney General, 1934–35; Attorney "C" of the Legal Department of the Secretariat of the Treasury, January, 1935, to December, 1935; head of the Legal Department of the National Bank of Ejido Credit in charge of the Nationalization of Properties Section, July, 1939, to August, 1941; representative of Capital (Group VII) on the Federal Board of Conciliation and Arbitration, 1942–47; adviser to the Secretary of the Presidency; *Supernumerary of the Supreme Court*, May 2, 1966 to June 27, 1967; *Justice of the Supreme Court*, 1967–75. g-None. h-Private law practice, 1943, 1947–66; attorney for Petroleos Mexicanos. i-Knew *Antonio Carrillo Flores* at the National School of Law; father was a federal deputy under Madero and a federal judge; married to Maria Santaella. j-None. k-Representative of the Federation of People's Parties to the Federal Electoral Commission; candidate of the Federation of People's Parties in Michoacan, 1952. l-Letter; DBM68, 86; DGF50, II, 347; Morton, 63; HA, 6 June 1952, 8; *Excelsior*, 7 Oct. 1975, 5; *Justicia*, Aug., 1968.

Bustamante (Vasconcelos), Eduardo

a-Oct. 12, 1904. b-Oaxaca, Oaxaca, *South, Urban*. c-Primary studies at the Colegio Union, Oaxaca, 1910–15; preparatory at the Colegio Union and the Institute of Arts and Sciences of Oaxaca, 1917–22; law degree, National School of Law, UNAM, October 6, 1926; Professor of Public Finance at the National School of Economics, UNAM, 1947–60. d-None. e-None. f-Technical consultant to the Technical Fiscal Department of the Secretariat of the Treasury, 1928, and head of that department in 1932; financial adviser to the State of Nuevo Leon, 1927-31; Director General of Revenues of the Secretariat of the Treasury, 1934; Director General of the Bank of Industry and Commerce, 1942–45; private secretary to the Secretary of Public Education, Puig Casauranc, 1930–31; private secretary to the Secre-

tary of Industry and Commerce, Aaron Saenz, 1931; *Subsecretary of the Treasury*, 1946–49; Mexican delegate to the United Nations with *Adolfo Lopez Mateos*, 1951; *Secretary of Government Properties*, 1958–64; member of the Advisory Council of the Bank of Commerce and the Bank of Industry and Commerce, 1965–70, g-None. h-Private law practice, 1934-46; first employment as fourth official of the Technical Fiscal Department of the Secretariat of the Treasury, 1925; author of articles on law; attended numerous conferences on economics. i-Friends with *Mario Ramon Beteta, Miguel Aleman, Manuel Gual Vidal, Jaime Torres Bodet, Antonio Garcia Lopez, Antonio Carrillo Flores* and *Alfonso Garcia Gonzalez* since college days at the National School of Law; father a self-made businessman; relative of *Juan I. Vasconcelos,* federal deputy from Oaxaca, 1964–67; brother of *Miguel E. Bustamante,* Subsecretary of Health, 1960–64; married Refugio Davila. j-None. k-None. l-Letter; WWM45, 16; HA, 3 June 1963; HA, 5 Oct. 1959; DBM68, 88; HA, 8 Dec . 1958, 30.

Bustamante (Vasconcelos), Miguel E.

a-May 2, 1898. b-Oaxaca, Oaxaca, *South, Urban*. c-Primary and secondary studies in Oaxaca; preparatory studies at the Institute of Arts and Sciences in Oaxaca, 1914–19; medical degree from the National School of Medicine, UNAM, 1925; Doctorate in Public Health, Johns Hopkins University, 1928; Professor of Hygiene at the National School of Medicine, UNAM, 1931-52; special lecturer, United States universities, 1942-43; Director of the Department of Social and Preventive Medicine, 1956–58. d-None. e-None. f-Director of the Health Training Station at Xochimilco, Secretariat of Public Health; assistant head of the Federal Health Bureau of the Secretariat of Public Health, 1931; head of the Federal Health Bureau, 1932-35; Director of the Cooperative Health Unit in Veracruz, 1930; Supervisor of Foreign Health Missions, 1938; Director General of the Institute of Health and Tropical Diseases of the Secretariat of Public Health, 1942–43, 1946–47; Secretary General of the Sanitation Bureau, Pan American Union, 1947–56; Director General of Health Services, Secretariat of Health, 1958–59; *Subsecretary of Public Health and Welfare,* Jan. 27, 1960 to 1964; Secretary General of the National Council of Health, 1965. g-None. h-Intern, General Hospital of Mexico, D.F., 1924–25; Fellow of the Rockefeller Foundation, 1926–28; Epidemiologist of the Institute of Health and Tropical Diseases of the Secretariat of Public Health, 1939–41; author of numerous articles and papers on public health which have appeared in North American journals. i-Brother of *Eduardo Bustamante,* Secretary of

Government Properties, 1958–64; father a self-made businessman; co-founder of the Institute of Health and Tropical Diseases with *Manuel Martinez Baez,* 1937; married Alicia Connolly. **j-**None. **k-**None. **l-**D de Y , 10 Dec. 1964, 20; DGF47, 199; *Annals, Mar.,* 1940, 161; WWM45, 16; WWW70-71; letter; Enc. Mex., II, 178.

Butron Casas, Sergio
(Deceased Feb. 25, 1973)
a-1941. **b-**Mineral del Chico, Hidalgo, *East Central, Rural.* **c-**Primary and secondary studies at Rafael Donde; teaching certificate at the Rural Normal School, Mexico, D.F.; law degree, National School of Law, UNAM. **d-***Federal Deputy* from the State of Hidalgo, Dist. 3, 1967–70, member of the Public Education Committee, the Small Agrarian Property Committee, the Social Security Committee, and the National Lands Committee. **e-**None. **f-**None. **g-**Founding member of the Agrarian Youth Vanguard; Secretary of Youth Action, CNC, 1965; state delegate of the CNC to Nayarit, Hidalgo, Michoacan, Chiapas, and Aguascalientes; Secretary of Labor Action of the CNC, 1970–73; President of the Federation of University Students, UNAM. **h-**None. **j-**None. **k-**None. **l-***Excelsior,* 30 Jan. 1973, 10; HA, 5 Feb. 1973, 11–12; C de D, 1967–69, 63, 82, 87 89.

Caamano Munoz, Enrique
a-July 13, 1911. **b-**Federal District, *Federal District, Urban.* **c-**Early education unknown; degree in business administration; certified public accountant. **d-**None. **e-**None. **f-**Accountant, Controller General, National Finance Bank, 1936–46; Director General of Expenditures, Secretariat of the Treasury, 1949–58; *Subsecretary of Expenditures,* Secretariat of the Treasury, 1958–64; *Subsecretariat of Expenditures,* 1964–70. **g-**None. **h-**Member of the board of directors of various companies, including Mexican Light and Power; Treasurer of the Mexican Tube Company, 1947–49. **i-**Married Isabel Rico. **k-**None. **l-**D del S, 2 Dec. 1964; DPE51, 147; DGF56, 164; *Siempre,* 14 Jan. 1959, 6; WNM, 30; DPE61, 40.

Caballero Aburto, Raul
b-Ometepec, Guerrero, *South, Rural.* **c-**Primary studies in Ometepec; secondary at the National Military College. **d-***Governor* of Guerrero, 1957–61. **d-**None. **f-**Military attache to El Salvador, 1961. **g-**None. **h-**None. **j-**Joined Francisco Madero, 1910; fought in the Constitutionalist Army during the Revolution; rank of brigadier general; career army officer; zone commander of the 26th Military Zone, Jalapa, Veracruz, 1956. **k-**Caballero Aburto's powers as governor were removed by the federal government after a student revolt and *Adolfo Lopez Mateos* sent in federal troops; he was accused of

corruption and opposed by the Civic Association of Guerrero of which *Genaro Vazquez Rojas* was a member; *Hispano Americano* accused him of putting 60 relatives into state offices as governor; the Secretary General of the CNC in Guerrero claimed he held illegal large landholdings in Guerrero in August, 1972. **l-**NYT, 31 Dec. 1960, 1; NYT, 5 Jan. 1961, 9; NYT, 15 Apr. 1959, 8; *Excelsior,* 29 Aug. 1972, 27; DGF56, 202; G of M, 19–20; HA, 14 Apr. 1958, 10; HA, 14 Feb. 1972, 15.

Cabanas (Barrientos), Lucio
(Deceased December, 1974)
a-1938. **b-**San Vicente de Benitez, Guerrero, *South, Rural.* **c-**Early education unknown; teaching certificate; sixth grade teacher in Atoyac, Guerrero. **d-**None. **e-**Member of the Civic Association of Guerrero with *Genaro Vazquez Rojas;* leader of *Vazquez Rojas'* guerrilla band after his death in 1972. **f-**None. **g-**None. **h-**Teacher, 1960–67. **i-***Nabor A. Ojeda* took him to Mexico City as a young child; left teaching in 1967 when his brother was killed in a teachers' strike in Atoyac de Alvarez, Guerrero. **j-**None. **k-**Led a band of guerrillas which rescued *Genaro Vazquez Rojas* from prison, April, 1968; attacked army patrols in Guerrero, June and August, 1971; allegedly kidnapped gubernatorial candidate *Ruben Figueroa* of Guerrero, 1974; killed under somewhat mysterious circumstances after the army attacked his group to rescue *Figueroa.* **l-**HA, 17 June 1974, 14; HA, 10 June 1974, 12; HA, 9 Dec. 1974, 6–7.

Cabrera Carrasquedo, Manuel
(Deceased 1955)
a-Aug. 6, 1885. **b-**Oaxaca, Oaxaca, *South, Urban.* **c-**Primary studies in Oaxaca; preparatory and professional studies at the Institute of Arts and Sciences in Oaxaca; engineering degree from the Military College at Chapultepec, Mexico, D.F., 1908; professor at the Military College. **d-***Governor of Oaxaca,* 1952–55, replacing Governor *Manuel Mayoral Heredia* who was removed from office by the federal government. **e-**None. **f-**Assistant head of the Commission of Military Studies of the Secretariat of National Defense, *Oficial Mayor of the Secretariat of National Defense,* 1946–52. **g-**None. **h-**None. **j-**Joined the federal army in 1908; member of the general staff of General Felipe Angeles; reached the rank of Brigadier General in 1939. **k-**In exile in the United States after the defeat of Victoriano Huerta, 1914. **l-**WWM45, 17; DP70, 315; DGF47, 109; Peral, 130; HA, 10 Oct. 1955, 15; NYT, 5 Aug. 1952, 4.

Cabrera Munoz Ledo, Jesus
a-Apr. 20, 1928. **b-**Apaseo de Grande, Guanajuato, *West Central, Rural.* **c-**Preparatory studies in Celaya, Guanajuato; law degree, National School of

Law, UNAM; advanced studies at the School of Law and Economic Sciences, Paris, France, 1950–52; special studies in international relations in France, Switzerland and the United States on fellowships from the French government and the United Nations; no degree; professor at the Colegio de Mexico. **d-**Senator from Guanajuato, 1976– . **e-**None. **f-**Career Foreign Service Officer, joined 1953; reached rank of ambassador; Assistant Permanent Delegate to UNESCO; Subdirector General of International Organizations, Secretariat of Foreign Relations, 1965; Director General of Cultural Relations, Secretariat of Foreign Relations, 1969; Director-in-Chief of Cultural Affairs, Secretariat of Foreign Relations, 1970–75. **g-**None. **j-**None. **k-**None. **l-**MGF69, 179; DPE71, 6; MGF73, 339; BdM, 79.

Cal y Mayor (Sauz), Octavio

a-Dec. 14, 1920. **b-**Pozo Colorado Cintalapa, Chiapas, *South, Rural.* **c-**Primary studies at the Escuela Benito Juarez, Cintalapa (three years), and in the Federal District (three years); secondary education at public School No. 3, Federal District; preparatory at the Preparatory School for Children of Workers, Coyoacan (two years); medical degree, National School of Medicine, UNAM (six years); Professor of World History; Professor of Medicine, UNAM. **d-**Federal Deputy from the State of Chiapas, Dist. 6, 1970–73; member of the Public Assistance Committee, the Indigenous Affairs Committee, and the Foreign Relations Committee. **e-**Vice President of the *Efrain Aranda Osorio* campaign for Governor of Chiapas, 1952; Secretary of Political Action for CNOP in Chiapas, 1952; Director of Public Commissions for the 1952 presidential campaign in Chiapas. **f-**Director of Otoneurology, General Hospital, Mexico City. **g-**None. **h-**Founding member of the Mexican Society of Neurological Sciences; author of several books. **i-**Half-brother of Rafael Cal y Mayor; son of General Rafael Cal y Mayor. **j-**None. **k-**None. **l-**Directorio, 70–72; C de D, 1960–72, 104.

Calcaneo, Tito Livio

a-Dec. 7, 1902. **b-**Villahermosa, Tabasco, *Gulf, Urban.* **c-**Primary and secondary studies at the Juarez Institute and the Simon Sarlat School, Tabasco; preparatory studies up to the fourth year, Colegio de Tabasco; no degree. **d-**Local Deputy to the State Legislature of Tabasco, 1937–38; *Alternate Federal Senator* (replaced the regular Senator) from Tabasco, 1940–46. **e-**None. **f-**First Director for Fiscal Services of the State of Tabasco. **g-**None. **h-**Director of the Machinery Department, National Irrigation Commission, 1935. **j-**Joined the Navy, 1916; active in the Army during the Revolution; rank of Colonel in the Army, 1927. **k-**One of the leaders in the Senate in favor of impounding Axis property in Mexico. **l-**EBW46, 66; Peral, 133; C de S, 1940–46.

Calderon, Esteban B.

(Deceased)
a-1876. **b-**Santa Maria del Oro, Nayarit, *West, Rural.* **c-**Primary, secondary and preparatory studies; assistant in the Higher School of Tepic, Nayarit. **d-**Deputy to the Constitutional Convention, 1916–17; Senator from Jalisco, 1920; *Senator* from Nayarit, 1952–58, member of the Rules Committee, first secretary of the Second National Defense Committee, the First Navy Committee and the Social Welfare Committee. **e-**Co-founder with General Manuel Dieguez of the Liberal Union of Humanity in Cananea, Sonora, which was affiliated with the Flores Magon brothers. **f-**Director General of Taxes, State of Jalisco; Chief of Purchases for the National Railroads of Mexico; Director of Customs in Nuevo Leon, 1929; President of the National Claims Commission, 1918. **g-**Leader of the Cananea mining strike, imprisoned with Manuel Dieguez in San Juan de Ulloa. **j-**Organizer of volunteers to oppose Victoriano Huerta, 1913; fought under General Obregon; fought against Villa, 1915. **k-**Opposed Venustiano Carranza's imposition of a successor in 1920. **l-**DGF56, 7, 9–12; IndBiog., 30–32.

Calderon Corona, Esvelia

a-Nov. 18, 1944. **b-**Morelia, Michoacan, *West Central, Urban.* **c-**Primary studies at the Jose Maria Morelos School, Morelia; secondary at the Adolfo Lopez Mateos School, Villa Jimenez, Michoacan. **d-**Alternate Local Deputy to the State Legislature of Michoacan; *Federal Deputy* from the State of Michoacan, Dist. 3, 1970–73, member of the Child Welfare Committee, the Second Section of the Agrarian Affairs Committee, the Colonization Committee and the Rural Electrification Committee. **e-**None. **f-**None. **g-**Secretary of Feminine Action of the Agrarian Communities of Michoacan; Alternate Secretary of Feminine Action of the CEN of the CNC. **j-**None. **k-**None. **l-**C de D, 1970–73, 105; *Directorio*, 1970–72.

Calderon Martinez, Antonio

a-Oct. 12, 1930. **b-**Parras, Coahuila, *North, Urban.* **c-**Economics degree from the National School of Economics, UNAM, 1952; attended the English Language Institute of the University of Michigan, 1954–55; worked on national income studies at the United States Department of Commerce, 1955; graduate studies at American University, Washington, D.C., on a Bank of Mexico scholarship, 1955–56, MA degree, 1956; Professor of Foreign Trade, Ibero-American University; Professor of Economics, UNAM. **d-**None. **e-**None. **f-**Head of the Department of Latin American Trade, Bank of Mexico, 1959–65; Director General of Statistics, Bank of Mexico, National Center of Information on Foreign Trade, Mortgage Bank of Public Works;

Subdirector of the National Bank of Foreign Commerce, 1965–70; Director General of Trade, Secretariat of Industry and Commerce, 1970–76; Technical Director of the Center for Specialization for International Trade, 1976– . **g-**None. **h-**Economist, National Urban and Public Works Mortgage Bank, 1952, Bank of Mexico, 1952–54, 1956–57, and economist for the Secretariat of the Treasury, 1957–59; author. **j-**None. **k-**None. **l-**DBM68, 92–93; BdM,80; Enc. Mex., II, 230; DPE71, 52.

Calderon Rodriguez, Enrique

b-Durango, *West.* **c-**Early education unknown; no degree. **d-***Governor of Durango,* 1936–40. **f-**Assistant Chief of Police of the Federal District, 1934–35; Consul General of the Mexican Foreign Service in San Francisco, California, 1940–43. **g-**None. **h-**None. **i-**Brother *Ernesto Calderon Rodriguez* was a federal deputy from Durango, 1937–40. **j-**Joined the Constitutional Army in 1916; career army officer; rank of Colonel, 1927; rank of Brigadier General, Oct. 1, 1943. **k-**Protests in the Mexican press against his being appointed consul general for alleged crimes he committed while serving as Governor of Durango; Presidential candidate in 1945, receiving a minor number of votes; reported by *The New York Times* to being held on charges of fraud by Mexican authorities, 1953. **l-**WWM45, 17; Peral, 47, 64; Correa 46, 68–69; NYT, 27 Sept. 1953, 23.

Calderon Velarde, Alfonso G.

a-Sept. 19, 1913. **b-**Calabacillas, Chihuahua, *North, Rural.* **c-**Primary studies in San Jose de Gracia and Los Mochis, Sinaloa; no degree. **d-***Federal Deputy* from the State of Sinaloa, Dist. No. 1, 1946–49, member of the First Ejido Committee, the Development of Cooperatives Committee and the Sugar Industry Committee; Mayor of Ahome, Sinaloa, 1962–65; *Federal Deputy* from the State of Sinaloa, Dist. No. 1, 1967–70, member of the Second Labor Committee and the First Treasury Committee; *Senator* from the State of Sinaloa, 1970–74; President of the Hydraulic Resources Committee, first secretary of the Industries Committee, second secretary of the Development of Cooperatives Committee and member of the First Balloting Group; *Governor of Sinaloa,* 1975– . **e-**Treasurer of PRI in Sinaloa, 1951; President of PRI in Sinaloa, 1951–57. **f-**None. **g-**Cofounder of the CTM, Sinaloa, 1936; Secretary of the Executive Committee of Section Fifty-three of the Union of Mechanics and Similar Occupations of Mexico, 1931; Secretary of the Union of Workers and Laborers of Northern Sinaloa, 1934; founding member of the Union of Sugar Industry workers of Mexico, 1937; Secretary General of Section Twelve of the Sugar Industry Workers Union, Los Mochis;

Secretary of Conflicts and Head of Medical Services, Sugar Industry Workers Union, Los Mochis, 1943–45; Assistant to the Secretary of Political Affairs of the CTM, 1946–49; Assistant to the National Committee of the CTM, 1960–62; Secretary General of the CTM of Sinaloa, 1966–67, 1974; Secretary of Organization of the CEN of the CTM, 1974. **h-**Electrician, United Sugar Company, Los Mochis, 1931; co-author of the constitution for the Union of Workers and Farmers of Sinaloa. **i-**Father was a carpenter. **j-**None. **k-**Unexpected choice for PRI candidate for governor, 1974. **l-**MGF73, 66; C de S, 1970–76, 71; C de D, 1946–49, 67; C de D, 1967–70, 69, 73; DGF47, 11; MGF69, 95; HA, 14 Oct. 1974, 33; *Excelsior,* 22 May 1978, 16; Enc. Mex., Annual, 1977. 550.

Calleja Garcia, Juan Moises

a-Sept. 4, 1915. **b-**Federal District, *Federal District, Urban.* **c-**Primary studies in public schools in the Federal District; secondary studies at Secondary School No. 5, Federal District; preparatory studies at the National Preparatory School; law degree, National School of Law, UNAM, 1941; professor of law, National School of Law, UNAM; professor at the National Polytechnic Institute; secondary school teacher. **d-***Federal Deputy* from the Federal District, Dist. 10, 1970–73, member of the Department of the Federal District Committee, the Labor Section of the Legislative Studies Committee, the First Government Committee, the General Accounting Office Committee and the First Labor Committee. **e-**None. **f-***Justice of the Supreme Court,* June 17, 1975–76, 1976– . **g-**Adviser to the CTM; adviser to the National Union of Radio and Television Workers; adviser to the National Electricians Union; representative of labor to the Federal Board of Conciliation and Arbitration; delegate to the International Labor Organization; Chief, Legal Department, CTM. **h-**Helped in rewriting reforms for Article 127 of the Constitution. **j-**None. **k-**None. **l-***Excelsior,* 18 June 1975, 18; *Directorio,* 1970–72, 30.

Calles Pordo, Aureo l.

(Deceased 1957)

a-Sept. 23, 1887. **b-**Huimanguillo, Tabasco, *Gulf, Rural.* **c-**Early education unknown; no degree. **d-***Interim Governor of Tabasco,* 1935–36. **f-**Director of Infantry of the Secretary of National Defense; Commander of the Legion of Honor of the Secretariat of National Defense; *Subsecretary of National Defense,* 1949–52. **g-**None. **h-**None. **j-**Joined the Revolution as an enlisted man under Ernesto Colorado, 1913; served in the Constitutional Army; became a career army officer, serving as Commander of Operations of the military zones of Chiapas, Tabasco, and Yucatan; rank of Brigadier General, July 16, 1932;

reached rank of Divisionary General. **k-**None. **l-**DGF56; Peral, 136; DP70, 333; DGF51, I, 177; NYT, 24 July 1935, 6.

Caloca, Lauro G.
(Deceased 1956)
a-1884. **b-**San Juan Bautista del Teul, Zacatecas, *East Central, Rural*. **c-**Primary studies in Zacatecas, Zacatecas; law degree from the Institute of Sciences of Zacatecas. **d-**Federal Deputy from the State of Zacatecas; *Senator* from Zacatecas, 1952–56. **e-**None. **f-**Secretary General of Government of the State of Puebla; Interim governor of Puebla; Advisor to the Secretary of Agriculture, 1920–24. **g-**None. **h-**Co-founder of the rural school program in Mexico, 1921; Director of *La Voz* of Zacatecas, 1913; Director of *El Independiente* of Zacatecas, 1920; writer for *El Universal*, Mexico City; poet and short story writer. **j-**Fought in the Revolution under Francisco Villa and Emiliano Zapata. **k-**None. **l-**DGF56, 8; Lopez, 142; Enc. Mex. 1977, II, 236.

Calzada, Antonio
a-Sept. 9, 1931. **b-**Queretaro, Queretaro, *East Central, Urban*. **c-**Primary studies at the Instituto Queretaro, Queretaro; secondary and preparatory studies at the Colegio Civil of Queretaro; architecture degree, School of Architecture, UNAM. **d-**Mayor of Queretaro, 1970–73; *Governor of Queretaro*, 1973–79. **e-**Director of the CEPES in Queretaro, 1968–70; accompanied *Luis Echeverria* on his 1969 presidential campaign in Queretaro; delegate of the IEPES of PRI to various cities; Secretary of the CEPES of PRI in Quintana Roo, 1962–64; Delegate to the General Assembly of PRI, 1968. **f-**Delegate of the Institute of Social Security in Queretaro, 1965–70; Manager of the Federal Potable Water Service, Cozumel, 1962–64; President of the Federal Board of Civil and Moral Improvements, Chetumal and Cozumel, Quintana Roo, 1960–64. **g-**None. **h-**Employee of the Secretary of Public Works; employee of the Secretariat of National Patrimony; Manager of the Mexican Works Construction Company, 1958–60. **i-**Impressed *Echeverria* with his organizational abilities during the 1969 presidential campaign; married to Teresa Rovirosa. **j-**None. **k-**None. **l-**HA, 15 Oct. 1973, 47; Enc. Mex., Annual, 1977, 548–49.

Camacho Lopez, Aaron
a-July 1, 1908. **b-**Tulyehualco, Federal District, *Federal District, Urban*. **c-**Primary studies in the Federal District; studied at the Normal School, Federal District; law degree, National School of Law, UNAM. **d-**Alternate Federal Deputy from the Federal District, Dist. 12, 1937–40; *Federal Deputy* from the Federal District, Dist. 12, 1940–43, member of the Department of the Federal District

Committee; *Federal Deputy* from the Federal District, Dist. 11, 1949–52, member of the Social Action Committee (second year), and alternate member of the First Public Education Committee and the Electric Industry Committee. **e-**None. **f-**Inspector General of Delegations, Department of the Federal District; Director of Control of Delegations, Department of the Federal District. **g-**None. **j-**None. **k-**None. **l-**Peral, 136; C de D, 1937–39; C de D, 1940–42, 48; C de D, 1949–51, 11; Lopez, 143.

Camarena Medina, Ramon
a-Dec. 14, 1907. **b-**Chihuahua, Chihuahua, *North, Urban*. **c-**Preparatory studies, Ciudad Juarez; agricultural engineering degree. **d-**Federal Deputy from the State of Veracruz, Dist. 10, 1940–43, member of the Administration Committee; *Federal Deputy* from the State of Veracruz, Dist. 6, 1946–49, member of the Committee on National Waters and Irrigation, alternate member of the First Ejido Committee. **e-**None. **f-**Delegate of the Department of Agrarian Affairs in Chiapas; Director of the Ejido Credit Bank, Veracruz. **g-**None. **j-**None. **k-**None. **l-**Peral, 37; C de D, 1940–42; C de D, 1946–48, 67.

Campa, Valentin
a-Feb. 14, 1904. **b-**Monterrey, Nuevo Leon, *North, Urban*. **c-**Primary studies in Torreon, Coahuila, 1910–16; completed first year of secondary; no degree. **d-**Candidate of the Workers Bloc for Governor of Nuevo Leon against Plutarco Calles, Jr. and General Zuazua, 1934; candidate of the Mexican Communist Party for president of Mexico, 1976. **e-**Member of the Mexican Communist Party. **f-**None. **g-**Co-founder of the Unitary Mexican Federation of Workers; attended the International Red Unions Meeting, Moscow, 1931; member of the Executive Committee of STFRM, 1943–47. **h-**Employed by La Corona, subsidiary of Royal Dutch Shell, Tampico, 1920–21; office worker, National Railroads of Mexico; shipping clerk, National Railroads of Mexico, Hipolito, Coahuila, 1922; employee, National Railroads of Mexico, Ciudad Victoria, 1927. **j-**None **k-**Imprisoned numerous times by the Mexican government for his leadership in railroad strikes and political opposition, including Lecumberri prison, 1930, 1949–52, and Lecumberri and Santa Maria prisons for the 1958–59 Railroad Strike, 1960–70. **l-**Campa; HA, 14 June 1946, 41–42.

Campero, Jose
a-Oct., 1893. **b-**Colima, Colima, *West, Urban*. **c-**Early education unknown; no degree. **d-**Senator from the State of Colima, 1932–34; *Provisional Governor of Colima*, Aug. 24, 1935, to Nov. 1, 1935, appointed by the Senate to replace Governor Saucedo until new elections could be held; *Federal*

Deputy from the State of Colima, Dist. 1, 1937–40. **f**-Secretary General of Government of the State of Colima, 1931–32; Oficial Mayor of the Senate, 1936–37. **g**-None. **h**-Newspaper reporter in San Luis Potosi, Chihuahua, and other parts of Mexico. **j**-Joined the Constitutionalist Army in Sonora, 1913. **k**-Remained loyal to Carranza in 1920. **l**-Peral 47, 67–68; letter; Correa 41, 47; Gonzalez Navarro, 117.

Campillo Sainz, Carlos

a-Aug. 7, 1919. **b**-Federal District, *Federal District, Urban*. **c**-Primary and secondary in the Federal District; medical degree from the National School of Medicine, UNAM; post graduate work in hospital administration at the World Health Organization; special studies at the National Institute of Cardiology, Mexico, D.F.; studies in virology in Boston and at University of California at Berkeley, 1946–47, 1952–53; received a Pan American Union scholarship for his studies in Boston; Professor of Infectious Diseases at the National School of Medicine, UNAM, 1947–60; Professor at the School of Public Health of the Secretariat of Health and Public Welfare, 1947–68; Professor of Virology at the National School of Medicine, UNAM, 1962–66; Rockefeller scholarship for virology studies at University of California, 1946–47; Director of the School of Medicine, UNAM, 1968–70. **d**-None. **e**-Member of the New Advisory Council of the IEPES, 1972. **f**-Director of the Laboratory of Virology of the Secretariat of Health and Welfare, 1968; member of the Investigating Committee on Health, Secretariat of Health and Public Welfare; *Subsecretary of Health*, 1970–76. **g**-None. **h**-Doctor for IMSS; scientific investigator for IMSS and the Secretariat of Health and Public Welfare; specialist in malaria for the Institute of Health and Tropical Diseases of the Secretariat of Health and Public Welfare; recipient of the United States Department of Health award for studies on polio, 1965; recognized specialist and author of over sixty scientific works. **i**-Brother of *Jose Campillo Sainz*; married Haydee Serrano; father an engineer. **j**-None. **k**-None. **l**-DGF69, 756; letter; HA, 20 Sept. 1971, 48; DBM68, 97–98; BdM, 81; DPE61, 111.

Campillo Sainz, Jose

a-Oct. 9, 1917. **b**-Tlalpan, Federal District, *Federal District, Urban*. **c**-Primary and secondary education in the Federal District; legal studies at the Escuela Libre de Derecho; law degree from the National School of Law, UNAM, 1941; specialized studies in Italy, 1938; Professor of Law at the National School of Law, UNAM, 1942–79. **d**-None. **e**-None. **f**-President of the National Center of Productivity; President of the Coordinating Committee of the International Activities of Private Enterprise in Mexico; Mexican representative to the United Na-

tions for industrial development; *Subsecretary of Industry, Secretariat of Industry and Commerce*, 1970–74; *Secretary of Industry and Commerce*, 1974–76; Director General of INFONAVIT, 1976– . **g**-Director of the Mining Chamber of Mexico; President of the National Federation of Industrial Chambers (CONCAMIN), 1966–68. **h**-Director of Legal, Economic, and Social Affairs for the Compania Fundidora de Fierro de Monterrey, 1962–70. **i**-Son of Engineer Jose G. Campillo; brother of *Carlos Campillo Sainz*; married Luz Garcia de la Torre. **j**-None. **k**-None. **l**-DBM68, 98; HA, 14 Dec. 1970, 21; DPE71; *Excelsior*, 18 Jan. 1974, 1, 13; HA, 28 Jan. 1974, 16.

Campillo Seyde, Arturo

(Deceased 1958)

a-Aug. 14, 1884. **b**-Paso del Macho, Orizaba, Veracruz, *Gulf, Rural*. **c**-Primary studies in Cordoba, Veracruz; no degree. **d**-Federal Deputy from the State of Veracruz, 1920–22, 1922–24, 1924–26, 1926–28; Senator from Veracruz, 1928–32, leader of the National Revolutionary Bloc, secretary of the Permanent Committee of Congress; Federal Deputy from the State of Veracruz, 1935–37. **f**-Governor of Quintana Roo, 1930; federal customs official, 1952. **j**-Supporter of Felix Diaz during the Revolution; joined Obregon against Carranza, 1920; rank of brigadier general, January 1, 1924; zone commander of various regions. **k**-Expelled from the PNR in 1930 as a leader of the "Whites" on the permanent committee of Congress. **l**-Peral, 138; DP70, 342; Lopez, 147; Meyer, No. 12, 114, 125.

Campos Ortiz, Pablo

(Deceased 1963)

a-Mar. 17, 1898. **b**-San Juan del Rio, Queretaro, *East Central, Rural*. **c**-Preparatory at the National Preparatory School, Mexico, D.F.; studies in law from the National Law School, 1916–18; law degree from the University of Rio de Janeiro, 1919–22; Professor of International Law at the National School of Law, UNAM. **d**-None. **e**-None. **f**-Joined the Mexican Foreign Service, Third Secretary of the Mexican legation in Brazil, 1921–23; Assistant to the Head of Protocol, Secretariat of Foreign Relations, 1923; Third Secretary to the Mexican legation in Spain, 1925–26; First Secretary and adviser to the Embassy in Washington, D.C.; Charge d'Affaires of the Embassy in Honduras, 1925; Charge d'Affaires in Madrid, Washington, The Hague, Nicaragua, and Chile; Director General of Political Affairs for the Secretariat of Foreign Relations, 1943–44; *Oficial Mayor of the Secretariat of Foreign Relations*, 1944–46; *Oficial Mayor of the Secretariat of Foreign Relations*, 1952–56; *Ambassador to Great Britain*, 1957–61; *Subsecretary (2) of Foreign Relations*,

1961–63. **g**-None. **h**-None. **i**-Knew *Rafael de la Colina* at the National Law School as a student; married Ivonne Lynch; son Pablo an engineer. **j**-None. **k**-None. **l**-WWM45, 18; DGF56, 123; DP70. 344–45; letter, EBW46, 25; Peral, 139–40; DPE61, 15; WB48, 962; DPE61, 15.

Campos Salas, Octaviano

a-Mar. 22, 1916. **b**-San Luis Potosi, San Luis Potosi, *East Central, Urban*. **c**-Primary studies in San Luis Potosi; attended Normal School in San Luis Potosi, 1926–32; economics degree from the National School of Economics, UNAM, 1940–44, with a thesis on the "Intervention of the State in the Wheat and Flour Market;" award for outstanding student in economics, 1942; graduate work in economics on a scholarship at the University of Chicago, 1944–47, and in the State of California, 1948; rural teacher, San Luis Potosi; inspector of rural schools, State of San Luis Potosi, 1934; Director of Elementary Schools of the Federal Government for the Federal District and for the States of San Luis Potosi, Guanajuato, Coahuila, 1940; in the field of education from 1931–44; most distinguished student of the United States Department of Commerce course on national income, 1950; Professor of Economics, National School of Economics, UNAM; Professor of Public Administration in Costa Rica, 1955; Director of the National School of Economics, UNAM, 1963–64. **d**-None. **e**-*Director of the Institute of Political, Social, and Economic Studies of PRI*, 1963–64. **f**-Director General of Statistics of the Secretariat of Industry and Commerce; head of the Department of Economic Studies for the Bank of Mexico, 1953; head of the Balance of Payments Department of the International Monetary Fund, 1950–52; Subdirector of Census and Statistics, Secretariat of the Treasury, 1942–49; Director General of Trade, Secretariat of Industry and Commerce, 1962–64; Gerente, Bank of Mexico, 1953–64; *Secretary of Industry and Commerce*, 1964–70; Ambassador to West Germany, 1979– . **g**-*Secretary General of the Mexican Teachers Union*, 1938–40. **h**-Assistant economist for the Secretariat of the Treasury; adviser to the Secretary of Industry and Commerce; economist for the United Nations; economist for the Center for Monetary Studies of Latin America, 1949; author of numerous articles on economic subjects; member of numerous economic commissions. **i**-Student of *Eduardo Bustamante* at the National School of Economics; friend of *Jorge Espinosa de los Reyes* at UNAM. **j**-None. **k**-Marxist as a student and normal teacher; supported *Narciso Bassols'* candidacy as a federal deputy in 1943. **l**-WWMG, 10; HA, 7 Dec. 1964, 19; DBM68, 99–100; Correa 41, 536; Por Que, 16 Oct. 1969, 14–17; Enc. Mex., 1977, II, 311–312.

Canale (Munoz), Eleazar

a-1906. **b**-Sonora, *North*. **c**-Early education unknown; law degree from the Free Law School, Mexico City, October 29, 1929. **d**-*Federal Deputy from the State of Hidalgo, Dist. 1, 1937–40*. **f**-Member of the Federal Board of Conciliation and Arbitration, Federal District; labor arbitrator for the Secretariat of Labor; head of the Legal Department of the Federal District, 1946–48; *Subsecretary of Labor*, 1948–52; Judge of the Fourth Chamber of the Federal Tax Court, 1952–70. **g**-None. **h**-Legal adviser to the Department of the Federal District. **i**-Brother of Senator *Antonio Canale*, 1946–52; served on Federal Board of conciliation with *Manuel Ramirez Vazquez*. **j**-None. **k**-None. **l**-HA, 15 Oct. 1948, 3; DGF56, 557; DGF69, 389; DPE51, 399.

Canales Valverde, Tristan

a-1909. **b**-Veracruz, Veracruz, *Gulf, Urban*. **c**-Law degree from the National School of Law, UNAM, 1933. **d**-None. **e**-None. **f**-Appeals judge of Matamoros, Tamaulipas, 1934; Secretary General of Government of the State of Tamaulipas; head of the Department of Plaints for the Federal District, 1951; Director General of the Division of Government, Secretariat of Government, 1952–62; *Oficial Mayor of the Secretariat of Labor*, 1964; *Subsecretary B of Labor*, 1964–70. **g**-First Secretary General of the Workers Union of the Office of the Attorney General of the Federal District and Federal Territories, 1939. **h**-Practicing lawyer; Assistant Secretary of the Federal Electricity Commission; technical adviser to the Mexican Social Security Institute; held numerous judicial posts. **i**-Father of *Tristan Canales Najjar*, federal deputy from the Federal District, 1979–82, and Secretary of Finances of the CEN of PRI, 1976. **j**-None. **k**-None. **l**-*Hoy*, 25 May 1968, 60; DGF56, 83; DGF51, 479; HA, 21 Dec. 1964, 10; DPE61, 12.

Candia (Galvan), Isidro

a-May 2, 1897. **b**-Sanctorun, Tlaxcala, *East Central, Rural*. **c**-Primary studies at Calpulalpan, Tlaxcala; teaching certificate. **d**-Local deputy to the State Legislature of Tlaxcala, 1934; Mayor of Tlaxcala; *Governor of Tlaxcala*, 1937–41. **e**-None. **f**-Director of the Department of Indigenous Affairs, 1941. **g**-None. **j**-Joined the Revolution under the Zapatista forces, 1912; colonel in the Army. **k**-Under investigation in 1971 by the government for alleged illicit land dealings in Tlaxcala. **l**-LAD, Oct. 1971; letter; D de Y, 3 Dec. 1940, 6; Peral, 142; PS, 0931.

Canto Carrillo, Nicolas

a-Dec. 7, 1917. **b**-Hecelchacan, Campeche, *Gulf, Rural*. **c**-Primary studies in Hecelchacan, Campeche; secondary studies in Campeche, Campeche; rural teaching certificate from the Normal Rural School,

Campeche; teacher in Calkini, Campeche and other towns. **d-**Mayor of Calkini, Campeche, 1942–44; Local Deputy to the State Legislature of Campeche, 1947–50; Mayor of Calkini, 1952; *Senator* from the State of Campeche, 1958–64, secretary of the Gran Comision (1st year), president of the Development of Cooperatives Committee, second secretary of the Second Naval Committee and the Insurance Committee, alternate member of the Second Labor Committee, the National Properties Committee and the Special Legislative Studies Committee. **e-**President of PRI in the State of Campeche, 1956–58; General Delegate of the CEN of PRI in Campeche, 1958. **f-**None. **g-**Active member of the CTM; Secretary General of the League of Agrarian Communities, State of Campeche. **h-**Began teaching in 1934. **i-**Parents were peasants. **j-**None. **k-**None. **l-**Func., 133; C de S, 1961–64, 14, 53.

Canto Echeverria, Humberto

a-1900. **b-**Merida, Yucatan, *Gulf, Urban*. **c-**Primary studies in Merida; professional studies from Rensselaer Polytechnic Institute and from the Brooklyn Polytechnic Institute; courses from Ohio Northern University; engineering degree. **d-***Governor of Yucatan*, 1938–42. **e-**None. **f-**Director, Department of Public Works, State of Yucatan, 1930–34. **g-**None. **h-**Manager of a sugar plantation in Cuba; business manager for a newspaper, 1931. **i-**Father a prominent attorney and public notary in Merida. **j-**None. **k-**None. **l-**HA, 12 June 1942, 30.

Cantu Estrada, Jose

(Deceased Nov. 28, 1938)
a-1904. **b-**Nuevo Laredo, Tamaulipas, *North, Rural*. **c-**Primary studies in Nuevo Laredo; preparatory studies in Ciudad Victoria; law degree, National School of Law, UNAM, 1928. **d-***Federal Deputy* from the State of Tamaulipas, Dist. 1, 1937–38, president of the chamber of deputies; answered President Cardenas' 3rd State of the Union address. **e-**None. **f-**Member of the Advisory Council to the President of Mexico; President of the Federal Conciliation and Arbitration Board, 1933; Chief of the Office of Publications, Secretariat of Foreign Relations; *Subsecretary of Labor*, 1935–37. **g-**None. **j-**None. **k-**None. **l-***Excelsior*, 24 Aug. 1979, 14A; C de D, 1935–37; PS, 954.

Cantu Jimenez, Esteban

(Deceased)
a-Nov. 27, 1880. **b-**Linares, Nuevo Leon, *North, Rural*. **c-**Primary studies in Linares, Nuevo Leon; special classes in Morelia, Michoacan; enrolled in the National Military College, 1897. **d-***Senator* from the State of Baja California del Norte, 1952–58, President of the Second Naval Committee, second secretary of the Military Health

Committee, member of the Second Balloting Group. **e-**None. **g-**None. **j-**Career Army officer; served in the 7th Cavalry Regiment, Mexico City; Instructor in the Second Army Reserve, Chihuahua, Jalisco and Zacatecas, 1902–03; fought against the Yaquis in Sonora, 1903–06; rank of major, 1911; fought in the Cuesta del Gato, Chihuahua; Chief of the Federal Garrison, Mexicali, 1914–17; Governor and Military Commander of Baja California del Norte, 1917–20; reached the rank of Colonel. **k-**Had to flee to the United States in 1914 for opposing the assassination of Madero. **l-**Ind. Biog., 32–33; DGF56, 5, 8, 10–13.

Cantu Pena, Fausto

a-May 12, 1941. **b-**Monterrey, Nuevo Leon, *North, Urban*. **c-**Economics degree, Technical Institute of Higher Studies, Monterrey, March 6, 1964; Eisenhower Fellowship in the United States for studying the theory and practice of industrial, agricultural, and tourist development, 1967; studies at the National Center of Productivity; Professor of General Economics and Business Economics, Technical Institute of Higher Studies, Monterrey. **d-**None. **e-**Director of the CEPES of PRI for Nuevo Leon. **f-**Economic investigator for the National Minimum Wage Commission; Director of the Commission for Industrial Growth and Economic Development of the State of Nuevo Leon, 1970; Gerente, Nacional Financiera; Director General of the Mexican Coffee Institute, 1971–77. **g-**Treasurer of the College of Economists for Nuevo Leon. **h-**Hone. **i-**Married Maria Felicitas. **j-**None. **k-**Convicted of fraud committed while Director General of the Mexican Coffee Institute, 1978. **l-**DBM68, 109; HA, 5 Nov. 1973, 21; DBM70, 111.

Canudas Orezza, Luis Felipe

(Deceased Oct. 21, 1978)
a-Sept. 8, 1911. **b-**Campeche, Campeche, *Gulf, Urban*. **c-**Primary studies at the Public School Modelo No. 3, Ciudad del Carmen; preparatory studies at the Liceo Carmelita, Ciudad del Carmen and at the National Preparatory School, 1928; law degree from the National School of Law, UNAM, Dec. 20, 1934, (honorable mention), with a thesis on "Lesions in Civil Law;" LLD from the National School of Law, UNAM, Apr. 10, 1950; Professor of General Theory of the State and Constitutional Law, UNAM, 1938–68; professor of graduate courses in law for the LLD, UNAM, 1950–68; guest professor at various state universities. **d-**None. **e-**None. **f-**Judge of the Second District, Civil Section, Federal District, 1932–34; Agent of the Ministerio Publico, Office of the Attorney General, 1935; Auxiliary Agent, Office of the Attorney General, 1936–37; Director, Office of Amparo, Department of the Federal District, 1938–40;

Subdirector of the Advisory Office of the Attorney General of Mexico, 1941–44; Director of the Advisory Office of the Attorney General of Mexico, 1944–49; *Assistant Attorney General of Mexico (2)*, 1949–51; *Assistant Attorney General of Mexico (1)*, 1951–52; Director, Legal Department, National Railroads of Mexico, 1953–56; Director of the Office of Amparo, Secretariat of the Treasury, 1959–65; Director General of the Legal and Advisory Department, Office of the Attorney General, 1965–68; *Justice (supernumerary) of the Supreme Court,* 1968–70; *Subsecretary General of Legal Affairs of the Department of Agrarian Affairs and Colonization,* 1971–75 (first appointee to this position); *Supernumerary Justice of the Supreme Court,* 1976–78. **g-**None. **h-**Judicial Porter, Third District, Federal District; Scribe and Section Chief for Amparos, Sixth District, Federal District; author of many articles and codes. **i-**Attended college with *Antonio Luna Arroyo*. **j-**None. **k-**None. **l-**HA, 26 July 1971, 16; DGF51, 535; DGF47, 309; DGF69, 120; DPE65, 210; D de Y, 26 July 1971; *Justicia*, 1968.

Cardenas (del Rio), Damaso

(Deceased Feb. 4, 1976)
a-1898. **b-**Jiquilpan de Juarez, Michoacan, *West Central, Rural*. **c-**Early education unknown, no degree. **d-***Senator* from the State of Michoacan, 1932–34; *Governor of Michoacan,* 1950–56. **e-**None. **f-**Interim Governor of Michoacan, 1930; Oficial Mayor of the Secretariat of the Treasury, 1934–35. **g-**None. **h-**Director of a construction firm. **i-**Father was a small groceryman; brother of President *Lazaro Cardenas*; married Baby Castellanos. **j-**Participated in the Revolution; reached rank of Divisionary General. **k-**Declined the nomination for governor, 1939. **l-**Strode, 302; Romero Flores, 72; Novo35, 339; DGF56, 96; Michaels, 8; DPE51, I, 90; *Excelsior*, 5 Feb. 1976.

Cardenas (del Rio), Lazaro

(Deceased Oct. 19, 1970)
a-May 21, 1895. **b-**Jiquilpan de Juarez, Michoacan, *West Central, Rural*. **c-**Primary studies in Jiquilpan de Juarez; no formal education after 1909. **d-**Governor of Michoacan, 1928–32, with numerous leaves of absence; *President of Mexico*, 1934–40. **e-**President of the CEN of the PNR, 1930–31. **f-**Interim Governor of Michoacan, 1920; Secretary of Government, August 28, 1931 to October 15, 1931; Secretary of War and Navy, 1933; Secretary of National Defense, 1942–45; Executive Director of the Cuenca del Tepalcatepec, 1947–60; Executive Director of the Cuenca del Rio Balsas, 1960–70. **g-**None. **h-**Worked as a printer, 1911–13. **i-**Brother of *Damaso Cardenas*; married Amalia Solorzano; father a small grocer; father of *Cuauhtemoc Cardenas*.

j-Joined the Revolution, 1913, under the forces of General Guillermo Garcia Aragon as a 2nd Captain and member of his staff; fought under General Obregon against Emiliano Zapata, 1941; Major in charge of a detail of the 22nd Cavalry Regiment; fought under the forces of Lucio Blanco, 1914; fought the forces of Francisco Villa under General Plutarco Calles, 1915; fought against the De la Huerta rebellion during which he was captured by *Enrique Estrada*, 1923; rank of brigadier general, 1924; Commander of the military zone of Tampico, 1925; rank of divisionary general, 1928; fought against the Cristeros, 1928; Commander of the 19th Military Zone, Puebla, November 1, 1933 to January 1, 1934; Commander of special Pacific Defense Zone, 1941–42. **k-**Saved the life of General *Enrique Estrada* from a military execution, 1924, who later served as a federal deputy during his presidency; active in the National Liberation Movement in the 1960s; leader of one of the largest political groups in Mexico until his death. **l-**WWM45, 18–19; DBM68, 114; EBW46, 29; DGF56, 414; *Hoy,* 31 Oct. 1970, 15–16; DP70, 362–63; 2374–75; Strode, 302; DGF50, II, 451; WB54, 162; IWW40, 172; Q es Q, 100–01; *Annals*, Mar., 1940; Morton, 88; Enc. Mex., 1977, II, 361–67; NYT, 20 Oct. 1970; *Justicia*, June, 1970.

Cardenas Gonzalez, Enrique

a-1927. **b-**Ciudad Victoria, Tamaulipas, *North, Urban*. **c-**Primary studies in Ciudad Victoria; secondary studies in Ciudad Victoria; engineering studies at the Escobar Brothers Agricultural School, Ciudad Juarez, Chihuahua. **d-**Mayor of Ciudad Victoria, 1969–70; *Senator* from the State of Tamaulipas, President of the Second Petroleum Committee, Second Secretary of the Industries and the Public Works Committees, member of the First Balloting Committee, member of the Fishing Committee, and Secretary of the First Instructive Section of the Grand Jury; *Governor of Tamaulipas*, 1975– . **e-**President of the Local Electoral Committee, Ciudad Victoria, 1963; *Secretary of Social Action of the CEN of PRI*, 1971–72; General Delegate of the CEN of PRI to Baja California del Sur, 1971–72. **f-***Subsecretary of Tax Investigation,* 1972–74. **g-**None. **h-**Owner of several radio stations. **i-**Boyhood friend of *Luis Echeverria* in Ciudad Victoria where *Echeverria's* father worked. **j-**None. **k-**Lost as a precandidate for governor of Tamaulipas to *Manuel Ravize*, 1967. **l-***Excelsior,* 1 June 1974, 16; *Excelsior,* 12 November 1973; Enc. Mex., Annual, 1977, 551; *Novedades de Yucatan*, 19 Jan. 1972, 1; HA, 31 Jan. 1972, 19; Loret de Mola, *91*, 146.

Cardenas Huerta, Gustavo

a-1905. **b-**Saltillo, Coahuila, *North, Urban*. **c-**Primary studies in Saltillo, Coahuila; preparatory studies at the Ateneo Fuente School, Saltillo; law degree, National School of Law, UNAM, 1930. **d-**Senator from the State of Coahuila, 1952–58, president of the Committee on Water and National Irrigation, first secretary of the Federal District Committee, secretary of the First Justice Committee, member of the Second Balloting Committee and the Special Legislative Studies Committee, and first secretary of the Second Instructive Group of the Grand Jury. **e-**Secretary General of the CEN of the PRM, 1940. **f-**Agent of the Ministerio Publico in the Federal District, 1930–36; Public Defender, 1936–37; Agent of the Ministerio Publico, 1937–38; Defense Attorney for Labor, 1938–39; Justice of the Superior Court of Justice of the Federal District, 1940–46; *Oficial Mayor of Hydraulic Resources*, 1946–52. **g-**None. **h-**Worked way through law school; author of several books. **j-**None. **k-**None. **l-**Ind. Biog., 34–35; DGF56, 5, 9–11, 13–14; DGF51, I, 413.

Cardenas Rodriguez, Antonio

(Deceased, 1969)

a-Oct. 6, 1903. **b-**Hacienda la Trinidad, Municipio General Cepeda, Coahuila, *North, Rural*. **c-**Early education unknown; enrolled in the National Military College, 1923; transferred to the Military Aeronautics School, graduating as an aviator in 1927; combat courses and air staff courses, United States, 1944. **d-**None. **e-**None. **f-**Chief of the Mexican Air Force, 1946–52. **g-**None. **h-**Flew for the Air Mail Service, 1927. **i-**Married Xochitl Zamora. **j-**Career Air Force officer; pilot of the Good Neighbor flight from San Francisco to Buenos Aires, 1940; observer of the Mexican Government attached to the United States forces in North Africa, 1943; Commander of the Mexican Expeditionary Air Forces, Squadron 201, 1945; participated in combat operations in the Pacific, 1945; rank of brigadier general, 1952. **k-**None. **l-**DP70, 363; DGF51, 180; Enc. Mex., 1977, II, 368; WWM45, 19.

Cardenas (Solorzano), Cuauhtemoc

a-May 1, 1934. **b-**Federal District, *Federal District, Urban*. **c-**Preparatory studies at the National Preparatory School; Civil Engineering degree, National School of Engineering, UNAM, January 22, 1957; special training at the Ministry of Reconstruction, Paris, France, 1957–58, and at Electricity of France, Paris, 1957–58; Bank of Mexico fellowship to work for Krupp in Germany, 1958; special studies in regional and urban planning. **d-**Senator from the State of Michoacan, 1976; *Governor* of Michoacan, 1980– . **e-**Member of the National Committee of the National Liberation Movement; student supporter of the presidential campaign of General Miguel Henriquez, 1951. **f-**Planner, Rio Balsas, Secretariat of Hydraulic

Resources; Subdirector of Las Truchas, 1970–73; *Subsecretary of Forest Resources and Fauna*, Secretariat of Agriculture, 1976–80. **g-**None. **h-**Director of Constructora Inde, S.A., 1956–57; practicing engineer, 1960. **i-**Son of President *Lazaro Cardenas*; nephew of Roberto Ruiz del Rio, secretary general of government in Michoacan. **j-**None. **k-**None. **l-**BdM, 84; C de S, 1976–82.

Cardiel Reyes, Raul

a-Nov. 1, 1915. **b-**Saltillo, Coahuila, *North, Urban*. **c-**Primary studies at the Colegio Roberts and the school attached to the State Normal School, 1921–26; secondary education at the Ateneo Fuente del Saltillo, 1927, and at the University of San Luis Potosi, 1933–34; preparatory studies at the University of San Luis Potosi, 1934–35; law degree, University of San Luis Potosi, Dec. 12, 1939; philosophy studies at UNAM, 1946–49; Master of Arts in Philosophy, 1961, magna cum laude; audited courses in law and political science from the University of Southampton, England, 1953; Professor of the History of Philosophical Doctrines, University of San Luis Potosi, 1939–44; Professor of Logic, National Preparatory School, 1947–62; Professor of Administrative Law at the School of Public Health, 1950; Professor of World History and of Political Theory, School of Political and Social Sciences, UNAM, 1956–72; Professor of Law, National School of Law, UNAM, 1958–61; many other teaching positions. **d-**None. **e-**None. **f-**Secretary General of the Board of Conciliation and Arbitration of the State of San Luis Potosi, 1934–38; consulting lawyer to the State of San Luis Potosi, 1940; Chief of Public Defenders for the State of San Luis Potosi, 1941; legal adviser, Movie Directors Union, 1945–48; Secretary of Scholarly Services of UNAM, 1954–56; Director General of Scholarly Services of UNAM, 1956–61; private secretary to the Subsecretary of the Presidency, 1962–63; legal advisor to the Subsecretary of the Presidency, Feb. 1962, to Sept., 1962; private secretary to the Secretary of Public Education, 1964–70; cultural adviser to the Secretary of Public Education, 1971–76; Director General of Channel 13 (Government television station), 1978. **g-**Secretary of Labor and Strikes of the National Union of Employees of the Secretariat of National Patrimony, 1951–54; founder and Auxiliary Secretary of the Executive Committee of the National Association of Universities and Institutions of Higher Learning. **h-**Lawyer for the Legal Department of the Secretariat of National Patrimony, 1947–48; lawyer for the Secretariat of National Patrimony, 1948–54; practicing lawyer, San Luis Potosi, 1939–45; practicing lawyer, Federal District, 1945–49. **i-**Friend of *Agustin Yanez*; father a small businessman. **j-**None. **k-**None. **l-**DPE70, 102; DBM68, 114–15; DGF47,

264; DBM70, 116–17; Enc. Mex., IV, 225; Enc. Mex., II, 162–63; letter.

Carranca y Trujillo, Raul
(Deceased, 1968)
a-Aug. 27, 1897. b-Campeche, Campeche, *Gulf, Urban*. c-Preparatory studies from the Literary Institute of Yucatan; law degree from the University of Madrid, Spain, on a private scholarship; LLD from the University of Madrid, 1925; studies at the University of Paris; professor, National School of Economics, UNAM; professor, National School of Law, UNAM, 1926–60; Dean, School of Political and Social Science, UNAM, 1953. d-None. e-Supporter of Jose Vasconcelos for president, 1929. f-Agent of the Ministerio Publico of the Federal District, 1928–29; Assistant to the Attorney General of the Federal District; Judge of the 8th Penal Court, Federal District, 1930; Justice of the Superior Court of the Federal District, 1940; First District Court Judge, 1944; Director of Cultural Dissemination, UNAM, 1948–52; *Secretary General of UNAM*, 1952–53, under Rector *Luis Garrido*; Chief, Legal Department, National Savings Bonds, 1953. g-None. h-Legal adviser to the President of Mexico; author of numerous works on penal law; co-founder of the review *Criminalia* with *Luis Garrido*, 1933. i-Friend and collaborator of *Luis Garrido* for many years. j-None. k-None. l-WWM45, 19–20; DP70, 372; Casasola, V, 2422; Enc. Mex., 1977, II, 382; Garrido.

Carranza Hernandez, Rafael
a-April 28, 1919. b-Federal District, *Federal District, Urban*. c-Primary studies in Mexico City; engineering degree. d-*Federal Deputy* from the State of Coahuila, Dist. 1, 1952–55, member of the Gran Comision, the Budget and Accounts Committee, the Foreign Relations Committee and the Administration Committee, secretary of the Preparatory Committee; *Alternate Senator* from the State of Coahuila, 1958–60; *Senator* from the State of Coahuila, 1960–64, President of the Colonization and the Public Works Committees, Second Secretary of the Consular and Diplomatic Service Committee and First Secretary of the Special Hydraulic Resources Committee. e-Member of the Presidium of PARM; Treasurer of the CEN of PARM, July 3, 1977– . f-*Secretary General of the Department of Agrarian Affairs*, 1955–58; Director General of the Agricultural Bank of the North West, 1965–68; General Adviser to the Director of the National Agricultural Bank, 1968–70; Coordinator General of the Agricultural Program for the Central Zone of the State of Coahuila, 1971–74. g-None. i-Son of Venustiano Carranza, president of Mexico. j-None. k-Replaced Senator *Vicente Davila Aguirre* who died in office,

1960. l-DGF56, 453; C de S, 1961–64; C de D, 1952–55, 7; HA, 26 Feb. 1979, V; *Excelsior*, 16 Apr. 1979, 16.

Carrasco Gutierrez, Victor Manuel
b-Toluca, Mexico, *West Central, Urban*. c-Normal certificate from the Normal School of Toluca; medical studies at the National Polytechnic Institute; medical degree; primary school teacher in rural schools and in night workers schools; high school teacher; normal school teacher; Professor of the History of the Mexican Labor Movement, Workers University, Mexico City. d-*Federal Deputy* from the State of Mexico, Dist. 11, 1976–79. e-Member of the Central Committee of the CEN of PRS. f-None. g-Official of the SNTE in the State of Mexico. i-Married Rosa Luz Fuentes R. j-None. k-None. l-D de C, 1976–79, 9; HA, 30 Apr. 1979, IV.

Carreno Gomez, Franco
a-May 16, 1898. b-Alaquines, San Luis Potosi, *East Central, Rural*. c-Primary studies in Alaquines; law degree from the National School of Law, UNAM, 1923; LLD, National School of Law, UNAM, 1961; Professor of law, National School of Law, UNAM; Professor at Night School, Mexico City, 1921. d-None. e-None. f-Consulting lawyer for the Department of the Federal District; Consulting lawyer for the Secretariat of Communications; Consulting lawyer for the National Agrarian Commission; Assistant Attorney General of the Federal District, 1929; Secretary General of Government of the State of San Luis Potosi under Governor *Genovevo Rivas Guillen*, 1938–39; *Justice of the Supreme Court*, 1941–46, 1947–52, 1953–58, 1959–64, president of the Administrative Division, 1943, 1948, 1953, 1958 and 1963. g-Co-founder of the Student Society of the National Preparatory School, 1915; Secretary General of the Union of Lawyers of the Federal District, 1935–37; President of the Society of Friends of Cuba, 1952–60. h-Student author for *Mexico Nuevo*; practicing lawyer with *Luis Garrido*, 1922–23; writer for *El Monitor Republicano*, 1924; practicing lawyer with *Manuel Moreno Sanchez*; author of numerous books on law. i-Close personal friend of *Luis Garrido* since law school days; married Lucia Garcia Valencia. j-None. k-Worked for many years to remove *Gonzalo Santos'* political influence in San Luis Potosi. l-WNM, 35; NYT, 26 Oct. 1958, 19; Garrido; DGF56, 567.

Carrillo Duran, Ricardo
a-Nov. 20, 1904. b-Zitacuaro, Michoacan, *West Central, Rural*. c-Law degree, National School of Law, UNAM, May 8, 1929. d-Federal Deputy from Zitacuaro, Michoacan, 1932–34; *Federal Deputy* from the State of Chihuahua, Dist. 3, 1961–64;

member of the Second Committee on Government, alternate member of the Committee on Taxes and the Committee on Public Works; Secretary of the Chamber of Deputies, 1962; *Alternate Senator* from the State of Chihuahua, 1964–70. **e-**President of PRI in Ciudad Juarez, 1957–61. **f-**Attorney General of the State of Michoacan, 1935; Judge of the First Instance, Ciudad Juarez, 1936–45; Secretary of the City Council of Ciudad Juarez, 1936–45, 1957–61; Subdirector of Loans and Pensions of the Institute of Security and Social Service for Federal Employees, 1964–70; *Administrative Subdirector of Petroleos Mexicanos*, 1970–76. **g-**None. **h-**Practicing lawyer in Mexico, D.F., 1947–57. **i-**Co-student with *Miguel Aleman, Antonio Carrillo Flores*, and *Hector Perez Martinez*. **j-**None. **k-**None. **l-**Letter, DGF69, 623,

Carrillo Flores, Antonio

a-June 23, 1909. **b-**Coyoacan, Federal District, *Federal District, Urban*. **c-**Primary education in Mexico, D.F., three years in New York City, 1914–17; preparatory at the National Preparatory School, 1921–24; law degree from the National School of Law, UNAM, Mar. 21, 1929; honorary LLD, UNAM, 1950; Professor of Administrative Law, National Law School, UNAM, 1936–52; Professor of General Theory, National School of Law, 1932–34; member of the Governing Council of UNAM, 1947–52; Director of the National School of Law, 1944–45; professor of special courses on "The State in Economic Life," Rector of the Autonomous Technological Institute of Mexico, 1971–72. **d-***Federal Deputy* from the Federal District, 1979–80. **e-**None. **f-**Agent of the Ministerio Publico of the Federal Attorney General, 1930–31; head of the Legal Department of the Attorney General of Mexico, 1931–32, 1934–35; Secretary of the Supreme Court of Justice, 1933; head of the Department of Legal Affairs of the Secretariat of the Treasury, 1935–36; adviser to the Consulting Department of the Bank of Mexico, 1938–41, 1946–52, 1971–72; *Director General of Nacional Financiera*, 1945–52; Founding President of the National Securities Commission, 1946–47; *Secretary of the Treasury*, 1952–58; *Ambassador to the United States*, 1958–64; *Secretary of Foreign Relations*, 1964–70; Director General of Fondo de Cultura Economica, 1970–72; Founding Judge of the Federal Tax Court, 1937–38; Mexican Governor of the International Bank for Reconstruction and Development; *Ambassador to the Soviet Union*, 1980– . **g-**None. **h-**Author of banking legislation and several books and numerous articles on law and economics; co-authored a book with *Ezequiel Burguete* in 1935; practicing lawyer, 1976– . **i-**Formed early friendships at the National School of Law with *Miguel Aleman, Ezequiel Burguete, Antonio Ortiz Mena, Alfonso Noriega, Angel Carvajal, Antonio Armendariz,*

Jose Castro Estrada, Salomon Gonzalez Blanco, Manuel Ramirez Vazquez, Ernesto Uruchurtu, Manuel Sanchez Cuen, and *Andres Serra Rojas*; studied at the National School of Law under *Luis Garrido Diaz*; son of the distinguished Mexican composer Julian Carrillo, discoverer of sound number 13 on the musical scale; brother of *Nabor Carrillo*, Rector of UNAM, 1952–61. **j-**None. **k-**None. **l-**DBM68, 121–22; letter; *El Univ.*, 2 Dec. 1964; *Hoy*, 11 Oct. 1969; WWMG, 11; Brandenburg, 113; HA, 5 Dec. 1952, 9; DGF56, 161; IWW, 197–98; Tucker, 437, Baker; NYT, 28 July 1957, 2.

Carrillo (Flores), Nabor

a-Feb. 23, 1911. **b-**Coyoacan, Federal District, *Federal District, Urban*. **c-**Primary and secondary education in the Federal District; preparatory at the National Preparatory School and at the George Washington High School, New York City; began university studies in New York; Engineering degree, National School of Engineering, UNAM, 1932; Master of Arts in Science from Harvard University, 1941; Ph.D. in science from Harvard University, 1942; Guggenheim Fellow; student assistant in math, 1932; Professor at the National Preparatory School; Professor of Math at UNAM, 1932–53. **d-**None. **e-**None. **f-**Employee, National Irrigation Commission, 1934–36; Chief of Engineers, National Irrigation Commission, 1936–45; member of the Mexican Commission of Scientific Investigation, 1943–45; Mexican representative to the atomic site on Bikini Island, 1946; *Rector of UNAM*, 1952–61; Director of the Atomic Energy Center in Mexico; executive member of the National Commission of Nuclear Energy; Director of the Mexican-North American Institute of Cultural Relations, Mexico, D.F., 1966–67. **g-**None. **h-**Internationally famous specialist in underground mechanics; promoter of the Atomic Energy Center in Mexico. **i-**Brother of *Antonio Carrillo Flores*; son of Julian Carrillo, distinguished Mexican composer and discoverer of sound number 13 on the musical scale; author of many scientific articles. **j-**None. **k-**None. **l-**WWM45, 21; *Excelsior*, 21 Aug. 1971, 7A; DP70, 380; Hayner, 169; DP70, 378–79; DGF50, II, 207; DGF51, II, 299; HA, 27 Feb. 1953, 35.

Carrillo Gamboa, Emilio

a-1938. **b-**Federal District, *Federal District, Urban*. **c-**Early education unknown; law degree from the National School of Law, UNAM, August, 1959. **d-**None. **e-**None. **f-**Assistant to the Director General of Telefonos de Mexico, 1960–62; Secretary of the Board of Telefonos de Mexico, 1962–67; Subdirector General of Telefonos de Mexico, 1967–75; Director General of Telefonos de Mexico, 1975– . **g-**None. **h-**None. **j-**None. **k-**None. **l-***Excelsior*, 1 June 1975, 1.

Carrillo (Marcor), Alejandro

a-Mar. 15, 1908. b-Hermosillo, Sonora, *North, Urban*. c-Primary studies in Hermosillo, Sonora; secondary studies in Texas; attended Tulane University, 1929; law degree, National School of Law, UNAM, 1934; Professor at the National Preparatory School, Mexico, D.F., 1930–60; Dean of the School of History, National War College; Professor at UNAM, 1930–33; Professor at the National War College, 1933–63; Director of Preparatory School Gabino Barreda; member of the National Board of Higher Education, 1935–39; Secretary of the Workers University, 1936–43; Assistant Director of the Workers University, 1943. d-*Federal Deputy* from the Federal District, Dist. 7, 1940–43, member of the Economy and Statistics Committee, the Social Works Committee, the Labor Committee, and the Editorial Committee; *Federal Deputy* from the Federal District, Dist. 17, 1964–66, member of the Second Committee on the Treasury, the Committee on Taxes, and the Committee on Budgets and Accounts; President of the Chamber of Deputies, December, 1966, and member of the Permanent Commission; *Senator* from Sonora, 1970–75; President of the First Foreign Relations Committee, First Secretary of the Federal District Department and the Second Constitutional Affairs Committee. e-Directed the national publicity for *Miguel Aleman's* campaign for President, 1946; cofounder of PPS, 1948; member of the National Council of PRI, 1972. f-*Secretary General of the Federal District*, 1946–51; head of special mission to Trinidad, 1962, accompanied *Adolfo Lopez Mateos* to Asia, 1958; publisher of the daily government newspaper *El Nacional*, 1968; Ambassador to the United Arab Republic, 1958–61; *Interim Governor of Sonora*, 1975–79. g-Member of the Executive Committee of the Mexican Federation of Workers, 1943–45. h-Adviser to PIPSA; publisher of the daily newspaper *El Popular*, 1943; author of many books on politics and economics. i-Close personal friend of *Vicente Lombardo Toledano*; son of Alejandro P. Carrillo, Consul General of Mexico in San Antonio, Texas; cousin of *Adolfo de la Huerta O.* j-None. k-Answered the State of the Union address in 1941; resigned as Secretary General of the Federal District to support *Vicente Lombardo Toledano*, 1951. l-HA, 28 Feb. 1972; DGF47, 293; DGF51; HA, 24 Apr. 1972; Correa 46, 71; Millon, 141; DBM68, 121; WWM45, 20; DPE61, 20; Kirk, 91; DGF51, 471; DGF50, II, 77, 317, 413; Peral, 154; HA, 12 Dec. 1947; Enc. Mex., 1977, II, 395; *Excelsior*, 4 Aug. 1978, 15; C de S, 1970–76, 75.

Carrillo Salinas, Gloria

a-Mar. 20, 1940. b-Zumpango, Mexico, *West Central, Rural*. c-Primary studies in public schools. Mexico City; no degree. d-*Alternate Federal Deputy* from the Federal District, Dist. 10, 1973–76; *Federal Deputy* from the Federal District, Dist. 10, 1976–79. e-Joined PRI, 1966; participated in *Luis Echeverria's* campaign for president, 1970; Secretary of Social Action of PRI in District No. 10, Federal District. f-None. g-Secretary of Relations of the Federation of Women Workers Organizations of the CTM, 1976; President of Feminine Action of the CEN of the National Meatworkers Union, 1976. h-Employee in a meatworkers industry; stenographer. j-None. k-None. l-*Excelsior*, 18 Aug. 1976,

Carrillo Torres, Francisco

(Deceased 1952)

a-1896. b-Comala, Colima, *West, Rural*. c-Early education unknown; no degree. d-*Governor of Colima*, 1935. f-Subdirector of the Department of Aviation, Secretariat of National Defense; Chief of Aviation for the North-East region. g-None. h-Responsible for the construction of Federal airports at Ensenada and La Paz; miner at Cananea before the Revolution. j-Joined the Revolution in 1913 under Obregon, aviator for the Secretariat of National Defense, 1923; fought with *Saturnino Cedillo*; rank of Colonel in the Air Force. k-Removed from the office of Governor by the federal government because of political ties with Calles. l-DP70, 381–82.

Carrion Valdes, Juan Francisco

a-Sept. 27, 1945. b-Gomez Palacio, Durango, *West, Urban*. c-Secondary studies in Torreon, Coahuila; preparatory studies in Torreon; degree in political science and administration, School of Political and Social Sciences, UNAM. d-None. e-Secretary General of the CEN of PARM in the Federal District, 1979; member of the Special Committee of the CEN of PARM, Tamaulipas, 1979. f-None. g-Student leader. j-None. k-None. l-HA, 12 Mar. 1979, VIII.

Carvajal, Angel

a-1900. b-Santiago Tuxtla, Veracruz, *Gulf, Rural*. c-Secondary studies at the National Preparatory School; preparatory studies at the National Preparatory School, 1921–24; studied law at the National School of Law, UNAM, 1925–27, degree in 1928, with a thesis on presidential resolutions on the agrarian question, which became a classic work; adviser at National Preparatory School; formed the Vasco de Quiroga Society to campaign against illiteracy; Director of a National Student Campaign, Secretariat of Public Education, 1923; professor, Law School, University of Veracruz, 1944–50; teacher in secondary and normal schools, 1944–50; professor at the National Preparatory School, 1930–44; Professor of Law, National School of Law, UNAM; Director of the Escuela de Iniciacion Universitaria, 1938–42. d-None. e-President of the Student Association at the

National Preparatory School; delegate to the student congress, 1928. **f-**Director of the Department of Prices, Secretariat of Communication and Public Works, 1934; Director of the Department of Administration, Secretariat of Public Education; Private Secretary to the Secretary of Public Education; agent of the Ministerio Publico attached to the Supreme Court; chief of the auxiliary agents of the Criminal Division of the Attorney General of Mexico; *Assistant Attorney General of Mexico*, 1936–40; *Assistant Attorney General of Mexico*, 1940–44; *Justice of the Supreme Court*, 1944; Secretary General of Government of the State of Veracruz, 1944–46; *Subsecretary of Government Properties*, 1946–47; *Governor of Veracruz*, 1948–50; *Secretary of Government Properties*, 1951–52; *Secretary of Government*, 1952–58; *Justice of the Supreme Court*, 1958–72 (retired). **g-**None. **h-**Lawyer, Department of Public Health; Secretary of the Intersectoral Board for Enemy Properties and Businesses, 1942. **i-**Friendships with *Antonio Carrillo Flores, Miguel Aleman, Adolfo Zamora, Alfonso Noriega, Ezequiel Burguete,* and *Jose Castro Estrada* at UNAM; close friend of *Adolfo Ruiz Cortines*; married Magda Moreno; son *Gustavo Carvajal Moreno* was Subsecretary of Labor, 1976–78, selected President of the CEN of PRI, 1979; father a small rancher. **j-**None. **k-**Precandidate for President, 1958, opposed by Cardenists; supported Jose Vasconcelos for President, 1929. **l-**HA, 5 Dec. 1952, 9; DGF56, 83; HA, 10 Aug. 1951, 14; WWMG, 12; D del Y, 2 Dec. 1952, 1; Scott, 222; Dulles, 473; letters, Morton, 92; *Justicia.*

Carvajal (Moreno), Gustavo

a-Oct. 29, 1940. **b-**Santiago Tuxtla, Veracruz, *Gulf, Urban.* **c-**Primary studies in Arnulfo Navarro, Jalapa and Veracruz, Veracruz and in the Chapultepec School, Mexico City; secondary studies at Secondary School No. 3, Mexico City; preparatory studies at the National Preparatory School No. 1; law degree from the National School of Law, UNAM, January 21, 1963; business administration degree from the School of Business and Administration, UNAM; Professor by Opposition of Civics, National Preparatory School, 1964; Professor by Opposition of Sociology, National Preparatory School, 1964; Professor of Political, Social and Economic Problems of Mexico, National Preparatory School; Professor of Political Society of Contemporary Mexico, School of Political and Social Sciences, UNAM. **d-**None. **e-**Private Secretary to *Jose Lopez Portillo* during presidential campaign, 1976; *Secretary General of the CEN of PRI,* August 11, 1978–79; *President of the CEN of PRI,* 1979– . **f-**Consulting lawyer to the Legal Consulting Office of the Secretariat of the Presidency; lawyer for the Department of Disputes of the Federal Tax Attorney's Office; lawyer, Department of Disputes for the Federal Income Tax Division, 1963; Agent of the Auxiliary Ministerio Publico of the Attorney General of the Federal District; Subdirector of Investigations of the Attorney General of the Federal District; Aide to the Attorney General of Mexico; Private Secretary to the Attorney General of Mexico; Legal Subdirector of Guanos and Fertilizantes; *Subsecretary (A) of Labor,* 1976–78. **g-**None. **h-**Director of the National Preparatory School No. 6, UNAM; Director General of Information and Relations, UNAM. **i-**Son of *Angel Carvajal,* Secretary of Government, 1952–58 and precandidate for president of Mexico, 1958. **j-**None. **k-**None. **l-**Letter; *Excelsior,* 11 Aug. 1978, 1.

Casas Aleman, Fernando
(Deceased Oct. 30, 1968)
a-July 8, 1905. **b-**Cordoba, Veracruz, *Gulf, Rural.* **c-**Primary and secondary studies in Cordoba; preparatory in Cordoba, law degree, National School of Law, UNAM, 1921–25. **d-**Provisional Governor of Veracruz, 1939–40; *Senator* from the State of Veracruz, 1946–52 (never held office). **e-**Personal representative and director of *Miguel Aleman's* campaign for President, 1945–46. **f-**Secretary of the Board of Conciliation and Arbitration, Dist. 5, 1930; agent of the Ministerio Publico in the State of Veracruz, 1926; judge in the State of Veracruz; consulting lawyer on the Labor Law for the Secretariat of Industry and Commerce, 1929; Secretary General of Government of the State of Veracruz, 1936–39; *Head of the Federal District,* 1946–52; *Subsecretary of Government,* 1940–45; Ambassador to Italy, Greece, China, 1953–64; Ambassador to Japan, 1964–68. **g-**None. **h-**Practicing lawyer in Veracruz, 1935–36. **i-**Intimate friend of *Miguel Aleman*; practiced labor law next to *Miguel Aleman* and *Gabriel Ramos Millan*; was a professor of *Miguel Aleman's* at the Law School; son Miguel married daughter of *Gilberto Limon,* Secretary of National Defense, 1946–52. **j-**None. **k-**Miguel Aleman's personal choice for the PRI candidate for President in 1946; rejected because of charges of excessive corruption in the Federal District. **l-**DPE65, 28; HA, 13 Oct. 1950, 15; DBM68, 125; G of M, 14; Greenburg, 24–25; DP70, 389; DGF47, 22; HA, 28 Feb. 1947, 11; DGF50, II, 317, 329; Q es Q, 108–09; Lopez, 173.

Caso Lombardo, Andres
b-Federal District, *Federal District, Urban.* **c-**Primary studies in the Federal District; secondary studies at Secondary School No. 3; preparatory studies at the National Preparatory School; economics degree, National School of Economics, UNAM; Professor of the National School of Economics, UNAM. **d-**None. **e-**None. **f-**Director,

Department of Personnel, Secretariat of Public Works, 1953–55; Director General of Administration, Secretariat of Public Works, 1956–58; technical adviser and Director of Administrative Services, Secretariat of Public Works, 1959–64; Director of Personnel, Petroleos Mexicanos, 1966–70; *Oficial Mayor, Secretariat of Public Works*, 1970–76. **g-**None. **h-**Executive Secretary, Technical Commission on General Means of Communication, Secretariat of Public Works; President of the Institute of Public Administration; Mexican representative to various international conferences on public administration. **i-**Son of *Alfonso Caso*. **j-**None. **k-**One of the two negotiators representing President *Gustavo Diaz Ordaz* in negotiations with the students, 1968; precandidate for Secretary General of CNOP, 1974. **l-**HA, 14 Dec. 1970, 22; HA, 9 Oct. 1972, 12; *Excelsior*, 13 Apr. 1977, 1; *Excelsior*, 8 Dec. 1974, 23.

Caso (y Andrade), Alfonso

(Deceased Nov. 30, 1970)
a-Feb. 1, 1896. **b-**Federal District, *Federal District, Urban*. **c-**Primary and secondary studies in Mexico, D.F.; preparatory studies at the National Preparatory School, Mexico, D.F.; law degree, National School of Law, UNAM, 1919; Professor of Philosophy, UNAM, 1918–40; professor at the National School of Law, 1919–29; professor at the University of Chicago, 1943; Director General of Graduate Studies and Scientific Investigation, UNAM, 1944; Director of the National Preparatory School, 1928–30. **d-**None. **e-**Joined the Mexican Labor Party founded by *Vicente Lombardo Toledano*, 1919. **f-**Director of Explorations at Monte Alban, 1931–43; head of the Department of Archaeology of the National Museum, 1930–33; head of the Welfare Section of the National Agrarian Commission; private secretary to the Secretary of Industry and Commerce; Director of the National Institute of History and Anthropology, 1939–44; *Rector of UNAM,* 1944–45; *Secretary of Government Propertites,* Dec., 1946, to Dec. 31, 1948 (first appointee to this position); Director of the National Indigenous Institute, 1949–70. **g-**None. **h-**Lawyer, Legal Department, Secretary of the Federal District; Director of the Mexican Journal of Historical Studies; author of numerous books and articles on indigenous peoples of Mexico. **i-**Taught *Miguel Aleman* at the National School of Law; son of engineer Antonio Caso and brother of the distinguished philosopher Antonio Caso; son *Andres Caso Lombardo*, was Oficial Mayor of Public Works, 1970–76; brother-in-law of *Vicente Lombardo Toledano*. **j-**None. **k-**Appointed Rector of UNAM in 1944 to supervise the writing of a new governing code and to settle campus disorders. **l-**Nicholson, 251; Simpson, 354; IWW, 201; HA, 25 Aug. 1944; HA, 28 May 1956, 12; WWM45, 21–22; DP70,

2375; Hayner, 266–67; WB48, 1017; WB54, 174; Enc. Mex., 1977, II, 409.

Castaneda Gutierrez, Jesus

a-1921. **b-**Federal District, *Federal District, Urban*. **c-**Early education unknown; enrolled in the National Military College, 1936; graduated from the National Military College, 1939, as a 2nd lieutenant; 1st place awards as an outstanding student; Professor, National Military College; Professor, Superior War College; special studies, Fort Leavenworth, Kansas; staff diploma from the Superior War College. **d-**None. **e-**None. **f-**Commander of the Cadets, National Military College; Commander of the 1st Batallion of Presidential Guards, 1964–70; Chief of the Presidential Staff, 1970–76. **g-**None. **h-**None. **j-**Career Army officer. **k-**None. **l-**Excelsior*, 1 Dec. 1970.

Castaneda, Jorge

c-Early education unknown; law degree, National School of Law, UNAM, 1943; professor of law at the National School of Law, UNAM, professor of law at the Free Law School and professor at the Colegio de Mexico. **d-**None. **e-**None. **f-**Career Foreign Service Officer, joined, 1950; legal adviser to the Secretariat of Foreign Relations, 1955–58; rank of minister, 1959–62; Director General of International Organizations, Secretariat of Foreign Relations, 1959–62; Alternate representative of Mexico to the United Nations, 1961–62; Ambassador to Egypt, 1962–65; Director-in-Chief of the Secretariat of Foreign Relations, 1965–70; Permanent Representative of Mexico to the United Nations and International Organizations in Geneva, 1970–76; *Subsecretary of Studies and Special International Affairs*, January 12. 1976–79; *Secretary of Foreign Relations,* 1979–. **g-**None. **j-**None. **k-**First appointee to this new subsecretaryship established in 1976. **l-**HA, 18 Jan. 1976, 14; *Excelsior*, 13 Jan. 1976, 4; DPE65, 18; *Excelsior*, 9 Jan. 1976, 18; *Excelsior*, 17 May 1979, 9.

Castanos Patoni, Fernando

a-Aug. 5, 1921. **b-**Durango, Durango, *West, Urban*. **c-**Primary studies in public and private schools; secondary studies at Secondary School No. 3, Mexico City; engineering degree, National School of Engineering, UNAM; studies in economics. **d-**None. **e-**None. **f-**Topographer, Department of the Federal District; planner, National Irrigation Commission; local engineer, National Railroads of Mexico; Director, Department of Planning and Promotion of Industrial Development, State of Queretaro; Director General of the Potable Water System, Secretariat of Hydraulic Resources; *Oficial Mayor of the Secretariat of Hydraulic Resources*, 1970–76. **g-**None. **h-**Director General of various private enterprises.

i-Studied under *Brito Foucher* and *Gustavo Baz* at UNAM; co-student with *Luis Echeverria* at secondary school. j-None. k-None. l-HA, 14 Dec. 1970, 22; DPE71; letter; *Excelsior*, 16 June 1976, 4.

Castellano (Jimenez), Jr., Raul

a-Nov. 3, 1902. b-Las Esperanzas, Coahuila, *North, Rural.* c-Primary and secondary studies at the Colegio Internacional, Monterrey, Nuevo Leon, 1912–17; secondary and preparatory studies, Colegio Civil, Monterrey, 1917–22; legal studies, School of Law, University of Guadalajara, 1923–28; law degree, Jan. 8, 1929. d-None. e-Leader of the movement supporting General *Miguel Henriquez Guzman* for President, 1952. f-Scribe, Second Civil Division, Monterrey, Nuevo Leon; public defender, Guadalajara, Jalisco; Secretary of the First District, Guadalajara; Secretary of the Superior Court of Justice, Morelia, Michoacan, 1929; Justice of the Civil Division of the State Superior Court of Michoacan, 1929–31; attorney for the Secretariat of the Treasury, 1932–34; Oficial Mayor of Baja California del Sur, 1931; *Attorney General for the Federal District and Federal Territories, 1934–37; Private Secretary to President Cardenas, 1938–39; Head of the Federal District, 1939–40;* Ambassador to Panama, 1940–46; *Supernumerary Justice of the Supreme Court,* 1963–72. g-None. h-Practicing lawyer in Mexico, D.F., 1946–63; delegate to the Eighth Pan American Conference. i-Knew *Antonio Martinez Baez* at UNAM; married Consuelo Martinez Baez. j-None. k-None. l-Letter, D del Y, 4 Jan. 1938, 1; D del Y, 2 Dec. 1935; EBW46, 161; *Justicia*; WB48, 1022; *Excelsior*, 28 July 1972, 1; *Excelsior*, 24 Feb. 1973, 17; *Hoy*, Nov. 1, 1939.

Castellanos, Everardo Milton

a-Mar. 23, 1920. b-Copainala, Chiapas, *South, Rural.* c-Primary and secondary studies at Tuxtla Gutierrez, Chiapas; preparatory studies at the National Preparatory School, Mexico, D.F.; law degree, National School of Law, UNAM, 1943, with a thesis on insufficient guarantees for individual public rights. d-Local deputy to the State Legislature of Chiapas; *Federal Deputy from the State of Chiapas,* 1949–52, member of the Economy and Statistics Committee and the First Balloting Committee; *Alternate Senator* for Baja California del Norte, 1964–70; *Governor of Baja California del Norte,* 1971–74. e-Joined PRI, 1946, President of the Regional Executive Committee, Chiapas; President of the State Committee of PRI, Baja California del Norte, 1952–58; Director of *Adolfo Ruiz Cortines'* campaign in Baja California del Norte, 1952; Director of *Braulio Maldonado Sanchez's* campaign for governor, 1953; Director of *Eligio Esquivel Mendez's* campaign for governor, 1959; adviser to the Regional

Committee of PRI and the CEPES, 1965–70. f-Director of the Legal Department, Secretariat of the Navy, 1952; President, Superior Tribunal of Justice, Baja California del Norte, 1960; Director General, Agricultural Credit Bank, 1965–70. g-None. h-Private law practice, Mexicali, 1953; founder of the *Judicial Bulletin of Baja California del Norte.* i-Personal representative of *Luis Echeverria* at the polls, 1970. j-None. k-CCI accused him of fraud as governor in January, 1978. l-DGF69, 105; C de D, 1949–51, 66; DGF51, 20, 31, 34; HA, 18 Oct. 1971; letter; *Excelsior*, 27 Jan. 1978, 12.

Castellanos, Jr., Francisco

a-1893. b-San Nicolas, Tamaulipas, *North, Rural.* c-Law degree. d-Governor of Tamaulipas, 1931; *Senator* from the State of Tamaulipas, 1934–40. f-Agent of the Ministerio Publico in Tamaulipas; Judge of the First Appellate Court, Tamaulipas; Attorney General of Tamaulipas; member of the Advisory Council to the President of Mexico; Secretary of the Presidency, 1940–41; *Attorney General of the Federal District and Federal Territories,* 1941–46; Administrator of Customs for Matamoros, Tamaulipas, 1952–58. g-None. i-Parents were peasants. j-None. k-President of the Opposition Socialist Party of Tamaulipas; split with state political boss *Emilio Portes Gil* after *Portes Gil* wanted to run for Governor a second time. l-*Hoy*, 20 Sept. 1941, 3; DGF56, 162; Correa, 77; NYT, 12 Sept. 1941, 8.

Castellanos Coutino, Horacio

a-July 7, 1929. b-Venustiano Carranza, Chiapas, *South, Rural.* c-Primary studies in Veracruz, secondary and preparatory studies in Mexico City; law degree, National School of Law, UNAM, 1950–54, graduated, July, 1955, with a thesis on the rule-making function of Mexican administrative law; Professor by Opposition, Constitutional Law and Administrative Law, National School of Law, UNAM. d-*Senator* from the State of Chiapas, 1976– , president, November, 1976. e-Delegate of the IEPES of PRI to Tamaulipas and Hidalgo, 1970. f-Director General of Legal Affairs and Legislation, Secretariat of the Presidency, 1970–72; *Attorney General of the Federal District and Federal Territories,* 1972–76. g-None. h-Practicing lawyer, 1955–70; author. i-Co-student at UNAM with *Jorge de la Vega Dominguez.* j-None. k-Assisted in helping to settle the 1966 student strike at UNAM. l-HA, 25 Dec. 1972, 40; HA, 15 Apr., 1974, 32; C de S, 1976–82; DBC, 32–33.

Castellot Madrazo, Gonzalo

a-Feb. 20, 1922. b-Federal District, *Federal District, Urban.* c-Primary and secondary studies in the Federal District; preparatory at the National Preparatory School in Mexico, D.F.; law degree from the National School of Law, UNAM, 1948. **d**-*Federal Deputy* from the Federal District, Dist. 7, 1961–64, member of the Committee on Radio and Television Industry and the Editorial Committee; *Federal Deputy* from the Federal District, Dist. 9, 1979–82. **e**-Official Orator for the PRI during the presidential campaigns of *Adolfo Lopez Mateos* and *Gustavo Diaz Ordaz*. **f**-Head of the Department of Radio, Television, and Movies of the Department of Information and Public Relations of the Office of President of Mexico, 1964–70. **g**-Secretary General of the National Industrial Union of Television Actors and Workers. **h**-Radio and television announcer; director of documentary movies and television programs. **i**-Co-student with *Jose Lopez Portillo*. **j**-None. **k**-None. **l**-DBM68, 131; C de D, 1961–63, 74.

Castillo Castillo, Fernando

a-Mar. 20, 1920. **b**-Oaxaca, Oaxaca, *South, Urban*. **c**-Primary studies at the Colegio Union, Oaxaca, 1920–25; secondary and preparatory at the Institute of Arts and Sciences, Oaxaca; law degree from the Autonomous Institute of Arts and Sciences, Oaxaca; Professor of Sociology and General Theory, School of Law, Benito Juarez University, Oaxaca. **d**-Local Deputy to the 41st and 45th State Legislatures of Oaxaca; *Alternate Federal Deputy* from the State of Oaxaca, Dist. 9, 1961–64; *Alternate Federal Deputy* from the State of Oaxaca, Dist. 9, 1967–70; *Federal Deputy* from the State of Oaxaca, Dist. 7, 1970–73, member of the Third Ejido Committee and the Naval Committee. **e**-President of the local electoral committee of Oaxaca, 1958–60; delegate of PRI from Oaxaca to the national PRI conventions. **f**-Director of the Office of Investigations, Department of Agrarian Affairs; Civil and Criminal Judge of the First Instance, Ejecutla and Juchitlan, Oaxaca; agent of the Ministerio Publico (Criminal Division) in Oaxaca. **g**-None. **h**-None. **j**-None. **k**-None. **l**-*Directorio* 1970–72; C de D, 1970–72; C de D, 1961–64; C de D, 1967–70; MGF69, 94.

Castillo Fernandez, Guillermo

a-June 25, 1902. **b**-Teziutlan, Puebla, *East Central, Urban*. **c**-Primary and secondary studies in Teziutlan; normal studies at the Normal Institute of Puebla on a scholarship from the Governor of Puebla, 1917–20; completed teaching certificate in Mexico City; teacher for seventeen years; director of primary and secondary schools; rural missionary teacher. **d**-Local deputy to the State Legislature of Puebla; *Senator* from the State of Puebla, 1952–58, President of the First Tariff Committee and the Foreign Affairs Committee; First Secretary of the Indigenous Affairs Committee; member of the First Public Education Committee and the Consular Service and Dip-

lomatic Committee. **e**-Secretary General of *Rafael Avila Camacho's* campaign for governor of Puebla, 1950. **f**-Federal Inspector of Education, Tlaxcala, Puebla, Oaxaca, Chihuahua, Coahuila, Durango and Chiapas; agent of the Secretariat of Agriculture in Puebla, Tlaxcala, Oaxaca and Veracruz; Oficial Mayor of the National Pawnshop; Director General of the National Pawnshop; Information Officer for the Mexican-North American Commission on Hoof and Mouth Disease; Oficial Mayor of the State of Puebla under Governor *Rafael Avila Camacho*, 1951–52. **g**-None. **i**-Knew *Rafael Avila Camacho* since they were children in Teziutlan. **j**-None. **k**-None. **l**-DGF56, 7, 9–13; Ind. Biog., 40.

Castillo Hernandez, Jose

a-Nov. 28, 1918. **b**-Leon de los Aldama, Guanajuato, *West Central, Urban*. **c**-Primary and secondary studies in Guanajuato; medical degree. **d**-Mayor of Leon, Guanajuato; *Federal Deputy* from the State of Guanajuato, Dist. 2, 1967–70; *Senator* from the State of Guanajuato, 1970–76, President of the National Properties and Resources Committee, First Secretary of the Foreign and Domestic Trade Committee, Second Secretary of the Industries, the Second Mines and the Health Committees. **e**-Member of PRI. **f**-Secretary General of Government of the State of Guanajuato. **g**-Secretary General of CNOP in Guanajuato. **i**-Married Celia Rio de Castillo. **j**-None. **k**-None. **l**-C de S, 1970–76, 74; C de D, 1967–70; PS, 1135.

Castillo Lanz, Angel

a-Nov. 1, 1898. **b**-Isla de Champoton, Campeche, *Gulf, Rural*. **c**-Primary studies in Champoton; law degree, School of Law, University of Campeche. **d**-Governor of Campeche, 1923–27; Federal Deputy from the State of Campeche, Dist. 2, 1928–30, member of the Gran Comision, secretary of the chamber; Federal Deputy from the State of Campeche, Dist. 1, 1930–32, member of the Gran Comision; Federal Deputy from the State of Campeche, Dist. 1, 1932–34, member of the Gran Comision; *Senator* from the State of Campeche, 1934–40. **e**-None. **f**-Official Mayor of the Chamber of Deputies, 1934; Director, Accounting Office, Chamber of Deputies, 1951–56. **g**-None. **j**-None. **k**-Some sources considered him to have been the political boss of Campeche. **l**-Enc. de Mex., II. 301; DGF56, 38; DGF51, I, 28; C de S, 1934–40; PS, 1138.

Castillo Larranaga, Jose

a-Feb. 5, 1899. **b**-Oaxaca, Oaxaca, *South, Urban*. **c**-Primary and secondary studies in Oaxaca, Oaxaca; preparatory studies at the Institute of Arts and Sciences of Oaxaca (four years) and completed at the University of Puebla and the National Preparatory

School; law degree from the National School of Law, UNAM, May 24, 1922, Professor of Procedural Law, National School of Law, UNAM, 1935 to 1960s; Professor of Amparo and Guarantees, National School of Law, UNAM, 1942; professor of Agrarian Law, National School of Law, UNAM, 1940 to 1960s; advisor to the University Council of UNAM; Director of the Division of Law, Post-graduate School, UNAM; Dean, National School of Law, UNAM, 1949–51. d-Federal Deputy from the State of Oaxaca, 1924–26, president of the Justice Committee, president of the political bloc. e-None. f-Actuary, 4th Supernumerary District, Federal District; Agent of the Ministerio Publico of the Attorney General of Tamaulipas; Secretary of the Third Correctional Judicial District, Federal District; First Supernumerary Judge of the District Court of Puebla; lawyer, Secretariat of Government, 1951; Justice of the Superior Tribunal of Justice of the Federal District and Federal Territories, 1951–52, 1953–58. g-None. h-Student scribe for the Second Justice of Peace of the Higher Military Tribunal; practicing lawyer, 1927–5⅟; author of numerous legal codes and books. j-None. k-None. l-Lopez, 180; DGF51, I, 487; DGF56, 513.

Castillo Ledon, Amalia (Gonzalez Caballero)

a-Aug. 18, 1902. b-San Jeronimo, Tamaulipas, *North, Rural*. c-Teaching certificate at the Normal School for Women, Ciudad Victoria, Tamaulipas; studies at UNAM; teacher at a girls' school in Ciudad Victoria, 1918; teacher at the Normal School for Men, Mexico, D.F., 1925–29. d-None. e-National Association for Child Welfare, 1929; founder of the Child Welfare Committee in Tepic, Nayarit, 1930; head of the Bureau of Educational Activities, General Administration of Civic Action, Mexico, D.F., 1933–45; adviser to the Mexican delegation to the United Nations Conference on International Organizations in San Francisco, 1945; Ambassador to Finland and Sweden, 1956; adviser to the Secretary of Foreign Relations, 1957; *Subsecretary of Public Education*, 1958–64; Ambassador and head of the permanent delegation to the International Organization of Atomic Energy, 1964–70; Ambassador to Austria, 1967. g-Founder of the Mexican Alliance for Women, 1953; President of the Revolutionary Federation of Women. h-Statistician of the Bureau of Education, State of Tamaulipas, 1918; joined the Foreign Service in 1953; President of the Inter-American Commission of Women; author of many dramatic works and numerous articles on the theater. i-Wife of the Mexican historian Luis Castillo Ledon, 1879–1944, who was Governor of Nayarit, 1930–31. j-None. k-First woman to address the Mexican Senate on women's suffrage; first woman to be appointed to a subsecretary position in the Mexican cabinet. l-WWMG, 12; WWM45, 2223; DGF56,

126, 129; Correa 46, 332; HA, 23 Feb. 1959, 17; Enc. Mex., II, 210.

Castillo Lopez, Jesus

a-May 16, 1905. b-Cuernavaca, *West Central, Urban*. c-Law degree, National School of Law, UNAM, 1928–32. d-*Senator* from Morelos, 1940–42; *Governor of Morelos*, 1942–46. e-None. f-Secretary General of Government of the State of Morelos, 1938–39; Director General of Cinematography, Secretariat of Government, 1951. i-Protege of General *Elpidio Perdomo*. j-None. k-None. l-HA, 15 May 1942, 3; HA, 18 Jan. 1946, IV; Peral, 162; DGF51, I, 69.

Castillo Mena, Ignacio

a-July 31, 1929. b-Durango, *West*. c-Primary studies at the Justo Sierra School, Monterrey and Secondary School No. 3, Mexico City; preparatory studies at the National Preparatory School; law degree, National School of Law, UNAM, July 9, 1951, with an honorable mention and a 9.6 average; professor of History and Literature, National Preparatory School. d-*Alternate Senator* from the State of Durango, 1964–67; *Federal Deputy* from the Federal District, Dist. 6, 1967–70, member of the Legislative Studies Committee, Second Section (Civil Law), Secretary to the President of the Legislative Studies Committee for the first year; member of the Federal District Committee; *Senator* from Durango, 1976– . e-Official orator for PRI, 1950–52, active during the presidential campaign of *Adolfo Ruiz Cortines*, 1952; *Director of Youth Action for PRI*, 1954–59; Subdirector General of Professions for PRI, 1949–61; Director of Legal Affairs for PRI, 1961–64; state committeeman from Durango to PRI, 1952–70; Private Secretary to the President of the CEN of PRI, 1966–68. f-Secretary to the President of the Superior Court of Justice of the Federal District and Federal Territories; Director of Public Relations for the Secretariat of Industry and Commerce; President of the Local Board of Conciliation and Arbitration, 1971–75, for the Federal District. g-President of the 1947 Generation of Law School students. Department of Agrarian Affairs and Colonization. i-Collaborator of *Lauro Ortega Martinez*; son of *Mariano Castillo Najera*, Senator from Durango, 1946–52. j-None. k-None. l-HA, 2 August 1971, 62; WWMG, 12; letter; C de D, 1967–69; DPE61, 101; MGF69, 105; C de S, 1964–70; *Excelsior*, 6 April 1973, 10; *Justicia*, Oct. 1973; HA, 27 Oct. 1975, 23.

Castillo Najera, Francisco

(Deceased 1954)

a-Nov. 25, 1886. b-Durango, Durango, *West, Urban*. c-Primary and secondary studies in Durango; preparatory at the Juarez Institute of Durango; medical degree from the National School of Medicine,

UNAM, 1903; advanced studies at the University of Paris and the University of Berlin; Professor of Urology at the Military Medical College, 1917–27; Professor of Forensic Medicine at the National School of Medicine, UNAM, 1920–22, 1924; Professor of General Pathology at the National School of Medicine, UNAM, 1927; Professor of Urology for postgraduate students, UNAM, 1927. **d-**None. **e-**None. **f-**Director of the Juarez Hospital, Mexico, D.F., 1918–19; Director of the Military Medical College, 1920; head of the Council of Legal Medicine for the Federal District, 1919–21; Minister to China, 1922–24; Ambassador to Belgium, 1927–30; Ambassador to Holland, 1930–32; head of the Department of Health and Welfare, 1932; Ambassador to Sweden, 1932; Ambassador to France, 1933–35; Ambassador to the League of Nations, 1934; *Ambassador to the United States*, 1935–45; *Secretary of Foreign Relations*, 1945–46; President of the National Securities Commission, 1946–54. **g-**None. **h-**Founding member of the Mexican Medical Association, President of the National Academy of Medicine. **i-**Close personal friend of *Lazaro Cardenas*; brother *Marino Castillo Najera* was Federal Deputy from Durango, 1943–45; and Senator, 1946–52; son Francisco is a Captain in the Navy and Subdirector of the Naval Medical Center; other son Guillermo was head of the Department of Security of the General Administration of the Consular Service of the Secretariat of Foreign Relations. **j-**Career army medical officer; Lt. Colonel and surgeon, Oct. 11, 1915; Colonel, July 21, 1916; Brigadier General, Jan. 21, 1922; and Major General, Jan. 11, 1939. **k-**Precandidate for President, 1939. **l-**DP70 403; Strode, 370; Peral, 162–63; DGF50, 83; EBW46, 34; DGF47, 20; DPE65, 19; DBM68, 133; Enc. Mex., II, 420; DGF51, II, 105; Kirk, 210–11; Michaels, 3; HA, 29 Mar. 1946.

Castillo Najera, Marino

a-July 18, 1890. **b-**Durango, Durango, *West, Urban*. **c-**Primary studies in Durango; preparatory studies at the National Preparatory School, Mexico, D.F.; law degree, National School of Law, UNAM. **d-**Federal Deputy from the State of Durango, 1918–20; Federal Deputy from the State of Durango, Dist. 1, 1922–24; *Federal Deputy* from the State of Durango, 1943–45; *Senator* from Durango, 1946–52. **e-**None. **f-**Consulting lawyer to the Secretariat of Agriculture; Director of the Legal Department of the Department of the Federal District; Justice of the Superior Tribunal of Justice of the Federal District, 1940–42. **g-**None. **h-**Practicing lawyer. **i-**Brother of *Francisco Castillo Najera*, Secretary of Foreign Relations, 1945–46; father of *Ignacio Castillo Mena*, Senator from Durango, 1976– . **j-**None. **k-**None. **l-**Peral; DGF47, 20; C de S, 1946–52; DGF51, I, 6, 9, 11, 12, 14.

Castillo Tielemans, Jose

a-1911. **b-**San Cristobal las Casas, Chiapas, *South, Urban*. **c-**Primary studies in San Cristobal las Casas; preparatory at the National Preparatory School, Mexico, D.F.; law degree, National School of Law, UNAM, 1937, with a thesis on reparations for damage in criminal law; Professor, University Extension of the Military College. **d-***Senator* from the State of Chiapas, 1958–64; Secretary of the Senate, 1959; President of the Committee on Immigration, President of the Third Committee on Labor; First Executive Secretary of the Second Committee on Justice and a member of the Special Committee on Legislative Studies; *Governor of Chiapas*, 1964–70. **e-**Active in the CEPES in support of *Manuel Avila Camacho* for President, 1940; private secretary to *Gabriel Leyva Velazquez*, President of PRI, 1952–56; private secretary to *Agustin Olachea Aviles*, 1956–58, President of PRI; member of the Regional Committee of PRI, Chiapas. **f-**Attorney General of the State of Hidalgo; agent of the Ministerio Publico attached to the Penal Courts, Federal District; Investigator, Secretariat of Agriculture; Substitute President of the Board of Conciliation and Arbitration for the Federal District. **g-**Delegate to the 5th National Student Congress, 1928; President of the National Law School Student Association, 1936; founder of an organization of Chiapan residents in Mexico, D.F. **j-**None. **k-**None. **l-**WWMG, 12; C de S, 1958–64, 54; DPE51, II, 210, 213; Func., 152.

Castillo Torre, Jose

a-1891. **b-**Merida, Yucatan, *Gulf, Urban*. **c-**Law degree, University of Yucatan, 1914; member of the University of the Southeast Council, 1922. **d-**Councilman for Merida, Yucatan, 1918; Federal Deputy from the State of Yucatan, 1918–24; President of the Chamber of Deputies, 1919; *Senator* from the State of Yucatan, 1926–30, President of the Senate, 1926; *Senator* from the State of Yucatan, 1940–46, Secretary of the Senate; President of the First Public Education Committee, President of the Second Foreign Relations Committee; *Federal Deputy* from the State of Yucatan, 1949–52, member of the Legislative Studies Committee (1st and 2nd years), the First Committee on Government, and the Foreign Relations Committee; member of the Gran Comision. **e-**None. **f-**Member of the State Commission to Revise the Legal Codes of Yucatan, 1916; assistant lawyer for the Secretary General of Government of the State of Yucatan, 1917; representative of the State of Yucatan in Mexico, D.F., 1922; President of the Editorial Commission of the Secretariat of Foreign Relations; legal adviser to the Mexican delegation to the United Nations Conference on International Organizations, San Francisco, 1945. **g-**None. **h-**Consulting lawyer to the State Government of Yucatan, 1918, 1924; lawyer for Railroads of Yucatan in Mexico, D.F., 1922; lawyer for the Secretariat of Foreign Relations, 1934, 1937; lawyer for the Consulting Office of the Attorney General of Mexico, 1938–39; author of many legal articles. j-None. k-None l-WWM45, 23; C de D, 1949–51, 67; DGF51, 27, 29, 32, 33, 36; Enc. Mex., II, 210; Peral, 164; WB48, 1026.

Castillon Coronado, Maria Regufio
a-Mar. 24, 1929. b-Guadalajara, Jalisco, *West, Urban*. c-Early education unknown; no degree. d-Councilwoman of the City Council of Guadalajara, 1956–58, under Mayor *Juan Gil Preciado*; Councilwoman of the City Council of Guadalajara, 1971–73, under Mayor *Guillermo Cosio Vidaurri; Federal Deputy* from the State of Jalisco, Dist. 7, 1976–79, member of the Social Action Committee, the Agricultural Development Committee, Section Three of the Education Development Committee, the Development of Natural and Energy Resources Committee, the Forest and Fauna Development Committee and the Maternal and Infant Section of the Development of Social Security and Public Welfare Committee. e-None. f-None. g-Member of the League of Small Industries of the City of Guadalajara, 1947; Secretary General of the Union of Unsalaried Workers of Jalisco; active feminist in Jalisco. j-None. k-None. l-*Excelsior*, 24 Aug. 1976, 18; Enc. Mex., 1977, IV, 579; D de C, 1976–79, 4, 11, 18, 19, 23, 31, 40.

Castorena Monterrubio, Saul
a-Aug. 22, 1942. b-Huejutla, Hidalgo, *East Central, Rural*. c-Studies at the Autonomous University of Puebla, law degree; studies toward an MA in education from the National Center of Industrial Technical Teaching. d-*Federal Deputy* from the Federal District, Dist. 15, 1976–79; minority coordinator of his party in the chamber, 1976–77. e-Representative of PARM to the Federal Electoral Commission; delegate of PARM to every state in Mexico; Coordinating Secretary of Legislation of the CEN of PARM, 1976–77. f-None. g-None. h-Practicing lawyer, notary and actuary. i-Married Maria de los Angeles Hidalga. j-None. k-None. l-D de C, 1976–79, 12; HA, 30 Apr. 1979, VIII.

Castorena (Zavala), Jose de Jesus
a-Nov. 6, 1901. b-Jaripito, Guanajuato, *West Central, Rural*. c-Early education unknown; law degree, National School of Law, UNAM, 1925, with a thesis on strike law in Mexico; professor of Labor Law, UNAM. d-None. e-None. f-*Oficial Mayor of Labor*, 1940; President of the Federal Conciliation and Arbitration Board; *Provisional Governor of Guanajuato*, 1947–48. g-None. h-Practicing lawyer;

author of several legal works. i-Attended UNAM with *Antonio Martinez Baez*; protege of *Jose Aguilar y Maya*; married to Luisa Bringas. j-None. k-Considered an outstanding authority on labor law; replaced *Vicente Lombardo Toledano* as professor of this subject at UNAM. l-DBM68, 134; HA, 16 Jan. 1948, 3–4; HA, 20 Feb. 1948, 11–12; Anderson; Lopez, 183.

Castrejon Diez, Jaime
a-May 22, 1931. b-Taxco, Guerrero, *South, Urban*. c-Studied at the University of Chicago, 1949–50; Bachelor of Science in Bacteriology, University of California, 1954; Master of Science in Bacteriology and Microbiology, University of Bristol, 1956, Ph.D. in Microbiology, Tulane University, 1961; post-graduate work in microbiology, 1961–62; Vice President of the National Association of Universities and Institutions of Higher Learning; Rector of the University of Guerrero, 1970–72. d-Mayor of Taxco, Guerrero, 1966–68. e-Adviser to the State Committee on Economic, Political, and Social Studies for PRI in Guerrero, 1968–70; Secretary of Finances of the National Confederation of Popular Organizations of Guerrero, 1968–70. f-None. g-None. h-Owner of numerous bottling companies; one of the wealthiest businessmen in Guerrero; author of various works in the field of microbiology and a history of Taxco. j-None. k-Precandidate for Governor of Guerrero several times, kidnapped by guerrillas in Guerrero in 1972. l-HA, 29 Nov. 1971, 54.

Castrejon y Chavez, Gustavo
a-June 11, 1910. b-Hacienda de San Pedro Jorullo, Municipio de la Huacana, Michoacan, *West Central, Rural*. c-Studied at the Colegio de San Nicolas de Hidalgo (University of Michoacan), and the University of LaSalle, Chicago. d-*Federal Deputy* from the Federal District, Dist. 2, 1946–49, member of the First Committee on Public Education, the Second Committee on Elections, and the Tourism Committee; member of the Social Welfare Committee, 1947. f-Tax representative of the State of Mexico; *Oficial Mayor of the Secretariat of Hydraulic Resources*, 1958–61. g-None. h-Cashier of the National Irrigation Commission; accountant for the National Irrigation Commission; Director General of National Schools in Los Angeles, California; Director General of the Radio Technical Institute of Mexico, S.A., 1966–68. i-Married Carmen Ulloa. j-None. k-None. l-DBM68, 134; C de D, 1946–48; DPE61, 90; WB48, 1028.

Castro, Jesus Agustin
(Deceased Mar. 22, 1954)
a-Aug. 15, 1887. b-Rancho de Eureka, Ciudad Lerdo, Durango, *West, Rural*. c-Primary in the pub-

lic schools of Durango, had to leave school for economic reasons; no degree. **d-**_Senator_ from the State of Durango, 1924–28; Governor of Durango, 1921–24. **e-**None. **f-**Governor of Chiapas, 1914–15; Governor of Oaxaca, 1915–16; Subsecretary of National Defense, 1917–18, in charge of the Secretaryship; _Secretary of National Defense_, 1939–40. **g-**None. **h-**Conductor for a streetcar company, 1910. **i-**Close friend of Enrique Najera, who followed _Castro_ as Governor of Durango, 1924–27, when _Castro_ was military commander of the State; _Castro's_ personal political organization supported Najera. **j-**Joined the Revolution, 1910; rank of Colonel, 1911; fought under Madero; Brigadier General 1914; Divisionary General, 1920; Military Commander of various states, 1918–20; head of the Fifth Military Zone, 1935–39. **k-**Ran for President of Mexico, 1946. **l-**Lieuwen, DP70, 406; Gruening, 423–25; Peral, 166–67; D de Y, 24 Jan. 1939, 1; EBW46, 1133; Q es Q, 115–16; Enc. Mex., II, 423; Lopez, 184; NYT, 28 Jan. 1946, 9.

Castro Estrada, Jose

a-Dec. 29, 1908. **b-**Morelia, Michoacan, _West Central, Urban_. **c-**Primary and secondary education in Morelia under Professor Vargas; preparatory in the National Preparatory School in Mexico, D.F.; law degree from the National School of Law, UNAM, Dec. 16, 1929; Professor of Administrative Law at the National School of Law, UNAM, for thirteen years; adviser to and member of the Governing Board of UNAM, 1962–72. **d-**None. **e-**Supporter of _Juan Andreu Almazan_ for president, 1940. **f-**Secretary of the Review Board for Fiscal Infractions, Secretariat of the Treasury, 1929; Agent of the Ministerio Publico of the Criminal Courts; _Subsecretary of Forest Resources of the Secretary of Agriculture_, 1952 (first appointee); _Justice of the Supreme Court_, 1952–67; Director General of Forest Products of Mexico, 1968–70. **g-**Founding member of the Socialist Lawyers Front, 1936. **h-**Adviser to financial institutions; adviser to the National Lottery; adviser to Latin American Life Insurance Company, S.A.; head of Legal Affairs for Private Charity; author of articles on legal and economic subjects; member of several committees in charge of writing new federal codes; practicing lawyer in Mexico, D.F., 1970–72. **i-**Friends with numerous members of the 1929 generation of lawyers at the National Law School, including _Miguel Aleman, Antonio Carrillo Flores, Angel Carvajal, Andres Serra Rojas, Manuel Gual Vidal, Antonio Garcia Lopez, Manuel Sanchez Cuen_, and _Carlos Franco Sodi_; father a lawyer and grandfather was a Justice of the Supreme Court. **j-**None. **k-**Briefly in exile after the 1940 election. **l-**Letter, DBM68, 135; WWMG, 12; DGF69, 129; DGF51, 203; _Justicia_, Feb., 1967.

Castro Leal, Antonio

a-Mar. 2, 1896. **b-**San Luis Potosi, San Luis Potosi, _East Central, Urban_. **c-**Primary, secondary and preparatory studies in Mexico, D.F.; member of the 1915 "Seven Wise Men" generation; law degree, National School of Law, UNAM; LLD, National School of Law, UNAM; Ph.D., Georgetown University; Professor of Spanish Literature, National Preparatory School; Professor of Mexican and South American Literature, Graduate College, UNAM; Professor of Public International Law, UNAM, 1929; Rector of UNAM, Dec. 9, 1928 to June 21, 1929. **d-**_Federal Deputy_ from the Federal District, Dist. 18, 1958–61, member of the Editorial Committee (first year), the Legislative Studies Committee (4th Section), the Cinematography Development Committee, and the Foreign Relations Committee. **e-**None. **f-**Private Secretary to the Rector of UNAM, 1920; First Secretary to Chile, 1920, 1923; Charge d'Affaires, Chile, 1922, 1924–25; First Secretary and Adviser to Mexican Embassy, Washington, D.C., 1925; inspector, Mexican Consulates in the United States, 1926; legal adviser, Commercial Aviation Commission, Washington, D.C., 1927; Secretary General and Technical Adviser, Mexican delegation to the Inter-American Conference, Havana, Cuba, 1928; official adviser to the League of Nations, 1930–31; Diplomatic Counselor to France, 1929; Mexican delegate to the First Conference on the Codification of International Law, The Hague, 1930; adviser to the Mexican Ambassador to Spain, 1931; Director, Department of Bellas Artes (first appointee), 1934; Director General, Cinematographic Supervision, Secretariat of Government, 1947; Ambassador to UNESCO, 1949–52. **g-**None. **h-**Founder and Director of the _Revista de Literatura Mexicana_, 1940; author and editor of many books. **i-**Knew _Jaime Torres Bodet_ and _Luis Garrido Diaz_ at the National Preparatory School; married Maria Rafaela Espino. **j-**None. **k-**None. **l-**DEM, 75; DGF47, 72; Enc. Mex., II, 213–14; Peral, 167; C de D, 1958–60, 74; Func., 193; Novo, 389; WWLA35, 88; Lopez, 185; HA, June, 1958; Enc. Mex., 1977, II, 425–26.

Castro Sanchez, Juventino

a-1921. **b-**Amealio, Queretaro, _East Central, Rural_. **c-**Early education unknown; accounting degree. **d-**Local deputy to the State Legislature of Queretaro, 34th legislature; Mayor of Queretaro, 1961–64; Local deputy to the 41st State Legislature of Queretaro, 1964–65; _Governor of Queretaro_, 1967–73. **e-**President of PRI of the State of Queretaro. **f-**Director of Traffic, Queretaro, 1946–49; Director of Transportation, State of Mexico, 1974. **g-**Secretary General of the Union of Millers, Queretaro, 1939–41; Secretary of Labor Conflicts, Federation of Mexican Workers in Queretaro, 1941–43; Secretary of Finances, CTM in Queretaro, 1943–46; Secretary of Interior, Federation of Bus Companies, Mexico, 1949–54. h-Started career as a millstone cutter for a private milling company; operated own bus company, 1954–61. j-None. k-*Por Que* accused his administration as governor as being dishonest; *Excelsior* said he and his secretary general of government were ordered to appear in court on charges of fraud involving 700,000 pesos while governor, in 1974. l-WWMG, 12; *Excelsior*, 28 Feb. 1974, 4; *Excelsior*, 1 Oct. 1974, 16; *Por Que*, 4 Dec. 1969, 21.

Castro Villagrana, Jose
(Deceased 1960)
a-Mar. 10. 1888. b-Zacatecas, Zacatecas, *East Central, Urban.* c-Primary and secondary studies in Zacatecas, Extension School of the Normal School of Zacatecas, preparatory at the Institute of Sciences at Zacatecas; medical degree from the National School of Medicine, UNAM, 1914, with a thesis on the treatment of acute peritonitis; Professor of Anatomy, National School of Medicine, UNAM, 1912–22; Professor of Therapeutics and Surgery, Juarez Hospital, Mexico, D.F.; Professor at the National School of Medicine, 1944–50; Director of the National School of Medicine, 1950–54. d-None. e-None. f-Director of the Juarez Hospital, 1929–39; head of Medical Services for the Union of Mexican Electricians, 1937–46; *Subsecretary of Health*, 1958–60. g-None. h-Intern, Juarez Hospital, 1914; preparer of cultivation mediums, Bacteriological Institute, Mexico, D.F., 1913–15; assistant at the Clinical Laboratory, National School of Medicine, 1915–18; prosector of Topographical Anatomy, National School of Medicine, 1919–22; surgeon at Juarez Hospital, 1946; President and co-founder of the Mexican Academy of Surgery, 1942–46, editor of the medical journal *Postoperative and Preoperative*; responsible for introducing televised instruction at the National School of Medicine; author of numerous articles on therapeutics and surgery. i-Son Xavier a doctor in Mexico City. j-None. k-None. l-HA, 22 Dec. 1958, 7; Peral 47, 81; EBW46; DP70, 409; HA, 4 Aug. 1944, 7; Enc. Mex., II, 214; WB48, 1029.

Castro y Castro, Fernando
c-Law degree from the National School of Law, UNAM; graduate studies from the School of Philosophy and Letters, UNAM; course in general administration from the Mexican Association of Scientific Administration; courses in budgeting and costs and organization of office work from the Center of Industrial Productivity; Professor of Sociology of the National School of Law, UNAM, 1962–64.

d-None. e-None. f-Legal adviser to the Department of the Federal District, 1948–50; Legal agent for PIPSA, 1949–52; Private Secretary to the Secretary of Public Health, 1951–52; Subdirector of the National Bank of Small Businesses, 1960–64; Secretary of the Council for the Institute of Social Security for Federal Employees, 1960; Secretary of the National Advisory Commission of Fishing, 1962–64; *Oficial Mayor of the Secretariat of Navy*, 1964–70; Director in Chief of the Secretariat of Foreign Relations with the rank of Ambassador, 1970–72; Director General of International Affairs, Secretariat of Labor, 1976– . g-None. h-Technical adviser to the Mexican Institute of Social Security, 1956; legal adviser to the Subsecretary of Credit of the Secretariat of the Treasury; member of the law firm Castro and Gonzalez Guevara, 1948; lawyer for the Legal Department of the National Lottery, 1957–58; technical adviser to CONASUPO, 1961. i-Friend of *Rafael P. Gamboa*, Secretary of Public Health, 1946–52; married Elena Estrada. j-None. k-None. l-DBM68, 135–36; DPE71, 6; letter.

Catalan Calvo, Gerardo Rafael
a-Oct. 3, 1894. b-Chilpancingo, Guerrero, *South, Urban.* c-Preparatory studies in Chilpancingo; industrial engineering degree, national School of Agriculture and the National Military College, 1923; studied in the United States, 1930–32; Professor of Math and Ballistics at the National Military College, 1926–27; Director of Military Studies, 1933–34. d-*Governor of Guerrero*, 1941–45. e-None. f-None. g-None. h-Technical consultant to the National Military College. i-Brother Felipe was Treasurer of the Federal District. j-Joined the Revolution in 1914; career army officer; rank of Lt. Colonel, 1930; Brigadier General, October 1, 1943; Commander of various military units, 1934–40. k-President *Manuel Avila Camacho* personally attended his inauguration as Governor of Guerrero. l-WWM45, 241; HA, 28 May 1943, 16; Peral, 169; HA, 15 Sept. 1944, ix; Correa, 51; EBW46, 60; WB48, 1030; *Excelsior*, 18 Feb. 1976, 5.

Cebreros, Alfonso
a-Jan. 15, 1946. b-Culiacan, Sinaloa, *West, Urban.* c-Primary and secondary studies in Culiacan; economic studies (two years) in Culiacan; economics degree from the National School of Economics, UNAM, 1967, with a thesis on "External Disequilibrium, the Task of Development and Economic Policy." d-None. e-None. f-Economist, Department of Petrochemicals, Division of Control and Inspection of Decentralized Agencies, Secretariat of Government Properties, 1966–68; Head, Department of Petrochemicals, Secretariat of Government Properties, 1968–69; Assistant to the Director of Control and

Inspection, Secretariat of Government Properties, *Horacio Flores de la Pena,* 1969–70; Private Secretary to the Secretary of Government Properties, *Horacio Flores de la Pena*, 1970–74; Director General of Studies and Projects, Secretariat of Government Properties, 1974–76; *Subsecretary of Government Properties*, 1976; Secretary General of the Department of Fishing, 1977–78; *Subsecretary of Programming,* Secretariat of Planning and Programming, 1978–. g-None. h-Member of the Technical Planning Committee, UNAM, 1968–70; author of various books and articles on economics. i-Student of *Horacio Flores de la Pena.* j-None. k-None. l-Letter, *Excelsior*, 6 Sept. 1977; *Excelsior*, 26 Jan. 1978.

Cedillo, Saturnino
(Deceased Jan. 11, 1939)
a-1890. b-Rancho de Palomas, San Luis Potosi, *East Central, Rural.* c-Only completed primary school. d-Governor of San Luis Potosi, 1927–31. e-Active member of the National Agrarian Party; head of the Agrarian Sector of the National Revolutionary Party, 1934. f-Secretary of Agriculture, 1931; *Secretary of Agriculture and Livestock*, 1935–37. g-None. h-Auxiliary judge in Palomas San Luis Potosi, 1912. i-Brothers Magdaleno and Cleofas both fought with *Saturnino* under Emiliano Zapata and were killed during the Revolution; longtime friend of *Gildardo Magana* since they were companions fighting under Zapata; tried to persuade *Magana* to support him in his fight against President *Cardenas*; parents were peasants. j-Joined the Revolution in 1911; Commander of Military Operations in San Luis Potosi, 1920–27; fought against the De la Huerta rebellion in 1923; supported the government against Escobar, 1929; Commander-in-Chief of the Central Division, 1926; Divisionary General, 1928; Commander of Military Operations in San Luis Potosi, 1935. k-Imprisoned by Victoriano Huerta, 1912–14; supporter and later political enemy of Governor Aurelio Manrique, 1924–25; gave *Lazaro Cardenas* the decisive help of the agrarian sectors, 1934–35; resigned his cabinet post to protest governmental policies and become head of a rebellious military movement, 1938; killed in the fighting, 1939; member of the Inner Circle, 1934–37. l-D de S, 17 June 1935, 1; Gruening, 311; DP70, 417; Kirk, 40, 66–67; Dulles; Brandenburg, 80; Gonzalez Navarro, 150–51; Weyl, 234; Novo35; Daniels, 259–60; Q es Q, 117–18.

Celis Campos, Jesus
a-Aug. 26, 1895. b-Bamoa, Sinaloa, *West, Rural.* c-Primary studies in Alamos and in Navajoa, Sonora; no degree. *Senator* from the State of Sinaloa, 1952–58, first secretary of the First National Defense Committee, the Military Health Committee and the First Instructive Section of the Grand Jury, second secretary of the Military Justice Committee, member of the First Balloting Group and President of the War Materiels Committee. e-None. f-Military Attache, Special Mission to Peru, 1921; Military Attache, Guatemala, 1922–23; Director of the Military Prison of Santiago Tlaltelolco, 1925; Commander of Infantry, Federal District Police; Subdirector of the Federal District Police, 1932; Director of Traffic in the Federal District; Ambassador to the Dominican Republic and Haiti. g-None. j-Joined the Army, 1913; 2nd Lieutenant on the General Staff of Benjamin Hill, September 13, 1913; career officer; rank of Lt. Colonel 1921; rank of Lt. Colonel in Artillery awarded by the Peruvian government, 1921; fought against the De la Huerta rebellion as Subdirector of the Department of Cavalry, Secretary of War, 1923; commander of various cavalry companies, 1932–42; commander of various military zones. k-None. l-Ind. Biog., 41–42; DGF56, 7, 9–13.

Ceniceros (Andonequi), Jose Angel
(Deceased Apr. 24, 1979)
a-June 8, 1900. b-Durango, Durango, *West, Urban.* c-Primary studies in Mexico City, 1906–11; teaching certificate from the Normal School of Mexico, 1921; law degree from the Escuela Libre de Derecho, April 25, 1925; Doctor of Laws, National School of Law, UNAM, 1950; Professor at the National Teachers School, 1921–40; Professor at the National School of Law, UNAM, 1937–44; the Free Law School, 1928–34 and at the Higher Normal School, Mexico City, 1928–34. d-None. e-Director of the publication *El Nacional* of the PRI, 1936. f-Agent of the Ministerio Publico; public defender, Secretariat of National Defense; Adviser, Secretary of the Navy; Oficial Mayor of the Secretariat of Foreign Relations; Attorney General of Military Justice, 1931–32; Assistant Attorney General of Mexico, 1932–34; *Subsecretary of Foreign Relations*, 1935–36; *Ambassador to Cuba*, 1944–47; *Secretary of Public Education*, 1952–58; Ambassador to Haiti. g-None. h-Adviser to Nacional Financiera; author of numerous articles; Director of the Industrial Company of Atentique, Guadalajara, 1941; President of Phillips Mexicana; practicing lawyer, 1970–79. i-Attended law school with *Ernesto Enriquez Coyro*; married Amalia Hernandez. j-Fought in the Revolution; joined Constitutionalist forces, 1914, as a Normal School student with *J. Jesus Gonzalez Lugo* and *Roberto T. Bonilla Cortes*; Captain of the Infantry, 1915. k-None. l-DBM68, 139; WWM45, 24–25; HA, 5 Dec. 1952, 9; DGF56, 299; HA, 13 Jan. 1958; HA, 25 Feb. 1956, 61; D de Y, 2 Dec., 1972; Enc. Mex., 1977, II, 450–51.

Ceniceros, Severino

(Deceased June 15, 1937)
b-Durango, Durango, *West, Urban*. c-Early education unknown; no degree. d-Senator from the State of Durango, 1920–22; Senator from the State of Durango, 1932–34. e-None. f-*Interim Governor* of Durango, 1936. g-None. j-Revolutionary soldier; took part in taking Durango from the federal forces, 1911; joined Carranza, 1911; supported Madero, 1910–11; fought with Calixto Contreras in Cuencame; governor and military commander of Durango, Sept. 28, 1914 to Oct. 13, 1915; officer under Francisco Villa; reached rank of divisionary general. k-None. l-Q es Q, 119; NYT, 17 Dec. 1935, 1.

Cepeda Flores, Ramon

(Deceased 1973)
a-Apr. 8, 1907. b-Saltillo, Coahuila, *North, Urban*. c-Primary studies at the public school, Arteaga, Coahuila; preparatory at Ateneo Fuente, Saltillo; no degree. d-Member of the City Council, Torreon, 1946; Mayor of Torreon, 1949–51; *Governor of Coahuila*, 1951–57. e-President of PRI in Torreon, Coahuila, 1944–45. g-None. h-Rancher, 1937. i-Father, Rafael Cepeda de la Fuente, fought in the Revolution; farmer by profession; Constitutional Deputy, 1916–17, Governor of San Luis Potosi; Ramon is a cousin of *Ignacio Cepeda Davila*. j-None. k-None. l-HA, 3 Dec. 1956, 12; DGF56, 91; HA, 29 Nov., 1954; Lopez, 192.

Cerdan (Lara), Jorge

(Deceased 1959)
a-July 23, 1897. b-Jalapa, Veracruz, *Gulf, Urban*. c-Primary and secondary studies in Jalapa, Veracruz; preparatory in Veracruz; law degree from the University of Veracruz, specializing in finance, June 7, 1935. d-Local Deputy to the State Legislature of Veracruz, 1930–32; *Governor of Veracruz*, 1940–44. f-Director of the Treasury of the State of Veracruz, 1916; Treasurer General of Veracruz, 1936–39. g-None. h-Economist for the State of Veracruz, 1916; practicing lawyer, Mexico City, 1945–59. k-None. l-WWM45, 25; DP70, 424; Peral, 174; EBW46, 74; WB48, 1042; Lopez, 193.

Cerecedo Lopez, Felipe

a-Feb. 5, 1921. b-Chicontepec, Veracruz, *Gulf, Rural*. c-Primary studies at the Rafael Valenzuela Primary School, Chicontepec; secondary studies at the National Teachers School; teaching certificate, Normal School of Chiapas; primary school teacher. d-*Federal Deputy* from the State of Veracruz, Dist. 2, 1970–73, member of the Public Assistance Committee, the Agrarian Affairs Committee, the Second Ejido Committee, the Railroads Committee, and the Committee on Subsistence and Supplies; *Federal*

Deputy from the State of Veracruz, Dist. 2, 1976–79, member of the Ejido and Communal Section of the Agrarian Affairs Committee. e-Founder and Coordinator General of the PPS in Veracruz. f-None. g-Founder and Secretary General of the Alliance of Farmers Groups of Northern Veracruz. h-Director of a primary boarding school (22 years). i-Married Ernestina Diaz. j-None. k-None. l-C de D, 1970–72; *Directorio*, 1970–72; D de C, 1976–79, 12.

Cervantes Corona, Jose Guadalupe

a-1925. b-Teul, Zacatecas, *East Central, Urban*. c-Teaching certificate, Zacatecas; law degree, School of Law, University of Zacatecas; teacher for many years; Professor of Pedagogy and Logic, Manuel Avila Camacho Normal School, Zacatecas. d-*Federal Deputy* from the State of Zacatecas, Dist. 3, 1961–64; *Senator* from the State of Zacatecas, 1976–80; *Governor* of Zacatecas, 1980– . e-General Delegate of the CEN of PRI to many states; delegate of the CEN of PRI to Campeche, 1974. f-Secretary General of Government of the State of Zacatecas; administrative official of the Department of the Federal District, 1970–71. g-Secretary of Organization of the CEN of the CNC, 1979. i-Considered close to the political group of *Oscar Ramirez Mijares*. j-None. k-Pre-candidate for governor of Zacatecas, 1974; selection as gubernatorial candidate in 1980 seen as a stimulus to politicians following PRI party careers. l-*Excelsior*, 17 Dec. 1979, 18; HA, 17 Mar. 1980, 25; *Excelsior*, 25 Feb. 1980, 22A; *Excelsior*, 19 July 1979, 19A; C de D, 1961–64; C de S, 1976–82.

Cervantes del Rio, Hugo

a-July 4, 1927. b-Federal District, *Federal District, Urban*. c-Primary and secondary education in Mexico, D.F.; preparatory from the National Preparatory School, 1944–46; law degree from the National School of Law, UNAM, 1951; Professor of Constitutional Law at the National School of Law, UNAM, 1960–65; Professor of Mexican History, National Preparatory School, 1950–59. d-*Senator* from the Federal District, 1976. e-Interim Head of the Legal Department of PRI, 1952; active in youth movement in PRI with *Luis Echeverria*, 1946–52; President of PRI in the Federal District, 1975–76. f-Private Secretary to *Rodolfo Sanchez Taboada*, Secretary of the Navy, 1952–54; Director of Accounting of the Secretariat of the Navy, 1954–55; Customs Administrator for Sonoita, Sonora; *Director General of Federal Highways and Bridges and Adjacent Entrances and Exits*, 1959–65; *Governor of Baja California del Sur*, 1965–70; *Secretary of the Presidency*, 1970–75; *Director General of the Federal Electric Commission*, 1976–80. g-Student leader in secondary, the National Preparatory

School, and at UNAM. **h-**Treasurer of Mexican Railroads, 1956–59; Director of Customs, Sonoita, Sonora, 1955–56. **i-**Friend of *Luis Echeverria* and *Rodolfo Sanchez Taboada*; studied under *Jose Lopez Portillo* at UNAM; married Maria Luisa Vallejo. **j-**None. **k-**Winner of the Lanz Duret Prize as the Best Student of Constitutional Law, 1949. **l-**HA, 7 Dec. 1970, 26; WWMG, 13; *Hoy*, 19 Dec. 1970; D de Y, 5 Dec. 1952, 1; HA, 29 Jan. 1973, 22; *Excelsior*, 18 Feb. 1977; *Excelsior*, 12 Mar. 1976; Cadena Z., 19–36; *Excelsior*, 10 Oct. 1975, 20; Enc. Mex., 1977, II, 467.

Cervantes Delgado, Alejandro

b-Chilpancingo, Guerrero, *South, Urban*. **c-**Teaching certificate, National Teachers College; economics degree, National School of Economics, UNAM, 1944–48, degree, June 26, 1958; Professor of the Theory of Finance and Public Finance, National School of Economics, UNAM; primary school teacher. **d-***Federal Deputy* from the State of Guerrero, Dist. 3, 1973–76; *Senator* from Guerrero, 1976– , Secretary of the Gran Comision, 1976– . **e-***Director General of the IEPES of the CEN of PRI*, 1978– . **f-**Subdirector of Planning, National Railroads of Mexico; Controller General of National Railroads of Mexico; Director of Treasury and Economy, State of Guerrero; Director, Office of Fiscal Policy, State of Guerrero; Director of Technical and Economic Studies, Secretariat of Government Properties; Technical Subdirector, Division of Internal Taxes, Secretariat of the Treasury, 1971–72. **g-**None. **j-**None. **k-**None. **l-**HA, 26 Mar. 1979, V; DPE71, 37; C de S, 1976–82; D de C, 1973–76.

Cervantes (Hernandez), Anselmo

a-Apr. 13, 1908. **b-**Texcoco, Tlaxcala, *East Central, Rural*. **c-**Preparatory studies at the National Preparatory School; law degree from the National School of Law, UNAM; professor at the National Normal School, Mexico City. **d-**Local deputy to the State Legislature of Tlaxcala, 1947–59; *Alternate Senator* from the State of Tlaxcala, 1952–58; Local deputy to the State Legislature of Tlaxcala, 1955–56; *Federal Deputy* from the State of Tlaxcala, Dist. No. 1, 1961–64, member of the Gran Comision, the Third Labor Committee and alternate member of the Social Welfare Committee; *Governor of Tlaxcala*, 1963–69. **e-**General delegate of the CEN of PRI. **f-**Oficial Mayor of the State of Tlaxcala, 1951–53. **g-**None. **j-**None. **k-**None. **l-**WWMG, 13; DGF56, 8; C de D, 1961–63.

Cervera Pacheco, Victor

a-Apr. 23, 1936. **b-**Merida, Yucatan, *Gulf, Urban*. **c-**Primary and secondary studies at the Colegio Americano, Merida, Yucatan; preparatory studies at the University of Yucatan; no degree. **d-**Local Deputy to the State Legislature of Yucatan, 1960–62; Local Deputy to the State Legislature of Yucatan, Dist. No. 3, 1968–70; Mayor of Merida, Yucatan, 1971–73; *Federal Deputy* from the State of Yucatan, Dist. No. 1, 1973–76; *Senator* from the State of Yucatan, 1976– . **e-**Campaigner for *Luis Torres Mesias* and *Agustin Franco Aguilar* during their gubernatorial campaigns in Yucatan; youth delegate of PRI to CNOP. **f-**None. **g-**Secretary General of the Society of Preparatory Students, University of Yucatan, 1953; President of the Society of Preparatory Students, 1954; Secretary General of the University Student Federation of Yucatan; Delegate of the University Student Federation to the National Convention, Jalapa, Veracruz, 1956; Secretary General of the League of Agrarian Communities and Peasant Unions of Yucatan, 1967–70; Secretary of Health and Social Services, CEN of the CNC, 1968. **h-**Owns own ranch; administrator of a printing company; advisor to ejido credit associations. **i-**Bitter political opponent of *Carlos Loret de Mola*, governor of Yucatan, 1970–76. **j-**None. **k-**Political infighting with *Loret de Mola* precipitated a public battle between the state and local government in Merida. **l-**C de D, 1973–76; Q es Qy, 77–78; C de S, 1976–82; Loret de Mola.

Chapital, Constantino

(Deceased 1943)
a-Feb. 12, 1897. **b-**Oaxaca, Oaxaca, *South, Urban*. **c-**Early education unknown; no degree. **d-**Federal Deputy from the State of Oaxaca, Dist. 11, 1934–36; *Governor* of Oaxaca, 1936–40. **e-**None. **f-**Director of the Santiago Tlatelolco Military Prison. **g-**None. **h-**None. **j-**Career Army officer; Constitutionalist; fought Victoriano Huerta under General Fernando Davila; accompanied President Carranza on his flight to Veracruz, 1920; rank of Brigadier General; Chief of Mounted Police in the Federal District; Chief of Judicial Police in the Federal District; Chief of Staff of the 6th Military Zone; Military Attache to London, England. **k-**Smith says he was separated from the military under an indictment for the disappearance of jewels under his jurisdiction while director of the judicial police. **l-**PS; C de D, 1934–37.

Chavez (Amparan), Alfredo

(Deceased June 16, 1972)
a-July 14, 1891. **b-**Chihuahua, *North*. **c-**Primary education in Parral, Chihuahua; attended a private agricultural school in Ciudad Juarez, Chihuahua; no degree. **d-**Local Deputy to the State Legislature of Chihuahua; Interim governor of Chihuahua; *Senator* from the State of Chihuahua, 1946–52, member of the Gran Comision; member of the National Waters and Irrigation Committee, the Second Committee on

Mines, and the Foreign and Domestic Trade Committee; substitute member of the Department of the Federal District Committee; *Governor of Chihuahua*, 1940–44. **e**-None. **f**-Tax collector for Parral, Chihuahua; police inspector, Chihuahua. **g**-None. **h**-Began career as an agriculturist; after retirement from political activity, engaged in cattle ranching on a ranch in Villa Matamoros. **i**-Son, *Alfredo*, served as Federal Deputy from the State of Chihuahua, Dist. 5, 1958–60. **j**-Rank of Colonel in the Mexican Army. **k**-None. **l**-HA, 31 July 1947, 16; letter; EBW46, 68; *Excelsior*, 17 June 1972; DGF51, I, 6, 9–11, 13; DGF47, 20.

Chavez Carrillo, Rodolfo

a-May 11, 1923. **b**-Colima, Colima, *West, Urban*. **c**-Primary studies and secondary studies in Colima; government scholarship recipient at the National Polytechnic School, 1938; attended Prevocational School No. 3, Mexico, D.F., 1939; attended Vocational School No. 1, 1941; architectural engineering degree from the School of Engineering and Architecture, IPN, 1943–47, with an honorary mention; Professor of Mathematics, University of Colima. **d**-Mayor of Colima, 1952–54; *Governor of Colima*, 1955–61. **e**-None. **f**-Subdirector of Public Works, State of Colima, 1948–50; Director General of Public Works, State of Colima, 1950; Director of Puerto Mexico, Tijuana, Baja California del Norte, 1963; Representative of the Secretariat of National Patrimony, Baja California del Norte, 1964–72; President of the Federal Board of Material Improvements, Tijuana, Baja California del Norte, 1963–73. **g**-None. **h**-Intern, Resident Architect, Guanos y Fertilizantes, S.A., Mexico, D.F., 1947; planner and constructor of several building projects, 1961–62; President of the Mexican Society of Geography and Statistics, 1966–72. **j**-None. **k**-None. **l**-Letters; DGF56, 91.

Chavez Hernandez, Jose Servando

a-1936. **b**-San Lucas, Michoacan, *West Central, Rural*. **c**-Early education unknown; law degree from the National School of Law, UNAM, 1964. **d**-*Federal Deputy* from the State of Michoacan, Dist. 7, 1964–67, member of the Agrarian Section of the Legislative Studies Committee, the Petroleum Committee and the Technical Section of the Ejido Committee. **e**-None. **f**-Secretary General of Government of Quintana Roo; Secretary General of Government of the State of Michoacan, 1968–71, under Governor *Carlos Galvez Betancourt*; Interim Governor of Michoacan, 1971–74. **g**-Member of the CNC. **h**-Practicing lawyer. **i**-Parents were peasants; brother Ausencio Chavez was Secretary General of Govern-

ment in Michoacan under Governor *Carlos Torres Manzo*. **j**-None. **k**-None. **l**-HA, 4 Oct. 1971, 45; C de D, 1964–67; *Excelsior*, 26 Nov. 1978, 6.

Chavez Orozco, Luis

(Deceased 1966)

a-April 28, 1901. **b**-Irapuato, Guanajuato, *West Central, Urban*. **c**-Primary studies at the Instituto Sollano; teaching certificate from the Leon Institute, Guanajuato; professor at UNAM; professor for the Secretariat of Public Education. **d**-None. **e**-None. **f**-Chief of the Department of Publicity of the Secretariat of Foreign Relations, 1930–32; head of the Department of Administration, Secretariat of Public Education, 1933–35; head of the Department of Libraries of the Secretariat of Public Education, 1935–36; *Subsecretary of Public Education*, 1936–38; head of the Department of Indian Affairs, 1939–40; Ambassador to Honduras, 1941; First President of the Institute of Mexican and Russian Cultural Interchange, 1944; adviser to the Presidency of Mexico. **g**-The first Secretary General of the National Teachers Union of Mexico. **h**-Writer for the major daily newspaper, *Excelsior*; prolific historian, author of a 12-volume history of Mexico, and of works on economic history, diplomatic history, and education. **j**-None. **k**-Noted for his anti-clerical position in the *Cardenas* administration. **l**-WWM45, 27; DP70, 592; Peral, 207; WB48, 1079; Villasenor, II, 38; Casasol, V; Raby, 52; Lopez, 255–56; Enc. Mex., 1977, II, 284; Michaels, 125.

Chavez Padron de Velazquez, Martha

a-1925. **b**-Tampico, Tamaulipas, *North, Urban*. **c**-Early education unknown; studies in literature, School of Philosophy and Letters, UNAM; law degree, National School of Law, UNAM, 1948; Ph.D. in law, UNAM, 1954 (first Mexican woman to receive a Ph.D. in Law); professor specializing in rural sociology at UNAM, the National School of Agriculture and at the Secretariat of Agriculture and the Secretariat of Public Education. **d**-*Senator* from Tamaulipas, 1976– . **e**-Joined PRI as a student activist, 1946; worked for PRI, 1959; Director of Social Action of the CEN of PRI, 1961; member of the National Council of Women of PRI; member of the Advisory Council to the IEPES of PRI, 1972. **f**-Director General of Agrarian Laws, Department of Agrarian Affairs; adviser to the Department of Agrarian Affairs; *Subsecretary of the New Centers of Ejido Populations*, Secretariat of Agrarian Reform, 1970–76. **g**-Member of the CEN of the CNC, 1976. **h**-Author of several law texts. **i**-Student of *Agustin Yanez* at UNAM. **j**-None. **k**-First female lawyer from Tamaulipas; first female professor at the National School of Law, UNAM. **l**-HA, 19 June 1972, 66;

HA, 20 Sept. 1971, 29; DGF71, 129; HA, 21 Dec. 1970, 24; HA, 7 June 1970, 11–13; Enc. Mex., Annual, 1977, 495.

Chavez (Ramirez), Eduardo

a-May 16, 1898. b-Federal District, *Federal District, Urban*. c-Engineering degree from the National School of Engineering, UNAM, 1922; professor of drawing at night school, 1912; left preparatory school in Mexico, D.F., in 1914 to help the cause of Carranza. d-None. e-None. f-Subchief of the Department of the Organization of Irrigation Systems; President of the Engineering Commission of the Secretariat of National Patrimony, 1947; chief of internal projects for the Rio Bravo project; secretary and member of the Papaloapan Commission, 1947–50; Executive Secretary of the Tepalcatepec Commission, 1950–52; *Secretary of Hydraulic Resources*, 1952–58. g-None. h-Began work for the National Irrigation Commission, 1926; technician for hydraulic and irrigation construction materials; engineer on various construction projects for the Department of Public Works, 1933; worked on hundreds of projects from 1933–52 in the field of irrigation and hydroelectric projects. i-Married Margarita Barragan. j-None. k-Resigned from the Secretaryship of Hydraulic Resources in 1958 because of disagreements with President *Ruiz Cortines* on the regional commission policies of the Secretariat of Hydraulic Resources. l-Greenberg, 25; *El Universal*, 2 Dec. 1958; DBM68, 167–68; DGF47, 256; HA, 5 Dec. 1952, 9; DGF56, 411; DGF50, II, 451; *Excelsior*, 2 Aug. 1972, 1, 16; NYT, 27 July, 1954, 10; Enc. Mex., Vol. III, 281–82.

Chavez (Sanchez), Ignacio

(Deceased July 12, 1979)
a-Jan. 31, 1897. b-Zirandaro, Guerrero, *South, Rural*. c-Secondary studies in Morelia, Michoacan, at the Colegio de San Nicolas de Hidalgo; two years of professional studies in medicine at Morelia, at the Colegio de San Nicolas de Hidalgo, 1914–16; medical degree from the National School of Medicine, UNAM, May 4, 1920; Ph.D. in Biological Sciences from UNAM, 1934; instructor at the Colegio de San Nicolas, 1914–15; Professor of Cardiology at the National School of Medicine, UNAM, 1946–66, also at the Graduate School; Professor of Medicine, 1923–50; Rector of the University of Michoacan, 1920–22; postgraduate work in Paris, 1926–27; Director of the National School of Medicine, UNAM, 1933–34; President of the Union of Latin American Universities; Professor at UNAM, 1966–70. d-None. e-Supporter of Jose Vasconcelos in 1929. f-Head of the Medical Clinic, UNAM, 1922–23; Director of the General Hospital of Mexico, D.F., 1936–39;

founder and Director of the National Institute of Cardiology, 1944–61; *Rector of UNAM*, 1961–66; Director of the National Institute of Cardiology, 1975–79. g-None. h-Author of numerous articles on medical subjects; Honorary Director of the National Institute of Cardiology, 1970–75. i-Brother of *Rodolfo Chavez Sanchez*, Justice of the Supreme Court, 1936–40; 1955–59; heart specialist to President Calles; daughter married to poet Jaime Garcia Terres; father a small farmer; co-student with *Manuel Martinez Baez, Gabino Fraga*, and *Eduardo Villasenor* at the Colegio de San Nicolas. j-None. k-Resigned the Rectorship of UNAM after a major student strike. l-DBM70, 155–56; DBM68, 168–69; WWM45, 26; Hayner, 269; IWW68, 220–21; Peral, 205–06, WWW70–71, 174; DGF51, 342; *Justicia*, May, 1971; letter.

Chavez (Sanchez), Rodolfo

a-May 8, 1895. b-Zirandaro, Guerrero, *South, Rural*. c-Primary studies in Morelia, Michoacan, 1904–07; preparatory studies in the Colegio de San Nicolas, Morelia; law degree from the Colegio de San Nicolas, Morelia, December 4, 1917. d-None. e-None. f-Syndic of the City Council of Morelia, 1918; Secretary to the District Court of Tuxpan, Veracruz, 1924–25; Consulting lawyer to the State of Veracruz, 1924–27; Attorney General of the State of Veracruz, 1928–36, under Governors Adalberto Tejada and *Gonzalo Vazquez Vela; Justice of the Supreme Court*, 1936–40; 1955–59. g-Student leader in support of Madero. h-Author of the Legal Code of the State of Veracruz. i-Brother of *Ignacio Chavez*, Rector of UNAM, 1961–66; parents were middle-class land owners; supporter of *Francisco Mugica*, 1920s. j-Fought in the Revolution; served under General Obregon; reached rank of brigadier general. k-None. l-Peral, 207; letters; DGF56, 567.

Chavez Vazquez, Alfredo

a-June 4, 1918. b-Hidalgo del Parral, Chihuahua, *North, Urban*. c-Primary studies at Public School No. 99, Parral; studies in business administration, Sanchez Celis Academy. d-Local deputy to the State Legislature of Chihuahua, 1944–46; *Federal Deputy from the State of Chihuahua*, Dist. 5, 1958–61, member of the Gran Comision, the Indigenous Affairs Committee, the Livestock Committee, and the Inspection Committee for the General Accounting Office. e-None. f-None. g-None. h-Founder and owner of Bodegas de Delicias, S.A.; owner of Construcciones y Trabajos Agriculturales, S.A. i-Son of *Alfredo Chavez*, Governor of Chihuahua, 1940–44. j-None. k-None. l-Func., 168; C de D, 1958–60, 41, 76.

Chavez Velazquez, Bernardo

a-Dec. 1, 1900. b-Puebla, Puebla, *East Central, Urban*. c-Preparatory studies in Puebla; professional studies at the University Palafoxiana, University of Puebla, and the Military Medical College; medical degree. d-Federal Deputy from the State of Puebla, 1930–32, 1932–34; *Federal Deputy* from the State of Puebla, Dist. 3, 1940–43, member of the Foreign Relations Committee and the Committee on Social Assistance for Infants; *Federal Deputy* from the State of Puebla, Dist. 6, 1946–49, member of the Child Welfare and Social Security Committee and the Military Health Committee. f-Chief of Health Inspections, Department of Health of the Federal District; Inspector General of the Attorney General of Mexico; Consul of Mexico in various European countries and in the United States; head of the Department of Justice and Government, State of Puebla; Director of the Federal Transit Department, 1946. g-None. h-Practicing surgeon. j-Lieutenant in the Army, 1914; Director of the Sanitation Sections, 2nd Division. k-None. l-EBW46, 108; C de D, 1942; WB48, 1078; DGF47, 11; C de D, 1946–48.

Chazaro Lara, Ricardo

a-Jan. 26, 1920. b-Veracruz, Veracruz, *Gulf, Urban*. c-Primary studies in the Justo Sierra School, Veracruz; secondary and preparatory studies at the Veracruz Institute, Veracruz; degree in mechanical engineering from the National Naval College, Veracruz, graduated as a Corvette Lieutenant, 1943; special course from the Subchaser Training Center, Miami, Florida, 1943; special course in electronics, Treasure Island, San Francisco, 1952. d-None. e-None. f-Assistant to President *Adolfo Ruiz Cortines*, 1953–58; *Subsecretary of the Navy*, 1970–76; *Secretary of the Navy*, 1976– . g-None. h-None. i-Married to Luz del Alva Iza; long-time friend of *Adolfo Ruiz Cortines*. j-Rank of Coastguardman, September 1, 1942; Corvette Lieutenant, May 16, 1943; Frigate Lieutenant, November 20, 1946; Naval Lieutenant, November 20, 1949; Corvette Captain, November 20, 1952; Frigate Captain, November 20, 1956; Naval Captain, November 20, 1961; Rear Admiral, November 20, 1964; Vice Admiral, April 21, 1971; Admiral, June 1, 1976; joined the Coastguard ship "Guanajuato", 1942; Chief of Machinery, Coastguard ship "1", 1943–44; Chief of Machinery, Coastguard ship "20", 1944–45; Chief of Fatigue Duty, "Queretaro", 1945–47; Chief of Machinery, Coastguard ship "2"; Chief of Machinery, ship "Baranda", 1951–52; Chief of Workshops for Naval Classes in Mazatlan, 1952; Subdirector of the Drydocks, Salina Cruz, Oaxaca, 1952–53; Inspector General of Machinery, Pacific, 1964–66; Technical Subdirector of the Navy, Pemex, 1966–70. k-Pre-candidate for Governor of Veracruz, 1973. l-DPE61, 39; D del S, 2 Dec. 1970; HA, 6 Dec.

1976, 22; HA, 4 Apr. 1977, 15; *Excelsior*, 1 Dec. 1976; *El Dia*, 1 Dec. 1976; *Hoy*, 19 Dec. 1970, 60; HA, 14 Dec. 1970, 20.

Chico Goerne, Luis

(Deceased Jan. 16, 1960)
a-Feb. 16, 1892. b-Guanajuato, Guanajuato, *West Central, Urban*. c-Primary and secondary education in Guanajuato; law degree from the University of Guanajuato, 1918; advanced studies in sociology in Paris, 1923; Professor of Law and Sociology at the Colegio de Guanajuato; Professor of Law at the Escuela Libre de Derecho; Professor of Sociology at the National School of Law, UNAM; Director of the National School of Law, UNAM, 1929–33. d-None. e-None. f-Judge of the Superior Military Court, 1920; *Rector of UNAM*, 1935–38; adviser to the Mexican legation in Paris, 1938–40; adviser to the Presidency of Mexico, 1941–46; *Justice of the Supreme Court*, 1947–52, 1952–58, and 1958–60. g-None. h-Assisted with the writing of the 1929 and 1931 penal codes of Mexico; author of several books on law and sociology. i-From a wealthy family background; son is an architect; professor of many prominent public men, including *Antonio Armendariz; Manuel Hinojosa Ortiz* practiced law with him in 1935–36. j-None. k-None. l-HA, 8 Oct. 1943; 37–38; WWM45, 27; DGF56, 567–68; DP70 598–99; Enc. Mex., Vol. 3, 24; Peral, 208; WB48, 1098.

Christlieb Ibarrola, Adolfo

(Deceased Dec. 6, 1969)
a-Mar. 12, 1919. b-Federal District, *Federal District, Urban*. c-Primary studies at Colegio Frances Puente de Alvarado and Jalisco; secondary studies at the Colegio Frances Morelos; law degree from the National School of Law, UNAM, Aug. 27, 1941; studied at the School of Philosophy and Letters, UNAM, 1936–40; adviser to the School of Philosophy and Letters, 1937–39; Professor of Constitutional Law, National School of Law, UNAM, 1954–57; Professor of Mexican History, Colegio Frances Morelos. d-*Federal Deputy* from the Federal District, Dist. 23, 1964–67, member of the Foreign Trade Committee, the Legislative Studies Committee (Seventh Section of Credit and Trade), the Second Government Committee, and the Committee on Mines; leader of the National Action Party delegation to Congress, 1964. e-*President of the CEN of PAN*, 1962–68; PAN representative to the Federal Electoral Commission; joined PAN in 1942. f-None. g-None. h-Practicing lawyer, 1941–69; Secretary of the Mexican Bar Association. i-Lawyer in the firm of *Roberto Cossio*, a student companion and later Secretary General of the CEN of PAN, 1939–51, j-None. k-None. l-DP70, 617; C de D, 1966; Enc. Mex., III, 97; WWMG, 13; HA, 7 Dec. 1964, 21; letter.

Chumacero Sanchez, Blas

a-Jan. 18, 1908. **b-**Puebla, Puebla, *East Central, Urban.* **c-**Primary and secondary studies in Puebla; studied labor law at night school in Puebla. **d-***Federal Deputy* from the State of Puebla, Dist. 2, 1940–43, member of the Administration Committee (2nd year), the First Balloting Committee, and the Gran Comision, 1942; *Federal Deputy* from the State of Puebla, Dist. 1, 1946–49, member of the Textile Industry Committee, the Committee on Credit, Money, and Credit Institutions, the First Credentials Committee, and the Health Committee; *Federal Deputy* from the State of Puebla, Dist. 1, 1952–55, Vice President of the Chamber, September, 1952; Secretary of the Chamber, September, 1954, member of the Library Committee (2nd year), the Editorial Committee (1st year), and the Budget Committee; *Federal Deputy* from the State of Puebla, Dist. 1, 1958–61, member of the Second Government Committee, the Inspection Committee of the General Accounting Office (2nd year), the First Budget Committee, the Rules Committee, the Second Credentials Committee and the Third Labor Committee; *Federal Deputy* from the State of Puebla, Dist. 1, 1967–70, member of the Legislative Studies Committee, Fifth Section on Labor and Ninth Section on General Affairs; the First Treasury Committee, the Steel Industry Committee, the Industries Committee, and the First Labor Committee; *Senator* from the State of Puebla, 1976– , president of the Senate, November, 1976. **e-***Secretary of Labor Action, CEN of PRI*, 1946; *Secretary of Labor Action, CEN of PRI*, 1964–80. **f-**None. **g-**Secretary General of the Union of the Industrial Plant of San Alfonso; Secretary General of the CTM for the State of Puebla; Secretary of Labor and Conflicts, National Council of the Federation of Laborers and Farmers, State of Mexico. **h-**Representative for labor on the Board of Conciliation and Arbitration, Puebla. **i-**Father was a laborer; Chumacero Sanchez worked for many years in textile plants in Puebla. **j-**None. **k-**As of 1979, had served as a Federal Deputy more times since 1940 than any other Mexican. **l-**C de D, 1946–48, 70; C de D, 1967–69, 66, 67, 73, 74; C de D, 1952–54; Func, 318; C de D, 1940–42, 9, 53; C de D, 1958–60, 76; *Excelsior*, 20 Jan. 1976, 5A.

Cisneros Molina, Joaquin (Francisco)

a-Aug. 1, 1907. **b-**Tlaxcala, Tlaxcala, *East Central, Urban.* **c-**Preparatory studies at the National Preparatory School, Mexico, D.F.; teaching certificate in primary education from the National Teachers School, 1928; law degree from the National School of Law, UNAM, Nov. 3, 1936; primary, secondary, and preparatory education teacher; Director of Preparatory Education for the State of Tlaxcala. **d-***Federal Deputy* from the State of Tlaxcala, Dist. 1, 1949–52, member of the Third Ejido Committee;

member of the Gran Comision; *Governor of Tlaxcala*, 1957–63. **f-**Director of Libraries for the Secretariat of the Treasury, 1935–36; Secretary of the Federal Tax Court, 1937–38; Director of the Department of Legal Consultants, Secretariat of the Treasury, 1942; Secretary General of the Department of Indigenous Affairs, 1941–42; Secretary General of Government of the State of Tlaxcala, 1952–57; *Private Secretary to President Gustavo Diaz Ordaz*, 1964–70; Delegate of the Secretariat of Public Education to the State of Tlaxcala, 1978– . **g-**None. **h-**None. **i-**Friend of *Gustavo Diaz Ordaz* since they served together in the Chamber of Deputies; son, Joaquin Cisneros Fernandez, was a pre-candidate for Federal Deputy, 1975. **j-**None. **k-**None. **l-**DBM68, 144; Hayner, 211; C de D, 1949–51; *Excelsior*, 8 Dec. 1975, 22; Enc. Mex., II, 488; *Excelsior*, 19 July, 1978, 9.

Coello (Ochoa), David

(Deceased 1959)
a-Aug. 20, 1885. **b-**Alvardo, Veracruz, *Gulf, Rural.* **c-**Degree from the Naval College of Veracruz, 1900. **d-**None. **e-**Co-founder of PARM, 1954. **f-***Oficial Mayor of the Secretariat of the Navy*, 1948–49; *Secretary of the Navy*, 1948–49; Inspector of Fishing for Tuxpan, Nayarit, 1952–58. **g-**None. **h-**Considered an expert on naval warfare. **j-**Joined the Navy in 1909; member of the Merchant Marine, 1917–27; rejoined the Navy, 1927; career naval officer; rescued a North American ship off the coast of Mexico, 1924; commander of various naval ships; Commander of the 4th Naval Zone, 1939–40; rank of Commodore, 1940; Subdirector of the Navy, 1940; Secretary General of the Merchant Fleet, 1940–41; Director of the Fleet, 1941–42; Commander of the 1st Naval Zone, 1942–43; Acting Commander of the 4th Naval Zone, 1944–45; Commandant, Islas Margaritas Naval Base, 1945–46; rank of Vice Admiral, 1949. **k-**None. **l-**DGF47, 233; DP70, 459; DGF56, 384; D de Y, 5 Dec. 1940, 1; HA, 15 Oct. 1948, 3; *Excelsior*, 20 Oct. 1949; PS, 1258.

Colin Sanchez, Mario

a-June 22, 1922. **b-**Atlacomulco, Mexico, *West Central, Rural.* **c-**Primary studies at the public school, Atlacomulco; secondary studies at a public school, Toluca, Mexico; preparatory studies at the National Preparatory School, 1940–41; law degree, National School of Law, UNAM, 1942–47, with a thesis on "The Municipality in Mexico;" Rector of the Scientific and Literary Institute of Mexico, 1951–52. **d-**Local Deputy to the State Legislature of Mexico, 1947–50; *Federal Deputy* from the State of Mexico, Dist. 4, 1955–58, alternate member of the Second Government Committee, and the Rules Committee; *Alternate Senator* from Mexico, 1958–64; *Federal Deputy* from the State of Mexico, Dist.

5, 1964–67, member of the Tariff Committee, and the First Ejido Committee; *Federal Deputy* from the State of Mexico, Dist. 8, 1970–73, member of the Industries Committee, the Gran Comision, the Cultural Affairs Committee, and the Editorial Committee (1st year). **e-**President of the Regional Committee of PRI, San Luis Potosi; delegate of PRI to various states. **f-**Private Secretary to the Governor of Mexico, 1945–47, *Alfredo del Mazo*; Judge of the First Instance; head of the Public Registry, Tlalnepantla. **h-**Created the multi-volume *Encyclopedia of the State of Mexico*; winner of the 1942 oratory contest at the National Law School. **i-**Brother of author and lawyer Guillermo Colin Sanchez, Justice of the Superior Tribunal of Justice of the Federal District; companion of *Luis Echeverria* at UNAM. **j-**None. **k-**None. **l-**DGF56, 25, 33, 36, 398; C de S, 1961–64, 14; C de D, 1955–57, 54; *Directorio*, 1970–72; C de D, 1970–72, 107; letters; Enc. Mex., 1977, III, 22–23; C de D, 1964–67, 77, 82.

Colomo y Corral, Jose

(Deceased 1969)

a-Oct. 6, 1894. **b-**Meoqui, Chihuahua, *North, Rural*. **c-**Secondary studies at the Scientific and Literary Institute of Chihuahua, 1907–12; engineering degree in petroleum engineering from the National School of Engineering, UNAM, 1920; Professor of Engineering at the National School of Engineering, UNAM, 1931–45. **d-**None. **e-**None. **f-**Subdirector of the Department of Petroleum, Secretariat of Industry and Commerce, 1927–37; Assistant Director of Mines and Petroleum, Secretariat of Industry and Commerce, 1939–40; Director, Department of Coordination and Technical Studies, Petroleos Mexicanos, 1941–45; *Subdirector of Production of PEMEX*, 1950–64; *Subdirector of Primary Production of PEMEX*, 1965–69. **g-**None. **h-**None. **j-**None. **k-**None. **l-**Letter, WWM45, 28; DGF50, II, 203, 279, 280; DGF51, II, 293, 383–84.

Conchello Davila, Jose Angel

a-Sept. 1, 1923. **b-**Monterrey, Nuevo Leon, *North, Urban*. **c-**Law degree, National School of Law, UNAM; studied industrial development in Canada on a United Nations scholarship; Professor of Economics, School of Banking and Business Administration, UNAM; Professor of Journalism. **d-**Candidate for Federal Deputy, 1955; *Federal Deputy* from the Federal District, Dist. 19, 1967–70, member of the Tariff Committee, the International Trade Committee, the Legislative Studies Committee, Seventh Section on Commerce and Credit, the Cinematographic Development Committee, the Television Industry Committee, and the Desert Zones Committee; *Federal Deputy* (PAN party deputy), 1973–76; head of the PAN delegation, 1974; member of the Tenth Interparliamentary Reunion,

1970. **e-**Joined PAN, 1955, member of the National Executive Committee of PAN, 1969; *President of the CEN of PAN*, 1972–75. **f-**Administrative Director, National Council of Productivity. **g-**Director, Economic Studies Department, CONCAMIN; represented Mexican employers at the Administrative Council of the International Labor Organization, Geneva, 1953. **h-**Director of a private public relations firm, 1974; Director of Public Relations, Cerveceria Moctezuma; writer for *La Nacion*, official publication of PAN; fluent in French, English, and Italian. **i-**Disciple of Federal Deputy *Antonio Rodriguez* when he joined PAN; *Jorge Garabito* and *Efrain Gonzalez Morfin* supported him for the presidency of PAN. **j-**None. **k-**Accused by dissident members of PAN of attempting to split the Party, 1978; lost leadership of PAN delegation to Congress when he defied new party leadership; PAN candidate for Governor of Nuevo Leon, 1979. **l-**Letter; *Excelsior*, 28 Feb. 1973, 19; *Excelsior*, 30 Mar. 1973, 22; HA, 18 Jan. 1973, 16; HA, 21 Feb. 1972, 13; MGF69, 91; C de D, 1967–69, 61, 70, 72, 75; *Proceso*, 17 Apr. 1978, 10–16; HA, 9 Apr. 1979, VI.

Contreras Camacho, Maximo

a-Sept. 7, 1913. **b-**Pichucalco, Chiapas, *South, Urban*. **c-**Primary studies at the public school, Pichucalco; secondary and preparatory studies at Secondary School No. 4, preparatory at the National Preparatory School, Mexico, D.F.; law degree, National School of Law, UNAM. **d-***Alternate Federal Deputy* from the State of Chiapas, Dist. 1, 1958–61; *Federal Deputy* from the State of Chiapas, Dist. 4, 1961–64, member of the Budget and Accounts Committee and the Second Labor Committee; *Federal Deputy* from the State of Chiapas, Dist. 3, 1970–73, member of the Second Constitutional Affairs Committee, the Foreign Trade and Tariff Committee, the Fiscal Section of the Legislative Studies Committee, and the Gran Comision. **e-**Delegate of CNOP; delegate of PRI in various states. **f-**Administrator of Customs, Nuevo Laredo; conciliator, Secretariat of Labor; Director of Legal Affairs, Secretariat of Health; Oficial Mayor of Government of the State of Guerrero; District Judge, Guerrero; judge in the State of Chiapas. **g-**None. **h-**Rector of the Institute of Arts and Sciences, Chiapas. **i-**Brother *Gregorio* was a Justice of the Superior Tribunal of Justice of the Federal District; son Maximo was head of the Legal Department of the Metro, 1974; married Amparo Barrera. **j-**None. **k-**None. **l-***Directorio*, 70–72; C de D, 1961–63, 75; C de D, 1970–72, 107; C de D, 1958–60.

Coquet Laguna, Benito

a-Aug. 26, 1913. **b-**Jalapa, Veracruz, *Gulf, Urban*. **c-**Primary and secondary studies in Jalapa; law degree from the University of Veracruz, Jalapa, 1935, with a thesis on labor legislation. **d-***Federal Deputy* from the State of Veracruz, Dist. 11, 1943–46, president of the Chamber, September, 1945, 1946. **e-**Orator for the presidential campaign of *Avila Camacho*, 1940; participant in Jose Vasconcelos' campaign for president, 1929. **f-**Agent of the Ministerio Publico in Coatepec, Veracruz; Chief of Legal Affairs, Agricultural Credit Bank, Veracruz, 1935–39; Public defender, Superior Tribunal of Justice of the State of Veracruz, 1935–39; Director of the National Institute of Bellas Artes, 1941–43; *Ambassador to Cuba*, 1947–52; *Oficial Mayor of the Secretariat of Government*, 1946–47; *Subsecretary of the Presidency*, 1952–56; *Secretary of the Presidency*, 1956–58; *Director General of the Mexican Institute of Social Security*, 1958–64. **g-**Delegate from Veracruz to the National Student Congress in San Luis Potosi, 1933; Vice-president and President, National Student Federation, 1934. **h-**None. **j-**None. **k-**None. **l-***El Universal*, 2 Dec. 1958; HA, 8 Dec. 1958, 32; DGF56, 53; D del S, 3 Dec. 1952, 1; DGF51, I, 104; Gomez Maganda, 106; *Quien Sera*, 145; Func, 103; Enc. Mex., 1977, III, 138–39.

Cordera (Ruiz), Miguel Angel

a-Oct. 10, 1912. **b-**Jalapa, Veracruz, *Gulf, Urban*. **c-**Early education unknown; law degree from the School of Law, University of Veracruz, Jalapa, 1935. **d-**None. **e-**None. **f-**Consulting lawyer to the State Government of Veracruz, 1940; President of the National Coffee Commission, 1954–59, (forerunner of the Mexican Institute of Coffee); Director General of the Mexican Institute of Coffee, 1959–66; Executive Coordinator of CONASUPO, 1976– . **g-**None. **h-**Industrial farmer in coffee and tropical agricultural crops. **i-**Father a lawyer; practiced law with him as a student. **j-**None. **k-**None. **l-**DBM68, 149.

Corella Gil Samaniego, Norberto

a-July 24, 1928. **b-**Douglas, Arizona, *Foreign, Urban*. **c-**Primary studies in Douglas, Arizona; secondary studies in Hermosillo, Sonora, at the University of Sonora; degree in business administration from the Institute of Technology and Higher Education of Monterrey, Monterrey, Nuevo Leon, May, 1950. **d-**None. **e-**President of the Executive Committee of the Regional Council of the National Action Party, 1963–65; Head of the National Action Party for the State of Baja California del Norte, 1968–70. **f-**None. **g-**Secretary of the Council of the National Chamber of Commerce of Mexicali, 1954–55; President of the National Chamber of Commerce of Mexicali, 1955–56; Founding President of the State Confederation of Chambers of Commerce of Baja California del Norte, 1956–59; Founding President of the Employer's Center of Baja California del Norte, 1958–63. **h-**Director of Sales, Cia. Maderera y Ganadera del Noroeste, Ciudad Juarez, Chihuahua, 1950; Subdirector of Proveedores de la Construccion, S.A., 1952–54; Director of Concretos de Mexicali, 1954; Director of Proveedores de la Construccion, S.A., 1954–70. **j-**None. **k-**National Action Party candidate for Governor of Baja California del Norte; pre-candidate for the PAN candidacy for president, 1975. **l-**DBM68, 150; Aguirre, 497.

Corella Molina, Emiliano

a-May 18, 1891. **b-**Banamichi, Sonora, *North, Rural*. **c-**Self-educated; no degree. **d-**Mayor of Banamichi, Sonora, 1912–13, 1916–19; Alternate Local Deputy to the State Legislature of Sonora, 1919–21; Local Deputy to the State Legislature of Sonora, 1924–26; Federal Deputy from the State of Sonora, 1930–32; Senator from the State of Sonora, 1932–36; *Federal Deputy* from the State of Sonora, Dist. No. 2, 1955–58, president of the Agricultural Development and Livestock Committee. **e-**None. **f-**Interim Governor of Sonora, 1934–35. **g-**President of the Livestock Union of Sonora, 1947; president of the Lions Club of Banamichi. **h-**Businessman; adviser to the Livestock and Agricultural Bank of Sonora, 1956. **j-**None. **k-**None. **l-**Ind. Biog., 44–45; DGF56, 28, 33; C de D, 1955–58.

Coria (Cano), Alberto

(Deceased, 1960)

a-July 4, 1892. **b-**Paracho, Michoacan, *West Central, Rural*. **c-**Primary studies in Paracho; secondary at the Colegio de San Nicolas, Morelia; abandoned studies in 1913 to fight against the forces of Victoriano Huerta; law degree, University of Michoacan, 1929; normal professor, Colegio de San Nicolas, 1916; Rector of the University of Michoacan, 1929. **d-**Councilman of the City Council of Morelia, 1916–17, 1924; Local Deputy, State of Michoacan, 1920–24; Federal Deputy from the State of Michoacan, 1932–34. **e-**None. **f-**Agent of the Ministerio Publico, 1928; Attorney General of the State of Michoacan, 1931–32; Justice of the Superior Tribunal of Justice of the Federal District and Federal Territories, 1935–40; Justice of the Federal Tax Court, 1951–58; Justice of the Federal Circuit Court, Mexico City, 1959–60. **g-**Co-founder of the World House of Labor; First Secretary General of Labor, Michoacan, under Governor *Lazaro Cardenas*. **i-**Close friend of *Alberto Bremauntz* during the 1920s. **j-**Captain in the Constitutionalist Forces in Michoacan, 1913–15. **k-**Co-author of the socialist revision of Article 3 of the 1917 Constitution with *Alberto Bremauntz*. **l-**DGF56, 551; DP70, 521; Enc. Mex., 1977, III, 152; DGF51, I, 549.

Corona Bandin, Salvador

a-1912. **b-**Guadalajara, Jalisco, *West, Urban*. **c-**Primary, secondary and preparatory studies in

Guadalajara; language specialist; professor of English and French in the Guadalajara schools. **d**-Local Deputy to the State Legislature of Jalisco; *Federal Deputy* from the State of Jalisco, Dist. 9, 1961–64, member of the Gran Comision; *Senator* from the State of Jalisco, 1964–70. **e**-General Delegate of the CEN of PRI to Veracruz, 1964; President of PRI in Jalisco. **f**-Oficial Mayor of the State Legislature of Jalisco; Director of the Complaints Department, Department of Agrarian Affairs, 1945–46; Private Secretary to *Silvano Barba Gonzalez*, Head of the Department of Agrarian Affairs, 1944–45. **g**-None. **i**-Member of *Barba Gonzalez*'s political group. **j**-None. **k**-None. **l**-C de S, 1964–70; MGF69; C de D, 1964–70.

Corona del Rosal, Alfonso

a-1906. **b**-Ixmiquilpan, Hidalgo, *East Central, Rural*. **c**-Early education unknown; law degree with honorable mention, National School of Law, UNAM, September 29, 1937; Bachelor of Science in Biology from the National Military College and commissioned a 2nd Lt. in the Cavalry, 1921; Professor of Labor Law at the National School of Law, UNAM; Professor of Military Morals at the National Military College. **d**-*Federal Deputy* from the State of Hidalgo, Dist. 5, 1940–43, member of the Committee on Libraries; *Federal Senator* from Hidalgo, 1946–52, member of the Committee on Legislative Studies, the Department of the Federal District Committee, the Special Forestry Committee, the First Justice Committee, the Second Balloting Committee, the First National Defense Committee, and the Military Justice Committee; substitute member of the First Committee on Constitutional Affairs; *Governor of Hidalgo*, 1957–58. **e**-Member of the Youth Section of the Mexican Revolutionary Party, 1938; Subsecretary of Military Action for the Mexican Revolutionary Party, 1940; President of the Regional Committee of the Federal District during the campaign of *Adolfo Ruiz Cortines*, 1951–52; *President of the CEN of PRI*, 1958–64. **f**-Private secretary to *Javier Rojo Gomez*, head of the Federal District, 1943–46; Director General of the National Army-Navy Bank; Director of Labor and Welfare for the Federal District; *Secretary of Government Properties*, 1964–66; *Head of the Department of the Federal District*, 1966–70. **g**-Student leader. **h**-None. **i**-Friend of *Javier Rojo Gomez*; father a school teacher; son *German* was a Senator from Hidalgo, 1970–76; married Carmen Alvarez. **j**-Career army officer; promoted to Lt. Colonel by *Manuel Avila Camacho* just before he left the presidency, 1946; participated in the campaigns of 1923, 1927, and 1929; Director of Military Industries, 1953–54; rank of Divisionary General. **k**-None. **l**-MacAlister, 223; DGF47, 20; HA, 7 Dec. 1964, 19; D del S, 1 Dec. 1940, 1; DBM68, 151; D del S, 3 Dec. 1946, 1;

Scott, 31, 306; DGF51, I, 6, 11–14; Enc. Mex., 1977, III, 155.

Corona del Rosal, German

a-Apr. 14, 1932. **b**-Ixmiquilpan, Hidalgo, *East Central, Rural*. **c**-Educated at the National Military College; graduated as a 2nd lieutenant, National Military College. **d**-*Senator* from the State of Hidalgo, 1970–76, Secretary of the Permanent Committee, December, 1973, President of the Indigenous Affairs Committee and First Secretary of the First National Defense Committee. **e**-None. **f**-Executive Secretary of the Indigenous Property of the Quezquital Valley; Delegate of the Department of the Federal District, 1976–77. **g**-None. **i**-Son of General *Alfonso Corona del Rosal*, president of the CEN of PRI, 1958–64. **j**-Career Army officer, reached rank of captain. **k**-Precandidate for governor of Hidalgo, 1973 and 1978. **l**-C de S, 1970–76, 74; PS, 1222; *Excelsior,* 28 June 1974, 4; HA, 7 Jan. 1974, 12.

Corona Mendioroz, Arturo

a-Dec. 18, 1915. **b**-Federal District, *Federal District, Urban*. **c**-School of Military Studies; graduated from the National Military College as a 2nd Lt. of Cavalry, Jan., 1931; graduated from the Superior War College as a Captain, 1942; attended the United States Command School; Professor of Cavalry Tactics at the National Military College; Professor at the United States Staff and Command School (Army), 1949; Professor of Spanish at West Point, 1950. **d**-None. **e**-None. **f**-*Oficial Mayor of the Secretariat of National Defense*, 1970–76. **g**-None. **h**-None. **j**-Career army officer; Commander of the 13th Cavalry Regiment, chief of Sections 2 and 4 of the General Staff of the Secretariat of National Defense, 1951; Director of the Superior War College, 1966–70. **k**-None. **l**-HA, 14 Dec. 1970, 20; DBM68, 157.

Coronado Organista, Saturnino

a-Feb. 19, 1892. **b**-Guadalajara, Jalisco, *West, Urban*. **c**-Primary and secondary studies in Guadalajara; preparatory studies in Guadalajara; law degree from the School of Law, University of Guadalajara; professor of civil and administrative law, School of Law, University of Guadalajara; Rector, University of Guadalajara. **d**-Vice-mayor of Guadalajara, Jalisco, 1947–48; *Federal Deputy* from the State of Guadalajara, Dist. 1, 1949–52, member of the Gran Comision, the Legislative Studies Committee, the Tax Committee and the Insurance Committee; *Senator* from the State of Jalisco, 1952–58, member of the Gran Comision, the Foreign and Domestic Trade Committee, the Second Government Committee, the First Constitutional Affairs Committee and the Legislative Studies Committee. **e**-President of the State Electoral Committee, Jalisco, 1946; campaigned for *Miguel Aleman*, 1946. **f**-Attorney for the State Planning Commission, Jalisco, 1947–51.

g-None. i-Held first political position under Governor *Marcelino Garcia Barragan*, 1946. j-None. k-None. l-DGF51, 22, 29, 32, 33, 36; C de D, 1949–52, 68; DGF56, 6, 9–12, 14; Enc. Mex., 1977, V, 579; Ind. Biog., 45–46.

Corral Martinez, Blas

(Deceased Apr. 29, 1947)
a-Feb. 11, 1883. b-Presidios, Durango, *West, Rural*. c-Early education unknown; no degree. d-*Governor of Durango*, 1944–47. e-None. f-*Oficial Mayor of the Secretariat of National Defense*, 1936–38; *Subsecretary of National Defense*, 1938–39; *Oficial Mayor of the Secretariat of National Defense*, 1941. g-None. h-None. i-Fought with *Jesus Agustin Castro* during the Revolution; married Josefina Ramirez. j-Joined the Revolution, 1911; fought against Huerta, 1913–14; organized the 21st Rural Guard; Governor and Military Commander of Chiapas, 1914; rank of Brigadier General, 1916; President of the Superior Military Tribunal; rank of Divisionary General, Apr. 1, 1938. k-None. l-D de Y. Jan. 1938; letter; Peral, 188; Q es Q, 135; Cadena, 139.

Corrales Ayala (Espinosa), Rafael

a-Sept. 14, 1905. b-Guanajuato, Guanajuato, *West Central, Urban*. c-Law degree, National School of Law, UNAM; Professor at the National School of Law, UNAM, 1930s–1960s. d-*Federal Deputy* from the State of Guanajuato, Dist. 1, 1949–52, member of the Gran Comision, the Committees on Legislative Studies (1st and 2nd year), Budgets and Accounting (2nd year), and Vice President of the Chamber, Nov., 1949; *Alternate Senator* from the State of Guanajuato, 1952–58; *Federal Deputy* from the State of Guanajuato, Dist. 1, 1955–58; member of the Committee on Money, Credit, and Credit Institutions, and the Committee on Foreign Relations; Secretary of the Introductory Council; President of the Chamber, Sept., 1956. e-*Secretary General of the CEN of PRI*, 1956–58. f-*Assistant Attorney General of Mexico (1)*, 1946–47; Chief of Press Relations, UNAM, 1948–49; Chief of the University Extension Department, UNAM, 1949; Head of the Press Department, Presidency of Mexico, 1953–54; Director of Information, Secretariat of Government, 1954–55; Director General of the National Lottery for Public Welfare, 1964–70; Adviser to the Secretary of the Treasury, 1976– . h-None. i-Part of the group recruited to PRI by *Rodolfo Sanchez Taboada*. j-None. k-Oratory champion, 1930s; precandidate for Governor of Guanajuato, 1978. l-DGF47, 309; DGF56, 6; *Siempre*, 7 Sept. 1956, 6; DGF69, 680; *Tiempo Mexicano*, 56; DGF51, 21, 29, 32, 35, 36.

Correa Racho, Victor Manuel

(Deceased, 1978)
a-Oct. 18, 1917. b-Merida, Yucatan, *Gulf, Urban*. c-Primary studies in Merida; secondary studies at the Bucareli School; preparatory studies at the Frances Morelos School, Mexico City; law degree, Law School, University of Yucatan, Dec., 1940; special studies in contract law. d-Mayor of Merida, Yucatan, 1966–70. e-Head of the regional committee for the National Action Party in the State of Yucatan; adviser to the National Executive Committee of PAN, 1972–73; f-None. g-Vice President of the College of Lawyers of Yucatan. h-Notary Public in Merida; lawyer for the National Chamber of Commerce in Merida; founder and first director of the Trust Department, Bank of the Southeast, Merida; practicing lawyer, 1972–78; Director General of Mutual Previsora Banhiner. A.C., 1972–73. i-Married Elvira Mena Peniche. j-None. k-Candidate of the National Action Party for Federal Deputy, Dist. 1, Yucatan, 1949; candidate of the National Action Party for Governor of Yucatan, 1969, in a highly disputed election; praised by *Loret de Mola* as an honest mayor. l-DBM70, 146–47; letters; Loret de Mola, 47.

Cortes Herrera, Vicente

(Deceased 1963)
a-July 10, 1889. b-Guanajuato, Guanajuato, *West Central, Urban*. c-Preparatory studies at the University of Guanajuato; engineering degree from the National School of Engineering, UNAM, 1913. d-Federal Deputy, 1926–28. e-None. f-Director of National Works, Department of the Federal District; Director of Buildings and Monuments, Department of the Federal District, 1922–24; Director of Public Works in Mexico, D.F., 1925–28; President of the National Commission of Highways, 1932; *Subsecretary of Public Works*, 1935–38; *Director General of Petroleos Mexicanos*, 1938–40; *Subsecretary of Public Works*, 1940–41; head of the Sixth Zone for the Secretariat of Public Works, 1946–52, 1952–58. g-None. h-Author of works on civil engineering in Europe. i-Brother Manuel served as Rector of the University of Guanajuato, 1936–43; married Luz Estrada. j-None. k-Came to the attention of *Lazaro Cardenas* after building a road through Michoacan, 1932. l-D de Y, 19 Apr. 1938, 1; letter; WWM45, 31; DGF56, 257–58; D del S, 2 Dec. 1940, 1, 6; DGF51, I, 255; Peral, 190; DP70, 535; Lopez, 237.

Cortes Muniz, Roberto A.

a-May 31, 1915. b-Monterrey, Nuevo Leon, *North, Urban*. c-Primary and secondary studies in Monterrey; no degree. d-Local Deputy to the State Legislature of Nuevo Leon, Dist. 2, 1946–49; *Senator* from the State of Nuevo Leon, 1952–58 (elected as an alternate, but replaced *Rodrigo Gomez*), member of the Gran Comision, the Mail and Telegraph Committee, the Rules Committee, the First Labor Committee, the First Petroleum Committee, the First Balloting Committee, and Secretary of the First Instructive Section of the Grand Jury. **e-**Joined the PNR youth section, 1935; president of the youth section for Nuevo Leon, 1939; Official Orator for the *Aleman* and *Ruiz Cortines* campaigns in Nuevo Leon; President of the State Committee of PRI of Nuevo Leon, 1947–52; President of PRI in Tabasco; delegate of the CEN of PRI in Tampico, Nayarit, **f-**Oficial Mayor of the City Council of Monterrey, 1941–42; Oficial Mayor of the State of Nuevo Leon, 1949–52; Subdirector General of the National Border Program, 1965–69; President of the National Commission of Medical Services, 1964–69. **g-**Secretary General of the 67th Section of the Miners Union; President of the Mixed National Commission of Medical Services for Sugar Cane Workers, 1959–64. **h-**Employee of the Cia. Fundidora de Fierro y Acero, Monterrey, 1933–56. **j-**None. **k-**None. **l-**Letters; DBM68, 153–54; DGF56, 7, 9, 11; Ind. Biog., 46.

Cortes Silva, Porfirio

a-July 22, 1918. **b-**Guadalajara, Jalisco, *West, Urban,* **c-**Primary and secondary studies in Guadalajara; law degree from the School of Law. University of Guadalajara; Professor of Political Economy, University of Guadalajara. **d-**Secretary of the City Council of Guadalajara; Local Deputy to the State Legislature of Jalisco (twice); *Federal Deputy* from the State of Jalisco, Dist. 3, 1958–61, Assistant Secretary of the Chamber, 1958, member of the Fifth Section of the Legislative Studies Committee, the Tax Committee, the First General Means of Communication Committee and the Industries Committee; *Federal Deputy* from the State of Jalisco, Dist. 4, 1970–73, Member of the Legislative Studies Committee, Fifth Section and the First Labor Committee; *Federal Deputy* from the State of Jalisco, Dist. 4, 1976–79, Member of the First Labor Committee, the First Section of Constitutional Affairs, the Section on Transformation and on the Automotive Industry of the Industrial Development Committee, the Border Zone Section of the Regional Development Committee, and the Constitutional, Administrative and Labor Sections of the Legislative Studies Committee. **e-**None. **f-**Agent of the Ministerio Publico; Justice of the Peace, Jalisco. **g-**Joined the CTM, 1937; President of the Student Society of the Law School, University of Guadalajara. **i-**Married Melida Garcia. **j-**None. **k-**None. **l-**C de D, 1970–73, 108; D de C, 1976–79, 21, 26, 27, 36, 50–51, 54, 73; C de D, 1976–79, 13; C de D, 1958–61, 75, 98; Func., 242.

Cosio Vidaurri, Guillermo

a-June 25, 1930. **b-**Jalisco, *West.* **c-**Early education unknown; law degree. **d-***Federal Deputy* from the State of Jalisco, Dist. 12, 1967–70, member of the Fourth Ejido Committee, the Fiscal Section of the Legislative Studies Committee, the First Tax Com-

mittee and the General Means of Communication Committee; Mayor of Guadalajara, 1971–73; *Federal Deputy* from the State of Jalisco, Dist. 1, 1976–79, Secretary of the Gran Comision, member of the Administration Committee. **e-**Joined PRI in 1949; General Delegate of the CEN of PRI to Baja California del Norte, Coahuila, Chihuahua, Yucatan. **f-**Judge, State of Jalisco; Director of Public Education, State of Jalisco; Director General of Administration, Secretariat of Agriculture. **g-**None. **i-**Married Idolina Gaona. **j-**None. **k-**None. **l-**D de C, 1976–79, 5; C de D, 1967–70, 65, 70, 73, 90; Enc. Mex., 1977, IV, 579; *Excelsior,* 3 Sept. 1976, 1C.

Cossio y Cossio, Roberto

a-Feb. 13, 1904. **b-**Federal District, *Federal District, Urban.* **c-**Early Education unknown; law degree from the National School of Law, UNAM, 1929, with a thesis on the "Influence of Francisco Cosentini on the New Civil Code"; professor of Mercantile and Civil Law, National School of Law, UNAM, 1930– . **d-**None. **e-**Member of the National Council of PAN, 1939; member of the CEN of PAN, 1939; *Secretary General* of the CEN of PAN, 1939–51. **f-**None. **g-**None. **h-**Lawyer for many small businesses; lawyer for the Chamber of Commerce of Mexico City. **i-**Son of Jose Lorenzo Cossio, lawyer and judge; brother Jose Lorenzo Cossio y Cossio was director of Legal Affairs, PNR and Secretary to *Antonio Villalobos,* President of the CEN of the PNR; close friend of *Manuel Gomez Morin* since law school days. **j-**None. **k-**None. **l-**Letter; *Excelsior,* 27 Sept. 1975, 1–2B.

Coudurier (Sayago), Luis

b-Federal District, *Federal District, Urban.* **c-**Primary and secondary studies in Mexico City; preparatory studies in Mexico City; law degree from the National School of Law, UNAM, 1947, with a thesis on industrial property. **d-**None. **e-**None. **f-**Auxiliary Secretry to the Head of the Department of the Federal District, *Ernesto P. Uruchurtu,* 1953–64; member of the Mixed Planning Commission of the Department of the Federal District; *Oficial Mayor of the Department of the Federal District,* 1964–66. **g-**None. **h-**Practicing lawyer, Mexico City, 1942–52, 1967– . **i-**Married Ana Maria Lascurain. **j-**None. **k-**None. **l-**HA, 21 Dec. 1958, 10; Libro de Oro, 1972, 54; DPE65, 191.

Coutino (de Cos), Amador

(Deceased March 6, 1966)
a-Apr. 30, 1895, **b-**Chiapa de Corzo, Chiapas, *South, Urban.* **c-**Primary studies in Chiapa de Corzo; preparatory studies in San Cristobal de Las Casas, Chiapas; law degree from the National School of Law, UNAM, **d-**Federal Deputy from the State of Chiapas, Dist. 4, 1934–37. **e-**None. **f-**Interim Gov-

ernor of Chiapas, 1928; Judge, Seventh Civil Court District, Mexico City; President of the Superior Tribunal of Justice of the State of Chiapas; *Interim Governor of Chiapas,* September 23, 1936 to December 14, 1936; *Attorney General for the Federal District and Federal Territories,* 1938–40. **g**-None. **k**-None. **l**-DBC. 51–52; Casasola, V, 2258; Navarette, 201; D de Y, 4 Jan. 1938, 2; Correa, 60.

Covian Perez, Miquel

a-Feb. 8, 1930. **b**-Merida, Yucatan, *Gulf, Urban.* **c**-Early education unknown; law degree, National School of Law, UNAM, 1956. **d**-*Federal Deputy* from the Federal District, Dist. 21, 1964–67. **e**-Oficial Mayor of the CEN of PRI, 1976–78. **f**-Administrative Subdirector of the ISSSTE; Consulting lawyer to the Secretary of Labor; Agent of the Ministerio Publico; *Ambassador to Cuba,* 1967–70. **g**-None. **j**-None. **k**-None. **l**-C de D, 1964–67; PS, 1973.

Cravioto, Alfonso

(Deceased Sept. 11, 1955)
a-Jan. 24, 1883, **b**-Pachuca, Hidalgo, *East Central, Urban.* **c**-Primary studies at the Fuentes y Bravo School, Pachuca; preparatory studies at the Scientific and Literary Institute of Pachuca and at the National Preparatory School, Mexico City; law degree, National School of Law, UNAM. **d**-Federal Deputy from the State of Hidalgo, Dist. 6, 1911–13; Federal Deputy from the State of Hidalgo, 1922–24; Deputy to the Constitutional Convention of Queretaro from Hidalgo, Dist. 7, 1916–17; Senator from the State of Hidalgo, 1922–24; *Senator* from the State of Hidalgo, 1952–58. **e**-Active in the anti-reelectionist movement. **f**-Secretary of the City Council of Mexico City, 1911; Director of the University Section of the Council on Higher Education, 1914; Director General of Fine Arts, 1914; Oficial Mayor of Public Education, 1915; Secretary of Public Education, 1915–17; Ambassador to Guatemala, 1925-26, 1927; Ambassador to Chile, 1926–27, 1928–32; Ambassador to Belgium, 1932–34; *Ambassador to Cuba,* 1934–38; Ambassador to Bolivia, 1939–43. **g**-None. **h**-Cofounder of several important magazines including *Savia Moderna* with Luis Castillo Ledon, 1906. **i**-Son of General Rafael Cravioto, prominent libera officer and politician, and governor of Hidalgo, 1895; married Elena Vazquez Sanchez. **j**-None. **k**-Imprisoned in Belem for articles which attacked President Diaz. **l**-WWM45, 32; Peral, 193; DGF56; C de S, 1952–58; DP70.

Cravioto Cisneros, Oswaldo

a-1919. **b**-Pachuca, Hidalgo, *East Central, Urban.* **c**-Graduated from the National Military College, Feb. 1, 1939, as a 2nd Lieutenant; Staff Officer Di-

ploma; Superior War College, 1948. **d**-*Senator* from the State of Hidalgo, 1964–70, Secretary of the Gran Comision. **e**-*Secretary of Organization of the CEN of PRI,* 1965–68, **f**-Chief of Security Services, State of Hidalgo, under Governor *Corona del Rosal,* 1957–58; Oficial Mayor of the State of Hidalgo under Governor *Corona del Rosal,* 1958; *Substitute Governor of Hidalgo,* 1958–61; Gerente, National Army-Navy Bank, 1970–76. **g**-None. **i**-Protege of *Alfonso Corona del Rosal.* **j**-Career army officer; rank of major; assigned to the 28th Military Zone, Pachuca, Hidalgo, 1949; served in various Infantry Battalions; cadet officer at the National Military College. **k**-None. **l**-WWMG, 14; HA, 15 Dec. 1958, 15–16; HA, 7 Mar. 1966, 17; MGF69, 105, *Excelsior,* 16 July 1972, 22.

Creel Lujan, Enrique

b-Chihuahua, *North.* **c**-Early education unknown; architecture degree. School of Architecture, UNAM; MA degree in architecture, University of Notre Dame **d**-None. **e**-Joined PAN, 1958; member of the CEN of PAN, 1959–75; Treasurer of PAN, 1959–75. **f**-None. **g**-None. **h**-Practicing architect. **i**-Grandson of Enrique Creel, Ambassador to the United States and a cabinet secretary under Porfirio Diaz; brother-in-law of *Hugo B. Margain.* **j**-None. **k**-None. **l**-Mabry, 237.

Cruickshank Garcia, Jorge

a-July 29, 1915. **b**-Tehuantepec, Oaxaca, *South, Urban.* **c**-Primary studies at the Escuela Morelos y Veracruzano, Veracruz; secondary and preparatory at the Secondary and Preparatory School of Veracruz; studied at the Superior School of Mechanical and Electrical Engineering and at the Municipal Engineering School; engineering degree. **d**-*Federal Deputy* from the State of Oaxaca, Dist. 1, 1964–67, member of the Cultural Affairs Committee, the Second Railroads Committee, and the Second General Means of Communication Committee; *Federal Deputy* from the PPS (party deputy), 1970–73, member of the Department of the Federal District Committee, the Government Committee, the Social Security Committee, and the Fish and Game Committee; *Senator* from Oaxaca, 1976– . **e**-Founding member of the Popular Party, 1948; Interim Secretary of the National Central Committee of the PPS, 1968; *Secretary General of the PPS,* 1969–79, 1979– . **f**-None. **g**-Secretary General of Section X, National Union of Educational Workers (SNTE); Auxiliary Secretary of the National Committee of Unified Socialist Youth of Mexico, 1937; co-founder of the National Union of Educational Workers. **h**-None. **j**-None. **k**-Candidate for Federal Deputy from Oaxaca, 1949, for the Popular Party; candidate for Governor of Oaxaca, 1968, for the PPS; critics accuse him of accepting PRI support as a candidate for Senator from Nayarit in exchange for recognizing the defeat of the PPS candidate *Gascon Mercado* for governor of Nayarit, 1975, l-*Directorio,* 1970–72; HA, 4 June 1973, 4; C de D, 1970–72, 108; C de D, 1964–66, 78, 84, 95; *Latin America,* 11 Nov. 1977, 349.

Cruz (Castillejos), Wilfrido
(Deceased Aug. 26, 1948)
a-Apr. 29, 1898. b-Espinal, Juchitan, Oaxaca, *South, Rural.* c-Primary and secondary studies at the Veracruz Institute; preparatory studies at the Veracruz Institute; law degree from the National School of Law, UNAM, Apr. 23, 1921; Professor of Law, University of Oaxaca; Professor of Law, University of Puebla; rural school teacher, 1916. d-Federal Deputy from the State of Oaxaca, Dist. 4, 1930–32; Federal Deputy from the State of Oaxaca, Dist. 11, 1932–34; *Senator* from the State of Oaxaca, 1934–40. e-None. f-Judge in the Federal District; judge in Oaxaca; judge in Hidalgo; Judge of the Superior Court of Puebla, 1926; Attorney General of the State of Oaxaca, 1927–28; Judge and President of the Superior Tribunal of Justice of the Federal District and Federal Territories, 1940–43. g-None. h-Author of several books; author of the reform of Article 27 of the Constitution.j-None. k-Member of the Executive Committee of the National Pre-Electoral Center for *Manuel Avila Camcho,* 1939; as a Senator, favored women's suffrage. l-WWM45, 32; Peral, 197; Morton, 32; Novo, 286; Casasola, V, 2422; Lopez, 243.

Cruz de Mora, Aurora
a-June 22, 1931. b-Ejido Buenos Aires, Municipio Altamira, Tamaulipas, *North, Rural.* c-Early education unknown; no degree. d-Mayor of Altamira, 1961–62; Local Deputy to the State Legislature of Tamaulipas, 1973; *Federal Deputy* from the State of Tamaulipas, Dist. 4, member of the Foreign Relations Committee, the Second Labor Committee, the Sugar Cane Products and the Social, Economic and Cultural Development of Peasant Women sections of the Agrarian Affairs Committee, the Section on Sugar of the Industrial Development Committee, the Social Security and Public Health Development Committee and the Gran Comision. e-None. f-None. g-Secretary of Feminine Action of the Regional Farmers Committee of the Altamira Ejido Zone; Secretary of Feminine Action of the League of Agrarian Communities of the State of Tamaulipas; Secretary of Feminine Action of the CNC. j-None. k-None. l-*Excelsior,* 21 Aug. 1976, 1C; D de C, 1976–79, 4, 8, 13, 26, 38, 71, 74.

Cue Merlo, Eduardo
a-Dec. 13, 1909, b-Puebla, Puebla, *East Central, Urban.* c-Primary education from the Ignacio Ramirez School, Puebla; studies in business ad-

ministration, El Portalillo School, Puebla; no degree. d-*Senator* from Puebla, 1964–70; First Councilman of Puebla; Mayor of Puebla, 1960–63. e-Secretary of Finances of the State Committee of PRI of Puebla, 1963–64. f-Executive Secretary of the Board of Public Welfare, Puebla, 1951–60; President of the Savings Fund of Employes and State Officials of Puebla, 1960–67; Treasurer of the City Council of Puebla, 1960. g-None. h-Industrialist. j-None. k-Donated salary as Mayor and Councilman of Puebla to charitable causes. l-C de S, 1964–70; MGF69, 106; CyT, 198–200.

Cuenca Diaz, Hermenegildo
(Deceased May 17, 1977)
a-Apr. 13, 1902. b-Puruandiro, Michoacan, *West Central, Urban.* c-Primary studies from father; preparatory studies at the National Polytechnical Institute; graduated in engineering from the Higher School of Mechanical and Electrical Engineering of the Military College with the rank of 2nd lieutenant, Feb. 1, 1922; graduated from the Superior War College, d-*Senator* from the State of Baja California del Norte, 1964–70. e-None. f-Chief of Staff of the Secretariat of National Defense, 1951–52; *Secretary of National Defense,* 1970–76. g-None. h-Author of various military works. i-Parents were rural teachers. j-Career army officer; fought in more than fifty battles, 1924; liaison officer between Mexico and the United States, San Antonio, Texas; Assistant Chief of Staff of the 17th Military Zone, head of the Special Intelligence Service of the Presidential Staff, 1940–46; rank of Colonel, February 12, 1946; Chief of Staff of the 3rd Division; Brigade General, November, 1952; Commander of the 23rd Military Zone in Tlaxcala, Tlaxcala, 1956; rank of Divisionary General, December 1, 1958. k-Formed part of the cadets who accompanied Carranza when he fled Mexico, D.F., to Veracruz, 1920; PRI candidate for governor of Baja California del Norte when he died, 1977. l-HA, 7 Dec. 1970, 23; *Hoy,* 14 Dec. 1970; DGF56, 202; DGF, 69; HA, 12 Dec. 1952, 6; DBM68, 160–61; *Excelsior,* 18 May 1977, 1, 11.

Cueto Fernandez, Fernando
a-Dec. 30, 1896, b-Puebla, Puebla, *East Central, Urban.* c-Primary studies in Hidalgo, Puebla (6 years); secondary studies in San Pedro y San Pedro, Puebla (2 years) attended the National Military College; no degree. d-Local Deputy to the State Legislature of San Luis Potosi, 1939–41; *Federal Deputy* from the State of Puebla, Dist. 7, 1955–58, member of the Second National Defense Committee, the First Balloting Committee and the Budget and Accounting Committee (2nd year), Vice President of the Chamber; *Federal Deputy* from the State of Puebla, Dist. 6, 1970–73, member of the First National Defense Committee and the Military Industry Commit-

tee. e-None. f-Treasurer General of San Luis Potosi, 1939–40; Department Director, Federal District Police Department, 1947; Director General of Traffic, State of Puebla, 1951; Oficial Mayor of the State of Puebla, 1954. g-None. i-Disciple of *Rafael Avila Camacho.* j-Joined the army at age thirteen under Colonel Epigmenio Martinez; 1st Sgt., 1913; fought in fifty-six battes during the Revolution, 1910–14; career army officer; Chief of Staff of the 25th Military District, Puebla, Puebla, 1956; rank of Brigadier General, 1953. k-None. l-*Directorio, 1970*–72; C de D, 1955–57, 48, 62; C de D, 1970–72, 108; CyT, 200–201; Ind. Biog., 47–48.

Cueto Ramirez, Luis
(Deceased Jan. 16, 1977)
a-1901. c-Early education unknown; distinguished cadet at the National Military College, 1924–28. d-None. e-None. f-Chief of Police of the Federal District, 1958–64, 1965–69, g-None. h-None. i-Married Graciela Garcia, son Jorge was medical subdirector of IMSS. j-Career army officer; joined the Revolution at age fourteen; fought against the Escobar rebellion, 1929; Commander of the 8th Military Zone, Tamaulipas, 1952–57. k-Removed as Police Chief after 1968 student movement demanded his resignation. l-DGF56, 201; DPE61, 141; *Proceso,* 22 Jan. 1977, 34; DPE65, 201.

Cuevas Canciano, Francisco
a-May 7, 1921. b-Federal District, *Federal District, Urban.* c-Law degree from the Escuela Libre de Derecho, 1943; graduate studies at McGill University, Montreal, Canada, L.L.D. in civil law; studies in Ottawa, London, and at Columbia University, New York; Professor at Mexico City College; Professor at the Escuela Libre de Derecho; Director of the Center of International Studies at the Colegio de Mexico. d-None. e-None. f-Third Secretary of the Mexican Embassy in London, 1946–49; adviser to the Secretary of Foreign Relations, 1954; Subdirector of International Organizations for the Secretariat of Foreign Relations, 1957; legal advisor to the Mexican delegation to the United Nations, 1960; Subsecretary General of the Mexican delegation to the Third General Assembly of the United Nations; *Mexican Ambassador to the United Nations,* 1965–70, 1976–79. g-None. h-Author of many articles on legal subjects and foreign affairs. i-Collaborator of *Luis Padilla Nervo* for many years. j-None. k-None. l-DGF69, 184; DBM68, 161–62; WWW70–71, 209; *El Universal,* 14 Sept. 1965.

Danzos Palomino, Ramon
a-Oct. 15, 1912. b-Bacadehuachi, Sonora, *North, Rural.* c-Primary studies in Bacadehuachi; secondary studies in Hermosillo, Sonora; rural teaching certificate. d-None. e-Joined the Mexican Communist Party, 1939; Alternate Member of the Central Com-

mittee of the Mexican Communist Party, 1954. f-None. g-Secretary General of the Federation of Workers of Southern Sonora, 1958; leader of the Independent Farmers Federation (CCI), 1970s. h-Teacher, Ciudad Buenavista, Sonora, j-None. k-Candidate for Federal Deputy from Sonora, Dist. No. 5, 1949, on the Popular Party ticket; candidate for Federal Deputy from Sonora, Dist. No. 3, on the Popular Party ticket; imprisoned in the 1960s for his political activities and leadership of peasant strikes; candidate for governor of Sonora; candidate of the Mexican Communist Party for Federal Deputy from Sonora, Dist. No. 7, 1979. l-*Excelsior,* 24 Nov. 1974, 4; Johnson, 1978, 94.

Davila, Jose Maria
a-Apr. 21, 1897. b-Mazatlan, Sinaloa, *West, Urban.* c-Secondary and preparatory education at the Literary and Scientific Institute of San Luis Potosi; graduated from the National Military College. d-Federal Deputy from the State of Sinaloa, 1930–32, 1932–34, and 1934–36; *Senator* from the Federal District, 1936–40, member of the Gran Comision. e-None. f-Head of the Office of Immigration of the Secretariat of Government, 1922–30; Mexican Ambassador to Guatemala, 1940; Mexican Ambassador to Brazil, 1940; member of the Administrative Council of the National Bonded Warehouses, 1946–52; Director General of the National Bank of Agricultural and Livestock Credit, 1946–52. g-None. i-Son of Doctor Jose M. Davila. j-Joined the Revolution in 1914; rank of Captain, 1915. k-Precandidate for Governor of Sinaloa, 1944. l-EBW46, 70; letter; DGF47, 356; DGF50, II, 130, 409; DGF, II, 166; WB48, 1361; Peral, 211; DGF49, 468; Kirk, 126; Lopez, 263.

Davila Aguirre, Vicente
(Deceased 1960)
a-Oct. 13, 1893. b-Ramos Arizpe, Coahuila, *North, Rural.* c-Primary and secondary studies in Ramos Arizpe; studied at the National Military College (3 years); degree in mechanical engineering, United States. d-Local deputy from Monclova to the State Legislature of Coahuila, 1912, and 1935; *Senator* from the State of Coahuila, 1958–60. e-None. f-Provisional Governor of San Luis Potosi, 1915; Secretary General of Government of the State of Coahuila, 1935. g-None. h-Practicing engineer. j-Career army officer; supported Madero in the Revolution, 1912–13; fought under General Maclovio Herrera, 1914, assumed command of his men when Herrera died, and supported Carranza; rank of Brigadier General, June 1, 1942; Commander of the Military Zones of Chihuahua, Guanajuato, and Sinaloa. k-Abandoned studies at the National Military College to fight in the Revolution; member of the State Legislature of Coahuila which disavowed Huerta as legal President of Mexico after the death of

Madero, 1914; supported the De la Huerta rebellion, 1923. l-DP70, 624; C de S, 1961–64, 14; Peral, 212; Func., 139; Lopez, 264.

de Alba, Pedro
(Deceased Nov. 10, 1960)
a-Dec. 17, 1887. b-San Juan de los Lagos, Jalisco, *West, Rural.* c-Primary in San Juan de los Lagos, Jalisco; secondary and preparatory studies at the Institute of Sciences, Aguascalientes; medical degree from the National School of Medicine, UNAM, graduated as a surgeon; studies in medicine at the Medical-Military Practical School of the Army, 1913; diploma in ophthalmology in Paris; Professor of General History and of Spanish Literature at the National Preparatory School and the School of Philosophy and Letters, UNAM; commissioned by the Secretary of Public Education of the State of Nuevo Leon to organize the University of Monterrey, 1933. d-Federal Deputy from the State of Aguascalientes, Dist. 1, 1920–22; Senator from Aguascalientes, 1922–26, President of the Senate, member of the Foreign Relations Committee; *Senator* from the State of Aguascalientes, 1952–58, member of the Gran Comision, the Public Welfare Committee, the First Public Education Committee, and the Health Committee. f-Counselor of Public Education in Aguascalientes, 1917; Director of the Health Service in Aguascalientes, 1918; Director of the Preparatory School in Aguascalientes, 1919; Director of the Institute of Sciences of Aguascalientes; Director of the National Preparatory School, 1929–33; member of the Technical Advisory Council to the Secretariat of Public Education, 1935; Assistant Director of the Pan American Union, 1936–47; Ambassador to Chile; Ambassador to the International Organization of Labor, 1948–51; Delegate to UNESCO, 1951. g-None. h-Author of several books. j-Major in the Mexican Army. k-None. l-WWM45, 3; DP70, 54; DGF56, 5, 8, 9, 10, 12; DGF51, 110, 117; WB48, 1383; IWW40, 22; Ind. Biog., 49–50.

de Dios Batiz, Juan
(Deceased May 20, 1979)
a-Apr. 2, 1890. b-Zataya, Sinaloa, *West, Rural.* c-Early education unknown; began engineering studies in Culiacan, completed at the National Military College. d-Federal Deputy from the State of Sinaloa, Dist. 1, 1922–24, member of the Gran Comision; Federal Deputy from the State of Sinaloa, Dist. 3, 1924–26; Federal Deputy from the State of Sinaloa, Dist. 2, 1930–32; Senator from the State of Sinaloa, 1932–34. e-Treasurer of the CEN of the PNR, 1931. f-Interim Governor of Sinaloa, 1926–27; Director of Technical Education, Secretariat of Public Education, 1934–36; founder of the IPN, 1936; Director of Social Welfare, Secretary of Labor, 1936–40; Director General of the National

Mortgage Bank, 1940–46. g-None. h-Manager of various private firms, 1946–70. i-Married Laura Perez de Batiz; son Juan de Dios was a director general in the Secretariat of Industry and Commerce, 1961. j-Participated in the Revolution; military governor of Nayarit. k-President Cardenas allegedly offered him the position of Secretary of Public Education in 1934, but he turned it down to found the IPN. l-HA, 28 May 1979, 14; *Excelsior,* 21 May 1979, 4; Peral, 97; *Excelsior,* 22 May 1979, 30; DPE61, 66.

de Icaza (Gonzalez), Antonio
a-Jan. 10, 1938. b-Mexican Legation, Berlin, Germany, *Foreign, Urban.* c-Preparatory studies at the Liceo Frances in London, 1955; law degree from the National School of Law, UNAM, 1956–60; postgraduate work at the Institute of Higher Labor Studies in Geneva. d-None. e-None. f-Vice Consul in La Paz, Bolivia; Assistant to the Secretary of Foreign Relations; head of the Department of Technical Assistance, the Department of European Political Affairs, and the Department of Treaties and Conventions, Secretariat of Foreign Relations; rank of Third Secretary, 1960; rank of Second Secretary and Private Secretary to the Subsecretary (2) of Foreign Relations, 1964–69, *Gabino Fraga Magana*; adviser to the Foreign Service, 1966–70; Private Secretary to the Subsecretary of Foreign Relations, *Ruben Gonzalez Sosa,* 1970–71; Ambassador to Nicaragua, 1971–74; Ambassador to Egypt, 1977– . g-None. h-Joined the Foreign Service, 1956; received vice consul rank based on results of Foreign Service Examination, 1958; member of delegation to various international conferences. i-Son of Ambassador *Francisco A. de Icaza.* j-None. k-None. l-DBM68, 169j DPE65, 17.

de Icaza (y Leon), Francisco A.
a-Dec. 31, 1904. b-Berlin, Germany, *Foreign, Urban.* c-Medical degree. d-None. e-None. f-Fourth official of the Secretariat of Foreign Relations, 1926; third official of the Secretariat of Foreign Relations, 1926; Third Secretary in charge of trade, Costa Rica, 1929; Third Secretary in charge of trade, El Salvador, 1930; Third Secretary to the legation in Havana, Cuba, 1931; First Secretary, Berlin, Germany, 1936–38; Counsellor to Argentina, 1940–41; Counsellor to Guatemala, 1942; Ambassador to Lebanon, 1947–49; Ambassador to Belgium and Luxemburg, 1949–52; *Ambassador to Great Britain,* 1952–55; Ambassador to Guatemala, 1956–58; Ambassador to Argentina, 1964–70. g-None. h-None. i-Son, *Antonio de Icaza* is a career foreign service officer; father, Francisco A. de Icaza was a poet and diplomat, serving in various European posts, including positions in Spain and Germany, 1863–1925; married Maria Gonzalez. j-None. k-None. l-DGF56, 126; DPE65, 23; Peral, 404; DP70, 1050; DGF51, 107–08; STYRBIWW, 1951, 692; DPE61, 20.

de Keratry Quintanilla, Pedro

a-Feb. 12, 1918. b-Tampico, Tamaulipas, *North, Urban*. c-Primary studies at the Public Schools of Ciudad Victoria, Tamaulipas; secondary studies at the Escuela Secundaria No. 4, Federal District; preparatory studies at the National Preparatory School; law degree from the National School of Law, UNAM, 1938-42, degree on Nov. 15, 1945; Professor of History, Preparatory School Jose de Escandon, Ciudad Reynosa, Tamaulipas, 1946-47; Professor of Civil Law, Technical Institute of Higher Studies, Monterrey, 1960-64; Professor of Guarantees and Amparo, School of Law, University of Nuevo Leon, 1962-64. d-None. e-Secretary of the Luis Echeverria Association of Nuevo Leon, 1969-70. f-Agent of the Ministerio Publico of the State of Tamaulipas, 1945-46; Civil and Penal Judge of the First Instance, Sixth District, State of Tamaulipas, 1947-48; legal advisor to the National Colonization Commission; legal adviser to the Administration of Hydraulic Resources for the Rio Bravo district, Tamaulipas; consulting lawyer to the Customs Agency, Ciudad Reynosa; legal adviser to the City Council of Ciudad Reynosa; Notary Public No. 43, Ciudad Reynosa, 1949-58; Agent of the Ministerio Publico, Monterrey, 1959-64; Secretary General of the State of Tamaulipas, 1965-69; Notary Public No. 37, Monterrey, 1969-72. g-Legal adviser to the Union of Restaurant Workers, Ciudad Reynosa. h-None. i-Father, a lawyer. j-None. k-None. l-Letter; DBM68, 179; P de M, 67, 83.

de la Colina (Riquelme), Rafael

a-Sept. 20, 1898. b-Tulancingo, Hidalgo, *East Central, Urban*. c-Preparatory studies at the National Preparatory School in Mexico, D.F.; Bachelor of Science from UNAM, 1916; Master of Science from UNAM; never taught because of career outside the country in the foreign service. d-None. e-None. f-Member of the Consulate in Philadelphia, Pennsylvania, 1918-22; Vice Counsul, St. Louis, Missouri, 1922, and Eagle Pass, Texas, 1922-23; Chief of the Administrative Department of the Consular Division of the Secretariat of Foreign Relations, 1923-24; Consul, Boston, Massachusetts, 1924-25, New Orleans, 1925-28, Laredo, Texas, 1928-30, and Los Angeles, 1930-32; Head of the Consular Department, Secretariat of Foreign Relations, 1932-33; Head of the License Bureau, Federal District, Secretariat of Foreign Relations, 1933; Consul General, San Antonio, Texas, 1934-35, New York, 1936-43; Minister, Washington, D.C., 1943-44; rank of Ambassador, 1944; *Ambassador to the United States*, 1949-52; *Ambassador to the United Nations*, 1952-58, to Canada, 1958-62, to Japan, 1962-64, and *Ambassador to the Organization of American States*, 1965-76, 1976- . g-None. h-Assistant Secretary General at the Inter-American Conference on War and Peace, 1945; technical advisor of the Mexican delegation to the United Nations, San Francisco, 1945; Envoy attached to the Mexican Embassy, Washington, D.C., 1946; delegate from Mexico to the First General Assembly of the United Nations, 1947. i-Attended National Preparatory School with several members of the famous "Seven Wise Men of Mexico" which included *Lombardo Toledano*, *Teofilo Olea y Leyva, Alfonso Caso*, also knew *Jaime Torres Bodet, Jose Gorostiza, Pablo Campos Ortiz, Narciso Bassols*, and *Daniel Cosio Villegas*; father a school teacher and supporter of Madero; grandfather founder of the Scientific and Literary Institute of Hidalgo; married Ruth Rosecrans. j-Private Secretary to General *Candido Aguilar*, 1917-18, reached rank of Lieutenant. k-None. l-Letter; WWM45, 28; Inf. Please, 189, 201 (1950-51); DGF56, 128; Peral, 179; DPE61, 20; DGF51, 105; WB48, 1417-18; STYRBIWW54, 693; WB54, 278; WWW70-71, 191; HA, 7 Oct. 1974, 6ff; NYT, 29 Dec. 1948, 9; Lopez, 273; Enc. Mex., 1977, III, 23.

de la Cueva (y de la Rosa), Mario

a-July 11, 1901. b-Federal District, *Federal District, Urban*. c-Preparatory studies at the National Preparatory School; law degree, National School of Law, UNAM, 1925; advanced studies in philosophy and law, University of Berlin, 1931-32; Professor of Introduction to the Study of Law, Theory of the State, Labor Law, and Constitutional Law, UNAM, 1929-70; professor emeritus, UNAM; Dean, National School of Law, UNAM, 1951-53. d-None. e-None. f-*Secretary General of UNAM*, 1938-40, under *Gustavo Baz*; *Rector of UNAM*, 1940-42; Coordinator of Humanities, UNAM; President of the Federal Board of Conciliation and Arbitration, 1946; Director General of the National Cinematographic Bank, 1946-52. g-None. h-Author of a classic work on Mexican labor law; author of many books. i-Professor of *Alfonso Pulido Islas*, *Jose Juan de Olloqui, Mario Colin Sanchez, Miguel de la Madrid*, *Jesus Reyes Heroles*, and *Fernando Zertuche Munoz*. j-None. k-None. l-*Hoy*, 21 Mar. 1970, 20; DGF47, 351; DGF51, II, 65, 421; DGF50, 292; Peral, 47, 96; letter; Enc. Mex., 1977, III, 227; WNM, 57-58.

de la Flor Casanova, Noe

a-May 29, 1904. b-Teapa, Tabasco, *Gulf, Rural*. c-Law degree from the National Law School, UNAM, 1930; professor at the National Law School, UNAM, 1937-42. d-*Governor of Tabasco*, 1943-46. e-None. f-Secretary of the Criminal Courts in the Federal District, 1930-36; Justice of the Peace, 1937-39; Judge of the Superior Tribunal of Justice of the Federal District and Federal Territories, 1940-42, 1955-58. g-Founding member of the Socialist Lawyers Front, 1936. h-Author. j-None. k-Removed from the office of Governor in February, 1946.

l-DGF56, 513; HA, 14 May 1943, 13; HA, 28 Sept. 1945, xii; WWM45, 42; EWB46, 174; Lopez, 362.

de la Fuente, Fernando
(Deceased 1965)

a-1889. b-Federal District, *Federal District, Urban*. c-Law degree, National School of Law, UNAM, 1915. d-None. e-Member of the Social Democratic Party, 1937; Secretary of Interior of the CEN of the National Independent Party, 1938. f-Penal judge, 1924; Judge of the Superior Tribunal of Justice of the Federal District and Federal Territories; Justice of the Supreme Court, 1929–34; *Justice of the Supreme Court*, 1940–46, and 1946–52. g-None. h-Assisted in writing the monetary law, 1930–31; helped to create the Bank of Mexico with *Manuel Gomez Morin*; founder of the Pension Department. j-None. k-Appointed Director of National School of Economics, but never accepted position. l-Enc. Mex., IV, 478; DP70, 795; letter; DGF47; DGF51, I; Novo35, 76.

de la Fuente Rodriguez, Juan Antonio
(Deceased, 1979)

a-Nov. 10, 1913. b-Saltillo, Coahuila, *North, Urban*. c-Primary and secondary studies in Saltillo; studies at the National Military College, 1931–35, graduated as a 2nd lieutenant of cavalry, Jan. 1, 1935; studies in biology, National Preparatory School, 1936–37; course in cavalry tactics, School of Applied Military Studies, 1939–40; attended the Staff and Command School, Higher War College, 1941–44; special studies in armored vehicles, Fort Knox, United States, 1950–51; instructor in armored vehicles, Higher War College; Director of the National Military College; Director of the Higher War College. d-None. e-None. f-Military Attache, Santiago, Chile; Director of Military Education, Secretariat of National Defense; *Subsecretary of National Defense*, 1976–79. g-None. h-None. i-Costudent at the National Military College and the Higher War College with *Felix Galvan Lopez*. j-Career Army officer; fought against rebel groups in Jalisco, 1935–36; fought against rebel groups in Putla, Oaxaca, 1940; Section Chief, Presidential Staff; Commander of the 18th Cavalry Regiment; Commander of the Mazatlan garrison; rank of Divisionary General, Nov. 20, 1975. k-Strongest precandidate for governor of Coahuila before his death in a helicopter crash. l-Enc. Mex., Annual, 1977, 535; *Excelsior*, 16 Mar. 1980, 21.

De la Fuentes Rodriguez, Jose

a-Apr. 20, 1920. b-General Zepeda, Coahuila, *North, Rural*. c-Early education unknown; law degree from the National School of Law, UNAM, 1939–44; Rector of the University of Coahuila, 1967–70, d-*Federal Deputy* from the State of Coahuila, Dist. 1, 1967–70, member of the Administration Committee (2nd year), Penal Section of

the Legislative Studies Committee, Second Justice Committee, Petroleum Committee, and the Public Security Committee; *Federal Deputy* from the State of Coahuila, Dist. 1, 1976–79, member of the Gran Comision, Section Four of the Educational Development Committee, the Higher Education Committee, the Electrical Section of the Industrial Development Committee, the Development of Natural and Energy Resources Committee, the Rural and Arid Zone Industry Section of the Regional Development Committee, the Development of Social Security and Public Health Committee, the Social Welfare Section of the Social Security and Public Health Committee, the Penal Section of the Constitution Studies Committee, the Government Committee, the Justice Committee and the Foreign Relations Committee. e-President of the State Committee of PRI of Coahuila; General Delegate of the CEN of PRI to Baja California del Norte; *Popular Secretary of the CEN of PRI*, 1976–79; *Secretary General of the CEN of PRI*, 1979– . f-Judge; Agent of the Ministerio Publico; Attorney General of the State of Coahuila. g-*Secretary General of the CNOP*, 1976–79. i-Co-student of *Jose Lopez Portillo* at UNAM. j-None. k-None. l-C de D, 1967–70, 56, 66, 79, 87; D de C, 1976–79, 19, 21, 25, 31, 32, 34, 38, 51, 56, 61, 71; *Excelsior*, 21 Aug. 1976, 1C; MGF69, 89.

de la Garza (Gonzalez), Arturo

a-Aug. 1, 1936. b-Monterrey, Nuevo Leon, *North, Urban*. c-Primary studies at the Simon de la Garza Melo School, Monterrey (6 years); secondary at the Moises Saenz School; preparatory at the Colegio Civil, Monterrey; studied law and social sciences for one year at the University of Nuevo Leon. d-*Federal Deputy* from the State of Nuevo Leon, Dist. 8, 1970–73, member of the Gran Comision, the Livestock Committee, the Small Agricultural Properties Committee, and the Hydraulic Resources Committee. e-Delegate of the CEN of PRI to Coahuila; President of PRI in Guadalupe, Nuevo Leon. f-Adviser to the National Agricultural Credit Bank of Nuevo Leon. g-Delegate from Nuevo Leon to the National Livestock Federation; adviser to the National Livestock Federation; President of the Regional Livestock Union for Nuevo Leon; Secretary of the Council for the Promotion of Livestock, Nuevo Leon. h-Rancher. i-Son of former Governor of Nuevo Leon, *Arturo B. de la Garza*; married De la Luz Tijerina. j-None. k-None. l-*Directorio*, 1970–72; C de D, 1970–72, 109.

de la Garza Gutierrez, Jesus B.

a-Oct. 1, 1895. b-Monterrey, Nuevo Leon, *North, Urban*. c-Primary in Nuevo Leon; secondary at the Colegio Civil, Monterrey; preparatory studies at the National Preparatory School, Mexico, D.F.; attended the Mining School of Mexico, Mexico, D.F.; degree in military construction, Military College, 1917; degree in civil engineering, National School of Engineering, UNAM, 1920. **d-**None. **e-**None. **f-***Subsecretary of Public Works*, 1940; *Secretary of Public Works*, 1940–41; Director General of War Materiels for the Secretariat of National Defense, 1941–46; Director General of Military Social Security, Secretariat of National Defense, 1964–70. **g-**None. **h-**None. **i-**Married Maria Casas. **j-**Career army officer; cadet at the National Military College, 1909; joined the Revolution as a Maderista in 1910; Inspector General of Police, Monterrey; head of Military Education, Secretariat of National Defense; Director of Agricultural Schools, Secretariat of National Defense; President of the First War Committee; rank of Brigadier General, 1940. **k-**Attended the Convention of Aguascalientes, 1914–15; precandidate for Governor of Nuevo Leon, 1943. **l-**DGF65, 44; WB48, 1419; EBW46, 1133; *Hoy*, 7 Dec. 1940, 3–4; Peral, 323; WWM45, 48.

de la Garza Ollervides, Eulogio

a-Jan. 29, 1905. **b-**Sierra Mojada, Coahuila, *North*, *Rural*. **c-**Primary studies in five different schools in Coahuila and Chihuahua; preparatory studies at the Scientific and Literary Institute of Chihuahua, Chihuahua; engineering degree from the National School of Agriculture, Chapingo; professor at the National Forestry School, Coyoacan, Federal District; Director of the Institute of Higher Forestry Education, Los Molinos, Perote, Veracruz. **d-**None. **e-**None. **f-**Inspector General of the Forestry Service, 1936; Inspector General in the Southeast, 1937; Alternate Director of the National Museum of Flora and Fauna, Chapultepec, Mexico, D.F., 1938; General Agent of the Secretariat of Agriculture in Toluca, Mexico, 1940; Chief of Services, Secretariat of Agriculture, 1941; head of the Legal Department, Secretariat of Agriculture, 1943; head of the Technical Forestry Council, 1945; Technical Director of the Department of Forests and Game, 1949; Director General of the Department of Forests and Game, Secretariat of Agriculture, 1949–51; adviser to National Railroads of Mexico, 1953; *Subsecretary of Forests and Fauna of the Secretary of Agriculture*, 1970 to June 7, 1972. **g-**Adviser to the National Chamber of Forest Industries; head of the Technical Union of the National Chamber of Industries (Cultivating Forests). **h-**Leave of absence to work for the National Urban Mortgage Bank of Public Works, 1947; consulting engineer to the Papaloapan Commission, 1957; practicing engineer in the Office of Private Forests, 1927–36; began career as a practicing student at the South East Forest Station, Xochimilco, Federal District, 1927; author of several articles on trees. **j-**None. **k-**Resigned from the Subsecretary position for personal reasons. **l-**Letter; HA, 14 Dec. 1970, 21; *Excelsior*, 8 June 1972, 1; DGF51, I, 204–05.

de la Huerta Oriol, Jr., Adolfo

a-Jan. 3, 1910. **b-**Guaymas, Sonora, *North*, *Urban*. **c-**Primary studies in Guaymas and in the Federal District; preparatory studies in Los Angeles, California; no degree. **d-***Senator* from Sonora, 1976– . **e-**None. **f-**Private Secretary to Adolfo de la Huerta, Inspector General of Consulates, Secretariat of Foreign Relations, 1936–43; Vice Consul, Tucson, Arizona, 1955; Director of the Department of Passports for the Secretariat of Foreign Relations, 1956–64; *Secretary General of Tourism*, 1964–70, and 1970–74. **g-**None. **h-**Worked for a newspaper in Los Angeles, California; joined the Foreign Service, 1943; reached the rank of first chancellor; visited all consulates in the United States as private secretary to his father. **i-**Son of the former Mexican President Adolfo de la Huerta; cousin of *Alejandro Carrillo M.*, Governor of Sonora, 1975–79. **j-**None. **k-**None. **l-**DGF56, 141; DPE70, 136; DPE65, 178; HA, 21 Dec. 1964, 9; letter; DPE61, 16; *Excelsior*, 4 Aug. 1978, 15.

de la Madrid (Hurtado), Miguel

a-Dec. 12, 1934. **b-**Colima, Colima, *West, Rural*. **c-**Primary and secondary studies in Mexico, D.F.; law degree with honorable mention from the National School of Law, UNAM, 1952–57, thesis on "Economic Thought of the 1857 Constitution;" Master's degree in Public Administration from Harvard University, 1964–65; Professor of Constitutional Law at the National School of Law, UNAM, on leave since 1968. **d-**None. **e-**Member of PRI since 1963. **f-**Advisor to the Administration of the Bank of Mexico, 1960–65; Subdirector General of Credit of the Secretariat of the Treasury, 1965–70; Subdirector of Finances of Petroleos Mexicanos, Dec., 1970 to Apr., 1972; Director General of Credit of the Secretariat of the Treasury, May 4, 1972 to 1975; *Subsecretary of Credit* of the Secretariat of the Treasury, 1975–76; 1976–79; *Secretary of Planning and Programming*, 1979–82. **g-**None. **h-**Employed in the Legal Department of the National Bank of Foreign Commerce, 1953–57; Secretary of the Mexican delegation to the first Annual Reunion of the Inter-American Economic and Social Council of the Organization of American States, 1962; attended many international economic conferences, 1963–69; author of various articles. **i-**Nephew of *Ernesto Fernandez Hurtado*, former Director General of the Bank of Mexico, who became his mentor; son of Miguel de la Madrid Castro, a public notary and lawyer; family prominent in Colima since the 1700s. **j-**None. **k-**Presidential candidate of PRI, 1981. **l-**Letters; HA, 15 May 1972; *Excelsior*, 4 May 1972, 4; *Excelsior*, 17 May 1979, 9; HA, 28 May 1979, 13.

De Lamadrid Romandia, Roberto

a-Feb. 3, 1922. **b-**Calexico, California, *Foreign*. **c-**Primary studies in the Cuauhtemoc Elementary

School, Mexicali; secondary at Southeast Junior High School, Nestor, California, and at Sweetwater Union High School, National City, California; degree in business administration from the Sweetwater Evening High School, National City, California. **d-***Senator* from Baja California del Norte, 1976; *Governor of Baja California del Norte*, 1977– . **e-**Member of the Advisory Council of *Adolfo Lopez Mateos'* presidential campaign, 1958; Coordinator of the Socio-Economic Study Groups, *Milton Castellanos'* campaign for Governor of Baja California, 1971; Secretary General of the CEPES of PRI in Tijuana and Tecate during the *Luis Echeverria* campaign, 1970; Chief of the Administrative Department of the IEPES of the CEN of PRI, 1975–76. **f-**President of the Federal Board for Moral and Material Betterment, Baja California del Norte, 1970–75; Director of Economic Development, Baja California del Norte, 1971; President of the Committee of Inter-Governmental Affairs, 1971; Director General of the National Lottery, 1976–77. **g-**President of the Federation of Border Towns, 1970–75. **h-**Employee of the National Chamber of Commerce and Industry, Tijuana, 1936; employee of the Bank of the Pacific, S.A., Assistant Cashier, Bank of Baja California; distributor for Pemex for Richfield Oil and Pennzoil, 1942–74; Vice-president of the San Diego Planning Commission. **i-**Long-time friend of *Jose Lopez Portillo;* married Elena Victoria. **j-**None. **k-**Pre-candidate for governor of Baja California del Norte, 1976; lost out to General *Cuenca Diaz*, but became the PRI candidate when *Cuenca Diaz* died during the campaign. **l-**HA, 30 May 1977, 21; HA, 14 Nov. 1977, 25; C de S, 1976–82.

De la Pena Porth, Luis
(Deceased Apr. 30, 1979)

a-1923. **b-**Tlapan, *Federal District, Urban*. **c-**Primary studies in Tlapan, Tampico, Tamaulipas, and in Sonora; secondary in Nogales, Sonora; preparatory studies at the National Preparatory School, 1938–39; Engineering degree from the National School of Engineering, UNAM, 1943. **d-**None. **e-**None. **f-**Program Director, Mining Development Commission, Saltillo and Hermosillo, 1956–58; Director General of Unrenewable Resources, Secretariat of Government Properties, 1958–60; Director General of Mines and Petroleum, Secretariat of Government Properties, 1965–66; Director of Engineering, Mining Development Commission, 1967–70; *Subsecretary of Renewable Resources*, 1970–73. **g-**None. **h-**Worked for a North American company, 1944–47; hydraulic geologist, Mexican government, 1947–52, 1952–54; operated own cotton farm, 1954–56; representative of international firm in Mexico, 1960–63; advisor to private and government firms, 1973–76; Director General of Roca Fosforica Mexicana, 1977–79. **i-**Student companion of *Manuel Franco Lopez*, Secretary of National Patrimony, 1964–70; student of *Mariano Moctezuma*, Subsecretary of Industry and Commerce, 1938–42; father was a mining and civil engineer; grandfather had a medical degree but went into mining. **j-**None. **k-**Resigned from Subsecretaryship in 1973 after a heart attack. **l-**Letters; DPE65, 83; HA, 14 Dec. 1970, 21; HA, 12 Mar. 1973, 21.

de la Selva y Escoto, Rogerio
(Deceased 1967)

a-1900. **b-**Leon, Nicaragua, *Foreign, Urban*. **c-**Law degree, National School of Law, UNAM, 1929–33; Professor at the National School of Law, UNAM. **d-**None. **e-**Member of the first National Advisory Council of the National Confederation of Popular Organizations of PRI, 1944. **f-**Private Secretary to *Miguel Aleman* as Justice of the State Supreme Court of Veracruz, 1934–36; private secretary to *Miguel Aleman* as Governor of Veracruz, 1936–40; private secretary to *Miguel Aleman* as Secretary of Government, 1940–45; *Secretary of the Presidency*, 1946–52; Judge of the Military Court; private secretary to *Miguel Aleman* as President of the National Council of Tourism, 1964–67. **g-**None. **h-**None. **i-**Long-time personal friend of *Miguel Aleman* since college days at the National School of Law; knew *Salvador Aceves Parra* at UNAM. **j-**Not a career officer; received a presidential appointment as a general in order to serve as a justice on the military court. **k-**Became a naturalized citizen of Mexico, one of the few naturalized citizens ever to hold such a high public office in Mexico; accused by Senator *David Franco Rodriguez* of trying to divide the PRI, 1954. **l-**DP70, 1976; D de S, 3 Dec. 1956, 1; HA, 6 Dec. 1946, 6; DGF47; DGF51, I, 55; Brandenburg, 102; Letters; *Excelsior*, 2 Aug. 1949; NYT, 30 July 1954, 3; Villasenor, II, 100.

de la Torre Grajales, Abelardo
(Deceased April 22, 1976)

a-Dec. 4, 1913. **b-**Chiapa de Corzo, Chiapas, *South, Urban*. **c-**Primary and secondary studies in San Cristobal de las Casas, Chiapas; no degree. **d-**Local Deputy to the State Legislature of Chiapas; Mayor of San Cristobal de las Casas; *Federal Deputy* from the State of Chiapas, Dist. 2, 1952–55; member of the Second Committee of the Treasury and the Committee on Budgets and Accounts; *Senator* from the State of Chiapas, 1958–64, member of the Gran Comision, the First Petroleum Committee, the First Labor Committee, and the First Balloting Committee; President of the First Instruction Section of the Grand Jury. **e-**Joined the PNR, 1931; candidate of the CNOP of PRI for Senator, 1958; *Secretary of Organization of the CEN of PRI*, 1959–64; *Secretary of Organization of the CEN of PRI*, 1964–65. **f-**Oficial *Mayor of the Secretariat of National Patrimony*, 1964–68; *Subsecretary of Government Properties*,

1968–70; Director General of Services, IMSS, 1970–76. **g**-Occupied various union positions, 1930s; Secretary General of the National Union of Treasury Workers; *Secretary General of the FSTSE*, 1952–58. **h**-Employee of the Secretariat of the Treasury, 1930s. **i**-Friend of *Alfonso Corona del Rosal*; married Juanita Delgado. **k**-PRI candidate for Senator from Chiapas, 1976, died prior to the election. **l**-C de S, 1964, 55; *Siempre*, 5 Feb. 1959, 6; DPE65, 76; HA, 21 Dec. 1964, 11; HA, 28 Dec. 1964, 4; DBM68, 185; C de D, 1955, 9; Scott, 165; Func., 153; *Excelsior*, 23 Apr. 1976, 10; DBdeC, 245.

de la Torre Padilla, Oscar

a-Feb. 8, 1932. **b**-Guadalajara, Jalisco, *West, Urban*. **c**-Primary studies at the Horacio Mann School, Mexico. D.F.; secondary studies at Secondary School No. 14, Mexico, D.F.; preparatory studies at the Centro Universitario de Mexico; studies for two years at the School of Political and Social Science, UNAM; Diploma in Tourism, International University of Official Tourist Organizations. **d**-Councilman, Guadalajara, Jalisco; local deputy to the state Legislature of Jalisco; *Federal Deputy* from the State of Jalisco, Dist. No. 9, 1970–73, member of the Crafts Committee, the Immigration Committee, and the Tourism Committee. **e**-None. **f**-Federal delegate of the Department of Tourism to the State of Jalisco; Director of Tourism for the State of Jalisco; *Secretary General "C" of the Department of the Federal District*, 1970–73; *Secretary General of the Department of Tourism*, 1974–76. **g**-None. **i**-Married Mary Ann Grillo. **j**-None. **k**-None. **l**-HA, 21 Jan. 1974, 14; *Directorio*, 1970–72.

de Lara Isaacs, Alfredo

a-Nov. 14, 1919. **b**-Calvillo, Aguascalientes, *West, Rural*. **c**-Preparatory studies at the National Preparatory Night School; law degree, National School of Law, UNAM, 1946. **d**-*Alternate Federal Deputy* from the State of Aguascalientes, Dist. No. 2, 1955–58; *Senator* from the State of Aguascalientes, 1958–64, Secretary of the Senate, 1958, President of the Protocol Committee; Executive Secretary of the Military Justice Committee; Second Secretary of the First Labor Committee and the Special Legislative Studies Committee. **e**-Official of the CNOP, 1953–58. **f**-Youth Delegate of the Youth Section of the Department of the Federal District, 1938; Director of the Federal Prosecutors Office for the Defense of Labor, Secretariat of Labor; Director of the Department of Inspection, Secretariat of Labor. **g**-Vice-president of the Federation of Intellectuals of the Federal District; student leader in the Law School Society, UNAM. **h**-Journalist; writer for *La Batalla*; editor. **j**-None. **k**-None. **l**-Func., 116; C de S, 1961–64, 54; DGF56, 21.

de Lascurain Obregon, Javier

a-Nov. 16, 1919. **b**-Federal District, *Federal District, Urban*. **c**-Law degree from the Escuela Libre de Derecho, Aug. 20, 1945. **d**-None. **f**-None. **g**-None. **h**-Joined the Cia. de Fianzas Lotonal, S.A., 1945; head of the criminal agency for that firm, 1945–47; head of the criminal agency for the Cia. General de Fianzas, 1947; Subdirector of Fianzas Modelo, 1954–66; Director of Fianzas Modelo, 1966–70. **i**-Father an engineer. **k**-Member of the National Action Party; candidate for Federal Deputy from the Federal District, Dist. 23, 1961, for the National Action Party. **l**-DBM70, 84.

de la Vega Dominguez, Jorge

a-Mar. 14, 1931. **b**-Comitan, Chiapas, *South, Urban*. **c**-Primary studies at the public school Belisario Dominguez, Comitan, Chiapas, 1940–45; secondary education in Comitan, 1946–48; preparatory at the National Preparatory School, 1949–50; degree in economics with honorable mention from the National School of Economics, UNAM, 1958, with his thesis on "Petroleum Industry in Mexico: Some Aspects of its Development and Financial Problems," received an honorable mention; professor of third year engineering at the Technological Institute of Ciudad Madero, Tamaulipas, 1957–58; Professor of the Theory of Public Finance at the National Polytechnic School, 1960–65; Director of the Graduate School of Economics, National Polytechnic School, 1963–64; President of his generation at the National Preparatory School and of the 1955 Generation of the National School of Economics. **d**-*Federal Deputy* from the State of Chiapas, Dist. 3, 1964–67, member of the Committee on National Properties and Resources and the Committee on Budgets and Accounts; member of the Interparliamentary Delegation to the United States; *Governor of Chiapas*, 1976–77. **e**-Director of the Institute of Economic, Political, and Social Studies of PRI, 1968–70; adviser to the IEPES of PRI during the national platform meeting, 1963. **f**-Economist for the Secretariat of Industry and Commerce, 1951–55; Gerente General of the Tampico Branch of the Small Business Bank, 1956–58; Subdirector of Diesel Nacional, S.A., 1959–61; Subdirector of the Small Business Bank, 1962; Head of the Department of Public Expenditures, Secretariat of the Presidency, 1963–64; Subdirector in charge of sales, CONASUPO, 1965–68; *Director General of CONASUPO*, 1971–76; *Secretary of Trade*, 1977– . **g**-President of the College of Economists of Mexico, Mar., 1961, to Apr., 1963. **h**-Organized the first Congress of Economics Students in Latin America, 1956; author of many articles and pamphlets. **i**-Attended the National School of Economics, UNAM, with *Julio Faesler*, Director of the Mexican Institute of Foreign Trade, 1970–76, and *Carlos Torres Manzo*; nephew of Belisario Dominguez, the Mexican Senator who publicly accused General Huerta of the murder of Francisco Madero; first helped in public career by his professor and mentor, *Gilberto Loyo*. **j-**None. **k-**Representative of President *Diaz Ordaz* to student leaders of the 1968 strike. **l-**Letter; C de D, 1964–66; *Excelsior*, Dec. 1970; *Excelsior*, 16 Dec. 1977, 6; *Excelsior*, 15 Apr. 1975, 7; *Excelsior*, 13 Apr. 1977, 1, 14; *Excelsior*, 10 Dec. 1977, 1, 13.

del Castillo Franco, Armando

a-1918. **b-**Durango, *West*. **c-**Early education unknown; law degree. **d-***Federal Deputy* from the State of Durango, Dist. 4, 1949–52, President of the Chamber, Sept., 1949, member of the Film Industry Committee and the Legislative Studies Committee; answered *Miguel Aleman's* 3rd State of the Union address, 1949; *Federal Deputy* from the State of Durango, Dist. 3, 1979–80, President of the Administration Committee; *Governor of Durango*, 1980– . **e-**Director of the National Youth Sector of PRI. **f-**Director of Public Defenders for the Department of the Federal District; Secretary General of the State of Durango. **g-**Coordinator of Federal Deputies of CNOP for Durango, 1979; Secretary of Legislative Promotion of CNOP, 1980. **j-**None. **k-**Politically inactive during most of the 1960's and 1970's. **l-**DGF51, I, 22, 32, 33; C de D, 1949–52, 66; *Excelsior*, 19 Feb. 1980, 4.

Delgado, Alfredo

a-Dec. 1, 1890. **b-**El Fuerte, Sinaloa, *West*, *Rural*. **c-**Primary studies in Oakland, California; no degree. **d-***Governor of Sinaloa*, 1937–40. **e-**None. **f-**Chief of the Mounted Police, Federal District, 1920–24. **g-**None. **h-**None. **j-**Fought in the Revolution; career Army officer; held various commands; rank of Brigadier General, June 1, 1941. **k-**None. **l-**Peral 47, 102; letter.

Delgado Valle, Jose

a-July 12, 1927. **b-**Federal District, *Federal District*, *Urban*. **c-**Primary at the Centro Escolar of the State of Michoacan, Mexico City; secondary studies from Secondary School No. 5, Mexico City; special course in mechanics from Vocational School No. 2, Mexico City; no degree. **d-**Local Deputy from Dist. 6 to the State Legislature of Mexico; *Federal Deputy* from the State of Mexico, Dist. 2, 1970–73, member of the Public Welfare Committee, the Tube Industry Committee and the First Balloting Committee; *Federal Deputy* from the State of Mexico, Dist. 3, 1976–79. **e-**Secretary of Political Action of PRI in the State of Mexico. **f-**Syndic of the City Council of Tlalnepantla, Mexico. **g-**Secretary of Political Action of the Union of Workers of the State of Mexico; Secretary General of the CTM of Tlalnepantla,

Mexico; member of the Tube Workers Union. **h-**Industrial maintenance employee. **i-**Married Jacoba Lopez Donez. **j-**None. **k-**None. **l-**C de D, 1970–73, 109; *Directorio*, 1970–72; D de C, 1976–79, 16.

del Mazo Velez, Alfredo
(Deceased Dec. 19, 1975)

a-Aug. 21, 1904. **b-**Atlacomulco, Mexico, *West Central*, *Rural*. **c-**Primary studies in Atlacomulco, Mexico; secondary in Mexico City; professional schools in Mexico, D.F.; no degree. **d-***Governor of Mexico*, 1945–51; *Senator* from the State of Mexico, 1952–58, member of the Gran Comision, the Colonization Committee, the Secondary Money, Credit, and Credit Institutions Committee, the Department of the Federal District Committee, and substitute member of the Committee on the Consular and Diplomatic Service; president of the Senate, October, 1954. **e-**Assisted PRI in the presidential campaign of *Adolfo Ruiz Cortines*, 1952; Political Secretary to *Adolfo Lopez Mateos* during his campaign, 1958; representative of the CEN of PRI to Sonora, Yucatan, Veracruz and Puebla. **f-**Director of the Administrative Department of the National Irrigation Commission, 1940–42; Director of Warehouses for the National Highway Commission, 1932–33; Director of Warehouses for the National Irrigation Commission, 1933; Treasurer of the State of Mexico, 1942–43; Secretary General of Government of the State of Mexico, 1943–45, under Governor *Isidro Fabela*; *Secretary of Hydraulic Resources*, 1958–64. **g-**None. **h-**Worked as an agricultural laborer; general laborer for the National Irrigation Commission, 1926. **i-**Father and grandfather both served as Mayors of Atlacomulco; father was a small rancher; political disciple of *Isidro Fabela*, who opposed him for the 1944 PRI nomination for Governor; personal friend of *Adolfo Lopez Mateos*; married Margarita Gonzalez; son Alfredo was Director General of the Workers Bank, 1979. **j-**None. **k-**Ran against *Francisco J. Gaxiola* and *Alfredo Navarrete* for the PRI nomination for governor, 1944. **l-**HA, 30 Nov. 1969, 21; HA, 8 Dec. 1958, 30; DGF56, 6, 9, 10; Greenberg, 26; Scott, 282; DGF51, I, 90; Colin, 201–31; HA, 14 Sept. 1951; HA, 4 June 1948; HA, 29 Dec. 1975, 14; Func., 89.

del Olmo Martinez, Joaquin

a-Aug. 16, 1904. **b-**Federal District, *Federal District*, *Urban*. **c-**Primary studies in public schools, Mexico City; no degree. **d-***Alternate Federal Deputy* from the Federal District, Dist. No. 4, 1955–58; *Federal Deputy* from the Federal District, Dist. No. 2, member of the Traffic Committee and the Library Committee; *Federal Deputy* from the Federal District, Dist. No. 18, 1967–70, member of the Department of the Federal District Committee, and the Pharmaceutical Industry Committee; *Federal Deputy* from the Federal District, Dist. No. 18, 1973–76. **e-**None. **f-**Representative of Labor to Special Group no. 4, Federal Board of Conciliation and Arbitration, 1961. **g-**Secretary of Organization and Statistics of the CTM, 1961. **h-**Auto mechanic. **i-**Married Maria Luisa Diaz. **j-**None. **k-**None. **l-**Func., 177; DGF56, 22; C de D, 1955–58; C de D, 1958–61, 9; C de D, 1967–70, 62, 75; C de D, 1973–76, 18.

de los Reyes, Jose Maria

a-Mar. 19, 1902. **b-**Tula, Hidalgo, *East Central, Rural.* **c-**Primary studies in the Federal District, 1918–21; preparatory at the Escuela Preparatoria Libre de Homeopatia, 1921–22, and at the National Preparatory School, 1923–27; law degree from the National School of Law, UNAM, 1928–32; founder of the National Preparatory Night School and other secondary schools in Mexico; professor of economic and social geography of Mexico (thirty-five years). **d-***Federal Deputy* from the State of Hidalgo, Dist. 3, 1952–55, member of the Budget and Accounts Committee (3rd year) and the Legislative Studies Committee (2nd year). **e-**Supporter of Jose Vasconcelos, 1929; Secretary of Political Education of PRI for the Federal District, 1975. **f-**Subdirector General of the National Preparatory School, 1936; Secretary of the National Preparatory School, 1930–35; Director General of Administration, UNAM, 1946–47; Technical advisor to the Rector, UNAM, 1948–60; Director of the Home School for Boys, Secretariat of Government, 1938–42; Director, Office of Cinematography and National Films, Secretariat of Public Education, 1943–46; Director of the publication *Educacion,* Secretariat of Public Education, 1946–49; Director of the National Preparatory Night School, 1924–55; member, National Technical Council of Education. 1957–63. **g-**President of the Student Society of the National Preparatory Night School; active student leader in the 1926, 1927, 1928 and 1929 Student Congresses; member of the National Strike Committee, for the National School of Law, UNAM, 1929. **h-**Assistant to Colonel Leonardo Torres during the Revolution. **i-**Attended primary school with *Roman Badillo.* **j-**None. **k-**Participant in Cuban Revolutionary activity, 1917–18. **l-**C de D, 1952–55, 52, 63; letter.

del Rincon Bernal, Jorge

a-Nov. 27, 1930. **b-**Guaymas, Sonora, *North, Urban.* **c-**Preparatory studies at the Scientific Institute of Guadalajara, Jalisco; professional studies at the Ibero-American University and UNAM, degree in business administration; professor at the University of Sonora. **d-**None. **e-**Member of PAN. **f-**None. **g-**President of the Employers Center of Sinaloa; ad-

viser to the Chamber of Commerce. **j-**None. **k-**Headed a civic movement in Culiacan which forced the federal government to expropriate the Sinaloa Electric Company; candidate for Federal Deputy from the Federal District, Dist. 2, as a member of the National Action Party. **l-**DBM70, 176.

del Valle, Alberto

a-Dec. 15, 1890. **b-**Aguascalientes, Aguascalientes, *West, Urban.* **c-**Primary studies in Aguascalientes; secondary studies at the Institute of Sciences of Aguascalientes, 1911–14; studied medicine at the Medical School of the University of San Luis Potosi (two years); medical degree from the National School of Medicine, UNAM, 1917; Professor of Chemistry at the Scientific Institute of Aguascalientes. **d-**Local deputy to the State Legislature of Aguascalientes, 1928–30; Mayor of Aguascalientes, 1937–38; *Senator* from Aguascalientes, Sept., 1934, to Aug., 1936; *Governor of Aguascalientes*, 1940–44. **f-**Founder and Director of the Antivenereal Clinic, 1920–21; Director of Education for Aguascalientes, 1917–20; Director of the Preparatory School for the State of Aguascalientes. **g-**None. **h-**Began career as a practicing surgeon, 1917. **j-**Head of the Sanitary Section of the Brigade Luis Moya, 1915. **k-**None. **l-**EBW46, 55; WWM45, 120; WB48, 1436; Peral, 825.

de Olloqui Labastida, Jose Juan

a-Nov. 5, 1931. **b-**Federal District, *Federal District, Urban.* **c-**Primary and secondary studies in the Federal District; law degree from the National School of Law, UNAM, Aug., 1956; Master of Arts in Economics, George Washington University, 1970; graduate work in law, National School of Law, UNAM; professor by competition, History of Economic Thought, National School of Law, UNAM, 1964–66; Professor of Economic Problems of Mexico and Economic Theory, UNAM and Ibero-American University; attended the English Language Institute, University of Michigan, 1957. **d-**None. **e-**None. **f-**Director of the Department of Currency, Banking, and Investment, Secretariat of the Treasury, 1958–66; Deputy General of Credit, Secretariat of the Treasury, 1966–70; President of the National Securities Commission, 1970–71; Executive Director of the Inter-American Development Bank, 1966–70; *Ambassador to the United States*, 1971–76; *Subsecretary (A) of the Secretariat of Foreign Relations*, 1976–79; *Ambassador to Great Britain*, 1979– . **g-**None. **h-**Joined the Bank of Mexico, 1951; author and translator of books, articles, and reviews. **i-**Father a banker; second cousin of *Oscar Flores Sanchez.* **j-**None. **k-**None. **l-**Letters; DPE65, 54; BdM, 102; DPE61, 41; NYT, 2 Dec. 1976.

Diaz Arias, Julian

c-Economics degree from the National School of Economics, UNAM, November 28, 1946; Professor and Superintendent of Technical Education at the National Polytechnical Institute, 1938–58; professor at the National School of Economics, UNAM, 1945–65; professor at the Scientific Institute, 1952–53; professor at the Higher Normal School, 1945–47. d-None. e-None. f-Head of the Department of Banks, Secretariat of the Treasury, 1947–51; President of the Executive Board of the Administration of Pensions, 1952–53; head of the Department of Properties and Construction of the Mexican Institute of Social Security, 1953–58; *Oficial Mayor of the Secretariat of Industry and Commerce,* 1959; *Subsecretary of Industry and Commerce,* 1959–61; business administrator and general attorney for Nacional Financiera, 1960–62; Director General of Financiera Nacional Azucarera, 1962–65; *Subdirector of National Finance Bank,* 1965–70, 1970–72; Director General of Financiera Nacional Azucarera, May, 1972, to 1976; Director of Collective Transportation, Department of the Federal District, 1976– . g-Participant in a student conference with *Luis Echeverria,* 1945. h-Attended conference in Central America. i-Friend of *Jorge Espinosa de los Reyes* at UNAM; married Isabel Gomez. j-None. k-None. l-HA, 15 May 1972, 31; letters; DBM66, 194–95; DGF50, II, 35, 409, 413; DGF51, II, 146, 570, 577, 43.

Diaz Ballesteros, Enrique

b-Morelia, Michoacan, *West Central, Urban.* c-Early education unknown; law degree, National School of Law, UNAM. d-None. e-None. f-Director of Legal Services, National Railroads of Mexico; Consulting Attorney to the Attorney General of Mexico; Director of Legal Services, Zacatepec Mill; General Counsel to the Director General of the National Railroads; Manager of the Administrative Division, CONASUPO, 1961–68; Subdirector of Operations, CONASUPO, 1971–75; *Director General of CONASUPO,* 1976; Director General of Metropolitan Services of the Federal District, 1977; *Subsecretary of Commercial Planning,* Secretariat of Trade, 1978; *Subsecretary of Regulations,* Secretariat of Trade, 1978–79; *Director General of CONASUPO,* 1979– . g-None. j-None. k-None. l-*Excelsior,* 5 May 1979, 1, 10; DPE71; DAPC.

Diaz de Cossio (Carvajal), Roger

a-Dec. 5, 1931. b-London, *Foreign, Urban.* c-Engineering degree from the National School of Engineering, UNAM, 1953; Master of Science in Civil Engineering from the University of Illinois, 1955–57; Ph.D. in Engineering from the University of Illinois, 1958–60; researcher, University of Illinois, 1958–60; Director of the Engineering Institute of UNAM, 1964–70. d-None. e-None. f-*Subsecretary of Planning of the Secretariat of Public Education,* 1971–76; Director General of Studies and Projects, Secretary of Commerce, 1976; Director General of Publications and Libraries, Secretariat of Public Education, 1978; *Subsecretary of Culture and Recreation,* November 15, 1978– . g-None. h-Assistant on construction works to Engineer Gonzalez Fernandez, 1953–54; calculator for the Division of Bridges, National Railroads of Mexico, 1955. j-None. k-None. l-DPE71, 103; BdM, 106; DGF69, 756.

Diaz Duran, Fernando

a-Nov. 4, 1905. b-Gomez Palacio, Durango, *West, Urban.* c-Secondary studies at the Escuela Zaragoza, Zacatecas, Zacatecas; graduated as an accountant from the Institute of Sciences, Zacatecas; licensed public accountant. d-Secretary of the City Council of Irapuato, 1928; Mayor of Irapuato; Local Deputy to the State Legislature of Guanajuato; *Federal Deputy* from the State of Guanajuato, Dist. 4, 1943–46, Secretary of the Chamber of Deputies, *Federal Deputy* from the State of Guanajuato, Dist. 5, 1958–61, member of the Administration Committee (2nd year); *Federal Deputy* from the State of Guanajuato, Dist. 4, 1967–70, member of the Public Education Committee and the Rules Committee. e-Secretary General of CNOP of PRI for Guanajuato; *Secretary of Organization of the CEN of PRI,* 1964–65; *Secretary General of the CEN of PRI,* 1965–68. f-Secretary of Education for the State of Guanajuato, 1940–43; Director of the Department of Labor, State of Guanajuato; President of the Board of Conciliation and Arbitration, Guanajuato. g-None. h-Employed in various positions by the Secretariat of the Treasury. i-Political disciple of *Enrique Fernandez Martinez* during early political career. j-None. k-Secretary of the Federation of Political Parties of Guanajuato. l-Peral, 220; C de D, 1943–45; C de D, 1958–60, 76; Func., 212; C de D, 1967–69, 64, 86.

Diaz Infante, Luis

a-Sept. 20, 1896. b-Leon, Guanajuato, *West Central, Urban.* c-Law degree, National School of Law, UNAM; Professor of Civil Law at the Escuela Libre de Derecho. d-*Federal Deputy* from the State of Guanajuato, Dist. 2, 1946–48, member of the Library Committee (1st year) and the First Committee on Balloting; President of the First Instructive Section of the Grand Jury, member of the Committee on Constitutional Affairs, substitute member of the Treasury Committee and the First Committee on General Channels of Communication. e-None. f-Judge of the

First Civil Court; Judge of the Superior Tribunal of the Federal District and Federal Territories; President of the Superior Tribunal of the Federal District and Federal Territories; *Justice of the Supreme Court*, 1948 and 1950–58; *Interim Governor of Guanajuato*, 1948–49. **g-**None. **h-**Member of the national commission charged with the writing of new civil codes. **j-**None. **k-**Member of the Sinarquista movement in Mexico; Simpson claims he was the first anti-revolutionary governor of Mexico. **l-**HA, 7 Oct. 1949, xxii; Peral 222; DGF47, 568; Simpson, 337; C de D, 1946–48, 70; DGF51, 568.

Diaz Lombardo, Antonio

a-Jan. 8, 1903. **b-**Federal District, *Federal District, Urban*. **c-**Primary studies in Mexico, D.F.; secondary studies at the English-French School, studied at the English School in Mexico, D.F.; preparatory at the National Preparatory School in Mexico, D.F.; studied at the Higher School of Mechanical and Electrical Engineering of the National Polytechnic Institute. **d-**None. **e-**None. **f-**Director General of the Bank of Transportation, 1943–46, 1953; *Director General of the Mexican Institute of Social Security*, 1946–52. **g-**Secretary General of the Alianza de Camioneros of Mexico. **h-**Employed by El Aguila; employed by Aeronaves de Mexico; President of the Latin American Bank; President of the Central Savings Bank; principle stockholder of El Popo, 1931. **j-**None. **k-***The New York Times* claims he was forced to resign as Director of the Bank of Transportation because of a conflict of interest from his financial control over bus companies. **l-**HA, 21 May 1943, 9; HA, 6 Dec. 1946, 6; WWM45, 35; Enc. Mex., Vol. 3, 236; Scott, 250; DGF50, II, 103; Brandenburg, 102; NYT, 12 July 1953, 26; Lopez, 291.

Diaz Munoz, Vidal

a-Mar. 21, 1900. **b-**Las Puentes, Veracruz, *Gulf, Rural*. **c-**Primary and secondary education at public schools; no degree. **d-***Senator* from Veracruz, 1940–46, member of the National Properties and Resources Committee, the Public Works Committee, First Secretary of the Third Labor Committee, and President of the Electrical Engineering Committee; *Federal Deputy* from the State of Veracruz, Dist. 11, 1946–49, Secretary of the Chamber, September, 1946, member of the Second Committee on the Treasury, the Committee on Taxes, the Committee on the Sugar Industry, and the Inspection Committee of the General Accounting Office (2nd year). **e-**Expelled from the PRI for joining the Popular Party, 1946; member of the Popular Socialist Party; member of the Finance Committee of the Popular Party, 1947; Secretary of the Electoral Affairs Committee, Popular Party, 1948; founder of the Veracruz

Socialist Party in 1957. **f-**None. **g-**Active in union organizations of the Regional Federation of Mexican Labor, 1925–32; served with the Federation of Latin American Workers, 1932–43; prominent leader of the sugar cane workers. **j-**Member of the Mexican Army, 1910–25; reached the rank of Lt. Colonel, 1925. **k-**Split with *Vicente Lombardo Toledano* in 1957 to found his own party with the support of sugar cane workers; supported *Adolfo Lopez Mateos* in the 1958 presidential election. **l-**EBW46, 37; Correa, 75; C de D, 1946–48, 70; Scott, 190–91; Morton, 104; Peral, 223; WB48, 1494.

Diaz Ordaz, Gustavo

(Deceased July 15, 1979)

a-Mar. 11, 1911. **b-**Ciudad Serdan (San Andres), Puebla, *East Central, Urban*. **c-**Primary studies in Oaxaca, Oaxaca, and in Guadalajara, Jalisco; preparatory studies at the Institute of Arts and Sciences, Oaxaca, Oaxaca; studied law at the University of Guadalajara and at the Institute of Arts and Sciences, Oaxaca; law degree from the University of Puebla, February 8, 1937; Professor of Law at the University of Puebla; Vice Rector of the University of Puebla, 1940–41. **d-***Federal Deputy* from the State of Puebla, Dist. 1, 1943–46; *Senator* from Puebla, 1946–52, member of the Administrative Committee, the Legislative Studies Committee, the Second Petroleum Committee, the First Government Committee, the First Constitutional Affairs Committee, and the Second Foreign Relations Committee; *President of Mexico*, 1964–70. **e-**None. **f-**Prosecuting Attorney for Tehuacan, Puebla; President of the Arbitration and Conciliation Board of Puebla; Agent of the Ministerio Publico for Tlatlahuqui, Puebla, 1943; Justice of the Superior Court of the State of Puebla; Secretary General of Government of the State of Puebla under *Gonzalo Bautista*, 1941–45; Director General of Legal Affairs of the Secretariat of Government, 1953–56; *Oficial Mayor of Government*, 1956–58; *Secretary of Government*, 1958–64; Ambassador to Spain, 1977. **g-**None. **h-**Employed as an office boy in the Palacio de Gobierno of Puebla; practicing attorney, 1937. **i-**Father was an accountant and his mother, a school teacher; brother-in-law of Guillermo Borja Osorno, Justice of the Tribunal Superior of Justice, Puebla; great-grandfather was lawyer and a general and Governor of Oaxaca; father-in-law of *Salim Nasta*, formerly his private secretary, 1964. **j-**None. **k-**Resigned from ambassadorship to Spain after strong protests from important political figures, 1977. **l-**D de Y, 1 Dec. 1964, 1; Enc. Mex., Vol. 3, 237–38; DGF56, 83; G of S, 14; WWMG, 14; DBM68, 197–98; HA, 8 Dec. 1958, 24; DP70, 2386–87; Covarrubias, 116; DGF47; C de D, 1943–45, 9; DGF51, I, 7, 10–13; NYT, 2 Dec. 1964, 16; IWW64–65; HA, 11 Apr. 1977, 7.

Diaz Serrano, Jorge

a-Feb. 6, 1921. **b-**Nogales, Sonora, *North*, *Urban*. **c-**Early education unknown; mechanical engineering degree from the Higher School of Mechanical and Electrical Engineering, IPN, 1941; MA degree in the history of art and Mexican history, School of Philosophy and Letters, UNAM, 1972–74; fellowship student to the United States to study internal combustion engines at private firms, 1943–45. **d-**None. **e-**None. **f-***Director General of PEMEX*, 1976– . **g-**None. **h-**Director of the Diesel and Locomotive Department, Fairbanks Morse, 1946–56; founded numerous companies, 1956–65; supervisor of a drilling company, Veracruz, 1962–64; Director and owner of the Golden Lane Drilling Company, 1965–70; representative of General Motors in electrical diesel engines and generators, 1969–73. **i-**Personal friend of *Jose Lopez Portillo* for many years; friend of *Octavio Senties*. **j-**None. **k-**Considered an international authority on the perforation and exploitation of petroleum. **l-***El Dia*, 1 Dec. 1976; *Excelsior*, 18 Mar. 1977, 6, 8; HA, 21 Mar. 1977, 12.

Diaz y Soto y Gama, Antonio

(Deceased, 1967)

a-1880. **b-**San Luis Potosi, San Luis Potosi, *East Central*, *Urban*. **c-**Primary studies in a public school in San Luis Potosi; law degree, Scientific and Literary Institute of San Luis Potosi, 1900; Professor of the History of the Mexican Revolution, National Preparatory School; Professor of Agrarian Law, National School of Law, UNAM, 1930's. **d-**Federal Deputy from Atlixco, Puebla, 1920–22, 1922–24, 1924–26, 1926–28. **e-**Founding member of the Liberal Club Ponciano Arriaga; active in the Liberal Party, 1904–1912; co-founder of the National Agrarian Party, 1920, in reality, a personal movement; Vice-president of the Mexican Democratic Party which ran *Ezequiel Padilla* for president, 1945; representative of the PDM to the Federal Electoral Commission, 1946. **f-**None. **g-**None. **h-**Wrote for *Renacimiento* and *El Universal*. **i-**Related to Valentin Gama, prominent educator at UNAM; son of lawyer Conrado Diaz Soto, a supporter of Sebastian Lerdo de Tejada. **j-**Joined Emiliano Zapata's forces, 1914–20. **k-**Notable orator during congressional debates in the 1920's. **l-**Letters; Medina, 20, 61; DP70, 2015; Enc. Mex., XI, 500.

Dominguez (Canabal), Jose Agapito

(Deceased Mar., 1970)

a-1913. **b-**Montecristo, Tabasco, *Gulf*, *Rural*. **c-**Completed primary, secondary and preparatory studies, attended the National Polytechnic Institute, no degree. **d-***Federal Deputy* from the State of Tabasco, Dist. 2, 1955–58, member of the Gran Comision, the Library Committee, and the First Committee on Balloting; *Federal Deputy* from the State of Tabasco, Dist. 2, 1967–70, member of the Gran Comision and the Committee on Budgets and Accounts (2nd year). **e-**Various positions in PRI; General Delegate of PRI to Yucatan. **f-**Adviser to the Secretary of Public Health; head of the Department of Health of the Department of the Federal District; Inspector General of the National Urban Mortgage Bank; advisor to the Secretary of Government; head of the Federal Office of the Treasury in San Luis Potosi, Yucatan, and Tabasco. **g-**Organized the First Congress of National Students in Frontera, Tabasco; First President of the National Federation of Technical Students at the National Polytechnic Institute. **i-**Nephew of the Tabascan political leader Garrido Canabal. **j-**None. **k-**Elected Governor of Tabasco in 1970, but died of a heart attack before taking office. **l-**DGF56, 28; DP70, 663; C de D, 1955–57, 42, 47, 56; C de D, 1967–69; DGF51, 337; Ind. Biog., 51.

Dominguez Cota, Isidro

a-May 15, 1907. **b-**Cananea, Sonora, *North*, *Urban*. **c-**Attended the National Military College. **d-***Federal Deputy* from Baja California del Sur, 1940–43. **e-**None. **f-**Private Secretary to the Governor of Baja California del Sur, 1932–37. **g-**None. **h-**Employed by the Light and Power Company of the Isthmus of Tehuantepec; author of articles on Baja California. **i-**Brother of Governor *Juan Dominguez Cota*. **k-**None. **l-**Peral, 229; C de D, 1940–42, 9.

Dominguez Cota, Juan

a-Dec. 16, 1888. **b-**La Purisima, Baja California, *Rural*. **c-**Early education unknown; none; no degree. **d-**None. **e-**None. **f-***Governor of Baja California del Sur*, 1935–37. **g-**None. **h-**Miner. **i-**Brother of *Isidro Dominguez Cota*. **j-**Joined the Revolution, 1910; fought against Huerta and Orozco; fought against Villa, 1914–15; fought against De la Huerta, 1923; commander of military operations in Morelos, 1927; fought against the Cristeros, 1928; supported the government against General Escobar, 1929; rank of Divisionary General, May 16, 1929; Commander of the 3rd Military Zone, La Paz, Baja California. **k-**Participated in the Cananea mining strike, 1906; commander of the troops who captured and executed General Serrano and his companions. **l-**Peral, 229; D de Y, 5 Sept. 1935; letter.

Dorado Baltazar, Emilia

a-Aug. 11, 1909. **b-**Guadalajara, Jalisco, *West*, *Urban*. **c-**Primary studies at the Three Friends School, Guadalajara, 1918–24; secondary studies, Normal School of Jalisco, Guadalajara, 1924–27; teaching certificate, Normal School of Jalisco, 1927–30; school teacher. **d-***Federal Deputy* from the State of

Jalisco, Dist. 3, 1970–73, member of the Social Action Committee (1st year), the Protocol Committee, the Sugar Industry Committee, and the Social Welfare Committee (1st year). e-Member of the PPS. f-None. g-Member of the SNTE. i-Married Leon Fernandez Caudillo. j-None. k-None. l-C de D, 1970–72, 111; *Directorio*, 1970–72.

Dovali Jaime, Antonio

a-Oct. 3, 1905. b-Zacatecas, Zacatecas, *East Central, Urban*. c-Preparatory studies at the National Preparatory School in Mexico, D.F., 1920–23; engineering studies at the National School of Engineering, UNAM, 1924–28; engineering degree, UNAM, June 18, 1930; Professor of Engineering (Bridges) at the National School of Engineering, UNAM, 1937–67; Director of the National School of Engineering, UNAM, 1959–66; member of the Governing Council of UNAM; Professor of Bridges at the Military College, 1954. d-None. e-None. f-Resident Subdirector of Construction of the Calles Railroad, Tamaulipas, 1929; Subdirector General of Railroad Construction, Secretariat of Public Works, 1941–42; Director General of Railroad Construction, Secretariat of Public Works, 1943–48; *Subsecretary of Public Works*, 1949–52; Director of Construction for the Chihuahua-Pacific Railroad, 1952–58; Director of the National Institute of Petroleum, 1966–70; *Director General of Petroleos Mexicanos*, 1970–76. g-None. h-Engineer of six different projects for the National Highway Commission, 1930–36; construction engineer for the National Railroads of Mexico, 1936–38. i-Brother of Alberto Dovali Jaime, a Mexican engineer who used innovative preformed concrete construction for public works projects; established numerous friendships during education at UNAM, including those with *Miguel Aleman, Antonio Carrillo Flores, Antonio Ortiz Mena, Raul Lopez Sanchez, Adolfo Orive Alba, Angel Carvajal, Javier Barros Sierra, Alfonso Guzman Neyra, Leopoldo Chavez, Jose Hernandez Teran, Gilberto Valenzuela* and *Luis E. Bracamontes*; son Antonio Dovali Ramos was Director General of Planning, Department of the Federal District, 1978. j-None. k-None. l-*Hoy*, 23 Jan. 1971, 10; DGF47, 143; Enc. Mex., Vol. III, 304; letter; HA, 22 Mar. 1971, 25; DP70, 668; DGF50, II, 377, 389; *Excelsior*, 31 Oct. 1978, 16.

Ducoing Gamba, Luis Humberto

a-May 15, 1937. b-San Luis de la Paz, Guanajuato, *West Central, Urban*. c-Primary studies at the San Luis Rey School, San Luis de la Paz (4 years); secondary studies at the Queretaro Institute, the Internado Mexico, Federal District, and the Lux Institute, Leon, Guanajuato; preparatory studies at the Leon Preparatory School, Leon; law degree with a specialty in administrative appeal, University of Guanajuato, 1960; Professor of Mexican History, World History and the Philosophy of History at the Preparatory School and University of Guanajuato, 1958–62. d-*Federal Deputy* from the State of Guanajuato, Dist. 6, 1964–67, member of the Bellas Artes Committee, the Sugar Industry Committee, and the First Instructive Section of the Grand Jury Committee; *Federal Deputy* from the State of Guanajuato, Dist. 9, 1970–73, Secretary of the Gran Comision, member of the First Section (Constitutional) of the Legislative Studies Committee, the First Government Committee, and the First Constitutional Affairs Committee; *Governor of Guanajuato*, 1973–79. e-Youth Director of PRI, Guanajuato; Secretary General of PRI, Guanajuato; special delegate of PRI to the municipal elections of Romita and Comonfort; general delegate of the CEN of PRI to Aguascalientes, Guerrero and Veracruz; Auxiliary Secretary to *Luis Echeverria* during presidential campaign, 1969–70; *Secretary of Political Action of the CEN of PRI*, 1970–73. f-Public Defender, Guanajuato; labor inspector for Guanajuato. g-President of the 1956–60 generation of lawyers, University of Guanajuato; student leader at the Leon Preparatory School; special delegate of the CNC to Veracruz, Sonora, and Nayarit; member of the National Committee of the CNC for Michoacan, Yucatan, Campeche, and Quintana Roo; private secretary to the Secretary General of the CNC; Secretary of Education Action, CEN of the CNC; President of the Political Committee of the CNC, 1972. h-None. i-Married Martha Nieto. j-None. k-None. l-C de D, 1964–66, 79, 87, 89; *Directorio*, 1970–72; *Excelsior*, 27 Feb. 1973, 12; C de D, 1970–72, 111; HA, 24 Sept. 1973, 32, 34, 36; Enc. Mex., Annual, 1977, 544.

Dupre Ceniceros, Enrique

a-1913. b-Durango, *West*. c-Eningeering degree, National School of Engineering, UNAM, 1932–36. d-*Federal Deputy* from the State of Durango, Dist. 2, 1952–55; member of the Committee on National Waters and Irrigation, the Committee on the Agrarian Department, and the Committee on Social Welfare; *Senator* from the State of Durango, 1958–62; member of the Gran Comision, President of the Senate (1st year); President of the First Committee on Government; President of the Special Committee on Forests and member of the Second Committee on Ejidos; *Governor of Durango*, 1962–66. e-Inactive in PRI since 1967. f-Employed in the Department of Agrarian Affairs. g-Member and official of the CNC. h-Attended the Inter-American Conference on Conservation, Washington, D.C., 1948; author of a pamphlet on Mexican forest problems published by the U.S. Department of State, 1949. j-None.

k-Resigned from the governorship, August 4, 1966. **l**-G of M, 10; C de D, 1952–54, 9; C de S, 1964, 55; Func., 198; NYT, 6 Aug. 1966, 3.

Dzib Cardozo, Jose de Jesus

a-Jan. 12, 1921. **b**-Campeche, Campeche, *Gulf, Urban*. **c**-Preparatory studies at the National Preparatory School in Mexico, D.F., 1940–44; law degree from the National School of Law, UNAM; studied French at the Alianza Francesa in Mexico, D.F.; Professor of Law, French, and Spanish Language and Literature at the University of Campeche; Professor of Oceanography, Meteorology, and Fishing Legislation, Campeche Practical School of Fishing; Professor of Spanish and Spanish Literature, Women's University of Veracruz; Rector of the University of Campeche, 1961–62. **d**-None. **e**-None. **f**-Private Secretary to *Rafael Matos Escobedo*, Justice of the Supreme Court of Mexico; Director of the Office of Regulation and Administration of Goods and Chattels, Secretariat of National Patrimony; Director of the Department for the Inspection of Goods and Chattels, Secretariat of National Patrimony; Agent of the Ministerio Publico (Auxiliary) of the Attorney General of Mexico, 1962–64; Secretary General of Government of the State of Campeche under Governor *Trueba Urbina*, 1955–61; Assistant Attorney General of the Federal District and Federal Territorities (2), 1964–70, and 1970–76. **g**-None. **h**-Author of several articles; librarian during student days in the Department of Social Action, Department of the Federal District. **j**-None. **k**-None. **l**-DPE70, 162; DBM68, 206; letter; DGF56, 90.

Echeverria Alvarez, Luis

a-Jan. 17, 1922. **b**-Federal District, *Federal District, Urban*. **c**-Primary studies in Mexico City and Ciudad Victoria, Tamaulipas; secondary in Mexico City; preparatory at the National Preparatory School, 1938–40; special studies in Chile, Argentina, Paris, and the United States on a scholarship, 1941; law studies from the National School of Law, UNAM, 1940–44; law degree, Aug., 1945, with a thesis on "The Balance of Power System and the Society of Nations;" Professor of Legal Theory at the National School of Law, UNAM, 1947–49. **d**-*President of Mexico*, 1970–76. **e**-Joined PRI in Mar., 1946; Private Secretary to the President of the National Executive Committee of PRI, *Rodolfo Sanchez Taboada*, Dec. 1946; Assistant Secretary to the Regional Director of PRI for the Federal District, *Rodolfo Sanchez Taboada*, Mar. to Dec., 1946; Platform Adviser to PRI, 1946; *Secretary of Press and Publicity of the CEN of PRI*, 1946–52; General Delegate of the CEN of PRI, 1948; President of the Regional Committee of the State of Guanajuato; Representative of the CEN of PRI to *Sanchez Colin's* campaign for Gover-

nor of Mexico, 1951; *Oficial Mayor of PRI*, 1957–58. **f**-Director of Accounts for the Secretariat of the Navy, 1952–54; *Oficial Mayor of the Secretariat of Public Education*, 1954–57; *Subsecretary of Government*, 1958–63; *Subsecretary in Charge of the Secretariat of Government*, 1964; *Secretary of Government*, 1964–70; Ambassador to UNESCO, 1977–78; Ambassador to Australia, 1978– . **g**-Student delegate to the Free World Youth Association, 1943; founder of Students for Revolutionary Action, 1947. **h**-None. **i**-Brother, Eduardo, was a member of the Advisory Council of the IEPES of PRI and President of the Technical Council of the Subsecretary of Public Health, 1974; brother, *Rodolfo*, was Director General of the National Cinema Bank; nephew, *Rodolfo Echeverria, Jr.*, was Oficial Mayor of PRI and a Federal Deputy; political disciple of *Rodolfo Sanchez Taboada*; studied under *Alfonso Noriega* and *Luis Garrido Diaz* at the National University; knew *Luis M. Farias* as a student at UNAM; son-in-law of Jose Zuno Hernandez, former governor of Jalisco. **j**-None. **k**-Delivered the nomination speech for *Adolfo Lopez Mateos* before PRI, Nov. 17, 1957. **l**-Enc. Mex., III, 354; DPE65, 13; G of S, 14; Fuentes Diaz, 265; DGF56, 299; WWMG, 15; DBM70, 191; HA, 17 Dec. 1964, 18; DPE61, 11; Morton, 93; LA, 27 Oct. 1978, 330; *Excelsior*, 18 Feb. 1977, 6.

Echeverria Alvarez, Rodolfo

b-Federal District, *Federal District, Urban*. **c**-Law degree from the Escuela Libre de Derecho, October 4, 1940, with a thesis on the intervention of the state in the functions of credit institutions; law degree from the National School of Law, UNAM, 1944. **d**-*Federal Deputy* from the Federal District, Dist. 18, 1952–55, Vice President of the Chamber of Deputies, Oct. 1953, member of the First Labor Committee, the Second Balloting Committee, the Film Industry Committee, and the Committee on Bellas Artes (3 years); substitute member of the Radio and Television Industry Committee; *Federal Deputy* from the Federal District, Dist. 6, 1961–64, President of the Chamber of Deputies, member of the Fifth Section of the Legislative Studies Committee (Labor), the Film Industry Committee; substitute member of the First Constitutional Affairs Committee; *Alternate Senator* for the Federal District, 1964–70. **e**-Member of the Advisory Council for Ideology and Program of the IEPES of PRI, 1972. **f**-Director General of the National Cinema Bank, 1970–76; Private Secretary to *Ernesto P. Uruchurtu*. **g**-Director General of the Mexican Actors Union. **h**-Professional actor, worked under the name Rodolfo Landa; co-founder of the University Theater at UNAM. **i**-Brother of President *Luis Echeverria*; father of *Rodolfo Echeverria Jr.*, Oficial Mayor of

PRI; student of *Alfonso Noriega* at UNAM; father a government employee. **j**-None. **k**-None. **l**-C de D, 1954, 9; C de D, 1961–63, 76; G of Nl, 17; DBM68, 368; letter; *Excelsior*, 16 Mar. 1973, 22.

Echeverria Castellot, Eugenio

a-1924. **b**-Ciudad del Carmen, Campeche, *Gulf, Urban*. **c**-Early education unknown; degree in petroleum engineering, University of Campeche, 1947, with a thesis on the "Cost of Building a Petroleum Pipeline from the Teapa, Tabasco, Oilfields to Campeche." **d**-Mayor of Campeche, 1961; *Governor of Campeche*, 1979– . **e**-Joined PRI, 1957. **f**-Began governmental career, 1947; Director of Public Works for the State of Campeche (25 years). **g**-None. **h**-None. **i**-Distinguished student of *Maria Lavalle Urbina*; student supporter of *Carlos Sansores Perez* when the latter was President of the Campeche Student Federation; *Rafael Rodriguez Barrera*, Governor of Campeche, 1973–79, was private secretary to Echeverria Castellot as mayor of Campeche. **j**-None. **k**-Precandidate for Governor of Campeche, 1961 and 1967. **l**-*Excelsior*, 19 Dec. 1978, 22; *Latin America*, 26 Jan. 1979, 30; *Excelsior*, 6 Jan. 1979, 1, 11.

Echeverria Ruiz, Jr., Rodolfo

c-Law degree from the National School of Law, UNAM; postgraduate work in the fields of politics and economics, London, England. **d**-*Federal Deputy* from the Federal District, Dist. 24, 1973–76. **e**-Joined PRI, 1961; Director of the Youth section for the sixth electoral district of the Federal District of PRI; Secretary of Social Action of Youth of PRI for the Federal District; Director of the Youth Section of PRI for the Federal District; official orator for the *Diaz Ordaz* campaign, 1964; Auxiliary Secretary to the National Executive Committee of PRI attached to the IEPES; *Director of the National Youth Sector of the CEN of PRI*, 1965; *Oficial Mayor of PRI*, 1970–76. **f**-Representative of the State of Hidalgo in Mexico, D.F., 1969–70; Secretary to Senator *Sanchez Vite* on the Federal Electoral Commission; Coordinating Secretary of the Gran Comision of the Senate; *Subsecretary of Government (2)*, 1976–78; *Subsecretary of Labor*, 1978– . **g**-None. **h**-Second place award for oratory, 1963. **i**-Son of *Rodolfo Echeverria* and nephew of *Luis Echeverria*; married De los Angeles Andrade. **j**-None. **k**-None. **l**-HA, 21 Dec. 1970, 21; G of NL, 17; *Excelsior*, 28 Feb. 1973, 19; *Excelsior*, 16 Mar. 1973, 22; *Excelsior*, 21 July 1973, 12.

Elizondo, Juan Manuel

a-1905. **b**-Monterrey, Nuevo Leon, *North, Leon*. **c**-Primary studies in Monterrey; law student at UNAM, 1930s, but did not complete his studies. **d**-*Senator* from Nuevo Leon, 1946–52, member of

the First Balloting Group, the Second Labor Committee and the Immigration Committee, alternate member of the Social Welfare Committee. **e**-One-time member of the Mexican Communist Party; member of the Executive Committee of the Popular Party (later the PPS), 1947. **f**-Delegate from Mexico to the International Labor Organization conference; advisor to the Mexican Labor delegation in Geneva, 1947. **g**-Secretary General of the Union of Metalurgical Miners. **i**-Friend of *Vicente Lombardo Toledano*; father a local politician in Monterrey. **j**-None. **k**-Tried to introduce agricultural reforms as a senator, but opposed openly by *Rodolfo Sanchez Taboada*, president of the CEN of PRI, 1946–52; expelled from PRI in Jan., 1946 for joining the Popular Party. **l**-*Excelsior*, 17 Nov. 1949; DGF47, 21; DGF51, 7, 13, 14; Morton, 59–60; C de S, 1946–52, 36; HA, 10 Oct. 1947, 5; *Excelsior*, 16 Nov. 1974, 9; letter; *Excelsior*, 15 Apr. 1976, 16; Medina, 20,138.

Elizondo (Lozano), Eduardo Angel

a-Dec. 7, 1922. **b**-Monterrey, Nuevo Leon, *North, Urban*. **c**-Law degree from the University of Nuevo Leon, 1945; Professor at the University of Nuevo Leon, 1945–50; Professor at the Institute of Technology and of Higher Education, Monterrey; Rector of the University of Nuevo Leon, 1965–67. **d**-*Governor of Nuevo Leon*, 1967–70. **e**-None. **f**-Agent of the Ministerio Publico, 1945–46; public defender, 1944; Treasurer General of the State of Nuevo Leon, 1961–65; Judge of the Superior Tribunal of Justice of the State of Nuevo Leon, 1973–74. **g**-None. **h**-Adviser to various industries in the field of taxation, 1945–67; practicing lawyer in the firm of Santos de la Garza, 1950; President of the Regional Banks of the North (Garza-Sada chain). **j**-None. **k**-Resigned from the Governorship of Nuevo Leon after major student riots in opposition to his imposing his own choice of Rector of the University of Nuevo Leon. **l**-PdM, 104; DBM68, 212–13; DBM70, 195; G of NL, 15; *Excelsior*, 12 Jan. 1973, 28; *Excelsior*, 24 Feb. 1967, 16.

Elorduy, Aquiles

(Deceased August, 1964)
a-Sept. 20, 1875. **b**-Aguascalientes, Aguascalientes, *West, Urban*. **c**-Primary studies in Sombrerete, Zacatecas, and at the Colegio Franco-Espanol, Mexico City; preparatory at the National Preparatory School; law degree from the National School of Law, UNAM, September 28, 1903; professor at the National School of Law, UNAM; Director of the National School of Law, UNAM, 1925, 1927–29. **d**-Federal deputy when the Chamber was dissolved by Victoriano Huerta, 1912–14; local deputy to the state legislature of Zacatecas; *Federal Deputy* from

the State of Aguascalientes, Dist. 1, 1946–49, member of the Committee on the Diplomatic Service; *Senator* from the State of Aguascalientes, 1952–58, member of the Second Committee on Justice and the Second Group of the Balloting Committee, and substitute member of the Colonization Committee and the First Committee on Tariffs and Foreign Trade. **e-**One of the few Mexican congressmen to be elected to the Congress on different party tickets, having been the candidate of the National Action Party as Federal Deputy and candidate of the PRI as Senator; joined PAN, 1940; founder of the anti-reelectionist center in Mexico, D.F., 1909. **f-**Delegate to the Sixth Pan American Conference in Havana, Cuba, 1928. **g-**None. **h-**Wrote for *Siempre* and *Excelsior* and author of a three-act comedy, 1931; founder of the magazine *La Reaccion*. **i-**Student of Justo Sierra; professor and friend of many prominent political leaders, including *Miguel Aleman*, *Mariano Ramirez Vazquez*, *Antonio Carrillo Flores* and *Alejandro Gomez Arias*. **j-**None. **k-**Donated salaries as a federal deputy and senator to the school system in Aguascalientes. **l-**WWM45, 36; C de D, 1946–48, 71; DGF56, 9, 10, 11, 13; DP70, 700; Enc. Mex., III, 417; Morton, 54–56, 73–75; HA, 26 Sept. 1976, 25.

Encinas Johnson, Luis

a-Oct. 23, 1912. **b-**Hermosillo, Sonora, *North*, *Urban*. **c-**Teaching certificate, 1922; law degree from the National School of Law, UNAM, June, 1935; Rector of the University of Sonora, 1956–61. **d-**Local deputy to the state legislature of Sonora, 1956; Mayor of Ciudad Obregon, Sonora; *Governor of Sonora*, 1961–67. **e-**President of the Regional Committee of PRM for the State of Sonora. **f-**Director of the State Department of Labor, State of Sonora; Deputy Prosecuting Attorney for the State of Sonora; Attorney General of Sonora; Justice of the Superior Tribunal of Justice of Sonora; Secretary General of Government of the State of Sonora under Governor *Ignacio Soto*, 1950–55; member of the Federal Board of Conciliation and Arbitration for the Federal District; Director General of the National Bank of Agricultural Credit, 1970–75. **g-**None. **h-**Practicing attorney, 1967–70; author of several books on political and social problems in Mexico. **i-**Father, Luis Encinas, was Mayor of Hermosillo, 1921–22. **j-**None. **k-**Retired from public life midway during his career because of health; defeated Fausto Acosta Romo for the PRI gubernatorial nomination, 1967; *Proceso* accused him of representing the interests of large landowners in Sonora. **l-**G of S, 23; DGF56, 100; HA, 14 Dec. 1970, 25; Tucker, 429; WWMG, 16; letter; Anderson, 112–13; HA, 29 Apr. 1974, 13; NYT, 24 Mar. 1967, 2; NYT, 27 Mar. 1967, 8; *Excelsior*, 11 Jan. 1975, 1; *Proceso*, 7 Aug. 1978, 17; Moncada, 12ff.

Enriquez Coyro Jr., Ernesto

a-Nov. 29, 1901. **b-**Federal District, *Federal District*, *Urban*. **c-**Primary studies in Mexico, D.F.; secondary studies at the Technical Institute in Mexico, D.F.; attended the University of Catalona; Bachelor of Science from the University of Barcelona, Spain, 1918; studied law at the Escuela Libre de Derecho, 1919–24, degree in Nov., 1924; Professor of Music History and of Esthetics at UNAM, 1931–44; Professor of International Public Law at the National School of Law, UNAM, 1941–50; participated in organizing the new faculty of music at the UNAM, 1930; founder and Director of the School of Political and Social Sciences, UNAM, 1950–52; Professor of the History of Political Ideas, 1961. **d-**None. **e-**None. **f-**Consultant to the Diplomatic Department of the Secretariat of Foreign Relations, 1938–40; advisor to the Secretary of Public Education; head of the Department of Legal Affairs of the Secretariat of Foreign Relations, 1941–45; *Oficial Mayor of the Secretariat of Public Education*, 1945–46; Director of Administrative Inspection of the Secretariat of National Patrimony; in charge of the reorganization of the Secretariat of National Patrimony, 1950; Subdirector (Administrative) of the Mexican Institute of Social Security, 1952–58; *Subsecretary of Public Education*, 1958–64. **g-**None. **h-**Private law practice, 1925–40; represented Mexico at various international conferences; assistant agent for the Mexican-United States Claims Commission, 1935–38; author of many books on international law and on Mexico. **i-**Attended the Escuela Libre de Derecho with *Javier Gaxiola* and *Jose Angel Ceniceros*; practiced law with *Ceniceros*, who helped him obtain his first job as an agent for the Mexican-United States claims commission; grandfather was Governor of Mexico and a Senator under Porfirio Diaz; served in various positions under *Jaime Torres Bodet*. **j-**None. **k-**None. **l-**Letter; HA, 22 Dec. 1958, 7; D de Y, 3 Dec. 1958, 10; Peral, 244; DGF47, 269; WWM45, 37; DBM68, 215–16; DBM70, 196–97.

Enriquez (Rodriguez), Enrique A.

(Deceased Mar. 22, 1974)
a-July 15, 1887. **b-**Toluca, Mexico, *West Central*, *Urban*. **c-**Primary and secondary studies in Toluca; law degree from the Institute of Arts and Sciences of Mexico, Toluca; professor of law at the Institute of Arts and Sciences of Mexico (19 years); Director of the Institute of Arts and Sciences of Mexico, 1923–25. **d-**Deputy to the Constitutional Convention from the State of Mexico, Dist. No. 14, 1916–17; Federal Deputy from the State of Mexico, 1926–28. **e-**None. **f-**Secretary of the Mexican legation to Colombia and Uruguay; Charge d'Affaires of the Mexican Embassy in Argentina; Agent of the Ministerio Publico; Minister to Costa Rica; Justice of the Superior Court of

the Federal District and Federal Territories, 1956. **g-**None. **h-**None. **i-**Married Maria de Jesus Escallon. **j-**Career army officer; military judge; reached rank of brigadier general; retired 1957; member of the Legion of Honor. **k-**None. **l-**HA, 1 Apr. 1974; DGF56, 514.

Enriquez Savignac, Antonio

a-Aug. 17, 1931. **b-**Mexico, D.F., *Federal District, Urban*. **c-**Early education unknown; degree in business administration from Ottawa University, June 5, 1955; MBA degree, Graduate School of Business Administration, Harvard University, June, 1957; studies on a Bank of Mexico Fellowship. **d-**None. **e-**None. **f-**Subdirector, Department of Economic Studies, Bank of Commerce, 1955; *Subsecretary of Tourism and Planning*, 1976–77. **g-**None. **h-**Subdirector of Public Relations, American Smelting, New York, 1957–60; Director of Research and Marketing, Young and Rubicon, S.A., 1960. **j-**None. **k-**None. **l-**BdM, 108; HA, 14 Nov. 1977, 22.

Escobar Munoz, Ernesto
(Deceased)
a-1902. **b-**Mexico, D.F., *Federal District, Urban*. **c-**Primary studies in Mexico City; law degree from the National School of Law, UNAM, 1928–32. **d-***Governor of Morelos*, 1946–52. **e-**None. **f-**Secretary General of Government of the state of Morelos, 1942–46, under Governor *Jesus Castillo Lopez*. **g-**None. **h-**Practicing lawyer. **i-**Co-student at UNAM with *Jesus Castillo Lopez*. **j-**None. **k-**None. **l-**Letters; DGF51, 90; Lopez, 320.

Escudero Alvarez, Hiram
a-Oct. 11, 1935. **b-**Morelia, Michoacan, *West Central, Urban*. **c-**Primary studies at the Instituto Patria, Federal District, 1943–49; secondary and preparatory studies, Instituto Patria, 1949–51, 1951–53; studied at the School of Philosophy, UNAM, 1953–55; studied law at Escuela Libre de Derecho, 1954–58, degree in 1960 with his thesis on "The Confession in Criminal Cases;" graduate studies in psychology; Professor of Penal Law. **d-***Alternate Federal Deputy* from the Federal District, Dist. 2, 1964–67; *Federal Deputy* (Party Deputy for PAN), 1970–73, member of the Cultural Affairs Committee; the Legislative Studies Committee (Seventh Section on Commerce and Credit), and the Small Agricultural Properties Committee. **e-**Member of PAN; President of the National Youth Section of PAN. **f-**None. **g-**None. **h-**Practicing lawyer specializing in banking matters; fluent in English. **i-**Father, an engineer; married Silvia Mendoza. **j-**None. **k-**None. **l-**C de D, 1970–72, 14; *Directorio*, 1970–72; DJBM, 41.

Esparza Reyes, J. Refugio
a-Aug. 23, 1921. **b-**Villa Juarez, Aguascalientes, *West, Rural*. **c-**Early education unknown; graduate of the Normal School of San Marcos, Zacatecas, 1938–43; advanced studies at the Higher Normal School in technical education; rural school teacher for many years; professor at the Normal School of San Marcos; Director of Rural Boarding School students. **d-**Local deputy to the State Legislature of Aguascalientes, 1962; *Federal Deputy* from the State of Aguascalientes, Dist. 2, 1967–70, member of the First Balloting Committee; *Governor of Aguascalientes*, 1974–80. **e-**Secretary General of PRI for the State of Aguascalientes, 1962–68. **f-**Private Secretary to *Augusto Gomez Villanueva*, Secretary General of the CNC, 1968–70; *Oficial Mayor of the Department of Agrarian Affairs and Colonization*, 1970–74. **g-**Secretary of the Third Delegation of the First Section of the SNTE, 1946–48; Secretary of Social Action of Section One, SNTE, 1948–50; Secretary General of Section One, SNTE, 1950–52; Secretary of the National Inspection Committee, SNTE, 1966–68; President of the Political Committee of the SNTE, 1963–65; member of the Executive Council of the SNTE, 1970–74. **h-**None. **i-**Parents were peasants. **j-**None. **k-**None. **l-**C de D, 1967–69, 77; *Excelsior*, 30 Jan. 1974, 1; HA, 11 Feb. 1974, 38; MGF69, 89; HA, 21 Dec. 1970, 24; *Excelsior*, 17 July, 1978, 1, 18–20; Enc. Mex., Annual, 1977.

Esperon, Roberto
a-1957. **b-**Puebla, Puebla, *East Central, Urban*. **c-**Primary and secondary studies; studies in the technical science of information; preparatory school teacher. **d-**None. **e-**Joined the Socialist Workers Party, 1974; Director of *El Insurgente Socialista* (official PST paper); Secretary of Information, Political Education and Publicity of the Executive Committee of the PST; President of the National Committee of Electoral Affairs of the Executive Committee of the PST, 1979; member of the Central Committee of the Executive Committee of the PST, 1979. **f-**None. **g-**None. **h-**Journalist; editorial writer for *Excelsior*. **j-**None. **k-**None. **l-**HA, 30 Apr. 1979, IX.

Espino de la O., Everardo
a-Aug. 5, 1938. **b-**Chihuahua, Chihuahua, *North, Urban*. **c-**Early education unknown; law degree from the National School of Law, UNAM; MA in economics and public administration, Harvard University. **d-**None. **e-**Subdirector of the IEPES of the CEN of PRI, 1975–76, under *Julio Rodolfo Moctezuma Cid*. **f-**Official of the International Monetary Fund; Subdirector of Finances, Pemex; Subdirector of Credit, Secretariat of the Treasury; Advisor to the National Sugar Commission; Advisor to the Secretariat of the Treasury; Director General of the Na-

tional Rural Credit Bank, 1976– . **g**-None. **j**-None. **k**-None. **l**-*Excelsior*, 1 Dec. 1976.

Espinosa de los Monteros, Antonio
(Deceased Sept. 19, 1959)
a-Jan. 15, 1903. **b**-Sinaloa, *West*. **c**-Preparatory at Gettysburg Academy, Pennsylvania; Sacred Heart College, Denver, Colorado; Bachelor of Science from Gettysburg College, 1925; Master's degree from Harvard University, 1927; Professor of Economics, 1927–31; Professor at the National University, 1929–34. **d**-None. **e**-None. **f**-Head of the Economics Library and Archives, Secretariat of the Treasury, 1929–30; head of the Department of Alcohol for the Secretariat of the Treasury, 1931–32; Chief of the Department of Economic Studies for the Secretariat of Industry and Commerce, 1933–36; Gerente of Nacional Financiera; *Director General of the National Finance Bank*, 1935–40 and 1940–45; *Subsecretary of the Treasury*, 1940; *Ambassador to the United States*, 1945–48. **g**-None. **h**-Economist, Secretariat of the Treasury, 1927–28; economist, Bureau of Statistics, 1928–29, 1932–33; one of the founders of Nacional Financiera; major investor in Altos Hornos, 1947; one of the founders of the National School of Economics, UNAM; author of several books. **i**-Father a druggist; roomed together at Harvard with *Daniel Cosio Villegas*; close friend of *Jesus Silva Herzog*. **j**-None. **k**-Director of General *Henriquez Guzman's* campaign for President of Mexico, 1951–52. **l**-WWM45, 37–38; DP731; HA, 21 Sept. 1945, 6; Enc. Mex., III, 532; Novo, 652; NYT, 9 Sept. 1940, 5; NYT, 29 Dec. 1948, 9; NYT, 15 July 1944, 11; Lopez, 326; Alonso, 227, 231, 167–68.

Espinosa de los Reyes Sanchez, Jorge
a-June 20, 1920. **b**-Federal District, *Federal District, Urban*. **c**-Economics degree from the National School of Economics, UNAM, 1940–44; London School of Economics, 1945–47; Professor of Economics at Mexico City College, 1948–49, 1952–53; Professor of Economics at UNAM, 1949, 1951–55; Professor of Economics at the Technical Institute of Mexico, 1953–54; Professor at CEMLA, 1954–59. **d**-None. **e**-None. **f**-Subchief of the Department of Credit in the National Bank of Agricultural Credit, 1953–54; Program Director for the National Investment Commission, 1954–58; Subdirector of the Investment Commission for the Secretariat of the Presidency, 1958–59; Director General of Industries, 1959–61; *Oficial Mayor of the Secretariat of Industry and Commerce*, 1961–64; *Subdirector of Petroleos Mexicanos*, 1965–70; *Subdirector of Petroleos Mexicanos*, 1971–76; Subdirector General of the Bank of Mexico (2), 1976–77; *Director General of the National Finance Bank*, 1977– . **g**-None.

h-Assistant Economist, Bank of Mexico, 1942–44; economist for the Department of Economic Statistics, Bank of Mexico, 1947–48; economist and investigator for the Department of Financial Studies, Nacional Financiera, 1948–51. **i**-Friends with *Octaviano Campos Salas*, *Alfredo Navarrete*, and *Julian Diaz Arias* at the National School of Economics; brother of *Mario Espinosa de los Reyes*. **j**-None. **k**-None. **l**-Enc. Mex., III, 532; HA, 4 Jan. 1965, 27; letters; DPE61, 66; BdeM, 115; WWMG, 16; DGF56, 59; DGF69; *Excelsior*, 24 Nov. 1977, 15.

Espinosa de los Reyes Sanchez, Mario
a-Feb. 2, 1930. **b**-Federal District, *Federal District, Urban*. **c**-Degree in economics from the Technological Institute of Mexico; attended the English Language Institute, Harvard University, 1957; advanced studies, Harvard University, 1958. **d**-None. **e**-None. **f**-Head of the Tariff Department, Secretariat of the Treasury, 1965; Ambassador to the Latin American Free Trade Zone and to Uruguay, 1965–70; Director-in-Chief of the Secretariat of Foreign Affairs, 1970–76. **g**-None. **h**-Investigator for the Bank of Mexico, 1955; Economist, Economic Commission for Latin America, 1956. **j**-None. **k**-None. **l**-DPE71, 6; DPE65, 60; DPE61, 42; BdM, 115–16.

Espinosa Gutierrez, Fernando
(Deceased Apr. 3, 1966)
a-Nov. 10, 1919. **b**-Queretaro, Queretaro, *East Central, Urban*. **c**-Primary and secondary schools in Queretaro, Queretaro; preparatory studies at the National Preparatory School, 1936–37; civil engineering degree from the National School of Engineering, UNAM, 1942; studies toward a Master of Arts in Mathematics, 1942; Professor of Laboratory Physics, National Preparatory School, 1938–42; Professor of Trigonometry, Analytical Geometry, and Calculus, National Preparatory School, 1940–44; Professor at the School of Engineering, UNAM, 1943–48; Professor of Mechanics and Fluids, School of Engineering, UNAM, 1944. **d**-*Alternate Senator* from the State of Queretaro, 1964. **e**-None. **f**-Engineer, Office of Experimental Engineering, National Irrigation Commission, 1942–44; Director General of Highways, Secretariat of Public Works, 1953; Technical Adviser to the Subsecretary of Public Works, 1954–55; Director of Technical Advisers, Secretariat of Public Works, 1956–58; Director General of Projects and Laboratories, Secretariat of Public Works, 1959–64; *Subsecretary of Public Works*, Dec. 23, 1964, to 1966. **g**-None. **h**-Engineer, Director of Construction, Gerente of Roads, Bridges, and Railroads for Ingenieros Civiles, S.A., 1944–53. **i**-Friends of *Javier Barros Sierra* and *Fernando Hiriart Balderama* at UNAM; son Enrique Espinosa works for the Bank of Mexico. **j**-None. **k**-None.

l-Letter; HA, 4 Jan. 1965, 7; *Libro de Oro*, xxiv; DPE65, 116; DPE61, 84; MGF69, 106; WWMG. 16; DGF56.

Espinosa Michel, J. Jesus
(Deceased 1959)
a-1901. b-Rancheria Agua Zarca, Coquimatlan, Colima, *West*, *Rural*. c-Early education unknown; none. d-Local deputy to the state legislature of Colima; Mayor of Coquimatlan, 1935; *Federal Deputy* from Colima, Dist. 2, 1940–43, member of the First Balloting Committee; *Federal Deputy* from Colima, Dist. 2, 1946–49, member of the Petroleum Committee, substitute member of the Second Ejido Committee. e-None. f-Inspector General of Police, Colima. g-None. h-Ejidatario for many years, retired from politics in 1949 to work his farm. j-Fought with Francisco Villa during the Revolution; fought against the De la Huerta rebellion under General Higinio Alvarez in 1923. l-Enc. Mex., III, 532; C de D, 1946–48, 71; C de D, 1940–42; DP70, 731; DGF47, 6.

Espinosa Porset, Ernesto
(Deceased July 25, 1972)
a-May 3, 1887. b-Zinapecuaro, Michoacan, *West Central*, *Rural*. c-Early education unknown; no degree. d-None. e-None. f-Auditor General of the Department of Pensions, Secretariat of the Treasury, 1932; Head of the Credit Department of the Bank of Mexico, 1932–38; *Subdirector General of the Bank of Mexico*, 1938–40, 1940–46, 1946–52, 1952–58, 1958–64, and 1964–70; Secretary of the Administrative Council of the Bank of Mexico, 1947–68. g-None. h-Probationer for the Central Bank of Mexico, 1904; Assistant in the Accounts and Checking Department, Central Bank of Mexico, 1906; Head of the Department of Cheques, El Descuente Espanol, S.A., Secretary to the Director, El Descuente Espanol, S.A.; Assistant Accountant, El Descuente Espanol, S.A.; Bookkeeper, El Descuente Espanol, S.A.; Cashier, Banco Espanol Refaccionario; Adviser to Financiera Bancamex, 1970–72; author of several books on banking in Mexico. j-None. k-None. l-Letter; DGF50, II, 10–11, 211, 197; DGF51, II, 585, 467; DBM68, 22–23.

Espinosa Rivera, Jose
a-1927. b-Federal District, *Federal District*, *Urban*. c-Certified Public Accountant, degree from the National University. d-None. e-*Secretary of Finances for the National Executive Committee of PRI*, 1964–69. f-Head of the Department for Regional Economic Investment for the Secretariat of the Treasury, 1970–72. g-None. h-Investigator for the Department of Treasury Studies, Secretariat of the Treasury; Fiscal Investigator for the Department of Treasury Studies; Head of the Economic Studies Department for the Patronato del Valle Mezquital; tax adviser to the State Governments of Durango, Sonora, Chihuahua, Tamaulipas, San Luis Potosi, Campeche, Tabasco, and Nayarit. j-None. l-HA, 21 Dec. 1964, 10; DPE70, 35; WWMG, 16.

Espinosa Sanchez, Juventino
a-Jan. 26, 1891. b-Tecuala, Nayarit, *West*, *Rural*. c-Early education unknown; no degree. d-*Governor of Nayarit*, 1938–41. e-None. f-Substitute Governor of Nayarit, 1931. g-None. h-None. i-Son, *Juventino Jr.*, served as an Alternate Federal Deputy for Nayarit, Dist. 1, 1952–55. j-Joined the Revolution, 1913; career military officer; Brigadier General, May 16, 1929; Military Zone Commander in the Northeast; Commander of the 14th Military Zone, Aguascalientes, Aguascalientes, 1956; Rank of Divisionary General. l-Peral, 253; DGF56, 202; Enc. Mex., III, 531; C de D, 1952–54, 10; Lopez, 327.

Esponda, Juan M.
a-1897. b-Tuxtla Gutierrez, Chiapas, *South*, *Urban*. c-Primary studies in Tuxtla Gutierrez; law degree. d-Federal Deputy from Chiapas, 1928–30; Federal Deputy from the State of Chiapas, 1930–32; Federal Deputy from the State of Chiapas, 1932–34; *Senator* from the State of Chiapas, 1934–40; *Federal Deputy* from the State of Chiapas, Dist. 2, 1943–44; *Governor of Chiapas*, 1944–46. e-None. f-Director of the office of Presidential Affairs under General Obregon; Judge of the Superior Tribunal of Justice of the State of Chiapas; Secretary General of Government of the State of Chiapas, 1940–43, under Governor *Rafael P. Gamboa*. g-None. j-Joined the Constitutionalists in 1915 under General *Jesus A. Castro*; served under *Blas Corral Martinez*. k-Did not complete term as Governor; Anderson suggests he resigned because of protests over his imposing municipal appointments. l-HA, 7 Dec. 1946, 30; HA, 15 Dec. 1944, viii; letter; C de D, 1943–45; HA, 29 Oct. 1943, 14; DBdeC, 79; Enc. Mex., 1977, III, 310; Anderson.

Esquivel de Quintana, Josefina
a-Mar. 19, 1918. b-Valle de Bravo, Mexico, *West Central*, *Urban*. c-Primary studies in the Valle de Bravo; completed 4th grade; no degree. d-*Federal Deputy* from the State of Mexico, Dist. No. 2, 1976–79, member of the Second Section of the Social Action Committee, and member of the Section of Female Peasant Development of the Agrarian Affairs Committee. e-None. f-None. g-Began participating in peasant organizations in 1932; Secretary of Feminine Action of the League of Agrarian Committees, State of Mexico; Secretary of Feminine Action of the Regional Peasant Committee, Valle de Bravo, 1963–70. i-Parents were peasants. j-None. k-None.

l-D de C, 1976–79, 4, 8; *Excelsior*, 22 Aug. 1976, 29; C de D, 1976–79, 21.

Esquivel Mendez, Eligio
(Deceased Dec. 17, 1964)
a-1908. b-Merida, Yucatan, *Gulf*, *Urban*. c-Engineering degree from the National School of Engineering, UNAM, 1933. d-*Governor of Baja California del Norte*, 1959–64. e-None. f-Director of Construction on the Morelos Dam, the Matamoros Dam, and other projects; engineer on hydroelectric project in Bolivia; Director of the engineering commission to provide South America with technical assistance, 1939–40; head of the Mexicali Irrigation District, including the Colorado River, for the Secretariat of Hydraulic Resources, 1943–57. g-None. h-None. j-None. k-Retired from 1957–59 for medical treatment resulting from a heart attack in 1957; won PRI nomination because of expertise with the irrigation problems in his state and his ties with ranchers' associations. l-G of M, 15–16; DP70, 733–34; DGF51, I, 434; Enc. Mex., III, 537; HA, 28 Dec. 1964, 14; NYT, 11 Aug. 1959, 8; NYT, 2 Nov. 1959, 28.

Estrada Iturbide, Miguel
a-Nov. 17, 1908. b-Morelia, Michoacan, *West Central*, *Urban*. c-Studies in law at the Colegio Libre del Derecho, Morelia; law degree, Colegio Civil of Guanajuato, Guanajuato, 1932. d-Candidate for Federal Deputy from Michoacan; candidate for Senator from Michoacan; *Federal Deputy* from the State of Michoacan, Dist. 5, 1964–67. e-Founder of PAN in Michoacan; founding member of PAN, 1939; member of the National Council of PAN; Director of the Regional Committee of PAN for the State of Michoacan (seventeen years); precandidate for the presidential nomination of PAN, 1964. f-None. g-Founder and member of the National Union of Catholic Students, 1931. h-Practicing lawyer; founding partner of General Hipotecaria, S.A.; distinguished orator. i-Descendant of Agustin Iturbide; members of his family from Michoacan for generations; active in Catholic student organizations with *Manuel Ulloa Ortiz*. j-None. k-None. l-*Excelsior*, 7 Nov. 1963, 1, 16; Mabry; letter.

Estrada Reynoso, Enrique
(Deceased Nov. 11, 1942)
a-1889. b-Mayahua, Zacatecas, *East Central, Rural*. c-Studied in Guadalajara; almost completed studies in civil engineering; no degree. d-*Federal deputy* from the State of Zacatecas, Dist. 3, 1937–40; *Senator* from the State of Zacatecas, 1940–42. e-None. f-Governor of Zacatecas, 1920; Subsecretary of War, 1921; Secretary of War, 1922; *Director General of the National Railroads of Mexico*,

1941–42. g-None. h-None. i-Brother of *Roque Estrada Reynoso*, President of the Supreme Court, 1952. j-Joined the Revolution under General Rafael Tapia, 1910; Constitutionalist; Chief of Operations in Michoacan and Colima, 1923; career army officer reaching rank of Divisionary General. k-Joined the De la Huerta Rebellion as a principal leader in 1923, when he was serving as Chief of Military Operations in Jalisco; defeated by General Obregon in Ocotlan and exiled to the United States; supported the Escobar rebellion in 1929, during which he captured the future President of Mexico, *Manuel Avila Camacho*, but allowed him to go free; one of the most prominent examples in recent Mexican politics of an opposition leader co-opted back into the system. l-C de D, 1937–39; C de S, 1946; DP70, 739; Michaels, 11; Enc. Mex., 1977, 563; Peral, 255–56; Q es Q, 200.

Estrada Reynoso, Roque
(Deceased Nov. 27, 1966)
a-Aug. 16, 1883. b-Moyahua, Zacatecas, *East Central, Rural*. c-Primary studies in Moyahua; secondary at the Martin Sousa School, Guadalajara; preparatory studies in Guadalajara, Jalisco; attended law school, forced into exile, but later completed his law degree at the University of Guadalajara, 1906. d-Federal Deputy from the State of Zacatecas, 1920–22. e-Member of the Anti-Reelectionist Center, 1909; *Secretary of Press and Publicity of the CEN of PRI*, June 19, 1935. f-Provisional Secretary to Francisco Madero, 1910; Private Secretary to Carranza, 1914; General Peace Delegate of Jalisco, 1911; Secretary of Justice, 1915–17; Temporary Secretary to Francisco Madero when he returned to Mexico; *Justice of the Supreme Court*, 1941–46, and 1946–51; *President of the Supreme Court*, 1952. g-Organized workers in a socialist party, 1904. i-Brother of General *Enrique Estrada Reynoso*, Senator from the State of Zacatecas. j-Participated in the Revolution; orator for Madero; Commanding Officer of the 2nd Cavalry Brigade, Western Division, 1914–15; rank of Brigadier General. k-Jailed with Francisco Madero in San Luis Potosi, 1909; turned down candidacy for governor of Jalisco because he did not meet the constitutional age requirement; candidate for President of Mexico against General Obregon, 1920; joined brother *Enrique* in support of the De la Huerta rebellion, 1923; exiled to the United States, 1923; 1927–29. l-Enc. Mex., III, 564; DP70, 740; D del S, 19 June 1935, 1; DGF51, I, 568; WB48, 1695; Peral, 257; Lopez, 334.

Ezeta Uribe Remedios, Albertina
a-Aug. 7, 1907. b-Toluca, Mexico, *West Central*, *Urban*. c-Primary and secondary studies in Toluca; preparatory studies from the Scientific and Literary

Institute of Mexico, Toluca; law degree from the National School of Law, UNAM; professor. **d-***Federal Deputy* from the State of Mexico, Dist. 6, 1955–58, member of the Tariff Committee, the Foreign Trade Committee, the Public Welfare Committee, the Legislative Studies Committee and the First Justice Committee. **e-**Member of the popular sector of PRI. **f-**Juvenile Court Judge, State of Mexico; public defender; judge, District 2, Toluca, Mexico, 1943–52; Notary Public No. 2, Toluca, Mexico. **g-**None. **j-**None. **k-**She was the only public notary in Mexico in 1955. **l-**Ind. Biog., 57; C de D, 1955–58.

Fabela, Isidro

(Deceased Aug. 12, 1964)
a-June 28, 1882. **b-**Atlacomulco, Mexico, *West Central*, *Rural*. **c-**Primary studies in Mexico, D.F.; preparatory at the National Preparatory School, Mexico, D.F.; law degree from the National School of Law, UNAM, 1908; Professor of History, National Institute, Chihuahua, 1911–13; Professor at the Literary Institute of Chihuahua, 1912–13; Professor of International Public Law, National School of Law, UNAM, 1921. **d-**Federal Deputy from the State of Chihuahua, 1913–14; Federal Deputy from the State of Chihuahua, 1922–23; *Governor of Mexico*, 1942–45; *Senator* from Mexico, 1946, but resigned to accept appointment to the International Court of Justice. **e-**None. **f-**Chief Public Defender for the Federal District, 1911; Adviser to and Director of the Federal Penitentiary, Federal District, 1911; Oficial Mayor and Secretary General of Government of the State of Chihuahua, 1911–13; Oficial Mayor and Secretary General of Government of the State of Sonora, 1913; Secretary of Foreign Relations, 1913–15; Special Diplomat to Italy and Spain, 1915; Minister to Argentina, Brazil, Chile, and Uruguay, 1916; Special Ambassador to Argentina, 1918–20; Judge for the Italian-Mexican International Arbitration Commission, 1928–32; Technical Commissioner, Secretariat of Foreign Relations, 1933; Legal Adviser to the French Legation in Mexico, 1933; President of the First Agricultural Conference, 1938; Mexican Delegate to the International Office of Labor, League of Nations, 1937–40; Judge of the International Court of Justice, 1946–52. **g-**None. **h-**Founded the newspaper, *La Verdad,* 1910, and *El Puebla,* 1914; practicing lawyer, 1921–28; attorney for several private companies, including Cauum Oil Company. **i-**Established early friendships with Jose Vasconcelos, *Alfonso Caso*, and Luis Castillo Ledon. **j-**None. **k-**One of the founders of the Ateneo de la Juventud, 1901; Kirk claims *Fabela* was very critical of *Ezequiel Padilla* as Secretary of Foreign Relations, because he himself did not receive the Secretaryship; his home has been turned into a public library in San Angel, Federal District. **l-**HAHR, Feb.

1972, 124–25; Kirk, 207; DP70, 747; Enc. Mex., III, 593; Peral, 258; EBW46, 71; WWM45, 38–39; letter, WB48, 1711–12; WB54, 350.

Fabre del Rivero, Carlos

a-Sept. 20, 1937. **b-**Puebla, Puebla, *East Central*, *Urban*. **c-**Primary and secondary studies at private schools in Puebla and Mexico, D.F.; law degree from the University of Puebla, Mar. 29, 1962, with his thesis on the ISSTE; studied at the National Center of Productivity; Professor of Economic Problems of Mexico and of Industrial Development (3rd and 5th years), School of Business Administration, University of Puebla. **d-**Substitute Mayor of Puebla, 1969–70. **e-**Joined PRI, 1955; state oratory champion, 1956 and 1957; third-place winner of the national PRI oratory contest, 1957; participated in *Luis Echeverria's* campaign in Puebla; member of the CEPES of PRI in Puebla; Auxiliary Secretary to *Luis Echeverria* during presidential campaign, 1970. **f-**Director General of Industrial and Commercial Development, State of Puebla, 1963–69; *Oficial Mayor of Industry and Commerce*, 1970–76. **g-**Student leader at the University of Puebla. **h-**Practicing lawyer; author of several works. **i-**Married Artemia Zardona. **j-**None. **k-**Precandidate for governor of Puebla, 1974. **l-**HA, 14 Dec. 1970, 21; letter; *Excelsior*, 9 May 1974, 19.

Faesler Carlisle, Julio

a-May 10, 1930. **b-**Chihuahua, Chihuahua, *North*, *Urban*. **c-**Primary studies at a Jesuit School; secondary studies at the Regional Institute, Chihuahua, Chihuahua; preparatory studies from a Jesuit school; law degree from the National School of Law, UNAM, 1955, thesis on "The Most Favored Nation Clause and International Treaties;" economics degree from the National School of Economics, UNAM, 1956, thesis on "The Intervention of the State in Economic Life;" Professor of Economic Theory and the History of Economic Doctrines, National School of Law, UNAM; Professor of Mexican Economic Problems, University of the Americas; Professor of Economic Theory; Escuela Libre de Derecho; Professor of Business Finance, Ibero-American University; Director of the Ph.D. Seminar in Foreign Trade, IPN. **d-**None. **e-**None. **f-**Assistant Economist, National Price Commission, 1952; Private Secretary to the Subsecretary of the Treasury, *Antonio Armendariz*, 1952–57; Commercial Attache, London; Commercial Attache, Brussels, 1964; Subdirector General of Trade, International Economic Affairs, Secretariat of Industry and Commerce, 1965–67; Director General of Latin American Economic Integration, Secretariat of Industry and Commerce, 1967–70; Director General of the

Mexican Institute of Foreign Trade, 1970–76; Director General of Exports of Mexico, 1977– . **g-**None. **h-**Self-employed, 1968–70. **i-**Attended UNAM with *Jorge de la Vega Dominguez*, *Mario Moya Palencia*, and *Carlos Torres Manzo*; parents from the middle class. **j-**None. **k-**None. **l-**Letter; HA, 21 Mar. 1977, 19.

Farell (Cubillas), Arsenio

a-June 30, 1921. **b-**Mexico, D.F., *Federal District*, *Urban*. **c-**Early education unknown; law degree from the National School of Law, UNAM, May 9, 1945; professor by competition in civil law, civil legal process and forensic law, National School of Law, UNAM (twenty-five years). **d-**None. **e-**None. **f-**Secretary of the Patronate of the National University, 1966; *Director General of the Federal Electric Commission*, May 29, 1973–76; *Director General of the Mexican Institute of Social Security*, 1976– . **g-**Consulting lawyer to the Society of Authors and Composers, to the Union of Cinematographic Production Workers, to the Mexican Union of Aviation Pilots and to the National Actors Association. **h-**Adviser to the Chapala Electric System Company; President of the National Chamber of Alcohol and Sugar Industries, 1973. **i-**Practiced law with *Rodolfo Echeverria*; co-student at the National School of Law with *Jose Lopez Portillo* and *Luis Echeverria*. **j-**None. **k-**None. **l-**HA, 4 June 1973, 16; HA, 3 June 1974, 24; *Excelsior*, 30 May 1973, 13.

Farias (Martinez), Luis M.

a-June 7, 1920. **b-**Monterrey, Nuevo Leon, *North*, *Urban*. **c-**Studied law at the National Law School, UNAM, 1941–45, degree, 1947, with a thesis on the 1950 constitutional reforms on amparo; Professor of Philosophy at the National Preparatory School, Mexico, D.F.; Professor of Philosophy at UNAM, 1954. **d-***Federal Deputy* from the Federal District, Dist. 16, 1955–58; member of the Committee on Bellas Artes, the Legislative Studies Committee, the Committee on the Radio and Television Industry; *Federal Deputy* from the State of Nuevo Leon, Dist. 2, 1967–70; President of the Gran Comision, PRI Majority Leader in the Chamber of Deputies, member of the First Committee of Government, the First Constitutional Affairs Committee; *Senator* from Nuevo Leon, 1970, 1973–76, member of the permanent committee, executive secretary of the Second Government and Justice Committees; *Federal Deputy* from the State of Nuevo Leon, Dist. 6, 1979–82, President of the Gran Comision. **e-**Joined PRI in 1951; General Delegate of the CEN of PRI to Sinaloa, 1973. **f-**Translator for Presidential Conferences, 1961; Oficial Mayor of the Department of Tourism, 1964–67; Director General of Information, Secretariat of Government, 1958–64; *Substitute*

Governor of Nuevo Leon, 1970–73. **g-**President of the National Federation of University Students, 1941–42; president of the Student Generation of UNAM, 1941; founder and first director of the National Association of Announcers, 1951–52; Secretary General of the Union of Artists and Workers of Station XEW, 1945–53, 1955–64. **h-**Television commentator, 1951–58; radio commentator, 1946–58; author of several books on politics in Mexico. **j-**None. **k-**Senator from Nuevo Leon before he was appointed Governor to replace *Eduardo Elizondo* in 1970. **l-**Enc. Mex., IV, 13–14; DBM68, 227; WWMG, 16; DGF56, 23, 31, 33–34; LAD, Oct. 1971, 2; G of NL, 16; PdM, 110–12; DBM70, 200; C de D, 1957; C de D, 1967–69; Ind. Biog., 57–58.

Faz Riza, Paz

a-April 18, 1893. **b-**Coahuila, *North*. **c-**Early education unknown, no degree. **d-**Federal Deputy from the State of Coahuila, 1932–34. **e-**None. **f-***Provisional Governor of Coahuila*, March to June, 1948. **g-**None. **j-**Joined the Revolution; fought under General Fortunato Maycotte in Hidalgo and Puebla; supported the Plan of Agua Prieta; joined the De la Huerta rebellion, 1923; rank of brigadier general, 1941. **k-**Replaced *Ricardo Ainslie* as governor until a special election could be held in which *Raul Lopez Sanchez* was selected as governor. **l-**Lopez, 339; Peral, 260.

Felix Serna, Faustino

a-May 14, 1913. **b-**Pitiquito, Sonora, *North*, *Rural*. **c-**Primary at the Colegio Sonora, Hermosillo, Sonora; teaching certificate from the State of Sonora Normal School. **d-**First Councilman of the City of Cajeme, Sonora, 1952; Interim Mayor of Cajeme, 1953; Mayor of Ciudad Obregon, Municipio of Cajeme, 1961–63; *Federal Deputy* from the State of Sonora, Dist. 2, 1964–67, member of the Gran Comision, the Public Works Committee, the Agricultural Development Committee and the First Committee on Taxes; *Governor of Sonora*, 1967–73. **e-**President of PRI during the gubernatorial campaign, 1961. **f-**None. **g-**Secretary General of the Agricultural Credit Union of Cajeme, 1936–40; President of the Agricultural Credit Union of Cajeme; President of the Political Revolutionary Group of Sonora, 1977. **h-**Private accountant for a local bank in Ciudad Obregon; operated trucking service in Sonora; founded the Sindicato de Fleteros del Valle del Yaqui, 1936; organized the company of Algodon y Semillas de Caborca. **i-**Friend of Rodolfo Elias Calles, Mayor of Cajeme, 1952; father was mayor of Cajeme; son-in-law *Javier R. Bours* was a federal deputy from Sonora, 1970–73, and pre-candidate for governor of Sonora, 1978. **j-**None. **k-***Proceso* accused him of representing the interests of large landowners in Sonora. l-Letter; C de D, 1964–66; WWMG, 17; *Excelsior*, 7 June, 1977, 23; *Excelsior*, 10 Sept. 1978, 14; *Proceso*, 7 Aug. 1978, 12–14; Moncada, 60.

Felix Valdes, Rodolfo

a-May 22, 1922. b-Nacozari, Sonora, *North*, *Rural*. c-Degree in civil engineering, National School of Engineering, UNAM, 1947; professor of general topography, National School of Engineering, UNAM, 1954; member of the University Council, UNAM, 1962–66; Auxiliary Secretary of the School of Engineering, 1954–59; Director of Planning, Graduate School of Engineering, UNAM. d-None. e-None. f-Head of the Department of Planning, Secretariat of Public Works, 1959–61; Director General of Planning and Programming, Secretariat of Public Works, 1961–64; Director General of Planning and Programming, Secretariat of Public Works, 1964–66; *Subsecretary of Public Works*, 1966–70, 1970–76; 1977– . g-President of the Student Society of the School of Engineering. h-Held many positions in the Department of the Federal District, the Secretariat of Hydraulic Resources and the Secretariat of National Defense. i-Married Gloria Flores. j-None. k-Precandidate for governor of Sonora, 1978. l-HA, 14 Dec. 1970, 22; DPE65, 117; DPE61, 84; letter; *Excelsior*, 23 Nov. 1977, 18; PS, 6150.

Fernandez, Rafael

a-1940. b-Federal District, *Federal District*, *Urban*. c-Early education unknown; sociology degree. d-None. e-Co-founder of the first National Committee to form an opposition political party; co-founder of the Socialist Workers Party, 1973; member of the Central Committee and the Executive Committee of the Socialist Workers Party. f-None. g-None. h-Writer for *El Universal*; writer for *Uno Mas Uno*. i-Parents were Spanish Republicans who emigrated from Spain; grandfather an Austrian miner. j-None. k-First became politically active in 1971. l-HA, 12 Feb. 1979, 20.

Fernandez Aguirre, Braulio

a-Nov. 21, 1912. b-San Pedro de las Colonias, Coahuila, *North*, *Urban*. c-Early education unknown; degree in business administration from the Zaragoza Academy, Monterrey, Nuevo Leon. d-Mayor of Torreon, Coahuila, 1945–48; *Alternate Federal Deputy* from the State of Coahuila, Dist. 2, 1949–52; Mayor of Torreon, Coahuila, 1950–58; *Federal Deputy* from the State of Coahuila, Dist. 2, 1961–63, member of the Gran Comision, the Waters and Irrigation Committee and the Sugar Industry Committee, Vice-president of the Chamber, Nov., 1961; *Governor of Coahuila*, 1963–69; *Senator* from the State of Coahuila, 1970–76, member of the Gran

Comision, President of the First Treasury Committee and the Small Agrarian Property Committee, First Secretary of the First Tariff and Foreign Trade Committee, and Second Secretary of the Second Government Committee; member of the Permanent Committee, Jan., 1973. e-General Delegate of the CEN of PRI, 1970; member of the Political Action Committee of the New Advisory Council to PRI, 1972. f-President of the National Arid Zones Committee, 1970. g-None. j-None. k-The CNC of Coahuila opposed his nomination as the PRI gubernatorial candidate, 1963. l-GofM, DGF51, I, 20; C de D, 1949–52; C de S, 1970–76, 73; HA, 10 July 1972, 10.

Fernandez Albarran, Juan

(Deceased Mar. 27, 1972)

a-Jan. 10, 1901. b-Toluca, Mexico, *West Central*, *Urban*. c-Law degree, National School of Law, UNAM. d-Mayor of Toluca, Mexico; *Federal Deputy* from the State of Mexico, Dist. 7, 1943–46; *Senator* from the State of Mexico, 1952–58, member of the Committee on Mines, the Second Balloting Committee; substitute member of the Committee on Foreign and Domestic Commerce, the Committee on Cooperative Development, and the Committee on Labor; *Governor of Mexico*, 1963–69. e-Representative to PRI from Toluca; *Secretary General of PRI*, 1959–63, under *Alfonso Corona del Rosal*. f-Agent of the Ministerio Publico, Mexico City; judge, Mexico City; Oficial Mayor of the State Legislature of Mexico; Secretary General of Government of the State of Mexico, 1937–41, under Governor *Wenceslao Labra*; member of the Federal Electoral Commission, 1946; *Oficial Mayor of the Department of Agrarian Affairs*, 1946–52; Judge of the Superior Tribunal of Justice of the State of Veracruz; Judge of the Superior Tribunal of Justice of the State of Durango. h-None. j-None. k-None. l-DGF51, I, 465; DGF56, 6, 10–13; letter; DBM68, 230; Correa, 447; WWMG, 17.

Fernandez Fernandez, Aurora

b-Mexico, *West Central*. c-Primary and secondary studies at the Colegio Sara L. King; teaching certificate; preparatory studies from the National Preparatory School; degree in political science from the School of Political and Social Sciences, UNAM, (second woman to receive this degree from the National University). d-*Federal Deputy* from the Federal District, Dist. 9, 1970–73, member of the Infant Welfare Committee, the Department of the Federal District Committee and the Second Balloting Committee. e-Joined the PNR, 1933; Oficial Mayor of the Women's Sector of the PNR; Secretary of Organization of the Women's Sector of PRI; Secretary General of the Women's Sector of PRI; Secretary of Organization of the Women's Sector of the PRI in the Federal District, 1937. **f-**Delegate of the Department of the Federal District to Milpa Alta, 1947–50; Head of the Office of Feminine Action, Department of the Federal District, 1950–69. **g-**Delegate of the Women's Section of the Federal District before the National Women's Committee, 1937; Representative of the Female Farmers of the State of Mexico, 1939; Secretary of Female Action, League of Agrarian Communities and Peasant Unions, 1939–42; co-founder of the National Women's Alliance during the *Miguel Aleman* presidential campaign, 1945–46; Secretary of Feminine Action, Mexican Federation of Labor, 1951; co-founder of the Mexican Alliance of Women, 1952. **i-**Mother was a rural school teacher; father died when she was a month old. **j-**None. **k-**None. **l-**Chumacero, 66–70; *Directorio*, 1970–72; C de D, 1970–73, 10, 39, 113; DGF51, I, 484; DGF56, 469; DPE61, 146; DPE65, 195.

Fernandez Flores, Manuel

a-Sept. 16, 1933. **b-**Nogales, Veracruz, *Gulf*, *Rural*. **c-**Early education unknown; no degree. **d-**None. **e-**Joined the Popular Socialist Party, 1952; member of the Central Committee of the PPS; Secretary of Labor Policy, Central Committee, PPS, 1979. **f-**None. **g-**Delegate of the Mexican Electricians Union to international conferences; Secretary of External Affairs, Central Committee, Mexican Union of Electricians, 1979. **h-**Laborer in the electrical industry, 1953– . **j-**None. **k-**None. **l-**HA, 12 Mar. 1979, V .

Fernandez Hurtado, Ernesto

a-Nov. 19, 1921. **b-**Colima, Colima, *West, Urban*. **c-**Preparatory studies at the National Preparatory School, 1939–40; degree in economics, National School of Economics, UNAM, 1941–45; Master's degree in public administration from Harvard University, June, 1948, with a thesis on "Income Elasticity of Foreign Commerce in Latin American Countries"; Professor of Money and Banking at Mexico City College; Professor of Money and Banking and International Trade at the National School of Economics, UNAM; Professor of International Trade at the Technological Institute of Mexico, 1956–59; Professor in the field of central banking at the Center for Monetary Studies of Latin America. **d-**None. **e-**None. **f-**Head of Balance of Payments Section, Department of Economic Studies, Bank of Mexico, 1950; Gerente of the Department of Economic and Foreign Studies, Bank of Mexico; head of the Technical Office of the Bank of Mexico; technical adviser to the Director General, *Rodrigo Gomez*, 1954; Subdirector of the Bank of Mexico, 1964–70; *Director General of the Bank of Mexico*, Sept. 18, 1970, to 1976. **g-**None. **h-**Assistant economist, Bank of Mexico, 1944; specialized economic studies at the International

Monetary Fund, 1948–49; investigator for the Department of Economic Studies, Bank of Mexico. **i-**Student of *Eduardo Bustamante* at the National School of Economics; married Evelyn Terovane. **j-**None. **k-**Precandidate for governor of Colima, 1977. **l-***Hoy*, 17 Apr. 1971, 12; letters; B de M, 119–20.

Fernandez MacGregor, Genaro
(Deceased Dec. 22, 1959)

a-May 4, 1883. **b-**Federal District, *Federal District, Urban*. **c-**Primary and secondary education at the Instituto Cientifico, Mexico City; preparatory studies at the Colegio de Mascarones, 1897–1900, Mexico City; law degree from the National School of Law, UNAM, 1901–07; Professor of International Private and Public Law at the National Law School, UNAM, 1918–25; Professor of Spanish Literature and General History, National Preparatory School, 1912–16; *Rector of UNAM*, Mar., 1945, to Feb., 1946. **d-**None. **e-**None. **f-**Private Secretary to the Secretary of Industry and Commerce, 1908–09; Assistant Director of the Office of Patents, 1909–11; Director of International Affairs, Secretariat of Foreign Relations, 1911–14; legal adviser to the Secretariat of Foreign Relations, 1917–24; member of the United States-Mexican Claims Commission, 1924–36; member of the International Tribunal of Arbitration, The Hague. **g-**None. **h-**Author of many novels; Founder and Director of the Mexican Journal of International Law. **i-**Father a mining engineer who administered Genaro Fernandez's grandfather's affairs; brother of Luis Fernandez MacGregor, member of the Mexican Foreign Service; the Fernandez MacGregor family has figured prominently in the history of the Mexican Foreign Service; related to *Eduardo Hay*; practiced law with Alejandro Quijano; close friend of Antonio Caso; related to Jose Maria Pino Suarez, Vice President of Mexico under Madero, and to Justo Sierra. **j-**None. **k-**Student strike in Nov., 1945, was instrumental in bringing about his resignation as Rector of UNAm three months later. **l-**DP70, 762; Hayner, 269; Peral, 269; Correa, 50; Enc. Mex., IV, 117; EWB46, 546; IWW40, 333; WB48, 1759.

Fernandez Manero, Victor

a-Nov. 17, 1898. **b-**Villahermosa, Tabasco, *Gulf, Urban*. **c-**Primary, secondary and preparatory studies in Villahermosa; medical degree, with a specialty as a surgeon, National School of Medicine, UNAM. **d-**Federal Deputy from the State of Tabasco, 1934–36; *Governor of Tabasco*, 1936–39. **e-**None. **f-**Head of the Department of Hygiene, Secretariat of Public Education, 1930–31; attache to the Mexican Embassy in Paris, 1931; *Head of the Department of Health*, 1940–43 (last director); *Ambassador to France*, 1946–51; and to Yugoslavia. **g-**None. **h-**Mexican representative to the International Medical Congress, Washington, D.C., 1930. **i**-Married Alicia Islas. **j**-None. **k**-Wealthiest member of the *Avila Camacho* cabinet in 1940 with over one million pesos in assets. **l**-D de Y, 1940; Correa 41, 2, 70; DGF51, 105, 109; Enc. Mex., IV, 117; Peral, 269.

Fernandez Martinez, Enrique

a-June 15, 1897. **b**-San Felipe Torres Mochas, Guanajuato, *West Central*, *Rural*. **c**-Early education unknown; no degree. **d**-Federal Deputy from the State of Guanajuato, 1922–23; Federal Deputy from the State of Guanajuato, 1924–25, 1926–27, 1928–30, 1934–35; became *Interim Governor of Guanajuato*, Dec. 13, 1935 to 1937, replacing *Jesus Yanez Maya*; *Governor of Guanajuato*, 1939–43. **g**-None. **h**-None. **i**-Friend of Governor Enrique Colunga and Governor *Arroyo Ch.*; intimate friend of *Luis I. Rodriguez*. **j**-None. **k**-Brandenburg gives him Inner Circle status; critics considered him an unconstitutional governor since he was the interim governor before being elected in 1939. **l**-Dulles, 662; Peral, 269; Gruening, 428; Correa 41, 78–79; Brandenburg, 80; NYT, 29 Apr. 1935, 8; NYT, 17 Dec. 1935, 1; Lopez, 497–98.

Fernandez Robert, Raul

a-1905. **b**-Tulancingo, Hidalgo, *East Central*, *Urban*. **c**-Primary and secondary studies in Pachuca, Hidalgo; preparatory and part of professional studies in Pachuca; completed law degree at the National School of Law, UNAM, 1929; Professor at the National Polytechnic Institute. **d**-*Senator* from the State of Hidalgo, 1952–58, secretary of the Economics and Statistics Committee, second secretary of the Second Mines Committee, president of the Military Justice Committee, member of the Gran Comision, and member of the Second Balloting and the Legislative Studies Committee. **e**-None. **f**-Consulting lawyer to the Chief of Police of the Federal District, 1932–37; Attorney General of Military Justice, 1946–52; Director of the Federal Custom's Office, Ciudad Juarez, Chihuahua, 1961; Director of the Federal Custom's Office, Tampico, Tamaulipas, 1965. **i**-Co-student of *Miguel Aleman* at UNAM. **j**-Career officer in military justice; reached rank of Brigade General. **k**-Prominent athlete; member of the Mexican Olympic Basketball Team, 1936. **l**-Ind. Biog., 60–61; MGF47, 110; DGF51, I, 178; DGF56, 6, 8, 10–14, DPE61, 45; DPE65, 58.

Fierro Villalobos, Roberto

a-Nov. 7, 1897. **b**-Ciudad Guerrero, Chihuahua, *North*, *Rural*. **c**-Primary studies in Ciudad Guerrero; graduated from the Military Aviation School as a First Captain of Auxiliary Cavalry; Director of the Military Aviation School, 1932. **d**-None. **e**-None. **f**-Chief, Department of Civil Aviation, 1930; Direc-

tor of Military Aviation, 1935–36; Interim Governor of Chihuahua, 1931–32; Director of Military Aviation, 1940; Military Attache to China and Japan, 1936–38; *Chief of the Mexican Air Force*. 1940–41, 1959–64. **g**-None. **h**-Employed at various jobs in his youth, including an employee at a pharmacy, a railroad lineman, a chauffeur and an auto mechanic; businessman, 1941–59. **i**-Friend of *Marcelino Garcia Barragan* since 1921, when he was an instructor at the National Military College; married Carmen Jasso; father a street vendor and mother washed clothes to support his family in El Paso during the Revolution. **j**-Joined the Revolution in 1913, under the forces of General Jesus Maria Rios; rejoined the Revolution in 1917, fighting under General Enriquez until 1920; Chief, First Air Regiment, 1929–30; rank of Brigadier General, 1938; reached rank of divisionary general. **k**-Worked in El Paso, Texas, 1911, at the Pierson Lumber Company; worked in Hollywood, California, 1913, as a movie extra; set world speed record from New York to Mexico City, 1930. **l**-Enc. Mex., IV, 1977, 168–69; DPE61, 33; DBM68, 218; WWM45, 42; letter.

Figueroa, Andres
(Deceased Oct. 17, 1936)

a-Jan. 13, 1884. **b**-Chaucingo, Municipio de Huitzuco, Departamento de Hidalgo, Guerrero, *South*, *Rural*. **c**-Primary studies at the Morelos Institute in Cuernavaca; no degree. **d**-Member of the City Council of Quetzalapa; Mayor of Quetzalapa; member of the City Council of Huitzuco, Guerrero. **e**-None. **f**-*Secretary of National Defense*, 1935–36. **g**-None. **h**-None. **i**-Brother, Romulo, fought in the Revolution with *Andres*; son of small landowners; uncle of *Manuel Avila Camacho*. **j**-Joined the Revolution in Aug., 1910; formed the "Figueroa Brigade" under General Obregon; fought against Carranza; commander of various military zones, 1920–35; Commander of the 22nd Military Zone, Toluca, Mexico; Commander of the 31st Military Zone, Chiapas, 1935. **k**-None. **l**-DP70, 770; D de S, 19 June 1935, 1; Enc. Mex., IV, 402; Q es Q, 207; HA, 28 May 1979, VI.

Figueroa Balvanera, Jose

b-Queretaro, Queretaro, *East Central*, *Urban*. **c**-Primary studies in Queretaro; secondary and preparatory studies at the Colegio Civil, Queretaro; veterinary doctor, National School of Agriculture, 1914; post graduate studies in Europe, Canada, Brazil, Argentina and the United States. **d**-*Senator* from Queretaro, 1952–58, member of the Balloting Committee; first secretary of the Special Committee on Livestock and the Committee on Health; president of the Agricultural and Development Committee and the Military Health Committee. **e**-None. **f**-Director General of Livestock, Secretariat of Agriculture and

Livestock, 1951. **g-**None. **j-**None. **k-**None.
l-DGF51, I, 208; DGF56, 7, 9–10, 12–14; Ind.
Biog., 61–62.

Figueroa Figueroa, Ruben

a-Nov. 9, 1908. **b-**Huitzuco de los Figueroa, Guerrero, *South*, *Rural*. **c-**Early education unknown;
self-educated as a librarian and bibliographer, National Library of Mexico; preparatory studies in engineering at the National Preparatory School; degree
in topographical and hydrological engineering, National Engineering School, UNAM. **d-***Federal Deputy* from the State of Guerrero, Dist. No. 2, 1940–
43, member of the Editorial Committee (1st year),
the Tax Committee, and the General Means of
Communication Committee; *Federal Deputy* from
the State of Guerrero, Dist. No. 2, 1964–67,
member of the Tariff Committee, the Automobile
Transportation Committee, and the First General
Means of Communication Committee; *Senator* from
the State of Guerrero, 1970–74, member of the Gran
Comision, president of the General Means of Communication Committee and the Public Works Committee; *Governor of Guerrero*, 1975– . **e-**Delegate
from Guerrero to the Constitutional Convention of
the PNR, 1928; delegate to the PNR National Convention, 1933. **f-**Porter, National Library, Mexico,
D.F.; Assistant Librarian, National Library; Director, Jose E. Rodo Public Library; Assistant Director,
Ibero-American Library, 1932; member, Mixed Agrarian Commission of Guerrero; topographical engineer, Guerrero; Inspecting Engineer, Railroad Department, Secretariat of Public Works, 1936; Sanitation Engineer, Secretariat of Public Health; Executive Director, Cuenca del Balsas Commission, 1974.
g-Student representative of the first year engineering
students; member of the Mixed Agrarian Commission in Guerrero; President of the Truckers Alliance
of Mexico, 1974. **h-**Director General of *Voz*.
i-Parents were peasants; uncles were murdered during the initial stages of the Revolution; brother of
Ruffo Figueroa; political ally of *Carlos Duffo*, Federal Deputy, 1973–76; son Ruben Figueroa Alcocer
is the Federal Deputy from the Federal District, Dist.
No. 17, 1979–82. **j-**None. **k-**Kidnapped by Guerrero
guerrilla leader, *Lucio Cabanas*, May 30, 1974, and
rescued by the Army on Sept. 8, 1974. **l-***Excelsior*,
16 Mar. 1973, 22; *Excelsior*, 17 Aug. 1972, 5; C de
D, 1964–66; C de D, 1940–42, 10, 48, 51; HA, 10
June 1974, 15–16; *Hoy*, 14 Mar. 1970, 4; *Excelsior*,
1 Feb. 1975, 6.

Figueroa Figueroa, Ruffo
(Deceased July 25, 1967)

a-1905. **b-**Huitzuco de los Figueros, Guerrero,
South, *Rural*. **c-**Early education unknown; no degree. **d-***Federal Deputy* from the Federal District,

Dist. 4, 1943–46; *Senator* from Guerrero, 1946–52,
member of the Committees on Public Welfare and
Social Security, and substitute member of the
Economy and Statistics Committee. **e-***Secretary
General of the National Confederation of Popular
Organizations*, 1964–65; important representative of
the bureaucratic sector in PRI delegations.
f-Subdirector of the ISSSTE, 1952–58; Subdirector
of the ISSSTE, 1959–64; *Governor of Quintana
Roo*, 1965–67. **g-**Delegate of Section 17 of the
Union of the Workers of the Federal District
(SUTDDF), 1935; Action Secretary of Section 17;
Secretary of Interior, SUTDDF; Secretary General of
Section 17, SUTDDF; Secretary of Labor and Strikes
of the Popular Sector of the Federal District, Secretary of Bureaucratic Action of the National Federation
of Popular Organizations, 1943; *Secretary General
of the FSTSE*, 1943–46. **h-**Assistant librarian, 1922;
librarian in the Jose Enrique Rodo Library. **i-**Brother
Ruben Figueroa has been a union leader of transportation workers, was Federal Deputy from Guerrero in
1940–42, 1964–66, and was Senator from Guerrero,
1970–74. **j-**None. **k-**The Figueroa brothers are from
a revolutionary family in Guerrero, their uncle Ambrosio initiated the Revolution in their native region
and was shot by General Huerta; precandidate for
governor of Guerrero, 1957, lost to *Raul Caballero
Aburto*. **l-**HA, 10 Dec. 1962, 21; HA 19 Jan. 1959,
11; HA, 15 Nov. 1946, 5; DGF47, 20; DP70, 771; G
of M, 10.

Figueroa Velasco, Juan

a-June 24, 1909. **b-**Coixtelhuaca, Puebla, *East Central*, *Rural*. **c-**Primary studies in the Benito Juarez
School, Puebla; three years of secondary studies,
University of Puebla; first year of preparatory studies
at the University of Puebla; no degre. **d-**Local Deputy to the State Legislature of Puebla; *Federal Deputy* from the State of Puebla, Dist. 2, 1961–64;
Federal Deputy from the State of Puebla, Dist. 2,
1970–73, member of the Mines and the National
Lands Committees. **e-**None. **f-**None. **g-**President of
the National Committee of CROC; Secretary of
Technical and Economic Affairs of the National
Committee of CROC; Secretary General of CROC in
Puebla; director of *Resurgimiento*, the official paper
of CROC in Puebla. **i-**Married Guadalupe Becerra.
j-None. **k-**None. **l-***Directorio*, 1970–72, 72–73; C
de D, 1970–73, 114; C de D, 1961–64.

Flores Betancourt, Dagoberto

a-Jan. 20, 1906. **b-**Silacayoapan, Oaxaca, *South*,
Rural. **c-**Primary studies in Silacayoapan and Mexico
City; secondary studies in Mexico City, 1925–27;
normal teaching certificate from the National
Teachers School. Mexico City. 1928–30; preparatory studies at the National Preparatory School,

Mexico City, 1930–31; law degree from the National School of Law, UNAM, 1932–36; school teacher. **d-**_Alternate Federal Deputy_ from the State of Oaxaca, Dist. 10, 1937–40; _Federal Deputy_ from the State of Oaxaca, Dist. 6, 1967–70, member of the Gran Comision. **e-**None. **f-**Agent of the Ministerio Publico. **g-**Leader in the National Union of Educational Workers. **i-**Father a peasant. **j-**None. **k-**None. **l-**D de Y, 4 Dec. 1970; C de D, 1967–70; MGF69, 94.

Flores Castellanos, Petronilo

(Deceased Apr. 4, 1957)
a-May 31, 1890. **b-**Union de Tula, Hidalgo, _East Central_, _Rural_. **c-**Primary and secondary studies in public schools, Guadalajara, Jalisco; no degree. **d-**None. **e-**None. **f-**_Governor of Baja California del Sur_. 1956–57. **g-**None. **h-**None. **j-**Joined the Revolution in 1913, under General Dieguez; career army officer; rank of Brigadier General, Feb. 16, 1914; Chief of Staff of the 3rd Military Zone, La Paz, Baja California del Sur, 1939–56; Chief of Staff of the 28th Military Zone, Oaxaca, Oaxaca; commander of various military zones; Commander of the 3rd Military Zone, La Paz, Baja California del Sur, 1956–57. **k-**Served as Chief of Staff under _General Olachea Aviles_ from 1946–56. **l-**_Siempre_, 19 Sept. 1956, 10; DP70, 781; Peral, 276; Casasola, V.

Flores Curiel, Rogelio

a-Mar. 3, 1923. **b-**Tepic, Nayarit, _West_, _Urban_. **c-**Primary studies at the Juan Escutia School, Tepic; secondary studies at the Institute of Science and Letters of Nayarit; graduated from the National Military College, 1941–44, graduated with distinction from the Staff School of the National War College, Mexico, D.F.; Professor and Chief of Curriculum at the National War College, Mexico, D.F., 1964–67; Subdirector of the National Military College, 1968–69. **d-**_Alternate Senator_ from the State of Nayarit, 1964–70; _Senator_ from Nayarit, 1970, 1971–75, member of the Gran Comision, president of the Military Justice Committee, member of the permanent committee, 1974; _Governor of Nayarit_, 1975– . **e-**Delegate of the CEN of PRI to CNOP, 1975; Secretary of Legislative Promotion, CNOP, 1975–76; special delegate of PRI to Chiapas, Durango and Nuevo Leon. **f-**Member of the Mexican delegation to the Inter-American Defense Board, 1953; Military Attache to El Salvador, 1959–61; Private Secretary to the Secretary of National Defense, 1961–64, _Agustin Olachea Aviles;_ member of the Mexican Delegation to the International Air and Space Reunion; Chief of Police for the Federal District, 1970–71. **g-**Secretary of Legislation, CEN of CNOP. 1975. **h-**Scribe. Nayarit Department of Public Works. **j-**Career army officer, 1st Sgt. of the Cadet Honor

Squad at the National Military College; rank of Colonel. **k-**Removed from his position as Chief of Police after student riots in Oct., 1971. **l-**HA, 14 Dec. 1970, 25; MGF69–70; C de S, 1964–70; _Excelsior_, 21 Feb. 1975, 12; _Excelsior_, 21 Mar. 1975, 4; Enc. Mex., Annual, 1977, 547.

Flores de la Pena, Horacio

a-July 24, 1923. **b-**Saltillo, Coahuila, _North_, _Urban_. **c-**Primary and preparatory studies in Saltillo; degree in economics from the National School of Economics, UNAM, 1946; postgraduate work at American University, Washington, D.C., 1947–49; Professor of Modern Economic Systems, National School of Economics, 1956–63; Professor of Theories of Economic Development, National School of Economics, 1964–66; Director of the National School of Economics, UNAM, 1965–66; Executive Coordinator of the Technical Planning Commission of UNAM, 1967–70. **d-**None. **e-**Technical adviser to the IEPES of PRI. **f-**Member of the Mexican delegation to the United Nations; Director of Administration and Inspection of Decentralized Agencies and Enterprises, Secretariat of Government Properties, 1959–70; _Secretary of Government Properties_, 1970–75; _Ambassador to France_, 1977–78; Ambassador to UNESCO, 1978. **g-**None. **h-**Head of the Tariff Committee, 1944–47; held numerous positions in the Ejido Credit Bank and the Agrarian Credit Bank. **i-**Student of _Eduardo Bustamante_ at the National School of Economics, UNAM; attended UNAM with _Raul Salinas Lozano_ and _Octaviano Campos Salas_; married Alena Justic. **j-**None. **k-**None. **l-**DGF69, 238; DPE61, 58, HA, 7 Dec. 1970, 24; letter; _Hoy_, Dec. 1970; HA, 13 Jan. 1975, 7–8; LA, 17 Jan. 1975, 20.

Flores Fuentes, Raymundo

a-Mar. 15, 1913. **b-**Chalma, Veracruz, _Gulf_, _Rural_. **c-**Normal teaching certificate; primary school teacher, Veracruz, 1933; secondary school teacher; Professor at the Night Institute for Workers, Jalapa, Veracruz. **d-**Local deputy to the State Legislature of Veracruz; City council member of Jalapa; _Federal Deputy_ from the State of Veracruz, Dist. 1, 1955–58, President of the Administration Committee, member of the Second Government Committee. **e-**President of PRI in the State of Veracruz. **f-**Director of Population, Secretariat of Government, Reynosa, Tamaulipas; founder and President of the Board of Civic and Moral Improvement, Reynosa; President of the Electoral Committee for Baja California del Norte; Director of Customs, Tampico. **g-**Secretary General of the Teachers Union of Jalapa; Secretary General of Section 30 of the Union of Education Workers of Mexico (STERM); Secretary General of STERM, 1940; Secretary General of the CTM in the State of Veracruz; Secretary of Education of the CTM; Executive Secretary of the Southern Zone for the CNC, 1975; *Secretary General of the CNC*, 1957–59. i-Son *Raymundo Flores Bernal* was Federal Deputy from the State of Veracruz, 1970–73; relative of *Guilbaldo Flores Fuentes*, Federal Deputy from the State of Veracruz, 1976–79. j-None. k-None. l-Ind. Biog., 62–63; *Excelsior*, 5 Jan. 1957; DGF56, 28, 30, 34; Navarro, 220; *Directorio*, 1970–72.

Flores Granados, Roberto

a-July 25, 1931. b-Ixtapalapa, *Federal District*, *Urban*. c-Primary studies at a private school in the Federal District; secondary and preparatory studies at the National Preparatory School No. 2, 1947–52; degree in dentistry from the School of Dentistry, UNAM, 1953–58; Professor of Surgical Techniques, UNAM; Secretary of the School of Odontology, UNAM, 1970. d-*Alternate Federal Deputy* from the Federal District, Dist. No. 21, 1967–70; *Federal Deputy* (Party) from the Federal District, Dist. 21, 1970–73. e-Joined PAN, 1948; Secretary of the PAN Committee for Dist. No. 21, Federal District, 1960; Regional adviser to PAN, 1973. f-None. g-None. h-Practicing dentist. j-None. k-Candidate for Alternate Federal Deputy from the Federal District, 1961. l-*Directorio*, 1970–72; MGF69, 91.

Flores M., Alfonso

a-Aug. 3, 1907. b-Ixtlahuaca, Mexico, *West Central*, *Rural*. c-Studies at the Scientific and Literary Institute of Mexico, Toluca; no degree. d-*Federal Deputy* from the State of Mexico, Dist. 7, 1937–40; *Senator* from the State of Mexico, 1940–46, President of the Tariffs and Foreign Trade Committee, First Secretary of the Development of Cooperatives Committee, member of the Gran Comision, First Secretary of the Tax Committee, President of the Public Works Committee, First Secretary of the Second Petroleum Committee and Second Secretary of the Foreign Relations Committee. f-Manager of the Workers Clothing and Equipment Cooperative, 1947–52. g-None. h-None. k-None. l-PS, 2112; Libro de Oro, 1946, 6; DGF51, I, 504; C de S, 1940–46; C de D, 1937–40.

Flores Mazari, Antonio

a-1908. b-Jojutla, Morelos, *West Central*, *Urban*. c-Studies at the School of Mechanical Engineering, Mexico City; studies in journalism at the Methodist Institute; completed preparatory studies; no degree. d-*Senator* from the State of Puebla, 1964–70. e-None. f-None. g-Secretary General of the National Union of Newspaper Editors, 1964. h-Journalist; sports editor, *La Aficion*; sports editor, *El Popular*; editor, *El Universal*. i-Member of *Emilio Riva*

Palacio's group. j-None. k-Outstanding football player on the champion Express Team, 1926. l-C de S, 1964–70; MGF69.

Flores Munoz, Gilberto

(Deceased Oct. 6, 1978)
a-May 4, 1906. b-Compostela, Nayarit, *West*, *Rural*. c-Studied at a military school in Guadalajara, Jalisco; no degree. d-Federal Deputy from the State of San Luis Potosi, 1930–32; Federal Deputy from the State of San Luis Potosi, 1934–37; *Senator* from the State of San Luis Potosi, 1940–46, president of the Second Public Education Committee, the General Means of Communication Committee; Executive Secretary of the Second Foreign Relations Committee and the Securities Committee; *Governor of Nayarit*, 1946–51. e-Campaign manager for *Reynaldo Perez Gallardo* for governor, 1939; Secretary of Labor Action, CEN of PNR, 1934–35; *Secretary of Education Action*, CEN of PNR, 1936–37; *Secretary General of the PNR*, 1937; National Coordinator of *Adolfo Ruiz Cortines'* campaign for President of Mexico, 1951–52. f-Labor Inspector for the State of San Luis Potosi, 1930; President of the Federal Conciliation and Arbitration Board, San Luis Potosi, 1928; *Secretary of Agriculture and Livestock*, 1952–58; Director General, National Sugar Industry Commission, 1977–78. g-None. h-None. i-Good friend of *Rodolfo Sanchez Taboada*; political disciple of *Gonzalo Santos*; son Gilberto Flores Izquierdo was medical subdirector of IMSS in 1978. j-Joined the Army in 1923; supported the De la Huerta rebellion, captured and imprisoned in San Luis Potosi; Captain of the Cavalry, 1928; member of the General Staff of Carrera Torres. k-Precandidate for the PRI presidential nomination, 1957; offered the position of Secretary of Agriculture in the Lopez Mateos administration. l-D de Y, 2 Dec. 1952, 1; Brandenburg, 112; HA, 5 Dec. 1952, 9; DGF56, 223; DGF51, I, 91; Peral, 47, 123; EBW46, 93; Enc. Mex., IV, 336; D del S, 2 Dec. 1952; HA, 9 May 1955, 3; WB54, 379; *Excelsior*, 12 Aug. 1977, 6; NYT, 28 July, 1957, 2; *Excelsior*, 11 Dec. 1969.

Flores Olea, Victor

a-Aug. 24, 1932. b-Toluca, Mexico, *West Central*, *Urban*. c-Early education unknown; law degree, National School of Law, UNAM, April 5, 1956; postgraduate work at the School of Law and Political Science, University of Rome, 1956–57, and at the Institute of Political Studies, Paris, 1957–58; Professor of Political and Social Sciences, School of Political and Social Sciences, UNAM, 1959–70; Dean, School of Political and Social Sciences, UNAM, 1970–75. d-None. e-None. f-*Ambassador to the Soviet Union*, 1975–76; *Subsecretary of Popular and Extracurricular Education*, 1976–78; *Subsecretary of Culture and Recreation*, Secretariat of Public Education, 1978; Ambassador to UNESCO, 1978– . **g**-Supporter of the 1968 student movement. **h**-Author of several books on Marxism and socialism; practicing lawyer in the law firm of Oscar Morineau; lawyer for American Smelting and Refining, 1953–56. **i**-Published *Medio Siglo* with *Porfirio Munoz Ledo*. **j**-None. **k**-None. **l**-HA, 17 Feb. 1975, 18; *Excelsior*, 7 Feb. 1975, 13; Enc. Mex., 1977, IV, 336; BdM, 123–24; HA, 27 Nov. 1978, 17–18.

Flores (Sanchez), Oscar

a-June 22, 1907. **b**-Chihuahua, Chihuahua, *North*, *Urban*. **c**-Primary, secondary and preparatory studies in Chihuahua; law degree, National School of Law, UNAM, 1930. **d**-*Senator* from the State of Chihuahua, 1952–58, member of the Committees on Agricultural Development, Legislative Studies, Livestock, General Routes of Communication, and the First Ejido and Second Petroleum Committtees; *Governor of Chihuahua*, 1968–74. **e**-None. **f**-Attorney for Labor, Chihuahua, 1931; Public Defender, Chihuahua; member of the Administrative Council of the National Bank of Agricultural and Livestock Credit, 1951; Director of the North American-Mexican Commission for the Eradication of Hoof and Mouth Disease, 1947–51; *Subsecretary of Livestock*, 1946–52; *Attorney General of Mexico*, 1976– . **g**-None. **h**-Practicing lawyer, Chihuahua. **j**-None. **k**-None. **l**-HA, 10 Aug. 1951, 15; DGF59, 149; DGF51, I, 203; II, 165, 219; HA, 5 April 1949, iii; DGF47, 123; DGF56, 6, 10–14; Ind. Biog., 63–64; *Excelsior*, 1 Dec. 1976; Lopez, 366.

Flores Tapia, Oscar

a-Feb. 5, 1917. **b**-Saltillo, Coahuila, *North*, *Urban*. **c**-Primary studies in Saltillo; teaching certificate; secondary teacher. **d**-*Senator* from the State of Coahuila, 1970–74, president of the Protocol Committee, first secretary of the Second Public Education Committee and the Second Treasury Committee; *Governor of Coahuila*, 1975– . **e**-Founder and President of the organization known as Culture and Political Science, which advocated *Luis Echeverria* for President of Mexico, 1968–70; President of PRI in Coahuila (twice); President of the Editorial Committee of the CEN of PRI, 1972–73; *Secretary of Popular Action of the CEN of PRI*, 1973. **f**-Director of Public Relations, Coahuila; Director of the Historical Archives, Coahuila; Private Secretary to the Governor of Coahuila. **g**-*Secretary General of the National Federation of Popular Organizations* (CNOP), Nov. 9, 1972–75. **h**-Poet, historian, and author of numerous books on Mexico. **i**-Son, director of public works, Arteaga, Coahuila, 1978. **j**-None. **k**-Founding member of the National Liberation Movement in Mexico. **l**-C de S, 1970–76; HA, 20

Nov. 1972, 13; letter; Enc. Mex., 1977, III, 336; HA, 24 Feb. 1975, 14; HA, 13 Jan. 1975, 29; *Excelsior*, 6 Jan. 1975, 7; *Excelsior*, 26 May 1978, 20.

Flores Torres, Juan

a-Jan. 31, 1896. **c**-Early education unknown; no degree. **d**-None. **e**-None. **f**-*Subsecretary of National Defense*, 1958–61; Director General of Personnel, Secretariat of National Defense, 1964–70. **g**-None. **h**-None. **j**-Joined the Revolution; career army officer; rank of Brigadier General, May 1, 1938; commander of various military zones; Commander of the 3rd Infantry Division for the State of Mexico and the Federal District; rank of Divisionary General. **k**-None. **l**-DPE61, 32; D del S, 1952; MGF69, 196; DPE65, 43; Peral, 47, 123; HA, 29 Dec. 1958, 8; *Siempre*, 7 Jan. 1959, 6; DGF47, 110.

Foglio Miramontes, Fernando

a-Dec. 8, 1906. **b**-Temosachic, Chihuahua, *North*, *Rural*. **c**-Preparatory studies at the Escuela Particular de Agricultura, Ciudad Juarez, Chihuahua; engineering degree in agronomy from the Escuela Particular de Agricultura, 1925. **d**-*Governor of Chihuahua*, 1944–49. **e**-None. **f**-Chief, Department of Agriculture, Department of Agrarian Affairs, 1934–35; Assistant Director General of National Statistics, 1935–36; Director General of National Statistics, Jan., 1936, to Jan. 4, 1937; *Subsecretary of Agriculture*, Jan. 5, 1937, to 1940; *Head of the Department of Agrarian Affairs and Colonization*, 1941–43; Agrarian Adviser for the Department of Agrarian Affairs, Consultant No. 2, 1964–65. **g**-None. **h**-Regional agronomist, 1926; author of works on the geography and agriculture of Michoacan. **j**-None. **k**-Precandidate for governor of Chihuahua, 1940, opposed by *Alfredo Chavez* and ex-governor *Gustavo Talamontes*; competed for the PRI nomination for Senator from Chihuahua, 1970; Gonzalez Navarro states that he had over 30,000 hectares of his own land in Laguna de Palomas, Chihuahua; supported *Javier Rojo Gomez* for president, 1946. **l**-DPE65, 171; EBW46, 48; Enc. Mex., IV, 343; Strode, 403; D de Y, 5 Jan. 1940, 1; *Hoy*, 21 Mar. 1971, 4; WWM45, 42; STYBIWW54, 738; Gonzalez Navarro, 268; Anderson, 75–76; Lopez, 367; Gaxiola, 318.

Fonseca Alvarez, Guillermo

a-1931. **b**-San Luis Potosi, San Luis Potosi, *East Central*, *Urban*. **c**-Primary and secondary studies in San Luis Potosi; preparatory studies in San Luis Potosi; law degree, University of San Luis Potosi; teacher in history, geography, and Spanish grammar; professor of the General Theory of the State, Introduction to the Study of Law, and Sociology, School of Law, University of San Luis Potosi. **d**-*Federal*

Deputy from the State of San Luis Potosi, Dist. 4, 1967–68; Mayor of San Luis Potosi, 1968–69; *Senator* from San Luis Potosi, 1970–73; *Governor of San Luis Potosi*, 1973–79. **e-**President of the Regional Committee of PRI of the State of San Luis Potosi; General Delegate of the CEN of PRI; Director of a San Luis Potosi committee to support the candidacy of *Luis Echeverria* for president, 1969; *Director General of the IEPES of PRI*, 1979– . **f-**Agent of the Ministerio Publico of the Office of the Attorney General; Clerk for the Board of Conciliation and Arbitration of the State of San Luis Potosi; President of the Board of Conciliation and Arbitration of the State of San Luis Potosi. **g-**Secretary of the Law Students Society of the University of San Luis Potosi; Secretary General of the Federation of University Students of San Luis Potosi. **h-**Participant in various oratory contests in San Luis Potosi. **i-**Met *Luis Echeverria* as a Federal Deputy. **j-**None. **k-**None. **l-**HA, 22 Jan. 1973, 37–38; C de D, 1967–69; HA, 1 Oct. 1973, 30; Enc. Mex., Annual, 1977, 549–50.

Fonseca Garcia, Francisco

b-Federal District, *Federal District, Urban*. **c-**Medical degree from the National School of Medicine, UNAM, 1925; professor, School of Medicine, UNAM, 1964. **d-***Federal Deputy* from the Federal District, Dist. 4, 1949–52, member of the Child Welfare and Social Services Committee, the Legislative Studies Committee, and the Health Committee. **e-**None. **f-**Director of the General Hospital of Mexico, D.F.; head of Medical Services for the Institute of Social Security for Government Employees, 1963; Subdirector General (Medical) of the Institute of Social Security for Government Employees, 1964–70. **h-**Surgeon in the General Hospital, Mexico, D.F., 1925. **j-**None. **k-**None. **l-**HA, 21 Dec. 1964, 10; DGF51, I, 21, 30, 32, 36; MGF69, 623.

Fraga (Magana), Gabino

a-Apr. 19, 1899. **b-**Morelia, Michoacan, *West Central, Urban*. **c-**Primary studies in Morelia; secondary studies at the Colegio Primitivo de San Nicolas de Hidalgo, Morelia, 1910–13; law degree from the National School of Law, UNAM, 1920; Doctor of Laws from the National School of Law, UNAM, 1950; Professor of Administrative Law, National School of Law, UNAM, 1925–64; member of the Governing Board of UNAM. **d-**None. **e-**None. **f-**Consulting lawyer to the Secretariat of the Treasury, 1920; Oficial Mayor of the Secretariat of the Treasury, 1920; head of the Consultative Department, Secretariat of the Treasury; head of the Legal Department, Secretariat of Labor, 1924; head of the Legal Department, Secretariat of Industry and Commerce, 1930; head of the Department of Consultation and Legisla-

tion, Secretariat of Agriculture and Livestock, 1930; President of the National Banking Commission, 1935–38; *Justice of the Supreme Court*, 1941–44, and President of the Second Chamber; *Subsecretary of Foreign Relations*, 1964–70. **g-**None. **h-**Practicing attorney in Mexico, D.F., 1920; practicing attorney, 1938–41; member of various commissions for new legal codes; founding member of the Institute of Public Administration; author of numerous legal works. **i-**Professor of numerous public men at UNAM, including *Hugo B. Margain*, *Jose Castro Estrada* and *Manuel R. Palacios*; law partner with *Antonio Martinez Baez* for many years; son Gabino Fraga Mouret was Director General of Government, 1977. **j-**None. **k-**None. **l-**DPE65, 17; HA, 21 Dec. 1974, 4; DBM66, 244–45; WWM45, 42; Enc. Mex., IV, 392; *Justicia*, Sept. 1966; DAPC, 1977, 3.

Franco Bencomo, Joaquin

b-Yucatan, *Gulf*. **c-**Agricultural engineering degree, National School of Agriculture, Chapingo. **d-**None. **e-**None. **f-**Advisor to the Department of Agrarian Affairs; Chief of Agricultural Advisory Service, Dist. 8, for Oaxaca, Michoacan, Tlaxcala, Department of Agrarian Affairs, 1952–58; Chief of Agricultural Advisory Service, Dist. 8, 1958–64; *Secretary General (2) of the Department of Agrarian Affairs and Colonization*, 1964–70. **g-**None. **h-**Agricultural engineer for the Department of Agrarian Affairs, 1930; member of various agrarian commissions. **i-**Married Teresa Gongora. **j-**None. **k-**None. **l-**HA, 11 Jan. 1965, 9; DGF56, 454; DPE61, 128.

Franco Lopez, Manuel

a-Apr. 10, 1921. **b-**Federal District, *Federal District, Urban*. **c-**Preparatory studies from the National Preparatory School; engineering degree from the National School of Engineering, UNAM, 1944; Professor of Geology and Mining Exploitation, School of Engineering, UNAM, 1954. **d-**None. **e-**None. **f-**Member of the National Council on Natural Resources; *Subsecretary of Unrenewable Resources of the Secretariat of Government Properties*; 1964–66; *Secretary of Government Properties*, 1966–70. **g-**None. **h-**Superintendent, Empresa Dos Estrellas, S.A.; Subdirector, Cia. Minera, S.A.; geologist for the Secretariat of Hydraulic Resources; Gerente, Metalurgicas de Guadalajara, S.A.; consulting engineer and contractor on many projects. **i-**Co-student with *Luis de la Pena Porth*; father a mining engineer. **j-**None. **k-**None. **l-**D del S, 21 Sept. 1966; DPE65, 76; DBM66, 245; Enc. Mex., 1977, IV, 402; letter.

Franco Rodriguez, David

a-Apr. 10, 1915. **b-**Pajacuaran, Michoacan, *West Central, Rural*. **c-**Primary studies in Pajacuaran; secondary and preparatory studies at the Colegio de San Nicolas; law studies, National School of Law, UNAM; law degree, Colegio de San Nicolas, 1940; Professor of law, University of Michoacan; Secretary, University of Michoacan. **d-***Federal Deputy* from Michoacan, Dist. 4, 1949–51, member of the Gran Comision, the Second Government Committee, the National Waters and Irrigation Committee, and the Legal Complaints Committee; *Senator* from Michoacan, 1952–58, member of the Gran Comision, 1954, substitute member of the First and Second Committees on Credit, Money, and Credit Institutions, and the Second Government Committee; member of the Small Private Farms Committee and the First Petroleum Committee; *Governor of Michoacan*, 1956–62. **f-**Appeals court judge, Cacoman, Tacambaro and Marauatio, Michoacan; consulting lawyer to the Secretary of Agriculture and the National Irrigation Commission; Director of the Consulting Department, Secretariat of Hydraulic Resources; *Assistant Attorney General (1) of Mexico*, 1964–70; *Assistant Attorney General of Mexico*, 1970–73; *Justice of the Supreme Court*, 1973–76, 1976– . **g-**None. **i-**Grandfather, David Franco, was a local deputy in Michoacan and orator. **j-**None. **k-**None. **l-**DPE65, 209; DGF51, I, 23, 30, 33; Enc. Mex., IV, 402; DGF56, 6, 9–12, 14; HA, 24 Sept. 1962, 28; DP70, 789; Ind. Biog., 64–65.

Franco Sodi, Carlos
(Deceased Apr. 16, 1961)
a-1904. **b-**Oaxaca, Oaxaca, *South, Urban*. **c-**Primary studies in Oaxaca; preparatory at the Institute of Science and Art of Oaxaca; law degree from the National School of Law, UNAM; Professor of Penal Law and the Penal Process, National School of Law, UNAM; Honorary Doctor of Laws, UNAM, **d-**None. **e-**None. **f-**Assistant Agent of the Ministerio Publico of the Attorney General's Office for the Federal District; Director of the *Diario Oficial* of the Federal Government; Judge of the Criminal Court, Pachuca, Hidalgo; Director of the Federal Penitentiary in the Federal District, 1935–36; Judge of the First Instance; *Attorney General of the Federal District and Federal Territories*, 1946–52; *Attorney General of Mexico*, 1952–56; *Justice of the Supreme Court*, 1956–58, and 1958–61. **g-**Member of the National Center of Anti-Reelectionist Students, National School of Law, UNAM, 1927, opposed to Obregon's election. **h-**Expert on criminal law; author of numerous books on legal subjects; editor of *Criminology*. **i-**Friend of *Jose Castro Estrada* and *Miguel Aleman* from college years. **j-**None. **k-**None. **l-***El Universal*, 2 Dec. 1958; DGF51, I, 487; DGF47, 294; Peral, 282; DP70, 790; Enc. Mex., IV, 403; DGF56, 539; D del S, 2 Dec. 1946, 1; Lopez, 369; Villasenor, I, 264.

Franco Urias, Salvador
b-Durango, *West*. **c-**Early education unknown; law degree. **d-**Federal Deputy from the State of Durango, 1920–22, 1922–24; *Senator* from the State of Durango, 1940–46, President of the Military Justice Committee, First Secretary of the Physical Education Committee, Second Secretary of the Development of Cooperatives Committee and member of the Gran Comision. **e-**None. **f-**None. **g-**None. **h-**Director of *El Continental*, El Paso, Texas; journalist for many years. **j-**Supported Adolfo de la Huerta against the government, 1923; supported the Escobar rebellion, 1929. **k-**None. **l-**Peral, 282; C de S, 1940–46; L de O, 1946, 6.

Fritsche Anda, Oscar
(Deceased 1965)
a-Apr. 10, 1906. **b-**Guanajuato, Guanajuato, *West Central, Urban*. **c-**Primary studies in Guanajuato; preparatory in Mexico, D.F.; graduated from the National Naval College, January, 1927; spent several years at the National War College, Mexico, D.F.; professor at the Naval College; Director of the Naval College of the Pacific. **d-**None. **e-**None. **f-**Chief of Naval Services for the Commander of the Navy, 1955–58; Naval Attache to Italy, 1958–61; *Subsecretary of the Navy*, 1964–65. **g-**None. **h-**Author of *Nomogramos Astronomicos*. **j-**Career naval officer; member of the Coast Guard, 1928–29; head of the Department of Information, Navy Department, 1933–34; Commander of the "Progreso," 1934–35; commander of various naval zones including the 3rd for Baja California, 1940–46; Commander of the 5th Naval Zone, Ciudad del Carmen, Campeche, 1951. **k-**Shipped arms to Republican Spain during the Civil War. **l-**DGF51, I, 389; Enc. Mex., IV, 414; DP70, 793–94; DGF47, 234; DGF56, 386; HA, 21 Dec. 1964, 9.

Fuentes Diaz, Vicente
a-1920. **b-**Chilpancingo, Guerrero, *South, Urban*. **c-**Early education unknown; teaching certificate, National Teachers School, 1939. **d-***Alternate Federal Deputy* from the State of Guerrero, Dist. 1, 1961–64; *Federal Deputy* from the State of Guerrero, Dist. 1, 1964–67, member of the Gran Comision, President of the Chamber, Oct., 1965; member of the Cultural Affairs Committee, the Editorial Committee, the First Treasury Committee, and the Legislative Studies Committee on General Affairs; *Senator* from the State of Guerrero, 1970–76, President of the Editorial and Library Committee, secretary of the First Foreign Relations and the First Tariff and Foreign Trade Committees; Secretary of the Gran Comision. **e-**Member of the Mexican Communist Party, expelled, 1943; Secretary of Press and Propaganda for the Popular Socialist Party; left the PPS in

1957; co-founder of the Youth Sector of PRI, 1938; member of the Regional Committee of PRI for the Federal District, 1954–61; Director of the National Editorial Commission of the CEN of PRI, 1969; *Secretary General of the CEN of PRI*, 1970–72. **f-**None. **g-**Director of Press for the CNOP. **h-**Author of many books on politics and history. **i-**Friend of *Enrique Ramirez y Ramirez*. **j-**None. **k-**None. **l-**Scott, 181; Enc. Mex., IV, 487; C de D, 1964, 66; letters; HA, 8 Jan. 1973, 11; *Politica*, Nov. 1969.

Galeano Sierra, Adalberto
(Deceased, 1957)
b-Campeche, Campeche, *Gulf, Urban*. **c-**Primary studies in Campeche, Campeche; law degree, School of Law, Instituto Campechano. **d-**Senator from the State of Campeche, 1924–28. **e-**None. **f-**Secretary of the District Court, Campeche; Judge of the Superior Tribunal of Justice of the State of Campeche; Attorney General of Campeche; Secretary General of Government of the State of Campeche; Justice of the Superior Tribunal of Justice of the Federal District and Federal Territories, 1929–57. **g-**None. **j-**None. **k-**None. **l-**DP70, 803; Casasola, V, 2442; DGF56, 513; DGF51, I, 486.

Galguera Torres, Hilario
a-Mar. 26, 1928. **b-**Federal District, *Federal District, Urban*. **c-**Architecture degree, National School of Architecture, UNAM, 1946–50; Professor of Composition, Universidad Femenina Motolinia; Assistant in Composition, National School of Architecture; Professor of Urbanism, School of City Engineers, 1955; Professor of Composition, University of Ibero-America, 1961. **d-***Federal Deputy* from the Federal District, Dist. 23, 1967–70, member of the Cultural Affairs Committee and the Department of the Federal District Committee. **e-**Director of *Luis Gonzalez Aparicio's* campaign for Federal Senator, 1964. **f-**Architectural foreman, National Hospital Commission, 1956; head of the Planning Subcommittee for Huixquilcuan, Mexico; head of the Technical Works Division for Nonoalco, 1960; Director General of Projects for the Construction Commission of the Secretariat of Health, 1965. **g-**President of the Student Association of the National School of Architecture, 1948; Secretary of the Federation of University Students and representative before the Gran Comision. **h-**Adviser to UNESCO; foreman for Mario Pani and Enrique del Moral, architects; supervisor of the construction of the rectory of the National University. **j-**None. **k-**None. **l-**DBM68, 249; C de D, 1967–69, 58; MGF69, 91.

Galindo Arce, Marcelina
a-Nov. 30, 1920. **b-**Pichucalco, Chiapas, *South, Urban*. **c-**Primary and secondary studies; preparatory

studies; normal teaching certificate; school teacher. **d-***Federal Deputy* from the State of Chiapas, Dist. 4, 1955–58, member of the Promotion and Development of Sports Committee, the Child Welfare Committee, the Social Security Committee and the Social Action Committee. **e-**None. **f-**None. **g-**None. **h-**Journalist. **j-**None. **k-**First female deputy elected from the State of Chiapas. **l-**Ind. Biog., 65–66; DGF56, 22, 30, 31, 36.

Galindo Ochoa, Francisco
a-Mar. 8, 1913. **b-**Tamazula de Gordiano, Jalisco, *West, Rural*. **c-**Early education unknown; no degree. **d-***Federal Deputy* from the State of Jalisco, Dist. 7, 1949–52, Secretary of the First Instructive Section of the Grand Jury and member of the First Balloting Committee; *Federal Deputy* from the State of Jalisco, Dist. 11, 1955–58, member of the Second Balloting Committee and the Editorial Committee (first year). **e-**Adviser to the PRM; Director of the Office of the Popular Sector of the PRM; Treasurer of PRI during the Ruiz Cortines presidential campaign, 1952; President of PRI in the Federal District; *Secretary of Political Action of the CEN of PRI*, 1956–58; *Secretary of Press and Publicity of the CEN of PRI*, 1958. **f-**Director General of the Department of Fishing; Director General of Press and Publicity, President of Mexico, 1965. **g-**Secretary of Organization of CNOP, Federal District; Secretary of the CEN of CNOP. **j-**None. **k-**None. **l-**DPE65, 11; Ind. Biog., 66–67; DGF56, 25, 32, 334; DGF51, I, 22, 34.

Gallastegui, Jose S.
a-Nov. 11, 1929. **b-**Federal District, *Federal District, Urban*. **c-**Law degree. **d-**None. **e-**None. **f-**Career foreign service officer; attached to the Mexican Embassy in France; Director General of Legal Affairs for the Secretariat of Foreign Relations; Director General of the Diplomatic Service; Director General of International Organizations; Director General of the Consular Service; Director General of Migratory Workers; head of the Office of Technical Advisers, Secretariat of Foreign Relations; Private Secretary to the Secretary of Foreign Relations under *Manuel Tello, Jose Gorostiza*, and *Antonio Carrillo Flores*, 1958–65; *Oficial Mayor of the Secretariat of Foreign Relations*, 1965–70; *Subsecretary of Foreign Relations*, 1970–76; Inspector General of the Diplomatic Missions, Secretariat of Foreign Relations, 1976– . **g-**None. **h-**Joined the Foreign Service, June 1, 1947; rank of ambassador. **i-**Married Luisa Paredes. **j-**None. **k-**None. **l-**DPE71, 6; DPE65, 17; DPE61, 15; HA, 14 Dec. 1970, 20.

Galvan (Bourel), Ferrer
a-1920. **b-**Veracruz, *Gulf*. **c-**Agricultural engineering degree, School of Agriculture, Ciudad Juarez,

Chihuahua, 1937. **d-**Local deputy to the State Legislature of Veracruz. **e-**None. **f-**Agronomist, Department of Agriculture, State of Veracruz, 1938; engineer, National Highway Department; *Subsecretary of Agrarian Action*, June 19, 1978– . **g-**Chief of the Agrarian Brigade, Acayucan, Veracruz; Substitute Secretary General of the Agrarian Commission of Veracruz, 1948; Alternate Secretary General of the CNC, 1952; *Secretary General of the CNC (substitute)*, 1952–53. **h-**None. **i-**Son of a distinguished Mexican agrarian leader, Ursulo Galvan, who was a carpenter by profession; mother worked in the Civil Hospital of Veracruz; grandparents were landless peasants; mother, *Irene*, was a federal deputy from Veracruz, 1961–64. **j-**None. **k-**None. **l-**HA, 1 Feb. 1952, 8–9; Enc. Mex., 1977, V, 74; *Excelsior*, 17 June 1978, 1, 10.

Galvan Campos, Fausto

a-1909. **b-**Cuernavaca, Morelos, *West Central*, *Urban*. **c-**Primary and secondary studies in Mexico City; preparatory studies completed in Mexico City, 1926; law degree, National School of Law, UNAM, June 3, 1932, with a thesis on the reforms in Article One, of the January 6, 1915 Agrarian Law. **d-***Senator* from the State of Morelos, 1952–58, President of the Agrarian Department Committee, member of the Second Balloting Committee, President of the Second Instructive Section of the Grand Jury, First Secretary of the Special Forest Committee and Second Secretary of the Agricultural Development Committee. **e-**President of PRI in Morelos, 1952. **f-**Director of the Congressional Library; Judge of the Fifth Penal Court, Mexico City; President of the Superior Tribunal of Justice of the State of Morelos; Secretary General of Government of the State of Morelos, 1951, under Governor *Ernesto Escobar Munoz*. **g-**Co-founder of the CNC; founder of the League of Agrarian Communities of the State of Morelos. **i-**Co-student at the National School of Law with *Ernesto Escobar Munoz* and *Jesus Castillo Lopez*, Governor of Morelos, 1942–46. **j-**None. **k-**None. **l-**Ind. Biog., 67; DGF51, I, 90; C de S, 1952–58; DGF56, 6, 9, 10, 11, 13, 14.

Galvan Lopez, Felix

a-Jan. 20, 1913. **b-**Villa de Santiago, Guanajuato, *West Central*, *Urban*. **c-**Primary studies in Villa de Santiago; preparatory studies in Mexico City and in Queretaro; enrolled at the National Military College, January 7, 1930, graduating as a 2nd Lieutenant in the Cavalry, January 1, 1934; distinguished cadet, served as a sergeant of the cadets; graduated from the Staff and Command School, Higher War College, 1941–44; course in military arms from the Applied Military School, 1937; lecturer at the Inter-American Defense College, Washington, D.C. **d-**None. **e-**None. **f-**Member of the Presidential Staff, 1946–

52; assistant to the military attache, Washington, D.C., January 1, 1952 to April 30, 1953; assistant to the Inspector General of the Army, October 1, 1959 to August 15, 1965; Private Secretary to the Secretary of National Defense, *Marcelino Garcia Barragan*, August 16, 1965 to January 15, 1969; Chief of Staff of the Secretariat of National Defense, January 16, 1969 to November 30, 1970; *Secretary of National Defense*, 1976– . **g-**None. **h-**None. **i-**Married Elisa Juarez. **j-**Career army officer; served in the 20th, 13th and 35th Regiments, 1934–40; fought against the rebellion of *Saturnino Cedillo* in San Luis Potosi, 1939; Section Chief of the 3rd Infantry Division, 1946; rank of 2nd Captain, 1946; rank of Colonel, November 16, 1952; rank of Brigade General, November 20, 1968; rank of divisionary general, November 20, 1970; Commander of the 6th Military Zone, Torreon, Coahuila, 1970–72; Commander of the 16th Military Zone, Irapuato, Guanajuato, 1973–74; Commander of the 5th Military Zone, Chihuahua, Chihuahua, 1974–76. **k-**Founded the first school for the Huichole Indians, Jalisco, 1939. **l-**HA, 6 Dec. 1976, 22; *El Dia*, 1 Dec. 1976; DPE65, 34; Enc. Mex., Annual, 1977, 536–37; *Excelsior*, 1 Dec. 1976, 13.

Galvan Maldonado, Rafael

a-1919. **b-**Uruapan, Michoacan, *West Central*, *Urban*. **c-**Primary studies in Jacona and Zamora, Michoacan; secondary and preparatory studies from the Colegio de San Nicolas, Morelia, Michoacan, and from Vocational School No. 2 of the IPN and the National Preparatory School No. 1; two years of studies at the Higher School of Mechanical and Electrical Engineering, IPN; four years of studies at the National School of Economics, UNAM. **d-***Senator* from the State of Michoacan, 1964–70, member of the Gran Comision. **e-**Founding member of the PRM. **f-**None. **g-**Student leader; founder of several student newspapers; Secretary General of the Union of Electrical Workers of Mexico; President of the National Workers Central. **h-**Employee of the Radio and Electric Industry; employee of the La Boquilla, Chihuahua Electric Plant. **j-**None. **k-**His senatorial nomination surprised most observers. **l-**PS, 2199; C de S, 1964–70; MGF69.

Galvez Betancourt, Carlos

a-Feb. 14, 1921. **b-**Jiquilpan, Michoacan, *West Central*, *Rural*. **c-**Preparatory studies from the National Preparatory School, 1939–40; law degree, National Law School, UNAM, 1946, with a special mention; professor of logic and ethics, National Preparatory and Normal School, 1949–64; Professor of Constitutional Law and the Philosophy of Law, National School of Law, UNAM. **d-***Governor of Michoacan*, 1968–70. **e-**Joined the PRM, 1940.

f-Subdirector of the Department of Professions, Secretariat of Public Education, 1950–56; Subdirector of the Department of Physical Education, Secretariat of Public Education, 1956–58; Subdirector and Director of Immigration, Secretariat of Goverment, 1958; Subdirector General of Government, Secretariat of Government, under *Tristan Canales Valverde*, 1958–61; Director General of Legal Affairs, Secretariat of Government, 1964; *Oficial Mayor of Government*, 1964–65; *Subsecretary of Government*, under *Luis Echeverria Alvarez*, 1965–68; *Director General of the Mexican Institute of Social Security*, 1970–75; *Secretary of Labor*, 1975–76. g-Secretary General of the Association of Professors and Intellectual Workers. h-Worked for the Department of Professions, Secretariat of Public Education, 1945–48. i-Student with *Alfonso Noriega*, *Jr*. at the National University; collaborator of *Luis Echeverria* in various positions, 1954–68; uncle of *Ignacio Galvez Rocha*, federal deputy from Michoacan, 1970–73. j-None. k-None. l-DPE61, 12; DPE65, 13; HA, 7 Dec. 1970, 26; DGF56, 302; HA, 21 Dec. 1964, 4; HA, 6 Oct. 1975; Cadena, 38.

Galvez Rocha, Ignacio

a-June 22, 1940. b-Jiquilpan, Michoacan, *West Central*, *Urban*. c-Primary studies at the Federal School Francisco Madero, Jiquilpan, 1949–54; preparatory studies at the National Preparatory School No. 2, Mexico, D.F., 1955–60; medical degree, National School of Medicine, UNAM, 1961–67. d-*Federal Deputy* from the State of Michoacan, Dist. 5, 1970–73, member of the Public Assistance Committee, the Social Welfare Committee (1st year), and the Health Committee. e-Delegate of the CNOP of PRI during *Gustavo Diaz Ordaz*'s campaign for President, 1964; Secretary of Political Action and Vice President of the National Committee of CNOP; Delegate for Internal Affairs, CNOP; Secretary of Social Action, CEN of CNOP, 1974. f-Director of Medical Services for Sports, Secretariat of Public Works; Auxiliary Secretary to Governor *Carlos Galvez Betancourt*, 1968–70. g-Secretary of Political Action of the Mexican Federation of University Students. h-None. i-Nephew of *Carlos Galvez Betancourt*. j-None. k-None. l-*Directorio*, 1970–72; C de D, 1970–72, 114; *Excelsior*, 20 Oct. 1974.

Gama (y Cruz), Valentin

(Deceased, 1942)
a-1868. b-San Luis Potosi, San Luis Potosi, *East Central*, *Urban*. c-Secondary and preparatory studies at the Scientific and Literary Institute of San Luis Potosi; degree in engineering, National School of Engineering, 1893; Professor, National School of Engineering, 1904–15; Dean, National School of Engineering. d-None. e-Co-founder of PAN, 1939.

f-Member of the International Boundary Commission Between Mexico and the United States, 1891–96; Subdirector of the National Observatory, 1903–10; Director of the National Observatory; Rector of UNAM, September to December, 1914 and April to June, 1915. g-None. h-None. i-Son of Dr. Ignacio Gama, Rector of the Scientific and Literary Institute of San Luis Potosi. j-None. k-None. l-DP70, 810; Lopez, 385.

Gamboa Pascasio, Noe

a-1905. b-Tuxtla Gutierrez, Chiapas, *South*, *Urban*. c-Medical degree from the National School of Medicine, UNAM; postgraduate work in medicine in France. d-Local deputy to the State Legislature of Chiapas. e-None. f-None. g-None. h-Practicing physician in the Federal District. i-Brother of *Rafael Gamboa Pascasio*, Governor of Chiapas and Secretary of Health. j-None. k-Precandidate for the Governorship of Chiapas, 1948; known for his altruism in the state of Chiapas, providing free medical service to the poor. l-HA, 6 Feb. 1948, 10.

Gamboa Pascasio, Rafael

(Deceased Aug. 2, 1979)
a-May 20,1897. b-Tuxtla Gutierrez, Chiapas, *South*, *Urban*. c-Primary studies in Tuxtla Gutierrez; secondary studies at the Prevocational and Industrial School; medical degree from the National Medical School, UNAM, 1923; studies in medicine in France; professor at the University of Chiapas. d-*Federal Deputy* from the State of Chiapas, Dist. 2, 1937–40; *Governor of Chiapas*, 1940–44. e-General Coordinator of *Miguel Aleman's* campaign for President; First President of the reorganized CEN of PRI, Jan. 19, to Dec. 5, 1946. f-Director General of Pensions of the Union of Government Bureaucrats, 1945; Secretary General of Government of the State of Chiapas, 1939–40, under Governor *Efrain Gutierrez*; *Secretary of Public Health*, 1946–52. g-None. h-Practicing physician in Tuxtla Gutierrez, 1923–35; entered state politics, 1935. i-Father-in-law of *Emilio Rabasa*, Secretary of Foreign Relations, 1970–75; son, *Rafael P*. *Gamboa Cano* was a Federal Deputy from Chiapas, 1961–64; married Carmen Cano; uncle of Humberto Gamboa Pascasio, federal deputy from Chiapas, 1943–45. j-None. k-Was imposed by *Miguel Aleman* as the President of PRI alienating other party leaders. l-*Polemica*, Vol. I, No. 1, 1969; *Hoy*, 21 Dec. 1940, 78; DGF50, II, 485; DPE51, I, 733, 335; DPE51, II, 713, etc.; *Excelsior*, 2 Dec. 1946; HA, 6 Dec. 1946, 6; Enc. Mex., V, 106–07; HA, 13 Aug. 1979, 11.

Gamboa Pascoe, Joaquin

c-Early education unknown; law degree, National School of Law, UNAM, 1939–44. d-*Alternate*

Senator from the Federal District under *Fidel Velazquez Sanchez*, 1958–64; *Federal Deputy* from the Federal District, Dist. 18, 1961–64, member of the Labor Section of the Legislative Studies Committee and the First Constitutional Affairs Committee; *Federal Deputy* from the Federal District, Dist. 13, 1967–70, member of the Administration Committee, the Second Instructive Section of the Grand Jury, the Budget and Accounts Committee (second year) and the Second Labor Committee; *Senator* from the Federal District, 1976– , President of the Gran Comision, 1976– . **e-**Auxiliary Secretary to the CEN of PRI. **f-**None. **g-**Secretary of Political Action of the Union of Workers of the Department of the Federal District; lawyer, Legal Office, Union of Workers of the Department of the Federal District; Secretary General of the Union of Workers of the Department of the Federal District, 1973–78; Secretary General of the CTM in the Federal District, 1977– . **i-**Long-time friend of *Jesus Yuren* whom he met at the Legal Office of the Union of Workers of the Department of the Federal District; son-in-law of *Fidel Velazquez*; son Joaquin Gamboa Enriquez was a precandidate for Federal Deputy, 1979; co-student with *Jose Lopez Portillo* at UNAM. **j-**None. **k-**PRI candidate for Federal Deputy from the Federal District, 1973, but defeated by *Javier Blanco Sanchez* of PAN. **l-**C de D, 1961–64, 78; C de D, 1967–70, 55, 79, 83; *Proceso*, 18 Dec. 1976, 8–9; *Proceso*, 11 Dec. 1976, 20–21.

Games Orozco, Edmundo

(Deceased 1953)

a-1902. **b-**Aguascalientes, Aguascalientes, *West*, *Urban*. **c-**Primary studies in Aguascalientes; teaching certificate from the San Carlos Academy, Mexico, D.F., 1919–23; secondary school teacher; Professor of Pedagogical Studies, 1936. **d-***Federal Senator* from the State of Aguascalientes, 1946–52, member of the First Committee on Tariffs and Foreign Commerce, the Agrarian Department Committee, the First Committee on Public Education, the Consulate and Diplomatic Service Committee, and the Protocol Committee; substitute member of the National Railroads Committee; *Governor of Aguascalientes*, 1950–53. **e-**None. **f-**Director General of Education, State of Aguascalientes, 1934–36; Secretary of the Federal Department of Education, Secretariat of Public Education; Director of Federal Schools in the State of Aguascalientes; Federal Inspector for the Secretariat of Public Education, State of Coahuila, 1937; Federal Inspector, Secretariat of Public Education, Ojo Caliente, Zacatecas, 1937–40; Federal Inspector, Secretariat of Public Education, Juchilpila, Zacatecas, 1941–44; Director of Education in Zacatecas for the Secretariat of Public Education, 1944–46. **g-**Director of the Teachers Union, 1940.

j-None. **k-**None. **l-**DGF47, 19; Enc. Mex., V, 109; DGF51, I, 5, 10, 11, 14, 88; C de S, 1946–52; DP70, 812; Anderson.

Gamiz Fernandez, Jr., Salvador

a-July 9, 1922. **b-**Durango, Durango, *West*, *Urban*. **c-**Primary studies in Durango; secondary studies at a public school in Durango; medical degree, IPN. **d-***Senator* from the State of Durango, 1970–76, member of the Gran Comision, President of the Health Committee, member of the First Balloting Group, First Secretary of the First Foreign Relations Committee, Second Secretary of the Public Welfare Committee. **e-**Joined PRI, 1958; aide to the President of the CEN of PRI, 1960–65; President of PRI in Durango; General Delegate of the CEN of PRI, 1964; *Secretary of Political Action of the CEN of PRI*, 1970–71; *Subsecretary of Political Action of the CEN of PRI*, 1973. **f-**Physician, Secretariat of Health, 1960–69; Director, ISSSTE Clinic; *Interim Governor of Durango*, Dec. 13, 1979– . **g-**Member of the Technical Council of the CNC; President of the Medical Association of the IPN; President of the National Association of Graduates of Schools for Workers' Sons. **i-**Father a peasant; brother *Maximo Gamiz Fernandez* was Secretary General of PRI in the Federal District and a federal deputy from Durango, 1952–55; originally a political disciple of *Vicente Lombardo Toledano*. **j-**None. **k-**None. **l-***Excelsior*, 16 Dec. 1979, 18; HA, 24 Dec. 1979, 10; C de S, 1970–76, 75.

Gandarilla Aviles, Emilio

a-Feb. 6, 1923. **b-**Federal District, *Federal District*, *Urban*. **c-**Early education unknown; no degree. **d-***Federal Deputy* from the Federal District, Dist. 8, 1958–61, member of the Department of the Federal District Committee, the General Accounting Office Committee and the Budget and Accounts Committee; *Federal Deputy* from the Federal District, Dist. 8, 1964–67, member of the Department of the Federal District Committee, the Complaints Committee, and the Foreign Relations Committee. **e-**President of PRI for the Eighth District, Federal District. **f-**Adviser to the Direction of Pensions; President of the National Housing Committee. **g-**Secretary of Interior of Section Fifteen, the Department of the Federal District Union; Press Secretary of the Department of the Federal District Union; Secretary of the Pension Fund of the Department of the Federal District Union. **h-**Journalist; graphic editor of *El Universal*. **j-**None. **k-**None. **l-**Func., 183; C de D, 1958–60, 77; C de D, 1964–67, 81, 92, 93.

Garabito Martinez, Jorge

a-Mar. 29, 1915. **b-**Guadalajara, Jalisco, *West*, *Urban*. **c-**Primary and secondary studies in Guadalajara;

preparatory studies in Guadalajara; law degree, School of Law, University of Guadalajara; studies in economics and philosophy. **d-**Federal Deputy from the Federal District, Dist. 16, 1964–67, member of the Penal Section of the Legislative Studies Committee; Federal Deputy from the Federal District, Dist. 1, 1970–73, member of the Department of the Federal District Committee, Social Security Committee, Fish and Game Committee and the Cinematographic Development Committee; Federal Deputy from the Federal District, Dist. 12, 1976–79. **e-**Founding member of PAN, 1939; represented PAN before the Federal Electoral Committee; President of PAN in the Federal District; member of the CEN of PAN. **f-**None. **g-**None. **h-**Practicing lawyer; entrepreneur in the glass industry. **i-**Married Maria Teresa Yanez. **j-**None. **k-**None. **l-**C de D, 1976–79, 23; C de D, 1964–67, 83; Directorio, 1970–72; C de D, 1970–73, 115; Mabry.

Garate (Legleu), Raul

a-Sept. 11, 1901. **b-**Matamoros, Tamaulipas, North, Rural. **c-**Primary studies at a public school, Matamoros; secondary studies in the United States; no degree. **d-**Federal Deputy to the Constitutional Convention, 1916–17; Senator from the State of Tamaulipas, 1952–58, member of the General Means of Communication Committee, the War Materiels Committee, and the Third National Defense Committee. **e-**None. **f-**Inspector General of Police, Mexico, D.F.; Provisional Governor of Tamaulipas, 1947–51. **g-**None. **h-**None. **j-**Joined the Revolution in 1913 under General Lucio Blanco; Governor and Military Commander of Tamaulipas, 1915–16; remained loyal to Carranza, 1920; rejoined the Army, 1923; Military Commander of the 22nd Zone, Toluca, Mexico, 1924; Brigadier General, 1924; Chief of Staff, 22nd Military Zone, 1924–33; Commander of the Garrison at Tapachula, Chiapas; Chief of Staff, 17th Military Zone, Queretaro; Commander of the 2nd Cavalry Regiment, 1941; rank of Divisionary General. **k-**Imposed by Miguel Aleman as Governor over the protests of local leaders and citizens; pre-candidate for governor, 1945, defeated by Hugo Gonzalez; opposed by Emilio Portes Gil and Magdaleno Aguilar for provisional governor. **l-**HA, 6 Sept. 1971, 19; Peral, 302; HA, 6 Oct. 1950, xiv; DGF56, 8, 10, 12, 13; Brandenburg, 103; NYT, 10 Apr. 1947, 5; Anderson, 348; Lopez, 391.

Garcia (Aguirre), Trinidad

(Deceased Feb. 2, 1981)
a-Dec. 11, 1895. **b-**Federal District, Federal District, Urban. **c-**Secondary studies from the Institute of Science and Letters of Mexico; preparatory studies at the Institute of Science and Letters of Mexico, Toluca, and at the National Preparatory School; law

degree from the National School of Law, UNAM, December 11, 1919; honorary LLD, National School of Law, UNAM, 1950; professor at the National Preparatory School; professor at the School of the Brothers of Mary; Professor of Civil Law, Mercantile Law and International Public Law, National School of Law, UNAM, 1919–70; Professor of Civil Law, LLD Program, National School of Law, UNAM, 1950–70; member, Board of Governors, UNAM, 1932–40; Dean of the National School of Law, UNAM, 1934–35. **d-**None. **e-**Founding member of the National Council of PAN, 1939; founding member of the CEN of PAN, 1939. **f-**General counsel for UNAM. **g-**None. **h-**Practicing lawyer, Mexico City; represented the petroleum companies in labor-management disputes, 1938. **i-**Son of lawyer and historian Genaro Garcia; married Elisa Terres; son Jaime Garcia Torres is a prominent poet and Subdirector of the Fondo de Cultura Economica; close friend of Manuel Gomez Morin. **j-**None. **k-**Emilio Portes Gil offered him an appointment as Justice of the Supreme Court in 1929, but he declined; participant in the 1929 Autonomy Movement at UNAM. **l-**WWM45, 44; letter; WNM, 87; Lopez, 410; DBM70, 242; Novo35, 423.

Garcia Barragan, Marcelino

(Deceased Sept. 3, 1979)
a-June 2, 1895. **b-**Cuauhtitlan, Jalisco, West, Rural. **c-**Primary studies in the Primary School of Autlan; military studies at the National Military College, 1920; Adjutant General of the National Military College, 1926–29; Director of the National Military College, 1941–42. **d-**Governor of Jalisco, 1943–46. **e-**President of the Federation of People's Parties, 1950–52. **f-**Secretary of National Defense, 1964–70. **g-**None. **h-**None. **i-**Friend of General Matias Ramos Santos, Secretary of National Defense, 1952–57, and of Francisco L. Urquizo Benavides, Secretary of National Defense, 1945–46; close friend and companion of Roberto Fierro at the National Military College; son Javier Garcia Paniagua was Senator from Jalisco, 1970–76 and Subsecretary of Government, 1978; brother of Sebastian Garcia Barragan. **j-**Participated in the Revolution as an enlisted man, 1913; rank of Major, 1921; military mission to Brazil and Argentina, 1921, 1924; Lt. Colonel, 1924; Colonel and Commanding Officer of the 11th Cavalry Regiment, 1928; rank of Brigadier General, 1940; not in the Army, 1950–58; reincorporated back into the Army in 1958 by President Lopez Mateos; commander of various military zones including the 11th, 17th, and 22nd; rank of Divisionary General. **k-**Leader of the candidacy of General Henriquez Guzman for President, 1951; example of the co-optation process by the political system in Mexico; forced out of the governorship for not putting into effect the constitutional six year term, February 17,

1947. l-Lieuwen, 147; Enc. Mex., V, 178; HA, 7 Dec. 1964, 18; EWB46, 123; McAlister, 224; WB48, 1921; DPE65, 33; WWW70–71, 335; *Siempre*, 4 Feb. 1959, 6; NYT, 18 Feb. 1947, 15; *Excelsior*, 14 Sept. 1976, 4; *Excelsior*, 17 Aug. 1978, 17; *Excelsior*, 5 Sept. 1979, 19; HA, 10 Sept. 1979, 27.

Garcia Barragan, Sebastian

a-1915. b-Autlan de Navarro, Jalisco, *West*, *Urban*. c-Primary studies in Autlan, Jalisco; no degree. d-Vice Mayor of Guadalajara, 1943–44; Mayor of Autlan; City Councilmember of Guadalajara, 1947–48; *Federal Deputy* from the State of Jalisco, Dist. 10, 1958–61, member of the Social Action Committee; *Federal Deputy* from the State of Jalisco, Dist. 11, 1967–70, member of the Agrarian Section of the Legislative Studies Committee, the Military Health Committee, the Sugar Industry Committee and the Small Agricultural Property Committee. e-None. f-Income tax official, Autlan. g-President of the Ejido Committee, Autlan. i-Brother of *Marcelino Garcia Barragan*, Secretary of National Defense, 1964–70. j-None. k-None. l-C de D, 1958–61, 77; Enc. Mex., 1977, V, 579; C de D, 1967–70, 69, 74, 82; Func., 249.

Garcia Correa, Bartolome

(Deceased 1978)

a-Apr. 2, 1893. b-Uman, Yucatan, *Gulf*, *Rural*. c-Primary studies at a private night school; secondary studies from the Literary Institute of Yucatan; primary school teacher; professor at the Modelo School. d-Deputy to the Constitutional Convention of Queretaro, 1916–17; Mayor of Uman, Yucatan; Mayor of Merida, Yucatan; Local Deputy to the State Legislature of Yucatan, 1917; Senator from the State of Yucatan, 1928–30; Governor of Yucatan, 1930–34; *Senator* from the State of Yucatan, 1934–40. e-Member of the Antireelectionist Party, 1910; Secretary of the Benito Juarez Political Club, 1913; founder and Vice-president of the Socialist Party of the Southeast, 1918; member of the organizing committee to establish the PNR, Dec., 1928. f-Interim Governor of Yucatan (3 times); Private Secretary to Felipe Carrillo Puerto as Mayor of Merida. g-Founder of the Mutualist Workers Unions, 1913. h-Laborer in a harness factory. j-Supported the Constitutionalists; opposed to Adolfo de la Huerta. k-Jailed for political activities; retired from politics in Cerro de Ortega, Tecoman, Colima, since 1940. l-PS, 2283; C de S, 1934–40; Loet de Mola, Caciques, 102.

Garcia Cruz, Miguel

(Deceased 1969)

a-Oct. 13, 1909. b-Cuanana, Oaxaca, *South*, *Rural*. c-Primary studies in Cuanana; preparatory studies at

the Central Agricultural School El Mexe, Hidalgo, 1927–29; engineering degree from the National School of Agriculture, Chapingo, 1936; Professor of Social Security, Demography, and Population Policy at the National School of Economics, UNAM, 1950–54. d-*Federal Deputy* from Oaxaca, Dist. 7, 1952. e-None. f-Section Chief and Cashier of the National Agricultural Credit Bank, 1935–36; head of the Department of Social Security, Secretariat of Labor, 1941–42; President of the Editorial Committee for the new Social Security Law, 1941–42; *Secretary General of the Mexican Institute of Social Security*, 1943–46, 1946–52, 1952–58. g-Member of the National Farmers Federation; member of the Political Action Committee of the Mexican Agronomy Society, 1953. h-Economist, National Ejido Credit Bank, 1936–37; economist, Department of Economic Studies, Bank of Mexico, 1937–38; economist, Technical Department, National Bank of Foreign Commerce, 1938; economist, Office of the Six Year Plan, 1939; technical adviser, National Urban Mortgage Bank, 1945; delegate to the Inter-American Conference on Social Security, 1942; President of the Social Welfare Commission, 1953; author of several books on social security in Mexico and over 265 articles. j-None. k-Joined PRI in 1945, two years after he was appointed to a subcabinet level position. l-Enc. Mex., IV, 183; DGF47; WB45, 411; WWM45, 45; WB48, 1921; DGF51, II, 103–04.

Garcia de Alba, Esteban

(Deceased 1959)

a-1887. b-Tecolotlan, Jalisco, *West*, *Rural*. c-Law degree from the University of Guadalajara, Guadalajara, Jalisco. d-Local deputy to the State Legislature of Jalisco (twice); Federal Deputy from the State of Jalisco, 1928–30, 1930–32; *Senator* from the State of Jalisco, 1940–46, President of the Senate, 1942, member of the Gran Comision, president of the Second Government Committee and the First Foreign Relations Committee, and member of the First Balloting Group. e-*Secretary General of PRI*, 1936–37. f-*Oficial Mayor of the Secretariat of Government*, 1935–40; Subsecretary of Labor; Ambassador to Colombia and Venezuela; *Director General of the ISSSTE*, 1946–52. i-Son of General Esteban Garcia de Alba, Governor of Baja California del Sur. j-None. k-Precandidate for Governor of Jalisco (twice). l-DGF51, II, 113; DGF50, II, 40; I, 91; DGF47, 392; D de Y, 24 June 1937, 1; D de Y, 28 Aug. 1936, 1; D de Y, 1 Jan. 1936, 3; D del S, 2 Dec. 1946, 1; WWM45, 45; C de S, 1940–46; DP70, 823; Enc. Mex., 1977, V, 184.

Garcia Escamilla de Santana, Consuelo

a-June 18, 1930. b-Federal District, *Federal District*, *Urban*. c-Primary studies in Mexico City; secondary studies in Mixcoac, Mexico City; normal school in Toluca, Mexico; two years of study in social work at UNAM. **d-***Federal Deputy* from the State of Queretaro, Dist. 1, 1970–73, member of the Infant Welfare Committee, the Fine Arts Committee and the Consular and Diplomatic Service Committee. **e-**None. **f-**None. **g-**None. **j-**None. **k-**None. **l-**C de D, 170–73, 115; *Directorio*, 1970–72.

Garcia Flores, Margarita

a-July 4, 1925. **b-**Monterrey, Nuevo Leon, *North*, *Urban*. **c-**Primary studies in the Serafin Pena Institute, Monterrey, Nuevo Leon; secondary studies in the Secondary School, No. 1, Monterrey; law degree from the School of Law, University of Nuevo Leon, Monterrey, 1945, with a thesis on the legal and economic situation of the working woman; advanced studies in social work and political economy; Professor of Economics, Ethics and Domestic Education, University of Nuevo Leon. **d-**Member of the City Council of Monterrey, 1951–52; *Federal Deputy* from the State of Nuevo Leon, Dist. 4, 1955–58, member of the Social Action Committee, the Legislative Studies Committee, the First Balloting Committee, the First Section of the Grand Jury, and the First Constitutional Affairs Committee; *Alternate Senator* from the State of Nuevo Leon, 1958–64; *Federal Deputy* from the State of Nuevo Leon, Dist. 1, 1973–76. **e-**Secretary of Feminine Action, PRM, State of Nuevo Leon, 1950; *Secretary of Feminine Action of the CEN of PRI*, 1946–52; 1952–58. **f-**Department Head in the Division of Rural Communities, State of Nuevo Leon, 1947–48; lawyer, League of Agrarian Communities, State of Nuevo Leon, 1949–52; Director of the Department of Social Services, Mexican Institute of Social Security, 1958; Delegate of the Department of the Federal District to Cuajimalpa, 1976–80. **g-**Representative of Mexican Women's Organizations to the International Labor Organization, 1954; Secretary of Women's Activities, CEN of CNOP, 1974–75. **i-**Father was a Colonel. **j-**None. **k-**None. **l-**Chumancero, 94–97; Ind. Biog., 69; DGF56, 26, 30, 33–36; C de D, 1973–76, 16.

Garcia Gonzalez, Alfonso

(Deceased Dec. 2, 1961)
a-Mar. 19, 1909. **b-**Toluca, Mexico, *West Central*, *Urban*. **c-**Primary studies at the Colegio Legorreta and the Colegio San Jose, Toluca, Mexico; secondary studies at the Scientific and Literary Institute of the State of Mexico; preparatory studies at the National Preparatory School, Mexico, D.F.; law degree, National School of Law, UNAM, 1931. **d-***Governor of Baja California del Norte*, 1952–53. **e-**None. **f-**Ambassador to Colombia, 1952–58; appointed *Governor of Baja California del Norte*, 1947–52, by *Miguel Aleman*; *Director General of*

Tourism, 1959–61; President of the Mexican Sports Federation, 1958. **h-**Practicing lawyer, 1931–47; Scribe, Eighth Correctional Court, Federal District; Public Defender, Tijuana, Baja California del Norte. **i-**Personal friend of *Miguel Aleman* who was present at *Garcia Gonzalez*'s bedside when he died; married Dolores Cacho. **j-**None. **k-**Winner of the Heavyweight Boxing Championship of the State of Mexico; member of the Boxing Team at UNAM, 1926–29; attended the Central American Games and the Ninth Olympics, 1927; first constitutionally elected governor of Baja California del Norte, 1952–53; precandidate for Senator, 1958. **l-**DP70, 827, 2386; Enc. Mex., V, 188; HA, 5 Jan. 1959, 7; DGF51, I, 88; DPE61, 129; *Tiempo*, 11 Dec. 1961, 38; STYRBIWW54, 748; Novo, 677–80; Villasenor, 267.

Garcia Leal, Dionisio

a-Nov. 1, 1894. **b-**China, Nuevo Leon, *North*, *Rural*. **c-**Primary studies only; no degree. **d-**Federal Deputy from the State of Nuevo Leon, Dist. 3, 1932–34; *Federal Deputy* from the State of Nuevo Leon, Dist. 3, 1937–40; *Senator* from the State of Nuevo Leon, 1940–46, President of the First Tariff and Foreign Trade Committee, and Credit Institutions Committee, and Second Secretary of the Treasury Committee. **e-**None. **f-**None. **g-**None. **j-**None. **k-**None. **l-**Libro do Oro, 1946, 7; PS, 2313; C de D, 1932–34; C de D, 1937–40; C de S, 1940–46.

Garcia Lopez, Agustin

(Deceased Jan. 15, 1976)
a-1901. **b-**Toluca, Mexico, *West Central*, *Urban*. **c-**Primary and secondary studies in Toluca; elementary studies at the Normal School, Toluca and the Mariano Riva Palacio School, Toluca; preparatory studies at the Scientific and Literary Institute, Toluca; law degree from the National Law School, UNAM, 1923; Doctorate in Law; professor at the Inter-American Institute of Constitutional Law, Cuba; Professor of Introduction to Law and Obligations and Contracts, National Law School, UNAM; Professor of Comparative Law, University of Washington; Dean of the National School of Law, UNAM, 1938–39; Director of the School of Comparative Law, UNAM, 1956–72. **d-**None. **e-**Director of the Revolutionary Unification Front of PRI; Secretary of Statistics for the presidential campaign of *Miguel Aleman*. **f-**Consulting lawyer to the Secretariat of the Treasury, 1924; technical adviser to the Mexican Institute of Social Security; Secretary of the Penal Division of the Supreme Court, 1929–31; Agent of the Ministerio Publico of the Attorney General in the State of Mexico; *Secretary of Public Works*, 1946–52. **g-**None. **h-**Assistant lawyer to the Revenue Division, 1921–22; member of the Mexican

delegation to UNESCO. **i-**Friends with *Jose Castro Estrada*, *Antonio Armendariz*, *Rodolfo Brito Foucher*, *Eduardo Bustamante*, and *Luis Garrido Diaz* at UNAM; student assistants included *Raul Martinez Ostos* and *Nicolas Pizarro Suarez*; professor of *Miguel Aleman*; married Julieta Galindo. **j-**None. **k-**Member of the De la Huerta group; founded a free law office to defend students and professors from government persecution, 1923. **l-**DBM68, 261; HA, 14 Oct., 1949; HA, 23 June 1950; Enc. Mex., V, 192; letter; DGF51, I, 239; II, 523, 553; DGF50, II, 377, 395; HA, 26 Jan. 1976; *Excelsior*, 16 Jan. 1976; *Justicia*, Sept., 1973.

Garcia Paniagua, Javier

a-Feb. 13, 1935. **b-**Casimiro Castillo, Jalisco, *West, Rural*. **c-**Primary and secondary studies; completed preparatory studies; no degree. **d-***Senator* from the State of Jalisco, 1970–76, President of the First Credit, Money and Credit Institutions Committee, Second Secretary of the Agricultural and Development Committee, the Economic and Statistics Committee and the First National Defense Committee. **e-**Member of PRI; *Subsecretary General of the CEN of PRI*, 1970; General Delegate of the CEN of PRI to fifteen states. **f-**General Agent of CEIMSA, Colima, 1958–59; Director, Seguro Agricola of Colima, 1958–65; Director of the Agricultural Bank, Michoacan, 1965–70; Director of the Department of Federal Security, Secretariat of Government, 1976–78; *Subsecretary (3) of Government*, 1978–80; *Secretary of Agrarian Reform*, 1980– . **g-**None. **h-**None. **i-**Son of General *Marcelino Garcia Barragan*; newphew of *Sebastian Garcia Barragan*; a long-time friend of *Lazaro Cardenas*. **j-**None. **k-**None. **l-***Excelsior*, 17 Aug. 1978, 7; *Excelsior*, 16 Aug. 1978, 1; *Excelsior*, 27 Apr. 1980, 20; C de S, 1970–76, 75; DAPC.

Garcia (Pujou), Leon

(Deceased Jan. 12, 1972)
a-Nov. 22, 1903. **b-**San Luis Potosi, San Luis Potosi, *East Central, Urban*. **c-**Primary studies in San Luis Potosi; no degree. **d-**Local Deputy to the State Legislature of San Luis Potosi; Federal Deputy from the State of Zacatecas, Dist. 4, 1928–30; *Federal Deputy* from the Federal District, Dist. 12, 1937–40; Secretary of the Permanent Commission, 1939; *Senator* from the State of San Luis Potosi, 1940–46, president of the Second Ejido Committee, member of the Gran Comision and the Second Balloting Group and first secretary of the Industry and the Agricultural Development Committee. **e-**Member of the National Agrarian Party headed by *Aurelio Manrique*; head of the Zapatista Front; *Secretary of Agrarian Action of the CEN of the PRM*, 1938.

f-Executive Director of the National Colonization Commission, 1952–58; President of the Federal Board of Conciliation and Arbitration; Director of the Office of Plaints, Secretariat of the Presidency, 1958–64; General Coordinator for the Secretariat of Agriculture and Livestock, 1964–72. **g-**Co-founder with *Graciano Sanchez* of the National Farmers Federation (CNC) in 1938; first Oficial Mayor of the CNC, 1938; Alternate Secretary General of the CNC. **h-**Mechanic before entering politics. **i-**Political supporter of *Aurelio Manrique*, former governor of San Luis Potosi, 1923. **j-**None. **k-**Precandidate for Governor of San Luis Potosi, lost to *Gonzalo Santos*; precandidate for Secretary General of the CNC, 1941, 1957, 1966; involved in a land scandal in the Federal District, 1964. **l-**Peral, 314; HA, 24 Jan. 1972, 16; C de D, 1937–39, 11; Gonzalez Navarro, 256, 266, 137, 168; *Excelsior*, 28 June 1942; Libro de Oro, 1946, 7.

Garcia Ramirez, Sergio

a-1938. **b-**Guadalajara, Jalisco, *West, Urban*. **c-**Primary and secondary studies in Guadalajara; preparatory studies in Mexico, D.F.; law degree from the National Law School, UNAM, 1955–59, received honorary mention for his thesis on "Repression and Penitentiary Treatment of Criminals," 1961; advanced studies in law at the National Law School, 1963–64; advanced studies of penal systems in Europe; LLD degree from the National Law School, UNAM, Apr. 24, 1971, on the subject of prisons without bars; Professor of Penal Law, National School of Law, UNAM, 1965–66, 1970; Professor of Advanced Studies in Penitentiary Law, 1970. **d-**None. **e-**None. **f-**Delegate of the Social Welfare Department to the Federal District Penitentiary, 1961–63; Judge of the Guardian Council for the Guardian School for the Rehabilitation of Children; Director General of the Central Penitentiary, Mexico, D.F.; head of the Department of Political Investigations, Secretariat of Government; Subdirector General of Government, Secretariat of Government, 1970; *Attorney General of the Federal District and Federal Territories*, 1970–72; *Subsecretary of Government Properties*, Aug. 9, 1972–73; *Subsecretary of Government*, Apr. 30, 1973–76; *Subsecretary of Youth, Recreation and Sports*, Secretariat of Public Education, 1976–78; *Subsecretary of State Industry*, Secretariat of Property and Industrial Development, 1978– . **g-**None. **h-**Founder of the first prison without bars in Mexico; investigator of the Institute of Comparative Law, 1965–70; author of nine books; considered an outstanding expert on penal institutions in Mexico. **i-**Worked under *Luis Echeverria* before he became president. **j-**None. **k-**None. **l-**HA, 7 Dec. 1970, 26; *Hoy*, 8 May 1971, 12; letter; *Excelsior*, 10 Aug. 1972, 10; HA, 21 Aug.

1972, 13; HA, 7 May 1973, 23; HA, 6 Feb. 1978, 15; HA, 17 May 1976, 12.

Garcia Reynoso, Placido

c-Primary and secondary studies unknown; studies at the National Teachers' College, Mexico, D.F.; law degree. National School of Law, UNAM, 1927–35; Professor, National Teachers' College, 1932. d-None. e-None. f-Private Secretary to the Secretary of the Treasury, *Narciso Bassols*, 1935; Head of the Legal Department, Bank of Mexico, 1946–49; Head of the Credit and Trust Department, Bank of Mexico, 1950; Gerente and Second Subdirector of the Bank of Mexico, 1951–52; Gerente of the Bank of Mexico, 1952–58; *Subsecretary of Industry and Commerce (A)*, 1958–64, 1964–70; Director General of the Asociacion Hipotecaria Mexicana, S.A., 1971–72; Ambassador and Permanent Delegate to the International Organizations in Geneva, Switzerland, 1979– . g-Director of the First Convention of Socialist Teachers, 1935. h-Official, Secretariat of Public Education, 1935; Head of the Permanent Mexican Delegation to LAFTA, Montevideo, Uruguay, 1965; Director General of Azucar, S.A. i-Married Alicia Corona. j-None. k-None. l-D de Y, 10 Dec. 1964, 1; DGF50, II, 12, 57, 413, 433; DPE61, 64; DGF51, 8; DPE65, 29; Justicia, Dec., 1971.

Garcia Robles, Alfonso

a-Mar. 20, 1911. b-Zamora, Michoacan, *West Central, Urban*. c-Law degree, Faculty of Law, University of Paris; graduate studies at the National Law School, UNAM and Academy of International Law, The Hague, LLD degree. d-None. e-Member of the IEPES advisory council of PRI, 1972. f-Career foreign service officer; rank of third secretary, 1939; member of the delegation to Sweden, 1939–41; Director General of Political Affairs and the Diplomatic Service, Secretariat of Foreign Relations, 1941–46; Mexican representative to the United Nations, 1946–57; Director of the Political Affairs Division, United Nations, 1946–57; head of the Department of International Organizations; Director in Chief of the European, Asian, and African Department, Secretariat of Foreign Relations, 1957–61; Ambassador to Brazil, 1962–64; *Subsecretary of Foreign Relations*, 1964–70; Ambassador to the United Nations, 1971–75; *Secretary of Foreign Relations*, 1975–76; Head of the Mexican Delegation to the Disarmament Conference, 1976– . g-None. h-Delegate to over forty international conferences; President of the Association for the Denuclearization of Latin America, 1964–67; joined the Foreign Service in 1939; rank of ambassador; author of 20 books and over 300 articles on foreign affairs and international law. j-None. k-None. l-Enc. Mex., V; *Polemica*, **I, 1969, 81;**

WWW70-71, 335; IWW66, 425; DBM70, 239–40; DBM68, 262–63; DPE65, 17; DPE61, 15; WWM45, 46; *Excelsior*, 30 Dec. 1975, 11.

Garcia Rojas, Antonio

a-Dec. 9, 1914. b-Tampico, Tamaulipas, *North, Urban*. c-Primary studies; business studies as a stenographer; no degree. d-*Federal Deputy* from the State of Tamaulipas, Dist. 2, 1961–64; *Senator* from the State of Tamaulipas, 1964–70. e-Joined the PRM, 1937; President of the Avila Camacho Youth Group, Tampico, Tamaulipas, 1939–40. f-Syndic of the City Council of Reynosa, Tamaulipas; Director of Public Works, Reynosa, Tamaulipas, 1952–54; Director of Administration, Pemex, Reynosa; member of the Administrative Council of Pemex, 1959–61. g-Founder and Director of Section 36, Petroleum Workers Union; adviser to the STPRM. i-Son of Cruz Garcia Rojas Avila, a lawyer; great great grandson of a founder of Tampico. j-None. k-Resigned as Director of Public Works of Reynosa because of a disagreement with Governor *Trevino Zapata*. l-C de S, 1964–70; MGF69; C de D, 1961–64; PS, 2347.

Garcia Rojas, (Jorge) Gabriel

a-May 12, 1893. b-Pinos, Zacatecas, *East Central, Rural*. c-Primary studies in San Luis Potosi; secondary studies in Aquascalientes; law degree from the National School of Law, UNAM, 1919; LLD, National School of Law, UNAM, 1950; Professor of the General Theory of Obligations and Contracts, National School of Law, UNAM, 1920–77; Director of the Seminar of Private Law, National School of Law, UNAM; Professor of Civil Law and Judicial Methodology, LLD Program, National School of Law, UNAM, 1977; Dean of the Law School Professors, UNAM, 1977. d-*Federal Deputy* from the Federal District, Dist. 6, 1949–51, member of the Gran Comision, the Department of the Federal District Committee, the Legislative Studies Committee and the First Justice Committee. e-None. f-*Supernumerary Justice of the Supreme Court*, 1951–52; *Justice of the Supreme Court*, 1952–58; *Justice of the Supreme Court*, 1959–61. g-None. i-Father of *Jorge Gabriel Garcia Rojas*, senator from Zacatecas, 1976– . j-Participated in the Revolution. k-None. l-Lopez, 408; DGF51, 21, 29, 31, 34; C de D, 1949–51, 72; *Excelsior*, 28 Mar. 1977, 4.

Garcia Ruiz, Ramon

a-Aug. 27, 1908. b-Guadalajara, Jalisco, *West, Urban*. c-Teaching certificate from the Normal School of Jalisco, 1926; certified as an expert in rural education by the National School of Philosophy, Superior Normal School, UNAM, 1928; educational adviser to the National Commission of Free Textbooks,

1959–64. **d-***Federal Deputy* from the State of Jalisco, Dist. 4, 1952–55, member of the Library Committee (2nd year), the Editorial Committee (1st year), the Second Public Education Committee, and the First Section of the Credentials Committee. **e-**None. **f-**Director of Inspection, Secretariat of Public Education, for the States of Mexico, Morelos, and Jalisco, 1931–36; Inspector General, Secretariat of Public Education, 1937; Director General of Primary Education, 1942–43; Private Secretary to the Governor of Jalisco, 1947–52, under *Jesus Gonzalez Gallo*; Coordinator General of Services for Preschool and Primary Education; Coordinator General of Secondary and Normal Education, Secretariat of Public Education, 1961–64; Co-director of the Center of Fundamental Education for Community Development in Latin America, UNESCO, 1964–70. **g-**None. **h-**First employment as an inspector, 1929–30; author of numerous books and articles on rural education. **j-**None. **k-**None. **l-**DBM68, 263–64; C de D, 1952–54, 45, 47, 49; WWM45, 47; DPE61, 108; Enc. Mex., V, 1977, 198.

Garcia Sainz, Ricardo

a-June 9, 1930. **b-**Federal District, *Federal District, Urban.* **c-**Law degree from the National Law School, UNAM, 1952. **d-**None. **e-**None. **f-**Secretary of the Qualifying Committee of the Income Tax, 1952–56, under Director *Hugo B. Margain*; Administrative Subdirector of CONDUMEX, 1956–57; Director General of CONDUMEX, 1958–60; Subdirector General of Administration of the Mexican Institute of Social Security, 1966–70; Subdirector General of Administration of the Mexican Institute of Social Security, 1970–76; *Subsecretary of Control of Government Properties and Industrial Development,* 1976–77; *Secretary of Planning and Programing,* 1977–78. **g-**None. **h-**Worked for the Department of Commercial Revenues, 1951–52; President of the National Association of Imports and Exports, 1960–63. **j-**None. **k-**None. **l-**HA, 14 Dec. 1970, 25; DGF56, 168; HA, 7 Mar. 1966, 13; MGF69; HA, 28 Nov. 1977, 16; HA, 13 Dec. 1976, 9; *Excelsior,* 17 Nov. 1977, 11.

Garcia Santacruz, J. Jesus

a-Dec. 28, 1910. **b-**Michoacan, *West Central.* **c-**Primary studies in Michoacan; engineering degree from the National School of Agriculture. **d-***Federal Deputy* from the State of Michoacan, Dist. 9, 1964–67; *Senator* from the State of Michoacan, 1970–76, member of the Gran Comision and the First Balloting Group, President of the National Waters and Irrigation Committee, Second Secretary of the Second Ejido Committee, the First Petroleum

Committee and the Third Labor Committee. **e-**Joined the PNR, 1936. **f-**Agent, Ejido Credit Bank; Executive Secretary, Regional Agricultural Committee, Sinaloa; Chief General Agent, Secretary of Agriculture, Sinaloa; Secretary, Forest Commission, Michoacan; Vice-president, National Agricultural Bank; General Agent, Secretary of Agriculture; Executive Secretary, Collective Society of Ejido Credit. **g-**None. **h-**None. **j-**None. **k-**None. **l-**C de D, 1964–67; C de S, 1970–76, 75; PS, 2352.

Garcia Sela, Miguel

(Deceased 1964)
a-1904. **b-**Hacienda de San Lucas, San Martin Texmelucan, Puebla, *East Central, Rural.* **c-**Primary and secondary studies at Angelopolis; preparatory studies at the National Preparatory School, Mexico, D.F.; law degree, National School of Law, UNAM. **d-**Local deputy to the State Legislature of Puebla; *Federal Deputy* from the State of Puebla, Dist. 3, 1958–61, member of the Library Committee (1st year) and the First Justice Committee, and substitute member of the Treasury Committee. **e-**Campaigned for Jose Vasconcelos for President of Mexico in 1929 with *Adolfo Lopez Mateos.* **f-**Head of the Department of Conservation, National Highway Commission, Secretariat of Public Works, 1951; Director General of Cooperative Highways, Secretariat of Public Works, 1961–64. **g-**None. **h-**Author of several books and articles on Puebla and the Mexican Revolution. **j-**None. **k-**Involved in local politics in Puebla for many years. **l-**C de D, 1958–60, 78; DPE61, 86; DGF51, I, 242; DP70, 833.

Garcia Sierra, Aurelio

a-Sept. 18, 1918. **b-**Ejido Laguna Larga, Municipio de Penjamo, Guanajuato, *West Central, Rural.* **c-**Primary studies in Penjamo, secondary and preparatory studies in Guanajuato; economics degree from the Higher School of Economic Science, University of Guanajuato. **d-**Local Deputy to the State Legislature of Guanajuato; Mayor of Penjamo; *Federal Deputy* from the State of Guanajuato, Dist. 4, 1958–61, member of the Agrarian Affairs Department Committee, the First Balloting Committee and the Insurance Committee; *Federal Deputy* from the State of Guanajuato, Dist. 5, 1976–79, member of the Agrarian Affairs Committee. **e-**President of PRI in the State of Guanajuato. **f-**Justice of the Peace, Guanajuato. **g-**Secretary General of the League of Agrarian Communities, State of Guanajuato, 1962; Oficial Mayor of the National Farmers Federation, 1965. **j-**None. **k-**None. **l-***Excelsior,* 19 Aug. 1976, 18; Func., 211; C de D, 1958–61, 78; D de C, 1976–79, 7.

Garcia Tellez, Ignacio

a-May 21, 1897. **b-**Leon, Guanajuato, *West Central*, *Urban*. **c-**Primary, secondary, and preparatory studies in Leon; law degree from the National School of Law, UNAM, 1921, with a thesis on taxes in Mexico; first Rector of UNAM, 1929–32. **d-**Federal Deputy from Leon, Guanajuato, 1922–24; Interim Governor of Guanajuato, 1924; *Senator* from Guanajuato, 1934. **e-**Secretary of the Campaign Committee for the presidential campaign of Lazaro Cardenas, 1933; *Secretary General of the CEN of PRI*, 1935–36. **f-**Attorney for the Technical Commission on Legislation, 1926; Oficial Mayor of the Secretariat of Government, 1924–28; Acting Subsecretary of Government, 1928; Secretary of Public Education, 1934–35; *Private Secretary* to President *Lazaro Cardenas*, 1937–38; *Secretary of Government*, Jan. 4, 1938 to 1940; head of the Department of Credit, Secretariat of the Treasury, 1925; *Secretary of labor*, 1940–43; *Director General of the Mexican Institute of Social Security*, 1944–46; Private Secretary to *Lazaro Cardenas*, 1948; practicing lawyer, 1970. **g-**None. **h-**None. **i-**Personal friend of *Lazaro Cardenas*, worked with him from 1934 until his death; married Manuela Madrazo. **j-**None. **k-**Candidate for the Governor of Guanajuato in 1943 for the Unified Guanajuato Front, lost to *Ernesto Hidalgo*; shifted cabinet-level positions in 1944 to bring IMSS out of financial disaster. **l-**WWM45, 47; Peral, 319; Kirk, 337; Strode, 302; DBM68, 265; Enc. Mex., V, 199–200; D del S, 19 June 1935, 1; letter; NYT, 4 Jan. 1944, 31; NYT, 24 Jan. 1943, 4.

Garcia Toledo, Anastasio

b-Oaxaca, *South*. **c-**Law degree. **d-**Federal Deputy from the State of Oaxaca, 1930–32; *Governor of Oaxaca*, 1934–36. **e-**None. **f-**Oficial Mayor of the Secretariat of Government; head of Infractions Section of the Transportation Department of the Federal District, 1944; head of the Public Registry Office for Property and Commerce, Federal District Palace Office, Department of the Federal District, 1951. **g-**None. **j-**None. **k-**None. **l-**Peral, 319; DPE51, I, 483.

Garcia y Gonzalez, Vicente

a-1909. **b-**Penjamo, Guanajuato, *West Central*, *Urban*. **c-**Primary and secondary studies in Penjamo and Guanajuato, Guanajuato. **d-***Senator* from the State of Guanajuato, 1958–64, member of the Gran Comision, First Secretary of the Cooperative Development Committee, Second Secretary of the Social Security Committee, and President of the Second Labor Committee. **e-**None. **f-**None. **g-**Founder of the Federation of Workers Unions of Irapuato, Guanajuato; militant strike leader in the labor movement. **h-**Journalist; writer for *El Nacional*. **i-**Parents were from the working class. **j-**None. **k-**None. **l-**Func., 206; C de S, 1961–64, 55–56.

Garizurieta (Ehrenzweig), Cesar
(Deceased 1961)

a-July 19, 1904. **b-**Tuxpan, Veracruz, *Gulf*, *Rural*. **c-**Law degree, National School of Law, UNAM, 1931. **d-***Federal Deputy* from the State of Veracruz, Dist. 3, 1940–43, member of the Budget and Accounting Committee (1st year) and the Tourism Committee; substitute member of the Constitutional Affairs Committee; *Federal Deputy* from the State of Veracruz, Dist. 3, 1949–52, member of the Protocol Committee, the Library Committee, and the Agrarian Department Committee, and substitute member of the First Justice Committee. **e-**None. **f-**Judge of the Court of First Instance, 1931–40; Judge of the Tribunal Superior of Justice of Veracruz; Presidential Adviser; Consultant for Area 6 of the Department of Agrarian Affairs, 1947; *Oficial Mayor of the Department of Agrarian Affairs*, 1952–58; Ambassador to Haiti and Honduras, 1958–61. **g-**Founding member of the Socialist Lawyers Front, 1936; leader in the 1929 strike movement of UNAM. **h-**Started private law practice in Mexico, D.F., 1931; author of many novels. **i-**Brother, Miguel, served as an administrator in the Agrarian Department, 1956. **j-**None. **k-**None. **l-**EBW46, 35; Peral, 47, 138; DGF47, 280; DPE51, I, 26, 30, 31, 34; DP70, 835; DGF56, 453; C de D, 1940–42; C de D, 1949–51, 73; DEM, 135; Enc. Mex., 1977, 208.

Garrido Diaz, Luis
(Deceased Oct. 19, 1973)

a-May 15, 1898. **b-**Federal District, *Federal District*, *Urban*. **c-**Primary studies at the Colegio Fournier and the Pablo Moreno School in Mexico, D.F.; preparatory studies at the National Preparatory School, Mexico, D.F.; law degree from the National School of Law, UNAM, 1922; LLD degree from the National School of Law, UNAM, 1942; Professor of Forensic Law, National School of Law, UNAM, 1929–72; Professor of Economic Doctrines, UNAM, 1929–72; Professor at the Colegio de San Nicolas de Hidalgo, Morelia; co-founder of the Mexican Association of Universities and Institutions of Higher Education; Professor of the History of Economic Doctrines, Graduate School, UNAM, Rector of the University of Michoacan, 1924; Director of the Faculty of Law, University of Michoacan, 1924. **d-**None. **e-**None. **f-**Auxiliary agent of the Ministerio Publico for the Federal District for the Office of the Attorney General, 1929–30; Prosecuting Attorney for the State of Michoacan, 1924–25; head of the Diplomatic Department for the Secretariat of Foreign Relations, 1935–36; Penal Judge for the Federal District, 1930–34; Director of Seguros de Mexico, S.A., 1939–48; Executive Secretary of National Savings Bonds; *Rector of UNAM*, 1948–52; Subdirector of *El Nacional*, government daily newspaper, 1936; President of the Superior Court of Michoacan, 1925–28. **g**-None. **h**-President of the National Lawyers Association, 1970–72; prolific author, co-authored a book with *Jose Ceniceros*. **i**-As a student at National Preparatory School and UNAM, knew *Jaime Torres Bodet* and *Manuel Gomez Morin*; friend of *Franco Carreno* for many years; father worked for Wells Fargo. **j**-None. **k**-None. **l**-WWM45, 47; IWW66-67, 428; DGF47, 381; EBW46, 422; WB48, 431; WB54, 414; DBM70, 253–54; letter.

Garza Cardenas, Fortino Alejandro

a-Sept. 4, 1917. **b**-Monterrey, Nuevo Leon, *North*, *Urban*. **c**-Early education unknown; no degree. **d**-*Federal deputy* from PARM (Party Deputy), 1970–73; member of the Second National Defense Committee, the Hunting and Fishing Committee and the Plaints Committee, *Federal Deputy* from PARM (Party Deputy), 1976–79. **e**-None. **f**-Employee of the State of Nuevo Leon, 1935–36; Employee of the Secretariat of Health, Nuevo Leon, 1938–40; Employee of the Police Department, Federal District, 1940–46; Employee of the Secretary of Agriculture and Captain of the Federal Forest Police, 1947–58; Commandant in the Customs Department, 1960–61; Employee of the Secretariat of Communications, 1963–68; Employee of the Department of Fishing, Secretariat of Industry and Trade in Monterrey, Nuevo Leon, 1968–70. **g**-None. **i**-Son of Colonel Fortino Garza Campos; married Ernestina Rodriguez. **j**-None. **k**-None. **l**-*Directorio*, 1970–72; C de D, 1970–73, 115; D de C, 1976–79.

Garza Tijerina, Julian

(Deceased 1976)
a-Jan. 28, 1900. **b**-General Bravo, Nuevo Leon, *North*, *Rural*. **c**-Primary studies in General Bravo; fifth and sixth years plus preparatory studies at Colegio Civil, Monterrey, Nuevo Leon; medical degree from the Military Medical School, Federal District, 1925, with the rank of Major; Professor of Internal Pathology. **d**-Local deputy to the State Legislature of Nuevo Leon; *Senator* from the State of Nuevo Leon, 1934–40, member of the permanent committee, 1938; *Federal Deputy* from the State of Nuevo Leon, Dist. 2, 1943–46. **e**-*Director of the IEPES of the PNR, 1936*. **f**-Director of Medical Services, Monterrey; Subdirector of the Military Hospital, Monterrey; Director of Medical Services for the Green Cross, Federal District; Director General of Hygiene and Welfare in States and Territories, Secretariat of Health, 1946. **g**-None. **h**-Author of books on medical

subjects and Nuevo Leon history. **i**-Studied under *Francisco Castillo Najera* and *Fernando Ocaranza*. **j**-Participated in various military battles; rank of Lt. Col. in the Medical Military Service. **k**-None. **l**-Peral, 324; C de D, 1943–45; C de S, 1934–40; letters; MGF47, 197.

Garza Zamora, Tiburicio

(Deceased Dec. 13, 1973)
a-1900. **b**-Rancho el Mezquite, Reynosa, Tamaulipas, *North*, *Rural*. **c**-Primary studies in Ciudad Victoria; no degree. **d**-*Federal Deputy* from the State of Tamaulipas, Dist. 1, 1958–61, member of the Gran Comision, the First National Defense Committee, the General Accounting Office Committee and the Military Justice Committee. **e**-None. **g**-None. **h**-None. **i**-Married Francisca Guajardo de Garza. **j**-Joined the Revolution, 1915; rank of Colonel, 1920; career army officer; reached rank of Divisionary General; Zone Commander of the 26th Military Zone, Veracruz, Veracruz; Zone Commander of the 20th Military Zone, Colima, Colima; Zone Commander of the 5th Military Zone, Chihuahua, Chihuahua; Zone Commander of the 7th Military Zone, Monterrey, Nuevo Leon, 1970; retired from active duty, 1970. **k**-None. **l**-*Excelsior*, 14 Dec. 1973, 21; Func., 374; C de D, 1958–61, 79.

Garzon Santibanez, Alfonso

a-Aug. 4, 1920. **b**-Ejido el Salto, Mazatlan, Sinaloa, *West*, *Urban*. **c**-Early education unknown; no degree. **d**-*Alternate Federal Deputy* from the State of Baja California del Norte, Dist. 1, 1961–64; *Federal Deputy* from the State of Baja California del Norte, Dist. 3, 1970–73, member of the Agricultural Committee, the Waters and Irrigation Committee and the First Balloting Committee; *Federal Deputy* from the State of Baja California del Norte, Dist. 3, 1976–79, member of the Ejido and Communal Organization Section of the Agrarian Affairs Committee, member of the Agricultural Committee and the Committee for the Development of Marine Resources. **e**-Joined the PNR, 1936; *Agrarian Subsecretary of the CEN of PRI*, 1978. **f**-None. **g**-Began activities in the agrarian union movement, 1936; Secretary General of the Independent Peasant Federation (CCI), 1976– . **i**-Parents were peasants. **j**-None. **k**-None. **l**-*Excelsior*, 21 Aug. 1976, 1C; C de D, 1976–79, 25; C de D, 1970–73, 116; D de C, 1976–79, 6, 12, 31; C de D, 1961–63, 12.

Gasca, Celestino

a-May 17, 1893. **b**-Cuitzeo de Abasolo, Guanajuato, *West Central*, *Rural*. **c**-Early education unknown; no degree. **d**-Deputy to the Constitutional Convention, 1916–17; *Federal Deputy* from the State of Guanajuato, Dist. 2, 1937–40; *Senator* from the

State of Guanajuato, 1940–46, President of the First National Defense Committee, member of the First Balloting Group, President of the Second Labor Committee and Second Secretary of the First Mines Committee. **e-**Secretary of Labor Action of the Pro Avila Camacho Committee, 1939–40; supporter of General *Miguel Henriquez Guzman* for president, 1951–52. **f-**Governor of the Federal District, 1921–23. **g-**Joined the House of the Workers of the World, 1913; active in the Red Labor Battalions which supported General Obregon; Secretary General of the Shoeworkers Union; important leader of CROM. **h-**Worked as a saddle maker before the Revolution of 1910; employee of United Shoe Leather. **i-**Father was a peasant and shoemaker. **j-**Joined the Revolution, 1910; supporter of Francisco Madero; fought De la Huerta's forces in Tabasco, Veracruz and Hidalgo, 1923; Quartermaster General of the Army, 1929; fought against the Escobar rebellion, 1929; rank of Brigadier General. **k-**Founder of the Federal Board of Conciliation and Arbitration as Governor of the Federal District; national government candidate for governor of Guanajuato, but lost to *Agustin Arroyo Ch.* backed by powerful state machine, 1927; precandidate for governor of Guanajuato, 1935; precandidate for Secretary General of the CTM; accused by the government of supporting a leftist insurrection against President *Adolfo Lopez Mateos*, 1962, and briefly imprisoned. **l-**Peral, 326; C de D, 1937–39, 11; C de S, 1940–46; Lopez, 414; Casasola, V; Enc. Mex., V, 1977, 277–78.

Gascon Mercado, Alejandro

a-Mar., 1932. **b-**Autan, Nayarit, *West*, *Rural*. **c-**Primary studies at the Francisco Madero Public School, Tepic, Nayarit; secondary studies at the Secondary Boarding School for Workers' Children, 1947–49; preparatory studies at the National Preparatory Night School, 1950–51. **d-**Federal Deputy from the State of Nayarit, Dist. 1, 1970–73, member of the Agriculture Committee, the Rural Electricity Committee, the Money and Credit Institutions Committee, and the Rules Committee; Mayor of Tepic, Nayarit, 1975. **e-**President of the Youth Division of the PPS for the Federal District, 1953; President of the National Committee of the Youth Division of the PPS, 1954–56; Secretary of Press and Publicity, National Central Committee of the PPS; Secretary of Organization, National Central Committee of the PPS; Secretary of Economic Studies of the National Central Committee of the PPS; Oficial Mayor of the PPS; founder of a splinter party from PPS called the Party of the Mexican People (PPM), 1976. **f-**Ambassador to Venezuela, 1978– . **g-**President of the National Federation of Boarding Schools for Workers' Children, 1949. **i-**Brother of *Julian Gascon Mercado*, Governor of Nayarit, 1964–70; parents

were peasants. **j-**None. **k-**Candidate of the PPS for Governor of Nayarit; lost to Rogelio Flores Curiel in what *Latin America* and critics termed a rigged election. **l-**C de D, 1970–72, 116; *Directorio*, 1970–72; LA, 11 Nov. 1978, 349–50; *Excelsior*, 21 Feb. 1975, 12; *Proceso*, 24 Apr. 1978, 23.

Gascon Mercado, Julian

a-Jan. 28, 1925. **b-**Ejido de Trapichillo, Tepic, Nayarit, *West*, *Urban*. **c-**Primary studies in Tepic; secondary studies on a peasant scholarship of the Socialist School for Workers in Tepic; medical degree from the National School of Medicine, UNAM. **d-**Governor of Nayarit, 1964–70. **e-**Member of PPS. **f-**Head of the Medical Services for the National Chemical and Pharmaceutical Industry, 1958–62; Director of the Hospital of the National University; Coordinator General of the Jesus Hospital, Mexico, D.F., 1971–73. **g-**Member and official of the National Farmers Federation. **h-**Surgeon at the Jesus Hospital, 1955–63, under the administration of *Gustavo Baz*; head of Social Work for the Center for Private Assistance in the Federal District and Territories, 1960–61; author of three books in the medical field. **i-**Co-authored a book on surgery with *Gustavo Baz*; brother of *Alejandro Gascon Mercado*, federal deputy from Nayarit, 1970–73; parents were peasants. **j-**None. **k-**Elected on the PPS and the PRI ticket; supported by the Cardenistas for the governorship but opposed by local PRI leaders. **l-**WWMG, 18; Enc. Mex., V, 228; *Por que*, 25 Sept. 1968, 41; Anderson, 114; *Excelsior*, 22 May 1973, 22.

Gastelum Salcido, Juan Jose

a-July 2, 1895. **b-**Hermosillo, Sonora, *North*, *Urban*. **c-**Early education unknown; no degree. **d-**Senator from the State of Sonora, 1976– . **e-**None. **f-**Subsecretary of National Defense, 1964–70. **g-**None. **h-**None. **j-**Career army officer; joined the Revolution in 1911 as a supporter of Madero; served under the Constitutionalists with General Benjamin Hill; commander of various military zones; rank of Brigadier General, Mar. 1, 1942; Director General of Social Services of the Army, Secretariat of National Defense, 1946–48; Inspector General of the Army, 1951–52; Commander of the 4th Military Zone, Hermosillo, Sonora, 1956; Director of the National Military College; rank of Divisionary General. **k-**None. **l-**DGF56, 201; DGF51, I, 180; DPE65, 33; HA, 21 Dec. 1964, 9; Peral, 47, 141; C de S, 1976–82.

Gavira, Gabriel

(Deceased)

a-1867. **b-**Orizaba, Veracruz, *Gulf*, *Urban*. **c-**Primary education only. **d-**None. **e-**None. **f-**President, Higher Tribunal of Military Justice; *Governor of Baja California del Norte*, 1936.

g-Active in the labor movement in Orizaba. h-Carpenter for many years. i-Parents were poor. j-Joined the Revolution under the Maderistas, 1911; supported General Obregon in 1920. k-Losing candidate for the governorship of the State of Veracruz. l-Lopez, 414; letter.

Gaxiola Urias, Marcario
(Deceased 1953)
a-1890. b-Angostura, Sinaloa, *West*, *Rural*. c-Early education unknown; no degree. d-Governor of Sinaloa, 1929–32; *Senator* from the State of Sinaloa, 1952–53. e-None. f-None. g-None. h-Miner before the Revolution. j-Joined the Revolution; Constitutionalist; fought against Victoriano Huerta, 1913; commander of the 1st Battalion under General Obregon, 1913–14; Brigadier General, Army of the Northeast, under General Obregon; supported the Plan of Agua Prieta. k-None. l-C de S, 1952–58; DGF56; PS, 2444.

Gaxiola (Zendejas), Jr., Francisco Javier
(Deceased Aug. 3, 1978)
a-Sept. 6, 1898. b-Toluca, Mexico, *West Central*, *Urban*. c-Primary studies at the School of Senorita Esther Cano and the Pestalozzi School, Toluca; secondary studies at the Scientific and Literary School of Toluca and the Liceo Fournier, Mexico, D.F.; preparatory studies at the National Preparatory School in Mexico, D.F., 1912–16; law degree from the Escuela Libre de Derecho, Apr. 15, 1922, with his thesis on "Jurisdictional Invasions in Constitutional Opinions;" Professor of Political Economy at the Escuela Libre de Derecho, 1923–28; won prizes as a student at the Escuela Libre de Derecho. d-None. e-None. f-Representative of the Secretariat of the Treasury to the State of Mexico, 1919; Envoy to the Spanish American Congress, Madrid, 1920; Agent of the Ministerio Publico (Auxiliary) for the Attorney General in the Federal District; Assistant District Attorney for the Federal District, 1926; Acting Governor of Baja California del Norte, 1929; Governor of Baja California del Norte, 1930–32; Private Secretary to President *Abelardo Rodriguez*, 1932–34; President of the Council of Arbitration and Conciliation for the Secretariat of Industry and Commerce, 1932; Secretary General of Government of Baja California del Norte, 1929–30; manager of the private fortunes of *Abelardo Rodriguez*, 1934–40; *Secretary of Industry and Commerce*, 1940–44; personal representative of *Manuel Avila Camacho* to Franklin D. Roosevelt, 1942. g-None. h-Founder of the Mexican Bar Association, 1923; Secretary General of the Mexican Bar Association, 1928; Oficial Mayor of the First Legal Congress, 1921; President of the Illustrious and National College of Lawyers, 1957–72; private law practice with son Francisco,

1945–78; founder of the National Bank of Cooperative Development; co-author with *Rodrigo Gomez* of the reform of Article 27. i-Attended the Escuela Libre de Derecho with *Emilio Portes Gil* and *Ezequiel Padilla* and taught *Felipe Tena Ramirez*, *Vicente Sanchez Gavito*, and *Abel Huitron y Aguado*; father, a well-known author, lawyer, and diplomat, who served as a local deputy and as Governor of Mexico, 1919–20; brother Jorge, an adviser to *Jaime Torres Bodet* as Secretary of Public Education, and General Counsel for *Abelardo Rodriguez*; married Clotilde Ochoa. j-None. k-Resigned as Secretary of Industry to run for Governor of Mexico; defeated for the nomination by *Alfredo del Mazo*, 1944. l-DP70, 843; DBM68, 282–83; WWM45, 48; Enc. Mex., V, 245; WB48, 1940; EBW46, 531; Peral, 328; letters; Strode, 370; HA, 11 June 1943, 38.

Gil Preciado, Juan
a-June 26, 1909. b-Juchitlan, Jalisco, *West*, *Rural*. c-Education degree from the Guadalajara International School; Professor of Mathematics, University of Guadalajara; secondary school principal, Ocotlan, Jalisco, 1927–28; Professor of Civics for the Federal Army, 32nd Regiment, 1929; founder and Director of the Workers and Farmer's School, 1935; Director of Extension, University of Guadalajara, 1936; Secretary General of the Polytechnical School of the University of Guadalajara. d-Local deputy to the State Legislature of Jalisco, 1955–56; *Federal Deputy* from the State of Jalisco, Dist. 13, 1940–43, member of the Tourism Committee; Secretary of the Chamber, Sept., 1940; Mayor of Guadalajara, 1956–58; *Governor of Jalisco,* 1959–64. e-Committee Chairman for the PNR, 1938; President of the State Committee of the PRM for Jalisco; member of the first council of the CNOP of the PRM, 1944; General Delegate of the CEN of PRI, 1978. f-Executive Secretary for General Garcia de Alba, Governor of Baja California del Sur; Oficial Mayor and Secretary General of Government, Baja California del Sur; Director of Planning for the Department of Agrarian Affairs, 1943; Director of Information, United States-Mexican Commission of Hoof and Mouth Disease, 1946–52; private secretary to the Subsecretary of Agriculture, *Oscar Flores Sanchez*, 1948–52; *Secretary of Agriculture*, 1964–70. g-Student leader at the Second Congress of Socialist Students, 1935. h-None. i-Married Aida Elizondo; son Juan Gil Elizondo active in Jalisco politics. j-None. k-Precandidate for President of Mexico, 1970. l-Enc. Mex., V, 372–73; *El Universal*, 1 Dec. 1964; WWMG, 18; HA, 7 Dec. 1964, 19; DGF51, II, 220; DPE65, 98; Peral, 330; DGF51, I, 203; DGF56, 95; HA, 4 Aug. 1944; Johnson, 193; *Excelsior*, 15 July 1977, 12; NYT, 6 Oct. 1969, 16; *Excelsior*, 12 Nov. 1978, 18.

Giner Duran, Praxedes

a-Feb. 15, 1893. b-Santa Rosalia de Conchos, Camargo, Chihuahua, *North, Rural*. c-Educated in public schools; no degree. d-Federal Deputy from the State of Chihuahua, Dist. 5, 1928–30, member of the Permanent Committee; Senator from the State of Chihuahua, 1930–34, President of the Senate; *Governor of Chihuahua*, 1962–68. e-President of the Administrative Commission of the Chamber of Deputies in charge of organizing a national political party, PNR; founding member of the PNR. f-None. g-None. h-None. k-Joined the Revolutionary forces, 1911; Chief of Staff under the forces of Francisco Villa; Chief of Staff of the 6th Brigade, Monclova, Coahuila, 1918; Chief of Staff of the 4th Military Zone, Hermosillo, Sonora, 1934; Subchief of Staff for the Federal District, 1935; Chief of Staff of the 6th Military Zone, Torreon, Coahuila, 1943; Chief of Staff of the 5th Military Zone, Chihuahua; Commander of the 2nd Military Zone, Mexicali, Baja California del Norte, 1953; Commander of the 17th Military Zone, Queretaro, Queretaro, 1953; Commander of the 18th Military Zone, Pachuca, Hidalgo, 1953–55; Commander of the 27th Military Zone, 1955–59, Acapulco, Guerrero; Commander of the 5th Military Zone, Chihuahua, 1959–61; rank of Divisionary General. l-WWMG, 17; DBM68, 284–85; DGF56, 202; Peral, 330–331; HA, 6 Sept. 1971, 19.

Godinez Bravo, Miguel Angel

a-April 4, 1931. b-Puebla, Puebla, *East Central, Urban*. c-Primary studies at the Manuel Avila Camacho School, Tezuitlan, Puebla; secondary studies at the Oriente Institute, Puebla; preparatory studies at the University of Puebla; graduated from the National Military College, 1953, as a 2nd Lieutenant of Cavalry; graduated as a staff officer, Higher War College; Professor of General Staff Materiels and Tactics, Higher War College. d-None. e-None. f-Chief of Section Four, Presidential Staff; Subchief of the Presidential Staff; Chief of the Presidential Staff, 1976– . g-None. h-None. i-Son of Miguel Angel Godinez, a school teacher. j-Career Army officer; officer in the 6th Cavalry Regiment, Atlixco, Puebla; officer in the 9th Cavalry Regiment, San Andres Tuxtla, Veracruz; officer in the 13th Cavalry Regiment, Hacienda Echegaray; officer in the 12th Armored Regiment of the Presidential Guards; Commander of the First Armored Squadron, Presidential Guards. k-None. l-*El Dia*, 1 Dec. 1976.

Gomar Suastegui, Jeronimo

(Deceased Jan. 21, 1972)
a-Sept. 30, 1908. b-Ayutla, Guerrero, *South, Rural*. c-Secondary education at the School of Administration, 1925; attended the Vocational School of the National Military College; graduated from the National Military College as a 2nd Lieutenant in the Infantry, Jan., 1930; graduated from the Superior War College, Mar., 1936, with a diploma in military staff administration. d-*Alternate Senator* from the State of Guerrero, 1964–70. e-None. f-Director of the National Military College, 1958–64; Director of the Department of Military Industry, 1964–70; *Subsecretary of National Defense*, 1970–72. g-None. h-None. j-Career army officer since Apr. 14, 1925; Subchief of Staff of the 1st and 2nd Infantry Divisions; Commander of the 8th Battalion of Infantry; head of the Inspection Commission for the Inspector General of the Army; Military Attache to Guatemala and Central America; rank of Divisionary General. k-None. l-DPE70, 113; DPE65, 35, 45; letter; HA, 26 Jan. 1939, 8; HA, 31 Jan. 1972, 14; MGF69, 568; HA, 14 Dec. 1970, 20.

Gomez Arias, Alejandro

b-Oaxaca, Oaxaca, *South, Urban*. c-Early education unknown; preparatory studies at the National Preparatory School; law degree cum laude from the National School of Law, UNAM, with a thesis on Hans Kelsen; professor at the National Preparatory School; professor at UNAM. d-None. e-Orator for the Jose Vasconcelos campaign, 1929; Vice President of the Popular Party (later the PPS), 1947; co-founder of the Mexican Civic Front of Revolutionary Affirmation, 1963. f-Private Secretary to Secretary of Public Education, *Octavio Vejar Vazquez*, 1941–43. g-President of the Student Federation of the Federal District, 1928; President of the National Student Federation, 1928–29. h-Co-founder of the National College; National Oratory Champion, 1928; member of the 1925 Committee to Reorganize the National University; author. i-Knew *Miguel Aleman* and *Salvador Novo* at UNAM; met *Adolfo Lopez Mateos* at night school; father a physician, Revolutionary and federal deputy, 1920. j-None. k-None. l-Letters; HA, 10 Oct. 1947, 5; HA, 27 Sept. 1976, 25; *Excelsior*, 29 Feb. 1960.

Gomez Esparza, Jose

a-1898. b-San Santomo, Hidalgo, *East Central, Rural*. c-Primary studies in San Santomo; secondary studies in San Santomo; medical degree, National School of Medicine, UNAM; special studies in medicine in France. d-Federal Deputy from the State of Hidalgo, Dist. 2, 1934–37; *Federal Deputy* from the State of Hidalgo, Dist. 3, 1940–43, member of the First Balloting Committee; president of the Chamber of Deputies, December, 1942; *Senator* from the State of Hidalgo, 1946–52, member of the Gran Comision, the Indigenous Affairs Committee and the First Balloting Committee. e-*Secretary Gen-*

eral of the CEN of PRI, 1952; *Secretary General of the CEN of PRI*, 1953. **f-**Ambassador to China (never went because of WWII), 1944; Ambassador to Bolivia, 1944–46; *Oficial Mayor of Government Properties*, 1953–58; Ambassador to El Salvador, 1958–59. **g-**None. **j-**None. **k-**Author of a PNR petition in Congress, June 14, 1935. **l-**C de D, 1940–43, 53; DGF51, I, 9, 10, 11, 14; DGF56; PS, 2498.

Gomez (Gomez), Rodrigo

(Deceased Aug. 14, 1970)
a-May 18, 1897. **b-**Linares, Nuevo Leon, *North*, *Rural*. **c-**Secondary studies in accounting at the General Zaragoza Commercial Academy, 1913–14. **d-***Senator* from Nuevo Leon, Sept. to Nov., 1952. **e-**None. **f-**Head of the Exchange Department, Bank of Mexico, 1933; First Gerente of the Bank of Mexico, 1941–47; *Subdirector General of the Bank of Mexico*, 1947–52; *Director General of the Bank of Mexico*, 1952–58, 1958–64, 1964–70. **g-**None. **h-**Employee of an electrical company, Monterrey, Nuevo Leon; accountant for various private businesses, 1915–18; employee of the Compania Fundidora de Fierro, Monterrey, 1918; Subgerente of the Branch Office, Merida, Yucatan, 1921; head of the Department of Exchanges, Mercantile Bank, Monterrey, 1922; Executive Director of the International Monetary Fund for Mexico and Central America, 1946–48. **j-**None. **k-**Prominent in the Mexican movement to join the Latin American Free Trade Association in 1960 with *Placido Garcia Reynoso*. **l-**DGF51, II, 11, 63, etc.; DP70, 880–81; D del S, 5 Dec. 1952, 1; IWW67, 451; DGF56, 7; HA, 5 May 1954; HA, 5 June 1957; DBM68, 293–94.

Gomez Gutierrez, Juan Manuel

b-Federal District, *Federal District*, *Urban*. **c-**Early education unknown; law degree from the National School of Law, UNAM; professor, National School of Law, UNAM. **d-**None. **e-**Joined the Mexican Communist Party, 1950; organizer, Mexican Peace Movement; organizer, National Liberation Movement. **f-**None. **g-**Organizer, Independent Union Front; advisor to various labor unions and housing groups. **h-**Practicing lawyer. **j-**None. **k-**Candidate for Federal Deputy from the Federal District, Dist. 7, of the Leftist Coalition, 1979; lawyer for various political prisoners. **l-**HA, 23 Apr. 1979, VI.

Gomez Maganda, Alejandro

a-Mar. 3, 1910. **b-**Arenal de Gomez, Galeana, Guerrero, *South*, *Rural*. **c-**Graduated from the National Teachers School, UNAM. **d-**Federal Deputy from the State of Guerrero, 1934–37, president of the government bloc of deputies, September, 1936; *Federal Deputy* from the State of Guerrero, Dist. 4, 1946–49, member of the Library Committee, the Second Balloting Committee, the Second Instructive Section for the Grand Jury, and the Gran Comision, 1946; President of the Chamber of Deputies, Sept., 1947; *Governor of Guerrero*, Apr. 1, 1951 to 1954. **e-**Coordinator for the Frente Civico Mexicano de Afirmacion Revolucionaria, 1961–65. **f-**Private Secretary to General *Matias Ramos Santos*; private secretary to Socialist Juan R. Escudero; member of the Technical Study Commission of the Secretary of the Presidency, 1939–40; Director General of Social Action for the Federal District, 1941–43; Administrator of Maritime Customs, Acapulco, Guerrero, 1944–45; Adviser to the Presidency; Consul in Los Angeles, California; Consul General in Spain and Portugal during the Spanish Civil War; Ambassador to Panama, 1965; Ambassador to Jamaica, 1968;; Oficial Mayor of the National Council of Tourism under *Miguel Aleman*, 1971–76. **g-**President of the Second Congress of Student Cooperative Representatives, 1926; President of the National Student Convention in Morelia, Michoacan, 1933. **h-**Author of numerous historical works. **i-**Longtime collaborator of *Miguel Aleman*; father was a Revolutionary. **j-**Participated with irregular forces in the Costa Chica, 1920s. **k-**Term as Governor of Guerrero was ended in 1954, when the Senate dissolved his powers after complaints of widespread corruption in the state. **l-**DPE65, 30; Scott, 275; Morton, 56; DGF51, I, 89; Enc. Mex., V, 445; Peral, 338; Brandenburg, 103; NYT, 23 May 1954, 37.

Gomez Maqueo, Roberto

a-1892. **b-**Orizaba, Veracruz, *Gulf*, *Urban*. **c-**Engineering degree specializing in engineering mechanics, National Naval College, graduated as a captain, November 1, 1929; professor at the National Naval College. **d-***Federal Deputy* from the State of Veracruz, Dist. 9, 1952–54, member of the Administrative Committee (1st and 3rd years), the First Committee on National Defense, the Budget and Accounts Committee, and the Naval Committee; Vice President of the Chamber of Deputies, Nov. 1952; *Senator* from Veracruz, 1958–64, member of the Second Section of the Balloting Committee and the General Means of Communication Committee; President of the Naval Committee. **e-**None. **f-**Head of the autonomous Navy Department, 1940; *Secretary of the Navy*, 1955–58. **g-**None. **h-**Author of many technical engineering studies. **j-**Career naval officer; Commodore, 1939; Chief of Staff for the Pacific Regiment, 1941–45; Commander of the Destroyers "Veracruz," "Democracia," and "Morelos"; Inspector General of the Navy, 1951; Intendant General of the Army; rank of Admiral. **k-**None. **l-**DGF51, I, 380; STYRBIWW58, 415; DGF56, 381; HA, 2 Jan. 1956, 6; letter; C de S, 1961–64; Func., 386.

Gomez Mont, Felipe

(Deceased 1970)
a-1916. b-Federal District, *Federal District, Urban*.
c-Law degree, Escuela Libre de Derecho, August 24,
1939; Professor of Penal Law at the Escuela Libre de
Derecho, 1941–52; Professor of Law at the Ibero-
American University; Professor of Penal Law in the
United States, France, and Europe. d-*Federal Deputy* from the Federal District, Dist. 3, 1952–55,
member of the Child Welfare and Social Security
Committee, the Legislative Studies Committee, the
First Balloting Committee, and the Second Constitutional Affairs Committee; *Federal Deputy* from the
Federal District, Dist. 3, 1958–61; *Federal Deputy*
from the Federal District, Dist. 2, 1964–67, member
of the Department of the Federal District Committee
and the First Justice Committee. e-Member of PAN.
f-Participated in writing the reforms of the federal
penal codes. g-President of the National Association
of Catholic Lawyers. h-Adviser to the National Bank
of Mexico; opened law firm with Raul F. Cardenas in
Mexico, D.F.; conducted penal law studies for Inter-
pol; writer for Mexican and foreign magazines and
newspapers. i-Brother Francisco, a medical doctor
and served as Director of Instruction, General Hospital, National Medical Center; his law partner, Raul F.
Cardenas, appointed Rector of the Escuela Libre de
Derecho, 1972. j-None. k-Distinguished congressional debator. l-DP70, 887; Morton, 69; C de D,
64–66, 81, 89; C de D, 1952–54, 43, 51–53, 65; C
de D, 1958–60.

Gomez Morin, Manuel

(Deceased Apr. 19, 1972)
a-Feb. 27, 1897. b-Batopilas, Chihuahua, *North*,
Rural. c-Primary studies at the Colegio del Sagrado
Corazon in Leon, Guanajuato; started preparatory
studies in Leon and completed at the National Preparatory School in Mexico, 1913–15; law degree
from the National Law School, UNAM, 1918;
member of the generation of the National Preparatory
School known as the Seven Sages, which included
Narciso Bassols, *Vicente Lombardo Toledano*, *Alfonso Caso*, *Octavio Medellin Ostos*, and *Teofilo
Olea*; courses in economics, Columbia University,
New York, 1921; Professor of Law, UNAM, 1919–
38. d-None. e-Supporter of Jose Vasconcelos, 1929;
founder and *President of the CEN of PAN* (National
Action Party), 1939–49. f-Member of the Governing
Council of UNAM; Secretary of the National Law
School, UNAM, 1918–19; Oficial Mayor of the Sec-
retariat of the Treasury, 1919–20; Subsecretary of
the Secretariat of the Treasury in charge of the Secretariat, 1920–21; financial agent for the Federal
Government in New York City, 1921–22; Dean of
the National School of Law, UNAM, 1922–24;

founder and first Chairman of the Board of the Bank
of Mexico, 1925; Rector of UNAM, 1933–34.
g-President of the Student Society of the National
Law School. h-Editor of *La Vanguardia*; Scribe of
the 4th Correctional Court, Mexico City, 1915; official of the Department of Statistics, 1916; practicing
lawyer, 1918–19, 1921–72; lawyer, Soviet Trade
Delegation, Mexico City, 1928; author of legislation
creating the Bank of Mexico; author of the first reform of Credit Institutions 1931; author of several
books. i-Longtime personal friendships maintained
with *Alfonso Caso* and *Vicente Lombardo Toledano*
despite different political views; married Lydia Torres; father a miner. j-None. k-Candidate for Federal
Deputy on the PAN ticket, 1946, 1958; considered
by some scholars to have been a secret supporter of
Adolfo de la Huerta, 1923. l-Kirk, 310–12;
WWM45, 50; Padgett, 67–70; WB48, 2014–15;
Hoy, 29 April 1972, 3; DBM68, 292; HA, 24 April
1972, 21; letters; Justicia, Jan., 1973.

Gomez Morin Torres, Juan Manuel

a-Oct. 31, 1924. b-Federal District, *Federal District, Urban*. c-Primary studies in Mexico, D.F.;
secondary studies at the Colegio Frances Morelos;
law degree from the National School of Law,
UNAM; attended Law School, Harvard University;
Professor of Mercantile Law, Ibero-American University. d-*Federal Deputy* from the Federal District,
Dist. 23, 1967–70, member of the Federal District
Department Committee, the Legislative Studies
Committee (4th Section, Administrative and 8th Section, Fiscal) for the 1st year; member of the Legislative Studies Committee (2nd Section, Civil) for the
2nd year; member of the United States-Mexican Interparliamentary Conference, 1968. e-President of
the Regional Committee for PAN for the Federal District; *Secretary General of the CEN of PAN*, 1969–
72; *Secretary General of PAN*, 1974–75; Secretary
of Promotion, CEN of PAN, 1975. f-None. g-None.
h-Practicing lawyer. i-Son of *Manuel Gomez Morin*,
founder and President of PAN; married Casil de Martinez del Rio. j-None. k-None. l-DBM70, 259; C de
D, 1967–69, 62; MGF69–70; letter.

Gomez Reyes, Roberto

a-Apr. 30, 1919. b-Ixtlan del Rio, Nayarit, *West*,
Rural. c-Primary studies at a public school, Ixtlan del
Rio; rural normal certificate, Normal School of
Jalisco, Nayarit, 1934–36; teaching certificate, National Teachers College, 1937–40; preparatory
studies in economics, National Preparatory School,
1942–43; degree in economics from the National
School of Economics, UNAM, 1944–49; instructor
in world history and teaching, secondary schools in

Nayarit, 1941; primary school teacher, 1942–49; Professor of Economic Thought, National School of Economics, UNAM, 1960–63; Professor of the History of Economic Doctrines, National School of Economics, UNAM, 1964–65; Professor of Public Finances, National School of Economics, UNAM, 1978– , Professor of Economic and Social Problems, University of the Valley of Mexico, 1978– . **d-***Federal Deputy* from the State of Nayarit, Dist. 1, 1967, President of the First Treasury Committee and First Secretary of the Budget Committee; *Governor of the State of Nayarit*, 1970–76. **e-**Joined the PRM, 1942. **f-**Economist, Secretariat of the Treasury, 1950–59; Director, Technical Office, Merchandise Division, Secretariat of Government Properties, 1954–58; Head of the Registration and Certificate Control Department, Secretariat of Government Properties, 1959–62; Head of the Department of Temporary Import Permits, Secretariat of Government Properties, 1963–64; Head of the Receiving Department, Division of Automobile Registration, 1965–77; Secretary General of Government of the State of Nayarit under Governor *Julian Gascon Mercado*, 1967–70. **g-**Secretary General of the Student Society of the Normal School of Jalisco, Nayarit, 1935; Secretary of Labor Action, Federation of Mexican Youth, 1940; Secretary General of Delegation 78, Section IX, Teachers Union of the Federal District, 1944–45; Auxiliary Secretary of the CEN of the SNTE, 1946–47. **h-**None. **i-**Student of *Alfonso Pulido Islas* at UNAM. **j-**None. **k-**Precandidate for Governor of Nayarit, 1963; precandidate from the Popular Sector for Senator from Nayarit, 1964. **l-**HA, 28 Aug. 1967, 5; DPE61, 40; DPE65, 70; *Excelsior*, 21 Feb. 1975, 12; Loret de Mola, *91*, 194.

Gomez Robleda, Jose

a-July 24, 1904. **b-**Orizaba, Veracruz, *Gulf*, *Urban*. **c-**Early education unknown; medical degree, National School of Medicine, UNAM, 1929; professor of biology, legal medicine and psychology, National School of Medicine, UNAM, 1930– ; Secretary, National School of Medicine, UNAM, 1934. **d-**None. **e-**Member of the Coordinating Committee of the Popular Party, 1947; Secretary General of the Popular Party, 1947. **f-**Director, Department of Medical Biological Studies, National School of Medicine, UNAM, 1942; Director, Department of Scientific Research, Secretariat of Public Education, 1940–41; Secretary of the Technical Studies Committee, Secretariat of Public Education, 1948; *Subsecretary of Education*, 1952–54. **g-**None. **h-**Author of numerous books. **i-**Student of *Octavio Vejar Vazquez* with whom he collaborated in the Secretariat of Public Education and the Popular Party; married Victoria Trujillo. **j-**None. **k-**Candidate for Federal Deputy

from the Federal District, Dist. 4, 1949, for the Popular Party. **l-**HA, 10 Oct. 1947, 5; WWM45, 51; Villasenor, II, 118; NYT, 20 Feb. 1953, 6; Beltran.

Gomez Robledo, Antonio

a-1908. **b-**Guadalajara, Jalisco, *West*, *Urban*. **c-**Law degree, University of Guadalajara; Ph.D. in Philosophy; special studies, School of Law, Paris, the Academy of International Law, The Hague, Fordham University, New York, and the University of Rio de Janeiro; Professor, National School of Law, UNAM and the Institute of Advanced Studies at Monterrey. **d-**None. **e-**None. **f-**Career Foreign Service Officer, joined the Foreign Service, 1936; member of the Ninth Inter-American Conference, Bogota, 1948; alternate Mexican representative to the Organization of American States, 1949–51; Legal Adviser to the Mexican Embassy, Washington, D.C., 1951–54; rank of ambassador, 1959; Ambassador to Brazil, 1959–61; member of the Permanent Delegation to International Organizations, Geneva, 1965; Mexican representative to the Disarmament Committee, Geneva, 1964–66; Ambassador to Italy, 1967–70; Legal Adviser to the Secretary of Foreign Relations, 1971–74, replacing Oscar Rabasa; Ambassador to Greece, 1974–76; Ambassador to Switzerland. **g-**Representative of Mexico to the Ibero-American Convention of Catholic Students, 1931, elected president of the National Federation of Catholic Students of Mexico; representative of Mexico to the Ibero-American Catholic Student Secretariat, Rome, Italy, 1933. **h-**Author of many diplomatic and legal works. **i-**Wrote for *Agustin Yanez's Bandera de Provincias*; private secretary to *Ezequiel Padilla*, Rio Conference. **j-**None. **k-**None. **l-**HA, 22 Feb. 1971, 31; DPE61, 20; DPE65, 29; *Excelsior*, 29 Nov. 1974.

Gomez Sada, Napoleon

a-1914. **b-**Municipio de Cadereyta, Nuevo Leon, *North*, *Rural*. **c-**Early education unknown; no degree. **d-***Alternate Senator* from the State of Nuevo Leon, 1958–64; *Senator* from the State of Nuevo Leon, 1964–70; *Senator* from the State of Nuevo Leon, 1976– . **e-**None. **f-**None. **g-**Alternate Secretary General of the Union of Mining and Metallurgical Industry Workers of Mexico (SITMMRM), 1958–59; Secretary General of the SITMMRM, 1960– . **h-**Employee of Metalurgica de Penoles, S.A. **j-**None. **k-**None. **l-**MGF69, 106; C de S, 1961–64, 16; C de S, 1964–70; C de S, 1976–82; *Excelsior*, 3 June 1979, 21; PS, 2524.

Gomez Sandoval, Fernando

a-1930. **b-**Oaxaca, Oaxaca, *South*, *Urban*. **c-**Primary studies at the Pestalozzi School, Oaxaca; secondary studies at the Institute of Arts and Sciences, Oaxaca (presently known as the Benito Juarez University); law degree from the Institute of Arts and Sciences, 1950; Director of the Preparatory School of the Benito Juarez University (twice); Professor of Sociology and Philosophy of Law, Benito Juarez University; Rector of the Benito Juarez University, 1959–62, 1977– . **d-***Alternate Federal Deputy* for the State of Oaxaca, Dist. 3, 1956–59; Local Deputy to the 43rd State Legislature of Oaxaca; *Substitute Governor of Oaxaca*, 1970–74 replacing *Victor Bravo Ahuja*, who became Secretary of Public Education. **e-**Secretary General of the State Executive Committee of PRI, Oaxaca (twice). **f-**Agent of the Ministerio Publico of the Attorney General's Office; Assistant Attorney General for Oaxaca; Penal and Civil Judge in the State of Oaxaca; Inspecting Judge of the Superior Tribunal of Justice of the State of Oaxaca; private secretary to Governor *Jose Pacheco Iturribarria*, 1955–56; legal adviser to the Federal Electric Commission; Secretary General of Government under Governor *Victor Bravo Ahuja*, 1968–70. **g-**None. **h-**Practicing lawyer, 1957–58. **i-**Father, an accountant; mother, a teacher; married Martha Audiffred Flores. **j-**None. **k-**Precandidate for senator from Oaxaca, 1976. **l-**DGF56, 26; letter; *Excelsior*, 8 Dec. 1975, 17.

Gomez (Segura), Marte Rodolfo

(Deceased December 16, 1973)
a-July 4, 1896. **b-**Ciudad Reynoso, Tamaulipas, *North*, *Urban*. **c-**Primary studies in Aguascalientes and at the Escuela Anexa a la Normal de Maestros, Mexico, D.F.; no secondary studies or preparatory; agricultural engineering studies from the National School of Agriculture, San Jacinto, 1909–14, degree, Sept., 1917; helped organize the Escuela Libre Ateneo Ceres; attended the Free Social Science School, Paris, 1916–17; Professor of Rural Economy, National School of Agriculture; Director of the National School of Agriculture, 1923–24. **d-**Local Deputy to the State Legislature of Tamaulipas, 1927; Federal Deputy from the State of Tamaulipas, 1928–30, President of the Chamber of Deputies, 1928; Senator from the State of Tamaulipas, 1930–32, President of the Senate, 1932; *Governor of Tamaulipas*, 1937–40. **e-**None. **f-**Topographer for the Agrarian Commission of Yautepec, Morelos, 1915; Director of the Department of Ejido Improvements, 1917–22; Auxiliary Director of the National Agrarian Commission, 1917–22; Subgerente of the National Agrarian Credit Bank, 1926–28; Secretary of Agriculture, Nov. 30, 1928, to Feb. 5, 1930; Subsecretary of the Treasury, 1933; Secretary of the Treasury, 1933–34; Gerente of the National Railroads of Mexico, 1934; *Ambassador to France*, 1935–36; *Secretary of Agriculture*, 1940–46; Ambassador to the League of Nations,

1935–36; President of the Council of Development and Coordination of National Productivity, 1954–56. **g-**President of the Local Agrarian Commission of Tamaulipas, 1925, appointed by *Emilio Portes Gil*. **h-**President of Worthington of Mexico, S.A., 1950–66; author of many books on Mexican agriculture. **i-**Political associate of *Emilio Portes Gil* since 1920; close friend of General Jesus M. Garza, who graduated from the National School of Agriculture; father was a colonel and graduate of the National Military College; son is a physician for IMSS; knew *Alfonso Gonzalez Gallardo* at the National School of Agriculture; close friend of *Jaime Torres Bodet* since 1935, when he served under Gomez in France; married Hilda Leal. **j-**Joined the Revolution in Morelos, 1915. **k-**Brandenburg considered him a member of the Inner Circle, 1940–46; important leader of the Calles bloc in the Chamber of Deputies, 1928–30. **l-**IWW67, 450–51; WWM45, 50; EBW46, 189; DBM68, 290; Brandenburg, 80; DGF56, 63; Peral, 338; WB48, 2015; Strode, 323–24; HA, 8 Sept. 1944, 27; Enc. Mex., V, 438–39; Kirk, 121–22; letter; HA, 24 Dec. 1973, 8; *Justicia*, Feb., 1973.

Gomez Velasco, Antonio

a-Sept. 3, 1897. **b-**Sayula, Jalisco, *West*, *Urban*. **c-**Completed business studies; no degree. **d-**None. **e-***President of the CEN of PARM*, 1975–79. **f-**Director of Physical Education and Premilitary Education, Secretariat of National Defense; Subdirector of Cavalry, Secretariat of National Defense, 1935–36; Chief of Foot Police, Department of the Federal District; Director of Traffic, Department of the Federal District. **g-**None. **h-**None. **j-**Career Army officer; joined the Constitutional Army, June 11, 1913 as a 2nd Captain of Cavalry in the 3rd Brigade of General Mariano Arrieta's forces; aide and secretary to General Mariano Arrieta, Chief of Instruction of the Escolta Brigade, under General Pablo Gonzalez; Chief of Staff, 4th Brigade, 21st Division, under General *Jesus Agustin Castro*; Chief of Staff, 2nd Division of the Army of the Northeast, under General *Enrique Estrada*; Chief of Staff under General Roberto Cruz; Chief of Staff to General Joaquin Amaro in Michoacan; Commander of the Bravos Battalion, 2nd Brigade, 21st Division; rank of Brigade General, Feb. 9, 1924; commander of the various military garrisons in Tlalnepantla, Mexico, Chalchimomula, Puebla, Esperanza, Puebla and Veracruz, Veracruz; Commander of the 30th Cavalry Regiment; zone commander of the 5th and 29th military zones; director, Civil Defense, Regional Guards and the Reserves, Secretariat of National Defense; Commander of the 2nd Infantry Division; reached rank of divisionary general. **k-**Resigned as President of PARM under disputed circumstances. **l-**DBM66, 295; HA, 28 May 1979, X.

Gomez Villanueva, Augusto

a-July 23, 1930. **b-**Aguascalientes, Aguascalientes, *West*, *Urban*. **c-**Primary studies in Aguascalientes; secondary studies in Durango in the School for the Children of Peasants and Laborers; political science degree from the National School of Social and Political Science, UNAM, 1965; professor at the National School of Social and Political Science, UNAM; professor at the Autonomous Institute of Sciences, Aguascalientes. **d-***Federal Deputy* from the State of Aguascalientes, Dist. 2, 1964–67, member of the Consular Service Committee, the Editorial Committee, the Second Balloting Committee, the Legislative Studies Committee (Agrarian Section), and the Gran Comision, President of the Chamber of Deputies, Sept., 1965, answered President *Diaz Ordaz's* first State of the Union Address, 1965; *Senator* from Aguascalientes, 1970, 1975–76; *Federal Deputy* from the State of Aguascalientes, 1976–77, President of the Gran Comision, 1976–77. **e-**Representative of the Agrarian Sector on the National Political Council of PRI; Technical Secretary of the IEPES of PRI; Technical Director of the pre-election campaign of *Enrique Olivares Santana* for Governor of Aguascalientes, 1961–62; Director of the Editorial Department of the Youth Sector of PRI; *Secretary of Agrarian Action of the CEN of PRI*, 1968–70, when *Olivares Santana* was Secretary General of PRI; *Secretary General of the CEN of PRI*, 1975–76. **f-**Coordinator of Planning Projects for the State of Aguascalientes; head of the Department of Publicity, State of Aguascalientes; Director of the Information Bulletin of the Secretariat of Communication and Transportation; head of the Office of Personnel Analysis, Secretariat of Communication and Transportation; Private Secretary to the Governor of Aguascalientes, *Enrique Olivares Santana*, 1962–64; *Secretary of the Department of Agrarian Affairs and Colonization*, 1970–75; Ambassador to Italy, 1977. **g-**Secretary of Organization of the National Farmers Federation, 1967–68; *Secretary General of the National Farmers Federation*, 1968–70. **h-**Worked as a laborer on the National Railroads of Mexico. **i-**Student of *Ernesto Enriquez Coyro* at the National School of Social and Political Science, UNAM; son of peasants; dedicated thesis to his political mentor, *Enrique Olivares*. **j-**None. **k-**Accused of fraud, Second Judicial District, Mexico City, 1977. **l-***Hoy*, 7 Dec. 1970, 26; WWMG, 19; HA, 11 Jan. 1971, 31; DPE71, 129; C de D, 1964–66; letters; LA, 12 Mar. 1976, 83; HA, 24 Oct. 1977; LA, 11 Nov. 1977, 349; Loret de Mola, 68.

Gomez Zepeda, Luis

a-Dec. 18, 1905. **b-**Aguascalientes, Aguascalientes, *West*, *Urban*. **c-**Primary studies in Aguascalientes; attended the Industrial School for Orphans; no degree. **d-***Senator* from the State of Aguascalientes, 1964–70. **e-**Coordinator of Social Affairs for the CEN of PRI, 1969; Secretary of Organization of the CEN of PRI, 1970. **f-**Director General of the Workers Cooperative Society of Clothing and Equipment, 1970–73; *Director General of the National Railroads of Mexico*, 1973–76, 1976– . **g-**Co-founder of the Railroad Workers Union of the Mexican Republic, 1933; Secretary of Organization of Section Seventeen of the Railroad Workers Union, 1933–36; Secretary of Organization and Education of the Union of Mexican Railroad Workers, 1940; Secretary of Conflicts of the CTM, 1940, 1944; Secretary General of the Union of Mexican Railroad Workers, 1944, 1962–64, 1965–68; member of the CEN of the Revolutionary Federation of Farmers and Workers (CROC), 1952–56; Secretary General of CROC, 1953–54, 1961–62. **h-**He became a railroad worker on the Constitutionalist railroads, 1917–18; messenger, Buenavista telegraph office, 1918; sold chocolates as a boy; worked for a butcher at age eleven; mimeographer, 1917–18; **i-**Distantly related to *Adolfo Lopez Mateos*, grandfather a physician, father a bookkeeper. **j-**None. **k-**Imprisoned in the Federal District for labor activities, 1948; attempted to become Secretary General of the STFRM, 1942. **l-**HA, 8 Apr. 1974, 16–17; *Excelsior*, 5 July 1973, 15; HA, 7 Dec. 1970, 27–28; HA, 14 May 1973, 25; C de S, 1964–70; MGF69; *Proceso*, 18 Dec. 1976, 18–21; Villasenor, II.

Gonzalez, Jesus B.

(Deceased 1955)

a-1887. **b-**Zacatecas, Zacatecas, *East Central*, *Urban*. **c-**Early education unknown; no degree. **d-**Federal Deputy from Zacatecas (twice); *Federal Senator* from Zacatecas, 1946–52, member of the Gran Comision, the Second Committee on Tariffs and Foreign Trade, the Second Instructive Section of the Grand Jury Committee, and the Securities Committee. **e-**None. **f-**Secretary of the Administration of the National Railroads of Mexico; Subdirector of PIPSA; Secretary of the Advisory Council of PIPSA; administrative official of National Patrimony. **g-**None. **h-**Newspaper reporter; writer for *Excelsior* and *Revista de Revistas*. **j-**None. **k-**None. **l-***Excelsior*, 11, May 1972; DP70, 891; DGF51, I, 8–10, 12, 14; letter.

Gonzalez Aparicio, Luis

(Deceased Sept. 23, 1969)

a-1907. **b-**Jalapa, Veracruz, *Gulf*, *Urban*. **c-**Architecture degree, National School of Architecture, 1933; Professor of Architecture, National School of Architecture, UNAM. **d-***Senator* from the

Federal District, 1964–69. e-Director of the Center of Economic, Political, and Social Studies of PRI. f-Head of the reconstruction project of the State Palace, Hermosillo, Sonora; constructed experimental agricultural stations in the Valle del Yaqui; constructed Workers Housing Projects on the Emiliano Zapata Ejido, Zacatepec, Morelos; Director of the Planning Commission for the Papaloapan Commission, 1950; instituted the Modern Market Construction Program for the Federal Government in Mexico, D.F.; Executive Secretary of the Papaloapan Commission, 1951–52; President of the Western Zone Planning Committee for the Valley of Mexico, 1958–59. g-None. h-President of the National College of Architects, 1959. j-None. l-Enc. Mex., V, 454; Correa, 105; DGF51, II, 615; DP70, 895.

Gonzalez Azcuaga, Pedro

a-Nov. 11, 1945. b-Palizada, Campeche, *Gulf*, *Rural*. c-Early education unknown; degree in political science, National School of Political and Social Sciences, UNAM; studies in international relations, Colegio de Mexico. d-*Federal Deputy* from the Federal District, Dist. 24, 1976–79; Vice-president of the Chamber of Deputies; member of the Permanent Committee. e-Joined PARM, May, 1971; *President of PARM*, February, 1973 to May, 1975; member of the Federal Electoral Commission. f-None. g-None. i-Married Rita H. Zozaya. j-None. k-None. l-HA, 12 Feb. 1979, 19; D de C, 1976–79, 28.

Gonzalez Beytia, Jose

a-June 17, 1908. b-Yucatan, *Gulf*. c-Teaching certificate from the Rodolfo Menendez de la Pena Normal School, Merida; studies at the National Teachers' College, Mexico City; attended the University of Yucatan; teacher of Spanish, Agustin Vadillo Cicero School; secondary school teacher in Mexico City; secretary of the Preparatory School for Children of Workers, Coyoacan, Federal District. d-Local Deputy to the State Legislature of Yucatan, 1943–46; *Governor of Yucatan*, 1946–51. e-None. f-Private Secretary to the Governor of Yucatan, *Ernesto Novelo Torres*, 1940–43. g-Representative of the Yucatan Socialist Students to the National Student Congress, Ciudad del Carmen; student leader in the first and second Socialist Student Congresses, 1934–35. h-None. i-Married Blanca Rosa Rodriguez Barrera; protege of the *Novelo Torres* political clique. j-None. k-Resigned as governor in 1952 in an attempt to prevent the imposition of *Tomas Marentes* as his successor; his attempt failed. l-STYBIWW54, 758; Anderson, 94; C de D, 1943–46; HA, 16 Feb. 1951, 9; D de S, 22 Jan. 1946, 1; DPE51, I, 93; HA, 8 Feb. 1946, 3.

Gonzalez Blanco, Alberto

(Deceased Nov. 1, 1974)
b-Tuxtla Gutierrez, Chiapas, *South*, *Urban*. c-Primary studies in the State of Chiapas; preparatory studies at the National Preparatory School, 1920–24; law degree, National School of Law, UNAM, Oct. 24, 1927; LLD, National School of Law, UNAM, 1958 (honorary mention); first thesis on the agrarian problem and LLD thesis on sexual crimes in Mexican doctrine and positive law. d-None. e-None. f-Consulting lawyer for the National Agrarian Commission; Director of the Department of Colonization, Secretariat of Agriculture; consulting lawyer, Secretariat of Agriculture; Secretary, First Civil Judicial District, Federal District; Sixth Judge, Second Penal Court, Federal District, 1941; Justice of the Superior Tribunal of Justice of the Federal District; Secretary of Studies, Supreme Court of Justice; District Court Judge, Yucatan and Queretaro; *Supernumerary Justice of the Supreme Court*, 1963–64, 1964–67. g-None. i-Brother of *Salomon Gonzalez Blanco*, Secretary of Labor, 1958–70; close friend of *Antonio Luna Arroyo* at graduate school. j-None. k-None. l-*Justicia*; letter.

Gonzalez Blanco, Salomon

a-Apr. 22, 1902. b-Playa de Catozaja, Chiapas, *South*, *Rural*. c-Primary studies in Salto de Agua, Tapachula, and Tuxtla Gutierrez, Chiapas; preparatory studies at the National Preparatory School, Mexico, D.F.; first three years of legal studies, Free Law School, 1922–24; law degree from the National Law School, UNAM, May 16, 1927, with a thesis on the social evolution of unions; LLD from the National Law School, UNAM; Professor of Labor Law, National School of Law, UNAM (15 years); Professor at the Escuela Libre de Derecho; Director of the Juarez Institute, Tabasco, 1931–32. d-*Alternate Senator* from Tabasco, 1934–40; *Senator* from the State of Chiapas, 1976–78, member of the Gran Comision and President of the Chamber, September 1977. e-None. f-Second Auxiliary Secretary of the Fourth Division of the Superior Tribunal of Justice of the Federal District, 1927–30; Judge of the First Appeals Court, Villahermosa, Tabasco, 1930; Magistrate of the Superior Tribunal of Justice for the State of Tabasco, 1931; Commissioner of the Agricultural Department of the National Agrarian Commission; Assistant Auditor, General Accounting Office, Secretariat of the Treasury; Magistrate of the Superior Tribunal of Justice of the Federal District and Territories, 1941–47; Director General of Conciliation, Secretariat of Labor, 1947; *Oficial Mayor*, *Secretariat of Labor*, September 20, 1947, to December 31, 1952; *Subsecretary of Labor*, Jan. 1, 1953, to Nov. 16, 1957; *Subsecretary in Charge of the Sec-*

retariat of Labor, Nov. 17, 1957, to Nov. 30, 1958; *Secretary of Labor*, 1958–64, 1964–70; *Substitute Governor of Chiapas*, December 9, 1978–80. **g-**None. **h-**Author of numerous works on labor law. **i-**Friend of *Antonio Carrillo Flores* and *Manuel Ramirez Vazquez* at the National Law School, UNAM; son, *Jose Gonzalez Blanco*, served as Secretary General of the Department of the Federal District; married Josefa Garrido. **j-**None. **k-**Precandidate for president of Mexico, 1963. **l-**EGF56, 397; Enc. Mex., V, 455; HA, 6 Feb. 1948, 10; IWW67, 452; WWMG, 19; DBM68, 296–97; HA, 8 Dec. 1958, 26; DPE61, 115; DPE65, 154; DGF51, I, 399; HA, 7 Dec. 1964, 20; Func., 87; Richmond, 375.

Gonzalez Blanco (Garrido), Jose

a-May 18, 1934. **b-**El Paraiso, Municipio de Catazaje, Chiapas, *South*, *Rural*. **c-**Law degree from the National School of Law, UNAM, Apr. 26, 1956; graduate work in law and economics at Trinity Hall, Cambridge University, 1957–59, graduating November, 1961; professor at secondary schools. **d-***Federal Deputy* from the State of Chiapas, Dist. 6, 1967–70, member of Industries Committee, the Fiscal Committee, the Tariff Committee, and the Gran Comision. **e-**General delegate of PRI to Oaxaca, Jalisco, and Guanajuato. **f-**Chancellor, Mexican Embassy, London, 1957–59; Secretary of the Directive Council of the ISSSTE; Director of Public Investments, Secretariat of the Presidency; Subgerente of the National Lottery; *Secretary General (B) of the Department of the Federal District*, 1970–73; Subdirector of the Department of Public Investments, Secretary of the Presidency, 1961; delegate of the Department of the Federal District, 1976. **g-**Student leader and President of the 1952 Generation of Lawyers. **h-**Author of various books. **i-**Son of *Salomon Gonzalez Blanco*, Secretary of Labor, 1958–70. **j-**None. **k-**None. **l-**HA, 14 Dec. 1970, 24; BdM, 135; DPE61, 124; DPE70.

Gonzalez Bustamante, Juan Jose

a-May 16, 1899. **b-**Matehuala, San Luis Potosi, *East Central*, *Urban*. **c-**Law degree from the Escuela Libre de Derecho, January 8, 1929; LLD from the National School of Law, UNAM; professor, National School of Law, UNAM, 1937. **d-***Senator* from San Luis Potosi, 1964–70, president of the Senate. **e-**None. **f-**Third Judge of the First Penal Court, 1936; judge of the Ninth Penal Court, 1940; Magistrate of the Superior Tribunal of Justice of the State of San Luis Potosi; Judge of the First District Criminal Court, 1947–52; *Assistant Attorney General of Mexico*, 1940–46; *Secretary General of UNAM*, 1948–52; *Supernumerary Justice of the Supreme Court*, 1958; *Justice of the Supreme Court*, 1959–64;

President of the First Division of the Supreme Court, 1959–64. **g-**None. **h-**Journalist for many years; author of numerous articles, writer for *Excelsior* since 1928. **i-**Son, Juan Jose Gonzalez Suarez, was a judge in the Fourth Penal District of the Federal District, 1969. **j-**Joined the Revolution, 1915; fought in Tampico. **k-**None. **l-**MGF69, 106; DGF51, I, 591; DGF47, 47; C de S, 1964–70; DBM68, 297; Correa, 60; *Por que*, 13 Nov. 1969, 17; Casasola, V; WNM, 98; Garrido, 266, 336; Peral, 343; Enc. Mex., V, 457.

Gonzalez Casanova, Pablo

a-Feb. 11, 1922. **b-**Toluca, Mexico, *West Central*, *Urban*. **c-**Preparatory studies at the National Preparatory School, 1939–40; studies from the National School of Law, UNAM, 1940–42; MA degree in history, 1943–46; Ph.D. in sociology from the University of Paris, 1947–50, with a thesis on French ideology toward Latin America; scholarship from the French government; scholarship from the Colegio de Mexico to study in Paris; Professor of Historical Sciences, UNAM; Professor of Sociology in various universities; Researcher, Institute of Social Investigations, UNAM, 1950; Reseacher, Colegio de Mexico, 1950; Researcher, Institute for Research in Economics, UNAM. **d-**None. **e-**None. **f-**Director of the Center for Development Studies; Dean, National School of Political and Social Sciences, UNAM, 1957–65; Director of the Institute of Social Investigations, UNAM, 1966–70; *Rector of UNAM*, 1970–72; Director of the Institute of Social Investigations, UNAM, 1977– . **g-**None. **h-**Author of works on sociology and Mexican politics. **i-**Son of Pablo Gonzalez Casanova, linguist and Professor of Anthropology at UNAM, who resigned in protest in 1935; originally a disciple of *Lucio Mendieta y Nunez* at UNAM. **j-**None. **k-**Resigned from rectorship Dec., 1972, after numerous strikes. **l-**Correa, 340; DP70, 896; DBM70, 263; Enc. Mex., V, 460.

Gonzalez Cavazos, Agapito

a-Dec. 22, 1915. **b-**China, Nuevo Leon, *North*, *Rural*. **c-**Early education unknown; no degree. **d-***Federal Deputy* from the State of Tamaulipas, Dist. 3, 1970–73, member of the Second Railroad Committee, the Petroleum Committee and the Second Public Housing Committee; *Federal Deputy* from the State of Tamaulipas, Dist. 3, 1976–79, member of the Agrarian Affairs Committee, the Small Property Section of the Agricultural Development Committee, the Industrial Development Committee, the Housing Development Committee and the Committee for Social and Economic Development Planning. **e-**Campaigner for PRI in many electoral campaigns. **f-**None. **g-**Joined the Union of Industrial

Employees and Workers, 1932; member of Section Sixteen of the Union of Oil Industry Workers. **i-**Married Eva Benavides. **j-**None. **k-**None. **l-**C de D, 1970–73, 116; C de D, 1976–79, 28; D de C, 1976–79, 5, 7, 13, 27, 45, 66.

Gonzalez Cortazar, Jose de Jesus

a-1934. **b-**Guadalajara, Jalisco, *West*, *Urban*. **c-**Law degree from the University of Guadalajara; postgraduate work at the City of London College. **d-***Federal Deputy* from the State of Jalisco, Dist. 7, 1961–64, member of the Second Balloting committee and the Committee on Foreign Relations, and substitute member of the Small Agricultural Property Committee; member of the Mexican Congressional Delegation to the Second, Third, and Fourth Interparliamentary Conferences between Mexico and the United States. **e-**Adviser to the Legal Studies Section and Historical Studies Section of the IEPES of PRI, 1968; delegate of PRI to Colima for the 1964 Presidential elections. **f-**Technical adviser to the Mexican Institute of Social Security; member of the Development Commission for the Chapala Lake Region. **g-**President of the Law School Student Association of the University of Guadalajara, 1953. **h-**Lawyer for PEMEX; President of the Agricultural and Industrial Credit Union of the West; Vice President of the Fourth Inter-American Consular Reunion. **i-**Son of *J. Jesus Gonzalez Gallo*, Governor of Jalisco, 1947–53. **j-**None. **k-**None. **l-**DBM68, 306–07; C de D, 1961–63, 70; Enc. Mex., V, 466.

Gonzalez Cosio, Manuel

a-Apr. 15, 1915. **b-**Queretaro, Queretaro, *East Central, Urban*. **c-**Primary studies in Queretaro; secondary and preparatory studies at the Colegio Frances and University of Queretaro; degree in chemical engineering from the School of Science, UNAM. **d-***Federal Deputy* from the State of Queretaro, Dist. 1, 1949–52, member of the Gran Comision, the National Waters and Irrigation Committee, the First and Second Legislative Studies Committee, the Industries Committee, the Public Works Committee, and the General Accounting Office Inspection Committee (2nd year); *Senator* from the State of Queretaro, 1952–58; member of the Gran Comision, the Second Ejido Committee, and the Forestry Committee; *Governor of Queretaro*, 1961–67; *Senator* from Queretaro, 1976. **e-**None. **f-**Director General of Desert Zones for the Federal Government, 1950–52; Director General of La Forestal, 1958–61; Ambassador to Venezuela, 1968–70; President of the Administrative Council of the National Laboratories of Industrial Development, 1971–72; Director General of Alimentos Balanceados de Mexico, S.A., 1968–71; *Director General of CONASUPO*, 1976–79. **g-**Secretary General of the Union of Federal

Employees for Queretaro, 1940–43; President of the Confederation of University Students for the Federal District, 1934; Secretary General of the National Union of Workers of the Secretary of Agriculture; Secretary of Conflicts and Technical Problems, FSTSE; President of the Student Society of the School of Chemical Sciences, UNAM. **i-**From a longtime politically active family in Queretaro; grandfather was a federal deputy and governor of Queretaro. **j-**None. **k-**None. **l-**Enc. Mex., V; DGF50, 9, 10, 14; DGF51, I, 204, 25, 29–35; C de D, 1949–51; C de S, 1952–58; Peral, 344; *Excelsior*, 15 Apr. 1977, 6; Ind. Biog., 74.

Gonzalez Cosio (Diaz), Arturo

a-May 3, 1930. **b-**Federal District, *Federal District, Urban*. **c-**Law degree from the National Law School, UNAM, Sept. 27, 1954; Ph.D. from Cologne, West Germany, 1954–56; Professor, National School of Law, UNAM, 1962– . **d-***Federal Deputy* from the Federal District, Dist. 22, 1973–76. **e-**Member of the Political Committee of the New Advisory Council of the IEPES of PRI, 1972; *Secretary of Political Education of the CEN of PRI*, 1972–76. **f-**Private Secretary to the Director of Ciudad Sahagun Industrial site, 1959–62; head of publicity and studies for the Private Secretary of the President of Mexico, *Humberto Romero Perez*, 1962–64; Auxiliary Secretary to the head of the Department of the Federal District, *Ernesto P. Uruchurtu*, 1964–66; Director General of Copyrights, Secretariat of Public Education, 1968–70; Director General of Industrial Property, Secretary of Industry and Commerce, 1970–73; Subdirector of Delegations, CONASUPO, 1976. **g-**Secretary General of the Association of University Professors of Mexico. **h-**Employee of the National Securities Commission, 1951-52. **i-**Published a literary review with *Victor Flores Olea*, *Porfirio Munoz Ledo* and others at UNAM, 1950s. **j-**None. **k-**None. **l-**HA, 21 Dec. 1964, 10; HA, 10 July 1972, 10; DPE70, 62; B de M, 135; *Excelsior*, 16 Mar. 1973, 27; *Excelsior*, 28 Feb. 1973, 19; Enc. Mex., V, 460.

Gonzalez de la Vega, Francisco

(Deceased Mar. 3, 1976)
a-Dec. 3, 1901. **b-**Durango, Durango, *West, Urban*. **c-**Studied at the National School of Law, UNAM, 1917–20, law degree, 1923; LLD in penal sciences from the School of Law, University of Veracruz; Professor of Penal Law, Escuela Libre de Derecho; professor at the National School of Law, UNAM, 1921–23; member of the Commission of Legal Studies, UNAM, 1944–45; founder of the University of Durango 1957. **d-***Senator* from the State of Durango, 1952–57, member of the Second Balloting Committee, the Legislative Studies Committee, and the First Committee on Credit, Money, and Credit

Institutions; substitute member of the Department of the Federal District Committee; *Governor of Durango*, 1957–61. **e-**Supported Jose Vasconcelos, 1929. **f-**Correctional Judge, 1929; Assistant Attorney General of Mexico, 1930–31; Penal Judge, 1931–38; President of the Legislative Commission on Education, 1942–43; *Attorney General of Mexico*, 1946–52; Director General of PIPSA, 1952–56; *Head of the Department of Tourism*, 1961–64; Ambassador to Argentina, 1969–70. **g-**None. **h-**Practiced law, Durango, 1923–29; President of the Mexican Academy of Penal Sciences; author of over fifteen books on penal law. **i-**Studied with *Luis Garrido Diaz* at UNAM; during his career as a professor of law, he taught four Mexican Presidents who attended the National Law School, *Miguel Aleman*, *Adolfo Lopez Mateos*, *Gustavo Diaz Ordaz*, and *Luis Echeverria*; father was a judge; brother of *Angel Gonzalez de la Vega*, Justice of the Supreme Court, 1951–65; married Angelita Zevada. **j-**None. **k-**Hayner considered him to be an extremely honest governor; offered Rectorship of UNAM in 1948 but remained as the Attorney General. **l-**Letter; Hayner, 221; Peral, 47, 148–49; DGF51, II, 653; I, 535; DGF50, II, 481; WWM45, 41; MGF69; DGF56, 6, 13, 14; HA, 8 Dec. 1948; *Quien Sera*, 140; HA, 15 Mar. 1976, 17; Ind. Biog., 74–75.

Gonzalez de la Vega (Iriarte), Angel

a-Sept. 26, 1895. **b-**La Paz, Baja California del Sur, *West*, *Urban*. **c-**Preparatory studies at the National Preparatory School; law degree from the National School of Law, UNAM, 1919. **d-**None. **e-**None. **f-**Director, Bureau of International Taxes, Secretariat of the Treasury; president of the revisory committee on the federal income tax; Director, Economic Archives, Secretariat of the Treasury; founding Justice of the Federal Tax Court; Assistant Attorney General of Mexico; *Subsecretary of the Treasury*, 1949–50; *Supernumerary Justice of the Supreme Court*, 1951–52; *Supernumerary Justice of the Supreme Court*, 1952–58; *Justice of the Supreme Court*, 1958–65. **g-**None. **i-**Brother of *Francisco Gonzalez de la Vega*, Attorney General of Mexico, 1946–52; son of lawyer Angel Gonzalez de la Vega; mother ran a boarding house for students at the National Preparatory School and the National University; co-student with *Ramon Beteta* at UNAM. **j-**None. **k-**None. **l-**DGF51, 568; WNM, 99; *Excelsior*, 18 Nov. 1949; Balboa.

Gonzalez Fernandez, Vicente
(Deceased 1959)
a-Jan. 17, 1885. **b-**Ocotlan de Morelos, Oaxaca, *South*, *Rural*. **c-**Attended the Escuela de Aspirantes, for military cadets, Mexico, D.F.; no degree. **d-***Governor of Oaxaca*, 1940–44. **e-**None. **f-**Chief of

Police for the Federal District, 1934–40; Director of the Department of Artillery, Secretariat of National Defense. **g-**None. **j-**Career military man; joined the Revolution, 1910; served in the Federal Army under General Carlos Tejada; served under General Pablo Gonzalez; rank of Brigadier General, 1920; rank of Divisionary General, Nov. 16, 1940; Chief of Military Operations in various states, including Guerrero, Puebla, and the Federal District; fought against the Escobar Rebellion, 1929; fought against the De la Huerta revolt in Tabasco, 1923; Commander of the 25th Military Zone, Puebla. **k-**None. **l-**DP70, 899; Enc. Mex., V, 464; Peral, 353; *Hoy*, 21 Dec. 1940, 68; D de Y, 1 Nov. 1940, 2.

Gonzalez Gallardo, Alfonso
a-Jan. 21, 1891. **b-**Lagos de Moreno, Jalisco, *West*, *Rural*. **c-**Engineering degree in agronomy and hydraulics, National School of Agriculture, San Jacinto, 1913; Professor of Geology, Mineralogy, and Topography at the National School of Agriculture, Chapingo. **d-**None. **e-**None. **f-**Head of the Technical Department, National Agricultural Credit Bank; Oficial Mayor of Agriculture, 1930–32; Oficial Mayor of the Treasury, 1932; Subsecretary of the Treasury, 1932–34; in charge of many Mexican delegations to international agricultural conferences; *Subsecretary of Agriculture*, 1940–46; Director of the Institute for the Improvement of Sugar Production, 1964–70. **g-**None. **h-**Began career as an engineer in the National Irrigation Works, 1913; helped to bring the Rockefeller Foundation to Mexico; founded the Institute for the Improvement of Sugar Production, 1949; author of many publications on the sugar industry in Mexico. **i-**Student with *Marte R. Gomez* and *Luis L. Leon* at the National School of Agriculture; collaborator of *Marte R. Gomez* for many years; married Eva Karg; son of a medical doctor. **j-**None. **k-**None. **l-**D del S, 2 Dec. 1940, 1, 6; letter; WB48, 2018; DBM68, 302; Peral, 345.

Gonzalez Gallo, J. Jesus
(Deceased Aug. 17, 1957)
a-Jan. 14, 1900. **b-**Yahualica, Jalisco, *West*, *Rural*. **c-**Primary studies in Yahualica; preparatory studies in Guadalajara; law degree from the University of Guadalajara, 1923. **d-**Federal Deputy from Jalisco, Teocaltiche District, 1930–32; *Senator* from Jalisco, 1934–40. **e-**President of the Revolutionary Party of Jalisco, part of the PNR; editor of the PNR newspaper for Jalisco, *El Jalisciense*; President of the PNR regional committee for the State of Jalisco, 1932–34. **f-**Judge of the First Instance, Jalostotitlan, Jalisco, 1923; Secretary of the Fifth Division of the Superior Tribunal of Justice, Jalisco; Criminal and Civil Judge, Guadalajara; Secretary of the Federal

Council of Conciliation and Arbitration; Subdirector of the Department of Government of the Federal District, 1927–30; *Private Secretary to the President of Mexico*, under *Manuel Avila Camacho*, 1940–46. g-None. h-None. i-Son, *Jose de Jesus*, was a Federal Deputy from Jalisco, 1961–64; married Paz Cortazar; knew *Efrain Gonzalez Luna* and *Agustin Yanez* from student days in the Mexican Association of Catholic Youth in Guadalajara. j-None. k-Political rival of *Marcelino Garcia Barragan*. l-DP70, 899; letter; Enc. Mex., V, 464–65; DGF51, II, 699; I, 90.

Gonzalez Guevara, Rodolfo

a-Dec. 22, 1918. b-Mazatlan, Sinaloa, *West*, *Urban*. c-Law degree, University of Guadalajara. d-Secretary of the City Council of Guadalajara, 1947–52; *Federal Deputy* from the State of Jalisco, Dist. 1, 1952–55, member of the Legislative Studies Committee (1st and 2nd years), the Balloting Committee, and the Administrative Committee (3rd year); President of the Chamber of Deputies, Dec., 1954; *Federal Deputy* from the Federal District, Dist. No. 13, 1976–79, President of the Gran Comision, 1977–79. e-*Secretary of Political Action for the CEN of PRI*, 1955; President of the PRI in the Federal District, 1955–59; President of PRI in the Federal District, 1959–64; *Secretary General of the CEN of PRI*, 1964; member of the New Advisory Council of the IEPES of PRI, the Ideology and Program Commission, June 28, 1972; General Delegate of the CEN of PRI to Sonora, 1972; Director of the CEPES of PRI of the Federal District, 1976. f-Director of the General Office for the Secretariat of Industry and Commerce, Guadalajara, Jalisco, 1951; *Subsecretary of Government Properties*, 1964–66, under *Corona del Rosal*; *Secretary General of the Federal District Department*, 1966–70, under *Corona del Rosal*; *Subsecretary of Government*, May 25, 1979– . g-President of the Federation of Socialist Students of the West, 1934. i-Collaborator of *Alfonso Corona del Rosal* since 1958; married Elisa Macias; brother Hector Gonzalez Guevara a federal deputy from Sinaloa, 1979–82. j-None. k-Resigned as the General Delegate of PRI in protest to *Carlos Biebrich's* selection as governor of Sonora, 1973. l-DGF51, I, 268; C de D, 1952–54; HA, 10 July 1972, 10; *Siempre*, Jan. 3, 1959, 6; Enc. Mex., V, 579; DPE65, 76; MGF69; HA, 21 Dec. 1964, 7; Johnson, 1978, 181; *Excelsior*, 30 July 1978, 23.

Gonzalez Hinojosa, Manuel

a-1912. b-San Luis Potosi, *East*, *Central*. c-Early education unknown; law degree; Professor of Agrarian Law, National School of Law, UNAM; Professor of Agrarian Law, Ibero-American University.

d-*Federal Deputy* from PAN (party deputy), 1967–70, 1973–76. e-Founding member of PAN, 1939; President of the Regional Committee of PAN for San Luis Potosi; *President of the CEN of PAN*, 1969–72. f-None. g-Member of the Catholic Action organization. h-Practicing lawyer in the Federal District; multilingual. i-Jose G. Minondo, Secretary General of the CEN of PAN, was a political disciple of *Gonzalez Hinojosa*; son, Alejandro, was a candidate for federal deputy for PAN in 1979, but resigned before the election. j-None. k-His opposition party activities forced him to leave San Luis Potosi in the 1950s; candidate of PAN for Federal Deputy in 1979 but resigned before the election. l-*Excelsior*, 28 Feb. 1973, 19; Mabry, 81, 153.

Gonzalez (Lugo), Hugo Pedro

b-Nuevo Laredo, Tamaulipas, *North*, *Rural*. c-Secondary studies at the Colegio Civil; law degree from the National School of Law, UNAM, 1928–32, degree, February, 1933. d-*Federal Deputy* from the State of Tamaulipas, Dist. 1, 1940–43, member of the Gran Comision, the Committee on Government, the Budget and Accounts Committee, and the Second Constitutional Affairs Committee; *Governor of Tamaulipas*, 1945–47. e-Secretary of the Center for his father's gubernatorial campaign, 1927. f-Scribe, 3rd Division of the Superior Court of Tamaulipas, 1927–28; scribe, 5th Civil District Court, Mexico City, 1928; scribe, 3rd Civil Court, Mexico City, 1931–32; scribe, 6th Penal Court, Mexico City, 1932–33; Judge of the Superior Tribunal of Justice of the Federal District, 1943; General Manager of the National Bonded Warehouses, 1949–52; Director General of Legal Services for the Department of Tourism, 1958–61; Ambassador to Bolivia, 1966–70; Ambassador to Indonesia, 1970–71. g-President of the Student Society of the National Preparatory School; Secretary of the Law School. h-Practicing lawyer, Tamaulipas, 1933. i-Father a lawyer and prominent politician in Tamaulipas, having served as Senator, State Attorney General and Secretary General of Government. j-None. k-Removed from the Governorship of Tamaulipas on the pretext that he allowed the murderer of the most outspoken critic of his administration, newspaper editor Vicente Villasana of *El Mundo*, to get away from the authorities after he was seen in the Governor's home in Ciudad Victoria; the murderer was the Police Chief of Ciudad Victoria, and was part of his administration; according to Medina, the real reason for his removal was his loyalty to Portes Gil and his sympathy to the presidential candidacy of *Javier Rojo Gomez* in 1945. l-*Excelsior*, 7 April 1947, 9; DGF51, II, 572; MGF69, 180; DGF50, 410; DPE61, 129; NYT, 10 April 1947, 5; Anderson; letter; Medina, 20, 98–99.

Gonzalez Lugo, J. Jesus

(Deceased 1965)
a-Dec. 27, 1892. **b-**Colima, Colima, *West, Urban.*
c-Secondary studies at the Normal School of Mexico,
D.F.; teaching certificate, 1914; Director of the
School for Dependents of the Army. **d-***Governor of
Colima*, 1949–55. **e-**None. **f-**Chief of Staff for the
Secretariat of National Defense, 1940–45; *Subsecretary of National Defense*, 1946–49. **g-**None.
h-None. **i-**Political protege of *Miguel Aleman*.
j-Career army officer; joined the Federalists, 1914;
fought against Carranza in the Federal Army, his
troops were incorporated into the Constitutional
Army under De la Huerta; rank of Divisionary General. **k-**As Governor of Colima, became one of the
rare cases in recent Mexican political history, in
which a governor was deprived of his powers by the
local legislature for alleged corruption and illegal
procedures; the Secretary of Government, *Adolfo
Ruiz Cortines* sent the Oficial Mayor to investigate
the legislature for not observing the proper legal procedures; the local legislature changed its mind and
recalled *Gonzalez Lugo* back to the Governorship; he
retired from politics in 1955. **l-**DP70, 901; DGF51,
I, 89; letter; DGF47, 109; Enc. Mex., V, 468; HA,
30 Mar. 1951, 10–11.

Gonzalez Luna, Efrain

(Deceased September 10, 1964)
a-Oct. 18, 1898. **b-**Autlan, Jalisco, *West, Rural.*
c-Primary studies at the Instituto del Sagrado Corazon in Autlan, 1906–08; secondary studies at the San
Jose Institute, 1908–11, and at the Morelos University, 1911–14; preparatory studies in Guadalajara,
1915–16; law degree from the University of
Guadalajara, 1916–20, degree, Oct. 19, 1920; Professor of Law at the University of Guadalajara; Professor of Law at the National School of Law,
UNAM. **d-**None. **e-**Founded the National Action
Party (PAN) with *Manuel Gomez Morin*, 1939.
f-None. **g-**Joined the Catholic Association for Mexican Youth (ACJM), 1921; orator for and President of
the ACJM. **h-**Author of many articles on social and
political subjects; participated in the National
Catholic Conference on Social Problems in the
United States, 1942; private law practice in Guadalajara, 1923–64. **i-**Son, *Efrain Gonzalez Morfin*, served
as a Federal Deputy from the National Action Party,
1967–70; son, Ignacio, a practicing attorney in
Guadalajara and a graduate of the 1949 Law School
Generation of UNAM; son, Adalberto, a Jesuit and
professor with a Ph.D. in Theology; father, Mauro
H. Gonzalez, was a lawyer; *Jesus Gonzalez Gallo*
and *Agustin Yanez* were also members of the ACJM
at the same time as *Gonzalez Luna*; married Amparo
Morfin. **k-**Presidential candidate of PAN, 1952.

l-DP70, 901; WWM45, 52; WWMG, 19; Morton,
63–64; Enc. Mex., 1977, V, 468.

Gonzalez Morfin, Efrain

a-June 5, 1929. **c-**Primary and secondary studies at
the Institute of Sciences, Guadalajara, Jalisco,
1936–48; preparatory studies, Institute of Sciences,
Guadalajara; studied Greek and Latin in the United
States, 1948–51; studied philosophy at the University of Innsbruck, Austria, 1955; studied economics,
political science, and sociology at the Sorbonne,
Paris, 1956–58; taught philosophy for four years.
d-*Federal Deputy* from the Federal District, Dist. 8,
1967–70, member of the Department of the Federal
District Committee, the Second Taxes Committee,
and the Money and Credit Institutions Committee.
e-Joined PAN, 1959; member of the National Executive Committee of PAN; member of the PAN youth
group as a student; member of the studies commission of PAN; Regional Director of PAN for the Federal District, 1969; Presidential Candidate for PAN,
1969–70. **f-**Professional translator for a series on
economic development for CEMLA. **g-**None.
h-Author of an administrative document for PAN approved at the 20th Annual Convention; author of
numerous articles for National Action, official PAN
publication; speaks eight languages. **i-**Son of *Efrain
Gonzalez Luna*; godson of *Manuel Gomez Morin*.
j-None. **k-**None. **l-**Letter; C de D, 1967–69, 62, 74,
81; Enc. Mex., 1977, V, 471.

Gonzalez (Parra), Emilio M.

a-May 23, 1913. **b-**Ixtlan del Rio, Nayarit, *West,
Urban.* **c-**Primary education only; no degree.
d-*Federal Deputy* from the State of Nayarit, Dist. 2,
1940–43; Local Deputy to the State Legislature of
Nayarit, 1945–48; *Federal Deputy* from the State of
Nayarit, Dist. 2, 1949–52, member of the Industries
Committee, the First Balloting Committee and the
Complaints Committee; *Senator* from the State of
Nayarit, 1952–58, President of the Social Action
Committee, First Secretary of the Second Labor
Committee; Secretary of the Second Instructive Sec-
tion of the Grand Jury and member of the Second
Balloting Group; *Federal Deputy* from the State of
Nayarit, Dist. 2, 1967–70, member of the Gran
Comision, member of the First Balloting Committee;
Senator from the State of Nayarit, 1970–76, Presi-
dent of the Mail and Telegraph Committee, First Sec-
retary of the Cooperative Development Committee,
Second Secretary of the National Resources and
Properties Committee and member of the Fishing
Committee; *Federal Deputy* from the State of
Nayarit, Dist. 2, 1979–82. **e-**None. **f-**Telegrapher
and Radio Telegrapher, Secretariat of Communica-
tions and Public Works, 1929. **g-**Leader in the Union

of Workers of the Secretariat of Communications and Public Works; First Secretary General of the Coordinating Committee of the Federation of Workers of the State of Nayarit; Secretary General of the Federation of Workers of the State of Nayarit, 1937–38; Secretary General of the Mexican Federation of Labor of the State of Nayarit, 1938–79; Secretary of Political Action of the CTM, 1978– . h-None. j-None. k-One of the few Mexican politicians to have become Senator and Deputy six times since 1935. l-C de D, 1967–70, 77; Ind. Biog., 75–76; *Excelsior*, 29 Dec. 1978, 12; C de D, 1940–43; C de S, 1970–76, 76; C de D, 1949–52, 74.

Gonzalez Parrodi, Carlos

a-Nov. 4, 1923. b-Federal District, *Federal District, Urban*. c-Law degree from the National School of Law, UNAM, 1947. d-None. e-None. f-Third Secretary, Mexican Embassy, London, 1948–49; Third Secretary, Mexican Embassy, Lisbon; head of the Central American and Caribbean Section, Secretariat of Foreign Relations, 1955–56; Second Secretary of the Mexican Embassy, London, July, 1957, to July, 1959; Mexican Embassy, Buenos Aires, 1959–60; First Secretary Rank, 1960; Subdirector General of Press and Publicity, Secretariat of Foreign Relations, 1960–62; Director of the Mexican International City, University of Paris, 1963–65; Director General of the Consular Service, Secretariat of Foreign Relations, 1965; rank of ambassador, February, 1966; private secretary to the Secretary of Foreign Relations, *Antonio Carrillo Flores*, Feb. 1966, to 1970; private Secretary to the Secretary of Foreign Relations, *Emilio Rabasa*, 1970–75; Director-in-Chief of Cooperative Cultural Affairs, Secretariat of Foreign relations, 1976–79; Ambassador to Panama, 1979– . g-None. h-Career Foreign Service Officer; joined the Foreign Service as an Assistant Protocol Officer, 1947; technical adviser to IMSS; technical adviser to the Department of Treasury Studies, Secretariat of the Treasury. i-Mother a teacher; father, Carlos Gonzalez Pena, a well-known journalist and educator; grandfather a physician; married Maria de los Angeles. j-None. k-None. l-DBM68, 313; DPE70, 6; DPE65, 18; DPE61, 18.

Gonzalez Pedrero, Enrique

a-Apr. 7, 1930. b-Villahermosa, Tabasco, *Gulf, Urban*. c-Law degree from the National School of Law, UNAM, 1950–56, degree, October 25, 1957; studies at the University of Paris in economics, and political and social sciences, 1953–54; Professor of the Sociology of Religion, National School of Political and Social Sciences, UNAM, 1956–58; Professor of the Sociology of Political Parties, School of Political and Social Sciences, UNAM, 1959–61; Professor of the Theory of the State, National School of Political

and Social Sciences, UNAM, 1960–70; Director of the School of Political and Social Sciences, UNAM, 1965–70. d-*Senator* from the State of Tabasco, 1970–74, member of the Gran Comision, president of the Second Committee on the Consular and Diplomatic Service, first secretary of the Second Foreign Relations Committee, and first secretary of the First Public Education Committee. e-Founder of the National Liberation Movement in Mexico; adviser to the IEPES of PRI, 1970; member of the Commission of Political Training for the IEPES of PRI, 1972; *Secretary General of the CEN of PRI*, 1972–74; participated in *Luis Echeverria's* campaign for President; Director of Political Training of PRI (preparing 200 young men in political speaking and policies), 1971–72. f-Adviser to the Directorship of PEMEX under *Jesus Reyes Heroles*; investigator for the Commission of Planning Studies (University), Secretariat of Public Education, 1961; lawyer for the Department of Mercantile Income, Secretariat of the Treasury; Director General of the Mexican Corporation of Radio and Television, 1974–76, President of the National Textbook Commission, 1979– . g-None. h-Secretary of the magazine *El Trimestre Economico*; member of the Technical Department, *El Trimestre Economico*; founder of the magazine, *Politica*; author of six books and translator of over a dozen books. i-Married Julieta Campos. j-None. k-Critic for many years of PRI and active political leftist. l-B de M, 137–38; HA, 28 Feb. 1972, 13; *Analisis Politico*, 3 July 1972, 4; *El Dia*, 22 Feb. 1972; MGF69, 756; HA, 10 July 1972, 10; HA, 21 Jan. 1974, 58; Enc. Mex., 1977, V, 473; *Excelsior*, 12 Jan. 1974, 12; *Excelsior*, 16 Nov. 1979, 20.

Gonzalez Roa, Fernando

(Deceased 1936)

a-1880. b-Salamanca, Guanajuato, *West Central, Rural*. c-Primary studies in Salamanca; secondary in Guanajuato; law degree, University of Guanajuato, 1904; Professor of Law, National School of Law, UNAM; Professor of Law at the Escuela Libre de Derecho; Director, School of Commerce, UNAM. d-None. e-None. f-Civil Judge, Guanajuato, 1904–05; Judge of the Correctional Courts, 1905; Secretary General of Government of the State of Guanajuato; Director of Government for the Federal District; Secretary of Justice, 1910–13; Judge of the Superior Tribunal of Justice, Federal District and Territories; Subsecretary of Government; adviser to the Secretary of the Treasury; President of the Executive Board of the Bank of Mexico; Mexican delegate to the World Monetary Conference, 1933; Ambassador to the United States, 1934; *Secretary of Foreign Relations*, June 17, 1935, to Nov. 30, 1935; Ambassador to Guatemala, 1935. g-None. h-Practicing attorney, 1906–09; author of several books on the Mexican agrarian problem. **i-**Students included *Emilio Portes Gil*, *Eduardo Villasenor*, and *Eduardo Bustamente*. **j-**None. **k-**Never functioned in the position of Secretary of Foreign Relations because of poor health. **l-**Enc. Mex., V, 474; WWLA35, 179; DP70, 905; DP64, 629; D del S, 27 June 1935, 1; Daniels, 98–99; Peral, 352.

Gonzalez Rodriguez, Jorge Carlos

a-Feb. 22, 1931. **b-**Merida, Yucatan, *Gulf*, *Urban*. **c-**Primary studies at the Aquiles Serdan School, Izamal (6 years); secondary studies at the Cisneros Colegio Americano, Merida; no degree. **d-**Local Deputy from the Fifth District to the State Legislature of Yucatan, 1967; Mayor of Izamal, Yucatan, 1959; *Federal Deputy* from the State of Yucatan, Dist. 3, 1970–73, member of the Auto Transportation Committee, the Public Security Committee, the Subsistence and Supplies Committee, and the Gran Comision. **e-**General coordinator of the campaign for federal deputies in Yucatan, 1964; general coordinator of the gubernatorial campaign in Yucatan, 1969; President of PRI for Yucatan. **f-**General agent of the ISSSTE in Yucatan, 1961. **g-**Secretary of Agrarian Action of the League of Agrarian Communities, 1968; member of the CNC. **h-**Truck driver. **j-**None. **k-**None. **l-**Q es Q, 119–20; *Directorio*, 1970–72; C de D, 1970–72, 117.

Gonzalez Saenz, Leopoldo

a-Feb. 6, 1924. **b-**Cienega de Flores, Nuevo Leon, *North*, *Rural*. **c-**Primary and secondary studies in Monterrey; law degree, National School of Law, UNAM, November 25, 1939; professor, School of Law, University of Nuevo Leon. **d-**Mayor of Monterrey, Nuevo Leon, 1974–76; *Federal Deputy* from the State of Nuevo Leon, Dist. 1, 1958–61, member of the Gran Comision; President of the Chamber of Deputies, Sept. 1959; Secretary of the Preparatory Council of the Chamber of Deputies, 1958, member of the Foreign Relations Committee (4th Section); *Federal Deputy* from the State of Nuevo Leon, Dist. 1, 1964–67, member of the Gran Comision and the Credentials Committee (4th Section); *Federal Deputy* from the State of Nuevo Leon, Dist. 4, 1973–74. **e-**Adviser to the National Council of PRI; adviser to the CNOP of PRI; State Director of the CNOP of PRI in Nuevo Leon; *Secretary of Organization of the CEN of PRI*, 1975–76. **f-**Agent of the Ministerio Publico, 1942; Judge in Nuevo Leon; Head of Legal Affairs for the City Council of Monterrey; Director of Construction for the Metro in Mexico, D.F., 1968; *Subsecretary of Public Works*, 1976– . **g-**None. **j-**None. **k-**Answered the Presidential State of the Union Address of *Adolfo Lopez Mateos*, 1958; considered by political observers to be a very powerful

political leader in Nuevo Leon; precandidate for governor of Nuevo Leon, 1978. **l-**DBM68, 315; PdM, 176–77; C de D, 1958–60, 42; *Excelsior*, 2 Apr. 1973, 13; C de D, 1964–66, 42, 66; HA, 25 Dec. 1972, 42; HA, 26 Nov. 1973, 34; Func., 294.

Gonzalez Schmal, Raul Jaime

a-1940. **b-**Federal District, *Federal District*, *Urban*. **c-**Early education unknown; law degree. **d-**None. **e-**President of the National Youth Organization of PAN; member of the CEN of PAN; *Secretary General of the CEN of PAN*, 1975–78. **f-**None. **g-**None. **h-**Practicing lawyer. **j-**None. **k-**Candidate for Federal Deputy from PAN, Federal District, Dist. 11, 1970. **l-***Excelsior*, 6 Apr. 1975, 9; *La Nacion*, 14 June 1970, 11; *Excelsior*, 30 Mar. 1975, 4.

Gonzalez Sosa, Ruben

a-Aug. 24, 1922. **b-**Zacatlan, Puebla, *East Central, Rural*. **c-**Primary studies at Ramon Marquez School, Zacatlan, Puebla; secondary studies in Mexico City; law degree, National School of Law, UNAM, 1942–46; advanced studies at the Graduate Institute of International Studies, Geneva; professor, National School of Law, UNAM. **d-**None. **e-**None. **f-**Ambassador to the OAS, 1957–58; in charge of the Mexican Embassy, London, 1965; rank of ambassador, 1969; Director General of Legal Affairs, Secretariat of Foreign Relations, 1969–70; Director in Chief of the Secretariat of Foreign Relations, 1970–71; *Subsecretary of Foreign Relations*, 1971–76, Ambassador to the Dominican Republic, 1979– . **g-**President of the first law generation of the class of 1942. **h-**Career Foreign Service officer; joined the Foreign Service, Apr., 1946; held posts in San Francisco, Geneva, Spain, and England. **i-**Friend of *Luis Echeverria* since youth; married Patricia Flavell. **k-**Precandidate for Governor of Puebla, 1974. **l-**DPE70, 6; letter; HA, 14 Dec. 1970, 20; MGF69, 179; CyT, 307–08; *Excelsior,* 12 Sept. 1974, 4.

Gonzalez Torres, Jose

a-Sept. 16, 1919. **b-**Cotija, Michoacan, *West Central, Rural*. **c-**Primary studies in the Colegio Jalisco, Guadalajara; secondary and preparatory studies at the Institute of Sciences, Guadalajara; law degree from the National School of Law, UNAM, August 20, 1945, with a thesis on tax powers; Professor of History at the Escuela Libre de Derecho; studied for a doctorate. **d-**None. **e-***Secretary General of the National Action Party*, 1956–58; *President of the CEN of the National Action Party*, 1959–62. **f-**None. **g-**President of the Catholic Association of Young Mexicans, 1944–49; President of National Catholic Action, 1949–52; International President of Pax Romana; Secretary General of the National Union of Parents. **h-**Representative of Catholic intellectuals in many international conferences. **i**-Father a prosperous rancher; recruited to PAN by *Manuel Ulloa Ortiz* and *Rafael Preciado Hernandez*, 1941. **j**-None. **k**-Candidate for Federal Deputy for the Eighth District in the Federal District, 1955; Candidate for President of Mexico, 1963–64, on the National Action ticket. **l**-Scott, 185; HA, 2 Dec. 1963, 7; *El Universal*, 2 Mar. 1964, 1; HA, 15 Apr. 1949, 5; Mabry, 155; *La Nacion*, 29 Mar. 1959, 19.

Gonzalez Varela, Jose

a-Aug. 15, 1911. **b**-Zacatecas, Zacatecas, *East Central*, *Urban*. **c**-Primary studies in Colegio Margil, Zacatecas; secondary studies at Secondary School No. 2, Mexico City; preparatory studies from the National Preparatory School; medical degree from the Military Medical College, 1932–36; advanced studies in physiotherapy, North Western University; advanced studies in electroencephalography, Illinois Neuro Psychiatry Institute; professor at the Military Medical College. **d**-*Senator* from the State of Zacatecas, 1964–70. **e**-Joined the PNR, 1936; campaigned for *Jose Elias Rodriguez* for governor, 1962; General Delegate of the CEN of PRI to Queretaro during *Luis Escheverria*'s presidential campaign, 1970; Director of the CEPES of PRI in Zacatecas, 1964. **f**-Director of Medical Services for the Department of Agrarian Affairs; Secretary of Finances of the FSTSE; Director of the Military School for Nurses; Director of the Central Military Hospital. **g**-Secretary General of the Union of Workers of the Department of Agrarian Affairs; Director of Social Promotion of the CEN of CNOP; Secretary of Legislative Promotion of CNOP. **i**-Compadre of *Jose Elias Rodriguez*. **j**-None. **k**-None. **l**-C de S, 1964–70; PS, 2678; MGF69.

Gonzalez Ventura, Salvador

(Deceased 1966)
a-1898. **b**-Colima, Colima, *West*, *Urban*. **c**-Primary and secondary studies in Colima; preparatory studies in Guadalajara; medical degree from the University of Guadalajara, 1925, with a thesis on the "Bismuth in Specific Therapeutics"; professor at preparatory and normal schools in Colima; professor for twenty years at the Dental School, University of Colima; Rector of the University of Colima, 1961–65. **d**-Mayor of Colima, 1927; *Federal Deputy* from the State of Colima, Dist. 2, 1949–52, member of the Social Action Committee (2nd year); substitute member of the Foreign Relations Committee. **e**-None. **f**-Director of the Civil Hospital of Colima. **g**-None. **h**-Practicing physician; President of the Coliman Doctors Society. **j**-None. **k**-None. **l**-DP70, 907; C de D, 1949–52, 74; DGF51, I, 20, 30, 36.

Gonzalez Villarreal, Marciano

(Deceased 1970)
a-Nov. 2, 1883. **b**-Cerralvo, Nuevo Leon, *North*, *Rural*. **c**-Studied in Ciudad Victoria, Tamaulipas, and Mexico, D.F.; no degree. **d**-Federal Deputy from Nuevo Leon, 1916–18; 1918–20; *Federal Deputy* from the Federal District, Dist. 19, 1964–67, member of the National Defense Committee (2nd); the Editorial Committee, and the Committee on Mines. **e**-None. **f**-Comptroller General of Mexico; high official of the Secretariat of the Treasury, 1935–37; *Oficial Mayor of the Federal District*, 1937–38; *Oficial Mayor of the Secretariat of National Defense*, 1939–40; *Subsecretary in charge of National Defense*, 1940; Director General of the Manufacturing of Supplies; Secretary General of Government of Quintana Roo; Secretary General of Government of the State of Puebla. **g**-None. **h**-None. **i**-Nephew of a former President of Mexico, General Manuel Gonzalez. **j**-Joined Carranza during the Revolution; jailed in 1907 for attacking President Diaz in a speech; Secretary of the Revolutionary Convention of Aguascalientes, 1915; career army officer; rank of General. **k**-Exiled from Mexico after the death of Carranza. **l**-Peral, 354; DP70, 907–08; C de D, 1964–66, 49.

Gorostiza, Celestino

(Deceased Jan. 11, 1967)
a-Jan. 31, 1904. **b**-Villahermosa, Tabasco, *Gulf*, *Urban*. **c**-Secondary studies at the Institute of Sciences, Aguascalientes, Aguascalientes, and at the Colegio Frances, Mexico, D.F.; preparatory studies at the National Preparatory School, Mexico, D.F.; professor at the School of Dramatic Art, Institute of Bellas Artes; Director of the School of Dramatic Art, Institute of Bellas Artes. **d**-None. **e**-None. **f**-Director of the Department of Bellas Artes, Secretariat of Public Education; Director of the Department of Theater, Secretariat of Public Education, 1952–58; Director of the National Institute of Bellas Artes, 1958–64; Secretary of the National Conservatory, Secretariat of Public Education. **g**-None. **h**-Distinguished Mexican author; member of the *Contemporaneos*, 1928–31; created the Teatro de Ulises with Xavier Villaurrutia and *Salvador Novo*, 1927–28; founder of the Teatro Orientacion, 1932. **i**-Brother of *Jose Gorostiza* and friend of *Jaime Torres Bodet*. **j**-None. **k**-None. **l**-DP70, 909; DPE61, 107; Peral, 354; DGF56, 305; DEM, 155–56; letter; Enc. Mex., 1977, V, 478.

Gorostiza, Jose

(Deceased Mar. 16, 1973)
a-Nov. 10, 1901. **b**-Villahermosa, Tabasco, *Gulf*, *Urban*. **c**-Primary studies in Queretaro, Queretaro

and Aguascalientes, Aguascalientes; preparatory studies at the National Preparatory School, Mexico, D.F., and the Colegio Frances de Mascarones; degree from UNAM; Professor of Literature at UNAM, 1929; Professor of Modern History, National School of Teachers, 1932. **d-**None. **e-**None. **f-**First Chancellor, Mexican Embassy, London, 1927; Secretary of the Department of Bellas Artes, Secretariat of Public Education, 1932–35; head of the Department of Publicity, Secretariat of Foreign Relations, 1935–37; Third Secretary in Copenhagen, 1937; Private Secretary to the Secretary of Foreign Relations *Eduardo Hay*, 1937–39, with the rank of Second Secretary; First Secretary, Mexican Embassy, Rome, 1939–40; First Secretary in Guatemala, 1940–41; First Secretary in Havana, Cuba, 1942; adviser in Cuba, 1942–44; Director General of Political Affairs, Secretariat of Foreign Relations, 1944; adviser to the Mexican Delegation to the United Nations Conference, San Francisco, 1945; adviser to the Mexican Delegation, First Session of the United Nations, New York, 1946; Director General of the Diplomatic Service, Secretariat of Foreign Relations, 1946–49; delegate to the Rio Conference, 1947; delegate to the Inter-American Conference, Bogota, 1948; Ambassador to Greece, 1950–51; Alternate Permanent Representative of Mexico under *Padilla Nervo* to the United Nations, 1951–53; *Subsecretary of Foreign Relations*, 1953–58; *Subsecretary of Foreign Relations*, 1958–64; *Secretary of Foreign Relations*, Apr., 1964, to Nov., 1964; head of the National Commission of Nuclear Energy, 1965–70. **g-**None. **h-**Distinguished Mexican writer and poet; published his first book of poems at age 24; member of the famous literary group, the *Contemporaneos*. **i-**Brother of *Celestino Gorostiza*, head of the Department of Theater, Secretariat of Public Education, 1952–58, Director of the National Institute of Bellas Artes, 1958–64, and one of Mexico's distinguished writers and intellectuals who also was a member of the *Contemporaneos*; *Jose* knew *Rafael de la Colina* at UNAM and served with him in the Foreign Service; friend of *Jaime Torres Bodet* at the National Preparatory School and at UNAM; married Josefina Ortega. **j-**None. **k-**None. **l-**DP70, 909; DPE61, 107; DGF56, 305; letters; DPE61, 15; WWM45, 53; DBM68, 320; DGF51, I, 110; DGF56, 123; DGF47, 89; *Libro de Oro*, xli; Peral, 354–55; *Justicia*, 6 May 1973; HA, 26 Mar. 1973, 11; *Excelsior*, 17 Mar. 1973, 11.

Grajales (Godoy), Francisco J.

a-Aug. 1, 1898. **b-**Chiapa de Corzo, Chiapas, *South*, *Urban*. **c-**Studies at the Military School, Tuxtla Gutierrez, Chiapas, and at the National Military College, 1924; professor at the National Military College; professor at the National War College; Director of the National Military College; engineering degree; studied in France and Germany before World War II. **d-***Governor of Chiapas*, Dec. 1, 1948, to Nov. 30, 1952. **e-**None. **f-**Military Attache in Berlin; Military Attache in Austria and Czechoslovakia; Chief of Staff of the Secretariat of National Defense, 1946–47; Director of the Superior War College, Secretariat of National Defense, 1958–64. **g-**None. **h-**Author of several books on military strategy. **j-**Joined the Revolution, 1914; career army officer; Subchief of Staff for the Isthmus Military Zone, 1941–45; rank of Brigadier General. **k-**Precandidate for Governor of Chiapas, 1943. **l-**DGF51, I, 89; HA, 6 Feb. 1948, 10; HA, 29 Oct. 1943, 14; DGF47, 109; HA, 10 Nov. 1950, 12–16; HA, 26 Jan. 1959, 8; DBdeC, 108.

Grant Munive, Maria de los Angeles

a-Mar. 10, 1929. **b-**Tlaxco, Tlaxcala, *East Central*, *Rural*. **c-**Primary studies at the Colegio Esparza, Puebla; secondary studies at the Carlos Gonzalez Vespertina Cooperative School, Tlaxco; studies in art and music at the Colegio Esparza, Puebla; secondary school teacher in art and music. **d-**Local Deputy to the State Legislature of Tlaxcala; Mayor of Tlaxco, Tlaxcala; *Federal Deputy* from the State of Tlaxcala, Dist. 2, 1970–73, member of the Gran Comision. **e-**Director of the Woman's Section of PRI, Tlaxcala. **f-**None. **g-**Secretary of Municipal Promotion, CNOP. **i-**Daughter of Carmine James Grant; widow. **j-**None. **k-**None. **l-***Directorio*, 1970–72; C de D, 1970–73.

Guajardo Hernandez, Gonzalo

a-May 16, 1919. **b-**Cuautla, Morelos, *West Central*, *Rural*. **c-**Preparatory studies at the University of Nuevo Leon, Monterrey; medical degree with a specialty in pediatrics, National School of Medicine, UNAM, 1943–48, degree in June, 1949; Temporary Assistant Professor of Pediatrics, University of Nuevo Leon, 1955. **d-**None. **e-**Head of the Regional Committee for the National Action Party of the State of Nuevo Leon; Secretary of the State Committee, 1968. **f-**None. **g-**None. **h-**Practicing physician in pediatrics. **i-**Attended school with *Javier de la Riva Rodriguez*, Federal Deputy from PRI and Medical Director of the ISSSTE; and with Rafael Campos, member of the PPS and Mayor of Teziutlan, Puebla, 1972. **j-**None. **k-**Candidate for Federal Deputy from the Federal District for PAN, 1949; candidate for Federal Deputy from Nuevo Leon for PAN, 1955 and 1961; candidate for Senator from Nuevo Leon for PAN, 1964; precandidate for governor of Nuevo Leon for PAN, 1973. **l-**Letter; DBM68, 324–25; PdM, 183.

Gual Castro, Carlos

a-1927. **b-**Villahermosa, Tabasco, *Gulf, Urban.* **c-**Early education unknown; graduated as a surgeon, National School of Medicine, UNAM, 1951; resident and Professor of Endocrinology, Diabetes and Nutrition, National Institute of Nutrition and the Graduate Division, National School of Medicine, UNAM, 1951–55; postgraduate studies in biochemistry of steroids, Clark University and the Worcester Foundation for Experimental Biology, Worcester, Massachusetts; Professor of the Biology of Human Reproduction, Graduate Division, National School of Medicine, UNAM; Professor of Clinical Endocrinology, National School of Medicine, UNAM, 1978– . **d-**None. **e-**None. **f-**Full-time researcher, National Institute of Nutrition, 1959; Director, Endocrinology Laboratory, National Institute of Nutrition; Director, Department of Endocrinology, National Institute of Nutrition; Director, Research Division, National Institute of Nutrition; Director, Department of Reproductive Biology, National Institute of Nutrition, 1976; *Subsecretary of Assistance,* 1976–80. **g-**None. **h-**None. **j-**None. **k-**None. **l-**Letter; DAPC, 33.

Gual Vidal, Manuel

(Deceased Jan. 22, 1954)

a-June 9, 1903. **b-**Campeche, Campeche, *Gulf, Urban.* **c-**Primary and secondary studies in Tampico; preparatory studies in Mexico, D.F., completed in 1920; law degree from the National School of Law, UNAM, 1926; professor of contract and civil law, National School of Law, UNAM, 1926–45; Director, National Law School, 1939–41; *Secretary General of UNAM,* 1938–39; *Interim Rector of UNAM,* 1944. **d-**None. **e-**None. **f-**Adviser to the Secretary of Agriculture, 1926–28; Secretary of the Civil Division of the Supreme Court, 1929–30; adviser to the Bank of Mexico, 1935; technical adviser, Department of General Credit, Secretariat of the Treasury, 1935; President of the Patrons of the National Lottery, 1944–46; *Secretary of Education,* 1946–52. **g-**Manager of the National Association of Bankers, 1941–45. **h-**Practiced law for a private firm in New York, 1936–38; attorney for a group of electric companies, 1931–45; private law practice, 1934–35; author of many articles on education. **i-**Went to the National University with *Jose Castro Estrada, Antonio Armendariz* and *Eduardo Bustamante*; personal friend of *Gustavo Baz*; brother *Rafael* was a lawyer and a judge for the Superior Tribunal of the Federal District, and also served as head of the Legal Department for the Oficial Mayor of the PRM; *Rafael* served under Manuel as head of the Legal Department for the Federal Committee on the Construction of Schools, 1950; taught *Miguel Aleman* at UNAM; practiced law with *Antonio Martinez Baez.* **j-**None. **k-**None. **l-**HA, 21 April 1950, 5; WWM45, 53;

DP70, 929; DGF51, II, 445; DGF51, I, 285; WB48, xvii; DGF50, II, 329, 455.

Gual Vidal, Rafael

a-Jan. 7, 1898. **b-**Campeche, Campeche, *Gulf, Urban.* **c-**Primary studies at the Colegio of the State of Campeche, preparatory studies at the National Preparatory School and at Tulane University; law degree from the National School of Law, UNAM; studies in languages; Professor of Sociology and Economic Policy, UNAM. **d-**None. **e-**Director of the Legal Department, Oficial Mayor's Office, PRM. **f-**Agent of the Ministerio Publico Militar; local judge; Judge of the First Appellate Court; Justice of the Superior Tribunal of Justice of the Federal District and Federal Territories; Director, Legal Department, National Committee for School Construction, Secretariat of Public Education. **g-**None. **h-**Co-author of the Civil Code. **i-**Married Maria Aguilar; brother of *Manuel Gual Vidal,* Secretary of Education, 1946–52. **j-**None. **l-**DBM70, 281–82.

Gudino Canela, Baltasar

a-Jan. 25, 1900. **b-**Jiquilpan, Michoacan, *West Central, Urban.* **c-**Primary studies at the public school in Jiquilpan; no degree. **d-**Mayor of Jiquilpan, Michoacan, 1935; *Federal Deputy* from the State of Michoacan, Dist. 6, 1937–40; Local Deputy to the State Legislature of Michoacan, 1942–44; *Federal Deputy* from the State of Michoacan, Dist. 5, 1958–61, member of the Fourth Ejido Committee and the First Balloting Committee, and substitute member of the First Instructive Section of the Grand Jury. **e-**Joined the Partido Democratico Jiquilpense (Socialist) in 1926; founding member of the PNR, 1929. **g-**Organized peasant groups for the Partido Democratico Jiquilpense; leader of the Agrarian Ejido Association, 1936. **j-**Joined the Revolution, 1916; left the Army as a 1st Captain, 1924. **k-**None. **l-**Func., 272; C de D, 1958–60, 80; C de D, 1937–39, 11.

Gudino (Diaz), Manuel

(Deceased Oct. 11, 1971)

a-1895. **b-**Colima, Colima, *West, Urban.* **c-**Primary studies in Colima; secondary studies at Normal School; normal certificate from the Normal School of Colima; law degree, National School of Law, UNAM; secondary school teacher. **d-**Alternate Federal Deputy from the State of Colima, 1922–24; *Senator* from the State of Colima, 1934–40, member of the Gran Comision; *Federal Deputy* from the State of Colima, 1940–43, member of the Second Government Committee and the Second Justice Committee; *Governor of Colima,* 1943–49. **e-***Secretary of Organization of the CEN of the PNR,* 1936. **f-**Judge in the State of Colima; Secretary General of Government of the State of Colima; President of the Superior Tribunal of Justice of the State of Colima, 1971. **g**-President of the Third National Student Congress. **h**-Librarian in Colima, Colima; journalist. **j**-None. **k**-Rival of *Daniel Cosio Villegas* for leader of the Second National Student Congress. **l**-HA, 19 Nov. 1943, 14; D del S, 1 Dec. 1940, 1; letter; C de D, 1940–42; Peral, 367.

Guel Jimenez, Francisco

a-Dec. 16, 1915. **b**-Aguascalientes, Aguascalientes, *West*, *Urban*. **c**-Primary studies in Aguascalientes, secondary and preparatory studies at the Preparatory School, Aguascalientes, 1930–34; medical studies at the National School of Medicine, UNAM, 1935–40, graduated as a surgeon, 1941. **d**-Member of the City Council of Rincon de Romos, Aguascalientes, 1954–56; Mayor of Aguascalientes, 1963–65; *Federal Deputy* from the State of Aguascalientes, Dist. 1, 1967–68, member of the Gran Comision and the General Accounting Office Inspection Committee; *Governor of Aguascalientes*, 1968–74. **e**-Director of the CEPES of Aguascalientes, 1962. **f**-Treasurer of the Board of Material and Moral Improvements, Pabellon, Aguascalientes, 1948; Director of the IMSS Hospital, Aguascalientes, 1958–62; Director General of the National Arid Zones Commission, 1976– . **g**-Secretary of Economic and Agricultural Affairs, CEN of CNOP, Aguascalientes, 1949; Secretary General of the ISSSTE Union of Aguascalientes, 1961; Advisor to CNOP, 1965; Secretary General of CNOP of Aguascalientes, 1966. **h**-Began medical practice in Pabellon de Arteaga, Aguascalientes, 1941. **j**-None. **k**-None. **l**-C de D, 1967–70, 78; MGF69, 89; *Excelsior*, 1 Dec. 1976.

Guerra Castanos, Gustavo

a-Sept, 10, 1926. **b**-Coahuila, *North*. **c**-Primary studies at the Apolonio M. Aviles School; secondary studies at the Lucio Blanco Secondary School, Muzquis, Coahuila; preparatory studies from the San Ildefonso Night School, Mexico City; law degree, School of Law, University of Coahuila. **d**-Local Deputy to the State Legislature of Coahuila; *Federal Deputy* from the State of Cohauila, Dist. 1, 1970–73; *Senator* from the State of Coahuila, 1976–82. **e**-Youth Director of PRI in Coahuila; Director of the IEPES of PRI in Coahuila; special delegate of the CEN of PRI to Durango. **f**-Adviser to the Treasury General of Coahuila; president of the State Electric Commission of Cohauila, 1963–69. **g**-Secretary General of CNOP in Coahuila; president of the National Federation of Small Property Owners, 1974. **h**-Lawyer; fruitgrower. **i**-Married Concepcion de Luna. **j**-None. **k**-Precandidate for the gubernatorial nomination of PRI in Coahuila, 1974. **l**-*Excelsior*, 30

Dec. 1974, 13; *Directorio*, 1970–72, 92; C de D, 1970–73.

Guerra (Olivares), Alfonso
(Deceased Oct., 1967)
a-1897. **b**-Tepic, Nayarit, *West*, *Urban*. **c**-Studied on a scholarship in Switzerland, Germany, and Europe in the fields of politics and economics. **d**-*Senator* from the State of Nayarit, 1964–67. **e**-None. **f**-Fourth Consul in Guatemala, 1923; rank of Vice Consul; Vice Consul, Zurich, 1923; Consul, Hamburg, Germany, 1924; Director General of the Consular Service, Secretariat of Foreign Relations, 1946; *Oficial Mayor of the Secretariat of Foreign Relations*, 1946–51; *Subsecretary of Foreign Relations*, 1951–53; Ambassador to Germany, 1953–58, 1958–64. **g**-None. **h**-Career Foreign Service Officer. **j**-None. **k**-None. **l**-*Hoy*, 28 Oct. 1967, 13; DGF51, II, 585; DGF51, I, 97; DGF50, II, 421; DPE61, 20; Peral, 360; DP70, 945; DGF56, 124.

Guerrero Briones, Alfonso
a-1915. **b**-San Luis Potosi, San Luis Potosi, *East Central*, *Urban*. **c**-Preparatory studies at the University of San Luis Potosi; law degree from the National School of Law, UNAM, professor at UNAM and at IPN. **d**-*Federal Deputy* from the State of San Luis Potosi, Dist. 1, 1961–64, member of the Civil Section, Legislative Studies Committee and of the Consular and Diplomatic Service Committee. **e**-Member of PAN. **f**-None. **g**-Prominent student leader at the University of San Luis Potosi; President of the National Student Federation; President of the Federation of Students of the Federal District; President of the Student Society of the National Preparatory School. **j**-None. **k**-Candidate for Federal Deputy for Dist. 4, State of San Luis Potosi, for PAN, 1970. **l**-*La Nacion*, 14 June 1970, 26; C de D, 1961–64, 13, 70; *Excelsior*, 28 May 1979, 27.

Guerrero (Guajardo), Anacleto
a-Aug. 5, 1892. **b**-Hacienda del Porvenir, Nuevo Leon, *North*, *Rural*. **c**-Early education unknown; no degree. **d**-*Governor of Nuevo Leon*, 1936–38; *Senator* from the State of Nuevo Leon, 1952–58, member of the Agricultural Development Committee, the War Materiels Committee, the Second Committee on National Defense, and the Administrative Committee (1st year). **e**-None. **f**-Head of the Department of Cavalry, Secretariat of National Defense; Chief of Staff of the Secretariat of National Defense, 1933. **g**-None. **i**-Son Pedro Armando Guerrero Garate was an agent of the Secretariat of Agriculture. **j**-Joined the Revolution, November 27, 1910, fought under the forces of Major Celedonio Villarreal; career army officer; head of the 21st Regiment of the Constitutional Army; fought against the

Escobar rebellion, 1929; head of the Army Garrison at Ciudad Juarez; Commander of the 82nd Infantry Batallion; Commander of the 1st Infantry Batallion, Guanajuato; Commander of the 3rd, 6th, 21st, 24th and 71st Calvary Regiments; Commander of the 5th Military Zone, Chihuahua, Chihuahua, 1936; Commander of the 15th Military Zone, Guadalajara, Jalisco, 1939; Commander of the 30th Military Zone, Tampico, Tamaulipas, 1952; Commander of the 20th Military Zone, Colima, Colima; rank of Brigadier General, 1929; reached rank of Divisionary General. k-None. l-DGF56, 7, 9–11; Dulles, 646; Peral, 362; Brandenburg, 80; Ind. Biog., 78–79.

Guerrero Mendoza, Jr., Niceforo

(Deceased 1969)
b-Guanajuato, Guanajuato, *West Central*, *Urban*. c-Law degree from the University of Guanajuato, 1920. d-*Alternate Senator* from the State of Guanajuato, 1934–37; *Senator* from the State of Guanajuato, acting as replacement for *Ignacio Garcia Tellez*, 1937–40, member of the Permanent Committee, 1938. e-None. f-Secretary of the Supreme Court of Mexico; Oficial Mayor of the State of Guanajuato; Secretary General of Government of the State of Guanajuato; private secretary to President Pascual Ortiz Rubio; Attorney General of the Federal District, Feb. 5, 1930, to July 1, 1931; *Justice of the Supreme Court of Mexico*, 1940–46, 1946–52, 1952–57; *Provisional Governor of Guanajuato*, 1946–47 (on leave from the Supreme Court). g-None. h-Assistant lawyer in Mexico, D.F.; practicing lawyer. i-Son of a distinguished Mexican lawyer. j-Volunteered to fight against the North American invasion of Veracruz, 1914. k-Anderson says he resigned because of a split in the state party, August, 1947; resigned from the PRM in May, 1940, because of Guanajuato election. l-DP70, 950; Morton, 32; DGF56, 567; DGF51, I, 567; HA, 18 Jan. 1946, 1; HA, 25 Jan. 1946, 8; letter; Peral, 363–64; Anderson, Casasola, V.

Guerrero Ortiz, Arturo

a-Sept. 7, 1911. b-Acambaro, Guanajuato, *West Central*, *Urban*. c-Primary studies from the Benito Juarez Public School, Acambaro; secondary studies from the Colegio Civil of Queretaro, 1926–29; preparatory studies from the Colegio de San Nicolas, Morelia, Michoacan, 1929–31; medical degree, School of Medicine, University of Michoacan, 1937; residency in Oklahoma, United States. d-*Federal Deputy* from the State of Queretaro, Dist. 1, 1964–67, member of the Gran Comision; *Senator* from the State of Queretaro, 1970–76, President of the Development of Cooperatives Committee, Second Secretary of the National Properties and the Second Labor committees, and member of the Gran Comi-

sion and of the First Balloting Group. e-Secretary of the CEPES of PRI in Queretaro. f-Director of Medical Services of the IMSS in Queretaro, 1970; Director of the IMSS Hospital, Queretaro, Queretaro, 1970. g-Joined the Union of Health and Welfare Workers, 1938; Secretary General of Section 32 of the Union of Health and Welfare Workers; Adviser to the League of Agrarian Communities in Aguascalientes; Secretary of Organization of CNOP in Queretaro, 1970. h-Lived in Queretaro since 1926. i-None. k-None. l-C de S, 1970–76, 76; C de D, 1964–67; PS, 2746.

Guerrero Lopez, Euquerio

a-Feb. 20, 1907. b-Guanajuato, *West Central*. c-Early education unknown; preparatory studies at the University of Guanajuato, 1920–24; law degree, University of Guanajuato, Nov. 16, 1929; Professor of Law, Law School, University of Guanajuato; Professor of Law, National School of Law, UNAM; Professor of Law, Ibero-American University; Professor of Law, Superior War College; Rector, University of Guanajuato, 1967–70; Secretary General of the University of Guanajuato under Rector *Luis I. Rodriguez*, 1930–31. d-*Senator* from the State of Guanajuato, 1976– . e-None. f-Agent of the Ministerio Publico in Guanajuato, 1931–32; Judge of the Superior Tribunal of Justice, State of Guanajuato, 1931, 1933, 1934–37; Chief of the Advisory Department of the Private Secretary to the President of Mexico, 1936–37; Director of the Department of Government, Secretariat of Government, 1938; Alternate President of the Federal Board of Conciliation and Arbitration, 1940–43; President of the Federal Board of Conciliation and Arbitration, 1943; *Supernumerary Justice of the Supreme Court*, 1970–73; *Justice of the Supreme Court*, 1973–76; *President of the Supreme Court*, 1974–76. g-None. h-Director, Department of Labor, Mexican Light and Power Company, 1943–54; Administrative Subdirector, Mexican Light and Power Company, 1954–70; author of many books. i-Student with *Luis I. Rodriguez* at the University of Guanajuato; longtime collaborator with *Luis I. Rodriguez*; married Alicia Reynoso. j-None. k-None. l-HA, 7 Jan. 1974, 26; *Excelsior*, 18 Nov. 1974.

Guerrero Martinez, Pedro

a-Sept. 16, 1905. b-Campeche, Campeche, *Gulf*, *Urban*. c-Primary studies at the Colegio Manuel R. Samperio and at the Model School No. 1, Campeche; preparatory studies at the Campeche Institute of Science and Letters; law degree, University of Campeche, Mar. 5, 1932; professor, School of Law, University of the Southeast, Merida, Yucatan. d-*Alternate Federal Deputy* from the State of Campeche, Dist. 1, 1937–40; *Federal Deputy* from the

State of Campeche, Dist. 1, 1943–46; *Senator* from the State of Campeche, 1946–52, member of the Gran Comision, the National Property and Resources Committee, the Legislative Studies Committee, the First Constitutional Affairs Committee, and the First Balloting Committee; substitute member of the Tax Committee. **e-**None. **f-**Secretary of the City Council of Campeche, 1927–28; agent of the Ministerio Publico (Criminal Division) in Campeche, 1929–30; Director of the Public Defender's Office, Campeche, 1931–32; Attorney General of the State of Campeche, 1932; Auxiliary Secretary of the First Judicial District of the Federal District, 1933; Treasurer General of the State of Campeche, 1936–38; Director, Department of Legal Affairs for the State of Campeche, 1940–42; Director, Public Registry of Property and Trade, Federal District, 1955–57; Judge of the Superior Tribunal of Justice for the Federal District, 1957–59; President of the Superior Tribunal of Justice for the Federal District, 1959–63; *Justice of the Supreme Court*, 1963–74. **g-**None. **h-**None. **i-**Political disciple of *Hector Perez Martinez*. **j-**None. **k-**None. **l-**C de D, 137–39, 11; C de D, 1943–45; *Justicia*, July, 1968; DGF51, 5, 9–15. •

Guerrero, Silvestre

(Deceased 1968)
a-Dec. 10, 1891. **b-**Acambaro, Guanajuato, *West Central, Urban.* **c-**Primary and secondary studies in Morelia, Michoacan; law degree. **d-**Federal Deputy from the State of Michoacan, Dist. 5, 1924–26; Federal Deputy from the State of Michoacan, Dist. 5, 1926–28; Senator from the State of Michoacan, 1930–34. **e-**Secretary General of the CEN of PNR, 1930–31. **f-**Private Secretary to *Lazaro Cardenas*, 1920; Secretary General of Government in the State of Michoacan, 1928–30, under *Lazaro Cardenas*; *Attorney General of Mexico*, Dec. 1, 1934, to Aug. 25, 1936; *Secretary of Government*, Aug. 25, 1936, to Dec., 1937; *Secretary of Health and Welfare*, Jan. 24, 1939, to 1940. **g-**None. **i-**Close friend of *Lazaro Cardenas*. **j-**None. **k-**None. **l-**Peral, 364; D de Y, 24 Jan. 1939, 1; DP70, 949; Enc. Mex., V, 44; *Excelsior*, 2 Dec. 1934; DBM68, 364.

Guevara, Gabriel R.

a-Mar. 13, 1887. **b-**Chilpancingo, Guerrero, *South, Urban.* **c-**Early education unknown; no degree. **d-**Governor of Guerrero, 1933–35; *Governor of Quintana Roo*, 1940–46. **e-**None. **f-**None. **g-**None. **i-**Longtime friend of *Manuel Avila Camacho*. **j-**Career army officer; military commander of various zones; rank of Brigadier General, Jan. 1, 1928; returned to active duty, 1935–40. **k-**When Governor of Guerrero, his powers were dissolved by the state legislature in order to replace *Guevara* with a gover-

nor loyal to President *Cardenas*. **l-**Peral, 366; D de Y, 7 Nov. 1935, 1; Gomez Maganda, 100.

Guillot Schiaffino, Alejandro

(Deceased 1966)
a-1913. **b-**Apizaco, Tlaxcala, *East Central, Rural.* **c-**Secondary education from the Methodist Institute of Puebla; engineering degree from the Superior School of Engineering, IPN, Mexico, D.F., 1937. **d-**None. **e-**None. **f-**Head of the Laboratory for the Superior School of Engineering; head of Special Instruction for the Federal District; head of the Laboratory Department for the National Polytechnical School; *Director General of the National Polytechnical School*, 1948–50; adviser to the Mexican Institute of Social Security; Director General of Technical, Industrial, and Commercial Education, Secretariat of Public Education, 1958–66. **g-**None. **h-**Founder of the College of Electrical and Mechanical Engineering. **j-**None. **k-**None. **l-**DP70, 953; DPE61, 105; DPE65, 140.

Guinart Lopez, Modesto A.

(Deceased Aug. 30, 1977)
a-June 15, 1897. **b-**Veracruz, Veracruz, *Gulf, Urban.* **c-**Early education unknown; no degree. **d-**Federal Deputy from the State of Veracruz, Dist. 10, 1963–76. **e-**Director of Administrative Services of the CEN of PRI, 1976. **f-**Subsecretary of National Defense, 1952–58. **g-**None. **j-**Career army officer; joined the Revolution under General *Candido Aguilar*, 1914; rank of Brigadier General, Sept. 16, 1943; Commander of the 27th Military Zone, Acapulco, Guerrero, 1946; Chief of Staff of the 1st Division, 1946; Commander in Chief of the 2nd Division, 1947; Director General of the Army; rank of Divisionary General. **k-**Accompanied Carranza on his flight from Mexico City, 1920. **l-**Peral, 47, 155; DGF47, 110; DGF56, 199; HA, 12 Dec. 1952, 6; D del Y, 2 Dec. 1952, 1; *Excelsior*, 8 Mar. 1973, 14; *Excelsior*, 30 Aug. 1977; *Excelsior*, 9 Dec. 1976.

Gurria Ordonez, Manuel

a-Oct. 31, 1931. **b-**Cunduacan, Tabasco, *Gulf, Rural.* **c-**Primary studies in Tabasco; secondary studies in public schools in Mexico City; preparatory studies at the National Preparatory School; law degree, National School of Law, UNAM. **d-**Federal Deputy from the State of Tabasco, Dist. 1, 1964–67, member of the Gran Comision; answered *Adolfo Lopez Mateos'* 6th State of the Union Address, 1964. **e-**None. **f-**Subsecretary of Government of the State of Tabasco, 1955–58; Secretary General of the State of Tabasco under Governor *Carlos Madrazo*, 1959–64; *Secretary General (B) of the Department of the Federal District*, 1978–79; *Secretary of Government of the Department of the Federal District*,

1979– . g-Student adviser to UNAM. j-None. l-*Excelsior,* 29 Aug. 1979, 14; C de D, 1964–67; DAPC.

Gurza Falfan, Alfonso
(Deceased 1965)
a-1905. b-Durango, Durango, *West, Urban.* c-Secondary at the National Military Academy, 1922; graduated from the Superior War College; Subdirector of the National Military College; Director of the Superior War College. d-None. e-None. f-Military Attache to Canada; Military Attache to the United States; *Oficial Mayor of the Secretariat of National Defense,* 1965. g-None. h-None. i-Son of Jaime Gurza, Subsecretary of the Treasury under President Madero. j-Career military officer; attached to the 14th Infantry Regiment, French Army, 29th Infantry Batallion, United States Army; member of the 1st Air Regiment, 2nd Belgium Army; attached to the Lancers, 6th Artillery, 2nd Belgium Army; Chief of Staff of the 201st Mexican Air Squadron; Chief of Staff of the Secretariat of National Defense; Chief of Military Details for the Chief of Police of the Federal District, 1950. k-None. l-DP70, 954; DGF51, I, 486.

Gutierrez Barrios, Fernando
a-October 26, 1927. b-Veracruz, Veracruz, *Gulf, Urban.* c-Early education unknown; graduated from the National Military College, 1943–47. d-None. e-None. f-Civilian employee and Control Officer, Federal Security Police, Secretariat of Government, 1950–58; Subdirector of the Federal Security Police, Secretariat of Government, 1958–64; Director, Federal Security Police, 1964–70; *Subsecretary of Government,* 1970–76; *Subsecretary of Government,* 1976– . g-None. h-None. j-Career army officer, 1947–50; resigned from the Army, 1950. l-DPE71, 2; DPE61, 14.

Gutierrez Cazares, Jesus
(Deceased 1959)
a-Oct. 28, 1895. b-Huatabampo, Sonora, *North, Rural.* c-Primary and secondary studies in Huatabampo, Sonora; no degree. d-*Governor of Sonora,* Dec. 17, 1935, to Jan., 1937. e-None. f-None. g-None. j-Career army officer; joined the Constitutional Army, 1913; Commander, Nogales Garrison, 1930–32; fought against the De la Huerta rebellion, 1923; commander of various army regiments; Chief of Staff of the Expeditionary Column to Sonora; reentered the Army Reserves, Apr., 1938, to 1939; Commander of the 4th Military Zone, Sonora, 1939. k-None. l-Peral, 369; HA, 15 May 1942, 15; D de Y, 1 Jan. 1936, 4; NYT, 17 Dec. 1935, 1, 6; Enc. Mex., 1977, VI, 333; PS, 2788.

Gutierrez Gurria, Alfonso
a-Mar. 27, 1902. b-Teapa, Tabasco, *Gulf, Rural.* c-Primary studies in Tabasco; no degree. d-*Federal Deputy* from the State of Tabasco, Dist. 1, 1937–40, member of the Gran Comision; *Senator* from the State of Tabasco, 1940–46, President of the First Credit, Money and Credit Institutions Committee, First Secretary of Foreign and Domestic Trade and the First Petroleum Committees, Second Secretary of the Economics and Statistics and the Tax Committees, and member of the Second Balloting Group. e-President of the PRM in Tabasco. f-None. g-None. i-Cousin of *Francisco Trujillo Gurria,* governor of Tabasco, 1939–43. j-None. k-None. l-Libro de Oro, 1946, 7; C de S, 1940–46; C de D, 1937–40; PS, 2797.

Gutierrez (y Gutierrez), Jose Luis
(Deceased 1967)
a-1900. b-Guanajuato, Guanajuato, *West Central, Urban.* c-Primary and secondary studies in Guanajuato; preparatory studies in Guanajuato; law degree from the University of Guanajuato. d-None. e-None. f-Penal Judge in Mexico, D.F.; Judge of the Superior Tribunal of Justice of the Federal District and Federal Territories; Secretary General of Government of the State of Mexico, 1941–45; *Acting Governor of Mexico,* 1942, after *Alfredo Zarate* was assassinated; Assistant Attorney General of the Federal District under Attorney General *Franco Sodi,* 1946–52; *First Assistant Attorney General of Mexico,* 1952–58; *Supernumerary Justice of the Supreme Court of Mexico,* 1964–67. g-None. h-None. j-None. k-None. l-DGF56, 539; DP70, 960; letter; DGF51, I, 487.

Gutierrez Hernandez, Arnaldo
a-1920. b-Guerrero, Chihuahua, *North, Rural.* c-Primary studies in Guerrero, Chihuahua; no degree. d-Member of the City Council of Guerrero, Chihuahua; *Federal Deputy* from the State of Chihuahua, Dist. 4, 1958–61, member of the Fishing and Hunting Committee and the Budget and Accounts Committee; *Federal Deputy* from the State of Chihuahua, Dist. 5, 1964–67, member of the Livestock Committee; *Senator* from the State of Chihuahua, 1970–76, President of the Second Ejido Committee, First Secretary of the National Properties Committee, the Department of Agrarian Affairs Committee and the Forest Committee. e-General Delegate of the CEN of PRI to Chihuahua; campaigned for *Teofilo Borunda* for governor of Chihuahua, 1956. f-None. g-Leader of the League of Agrarian Committees, Chihuahua. h-Farmer and small businessman. i-Parents were campesinos; collaborator of *Teofilo Borunda.* j-None. k-None.

l-Func., 167; C de D, 1958–61, 80; C de D, 1964–67, 50, 85; C de S, 1970–76, 76.

Gutierrez Herrera, Magdaleno

a-July 22, 1918. b-Suchitepec, Oaxaca, *South, Rural*. c-Primary studies at the Public School of Suchitepec, 1927–28; secondary studies at the Public School for Children of Agricultural Industry Workers, 1929–32, and at Tehuacan, Puebla; Secondary Night School for Workers No. 15, Federal District, 1947–49; vocational studies at Vocational School No. 3, IPN, 1950–51; studies at the Higher School of Commerce and Administration, IPN, 1952–55; Professor of Applied Costs, Higher School of Commerce and Administration, 1959–70; taught at the University of Veracruz. d-*Federal Deputy* from the Federal District, Dist. 14, 1970–73, member of the Agrarian Affairs Committee (1st Section), the Department of the Federal District Committee, and the Electric Industry Committee. e-Joined PAN in 1940; adviser to PAN; candidate for Federal Deputy from Oaxaca, 1952; candidate for Senator from Oaxaca, 1958. f-None. g-None. j-None. k-None. l-C de D, 1970–72, 118; Directorio, 1970–72.

Gutierrez Lascurain, Juan

(Deceased Mar. 5, 1959)
a-1911. b-Federal District, *Federal District, Urban*. c-Engineering degree from the National School of Engineering, UNAM. d-*Federal Deputy* from the Federal District, Dist. 7, 1946–49, member of the Second Committee on the Treasury and the Industries Committee. e-Joined PAN, 1943; member of the National Council of the National Action Party, 1956–59; *President of the CEN of PAN*, 1949–56. f-None. g-Active member of the Catholic Association of Mexican Youth. h-Practicing engineer. j-None. k-As a Federal Deputy, proposed reform projects for Articles 27 and 115 of the Constitution, including amendments providing women with rights of suffrage. l-DP70, 960; Morton, 56–57; C de D, 1946–48; DGF47, 7; Mabry, 51.

Gutierrez (Rincon), Efrain A.

a-Aug. 24, 1897. b-Tuxtla Gutierrez, Chiapas, *South, Urban*. c-Engineering degree from the National School of Engineering, UNAM. d-*Governor of Chiapas*, 1937–40. e-None. f-Director General of Waters, Lands, and Colonization, Department of Agrarian Affairs; adviser to the Department of Agrarian Affairs; Secretary General of the Department of Agrarian Affairs; Director General of the National Bank of Agricultural Credit. g-None. h-Member of the Administrative Council of Inmobiliaria Fenix, S.A. i-Brother Gustavo was a local deputy and Treasurer of the State during the governorship of *Efrain*, and

later became a precandidate for Governor of Chiapas, 1943. j-Fought in the Revolution under General Emiliano Zapata in Morelos; rank of Captain, 1915; returned to Mexico, D.F., to finish studies in 1916. k-None. l-DP70, 1845; DBM68, 330–31; HA, 29 Oct. 1943, 14.

Gutierrez Roldan, Emilio

(Deceased Jan. 20, 1977)
a-May 8, 1905. b-Tlalpujahua, Michoacan, *West Central, Rural*. c-Engineering degree from the National School of Agriculture; Director of the De la Huerta Agricultural School, Michoacan. d-*Federal Deputy* from the State of Puebla, Dist. 11, 1940–43, member of the Committee on Credit, Money, and Credit Institutions, and the Polling Committee for the election of a senator from the Federal District; Secretary of the Gran Comision, Sept., 1942; member of the Permanent Commission, 1940; President of the Chamber of Deputies. e-None. f-Member of the Executive Council of the National Ejido Credit Bank; Agent of the National Agricultural Bank; Director General of National Seed Production, Secretariat of Agriculture and Livestock, 1964–70; Director of Agents for the National Ejido Credit Bank. g-Secretary of Political Control for the CNC. h-Author of articles on ejido credit; Secretary General of the Mexican Economic Society. i-Brother of *Pascual Gutierrez Roldan*, Director General of PEMEX, 1958–64. j-None. k-None. l-DBM68, 287–88; DPE65, 102; C de D, 1940–42, 47, 50; MGF69, 264; Peral, 373.

Gutierrez Roldan, Pascual

(Deceased June 19, 1979)
a-May 29, 1903. b-Mazatlan, Sinaloa, *West, Urban*. c-Secondary studies at the Colegio Frances until 1918; preparatory studies at Forestry School, 1918–21; engineering degree in agronomy and forestry, National School of Agriculture, 1925; degree in economics, National School of Economics, UNAM, 1935; Ph.D. in Economics in the United States; Professor of Monetary Theory and Credit, National School of Economics, UNAM, 1938–42; Professor at the National School of Banking, 1937. d-None. e-None. f-Subchief of the Department of Agricultural Organizations, National Agrarian Commission, 1929; Agricultural Attache to the Mexican Embassy, Washington, D.C., 1930–31; Office of Economic Investigations, Secretariat of the Treasury, 1932; Director General of Credit, Secretariat of the Treasury, 1933–34; technical advisor to the Secretariat of the Treasury, 1934–35; Director General of Credit, Secretariat of the Treasury, 1936–40; Director General of the Bank of Popular Credit, 1935–36; Director General of the Savings Promotion Bank, 1941–45;

Director General of National Steel Industry, 1952–58; *Director General of PEMEX*, 1958–64. **g-**None. **h-**Organized the National Mortgage Bank of Public Works, 1935; vice-president of a private firm, 1977. **i-**Brother *Emilio*, Federal Deputy, 1940–43; daughter married to *Gustavo Baz's* son; married Elisa Saldivar. **j-**None. **k-**None. **l-**HA, 4 Jan. 1960, 41; IWW66, 484; WB48, 2106; EBW46, 408; HA 5 Oct. 1945, xxvi; DGF51, II; *Quien Sera*, 148–49.

Gutierrez Ruiz, David Gustavo

a-1940. **b-**Tabasco, *Gulf*. **c-**Economics degree from the National School of Economics, UNAM; special studies at the Institute of Economic Development, Paris; special studies in the rural provinces of France on Agricultural Credit; Professor of Economic Problems of Mexico, National School of Economics, UNAM. **d-***Senator* from Tabasco, 1976. **e-***Secretary General of the CNOP*, 1975–76. **f-**Represented Mexico before the Common Market, 1963; Treasurer of Tabasco, 1965; Secretary General of Government of the State of Tabasco; *Governor of Quintana Roo*, 1971–75; Director General of Guanos and Fertilizers, 1976– . **g-**None. **j-**None. **k-**None. **l-***Excelsior*, 8 Dec. 1974, 23; *Excelsior*, 30 Jan. 1975, 13; HA, 24 Feb. 1975, 14.

Gutierrez Trevino, Eulalio

(Deceased Jan. 14, 1977)
a-Oct. 23, 1916. **b-**Saltillo, Coahuila, *North*, *Urban*. **c-**Primary and secondary studies from the Colegio Robert, Saltillo; agricultural engineering degree from the Antonio Narro Agricultural School, Saltillo, 1937. **d-**Mayor of Saltillo, Coahuila; *Senator* from the State of Coahuila, 1964–70; *Governor of Coahuila*, 1970–76. **e-**None. **f-**Director of Agriculture, Papaloapan, Veracruz; President of the Board of Material and Moral Improvements, Saltillo. **g-**None. **h-**Director, Noche Buena Mining Company, Ramos Arizpe, Coahuila; involved in the mining construction business, 1976–77. **i-**Son of General Eulalio Gutierrez, interim president of Mexico, 1914. **j-**None. **k-**His successor, Governor *Oscar Flores Tapia*, accused him of misusing more than 500 million pesos as governor; his nomination as the PRI gubernatorial candidate in 1969 came as a surprise since *Federico Berrueto Ramon* was thought to be a shoo-in for the nomination. **l-**WWMG, 20; DGF69, 105; *Excelsior*, 15 Jan. 1977, 27; *Proceso*, 22 Jan. 1977, 34.

Gutierrez Zorrilla, Felipe

a-Aug. 21, 1923. **b-**Monterrey, Nuevo Leon, *North*, *Urban*. **c-**Studied at New York University; law degree from the National School of Law, UNAM; Professor of Constitutional Law, Technological Institute of Higher Studies, Monterrey. **d-***Federal Deputy*

from the State of Nuevo Leon, Dist. 1, 1967–70, member of the Committee on Agricultural Development and the Committee on Small Agricultural Property. **e-**Member of the Regional Committee of PAN, Nuevo Leon. **f-**None. **g-**None. **h-**Secretary of the Institute of Social Studies, Monterrey; private law practice, Monterrey. **j-**None. **k-**Candidate for Federal Deputy on the PAN ticket, 1970. **l-**DBM68, 332; C de D, 1967–69; MGF69, 94; *La Nacion*, 14 June 1970, 21.

Guzman, Martin Luis

(Deceased Dec. 22, 1976)
a-Oct. 6, 1887. **b-**Chihuahua, Chihuahua, *North*, *Urban*. **c-**Primary studies in Tacubaya, Federal District; preparatory studies at the National Preparatory School, Mexico, D.F.; law degree from the School of Law, UNAM, January 7, 1909; Professor of Graduate Studies, UNAM, 1911; professor at the School of Commerce, UNAM, 1911; Professor of Spanish, University of Minnesota, 1917. **d-**Federal Deputy from the Federal District, Dist. No. 6, 1922–23; *Senator* from the Federal District, 1970–76. **e-**Member of the Political Education Section of the New Advisory Council of the IEPES of PRI, 1972. **f-**Librarian at the National School of Graduate Studies, 1911; Chancellor of the Mexican Consulate, Phoenix, Arizona, 1909–10; Secretary of the Popular University, 1912; Director of the National Library; adviser to the Secretary of War, 1914–15; Ambassador to the United Nations, 1941; President of the National Commission on Free Textbooks, 1959–76; Executive Member of the National Planning Commission for Hospitals, 1961. **g-**None. **h-**Member of the Literary Group El Ateneo, 1911; Director of *El Grafico* in New York, 1917; Chief of the editorial section of *El Heraldo de Mexico*; founded the Mexico, D.F., evening paper *El Mundo*, 1922; director of various newspapers, 1925–34; worked for *El Universal*, 1936–41; co-founder with *Adolfo Lopez Mateos* and *Pascual Gutierrez Roldan* of the publishing firm which is today Libreria Cristal, S.A.; founder and Director of the magazine *Tiempo*, 1942–76; winner of the National Prize in Literature, 1958; author of *The Memoirs of Pancho Villa* and the autobiographical book of the Revolution, *El Aguila y la Serpiente*. **i-**Close friend of *Adolfo Lopez Mateos*; son of Colonel Martin Luis Guzman. **j-**Joined the Revolution in 1911 under Francisco Madero; attached to the forces of *Ramon F. Iturbe*, 1913–14; joined Francisco Villa, 1914; carried out numerous assignments as a civilian; reached rank of colonel. **k-**Jailed briefly, 1914; exiled in Spain, 1915–16, 1924–36; and in the United States, 1916–20; delegate of the Progressive Constitutional Party. **l-**Letters; DBM68, 333–34; DPE61, 113; WWM45, 54–55; Strode, 215; DPE70, 104; DPE65, 136;

WB54, 467; WB48, 2109; *Proceso*, 1 Jan. 1977, 77; HA, 3 Jan. 1977, 523; *Excelsior*, 27 Dec. 1976, 2B; Enc. Mex., 1977, VI, 339–40.

Guzman Araujo, Roberto
(Deceased 1969)
a-1911. **b**-Guanajuato, Guanajuato, *West Central, Urban*. **c**-Primary studies in Guanajuato; law degree from the National School of Law, UNAM. **d**-*Senator* from the State of Guanajuato, 1946–52, member of the Mail and Telegraph Committee, the Second Justice Committee, the Military Justice Committee, the Second Mines Committee, and the Committee on the Consular and Diplomatic Service. **e**-Orator for *Avila Camacho*, 1940. **f**-Mexican delegate to the Brussels Peace Conference, 1936; Assistant Attorney General of the Federal District and Federal Territories, 1941–45; *Oficial Mayor of the Secretariat of Government*, June 18, 1945, to 1946; adviser to the President of Mexico, 1966–69. **g**-Representative of the Federal District to the Cardenas Student Youth Group, 1933; Secretary of Publicity, Cardenas Student Youth Group, 1933. **h**-Director of the *Revista America*, 1942–59; founder with Pablo Neruda of *Nuestro Espana*; author of numerous plays, novels and books on history. **j**-None. **k**-None. **l**-DGF47, 20; Peral, 47, 158; Correa, 360; DGF51, I, 6, 10, 12–14; DP70, 963–64; C de S, 1946–52; Gomez Maganda, 106; Enc. Mex., 1977, VI, 344.

Guzman Bracho, Roberto
a-Feb. 15, 1932. **c**-Law degree from the National Law School, UNAM, 1954. **d**-None. **e**-None. **f**-Auxiliary lawyer to Public Notaries No. 10, No. 71, Mexico, D.F.; Private Secretary to the Subsecretary of Unrenewable Resources, Secretariat of National Patrimony, *Manuel Franco Lopez*, 1964–66; Private Secretary to the Secretary of Government Properties, *Manuel Franco Lopez*, 1967–70; *Oficial Mayor of Government Properties*, 1970–75; Director General of Tracto-Sidena, S.A., 1975–76. **g**-None. **h**-Practicing attorney in firm of Guzman Bracho and Ruiz, Mexico, D.F. **j**-None. **k**-None. **l**-HA, 14 Dec. 1970, 20–21; DPE70, 44; HA, 24 Feb. 1975, 30; HA, 21 Apr. 1975, 31.

Guzman Cardenas, Cristobal
a-Mar. 2, 1898. **b**-Santa Maria del Oro, Durango, *West, Rural*. **c**-Graduate of the Military Staff Academy. **d**-*Senator* from Durango, 1964–70. **e**-*Secretary of Political Action of the CEN of PRI*, 1964–70. **f**-Director General of Military Education, 1958–61; Chief of Staff of the Secretariat of National Defense, 1944–46; military adviser to the Mexican Delegation to the United Nations, 1945; military attache to the Mexican Embassy, Washington, D.C., 1941–42. **g**-None. **h**-Author of several works on ar-

tillery. **i**-Married Carmen Chazaro. **j**-Career army officer; 2nd lieutenant, 1914; commander of an artillery regiment, 1938–40; commander of a mechanized brigade, 1943; rank of Brigadier General, 1942; reached rank of Divisionary General. **k**-None. **l**-WWM45, 55; C de S, 1964–70; DPE61, 33; MGF69, 105; Peral, 373.

Guzman Guzman, Carlos
a-Nov. 26, 1903. **b**-Mascota, Jalisco, *West, Rural*. **c**-Primary studies in Mascota; preparatory studies at the University of Guadalajara; law degree from the University of Guadalajara, 1926, with a thesis on *amparo*. **d**-Federal Deputy from the State of Jalisco, 1935–37; Local Deputy to the Fortieth State Legislature of Jalisco; *Federal Deputy* from the State of Jalisco, Dist. 4, 1958–61, member of the Second Section of the Legislative Studies Committee, the Second Constitutional Affairs Committee, and the First Credentials Committee. **e**-None. **f**-Secretary of the Judiciary, Jalisco; Judge of the Superior Tribunal of Justice of the State of Jalisco; Agent of the Ministerio Publico of the Office of the Attorney General in the Federal District; Secretary to the Chief of Police of the Federal District; Secretary General of Government of the State of Jalisco; Private Secretary to the Private Secretary of the President of Mexico, *J. Jesus Gonzalez Gallo*, 1940; Oficial Mayor of the Presidency, 1946. **g**-None. **j**-None. **k**-None. **l**-Func., 243; C de D, 1958–60, 80.

Guzman Neyra, Alfonso
a-1906. **b**-Panuco, Veracruz, *Gulf, Rural*. **c**-Primary studies in Panuco, completed in Tampico; preparatory studies at the National Preparatory School, Mexico, D.F.; law degree from the National School of Law, UNAM, 1929–33, with his thesis on "Insurance against Unemployment;" Professor of Labor Law, School of Law, University of Veracruz, Jalapa. **d**-Local Deputy to the State Legislature of Veracruz. **e**-Director of *Manuel Avila Camacho's* campaign for President in the State of Veracruz, 1939; Director of *Miguel Aleman's* campaign for President in the State of Veracruz, 1945–46; President of the Regional Committee of PRI for the Federal District, 1951–52. **f**-Agent of the Ministerio Publico in the State of Aguascalientes, 1934; President of the Superior Tribunal of Justice of the State of Veracruz; consulting lawyer to the Secretariat of Public Works; President of the Federal Council of Conciliation and Arbitration, 1947–50; Director General of Labor and Social Welfare, Department of the Federal District, 1951; Director General of Public Works, Department of the Federal District, 1952; *Justice of the Supreme Court of Mexico*, 1952–58, 1965–69; *President of the Supreme Court of Justice*, 1959–64, 1969–74. **g**-Student

participant in the 1929 Autonomy Movement; representative of the National Law School, 1930. h-Practicing attorney, 1946–49; President of the Administrative Council of Braniff Airlines, 1940–46. i-Father, a pharmacist and a graduate of the National Medical School, became a small cattle rancher and a supporter of Madero; family has resided in the Panuco area since 1750; knew *Antonio Armendariz* and *Antonio Dovali Jaime* at UNAM; related to *Manuel Guzman Willis*, senator from Tamaulipas, 1952–58. j-None. k-None. l-Letter; DGF56, 568; *Hoy*, 17 Jan. 1970, 53; IWW66, 485; WWW70–71, 300; DGF51, I, 481; *Justicia*, Jan., 1967.

Guzman Orozco, Renaldo

a-June 7, 1920. b-Arandas, Jalisco, *West, Urban*. c-Medical degree from the National School of Medicine, UNAM; postgraduate work at the Children's Hospital, University of Iowa. d-*Federal Deputy* from the Federal District, Dist. 20, 1961–64, member of the Social Security and Child Welfare Committee and the Editorial Committee; *Federal Deputy* from the State of Jalisco, Dist. 7, 1967–70, member of the Second Treasury Committee, the Social Security Committee, and the Public Welfare Committee; *Alternate Senator* from the Federal District, 1964–67; *Senator* from Jalisco, 1970. e-*Secretary of Popular Action of the CEN of PRI*, 1965–70; *Secretary General of the National Confederation of Popular Organizations of PRI*, 1965–70. f-Surgeon in IMSS hospitals; *Subsecretary of Health*, 1970–76. g-Various administrative positions in the IMSS Employees Union. h-None. i-Married Dolores Garcia Jurado; student of *Enrique Beltran*. j-None. k-None. l-MGF69, 105; C de D, 1967–69, 57; C de D, 1961–64; letter; *Hoy*, 31 Jan. 1971, 4; WWMG, 20; HA, 14 Dec. 1970, 23.

Guzman Willis, Manuel

(Deceased May 13, 1973)

a-Aug. 19, 1900. b-Panuco, Veracruz, *Gulf, Rural*. c-Primary studies in Tampico and Mexico, D.F.; secondary studies at the Williams Institute, Tacubaya, Federal District; preparatory studies at the National Preparatory School, Mexico, D.F.; no degree. d-Mayor of Tampico, 1948; *Senator* from the State of Tamaulipas, 1952–58, member of the Gran Comision, 1954, the Committee on National Property, and the First Committee on Mines, substitute member of the Second Committee on the Navy and the Agricultural and Development Committee. e-One-time member of PAN. f-Representative of the Secretariat of National Patrimony on the Federal Board for Material Improvement, Tampico, Tamaulipas (15 years); Delegate of the Technical In-

spection Office of the Secretariat of National Patrimony, Tampico, 1951; *Subsecretary of Livestock*, 1965–70. g-Founder of the Regional Union of Cattle Ranchers of Huastecas; President of the Livestock Association of Cebu Cattle Ranchers. h-Operated father's business at age 20; organizer of the Second Pan American Games; discus champion of Central America, 1926; President and founder of the Livestock Bank of Tampico. i-Father an entrepreneur in petroleum and cattle; married Maltilda Maya; related to *Alfonso Guzman Neyra*. j-None. k-None. l-DGF56, 9, 8, 11–13, 437; DGF51, 456; letter; *Excelsior*, 14 May 1973, 2; *El Universal*, 14 Sept. 1965; HA, 14 Mar. 1955; Ind. Biog., 80–81.

Hank Gonzalez, Carlos

a-Aug. 28, 1927. b-Tiangustenco de Galeana, Mexico, *West Central, Rural*. c-Primary and secondary studies at Tianguistenco, completed 1940; teaching certificate from the Superior Normal School of Mexico, Toluca, 1947–50, with a field specialty in biology and history; Professor of Primary Education, 1941–46; secondary teacher in Atlacomulco, Mexico, 1947–51. d-Mayor of Toluca, 1955–57; *Federal Deputy* from the State of Mexico, Dist. 6, 1958–61, member of the Editorial Committee (1st year), Secretary of the Chamber (2nd year); *Governor of Mexico*, 1969–75. e-Member of PRI since 1944; head of the state delegation from CNOP to the PRI Convention, 1952; delegate of PRI to the State of Tabasco, 1961; delegate of CNOP in San Luis Potosi, 1961; member of the Policy Committee of the CEN of CNOP; assistant to the President of the CEN of PRI. f-Director of the Department of Secondary Education, Toluca, Mexico, 1952; Director of the Board of Material and Moral Improvements, Toluca, Mexico, 1952; Treasury of Toluca, 1954; Director General of Government of the State of Mexico, 1957–58; Subdirector of Sales, CONASUPO, 1961–64; *Director General of CONASUPO*, 1964–69; *Head of the Department of the Federal District*, 1976– . g-President of the Student Association of the Normal School of Mexico; Secretary General of the Youth Federation for the State of Mexico, PRM, 1944; Secretary General of the 27th Delegation of the National Union of Teachers, 1947–51. h-None. i-Father an officer in the German Army; colonel in the Mexican Army under General Amaro, but died in 1929; step-father a shoemaker and owner of a small store; disciple of *Isidro Fabela*; supported *Mario Moya Palencia* for president, 1975. j-Owner of various enterprises, including the White Truck Company. k-None. l-HA, 21 Dec. 1964, 9; C de D, 1958–60; HA, 31 Jan. 1972, 31, 34; WWMG, 20; letter; Func., 261; LA, 3 Dec. 1976; Enc. Mex., 1977, VI, 636–64; HA, 20 Dec. 1976, 22; LA, 12

Mar. 1976, 83; *Excelsior*, 28 Feb. 1974; *Excelsior*, 13 Dec. 1974; HA, 24 June 1974, 38; *Excelsior*, 22 Apr. 1977, 6.

Hay, Eduardo
(Deceased Dec. 27, 1941)
a-Jan. 29, 1877. **b-**Federal District, *Federal District*, *Urban*. **c-**Engineering degree from the University of Notre Dame, 1901. **d-**Federal Deputy, 1914–16, 1916–18. **e-**None. **f-**Inspector General of Consulates for Europe, Secretariat of Foreign Relations, 1911; Confidential Agent to South America, 1911–12; Inspector General of Police, 1912–13; Subsecretary of Agriculture and Development, 1916; Minister to Italy, 1918–23; Minister to Japan, 1924–25; Subsecretary of Trade and Public Works, Aug. 27, 1927 to Dec. 1, 1928; Director General of Public Welfare for the Federal District, 1929; Ambassador to Guatemala, 1929; Director General of Customs, 1932–33; Consul General Paris, 1933–34; *Secretary of Foreign Relations*, 1935–40. **g-**None. **h-**Author. **i-**Close friend of President Carranza and General Obregon; married Angelina Sais. **j-**Joined the Revolution in January, 1911; Chief of Staff for Francisco Madero, 1911; Chief of Staff under General Villarreal and General *Ramon Iturbe*, 1913; rank of Brigadier General, 1913. **k-**None. **l-**DP70, 968; Peral, 377; WWLA40, 239; Daniels, 105ff; Enc. Mex., 1977, VI, 368; Lopez, 486–87; Garrido, 213.

Henestrosa (Morales), Andres
a-1906. **b-**Ixhuatan, Oaxaca, *South*, *Rural*. **c-**Teaching certificate; Professor of Mexican Literature and Spanish American Literature, Higher Normal School and the National Preparatory School, Mexico City; advanced studies in linguistics, United States, on a Guggenheim fellowship. **d-***Federal Deputy* from the State of Oaxaca, Dist. 1, 1958–61, member of the Protocol Committee, the Indigenous Affairs Committee, the Editorial Committee (1st year), the Tourism Committee, and the Inspection Committee of the General Accounting Office; *Federal Deputy* from the State of Oaxaca, Dist. 1, 1964–67, member of the Committee on Fine Arts, the Library Committee (1st year), the Protocol Committee, and the Television Industry Committee. **e-**Member of the Cultural Committee of the Popular Party, 1947; Secretary of Press and Publicity of the Popular Party, 1948. **f-**Chairman, Department of Literature, National Institute of Fine Arts, 1952–58. **g-**None. **h-**Director of *El Libro y el pueblo* and *Letras patrias*; well-known author of short stories. **j-**None. **k-**Participated in the 1929 strike at the National University with *Adolfo Lopez Mateos*; campaigned for Jose Vasconcelos in 1929 along with *Angel Carvajal*. **l-**C de D, 1958–60, 81; C de D,

1964–66, 79, 80, 87; Enc. Mex., 1977, VI, 378; Lopez, 487.

Henriquez Guzman, Miguel
(Deceased Aug. 29, 1972)
a-Aug. 4, 1898. **b-**Piedras Negras, Coahuila, *North*, *Rural*. **c-**Began studies as a cadet at the Military College, Mexico, D.F., engineering degree, 1913. **d-**None. **e-**None. **f-**None. **g-**None. **h-**None. **j-**Career army officer; joined the Revolution, 1914, as a 2nd lieutenant, 10th Army Brigade of the Army of the Northeast under General Andres Saucedo; member of the General Staff of the 2nd Division, Army of the Center, 1914; fought under General Jesus Carranza, 1914; Chief of Staff of the 1st Infantry Brigade under General Vicente Gonzalez, 1920; Lt. Colonel, 1920; Commander of the 74th Cavalry Regiment; rank of Brigadier General, May 16, 1929; Commander of Military Operations for the State of San Luis Potosi, 1938; Commander of the 7th Military Zone, Monterrey, Nuevo Leon, 1940; Commander of the 1st Military Zone, Guadalajara, Jalisco, 1943; head of the 4th Army Regiment; rank of Divisionary General, Aug. 1, 1942. **k-**Member of the group of cadets who protected President Madero on his trip from Chapultepec Castle to the National Palace during the Felix Diaz uprising, Feb. 1913; supported President *Cardenas* during the *Cedillo* revolt in San Luis Potosi, 1938–39; precandidate for President of Mexico, 1946; candidate for President of Mexico, 1952, for the Federation of People's Parties of Mexico; expelled from PRI in 1951 for his premature campaigning for President. **l-**WWM45, 56; Scott; Padgett, 66; HA, 11 Sept. 1972, 16; Peral, 377; Enc. Mex., 1977, VI, 386; Lopez, 487.

Heredia Ferraez, Jorge
c-Law degree, National School of Law, UNAM, May 30, 1947. **d-**None. **e-**None. **f-**Agent of the Ministerio Publico of the Attorney General of Mexico, Tampico, Tamaulipas; head of the Technical Department of the Division of Professions; Legal Adviser to the National Housing Institute; Director General of Legal Affairs, Secretariat of Government, 1968; *Oficial Mayor of Government*, 1968–70; Oficial Mayor of the Federal Electric Commission, 1970–73. **g-**None. **h-**Attorney for PEMEX. **j-**None. **k-**None. **l-**HA, 14 Dec. 1970, 25.

Hernandez, Pablo Mario
(Deceased Jan. 8, 1974)
a-July 1, 1894. **b-**Lagos de Moreno, Jalisco, *West*, *Urban*. **c-**Primary and secondary education at Morenci and Clifton, Arizona; no degree. **d-**None. **e-**None. **f-**Chief of Trains, National Railroads of Mexico; Assistant Director General of the Railroads

of Mexico, 1941; *Acting Director General of the National Railroads of Mexico*, 1941; Assistant Director General of the National Railroads, 1943–45; *Director General of the National Railroads of Mexico*, 1945–46. **g**-None. **h**-Joined the National Railroads as a laborer; machinist; superintendent of various divisions in the National Railroads of Mexico, 1921–41. **i**-Married Graciela Trevino. **j**-None. **k**-None. **l**-WWM45, 56; *Excelsior*, 9 Jan. 1974, 14; HA, 21 Dec. 1945.

Hernandez Alvarez, Enrique
(Deceased Nov. 2, 1938)
a-June 24, 1892. **b**-Gonzalez, Guanajuato, *West Central*, *Rural*. **c**-Primary studies in Ciudad Gonzalez; secondary studies in Leon, Guanajuato; medical degree, National School of Medicine, UNAM, 1917; student professor at the Guanajuato Studies Center, 1917. **d**-Governor of Guanajuato, 1931; Federal Deputy from Guanajuato, Dist. 16, 1920–22, Dist. 16, 1922–24, Dist. 16, 1928–30, and 1930–31. **e**-President of PNR in Guanajuato; President of the Federation of Revolutionary Parties of Guanajuato. **f**-President of the Board of Directors for Public Welfare; representative of the Federal Government before the Henequen Cooperative; *Secretary of Health and Public Welfare*, Jan. 3, 1938, to Nov. 2, 1938. **g**-None. **i**-Co-student at the Guanajuato Studies Center with *Ignacio Garcia Tellez*, Secretary of Government, 1938–40, and with *Luis Diaz Infante*, Governor of Guanajuato, 1948–49; supported for governor by *Agustin Arroyo Ch.* and *Enrique Fernandez Martinez*. **k**-First Secretary of the Secretariat of Health; removed from the governorship of Guanajuato after the Congress declared his powers dissolved, June 4, 1931; this movement was led by a political faction of Manuel Ortega. **l**-D de Y, 3 Nov. 1938, 1; *Hoy*, 12 Nov. 1938, 17; Peral, 47, 161; Novo, 35, 195.

Hernandez Cervantes, Hector
a-1926. **b**-Federal District, *Federal District*, *Urban*. **c**-Early education unknown; economics degree from the National School of Economics, UNAM, 1941–45; masters degree in economics from the University of Melbourne, Australia, 1949–50; Assistant Professor of Economic Theory, National School of Economics, UNAM, 1958; Professor at CEMLA. **d**-None. **e**-None. **f**-Economist, Bank of Mexico, 1946–47; Assistant to the Director of the National Committee to Control Imports, 1947–48; Secretary of the Committee on Export Prices, 1951–52; Subdirector of Economic Research, National Finance Bank; Subdirector of Economic Studies, Secretariat of the Treasury, 1958; Director General of Trade, Secretariat of Industry and Commerce, 1961; Director General of International Studies, Secretariat of the Treasury, 1970–76; *Subsecretary of Trade*, February 24, 1976 to November 30, 1976; *Subsecretary of Foreign Trade*, Secretariat of Commerce, 1976– . **g**-None. **i**-Co-student at UNAM with *Octaviano Campos Salas* and *Horacio Flores de la Pena*. **j**-None. **k**-None. **l**-B de M, 146; DGF61, 66; EN de E, 1958, 108; *Excelsior*, 25 Feb. 1976, 4; HA, 8 Mar. 1976, 26.

Hernandez Chazaro, Eduardo
(Deceased Nov. 23, 1957)
a-May 4, 1898. **b**-Tlacotalpan, Veracruz, *Gulf*, *Rural*, **c**-Early education unknown; no degree. **d**-Federal Deputy from the State of Veracruz, 1918–20; *Federal Deputy* from the State of Veracruz, Dist. 12, 1940–43, member of the Gran Comision, the First National Defense Committee, and the Second Credentials Committee; Secretary of the Political Control Committee. **e**-Member of the Executive Committee of the National Pre-Electoral Center of *Avila Camacho*, 1939. **f**-Member of the Chief of Staff, President Obregon, 1920–24; Assistant Chief of Staff to President Calles, 1924–28; Chief of Staff for President Ortiz Rubio, 1928–29; Secretary to President Ortiz Rubio, 1929–30; head of the Department of the Federal District, 1930; Consul in San Antonio, Texas, 1931–35; Inspector of Military Attaches, 1930–31. **g**-None. **h**-None. **i**-Son Eduardo, an engineer and director of several construction firms; married Sofia Lemus. **j**-Joined the Army, May 23, 1914, as a 2nd Lieutenant of Cavalry; 2nd Captain, 1915; 1st Captain, 1920; Major, 1924; Lt. Colonel, 1927; Brigadier General, 1944; Brigade General, 1949; Commander of the 23rd Military Zone, Tlaxcala, Tlaxcala, 1950–51; Commander of the 22nd Military Zone, Toluca, Mexico, 1951–57; rank of Divisionary General, 1952. **k**-Precandidate for Governor of Veracruz, 1936. **l**-DP70, 980; C de D, 1940–42; Peral, 379; letter; Novo35, 286.

Hernandez Corzo, Rodolfo
a-Oct. 4, 1909. **b**-Comitan, Chiapas, *South*, *Urban*. **c**-Primary studies in Chiapas; secondary studies at the Chiapas State Normal and Preparatory School, graduating as a normal teacher, Mar., 1928; Bachelor of Science in Biology, National Preparatory School, 1934; studies at Northwestern University, Master of Science, 1939–40; degree in chemistry, IPN, Nov. 19, 1940; Ph.D. from Stanford University, 1949–52, with a dissertation on the Biogenesis of Itacomic Acid; normal teacher, 1928–31; assistant professor in higher technical education; Professor of Graduate School; Professor of Cinematography, Military Communications School; founder and organizer of courses in applied mathematics in chemistry and biology, IPN, 1940–49; Professor of Chemi-

cal and Physical Biology, 1940–49; originator of the Microbiology Warfare Course, Superior War College, 1940–49; Director General of the National School of Biological Sciences, IPN, 1952–55. **d-**None. **e-**None. **f-**Scientific adviser to the Federal Government; adviser to the Bank of Mexico; adviser to UNESCO; *Director General of IPN*, 1953–56; Director General of Standards, Secretariat of Industry and Commerce, 1961; Director General of the Division of Wild Fauna, Secretariat of Agriculture and Livestock, 1964–70. **g-**None. **h-**Investigator for the Radon Emanation Corporation, 1940–41; author of numerous technical and scientific works. **i-**Brother Antonio, professor and investigator for the National School of Biological Sciences, IPN. **j-**None. **k-**None. **l-**DGF56, 304; B de M, 147–48; DGF65, 101; MGF69, 264; Enc. Mex., 1977, VI, 406–07.

Hernandez (de Galindo), Silvia

a-Sept. 12, 1951. **b-**Queretaro, Queretaro, *East Central, Urban*. **c-**Early education unknown; degree in political science and public administration, School of Political and Social Sciences, UNAM; MA degree in public administration in England; post graduate studies at the Sorbonne, Paris, in French and French Civilization. **d-***Federal Deputy* from the Federal District, Dist. 16, 1976–79; *Alternate Federal Deputy* from the Federal District, Dist. 7, 1973–76. **e-**Joined PRI in secondary school in 1962. **f-**Employee of the assistant secretary to the governor of the State of Guanajuato; Assistant Secretary to *Oscar Flores Tapia*; adviser to the Chamber of Deputies; Director General of the National Institute of Mexican Youth (INJUVE), 1976– . **g-**Founder of the National Insurgency of Women; adviser to the Mexican delegation to the World Conference of Women. **h-**Fluent in French and English. **j-**None. **k-**None. **l-**C de D, 1973–76, 7; HA, 31 Oct. 1977, 7; *Excelsior*, 29 Aug. 1976, 26; C de D, 1976–79.

Hernandez Delgado, Jose

a-Sept. 7, 1904. **b-**Guanajuato, Guanajuato, *West Central, Urban*. **c-**Law degree, School of Law, University of Guanajuato, Feb. 20, 1926; Professor of Law, National School of Law, 1931–34. **d-***Federal Deputy* from the State of Guanajuato, Dist. 3, 1937–40. **e-**None. **f-**Auxiliary Agent of the Attorney General of the Federal District and Federal Territories, March 29, 1930 to March 30, 1931; Second Assistant Attorney General of Mexico; Oficial Mayor of the Secretariat of the Presidency, 1934–37; Attorney General of the Federal District and Federal Territories, July 13, 1931, to Sept. 4, 1932; Director General of the National Workers Bank, 1941–42; President of the Liquidating Committee for the National Workers Bank, 1942–44; Director General of the National Bank of Cooperative Development,

1944–46, 1946–52; *Director General of Nacional Financiera*, 1952–58, 1958–64, and 1964–70. **g-**None. **i-**Brother *Herculano Hernandez Delgado* was a federal deputy from Guanajuato, 1952–55, and a founder of the Sinarquista movement. **j-**None. **k-**None. **l-**Letter; DGF50, II, 190; DGF51, II, 278; DGF47, 364; D de Y, 5 Dec. 1952, 1; C de D, 1937–39, 12; *Justicia*, Jan., 1966; Michaels, 102; Enc. Mex., 1977, VI, 402.

Hernandez Gomez, Tulio

a-May 26, 1938. **b-**Tlaxcala, Tlaxcala, *East Central, Urban*. **c-**Early education unknown; law degree, National School of Law, UNAM, 1962. **d-***Federal Deputy* from the State of Tlaxcala, Dist. 1, 1964–67, member of the Gran Comision; *Governor of Tlaxcala*, 1981– . **e-**Joined the Youth Sector of PRI, 1953; member of the Youth Leadership of PRI, Federal District, 1954; Director of Youth of PRI, Tlaxcala, 1957–60; Subdirector of the National Youth of the CEN of PRI, 1959–64. **f-**Director of the Department of Citizen Education, National Institute of Mexican Youth, 1959; Coordinator of Housing, National Institute of Mexican Youth, 1962; Adviser to the Director of the National Institute of Mexican Youth, 1964; *Oficial Mayor of Government*, 1979–80. **g-**Member of the Youth Sector of the CNC, 1960–61. **i-**Son of *Francisco Hernandez y Hernandez*, Secretary General of the CNC, 1959–62. **j-**None. **k-**None. **l-**C de D, 1964–67; *Excelsior*, 19 July 1979, 19; *Excelsior*, 17 Dec. 1979, 18; *Excelsior*, 6 May 1980, 4.

Hernandez (Gonzalez), Amador

a-May 14, 1925. **b-**Rancheria de Nicolas Bravo, Tehuacan, Puebla, *East Central, Rural*. **c-**Primary studies in Actzingo and Ciudad Mendoza, Puebla; secondary studies in Jalapa. **d-**Deputy to the State Legislature of Puebla, 1951–54; *Federal Deputy* from the State of Puebla, Dist. 6, 1955–58, member of the Second Ejido Committee and the Editorial Committee; *Federal Deputy* from the State of Puebla, Dist. 6, 1961–64, member of the First Ejido Committee and the Agriculture and Development Committee; *Federal Deputy* from the State of Puebla, 1979–82. **e-**Coordinator of the State Political Committee for *Miguel Aleman* for President, 1946; Secretary General of the State Committee for *Adolfo Ruiz Cortines* for President, 1952; Secretary General of PRI for Puebla, 1953–55; *Secretary of Agrarian Action of the CEN of PRI*, 1965–68. **f-**None. **g-**Secretary of Health and Social Security of the CEN of the CNC, 1956–59; Coordinating Secretary of the League of Agrarian Communities of the CNC, 1960–65; *Secretary General of the CNC*, August 28, 1965 to September 21, 1967; General Delegate of the CNC to Baja California del Norte, 1977. **h-**Worked as an ejidatario in Tehuacan, Puebla. **j**-None. **k**-Johnson suggests he resigned as Secretary General of the CNC under pressure from President *Diaz Ordaz* after armed clashes among CNC members; *Excelsior* accused him of being a cacique in Tehuacan in 1978; split PRI into two factions in Tehuacan, 1977. **l**-*Excelsior*, 11 Nov. 1978, 23; Ind. Biog., 82; Navarro Gonzalez, 267; Johnson, 35; D de Y, 29 Aug. 1965, 1; *Excelsior*, 8 Sept. 1977; C de D, 1961–64, 80; DGF56, 27, 32.

Hernandez (Gonzalez), Octavio Andres

a-Nov. 10, 1917. **b**-Federal District, *Federal District*, *Urban*. **c**-Primary studies in Mexico, D.F.; studied at the School of Banking and Commerce, 1939–41; accounting degree; law degree from the National School of Law, UNAM, 1946, with special mention; LLD degree from the National School of Law, UNAM, 1950–52; academic posts, 1938. **d**-*Federal Deputy* from the Federal District, Dist. 4, 1967–70, member of the Gran Comision, President of the Legislative Studies Committee. **e**-Member of PRI and the PRI sponsored National Conference on Political and Ideological Analysis of the Revolution. **f**-Notary Public No. 10, Mexico, D.F.; private secretary to the Secretary of Industry and Commerce, *Gustavo P. Serrano*, 1944–46; private secretary to the Secretary of Industry and Commerce, *Antonio Ruiz Galindo*, 1946–48; legal adviser to the Secretary of Industry and Commerce, 1948–52; head of the Department of Social Security, Secretariat of Industry and Commerce, 1952–58; head of the Department of Minimum Salaries, Department of the Federal District; legal adviser to the head of the Federal District, *Corona del Rosal*; attorney for the Mexican Institute of Social Security; legal adviser to the Oficial Mayor of the Secretariat of Public Works, 1966–67; Legal Gerente of the National Bank of Public Works, 1966–67; *Secretary General of the Department of the Federal District*, 1970–76; *Secretary General of the Department of the Federal District*, 1976–79; Director General of the Public Works Bank, 1979– . **g**-President of the Student University Federation at the National University which opposed *Chico Goerne* as rector, 1938. **h**-Practicing lawyer; lawyer for CONCAMIN. **i**-Second nephew of Francisco Madero; father Lorenzo L. Hernandez was the former Treasurer General of Mexico, 1923–31, 1932–33, head of the Department of the Federal District, Oct. 31, 1931, to Jan. 20, 1932, and founder and first Gerente of Nacional Financiera, 1934; student of *Alfonso Noriega* at the National University; author of many works on international law and economic and banking problems in Mexico; received second place in a contest for private accountants among over six thousand competitors, 1943. **j**-None.

k-None. **l**-DGF51, I, 265, II, 56; DPE65, 117; DGF56, 285; MGF69, 517, 90; HA, 1 Nov. 1946, 6; HA, 22 Nov. 1971, 23; DBM70, 306; DBM68, 40–41; DBM68, 339–40; WWM45, 56; DPE61, 18; letters; C de D, 1967–69; Enc. Mex., 1977, VI, 404.

Hernandez Hernandez, Manuel

a-Oct. 18, 1909. **b**-San Miguel Tixac, Oaxaca, *South*, *Rural*. **c**-Primary studies in Tlaxiaco, Oaxaca; preparatory studies in Oaxaca, Oaxaca; medical degree, National School of Medicine, UNAM; Professor of Philological Studies, National Preparatory School No. 2 and 5 **d**-*Federal Deputy* from the State of Oaxaca, Dist. 7, 1958–61, member of the Library and the Military Health Committees; *Federal Deputy* from the State of Oaxaca, Dist. 7, 1967–70, member of the Indigenous Affairs Committee. **e**-None. **f**-Employee, Secretariat of Public Health in Coahuila, Hidalgo, Michoacan and Mexico; Chief of Surgical Clinic, National School of Medicine, UNAM. **g**-Founder and President of the Coalition of the Mixtec Oaxacan People, 1951. **j**-None. **k**-None. **l**-Func., 310; C de D, 1958–61, 81; C de D, 1967–70, 59.

Hernandez (Jimenez), Antonio J.

a-Jan. 6, 1904. **b**-San Jeronimo Tequinapa, Municipio of Cholula, Puebla, *West Central*, *Rural*. **c**-Primary and secondary studies in the Madero Institute, Puebla; no degree. **d**-Member of the City Council of Atlixco, Puebla; *Federal Deputy* from the State of Puebla, Dist. 3, 1943–46; *Federal Deputy* from the State of Puebla, Dist. 4, 1955–58, member of the First Balloting Committee; *Federal Deputy* from the State of Puebla, Dist. 4, 1961–64, member of the Mail and Telegraph Committee; *Federal Deputy* from the State of Puebla, Dist. 4, 1967–70, member of the Textile Industry Committee; *Federal Deputy* from the State of Puebla, Dist. 3, 1976–79. **e**-*Subsecretary of Labor of the CEN of PRI*, 1978. **f**-Employee of the Board of Material and Moral Improvements, Atlixco, Puebla. **g**-Delegate of the Central Committee of CROM to the states of Puebla and Tlaxcala; member of the Union of Revolutionary Workers of Omtepec; Secretary General of the Federation of Workers and Farmers of Puebla (later CTM), 1935– . **h**-Worked as a youngster in the Couadonga Thread Factory; employee of the Metepex Textile Factory. **i**-Father was an employee in the Hercules Textile Factory, Queretaro. **j**-None. **k**-Antonio Hernandez has repeated as a federal deputy more times since 1943 than almost any other Mexican public figure. **l**-DGF56, 27, 33, 74; C de D, 1967–70, 76; *Excelsior*, 20 Aug. 1976, 1C; Ind. Biog., 83; C de D, 1961–64, 80.

Hernandez Juarez, Francisco

a-Oct. 16, 1925. b-Tlacochahuaya, Oaxaca, *South, Rural*. c-Primary studies at the Felipe Carrillo Puerto School, Tlacochahuaya; secondary studies at the Rural Normal School, Comitancillo, Oaxaca, 1944–45, and at the Rural Normal School El Mexe, Hidalgo, 1946; teaching certificate, National Teachers School, 1947–49; preparatory studies at the National Preparatory School, 1950–51; studied law, National School of Law, UNAM, 1952–57; primary school teacher, Federal District (7 years); secondary teacher at the Isthmus of Tehuantepec Secondary and Preparatory School (9 years); Professor at the Regional Technological Institute of the Isthmus of Tehuantepec, Oaxaca (2 years). d-*Federal Deputy* from the State of Oaxaca, Dist. 1, 1970–73, member of the Waters and Irrigation Committee, the Second Public Education Committee, the Second Justice Committee, and the Legislative Studies Committee, Ninth Section on General Affairs; *Federal Deputy* from the State of Oaxaca, Dist. 1, 1976–79, member of the Section on Commercialization and Industrialization of the Agrarian Affairs Committee and member of the Higher Education Section of the Educational Development Committee. e-Secretary General of the PPS in Oaxaca; member of the National Central Executive Committee of PPS; member of the Popular Youth Association. f-None. g-Director of the National Teachers School Student Association; leader of the SNTE; organized the Union of Construction Workers of Juchitan, Oaxaca. h-Practicing attorney. i-Married Dr. Silva Arteaga. j-None. k-None. l-C de D, 1970–72, 119; *Directorio*, 1970–72; D de C, 1976–79, 7, 21; HA, 5 Mar. 1979, V.

Hernandez Labastida, Miguel

a-Sept. 5, 1935. b-Veracruz, Veracruz, *Gulf, Urban*. c-Primary studies at the Republic of Guatemala Primary School, Coyoacan, Federal District; secondary studies at the Columbus Grammar School, Columbus, New Mexico, and Deming High School, Deming, New Mexico; Certified Public Accountant, with a degree from the Public Accountants School; taught courses in accounting. d-*Alternate Federal Deputy* from the Federal District, Dist. 22, 1967–70; *Federal Deputy* from the Federal District, Dist. 22, 1970–73, member of the Auto Transportation Committee and the Livestock Committee; *Federal Deputy* from the Federal District, Dist. 12, 1976–79, member of the Foreign Relations Committee and the Insurance and Finance Section of the Treasury Committee. e-Member of the National Organizing Commission of PAN; member of the Regional Committee for the Federal District of PAN, 1968–69; Director of PAN for the 22nd District, Federal District, 1963–70; joined PAN, 1950. f-None. g-None. h-Public accountant. i-Married Ana Maria Meixueiro. j-None. k-Candidate for Federal Deputy, 1967. l-C de D, 1970–72, 119; *Directorio*, 1970–72; C de D, 1976–79, 33; D de C, 1976–79, 71, 59, 57.

Hernandez Mendoza, Leonardo M.

a-Nov. 6, 1888. b-Atotonilco el Grande, Hidalgo, *East Central, Rural*. c-Primary studies in Atotonilco el Grande; no degree. d-*Federal Deputy* from the State of Hidalgo, Dist. 2, 1940–43, member of the Gran Comision, the Inspection Committee of the General Accounting Office, and the Social Welfare Committee; local deputy to the State Legislature of Hidalgo, 1922–24; Federal Deputy from the State of Hidalgo, 1924–26; *Senator* from the State of Hidalgo, 1958–64; Executive Secretary of the Colonization Committee, member of the First Committee on National Defense and the Second Committee on Mines, and substitute member of the Committee on Taxes. e-None. f-Director of Public Welfare for the State of Puebla, 1927–28. g-None. h-Involved in cattle ranching and agriculture. j-Joined the Revolution as a noncommissioned officer, serving under Gabriel Hernandez; career army officer; Commander of military zones in Coahuila, Sonora, Hidalgo, and Jalisco; rank of Divisionary General. k-None. l-EBW46, 56; C de D, 1940–42, 54, 58; letter; C de S, 1961–64, 57; Func., 228.

Hernandez Netro, Mateo

(Deceased 1946)

a-1890. b-San Luis Potosi, *East Central*. c-Early education unknown; no degree. d-*Governor of San Luis Potosi*, 1935–38. e-None. f-None. g-None. h-Involved in ranching after 1938. i-Longtime friend and supporter of *Saturnino Cedillo*. j-Joined the Revolution in 1910; fought with *Saturnino Cedillo*, 1913; fought against Victoriano Huerta, 1914; fought under Zapata; career army officer; supported the De la Huerta rebellion, 1923; fought against the Escobar rebellion, 1929; rank of Colonel in the Army. k-Abandoned the governorship of San Luis Potosi, May 22, 1938, to support the *Cedillo* rebellion against the government; received amnesty from President *Cardenas* after General *Cedillo's* death, 1938. l-Peral, 47, 163; DP70, 982; D de Y, May 22, 1938, 1; Peral, 382.

Hernandez Ochoa, Rafael

a-June 4, 1915. b-Municipio Vega de la Torre, Santa Gertrudis, Veracruz, *Gulf, Rural*. c-Primary studies in the Enrique C. Rebsamen Public School, Jalapa, Veracruz; secondary and preparatory studies in Jalapa; law degree from the National School of Law,

UNAM, 1944, thesis on state intervention; attended the University of Veracruz. **d-***Federal Deputy* from the State of Veracruz, Dist. 5, 1973–74; *Governor of Veracruz,* 1974–80. **e-**None. **f-**Municipal Judge, Veracruz; Agent of the Ministerio Publico of the Office of the Attorney General; Director of the Legal Department of the State of Veracruz; Subdirector General of Administration, Secretariat of Government, 1962; Subdirector of Population, Secretariat of Government, 1958–61; Auxiliary Secretary to *Luis Echeverria,* 1958; Director of Political and Social Investigations, Secretariat of Government, 1964; *Subsecretary of Government,* 1964–70; *Secretary of Labor,* 1970–72. **g-**President of the National Livestock Federation. **h-**Practiced law since 1940; member of the National Council of Tourism. **i-**Student of *Alfonso Noriega* at UNAM; married Teresa Penafiel. **j-**None. **k-**Resigned from the Secretaryship of Labor, Sept. 11, 1972, after two operations; his popularity among PRI members in Veracruz as a candidate for Federal Deputy in 1973 surprised many PRI officials; precandidate for PRI Majority Leader of the Chamber of Deputies, 1973. **l-**D de Y, 1 Dec. 1970, 2; DPE61, 13; DPE65, 13; *Hoy,* 21 Dec. 1964; HA, 7 Dec. 1970; HA, 3 May 1971, 12; HA, 18 Sept. 1972, 10–11; *Excelsior,* 8 Mar. 1973, 14; HA, 7 Jan. 1973, 12; *Excelsior,* 18 Dec. 1973, 15; HA, 6 May 1974, 39–40; Enc. Mex., 1977, VI, 410.

Hernandez Partida, Leopoldo

a-Aug. 26, 1908. **c-**Primary studies in Guadalajara, Jalisco; preparatory studies at the National Preparatory School; law degree from the National School of Law, UNAM, 1928–32. **d-***Federal Deputy* from the Federal District, Dist. 12, 1943–46; *Federal Deputy* from the State of Jalisco, Dist. 5, 1967–70, member of the Indigenous Affairs Committee and the Money and Credit Institutions Committee. **e-**Joined the PNR, 1932; *Secretary of Popular Action of the CEN of the PRM,* 1938–39; *Secretary of Agrarian Action of the CEN of PRI,* 1964; interim president of PRI for the Federal District. **f-**Secretary of the District Court of the Federal District; Attorney General of the State of Hidalgo under Governor *Javier Rojo Gomez,* 1937–38; Private Secretary to *Javier Rojo Gomez,* Head of the Federal District Department, 1940–43; Delegate of the IMSS to Jalisco; Director General of Central Agricultural Bank, 1974– . **g-**Student supporter of General Alvaro Obregon for president, 1928; founding member of the CNC, 1938; Private Secretary to Graciano Sanchez, Secretary General of the CNC, 1938–40; Private Secretary to *Javier Rojo Gomez,* Secretary General of the CNC, 1962–66. **h-**Campaigned for General Obregon with *Luis I. Rodriguez* and *Alfonso Pulido Islas.* **j-**None. **k-**None. **l-**Letter, C de D, 1967–70, 59, 81; C de D, 1943–46; MGF69, 92

Hernandez Teran, Jose M.

a-Dec., 1921. **b-**Merida, Yucatan, *Gulf, Urban.* **c-**Primary studies in Saltillo, Coahuila, Mexico, D.F., and Merida, Yucatan; secondary studies at the Evening Extension School, UNAM, Mexico, D.F.; engineering degree, National School of Engineering, UNAM, 1946. **d-**None. **e-**None. **f-**Secretary of Public Works for the Chihuahua-Pacific Railroad, 1960; joined the National Irrigation Commission, 1944; Project Chief for the Office of Structural Engineering, Secretariat of Hydraulic Resources; manager of the Rio Yaqui, Naucalpan-Zaragoza-Tlalnepantla projects; Director of Construction for the Rio Yaqui; technical adviser to the Federal Electric Commission for the 27th of September Hydroelectric Plant, 1958–60; Director of Construction, Rio Yaqui; Executive Secretary of the Rio Fuerte Commission, Secretariat of Hydraulic Resources; Director of the Rio Fuerte Commission, 1955–64; *Secretary of Hydraulic Resources,* 1964–70. **g-**President of the Executive Council of the College of Mexican Civil Engineers. **h-**Arbitrator for the El Aguila Construction Company with the government of El Salvador; engineering consultant, 1971. **i-**Student of *Javier Barros Sierra* and *Agustin Yanez* at the National Preparatory School; student of *Antonio Dovali Jaime* at UNAM; knew *Leandro Rovirosa Wade, Manuel Franco Lopez, Gilberto Valenzuela,* and *Luis Enrique Bracamontes* at UNAM. **j-**None. **k-**None. **l-**Letter; WWMG, 21; D de Y, 2 Dec. 1964, 2; IWW70–71, 423; *El Universal,* 2 Dec. 1964; *Libro de Oro,* 1967, xxxiv; DPE65, 126; *Excelsior,* 21 Aug. 1973, 1.

Hernandez Vela, Salvador

a-Dec. 31, 1908. **b-**Zaragoza, Coahuila, *North, Rural.* **c-**Primary studies at the Juan Antonio de la Fuente School, Zaragoza, Coahuila; secondary studies at the Ateneo Fuente, Saltillo, Coahuila; studied at Harvard Medical School, Walter Reed Hospital, and Brook Medical Center; medical degree; graduated from the Staff School of the Superior War College; professor at the Military Medical School; head of the Teaching Council at the Military Medical School. **d-***Alternate Senator* from Coahuila, 1958–64; *Federal Deputy* from the State of Coahuila, Dist. 4, 1970–73, member of the First Committee on National Defense and the Committee on Military Health. **e-**None. **f-**Subdirector General of Military Health, Secretariat of National Defense; member of the Directive Council of the Chief of Staff, Secretariat of National Defense. **g-**None. **h-**Founded the *Magazine of Military Health*; author of numerous books and articles. **j-**Career army medical officer; rank of Brigadier General; member of the Legion of Honor. **k-**None. **l-**C de D, 1970–72, 12, 120; C de S, 1961–64; DBM68, 343; *Directorio,* 1970–72.

Hernandez y Hernandez, Francisco

a-1908. b-Calpulalpan, Tlaxcala, *East Central, Rural*. c-Teaching certificate; school teacher. d-*Federal Deputy* from the State of Tlaxcala, Dist. 2, 1949–52, member of the Indigenous Affairs Committee, the First Public Education Committee, the Legislative Studies Committee, and the Second Balloting Committee; President of the Second Instructive Section of the Grand Jury and President of the Chamber of Deputies, Dec., 1949; *Senator* from the State of Tlaxcala, 1958–64, member of the Gran Comision, the Indigenous Affairs Committee, the National Lands Committee, and substitute member of the Agrarian Department Committee. e-None. f-Director of the *Diario Oficial*; Director of the Congressional Library; Director General of the National Ejido Credit Bank, 1964. g-*Secretary General of the CNC*, 1959–62. h-Author of articles on peasants. i-Supported for the position of Secretary General of the CNC by *Roberto Barrios*, *Raymundo Flores Fuentes* and *Gabriel Leyva Velazquez*; father of *Tulio Hernandez Gomez*, Oficial Mayor of the Secretariat of Government, 1979– . j-None. k-Critical of local agrarian leaders who had held their positions for more than twenty years; changed 445 of the 480 regional committees of the CNC. l-*Excelsior,* 27 Aug. 1959; C de D, 1949–51, 75; C de S. 1961–64, 57; Func., 380; Gonzalez Navarro, 266; Ronfeldt, 193.

Herrera, Enrique

a-Oct. 2, 1938. b-Federal District, *Federal District, Urban*. c-Degree in political science from the National School of Political and Social Sciences, UNAM, 1963; postgraduate studies abroad in mass communications; Professor of the Sociology and Philosophy of Law, National School of Law, UNAM; Professor of Economic and Social Analysis; Ibero-American University, Mexico, D.F.; Professor of Economic Analysis, National Polytechnic Institute. d-None. e-None. f-President of the National Broadcasting Commission, 1969–70; Subdirector of Information, Secretariat of Government, 1967–70; *Subsecretary of Broadcasting*, Secretariat of Communications and Transportation, 1970–72. g-None. h-Founded the Mexican News and Information Agency (NOTIMEX), 1968. j-None. k-None. l-HA, 14 Dec. 1970, 22; DPE71.

Herrera, Maria Guadalupe Calderon de

a-Feb. 14, 1938. b-Morelia, Michoacan, *West Central, Urban*. c-Primary studies in a public school and the Plancarte Institute; preparatory studies from the Colegio San Nicolas de Hidalgo; law degree from the School of Law and Social Science, University of Michoacan; criminology course from the Office of the Attorney General of the Federal District. d-*Federal Deputy* from the State of Michoacan, Dist.

1, 1967–70, member of the Inspection Committee of the General Accounting Office; the Social Action Committee (1st year), the Public Welfare Committee (1st year), the Editorial Committee (2nd year), the Legislative Studies Committee (Third Section on Penal Affairs), and the Subsistence and Supplies Committee. e-Director of the Women's Sector of PRI for Michoacan, 1963–70. f-Official of the Attorney General's Office; agent of the Ministerio Publico of the Attorney General in the State of Michoacan, 1961–63; laboratory expert in criminal cases for the Attorney General of Michoacan; Director of the Social Security Center for Family Welfare, Institute of Social Security, 1966–67. g-None. h-Pianist for a nursery school; social worker for the Mexican Institute of Social Security, 1964–66. j-None. k-None. l-DBM68, 344; C de D, 1967–69, 55, 57, 63, 66, 78, 88; MGF69; PS, 0854.

Herrera y Lasso, Manuel

a-1890. b-San Luis Potosi, San Luis Potosi, *East Central, Urban*. c-Primary studies in San Luis Potosi; began his secondary studies in 1900 at the Conciliar Seminary, San Luis Potosi; preparatory studies completed at the Scientific and Literary Institute of San Luis Potosi; studies in law at the National School of Law, UNAM; studies in law completed at the Free Law School, Mexico City, July 24, 1912 to March 17, 1914, law degree from the Free Law School, June 29, 1915, with a thesis on the 1917 Constitution; professor of Spanish, National Preparatory School, 1914; Professor of Sociology, Free Law School, 1914–22; Professor of Constitutional Law, Free Law School; Professor Emeritus of the Free Law School. d-None. e-Co-founder of PAN, 1939. f-Private Secretary to Eduardo Tamariz, Secretary of Agriculture, 1914; consulting lawyer to the City Government of Mexico City, 1919; adviser to the President of Mexico, 1947–64; adviser to the Chamber of Deputies, 1964–67. g-Student co-founder of the Free School of Law, 1912. h-Practicing lawyer with Agustin Rodriguez, 1914–19. i-Son of Engineer Manuel Herrera y Raso; married Raquel Mendez Armendariz; student of Emilio Rabasa. j-None. k-Recruited many future leaders of PAN from his students. l-Enc. Mex., VI, 421; Lemus, 38; ELD, 65.

Herrera y Tejeda, Ignacio

a-Oct. 21, 1893. b-Queretaro, Queretaro, *East Central, Urban*. c-Preparatory studies from the Conciliar Seminary, Queretaro, 1911–12; studies in medicine, National School of Medicine, UNAM, 1912–13; studies at the University of California, Berkeley, 1919; law degree from the School of Law, Colegio Civil of Queretaro, 1928; professor at the Normal School for Women, 1921–22; professor at the Colegio Civil of Queretaro, 1929; secondary school teacher, Guanajuato, 1930; professor at the Preparatory School of Celaya, 1930; professor at the Conciliar Seminary of Queretaro, 1946–50. **d**-None. **e**-None. **f**-Official of the Mexican Embassy in Guatemala, 1922–23; official of the Mexican Embassy in Peru, 1924–26; Interim Governor of Veracruz; judge in the State of Queretaro and the State of Guanajuato, 1929–31; Judge of the Superior Tribunal of Justice of the Federal District and Federal Territories, 1935–40. **g**-None. **i**-Son of Doctor Ponciano Herrera. **j**-Joined the Revolution as a student; fought with Emiliano Zapata, 1913–14; fought with the forces of Francisco Villa, 1914–15. **l**-WNM, 115–16.

Hidalgo, Ernesto
(Deceased 1955)
a-Aug. 5, 1896. **b**-San Jose Iturbide, Ciudad Obregon, Guanajuato, *West Central*, *Rural*. **c**-Early education unknown; no degree. **d**-Federal Deputy from the State of Guanajuato, 1928–30; 1930–32; *Governor of Guanajuato*, 1943–46. **e**-None. **f**-Press attache in the United States for the Mexican Foreign Service, 1916; Mexican delegate to a commercial congress in Argentina, 1917; private secretary to Secretary of the Treasury, Luis Cabrera, 1915; *Oficial Mayor of the Secretariat of Foreign Relations*, 1936–40; *Oficial Mayor of the Secretariat of Foreign Relations*, 1940–42; Minister to Poland, 1946–52. **g**-None. **h**-Journalist; wrote for *El Imparcial*; Director of *El Universal Grafico*, 1921–36; writer for *Excelsior*; author of a book criticizing Federal intervention in the States. **i**-Part of *Jose Aguilar y Maya's* political clique in Guanajuato. **j**-None. **k**-Was removed from the Governorship when his powers were dissolved on Jan. 8, 1946, after a riot occurred on Jan. 2, 1946, in which many people were killed; Scott claims he was removed to placate public opinion which reacted strongly against the killing of many rioters in Leon by troops called in by the Governor; the cause of the riots was attributed to rigged elections; *Hidalgo* wrote a book defending his position. **l**-DP70, 992–93; Peral, 389; Scott, 138; Simpson, 337; DGF51, I, 108; NYT, 9 Jan. 1946, 10; Anderson, 85–86; Enc. Mex., 1977, VI, 426.

Hinojosa (Hinojosa), Juan Jose
a-Sept. 3, 1921. **b**-General Garcia Trevino, Nuevo Leon, *North*, *Rural*. **c**-Early education unknown; law degree. **d**-*Federal Deputy* from the State of Nuevo Leon, Dist. 3, 1949–52, member of the Industries Committee and the Cooperative Development Committee; *Federal Deputy* from the Federal District, Dist. 11, 1973–76. **e**-Joined PAN, 1940; Secretary of the CEN of PAN (several times). **f**-None. **g**-None. **h**-Practicing lawyer; manager, National Distributor

Company, Mexico City; Sales Director, Vidriera Monterrey, S.A., 1972; editorial writer for *Excelsior*, 1975. **j**-None. **k**-One of the first members of PAN to win a seat in the Chamber of Deputies. **l**-C de D, 1949–52, 76; C de D, 1973–76, 7; Enc. Mex., VI, 532; *Directorio*, 1973; DGF51; WNM, 116; Lopez, 511.

Hinojosa, Jr., Cosme R.
(Deceased Dec., 1965)
a-1879. **b**-Tacupeto, Sonora, *North*, *Rural*. **c**-Early education unknown; no degree. **d**-Local deputy to the State Legislature of Sonora, 1911–13. **e**-Member of the Anti-Reelectionist Party with Benjamin Hill. **f**-Director of Mails, Hermosillo, Sonora; Director General of the Mails, 1920–28; Director General of the ISSSTE, 1928–34; Director General of the Mails and Telegraph, 1934–35; *Head of the Department of the Federal District*, 1935–38; Consul in San Antonio, Texas; Consul in Naco, Arizona, 1951; Consul in Tucson, Arizona, 1956–58; President of the Patronate of the National Pawnshop. **g**-None. **h**-Involved in the private banking field, 1938. **j**-Joined the Revolution in 1910; fought against Carranza in 1920. **k**-As Secretary of the State Legislature of Sonora, led the vote to not recognize the government of Victoriano Huerta, 1913. **l**-Q es Q, 283; DP70, 1001; DGF56, 141; Peral, 393–94; DGF51, I, 128; Lopez, 511; Enc. Mex., 1977, VI, 532.

Hinojosa Ortiz, Manuel
a-1910. **b**-Parangaricutiro, Michoacan, *West Central*, *Rural*. **c**-Primary and secondary studies at private schools in Michoacan; preparatory studies at the Colegio San Nicolas de Hidalgo; preparatory studies in physics at the National Preparatory School, 1931; preparatory studies in chemical engineering, 1932; studies in law, literature, and philosophy, UNAM, 1932–36; law degree, National School of Law, UNAM, with an honorable mention, 1937, and a thesis on administrative action; Professor of Civics, secondary school in the Federal District; Professor of Constitutional Law, University of Michoacan, 1951. **d**-*Federal Deputy* from the State of Michoacan, Dist. 6, 1952–53, member of the Legislative Studies Committee, the Budget and Accounts Committee, and the Credentials Committee; *Senator* from the State of Michoacan, 1958–64, President of the Committee on National Waters and Irrigation, member of the Second Balloting Committee, the Special Forestry Committee, and the Special Hydraulic Resources Committee; substitute member of the Third Committee on Labor and the Consular and Diplomatic Service Committee. **e**-General coordinator for the gubernatorial campaign of *Damaso Cardenas*, 1949–50; Director of Legal Affairs, PRI,

1948–49; lawyer for PRM, 1937. **f-**Lawyer for the Department of Agrarian Affairs, 1937–43; Secretary General of Government of the State of Aguascalientes, 1944–47, Secretary General of Government of the State of Michoacan under *Damaso Cardenas*, 1950–52; *Subsecretary of Forest Resources*, *Secretary of Agriculture*, 1953–58; Secretary of Colonization, Department of Agrarian Affairs, 1958; Representative of CORDEMEX in Mexico City, 1965–70; Director General of Forest Industry and Production, State of Mexico, 1970–71. **g-**Secretary of Planning and Organization of the CEN of the CNC, 1961–64. **h-**Author of many books on agricultural problems; practicing lawyer, 1937–43, 1972– . **i-**Political protege of *Damaso Cardenas*; father a small businessman; practiced law with *Luis Chico Goerne*, 1935–36. **j-**None. **k-**Recognized expert on Mexican forestation problems; favored the women suffrage proposal as a Federal Deputy. **l-**Letters; C de S, 1961–64, 57; D de Y, 12 Dec. 1964; Morton, 70–71; DGF51, I, 90; Func., 266; DGF56, 223; *Hoy*, 17 Jan. 1970, 4; C de D, 1952–54, 12.

Hiriart Balderrama, Fernando

a-Oct. 21, 1914. **b-**Santa Barbara, Chihuahua, *North*, *Urban*. **c-**Primary and secondary studies in Santa Barbara; preparatory studies from the National Preparatory School, 1932–34; studies in civil engineering, National School of Engineering, UNAM, 1934–37, engineering degree, 1938; Director, Engineering Institute, UNAM, 1955–58; member of the Governing Board of UNAM, 1963–71. **d-**None. **e-**None. **f-**Project designer, National Irrigation Commission, 1938–40; Subdirector of the Engineering Labs, National Irrigation Commission, 1940–41; Chief Engineer, Federal Electric Commission, 1950–53; Director General of Hydraulic Works, Department of the Federal District, 1953–58; Technical Director of Construction, ISSSTE Clinics, 1959–63; Subdirector General of the Federal Electric Commission, 1959–70; Adviser to *Jose Lopez Portillo*, Director General of the Federal Electric Commission, 1972–73; Director of Public Investment, Secretariat of the Presidency, 1971–76; Adviser to the Federal Electric Commission, 1976–77; *Subsecretary of Decentralized Industry of the Secretariat of Patrimony and Industrial Development*, 1977– . **g-**None. **h-**Author of many articles; Technical Director of Hydraulic Resources, ICA, S.A., 1942–50; technical consultant to the IMSS, 1955–66. **i-**Father of *Humberto Hiriart Urdanivia*, federal deputy from Jalisco, 1970–73. **j-**None. **k-**None. **l-**HA, 5 Dec. 1977, 28; *Justicia*, Oct. 1977; MGF69, 537.

Hiriart Urdanivia, Humberto

a-Oct. 31, 1939. **b-**Federal District, *Federal District*, *Urban*. **c-**Primary studies in the Benito Juarez School, Mexico City; secondary studies at Secondary School No. 3, Mexico City; preparatory studies at the National Preparatory School, economics degree from the National School of Economics, UNAM. **d-***Federal Deputy* from the State of Jalisco, Dist. 5, 1970–73, member of the Tax Committee, the General Accounting Office Committee, the Money and Credit Institutions Committee and the Budget and Accounts Committee. **e-***Subsecretary of Political Action of the CEN of PRI*, 1973. **g-**None. **i-**Son of Engineer *Fernando Hiriart Balderrama*, Subsecretary of Decentralized Industry, 1977. **j-**None. **k-**None. **l-**C de D, 1970–73, 120; *Directorio*, 1970–73.

Hirschfield Almada, Julio

a-Feb. 11, 1917. **b-**Federal District, *Federal District*, *Urban*. **c-**Most of his primary and secondary studies in the Federal District; studied at the University of Michigan and the National School of Engineering, UNAM; no degree. **d-**None. **e-**None. **f-**Director General of Airports and Auxiliary Services, 1970–73; *Head of the Tourism Department*, 1973–76. **g-**None. **h-**Sales agent, Vice President, and Gerente General of H. Steel Company, S.A., 1949–64; President and Director General of Productos Metalicos Steel, S.A., 1964–70. **i-**Married to the daughter of the important Sonoran politician, Aaron Saenz, Dora Saenz; son Julio is married to Patricia Torreblanco Calles, a grand-daughter of President Calles. **j-**None. **k-**Kidnapped on Sept. 27, 1971; released by the Frente Urbano Zapatista after they were paid a 3 million peso ransom which the group supposedly wanted to distribute to the urban poor in Mexico, D.F.; Carlos Fuentes commented on the possibility of the group being a front organization for right-wing officials in the *Echeverria* administration. **l-**HA, 7 Dec. 1970, 28; HA, 4 Oct. 1971, 22; HA, 7 Feb. 1972, 33–34; LAD, Jan. 1972, 2.

Hori Robaina, Guillermo

a-Oct. 16, 1932. **b-**Villa Flores, Chihuahua, *North*, *Rural*. **c-**Primary and secondary studies at the Williams School; preparatory studies at the University Center of Mexico; law degree at the National Law School, UNAM, 1952–56; studied social security systems in Europe under PEMEX and the Secretariat of Labor; Professor of Labor Law at the School for the Education of Workers of the Regional Confederation of Mexican Workers; Professor of Personnel Administration, School of Commerce and Administration, UNAM, 1965–68. **d-**None. **e-**None. **f-**Clerk, 1952–54, Secretary of Hearings, 1954–57, and counsel, 1958, of the Federal Board of Conciliation and Arbitration; head of the Department of Social Security, Secretariat of Labor, 1962; head of the Federal Department of Labor Inspection, Secretariat of Labor, 1963; Substitute President of the Federal

Conciliation Board, 1964; *Oficial Mayor of the Sec-retariat of Labor and Social Welfare*, Jan. 18, 1965 to 1970. **g-**None. **h-**Representative of the President before many labor conventions. **i-**Son of Dr. Mario D. Hori. **j-**None. **k-**None. **l-**DBM68, 349; DPE61, 154; *Libro de Oro*, xxxvi; MGF69.

Hoyos Schalamme, Myrna E.

a-Sept. 15, 1944. **b-**Merida, Yucatan, *Gulf, Urban.* **c-**Early education unknown; law degree, School of Law, University of Yucatan; advanced courses in human communications and human relations. **d-**Federal Deputy from the State of Yucatan, Dist. 1, 1976–79. **e-**Subdirector of Electoral Action of PRI in the Federal District. **f-**Director, Office of General Studies, Division of Fares, Secretariat of Communications and Transportation. **g-**Secretary General of the Gomez Farias Association. **i-**Married to Agrarian Engineer Jose Alberto Navarrete; daughter of Luis H. Villanueva, health education teacher and local PRI leader. **j-**None. **k-**None. **l-**D de C, 1976–79, 35; *Excelsior,* 28 Aug. 1976, 1C; Q es QY, 130–31.

Huerta Sanchez, Luciano

a-Jan. 7, 1906. **b-**Ixtenco, Tlaxcala, *East Central, Rural.* **c-**Primary studies at the Colegio Pensador Mexicano, Tlaxcala; preparatory studies at the National Preparatory School, 1920–24; medical degree from the National School of Medicine, UNAM, 1931; Professor of Clinical Surgery, National School of Medicine, UNAM, 1937–70; Director of Medical Services, UNAM, 1958–66, under Rector *Nabor Carrillo Flores.* **d-**Senator from the State of Tlaxcala, 1964–70; *Governor of Tlaxcala,* 1970–76. **e-**Entered politics in 1956; State committeeman for PRI. **f-**Physician, National School for the Deaf and Blind; Intern, General Hospital, Mexico City; Subdirector of the Hospital of the Secretariat of the Treasury; Director of Medical Services, Constructora Industrial, Ciudad Sahagun; Director of Medical Services, Secretariat of the Treasury, 1954–58. **g-**Physician, National Sugarworkers Union. **i-**Knew *Antonio Armendariz* and *Antonio Carrillo Flores* while a student at UNAM; father was a businessman and Mayor of Ixtenco. **j-**None. **k-**None. **l-**MGF69, 106; letter; C de S, 1964–70; PS, 3025.

Huitron y Aguado, Abel

(Deceased Apr. 19, 1980)
a-July 20, 1908. **b-**Jilotepec, Mexico, *West Central, Rural.* **c-**Primary studies at a public school, Federal District; attended the Normal School of Toluca on an academic scholarship; secondary and preparatory studies at the Colegio Frances Morelos, Mexico. D.F.; law degree, Escuela Libre de Derecho, October 24, 1934, with a thesis on the new law in Mexican criminal legislation; law degree, National School

of Law, UNAM, Aug. 14, 1935, with a thesis on resolutions in punitive law; Professor of Amparo and Constitutional Law, National School of Law, UNAM (12 years). **d-**Local Deputy to the State Legislature of Mexico; *Federal Deputy* from the State of Mexico, Dist. 7, 1949–52, member of the Credit, Money and Credit Institutions Committee and substitute member of the Rules Committee; *Senator* from the State of Mexico, 1958–64, President of the Department of the Federal District Committee, member of the Second Labor Committee, the First Industries Committee, and the Second Committee on Tariffs and Foreign Trade, substitute member of the Second Committee on Credit, Money, and Credit Institutions, Vice President of the Senate (twice), and Secretary of the Senate, 1962. **e-**General delegate of PRI to Oaxaca, Puebla, and Nayarit. **f-**Agent of the Ministerio Publico, Toluca, Mexico; Justice of the Superior Court of the State of Mexico; Director of Social Action, State of Mexico, 1942–44; Secretary General of Government of the State of Mexico, 1944–51; Director of the Legal Department of the Department of the Federal District, 1952–58; *Justice of the Supreme Court*, 1964–70 and 1970–75; President of the First Division of the Supreme Court, 1966. **g-**None. **h-**Practiced law for ten years; consulting lawyer to the State of Mexico. **i-**Personal friend of *Adolfo Lopez Mateos* since secondary school days; studied under *Francisco Javier Gaxiola* at the Escuela Libre de Derecho; brother *Manuel Huitron y Aguado* was an Alternate Senator from the State of Mexico, 1970–76. **j-**None. **k-**None. **l-**Letter; C de D, 1949–51; DGF56, 468; DGF51, I, 23, 31, 36, 90; C de S, 1961–64, 16; *Justicia*; Func., 254; *Excelsior*, 22 Apr. 1980.

Ibanez Llamas, Santiago

c-Early education unknown; law degree, National School of Law, UNAM, 1945. **d-**None. **e-**None. **f-**Consultant to the Division of Professions, Secretariat of Public Education; head of the Technical Advisory Department, 1948; Secretariat of Public Education, 1951–53; assistant head of the Department of Immigration, Secretariat of Government, 1955–64; Director General of the National Institute for Child Care, 1964–70. **g-**None. **j-**None. **k-**None. **l-**HA, 21 Dec. 1964, 9; DGF51, I, 289; DGF56, 84; DPE61, 13.

Ibarra Herrera, Manuel

a-Jan. 8, 1932. **b-**Tampico, Tamaulipas, *North, Urban.* **c-**Early education unknown; law degree; Professor of Agrarian Law, National School of Law, UNAM. **d-**None. **e-**None. **f-**Head of the Department of Presidential Resolutions, Department of Agrarian Affairs; Director General of Political and Social Investigations, Secretariat of Government; Private Secretary to the Subsecretary of Government, *Rafael Hernandez Ochoa*, 1964–70; *Oficial Mayor of the Secretariat of Government*, 1970–76. **g-**None. **h-**Employee of the Office of the Attorney General of Mexico; employee of the Income Tax Division. **j-**None. **k-**Pre-candidate for governor of Tamaulipas, 1974. **l-**HA, 14 Dec. 1970, 20; DPE65, 13; DPE71, 2.

Ibarra (Ibarra), Guillermo
(Deceased Apr. 17, 1980)
a-Nov. 28, 1911. **b-**Alamos, Sonora, *North, Urban*. **c-**Normal and preparatory studies in Hermosillo, Sonora; teaching certificate, Hermosillo, 1928; law degree, National School of Law, UNAM, 1937; teacher, 1928–43; Founder and Director, School for Children of Workers, Culiacan, 1937; Director of the Preparatory School of Coyoacan for Children of Workers, 1941. **d-***Senator* from the State of Sonora, 1958–64, member of the Gran Comision, President of the Second Committee on Public Education; member of the First Committee on National Defense, the First Committee on Constitutional Affairs, the Special Committee on Legislative Studies, and the Second Committee on Credit, Money, and Credit Institutions. **e-**None. **f-**Director General of Secondary Education, Secretariat of Public Education, 1940–41; President of Group No. 10 of the Federal Board of Conciliation and Arbitration, 1942; Judge of the Federal Tax Court, 1943–48; director of the official government newspaper, *El Nacional*, 1948–56; Gerente General of PIPSA, 1956–58; *Oficial Mayor of the Secretariat of Hydraulic Resources*, 1964–70. **g-**President of the National Student Federation of Mexico, 1933; representative of the Mexican Federation of Labor in Santiago, Chile, 1939; member of the National Executive Committee of STERM, 1938–40; Editor of the STERM newspaper. **h-**Member of the Administrative Board of PIPSA, 1951–56; author of numerous articles. **j-**None. **k-**None. **l-**C de S, 1961–64, 58; *Libro de Oro*, xxxv; DBM68, 354; DGF51, II, 495; DPE65, 126; *Hoy*, 31 Jan. 1970, 4; Func., 358; HA, 19 Nov. 1956, 15; Enc. Mex., 1977, VII, 108–09; *Excelsior*, 19 Apr. 1980, 2.

Ibarra Munoz, David
a-Jan. 14, 1930. **b-**Queretaro, Queretaro, *East Central, Urban*. **c-**Early education unknown; studies in auditing and public accounting, UNAM, 1947–51, public accounting degree, 1952, with a thesis on internal accounting; economics degree, National School of Economics, UNAM, 1953–57; Ph.D. in economics, Stanford University, 1959–61; Professor of Finance Math, School of Business Administration, UNAM, 1955–56; Professor of Financial Analysis, National School of Economics, 1955–56; Secretary

of Social Services, UNAM, 1955–57; Researcher, Planning Committee, University Student Association of UNAM, 1957–58; Professor of Techniques of Economic Research, National School of Economics, UNAM, 1957; Professor of Methods of Planning, Secretariat of Public Works, 1959; Professor of Applied Economics, UNAM, 1961–62; Professor of Theory and Methods of Planning, National School of Economics, UNAM, 1964–70; Director of Graduate Studies, National School of Economics, UNAM, 1967–69. **d-**None. **e-**None. **f-**Auditor, Bank of Mexico; economist, Economic Commission for Latin America (ECLA), Santiago, Chile, 1958–59; Chief of the Development Section, ECLA, Mexico City, 1961–63; Coordinator of Research, ECLA, Mexico City, 1964–66; Assistant Director of ECLA, Mexico City, 1966–66; Director of ECLA, Mexico City, 1970–73; Assistant Director of the National Finance Bank, 1974–76; *Subdirector General of the National Finance Bank*, 1976; *Director General of the National Finance Bank*, 1976–77; *Secretary of the Treasury*, November 17, 1977– . **g-**None. **h-**Chief of auditors, *Manuel Gomez Morin's* law firm. **i-**Son of Engineer David Ibarra; married Olga Cardona. **j-**None. **k-**None. **l-**B de M, 153; *El Dia*, 1 Dec. 1976; *Excelsior*, 17 Nov. 1977, 11; *Excelsior*, 28 Nov. 1977, 16; HA, 19 July 1976, 32.

Ibarrola Santoyo, Eugenio
a-Sept. 8, 1923. **b-**Morelia, Michoacan, *West Central, Urban*. **c-**Secondary studies at the Escuela Apostolica y Escoldasticado de los Misioneros del Espiritu Santo, 1935–45; law degree from the Escuela Libre de Derecho, 1947–51, degree, Apr. 30, 1953, with a thesis on political power. **d-***Federal Deputy* from the Federal District, Dist. 11, 1952–55, member of the Rules Committee, the Legislative Studies Committee (1st year), and the First Balloting Committee. **e-**None. **f-**Candidate for Notary Public, 1958–59; Notary Public No. 122 of the Federal District, 1959–80. **g-**Member of the Council of Notaries of the Federal District, Jan. 1, 1964, to Dec. 31, 1965. **h-**Businessman in Morelia, Michoacan; member of the Board of Directors of Mutualidad Notarial, A.C., 1965–69. **i-**Brother Roberto is an architect, professor at UNAM, and was head of projects for the Office of Buildings and Monuments, Department of the Federal District; married Maria Bertha Urquiaga. **j-**None. **k-**None. **l-**DBM68, 355–56; C de D, 52–54, 51, 66; DJBM, 70.

Icaza y Lopez Negrete, Xavier
(Deceased 1969)
a-Oct. 2, 1892. **b-**Durango, Durango, *West, Urban*. **c-**Preparatory studies at the National Preparatory School; law degree from the Free Law School, August 10, 1917, with a thesis on Constitutionalism;

Professor of Law and Literature, University of Veracruz, Jalapa, Veracruz; Professor of History and Literature, UNAM; Director of the School of Labor Law, 1939; member of the Board of Directors of the Workers University. **d**-None. **e**-None. **f**-*Justice of the Supreme Court*, 1935–40. **g**-None. **h**-Attorney for many private firms in Mexico, including Financiera de Mexico and the Compania Mexicana de Petroleo El Aguila, 1919; representative of El Aguila to the state government of Veracruz, 1922. **i**-Married Ana Guido. **j**-None. **k**-Refused to review the Arbitration Board findings in the well-known petroleum case, 1938. **l**-WWM45, 58; Kirk, 164; DP70, 2403; IWW40, 525; Peral, 404; ELD, 85–86.

Iduarte Foucher, Andres

a-May 1, 1907. **b**-Villahermosa, Tabasco, *Gulf*, *Urban*. **c**-Primary studies in Villahermosa and in Mexico, D.F., Dr. Hugo Topf's School; secondary studies at the Colegio Mexicano, Mexico, D.F.; preparatory studies at the National Preparatory School, Mexico, D.F., 1922–26; studied at UNAM, 1926–28, 1930–32; studied at the University of Paris, 1928–30; law degree from the University of Madrid, 1935; LLD degree, 1936; Ph.D. from Columbia University, 1944; LLD from the National School of Law, UNAM, 1953; Professor of General History, National Preparatory School; Professor at UNAM, 1930–32, 1953; Secretary of the Ateneo de Madrid, 1933–38; Professor of Spanish American Literature, Columbia University, 1939–72; instructor at Barnard College, 1941–45; professor at the University of California, Berkeley, 1947; professor at the University of Caracas, 1945; professor at the University of the Oriente, 1955. **d**-None. **e**-None. **f**-Director General of the National Institute of Bellas Artes, 1952–54. **g**-Editor of student paper *Angora*, National Preparatory School, 1924; writer for student magazine, *Avalanche*, 1923. **h**-Author. **i**-From a very important political family in Tabasco; father was a judge; cousin of *Rodulfo Brito Foucher*. **j**-None. **k**-Scott says that Professor Iduarte was dismissed from his position as Director General of Bellas Artes in 1954, for not prohibiting the use of a Communist flag which was draped over the coffin of the famous Mexican painter, Frida Kahlo, as the body lay in state at the Institute. **l**-Scott, 335; DEM, 180; letter.

Inarritu (y Ramirez), Jorge

a-Apr. 27, 1916. **b**-Tacubaya, Mexico, D.F., *Federal District*, *Urban*. **c**-Primary studies in Mexico City; law degree, National School of Law, UNAM, Nov. 13, 1939. **d**-None. **e**-None. **f**-Head of the Judicial Section, Supreme Court, 1945; Subdirector and Director of the *Judicial Weekly* of the Supreme Court, 1945–58; Oficial Mayor of the Supreme Court, 1958–59; Subsecretary of Resolutions, Supreme Court, 1959–60; Secretary General of Resolutions, Supreme Court, 1960–64; *Justice of the Supreme Court*, 1964–70, 1970–76, 1977. **g**-None. **h**-Author of many works on *amparo*; consulting lawyer to the Secretariat of Communications and Public Works and to the Secretariat of Health and Public Assistance. **i**-Married Holda Rodriguez. **j**-None. **k**-None. **l**-*Justicia*, Oct., 1968; letter; WNM, 119.

Inurreta, Marcelino

a-June 29, 1901. **b**-Cunduacan, Tabasco, *Gulf*, *Rural*. **c**-Primary studies in Oaxaca; preparatory studies at the National Preparatory School; enrolled in the National Military College, but left without completing studies to join the Revolution. **d**-*Federal Deputy* from the Federal District, Dist. 2, 1943–46, elected as an Alternate but replaced *Carlos Madrazo* when he was suspended; *Senator* from the State of Tabasco, 1952–58, member of the Rules Committee, the National Lands Committee, the Second National Defense Committee and the Balloting Committee. **e**-None. **f**-Subdirector of the Military Judicial Police; presidential adviser in public health; Paymaster General of the Federal District Police Department, 1943; first Director of the Federal Department of Security, 1946–52. **g**-None. **h**-Champion in various sports; expert pistol shot. **j**-Joined the Juan Antonio de la Fuente Brigade as a private; reached rank of Brigade General in the Army. **k**-None. **l**-Ind. Biog., 88–89; DGF51, 69; DGF56, 7, 9, 10, 12, 13.

Ireta (Viveros), Felix
(Deceased Oct. 26, 1978)
a-Nov. 20, 1893. **b**-Zinapecuaro, Michoacan, *West Central*, *Rural*. **c**-Primary studies in Zinapecuaro; none; no degree. **d**-*Senator* from the State of Michoacan, 1946–52; *Governor of Michoacan*, 1940–44. **e**-None. **g**-None. **i**-Fought with the *Avila Camacho* brothers during the Revolution. **j**-Joined the Revolution; Constitutionalist, 1913; commander of various military zones; fought against the Escobar Rebellion, 1929; Commander of the 21st Military Zone, Morelia, Michoacan, 1952–56; rank of Brigadier General. **k**-Strongly attacked in the press for various abuses committed by his government in Michoacan. **l**-DGF56, 202; DGF51, 6; Peral, 406; HA, 22 May 1942; HA, 25 Sept. 1942, 9; C de S, 1946–52; Gomez Maganda, 102; *Excelsior*, 28 Oct. 1978, 2; Lopez, 536.

Islas Bravo, Antonio
(Deceased 1949)
a-1885. **b**-Atlixco, Puebla, *East Central*, *Rural*. **c**-Law degree, National School of Law, UNAM, 1910. **d**-Federal Deputy, 1924-26. **e**-None. **f**-Agent of the Ministerio Publico; civil judge, Chihuahua;

consulting lawyer to the Secretary of Agriculture; Head of the Legal Department of the Secretariat of Agrarian Affairs; *Justice of the Supreme Court of Mexico*, 1940–46 and 1946–49; President of the Third Division of the Supreme Court, 1944. **g-**None. **h-**Author of the book *Presidential Succession in 1928*. **j-**Joined the Revolution; supporter of Francisco Madero; fought under General Villa, 1914–18. **k-**Opposed the reelection of General Obregon. **l-**Letter; DP70, 2406; Lopez, 539.

Islas Olguin, Guillermo

a-June 25, 1928. **b-**Federal District, *Federal District, Urban*. **c-**Primary studies at the Francisco Figueroa School, Tacuba, Federal District, 1934–40; secondary studies at the Manuel Acosta School, Tacuba, 1941–43; preparatory studies at the National Preparatory School, San Ildefonso, Mexico, D.F., 1944–46; medical degree, National School of Medicine, UNAM, 1948–53. **d-***Federal Deputy* from the Federal District, Dist. 19, 1970–73, member of the Bellas Artes Committee, the Small Industries Committee, and the Health Committee; *Federal Deputy* from the Federal District, Dist. No. 19, 1976–79. **e-**Joined PAN, 1951; Director of PAN for the Federal District, 1952–54. **f-**None. **g-**Member of the Mexican Academy of Sciences. **h-**Practicing physician. **i-**Married Lydia Leon. **j-**None. **k-**Candidate for Alternate Federal Deputy, Federal District, 1958. **l-**C de D, 1970–72, 121; *Directorio*, 1970–72.

Ituarte Servin, Alfonso

a-Oct. 30, 1914. **b-**Tacubaya, *Federal District, Urban*. **c-**Primary studies at Luz Savinon School, Mexico City and at a public school, Mexico City; two years of study in business school; private accounting degree, School of Banking and Business, 1936; CPA degree, National Polytechnic School. **d-***Federal Deputy* from the Federal District, Dist. 17, 1955–58, member of the First Balloting Committee and the Second General Means of Communication Committee; *Federal Deputy* (Party Deputy), 1967–70, member of Trade and Credit Section and the Tax Section of the Legislative Studies Committee; the First Government Committee, the Industries Committee, the Second Balloting Committee, and the Small Industries Committee. **e-**Member of PAN; *President of the CEN of PAN*, 1956–57. **f-**None. **g-**Member of various religious defense groups; propagandist for the League for Religious Defense; founder and President of the Civic Center of the Federal District; member of the CNIT; President of Catholic Action. **h-**Accountant. **j-**None. **k-**Candidate of PAN for Federal Deputy from the Federal District, Dist. 17, 1952. **l-**DGF56, 23, 34, 37; Ind. Biog., 89; *La*

Nacion, 29 Mar. 1959, 18; C de D, 1967–70, 67, 70, 72, 76, 77, 81.

Iturbe, Ramon F.

(Deceased 1970)
a-Nov. 7, 1889. **b-**Mazatlan, Sinaloa, *West, Urban*. **c-**Primary studies in Mazatlan; no degree. **d-***Federal Deputy* from the State of Sinaloa, Dist. 3, 1937–40, President of the Chamber. **e-**Founder of the Mexican Constitutional Front to support a presidential candidate in 1939. **f-**Provisional Governor of the State of Sinaloa, 1917–20; Director of the Cooperative Development, Secretariat of Industry and Commerce; Military Attache to Japan, 1941; Commander of the Mexican Legion of Honor, Secretariat of National Defense, 1958–64, 1964–66. **g-**None. **h-**None. **j-**Career army officer; joined the Revolution in 1909; commander of the forces that captured Mazatlan, 1914; commander of the forces that captured Culiacan under General Obregon, 1913; rank of Brigadier General, 1912; rank of Brigade General, October 28, 1913; Commander of Military Operations in Jalisco, Colima; rank of Divisionary General. **k-**Supported the Escobar movement, 1929; in exile in the United States, 1929–35; expelled from the PRM for his activities in support of the candidacy of General *Almazan* for President, 1938–39; later supported the candidacy of *Rafael Sanchez Tapia* in the 1940 campaign for President; received the Belisario Dominguez Medal from the Mexican Senate, 1966. **l-**DPE65, 42; DPE61, 34; C de D, 1937–39; *El Universal*, 18 Jan. 1939; Michaels, 22; *Annals*, Mar, 1940, 21; DP70, 2406; Peral, 407; Novo35, 271; Enc. Mex., VII, 1977, 363.

Iturriaga (Sauco), Jose E.

a-April 10, 1914. **c-**Preparatory studies at the National Preparatory School; studies in law at the Free Law School; studies in philosophy and history, School of Philosophy and Letters, UNAM; economic studies at the National School of Economics, no degree; fellow at the Colegio de Mexico, 1944; Professor of the History of the Mexican Revolution, Colegio de Mexico, 1949. **d-**None. **e-**Member of the Advisory Council to the IEPES of PRI, 1972. **f-**Employee of the National Finance Bank, 1934–64; official of the Historical Archives of the Secretariat of the Treasury, 1943–46; Director, Institution and Agency Inspection Department, Secretariat of National Patrimony, 1947–48; advisor to the President of Mexico, 1952–58, 1958–64; Subdirector of the National Finance Bank, 1959–64; *Ambassador to the USSR*, 1965–66; advisor to Luis Echeverria, 1971. **g-**None. **h-**Editorial writer, *Novedades*; editorial writer, *Manana*. **j-**None. **k-**Candidate for Federal Deputy for the Popular Party (later the PPS) with *Narciso Bassols* and *Victor Manuel Villasenor*, 1943.

l-*Siempre*, 28 Jan. 1959, 6; DGF47, 269; DPE65, 31; Villasenor, II, 33; Enc. Mex., VII, pp.365–66.

Iturribarria (Martinez), Jorge Fernando

a-Apr. 5, 1902. b-Oaxaca, Oaxaca, *South*, *Urban*. c-Secondary education at the Institute of Arts and Sciences, Oaxaca; teaching certificate; professor of normal school; professor at the Institute of Arts and Sciences. d-*Federal Deputy* from the State of Oaxaca, Dist. 3, 1967–70, member of the Library Committee (2nd year). e-None. f-Oficial Mayor of the Legislature of the State of Oaxaca. g-None. h-Director and editor of various newspapers; author of many books on the history of Oaxaca. i-Related to Governor *Jose Pacheco Iturribarria*. j-None. k-None. l-WWM45, 59; C de D, 1967–69, 60; Peral, 410.

Jara (Rodriguez), Heriberto

(Deceased Apr. 17, 1968)

a-July 10, 1884. b-Orizaba, Veracruz, *Gulf*, *Rural*. c-Primary and secondary studies, Escuela Modelo, in Orizaba; secondary studies at the Scientific and Literary Institute of Hidalgo; attended the Escuela Naval de Anton Lizardo. d-Federal Deputy from the State of Veracruz, 1910–13; Deputy to the Constitutional Congress from the State of Veracruz, 1916–17; Senator from the State of Veracruz, 1920–24; Governor of Veracruz, December 18, 1924 to October 31, 1927. e-Member of the Constitutional Party, 1913; *President of the CEN of PRI*, 1939–40. f-Minister to Cuba, 1917–20; Governor of the Federal District, 1914; *Secretary of the Navy*, 1941–46. g-None. h-Writer for many magazines and newspapers at the beginning of his career and after his retirement in 1946. i-Married Ana Maria Avalos; from very humble background. j-Career military officer; rank of Colonel, 1913; rank of Brigadier General, 1914; directed the Cadets against the North American invasion of Veracruz, 1914; rank of Brigade General, 1915; Divisionary General, 1924; joined the Revolution in 1910, fighting under General Camerino Mendoza; Commander of the 26th Military Zone, Veracruz, Veracruz, 1935–37; Assistant Inspector General of the Army; Inspector General of the Army, 1935; Commander of the 28th Military Zone, Oaxaca, Oaxaca, 1938; Director General of Military Education, Secretariat of National Defense, 1938–39. k-Participated in the Rio Blanco Mill Strike when he was a bookkeeper, 1907; voted against the renunciation of Madero and Pino Suarez as a federal deputy, 1913; one of the extreme radicals at the Constitutional Convention; opposed the candidacy of *Angel Carvajal* for President in an open letter signed by *Silvano Barba Gonzalez* and *Luis I. Rodriguez*; manager for *Avila Camacho's* campaign for President, 1940; his appointment as Secretary of

Navy strongly criticized by naval officers who felt a Navy rather than an Army officer should have been appointed; newspapers were also critical, calling Jara "General of the Ocean Cavalry." l-D de Y, 20 June 1939, 1; Daniels, 89; Peral, 414–15; D de Y, 1 Jan. 1936, 4; Kirk, 239–40; Morton, 41–42, 92; *Polemica*, April, 69, 70; DGF51, II, 699; DP70, 1110; *Hoy*, 27 April 1968, 4; WWM45, 60; Enc. Mex., VII, 1977, 450.

Jaramillo Gonzalez, Candido

(Deceased 1970)

a-1910. b-Zongolica, Veracruz, *Gulf*, *Rural*. c-Primary studies in Jalapa, Veracruz; teaching certificate in Veracruz; normal teacher in the State of Veracruz. d-None. e-Founder of the Popular Socialist Party with *Vicente Lombardo Toledano*, 1947. f-Comptroller General of the Secretariat of Industry and Commerce. g-Director General of the Mexican Federation of Teachers, 1937–38; *Secretary General of the FSTSE*, 1940–42. i-Brother Julio was a Mexican musician. j-None. k-None. l-DP70, 1112; Correa, 12; Raby, 76.

Jimenez, Antolin

a-Apr. 14, 1890. b-Villahermosa, Tabasco, *Gulf*, *Urban*. c-Primary and secondary studies at the Institute Juarez, Oaxaca; no degree. d-Federal Deputy from the State of Oaxaca, Dist. 13, 1928–30; *Federal Deputy* from the State of Oaxaca, Dist. 7, 1937–40. e-None. f-Director of Currency, Secretariat of the Treasury, 1923–24. g-None. h-Author and editor of banking and tax laws. j-None. k-Supported Jose Vasconcelos for governor of Oaxaca, 1923. l-EBW46, 119; C de D, 1937–39; Peral, 415.

Jimenez Cantu, Jorge

a-Oct. 27, 1914. b-Villa del Carbon, *Federal District*, *Urban*. c-Primary studies at the Centro Escolar Belisario Dominguez, Mexico City, 1922–28; secondary at Secondary School No. 1 and No. 7, 1929–31; preparatory studies in biological sciences, National Preparatory School, 1932–33; medical degree, National School of Medicine, UNAM, 1940; Professor of Clinical Surgery, National School of Medicine, UNAM, 1941–57; Professor of Biology, Instituto Mexico and the Centro Universitario Mexico. d-*Governor of Mexico*, 1975– . e-None. f-Secretary of Organization for the National Commission for the Campaign for School Construction, 1948–51; Administrative Committee of the Federal School Construction Program, 1951; Adviser to the National Institute of Youth, 1952–57; Director General of Medical Services, Secretariat of Public Works, 1952–56; Secretary General of Government of the State of Mexico, 1957–63, under Governor

Gustavo Baz; Gerente of CONASUPO, 1964–68, under *Carlos Hank Gonzalez*; Secretary General of Government of the State of Mexico, 1969–70, under Governor *Hank Gonzalez*; *Secretary of Health and Welfare*, 1970–75. **g**-President of the Student Society of the National School of Medicine; president of the Federation of University Students; student member of the University Council, 1937–38. **h**-Secretary General of the Commission of CONASUPO to promote rural improvements; founder of the College Military Pentathlon, 1938, commander of this organization. **i**-Married Luisa Isabel Campos. **j**-None. **k**-None. **l**-DPE71, 113; MGF69, 551; HA, 7 Dec. 1970, 25; DGF56, 259; DPE51, II, 446; *Hoy*, Dec. 1970; HA, 3 Feb. 1975, 34; Cadena Z., 41–42; HA, 6 Oct. 1975, 35.

Jimenez Cardenas, Simon

a-May 16, 1909. **b**-Armadillo, Mazatlan, Sinaloa, *West*, *Rural*. **c**-Primary studies at the Jose Maria Morelos School, 1919–25; secondary studies at the Federal Teacher Education Institute, 1952–57; teaching certificate from the Higher Normal School of Nayarit, 1963, with a speciality in Mexican and world history; Professor of Geography in the Public Secondary School, Mazatlan; Professor of Civics, Public Secondary School of Guamuchil, Sinaloa. **d**-*Federal Deputy* from the Popular Socialist Party (party deputy), 1970–73, member of the Waters and Irrigation Committee, the First Section of the Agrarian Affairs Committee, the Cultural Affairs Committee, and the Securities Committee. **e**-Member of the Central Committee of the PPS; Secretary of Electoral Affairs, Regional Committee of the PPS for Sinaloa; representative of the PPS on the Sinaloa Electoral Commission. **f**-Director of Rural Schools; Director of Urban Schools; Federal Inspector of Primary Education. **g**-Secretary General of the Workers and Farmers Federation of the South of Sinaloa. **h**-None. **j**-None. **k**-None. **l**-C de D, 1970–72, 121; *Directorio*, 1970–72.

Jimenez (Delgado), Ramon

a-Dec. 21, 1895. **b**-San Luis Potosi, San Luis Potosi, *East Central*, *Urban*. **c**-Educated at the Model School of San Luis Potosi; no degree. **d**-*Interim Governor of San Luis Potosi*, 1941–43. **e**-None. **f**-Head of the Federal Judicial Police for the Office of the Attorney General of Mexico, 1965. **g**-None. **h**-None. **j**-Career army officer; supported the Federal Government against the Cristero Revolt, 1927; Commander of the 4th Army Regiment (Cavalry); Director of the Military Hospital, Mexico, D.F.; Commander of the 15th Military Zone, Guadalajara, Jalisco, 1946; Commander of the 17th Military Zone, Queretaro, Queretaro, 1952–55; rank of Brigadier General, Aug. 1, 1942. **k**-None. **l**-HA, 7 May 1943,

12; DPE65, 210; Peral, 415; DGF56, 202; NYT, 20 Aug., 1941; Casasola, V.

Jimenez de Palacios, Aurora

a-1922. **b**-Tecuala, Nayarit, *West*, *Rural*. **c**-Early education unknown; economics degree from the School of Economics, University of Guadalajara, 1941–46; graduated in 1947 with a thesis on ''Social Welfare in Mexico.'' **d**-*Federal Deputy* from Baja California del Norte, Dist. 2, 1952–55. **e**-None. **f**-None. **g**-None. **j**-None. **k**-First female federal deputy in Mexico. **l**-ENE, 118; C de D, 1952–55.

Jimenez Lazcano, Mauro

a-July 10, 1942. **b**-Federal District, *Federal District*, *Urban*. **c**-Economics degree from the National School of Economics, UNAM, thesis on ''Principal Obstacles to Economic Integration of Latin America''; Assistant Professor of Economic Problems of Latin America, National School of Economics, UNAM; Professor, Graduate Program in Economics, Colegio de Mexico, 1977; Professor of Planning and Development, National School of Economics, 1967–68. **d**-None. **e**-None. **f**-Director of Information and Public Relations for the President of Mexico, 1970–76; *Subsecretary of the Presidency*, February 26, 1976–November 30, 1976. **g**-None. **h**-Reporter for *El Mexicano*, attached to the Presidency, 1961–63; reporter on political affairs for the newspaper *La Prensa*, 1964–69. **j**-None. **k**-Press assistant for *Luis Echeverria* during his campaign for President, 1969–70. **l**-HA, 14 Dec. 1970, 23; DPE71, 124; *Excelsior*, 27 Feb. 1976, 4; HA, 8 Mar. 1976, 6.

Jimenez O'Farrell, Federico

(Deceased)
a-Dec. 20, 1890. **b**-Chalchicomulca, Puebla, *East Central*, *Rural*. **c**-Law degree; graduate studies at UNAM; Professor of Civics, Common Law, and Political Economy, Puebla. **d**-None. **e**-None. **f**-Career Foreign Service Officer; Director of the Federal Office of the Treasury, Puebla; Librarian, UNAM; private secretary to the Secretary of Foreign Relations, 1919; Charge d'Affaires, San Jose, Costa Rica, and Managua, Nicaragua, 1921; *Ambassador to Great Britain*, 1945–51; *Ambassador to France*, 1951–54. **g**-Member of the Agrarian Commission of Puebla. **i**-Brother Alberto served as a military surgeon during the Revolution. **k**-None. **l**-DGF51, I, 105; Novo35, 37; STYRBIWW54, 817; Peral, 418; DP70, 1122.

Jimenez Rueda, Julio

(Deceased June 25, 1960)
a-Apr. 10, 1896. **b**-Federal District, *Federal District*, *Urban*. **c**-Preparatory studies from the National

Preparatory School; law degree, National School of Law, UNAM, 1919; Ph.D. in letters, School of Philosophy and Letters, UNAM, 1935; Dean of the School of Philosophy and Letters, UNAM; 1942–44, 1953–54; Professor Emeritus, School of Philosophy and Letters, UNAM; Dean of the National School of Archeology, UNAM; Director of Summer School, UNAM, 1928–32; Secretary General of UNAM, 1932–33; *Secretary General of UNAM*, 1944. **e-**None. **f-**Secretary of the Mexican Delegation to Buenos Aires, 1921–22; Secretary of the Mexican Delegation to Montevideo, 1920; Director of the School of Theatrical Arts, Secretariat of Public Education, 1917–20; Director of the National Archives, 1943–52. **g-**None. **h-**Director of *El Estudiantil*, 1913; Editor of the *Bulletin of Archeology*, 1943–52; Director of the Center for Mexican Writers, 1955–60; writer for many newspapers; novelist and dramatist. **i-**Student of poet Luis Urbina; married Guadalupe Ortiz de Montellano, sister of poet Bernardo Ortiz de Montellano; son Bernardo Jimenez Montellano was a successful poet and writer. **j-**None. **k-**None. **l-**DP70, 1122–23; WWM45, 60; DEM, 183–85; letter.

Jimenez Ruiz, Eliseo

a-Nov. 8, 1912. **b-**Xiacui, Ixtlan de Juarez, Oaxaca, *South*, *Rural*. **c-**Primary studies in Xiacui; secondary studies in Oaxaca; cadet at the National Military College, 1931–34, graduated as a 2nd Lieutenant; studies at the Applied Military School, 1937–38; graduated from the Superior War College as a Second Captain, 1942–45; instructor, Superior War College, 1947–48. **d-***Federal Deputy* from the State of Oaxaca, Dist. 2, 1964–67, member of the Indigenous Affairs Committee and the First National Defense Committee; *Senator* from the State of Oaxaca, 1976–77. **e-**None. **f-**Command Chief, Federal Highway Police; Subdirector and Director of Public Safety, State of Guerrero; Director of the Division of Traffic Inspection, Department of the Federal District; *Interim Governor of Oaxaca*, March 3, 1977–80. **g-**None. **h-**Worked as an agricultural laborer and miner in the Natividad Mine. **i-**Married Paz Migueles Navarro; brother Fidel was Director of Public Works, State of Oaxaca, 1978; daughter, Ana Maria Jimenez was a precandidate for Federal Deputy from Oaxaca, 1979. **j-**Career Army officer; 2nd Lieutenant, 28th Armed Battalion, 1935–36; commander, machine gun company, 48th Battalion, 1938–42; 2nd Captain, staff of a mechanized brigade; rank of 1st Captain, August 1, 1948; rank of Major in the Infantry, January 1, 1951; Commander, Light Mechanized Brigade, 1951–53; rank of Lt. Col., 1952; Chief of Staff, 18th Military Zone, 1960; Commander, 20th Infantry Battalion, Tapachula, Chiapas, 1961–63; Military Attache to Guatemala and Honduras,

1968–71; rank of Brigadier General, July 1, 1970; Chief of Staff, 7th Military Zone, Monterrey, Nuevo Leon, 1971–72; Commander of the 35th Military Zone, Chilpancingo, Guerrero, 1972–74; Commander of the 27th Military Zone, Acapulco, Guerrero, 1974–76; rank of Brigade General, 1974. **k-**Promoted to Brigadier General for helping to rescue the Guatemalan Foreign Secretary from kidnappers; according to government sources, he commanded the forces who rescued *Ruben Figueroa* from *Lucio Cabanas*, 1974, but critics claim the government paid the ransom without a military rescue. **l-**HA, 14 Mar. 1977, 22; C de D, 1964–67, 79, 81; Enc. Mex., Annual, 1977, 548; *Excelsior*, 11 Aug. 1978, 4; *Excelsior*, 10 Nov. 1978, 12.

Jimenez Segura, Javier

a-Nov. 13, 1905. **b-**Federal District, *Federal District*, *Urban*. **c-**Primary and secondary studies in the public schools of Mexico City; enrolled at the National Military College, February 10, 1920, graduating as an artillery lieutenant, December 21, 1924, and as a military industrial engineer, October 1, 1925; professor at IPN. **d-**None. **f-**Chief, Proving Section, Mexican Air Force; Chief, Mechanical Laboratories, Military Industry; Director of the Army Cartridge Factory; Inspector of Army Warehouses and Parks; Oficial Mayor of Military Industry; Secretary General of Military Industry, 1966–71; Director General of War Materiels, Secretariat of National Defense, 1971–73; Director General of Military Industry, July 16, 1973–76; 1976– . **g-**President of the National Military College Association; President of the College of Military Engineers. **h-**None. **j-**Career Army officer; rank of 2nd Captain, August 1, 1936; officer, 3rd Artillery Regiment; officer, artillery battery, National Military College; rank of Captain, August 16, 1941; rank of Major, March 16, 1944; rank of Lt. Colonel, September 16, 1946; rank of Colonel, November 20, 1950; rank of Brigadier General, November 20, 1953; rank of Brigade General, November 20, 1965; rank of Divisionary General, November 20, 1972. **k-**None. **l-**El Dia, 1 Dec. 1976, 10; DGF56, 529.

Jofre Vazquez, Sacramento

a-May 12, 1910. **b-**San Francisco Cuautlacingo, Puebla, *East Central*, *Rural*. **c-**Primary and secondary studies in Ciudad Serdan; no degree. **d-**Local Deputy to the State Legislature of Puebla; *Alternate Federal Deputy* from the State of Puebla, Dist. 8, 1937–40; *Federal Deputy* from the Federal District, Dist. 11, 1943–46; *Federal Deputy* from the State of Puebla, Dist. 5, 1976–79, member of the Social Action Committee, the National Defense Committee, the Chontalpa Southeast Zone Section of the Regional Development Committee, the Disaster Zone

Section of the Regional Development Committee, the National Properties Committee and the Committee for Civic Programs and Special Acts. **e-***Secretary of Agrarian Action of the CEN of the PRM*, 1940. **f-**None. **g-**Ejido organizer in Puebla, 1922; founder of the Union of Agrarian Communities of Ciudad Serdan, Puebla; cofounder of the CNC; Secretary General of the Old Guard Agraristas. **h-**Worked as a peasant and small businessman. **i-**Father was a peasant and ejido organizer. **j-**None. **k-**The government initiated criminal charges against him and *Carlos Madrazo*as an attack on the left, 1944. **l-**D de C, 1976–79, 4, 10, 36, 37, 63, 67; *Excelsior*, 22 Aug. 1976, 29; C de D, 1937–40; C de D, 1943–46. Medina, 20, 19; *Excelsior*, 4 June 1979, 22.

Jonguitud Barrios, Carlos
b-Coxcatlan, San Luis Potosi, *East Central*, *Rural*. **c-**Teaching certificate, Normal Rural School, Teneria, Mexico; preparatory studies at the National Preparatory School; studies in law at the National School of Law, UNAM; no degree; primary school teacher; civics teacher, Toluca, Mexico; history teacher, secondary schools and the prevocational school of IPN; professor of law at the Technological Institute of Mexico. **d-***Alternate Federal Deputy* from the Federal District, Dist. 14, 1967–70; *Senator* from the State of San Luis Potosi, 1976–77; *Governor of San Luis Potosi*, 1979– . **e-***Secretary of Organization of the CEN of PRI*, 1970; *Secretary of Social Action of the CEN of PRI*, 1976. **f-***Director General of the ISSSTE*, 1976–78. **g-**Student leader in the Normal Rural School, Teneria, Mexico; representative of the Normal Rural School of Ozuluoma to the National Congress of the Federation of Socialist Students; Secretary General of the Federation of University Students at UNAM; president of the Society of Students at the National Preparatory School; Auxiliary Secretary of the Secretary of Organization of the SNTE; Secretary of Press and Publicity, Section IX, SNTE; Private Secretary to *Manuel Sanchez Vite*, 1952–55; Secretary of Labor and Conflicts, Section XV, SNTE; Secretary General of the Thirty-first Delegation of Section IX, SNTE; Auxiliary Secretary of Labor and Conflicts of the CEN of the SNTE; Director General of Publishing of the CEN of the SNTE; President of the Congress of Labor. **h-**None. **i-**Political disciple of *Manuel Sanchez Vite*. **j-**None. **k-**Reputedly remained with *Luis Echeverria*when he and his mentor *Manuel Sanchez Vite*split politically. **l-***Excelsior*, 21 Dec. 1978, 29; *Excelsior*, 15 July 1977, 6, 8; LA, 15 Dec. 1978, 388.

Joublanc Rivas, Luciano
(Deceased 1959)
a-1896. **b-**Federal District, *Federal District*, *Urban*. **c-**Early education unknown; no degree. **d-**None.

e-None. **f-**Career Foreign Service officer; joined the Foreign Service, 1923; Ambassador to Portugal, 1940; Ambassador to Poland, 1944–46; *Ambassador to the Soviet Union*, 1946–48. **g-**None. **h-**Author of many works; founder and Director of *El Fifi*, San Luis Potosi; wrote for *El Universal Illustrado*. **j-**None. **k-**None. **l-**Q es Q, 302; letter.

Juarez Carro, Vicente
a-June 24, 1924. **b-**Panotla, Tlaxcala, *East Central*, *Rural*. **c-**Primary and secondary studies in Puebla; preparatory studies from the National Preparatory School; law degree, National School of Law, UNAM. **d-***Senator* from the State of Tlaxcala, 1970–76, member of the Gran Comision, President of the Military Justice Committee and the National Lands Committee, Second Secretary of the First Justice Committee and member of the Fourth Section of the Legislative Studies Committee. **e-**Joined the PRM, 1950; Director of the CEPES of PRI in Tlaxcala, 1962–64; Director of the magazine *Justicia Social* of PRI, 1956–57; President of the Assembly of the National Council of PRI, 1957. **f-**Public Defender, 1954–56; Judge of the Mixed Court of Appeals, Tlaxcala, 1957; Public Defender, Federal Jurisdiction, Tlaxcala, 1957–59; Consulting Lawyer, City Council of Tlaxcala, 1958–61. **g-**Secretary General of the College of Lawyers of Tlaxcala; Secretary General of CNOP in Tlaxcala, 1957; delegate of CNOP, 1957. **h-**Employee of the Secretariat of the Treasury, 1946–53. **j-**None. **k-**None. **l-**C de S, 1970–76, 77; PS, 3155.

Junco, Alfonso
a-Feb. 25, 1896. **b-**Monterrey, Nuevo Leon, *North*, *Urban*. **c-**Secondary studies at the Institute of the Sacred Heart; no degree. **d-**None. **e-**Co-founder of PAN, 1939. **f-**None. **g-**None. **h-**Weekly contributor to *El Universal*, 1928; weekly contributor to *Excelsior*, 1926–28; poet and author of numerous works. **i-**Son of Celedonio Junco de la Vega, noted poet and playwright; brother Humberto was Mayor of Garza Garcia, Nuevo Leon, 1964–66; married Mercedes Palacio. **j-**None. **k-**Candidate of PAN for federal deputy numerous times. **l-**Lemus, 38; Lopez, 563; WWM45, 61.

Kuri Brena, Daniel
c-Preparatory studies at the National Preparatory School; law degree, National School of Law, UNAM; Professor of the Philosophy of Law, National School of Law, UNAM. **d-**None. **e-**Member of the CEN of PAN, 1939–49. **f-**None. **g-**President of the National Federation of Students, 1934–35; cofounder of the National Federation of Catholic Students of Mexico, 1926. **h-**Manager of the Industrial

Bank, 1948– ; author of many books and contemporary Catholic philosopher. **i-**Catholic student leader with *Manuel Ulloa Ortiz* and *Carlos Septien Garcia*, co-members of the CEN of PAN, 1939. **j-**None. **k-**None. **l-**Lopez, 569; Mabry, 21.

Labastida (Munoz), Horacio

a-1918. **b-**Puebla, Puebla, *East Central*, *Urban*. **c-**Early education unknown; law degree from the University of Puebla, 1942; special studies at the School of Philosophy and Letters, UNAM, 1952–54; graduate studies at the University of California, Berkeley, 1963; Director of the Preparatory School, University of Puebla, 1945; Rector, University of Puebla, 1946–50; adviser to the Rector of UNAM, 1951; founding Professor of the History of Sociology, School of Political and Social Sciences, UNAM, 1954. **d-***Federal Deputy* from the State of Puebla, Dist. 9, 1973–76; *Senator* from the State of Puebla, 1976– . **e-***Director of the IEPES of the CEN of PRI*, 1972–75. **f-**Director of Cultural Diffusion, *Universidad de Mexico*, UNAM, 1952; Director of Scholarly Services, UNAM, 1953; Director of Social Services, UNAM, 1954; Secretary, District Court, Puebla; local judge, Puebla; Judge of the Superior Tribunal of Justice of the State of Puebla; Director of Information, Secretariat of Public Works, 1959–63; Director of Information, Secretariat of Communications, 1966–70; Ambassador to Nicaragua, 1979– . **g-**None. **h-**None. **i-**Son of Roberto Labastida Meza, lawyer and Interim Governor of Puebla, 1921–22. **j-**None. **k-**None. **l-**HA, 5 Mar. 1979, I; Enc. Mex., 7, 568; DPE, 1961, 86; DPE, 1965, 110.

Labra (Garcia), Wenceslao

a-Sept. 28, 1895. **b-**Zumpango, Mexico, *West Central*, *Rural*. **c-**Attended the Military Preparatory Academy, graduate of the National Military Academy as a 2nd lieutenant of cavalry, March 10, 1913. **d-**Local deputy to the State Legislature of Mexico; Federal Deputy from the State of Mexico, 1926–28, 1928–30, 1930–32, 1932–34; *Senator* from Mexico, 1934–37; *Governor of Mexico*, 1937–41. **e-***Secretary of Organization and Statistics of the CEN of PRI*, 1936–37. **f-**Director of the National Lottery. **g-**One of the founders of the National Farmers Federation, 1938; considered as a candidate for Secretary General of the CNC, 1941. **i-**Relative, *Armando Labra Manjarez*, was a federal deputy, 1976–79. **j-**Joined the Revolution; 2nd lieutenant of the Cavalry, 27th Irregular Regiment, 1913; rank of Colonel, 1940. **k-**Brandenburg considered *Labra* in the Inner Circle status as Governor of Mexico; supported *Miguel Henriquez Guzman* for president, 1951. **l-**Brandenburg, 80; Peral, 426–27; *Hoy*, 21 Dec. 1940, 64–65; *Hoy*, 13 Jan. 1940, 8–9, 60–61; Gonzalez Navarro, 168.

Lajous Martinez, Adrian

a-1920. **b-**Buenos Aires, Argentina, *Foreign*, *Urban*. **c-**Early education unknown; degree. **d-**None. **e-**None. **f-**Counselor, Mexican Embassy, Washington, D.C.; Executive Director, World Bank, Washington, D.C.; Director, Fund for Industrial Development, 1974–76; Director General of the Mexican Institute of Foreign Trade, 1976–79; *Director General of the National Bank of Foreign Trade*, 1979– . **g-**Manager, Inter-American Cotton Federation; President, International Sugar Council. **h-**Manager, Radio Programs of Mexico, S.A. **i-**Father a successful Ford car dealer of French birth. **j-**None. **k-**None. **l-**Letter.

Lamadrid (Sauza), Jose Luis

a-Feb., 1931. **b-**Guadalajara, Jalisco, *West*, *Urban*. **c-**Preparatory studies in Guadalajara; law degree from the University of Guadalajara; professor at the Preparatory School of Guadalajara; professor at the School of Law, Philosophy, and Liberal Arts, University of Guadalajara. **d-***Federal Deputy* from the State of Jalisco, Dist. 1, 1961–63, member of the Legislative Studies Committee (First Section on Constitutional Affairs), the First Treasury Committee, and the First Justice Committee; *Federal Deputy* from the State of Jalisco, Dist. 11, 1973–76. **e-***Secretary of Press and Publicity of the CEN of PRI*, 1964; *Secretary of Social Action of the CEN of PRI*, 1973–75; representative of PRI on the Federal Electoral Commission, 1975–76. **f-**Oficial Mayor of the Department of Education, State of Jalisco; *Oficial Mayor of the Secretariat of Government*, 1976–78; *Subsecretary of Government*, August 14, 1978 to May 24, 1979. **g-**President of the Federation of University Students of Guadalajara. **j-**None. **k-**None. **l-**HA, 21 Dec. 1964; C de D, 1961–63; 81; *Excelsior*, 13 July 1973, 4; C de D, 19, 73–76, 13; HA, 13 Oct. 1975, 17.

Lameiras Olvera, Esteban

a-1947. **b-**Federal District, *Federal District*, *Urban*. **c-**Early education unknown; studies at the School of Philosophy and Letters, UNAM, but left because of the 1968 student strike; studies in communication; Professor of Communication, College of Sciences and Humanities, Ibero-American University. **d-**None. **e-**Member of the PST since its founding; member of the Central Committee and the Executive Committee of the PST, 1975–76. **f-**None. **g-**None. **j-**None. **k-**Candidate of the PST for Federal Deputy from Dist. 18, State of Mexico, 1979. **l-**HA, 14 May 1979, VIII.

Landeros Gallegos, Rodolfo

a-1931. **b-**Calvillo, Aguascalientes, *West*, *Rural*. **c-**Early education unknown; no degree. **d-***Senator* from the State of Aguascalientes, 1976–80; *Governor of Aguascalienes*, 1980– . **e-**Director of Press for *Jose Lopez Portillo's* campaign for president, 1976; *Secretary of Press and Publicity, of the CEN of PRI*, 1978–80. **f-**Employee, Press Department, Secretariat of Agriculture; employee, Press Department, Secretariat of Industry and Commerce; Director of Public Relations, Secretariat of the Treasury, 1958–76; Acting Director of Information, President of Mexico, 1976–77; Advisor on Special Affairs, President *Jose Lopez Portillo*, 1977. **g-**None. **h-**Journalist; editor of *El Sol del Centro*, Aguascalientes. **j-**None. **k-**None. **l-***Excelsior*, 21 Mar. 1980, 18; *Excelsior*, 17 Dec. 1979, 19; Hoy, 12 Nov. 1977, 11; HA, 31 Mar. 1980, 26; C de S, 1976–82; DPE61; DPE65; MGF69.

Landerreche Obregon, Juan

a-Nov. 1, 1914. **b-**Federal District, *Federal District, Urban*. **c-**Secondary and preparatory studies at the Colegio Frances Morelos; law degree with honorable mention, National School of Law, UNAM, May 6, 1936, with his thesis on "Constitutional Theory and Real Estate"; LLD, with an honorable mention, June 24, 1955, with a thesis on "The Participation of Workers in Business Utilities." **d-***Federal Deputy* from the Federal District, Dist. 8, 1964–67, member of the Committee on Money and Credit Institutions; *Federal Deputy* from PAN (party deputy), 1970–73, member of the First Section of the Legislative Studies Committee, the Second Government Committee, the Second Constitutional Affairs Committee, and the Tourism Committee. **e-**Candidate for Federal Deputy from PAN four times before winning in 1964; founding member of PAN, 1939; member of the Legislative Studies Committee of PAN; member of the National Committee of PAN, 1975; Secretary of Policy of the National Executive Committee of PAN, 1975. **f-**None. **g-**Active in the 1933 student movement; Director of the National Catholic Student Union. **h-**Co-founder of Jus, a law and social science review; Director of Jus, 1941–57. **i-**Married Gabriela Gomez Morin, daughter of *Manuel Gomez Morin*; Catholic student leader with *Manuel Ulloa Ortiz*. **j-**None. **k-**None. **l-**Mabry; C de D, 1970–72, 121; C de D, 1967–69, 90.

Lang Islas, Jorge

a-Nov. 6, 1904. **b-**Texcoco, Mexico, *West Central, Rural*. **c-**Primary studies in Texcoco, Mexico; secondary studies at the Melchor Ocampo Center, Pachuca, Hidalgo; completed secondary studies at the Scientific and Literary Institute of Pachuca; graduated from the Naval Military College, as a coastguardsman, November 26, 1924; studied submarine warfare in Chile, 1938–40; advanced studies in engineering in Mexico; professor at the Naval College (4 years); Subdirector and Director of the Naval College of the Gulf, Veracruz, 1947. **d-***Federal Deputy* from the State of Colima, Dist. 2, 1958–61, member of the Fish and Game Committee, the Second Committee on National Defense, and the Naval Committee. **e-**None. **f-**Commanding General of the Fleet, Secretariat of the Navy, 1964–65. **g-**None. **h-**None. **j-**Career naval officer; rank of Corvette Lieutenant, 1927; Commander of the Coast Guard Cutter "28," 1940–41; Commander of the Destroyer "Guanajuato," 1941–42; Commander of the 1st Naval Zone, Tampico, Tamaulipas, 1951; Commander of the 6th Naval Zone, Manzanillo, Colima, 1955–58; Commander of the Attack Force, 1958; rank of Vice Admiral. **k-**None. **l-**HA, 21 Dec. 1964, 9–10; DGF51, I, 388; DPE65, 51; DGF56, 386; DGF47, 230; Func., 149.

Lanz Duret, Fernando

a-Jan. 19, 1916. **b-**Campeche, Campeche, *Gulf, Urban*. **c-**Preparatory studies at the National Preparatory School, Mexico, D.F.; law degree from the National School of Law, UNAM, 1940, with a thesis on the general subject of law. **d-***Federal Deputy* from the State of Campeche, Dist. 1, 1952–55, member of the Permanent Committee, 1952, Vice President, Dec. 1952, member of the Second Constitutional Affairs Committee, the Second Instructive Section of the Grand Jury, and the Second Balloting Committee; *Senator* from the State of Campeche, 1958–64, member of the Foreign and Domestic Trade Committee, the Second Constitutional Affairs Committee, the Second Foreign Relations Committee, and the Special Legislative Studies Committee; President of the First Credit, Money, and Credit Institutions Committee. **e-**Member of the Program Committee of the PRI; PRI delegate to Guanajuato, 1955. **f-**Director General of the Department of Legal Affairs, Secretariat of Health, 1964–71. **g-**Member of the University Council, UNAM; President of the Student Association, UNAM. **h-**Newspaperman, 1941; writer for *El Universal*; war correspondent in England, 1942–45; correspondent on European Reconstruction, 1945–46. **i-**Father and grandfather well-known lawyers; classmate of *Rafael Moreno Valle* at the National Preparatory School. **j-**None. **k-**None. **l-**Func., 132; DPE71, 116; C de D, 1952–54, 60, 58, 52, 53, 51, 50; C de S, 1961–64, 58; DPE65, 163.

Lanz Galera, Joaquin

(Deceased 1965)
a-1884. **b-**Campeche, Campeche, *Gulf, Urban*. **c-**Primary and secondary studies in Campeche; law degree, School of Law, University of Campeche. **d-**Deputy from the State of Campeche to the Constitutional Convention, 1916–17; Federal Deputy

from the State of Campeche, 1918–20; Senator from the State of Campeche, e-None. f-Secretary, local court of Campeche; Judge, First Circuit Court District, Federal District; Judge, District Court, Queretaro, Queretaro, 1951; Judge, Second Circuit Court District, Puebla, Puebla, 1956; Justice of the Superior Tribunal of Justice of the Federal District and Federal Territories, g-None. h-None. j-None. k-None. l-DP70, 1157; DGF51, I, 594; DGF56, 585.

Lara (Ramo), Cesar Agusto
(Deceased Jan. 10, 1962)
a-Nov. 24, 1896. b-Pichucalco, Chiapas, *South*, *Rural*. c-Primary studies in Pichucalco and in the Liceo of Chiapas, San Cristobal de las Casas. d-Mayor of Tuxtla Gutierrez, Chiapas, 1926–27; Federal Deputy from the State of Chiapas, 1918–20; Mayor of Arriaga, Chiapas; *Interim Governor of Chiapas*, 1947–48. e-None. f-Assistant Chief of Police, Federal District, 1938–40; Director, Department of Press and Tourism, State of Chiapas. g-None. h-Journalist and poet. j-Joined the Maderistas as a student under Col. Ignacio Gutierrez, 1910; fought against Pascual Orozco; reached rank of Brigadier General, 1924. k-Simpson credits him with ending pistolerismo in Chiapas. l-Simpson, 342; letter; Peral, 431; DBC, 132.

Lavalle Urbina, Eduardo J.
a-1910. b-Campeche, Campeche, *Gulf, Urban*. c-Secondary education at the Campeche Institute, Campeche; law degree, Dec. 24, 1934. d-Mayor of Campeche; *Governor of Campeche*, 1944–49. e-President of the Regional Committee of the PNR in Campeche. f-Agent of the Ministerio Publico of the Office of the Attorney General (in civil affairs), Campeche; Secretary of the Campeche Board of Conciliation and Arbitration; Judge of the Superior Tribunal of Justice of the State of Campeche; Attorney General of Campeche. g-None. i-Brother of *Maria Lavalle Urbina*; father a lawyer. j-None. k-Elected governor as the candidate of the Popular Electoral Front of Campeche. l-HA, 7 Oct. 1949, xxviii; Peral, 436.

Lavalle Urbina, Maria
a-1908. b-Campeche, Campeche, *Gulf, Urban*. c-Primary studies in Campeche; secondary studies in Campeche; teaching certificate from the Normal School of Campeche, 1927; law degree, School of Law, Campeche Institute, 1944; Professor of the Science of Education, Normal School of Campeche; primary school director. d-*Senator* from the State of Campeche, 1964–70. e-Director of the National Feminine Organizations of the CEN of PRI, 1965–70. f-Director of the State Literacy Campaign, Campeche; Judge of the Tribunal Superior of Justice of the Federal District, 1947–54 (first woman appointed

to this position); Director of the Department of Social Welfare, Secretariat of Government, 1954–63; Director of the Civil Registry, 1970–73; *Subsecretary of Primary and Normal Education*, 1976– . g-President of the Mexican Women's Alliance. h-None. i-Helped *Rafael Murillo Vidal* defend squatters' rights to colonize in a section known as the 201st Squadron; sister of *Eduardo J. Lavalle Urbina*; father a lawyer. j-None. k-First woman senator from Campeche. l-DPE61; DGF51, I, 487; Q es Q, 318; C de S, 1964–70; DGF56, 84; HA, 3 Feb. 1975, 9; Enc. Mex., VIII, 1977, 2; HA, 31 Oct. 1977, 8.

Lazo (Barreiro), Jr., Carlos
(Deceased Nov, 5, 1955)
a-Aug. 19, 1914. b-Federal District, *Federal District, Urban*. c-Primary studies at the San Borja Institute, Mexico, D.F.; secondary and preparatory studies at the Colegio Frances Morelos; architecture degree from the National School of Architecture, UNAM, 1934–39, with a thesis on "Planning and Rural Architecture in Mexico;" studied planning in the United States, 1940–42, on a scholarship from the United States Department of Defense; studied Planning in Canada, 1942–43; Professor of Drawing, Instituto Bachillerato, 1934; professor at the School of Architecture, UNAM; professor at the National Polytechnic Institute. d-None. e-Contributor to *Miguel Aleman*'s program of government during the 1945 presidential campaign. f-Adviser to the President of Mexico, 1949; *Oficial Mayor of the Secretariat of National Patrimony*, 1947, under *Alfonso Caso*; representative of the Secretariat of the Treasury to the Planning Commission for the Federal District, 1948; President of the Technical Architectural Commission, Secretariat of National Patrimony, 1947; President of the Federal Commission for Planning, Secretariat of National Planning, 1947; Director General of the University City, 1950; *Secretary of Public Works*, 1952–55. g-None. h-Representative of the Society of Architects to the Congress of Social Assistance, 1938; architectural adviser to Catholic Action, 1937; professional architect for the University City Project, Mexico, D.F., 1949–50; Co-director for the Congress for the Promotion of Popular Dwellings, 1946; author of several studies on planning; Co-director of the magazine, *Construction Review*. i-Son of an architect and former director of the School of Architecture, UNAM; married Yolanda Margain. j-None. k-Winner of many architecture prizes; died in an aviation accident. l-WWM45, 63; STYRBIWW54, 848, 1113; DGF47, 269; HA, 5 Dec. 1952, 9; DP70, 1165; Lopez, 583; Enc. Mex., VIII, 1977, 5.

Lazos, Efrain
a-1906. b-Tuxtla, Gutierrez, *South, Urban*. c-Early education unknown; law degree, National School of

Law, UNAM, 1930. **d-**Mayor of Tapachula, Chiapas; *Senator* from the State of Chiapas, 1946–52, member of the Legislative Studies Committee, the Public Welfare Committee and the Gran Comision. **e-**None. **f-**Civil judge, Tapachula; Justice of the Superior Tribunal of Justice of Chiapas. **g-**None. **i-**Co-student with *Miguel Aleman* at UNAM. **j-**None. **k-**None. **l-**DGF51, I, 5, 9–11; PS, 3229.

Lecona Soto, Noe
(Deceased 1945)
a-Dec. 6, 1903. **b-**Huachinango, Zacatlan, Puebla, *East Central*, *Rural*. **c-**Law degree from the National School of Law, UNAM. **d-**Local deputy to the 31st Legislature of the State of Puebla; *Senator* from the State of Puebla, 1940–45. **e-**None. **f-**Agent of the Ministerio Publico of the Office of the Attorney General for the Federal District; Secretary of the Mixed Agrarian Commission, Veracruz; head of the Legal Department of the Office of Public Works for the State of Puebla; Judge of the Civil Division in the State of Puebla; Secretary General of Government of the State of Puebla under Governor *Maximino Avila Camacho*, 1937–40. **g-**None. **h-**Author of a book on agrarian legislation, 1932. **j-**None. **k-**None. **l-**EBW46, 103; DP70, I, 1166; C de S, 1940–46; Peral, 438.

Leff Zimmerman, Gloria
a-Jan. 13, 1949. **b-**Federal District, *Federal District*, *Urban*. **c-**Early education unknown; sociology degree, School of Political and Social Sciences, UNAM; MA from the Colegio de Mexico; Ph.D. in the social sciences, Colegio de Mexico; Professor and Coordinator of the Sociology Curriculum, Autonomous University of Mexico in Unidad Azcapotzalco. **d-**None. **e-**Member of the Executive Committee of the PST. **f-**None. **g-**Director of the Intellectual Workers Front, 1979. **j-**None. **k-**Candidate for Federal Deputy from the PST for Round III, 1979. **l-**HA, 7 May 1979, VI.

Leipen Garay, Jorge
a-1937. **c-**Early education unknown; economics degree, National School of Economics, UNAM. **d-**None. **e-**None. **f-**Subdirector of the Mining Development Commission; Private Secretary to the Subsecretary of Nonrenewable Resources, Secretariat of Government Properties, *Manuel Franco Lopez*, 1965–66; Director General of ZINCAMEX, S.A., 1970–71; Director General of Foforitas Mexicanas, S.A., 1970–71; Director General of the Mining Development Commission, 1971–73; *Subsecretary of Nonrenewable Resources*, Secretariat of Government Properties, 1973–76, 1976–78; Director General of Siderurigca Lazaro Cardenas-Las Truchas, Altos Hornos de Mexico and the Compania Fundidadora de Fierro y Acero, 1978– . **g-**None.

h-Director General of Phibro de Mexico, S.A. **j-**None. **k-**None. **l-**HA, 12 Mar. 1973, 21; *Excelsior*, 29 Jan. 1978, 1.

Lenero (Ruiz), Agustin
a-Dec. 5, 1904. **b-**Villamar, Michoacan, *West Central*, *Rural*. **c-**Preparatory studies, University of Guadalajara; law degree, School of Law, University of Guadalajara; professor, School of Law, University of Michoacan; Dean, School of Law, University of Michoacan, 1927–30. **d-**Federal Deputy from the State of Michoacan, 1932–34. **e-**Director, Legal Department, PNR, 1930–31. **f-**Attorney General, State of Michoacan, 1927–28; President, Superior Court of Justice of the State of Michoacan, 1928–29; Secretary General of Government of the State of Michoacan under Governor *Lazaro Cardenas*, 1929–30; Director, Legal Department, Secretariat of Government, 1931–32; General Consul of Mexico to Paris, France, 1935–37; Ambassador to Czechslovakia, 1937–38; founder and Director, Legal Department, PEMEX, 1938–39; *Private Secretary* to President *Lazaro Cardenas*, 1939–40; Ambassador to Argentina, 1940–42; Ambassador to Sweden and Finland, 1958–62; Ambassador to Costa Rica, 1964–70. **g-**None. **h-**Author of various works. **i-**Close friend of *Damaso Cardenas*; collaborator of *Lazaro Cardenas* in numerous state and federal positions, 1927 to 1940; attended the University of Guadalajara with *Luis I. Rodriguez* and *Raul Castellano;* married Milagros Bores Bustamante; befriended *Alberto Bremauntz* early in his career. **j-**None. **k-**Supported General *Miguel Henriquez Guzman* for president, 1951–52. **l-**Enc. Mex., 8, 18; D de Y, 25 Jan. 1939, 1; DPE61, 21; Daniels, 76; Lopez, 588; WNM, 27–28; Cadena Z., 143.

Leon Bejarano, Armando
a-1916. **b-**Cuautla, Morelos, *West Central*, *Urban*. **c-**Early education unknown; graduated as a surgeon, National Medical School, UNAM, 1939; Professor of Clinical Medicine, Graduate School, National School of Medicine, UNAM, 1940–75; professor of special orthopedic courses, National School of Medicine, UNAM, 1940–75. **d-***Governor of Morelos*, 1976– . **e-**Joined PRM, 1940. **f-**Chief of Orthopedics and Traumatology, and Subdirector, Central Hospital, Secretariat of Communications and Transportation, 1946–61; Assistant Coordinator of Medical Services, Secretariat of Communications and Transportation, 1958–61; Chief of Orthopedic Services and Subdirector, Balbuena Hospital, Mexico City, 1961–63; Director of the Clinical Department of Traumatology Instruction, National Medical Center, 1963–70; Director of the Department of Regulation of Food and Drink, Secretariat of Health, 1975. **g-**Founder and President of the Mexican Orthopedic and Traumatology Association of the

IMSS. **h-**Author of many works. **j-**None. **k-**None. **l-**Enc. Mex., Annual, 1977, 546–47; *Excelsior*, 8 Feb. 1975, 21; HA, 19 Jan. 1976, 15.

Leon Brindis, Samuel

a-1896. **b-**Chiapas, *South*. **c-**Early education unknown; medical degree; professor, Institute of Arts and Sciences, Chiapas; Rector, Institute of Arts and Sciences, Chiapas. **d-***Governor of Chiapas*, 1958–64. **e-**None. **f-**Director of the Federal Office of Public Health, Chiapas, 1951–52. **g-**None. **h-**Practicing physician. **j-**None. **k-**Anderson suggests that he was very popular in Chiapas and was selected as the gubernatorial candidate in opposition to the national PRI choice. **l-**Anderson, 103; DGF51, 356; DBM, 375; Enc. Mex., 1977, III, 310.

Leon Murillo, Maximiliano **a-**Feb. 13, 1925.

b-Tecario, Michoacan, *West Central*, *Rural*. **c-**Primary studies at the Republic of Brazil Primary School, Mexico, D.F., 1935–40; secondary studies at the National School of Teachers, 1941–46; preparatory at the National Preparatory School, Mexico, D.F., 1953–54; teaching certificate in Mexican and World History, Higher Normal School, 1955–59; studied archaeology at the National School of Anthropology and History, 1960–65; primary and secondary school teacher, Federal District (25 years); professor at the National Preparatory School. **d-***Federal Deputy* from the PPS (party deputy), 1970–73, member of the Indigenous Affairs Committee, the First National Defense Committee, the Television Industry Committee, the Petroleum Committee, and the Second Labor Committee. **e-**Member of the PPS. **f-**None. **g-**Leader of the SNTE. **h-**None. **j-**None. **k-**None. **l-***Directorio*, 1970–72; C de D, 1970–72, 122.

Leon Orantes, Gloria

b-Tuxtla Gutierrez, Chiapas, *South, Urban*. **c-**Primary studies in Tuxtla Gutierrez, Chiapas; secondary studies in Secondary School No. 6, Mexico City; preparatory studies (first year) at the Scientific and Literary Institute of Mexico, Toluca, Mexico, and at the National Preparatory School; law degree, National School of Law, UNAM, July 18, 1940, with a thesis on the social and legal functions of the federal agent. **d-**None. **e-**None. **f-**Lawyer attached to the Consulting Department of the Attorney General's Office, 1940–41; investigating agent of the Ministerio Publico of the Attorney General of the Federal District, 1947; Agent of the Ministerio Publico, attached to the penal division of the Superior Tribunal of Justice of the Federal District, 1948–52; Agent of the Ministerio Publico, attached to the 8th and 9th Districts of the Third Penal Court and the 6th District of the Second Penal Court of Mexico City, 1952–53;

Judge, First Court of Appeals (mixed jurisdiction), Coyoacan, Federal District, 1953–54; Judge of the Superior Tribunal of Justice of the Federal District and Federal Territories, 1954–77; *Justice of the Supreme Court*, 1977– . **g-**None. **h-**Practicing lawyer, 1941–43. **i-**Daughter of Juan Jose Leon, a lawyer; widow of Engineer Francisco Pelaez. **j-**None. **k-**Second woman ever to be appointed to the Mexican Supreme Court. **l-**DBM70, 325; DBC, 137–38; DGF56, 513; MGF73, 111.

Leon (Uranga), Luis I.

a-July 4, 1890. **b-**Ciudad Juarez, Chihuahua, *North, Urban*. **c-**First five years of primary studies in Ciudad Juarez; last year of primary in a normal school, Mexico City; enrolled in the veterinary program at the National School of Agriculture; agricultural engineering degree, National School of Agriculture. **d-**Alternate Deputy to the Constitutional Convention, 1916–17; Federal Deputy from the State of Sonora, 1918–20; Federal Deputy from Chihuahua, 1920–22, 1922–24; Federal Deputy from the Federal District, 1924; *Senator* from the State of Chihuahua, 1964–70. **e-**Co-founder of the Mexican Civic Front for Revolutionary Affirmation, 1963. **f-**Director, Agricultural Department, State of Sonora, 1915–17; Subsecretary of the Treasury under Provisional President Adolfo de la Huerta, June 1, 1920 to December 1, 1920; Secretary of Agriculture, December 1, 1924 to November 30, 1928; Secretary of Industry and Commerce, February 5, 1928 to October 30, 1930; Interim Governor of Chihuahua, 1929–30; Executive Director, Northern Zone, National Colonization Commission, Secretariat of Agriculture, 1951. **g-**President of the local agrarian committee. **h-**Director of the Mexico City daily, *El Nacional*. **i-**Son of Marcelo Leon, a Juarista who fought the French at age 16 and reached the rank of Lt. Col. in the National Guard; later was director of customs in Ciudad Juarez and himself a federal deputy; mother, Dolores Uranga, was the granddaughter of a Juarista who was Mayor of Paso del Norte and a military commander. **j-**Supported General Obregon against Venustiano Carranza, 1919. **k-**In exile, 1935–40. **l-**Cadena Z.; Enc. Mex., 8, 50; Dulles; Uriostegui, 477ff; DGF51, I, 210.

Leonel Posasa, Marcos

a-Oct. 8, 1938. **b-**Tampico, Tamaulipas, *North, Urban*. **c-**Early education unknown; no degree. **d-**None. **e-**Joined the Mexican Communist Party, April, 1956; member of the Central Committee of the PCM, 1964–79; member of the Executive Committee of the PCM, 1979; Director of *Oposicion*, official newspaper of the PCM, 1973–78. **f-**None. **g-**Secretary General of the Mexican Communist

Youth, 1965–70. **h-**Electrician in the petroleum industry. **j-**None. **k-**None. **l-**HA, 19 Mar. 1979, X.

Leyva Mancilla, Baltasar R.
a-Jan. 6, 1896. **b-**Chilpancingo, Guerrero, *South*, *Urban*. **c-**Early education unknown; preparatory studies at the National Preparatory School; enrolled at the National Military College, 1912, left when it closed. **d-***Governor of Guerrero*, 1945–51; *Senator* from Guerrero, 1964–70. **e-**President of PRI in Guerrero. **f-***Oficial Mayor of the Secretariat of National Defense*, 1952–56. **g-**None. **h-**None. **i-**Married Fermina V. Pitagoras. **j-**Joined the Revolution in the Aquiles Serdan Brigade, Puebla; Chief of Staff of General Antonio Guerrero in Chihuahua; Commander of the Military Zones of Guanajuato, San Luis Potosi, and Tamaulipas; career army officer; rank of Brigadier General, Apr. 1, 1941. **k-**Accused of illegal landholdings by the Secretary General of the CNC of the State of Guerrero, 1972. **l-**DGF56, 199; letter; HA, 1 Nov. 1946; *Hoy*, 1 May 1971, 10; MGF69, 105; *Excelsior*, 29 Aug. 1972, 27; PS, 3281.

Leyva Velazquez, Gabriel
a-June 30, 1896. **b-**Los Humayes, Municipio San Ignacio, Sinaloa, *West*, *Rural*. **c-**Primary studies in Culiacan, Sinaloa; studied at normal school in Mexico, D.F., under a scholarship from President Madero; no degree. **d-***Federal Deputy* from the State of Sinaloa, Dist. 2, 1937–40; President of the Permanent Commission, Dec. 1940; Oficial Mayor of the Chamber of Deputies; *Senator* from the State of Sinaloa, 1940–46, president of the Administration Committee and the Department of Agrarian Affairs Committee; member of the Second Balloting Committee; *Governor of Sinaloa*, 1957–62; *Senator* from the State of Sinaloa, 1970–76, member of the Gran Comision, president of the First National Defense Committee, president of the Military Retirement and Pension Committee, executive secretary of the Livestock Committee and member of the Second Balloting Committee. **e-**President of the Congressional electoral commission for the 1940 presidential election; *President of the CEN of PRI*, 1952–56; member of the Political Action Committee of the New Advisory Commission of PRI, 1972. **f-***Provisional Governor of Sinaloa*, 1935–37. **g-***Secretary General of the National Farmers Federation*, 1942–47. **h-**Author of several books. **i-***Leyva* family were friends of the Maderos; Gabriel's father, a rural school teacher and court scribe in Culiacan, was a precursor of the Revolution and became the first martyr of the movement in Sinaloa, 1910; Gabriel's uncle, Jose Maria Leyva, also was a precursor of the Revolution, who was active in the Cananea mining strike in Sonora. **j-**Career army officer; commissioned by Francisco

Madero, 1911; joined the forces of General Obregon as a 2nd Lieutenant, 1914; rank of Colonel, 1927; rank of Brigadier General, Dec., 1934; reached the rank of Divisionary General. **k-**Brandenburg considers *Leyva Velazquez* to have been one of the strongest regional leaders in Mexico as Governor of Sinaloa; criticized by peasants who invaded his property in Sinaloa during the summer of 1972. **l-**WWM45, 63; letter; HA, 5 Nov. 1943, 35; Peral, 446–47; *Polemica*, Vol. 1, 1969, 74; McAlister, 223–24; Brandenburg, 108, 111, 151; EBW46, 200; HA, 10 July 1972, 10; *El Universal*, 1 July 1972; Morton, 77–78; Novo35, 235; Q es Q, 327; Lopez, 590; HA, June 1945; WNM, 129–30; C de S, 1970–76, 80; Enc. Mex., VIII, 1977, 67.

Liera B., Guillermo
a-Apr. 6, 1905. **b-**Ahome, Sinaloa, *West*, *Rural*. **c-**Agricultural engineering degree, College of Agriculture, Ciudad Juarez, Chihuahua. **d-**Federal Deputy from the State of Chihuahua, Dist. 2, 1934–37. **e-***Subsecretary of Political Action of the CEN of PRI*, 1962. **f-**Engineer, National Irrigation Commission; Director General of Agriculture, Secretariat of Agriculture; *Oficial Mayor*, *Secretariat of Agriculture*, 1940; *Subsecretary of Livestock*, *Secretariat of Agriculture*, 1940–46; Director, Department of Indigenous Affairs, 1946–49; Executive Secretary of the National Olive Commission, 1947–60. **g-**None. **j-**None. **k-**None. **l-**DGF51, II, 237; D de Y, 3 Dec. 1940, 1; DGF50, 163; Peral, 458; letter; HA, 26 Dec. 1952, 3; Maldonado, 92.

Liekens, Enrique
a-July 4, 1882. **b-**Juchitan, Oaxaca, *South*, *Rural*. **c-**Early education unknown; no degree. **d-**Federal Deputy from the State of Oaxaca, 1920–22; Dist. 2, 1930–32; Dist. 4, 1932–34. **e-**Member of the PNR. **f-**Employee, Department of Statistics, 1912; Assistant Consul General, San Francisco, California, 1920–21; Secretary of the Mexican Delegation to Rome, 1921–22; Assistant Consul General, Vienna, Austria, 1922–23; Assistant Consul General, Hamburg, Germany, 1923–24; Consul General, El Paso, Texas, 1927; *Director General of the ISSSTE*, 1935–40. **g-**None. **h-**Poet. **j-**Joined the Constitutional Army with a rank of major, 1914; fought, 1914–17; rejoined the army, 1920, with a rank of Lt. Colonel. **k-**None. **l-**Lopez, 601.

Limon Guzman, Jose
a-June 20, 1898. **b-**Amatlan de Canas, Nayarit, *West*, *Rural*. **c-**Primary studies; studied accounting; degree. **d-**Secretary of the City Council of Tepic, Nayarit; Secretary of the City Council of Ixtlan, Nayarit; *Senator* from the State of Nayarit, 1946–52, member of the Gran Comision, the Agricultural and

Livestock Committee, the Legislative Studies Committee, the Social Welfare Committee, the First Balloting Committee and the Special Committee on Tourist Affairs; *Governor of Nayarit*, 1952–56. **e-**Campaigner, presidential campaigns of *Lazaro Cardenas* and *Manuel Avila Camacho*; paymaster for the Secretary of Administrative Action of the PNR. **f-**Oficial Mayor of the Legislature of the State of Nayarit. **g-**None. **h-**Worked as a carpenter; scribe and later a small businessman. **i-***Excelsior* says he was the political disciple of *Gilberto Flores Munoz*, his gubernatorial predecessor. **j-**None. **k-**None. **l-**DGF51, I, 7, 9, 10, 11, 12–14; C de S, 1946–52; DGF56, 97; DGF47, 21; *Excelsior*, 21 Feb. 1975, 12.

Limon (Marques), Gilberto R.

a-Mar. 15, 1895. **b-**Alamos, Sonora, *North*, *Urban*. **c-**Secondary studies at the Colegio de Sonora; no degree. **d-**None. **e-**None. **f-***Subsecretary of National Defense*, 1945–46; *Secretary of National Defense*, 1946–52. **g-**None. **h-**None. **i-**Daughter Cristina married the son of *Fernando Casas Aleman*; married Maria Manlay. **j-**Career army officer; joined the Revolution under General Obregon as an enlisted man, member of the 10th Sonoran Battalion, Army of the North, 1914; fought against Francisco Villa, 1914–15; Chief of Staff, 1st Infantry Brigade under General Chavez, 1917; rank of Lt. Colonel, 1917; commander of the 44th line battalion; rank of Colonel, 1920; fought against the De la Huerta rebellion, 1923; rank of Brigadier General, 1924; head of the Presidential Guards, 1924–28; fought against the Escobar Rebellion, 1929; Director of the National Military College, 1931, 1942–46; head of the Department of Manufacturing Industries, 1932–34; Director of Military Education, Secretariat of National Defense, 1936–42; Brigade General, Oct. 11, 1927; rank of Divisionary General, Aug. 1, 1942; President of the National Unification of Revolutionary Veterans, 1979. **k-**None. **l-**WWM45, 63–64; Peral, 449; DGF51, I, 177; STYRBIWW54, 856; Lopez, 602; Enc. Mex., VIII, 1977, 96; *Excelsior*, 31 Mar. 1979, 10.

Livas Villarreal, Eduardo

a-Jan. 21, 1911. **b-**Monterrey, Nuevo Leon, *North*, *Urban*. **c-**Primary studies at Escuela Livas, Monterrey, 1918–23; secondary and preparatory studies from the Colegio Civil, Monterrey; law degree from the Escuela de Leyes, 1927–32, degree in 1933; one of the student members of an organization which founded the University of Nuevo Leon, 1933; member of the Board of Regents of the University of Nuevo Leon. **d-***Senator* from the State of Nuevo Leon, 1958–61; President of the Committee on Industries, President of the Second Instructive Section

for the Grand Jury; member of the Social Welfare Committee, the Social Security Committee, the Second Balloting Committee, the First Constitutional Affairs Committee, and substitute member of the Economics and Statistics Committee; *Governor of Nuevo Leon*, 1961–67. **e-**Director of the Council for Economic Planning in Nuevo Leon during the Presidential campaign of *Adolfo Lopez Mateos*, 1958. **f-**Agent of the Ministerio Publico of the Office of the Attorney General in Nuevo Leon, 1933–35; private secretary to the Governor of Nuevo Leon, General *Bonifacio Salinas Leal*, 1939–43; Secretary General of Government of the State of Nuevo Leon under Governor *Arturo B. de la Garza*, 1943; private secretary to the Governor of Nuevo Leon, *Luis Morones Prieto*, 1949. **g-**Member of the Cardenas Youth Group from Nuevo Leon, 1933. **h-**Practicing attorney, 1950–52; newspaperman, 1952; Director of *El Porvenir*, 1953–55. **i-**Son of Professor Pablo Livas, distinguished Nuevo Leon educator who operated the primary school which Eduardo attended; brother, Alfredo, director of bus lines in Nuevo Leon; brother, Enrique, a heart specialist, professor and former Rector of the University of Nuevo Leon; and brother, Juan, a businessman in Monterrey. **j-**None. **k-**Precandidate for Governor of Nuevo Leon, 1949. **l-**DBM68, 378; DBM70, 327; PdM, 221; C de S, 1961–64, 59; G of N1, 15; Func., 191; Enc. Mex. VIII, 1977, 123.

Llorente Gonzalez, Arturo

a-1920. **b-**Veracruz, Veracruz, *Gulf*, *Urban*. **c-**Primary studies in Veracruz; secondary and preparatory studies at the Escuela Civil, Veracruz; law degree from the National School of Law, UNAM, 1944, with a thesis on the rights of authors, artists, and writers; Rector of the University of Veracruz, 1946–50. **d-***Federal Deputy* from the State of Veracruz, Dist. 9, 1958–61, member of the Editorial Committee and the Gran Comision; President of the Legislative Studies Committee (first and second years); *Senator* from Veracruz, 1964–70; Mayor of Veracruz, 1953–55. **e-**None. **f-**Legal advisor to the Secretary of Public Works, 1943–46; legal advisor to the head of the Department of the Federal District, 1943–46; Director General of the Coordinating Division of the Boards of Civic, Moral, and Material Improvements, Secretariat of Government, 1955–56; *Oficial Mayor of the Federal District*, 1956–58; Director General of Professions, Secretariat of Public Education, 1961–64; *Subsecretary of Labor (A)*, 1970–76; Delegate of the Department of the Federal District to the Benito Juarez Delegation, 1976– . **g-**None. **h-**His law thesis was one of the first on that topic in Mexico and was published as a monograph. **i-**Student of *Alfonso Noriega* at the National Law School; married Bertha Lilia Martinez. **j-**None.

k-Precandidate for Governor of Veracruz, 1974; precandidate for federal deputy from Veracruz, 1976. l-DPE70-71, 119; WWMG, 22; DGF56, 89; HA, 14 Dec. 1970, 223; letter; Morton, 124; Func., 396; *Excelsior*, 13 Mar. 1973, 11; *Excelsior*, 8 Dec. 1975, 17; Enc. Mex., Annual, 1977, 575.

Loaeza, Enrique M.

a-May 10, 1944. c-Early education unknown; law degree, National School of Law, UNAM; MA degree in International Law, University of London; diploma in Air Space Law, London Institute of World Affairs. d-None. e-Advisor to presidential candidate, *Jose Lopez Portillo*, 1975–76. f-Auxiliary Secretary to the Subsecretary of the Presidency, *Jose Lopez Portillo*, 1970–71; Auxiliary Secretary to the Subsecretary of Government Properties, *Jose Lopez Portillo*, 1971–72; Auxiliary Secretary to the Director General of the Federal Electric Commission, *Jose Lopez Portillo*, 1973–75; Director General of Airports and Auxiliary Services, 1976– . g-None. h-None. i-Son of lawyer Enrique M. Loaeza, representative of Mexico to the International Civil Aviation Organization, 1951; distant nephew of *Jose Lopez Portillo*; sister married *Jose Lopez Portillo*'s son, 1980. j-None. k-None. l-HA, 23 Jan. 1978, 17; Smith, 301; DGF51, I, 111.

Loaiza, Rodolfo Tirado
(Deceased Feb. 20, 1944)
a-Dec. 18, 1894. b-San Javier, Sinaloa, *West*, *Rural*. c-Educated in the public schools of San Javier, Sinaloa; secondary education in Mazatlan, Sinaloa; no degree. d-Federal Deputy from the State of Sinaloa, 1934–36; *Senator* from the State of Sinaloa, 1936–40, member of the permanent committee, 1938; *Governor of Sinaloa*, 1940–44. e-*Treasurer of the CEN of PRI*, June 19, 1935. f-Assistant Chief of Staff of the Secretariat of National Defense, 1929–32; Chief of Staff of the Secretariat of National Defense, 1932–33. g-None. h-Author of several economic and social projects. i-From a very humble background; son was active in the 1929 student strike at UNAM. j-Joined the Revolution as a private, 1911; Paymaster General of the Army; reached the rank of Colonel. k-Assassinated at the Hotel Belmar, Mazatlan, Sinaloa. l-Peral, 451; D de S, 19 June 1935, 1; letter; EBW46, 145; DP70, 1196.

Lombardo de Gutierrez, Marcela
b-Federal District, *Federal District*, *Urban*. c-Primary teaching certificate; secondary teaching certificate; studies in French and French literature; studies at the National School of Economics, UNAM; studies in arts and sciences, McGill University; member of the governing board and General Coordinator of the Vicente Lombardo Toledano Center for Philosophical, Economic and Political Studies. d-*Federal Deputy* from the Federal District, Dist. 15, 1976–79. e-Founding member of the Popular Party, 1948. f-None. g-Founder of the Popular Youth. i-Daughter of *Vicente Lombardo Toledano*; married Raul Gutierrez. j-None. k-None. l-HA, 19 Mar. 1979, III; C de D, 1976–79, 40.

Lombardo Toledano, Vicente
(Deceased Nov. 19, 1968)
a-July 16, 1894. b-Teziutlan, Puebla, *East Central*, *Urban*. c-Primary education at the Liceo Teziuteco in Teziutlan; preparatory studies at the National Preparatory School in Mexico, D.F., 1911–15; law degree from the National School of Law, UNAM, 1919; Master of Arts, UNAM, 1919, with a thesis on public law and new philosophical currents; Ph.D., UNAM, 1933; professor at the National Preparatory School, 1922–23; founder and Director of the Gabino Barreda University, 1934; professor at the Gabino Barreda University, 1933–50; founder and Director of the Workers University of Mexico, 1936–68; Professor of Law at the National Law School, UNAM, 1918–33; Secretary of the School of Law, UNAM, 1919; Director of the National Preparatory School, 1922; founder and Director of the National Preparatory School Night Classes, 1923. d-Member of the City Council of the Federal District, 1924–25; Federal Deputy, 1926–28; *Federal Deputy* from the State of Puebla, Dist. 8, 1964–67, member of the Legislative Studies Committee (1st Section on Constitutional Affairs), and the Cultural Affairs Committee. e-Member of the Mexican Labor Party, 1921–32; leading organizer of the PRM, 1938; founder and *President of the Popular Party*, 1948–68, which later became the Popular Socialist Party, 1960. f-Chief Clerk of the Federal District, 1921; head of the Department of Libraries, Secretariat of Public Education, 1921; Interim Governor of Puebla, 1923. g-Alternate delegate of the Student University Federation to the First International Student Congress, 1921; member of the Regional Committee of the Revolutionary Federation of Mexican Workers, 1923–32; organizer and *Secretary General of the Federation of Mexican Workers*, 1936–40; organizer and President of the Latin American Federation of Workers, 1938–63; Secretary General of the Federation of Labor Unions of the Federal District, 1932; Secretary General of the Mexican Socialist League, 1944. h-Founder of many literary magazines and reviews; author of many articles. i-Son of a wealthy industrialist ruined by the Revolution; father was mayor of Teziutlan, and an alternate deputy, 1912; longtime friend of *Manuel Avila Camacho* and *Manuel Gomez Morin*; longtime friend of *Alejandro Carrillo*; friend of *Rafael de la Colina* at the National Preparatory School and at UNAM. j-None.

k-Expelled from the National University for his radical views, 1933; member of the ''Seven Wisemen'' generation of the National Preparatory School; had Inner Circle status 1934–38; presidential candidate on the Popular Party ticket, 1952. l-WWM45, 65; DP70, 1199; Peral, 453; NYT, 19 Nov. 1968, 40; *Annals*, Mar. 1940, 54; Padgett, 73–79; Millon, 199–203; Strode, 288–89, 324–25; IWW40, 686; DBM68, 380–81; Johnson, 83–84; Brandenburg, 82–85; Scott, 141–42, 190–91; letter; Kirk, 84–96; Enc. Mex., VIII, 1977, 128.

Lopez, Jose Dolores

a-Mar. 31, 1939. b-Fresnillo, Zacatecas, *East Central, Urban.* c-Early education unknown; no degree. d-None. e-Joined the PCM, 1958; Secretary General of the PCM for the State of Zacatecas, 1965–73; member of the Executive Committee of the PCM, 1979. f-None. g-Secretary of Union Action of the Independent Central of Agricultural Workers and Peasants (CIOAC), 1979. h-Worked as an agricultural laborer until he was 16. j-None. k-Imprisoned for political reasons, 1964, 1969, 1970. l-HA, 2 Apr. 1979, VII.

Lopez Arias, Fernando

(Deceased July 3, 1978)
a-Aug. 8, 1905. b-Zuchilapan, Coatzacoalcos, Veracruz, *Gulf, Rural.* c-Law degree, National School of Law, UNAM, 1929–34. d-Local deputy to the State of Veracruz, 1943–46; *Federal Deputy* from the State of Veracruz, Dist. 7, 1940–43, member of the First Justice Committee, the Second Balloting Committee, and the Library Committee (2nd year); *Senator* from Veracruz, 1946–52, member of the Gran Comision, the National Waters and Irrigation Committee, the Naval Committee, the First Committee on Constitutional Affairs, the Second Labor Committee, and the First Balloting Committee; *Governor of Veracruz*, 1962–68. e-Youth leader of PRI; *Secretary of Political Action of the CEN of PRI*, 1946–48. f-Agent of the Ministerio Publico of the Office of the Attorney General of Mexico in Coatzacoalcos, Veracruz; Judge in Coatzacoalcos; *Oficial Mayor of the Department of the Federal District*, 1952; *Oficial Mayor of the Secretariat of Government Properties*, 1952–53; *Subsecretary of Government Properties*, 1953; *Attorney General of Mexico*, 1958–62. g-Co-founder of CNOP; Secretary General of the Socialist Lawyers Front, 1938. h-Author of articles on Veracruz. i-Father, a peasant; married Carmen Bouzas; knew *Adolfo Lopez Mateos* at UNAM; son Fernando Lopez Valenzuela was interim president of PRI in the city of Veracruz. j-None. k-Student supporter, along with *Adolfo Lopez Mateos*, of Jose Vasconcelos for President, 1929. l-DGF47, 22; HA, 23 Jan. 1948, 15; D de Y, Dec. 2, 1958, 7; *El Universal*, 2 Dec. 1958, 8; HA, 8 Dec.

1958, 30; WWMG, 23; letter; DGF51, I, 8–10, 12–14; Func., 87; *Excelsior*, 4 July 1978, 4; *Excelsior*, 7 Feb. 1950, 1; *Excelsior*, 21 Apr. 1973, 1; *Excelsior*, 18 Jan. 1980, 1.

Lopez Avelar, Norberto

a-June 6, 1900. b-Totolapan, Morelos, *West Central, Rural.* c-Primary studies in the public schools of Totolapan and Mexico City; secondary in the army; no degree. d-*Federal Deputy* from the State of Morelos, Dist. 2, 1949–51, member of the Gran Comision and the Second Committee on National Defense; *Senator* from the State of Morelos, 1952–58, member of the Gran Comision, the Third Committee on National Defense, the War Materiels Committee, and the Electric Industry Committee; substitute member of the Military Health Committee; *Governor of Morelos*, 1958–64. e-*Secretary of Political Action of the CEN of PRI*, 1952. f-Inspector General of Police; Delegate of the government of Baja California del Norte to Ensenada and Tijuana; Oficial Mayor of the State of Baja California del Norte under *Rodolfo Sanchez Taboada*. g-None. h-Parents were peasants. j-Joined the Revolution; fought with the Constitutionalists; reached the rank of Colonel; assistant to *Rodolfo Sanchez Taboada*. k-Scott indicates that there was strong opposition to Lopez Avelar's nomination as Governor because of his supposed connection with the assassination of Zapata; one of Zapata's daughters spoke in his defense. l-Scott, 235; C de D, 1949–51, 77; DGF51, I, 23, 29, 31; letter; DGF56, 6, 9–12; HA, 8 Dec. 1958, 42; Ind. Biog., 91–92.

Lopez Bermudez, Jose

(Deceased July 19, 1971)
a-Dec. 19, 1910. b-Moroleon, Guanajuato, *West Central, Rural.* c-Engineering degree from the Agricultural School of Ciudad Juarez, 1933. d-*Federal Deputy* from the State of Chihuahua, Dist. 4, 1946–49, member of the Credits Committee, the Agrarian Department Committee, the Livestock Committee, and the Inspection Committee for the General Accounting Office (first year); *Federal Deputy* from the State of Guanajuato, Dist. 6, 1955–58, member of the Agrarian Department Committee and the Inspection Committee for the General Accounting Office; President of the Preparatory Council; President of the Chamber of Deputies, December, 1946; *Alternate Senator* from Guanajuato, 1958–61; *Federal Deputy* from the State of Guanajuato, Dist. 8, 1961–64, member of the Legislative Studies Committee (Agrarian Section), the Foreign Relations Committee, and the Protocol Committee; member of the Mexican-American Interparliamentary Conference. e-*Secretary General of PRI*, 1949–52; Director of Orators for PRI in the Presidential campaign of *Adolfo Ruiz Cortines*. f-Rural organizer for Cultural

Missions of the Secretariat of Public Education, 1934–36; Private Secretary to *Alfredo Chavez*, Governor of Chihuahua, 1943–44; Director "D" of the Department of Railroad Construction, Secretariat of Communications and Public Works, 1936–40; Assistant Director of Planning, Department of Agrarian Affairs, 1940–43; technical advisor to the Secretary of Agriculture and Livestock; Oficial Mayor of the Secretariat of Hydraulic Resources; *Secretary General of the Department of Agrarian Affairs and Colonization*, 1952–55. g-None. h-Started government career working in the Cultural Missions Program of the Secretariat of Public Education; author of numerous books and biographies of Mexican leaders; member of the Mexican delegation under *Jaime Torres Bodet* to the Inter-American Assembly, 1947. j-None. k-Precandidate for Governor of Guanajuato, 1955. l-Peral, 454; *Polemica*, Vol. I, 1969, 21; *Siempre*, Dec. 3, 1958, 6; C de D, 1946–48, 76; letter; DGF47, 6; DGF56, 24, 30, 32, 35; HA, 26 July 1971, 72; C de D, 1961–63, 81; C de D, 1956–58; *Excelsior*, 11 Aug. 1947; Gonzalez Navarro, 213; Lopez, 608; Enc. Mex., VIII, 1977, 135; Ind. Biog., 92–93.

Lopez Breton, Guadalupe

a-Dec. 7, 1935. b-Puebla, Puebla, *East Central*, *Urban*. c-Primary and secondary studies in Puebla; teaching certificate in Puebla; teacher in various schools in Puebla. d-*Alternate Senator* from the State of Puebla, 1970–73, but replaced Senator *Guillermo Morales Blumenkron*, 1973–76, president of the Second Credit Committee and the Money and Credit Institutions Committee; First Secretary of the Property and Natural Resources Committee; Second Secretary of the Second Consular and Diplomatic Services Committee; *Federal Deputy* from the State of Puebla, Dist. 7, 1976–79, member of the Agricultural Development Committee, the Section on Maternal-Infant Welfare of the Public Health Committee, the Second Government Committee and the Immigration Committee. e-None. f-None. g-Secretary of Education Action of the CEN of CNOP; active in the SNTE of Puebla, Puebla. h-None. j-None. k-First female senator from the State of Puebla. l-D de C, 1976–79, 11, 20, 38, 56, 62; *Excelsior*, 18 Aug. 1976, 29; C de S, 1970–76, 80.

Lopez Cardenas, Fernando

b-Yucatan, *Gulf*. c-Early education unknown; law degree, National School of Law, UNAM; Professor of Logic, National School of Law, UNAM. d-Federal Deputy from the State of Yucatan, Dist. 1, 1932–34; *Governor of Yucatan*, Oct. 5, 1935 to July 1, 1936. e-None. f-Secretary General of Government of the State of Yucatan under Governor *Cesar Alayola Barrera*, 1934–35; *Justice of the Supreme*

Court of Mexico, 1938–40. g-None. j-None. k-Resigned the governorship of Yucatan because of several violent workers' strikes. l-Daniels, 487; C de D, 1932–34.

Lopez Cortes, Francisco

a-1895. b-Ixtepec, Oaxaca, *South*, *Rural*. c-Early education unknown; law degree. d-Federal Deputy from the State of Oaxaca, Dist. 16, 1924–26; Federal Deputy from the State of Oaxaca, Dist. 16, 1928; Governor of Oaxaca, 1928–32; *Senator* from the State of Oaxaca, 1934–40; *Federal Deputy* from the State of Oaxaca, Dist. 6, 1943–46. e-None. f-Secretary of Government of the State of Baja California del Sur, 1920. g-None. j-None. k-None. l-C de D, 1924–26; C de D, 1928–30; C de S, 1934–40; C de D, 1943–46, 14.

Lopez Davila, Manuel

(Deceased Oct., 1974)
b-Ahualulco, San Luis Potosi, *East Central*, *Rural*. c-Primary studies in San Luis Potosi; secondary studies at the Urban Normal School, San Luis Potosi; teaching certificate; graduate studies in psychology and educational administration; professor of secondary schools in San Luis Potosi, Rector of the Scientific and Literary Institute of Chihuahua. d-*Alternate Senator* from Chihuahua, 1946–52, but replaced Senator *Antonio J. Bermudez* during the entire term; member of the Second Committee on Credit, Money, and Credit Institutions, the National Properties Committee, the Second Committee on Public Education, and the Second Petroleum Committee; *Governor of San Luis Potosi*, 1961–67. e-Representative of the CNOP on the National Advisory Council of PRI, 1946; state committeeman for PRI in San Luis Potosi. f-Director of Federal Education, State of San Luis Potosi, Secretariat of Public Education; Inspector General, Secretariat of Public Education; head of the Department of Libraries, Secretariat of Public Education; Director General of Literacy and Education, Secretariat of Public Education; Oficial Mayor of the Chihuahua State Department of Public Education, 1958–61. h-None. i-Married Maria del Carmen Chacon. j-None. k-Robert Bezdek believes he lost the gubernatorial election to the PAN candidate. l-WWMG, 23; DBM68, 383; DBM70, 332; DGF47, 20; DGF51, I, 6, 10, 11, 13, 294; D del S, 22 Jan. 1946, 1; letter; *Excelsior*, 18 Nov. 1974; NYT, 3 July, 1961, 2; Bezdek, 70–72.

Lopez de Nava (y Baltierra), Rodolfo

(Deceased 1965)
a-Dec. 1, 1893. b-Cuernavaca, Morelos, *West Central, Urban*. c-Primary studies at the Porfirio Diaz School, Cuernavaca; secondary studies at the Pape Carpentier Institute, Cuernavaca; no degree. d-*Governor of Morelos*, 1952–58. e-None. g-None.

h-Author of a standard military text. i-Son, Rodolfo, was in 1974 a department head in the Secretariat of National Patrimony. j-Career army officer; Commander of the Military Zones of Jalisco and Veracruz; Director of Army Supply Warehouses; rank of Brigadier General. k-None. l-DGF56, 96; DP70, 1207; DPE71, 47; Lopez, 615.

Lopez Faudoa, Eduardo

a-Sept. 6, 1939. b-Ciudad Lerdo, Durango, *West, Rural*. c-Medical degree from the National School of Medicine, UNAM, 1963; Professor of Anatomy, National School of Medicine, UNAM; special studies in medicine for burns, England, 1970. d-*Federal Deputy* from the State of Durango, Dist. 2, 1979–82. e-None. f-*Oficial Mayor of the Secretariat of Health*, 1970; *Secretary General of the Mexican Institute of Social Security*, September 27, 1971 to December 7, 1976. g-None. h-Consultant for the Pascua Dermatology Center; Chief of Services for the Surgery Section for Rehabilitation of Burns, Ruben Lenero Hospital. i-Personal physician to *Luis Echeverria* during his presidential campaign. j-None. k-Precandidate for Governor of Durango, 1974. l-DPE71, 113; HA, 14 Dec. 1970, 23; HA, 4 Oct. 1971, 34; HA, 20 Sept. 1971, 48; *Excelsior*, 29 Dec. 1973, 5.

Lopez Gonzalez Pacheco, Miguel

a-Oct. 2, 1925. b-Puebla, Puebla, *East Central, Urban*. c-Primary studies at the Colegio Benavente, Puebla; secondary studies at the Colegio Benavente, Puebla; preparatory studies at the Instituto Oriente, Puebla; law degree, University of Puebla; Professor of Private International Law and Mercantile Law, University of Puebla. d-*Federal Deputy* from PAN (party deputy), 1970–73, member of the Domestic Trade Committee and the Administrative Section of the Legislative Studies Committee. e-Director of the Youth Group of PAN, 1950; Director of the Study Commission of the Regional Committee of PAN; regional adviser to PAN. f-Employer's representative before the Central Board of Conciliation and Arbitration of Puebla, 1953. g-President of the Student Association of the University of Puebla; coordinator of lawyers for the Bank of Puebla. h-Practicing attorney; attorney for the University of Puebla; Chief of the Legal Department, Bank of Puebla, 1974. i-Father, a lawyer; married Marcela Arta Sanchez. j-None. k-Twice a candidate of PAN for Federal Deputy. l-*Directorio*, 1970–72; C de D, 1970–72, 122.

Lopez Hernandez, Manuel J.

a-Dec. 7, 1912. b-Campeche, Campeche, *Gulf, Urban*. c-Primary and secondary studies in Campeche; preparatory studies in Campeche; law degree, Institute of Campeche, October 8, 1938; Professor of history, Institute of Campeche. d-*Federal Deputy* from

the State of Campeche, Dist. 1, 1946–49, member of the Navy Committee, the Foreign Relations Committee and the Protocol Committee; *Governor of Campeche*, 1949–55. e-None. f-President of the Superior Tribunal of Justice of the State of Chiapas. g-None. h-Practicing lawyer, Campeche, Campeche. j-None. k-None. l-DGF51, I, 88; DGF47, 5; HA, 7 Oct. 1949, xxviii; C de D, 1946–49, 76; Crowson.

Lopez Lira, Jesus

(Deceased Sept. 2, 1961)

a-Aug. 26, 1888. b-Salamanca, Guanajuato, *West Central, Urban*. c-Scholarship student to the University of Guanajuato; preparatory studies in Mexico City; medical degree in dental surgery from the University of Puebla; professor of the Superior Normal School; secondary teacher in the Federal District until 1953. d-Mayor of Guanajuato; local deputy to the 40th State Legislature of Guanajuato; Federal Deputy from Guanajuato to the Constitutional Convention at Queretaro, 1916–18; Federal Deputy from the State of Guanajuato, Dist. 2, 1922–24; *Senator* from Guanajuato, 1958–64. e-None. f-Physician for the Secretariat of Health (ten years); adviser to the Governor of the State of Guanajuato; Administrator of Customs, Nuevo Laredo, Tamaulipas, 1953–58. g-None. h-Practicing surgeon. i-Brother of *Jose Lopez Lira*; father a physician; collaborator of *Jose Siurob*. j-Fought in the Revolution, 1910; a Constitutionalist, under the forces of General Jesus Carranza, 1913; rank of Lt. Col., 1915. k-In the United States, 1927–31. l-Func., 207; C de S, 1961–64, 17; DGF56, 153; PS, 3382.

Lopez Lira, Jose

(Deceased 1965)

a-Oct. 7, 1892. b-Salamanca, Guanajuato, *West Central, Urban*. c-Primary and secondary studies in Guanajuato; law degree from the University of Guanajuato; Professor of Sociology, National School of Law, UNAM; Professor of Amparo and Guarantees, National School of Law, UNAM; Interim Rector of UNAM, Aug. 2, 1929, to Sept. 4, 1929; Secretary General of UNAM, 1930. d-None. e-None. f-First Head of the Advisory Department of the Office of the Attorney General, 1931; Attorney General of the State of Guanajuato; Justice of the Superior Tribunal of Justice of the State of Guanajuato; Assistant Attorney General of Mexico; *Oficial Mayor of Health*, 1938–40; Secretary General of Government of the State of Tlaxcala, 1942–45, under Governor *Manuel Santillan*; Director of the Legal Department, Secretariat of Government, 1948–52; Prosecretary of the Board of Administration and Protection of Foreign Property, 1946; *Secretary Of Government Properties*; 1952–58; *Justice of the Supreme Court of Mexico*, 1958–62. g-None.

h-Administrative official of the Secretariat of Health and Welfare, 1938. i-Brother, Dr. *Jesus Lopez Lira*, served as a Senator from Guanajuato, 1958–64; father a physician. j-None. k-None. l-Peral, 458; HA, 5 Dec. 1958, 10; DGF56, 431; DGF51, I, 68; DP70, 1208; Enc. Mex., VIII, 1977, 147.

Lopez Lliteras, Jose Manuel

a-Aug. 18, 1915. b-Merida, Yucatan, *Gulf*, *Urban*. c-Primary and secondary studies at the Alcala y Alcala Institute; preparatory studies at the Preparatory School of Yucatan, University of Yucatan, Merida. d-*Federal Deputy* from the State of Yucatan, Dist. 3, 1955–58, member of the Second Railroads Committee and the Inspection Committee of the General Accounting Office (1st year); local deputy to the State Legislature of Yucatan; councilman of the City Council of Merida. e-None. f-None. g-President of the Truckers Alliance of Yucatan, 1954–72. h-Businessman in Merida. j-None. k-None. l-Q es QY, 146; C de D, 1955–57, 53; DGF56, 29, 33, 35.

Lopez Manzanero, Gonzalo

b-Yucatan, *Gulf*. c-Early education unknown; no degree. d-Mayor of Merida, Yucatan; Local Deputy to the State Legislature of Yucatan; *Senator* from the State of Yucatan, 1946–52, member of the Gran Comision and the Industries Committee; alternate member of the First Labor Committee. e-None. f-Secretary General of Government of the State of Yucatan. g-President of the Union of Workers Leagues of Yucatan; cofounder and leader of the Truckdrivers Alliance of Yucatan, 1930. j-None. k-None. l-DGF51, I, 8–12, 14; PS, 3387.

Lopez Mateos, Adolfo

a-May 26, 1910. b-Atizapan de Zaragoza, Mexico, *West Central*, *Rural*. c-Primary studies on scholarship at the Colegio Frances, Mexico, D.F.; secondary studies in Toluca; preparatory and law studies at the Literary Institute of Toluca; completed preparatory from the National Preparatory School and the Scientific and Literary Institute of Toluca, 1924–25; law degree from the National School of Law, UNAM, 1934, with a thesis on crimes against economic policy; professor of World History and Ibero-American Literature at the Normal School; professor at the Literary Institute of Toluca; Rector of the Literary Institute of Toluca, 1944–46. d-*Senator* from the State of Mexico, 1946–52, replacing *Isidro Fabela* who resigned to join the International Court of Justice, member of the Gran Comision, the First Committee on Credit, Money, and Credit Institutions, the Legislative Studies Committee, the Special Forestry Committee, the Treasury Committee, the Tax Committee, the First Balloting Committee, the Second Foreign Relations Committee, and the First

Section of the Instructive Committee for the Grand Jury. e-Delegate and student leader of the Socialist Labor Party, 1929; Secretary of the Regional Committee for the PNR in Toluca, Mexico, 1931–34; orator for the Presidential campaign of *Miguel Aleman*; Secretary General of the PNR for the Federal District; *Secretary General of PRI*, 1951–52; campaign manager for the Presidential campaign of *Adolfo Ruiz Cortines*, 1952. f-Agent of the Ministerio Publico of the Office of the Attorney General; private secretary to the Governor of Mexico, Colonel Filiberto Gomez, 1928; Private Secretary to Carlos Riva Palacio, President of the CEN of PRN, 1931–33; delegate of the National Workers Bank of Development to the Government Printing Office, 1933–43; head of the Publications Committee for the Secretariat of Public Education; Assistant Director of Bellas Artes, Secretariat of Public Education; Chairman of the Mexican Delegation to the International Economic Convention, Geneva, 1951; member of the Federal Electoral Commission, 1952; *Secretary of Labor*, 1952–58; *President of Mexico*, 1958–64. g-Secretary General of the Teachers Union. h-Worked in a library to support himself during secondary school; founded the magazine *Impetu*, 1927. i-Carlos Riva Palacio convinced him to join the official party; son of a dentist who died when he was very young; his mother supported five children on a very small income. j-None. k-As a student leader, he supported Jose Vasconcelos in his campaign against Pascual Ortiz Rubio in 1929; voluntarily went into exile in Guatemala, 1929; he led a 136-day walk to Guatemala, 1926. l-HA, 28 Dec. 1964, 4; Cline, 162; HA, 19 Jan. 1959; DGF51, I, 6, 9–14; Scott, 214, 218–20; DP70, 1208–09; Brandenburg, 3–6, 113–18; HA, 12 Dec. 1952, 5; WWMG, 23–24; HA, 5 Dec. 1952, 9; DGF56, 397; Covarrubias, 140; Johnson, 32–35; letter; STYRBIWW60, 1210; Enc. Mex., VIII, 1977, 147–48; *Justicia*, Feb., 1970.

Lopez (Mena), Hector F.

(Deceased 1957)
a-1880. b-Coahuayutla, Guerrero, *South*, *Rural*. c-Primary studies in La Huacana, Michoacan; enrolled in the Colegio de San Nicolas, Morelia; no degree. d-City councilman of Coahuayutla; Senator from the State of Guerrero, 1920; Governor of Guerrero, 1925. e-Director of General *Juan Andreu Almazan's* campaign for president, 1940; Vice-president of the Revolutionary Party of National Unification, 1940; Vice-president of the Mexican Democratic Party, 1945, which supported *Ezequiel Padilla* for president. f-Subdirector, Department of Infantry, Secretariat of War; Subdirector, Chief of Staff, Secretariat of War; Interim Governor of Michoacan. g-None. j-Joined the Revolution, 1910; career Army officer; military commander of Orizaba; rank of Brigade General. k-None. l-DP70, 1209–10.

Lopez Moctezuma, Jose

a-1926. b-Sonora, *North*. c-Early education unknown; degree in civil engineering, University of Sonora; professor of engineering, University of Sonora. d-None. e-Member of PAN. f-City agent, Hermosillo, Sonora, 1970. g-None. j-None. k-Candidate for Federal Deputy from the State of Sonora, 1958; candidate for Federal Deputy from the State of Sonora, Dist. 4, 1970. l-*La Nacion*, 14 June 1970, 28.

Lopez Munguia, Agustin

a-Aug. 12, 1920. b-Federal District, *Federal District, Urban*. c-Primary and secondary in Mexico, D.F.; preparatory at the National Preparatory School; economics degree from the National School of Economics, UNAM, 1940–44; Master of Arts in Public Administration from Harvard University, 1950–51; advanced studies in budgetary problems at the London School of Economics and Political Science, University of London, 1956; attended the English Language Institute, University of Michigan, 1950; Professor of Money and Banking, Mexico City College, 1953–55; Professor of Public Finance, National Polytechnical School, 1959; Professor of the Theory of Public Finance, National School of Economics, UNAM, 1953–71. d-None. e-None. f-Economist for the Department of Economic Studies, Bank of Mexico, 1943–48; head of Statistics, National Commission for the Control of Imports, 1943–48; Secretary of the Export Price Commission, 1949; head of the Department of Economic Studies, 1952–58; Assistant Director General of Treasury Studies, Secretariat of the Treasury, 1959–76; Subdirector General of the Bank of Mexico, 1977– . g-None. h-None. i-Attended the National School of Economics with *Julian Diaz Arias*, *Jorge Espinosa de los Reyes*, and *Octaviano Campos Salas*; during his long teaching career, among those he taught were *Carlos Torres Manzo*, *Jorge de la Vega Dominguez* and *Carlos Bermudez Limon*. j-None. k-None. l-Letter; DGF56, 164; BdM, 166; DPE65, 142; DPE71, 24, *Excelsior*, 21 Dec. 1977, 23.

Lopez Munoz, Jose Arturo

a-1906. b-Sinaloa, *West*. c-Early education unknown; no degree. d-None. e-President of PAN for the State of Sinaloa; adviser to the National Council of PAN. f-None. g-Adviser to the Sinaloan Union of Industry, Livestock and Agricultural Credit. h-Broker. j-None. k-Candidate of PAN for Mayor of Culiacan, Sinaloa, 1968; candidate of PAN for Senator from the State of Sinaloa, 1958; candidate of PAN for Senator from the State of Sinaloa, 1970. l-*La Nacion*, 14 June 1970, 26.

Lopez Padilla, Benecio

a-Aug. 23, 1888. b-Zaragoza, Coahuila, *North, Rural*. c-Early education unknown; no degree. d-*Governor of Coahuila*, 1941–45. e-None. f-Interim Governor of Tamaulipas; head of the Department of Archives, Correspondence, and History, Secretariat of National Defense, 1958–70. g-Organizer and Secretary General of the Mexican Mining Union, 1909. h-Employed as a miner in Nueva Rosita, Coahuila, before the Revolution. i-Married Carlota Duarte. j-Joined the Revolution as a private in the army of Arnulfo Gomez; Governor and Commander of Military Operations in the State of Tamaulipas, December 9, 1923–February 1, 1924; rank of Brigadier General, Sept. 1, 1922; fought against Carranza, 1920; Commander of the 18th Military Zone, Venta Prieta, Hidalgo; Commander of the 21st Military Zone, Morelia, Michoacan, 1935; Commander of the 11th Military Zone, Zacatecas, Zacatecas, 1936; Commander of the 1st Military Zone, Mexico, D.F., 1936; Inspector General of the Army; rank of Divisionary General, Oct. 16, 1937. k-None. l-WWM45, 66; DPE61, 32; HA, 14 Aug. 1942, 14; Peral, 453–54; MGF69, 196; DPE65, 45; Lopez, 618.

Lopez Portillo, Jose

a-June 16, 1920. b-Federal District, *Federal District, Urban*. c-Primary studies at the Benito Juarez Public School, Federal District; secondary studies completed in the Federal District, 1935; preparatory studies at the National Preparatory School, Mexico, D.F., 1937; law degree from the University of Santiago, Chile, on a political science scholarship from the Chilean government, 1942–45; law degree from the National School of Law, UNAM 1946; LLD from the National School of Law, UNAM, 1950; Professor of Law at the National School of Law, UNAM, 1947–58; Founder of the University Extension Program; founding Professor of Political Science and Government Policy, Ph.D. Program in Administrative Sciences, Graduate School of Business and Administration, UNAM. d-*President of Mexico*, 1976–82. e-Member of the Social and Economic Council during the Presidential campaign of *Adolfo Lopez Mateos*, 1958; member of the New Advisory Council of the IEPES of PRI, 1972. f-Technical adviser to the Oficial Mayor of the Secretariat of National Patrimony, 1959-60; member of the Revisory Committee of Article 3 of the Constitution, 1959; Director General of the Federal Boards of Material Improvement, Secretariat of Government Properties, 1960–65; Director of Legal Counsel to the Secretariat of the Presidency, 1965–68; *Subsecretary of the Presidency*, 1968–70; *Subsecretary of Government Properties*, 1970–72; *Director General of the Federal Electric Commission*, 1972–73; *Sec-*

retary of the Treasury, May 29, 1973, to 1975. **g-**None. **h-**Practicing lawyer, 1946–59; author of several books. **i-***Pedro Ojeda Paullada* served as Subdirector of the Federal Boards of Material Improvement under *Lopez Portillo*; friend of *Luis Echeverria* since grammar school days; grandson of Jose Lopez Portillo y Rojas, Secretary of Foreign Relations under Victoriano Huerta and governor of Jalisco, 1911–13; son of engineer Jose Lopez Portillo y Weber, historian and member of the Board of Directors of PEMEX. **j-**None. **k-**None. **l-**HA, 14 Dec. 1970, 21; HA, 21 Aug. 1972, 12; DPE61, 61; *Excelsior*, 19 June 1970, 4; HA, 18 Nov. 1968; *Excelsior*, 10 Aug. 1972, 10; WWMG, 24; HA, 11 June 1973, 13–14; Latin America, 26 Sept. 1975, 297; HA, 29 Sept. 1975, 7; Enc. Mex., VIII, 1977, 154D–55.

Lopez Portillo Brizuela, Arturo

a-July 7, 1908. **b-**Guadalajara, Jalisco, *West*, *Urban*. **c-**Primary and secondary studies in Guadalajara; preparatory studies in Aguascalientes; law degree, National School of Law, UNAM. **d-***Federal Deputy* from the Federal District, Dist. 9, 1958–61, member of the First Section of the Legislative Studies Committee; *Federal Deputy* from the Federal District, Dist. 1, 1964–67, member of the Tariff Committee and the Second Treasury Committee. **e-**None. **f-**Official, Federal Income Tax Department, Secretariat of the Treasury. **g-**Member of the Treasury Workers Union. **j-**None. **k-**None. **l-**Func., 184; C de D, 1958–61, 83; C de D, 1964–67, 77, 86.

Lopez Rea, Filomeno

a-July 5, 1909. **b-**La Puerta, Municipio of Tonantico, Mexico, *West Central*, *Rural*. **c-**Self-educated; no degree. **d-***Federal Deputy* from the State of Morelos, Dist. 2, 1970–73, member of the Sugar Industry Committee, the Second Balloting Committee and the Supplies and Foodstuffs Committee; *Federal Deputy* from the State of Morelos, Dist. 2, 1976–79, Dist. 2, member of the Section on Sugar Cane Production of the Agricultural Development Committee; member of the Primary Products Section of the Development of Foreign Trade Committee; member of the Sugar Section of the Industrial Development Committee and member of the Rural Industry and Arid Zones Section of the Development of Natural Resources Committee. **e-**None. **f-**President of the Administrative and the Inspection Committees, Emiliano Zapata Mill, Cacatepec, Morelos. **g-**Secretary General of the League of Agrarian Communities and Agrarian Unions, 1963–71. **j-**None. **k-**None. **l-**D de C, 1976–79, 13, 16, 26, 34; *Excelsior*, 27 Aug. 1976, 1C; C de D, 1970–73, 48, 122.

Lopez Sanabria, Juan Manuel

a-May 31, 1920. **b-**Angangueo, Michoacan, *West Central*, *Rural*. **c-**Primary studies at a private school in Morelia, Michoacan; preparatory studies at the University of Guanajuato; medical degree from the University of San Luis Potosi, Dec. 22, 1945; graduate studies at the New York General Hospital under Dr. Fernando Latapi, Mt. Sinai, New York, 1947–48; professor at the School of Medicine, University of Guanajuato. **d-***Federal Deputy* from PAN (party deputy), 1970–73, member of the Artisans Committee, the Legislative Studies Committee, the Tenth Section on General Means of Communication and Transportation, and the Chemical Pharmaceutical Industries Committee; Mayor of Ojuelos, Jalisco. **e-**Director of the Guanajuato State Committee of PAN; member of the National Executive Committee of PAN. **f-**None. **g-**None. **h-**Practicing dermatologist; Chief of the Dermatology and Allergy Service, Central Regional Hospital, Leon, Guanajuato. **i-**Son of engineer Maurilio Lopez Munoz. **j-**None. **k-**None. **l-**C de D, 1970–72, 122; DBM70, 338; *Directorio*, 1970–72.

Lopez Sanchez, Hermilo

a-1892. **b-**Chiapas, *South*. **c-**Law degree. **d-**None. **e-**None. **f-**District Judge; Criminal Judge; Interim Judge of the Tribunal Superior of Justice of the Federal District; Secretary of the Court of Justice of Tlalpan; Correctional Judge; Agent of the Ministerio Publico of the Office of the Attorney General; *Justice of the Supreme Court*, 1935–40, 1940–46, and 1946–51. **g-**None. **j-**None. **k-**None. **l-**Novo35, 216; letter.

Lopez Sanchez, Raul

(Deceased Jan. 11, 1957)
a-Dec. 28, 1904. **b-**Torreon, Coahuila, *North*, *Urban*. **c-**Primary studies at the Colegio Modelo de Elvirita Vargas, 1910–16, Torreon; secondary and preparatory studies in Mexico, D.F., preparatory studies from the National Preparatory School; law degree from the National School of Law, UNAM, 1925–29. **d-***Federal Deputy* from the State of Coahuila, Dist. 3, 1943–46; *Senator* from Coahuila, 1946–48, Secretary of the Gran Comision. **e-**None. **f-***Interim Governor of Coahuila*, June 1, 1948, to 1951; *Secretary of the Navy*, Feb. 7, 1952, to Nov. 30, 1952; head of the Department of Labor for the State of Veracruz, 1936–39, under Governor *Miguel Aleman*. **g-**None. **h-**Practicing attorney for labor unions, 1929–32. **i-**Son of General Mario Lopez Ortiz; knew *Mariano Ramirez Vazquez, Gabriel Ramos Millan*, *Miguel Aleman*, and *Antonio Dovali Jaime* at UNAM; attended school with *Salvador Novo*, who was a boyhood friend; son Mariano Lopez Mercado was defeated for federal deputy from Dist. 2, State of

Coahuila, 1979. **j-**None. **k-**None. **l-**DP70, 1212; HA, 15 Feb. 1952, 4; DGF51, I, 5, 88; Enc. Mex., Vol. 5, 46; letter; C de D, 1946–48; C de S, 1946–52; DGF47, 22; Novo, 204; HA, 21 Jan. 1957; Enc. Mex., VIII, 1977, 157.

Lopez Serrano, Francisco

a-Jan. 28, 1912. **b-**Monclova, Coahuila, *North*, *Urban*. **c-**Secondary at the Ateneo Fuente of Saltillo, Coahuila; law degree from the National School of Law, UNAM. **d-***Federal Deputy* from the State of Coahuila, Dist. 1, 1943–46. **e-**Director of *Miguel Aleman's* campaign for President in the State of Coahuila, 1946. **f-**Member of the UNAM Legal Committee which was sent to Tabasco to investigate student deaths, 1935; alternate member of the Federal Board of Conciliation and Arbitration, Federal District; Chief of the Public Defenders of the Federal District; President of the Central Board of Conciliation and Arbitration, Federal District; *Secretary General of Colonization*, *Department of Agrarian Affairs*, 1958–63. **g-**President of the Student University Federation, 1934. **h-**Author of several works on agrarian law and the University of Mexico. **j-**None. **k-**Precandidate for Governor of Coahuila, 1963. **l-***Siempre*, 4 Feb. 1959, 6; Correa, 363; DPE61, 126; Peral, 463.

Loret de Mola (Mediz), Carlos

a-July 30, 1921. **b-**Merida, Yucatan, *Gulf*, *Urban*. **c-**Primary and secondary studies in Merida; preparatory studies at the Colegio Montejo of Merida; degree in journalism from the University of Yucatan. **d-***Federal Deputy* from the State of Yucatan, Dist. 3, 1961–63, Prosecretary of the Chamber, Sept. 1963; member of the Committee on the Radio and Television Industry, the Protocol Committee, the Inspection Committee of the General Accounting Office, and the Gran Comision; *Senator* from the State of Yucatan, 1964–70; *Governor of Yucatan*, 1970–76. **e-**Member of the National Council of PRI; PRI delegate to the State of Durango, 1965. **g-**None. **h-**Journalist; began career with *Diario de Yucatan*, 1939; reporter for many newspapers; editor of *El Heraldo*, San Luis Potosi, 1951–55; *El Diario de Yucatan*, *Novedades*, Mexico City, 1946–51; and *El Mundo*, Tamaulipas, 1951–55; founder of *El Heraldo*, Aguascalientes; editor of *El Heraldo*, Chihuahua, 1955–57; Director of *Noticero Mexicano*, Mexico City, 1957–60; writer for *Excelsior*, 1976– ; author of numerous biographies and books on Mexican history. **i-**Father an agent of the Ejido Bank in Yucatan; *Adolfo Lopez Mateos* initiated his career after meeting him during his presidential campaign, 1958. **j-**None. **k-**None. **l-**HA, 11 Jan. 1965, 8; DBM68, 388; D de Y, 1970; Q es QY,

150–51; Enc. Mex., VIII, 1977, 160–61; Loret de Mola; Lopez, 625.

Loyo (Gonzalez), Gilberto

(Deceased Apr. 10, 1973)
a-Feb. 4, 1901. **b-**Orizaba, Veracruz, *Gulf*, *Urban*. **c-**Primary, secondary and preparatory studies at the Preparatory School of Orizaba; degree in economics from the National School of Economics, UNAM; law studies at UNAM; degree in statistics, University of Rome, 1932; professor at the National School of Economics, UNAM 1936–53, 1958–66; Director of the National School of Economics, 1944–52; Professor of Statistics and Demography and the founder of the first Professorship of Demography at UNAM; Professor of Economic History at the National Polytechnical School; Professor of Agricultural Economics at the National School of Agriculture; member of the Governing Board of UNAM, 1971–73. **d-**None. **e-**Member of the New Advisory Council of the IEPES of PRI, 1972. **f-**Director of the National Census, 1939–40; Director General of Credit and Statistics, Secretariat of Industry and Commerce, 1946–52; Director of Social Welfare; member of the First Mexican Delegation to the Economic Commission for Latin America, 1948; Director General of the Census, 1950; *Secretary of Industry and Commerce*, 1952–58; Chairman of the National Commission for Minimum Wages, 1963–72; Chairman of the Center for Agrarian Investigations, Department of Agrarian Affairs, 1968; adviser to the National Bank of Foreign Commerce; adviser to the Secretary of National Patrimony. **g-**None. **h-**Member of many statistical and census committees in the United States and Latin America; author of numerous books on economic and demographic subjects. **i-**Friends with many future public leaders in Mexico while studying at UNAM, including *Javier Rojo Gomez*, *Ignacio Garcia Tellez*, *Narciso Bassols*, *Ramon Beteta*, *Jaime Torres Bodet*, *Rodulfo Brito Foucher*, and *Salvador Novo*; long-time friend of *Jesus Silva Herzog*. **j-**None. **l-**Letter; WWM45, 66; DBM68, 388–89; HA, 5 Dec. 1952, 9; HA, 8 May 1972, 19; Peral, 465; DGF47, 155; DGF56, 277; DBM70, 339–40; HA, 10 July 1972, 10; Scott, 99; Brandenburg, 108; STYRBIWW54, 863; HA, 23 Apr. 1973, 36; *Excelsior*, 11 Apr. 1973, 16; Enc. Mex., VIII, 1977, 164–65; NYT, 27 July 1954, 10.

Lozano Ramirez, Raul

a-Mar. 9, 1911. **b-**Molango, Hidalgo, *East Central*, *Rural*. **c-**Secondary at the Rural School of Molango; preparatory studies from the Scientific and Literary Institute of Pachuca, Hidalgo; law degree, National School of Law, UNAM. **d-**Local Deputy to the State Legislature of Hidalgo; *Federal Deputy* from the State of Hidalgo, Dist. 4, 1943–46; *Federal Deputy* from the State of Hidalgo, Dist. 4, 1964–67; *Senator* from the State of Hidalgo, 1970–76, member of the Gran Comision, the Second Balloting Group and the First Section of the Legislative Studies Committee; President of the National Lands and Resources Committee; Second Secretary of the Waters and National Irrigation and the Second Justice Committees. **e-**None. **f-**Private Secretary to the Governor of Hidalgo, *Javier Rojo Gomez*, 1937–40; Secretary of the State Board of Conciliation and Arbitration of Hidalgo; Oficial Mayor of the State of Hidalgo; Attorney General of the State of Hidalgo; Secretary General of Government of the State of Hidalgo under Governor *Jose Lugo Guerrero*, 1941–43; Justice of the Superior Tribunal of Justice of Hidalgo; *Provisional Governor of Hidalgo*, May–August, 1975; *Justice of the Supreme Court of Mexico*, 1975– . **g-**None. **h-**Director of Legal Services of the Blue Cross Cement Cooperative, 1964. **i-**Political disciple of *Javier Rojo Gomez*; has known *Manuel Sanchez Vite* since childhood in Molango. **j-**None. **k-**Precandidate for the gubernatorial nomination of PRI in Hidalgo, 1974, 1978. **l-**C de S, 1970–76, 78; HA, 12 May 1975, 41; HA, 5 May 1975, 43; *Excelsior*, 27 Oct. 1975, 19; *Excelsior*, 18 Oct. 1974, 1; C de D, 1943–46; C de D, 1964–67.

Lugo, Jose Inocencio
(Deceased 1963)

a-1871. **b-**Santa Ana del Aguila, Guerrero, *South*, *Rural*. **c-**Primary and secondary studies in Morelia, Michoacan; preparatory studies in Morelia; law degree in Morelia; professor at the National Military College. **d-**Deputy to the Constitutional Convention at Queretaro, 1916–17; Federal Deputy from Guerrero; Senator from Guerrero. **e-**Member of the Anti-Reelectionist Party, 1909. **f-**Governor of Baja California del Norte; Governor of Guerrero, Dec., 1910, to Mar., 1913; Subsecretary of Government, June 1, 1920, to Aug. 4, 1920; Secretary of Government, Aug. 4, 1920, to Nov. 30, 1920; head of the Department of Justice, Secretariat of War and Navy; *Interim Governor of Guerrero*, Nov. 5, 1935, to 1936, replacing Governor *Gabriel R. Guevara*. **g-**President of the Student Nicolaita Committee in rebellion against the reelection of the state governor, 1895. **i-**Son, *Jose Inocente Lugo Lagunas*, served as Federal Deputy from Guerrero, Dist. 1, 1955–57, and President of the Fourth Division of the National Tax Court, 1964–70. **j-**Coordinated Revolutionary activities in Guerrero, 1910; imprisoned by General Huerta; fought against Huerta in the forces of General Gertrudis Sanchez; rank of Brigadier General, Feb. 16, 1921. **k-**Took an active part in writing Article 123 of the 1917 Constitution at the Queretaro Convention. **l-**D de Y, 6 Nov. 1935, 1; DP70,

1219–20; Peral, 468; DGF56, 24, 31, 33, 36; MGF69, 389; Enc. Mex., VIII, 1977, 170.

Lugo Gil, Humberto Alejandro

a-May 4, 1937. **b-**Huichapan, Hidalgo, *East Central, Urban*. **c-**Preparatory studies from the National Preparatory School; law degree, National School of Law, UNAM. **d-***Federal Deputy* from the State of Hidalgo, Dist. 5, 1967–70; *Senator* from the State of Hidalgo, 1976– . **e-**Delegate of the CEN of PRI to various states, 1957–58; President of PRI in Huichapan, Hidalgo, 1958–61; Director of the CEPES of PRI in Hidalgo, 1963; *Secretary of Press and Publicity of the CEN of PRI*, 1968; *Secretary of Press and Publicity of the CEN of PRI*, 1976–78; *Secretary of Organization of the CEN of PRI*, 1978. **f-**Agent of the Ministerio Publico, Pachuco, Hidalgo, 1957–58; Director of the Department of Prelimimary Accusations, Attorney General of Hidalgo, 1958; Director of Economic Studies, Department of Treasury Studies, Secretariat of the Treasury, 1960; Director General of Offices and Apartments of the Chamber of Deputies, 1964; Private Secretary to the President of the Gran Comision of the Chamber of Deputies, *Alfonso Martinez Dominguez*, 1965–67. **g-**President of the Student Society of the National Preparatory School, 1954; Vice-president of the 1957 Law School Generation; Secretary General of the Student Society of the National School of Law, UNAM, 1958; Delegate of the CEN of CNOP to various states, 1963–65; Vice-president of the National Policy Committee of the CEN of CNOP, 1966. **h-**None. **i-**Son of *Jose Lugo Guerrero*, Governor of Hidalgo, 1941–45; nephew of *Adolfo Lugo Guerrero*, federal deputy from Hidalgo, 1943–46; cousin of *Jorge Rojo Lugo*, Governor of Hidalgo, 1975–76; nephew of *Javier Rojo Gomez*, Governor of Hidalgo, 1937–40. **j-**None. **k-**None. **l-**C de D, 1967–70; C de S, 1976–82; MGF69.

Lugo Guerrero, Jose

a-Sept. 17, 1899. **b-**Huichapan, Hidalgo, *East Central, Rural*. **c-**Primary in the public schools of Huichapan; secondary studies in Pachuca, Hidalgo; law degree, National School of Law, UNAM, 1926. **d-**Local deputy to the State Legislature of Hidalgo; Mayor of Huichapan; Mayor of Pachuca, Hidalgo; Federal Deputy from the State of Hidalgo, Dist. 5, 1932–34; *Federal Deputy* from the State of Hidalgo, Dist. 5, 1937–40; *Senator* from the State of Hidalgo, 1940–41; *Governor of Hidalgo*, 1941–45. **e-**None. **g-**Member of the CNC. **i-**Related to *Javier Rojo Gomez*; son *Humberto A. Lugo* was a federal deputy from Hidalgo, 1967–70; brother *Adolfo Lugo Guerrero* was a federal deputy from Hidalgo, 1943–46; protege of *Rojo Gomez*. **j-**Joined the Revolution under General Martinez y Martinez, 1915. **k-**None.

l-HA, 12 Mar. 1943, 41; Peral, 468; Gonzalez Navarro, 177; Lopez, 629.

Lujan Gutierrez, Jesus

a-Apr. 26, 1934. b-Villa Lopez, Chihuahua, *North*, *Rural*. c-Primary studies in Public School No. 192, Ciudad Juarez, Chihuahua, 1941–47; secondary studies at the Rural Normal School, Salaices, Chihuahua, 1948–53; teaching certificate, Higher Normal School, Chihuahua, Chihuahua, 1961–64; primary school teacher; secondary school teacher; director of various primary and secondary schools. d-*Federal Deputy* (Party Deputy) from the PPS, 1970–73, member of the Forest Affairs Committee, the Agricultural Development Committee, the Electric Industry Committee and the Hydraulic Resources Committee; *Federal Deputy* from the Federal District, Dist. 14, 1976–79, member of the Physical Education Section of the Educational Development Committee, the Development of the Fishing Industry Committee, the Department of the Federal District Committee and the Complaints Committee. e-Joined the PPS, 1950; member of the Central Committee of the PPS, 1965; official of the Executive Secretariat of the PPS, 1972; Secretary of Electoral Policy of the PPS, 1979. f-Federal Inspector of primary schools. g-None. i-Married Esther Ponce. j-None. k-Candidate for Federal Deputy from the State of Chihuahua, 1964, 1967; candidate for Governor of Chihuahua, 1968, 1974. l-C de D, 1970–73, 123, 146; C de D, 1976–79; D de C, 1976–79, 22, 42, 46, 48, 70; HA, 12 Feb. 1979, 22.

Luna Arroyo, Antonio

a-June 13, 1910. b-Federal District, *Federal District*, *Urban*. c-Primary and secondary studies in the Federal District; teaching certificate from the National Teachers College, 1929; law degree from the National School of Law, 1933; professor of civics in secondary schools; director of curriculum in secondary schools; professor at the National School of Economics, 1937; professor at the National Teachers College, 1932–46. d-None. e-Secretary of Press and Publicity for the CEN of the PNR, 1935. f-Member of the Jury for Tax Infractions, Secretariat of the Treasury, 1935–36; President of the Publishing Commission, Secretariat of Education; head of the Department of Economic Studies, Secretariat of Labor; adviser to the Secretariat of Education, 1935; member of the National Population Council, 1939; Assistant Attorney General of Mexico, 1939–42; adviser to President *Manuel Avila Camacho*; Secretary General of CONASUPO, 1946; Director General of the Advisory and Legislative Division, Secretariat of Agriculture and Livestock, 1946–52. g-None. h-Author of school texts; Director General of *La Justicia*. i-Knew *Salvador Mondragon Guerra*, *Enrique*

Martinez Ulloa, *Mariano Ramirez Vazquez*, *Rafael Rojina Villegas*, and *Luis Felipe Canudas Orezza* at UNAM. j-None. k-None. l-EBW46, 516; DGF51, I, 206; DGF47, 123; Enc. Mex., VIII, 1977, 170; Lopez, 630.

Luna Bracamontes, Luis Javier

a-Oct. 11, 1917. b-Tamazula de Gordiano, Jalisco, *West*, *Rural*. c-Early education unknown; no degree. d-*Alternate Federal Deputy* from the State of Jalisco, Dist. 9, 1955–58; Mayor of Tamazula, Jalisco; *Federal Deputy* from the Federal District, Dist. 10, 1967–70, member of the Auto Transportation Committee, the Second Balloting Committee, and the National Properties Committee. e-None. f-None. g-Member of the Union of Sugar Industry Workers. h-Treasurer of the Obrero del Ingenio Tamazula, S.A. j-None. k-None. l-C de D, 1967–69, 59, 77, 89; DBM68, 392; C de D, 1955–57; DGF56, 25; MGF69, 93.

Luna Kan, Francisco

a-Dec. 3, 1925. b-Noc-Ac Hacienda, Municipio of Merida, Yucatan, *Gulf*, *Rural*. c-Primary studies in the Juan N. Alvarez School, Merida; two years of secondary studies at the Rural Normal School, Hecelchacan, Campeche, 1939–40; completed secondary at Public School No. 5, Merida, 1943; studies at Vocational School No. 4, IPN, Mexico City, in biological sciences, 1944–51; medical degree, Higher School of Rural Medicine, IPN, with a thesis on epidemiology and social characteristics of tubercular patients, 1952; MA in health sciences, Secretariat of Health, December, 1953, with a thesis on "Health Zoning in Yucatan"; professor of health sciences at various institutions. d-*Federal Deputy* from the State of Yucatan, Dist. 3, 1964–67, member of the Library Committee; *Senator* from the State of Yucatan, 1970–75, President of the Senate, December, 1974, President of the Colonization Committee and First Secretary of the Public Welfare Committee; *Governor of Yucatan*, 1976– . e-Agrarian sub-delegate of the CEN of PRI to Yucatan, 1965; General Delegate of the CEN of PRI to Yucatan, 1970; President of PRI in Yucatan, 1965–68. f-Divisional Director, Coordinated Health and Welfare Services, Yucatan, 1953–55; Technical Adviser, Division of Experimental Studies, Secretariat of Health, 1956–60; Physician, Federal Services, State of Yucatan, 1956; Director of Coordinated Health and Welfare Services, State of Yucatan, 1960–63; Chief of the Department of Sanitation, State of Yucatan, 1967–68. g-Member of the Political Action Committee of the CEN of the National Union of Health and Welfare Workers, 1964; Secretary General of the CNC in Yucatan, 1971–74. j-None. k-None. l-Q es QY, 152–53; C de S,

1970–76, 78; Enc. Mex., Annual, 1977, 552–53; C de D, 1964–67, 79.

Luque Loyola, Eduardo

a-Sept. 5, 1910. b-Queretaro, Queretaro, *East Central, Urban.* c-Preparatory studies at the Colegio Civil of Queretaro; law degree from the National School of Law, UNAM, 1935. d-*Federal Deputy* from the State of Queretaro, Dist. 1, 1943–46; *Senator* from the State of Queretaro, 1946–52, member of the Gran Comision, the Second Committee on Credit, Money, and Credit Institutions, the Agricultural Development Committee, and the Third Labor Committee; *Federal Deputy* from the State of Queretaro, Dist. 1, 1961–64, member of the Legislative Studies Committee, First Section on Constitutional Affairs, and the Gran Comision; *Senator* from the State of Queretaro, 1964–70, President of the Senate. e-President of the Regional Committee of PRI for the State of Queretaro. f-*Interim Governor of Queretaro*, 1949; Administrator of Customs, Chetumal, Quintana Roo, 1958–61; President of the Federal Board of Conciliation and Arbitration; Public Defender for Labor; Attorney General of Queretaro; Advisor to the Secretary of Government, 1977– . g-Member of the National Campesino Federation. h-None. i-Son Ernesto was a leader in the 1966 strike at UNAM. j-None. k-Precandidate for governor of Queretaro, 1979. l-DBM66, 393; C de S, 1964–70; C de S, 1946–52; C de D, 1961–63, 82; MGF69, 106; C de D, 1943–45; DGF51, I, 7, 9, 10, 12, 14; CyT, 91.

Luna Lugo, Arturo

b-Ascencion, Municipio of Aramberri, Nuevo Leon, *North, Rural.* c-Early education unknown; teaching certificate, Nuevo Leon. d-*Federal Deputy* from the State of Nuevo Leon, Dist. 5, 1952–55, member of Colonization Committee, the First Ejido Committee, and Vice-President of the Chamber, December, 1953; *Federal Deputy* from the State of Nuevo Leon, Dist. 5, 1976–79, member of the Agrarian Affairs Committee; member of the Agricultural Section of the Agricultural Development Committee; member of the Manufactured Products Section of the Foreign Trade Development Committee; member of the Transformation Section, Industrial Development Committee; member of the Mineral Section of the Natural Resources Development Committee; member of the Administrative Section of the Legislative Studies Committee and member of the Tax Section of the Treasury Committee. e-None. f-Agrarian Consultant, Department of Agrarian Affairs, 1971. g-Secretary of Organization, Revolutionary Agrarian Peasant Committee, Aramberri and Zaragoza, Nuevo Leon, 1941–43; Secretary of Youth Action, League of Agrarian Communities and Peasant Unions, Nuevo Leon; Alternate Secretary General of the

CNC, 1953–54; *Secretary General of the CNC*, 1954–57. i-Parents were ejidatarios. j-None. k-None. l-*Excelsior*, 23 Aug. 1976, 8; C de D, 1952–55, 46, 50; D de C, 1976–79, 5, 12, 17, 24, 32, 51, 58; C de D, 1976–79, 43.

Macedo Valdez, Eleuterio

c-Early education unknown; no degree. d-*Federal Deputy* from the Federal District, Dist. 8, 1967–70, member of the Second Treasury Committee, the Second Tax Committee, and the Public Housing Committee. e-Head of the 1st District Committee of PRI in the campaign of *Diaz Ordaz*, 1964. f-Alternate Judge of the Federal Tribunal of Arbitration and Conciliation of the FSTSE. g-Secretary of Acts and Agreements of the Union of Workers of the National Mint; delegate to the National Convention from the National Mint Workers' Union, 1939–41, 1943; Secretary General of the 2nd Section of the National Mint Workers' Union, 1941–43, 1952; Secretary of Labor and Conflicts, 1943–45, 1947–49; Secretary General of Section 26 of the Workers of the Federal Treasury. h-Began government career as a 20th-class level worker in the National Mint, 1935. j-None. k-None. l-C de D, 1967–69, 73, 74, 91; DBM68, 395.

Macias Valenzuela, Anselmo

(Deceased Jan., 1965)
a-Apr. 5, 1896. b-Agiabampo, Sonora, *North, Rural.* c-Primary studies in Alamos, Sonora; no degree. d-*Governor of Sonora*, Sept. 1, 1939, to Aug. 30, 1943. e-None. f-None. g-None. h-None. j-Joined the Revolution on Feb. 10, 1914, fighting with the 10th Battalion; Brigadier General, Sept. 1, 1929; Commander of the 11th Military Zone, Zacatecas, Zacatecas; Commander of the 13th Military Zone, Tepic, Nayarit; Commander of the 22nd Military Zone, Toluca, Mexico; Commander of the 2nd Regiment of Presidential Guards. k-None. l-WWM45, 67; Peral, 474; Lopez, 636.

Macias Valenzuela, Pablo E.

(Deceased May 3, 1975)
a-Nov. 15, 1891. b-El Fuerte, Las Cabras, Sinaloa, *West, Rural.* c-Early education unknown; no degree. d-*Governor of Sinaloa*, 1945–50. e-None. f-*Secretary of National Defense*, 1940–42; Director of Military Pensions, 1957–70; official in the Personnel Office, Secretariat of National Defense, 1975. g-None. h-None. i-Personal friend of *Manuel Avila Camacho*. j-Joined the Revolution under General Obregon as a Lieutenant in the 4th Battalion of Sonora, 1912; fought in eighty-six battles against the forces of Victoriano Huerta; fought against Pascual Orozco, 1912–13; fought Villa's forces as an officer in the 6th Sonoran Battalion, 1915; fought the Yaquis

as commander of the 8th Sonoran Battalion; Commander of the 23rd Cavalry Regiment, 1917–18; rank of Colonel, Dec. 15, 1915; rank of Brigadier General, Aug. 1, 1920; commander of military operations, Baja California del Norte, 1922; commander of military operations, Sinaloa, 1923; fought against the De la Huerta rebellion, 1923; rank of Brigade General, Jan. 16, 1924; fought against the Escobar rebellion, 1929; reached rank of Divisionary General, Oct. 16, 1937; Commander of the 4th Military Zone, Hermosillo, Sonora; Commander of the 17th Military Zone, Queretaro, Queretaro; Commander of the 15th Military Zone, Guadalajara, Jalisco; Commander of the 7th Military Zone, Monterrey, Nuevo Leon; Commander of the Pacific Military Region, 1942–45; Commander of the 1st Military Zone, Mexico, D.F., 1951–56. k-Supposedly appointed as Secretary of National Defense to represent the interests of the Veterans of the Revolution; awarded the Belisario Dominguez Award, 1973; Medina says the Left accused him of being the intellectual author of the murder of *Rodolfo T. Loaiza*, governor of Sinaloa, in 1945. l-*Informe*, 1949–50; *Hoy*, 7 Dec. 1940; WWM45, 67; DGF51, I, 182; Peral, 474; DGF56, 201; HA, 20 Dec. 1946, 9; HA, 19 Jan. 1951, 13–16; *Excelsior*, 4 May 1975, 4, 32; Anderson, 341; HA, 8 Oct. 1973, 13; Medina, 20, 20.

Maciel Salcedo, Ignacio

a-Sept. 29, 1910. b-Guadalajara, Jalisco, *West*, *Urban*. c-Primary studies in a public school, Guadalajara; secondary and preparatory studies in the Preparatory School, University of Guadalajara; law degree, School of Law, University of Guadalajara; Secretary General of the University of Guadalajara, 1953–59; Director of the School of Law, University of Guadalajara. d-*Senator* from the State of Jalisco, 1970–76, President of the Second Treasury and the First Consular and Diplomatic Service Committee; First Secretary of the First Government Committee, and member of the First Section of the Legislative Studies Committee. e-None. f-Assistant President of the Board of Conciliation and Arbitration, State of Jalisco; Judge in Atotonelco de Alto, Jalisco; Assistant Attorney General of Jalisco; Judge, Traffic Department, Guadalajara, Jalisco; Legal Adviser to the Chief of Police, Guadalajara; Director, Department of Labor and Social Welfare, Jalisco. g-None. j-None. k-None. l-C de S, 1970–76, 79; PS, 3514.

Madero (Gonzalez), Raul

a-Sept. 16, 1888. b-Parras, Coahuila, *North*, *Urban*. c-Early education unknown; no degree. d-*Governor of Coahuila*, 1957–63. e-Prominent member and co-founder of the Authentic Party of the Mexican Revolution (PARM), 1954. f-Provisional Governor of Coahuila, June 15–20, 1915; member of the

Board of the National Army-Navy Bank as a representative of the Secretariat of National Defense, 1952–57. g-Member of the Veterans of the Revolution who participated in honoring President *Echeverria*, 1971; Commander of the Legion of Honor, 1975– . i-Brother of Francisco Madero; great-grandfather was Governor of Coahuila, 1880–84; father was a millionaire; brother Emilio became a prominent Coahuilan industrialist; son Francisco was a precandidate for Mayor of Torreon, 1975; close friend of *Antonio I. Villarreal*. j-Joined the Revolution as a close collaborator of brother Francisco; involved in his brother's flight from Morelos, 1911; fought with Villa under Col. Eugenio Aquirre Benavides, 1913–14; rank of Col., Nov. 16, 1914; rank of Brigadier General, Apr. 2, 1915; fought Obregon with Villa, 1914–15; rejoined Army as a Brigadier General, 1939; rank of Division General, April 1, 1944; retired 1961; Chief of Arms for Zapata's surrender. k-Noted in the Revolution for saving Francisco Villa's life from a firing squad, 1912; fled into exile in the United States, 1913; supported the Escobar rebellion, 1929; Scott suggests that Madero may have been given the PRI nomination for Governor of Coahuila in return for PARM's recognition and support of *Adolfo Lopez Mateos* in 1958. l-DP70, 1230; Scott, 188; DGF, II, 35; HA, 17 Dec. 1962, 25; HA, 10 Sept. 1971, 18; Michaels, 40; Dulles, 441; Lopez, 640; *Excelsior*, 15 Apr. 1975, 16; Enc. Mex., Annual, 1977, 576.

Madrazo (Becerra), Carlos A.

(Deceased June 4, 1969)

a-1915. b-Villahermosa, Tabasco, *Gulf*, *Urban*. c-Primary and secondary studies in Villahermosa; preparatory studies from the National Preparatory School; law degree from the National School of Law, UNAM, 1937; professor of history in secondary schools. d-*Federal Deputy* from the Federal District, Dist. 2, 1943–46; president of the Chamber of Deputies, September, 1944; *Governor of Tabasco*, 1959–64. e-Founder of the National Federation of Popular Organizations (CNOP) of the PRM, Jan. 18, 1942, with *Ramon G. Bonfil* and *Lauro Ortega*; principal leader of the Bloc of Revolutionary Youth of the Red Shirts under Garrido Canabal, 1933–35; director of the Federation of Mexican Youth, 1939; member of the First National Council of the CNOP, 1944; *President of the CEN of PRI*, 1954–65. f-Private Secretary to the Governor of Guanajuato, *Luis I. Rodriguez*, 1937–38; Private Secretary to the President of the CEN of the PRM, *Luis I. Rodriguez*, 1938–39; official of the Secretariat of Public Education, 1941; head of the Department of Economic Statistics, Department of the Federal District; Director of Social Action of the Department of the Federal District, 1942–43; head of the Legal Department of the National Sugar Cane Commission. **g-**President of the Student Society of the National Preparatory School, 1933; President of the Federation of Mexican Youth, 1939; member of the Technical Council of Education of the Federation of Socialist Students of Tabasco, 1933–35. **h-**None. **i-**Son, *Carlos Madrazo Pintado*, was Assistant Secretary to *Alfonso Martinez Dominguez*, and was elected Federal Deputy from the Federal District, 1973–76 and became Oficial Mayor of Public Works, 1976– ; son Roberto important leader in the National Youth Sector of PRI; married Gabriela Pintado. **j-**None. **k-**Involved in a major political scandal as a Federal Deputy and was forced to resign; *Madrazo* was later exonerated and was reinstated as a Federal Deputy; the reason for his involvement was attributed to his support of *Javier Rojo Gomez* for president, 1945; resigned as President of the CEN of PRI after failing to bring about reforms; many of his supporters believe that the airplane crash in which he died was the result of sabotage. **l-**WWMG, 25; DP70, 1232; Enc. Mex., V, 220; Johnson, 45–47; Correa, 36, 114, 118; HA, 26 Jan. 1945, 5; HA, 4 Aug. 1944; *Por que*, 25 Sept. 1969, 12ff; Cadena Z., 129; NYT, 2 Sept. 1944, 9; CyT, 91; *Excelsior*, 5 June 1977, 4; Enc. Mex., VIII, 1977, 198.

Madrazo Pintado, Carlos Armando

a-Aug. 22, 1940. **b-**Federal District, *Federal District, Urban*. **c-**Law degree, National School of Law, UNAM, 1958–62, completed his thesis in 1963 on divestiture. **d-***Federal Deputy* from the Federal District, Dist. 23, 1973–76. **e-**None. **f-**Auxiliary Secretary to *Alfonso Martinez Dominguez*, 1970–71; delegate of the Department of the Federal District to San Angel, 1973; *Oficial Mayor of the Secretariat of Public Works*, 1976– . **g-**None. **h-**Practicing lawyer in the firm of Madrazo and De Buen, 1963–70. **i-**Son of *Carlos Madrazo*. **j-**None. **k-**None. **l-***Excelsior*, 16 Mar. 1973, 22; DJBM, 83; *Hoy*, 14 Mar. 1970, 4; *Excelsior*, 28 Feb. 1973, 19; *Excelsior*, 21 Jan. 1975, 5.

Magana, Gildardo

(Deceased Dec. 13, 1939)

a-June 8, 1891. **b-**Zamora, Michoacan, *West Central, Urban*. **c-**Studied at the Colegio de Jacona seminary in Zamora; studied business administration in San Antonio, Texas; studied accounting in Mexico, D.F.; no degree. **d-***Governor of Michoacan*, 1936–39. **f-**Governor of the Federal District and Secretary of Government during the Convention of Aguascalientes, 1914; *Governor of Baja California del Norte*, 1934–35. **g-**Secretary General of the Union of Small Property Owners; organizer of the National Agrarian Federation. **h-**Practicing accountant; author of a major work on Zapata and agrarianism in Mexico. **i-**Companion and longtime friend of *Saturnino Cedillo* since Revolutionary days under Zapata; precursor of the Revolution in a group which included Camilo Arriaga, Jose Vasconcelos, and *Francisco Mugica*. **j-**Joined the Revolution; instrumental in briefly uniting Villa and Zapata; became Chief of Staff of the Army of the South on the death of Zapata, 1919; Commanding General of the Liberating Army of the South, 1919; head of the Agrarian Settlement Program, 1920–24; career army officer, 1924–34; Commander of the 24th Military Zone, Cuernavaca, Morelos. **k-**Important intellectual in the Zapatista movement; Brandenburg considered *Magana* in the Inner Circle status as Governor of Michoacan; precandidate for President of Mexico, 1939. **l-**Brandenburg, 90; Kirk, 86, 118; DP70, 1233; *Heroic Mexico*, 163, 173, 330; D de Y, 5 Sept. 1935; Michaels, 3; Bermudez, 80–81; Gonzalez Navarro, 150; Enc. Mex., VIII, 1977, 201–02; Raby, 215.

Magdaleno (Cardona), Mauricio

a-May 13, 1906. **b-**Villa de Refugio, Zacatecas, *East Central, Rural*. **c-**Primary and secondary studies in Aguascalientes, Aguascalientes; preparatory studies at the National Preparatory School, 1920–23; studied at the Graduate School of UNAM, 1923–25; studied at the University of Madrid, 1932–33; Professor of History and Literature, UNAM, 1934–35. **d-***Federal Deputy* from the State of Zacatecas, Dist. 3, 1949–52, member of the Legislative Studies Committee (2nd year); *Senator* from the State of Zacatecas, 1958–64, member of the Gran Comision, President of the First Committee on Public Education, member of the First Committee on Foreign Relations, the First Balloting Committee, the First Instructive Section of the Grand Jury; substitute member of the Tourist Affairs Committee and the Legislative Studies Committee. **e-**None. **f-**President of the Revisory Committee on Income Taxes, 1934–36, Secretariat of the Treasury; member of the Technical Council for Theaters, Mexico, D.F., 1936–39; correspondent for the National Institute for the Investigation of Theaters; head of the Library and Archives, Secretariat of the Treasury, 1936–45; writer for the newspaper, *El Universal*, 1934–64; Director General of the Division of Social Action, Department of the Federal District, 1952–58; *Subsecretary of Cultural Affairs of the Secretariat of Public Education*, 1964–70. **g-**None. **h-**Well-known author of numerous plays, books, and movie scripts. **i-**Became friend of *Adolfo Lopez Mateos* and *Manuel Moreno Sanchez* during Vasconcelos campaign, 1929; brother Vicente a well-known poet; married Rosario Rios. **j-**None. **k-**Campaign aide to Jose Vasconcelos, 1929. **l-***Libro de Oro*, xxxv; DGF51, I, 27; C de D, 1949–51, 77; DPE65, 135; C de S, 1961–

64, 59–60; DBM68, 399; DBM70, 349; C de S, 1964, 12; WWM45, 68; Strode, 415; DEM, 207–08; HA, 21 Dec. 1964, 4; Haddox, 8; Func., 410; letter; Lopez, 642; Enc. Mex., VIII, 1977, 203.

Maldonado Lopez, Carlos B.

a-Aug. 15, 1911. b-Hermosillo, Sonora, *North*, *Urban*. c-Primary studies in Hermosillo; some secondary studies in Hermosillo and in Mexico City; no degree. d-*Senator* from the State of Sonora, 1958–64, Second Secretary of the Special Forestry Committee, Alternate member of the First Petroleum, Special Livestock and First Ejido Committees. e-Participated in the presidential campaign of General Alvaro Obregon, 1928; participated in the presidential campaign of *Adolfo Lopez Mateos*, 1958; General Delegate of the CEN of PRI to the states of Jalisco, Colima, Guanajuato and Sonora. f-None. g-Founding member of the CTM, 1936; President of the CTM in the State of Sonora. h-Laborer for many years. j-None. k-None. l-C de S, 1961–64, 60; Func., 359.

Maldonado Perez, Caritino

(Deceased Apr. 17, 1971)
a-1915. b-Tlalixtaquilla, Guerrero, *South*, *Rural*. c-Teaching certificate; school teacher. d-*Federal Deputy* from the State of Guerrero, Dist. 5, 1949–51, member of the Gran Comision, the First Committee on Public Education, and the Second Balloting Committee; substitute member of the Committee on Forest Affairs; *Alternate Senator* from Guerrero, 1952–58; *Senator* from the State of Guerrero, 1958–64, President of the Special Committee on Small Agricultural Property, member of the First Committee on Public Education, substitute member of the Internal and Foreign Trade Committee, the Protocol Committee, and the Industries Committee; *Governor of Guerrero*, 1969–71. e-*Secretary of Popular Action of the CEN of PRI*, 1952–56. f-Head of the Department of Inspection, Secretariat of Labor, 1952–58; *Oficial Mayor of the Secretariat of Health*, 1965–69. g-*Secretary General of the CNOP of PRI*, 1952–58. h-None. j-None. k-Considered a cacique of the local region he represented in Guerrero; *Por que* states that he was denounced in 1950 for being connected with the murder of three persons. l-C de S, 1961–64, 60; *Libro de Oro*, xxxvi; DGF56, 6, 399; DPE65, 148; C de D, 1949–51, 78; DGF51, I, 22, 30, 32, 34; *Siempre*, 19 Sept. 1956, 10; 21 Dec. 1964, 4; *Por que*, 4 Oct. 1968, 35; HA, 10 June 1974, 13.

Maldonado Sanchez, Braulio

a-1903. b-San Jose del Cabo, Baja California del Norte, *North*, *Rural*. c-Primary studies in Baja California; preparatory studies at the National Pre-

paratory School; special studies in the Army; enrolled in UNAM, 1924; law degree. d-*Federal Deputy* from Baja California del Norte, 1946–49, member of the Gran Comision, the Second Treasury Committee, the Second Balloting Committee, the Budget and Accounts Committee, and the First Constitutional Affairs Committee; secretary to the President of the Preparatory Committee; *Federal Deputy* from Baja California del Norte, 1952–53, member of the Third Section of the Credentials Committee and the Social Action Committee (1st year); *Governor of Baja California del Norte*, 1953–59. e-Leader of the Popular Electoral Front; co-founder of the Leftist Socialist Party, 1931; Secretary General of the Leftist Socialist Party; member of the National Advisory Council of PRI; attempted to found a new party, the Coordinating Revolutionary Movement of the Mexican Republic, 1977. f-Adviser to the Independent Farmers Central (CCI), 1966. g-Gonzalez Navarro states that the CCI was financed by *Maldonado Sanchez*; active in the National Students League. h-Worked as a laborer in the United States; author of a political commentary on Baja California and his regime. i-Former Federal Deputy *Leopoldo Sales Rovira* was part of his political organization in Baja California. j-1st sgt. in the army. k-Student participant in 1927 presidential campaign in support of General Serrano with *Miguel Aleman* and *Efrain Brito Rosado*; deported as a result of his supposed participation in the Popular Electoral Front's attempt to disrupt the *Diaz Ordaz* campaign, 1964; Johnson and *Por Que* claim his regime as governor was characterized by extensive corruption and that he was responsible for the development of a huge prostitution ring in Tijuana. l-C de D, 1946–48, 77; C de D, 1952–54, 14; Johnson, 134; *Por Que*, 2 July 1968, 2; DGF56, 90; DGF47, 4; D del S, 22 Jan. 1946, 1; *Por Que*, 4 Oct. 1968, 46–48; Gonzalez Navarro, 238, 241; HA, 28 Sept. 1953, 25; *Excelsior*, 17 June 1977, 10; HA, 5 July 1954, 9.

Mancera Ortiz, Rafael

(Deceased Sept. 30, 1968)
a-1895. b-Federal District, *Federal District*, *Urban*. c-Preparatory studies at the National Preparatory School, CPA degree from the National School of Business Administration, UNAM, 1917; Professor of Accounting at the Graduate School of Business and Administration, UNAM, 1932–36; and the School of Economics and Social Sciences, IPN, 1925–36. d-None. e-None. f-Oficial Mayor of the Controller General's office, 1925, 1927; Subsecretary of the Treasury, 1930–32; adviser to Nacional Financiera; *Subsecretary of the Treasury*, 1946–52, 1952–58. g-First President of the National Association of Public Accountants in Mexico. h-Organized a private accounting firm of Mancera and Sons; author of a

book on public administration and economic development in Mexico, 1953. **i-**Son Miguel was Gerente of the Bank of Mexico, 1964–70; son Gabriel is a CPA, managing the firm of Mancera and Sons; married Maria Luisa Aguayo. **j-**Participated in the Revolution, 1913–20. **k-**One of the initiators of the certified public accounting system in Mexico. **l-**DGF47; DGF51, II, 231, 303, 487, 359; DGF56, 161; DP70, 2413; HA, 12 Dec. 1952, 5; WNM, 139; Enc. Mex., VIII, 1977, 239.

Manero, Antonio
(Deceased 1964)
a-1885. **b-**Toluca, Mexico, *West Central, Urban*. **c-**Primary and secondary studies in Mexico, D.F.; Professor of Business Organization, National School of Economics, UNAM, 1945–48. **d-***Federal Deputy* from the State of Mexico, Dist. 2, 1943–46, president of economic commissions as a Federal Deputy, 1943. **e-**None. **f-**Member of the Inspection and Regulatory Commission of the Banking System; President of the Treasury and Public Credit Commission, 1920; member of the commission formed to found the Bank of Mexico; founder and Director General of the National Labor Bank, 1929; financial adviser to the bloc of Senators from the official party, 1935; Director of Finances for the Department of the Federal District, 1939–40; founder and President of the Industrial Bank of the State of Mexico, 1943; Director General of PIPSA, 1940; Director of Financial Studies of the Secretariat of the Treasury, 1944. **g-**None. **h-**Author of many books on Revolutionary banking institutions. **i-**Father, a well-known lawyer. **j-**Joined the Revolution, 1913; fought under Carranza. **l-**C de D, 1943–45, 15; DP70, 1246; Lopez, 648; Casasola, V; Enc. Mex., VIII, 1977, 242.

Manjarrez, Luis Cruz
b-Tochimilco, Municipio of Atlixco, Puebla, *East Central, Rural*. **c-**Primary studies in Puebla, Puebla; secondary and preparatory studies in Mexico City; began studies at the Higher School of Construction and Engineering. **d-**Local deputy to the State Legislature of Puebla; *Federal Deputy* from the State of Puebla, Dist. 2, 1949–52, member of the Editorial Committee, the Cinematographic Development Committee, and the Complaints Committee; *Senator* from the State of Puebla, 1952–58, member of the Second Tariff and Foreign Trade Committee, the Immigration Committee and the Special Legislative Studies Committee. **e-**President of PRI in the State of Puebla, 1952. **f-**Subdirector, Office of Public Entertainment, Department of the Federal District; Director of Press and Publicity, Secretariat of Communications; Director of Press and Publicity, Secretariat of Agriculture and Livestock. **g-**None. **h-**Journalist; founding Editor of *El Nacional* (official government

paper), Mexico City. **j-**None. **k-**Founder of the Casa del Campesino, Atlixco, Puebla, 1935; founder of the first Casa Materno-Infantil, 1947. **l-**DGF51, I, 29, 31, 33; C de D, 1949–51, 78; Ind. Biog., 99–100; DGF56, 7, 9–12, 14.

Manrique de Lara Hernandez, Aurelio
(Deceased 1967)
a-Apr. 27, 1891. **b-**San Luis Potosi, San Luis Potosi, *East Central, Urban*. **c-**Primary studies in the Scientific and Literary Institute of San Luis Potosi, San Luis Potosi; normal teaching certificate from the National Teachers College, Mexico, D.F.; completed 4th year of medical studies; professor at the National Preparatory School, 1912–17. **d-**Federal Deputy from the State of San Luis Potosi, 1916–18; Governor of San Luis Potosi, 1923–25; Federal Deputy from the State of San Luis Potosi, 1928–30. **e-**Founder of the National Agrarian Party, 1920; orator for General Obregon, 1920; President of the Revolutionary Federation of Independent Parties, 1933. **f-**Director of Information of the Secretariat of Government, 1934–40; *Director General of the ISSSTE*, 1940–46; Ambassador to Sweden, 1946–51 and 1952–55; Ambassador to Norway, 1951–52; Ambassador to Denmark, 1956; Director of the National Library, Secretariat of Public Education. **g-**None. **h-**Author of numerous articles. **i-**Active in the precursor movement to the Revolution with Ricardo Flores Magon, Juan Sarabia, *Antonio Diaz Soto y Gama, Juan Barragan* and others; jailed in San Luis Potosi during the Porfiriato; boyhood friend of *Jesus Silva Herzog*; son of a well-known lawyer. **j-**Fought under Obregon against Huerta, 1914. **k-**Rebuked President Calles in answer to his State of the Union Message; forced into exile, 1929–33; supported the Escobar rebellion, 1929; known for his dramatic debates with *Soto y Gama* in the Federal Chamber of Deputies. **l-**B de M, 170–71; DP70, 1248; DGF51, I, 107; DGF56, 125; Lopez, 649; Enc. Mex., VIII, 1977, 250.

Mantilla Molina, Roberto
a-Dec. 9, 1910. **b-**San Juan Bautista (Villahermosa), Tabasco, *Gulf, Urban*. **c-**Secondary studies in Tampico, Tamaulipas, Mexico and Veracruz; preparatory studies at the Preparatory School of Veracruz; law degree, National School of Law, UNAM, 1934; completed studies for a degree in philosophy, School of Philosophy and Letters, 1930–33, but did not take exam; secondary school teacher, Secondary School No. 4 and 1, 1933–34; professor of the History of Philosophic Doctrines and Logic, National Preparatory School, 1933–49; professor of Mercantile Law, National School of Law, UNAM, 1934–75; professor of Mercantile Law, School of Business and Administration, UNAM, 1935–50; professor, Mexican

Technological Institute, 1948; professor of Mercantile Societies, LLD Program, UNAM; Member of the Governing Board of UNAM, 1976– ; Director, National School of Law, UNAM, 1954–58; Director, Institute of Comparative Law, UNAM, 1959–66; *Secretary General of UNAM*, 1961–66. d-None. e-None. f-Agent of the Ministerio Publico, civil matters, Cordoba and Orizaba, Veracruz; Director, Legal Department, Secretary of Industry and Commerce, 1946–47; president, legislative committee, Secretary of Industry and Commerce. g-President of the Student Society of the School of Philosophy and Letters, UNAM, 1932–33; Secretary General of the Mexican Bar Association, 1944. h-Practicing lawyer, 1934– . i-Related to *Antonio Ruiz Galindo*, Secretary of Industry and Commerce, 1946–48. j-None. k-None. l-Letters; Lopez, 651.

Manzanilla Schaffer, Victor

a-Nov. 13, 1924. b-Federal District, *Federal District*, *Urban*. c-Primary studies at the Benito Juarez School, Mexico, D.F.; secondary studies at Public School No. 3, Mexico, D.F.; preparatory studies, National Preparatory School, Mexico, D.F.; law degree with honorable mention from the National School of Law, UNAM, 1948; LLD studies except the examination; postgraduate work in sociology at the New School of Social Research, New York, 1949; Professor by Competitive Appointment in Sociology, National School of Law, UNAM, 1955–70; Professor of Civics for the National Farmers Federation (CNC), 1963–64; Professor of Agrarian Reform, Institute of Comparative Law, UNAM, Professor of Economic Problems, UNAM; Professor of Introductory Law, School of Administration, National School of Economics, UNAM; Professor of Mercantile Law, School for the National Chambers of Commerce. d-*Federal Deputy* from the State of Yucatan, Dist. 3, 1967–69, member of the First Section of the Agrarian Affairs Committee, the Legislative Studies Committee (6th Section of Agrarian Affairs), the Livestock Committee, the Constitutional Affairs Committee, and the Desert Zones Committee; President of the Chamber of Deputies, Sept., 1967, answered *Diaz Ordaz's* third State of the Union address; *Senator* from the State of Yucatan, 1970–76, member of the Gran Comision, President of the Agriculture and Development Committee and the Agrarian Department Committee; *Federal Deputy* from the State of Yucatan, Dist. 3, 1976–79. e-*Secretary of Press and Publicity of the CEN of PRI*, 1970 to Aug. 2, 1972; assistant secretary to the President of the CEN of PRI, *Jesus Reyes Heroles*, Aug. 2, 1972–74; President of the National Revolutionary Coalition; adviser to the IEPES of PRI; President of the National Commission on Legislative Studies of PRI, 1963. f-Lawyer for the Office of the Assistant

Attorney General of Mexico; Legal Assistant to the International Division of Narcotics, United Nations, 1949–51; Director of the Department of the Press, Department of Agrarian Affairs, 1961; Director of Social Agrarian Action and Information, Department of Agrarian Affairs, 1965; agrarian adviser, Advisory Section, Department of Agrarian Affairs. g-President of the Junior Chamber of Commerce of Mexico, D.F., 1954; President of the 1942 Generation of Law Students, National School of Law, UNAM, 1942–46. h-Writer for *La Republica*, official PRI magazine; author of numerous articles. i-Father a prominent lawyer and revolutionary leader in Yucatan. j-None. k-*Por Que* claims that he turned down the PRI nomination for Governor of Yucatan in 1969, because he would accept only if the Governor had direct control over the appointments of the Directors of CORDEMEX and the Agricultural Bank of Yucatan; voted against a presidential sponsored amendment to Article 27, 1977. l-DBM68, 405–06; DPE65, 177; DPE61, 127; HA, 14 Aug. 1972, 11; C de D, 1967–69, 57, 67, 72, 84, 91; *Por Que*, 23 Oct. 1969, 22; C de S, 1970–76, 79; Enc. Mex., VIII, 1977, 256.

Manzur Ocana, Julian Alejandro

b-Tabasco, *Gulf*. c-Primary and secondary studies in Villahermosa; preparatory studies at the National Preparatory School; medical degree from the National School of Medicine, UNAM; professor of medicine, School of Medicine, University of Tabasco. d-*Senator* from the State of Tabasco, 1958–64, President of the Public Welfare Committee, member of the Treasury Committee and the Gran Comision, Secretary of the First Navy Committee. e-None. f-None. g-None. h-Practicing physician for many years. j-None. k-None. l-Func., 366; C de S, 1961–64, 61.

Mar de la Rosa, J. Refugio

a-July 4, 1924. b-Chihuahua, Chihuahua, *North*, *Urban*. c-Secondary studies at the Institute of Sciences and Letters, Chihuahua; no degree. d-*Federal Deputy* from the State of Chihuahua, Dist. 6, 1970–73, member of the Second Instructive Section of the Grand Jury, the Second Labor Committee and the Second General Means of Communication Committee; *Federal Deputy* from the State of Chihuahua, Dist. 6, 1976–79, member of the Machinery Section of the Industrial Development Committee, the Border Zones Section of the Regional Development Committee, the Third Section of the Development of Social Security and Public Health Committee, the First Section of the Development of Tourism Committee, and the Labor Section of the Legislative Studies Committee. e-Joined PRI, 1947; state PRI official. **f-**None. **g-**Secretary General of Section 32 of the Union of Hotel and Restaurant Workers; Secretary General of the CTM of the State of Chihuahua, 1976– . **j-**None. **k-**None. **l-**D de C, 1976–79, 27, 36, 38, 41, 54; *Excelsior*, 28 Aug. 1976, 1C; C de D, 1970–73, 123.

Marentes Miranda, Tomas

a-Apr. 1, 1904. **b-**Villa de Munucma, Yucatan, *Gulf, Rural*. **c-**Early education unknown; no degree. **d-***Governor of Yucatan*, 1952–53. **e-**None. **f-**Subdirector of the National Lottery, 1946–52. **g-**None. **i-**Protege of *Miguel Aleman*. **j-**None. **k-**Scott says he was imposed as governor of Yucatan over public protests; deposed by the state legislature, June 15, 1953, one of the rare cases of this occurring in Mexican politics; students and henequen producers sent complaints to President *Ruiz Cortines* about his performance as governor. **l-**Anerson; Scott, 276; DGF47, 410; DGF51, I, 657; HA, 29 June 1953, 10; letter.

Margain (Gleason), Hugo B.

a-Feb. 13, 1913. **b-**Federal District, *Federal District, Urban*. **c-**Secondary studies at the Colegio Frances Morelos, Mexico, D.F.; preparatory studies at the National Preparatory School; law degree from the National School of Law, UNAM, 1938, with a thesis on "The Law and Reality in Mexico"; Professor of Constitutional Law, 1947, Professor of Constitutional Writs, 1951–56, National School of Law, UNAM; Professor of Fiscal Law, 1952–56, School of Business Administration, UNAM. **d-**None. **e-**None. **f-**Director General of the Federal Retail Merchants Tax Division, Secretariat of the Treasury, 1947–52; Director General of the Federal Income Tax Bureau, Secretariat of the Treasury, 1952–59; *Oficial Mayor of the Secretariat of Industry and Commerce*, 1959–61; *Subsecretary of Industry and Commerce*, 1961–64; Director General of the National Commission on Profit Sharing, 1963–64; executive member of the National Institute of Scientific Investigation, 1962–64; *Ambassador to the United States,* 1965–70; *Secretary of the Treasury,* 1970–73; *Ambassador to Great Britain*, 1973–76; *Ambassador to the United States*, 1976– . **g-**None. **h-**Author of several books on fiscal law and public administration; practicing lawyer, 1938–47. **i-**Father, Cesar Margain, a well-known doctor; studied under *Antonio Carrillo Flores*, *Ramon Beteta*, and *Alfonso Noriega* at UNAM; married Margarita Charles; sister Maria Luisa married *Manuel Sandoval Vallarta*; brother-in-law of industrialist Carlos Phillips Olmedo. **j-**None. **k-**Resigned as Secretary of the Treasury because of economic policy differences with President *Echeverria*. **l-**IWW67, 789; WWW70–71, 607; DPE61, 64; DGF51, I, 149; DPE65, 26; *Hoy*, Dec. 1970; DGF56, 168; HA, 4 Jan. 1971, 15; HA, 7 Dec. 1970; WWMG, 25–26; letters; *Justicia*, Aug., 1973; Enc. Mex., VIII, 1977, 271–72.

Marin Ramos, J. Ricardo

b-Tepic, Nayarit, *West, Urban*. **c-**Early education unknown; studies at the School of Cavalry, National Military College; Industrial Subdirector of the National School of Agriculture. **d-***Alternate Senator* from the State of Nayarit, 1946–52; *Senator* from the State of Nayarit, 1964–70. **e-**Joined the PNR, 1929. **f-**Director of the Department of Rural Defenses, Secretariat of National Defense; Director General of Physical Education, Secretariat of Public Education, 1946–52. **g-**None. **j-**Career Army officer; joined the Revolution as an ordinary soldier; fought in eighty-six battles; reached rank of Divisionary General. **k-**Precandidate for the gubernatorial nomination of PRI in Zacatecas many times. **l-**C de S, 1964–70; DGF51, I, 7, 289; C de S, 1946–52; MGF69.

Marquez Padilla, Tarciso

a-Dec. 15, 1915. **b-**Federal District, *Federal District, Urban*. **c-**Enrolled in the National Military College, January 1, 1933, graduating as a 2nd Lieutenant of Artillery, January 1, 1937; graduate of the Applied Military School, 1938–39; preparatory studies at the National Preparatory Night School, 1938–39; law degree, National School of Law, UNAM, 1940–44. **d-**None. **e-**None. **f-**Adjutant, President of Mexico, 1940–41; Assistant Military Attache, Mexican Embassy, Washington, D.C., 1941; Assistant Director, Legal Department, PEMEX, 1945; Military Adviser, Mexican Delegation, United Nations Conference on International Organizations, San Francisco, 1945; *Oficial Mayor of the Secretariat of Industry and Commerce*, 1948–52; *Justice of the Supreme Court*, 1979– . **g-**None. **h-**None. **i-**Co-student with *Jose Lopez Portillo* at the National School of Law. **j-**Career army officer; reached rank of Brigade General. **k-**None. **l-**HA, 8 Jan. 1979, 14; WWM45, 71; DGF51, I, 263.

Martinez Adame, Arturo

(Deceased)
a-Dec. 11, 1896. **b-**Ciudad Bravo, Guerrero, *South, Rural*. **c-**Preparatory studies at the National Preparatory School; law degree, National School of Law, UNAM. **d-**Federal Deputy from the State of Guerrero, 1922–24; *Senator* from the State of Guerrero, 1940–46, President of the Third Labor Committee, First Secretary of the Second Government Committee, the First Mines Committee, the Railroad Committee, and the Administrative Committee; Second Secretary of the Second Justice Committee, and

member of the 1st Balloting Committee. e-None. f-Federal District Court Judge; President of the Federal Board of Conciliation and Arbitration, 1951; *Justice of the Supreme Court*, 1951–52, 1952–58, and 1958–61; *Provisional Governor of Guerrero*, 1961–63. g-Student representative of the Federation of University Students to the First International Student Congress, Mexico City, 1921. h-Author of several works on labor and government administration. i-Brother *Emigdio* served as a secretary of the CEN of PRI; student of Antonio Caso; co-student with *Vicente Lombardo Toledano* and *Teofilo Olea y Leyva* at the National Preparatory School. j-None. k-None. l-Peral, 496; DGF56, 568; G of M, 20; DGF51, I, 482; C de S, 1940–46; Casasola, V.

Martinez Adame, Emigdio

a-Aug. 5, 1905. b-Chilpancingo, Guerrero, *South, Urban.* c-Primary studies in Chilpancingo; preparatory studies at the National Preparatory School, Mexico City; law degree from the National School of Law, UNAM, 1929; studies in economics from the School of Economics, University of London, 1935–36; law studies in Paris; studies at the National School of Economics, UNAM, 1931–32; Professor of Economics, National School of Economics, UNAM, 1937–44. d-*Senator* from the State of Guerrero, 1952–58, member of the Permanent Commission of Congress, 1954; member of the Gran Comision, the Second Committee on Tariffs and Foreign Trade, the Protocol Committee, the Second Committee on Credit, Money, and Institutions of Credit, the First Constitutional Affairs Committee, and the Legislative Studies Committee. e-*Secretary of Political Action of the CEN of PRI*, 1953–56. f-Director General of Expenditures, Secretariat of the Treasury, 1934–35; Chief, Department of Credit, National Ejido Credit Bank; Consulting Minister, Mexican Embassy in Moscow, under Ambassador *Narciso Bassols*, 1944–46; Postmaster General of Mexico, 1947–52; Director General of the National Commerce Bank, 1958–64. g-President of the Student Society of the National School of Economics, 1932. h-Co-founder of the Fondo de Cultura Economica with *Eduardo Villasenor*, *Eduardo Suarez*, *Ramon Beteta*, and others, 1934; editor of the *Revista Trimestre Economico*. i-Brother *Arturo* served as a Senator from Guerrero, 1940–46; student assistant to *Manuel Gomez Morin*; member of the *Combate* group under *Narciso Bassols* opposed to the government of *Manuel Avila Camacho*, 1940–42. j-None. k-Precandidate for Governor of Guerrero, 1950. l-DGF51, I, 240; DGF47, 143; Correa, 59; *Excelsior*, 15 Aug. 1972, 7D; DGF56, 6, 8, 9, 10, 12, 14; D de Y, Dec. 1958; HA, 15 Dec. 1958, 5; C de S, 1952–58; HA, 28 Feb. 1947; Ind. Biog., 100–01.

Martinez Aguilar, Rogelio

a-1941. b-Federal District, *Federal District, Urban.* c-Economics degree from the National School of Economics, UNAM; postgraduate work in economic planning in developing countries; Professor of Economic and Social Problems of Mexico. d-None. e-None. f-Economist for the National Agricultural Credit Bank; economist in the Secretariat of the Treasury; Subdirector General of Administrative Affairs, Secretariat of the Presidency, 1970–72; Ambassador to Costa Rica, July 31, 1972–74. g-None. h-Author of economic and social essays. j-None. k-None. l-HA, 14 Aug. 1972, 9; *Excelsior*, 1 Aug. 1972, 9; DAPC, 11.

Martinez Baez, Antonio

a-July 18, 1901. b-Morelia, Michoacan, *West Central, Urban.* c-Primary studies in Morelia; preparatory studies at the Colegio Primitivo de San Nicolas de Hidalgo, Morelia, 1913–19; legal studies at the University of Michoacan, 1920; studied at the National School of Law, UNAM, 1921–15, law degree, July 21, 1926; Professor of Constitutional Law at the National Law School, UNAM, 1929–48, 1953–67; professor at the National Preparatory School, 1928; professor of special courses at the Escuela Libre de Derecho; professor at the Colegio de Mexico, 1944; professor of graduate law courses at the National University; LLD from the National School of Law, UNAM, 1950; Professor Emeritus, National School of Law, UNAM, 1966; member of the Governing Junta of UNAM (Secretary), 1945–66. d-*Federal Deputy* from the State of Michoacan, Dist. 3, 1973–76. e-Member of the Statutes Section of the Advisory Council to the IEPES of PRI, 1972. f-President of the Economic Commission for Latin America in Mexico, City., 1951; consulting lawyer for the National Agrarian Commission; head of the Legal Department for the National Urban Mortgage Bank, 1935–41; head of the Department of Indemnifications, Secretariat of Agriculture, 1935–41; President of the National Banking Commission, 1941–43; Director General of the Financiera Industrial Azucarera, 1943–46; *Secretary of Industry and Commerce*, Oct. 21, 1948, to Nov. 30, 1952; Director General of Guanos and Fertilizers, 1952–54; head of the National Securities Commission, 1953–59; member of the Permanent Tribunal of Arbitration, The Hague, 1965; arbitrator for LAFTA, 1968. g-President of the Mexican Bar Association, 1959–60. h-Practicing lawyer, in practice for many years with *Manuel Gual Vidal* and *Gabino Fraga*; author of many articles. i-Student at UNAM with *Eduardo Bustamante*, *Ramon Beteta*, *Manuel Gual Vidal*, *Carlos Novoa*, *J. Jesus Castorena*, *Ricardo J. Zevada*, and *Manuel Ramirez Vazquez*; father, Dr.

Manuel Martinez Solorzano, served as Director of the Michoacan Museum, 1900–20, was a Deputy to the Constitutional Congress, 1916–17, and taught at the Colegio San Nicolas in Morelia for 15 years; grandfather, Ramon Martinez Aviles, lawyer and noted composer; brother *Manuel* served as Subsecretary of Health, 1943–46; student assistant to *Narciso Bassols*, 1925; married Alicia Flores Magon. **j-**None. **k-**None. **l-**D de S, 21 Oct. 1948; D de Y, Oct. 1948, 1; HA, 29 Oct. 1948, 17; DGF51, I, 263; DGF51, II, 95, etc.; letters; Enc. Mec., VIII, 1977, 307–08.

Martinez Baez, Manuel

a-Sept. 26, 1894. **b-**Morelia, Michoacan, *West Central, Urban*. **c-**Primary studies in Morelia; preparatory studies at the Colegio de San Nicolas, Morelia, 1911; medical degree from the Medical School, Morelia, Jan. 2, 1916; graduate studies in Malaria at the University of Paris, 1934; Professor of Histology, Anatomy, and Pathology at the University of Michoacan, Morelia, 1922–25; Secretary General of the University of Michoacan, 1922–24; Rector of the University of Michoacan, 1924–25; lab assistant in the School of Medicine, University of Paris, 1933–34; special studies in tropical diseases, Department of Public Health; Professor of Natural and Physical Sciences, National Teachers College, 1917–20; Assistant Professor of Clinical Medicine, National School of Medicine, UNAM 1925–32; Professor of Parasitology, UNAM, 1933–40. **d-**None. **e-**None. **f-**Head of the Department of Publicity and Hygenic Education, Department of Public Health, 1926; First Director of the Institute of Tropical Diseases, Secretariat of Public Health, 1939, 1942–43, 1952–58; Director General of Epidemiology, Secretariat of Public Health, 1941–42; supervisory official, Secretariat of Health, 1943; *Subsecretary of Health,* 1943–46. **g-**None. **h-**Author of many articles on tropical diseases. **i-**Brother of *Antonio Martinez Baez,* Secretary of Industry and Commerce, 1948–52; son of Dr. Manuel Martinez Solorzano; married Aurora Palomo Gonzalez. **j-**None. **k-**None. **l-**EBW46, 693; Peral, 47, 205; WWM45, 72; Enc. Mex. VIII, 1977, 308–09; Lopez, 662.

Martinez Chavarria, Joaquin

a-May 21, 1924. **b-**Torreon, Coahuila, *North, Urban*. **c-**Degree in Architecture, 1947, National School of Architecture, UNAM, 1947; Professor of Architecture, National School of Architecture, UNAM, 1962–66. **d-**None. **e-**Coordinator of the National Reunion for the Study of Public Housing during the presidential campaign of *Luis Echeverria,* 1970, sponsored by PRI. **f-**Director General of construction of the Lopez Mateos Urban Center, 1960;

head of the Office of Construction, Department of Architecture and Planning, ISSSTE, 1962; member of the Commission for the Study of Housing and Social Interest (from the public sector), 1968; Director General of the National Institute of Housing, 1970–76. **g-**Member of the College of Architects. **j-**None. **k-**None. **l-**HA, 7 Dec. 1970, 27.

Martinez Corbala, Gonzalo

a-1928. **b-**San Luis Potosi, San Luis Potosi, *East Central, Urban*. **c-**Degree in Civil Engineering, National School of Engineering, UNAM; Master of Arts in Political Science, National School of Political and Social Sciences, UNAM. **d-***Federal Deputy* from the Federal District, Dist. 22, 1964–67, member of the Committee on National Properties and Resources, the Committee on the Department of the Federal District, the Committee on Public Works, and the Second Public Housing Committee; President of the Committee on Foreign Relations. **e-**President of the Regional Executive Committee of PRI in the Federal District. **f-**Ambassador to Chile, July 31, 1972, to 1974; Special Ambassador for South American Affairs, 1974–75; Director General of the Sahagun Industrial Complex, 1975–76; *Subsecretary of National Properties,* Secretariat of Public Works, 1976–77. **g-**President of the Mexican Society of Engineers. **h-**Director of the magazine *Civil Engineering CIC*; President of the Mexican Planning Society. **j-**None. **k-**As a Federal Deputy, made the protest speech which aroused public opinion against *Ernesto P. Uruchurtu* as head of the Department of the Federal District, culminating in his resignation, 1966; precandidate for Senator from San Luis Potosi, 1976. **l-**HA, 14 Aug. 1972, 9; *Excelsior*, 1 Aug. 1972, 1, 9; C de D, 1964–66, 52, 81, 90; *Excelsior*, 5 Jan. 1977, 22; *Excelsior*, 1 Apr. 1977; HA, 5 May 1975, 20.

Martinez de Hernandez Loza, Guadalupe

a-Feb. 11, 1906. **b-**Guadalajara, Jalisco, *West, Urban*. **c-**Primary studies at the Josefa O. de Dominguez School, Guadalajara; secondary studies at normal school; teaching certificate, normal school; studies in social work, University of Guadalajara (3 years); seminars on union education for women; primary school teacher; secondary school teacher; teacher at the Secondary Night School for Workers; Director of the 47th Urban School of Guadalajara. **d-***Federal Deputy* from the State of Jalisco, Dist. 2, 1958–61; *Federal Deputy* from the State of Jalisco, Dist. 2, 1970–73, member of the First Public Education Committee and the Social Welfare Committee (1st year); President of the State Legislature of Jalisco, 1979–80; *Alternate Senator* from the State of

Jalisco, 1976–82. e-Director of Feminine Action of PRI for the State of Jalisco; President of PRI in Jalisco. f-Oficial Mayor of the Cultural Department of the State of Jalisco. g-Secretary of Social Action of the Federation of Workers of Jalisco; Secretary of Press and Publicity of the CTM in Jalisco; Secretary of Political Action of the Women's Federation of the CTM of the Federal District. h-None. i-Husband *Heliodoro Hernandez Loza* was a Federal Deputy from Jalisco, 1943–46. j-None. k-None. l-C de D, 1958–60; C de D, 1970–72, 124; *Directorio*, 1970–72; Func., 241.

Martinez de la Vega, Francisco

a-Aug. 26, 1909. b-San Luis Potosi, San Luis Potosi, *East Central*, *Urban*. c-Primary and secondary studies at the Colegio Frances de Alvarado; preparatory studies at the National Preparatory School (distinguished student); no degree. d-*Federal Deputy* from the State of San Luis Potosi, Dist. 1, 1958–59, member of the Library Committee (1st year). e-Secretary General of the Popular Party (later PPS), 1951–55; joined PRI, 1957. f-Assistant to the Editor of *El Nacional*, 1930; chief of the editorial staff, *El Nacional*, 1944; Private Secretary to *Vicente Lombardo Toledano*, 1945; Private Secretary to *Cesar Martino Torres*, Director General of the National Ejido Bank; Private Secretary to General *Miguel Hernandez*, 1952; *Provisional Governor of San Luis Potosi*, 1959–61. g-None. h-Writer and journalist, began his journalism career in 1930; sports correspondent in South America and the United States; cofounder of *Siempre*; political affairs writer for *Hoy*. j-None. k-Expelled from the PPS for supporting *Enrique Ramirez y Ramirez*. l-HA, 2 Oct. 1961, 13; *Siempre*, 4 Feb. 1959, 6; Peral, 499; Func., 342; C de D, 1958–60, 83; Enc. Mex., VIII, 1977, 317.

Martinez Dominguez, Alfonso

a-Jan. 7, 1922. b-Monterrey, Nuevo Leon, *North*, *Urban*. c-Primary studies in Monterrey; secondary studies in Mexico, D.F.; Bachelor of Arts from the Franco-Mexican College, Mexico, D.F. d-*Federal Deputy* from the Federal District, Dist. 4, 1946–49, member of the Committee for the Department of the Federal District, the Second Balloting Committee, the Public Works Committee, and the Securities Committee; *Federal Deputy* from the Federal District, Dist. 17, 1952–55, member of the Legislative Studies Committee, and the Tourism Committee; *Federal Deputy* from the State of Nuevo Leon, 1964–67, Dist. 4, President of the Chamber of Deputies, Dec., 1964; President of the Gran Comision, member of the First Committee on Government, the Constitutional Affairs Committee; *Governor of Nuevo Leon*, 1979– . e-Secretary of Organization for the Regional PRI Committee of the Federal District, 1955; *Secretary of Popular Action of the CEN of PRI*; *President of the CEN of PRI*, 1968–70; *Secretary General of CNOP of PRI*, 1961–65. f-Began governmental career as a clerk (5th category) in the Department of the Federal District, 1937; Chief Editor of the Department of Public Relations, Department of the Federal District, 1943; *Head of the Department of the Federal District*, 1970–71. g-Secretary General of the Union of Workers of the Department of the Federal District, 1943–46; *Secretary General of the FSTSE*, 1949–52; Coordinator General of the ISSSTE; Secretary General of the 15th Section of the Union of Workers of the Department of the Federal District, 1942–43. h-Author of two books on history. i-Son of a doctor; brother *Guillermo Martinez Dominguez*, Director General of Nacional Financiera, 1970–74. j-None. k-Resigned from the Department of the Federal District after the 1971 student riots in Mexico, D.F.; most observers see the resignation as a result of internal power struggles within the ruling circle rather than just the result of the riots; precandidate for Governor of Nuevo Leon, 1972. l-C de D, 1952–54, 14; WWMG, 26; HA, 7 Dec. 1970, 26; *Hoy*, Dec. 1970; DBM70, 359–60; DGF47, 6; *Polemica*, I, 1969, 79; DBM68, 414–15; C de D, 1964–66, 52; C de D, 1946–48, 78; *Analisis Politico*, 26 Aug. 1972, 7; *Excelsior*, 10 Dec. 1978, 18.

Martinez Dominguez, Guillermo

a-1924. b-Monterrey, Nuevo Leon, *North*, *Urban*. c-Degree in Economics from the National School of Economics, UNAM; professor at the National School of Economics, UNAM, 1948–64; representative of the National School of Economics on the UNAM Council, 1954–56. d-None. e-None. f-Director of Prices, Secretariat of Industry and Commerce; Director General of the Small Business Bank; Oficial Mayor of the Federal Electric Commission, 1955–59; *Director General of the Federal Electric Commission*, 1964–70; *Director General of National Finance Bank*, 1970–74. g-President of the Student Society of the National School of Economics, 1947–48. h-Reporter for *Excelsior* and *La Prensa*; editorial writer for *Excelsior*, *La Prensa*, and *Hoy*; President of the National College of Economists; winner of the National Prize for Journalism, 1953. i-Brother of *Alfonso Martinez Dominguez*, head of the Federal District, 1970–71; son of a doctor, but orphaned at a young age; studied under *Eduardo Bustamante* at UNAM. j-None. k-As a journalist, exposed a fraud in the IMSS, 1953; resigned from NAFIN, 1974. l-WWMG, 26; HA, 7 Dec. 1970, 27; *Hoy*, 10 April 1971, 12; DBM70, 360; *Justicia*, Aug., 1971.

Martinez Garcia, Pedro Daniel

a-1906. b-Purepero, Michoacan, *West Central*, *Rural*. c-Primary studies at a school associated with the Normal School, Mexico City, 1912–19; preparatory studies at the National Preparatory School, 1920–24; medical degree, National School of Medicine, 1929; advanced studies in pediatrics, Children's Memorial Hospital, Chicago; Professor of Pediatrics, National School of Medicine, UNAM; professor of the School of Health and Welfare; professor of Public Hygiene, Johns Hopkins University, 1940; Director of the School of Health and Welfare, 1958–64; Professor of Infectious Diseases, National School of Medicine, UNAM, 1956–64; Professor of Pediatrics, National School of Medicine, UNAM, 1944–65. d-None. e-None. f-Subdirector and Director of the Children's Hospital of Mexico, Secretariat of Health, 1951; Director General of Maternal and Infant Hygiene, Secretariat of Health; Chief, Coordinated Health and Welfare Services, State of Michoacan; Subdirector of Education and Instruction in Public Health, Secretariat of Health, 1957; Director General of Education and Instruction in Public Health, 1958–64; Director of Services, Secretariat of Health; *Subsecretary of Health*, 1964–70; Medical Director, National Indigenous Institute, 1976. g-None. h-Health adviser to World Health Organization; member of expert committees on health. i-Friend of *Manuel Martinez Baez*, *Ignacio Chavez* and *Eduardo Villasenor*. j-None. k-None. l-HA, 21 Dec. 1964, 4; DPE65, 148; DPE61, 110; DGF51, II, 699–700; DGF51, I, 342; letters; Enc. Mex., VIII, 1977, 306.

Martinez Gil, Jose de Jesus

a-1935. b-Tampico, Tamaulipas, *North*, *Urban*. c-Early education unknown; law degree; teacher, Patriotic Institute; high school business teacher. d-*Federal Deputy* (Party Deputy) from PAN, 1973–76. e-Joined PAN, 1956; President of PAN in the Federal District; director of the presidential campaign for *Efrain Gonzalez Morfin*, 1969–70; member of the CEN of PAN, 1979; regional adviser to the CEN of PAN, 1979; Secretary of National Coordination of the CEN of PAN, 1979. f-None. g-None. h-Practicing lawyer. j-None. k-Candidate for Federal Deputy, 1970; candidate for Senator, 1976; candidate for Federal Deputy, 1979; resigned from PAN during his campaign for deputy, April, 1979. l-*Excelsior*, 24 Apr. 1979, 10; C de D, 1973–76, 29; HA, 19 Mar. 1979, VII.

Martinez Gortari, Jesus

a-May 23, 1919. b-Aguascalientes, Aguascalientes, *West*, *Urban*. c-Primary studies in a public school in Aguascalientes; secondary studies in a public school in Aguascalientes; no degree. d-*Federal Deputy* from the State of Aguascalientes, Dist. 1, 1976–79, member of the Social Action Committee, the Machinery Section of the Industrial Development Committee, the Development of Social Security and Public Health Committee, the Development of Tourism Committee and member of the Railroad Section of the Transportation and General Means of Communication Committee. e-Joined PRI, 1956. f-None. g-Director of the Cooperative of the Union of Mexican Railroad Workers (STFRM), Secretary General of Section 2, STFRM, 1968; Treasurer General of the STFRM, 1971–76; Secretary General of the STFRM, August 28, 1976– . h-Began railroad career as a laborer for the National Railroads of Mexico, 1936. i-Married Refugio Macias. j-None. k-None. l-*Excelsior*, 22 Aug. 1976, 29; D de D, 1976–79, 4, 38, 41, 76; C de D, 1976–79, 47.

Martinez Hernandez, Ifigenia (Navarrete)

a-June 16, 1924. b-Federal District, *Federal District*, *Urban*. c-Early education unknown; economics degree, National School of Economics, UNAM, 1946; MA in economics, Harvard University, 1949; researcher in economics, National School of Economics, UNAM, 1957–67; professor of economics, National School of Economics, UNAM, 1955–62; Director, National School of Economics, UNAM, 1967–70; professor of economics, CEMLA, 1955–62. d-*Federal Deputy* from the Federal District, Dist. 22, 1976–79, member of the Section on Improving Rural Living of the Agrarian Affairs Committee, the Section on Development of the Peasant Woman of the Agrarian Affairs Committee, the Committee of Agricultural Development, member of Section Three of the Educational Development Committee, the Television Section of the Development of the Means of Communication Committee, of the Social Welfare of the Development of Social Security and Public Health Committee, the Development of Housing Committee, the Department of the Federal District Committee and the Fiscal Section of the Legislative Studies Committee. e-None. f-Economist, Economic Commission for Latin America, 1949–50; economist, Department of Economic Studies, Pan American Union, 1951–52; Subdirector, Department of Subsidies, Secretariat of the Treasury, 1953–56; Director of the Office of Fiscal Policy, Secretariat of the Treasury, 1953–56; Director of the Office of the Fiscal Analysis, Secretariat of the Treasury, 1956–58; Adviser, Subsecretary of Revenues, Secretariat of the Treasury, 1961–65; Director of Economic Advisers, Secretariat of the Presidency, 1965–70; Director of Administrative Programs, Secretariat of the Treasury, 1970–76. g-None. h-None. i-Divorced from *Al-*

fredo Navarrete Romero, Subdirector of Finances of Pemex, 1972–76. **j-**None. **k-**One of Mexico's most prominent female economists. **l-**C de D, 1976–79, 46; D de C, 1976–79, 6, 8, 11, 18, 21, 29, 38, 40, 44, 47; HA, 5 Apr. 1976, 10; Enc. Mex., VIII, 1977, 313.

Martinez Lavalle, Arnulfo

(Deceased 1967)
a-1912. **b-**Federal District, *Federal District*, *Urban*. **c-**Early education unknown; law degree, National School of Law, UNAM, 1937; Professor of Criminal Procedures, National School of Law, UNAM; Professor of Sociology, School of Political and Social Sciences, UNAM. **d-**None. **e-**None. **f-**Secretary of the District Court, Federal District; official of the Superior Tribunal of Justice of the Federal District; Director of Preparatory Investigations, Attorney General of Mexico; Director, Inspector General's Office, Attorney General of Mexico, 1951; Justice of the Superior Tribunal of Justice of the Federal District and Federal Territories, 1956–67. **g-**None. **h-**Alternate Delegate to the Narcotics Commission, UNESCO; author of many works. **j-**None. **k-**None. **l-**DP70, 1275; DGF56, 514; DGF51, I, 435.

Martinez Manautou, Emilio

a-July 30, 1919. **b-**Ciudad Victoria, Tamaulipas, *North*, *Urban*. **c-**Primary and secondary studies in Ciudad Victoria; preparatory studies at the National Preparatory School, Mexico City, 1937–39; medical degree from the National School of Medicine, UNAM, 1944; postgraduate work in internal medicine in New York and Massachusetts. **d-***Federal Deputy* from the State of Tamaulipas, Dist. 2, 1955–58, member of the Gran Comision, the Committee on Forestry Affairs, the Inspection Committee for the General Accounting Office, the Committee on Public Works, and the Budget and Accounts Committee; member of the City Council of Matamoros, Tamaulipas, 1951; *Senator* from the State of Tamaulipas, 1958–64, member of the Public Welfare Committee, the Health Committee, the First Balloting Committee and the First Naval Committee; alternate member of the Second Committee on National Defense. **e-**State delegate of the CEN of PRI; head physician to *Gustavo Diaz Ordaz* during his presidential campaign, 1964. **f-**Chief of Medical Services, Chamber of Deputies, 1952–53; Private Secretary to *Norberto Trevino Zapata*, President of the Gran Comision, 1953–55; *Secretary of the Presidency*, 1964–70; *Secretary of Public Health*, 1976– . **g-**President of the Medical Association of Matamoros, 1951–52; Secretary General of CNOP in Matamoros. **h-**Director of the Civil Hospital, Matamoros, 1953; medical practice in Matamoros, 1946–55. **i-**Early political protege of *Norberto Tre-*

vino Zapata; father was a local deputy under *Emilio Portes Gil*; brother Alfredo was Secretary General of Government in Baja California del Norte, 1965–71. **j-**None. **k-**Precandidate for governor of Tamaulipas, 1962; precandidate for President of Mexico, 1970. **l-**DPE65, 169; C de D, 1955–57; HA, 7 Dec. 1964, 20; Johnson, 183–84; D de Y, 2 Dec. 1964, 2; DGF56; C de S, 1961–64, 61; Func., 372; LA, 3 Dec. 1976; Ind. Biog., 101–02; *Excelsior*, 25 Feb. 1977, 6, 8; *Excelsior*, 4 July 1974, 15.

Martinez Medina, Lorenzo

a-1918. **b-**Saltillo, Coahuila, *North*, *Urban*. **c-**Early education unknown; engineering degree from the Antonio Narro Higher School of Agriculture, Saltillo; Master of Science in Agriculture, University of Iowa; Doctorate in Agricultural Sciences, University of Minnesota, 1951; teacher in the regional peasant school, La Huerta, Michoacan; Subdirector of the Agricultural Vocational School, Champusco, Puebla; Director of the Antonio Narro Higher School of Agriculture, 1952–58. **d-**None. **e-**None. **f-**Researcher, Agricultural Field Station, Leon, Guanajuato; Chief, Division of Agricultural Investigations, Secretariat of Agriculture; Director General of Agriculture and Livestock, State of Coahuila; general agent of the Secretariat of Agriculture, Saltillo, Coahuila; President of the Board of Directors, Agricultural Credit Bank, Saltillo, Coahuila; Director General of National Seed Production, 1970–73; *Subsecretary of Agriculture*, Jan. 2, 1974–76. **g-**None. **h-**None. **j-**None. **k-**None. **l-**HA, 14 Jan. 1974, 15.

Martinez Ostos, Raul

a-Sept. 22, 1907. **b-**Tantoyuca, Veracruz, *Gulf*, *Rural*. **c-**Law degree from the National School of Law, UNAM, 1932; Professor of Civil Contracts, National School of Law, UNAM, 1934–35. **d-**None. **e-**None. **f-**Consulting lawyer to the Secretary of Public Works, 1935; consulting lawyer to the Department of Credit, Secretariat of the Treasury, 1936–40; consulting lawyer to the Federal Electric Commission, 1937; head of the Department of Credit, Bank of Mexico, 1940–45; Alternate Executive Director of the International Monetary Fund as a representative of Mexico, 1946–48; Director of Treasury Studies, Secretariat of the Treasury, 1949–50; *Subdirector of National Finance Bank*, 1945–46, 1952–58, 1958–64, 1964–65; Executive Director of the Inter-American Development Bank, 1960–63. **g-**None. **i-**Son of a doctor; student of and assistant to *Agustin Garcia Lopez*. **j-**None. **k-**None. **l-**Letter; DBM68, 419.

Martinez Peralta, Francisco

a-Aug. 24, 1895. **b-**Aconchi, Sonora, *North*, *Rural*. **c-**Primary studies in Sonora; no degree. **d-***Federal*

Deputy from the State of Sonora, Dist. 2, 1937–40; *Federal Deputy* from the State of Sonora, Dist. 1, 1946–49, member of the Second National Defense Committee and the Military Justice Committee, substitute member of the Foreign Relations Committee; *Senator* from the State of Sonora, 1940–46, President of the Second National Defense Committee, Second Secretary of the Ejido Committee, member of the Gran Comision, and alternate member of the Railroad and the Government Committees. e-*Secretary of Agrarian Action of the CEN of PRI*, 1946; Director of Traffic, Department of the Federal District, 1962–65. h-None. i-Uncle of *Ernesto P. Uruchurtu*. j-Career army officer; joined, 1910; Paymaster of the Army; rank of Colonel, 1940; reached rank of division general. k-None. l-C de D, 1946–48, 78; C de D, 1937–39, 14; Peral, 504; Libro de Oro, 1946, 9.

Martinez (Rodriguez), Jose Luis

a-Jan. 19, 1918. b-Atoyac, Jalisco, *West*, *Rural*. c-Primary studies at the Colegio Renacimiento, Ciudad Guzman, Jalisco, 1924–30, and at the Frances La Salle de Mexico, 1931; secondary and preparatory studies at the University of Guadalajara, 1932–37; studies in medicine, National School of Medicine, UNAM, 1938–39; degree in letters from the School of Philosophy and Letters, UNAM, 1938–43; professor of Mexican Literature, National Preparatory School, 1940–43, 1947–50; professor of Advanced Spanish, Summer School, UNAM, 1942–44; professor of Spanish Literature, Higher Normal School, Mexico City, 1945–51. d-*Federal Deputy* from the State of Jalisco, Dist. 8, 1958–61, member of the Protocol Committee, the Editorial Committee, the Public Education Committee, the Railroads Committee, the Foreign Relations Committee and the Consular and Diplomatic Service Committee. e-None. f-Private Secretary to the Secretary of Public Education, *Jaime Torres Bodet*, 1943–46; Secretary of the National College, 1947–51; Private Secretary to the Director General of the National Railroads of Mexico, *Roberto Amoros*, 1952–53; Administrative Assistant to the Director General of the National Railroads of Mexico, 1953–55; Director of Public Relations, National Railroads of Mexico, 1955–58; adviser to PIPSA, 1956–61; Ambassador to Peru, 1961–62; Ambassador to UNESCO, 1963–64; Director General of the National Institute of Fine Arts, 1965–70; Ambassador to Greece, 1971–76; Director General of the Fondo de Cultura Economica, 1977– . g-None. h-Member of the Governing Board, Colegio de Mexico, 1967– . i-Son of Doctor Juan R. Martinez. j-None. k-None. l-Func., 247; Enc. Mex., VIII, 304; letter; WWM45, 73; C de D, 1958–61, 84; DPE61, 24.

Martinez Rodriguez, Jose Maria

a-Jan. 9, 1912. b-Hacienda de San Lazaro, Tamazula, Jalisco, *West*, *Rural*. c-Primary studies (4 years); none; no degree. d-City Councilman, Guadalajara, Jalisco, 1944; Vice Mayor of Guadalajara, 1945–46; local deputy to the State Legislature of Jalisco, 1943–44; *Federal Deputy* from the State of Jalisco, Dist. 9, 1958–61, member of the Sugar Industry Committee; *Federal Deputy* from the State of Jalisco, Dist. 10, 1964–67; *Federal Deputy* from the State of Jalisco, Dist. 10, 1970–73, member of the Sugar Industry Committee and the Second Labor Committee; *Senator* from the State of Jalisco, 1976– . e-None. -None. g-Secretary General of Section 80 of the Sugar Cane Workers Union; Secretary of Correspondence and Agreements, National Sugar Cane Workers Union, 1941–42; Secretary General of the Federation of Workers of the State of Jalisco, 1943–46; Secretary of Conflicts, National Sugar Cane Workers Union, 1951–53; Secretary General of the National Sugar Cane Workers Union, 1953–59. h-None. j-None. k-None. l-C de D, 1964–66, 52; C de D, 1958–60, 84; C de D, 1970–72, 124; *Directorio*, 1970–72; Func., 248.

Martinez (Rodriguez), Miguel Z.

a-Sept. 29, 1888. b-Lampazos, Nuevo Leon, *North*, *Rural*. c-Primary studies in Lampazos; student at the National Military Cadet School, 1909. d-*Federal Deputy* from the State of Nuevo Leon, Dist. 2, 1937–40. e-None. f-Chief of Police for the Federal District, 1941–43. g-None. j-Constitutionalist during the Revolution; rank of Brigadier General, Nov. 16, 1940; Commander of the 10th Military Region, Irapuato, Guanajuato, 1956; reached rank of Divisionary General. k-Candidate for Governor of Nuevo Leon, 1943. l-EBW46, 185; C de D, 1937–39, 14; Peral, 504; NYT, 2 Apr. 1943, 6; Lopez, 669.

Martinez Ross, Jesus

a-May 8, 1934. b-Ciudad Chetumal, Quintana Roo, *Gulf*, *Rural*. c-Early education unknown; law degree, National School of Law, UNAM; Professor of the History of Culture, Center of Technological and Agricultural Studies, Chetumal; Professor of Language and Literature, Center of Technological Studies No. 62, Chetumal. d-*Federal Deputy* from Quintana Roo, Dist. 1, 1973–75, president of the Administrative Committee; *Governor of Quintana Roo*, April 5, 1975– . e-Secretary General of PRI for Quintana Roo, 1968; President of the Quintana Roo Committee of the National Council for Voter Registration, 1969. f-Agent of the Ministerio Publico, Chetumal, 1965–71; Oficial Mayor of Quintana Roo under Governor *David G. Gutierrez Ruiz*, 1971–72. g-Founder of the Civic and Social Front of Quintana

Roo, 1955; Secretary of Legislative Promotion of the CNOP of Quintana Roo; founder of the Quintanaroonian Fraternity, 1961; President of the Mexican Association for the Promotion and Publishing of Music, 1958–65; adviser to the Federation of Workers of Quintana Roo of the CTM, 1969. h-Director General of the music publishing firm Compas, 1958–65. i-Married Alicia Marquez. j-None. k-First constitutional governor of the State of Quintana Roo. l-*Excelsior*, 18 Jan. 1975, 4; HA, 14 Apr. 1975, 5; C de D, 1973–76, 19; Enc. Mex., Annual, 1977, 549; HA, 11 Dec. 1978, 38; HA, 23 Feb. 1976, 31; HA, 20 Jan. 1975, 29.

Martinez Tornel, Pedro
(Deceased 1957)
a-Oct. 29, 1889. b-Jalapa, Veracruz, *Gulf*, *Urban*. c-Preparatory studies at the National Preparatory School, Mexico, D.F.; engineering degree, UNAM, 1918; Professor of Engineering, UNAM; Director of the National School of Engineering, UNAM, 1942–46. d-None. e-None. f-Engineering adviser and technical inspector, Secretariat of Public Works, 1919–22; Superintendent, Port of Salina Cruz, Oaxaca, 1923; head of the Drainage Section, Secretariat of Public Works, 1924, 1925–32; technical inspector, Secretariat of Public Works; Assistant Director, Ports and Telegraphs, Secretariat of Public Works, 1933–34; Assistant Chief Engineer, National Railroads of Mexico, 1935–37; head of the Construction Department, National Irrigation Commission, 1938–40; Director General of Construction, National Railroads of Mexico, 1941–43; *Subsecretary of Public Works*, 1943–45; *Secretary of Public Works*, 1945–46. g-None. h-Member of the Board of the Mexican Tube Company and other firms. j-None. k-Director of *Juan Andreu Almazan's* campaign for President, 1940; supported General *Henriquez Guzman* for president, 1951. l-WWM45, 74; DP70, 1277; D de Y, 3 Oct. 1941, 2; Correa, 319; Lopez, 670; Enc. Mex., VIII, 324.

Martinez Ulloa, Enrique
b-Ixtlan del Rio, Nayarit, *West*, *Urban*. c-Primary and secondary studies in Guadalajara, Jalisco; preparatory studies at the Preparatory School of the State of Jalisco; law degree, University of Guadalajara; Secretary, University of Guadalajara. d-None. e-None. f-Actuary for the 2nd Judicial District, Guadalajara; Secretary of Studies and Accounts, Supreme Court of Justice; consulting lawyer, Secretariat of Communications and Public Works, Secretariat of Industry and Commerce, and the Secretariat of Agriculture; fiscal attorney for the Federal Government, 1948–49, 1960–64; Director of the Department of Legal Affairs, Institute of Social Security; *Justice of the Supreme Court*, 1964–70, 1970–74. g-None. h-None. j-None. k-None. l-*Justicia*, June, 1967; DPE61, 53.

Martino Torres, Cesar
(Deceased 1969)
a-1905. b-Sacramento, Durango, *West*, *Rural*. c-Agricultural engineering degree, School of Agriculture, Ciudad Juarez, Chihuahua, 1927. d-*Federal Deputy* from the State of Jalisco, Dist. 9, 1937–40. e-*Secretary of Agrarian Action of the CEN of the PRM*, 1938. f-Member of the Cultural Missions Program, Secretariat of Public Education, 1929–32; Director General of the Workers Bank, 1940; Director General of the National Bank of Agricultural Credit, 1940–46; head of the 5th Advisory Office of the Department of Agrarian Affairs, 1964–69; adviser to the Presidency, 1969. g-Founding member of the National Farmers Federation; First Secretary of Union Action of the National Farmers Federation; founder and President of the Mexican Agronomy Society. h-Founder and Director General of Constructora el Guadiana, S.A.; writer for *Hoy*, *Siempre* and *Excelsior*. j-None. k-Precandidate for Secretary General of the CNC, 1941, 1962; supporter of General *Henriquez Guzman* for president, 1952. l-DP70, 1277; DPE65, 171; Gonzalez Navarro, 137, 168, 232; C de D, 1937–39; Cadena Z., 143; Casasola, V; Enc. Mex., VIII, 1977, 324.

Massieu, Wilfrido
(Deceased 1944)
a-1878. b-Tacubaya, Federal District, *Federal District*, *Urban*. c-Engineering degree from the National Military College, 1896 to Dec. 6, 1903, graduating as a lieutenant; professor, National Polytechnic Institute. d-None. e-None. f-Director of the Military Industry College, San Luis Potosi, 1920–21; Director of the College of Railroad Workers, Secretariat of Public Education, 1921 (which became the Technical Industrial Institute and then the National Polytechnic Institute in 1937); *Director General of the National Polytechnic Institute*, 1940–42. g-None. h-None. i-Son, *Guillermo*, became Director General of IPN, 1964–70; close friend and colleague of Jose Vasconcelos. j-Graduated from the National Military College as a 2nd Lieutenant of Engineers; commander of a bridge-building company, 1910–11; officer in the Corps of Engineers, 1903–13; head of numerous engineering projects in the army; rank of Lt. Col., 1913; rank of Colonel, June, 1913; served under General Huerta against Carranza; rank of Brigadier General, Feb., 1914; opposed the Revolutionary forces of Pablo Gonzalez in Monterrey, Nuevo Leon. k-None. l-DP70, 1280–81.

Massieu (Helguera), Guillermo

a-Oct. 7, 1920. **b-**San Luis Potosi, San Luis Potosi, *East Central*, *Urban*. **c-**Primary studies at the Colegio Luis G. Leon and the Colegio San Borja, Mexico City, 1926–34; secondary and preparatory studies at Vocational School No. 1, 1935–40; engineering degree in chemical sciences, National School of Biological Sciences, IPN, with a specialty in Chemical Bacteriology, Nov. 21, 1946; graduate studies at Oxford, England, 1954–55; Ph.D. in Biochemistry, National School of Biological Sciences, IPN, 1963; Subdirector of the National School of Biological Sciences, IPN, 1956–57; professor at the National Polytechnic Institute, 1943–50; professor at the National University of Mexico, 1951–56; Professor of Medical Chemistry, UNAM, 1957–58. **d-**None. **e-**None. **f-**Head of Laboratories, National School of Medicine, UNAM, 1945–53; investigator, Department of Physiology, UNAM, 1947–53; head of the Laboratory, National Institute of Nutriology, 1956; investigator, Institute of Biology, UNAM, 1958–61; *Director General of the National Polytechnic School*, 1964–70; Director, Center for Research and Advanced Studies, IPN, 1970–77; *Subsecretary of Scientific Research and Education*, 1978– . **g-**None. **h-**Author of hundreds of articles on the biological sciences. **i-**Son of *Wilfrido Massieu*, Director General of IPN, 1940–42. **j-**None. **k-**None. **l-***Hoy*, 21 Jan. 1967, 60; B de M, 175–78; HA, 21 Dec. 1964, 7; MGF69; Enc. Mex., VIII, 1977, 333–34; HA, 17 Apr. 1978, 10; HA, 8 Dec. 1975, 13; DAPC, 46.

Matos Escobedo, Rafael
(Deceased 1967)

a-July 28, 1893. **b-**Oxkutzcab, Yucatan, *Gulf*, *Rural*. **c-**Primary and secondary studies in Oxkutzcab; preparatory studies in Yucatan; professional studies in law at the University of the Southeast, Merida, Yucatan; law degree from the National School of Law, UNAM, Sept. 20, 1922; professor at the University of Veracruz; Professor of Law, National School of Law, UNAM; Professor of Graduate Studies in Law, UNAM, 1967. **d-***Senator* from the State of Yucatan, 1964–70. **e-**None. **f-**Oficial Mayor of the State Legislature of Yucatan; Secretary of the 3rd Civil Court, Mexico, D.F., 1923; Judge of the 8th Correctional Tribunal, 1930; Judge of the 3rd Correctional Tribunal, 1930; Judge of the 6th Penal Court, 1931; District Judge of the State of Veracruz, 1941–46; *Assistant Attorney General of Mexico*, 1946–50; *Supernumerary Justice of the Supreme Court*, 1951–52, 1952–58; *Justice of the Supreme Court*, 1959–64. **g-**None. **h-**Author of numerous articles on penal law and a book on law. **i-**Graduated with *Francisco Gonzalez de la Vega* from the Na-

tional Law School, 1922; served with or under *Gonzalez de la Vega* in many government positions. **j-**None. **k-**None. **l-**DBM68, 424; DGF51, 568; DP70, 1285; MGF69, 106; WWMG, 26.

Mayagoitia Dominguez, Hector

a-Jan. 7, 1923. **b-**Federal District, *Federal District*, *Urban*. **c-**Primary studies in Gomez Palacio, Durango; Jimenez, Chihuahua; Torreon, Coahuila; secondary studies at the School for Workers' Children, Lerdo, Durango; preparatory studies at the National Preparatory School, Coyoacan, Federal District; attended the National Polytechnical Institute, 1942–46, chemistry degree in bacteriology and parasitology, IPN, 1946; soil chemistry studies, Rutgers University, 1948; Doctorate in Chemistry, IPN; Professor of Chemical Sciences, IPN, 1948–65; Subdirector of the National School of Biological Sciences, IPN, 1948–52; *Director General of IPN*, Dec. 14, 1979– . **d-***Governor of Durango*, 1974–79. **e-**Member of the Youth Action Committee of PRI; Secretary of External and Internal Affairs for the Federation of Mexican Youth, 1945; member of the IEPES of PRI. **f-**Founder and Director of the Chemical Laboratory for Soils and Plants, National School of Biological Sciences, IPN, 1952; Director General of Technological Instruction, Secretariat of Public Education, 1966–70; *Subsecretary of Technical Instruction and Graduate Studies*, *Secretariat of Public Education*, 1970–74. **g-**Secretary General of the Student Society of the National School of Biological Sciences, 1945; Secretary General of SNTE Delegation to IPN, 1951; Alternate Secretary General of Section Ten of the SNTE, 1958–60; Secretary of the Editorial Committee, CEN, SNTE, 1960–66. **h-**Representative of the Secretariat of Public Education on the National Commission of Productivity. **i-**Married Maria Luisa Prado. **j-**None. **k-**Defeated Senator *Gamiz Fernandez* for the gubernatorial nomination. **l-**HA, 14 Dec. 1970, 22; *Excelsior*, 12 Mar. 1974, 12; *Excelsior*, 25 Jan. 1974; MGF69, 312; HA, 11 Mar. 1974, 36; Enc. Mex., Annual, 1977; HA, 24 Dec. 1979, 10.

Mayes Navarro, Antonio

a-Oct. 7, 1905. **b-**Jiquilpan, Michoacan, *West Central*, *Urban*. **c-**Early education unknown; secondary studies at the Colegio de San Nicolas; no degree. **d-**Federal Deputy from the State of Michoacan, 1934–37; president of the left wing of the Chamber of Deputies, 1935; president of the Permanent Committee of Congress, 1935–37; local deputy to the State Legislature of Michoacan; *Senator* from the State of Michoacan, 1940–46, president of the Insurance Committee, First Secretary of the National

Properties and the Credit, Money, and Credit Institutions Committees and alternate member of the Waters and Irrigation Committee. e-*Secretary of Agrarian Action of the CEN of the PNR*, 1936; member of the Policy Directorate, Popular Party, 1949. f-None. g-None. h-Journalist. j-None. k-None. l-Libro de Oro, 1946, 9; Lopez, 675–76; Casasola, V; Villasenor, II, 175.

Mayoral Heredia, Manuel

a-1898. b-Oaxaca, Oaxaca, *South*, *Urban*. c-Primary and secondary studies in Oaxaca; preparatory studies in Oaxaca; engineering degree, University of Oaxaca; post-graduate studies at Stanford University. d-*Governor of Oaxaca*, 1950 to July 31, 1952. e-None. f-*Subsecretary of Public Works*, 1946–50. g-None. j-None. k-Resigned under pressure after an unpopular tax law caused a riot and a general strike resulting in the deaths of several people. l-DGF51, II, 523; Scott, 276; NYT, 3 July 1952, 5; NYT, 5 Aug. 1952, 4; DGF47, 143; DGF51, I, 91; Brandenburg, 103; Anderson.

Medellin, Jorge L.

a-May, 1916. b-Federal District, *Federal District*, *Urban*. c-Architecture degree, National School of Architecture, UNAM, 1939. d-None. e-None. f-Architect for the Department of Prehispanic Monuments, Federal District, 1939; technical positions in National Railroads of Mexico; Subdirector of Studies and Programs, National Railroads of Mexico; Director General of the Construction Commission for National Medical Centers; designer of highways in the Federal District; urban adviser to the head of the Department of the Federal District; *Subsecretary of Government Properties*, 1966–70; head of construction for the Mexican Institute of Social Security, 1970–72. g-President of various architectural associations. h-None. i-Married Enriqueta Ortega. j-None. k-None. l-DPE65, 76; DBM68, 426; DBM70, 372; HA, 21 Dec. 1970, 23; Enc. Mex., VIII, 1977, 395.

Medellin Ostos, Octavio

(Deceased 1952)
a-1896. b-Ozuluama, Veracruz, *Gulf*, *Rural*. c-Preparatory studies in Jalapa and at the National Preparatory School; law degree, National School of Law, UNAM; Professor of Law at the National School of Law, UNAM; Professor of Economics at the National School of Economics, UNAM; Professor of Ethics at the National Preparatory School; normal school teacher. d-None. e-Leader of the Vasconcelos party movement with *Adolfo Lopez Mateos*, 1928–29. f-Secretary General of Government of the Department of the Federal District, 1945. g-None. h-Author of many works; director of the magazine *Social Action*; director of the law association

magazine. i-Brother of *Roberto Medellin Ostos*, Secretary General of Health, 1935–37; practiced law with *Julio Rodolfo Moctezuma Cid*. j-None. k-Member of the "Seven Wisemen" Generation of the National Preparatory School and the National Law School; formed a campaign group to support the candidacy of *Adolfo Ruiz Cortines*; defended *Vatentin Campa* against government indictment, 1947. l-DP70, 1296; WWM45, 75; Peral, 512; *Hoy*, 29 April 1972, 3; Enc. Mex., VIII, 1977, 395; Campa, 221.

Medellin Ostos, Roberto

(Deceased Mar. 5, 1941)
a-Apr. 29, 1881. b-Finca Repartidero, Tantoyuca, Veracruz, *Gulf*, *Rural*. c-Primary studies in Tantoyuca; preparatory studies at the National Preparatory School; engineering degree, National School of Engineering, UNAM, 1908; Professor of Chemistry, National Preparatory School; professor at the National School of Medicine, UNAM; Secretary of the National University; Professor of Graduate Studies, UNAM; Director of Natural Sciences at the National Preparatory School; Director of Technical Instruction, School of Chemical Sciences, UNAM; Secretary General and Rector, UNAM, Sept. 12, 1932, to Oct. 15, 1933; *Director General of IPN*, 1937. d-None. e-Supporter of Jose Vasconcelos, 1928–29. f-Prosector of Botany, National Preparatory School; head of the Chemistry Department, National Medical Institute; Oficial Mayor of the Secretariat of Public Education, 1934–35, under *Eduardo Vasconcelos*; Secretary General of the Department of Public Health, 1935–37. g-None. h-Author of numerous works on botany. i-Brother of *Octavio Medellin Ostos*. j-None. k-Organizer of the school breakfast program. l-WWLA40, 316; Gruening, 535; Lopez, 678; Enc. Mex., VIII, 1977, 395; WWLA35, 244; Raby, 23; Skirius, 205.

Medina Alonso, Edgardo

a-July 13, 1913. b-Merida, Yucatan, *Gulf*, *Urban*. c-Primary studies in Merida; preparatory studies in Merida, 1927–32; medical degree, School of Medicine, University of Yucatan, 1933–39; member of the University Council of the University of Yucatan; Secretary, School of Medicine, University of Yucatan. d-Local Deputy to the State Legislature of Yucatan; *Senator* from the State of Yucatan, 1958–64, President of the Administrative Committee, First Secretary of the Health and the Military Sanitation Committees, President of the Insurance Committee, and member of the Second Balloting Group and the Special Legislative Studies Committees. e-None. f-Physician, Medical Services, Isla Mujeres, Quintana Roo, 1939–41. g-President of the Circle of Preparatory Students of Yucatan; co-founder of the Student Revolutionary Party of Yucatan; founder and director of the student newspaper, University of Yucatan, *El Preparatoriano*; President of the Circle of Medical Students, 1933–39. **h**-Department head, O'Horan Hospital, Merida. **j**-None. **k**-None. **l**-Func., 402; C de S, 1961–64, 61.

Medina Asencio, Francisco

a-Oct. 22, 1910. **b**-Arandas, Jalisco, *West*, *Urban*. **c**-Preparatory studies at the University of Guadalajara; law degree, University of Guadalajara, 1933; teacher of secondary night school in the Federal District; professor at the School of Economics, University of Guadalajara; founding teacher of the Night School for Workers in the Federal District. **d**-Councilman of Guadalajara, Jalisco, 1956–58; Mayor of Guadalajara, 1962–64; *Governor of Jalisco*, 1965–71. **e**-None. **f**-Judge of the 3rd Court of Appeals, Guadalajara; Secretary of the 8th Judicial District, Federal District; lawyer for the Director of Pensions, ISSSTE; Secretary for the Arbitration Tribunal for Federal Employees, Federal District; Treasurer of Jalisco, 1953–61; Director of National Properties, Jalisco, 1958; Ambassador to Italy, 1971–75. **g**-None. **h**-Employed as a porter in the 1st Criminal Court of the Federal District; scribe of the 1st Criminal Court of the Federal District; practicing lawyer, 1977– . **j**-None. **k**-None. **l**-WWW70–71, 630; Enc. Mex., V, 579; *Siempre*, 14 Jan. 1959, 6; DBM70, 372–73; *Hoy*, 13 Mar. 1971, 10; DBM68, 427; DGF56, 95; *Excelsior*, 22 Aug. 1978, 22.

Medina (Gaona), Hilario

(Deceased 1964)
a-1893. **b**-Leon, Guanajuato, *West Central*, *Urban*. **c**-Primary studies in Leon, preparatory studies from the National Preparatory School, 1918; law degree from the National School of Law, UNAM; Professor of History at the National Preparatory School; Professor of Constitutional Law, National School of Law, UNAM, 1930. **d**-Deputy to the Constitutional Convention, 1916–17; *Senator* from the Federal District, 1958–64, member of the Gran Comision, the Committee on the Department of the Federal District, the Rules Committee; President of the Second Justice Committee; member of the First Committee on Government, and the First Constitutional Affairs Committee. **e**-None. **f**-*Justice of the Supreme Court*, 1941–57; *Chief Justice of the Supreme Court*, 1953, 1957–58; Subsecretary in charge of Foreign Relations, 1919–20. **g**-None. **h**-Librarian during last year in law school to earn money to finish degree. **j**-Active in the Revolution. **k**-Important member of the Carranza administration; his public career suffered after Carranza was murdered in 1920.

l-DGF51, I, 568; C de S, 1961–64, 61; STYR-BIWW, 54, 892; Enc. Mex., V, 36; Peral, 513; DGF47, 29; DP70, 1299; WWM45, 75; DGF56, 567; Func., 174; Enc. Mex., VIII, 1977, 414.

Medina Medina, Calixto

a-Jan. 22, 1923. **b**-Huanusco, Zacatecas, *East Central, Rural*. **c**-Primary studies in public schools in Aguascalientes and in Zacatecas; secondary studies at the Institute of Sciences of Aguascalientes; preparatory studies at the Institute of Sciences of Aguascalientes; medical degree, National School of Medicine, UNAM. **d**-Local deputy to the State Legislature of Zacatecas; *Federal Deputy* from the State of Zacatecas, Dist. 1, 1967–70, member of the Gran Comision; *Senator* from the State of Zacatecas, 1970–76, President of the Second Mines Committee, member of the Gran Comision. **e**-Joined PRI, 1952; participant in various PRI campaigns. **f**-None. **g**-Secretary of Professional Action, CNOP, Zacatecas; Secretary of Organization of CNOP, Zacatecas; Secretary General of CNOP in the State of Zacatecas. **h**-Director of the Health Center, General Hospital, Jalapa, Zacatecas. **i**-Married Jovita Llamas. **j**-None. **k**-None. **l**-C de D, 1967–70; C de S, 1970–76, 79; PS, 3920.

Medina Munoz, Alberto

a-Aug. 7, 1922. **b**-Zapotan, Municipio of Compostela, Nayarit, *West*, *Rural*. **c**-Primary studies in Compostela, Nayarit; normal studies in Guadalajara, Jalisco; teaching certificate. **d**-Mayor of Tepic, Nayarit; Local Deputy to the State Legislature of Nayarit; *Senator* from the State of Nayarit, 1958–64, Secretary of the Gran Comision, President of the Second Credit, Money and Credit Institutions Committee, Second Secretary of the Rules and the Foreign and Domestic Trade Committees. **e**-President of PRI in Nayarit. **f**-None. **g**-Secretary General of the League of Agrarian Communities of Nayarit; member of the National Committee of the CNC. **j**-None. **k**-None. **l**-Func., 287; C de S, 1961–64, 62.

Medina Neri, Hector

a-Dec. 25, 1921. **b**-Federal District, *Federal District, Urban*. **c**-Early education unknown; engineering degree. **d**-None. **e**-None. **f**-Director of Tourism Delegations, Toluca, Mexico, 1961; Manager of Refrigeradora de Tepepan, Secretariat of Industry and Commerce; *Subsecretary of Fishing*, Secretariat of Industry and Commerce, 1970–76. **g**-None. **h**-Employee of *El Heraldo de Mexico*. **j**-None. **k**-Helped to promote the development of fish products in Mexico. **l**-HA, 14 Dec. 1970, 21; DPE61, 131.

Medina Valdes, Gerardo

a-1929. b-El Oro, Mexico, *West Central*, *Rural*. c-Early education unknown; journalism degree, Carlos Septien Garcia School of Journalism; Professor of Journalism, Carlos Septien Garcia School of Journalism. d-None. e-Member of the Regional Council of PAN for the Federal District, 1979; member of the National Council of PAN, 1979; member of the CEN of PAN, 1979; Secretary of Press and Publicity of the CEN of PAN; Director of *La Nacion*, official paper of PAN, 1963- . f-None. g-None. h-Author. j-None. k-Candidate for federal deputy from PAN from Dist. 20, Federal District (twice); candidate for federal deputy from PAN from Dist. 28, Federal District, 1979. l-HA, 14 May 1979, X.

Mediz Bolio (Contarell), Antonio

(Deceased Sept. 15, 1957)

a-Oct. 13, 1884. b-Merida, Yucatan, *Gulf*, *Urban*. c-Primary studies in Merida; secondary studies at the Seminario Conciliar Universitario de Merida and the Colegio Catolico de San Ildefonso; law degree from the School of Law, University of Yucatan, 1907, with a thesis on strikes. d-Federal Deputy from the State of Yucatan, 1912-14, 1928-30; *Senator* from the State of Yucatan, 1952-57, member of the Indigenous Affairs Committee, the First Public Education Committee, the First Foreign Relations Committee, the First Balloting Committee, and substitute member of the National Properties Committee; President of the First Instructive Committee for the Grand Jury. e-Director of Popular Culture, PNR, 1936. f-Private secretary to the Governor of Yucatan, 1903; Secretary to the 2nd Civil Court of Merida, 1905; Director of the Bulletin of the Secretariat of Public Education and Bellas Artes of Yucatan, 1912-13, 1915-18; Director General of Fine Arts, State of Yucatan, 1918-19; Second Secretary of the Mexican legation in Spain, 1919; Charge d'Affaires, Mexican legation in Spain, 1920; Second Secretary and Charge d'Affaires, Colombia, 1921; First Secretary and Charge d'Affaires, Argentina, 1921-22; First Secretary, Sweden, 1923-24; Ambassador to Costa Rica and Nicaragua, 1925-32; Director of the Department of Civic Action, 1932-34; Director of the Archeology Department, National Museum, 1937-39. g-None. h-Important figure in the development of Yucatan theater. i-Married Lucrecia Cuartas. j-Supported Madero during the Revolution. k-Exiled by Huerta and lived in Havana, 1914-15. l-DP70, 130; WWM45, 75; DGF56, 8, 9, 10, 12, 13; Peral, 514-15; C de S, 1952-58; Novo, 543; Lopez, 688; Enc. Mex., VIII, 1977, 416.

Medrano (Valdivia), Federico

(Deceased 1959)

a-Mar. 2, 1896. b-Union de San Antonio, Jalisco, *West*, *Rural*. c-Primary studies in San Francisco del Rincon; preparatory studies at the Colegio de Leon, 1913-17; law degree from the National School of Law, UNAM, 1918-22; taught at the Studies Center, University of Guanajuato, 1917. d-Federal Deputy from the State of Guanajuato, 1922-30; *Senator* from the State of Guanajuato, 1936-40; *Federal Deputy* from the State of Guanajuato, Dist. 3, 1940-43, President of the Chamber of Deputies and Party Majority Leader; *Senator* from the State of Guanajuato, 1946-52, member of the Gran Comision, the First Petroleum Committee, the Second Balloting Committee, the Second Labor Committee, the Agricultural and Development Committee; substitute member of the First Committee on National Defense. e-Secretary of Education of the CEN of the PNR; Secretary General of the PNR. f-None. g-Student leader during preparatory school days. h-None. i-Close friend of *Octavio Vejar Vazquez* at Law School. j-None. k-Retired from politics in 1952 to raise race horses; political enemy of *Gonzalo N. Santos*, who prevented him from holding his position as federal deputy, 1926-28; precandidate for Governor of Guanajuato, 1935; expelled from PNR by *Matias Ramos Santos*, 1935. l-WWM45, 76; DP70, 1301; C de S, 1946-52; DBM70, 376; Peral, 515; DGF51, I, 6, 9, 10, 11, 13, 14; HA, 20 Aug. 1943, 7-8.

Meixueiro Alexandre, Hector

a-Mar. 12, 1900. b-Santiago Xiacui de Ixtlan de Juarez, Oaxaca, *South*, *Rural*. c-Graduated from the Naval College at Veracruz, Veracruz. d-None. e-None. f-*Oficial Mayor of the Secretariat of the Navy*, 1952-58; *Oficial Mayor in charge of the Secretariat of the Navy*, Apr. 7, 1958, to Nov. 30, 1958. g-None. h-None. j-Career naval officer; Subdirector of the Naval School of the Pacific; commander of various destroyers; Chief of Staff of the 2nd Naval Zone, Ciudad Carmen, 1947; Chief of Staff of the 4th Naval Zone, Guaymas, Sonora, 1951-52; Chief of Staff of the Secretariat of the Navy; Interim Director of the Fleet; reached the rank of Admiral. k-None. l-HA, 8 Dec. 1958, 41; Enc. Mex., V, 47; HA, 14 April 1958, 6; DGF51, I, 386; DGF56, 381; DGF47, 234.

Melgar, Rafael E.

(Deceased Mar. 21, 1959)

a-Mar. 14, 1887. b-Yanhuitlan, Oaxaca, *South*, *Rural*. c-Primary studies in Yanhuitlan and in Seminary School, Oaxaca, Oaxaca; no degree. d-Federal Deputy from the State of Oaxaca, Dist. 7, 1926-28, president of the Balloting Committee; Federal Deputy from the State of Oaxaca, 1928-30, president of the Administrative Committee; President of the Obregonista Bloc and Federal Deputy from the State of Oaxaca, 1932-34; Local Deputy to the State Legislature of Oaxaca; *Senator* from the State of Oaxaca, 1952-58, member of the First Committee on National Defense, the Second Foreign Relations Committee, and the First Balloting Committee. **e-**Founding member of the PNR. **f-***Governor of Quintana Roo*, 1935–40; Ambassador to Holland, 1946–48. **g-**None. **h-**Administrator, *El Economista Mexicano*, 1907; Second Paymaster, Secretariat of Development, 1911–12; First Paymaster, Secretariat of Development, 1912; special mission to the United States, 1918. **j-**Joined the Revolution, 1913; career army officer; reached the rank of Brigade General, 1916. **k-**Head of the Nationalist Campaign, 1930. **l-**DGF56, 7, 10, 12–14; Peral, 517; DP70, 1304; Daniels, 490; C de S, 1952–58; Lopez, 683; Bremauntz, 116; Ind. Biog., 171–74.

Melgarejo Gomez, Jose

a-Sept. 8, 1912. **b-**Puebla, Puebla, *East Central*, *Urban*. **c-**Studied under a tutor, 1920; primary at the Colegio Frances de la Perpetua, 1921–22, the Colegio Luz Savinon, 1923, and the Colegio Frances La Salle, 1924–25, in Mexico, D.F.; secondary and preparatory at the Colegio Frances La Salle, 1926–28, 1929–30; degree in chemistry from the School of Chemical Sciences, Tacuba, Federal District, 1931–33; Professor of Experimental Physics and Higher Algebra, University of San Luis Potosi (3 years). **d-***Federal Deputy* from the PAN (party deputy), 1970–73, member of the Artisans Committee and the Subsistence and Supplies Committee. **e-**None. **f-**None. **g-**None. **h-**Businessman. **j-**None. **k-**Candidate of PAN for the 1st Councilman of Naucalpan, Mexico. **l-***Directorio*, 1970–72; C de D, 1970–72, 125.

Mena, Anselmo

(Deceased 1958)
a-1899. **b-**Federal District, *Federal District*, *Urban*. **c-**Early education unknown; law degree, National School of Law, UNAM; graduate studies in London and in Paris. **d-**None. **e-**Founding member of the Popular Party, 1947; Vice-president of the Popular Party. **f-**Director of the Consular Department, Secretariat of Foreign Relations; Ambassador to Honduras; Ambassador to Nicaragua; Director General of Political Affairs, Secretariat of Foreign Relations, 1937–42; Consul General to London, England; Ambassador to Czechoslovakia, 1956–58. **g-**None. **h-**Author of several books. **i-**Classmate of *Jaime Torres Bodet*, School of Law, 1918–19. **j-**None. **k-**None. **l-**DP70, 1305; Enc. Mex., VIII, 423; DGF56, 125; Lopez, 684; DGF51, I, 131.

Mena Brito, Antonio

a-Feb. 22, 1919. **b-**Merida, Yucatan, *Gulf*, *Urban*. **c-**Primary studies in Merida; secondary and preparatory studies in the Federal District; law degree, National School of Law, UNAM; Professor of Law, National Preparatory School and the University Ex-

tension, UNAM; Professor of Literature in public and private schools; Secretary General of the Night Program, National Preparatory School, Federal District. **d-***Senator* from the State of Yucatan, 1958–64, Secretary of the Gran Comision, member of the Foreign and Domestic Trade Committee, the Special Legislative Studies Committee, and the Tourist Affairs Committee; President of the Second Credit, Money, and Credit Institutions Committee; member of the Rules Committee; alternate member of the Second Constitutional Affairs Committee and the Second Committee on Tariffs and Foreign Trade. **e-**Active in the presidential campaign of *Miguel Aleman*, 1946; *Secretary of Youth Action of the CEN of PRI*, 1946–52; *Secretary of Popular Action of the CEN of PRI*, 1952–58. **f-**Director General of the National Youth Institute, Secretariat of Public Education, 1952–58. **g-**Student leader in secondary school; President of the Federation of University Students of Mexico. **j-**None. **k-**None. **l-**Func., 403; C de S, 1961–64, 62; DGF56, 306.

Mena Cordoba, Eduardo R.

b-Campeche, *Gulf*. **c-**Early education unknown; no degree. **d-**Federal Deputy from the State of Campeche, Dist. 1, 1922–24, member of the Gran Comision; Federal Deputy from the State of Campeche, Dist. 2, 1924–26, member of the Gran Comision; Federal Deputy from the State of Campeche, Dist. 2, 1926–28, member of the Gran Comision; *Governor of Campeche*, 1935–39; *Senator* from the State of Campeche, 1940–46, President of the Industries Committee, First Secretary of the First Tariff and Foreign Trade Committee, and Secretary of the Gran Comision. **e-**None. **f-**Director of the Federal Treasury Office, San Pedro de las Colonias, Coahuila, 1951. **g-**None. **j-**None. **k-**Raby says he had many problems with leftists and the teachers unions during his term as governor because of his conservative views; forced by President Cardenas to enforce the agrarian legislation in Campeche; the *Diario del Sureste* believes that the loss of his candidate for the senate against *Carlos Gongora Gala* in 1936 was the first defeat for the official party in a senatorial race. **l-**Letter; D de Y, 1 Jan. 1936, 4; Daniels, 488; D del S, 24 Aug. 1936, 25, 27; Raby, 226; DGF51, I, 167, Libro de Oro, 1940, 9.

Mena Palomo, Victor

b-Izamal, Yucatan, *Gulf*, *Urban*. **c-**Teaching certificate; no degree. **d-**Local Deputy to the State Legislature of Yucatan; Secretary of the City Council of Merida; *Federal Deputy* from the State of Yucatan, Dist. 2, 1937–40; *Alternate Senator* from the State of Yucatan, 1952–53. **e-**President of the Socialist Party of the Southeast. **f-***Interim Governor of Yucatan*, 1953–58. **g-**None. **h-**Owner of a PEMEX station,

Merida. **j**-None. **k**-None. **l**-HA, 29 June 1953; DGF56, 8, 102; C de D, 1937–39; C de S, 1952–58.

Mendez Aguilar, Benjamin

a-Nov. 10, 1886. **b**-Jerecuaro, Guanajuato, *West Central*, *Rural*. **c**-Primary and secondary studies in Guanajuato, Guanajuato; no degree. **d**-Federal Deputy from the State of Guanajuato, 1926–28 and 1930–32; *Federal Deputy* from the State of Guanajuato, Dist. 5, 1949–52, member of the First Committee on Railroads and the First Committee on General Means of Transportation. **e**-None. **f**-Telegrapher, Carneros, Coahuila, 1901; station master, Coahuila, 1901–03; telegrapher, Office of the Superintendent of Car Service, Federal District, 1904–08; first class telegrapher, 1908–09; dispatcher, 1909–17; chief of dispatchers, 1917–18; President of the Price Commission, Railroad Service, 1918–28; member of the Board of Directors, National Railroads of Mexico, 1918–28; Superintendent of Passenger Service, 1918–24; Director of the Railroad of Desague del Valle de Mexico, 1918–24; Oficial Mayor of the National Railroads of Mexico, 1918–24; Director of Traffic, National Railroads of Mexico, 1943–51; Representative of the National Railroads in Texas, 1951–54; Director General of the Railroad of the Pacific, 1954–58; *Director General of the National Railroads of Mexico*, 1958–64. **g**-None. **h**-None. **i**-Son of a doctor; son, Roberto, an engineer; son, *Benjamin Mendez Luna*, *Jr.*, served as a Federal Deputy from Puebla, 1961–64; formed a political group called "Los Compadres," 1958–64, included *Eufrasio Sandoval Rodriguez*. **j**-None. **k**-None. **l**-HA, 8 Dec. 1958, 32; DBM68, 429–30; D de Y, 2 Dec. 1958, 7; C de D, 1949–51, 79; DGF51, II, 451; DGF50, II, 390; Func., 105.

Mendez Docurro, Eugenio

a-Apr. 17, 1923. **b**-Veracruz, Veracruz, *Gulf*, *Urban*. **c**-Engineering degree in electrical communications from the National Polytechnic Institute, 1948; Master of Science from Harvard University, 1949; graduate studies at Harvard University on a scholarship from the Secretariat of Public Education; graduate studies at the School of Science, University of Paris, 1949–50; studies at the Royal College of Science and Technology, London, 1962–63; Subdirector General of the National Polytechnic Institute, 1950–53; *Director General of the Polytechnic Institute*, 1959–62. **d**-None. **e**-None. **f**-Director General of Telecommunications, Secretariat of Communications and Transportation, 1953–59; *Subsecretary of Communications and Transportation*, 1964–70; *Secretary of Communications and Transportation*, 1970–76; Coordinator General of Scientific and Technical Education, Secretariat of Public Education, 1976–77; *Subsecretary of Education and*

Scientific Investigation, 1976–78. **g**-None. **h**-President of the Consulting Commission on Broadcasting; member of the Mexican Delegation to UNESCO, 1960. **i**-Son of Eugenio Mendez, a lawyer and leftist who served as a Federal Deputy in the 1930s; godson of *Miguel Aleman*. **j**-None. **k**-Precandidate for the Governor of Veracruz, 1974; precandidate for Federal Deputy from Veracruz, 1976; prosecuted by the Attorney General for fraud; found guilty, 1978. **l**-DGF56, 252; *Libro de Oro*, xxxiv; DPE65, 104; DBM68, 430; DGF51, I, 292; *Hoy*, December, 1970; HA, 7 Dec. 1970; *Excelsior*, 13 April 1973, 11; Enc. Mex., VIII, 1977, 428; *Excelsior*, 8 Dec. 1975, 17; HA, 3 April 1978, 11–12; HA, 17 April 1978, 10.

Mendieta y Nunez, Lucio

a-Jan. 11, 1895. **b**-Federal District, *Federal District*, *Urban*. **c**-Primary studies at the Normal School, Oaxaca, Oaxaca; secondary studies at the Institute of Oaxaca, 1909–10; preparatory studies at the National Preparatory School, 1911–15; law degree from the National School of Law, UNAM, May 1, 1920; LLD, National School of Law, UNAM, 1950; Professor of Agrarian Law, Administrative Law, and Sociology, UNAM (25 years); Professor of Sociology, Technological Institute of Mexico, 1947–54; Director of the Institute of Social Investigations, UNAM, 1939–66; Professor at the Institute of Social Investigations, UNAM, 1970; co-founder with *Luis Garrido Diaz* of the School of Political and Social Science at UNAM; founder of the School of Economics, UNAM. **d**-None. **e**-Director of the Institute of Social Studies for the PNR, 1935. **f**-Chief of the Department of Population, Bureau of Anthropology, Secretariat of Agriculture, 1921; Director of the Institute of Social Investigations, Bureau of Population, Secretariat of Agriculture, 1934; adviser to the Department of Indian Affairs, 1936; *Oficial Mayor* of the Department of Agrarian Affairs and Colonization, 1946–48; Director of Educational and Cultural Affairs, National Council of Tourism, 1976– . **g**-None. **h**-Director of the magazine, *Social Policy*, 1935; Director of *Mexican Sociology Review*, 1939–46. **i**-Attended UNAM with *Manuel Gomez Morin*, Angel Alanis Fuentes, *Manuel Bartlett*, and Alberto Vazquez del Mercado; disciple of Manuel Gamio; married Josefina Escalante. **j**-None. **k**-Outspoken critic of the Mexican bureaucracy; prolific author and authority on agrarian reform and sociological studies of Mexico. **l**-DGF47, 285; WWM45, 76; Peral, 521; letters; Enc. Mex., VIII, 1977, 431–32.

Mendiola (Miranda), Carlos C.

a-Oct. 25, 1903. **b**-Matamoros, Tamaulipas, *North*, *Rural*. **c**-Studied at the Internado Nacional, 1918–19; studies from the La Salle Extension University,

1930–33; no degree. **d-**None. **e-**None. **f-**Banking inspector for the National Banking Commission; *Subdirector General of the National Bank of Foreign Commerce*, 1940–42; Subdirector General of the Bank of Commerce, 1942–46. **g-**None. **i-**Brother of *Mario Mendiola*, Subdirector General of the National Bank of Foreign Commerce, 1942–53; married Rosa Murga. **j-**None. **k-**None. **l-**WWM45, 76.

Mendiola (Miranda), Mario

a-Aug. 4, 1910. **c-**Professional studies in business administration, commerce and electrical engineering; no degree. **d-**None. **e-**None. **f-***Subdirector General of the National Bank of Foreign Commerce*, 1942–46, 1946–52, 1952–53; Administrative Director of CONCAMIN, 1970; Director General of the National Savings Bank. **g-**None. **i-**Brother of *Carlos Mendiola*, Subdirector General of the National Bank of Foreign Commerce, 1940–42; married Enriqueta Gedovius. **j-**None. **k-**None. **l-**DBM70, 378; DGF51, II, 29, 95, 195, etc.

Mendoza Aramburo, Angel Cesar

a-Dec. 15, 1934. **b-**La Paz, Baja California del Sur, *West, Urban*. **c-**Primary studies in the Venustiano Carranza School, La Paz; secondary studies at the Jose Maria Morelos School, La Paz; preparatory studies at the National Preparatory School; law degree, National School of Law, UNAM, 1953–57. **d-***Federal Deputy* from Baja California del Sur, Dist. 1, 1967–70, member of the General Affairs Section of the Legislative Studies Committee and member of the Hydraulic Resources Committee; *Governor of Baja California del Sur*, 1975– . **e-**Secretary General of Youth of PRI in Baja California del Sur, 1950; Secretary of Political Action of PRI in Baja California del Sur, 1967–70, 1974; President of the Electoral Committee of Baja California del Sur, 1967–70, 1974. **f-**Assistant to the President and judicial official of the Superior Tribunal of Justice of the Federal District, 1958–66; Private Secretary to the Secretary of Hydraulic Resources, *Jose Hernandez Teran*, 1964–65; Secretary General of Government of Baja California del Sur, under Governor *Hugo Cervantes del Rio*, 1965–67; Secretary General of Government of Baja California del Sur, March to January, 1970; Secretary General of Government of Baja California del Sur, under Governor *Felix Agramont Cota*, October, 1974 to January, 1975. **g-**President of the Southern California Student Society of Mexico, 1953. **h-**Practicing lawyer. **i-**Cousin of *Alberto Alvarado Aramburo,* Federal Deputy from Baja California del Sur, 1964–67. **j-**None. **k-**Defeated cousin for gubernatorial nomination, 1975; first constitutional governor of the State of Baja California del Sur. **l-**Enc. Mex., Annual, 1977, 540; C de D, 1967–70, 67, 85; DPE65, 125; *Excel-*

sior, 4 Jan. 1975, 3; *Excelsior*, 17 Jan. 1975; HA, 15 Apr. 1975, 7.

Mendoza Berrueto, Eliseo

a-Apr. 13, 1931. **b-**San Pedro, Coahuila, *North, Urban*. **c-**Teaching certificate; degree in economics from the National School of Economics, UNAM, 1962, with a thesis on "Regional Planning and Economic Development: The Case of Mexico"; graduate studies at the Institute of Social Studies, Holland, 1962, received a diploma; graduate studies in economic planning, integral planning and national accounts at the National School of Economics, UNAM; graduate studies in regional planning in Paris; visiting investigator to the Institute of Economics, Holland, 1962; professor at the National School of Economics, UNAM; professor at the National Polytechnical School; professor at the School of Economics, University of Guadalajara; professor at the Colegio de Mexico; professor at the School of Architecture (graduate program), UNAM; Director of the Center for Economic and Demographic Studies, Colegio de Mexico, 1967–70. **d-***Senator* from Coahuila, 1976–78. **e-**Technical adviser to the IEPES of PRI. **f-**Head of the Statistics Section for the Cooperative Industries Administration, 1953–56; Economic Investigator for the National Bank of Foreign Commerce, 1958–59; head of Administrative Budgets for the National Bank of Ejido Credit, 1959; Assistant Director of the Administrative Department, National Ejido Credit Bank, 1960; adviser to the National Chemical-Pharmaceutical Industry, 1963; Director of Economic and Social Planning for the Plan Lerma, 1963–66; adviser to the Subsecretary of Industry and Commerce, 1956–58; adviser to the Government of the State of Jalisco, 1965–66; *Subsecretary of Commerce, Secretary of Industry and Commerce*, 1970–76; *Subsecretary of Higher Education, Science and Technology*, 1978– . **g-**None. **h-**None. **i-**Attended the National School of Economics with *Carlos Bermudez Limon*; married Maria Guadalupe Altamira. **j-**None. **k-**None. **l-**HA, 14 Dec. 1970, 21; letter ; DPE71; HA, 9 Jan. 1978, 13.

Mendoza Gonzalez, Octavio

a-Dec. 1, 1900. **b-**Leon, Guanajuato, *West Central, Urban*. **c-**Primary and secondary studies in Leon, Guanajuato; preparatory studies at the University of Guanajuato, 1913–18; law degree, National School of Law, 1918–22, with a thesis on administration and administrators, Aug. 29, 1923; Assistant to the Secretary of the Preparatory School, Leon, Guanajuato, 1916. **d-**Federal Deputy from the State of Guanajuato, 1928–29. **e-**None. **f-**Secretary of the Justice of the Peace, Dist. 8; Commissioner of the First Justice of the Peace, 1917–19; secretary of the first cooperative founded by President Obregon, 1920; consulting lawyer to the Secretariat of the Government, 1924; Secretary General of Government of the State of Guanajuato, 1926; Interim Governor of Guanajuato, 1927; Subsecretary in charge of the Secretariat of Government, 1929; Ambassador to Germany and Austria, 1930–32; Oficial Mayor of the Secretariat of Foreign Relations, 1932; Secretary of the Board of Private Welfare, 1934–36; Director of the Legal Department, Department of the Federal District, 1936–38; *Justice of the Supreme Court*, 1941–46, 1947–52, 1953–58, 1959–64, 1965–68. g-None. h-None. i-Great grandfather served as a federal deputy under President Juarez; married Magdalena Causier. j-None. k-None. l-*Justicia*; letter.

Mendoza Pardo, Jose Maria

b-Michoacan, *West Central*. c-Early education unknown; law degree, School of Law, Colegio de San Nicolas, Morelia, Michoacan, 1925–29; Professor of History, Colegio de San Nicolas. d-*Governor of Michoacan*, 1944–49. e-None. f-Secretary General of Government of the State of Baja California del Norte; Attorney General of the State of Michoacan under Governor *Lazaro Cardenas*; Secretary General of Government of the State of Michoacan under Governor *Lazaro Cardenas*; *Justice of the Supreme Court*, 1941–44. g-None. h-Practicing lawyer. i-As a student visited *Lazaro Cardenas'* home as part of a regular discussion group; brother-in-law of *Alberto Bremauntz*, Federal Deputy from Michoacan, 1932–34. j-None. k-Resigned August 26, 1949, as governor, because of difficulties resulting from student unrest at the Colegio de San Nicolas over government subsidies. l-HA, 21 Sept. 1945; letter; Anderson; Bremauntz, 93; Romero Flores, 267; NYT, 20 May 1962, 30.

Meraz Nevarez, Braulio

a-Feb. 9, 1911. b-Santiago Papasquiaro, Durango, *West*, *Rural*. c-Professional studies at the Agricultural School of Santa Lucia of Durango; attended the National Military College. d-*Federal Deputy* from the State of Durango, Dist. 3, 1940–43, member of the Gran Comision, member of the Agricultural Development Committee; *Federal Deputy* from the State of Durango, Dist. 4, 1952–55, member of the War Materiels Committee; *Federal Deputy* from the State of Durango, Dist. 4, 1964–67, member of the Gran Comision, the Second Committee on National Defense, the Hydraulic Resources Committee, and the Livestock Committee. e-None. f-None. g-None. h-Accountant. j-Career army officer; Field Marshal for the Army Veterinary Medical School; Captain of the Cavalry; reached the rank of Major. k-None. l-Peral, 525–26; C de D, 1940–42, 10, 51; C de D, 1852–54, 61; C de D, 1964–66.

Merino Fernandez, Aaron

(Deceased Dec., 1976)
a-Mar. 31, 1908. b-Ixcaquixtla, Puebla, *East Central, Rural*. c-Agricultural engineering degree from the National School of Agriculture, with a specialty in irrigation; Professor of Topography, UNAM, 1929. d-*Federal Deputy* from the State of Puebla, Dist. 6, 1940–43, substitute member of the First Justice Committee, the Health Committee. e-None. f-Engineer in the Department of Agrarian Affairs, 1928–38; Director of General Services for the Department of the Federal District; delegate of the Department of Agrarian Affairs in Puebla, 1938–40; President of the Agrarian Commission in Puebla, 1940; Head of the Technical Consulting Corporation, 1943; Director General of Public Works, Secretariat of Public Works; *Oficial Mayor of the Secretariat of Public Education*, 1946–48; *Subsecretary of Public Education*, 1948–52; *Governor of Quintana Roo*, 1959–64; *Interim Governor of Puebla*, 1964–69. g-Secretary of the Mexican Agronomy Society; founder of the Platform of Professionals Group which served as a political base for *Mario Moya Palencia*, *Antonio Calzada* and *Pedro Ojeda Paullada's* careers. h-Author of a book on agriculture in Puebla. i-Brother of *Jesus Merino Fernandez*, Subsecretary of Agriculture and Livestock, 1946–54. j-None. k-One of the few examples in recent Mexican cabinet history where two brothers simultaneously held subsecretary positions. l-HA, 16 Jan. 1948, 7; DGF51, I, 285; EBW46, 115; D de S, 1 Dec. 1940, 1; C de D, 1940–42, 16, 61; Peral, 527; DGF47, 171; CyT, 441; HA, 13 Dec. 1976, 49; Lopez, 695.

Merino Fernandez, Jesus

a-1905. b-Ixcaquixtla, Puebla, *East Central, Rural*. c-Early education unknown; studies in agricultural engineering, National School of Agriculture, 1922–27, degree, 1929, with a thesis on the "Regulation of the Rio Coatzala Waters in Puebla"; Professor of Engineering, 1934–38; Professor of Agricultural Economics, School of Social Science, UNAM, 1934–37. d-None. e-None. f-Auxiliary engineer to the National Irrigation Commission, Morelos, 1928; Chief of Topography, Department of Agricultural Waters, La Laguna, Puebla and in Morelos, 1929; adviser to the presidency, 1934–40; delegate of the Department of Agrarian Affairs and Colonization to Morelos, 1939–40; Director of Public Works, State of Morelos, 1939–40; Executive Secretary of the National Irrigation Commission, 1941; adviser to NAFIN, 1942–46; Director General of the National Resources, Secretariat of the Treasury, 1942–46; *Subsecretary of Agriculture*, 1946–52; 1952–54; Gerente General of the National Bank of Cooperative Development, 1969. g-President of the Mixed Agrarian Commission, Morelos, 1930–33. **h-**Author of agrarian laws; Secretary General of the Mexican Agronomy Society. **i-**Brother of *Aaron Merino Fernandez*, Governor of Puebla, 1964–69. **j-**None. **k-**None. **l-**DBP, 441–42; DGF56, 223; DP70, 213; DGF47, 123; DGF51, I, 203; CyT, 441–42.

Merino Rabago, Francisco

a-1919. **b-**Irapuato, Guanajuato, *West Central*, *Urban*. **c-**Early education unknown; no degree. **d-**None. **e-**None. **f-**Rural Inspector, National Ejido Credit Bank, 1938; assistant to a zone director, National Ejido Credit Bank; adviser, director of the National Ejido Credit Bank, 1938–54; Director of Credit, National Ejido Credit Bank, 1954–56; Subdirector, National Ejido Credit Bank, 1956–58; Director of Credit, National Ejido Credit Bank, 1959–65; adviser, Secretary of Agriculture, 1959–60; Subdirector, National Ejido Credit Bank, 1968–70; Coordinator General of the National Ejido Bank, 1970–72; Manager, La Laguna Ejido Bank, 1972–74; Manager, Michoacan Ejido Bank, 1975; Subdirector General of the National Bank of Rural Credit, 1975; Director General of the National Bank of Rural Credit, 1975–76; *Secretary of Agriculture*, 1976– . **g-**Member of the CNC, 1939– . **i-**First political mentor was *Gilberto Flores Munoz*, Secretariat of Agriculture, 1952–58. **j-**None. **k-**None. **l-***Excelsior*, 1 Dec. 1976, 1; *Excelsior*, 25 Mar. 1977, 8; HA, 6 Dec. 1976, 23; *El Dia*, 1 Dec. 1976, 1; HA, 8 Aug. 1977, 18.

Mijares Palencia, Jose

(Deceased 1965)
a-Mar. 1, 1895. **b-**Villahermosa, Tabasco, *Gulf*, *Urban*. **c-**Primary studies at the Colegio Ayala and the Colegio San Bernardo, Puebla, 1902–07; secondary studies at the Colegio San Pedro and the Colegio San Pablo, and at the La Salle Christian School, Puebla, 1907–10; Cadet at the National Military College, Chapultepec, 1910–11; graduated, 1912, as a 2nd Lieutenant of Infantry; founder and Director of the Ignacio Zaragoza School, Puebla, Puebla, which later became a military academy. **d-***Governor of Puebla*, 1933–37. **e-**Campaign manager for *General Almazan's* presidential campaign, 1940. **f-**Chief of Mounted Police for the Federal District, 1929–31; Director General of Agricultural Education, Secretariat of Public Education, 1946–52. **g-**None. **h-**Director of a private military academy, 1946; author of an organizational manual for the federal government, 1936, and other works. **j-**Joined the Revolution as a 2nd lieutenant, 1912; rank of Captain, 1914; Brigadier General, 1927; Brigade General, 1931; Commander of the 17th Military Zone, Queretaro, Queretaro; Commander of the 27th Military Zone, Acapulco, Guerrero, **k-**Founder of the first

private military academy in Mexico. **l-**D de Y, 8 Nov. 1935, 1; D de Y, 5 Sept. 1935, 1; DGF51, I, 290; DGF47, 172; EBW46, 1136; CyT, 444–45; Enc. Mex., IX, 1977, 68; NYT, 21 Aug. 1940, 8.

Minero Roque, Jose

a-1907. **b-**Nochistlan, Zacatecas, *East Central*, *Rural*. **c-**Primary studies in Nochistlan; secondary and preparatory studies in Guadalajara, Jalisco; scholarship student in Rome (two years); law degree. **d-***Federal Deputy* from the State of Zacatecas, Dist. 3, 1949–50, member of the Library Committee; local deputy to the State Legislature of Zacatecas, 1946–47; *Governor of Zacatecas*, 1950–56. **e-**None. **f-**Private Secretary to *Leobardo Reynoso*, Governor of Zacatecas, 1944–45; Oficial Mayor of Zacatecas, 1945–46; Secretary General of Government of Zacatecas, 1947. **g-**None. **i-**Political protege of Governor *Leobardo Reynoso*. **j-**None. **k-**None. **l-**HA, 26 Sept. 1955, 10; DGF56, 103; HA, 29 Sept. 1950, xxiv; C de D, 1949–51, 80; DGF51, I, 27, 93.

Miramontes (Briseno), Candelario

a-July 2, 1902. **b-**Tepic, Nayarit, *West*, *Urban*. **c-**Primary education in Tepic; no degree. **d-***Federal Deputy* from the State of Nayarit, Dist. 1, 1940–43, member of the Balloting Committee, and the Third Ejido Committee; *Substitute Federal Deputy* from the State of Nayarit, Dist. 1, 1937–40; *Governor of Nayarit*, 1942–46; *Senator* from the State of Nayarit, 1946–52, substitute member of the Labor Committee (2nd). **e-**None. **f-**None. **g-**Member of the National Chamber of Commerce. **h-**Merchant, 1924–40. **j-**None. **k-**None. **l-**Letter; EBW46, 204; DGF51, I, 14; C de D, 1937–39, 14; C de D, 1940–42, 14, 53.

Miranda Andrade, Otoniel

a-1915. **b-**Molango, Hidalgo, *East Central*, *Rural*. **c-**Early education unknown; medical degree; advanced studies abroad. **d-***Governor of Hidalgo*, April 1, 1975 to April 29, 1975. **e-**None. **f-**Head physician to *Manuel Sanchez Vite*, Governor of Hidalgo, 1969–70, 1972–75; Coordinator, Institutions for the Protection of Children, State of Hidalgo; Director, Civil Hospital, Pachuca, Hidalgo; Director, ISSSTE in Hidalgo; Director, Medical Services for the Public Health Department, Hidalgo, 1974. **g-**Secretary General of CNOP in Hidalgo. **h-**Practicing physician. **i-**Born in the same year and in the same village as his mentor, *Manuel Sanchez Vite*. **k-**Served as a constitutionally elected governor for the shortest period of any Mexican governor since 1935; deposed by the Permanent Committee of Congress in what some political observers considered a move to further discredit his mentor, *Manuel Sanchez Vite*. **l-***Excelsior*, 12 Oct. 1974, 1; HA, 21 Oct. 1974, 40; LA, 9 May 1975, 141; HA, 5 May 1975, 42.

Miranda Fonseca, Donato

a-June 28, 1908. b-Chilapa, Guerrero, *South*, *Urban*. c-Primary studies in Chilapa; secondary studies at a normal school; law degree from the Escuela Libre de Derecho, Apr. 12, 1935, with a thesis on "Public Liberties and Article Three." d-Local deputy to the State Legislature of Guerrero; *Federal Deputy* from the State of Guerrero, Dist. 5, 1943–46; *Senator* from the State of Guerrero, 1946–52, member of the Gran Comision, the Third Committee on National Defense, the Legislative Studies Committee, the First Balloting Committee, substitute member of the Second Public Education Committee, and the Special Forestry Committee; Mayor of Acapulco, Guerrero. e-Head of *Miguel Aleman*'s campaign for president in the State of Guerrero, 1946. f-Judge of the Superior Tribunal of Justice of Guerrero, 1947; Representative to Petropolis, Brazil; Representative to Caracas, Venezuela; member of the Mexican delegation to the Inter-American Assembly of Mutual Defense, 1947, with *Jose Lopez Bermudez*; Justice of the Superior Tribunal of Justice of the Federal District and Federal Territories; President of the Superior Tribunal of Justice of the Federal District and Federal Territories, 1956–58; *Secretary of the Presidency*, 1958–64. g-Student leader and founder of the National Organization of Normal Students, 1927. h-Practicing lawyer, 1935. i-Married Maria Luisa Acosta. j-None. k-Precandidate for President of Mexico, 1964, reportedly *Lopez Mateos*' first choice; participated in 1929 student strike with *Lopez Mateos*; spoke at the PRI nominating assembly for *Miguel Aleman* in 1946; precandidate for governor of Guerrero, 1956. l-D del S, 20 Jan. 1946; *Excelsior*, 11 Aug. 1947; CB, 13 May 1965; *Excelsior*, 8 May 1972, B-2; *El Universal*, 2 Dec. 1958, 1; HA, 2 Dec. 1958, 32; DGF56, 513; Func.; NYT, 11 Aug. 1963, 34; HA, 10 June 1974, 13.

Miravete, Manuel E.

a-1894. b-San Andres Tuxtla, Veracruz, *Gulf*, *Urban*. c-Primary studies at the Escuela Cantonal, San Andres, Tuxtla; no degree. d-Local deputy to the 23rd Legislature of the State of Veracruz; Federal Deputy from the State of Veracruz, 1920–22, 1922–24, 1930–32; *Federal Deputy* from the State of Veracruz, Dist. 1, 1937–40. e-Director of various gubernatorial campaigns in the State of Veracruz. h-None. j-Private secretary to various Revolutionary leaders. k-None. l-Peral, 535; C de D, 1937–39, 15.

Moctezuma, Fernando

a-1895. b-Ciudad del Maiz, San Luis Potosi, *East Central*, *Rural*. c-Early education unknown; law degree; Professor of Law, School of Law, University of San Luis Potosi, 1922–25. d-*Federal Deputy* from the State of San Luis Potosi, Dist. 4, 1943–46; *Senator* from the State of San Luis Potosi, 1946–52, member of the Gran Comision, the Legislative Studies Committee, the Second Government Committee and the Tax Committee. e-Secretary General of the PNR, 1931–34. f-Legal adviser, Secretary of Public Health, 1952–58. g-None. i-Brother of *Mariano Moctezuma*, Subsecretary of Industry and Commerce, 1936–38; early political mentor of *Antonio Rocha*, who was his alternate as senator; his sister-in-law was the sister of *Juan Barragan*. k-None. l-Lopez, 713; DGF51, I, 7–12; DGF56, 331; C de S, 1946–52; C de D, 1943–46.

Moctezuma, Mariano

(Deceased July 28, 1942)

a-Feb. 15, 1877. b-Ciudad del Maiz, San Luis Potosi, *East Central*, *Rural*. c-Engineering degree in geology, August 23, 1905, School of Mines; professor at the National School of Engineering, UNAM, 1936–42; Director of the School of Engineering, UNAM, 1915–23, 1929–33, 1938–42; Director of the National Mining School. d-None. e-None. f-*Subsecretary of Industry and Commerce*, 1936–38; Subsecretary of Public Works, 1932–34, in charge of the Secretariat, Nov., 1934; *Subsecretary of Public Education*, 1934–36; Director of the National Observatory, Tacubaya, Federal District. g-None. h-None. i-Brother *Fernando* served as a Senator from San Luis Potosi, 1946–52. j-None. k-None. l-DP70, 1372; Peral, 537; HA, 7 Aug. 1942, 40; Lopez, 714.

Moctezuma Cid, Julio Rodolfo

a-1927. b-Federal District, *Federal District*, *Urban*. c-Early education unknown; law degree, National School of Law, UNAM; Professor of Political Science, School of Political and Social Science, UNAM. d-None. e-*Director General of the IEPES of the CEN of PRI*, January, 1975 to September, 1976. f-Private Secretary to *Raul Ortiz Mena*, Subsecretary of the Presidency, 1959–61; Subdirector of Planning, Secretariat of the Presidency, 1964–65; Director of Public Investments, Secretariat of the Presidency, 1965–70; adviser to the Secretariat of the Presidency, the Treasury and to CONASUPO, 1971–73; *Oficial Mayor of the Treasury*, 1974–75; *Secretary of the Treasury*, 1976–77; Coordinator of Special Projects, President of Mexico, 1979– . g-None. h-Practicing lawyer with *Octavio Medellin Ostos*; Director of the consulting firm Preinversion de Mexico, 1971–73. i-Friend of *Jose Lopez Portillo* since the 1950s. j-None. k-Fired by *Lopez Portillo* because of his inability to settle policy disagreements with *Carlos Tello Macias*. l-DPE61, 124; *El Dia*, 1 Dec. 1976; *Excelsior*, 17 Nov. 1977, 11; LA, Nov.

1977; *Excelsior*, 1 Dec. 1976; HA, 6 Dec. 1976, 22; MGF69, 345.

Moctezuma Diaz Infante, Pedro

a-Aug. 24, 1923. **b-**San Luis Potosi, *East Central, Urban.* **c-**Architecture degree, National School of Architecture, UNAM, 1950; Professor of the Theory of Architecture, National School of Architecture, UNAM, 1948–59; Professor of Program Analyses, Ibero-American University, 1957–58. **d-**None. **e-**None. **f-**Engineer for the Department of the Federal District; head of the Architecture Department, Secretariat of Public Works; member of the Commission for Colonial Monuments, National Institute of Anthropology and History; head of the Department of Urbanism and Architecture, Secretariat of Public Works, 1960–65; worked with *Mario Moya Palencia*, Subsecretary of Government, 1969–70; *Subsecretary of Real Property and Urbanism, Secretariat of Government Properties*, 1970–76. **g-**None. **h-**Practicing civil engineer; built the central office of PRI, Mexico City, 1968; constructed the Rectory of the University of Tamaulipas, 1967, and many other well-known public buildings. **j-**None. **k-**None. **l-**HA, 4 Oct. 1971, 9; HA, 14 Dec. 1970, 21; DPE71, 44; Enc. Mex., IX, 1977, 108–09.

Moguel Esponda, Arturo

a-1915. **b-**Cintalapa, Chiapas, *South, Rural.* **c-**Primary and secondary studies in Cintalapa; preparatory studies from the National Preparatory School; law degree, National School of Law, UNAM, 1937. **d-***Federal Deputy* from the State of Chiapas, Dist. 6, 1961–64, member of the Gran Comision, Secretary of the Chamber; *Senator* from the State of Chiapas, 1964–70. **e-**None. **f-**Agent of the Ministerio Publico, Federal District, 1938–42; Judge of the Superior Tribunal of Justice of the State of Chiapas, 1947–51; Private Secretary to *Rafael P. Gamboa*, Secretary of Health, 1952. **g-**None. **j-**None. **k-**None. **l-**C de S, 1964–70; MGF69; C de D, 1961–64; PS, 4086.

Moheno Velasco, Ruben

a-May 14, 1910. **b-**Guadalajara, Jalisco, *West, Urban.* **c-**Primary studies at the Manuel M. Villasenor School, Federal District; secondary and preparatory studies at public schools in the Federal District; studied law, National School of Law, UNAM (3 years); no degree. **d-***Federal Deputy* from the State of Jalisco, Dist. 3, 1964–67, member of the Legislative Studies Committee (the Second Section on Civil Affairs), the First Railroads Committee, and the Electric Industry Committee; *Federal Deputy* from the State of Jalisco, Dist. 6, 1970–73, member of the Legislative Studies Committee (Nineteenth Section on General Means of Communication and Transportation, and the Second General Means of Communication Committee). **e-**Member of the National Committee of PRI; *Secretary of Political Action of the CEN of PRI*, 1965. **f-**Employee of the National Railroads of Mexico, 1925–73. **g-**Official of the Railroad Workers Union of the Federal District. **h-**None. **i-**Married Celia Verduzco. **j-**None. **k-**None. **l-**C de D, 1964–67, 52, 73, 87; C de D, 1970–73, 126; *Directorio*, 1970–72.

Molina Betancourt, Rafael

(Deceased Aug. 24, 1957)

a-Nov. 16, 1901. **b-**Zacapoxtla, Puebla, *East Central, Rural.* **c-**Primary studies at the public school in Zacapoxtla, 1913; secondary studies at the Normal Institute of Puebla, 1918; teaching certificate from the Normal School of Mexico, D.F., June, 1921; Professor of Civics, Spanish, and World History. **d-***Federal Deputy* from the State of Puebla, Dist. 10, 1937–40. **e-**None. **f-**Director of Federal Schools, Chilpancingo, Guerrero, 1928–33; Inspector General of Federal Education, Celaya, Guanajuato, 1933–34; *Oficial Mayor of Public Education*, 1934–36; adviser to the Agricultural and Ejido Bank, 1936–37; Director General of Population, Secretariat of Government, 1941–47; Director General of Primary Education, Secretariat of Public Education, 1947–48; Director General of Indigenous Affairs, 1948–50. **g-**President of the Revolutionary Fraternal Bloc; member of the SNTE, 1941–54; adviser to the National Union of Technical Supervisors, 1952–54. **h-**Author of various books on education; Secretary General of the First Inter-American Demographic Congress, 1946. **j-**None. **k-**None. **l-**C de D, 1937–39; DGF47, 171; DBP, 449–50; CyT, 449–50.

Molina Castillo, Eduardo Jose

a-Dec. 25, 1903. **b-**Merida, Yucatan, *Gulf, Urban.* **c-**Primary studies in England and in Europe; secondary studies in the United States; no degree. **d-***Federal Deputy* from the State of Yucatan, Dist. 1, 1958–61, member of the Second Section of the Legislative Studies Committee, the Textile Industry Committee, and the Second Balloting Committee. **e-**President of the Regional Committee of PAN for Yucatan. **f-**None. **g-**None. **h-**Farmer; businessman; Director of Cordeleros de Mexico, S.A., 1958. **j-**None. **k-**Candidate for Federal Deputy from PAN (twice). **l-**Func., 404; C de D, 1958–60, 84.

Molinar (Simondy), Miguel

(Deceased 1964)

a-May 18, 1892. **b-**Chihuahua, Chihuahua, *North, Urban.* **c-**Primary, secondary and preparatory studies at the Scientific and Literary Institute of Chihuahua, Chihuahua; no degree. **d-**None. **e-**None. **f-***Oficial*

Mayor of the Secretariat of Communications and Public Works, 1941; Chief of Police of the Federal District, 1952–58; Director of Social Services of the Army, 1959–64. **g-**None. **j-**Career Army officer; joined the Revolution in the Huaxteco region, 1913; opposed the De la Huerta forces in Morelia, Michoacan, 1924; commander of the 13th infantry regiment; commander of the 16th cavalry regiment; Chief of Staff for the military zones of Mexico, Guanajuato, Jalisco, Baja California del Norte, Chihuahua, Oaxaca and Veracruz; Zone Commander of Guadalajara, San Luis Potosi, Veracruz and Queretaro; rank of Brigade General, January 1, 1939; Zone Commander of Oaxaca, Oaxaca, 1939–41. **k-**Saved General Miguel Dieguez from being executed by General Ramon B. Arnaiz. **l-**Lopez, 717–18; DP70, 1376; DGF61, 34; WWM45, 78.

Mondragon (Guerra), Octavio S.

a-June 20, 1908. **b-**Queretaro, Queretaro, *East Central, Urban.* **c-**Primary studies in Queretaro; secondary studies and preparatory studies at the Colegio Civil, Queretaro, 1925; medical degree from the Military Medical School, 1932. **d-***Governor of Queretaro*, 1949–55. **e-**None. **f-***Oficial Mayor of the Department of Health*, 1940–43, under *Fernandez Manero*; *Oficial Mayor of the Secretariat of Health and Public Welfare*, 1943–45, under *Gustavo Baz*; personal physician to the President of Mexico, *Manuel Avila Camacho*, 1940–46; *Subsecretary of Health and Public Welfare*, 1946. **g-**None. **h-**None. **i-**Personal friend of *Andres Serra Rojas*; married Alejandrina Gaytan; brother of *Salvador Mondragon Guerra*, Justice of the Supreme Court, 1968–77. **j-**Head of the Sanitary Division for the 34th Army Battalion, 1932–34; Director of the Infirmary, National Military College, 1934; Director of the Medical and Chemical Laboratory for the Army, 1935–39. **k-**None. **l-**WWM45, 79; letter; DGF51, I, 91; HA, 29 Oct. 1943, 14; Lopez, 718.

Mondragon Guerra, Salvador

a-1905. **b-**Queretaro, Queretaro, *East Central, Urban.* **c-**Primary studies at the Luis Hernandez and Benjamin Campa Schools, Queretaro; secondary and preparatory studies at the Colegio Civil of Queretaro; law degree, National School of Law, UNAM, Jan. 19, 1935; Professor by Competition of Mercantile Law (25 years), National School of Commerce and Administration; Professor of Mercantile Law, Ibero-American University; Professor of Mercantile Law, University of Morelos. **d-**None. **e-**None. **f-**Secretary of Resolutions, Civil Division, Judge of the 1st Instance, Villa Obregon, Federal District; Judge of the 1st Instance, Villa Obregon; Auxiliary Secretary of the 5th Division, Superior Tribunal of Justice of the Federal District; Second Secretary of

Resolutions, 4th Division, Superior Tribunal of Justice of the Federal District; First Secretary of Resolutions, 4th Division, Superior Tribunal of Justice of the Federal District; Judge of the 12th Civil District, Federal District; Judge of the Superior Tribunal of Justice of the Federal District, 1943–56; President of the Tribunal Superior of Justice of the Federal District, 1945; Justice of the 1st Circuit, Collegiate Tribunal of the Federal District, 1956; *Justice of the Supreme Court*, 1968–70, 1971–76; 1977. **g-**None. **h-**None. **i-**Classmate of *Antonio Luna Arroyo* at UNAM; brother of *Octavio S. Mondragon*, Governor of Queretaro, 1949–55. **j-**None. **k-**None. **l-***Justicia*, Nov. 1968; letter.

Mondragon Hidalgo (Mora), Gustavo

c-Accounting degree; CPA; professor at UNAM. **d-**None. **e-**None. **f-**Accountant for the Federal Electric Commission, 1964–65; Gerente of Finances, CONASUPO, 1965–69; *Substitute Director General of CONASUPO*, 1969–70; Director of the Cuatitlan-Izcalli Project, State of Mexico, 1972; Comptroller General of the Department of the Federal District, 1976–79; *Secretary General "B"*, Department of the Federal District, May 30, 1979– . **g-**President of the National College of Public Accountants. **i-**Collaborator with *Carlos Hank Gonzalez*, Director General of CONASUPO, 1964–69, and Governor of the State of Mexico, 1969–75. **j-**None. **k-**None. **l-***Hoy*, 19 April 1969, 8; HA, 11 Sept. 1972. 54; DAPC, 1977, 48.

Montes Alanis, Federico

(Deceased Dec. 1, 1950)

a-1884. **b-**San Miguel de Allende, Guanajuato, *West Central, Urban.* **c-**Primary and preparatory studies in Queretaro; enrolled in the Military School, Jan. 3, 1905, graduated as a 2nd Lieutenant of Artillery, Aug. 1, 1906. **d-**Federal Deputy to the Constitutional Convention at Queretaro, 1916–17; Governor of Queretaro, 1919–20; Federal Deputy from the State of Queretaro, 1932–34. **e-**None. **f-**Chief of Police of the Federal District, May 1, 1938 to Aug. 15, 1939; *Oficial Mayor of the Secretariat of National Defense*, Nov. 1–30, 1940; Ambassador to Columbia, 1941–42; Commander of the Legion of Honor, 1950. **g-**None. **h-**None. **j-**Career Army officer; rank of 1st Lieutenant of Artillery, Mar. 18, 1909; rank of 2nd Captain, Sept. 12, 1911; member of the presidential staff, 1911; fought the Carranzistas under General Guillermo Rubio Navarrete in Candela, Coahuila, 1913; rank of 1st Captain, July 10, 1913; joined the Constitutionalists, December 23, 1913; commander of a machine gun regiment, Northeast Division, 1914; rank of Colonel, Aug. 2, 1914; Commander of the 24th Brigade of the Army of the Northeast, 1914–17; rank of Brigadier General, Dec. 1, 1914; rank of Brigade General, 25 Nov. 1916; commander of various military zones, 1934–38; retired from active duty, 1950. **k-**As an aide to Madero, defended him by killing several officers when troops came to seize the president, 1913; imprisoned, 1913; accompanied Carranza to Tlaxcalantongo, 1920; imprisoned in Mexico City and accused of complicity in Carranza's murder, 1920–23. **l-**Enc. Mex., Annual, 1977, 580–81.

Montes de Oca, Luis
(Deceased Dec. 4, 1958)
a-1894. **b-**Federal District, *Federal District, Urban.* **c-**Accounting degree; CPA; Superior School of Business, Administration, and Consular Affairs, Mexico, D.F.; Professor of Public Accounting, School of Business, UNAM 1916–21. **d-**None. **e-**Campaigned for *General Almazan*, 1940. **f-**Consul General to El Paso, Texas; Hamburg, Germany; Paris; 1914–20; Comptroller General of Mexico, 1924–27; Secretary of the Treasury, 1927–32; *Director General of the Bank of Mexico*, 1935–40; Presidential adviser to the National Banking Council. **g-**None. **h-**First employment as a public accountant for the federal government; financial agent to the United States for Carranza; author of the important 1931 monetary reform; founder and President of the International Bank of Mexico, 1958; founder with *Eduardo Suarez* of the National Bank of Foreign Commerce. **j-**Served in civilian posts as a consulate during the Revolution. **k-**Opposed General Huerta as a student; initiator of the use of CPA's in the Comptroller's office; resigned from the directorship of the Bank of Mexico to support *General Almazan*, September 7, 1940. **l-**HA, 15 Dec. 1958, 10; Kirk, 19, 39; Peral, 545; DP70, 1398; DP64, 964; WWM45, 80; DBM68, 545; Enc. Mex., IX, 1977, 171; NYT, 8 Sept. 1940, 28; Enc. Mex., IX, 1977, 171.

Montes (Garcia), Antonio
a-Jan. 17, 1910. **b-**El Moral, Puebla, *East Central, Rural.* **c-**Early education unknown; no degree. **d-**Local Deputy to the State Legislature of Puebla; Federal Deputy from the State of Puebla, 1930–32; *Federal Deputy* from the State of Puebla, Dist. 3, 1952–55, member of the Fourth Ejido Committee; *Federal Deputy* from the State of Puebla, Dist. 3, 1976–79, member of the Ejido and Communal Organization Section of the Agrarian Affairs Committee, the Library Committee; and the Rio Balsas Section of the Regional Development Committee. **e-**Joined the PNR, 1929; Secretary General of the Agrarian Party of Puebla, 1928. **f-**None. **g-**Secretary of Organization of the League of Agrarian Communities of the State of Puebla; Secretary General of the League of Agrarian Communities and Agrarian Unions of the State of Puebla, 1975. **i-**Married Maria

Josefina Lezama. **j-**None. **k-***Excelsior* considers him to be a peasant cacique in Puebla since the 1930s. **l-***Excelsior*, 16 July 1978, 22; C de D, 1952–55, 51; D de C, 1976–79, 6, 9, 36; *Excelsior*, 21 Aug. 1976, 1C; C de D, 1976, 51.

Mora Plancarte, Norberto
a-May 23, 1923. **b-**Morelia, Michoacan, *West Central, Urban.* **c-**Early education unknown; law degree, National School of Law, UNAM. **d-***Alternate Federal Deputy* from the Federal District, Dist. 14, 1961–63; *Federal Deputy* from the State of Michoacan, Dist. 7, 1967–70, member of the Gran Comision, member of the Tariff Committee, the Forest Affairs Committee, the Administrative Section of the Legislative Studies Committee, and the Complaints Committee; *Senator* from the State of Michoacan, 1970–76, President of the Rules Committee, First Secretary of the Agricultural Development Committee, Second Secretary of the Indigenous Affairs and the Third National Defense Committees, and member of the Fishing Committee. **e-**None. **f-**Administrative official of the Chamber of Deputies, 1937–64; Oficial Mayor of the Chamber of Deputies, 1964–67. **g-**Secretary General of the Union of Employees of the Chamber of Deputies and the Senate; delegate of the FSTSE to the State of Michoacan; Secretary of Legislative Proposals of the CEN of CNOP, 1974. **i-**Son of Dr. Ignacio Mora Plancarte; brother *Francisco Mora Plancarte* was a Federal Deputy from Michoacan, 1946–49. **j-**None. **k-**Precandidate for Governor of Michoacan, 1974. **l-**C de D, 1967–70, 56, 58, 69, 85; DBM68, 444; *Excelsior*, 16 Sept. 1974; C de S, 1970–76, 80.

Mora Ramos, Daniel
a-Aug. 4, 1908. **b-**Tanhuato, Michoacan, *West Central, Rural.* **c-**Primary studies at the Centro Escolar Jose Maria Morelos, Tanhuato, Michoacan (six years); secondary at the Urban Normal School of Morelia, Michoacan (three years); teaching certificate from the Urban Normal School of Morelia; advanced studies in language and literature from the Higher Normal School; Professor of the Science of Education, Oral Intensive Center No. 15 of the Federal Institute for Teacher Education. **d-***Federal Deputy* from the State of Michoacan, Dist. 4, 1952–55, member of the Protocol Committee, the Editorial Committee (2nd and 3rd years), the First Public Education Committee and the First Balloting Committee; *Federal Deputy* from the State of Michoacan, Dist. 4, 1970–73, member of the Waters and Irrigation Committee, the Library Committee (1st year), and the First Public Education Committee. **e-**President of the State Committee of PRI for Michoacan; Secretary of Social Action of PRI for Michoacan, 1970. **f-**Federal School Inspector for the Morelia,

Michoacan, region; Director of Federal and State Education in Michoacan. **g-**Member of the SNTE. **h-**None. **i-**Cousin of *Luis Mora Tovar*. **j-**None. **k-**None. **l-**C de D, 1970–72, 126; *Directorio*, 1970–72; C de D, 1952–54, 47, 49, 50, 57.

Mora Tovar, Luis
(Deceased Dec. 27, 1943)
a-Aug. 25, 1895. **b-**Tanhuato, Michoacan, *West Central*, *Rural*. **c-**Primary and secondary studies at the Seminario Conciliar, Morelia, Michoacan, law degree. **d-**Local deputy to the State of Michoacan; Federal Deputy from the State of Michoacan, 1934–36, head of the leftist bloc, President of the Chamber, 1935; *Senator* from the State of Michoacan, 1937–40. **e-**Founding member of the Michoacan Socialist Party, 1917. **f-**Secretary of the Agrarian Commission for the State of Michoacan; President of the Conciliation and Arbitration Board of the State of Michoacan. **g-**Co-founder of the League of Agrarian Communities in Michoacan; co-founder of the Revolutionary Federation of Labor of Michoacan. **h-**Poet; founder of *La Lucha*, Morelia, 1928. **i-**Cousin of *Daniel Mora Ramos*. **j-**Joined the Revolution. **k-**Jailed for political ideas. **l-**DP70, 1404; Peral, 548; Novo35, 29; Enc. Mex., IX, 1977, 360.

Morales Blumenkron, Guillermo
(Deceased Aug. 24, 1979)
a-Apr. 27, 1908. **b-**Puebla, Puebla, *East Central*, *Urban*. **c-**Primary studies at the Escuela Pias and La Nueva Escuela, Puebla; secondary studies at the Colegio Ingles y Frances de San Borja; studies as a bookkeeper, Peralta and Berlitz Academies, Mexico, D. F. **d-***Federal Deputy* from the State of Puebla, Dist. 10, 1964–67; member of the Television Industries Committee and the Cinematographic Industries Committee; *Senator* from the State of Puebla, 1970–73, 1974–76, President of the Second Committee on Credit, Money and Institutions of Credit, First Secretary of the National Property and Resources Committee and the Tax Committee. **e-**National coordinator for radio during the *Diaz Ordaz* campaign, 1964; head of the official PNR radio station, XEFO, 1934–36; Secretary of Relations for CNOP, 1967. **f-**Covered the Presidential campaign for XEFO, 1933–34; covered the inauguration of President *Cardenas*, 1934; originated the National Hour Radio Program for the Federal Government; *Provisional Governor of Puebla*, May 9, 1973, to 1974. **g-**President of the National Chamber of Broadcasting Industries, 1968; President of the Association of Mexican Publicity Agencies, 1952–54, 1957–59. **h-**Head of the Accounting Department, Bank of Monterrey, Puebla branch, 1923; involved in the private antique and furniture business,

Mexico, D.F., 1924–26; correspondent for Mexican newspapers in Havana, Cuba, 1927; began publishing the magazine *Reembolso*, 1927; publisher of *Variedades*, 1929; joined radio station XEW, 1938–49; owner of various Mexican radio stations, including XEQK and XEDA; founder and Director of the Morkron Publicity Agency, S.A., 1949–72. **i-**Married Josefina Montesinos. **j-**None. **k-**None. **l-**DBM68, 440–42; C de S, 1970–76, 80; C de D, 196–66, 52, 85, 87, 88; HA, 21 May 1973, 25; *Excelsior*, 26 Dec. 1974, 12.

Morales Cruz, Jose Ignacio
a-Mar. 19, 1911. **b-**Huauchinango, Puebla, *East Central*, *Rural*. **c-**Primary studies at the Benito Juarez Public School, 1918–23; secondary studies at the Normal Institute of Puebla, 1928–30; studied law at the University of Puebla, 1942–47; law degree, July 14, 1948; professor at numerous secondary schools throughout Puebla, Veracruz, and other states; Director of the Venustiano Carranza Secondary School and the Normal Institute of Puebla; Professor of Constitutional Law and Roman Law, University of Puebla. **d-***Federal Deputy* from the State of Puebla, Dist. 10, 1955–58, member of the Gran Comision, the Protocol Committee, the First Public Education Committee, and the Consular and Diplomatic Service Committee; *Alternate Senator* from Puebla, 1958–64. **e-**Joined the PNR, 1935. **g-**Representative of several labor organizations. **h-**Director of the student publication, *Alma estudiante*, 1929. **j-**None. **k-**None. **l-**DBP, 467–68; DGF56, 27, 30–32, 37; C de D, 1955–57; C de S, 1961–64.

Morales Farias, Carolina
a-Jan. 28, 1917. **b-**Monterrey, Nuevo Leon, *North*, *Urban*. **c-**Primary studies in Monterrey; secondary studies and accounting courses, Colegio de la Paz, Monterrey; studies in social work in Puerto Rico; certified public accountant. **d-***Alternate Federal Deputy* from the State of Nuevo Leon, Dist. 4, 1958–61; *Federal Deputy* from the State of Nuevo Leon, Dist. 5, 1970–73, member of the Artesans Committee, the Second Ejido Committee and the Desert Zones Committee. **e-**None. **f-**Social worker, Secretariat of Agriculture. **g-**Secretary of Feminine Action of the CNC; Secretary of Feminine Action of the League of Agrarian Communities of the State of Nuevo Leon. **i-**Widow. **j-**None. **k-**None. **l-**C de D, 1958–61; C de D, 1970–73, 126.

Morales Salas, Adrian
a-July 1, 1896. **b-**San Miguel de Mesquital, Zacatecas, *East Central*, *Rural*. **c-**Primary and secondary studies in public schools; no degree. **d-***Senator* from the State of Zacatecas, 1940–46,

Second Secretary of the First Tariff and Foreign Trade Committee, member of the Gran Comision. **e-**None. **f-**None. **g-**None. **h-**None. **j-**Joined the Revolution in support of Madero, 1911; 2nd lieutenant, 1911; 1st lieutenant, 1913; Major, 1915; career army officer, reached the rank of Colonel, 1926. **k-**None. **l-**C de S, 1940–46; EBW46, 178; Libro de Oro, 1946, 9.

Moreno Cruz, Everardo

a-Nov. 17, 1946. **b-**Federal District, *Federal District, Urban*. **c-**Primary and secondary studies in Mexico, D.F.; preparatory studies at the National Preparatory School, Mexico, D.F.; law degree with an honorable mention from the National School of Law, UNAM, 1969. **d-**None. **e-**Director of Cultural Action for the Youth Division of PRI, IV District, Federal District, 1963; coordinator of Civil Action Conferences of PRI in the Federal District, 1965–66; Secretary of the PRI delegation from Villa Obregon, Federal District, 1967–70. **f-**Assistant secretary of the Secretary of the Presidency, 1970–71; private secretary to the Secretary of the Presidency, 1971–76. **g-**None. **h-**Author of various books on law. **j-**None. **k-**None. **l-**HA, 1 Nov. 1971, 5; DPE71.

Moreno (Moreno), Manuel M.

a-May 21, 1907. **b-**Guanajuato, Guanajuato, *West Central, Urban*. **c-**Law degree, School of Law, University of Guanajuato, 1931; MA in history from UNAM, with a thesis on "The Political and Social Organization of the Aztecs;" Professor of Sociology and History at the University of Guanajuato. **d-***Federal Deputy* from the State of Guanajuato, Dist. 7, 1961–64; President of the Legislative Studies Committee; member of the Second Constitutional Affairs Committee; President of the Chamber of Deputies, Oct., 1962; *Senator* from the State of Guanajuato, 1964–67; *Governor of Guanajuato*, 1967–73. **e-**President of the Regional Committee of PRI for the State of Guanajuato; Director of Legal Affairs for PRI; head of the Consultative Department, PRI, 1953; Secretary of Political Action of the CEN of PRI; Secretary General of the CEN of PRI. **f-**Director of Public Education for the State of Guanajuato, 1934–35; Attorney General of the State of Guanajuato, 1932–34; Secretary General of Government of the State of Guanajuato, 1935; head of the Legal Office for the Department of the Federal District, 1945; Director General of Labor; Secretariat of Labor, 1953–58; Director General of Professions, Secretariat of Public Education, 1958–61; head of the Association Registration Department, Secretariat of Labor, 1956–58. **g-**Leader of the Student Union of Guanajuato, 1927. **h-**Worked as a porter and scribe at the Superior Court of Justice of Guanajuato as a student. **i-**Married Carmen Contreras. **j-**None.

k-None. **l-**HA, Sept. 1971; C de D, 1961–63, 84; DPE61, 101; C de S, 1964–70, 19; DGF56, 398; DBM68, 445; HA, 9 Oct. 1972, 35; WNM, 153; *Excelsior*, 19 Oct. 1975, 1; Enc. Mex., IX, 1977, 257–58.

Moreno Sanchez, Manuel

a-July 11, 1908. **b-**Rancheria Tierra Dura, Aguascalientes, Aguascalientes, *West, Urban*. **c-**Primary studies in Aguascalientes; preparatory studies at the National Preparatory School, 1926; law degree from the National School of Law, UNAM, 1932, with a thesis on *amparo*; Professor of International Public Law, UNAM, 1935–36; professor at the Institute of San Luis Potosi; professor at the University of Michoacan, 1933–34; Director of the School of Plastic Arts, UNAM, 1936; Secretary of the Institute of Esthetic Investigations, UNAM, 1936–38. **d-***Federal Deputy* from the State of Aguascalientes, 1943–46; *Senator* from the State of Aguascalientes, 1958–64, President of the Gran Comision, President of the First Committee on Foreign Relations, President of the Committee on Foreign and Domestic Commerce, member of the First Committee on Tariffs and Foreign Trade, substitute member of the First Constitutional Affairs Committee. **e-**Orator for the 1940, 1946, and 1952 presidential campaigns. **f-**Judge of the Superior Tribunal of Justice of the State of Michoacan, 1933–34; Judge of the Superior Tribunal of Justice of the Federal District, 1940–43; adviser to the state government of San Luis Potosi, 1939; Director, Legal Department, National Bank of Agricultural and Livestock Credit, 1946–52; Director of Traffic, Department of the Federal District, 1952. **g-**None. **h-**Author of many books and articles; practicing lawyer in the Federal District, 1943–58. **i-**Personal friend of *Adolfo Lopez Mateos*; married Carmen Toscano; Assistant to Professor Antonio Caso. **j-**None. **k-**Orator during the 1929 campaign with *Adolfo Lopez Mateos*. **l-**C de S, 1961–64, 63; Brandenburg, 114; Peral, 557; WWM45, 81; Enc. Mex., I, 104; C de D, 1943–45, 16; Func., 117; Gomez Maganda, 106; Lopez, 741; HA, 1 Feb. 1952; Enc. Mex., IX, 1977, 261.

Moreno Torres, Manuel

(Deceased May 22, 1980)
a-Feb. 22, 1912. **b-**Matehuala, San Luis Potosi, *East Central, Urban*. **c-**Primary and secondary studies in Matehuala; electrical engineering degree from the National Polytechnic Institute, 1935; studies in civil engineering, National School of Engineering, UNAM. **d-***Federal Deputy* from the State of San Luis Potosi, Dist. 2, 1958–61, member of the Department of the Federal District Committee, the Fourth Section of the Legislative Studies Committee,

the Electrical Industry Committee, the Public Works Committee, and the General Means of Communication Committee. **e**-None. **f**-Chief Engineer, construction of the Ferrocarril del Sureste Project; Director General of the Department of Public Works, Secretariat of Public Works; *Director General of the Federal Electric Commission*, 1958–64; Subdirector General of the Federal Electric Commission, 1976–80. **g**-Member of the Student Association of the National Polytechnic Institute. **h**-Many technical and administrative positions in public works. **i**-Married Cristina Gonzalez. **j**-None. **k**-None. **l**-HA, 10 Dec. 1962, 3; DGF56, 467; C de D, 1958–60, 85; Func., 343; HA, 2 June 1980, 15.

Moreno Valle, Rafael

a-Aug. 23, 1917. **b**-Atlixco, Puebla, *East Central, Urban*. **c**-Primary studies in Atlixco; secondary and preparatory studies at the National Preparatory School; medical degree and military surgeon training from the Military Medical School, December 9, 1940, graduating with the rank of Major; advanced studies, United States Department of Defense, 1941; Professor of Orthopedics at the National Medical School, UNAM (ten years); professor at the Military Medical School, 1944–64; studies in the United States. **d**-*Senator* from the State of Puebla, 1958–64; President of the Senate, member of the Gran Comision, the Public Health Committee, the Second Foreign Relations Committee, the Second National Defense Committee, substitute member of the Public Welfare Committee, President of the Military Health Committee; *Governor of Puebla*, 1969–72. **e**-Secretary of Political Action of the CEN of PRI, 1962–64. **f**-Head of Medical Services, Central Military Hospital, 1956; Director of the Central Military Hospital; *Secretary of Health and Public Welfare*, 1964–68. **g**-None. **h**-Founding member with *Salvador Aceves Parra* of the Mexican Orthopedic Society; president of many advisory health commissions. **i**-From a humble family background; supported *Emilio Martinez Manautou* for president, 1964. **j**-Career military medical officer; rank of Brigadier General, 1952. **k**-First graduate of the Military Medical School to become Secretary of Health; requested a leave of absence as Governor of Puebla, Apr., 1972, and never returned to office. **l**-HA, 24 Apr. 1972, 53; *Libro de Oro*, xxxv; DPE65, 148; *El Universal*, 1 Dec. 1964; DBM70, 395–96; C de S, 1961–64, 64; HA, 7 Dec. 1964, 20; CyT, 475; *Excelsior*, 26 Dec. 1974, 12.

Morones Prieto, Ignacio

(Deceased Oct. 30, 1974)

a-1900. **b**-Ciudad Linares, Nuevo Leon, *North, Rural*. **c**-Preparatory studies from the Colegio Civil of Monterrey and from the Scientific and Literary Institute of San Luis Potosi; medical degree from the University of San Luis Potosi, 1923; medical degree from the Sorbonne, 1923–28; Professor of Medicine, University of San Luis Potosi; professor at the Scientific and Literary Institute of San Luis Potosi; professor at the Colegio Civil, Monterrey, Nuevo Leon; Dean of the School of Medicine, University of San Luis Potosi; Rector of the University of San Luis Potosi (6 years). **d**-*Governor of Nuevo Leon*, 1949–52. **e**-None. **f**-*Oficial Mayor of the Secretariat of Health*, 1946; *Subsecretary of Health*, 1946–49; *Secretary of Health and Public Welfare*, 1952–58; *Ambassador to France*, 1961–65; *Director General of the Mexican Institute of Social Security*, 1966–70. **g**-None. **h**-Practiced medicine, 1928–45. **i**-Married Francisca Caballero; member of *Gonzalo N. Santos'* camarilla. **j**-None. **k**-Precandidate for president of Mexico, 1958. **l**-DPE65, 26; HA, 21 Sept. 1953, 7; *Libro de Oro*, xli; HA, 21 Sept. 1953; HA, 12 July 1954; WWMG, 27; HA, 5 Dec. 1962, 9; DGF56, 329, 331; DGF47, 197; DGF51, I, 91; G of NL, 15; DPE61, 22; Lopez, 743; Enc. Mex., IX, 1977, 263; HA, 11 Nov. 1974, 11, WNM, 152; NYT, 28 July 1957, 2.

Moya Palencia, Mario

a-1933. **b**-Federal District, *Federal District, Urban*. **c**-Law studies at the National School of Law, UNAM, 1950–54, degree in 1955; graduate studies in Mexican history at the School of Philosophy and Liberal Arts, UNAM; Professor of Constitutional Law at the National School of Political Studies, Acatlan Branch, UNAM, 1976– . **d**-None. **e**-None. **f**-Assistant in the Office of Public Relations, National Railroads of Mexico, 1955–58; Subdirector of the Public Domain in the Division of Real Property, Secretariat of National Patrimony, 1959–61; Director General of the Bureau of Cinematography, Secretariat of Government, 1964–68; *Subsecretary of Government*, 1969–70, under *Luis Echeverria*; *Secretary of Government*, 1970–76; President of the Administrative Board of PIPSA, 1968. **g**-President of the Platform of Mexican Professions, 1961–65. **h**-Co-founder of the magazine *Voz* with Jorge Villa Trevino; editor, 1950–53; editor of *Ferronales*, 1954–57; wrote for *Novedades*, 1957–59. **i**-Student of *Alfonso Noriega* at UNAM; knew *Jorge de la Vega Dominguez* at UNAM; member of the student generation which included *Pedro Ojeda Paullada* and *Pedro Zorrilla*; married Marcela Ibanez. **j**-None. **k**-Precandidate for president of Mexico, 1976. **l**-HA, 7 Dec. 1970, 23; DPE65, 14; DPE61, 60; HA, 14 Aug. 1972, 12; HA, 15 Jan. 1973, 10; HA, 17 Oct. 1977, 12–13; Enc. Mex., IX, 1977, 272; *Excelsior*, 24 Jan. 1974, 14; *Proceso*, 8 Jan. 1977, 29.

Mugica, Francisco Jose

(Deceased April 12, 1954)
a-Sept. 2, 1884. **b-**Tinguindin, Michoacan, *West Central*, *Rural*. **c-**Primary and secondary studies at the Seminary of Zamora, Michoacan; school teacher; no degree. **d-**Deputy to the Constitutional Convention, 1916–17; Governor of Michoacan, 1920–22. **e-**Leader of the Cardenas campaign for president, 1934; Director of the leftist Constitutional Party, 1952. **f-**Head of the Port of Tampico, 1914; President of the Superior Tribunal of Justice, 1915; Governor and Military Commander of the State of Tabasco, 1916; Director of the Department of General Provisions, 1918–20; Director of the Federal Prison on Islas Marias, 1927–33; head of the Administrative Department, Secretariat of National Defense, May, 1933; Secretary of the Secretariat of Industry and Commerce, 1934–35; *Secretary of Public Works*, June 18, 1935, to Jan. 23, 1939; *Governor of Baja California del Sur*, 1940–46. **g-**None. **h-**Tax collector, Chauinda, Michoacan; postal employee, Zamora, Michoacan; journalist; member of the Luis Cabrera law firm, 1924. **i-**Longtime enemy of General Obregon and Melchor Ortega; close friend and supporter of *Lazaro Cardenas*, 1925–39; father, a school teacher; married Doctor Matilde Rodriguez Cabo; members of his political group included *Luis Mora Tovar*, *Jesus Romero Flores*, and *Agustin Arroyo Ch*; son Janitzio Mugica Rodriguez Cabo was Director of Forests and Ejidos, Secretariat of Agrarian Reform, 1979. **j-**Joined the Revolution under Madero, Nov. 20, 1910, as a 2nd lieutenant; Captain of the Constitutional forces under General Lucio Blanco; Chief of Military Operations of various states; Brigadier General, 1932; Military Zone Commander, 32nd Zone, Merida, Yucatan, 1933; Commander of the 21st Military Zone, Morelia, Michoacan, 1939; Divisionary General, 1939. **k-**Precandidate for President of Mexico, 1939; considered too radical; identified with Leon Trotsky, whom he helped bring to Mexico; Gruening states that *Mugica* was imposed over other candidates as Governor of Michoacan, 1920; supported the candidacy of *Miguel Henriquez Guzman* for President, 1952. **l-**Morton, 40; WWM45, 81–82; Kirk, 89, 118, 234; DP70, 1425–26; DP64, 985; Peral, 560–61; Gruening, 461; Michaels, 4, 32; Scott, 238–39; Brandenburg, 92–93, 80–82; Strode, 357–59; Enc. Mex., IX, 1977, 273; Q es Q, 401–02.

Mujica Montoya, Emilio

a-May, 1926. **b-**Federal District, *Federal District, Urban*. **c-**Preparatory studies at the National Preparatory School, 1942–44; studies in economics, National School of Economics, UNAM, 1944–48, with an honorable mention for his thesis on economic cy-

cles and economic development; Ph.D. in economics, Alexander Humboldt University, Berlin, Germany, 1956, with a thesis on Marxist analysis; Professor of the Theory of Economic Cycles, Economic Problems of Mexico, Mexican Foreign Trade, Planning and Development and International Economics, National School of Economics, UNAM, 1951–73; Coordinator of Studies on the Economy and Education, Colegio de Mexico, 1972–73; Dean, National School of Economics, UNAM, 1959–63. **d-**None. **e-**Participant, PRI presidential campaigns, 1952, 1958, 1964; member of the Advisory Council of the IEPES of PRI, 1975–76; Coordinator of the Communications and Transportation Sections of the *Lopez Portillo* presidential campaign committees, 1976. **f-**Economist, Secretariat of Communications, 1948–50; economist, Secretariat of National Properties, 1950; economist, Secretariat of Industry and Commerce, 1951–52; economist, National Finance Bank, 1952–53; analyst, National Warehouses, 1953–58; Secretary of the Council of Advisers to the Director of CONASUPO, 1959–62; Director of Sectoral Planning, Secretariat of the Presidency, 1965–70; Director of Planning and Organization, National Railroads of Mexico, 1971; adviser to *Jose Lopez Portillo*, Secretary of the Treasury, 1973–75; Executive Secretary of the Coordinating Committee of the Public Sector Industrial Policy, 1975–76; Director of the Public Sector, Secretariat of Government Properties, 1975–76; *Secretary of Communications and Transportation*, 1976– . **g-**None. **h-**Laborer, Waters and Sanitation Division, Department of the Federal District, 1943–48. **i-**Some of his more prominent students at the National School of Economics include *Julio Faesler* and *Jorge Tamayo*; disciple of Professor Eduardo Botas; founded a political group of co-students at UNAM called the Enrique Gonzalez Aparicio Group; among its members were *Alejandro Cervantes Delgado*, *Marcela Lombardo*, *Agustin Acosta Lagunes*, *Nathan Warman* and *Sergio Luis Cano*; rivalry with *Jorge de la Vega Dominguez* stems from their days as student activists at UNAM. **j-**None. **k-**None. **l-***Excelsior*, 1 Dec. 1976; letter; HA, 6 Dec. 1976, 23; *El Dia*, 1 Dec. 1976; HA, 25 July 1972, 17; DAPC, 49; *Excelsior*, 29 Feb. 1980, 13.

Munoz Ledo (Lazo de la Vega), Porfirio

a-July 23, 1933. **b-**Federal District, *Federal District, Urban*. **c-**Primary and secondary studies in Mexico, D.F.; preparatory studies at the National Preparatory School; law studies, National School of Law, UNAM, 1950–54, law degree, 1955; LLD, University of Toulouse, France, 1958; Lecturer in Hispanic Literature, University of Paris, 1959–60; professor at the National Preparatory School, 1950; professor at the Women's University of Mexico, 1950; studies in economics and political science, University of Paris, 1956–59; Professor of Mexican Political Institutions, Higher Normal School, 1962–63; Professor of the Mexican Political Process, Colegio de Mexico, 1964– ; Professor of the Theory of the State, School of Political Sciences, UNAM, 1962–63. d-None. e-Adviser to the Section for Political Studies of the IEPES of PRI; member of the Section on Ideological and Political Analysis of the Mexican Revolution, PRI, 1972; *President of the CEN of PRI*, 1975–76. f-Assistant in the Public Relations Office of the Secretariat of National Patrimony, 1950–53; adviser to UNESCO; technical adviser to the Presidency, 1960–64; Subdirector General of Graduate Education and Scientific Investigation, Secretariat of Public Education, 1961–65; cultural adviser to the Mexican Embassy, Paris, 1965; *Secretary General of the Mexican Institute of Social Security*, 1966–70; *Subsecretary of the Presidency*, 1970–72; *Secretary of Labor*, Sept. 12, 1972, to 1975; *Secretary of Public Education*, 1976–77; *Ambassador to the United Nations*, 1979– . g-President of the Student Society of the National School of Law. h-Author of legal articles; member of the Board of Fondo de Cultura Economica; adviser to the National Housing Institute. i-Political disciple of *Ignacio Morones Prieto*. j-None. k-None. l-B de M, 87; HA, 14 Dec. 1970, 23; HA, 18 Sept. 1972, 11; HA, 22 Nov. 1971, 23; Enc. Mex., IX, 1977, 278; HA, 6 Dec. 1976, 23; HA, 29 Dec. 1975, 7; *Excelsior*, 4 Feb. 1977, 6; LA, 3 Dec. 1976.

Murillo Vidal, Rafael

a-Oct. 29, 1904. b-San Andres Tuxtla, Veracruz, *Gulf*, *Urban*. c-Primary studies in Cordoba; secondary and preparatory studies in Cordoba; law degree, National School of Law, UNAM, 1925. d-*Federal Deputy* from the State of Veracruz, Dist. 2, 1943–46; *Federal Deputy* from the State of Veracruz, Dist. 4, 1949–52, President of the Chamber, Nov., 1949; member of the Legislative Studies Committee (2nd year); *Senator* from the State of Veracruz, 1964–65; *Governor of Veracruz*, 1968–74. e-Member of the National Advisory Committee to PRI from the CNOP, Jan., 1946; *Popular Secretary of the CEN of PRI*, 1946. f-Judge of the 1st Instance in Tuxpan, Nayarit; Judge of the 1st Instance in Panuco, Veracruz; Justice of the Superior Tribunal of Veracruz; Oficial Mayor of the Senate, 1946–49; Secretary General of Government of the State of Veracruz; *Oficial Mayor of the Secretariat of Government*, 1965–68; Director General of Government, Secretariat of Government; Postmaster General of Mexico, 1952–64. g-*Secretary General of CNOP*, 1946. h-None. i-Knew *Eduardo Bustamante* at UNAM. j-None. k-None. l-HA, 22 Dec. 1958, 7; D

de S, 22 Jan. 1946, 1; DGF51, I, 26, 32; DPE61, 81; WWW70–71, 663; *Hoy*, 22 June 1958, 64; DGF56, 254; DGF47, 22; C de D, 1949–51, 80; Q es Q, 403–04.

Narvaez Angulo, Fernando

a-1910. c-Early education unknown; law degree. d-None. e-None. f-Chief of the Board of Prior Investigations, Office of the Attorney General of the Federal District, 1947; Chief of Agents of the Ministerio Publico, Criminal Division, Federal District; Private Secretary to the Attorney General of Mexico, *Carlos Franco S.*, 1952–58; official of the Supreme Court of Mexico; Director General of the Office of Prior Investigations, Office of the Attorney General of Mexico, 1968–76; *Attorney General of the Federal District*, 1976. g-None. j-None. k-None. l-DPE71, 160; MGF69, 329; *Excelsior*, 5 Mar. 1976, 16; DGF56, 539; MGF73, 429.

Nasta (Haik), Salim

a-Jan. 21, 1938. b-Federal District, *Federal District*, *Urban*. c-Preparatory studies at the Centro Universitario Mexico, Mexico, D.F.; member of the 1957 generation at the National School of Law, UNAM, completing his thesis on Nov. 10, 1961, on the subject of welfare obligations under the law. d-None. e-Private Secretary to *Diaz Ordaz* during his campaign for President, 1964; adviser to the IEPES of PRI. f-Head of the Legal Department for the Federal District Police; Assistant Private Secretary to the Secretary of the Presidency, 1963–64; Director General of Guanos y Fertilizantes de Mexico, S.A., 1964–72. g-None. h-Fluent in French and English. i-Son-in-law of *Gustavo Diaz Ordaz*; married Guadalupe Diaz. j-None. k-*Nasta* resigned as Director General of Guanos y Fertilizantes de Mexico on Aug. 25, 1972. l-HA, 7 Dec. 1970, 27; DJBM, 93; *Excelsior*, 26 Aug. 1972, 1; *Politica*, Nov. 1969, 103; WNM, 158.

Natera, Panfilo

(Deceased 1951)

a-June 1, 1882. b-Hacienda de la Noria, Nieves, Zacatecas, *East Central*, *Rural*. c-No secondary education or degree. d-*Governor of Zacatecas*, 1940–44. e-None. f-None. g-None. h-Before the Revolution, Natera worked as a water carrier. i-Father Francisco was a Colonel in the Revolution, and *Panfilo* fought under him; son, *Panfilo Jr.*, served as a Federal Deputy from Zacatecas during his father's term as governor, 1943–45. j-Served in the Revolution from 1910–11, 1913–15 under Generals Luis Moya and Villa; rank of Brigadier General, Dec. 20, 1913; became a constitutionalist in 1915; Provisional Governor and Military Commander of Zacatecas; fought against De la Huerta, 1923; head of the Army Inspection Commission, 1925; Alternate President of the Second Council of War; Commander of the 27th Military Zone, Acapulco, Guerrero; Commander of the 11th Military Zone, Zacatecas, Zacatecas; rank of Divisionary General, Oct. 16, 1937. **k-**None. **l-**DP70, 1450; Peral, 566; *Heroic Mexico*, 198–202, 25–06; D de Y, 7 Dec. 1940, 1; Enc. Mex., IX, 1977, 316–17; Lopez, 758.

Nava, Alfonso L.

a-July 7, 1900. **b-**Iguala, Guerrero, *South, Urban*. **c-**Primary studies in Mexico City; secondary studies in business administration; professional studies in Boston, Massachusetts; no degree. **d-**Mayor of Iguala, Guerrero; Federal Deputy from the State of Guerrero, 1926–28; Federal Deputy from the State of Guerrero, 1930–32; *Federal Deputy* from the State of Guerrero, Dist. 2, 1949–52, member of the Colonization Committee, the Fourth Ejido Committee, the General Accounting Office Committee and Vice-President of the Chamber of Deputies, September, 1950; *Senator* from the State of Guerrero, 1952–58, Second Secretary of the Development of Cooperatives Committee and the Second Instructive Section of the Grand Jury, member of the Second Balloting Committee. **e-**None. **f-**None. **g-**President of the Guerrero Society of Youth, 1923–26. **h-**Author of numerous articles. **j-**None. **k-**None. **l-**Ind. Biog., 107–08; C de D, 1949–52, 80; DGF56, 6, 10–14; C de S, 1952–58.

Nava Castillo, Antonio

a-Sept. 9, 1906. **b-**San Juan Ixcaquixtla, Puebla, *East Central, Rural*. **c-**Primary studies in San Juan Ixcaquixtla; secondary studies at the Colegio Lafragua, Puebla, Puebla; enrolled at the National Military College, 1921, graduated as a lieutenant, 1922; Cadet Commander of the Cavalry Squadron, National Military College. **d-**Federal Deputy from the State of Puebla, 1935–37; *Federal Deputy* from the State of Puebla, Dist. 12, 1940–43, President of the Second Instructive Section of the Grand Jury, member of the Committee on the Electric Industry, the Second Committee on National Defense, and the Gran Comision; *Governor of Puebla*, 1963–64. **e-***Secretary General of the National Federation of Popular Organizations of PRI*, 1944–46. **f-**Director of the Federal Penitentiary, Federal District, 1955–58; Director General of Traffic, Department of the Federal District, 1961–63; Director of Iron Works, Secretariat of Industry and Commerce, 1969. **g-**Co-founder of CNOP. **h-**Member of the Mexican Olympic Polo Team, 1936. **i-**Married Maria Lopez. **j-**Career army officer; Second Captain, 1923; fought against the rebellions of 1923, 1927, and 1929; First Captain, 1929; Major, 1936; Commander of the 7th Military Zone; Colonel, 1946; Brigadier General,

1948; Brigade General, 1952; Divisionary General, November 20, 1960. **k-**Received a last-minute political promotion from *Avila Camacho*, along with *Corona del Rosal*, in Nov., 1946; forced to resign as Governor of Puebla after student strikes brought pressure on the federal government to dissolve his powers in 1964; *Por Que* claims he was involved in scandals in the meat-packing industry; supported *Miguel Henriquez Guzman* for president, 1946. **l-**G of M, 31; DGF56, 466; Wences Reza, 55; HA, 27 Nov. 1961, 61; C de D, 1940–42, 17; DPE61, 145; D de Y, Jan. 1946, 1; D del S, 3 Dec. 1946, 1; *Por Que*, 6 Nov. 1969, 10; *Excelsior*, 26 Dec. 1974, 12; CyT, 483; *Excelsior*, 5 June 1945; Medina, 20, 29.

Navarrete, Alfredo

a-1893. **b-**Valle de Acambay, Morelos, *West Central, Rural*. **c-**Primary studies in Valle de Acambay; no degree. **d-***Federal Deputy* from the State of Mexico, Dist. 7, 1952–55, member of the First Railroad Committee, the Inspection Committee of the General Accounting Office (2nd year), the First Labor Committee, the Petroleum Committee, and the Social Action Committee (3rd year). **e-**None. **f-**None. **g-**Early labor organizer and leader; member of the Railroad Workers Union, 1932; Secretary General of the Railroad Workers Union (STFRM), 1934–35; head of the Transportation Workers Organization in the Zacatepec Mill, Morelos, 1938. **h-**At age 11, was working on an ejido in Morelos; moved to Mexico, D.F., 1904, where he worked as a laborer at the San Lazaro Station, 1907–14; employed on the Interoceanic Railroad, 1910. **i-**Friend of *Ignacio Garcia Tellez* and *Graciano Sanchez*, first Secretary General of the National Farmers Federation. **j-**Train conductor during the Revolution. **k-**Participant in the precursor movement; member of the Club Reyes for a short time; joined the Anti-Reelectionist Club. **l-**Kirk, 93; C de D, 1952–54, 15, 41, 53, 62.

Navarrete, Jorge Eduardo

a-1940. **b-**Federal District, *Federal District, Urban*. **c-**Early education unknown; economics degree, National School of Economics, UNAM; special studies in export development, Switzerland, Norway, Denmark, Belgium, Sweden and Israel; normal teacher. **d-**None. **e-**None. **f-**Director of the Department of Statistics and Information, National Foreign Trade Bank; economist, CEMLA; economist, Secretariat of the Treasury; Ambassador to Venezuela, 1972; *Subsecretary of Foreign Relations "D"*, 1979–. **g-**None. **h-**Economist, National Foreign Trade Bank; Director, *Comercio Exterior*. **j-**None. **k-**None. **l-**HA, 14 Aug. 1972, 9; *Excelsior*, 1 Aug. 1972, 1, 9; HA, 11 June 1979, 9.

Navarrete (Romero), Alfredo

a-July 24, 1923. b-Federal District, *Federal District, Urban*. c-Degree in economics from the National School of Economics, UNAM, 1942–46; MA in Public Administration, Harvard University, 1947; Ph.D. in economics from Harvard University, 1950; Professor, Advanced Economic Theory, National School of Economics, UNAM, 1953–61. d-None. e-None. f-Economist for the Secretariat of the Treasury, 1944; economist for the Latin American Contributions Committee, United Nations, 1946; Alternate Executive Director of the World Bank, 1963–65; Director of the Department of Financial Research, National Finance Bank, 1953–58; manager of the National Finance Bank, 1959–61; Subdirector of the National Finance Bank, 1961–65; Director, the National Finance Bank, 1965–68; *Assistant Director General of the National Finance Bank*, 1968–70; Director General of the Financiera Nacional Azucarera, 1970–72; *Subdirector General of Finances of PEMEX*, May 4, 1972, to 1976; Director General of the Financiera Nacional Azucarera, 1976– . g-None. h-Served on advisory commissions to Latin America for the Secretary General of the OAS; special adviser to the Secretary of the Treasury, 1953–70; winner of the National Prize in Economics, 1951. i-Formerly married to *Ifigenia Martinez*, who served as an economic adviser to the Secretary of the Presidency, 1964–70; she also was Director of the National School of Economics and a member of the Advisory Council of the IEPES of PRI, 1972; brother Victor was head of economic investigations for Nacional Financiera, 1959. j-None. k-None. l-DBM68, 453; DBM70, 405–06; B de M, 189; letter; *Excelsior*, 4 May 1972, 4; HA, 15 May 1972, 31; Enc. Mex., IX, 1977, 322; WNM, 158.

Navarro Cortina, Rodolfo

a-Sept. 8, 1889. b-Durango, *West*. c-Early education unknown; no degree. d-None. e-None. f-*Governor of Baja California del Norte*, August 16, 1936 to February 22, 1937. g-None. h-None. j-Career Army officer; joined the Revolution, 1913; fought against the forces of General Adolfo de la Huerta, 1923; fought against the forces of General Escobar, 1929; rank of Brigade General, May 16, 1929; Director of the General Artillery Warehouses; Commander of the Second Military Zone, El Cipres, Baja California del Norte, 1935–37. k-Escorted ex-president Calles from Mexico during his forced departure by *Lazaro Cardenas*, 1935; removed from the governorship by President *Cardenas*. l-DP70, 1454; Casasola, V, 2342; Lopez, 760.

Navarro Diaz de Leon, Gines

a-1917. b-Federal District, *Federal District, Urban*. c-Early education unknown; medical degree as a sur-

geon, National School of Medicine, UNAM, 1940; professor, National School of Medicine, UNAM, eighteen years. d-None. e-None. f-Director General of Health for the Federal District, 1970–75; *Secretary of Health*, 1975–76. g-None. h-Secretary, Private Charities Board; various positions in the private sector; co-author, National Health Plan. j-None. k-None. l-HA, 10 Mar. 1975, 16; *Excelsior*, 3 Mar. 1975, 4.

Navarro Encinas, Antonio

a-1910. c-Early education unknown; graduated from the National Military College, 1928; graduate of the Military Aviation School; special studies in Spain; professor, Military Aviation School. d-*Federal Deputy* from the State of Baja California del Sur, Dist. 1, 1946–49, member of the Gran Comision; *Federal Deputy* from Baja California del Sur, Dist. 1, 1961–64, member of the Gran Comision, Secretary of the Chamber. e-None. f-Member of the Chief of Staff under Secretary of National Defense, *Lazaro Cardenas*, 1942–45; military attache to various embassies. g-None. i-*Alberto Alvarado Aramburo* was his alternate deputy in 1961–64. j-Career Air Force officer. k-None. l-C de D, 1946–49; C de D, 1961–64.

Neri Arizmendi, Porfirio

(Deceased 1965)

a-Feb. 28, 1894. b-Tehuixtla, Morelos, *West Central, Rural*. c-No degree. d-Federal Deputy from the State of Morelos, 1926–28; local deputy to the State Legislature of Morelos; *Federal Deputy* from the State of Morelos, Dist. 1, 1940–43, member of the Gran Comision, the Fifth Ejidal Commission; *Senator* from the State of Morelos, 1958–64, member of the Agrarian Department Committee, the Special Small Agricultural Property Committee, and substitute member of the Second Ejido Committee and the National Properties Committee. e-None. f-Oficial Mayor of the State of Morelos, 1936. g-Founding member and President of the Zapatista Front, 1965. h-None. j-Joined the Revolution, 1910; supported Madero; served under Zapata; fought against Huerta; attended the Convention of Aguascalientes, 1914; opposed Carranza; reached the rank of Brigadier General, 1913. k-None. l-DP70, 1464; C de S, 1961–64, 64; C de D, 1940–42, 17; Func., 281.

Nogueda Otero, Israel

a-Jan. 16, 1935. b-Atoyac de Alvarez, Guerrero, *South, Rural*. c-Primary studies at the English Academy; secondary studies at the Colegio Williams; preparatory studies at the Centro Universitario Mexico; degree in economics from the National

School of Economics, UNAM, 1960. **d-***Federal Deputy* from Guerrero, Dist. 4, 1967–68; Mayor of Acapulco, Guerrero, 1969–71; *Substitute Governor of Guerrero*, 1971–75. **e-**Secretary of Professional-Technical Action, CNOP, PRI, 1967. **f-**Investigator for the Tariff Department, Secretariat of the Treasury; Chairman of the Minimum Wage Regulatory Commission; President of the Committee for the Sports Center, Acapulco, 1963–67. **g-**Vice President of the Chamber of Commerce, Acapulco, Guerrero; President of the Chamber of Commerce, Acapulco. **i-**Knew *Jesus Silva Herzog F*. at UNAM; brother-in-law of *Agustin Olachea Borbon*, Head of the Department of Tourism, 1970–73. **j-**None. **k-**Campaign for Federal Deputy was in a hotly contested district; removed by the Permanent Committee of Congress as Governor, January 31, 1975. **l-***Hoy*, 15 May 1971, 12; MGF69, 92; C de D, 1967–69; letter; HA, 10 Feb. 1975, 27–28; LA, 7 Feb. 1975, 45; *Excelsior*, 31 Jan. 1975, 1.

Noriega (Cantu), Jr., Alfonso

a-Jan. 21, 1909. **b-**Federal District, *Federal District, Urban*. **c-**Primary, secondary, and preparatory studies at the Colegio Frances Morelos; law degree from the National School of Law, UNAM, Dec. 27, 1929, with a thesis on amparo; LLD, National School of Law, UNAM; Professor of Law, National School of Law, UNAM, 1939–71; Professor Emeritus of Guarantees and Appeals, UNAM, 1971–79; Professor of Guarantees and Appeals, Ibero-American University; Professor of Constitutional Law, Escuela Libre de Derecho; Professor at the National Preparatory School; Director of the National School of Law, UNAM, 1943–44; Secretary General of UNAM, 1944; member of the Governing Council of UNAM (12 years); Oficial Mayor of UNAM. **d-**None. **e-**None. **f-**Member of the Advisory Council for the Department of the Federal District, 1958–64; Secretary of the Advisory Council of the Department of the Federal District, 1964–70; Secretary General of the Advisory Council of the Federal District, 1970–72; Director General of the Financiera Nacional Azucarera; Director General of Higher Education and Scientific Research, Secretariat of Public Education; Gerente of CONCAMIN. **g-**Consultant for the Chamber of Industries of the Federal District, 1956. **h-**Author of articles and books on law; President of the National Association of Lawyers. **i-**Knew *Antonio Carrillo Flores, Manuel Ramirez Vazquez, Ernesto P. Uruchurtu, Antonio Ortiz Mena, Angel Carvajal, Manuel Sanchez Cuen, Andres Serra Rojas* at UNAM; studied under *Alfonso Caso*; married Maria del Carmen Fernandez. **j-**None. **k-**None. **l-**WWM45, 83; DGF56, 470; Correa, 255; letter; DPE61, 134; *Excelsior*, 15 Jan. 1976; Lopez, 769.

Noriega (Ondovilla), Raul

(Deceased Apr. 22, 1975)
a-July 27, 1907. **b-**Federal District, *Federal District, Urban*. **c-**Primary and secondary studies in the Federal District; preparatory studies at the National Preparatory School, 1920–24; studies, National School of Law, UNAM, 1924–28, receiving his degree March 1, 1947; Professor of the History of Mexico, National Preparatory School, 1934–36; Professor of World History, National Preparatory School, 1934–36. **d-***Federal Deputy* from the Federal District, Dist. 17, 1967–70, member of the Department of the Federal District Committee, the Editorial Committee (1st and 2nd year), the First Treasury Committee. **e-**None. **f-**Alternate Mexican delegate to the United Nations, 1947–51; *Oficial Mayor of the Secretariat of the Treasury*, 1951–58; Director General of PIPSA, 1958–59; Coordinator of Audiovisual Teaching, Secretariat of Public Education, 1958–64; Director of the Legal Department, Altos Hornos, 1971–74; Director General of the Government Printing Office, 1974–75. **g-**None. **h-**Director of the student newspapers *Agora, Policromias* and *La Huelga*, 1920–29; editor of the Sunday supplement, *El Nacional*, 1929; Editor-in-Chief of *Izquierdas*, 1935–39; Director of the Radio Station XEFO, 1935; founder and Director of the Publishing House, Biblioteca del Maestro; founder of the publishing series, 20th Century Collection; Director of *El Nacional*, 1938–47; President of the Permanent Commission of the First Latin American Press Congress, 1934–44; Director of the supplement section to *Novedades*, 1961–70. **i-**Friend of *Miguel Aleman* at the National Law School. **j-**None. **k-**None. **l-**MGF69, 91; DGF51, I, 145; DBM68, 456; WWM45, 84; letter; C de D, 1967–69, 62, 73; Novo, 746–47; Enc. Mex., IX, 1977, 403; HA, 12 Aug. 1974, 17; HA, 28 Apr. 1975, 11; *Excelsior*, 20 Oct. 1949; Lopez, 769.

Noriega Pizano, Arturo

a-Apr. 10, 1915. **b-**Colima, Colima, *West, Urban*. **c-**Primary studies at the Gabino Barreda and the Benito Juarez Schools, Colima; secondary and preparatory studies, Normal School, Colima; law degree, School of Law, University of Guadalajara, June, 1942, with a thesis on "Amparo Before the State Supreme Courts on Articles 16, 18, 20 of the Federal Constitution"; secondary teacher in civics and economics, 1936; Professor of Sociology and Ethics, Normal School, Colima, 1944; Director of the Preparatory School of Colima. **d-**Mayor of Colima, January 1, 1971 to September 19, 1973; *Governor of Colima*, January 1, 1974–80. **e-**None. **f-**Civil Judge and Director of the Public Property Registry, Colima, 1943–51; Public Notary, 1951–73; Judge of the Superior Tribunal of Justice of the State of Colima, 1951–52; President of the Superior Tribunal of Justice of the State of Colima, 1953–55; Attorney General of Colima, 1955–61; Secretary General of Government of the State of Colima under Governor *Pablo Silva Garcia*, 1967–70. **g-**None. **h-**Practicing lawyer, 1961–66. **j-**None. **k-**Elected governor in a special election after the governor-elect, *Antonio Barbosa Heldt*, committed suicide. **l-**Enc. Mex., Annual, 1977, 541–42; HA, 1 Oct. 1973, 35; *Excelsior*, 25 Sept. 1973, 4; *Excelsior*, 17 Dec. 1973, 6.

Norzagaray (Angulo), Bernardo

a-July 1, 1910. **b-**Guasave, Sinaloa, *West*, *Rural*. **c-**Preparatory at the French-English Institute, Mexico, D.F.; degree in agricultural engineering, Agricultural College, Ciudad Juarez, Chihuahua. **d-***Federal Deputy* from the State of Sinaloa, Dist. 3, 1943–46; *Federal Deputy* from the State of Sinaloa, Dist. 4, 1952–55, member of the Waters and Irrigation Committee, the Second Credentials Committee, the Budget and Accounts Committee (1st year), and substitute member of the Agrarian Department Committee, the Properties and Natural Resouces Committee, and the Colonization Committee; Mayor of Ciudad Juarez, 1968–71. **e-**Representative of the National Farmers Federation on the CEN of PRI. **f-**Administrator of the Ejido Bank of Culiacan and Mazatlan, Sinaloa; Administrator of the Agricultural Bank of Culiacan; Director of Farm Loans of the Bank of Sinaloa; head of the Department of Operations, National Army-Navy Bank, 1950–51; head of the Agricultural Credit Department, National Army-Navy Bank; Secretary General of Government for the State of Sinaloa; President of the Federal Improvement Board, Ciudad Juarez, Chihuahua, 1958–64. **h-**None. **j-**None. **k-***Por Que* holds him responsible for the rapid expansion of prostitution in Ciudad Juarez during his term as mayor. **l-**C de D, 1952–54, 116, 46, 63; DGF51, II, 34; C de D, 1943–45, 17; WWMG, 28–29; *Por Que*, 20 Nov. 1969; Peral, 574; DGF50, II, 36.

Novelo Torres, Ernesto

(Deceased 1968)

a-1895. **b-**Valladolid, Yucatan, *Gulf*, *Rural*. **c-**Studied for the priesthood in the Seminario Conciliar, Merida; studied at the Literary Institute of Yucatan, Merida, Yucatan. **d-**Mayor of Progreso, 1935; local deputy to the State Legislature of Yucatan, 1935–36; *Governor of Yucatan*, 1942–46; *Senator* from the State of Yucatan, 1946–52, member of the Mail and Telegraph Committee, the Second Balloting Committee, and the National Lands Committee. **e-**None. **f-**General accountant for National Telegraphs of Mexico, Mexico, D.F., 1927; head of Telegraph and Mail Office, Progreso, Yucatan; Treasurer General of Yucatan under Governor *Canto*

Echeverria, 1938–40; Oficial Mayor of Yucatan, 1940–42. **g-**None. **h-**Telegrapher, Merida, 1924–27; founder of the Fomento de Yucatan. **i-**Relative of Jose Ines Novelo, deputy to the Constitutional Convention, 1916–17; married Candelaria Serrano Cetina. **j-**None. **k-***Novedades* claims he dominated the selection of Yucatan governors until 1963. **l-**DP70, 1478; WWM45, 84; HA, 12 June 1942, 30; DGF51, I, i, 10, 14; Informes, 1943, 1944; HA, 28 Apr. 1945, 23; Enc. Mex., IX, 1977, 408; *Novedades*, 5 Aug. 1963.

Novo (Lopez), Salvador

(Deceased Jan 13, 1974)

a-July 30, 1904. **b-**Federal District, *Federal District*, *Urban*. **c-**Primary studies in Chihuahua and Torreon; secondary studies in Mexico, D.F.; preparatory at the National Preparatory School, 1920; began studies in law, UNAM, but changed to literature; MA, UNAM; Professor of Italian Literature, School of Philosophy and Liberal Arts, UNAM; Professor of Spanish, 1923–28; National Preparatory School; Professor of Spanish Literature, secondary schools; Professor of the History of Theater, National Conservatory, 1930–33; Professor of English, secondary schools. **d-**None. **e-**Member of the CEN of the Popular Party, 1947–48. **f-**Head of the Editorial Department, Secretariat of Public Education, 1924–28; head of the Department of Publicity, Secretariat of Foreign Relations, 1930–34; head of the Department of Theatrical Productions, National Institute of Bellas Artes, 1946–52; Director of the School of Dramatic Art, National Institute of Bellas Artes, 1956; Official Historian of Mexico, D.F., 1965–74. **g-**None. **h-**Prolific author of poems, plays, and books; author of books on the *Aleman* and *Cardenas* periods in Mexico; Director of the magazine, *Ulysses*, with the poet Xavier Villaurrutia, 1927–28. **i-**Boyhood friend of *Raul Lopez Sanchez*, Governor of Coahuila, 1948–51; attended the National Preparatory School with *Jose Gorostiza*, *Raul Noriega*, and *Mariano Ramirez Vazquez*; longtime friend of *Jaime Torres Bodet*. **j-**None. **k-**Supported Jose Vasconcelos for president, 1928–29. **l-**DGF51, I, 293; DPE61, 107; WWM45, 84; DBM68, 458–59; letter; Novo, 749, 757–58; *Excelsior*, 15 Jan. 1974, 10; HA, 21 Jan. 1974, 9–10; *Q es Q*, 417–18; Enc. Mex., IX, 1977, 408.

Novoa, Carlos

a-June 30, 1900. **b-**Federal District, *Federal District*, *Urban*. **c-**Secondary at the Colegio de Mascarones (Jesuit); preparatory at the National Preparatory School, Mexico, D.F.; law degree from the National School of Law, UNAM, 1926; Professor of Money and Credit at the School of Commerce, UNAM, 1930–36. **d-**None. **e-**Founder of PAN, 1939. **f-**Consulting lawyer to the Secretariat of

Treasury, 1926–35; President of the Public Debt Commission, 1932–33; President of the National Banking Commission, 1933; Director General of the Industrial Bank, 1940–46; *Director General of the Bank of Mexico*, 1946–52. **g-**Director, 1937–41, and President, 1945–46, of the Bankers Association of Mexico. **h-**Mexican delegate to the International Monetary Fund, 1946–52; President of Patronage for UNAM, 1968. **i-**Knew *Antonio Martinez Baez* at the National School of Law; son of lawyer Eduardo Novoa, Subsecretary of Justice under Porfirio Diaz; married Eugenia Allard. **j-**None. **k-**Supported Jose Vasconcelos for president, 1928–29. **l-***El Universal*, 2 Dec. 1946; DBM68, 458; WWM45, 84; DGF51, II, 6, 65, 77; DGF50, 71; Mabry, 35–36; letter; Skirius, 105; HA, 18 Apr. 1947, 30.

Noyola (Zepeda), J. Jesus M.

a-Sept. 7, 1898. **b-**Cerritos, San Luis Potosi, *East Central*, *Rural*. **c-**Primary and secondary studies in San Luis Potosi; preparatory studies at the University of San Luis Potosi; medical studies, Sorbonne, Paris; medical degree, University of San Luis Potosi; Director of the School of Medicine, University of San Luis Potosi, 1946–52; Rector of the University of San Luis Potosi, 1958–64. **d-***Alternate Senator* from the State of San Luis Potosi, 1952–58; *Federal Deputy* from the State of San Luis Potosi, Dist. 6, 1949–52; *Senator* from the State of San Luis Potosi, 1964–70. **e-**None. **f-**None. **g-**None. **i-**Alternate senator under *Antonio Rocha*, 1952–58. **j-**None. **k-**None. **l-**C de D, 1949–52; DGF51, I, MGF69; C de S, 1952–58; DGF56; C de S, 1964–70.

Nunez Keith, Guillermo

a-Feb. 7, 1921. **b-**Guaymas, Sonora, *North*, *Rural*. **c-**Primary and secondary studies; no degree; studies in private accounting. **d-***Federal Deputy* from the State of Sonora, Dist. 2, 1967–70; member of the Committee on Arid Zones, the Administration Committee (1st year), the Radio Industry Committee, the Television Industry Committee, the Development Committee, and the Budget Committee (2nd year). **e-**Official announcer for *Diaz Ordaz* during the campaign. **f-**Official announcer for the President, Department of Information and Public Relations, 1964–70. **g-**None. **h-**Announcer for station XEBH, Hermosillo, Sonora, 1936; radio announcer in Puebla and Mexico, D.F.; coordinator of the 1st Inter-American Congress of Announcers, 1952; delegate to the 2nd-5th Inter-American Congresses of Announcers. **j-**None. **k-**None. **l-**DBM68, 459; MGF69, 95; C de D, 1967–69, 74, 75, 84, 85, 91.

Ocana Garcia, Samuel

a-1932. **b-**Aribechi, Sonora, *North*, *Rural*. **c-**Early education unknown; medical degree, National School of Medicine, UNAM. **d-**Mayor of Navojoa,

Sonora, 1975; *Governor of Sonora,* 1979– . **e-**Director of the CEPES of PRI, Navojoa; President of PRI in the State of Sonora, 1978–79. **f-**Subsecretary of Government of the State of Sonora, 1973–74; Secretary General of Government of the State of Sonora, 1976–77. **g-**Leader of the medical students at UNAM; president of the ex-fellowship students of the National Institute of Pneumology; founder of the Union of Textile Workers of Sonora, 1949. **h-**Textile worker, 1948–49; founder and director of the Regional Hospital of Pulmonary and Thoracic Surgery, Navojoa, Sonora. **i-**Collaborator of *Alejandro Carrillo M.*, Governor of Sonora, 1975–79. **k-**Reportedly dismissed his entire police force as Mayor of Navojoa when a prisoner died under torture. **l-**LA, 26 Jan. 1979, 30; *Excelsior*, 18 Jan. 1979, 4, 18, 23; *Excelsior*, 17 Jan. 1979, 10.

Ocaranza Carmona, Fernando
(Deceased Feb. 12, 1965)

a-May 30, 1876. **b-**Federal District, *Federal District*, *Urban*. **c-**Secondary at the Scientific and Literary Institute of Toluca, Mexico, and at the Colegio Hispano-Mexico, Toluca; medical studies at the National Medical School, UNAM, 1895–97; transferred to the Military Medical School, medical degree, May 8, 1900, graduating as a Surgeon and Major in the Army; professor at the Military Medical School, 1917; Professor of Physiology at the National School of Medicine, UNAM, 1915–46; secretary at the National School of Medicine, 1917–20, UNAM; Director of the National School of Medicine, UNAM, 1925–32, 1934; professor at normal schools; Professor of Clinical Medicine, UNAM, 1926–46. **d-**None. **e-**Founder of PAN, 1939. **f-**Director of the Municipal Hospital, Guaymas, Sonora, 1914–15; head of the Department of Health, Guaymas, Sonora, 1908–10; emergency physician, Southern Pacific Railroads of Mexico, 1915; physician for the National Shipyards, 1916; head of the Laboratory of Comparative Physiology, Institute of Biology, 1915–18; Director of the Institute of Hygiene, 1922–23; adviser to the Secretary of Health, 1921–24; *Rector of UNAM*, 1934–35; member of the General Health Council of Mexico, 1952–58. **g-**None. **h-**Surgeon, Red Cross, Tacubaya; author of many books and over 150 articles on medical subjects. **i-**Great-grandfather was a Colonel in the Spanish Army of New Spain; married Loreto Esquer. **j-**Head of the Military Hospital, Jalapa, Veracruz, 1904; head of the 2nd Surgery Section, Military Hospital, Jalapa, Veracruz; joined the 19th Battalion, Sonora, 1900; left the Army with the rank of Lt. Colonel to go into private practice in Sonora. **k-**None. **l-**DGF51, II, 687; DGF56, 329; DP70, 1499–1500; Peral, 581–82; DGF447, 199; DGF51, 333, 335; Lopez, 784; Enc. Mex., IX, 543.

Ochoa Campos, Moises

a-Aug. 10, 1917. b-Iguala, Guerrero, *South*, *Urban*.
c-Primary studies at the Public School of Chilpan-
cingo; secondary studies at Colegio of Guerrero,
Chilpancingo; degree in political science, National
School of Political and Social Sciences, UNAM,
May, 1955, with a thesis on municipal reform;
studied at the School of Political Science, Degli Studi
University, Rome, 1955–56, and other studies in
Rome; professor at the School of Political and Social
Sciences, UNAM, 1957–59, in the field of theory;
Director of the Seminar on Political Investigations,
1955–59. d-*Federal Deputy* from the State of Guer-
rero, 1958–61, Dist. 1, member of the Radio and
Television Committee, the Budget and Accounts
Committee (2nd year), substitute member of the
Military Justice Committee; *Alternate Senator* from
the State of Guerrero, 1964–70; *Federal Deputy*
from the State of Guerrero, Dist. 1, 1970–73,
member of the Cultural Affairs Committee, the
Editorial Committee (1st year), the Money and
Credit Institutions Committee, and the First Section
of the Constitutional Affairs Committee. e-Private
secretary to the Director of Press and Publicity, CEN of
PRI; *Secretary of Press and Publicity of the CEN of
PRI*, 1952–58. f-Private secretary to the Secretary of
the Agrarian Department; Coordinating Director of
the Civic Improvement Boards, Secretariat of Government, 1958; Assistant Director, Office of Intellectual Cooperation, Secretariat of Public Education;
General Coordinator of Planning and Statistics, Secretariat of Public Education, 1965. g-None.
h-Director of the periodical, *La Republica*, 1958; author of several works. i-Son of engineer Lorenzo
Ricardo Ochoa. j-None. k-First graduate of the
School of Political and Social Science, UNAM. l-B
de M, 192; C de D, 1970–72, 127; C de D, 1958–
60, 86; Func., 220.

Odorica Inclan, Fernando

b-Toluca, Mexico, *West Central*, *Urban*. c-Primary
and secondary studies in Toluca; law degree, National School of Law, UNAM; Rector of the University of Mexico, Toluca. d-*Senator* from the State of
Mexico, 1964–70. e-None. f-Official of the Department of Alcohol, Secretariat of the Treasury.
g-None. j-None. k-None. l-PS, 4453; C de S,
1964–70; MGF69.

Ogaz Pierce, Jose Abel

a-November 16, 1949. b-Federal District, *Federal
District*, *Urban*. c-Preparatory studies at the National
Preparatory School No. 7; studies in economics, Na-
tional School of Economics, UNAM. d-None.
e-Secretary of Political Education of the PPS in the
Federal District, 1979; Director of the National
Committee of Political, Economic and Social Studies

of the PPS, 1979; Director, PPS Platform Committee, 1979. f-None. g-President of the Society of Students of the National Preparatory School No. 7;
leader of the Popular Socialist Youth, 1970; delegate
to the 7th Assembly of the World Confederations of
Democratic Youth, 1970. j-None. k-None. l-HA, 26
Mar. 1979, I.

Ojeda, Nabor A.

a-June 12, 1894. b-Ometepec, Guerrero, *South*,
Rural. c-Secondary at the Institute of Arts and Sciences, Oaxaca, Oaxaca; no degree. d-Local deputy
to the State Legislature of Guerrero; *Federal Deputy*
from the State of Guerrero, Dist. 5, 1937–40;
Senator from the State of Guerrero, 1940–46, President of the Indigenous Affairs Committee, member
of the Gran Comision, First Secretary of the Second
National Defense Committee, Second Secretary of
the Agrarian Affairs Department Committee; *Federal
Deputy* from the State of Guerrero, Dist. 2, 1967–
70, member of the Second National Defense Committee and the Military Justice Committee. e-None.
g-First Secretary of Conflicts of the CNC. h-Author
of federal laws dealing with communal lands and
benefits for Revolutionary veterans. i-Son *Gustavo
Nabor Ojeda* was a Federal Deputy from Guerrero,
1973–76. j-Joined the Revolution in support of Madero, 1911. k-Peral states that the Mexican press published articles accusing Ojeda of responsibility for
political murders in Guerrero. l-Peral, 584; C de S,
40–46; C de D, 1946–48, 81; C de D, 1937–39;
Gonzalez Navarro; Lopez, 787.

Ojeda Paullada, Pedro

a-Jan. 19, 1934. b-Federal District, *Federal District*,
Urban. c-Primary studies in Mexico City, 1940–44;
secondary studies in Mexico City, 1945–47; preparatory studies at the National Preparatory School,
1948–49; studied at the National School of Law,
UNAM, 1950–54, law degree, 1955, with a thesis
on Federal Boards of Moral and Material Improvement. d-None. e-None. f-Merit employee, Seventh
Civil Judicial District, Federal District, 1950–51;
employee, Personnel Department, PEMEX, 1952;
legal intern, Secretariat of Health and Welfare, 1953;
Subdirector General of the Federal Boards for Material Improvements, Secretariat of National Patrimony, under *Jose Lopez Portillo*, 1959–65; adviser
to the Chihuahua-Pacific Railroad; Director General
of Legal Affairs, Secretariat of Communication and
Transportation; Director of the Technical Advisory
Commission of General Means of Communication,
Secretariat of Communication and Transportation,
1966–70; *Oficial Mayor of the Presidency*, 1970–71;
Attorney General of Mexico, 1971–76; *Secretary of
Labor*, 1976– . g-Founder and President of the Platform of Mexican Professionals. h-Practiced law,

1955–59. **i-**Personal friend of *Luis Echeverria*; knew *Jorge de la Vega Dominguez* as a student at Law School; married Olga Cardenas. **j-**None. **k-**None. **l-**HA, 30 Aug. 1971, 10; MGF69, 278; HA, 14 Dec. 1970, 23; DPE61, 61; DPE71, 124; LA, 3 Dec. 1976; HA, 2 May 1977, 18; *Excelsior*, 1 Dec. 1976; HA, 6 Dec. 1976, 23.

Olachea Aviles, Agustin
(Deceased Apr. 13, 1974)
a-Sept. 3, 1892. **b-**Todos Santos, San Venancio, Baja California del Sur, *West*, *Rural*. **c-**No formal education. **d-**None. **e-***President of the CEN of PRI*, April 26, to December 3, 1958. **f-**Governor of Baja California del Sur, 1929–31; Governor of Baja California del Norte, 1931–35; *Governor of Baja California del Sur,* 1945–52, and 1952–56; *Secretary of National Defense,* 1958–64. **g-**None. **h-**Before the Revolution, worked as a miner. **i-**Parents were rural laborers; son, *Agustin Olachea Borbon*, was Director of the Department of Tourism, 1970–73; married Ana Maria Borbon. **j-**Joined the Revolution as a private, 1913, under the forces of General Manuel Dieguez; head of Military Operations in Yucatan and Quintana Roo, 1925–26; fought the Yaquis in Sonora, 1926; rank of Brigadier General, May 16, 1929; Commander of the 13th Military Zone, Tepic, Nayarit, 1940–46; Divisionary General. **k-**Brandenburg considers Olachea Aviles in the Inner Circle of decision-making in Mexico from 1946 to 1958; as a young boy, he participated in the Cananea mining strike in 1906; supported *Cardenas* for President in 1934. **l-***Hoy*, Dec. 1958; HA, 8 Dec. 1958, 25; DGF56, 103, 201; Brandenburg, 102; DGF51, I, 88; Scott, 171; Peral, 584; Morton, 93, 100, 110, 117–18; *Polemica*, Vol. 1, 1969, 75; Gaxiola, 177–78; Enc. Mex., IX, 1977, 569; *Excelsior*, 14 Apr. 1974, 4; HA, 22 Apr. 1974, 19; Lopez, 787.

Olachea Borbon, Agustin
a-May 2, 1933. **b-**Tijuana, Baja California del Norte, *North*, *Rural*. **c-**Studied at the National School of Economics, UNAM, 1954–58, economics degree in 1960. **d-**None. **e-**Coordinator of Economic Advisers for the Presidential campaign of *Adolfo Lopez Mateos*, 1958, while his father was President of the CEN of PRI. **f-**Member of the Advisory Commission for the Mexican-United States Border; Director of Publications for the Bureau of Tourist Studies, 1966–70; *Head of Tourism Department*, 1970–73; Ambassador to Rumania, 1973. **g-**None. **h-**Employed in the Administration of Treasury Studies, Secretariat of the Treasury, 1954; author of many works on tourism in Mexico. **i-**Attended law school with *Jose Bermudez Limon* at UNAM; son of *Agustin Olachea Aviles*, President of the CEN of

PRI, 1956–58, and Secretary of National Defense, 1958–64; brother-in-law of *Israel Nogueda Otero*, Governor of Guerrero, 1971–75. **j-**None. **k-**None. **l-**HA, 7 Dec. 1970, 26; *Hoy*, Dec. 1970.

Olamendi Torres, Carlos
a-Oct. 17, 1955. **b-**Cholula, Puebla, *East Central*, *Urban*. **c-**Primary and secondary studies in Cuautla, Morelos; preparatory studies in Puebla, Puebla; studies in law at the University of Morelos, Cuautla, and at the National School of Law, UNAM. **d-**None. **e-**Secretary of Relations, Central Committee of the Socialist Workers Party; member of the Executive Committee of the Central Committee of the Socialist Workers Party, 1979. **f-**None. **g-**None. **j-**None. **k-**None. **l-**HA, 19 Mar. 1979, IV.

Olea Munoz, Javier
b-Guerrero, *South*. **c-**Early education unknown; law degree, National School of Law, UNAM, 1954. **d-**None. **e-**None. **f-**Attorney General of the State of Guerrero under Governor *Raul Caballero Aburto*, 1961; Private Secretary to the Governor of Guerrero; *Governor of Guerrero*, January 31, 1975 to May 31, 1975; Ambassador to Japan, 1977–79. **g-**None. **h-**Practicing lawyer in criminal law, Mexico City. **j-**None. **k-**Resisted the Permanent Committee's decision to dissolve state powers under *Raul Caballero*, 1961; held responsible by some for ordering the army to shoot student strikers in Guerrero, 1961; appointed interim governor of Guerrero by the Permanent Committee after *Israel Nogueda Otero*'s powers as governor were dissolved. **l-**DJBM, 99; HA, 11 Apr. 1977, 6; HA, 10 Feb. 1975, 27; *Excelsior*, 3 Feb. 1975, 9; *Excelsior*, 2 Feb. 1975, 9.

Olea y Leyva, Sabino M.
(Deceased 1950)
b-Ajuchitlan, Guerrero, *South*, *Rural*. **c-**Early education unknown; preparatory studies at the Colegio de San Nicolas, Morelia, Michoacan; law degree, National School of Law, UNAM, 1907. **d-**None. **e-**None. **f-**Justice of the Superior Tribunal of Justice of the Federal District and Federal Territories; Justice of the Supreme Court, 1923–35, *Justice of the Supreme Court,* 1935–40. **g-**None. **h-**Poet. **i-**Father, an administrator of haciendas; nephew of Agustin Aragon, the foremost positivist in Mexico in 1900; brother of *Teofilo Olea y Leyva,* Justice of the Supreme Court, 1940–56. **j-**None. **k-**None. **l-**DP70, 1510; Lopez, 788.

Olea y Leyva, Teofilo
(Deceased Sept. 5, 1956)
a-Jan. 8, 1895. **b-**Miacatlan, Morelos, *West Central*, *Rural*. **c-**Preparatory studies at the National Preparatory School, Mexico, D.F., 1911–15; law de-

gree from the National School of Law, UNAM, August 19, 1919; Ph.D. from the School of Higher Studies, UNAM; professor of logic, ethics, penal law and legal procedures, School of Higher Studies and the Law School, UNAM; co-founder of the Popular University; professor of law, Free Law School. d-Local deputy to the State Legislature of Guerrero; president of the State Legislature of Guerrero, 1920. e-Prominent member of the National Action Party; supporter of General *Almazan*, 1939–40. f-Secretary General of Government of the State of Guerrero; Agent of the Military Ministerio Publico; Justice of the Tribunal Superior of the Federal District and Territories; *Justice of the Supreme Court*, 1941–46, 1946–52, and 1952–56. g-Founder of the National Association of Legal Employees. h-Author of many major works on Mexican law; writer for *El Universal*. i-Classmate of *Trinidad Garcia* at law school, who later became Director of the Law School, 1934–35; nephew of Agustin Aragon; father was an administrator of a hacienda; brother *Sabino* was a Justice of the Supreme Court, 1935–40. j-Served in the Revolution. k-Part of the "Seven Wisemen" generation at National Preparatory School, which included *Manuel Gomez Morin*, founder and President of the National Action Party. l-Peral, 585; DP70, 1510; WWM45, 86; DGF56, 567; DGF51, I, 567; HA, 17 Sept. 1956, 15; Enc. Mex., IX, 1977, 570; Lopez, 788; Krauze, 93; Cadena, 120.

Olivares Santana, Enrique

a-Aug. 22, 1920. b-San Luis de Letras, Rincon de Romos, Aguascalientes, *West*, *Rural*. c-Primary and secondary studies in Aguascalientes; secondary studies at the Normal School, San Marcos, Zacatecas; teaching certificate as a rural teacher, Regional Peasant School, 1938; normal teaching certificate, 1951; teacher at the Escuela de Jesus Maria, Aguascalientes; teacher at the Escuela de San Jose de Gracia; group teacher, Secretariat of Public Education. d-Local deputy to the State Legislature of Aguascalientes, 1950–53; *Federal Deputy* from the State of Aguascalientes, Dist. 2, 1958–61, member of the Administration Committee, the Legislative Studies Committee, the First Government Committee, and the Foreign Relations Committee; *Governor of Aguascalientes*, 1962–68; *Senator* from the State of Aguascalientes, 1970–76, President of the Gran Comision, President of the First Government Committee and the First Constitutional Affairs Committee. e-President of the State Regional Committee of PRI in Aguascalientes, 1952–53; delegate of the CEN of PRI to San Luis Potosi, Yucatan, and Colima, 1958–62; head of the State Planning Council of Aguascalientes for the presidential campaign of *Adolfo Lopez Mateos*, 1958; *Secretary General of the CEN of PRI* under *Alfonso Martinez Dominguez*,

1968–70; *Secretary of Political Action of the CEN of PRI*, 1972–74; member of the Political Action Commission of the IEPES of PRI, 1972. f-Director of Group Teachers, Secretariat of Public Education; Federal Inspector for the Secretariat of Public Education in Zacatecas and Aguascalientes; Director General of the National Public Works Bank, 1976–79; *Secretary of Government*, 1979– . g-Secretary General of the National Teachers Union (Section 1); Secretary of Organization of the National Teachers Union; leader of the League of Agrarian Communities and Farmers Unions, 1948. h-None. i-Son of peasants; father, an agrarian leader in Aguascalientes; married Belam Ventura; *Augusto Gomez Villanueva* was his private secretary as governor; son *Hector Hugo Olivares* was Oficial Mayor of the Department of Agrarian Affairs and Senator from Aguascalientes, 1976– . j-None. k-None. l-HA, 18 Jan. 1971, 18; DBM68, 464; *Hoy*, 20 Feb. 1971, 10; DBM70, 414–15; C de S, 1970–76; HA, 2 Jan. 1978; Func., 119; *Excelsior*, 7 June 1977, 6; HA, 10 July 1972, 10.

Olive, Issac

b-Paraiso, Tabasco, *Gulf*, *Rural*. c-Early education unknown; law degree, National School of Law, UNAM. d-Federal Deputy from the State of Tabasco, Dist. 3, 1922–24, member of the Gran Comision; Federal Deputy from the State of Oaxaca, Dist. 11, 1918–20, member of the Gran Comision; Federal Deputy from the State of Oaxaca; Dist. 2, 1917–18. e-None. f-Secretary of Government of the State of Oaxaca; Judge, Criminal Jurisdiction, Fifth Judicial District, Mexico City; District Court Judge; *Oficial Mayor of the Secretariat of Labor*, 1937–39. g-None. i-Political collaborator of *Antonio Villalobos*, Secretary of Labor, 1937–40. j-Joined the Constitutionalists as a law school student. k-Supported General Obregon in 1920. l-C de D, 1917–18; C de D, 1918–20; C de D, 1922–24; PS, 4430.

Olivo Solis, Angel

a-Jan. 21, 1917. b-Tuxtla, Veracruz, *Gulf*, *Rural*. c-Early education unknown; no degree. d-*Federal Deputy* from the Federal District, Dist. 2, 1973–76; *Federal Deputy* from the Federal District, 1979–82. e-None. f-None. g-Co-founder of the CTM, 1936; Secretary General of the Union Lonas La Providencia, 1936; member of the executive board, The Federation of Workers, 1947; member of the executive committee, Federation of Working Groups, 1949; founder and leader of the National Revolutionary Coalition, 1950; director of the Revolutionary Federation of Workers, 1952; founder and leader of the Revolutionary Workers Federation, 1959; founder of the National Workers Central, 1960; Secretary General of the National Workers Central, 1963; founder of the Congress of Labor, 1966; Secretary General of the Revolutionary Workers Federation, 1967–79. **j**-None. **k**-None. **l**-HA, 10 July 1978, 9; C de D, 1973–76, 6.

Olmos (Hernandez), Salvador
(Deceased July 10, 1978)
a-1917. **b**-Jalapa, Veracruz, *Gulf, Urban*. **c**-Teaching certificate. **d**-Councilman of Jalapa, Veracruz; local deputy to the State Legislature of Veracruz; *Federal Deputy* from the State of Veracruz, Dist. 5, 1958–61, member of the Colonization Committee, the Budget and Accounts Committee, the Securities Committee, and the First General Means of Communication and Transportation Committee. **e**-None. **f**-Private Secretary to *Adolfo Ruiz Cortines*, Secretary of Government, 1946–52; *Private Secretary to the President of Mexico*, *Adolfo Ruiz Cortines*, 1952–58. **g**-Representative of the CTM. **h**-Personal Secretary to *Adolfo Ruiz Cortines*, 1961–73. **j**-None. **k**-None. **l**-DGF56, 67; C de D, 1958–60, 86; Func., 392.

Olvera Gamez, Domingo
a-May 9, 1902. **b**-Villa del Pueblito, Queretaro, *East Central, Rural*. **c**-Primary studies in the Colegio Arana, Queretaro, Queretaro; secondary studies in the Colegio Civil of Queretaro; no degree. **d**-*Alternate Federal Deputy* from the State of Queretaro, Dist. 2, 1943–46; Local Deputy to the 36th Session of the State Legislature of Queretaro; *Federal Deputy* from the State of Queretaro, Dist. 1, 1955–58; *Senator* from the State of Queretaro, 1958–64, member of the Second Balloting Group, Second Secretary of the Second Ejido Committee and President of the Electrical Industry Committee. **e**-Oficial Mayor of PRI in Queretaro (twenty years). **f**-Oficial Mayor of the State Government of Queretaro, 1925; Secretary General of Government of the State of Queretaro; Treasurer of the City of Queretaro. **g**-None. **h**-Farmer until 1925. **j**-None. **k**-Elected as an Alternate Federal Deputy in 1955 but replaced the regular deputy in 1956. **l**-Func., 331; DGF56, 27; C de S, 1961–64, 65.

Olvera Reyes, Alfonso
b-Ozumba, Mexico, *West Central, Rural*. **c**-Early education unknown; law degree, National School of Law, UNAM, with a specialty in constitutional and administrative law. **d**-None. **e**-General Delegate of the CEN of PRI to the municipal elections in Veracruz, Zacatecas and Nuevo Leon, 1976; General Delegate of the CEN of PRI to the Sixth District, Pue-

bla, during the elections for deputies, 1976; Subsecretary of Electoral Action of the CEN of PRI, 1978. **f**-Political Subdelegate and General Coordinator of the Alvaro Obregon Delegation, Department of the Federal District, 1967; adviser to the Department of Ejido and Communal Services, Secretariat of Agrarian Reform, 1977; Director of Governmental and Juridical Unity, Tlalpan Delegation, Department of the Federal District, 1977. **g**-President of the Federation of University Students, 1960–61. **j**-None. **k**-None. **l**-HA, 20 Nov. 1978, 21.

Orijel Salazar, Manuel
a-July 29, 1913. **b**-Federal District, *Federal District, Urban*. **c**-Primary studies under Dr. Agustin Rivera, Mexico, D.F., 1920–27; secondary studies at the Centro Escolar Revolucionario, Mexico, D.F., 1941–43; preparatory studies at the National Preparatory School No. 3, 1944–45 and No. 1, 1957; law degree from the National School of Law, UNAM, 1958–62; professor at the National Preparatory School No. 2, Mexico, D.F., 1963–66. **d**-*Federal Deputy* from the Federal District, Dist. 9, 1946–49, member of the Second Balloting Committee, the War Materiels Committee, the Third Labor Committee, the Second General Means of Communication Committee, and the Inspection Committee of the General Accounting Office; *Federal Deputy* from the Federal District, Dist. 8, 1964–67, member of the Administration Committee (1st year), the Department of the Federal District Committee, the 4th Section on Administration of the Legislative Studies Committee, and the Public Works Committee; *Federal Deputy* from the Federal District, Dist. 8, 1970–73, member of the Domestic Trade Committee, the Department of the Federal District Committee, the Seventh Section on Commerce and Credit of the Legislative Studies Committee, the Military Industry Committee, and the Rules Committee. **e**-Secretary of Bureaucratic Action, PRI; Secretary of the Youth Commission of the CEN of PRI; Secretary of Press and Publicity of the Regional Committee of PRI for the Federal District; general delegate of the CNOP of PRI to various states; Treasurer and Secretary General of CNOP in the Federal District; member of the National Council of PRI; Director of Popular Action of PRI in the Federal District, 1976. **f**-Chief of lawyers of the Board of Arbitration of the FSTSE; delegate of the Department of the Federal District to Ixtapalpa. **g**-Secretary of the National Policy Commission of the FSTSE; member of the Legal Studies Committee, FSTSE; Secretary of Resolutions, FSTSE. **h**-Special studies of public administration, union organizations, and labor relations in the United States. **j**-None. **k**-None. **l**-C de D, 1946–48, 84; C de D, 1964–66, 63, 81, 83, 90; C de D, 1970–72, 128; *Directorio*, 1970–72.

Orive Alba, Adolfo
a-Dec. 9, 1907. b-Federal District, *Federal District, Urban*. c-Primary and secondary studies in Mexico, D.F.; engineering degree from the National School of Engineering, UNAM, 1927; studied irrigation in the United States on a scholarship from the National Irrigation Commission, 1928; Professor of Engineering, UNAM, 1968. d-None. e-None. f-Subdirector of the Department of Hydraulic Resources, Secretariat of Public Works, 1929–31; Chief Engineer, National Irrigation Commission, 1932–35; engineer in charge of construction of the Rodriguez Dam, 1935–36; Director of Irrigation of the Rodriguez Dam, 1936–38; member of the United States-Mexican International Boundary and Waters Commission for the Colorado and Bravo Rivers, 1939–40; Executive Director of the National Irrigation Commission, 1940–46; *Secretary of Hydraulic Resources*, 1947–52; Director General of Siderurgica las Truchas, S.A., 1969–78. g-None. h-Since 1932, author of numerous books and articles on irrigation in Mexico; consulting engineer to Latin American countries, 1952; founded a consulting engineering firm, 1961, president of the irrigation consulting firm, CIEPS, 1966–68. i-Close friend of *Miguel Aleman*; knew *Antonio Dovali Jaime* as a student at UNAM. j-None. k-Founder and first Secretary of the Secretariat of Hydraulic Resources. l-HA, 7 Aug. 1972; letter; DBM68, 466–67; HA, 21 Nov. 1952; DGF51, II, 615; Greenberg, 23; IWW67, 917; DGF50, II, 317, 455, etc.; DGF51, I, 413; Enc. Mex., IX, 1977, 602.

Orlaineta, Carlo M.
a-Feb. 13, 1906. b-Villahermosa, Tabasco, *Gulf, Urban*. c-Primary and secondary studies in Villahermosa; preparatory studies in Villahermosa; no degree. d-*Federal Deputy* from the Federal District, Dist. 5, 1940–43, member of the Rules Committee, substitute Member of the Department of the Federal District Committee. e-None. g-None. h-Began career as a bank employee; cashier for the Cia. Hipotecaria, 1931–35; staff writer and reporter for the *Universal Grafico*, the *Revista de Revistas*, *El Dia*, and other newspapers. i-Father, a doctor. j-None. k-None. l-EBW46, 69; C de D, 1940–42, 48, 59.

Ornelas Kuckle, Oscar
a-1922. b-Chihuahua, *North*. c-Early education unknown; law degree; Rector of the University of Chihuahua, 1964–70, 1970–74. d-Mayor of Chihuahua, Chihuahua; *Senator* from the State of Chihuahua, 1976–80; *Governor of Chihuahua*, 1980– . e-None. f-None. i-Has strong political ties to *Carlos Sansores Perez*. j-None. k-None. l-*Excelsior*, 15 Feb. 1980, 16; C de S, 1976–82.

Orozco Camacho, Miguel
(Deceased 1945)
a-May 5, 1886. b-Zapopan, Jalisco, *West, Rural*. c-Primary studies in Guadalajara; no degree. d-None. e-None. f-Head of the Department of Infantry, Secretariat of National Defense, 1932–33; head of the Department of Engineers, Secretariat of National Defense, 1934–35; Chief of Staff of the Secretariat of National Defense, 1936–37; *Oficial Mayor of the Secretariat of National Defense*, 1937–39; Director of the Federal Penitentiary, 1941–45. g-None. h-None. j-Joined the Revolution, 1911; served under the Constitutional Army of the North and the Army of the West, 1913; rank of Brigadier General, Mar. 21, 1925; reached rank of Divisionary General. k-None. l-DP70, 1549; Lopez, 796.

Orozco Romero, Alberto
a-Apr., 1925. b-Guadalajara, Jalisco, *West, Urban*. c-Primary studies at public schools, Guadalajara; secondary studies at the Secondary School No. 1 for Boys, Guadalajara; preparatory studies at the Preparatory School of Jalisco, Guadalajara; law degree, School of Law, University of Guadalajara, 1944–49, completing his thesis in 1950; Professor of Private Law, University of Guadalajara, 1953; Professor of General Theory of Obligations, University of Guadalajara, 1954. d-*Governor of Jalisco*, 1971–77. e-None. f-Secretary of the 6th Tribunal of the 1st Civil Court, Jalisco, 1951–52; 3rd Judge of the 1st Civil Court, 1952–54; Judge of the 6th Tribunal, 1st Civil Court, 1954–58; interim Judge of the 1st Division of the Superior Tribunal of Justice of the State of Jalisco, 1958–59; Alternate Justice of the Superior Tribunal of Justice of the State of Jalisco, 1959–60; Justice of the 1st Division, Superior Tribunal of Justice, Jalisco, 1960–65; President of the Superior Tribunal of Justice, Jalisco, 1965–67; *Supernumerary Justice of the Supreme Court*, 1967–70; *Justice of the Supreme Court*, 1970. g-None. h-None. j-None. k-None. l-Letter; G of NL, 42; *Justicia*, Sept. 1968; Enc. Mex., IX, 1977, 618.

Orozco Rosales, Alfonso
a-Aug. 4, 1916. b-Guadalajara, Jalisco, *West, Urban*. c-Primary studies at the Colegio Inmaculada Concepcion, Guadalajara, 1923–29; secondary studies at the Colegio del Espiritu Santo, Guadalajara, 1929–32; preparatory studies at the Notre Dame des Anges, Espira de L'Agly, France, 1932–36; studies in mathematics, National School of Engineering, UNAM, 1937–42; Professor of Mathematics. d-*Federal Deputy* from PAN (party deputy), 1970–73, member of the Public Welfare Committee and the Fiscal Section of the Legislative Studies Committee.

e-Member of PAN. f-None. g-None. h-Businessman. j-None. k-None. l-*Directorio*, 1970–72; C de D, 1970–72, 128.

Orrico de los Llanos, Miguel

a-Sept. 18, 1894. b-Villahermosa, Tabasco, *Gulf*, *Urban*. c-Primary studies in Macuspana, Tabasco; graduated from the National Military College. d-None. e-None. f-*Interim Governor of Tabasco*, 1955–58. g-None. h-None. j-Fought under Carranza during the Revolution; became a member of his staff; Commander of the 7th Military Zone of Nuevo Leon; Commander of the 4th Military Zone, Hermosillo, Sonora; commander of the garrison at Mexicali; rank of Brigadier General, Nov. 1, 1940; rank of Divisionary General. k-None. l-Peral, 601; DGF56, 101; HA, 28 Mar. 1955, 5; Scott, 276.

Ortega Cantero, Benjamin

a-April 16, 1919. b-Coyoacan, *Federal District*, *Urban*. c-Primary and secondary studies at the Escuela Heroes de Churubusco, Coyoacan; and at Secondary School No. 1, Mexico City; agricultural engineering studies in agricultural parasitology, National School of Agriculture, 1936–41, completed his thesis in 1945, on the cotton plant; fellowship student of the Rockefeller Foundation and the Secretariat of Agriculture, University of Minnesota, MS degree in phytology, 1946. d-None. e-None. f-Employee of the Secretariat of Agriculture in the Office of Special Studies, Rockefeller Foundation, 1944–45; researcher, hybrid wheat seeds, Don Martin, Coahuila, 1945; member of the Committee to Increase Improved Seeds, 1946; Director, Northern Agricultural Zone, Secretariat of Agriculture, Torreon, Coahuila; Representative of the Lagunera Delegation for Vegetable Cleanliness, Torreon, Coahuila, 1950–25; representative of the Secretariat of Agriculture to Comarca, 1952–58; Manager, Secretariat of Hydraulic Resources, 1958–72; Director General of Vegetable Cleanliness, Secretariat of Agriculture, 1972–76; *Subsecretary of Agriculture and Operations*, 1976– . g-Organized Agricultural Defense Groups, Coatzacoalcos, Veracruz. j-None. k-None. l-Letter, DAPC, 54.

Ortega, Fausto M.

(Deceased Aug. 25, 1971)
a-1905. b-Tezuitlan, Puebla, *East Central*, *Urban*. c-No degree. d-*Alternate Federal Deputy* from the State of Puebla, Dist. 9, 1937–40; *Federal Deputy* from the State of Puebla, Dist. 7, 1946–49, member of the Gran Comision and the Budget and Accounts Committee (1st year), substitute member of the Petroleum Committee; *Governor of Puebla*, 1957–62. e-None. f-*Oficial Mayor of Communications and Public Works*, 1942–45; Director of the Tax De-

partment, State of Puebla, 1951; Oficial Mayor of the Government of Puebla, 1951–57, under Governor *Rafael Avila Camacho*. g-None j-None. k-Originally a close collaborator of *Rafael Avila Camacho* but broke with him after Ortega was elected governor. l-C de D, 1946–48, 82; HA, 6 Sept. 1971, 104; DGF56, 98; DGF51, I, 91; NYT, 5 Aug. 1961, 14; NYT, 22 Sept. 1961, 16; *Excelsior*, 26 Dec. 1974, 12.

Ortega Hernandez, Samuel

a-1905. b-Torreon, Coahuila, *North*, *Urban*. c-No degree. d-*Federal Deputy* from the State of Tlaxcala, Dist. 2, 1955–58, member of the Library Committee (1st year) and the Textile Industry Committee, substitute member of the First Railroad Committee; *Senator* from the State of Tlaxcala, 1958–64, member of the Railroad Committee and the General Means of Communication Committee, substitute member of the Indian Affairs Committee and the Public Works Committee; local deputy to the State Legislature of Coahuila. e-None. f-Secretary General of Government of the State of Coahuila, under *Pedro Rodriguez Triana*, 1940; President of the National Committee on Railroad Policy, 1956. g-Secretary General of the National Railroad Workers Union, 1956–58. h-Employee of the National Railroads of Mexico (30 years); author of several books. j-None. k-None. l-Func., 381; C de S, 65; DGF56, 28, 31, 33, 34; C de D, 1955–57; Ind. Biog., 109.

Ortega Martinez, Lauro

a-1910. b-Federal District, *Federal District*, *Urban*. c-Medical degree from the National School of Medicine, UNAM, 1935. d-*Federal deputy* from the Federal District, Dist. 2, 1946–49, member of the Social Action Committee, the Child Welfare and Social Security Committee, the Foreign Relations Committee, the Military Health Committee, and the 3rd Section of the Credit Committee; *Federal Deputy* from the State of Morelos, Dist. 4, 1979–82. e-Secretary of Popular Action of PRM in the Federal District, 1929; co-founder of the CNOP of PRI with *Carlos Madrazo* and *Ramon Bonfil*, 1942; Secretary General of the CNOP of the Federal District, 1942–45; *Secretary General of the CEN of PRI*, 1964–65; *Interim President of the CEN of PRI*, 1965–68. f-Head of the Department of Psychology and Student Hygiene, Secretariat of Public Education, 1935–38; *Oficial Mayor of Health*, 1938–40; Assistant Treasurer of the Federal District, 1940–44; Subdirector and Director of the Mexican-United States Commission for the Eradication of Hoof and Mouth Disease, 1946–52; *Subsecretary of Agriculture and Livestock*, 1952–58; personal representative of President *Adolfo Lopez Mateos* to the United States in the field of communication problems. **g-**Secretary General of the National Student Cardenista Party, 1933–34; director of the Socialist Youth of Mexico in the Federal District, 1936. **h-**None. **i-**Close friend of *Fidel Velazquez Sanchez*, Secretary General of the Federation of Mexican Labor, 1949–81; knew *Carlos Madrazo* as a student leader in the 1930s. **j-**None. **k-**None. **l-**HA, 23 Dec. 1964, 4; *Polemica*, Vol. 1, No. 1, 28, 1969; DGF50, 149; Johnson, 68; C de D, 1946–48, 82; Fuentes Diaz, 281; DGF56, 223; Loret de Mola, 17.

Ortiz, Andres
(Deceased Feb. 5, 1945)
a-Oct. 28, 1890. **b-**Chihuahua, Chihuahua, *North, Urban.* **c-**Engineering degree in the field of hydraulics and topography, National School of Engineering, UNAM, 1913. **d-**Local deputy in Chihuahua, 1917–18; Provisional Governor of Chihuahua, Nov. 15, 1918 to Feb. 29, 1920; Governor of Chihuahua, Sept. 8, 1930, to Nov. 2, 1931. **e-**None. **f-**Chief of the Department of Bridges and Highways, Secretariat of Communication; Director of the Trolley Company of Mexico City; *Director General of the National Railroads of Mexico*, Feb., 1944, to Jan., 1945; member of the Committee for the Administration and Inspection of Foreign Properties, 1941–44. **g-**None. **h-**Author of the National Highway Law. **j-**Remained loyal to Carranza. **k-**As Provisional Governor of Chihuahua, put a price of 50,000 pesos for the capture of Francisco Villa. **l-**DP70, 1534; Peral, 596; HA, 10 Mar. 1944; Lopez, 802; Enc. Mex., X, 1977, 10.

Ortiz Armengol, Federico
a-Feb. 12, 1898. **b-**Oaxaca, Oaxaca, *South, Urban.* **c-**Primary studies in Oaxaca; secondary studies in Oaxaca; preparatory studies at the National Preparatory School; medical degree, National School of Medicine, October 3, 1925, with an honorable mention; professor of Physiology, National School of Medicine, UNAM; Rector, University of Oaxaca, 1954–58. **d-***Federal Deputy* from the State of Oaxaca, No. 3, 1958–61, member of the public health committee, the Fifth Section of the Legislative Studies Committee, the First Balloting Group and the First Instructive Section of the Grand Jury. **e-**None. **f-**Director, Anti-Rabies Institute, Mexico City, 1930–35; *Oficial Mayor of Labor*, 1935–36; Delegate of the Secretariat of Health, Merida, Yucatan, 1943–44; Delegate of the Secretariat of Health, Durango, 1947; Director of Hygiene Center No. 3, Mexico City; Director of the General Hospital, Oaxaca, Oaxaca, 1954–58. **g-**None. **h-**Practicing physician, 1925–30. **j-**None. **k-**Graduated from the National Medical School with the best grade point average of his class. **l-**Func., 306; C de D, 1958–61, 87.

Ortiz Avila (del Carmen), Jose
a-Mar. 4, 1919. **b-**Campeche, Campeche, *Gulf, Urban.* **c-**Early education unknown; student at the Cadet Military School; graduated from the National Military College; graduate of the Higher War College; diploma as a staff officer. **d-***Federal Deputy* from the State of Campeche, Dist. 1, 1958–61, member of the Property and National Resources Committee, the Second Committee on National Defense, the Second and Sixth Sections of the Legislative Studies Committee, the Military Justice Committee, the Inspection Committee of the General Accounting Office (2nd year), and the First and Second Sections of the Credentials Committee; *Governor of Campeche*, 1961–66. **e-**None. **f-**None. **g-**None. **j-**Career army officer; Assistant Chief of Staff of the 5th Military District, Chihuahua, Chihuahua, 1951, under General *Bonifacio Salinas Leal*; reached the rank of Colonel. **k-**None. **l-**G of M, 8; DGF51, I, 183; C de D, 1958–60, 87; Func., 134; *Excelsior*, 18 Dec. 1973, 15.

Ortiz Garza, Nazario S.
a-Dec. 31, 1893. **b-**Saltillo, Coahuila, *North, Urban.* **c-**Primary studies in Public School No. 2, Saltillo (completed 4th year); preparatory studies at the Ateneo Fuente, Saltillo; no degree. **d-**Councilman of Torreon, 1920, 1921–22; Mayor of Torreon, 1922; Mayor of Torreon, 1927–28; local deputy to the State Legislature of Coahuila, 1925; President of the State Legislature; Mayor of Torreon, Coahuila, 1927–28; Governor of Coahuila, 1930–34; *Senator from the State of Coahuila*, 1934–40. **e-**Campaign director for General Manuel Perez Trevino for governor of Coahuila, 1924. **f-**Appointed Mayor of Saltillo, Coahuila, 1928; appointed Mayor of Torreon, 1926; *Director General of CONASUPO*, 1943–46; *Secretary of Agriculture*, 1946–52. **g-**President of the National Association of Winegrowers, 1954–63, 1969–71. **h-**Began working at age 14; businessman. **i-**Protege of Manuel Perez Trevino, President of the PNR; father a small businessman; married Rebeca Rodriguez. **j-**Fought with General Francisco Murguia without military rank, 1915–17; purveyor of military trains, Chihuahua, Chihuahua, 1917. **k-**Won elections as Federal Deputy, 1923, but did not hold office; *New York Times* claimed the government expropriated his land holdings in Tampico in 1953 in a move against former Alemanistas. **l-**HA, 5 Nov. 1943, 34; DGF51, II, 165; DGF51, I, 203–04; Ha, 6 Dec. 1946, 5; HA, 26 Jan. 1951; Peral, 598; NYT, 25 June 1953, 17; letter; Enc. Mex., X, 1977, 14–15; Lopez, 804; *Justicia*, Mar., 1973.

Ortiz Macedo, Luis
a-1933. **b-**Federal District, *Federal District, Urban.* **c-**Early education unknown; degree in Architecture

with honorable mention, National School of Architecture, UNAM, 1960; studied monument restoration in France on a scholarship from the Bank of Mexico and the French Government; founder and director of the first Institute of Monument Restoration at the University of Guanajuato, 1963–67; Professor of the History of Architecture, National School of Architecture, UNAM, 1955–66. d-None. e-None. f-Executive Secretary of the Pro Guanajuato Committee, 1963–66; Head of the Department of Colonial Monuments, National Institute of Anthropology and History, 1966–68; *Subsecretary of Cultural Affairs of the Secretariat of Public Education, 1969–70*; Secretary General of the National Institute of Anthropology and History, 1968–69; director of projects in Washington, D.C., Rome, and Guatemala; Director of the National Institute of Anthropology and History, 1970–72; Director General of the Institute of Bellas Artes, January 11, 1972, to 1973. g-Representative of the Mexican Architectural Society in Rio de Janeiro, 1960. h-Author of many historical works on art; member of restoration groups for six different sites in Mexico, D.F. j-None. k-Received world recognition for his restoration of monuments. l-HA, 11 Jan. 1972; *Hoy*, 29 Apr. 1972, 62; *Excelsior*, 12 Jan. 1972, 9; D del S, 12 Jan. 1972, 1; DPE71, 108; Enc. Mex., X, 1977, 16.

Ortiz Mena, Antonio

a-Sept. 22, 1908. b-Parral, Chihuahua, *North*, *Urban*. c-Primary studies at the Colegio Aleman and the Colegio Franco-Ingles; secondary and preparatory studies at the National Preparatory School; law degree from the National School of Law, UNAM, 1925–28; studies in philosophy and economics at UNAM. d-None. e-None. f-Adviser, Department of the Federal District, 1930–32; head of the Legal Department, Department of the Federal District, 1932–36; assistant to the Director of the National Urban Mortgage Bank, 1936–45; head of the Department for the Nationalization of Properties, Office of the Attorney General of Mexico, 1940–45; Subdirector of the National Mortgage Bank, 1946–52; First Director General of the Division of Professions, Secretariat of Public Education, 1945–46; *Director General of the IMSS*, 1952–58; *Secretary of the Treasury*, 1958–64, 1964–70; President of the Inter-American Development Bank, 1971– . g-None. h-Founding Governor of the Inter-American Development Bank; Governor of the International Monetary Fund, 1959–70; member of the Revisory Committee on the Law of Enemy Properties and Businesses; member of the Political Defense Committee, 1940–45; practiced law upon graduating from law school, Mexico, D.F. i-While attending the National Law School, 1925–28, knew *Miguel Aleman*, *Antonio Carrillo Flores*, *Alfonso Noriega* and

Eduardo Bustamante; from well-to-do family; father and grandfather in politics, brother of *Raul Ortiz Mena*; married Martha Salinas. j-None. k-Precandidate for President of Mexico, 1970. l-HA, 27 April 1964, 56; 8 Dec. 1958, 25; WWMG, 29; *Hoy*, 17 May 1969, 13; HA, 8 Mar. 1971, 43; DGF47, 352; DGF51, II, 65, 77, etc.; DGF50, 318; letters; Enc. Mex., X, 1977, 16–17; *Justicia*, Jan., 1971; NYT, 6 Oct. 1969, 16.

Ortiz Mena, Raul

a-Aug. 31, 1917. b-Federal District, *Federal District*, *Urban*. c-Preparatory studies in the Federal District; economics degree from the National School of Economics, UNAM, June 5, 1942, with a thesis on "Mexican Money, a Historical Analysis of the Causes in its Fluctuations and Depreciations;" graduate studies in economics at Harvard University on a scholarship from the Bank of Mexico, Nov., 1943, to June, 1944; advanced studies at the Department of Commerce, Washington, D.C., 1944; advanced studies at the Federal Reserve Bank, Washington, D.C., 1945. d-None. e-None. f-Intern in economics, Secretariat of Industry and Commerce, 1942; economist, Secretariat of Industry and Commerce, 1943; economist for the Secretariat of the Treasury and the Bank of Mexico, 1943; head of the Department of Economic Studies, Bank of Mexico, 1946; head of Financial Studies, Nacional Financiera, 1946–50; Director of the Department of Economic Investigations, Nacional Financiera, 1950–52; Director General of Credit, Secretariat of the Treasury, 1952–58; *Subsecretary of the Presidency*, 1958–61, 1964–68. g-None. h-Author of many articles on monetary subjects; Director of the *Revista de Economia*, Secretariat of Industry and Commerce. i-Brother of *Antonio Ortiz Mena*, Secretary of the Treasury, 1958–70; married Clementina Garcia. j-None. k-The *Ortiz Mena* brothers are one of the few examples in recent Mexican cabinet history where two brothers have simultaneously held a Secretaryship and Subsecretaryship; *Raul* resigned from the Subsecretary of the Presidency for reasons of health, Nov. 6, 1968, and has assumed no public positions since that date. l-DGF56, 563; DGF51, II, 304; DGF50, II, B de M, 198; HA, 5 Jan. 1959, 4.

Ortiz Mendoza, Francisco

a-Mar. 27, 1921. b-San Luis Potosi, San Luis Potosi, *East Central*, *Urban*. c-Primary studies at the Rodolfo Menendez School, Federal District (6 years); prevocational studies at the Prevocational School No. 1 and Vocational School No. 1 and No. 2, Federal District (5 years); electronic engineering degree from the Higher School of Mechanical and Electrical Engineering, IPN, 1947; studied under a scholarship at the University of Cuyo, Mendoza,

Argentina; Professor of Physics and Cultural History, IPN; member of the Technical Advisory Council of IPN. d-*Federal Deputy* from the Federal District, Dist. 7, 1964–67, member of the Rural Electrification Committee and the Promotion and Development of Sports Committee; *Federal Deputy* from the PPS (party deputy), 1970–73, member of the Department of the Federal District Committee, the Constitutional Section of the Legislative Studies Committee, the General Means of Communication and Transportation Section of the Legislative Studies Committee, the Livestock Committee, the First Balloting Committee, the Mines Committee, the Small Agricultural Property Committee, and the Second Constitutional Affairs Committee; *Federal Deputy* from the PPS (party deputy), 1976–79. e-Founding member of the PPS, 1948; Secretary General of the PPS for the Federal District; Secretary of Political Education of the National Central Committee of the PPS; Secretary of Press of the Central Committee of the PPS, 1979. f-Chief Assessor, Department of Telecommunications, Secretariat of Communications and Transportation. g-Member of the Unified Socialist Youth of Mexico, 1947; Secretary General of the Federation of Mexican Youth, 1954; Secretary General of the Television Union of Mexico; member of the Executive Committee of the 10th Section of the SNTE, 1968. h-None. i-Married Eva Perez de Ortiz. j-None. k-None. l-C de D, 1964–66, 53, 83, 92; C de D, 1970–72, 129; *Directorio*, 1970–72; HA, 26 Feb. 1979, III.

Ortiz Rodriguez, Jose

(Deceased 1962)

a-1871. b-Taretan, Michoacan, *West Central*, *Rural*. c-Primary and secondary studies at the Zamora Seminary, Morelia, Michoacan; law degree, Colegio de San Nicolas, Morelia. d-Federal Deputy from the State of Michoacan, 1912–13; Senator from the State of Michoacan, 1920–24, 1924–28. e-Secretary General of the Peace and Union Political Group, 1912. f-Secretary of Foreign Relations, January, 1915, under President Eulalio Gutierrez; Justice of the Superior Tribunal of Justice of the Federal District and Federal Territories, 1930–34, 1935–40, 1941–46, 1947–51. g-None. j-Supporter of Francisco Madero. k-Imprisoned by Victoriano Huerta, 1913; candidate for the governorship of Michoacan. l-DP70, 1539–40; Casasola, V, 2422.

Ortiz Salinas, Antonio

a-July 2, 1935. b-Federal District, *Federal District*, *Urban*. c-Primary studies in the public schools of Mexico City; secondary studies from Secondary School No. 1, Mexico City; preparatory studies from the Vasco de Quiroga Institute, Mexico City; law degree, National School of Law, UNAM, 1958, with

a thesis on the Mexican tax system; CEMLA fellow, 1958; United Nations fellow, Harvard University, 1959–60, advanced studies in taxation and economic development, Harvard University and MIT, 1959–60. d-None. e-None. f-Lawyer, Legal Department, Mexican Institute of Social Security, 1953–56; lawyer, Ministerio Publico, Attorney General of Mexico, 1957–58; economic researcher, Technical Office, Bank of Mexico, 1958–59; member, Committee on Fiscal Reforms, 1960; Assistant Manager, National Pawnshop Bank, 1961–63; Subdirector, Department of Economic Affairs and Statistics, Secretariat of the Treasury, 1964–67; Oficial Mayor of the Secretariat of Tourism, 1976–77; *Subsecretary of Tourism*, 1977– . g-None. h-Engaged in private activities, 1970–76. j-None. k-None. l-HA, 14 Nov. 1977; letter; DAPC, 54.

Ortiz Tirado, Jose Maria

(Deceased 1968)

a-Aug. 8, 1894. b-Alamos, Sonora, *North*, *Urban*. c-Preparatory studies at the Colegio de Mascarones and the National Preparatory School, Mexico, D.F.; law degree, National School of Law, UNAM; Professor of Penal Law, UNAM, 1922–30. d-None. e-None. f-Public Defender, 1918–24; consulting lawyer to the Department of the Federal District, 1919; councilman, Mexico, D.F., 1924; agent of the Ministerio Publico of the Office of the Attorney General, 1924–29; Justice of the Superior Tribunal of Justice of the Federal District and Territories, 1929–32, President, 1932–34; *Justice of the Supreme Court of Mexico*, 1934–40, 1940–46, 1947, 1953–54, 1955–56; *President of the Supreme Court of Mexico*, 1954–55; Ambassador to Colombia, 1948–52; *Subsecretary of Government*, 1952; President of the National Commission of Nuclear Energy, 1956–58. g-None. h-None. i-Parents were wealthy; cousin, Alfonso Ortiz Tirado, 1894–1960, was a medical doctor and well-known Mexican singer; married Maria Antonieta Necchi. j-None. k-None. l-DP70, 1540; DGF51, I, 106; WWM45, 88; HA, 15 Feb. 1952, 3; STYRIWW54, 933; Enc. Mex., X, 21; Lopez, 808.

Ortiz Walls, Eugenio

a-July 4, 1931. b-Oaxaca, Oaxaca, *South*, *Urban*. c-Primary and secondary studies, University of Oaxaca, Oaxaca; law degree, University of Oaxaca, Oaxaca; professor of sociology, law, literature and history at various institutions in Mexico City. d-*Alternate Federal Deputy* (PAN party deputy), 1967–70; *Federal Deputy* (PAN party deputy), 1973–76. e-Joined PAN, 1952; Oficial Mayor of PAN; member of the CEN of PAN, 1969. f-None. g-Student leader. i-Married Maria Teresa Castro de Ortiz. j-None. k-Seen by some observers of PAN as a progressive Christian Democrat ideologically. l-C de D, 1973–76, 29; HA, 12 Feb. 1979, 17.

Osorio Marban, Miguel

a-Dec. 10, 1936. b-Chaucingo, Guerrero, *South*, *Rural*. c-Teaching certificate, National Normal School, 1948–53; preparatory studies in social sciences, National Preparatory School, 1954–56; law degree, National School of Law, UNAM, graduating with the highest GPA of his class; received an honorary mention for his thesis on ''Public Administration and the Educational Obligations of the State.'' d-*Federal Deputy* from the State of Guerrero, Dist. 3, 1964–67, member of the Second Ejido Committee, the Second Constitutional Affairs Committee and the Complaints Committee. e-Joined PRM, August 8, 1950; participated in *Adolfo Ruiz Cortines'* presidential campaign, 1952; Director of the National Youth of PRI, 1959–64; orator for the *Gustavo Diaz Ordaz* presidential campaign, 1964; General Delegate of the CEN of PRI to Morelos and Nayarit, 1964; President of PRI in Nayarit, 1964; representative of PRI before the Federal Electoral Commission, 1966–67; Private Secretary to *Lauro Ortega Martinez*, President of the CEN of PRI, 1966–68; Director of *Jose Lopez Portillo*'s campaign in the desert zones of Coahuila, Nuevo Leon, San Luis Potosi, Tamaulipas and Zacatecas, 1975–76. f-Technical adviser to the Director General of CONASUPO, 1968; Manager General of La Forestal, 1968–76; *Subsecretary of Agrarian Reform*, 1976–78. g-Secretary of Political Action of the Student Society of the National Teachers School, 1951–52; Secretary General of the Student Society of the National Teachers School, 1952–53; President of the Student Council of the National Preparatory School, 1955; Secretary General of the Federation of University Students, 1955–56; Representative of the National School of Law to the First National Congress of Law Students. h-Secondary school oratory champion, *El Universal* contest, 1950; Director of *Accion*, National Teachers School paper, 1950. i-Protege of *Lauro Ortega Martinez*. j-None. k-None. l-Letter; *Proceso*, 12 June 1978, 25; C de D, 1964–67, 82, 92; DAPC, 54.

Osorio Palacios, Juan Jose

a-Jan. 21, 1920. b-Federal District, *Federal District*, *Urban*. c-Primary and secondary studies in the Federal District; preparatory studies in the Federal District; studies at the National Conservatory of Music, 1938–45. d-*Federal Deputy* from the Federal District, Dist. 20, 1952–55, Vice President of the Chamber of Deputies, Dec., 1952, member of the Department of the Federal District Committee, the Inspection Committee of the General Accounting Of-

fice (3rd year), and the First Labor Committee; *Federal Deputy* from the Federal District, Dist. 15, 1958–61, member of the Library Committee (1st year), the Fifth Section of the Legislative Studies Committee, the Second Section of the First Credentials Committee, and the Committee on Bellas Artes; *Federal Deputy* from the Federal District, Dist. 15, 1976–79. e-Director of Political Action of PRI in the Federal District, 1976. f-Member of the National Symphony Orchestra of Mexico, 1939–48. g-Joined the Music Workers Union, 1945; Secretary General of the Music Workers Union of Mexico, 1946; member of the Board of Directors of the Student Society of the National Conservatory of Mexico; Secretary of Organization of the CTM, 1956. h-Violinist; member of the Orchestra at UNAM; member of the Classic Quartet and the Opera Orchestra of the National Symphony Orchestra; delegate to the International Music Congress, Geneva, 1954, 1957. i-Married Luz Maria Puente. j-None. k-None. l-Func., 190; C de D, 1958–60, 88; C de D, 1952–54, 48, 59, 69; *Excelsior*, 9 Dec. 1976; *Excelsior*, 20 Aug. 1976, 1C.

Osorio Ramirez, Miguel

a-1915. b-Xicohzingo, Tlaxcala, *East Central*, *Rural*. c-Primary studies in Xicohzingo; secondary studies at Secondary School No. 4, Mexico City; preparatory studies at the National Preparatory Night School; law degree, National School of Law, UNAM, March 20, 1935; one year of advanced studies, School of Philosophy and Letters, UNAM; one semester of studies toward an LLD degree. d-*Senator* from the State of Tlaxcala, 1952–58, President of the Administration Committee, Second Secretary of the Agrarian Department Committee, President of the Second Justice Committee, First Secretary of the First Petroleum Committee and Second Secretary of the Special Committee on Tourist Affairs. e-Secretary General of the CEN of PRI. f-Lawyer, Legal Office of Banks and Money, Secretariat of the Treasury; Director, Legal Office of Banks and Money; Secretary General of the Committee to Control Prices in the Federal District; Judge of the Superior Tribunal of Justice of the State of Tlaxcala; Director of Legal Affairs Secretariat of Hydraulic Resources, 1958–61. g-None. h-Worked as an agricultural laborer on the San Jacinto, Cuacualoya, and Santa Agueda haciendas; textile worker in the Covadonga Factory, Puebla; weaver, La Tlaxcalteca Factory, Tlaxcala. i-Helped by *Alfonso Caso* as a law school student; worked under *Ricardo Jose Zevada* in the Legal Office of Banks and Money, 1930; son, Federico Osorio Espinosa, was a precandidate for federal deputy from Tlaxcala. j-None. k-None. l-DPE61, 95; *Excelsior,* 12 Nov. 1978, 14; Ind. Biog., 109–10.

Osorio y Carvajal, Ramon

a-1914. b- Valladolid, Yucatan, *Gulf*, *Urban*. c-Preparatory in Merida; Ph.D. in Philosophy and Letters, Latin American University of Havana, 1954; medical degree, University of Yucatan; Doctorate in Psychology, School of Sciences, National Technical University of Cuba, 1947; Professor of Medicine, University of Yucatan, 1930– ; Director of the School of Medicine, University of Yucatan, 1943–44; Rector of the University of Yucatan, 1943. d-*Federal Deputy* from the State of Yucatan, Dist. 1, 1952–55, member of the Library Committee, the Editorial Committee (3rd year); *Senator* from the State of Yucatan, 1967–70. e-Delegate of PRI to many districts; Secretary General of Social Action of the CEN of CNOP of PRI. f-Director of the National Naval Clinic, ISSSTE; representative of the Agrarian Department; Director General of Coordination, Department of Tourism; representative from the Department of Tourism to the Organization of American States, 1967; Delegate of the Department of the Federal District in Cuajimalpa de Morelos, 1971. g-None. h-Director of the O'Horan Hospital, Merida, Yucatan; director of the sports section of the newspaper, *Voz*; author of many books. j-None. k-Originally elected as a Substitute Senator in 1964, but replaced *Matos Escobedo* when he died in 1967. l-*Hoy*, 21 Mar. 1970, 20; C de D, 1952–54, 16, 49; C de S, 1964–70; Enc. Mex., X, 1977, 24.

Osornio (Camarena), Enrique C.

(Deceased 1946)
a-1868. b-Queretaro, Queretaro, *East Central*, *Urban*. c-Early education unknown; medical degree; professor, Medical Military College; Director, Medical Military College. d-Senator from the State of Queretaro, 1928–30; *Governor of Aguascalientes*, 1932–36; *Senator* from the State of Aguascalientes, 1940–46, member of the Second Balloting Group, Second Secretary of the Foreign Trade Committee, the Social Welfare Committee, the Second Instructive Section of the Grand Jury and the Third Labor Committee, First Secretary of the Third National Defense Committee and President of the Military Health Committee. e-None. f-Chief of Medical Services on a special mission to Brazil, 1922; delegate of the Secretariat of Public Health to Baja California and Aguascalientes, 1924–30; director of various hospitals. g-None. h-None. j-Career army officer; fought under General Obregon during the Revolution; rank of Brigade General; Chief of the Medical Military Corps. k-Amputated General Obregon's arm at the Battle of Celaya; founder of the practical Medical Military College; the *New York Times* alleges he was charged with the murder of the manager of the state lottery, 1935. l-NYT, 27 July, 1935, 14; Libro de Oro, 1946, 9–10; D de Y, 5 Sept. 1935, 1; Peral, 603.

Otal Briseno, Rigoberto

a-Jan. 4, 1905. b-Campeche, Campeche, *Gulf*, *Urban*. c-Primary studies in Campeche; teaching certificate from the National Normal School; graduated from the Naval College, Veracruz. d-*Senator* from the State of Campeche, 1952–58, President of the First Naval Committee, First Secretary of the Public Works Committee, First Secretary of the Second Petroleum Committee and First Secretary of the National Defense Committee. e-None. f-Naval Attache to the Mexican Embassy in Argentina; *Oficial Mayor of the Secretariat of the Navy*, 1958–61. g-None. h-None. j-Career naval officer; coastguardman on the Progreso; fought the Cristeros, 1938; commander of the Coastguard ship G28; commander of the Mazatlan; commander of the Queretaro; commander of the transport ship, Durango; Subdirector of the National Fleet; Chief of Adjutants, Secretariat of the Navy; commander of the 6th Naval Zone, 1951; rank of rear admiral. k-Regarded as a hero during action against the Cristeros when he saved numerous noncombatant women and children. l-Ind. Biog., 111–12; DGF51, I, 389; DPE61, 37.

Oteyza, Jose Andres de

a-Nov. 21, 1942. b-Federal District, *Federal District*, *Urban*. c-Early education unknown; economics degree from the National School of Economics, UNAM, 1961–65, graduating with the best GPA in his class and an honorary mention, March 30, 1966; MA in economics, Kings College, Cambridge University, 1966–68; Professor of Economic Theory, Balance of Payments and International Liquidity, National School of Economics, 1968–71. d-None. e-Coordinator of the Advisory Council of the IEPES for *Lopez Portillo*'s presidential campaign, 1975–76. f-Economist for the Department of Economic Studies, Division of Control of State Agencies and Enterprises, Secretariat of National Patrimony, 1965–66; analyst, Department of Economic Studies, Bank of Mexico, 1968–70; Subdirector of Analysis of Operations, Division of Control of State Agencies and Enterprises, Secretariat of Government Properties, 1970–71; Director of the Division of Studies and Projects, Secretariat of Government Properties, 1972–74; Director General of the National Sugar Industry Bank, 1974–75; *Secretary of Government Properties*, 1976– . g-President of the Society of Latin American Students in Cambridge, England. h-Author of several books. i-Student of *Horacio Flores de la Pena*. j-None. k-Youngest member of *Jose Lopez Portillo*'s cabinet. l-Letter; *El Dia*, 1 Dec. 1976; HA, 13 Oct. 1975, 17; HA, 7 Feb. 1977, 17; HA, 6 Dec. 1976, 22.

Ovalle Fernandez, Ignacio

a-1944. b-Federal District, *Federal District*, *Urban*. c-Primary and secondary studies in Mexico, D.F.;

preparatory studies at the National Preparatory School; studied law, National School of Law, 1962–66, with a grade average of 9.8; law degree, 1968. d-None. e-Secretary of Cultural Action of the National Directorate of Youth Action of PRI; Secretary of Political Action of the National Directorate of Youth Action of PRI, 1965; Auxiliary Secretary of Organization of the CEN of PRI, 1966–67. f-Director, Office of Sidewalk Vendors, Department of the Federal District, 1967; private secretary to *Rafael Hernandez Ochoa*, Subsecretary of Government 1968–69; private secretary to *Rodolfo Gonzalez Guevara*; *Private Secretary to the President of Mexico*, 1970–72; *Subsecretary of the Presidency*, Nov. 14, 1972, to 1975; *Secretary of the Presidency*, 1975–76; Director, National Indigenous Institute, 1977– . g-None. h-Won first place in the 1967 National Literary Contest sponsored by the National Institute of Mexican Youth. i-Married Maria Luisa Cavazos. j-None. k-At age 28, *Ovalle Fernandez* became one of the youngest subsecretaries in recent cabinet history. l-HA, 7 Dec. 1970, 28; HA, 25 Sept. 1972; DPE71, 1; Enc. Mex., X, 1977, 38; DAPC, 1977, 3.

Pacheco Iturribarria, Jose

a-Apr. 29, 1894. b-Oaxaca, *South*. c-Early education unknown; no degree. d-*Senator* from the State of Oaxaca, 1964–69. e-None. f-*Substitute Governor of Oaxaca*, 1955–56; Director General of the Administrative Division, Secretariat of National Defense, 1965. g-None. h-None. j-Joined the Revolution; head of various army units; rank of Brigadier General, Dec. 16, 1940. k-*Por Que* claims he made 500,000 pesos a year in commissions in the purchase of military uniforms; took a leave of absence from his position as Federal Senator from Oaxaca. l-DGF56, 97; Peral 47, 246; DPE65, 40; MGF69, 106; *Por Que*, 4 July 1969, 5.

Padilla, Mariano

a-July 26, 1904. b-Arcinas, Gomez Palacio, Durango, *West, Rural*. c-Primary studies in Matamoros, Coahuila; no degree. d-*Federal Deputy* from the State of Durango, Dist. 2, 1940–43. e-None. f-None. g-Secretary of Peasant Action, Mexican Federation of Labor; Secretary General of the Mexican Federation of Labor for the State of Durango. j-None. k-None. l-Peral, 608; C de D, 1940–42, 17.

Padilla Nervo, Luis

a-Aug. 19, 1898. b-Zamora, Michoacan, *West Central, Urban*. c-Early education unknown; graduate of the school of Law, UNAM; attended the School of Economics and Political Science, University of London; attended the George Washington University, Washington, D.C.; and the School of Law and Social Science, University of Buenos Aires. d-None. e-None. f-Assistant Protocol Officer, Foreign Service, 1918; Assistant Secretary of the Mexican Legation to Buenos Aires, 1923; Secretary of the Mexican Legation to Buenos Aires; Charge d'Affaires, Havana; Minister to El Salvador, 1934; legal adviser to the Mexican Embassy in Washington, Madrid, and London; Second Secretary to the Legation in Madrid, 1931; Minister to Uruguay, El Salvador, Panama, Costa Rica, Denmark, and the Netherlands; adviser to the Mexican delegation to the United Nations Conference, San Francisco, 1945; President of the Mexican Delegation to the United Nations, 1945–52; *Secretary of Foreign Relations*, 1952–58; *Mexican Ambassador to the United Nations*, 1958–63; Justice of the International Court of Justice, 1963–73. g-None. h-Oficial Mayor of the Secretariat of Labor; Subsecretary of Labor; Subsecretary of Education and Fine Arts; President of the General Assembly of the United Nations, 1951–52; Chairman of the United States Disarmament Commission, 1959; adviser to many international commissions. i-Married Cecilia Winston. j-None. k-None. l-*Excelsior*, 18 Aug. 1972, 15; WB54, 911; WWM45, 89; HA, 15 Jan. 1959; WWMG, 30; HA, 5 Dec. 1952, 9; WWW70–71, 675; DGF56, 123; HA, 5 Jan. 1959; IWW67, 925; DPE61, 25; Peral, 608; STYR-BIWW54, 919; DGF51, I, 110; Enc. Mex., X, 1977, 74–75; Lopez, 817; NYT, 27 July 1954, 10.

Padilla (Penalosa), Ezequiel

(Deceased Sept. 6, 1971)

a-Dec. 31, 1890. b-Coyuca de Catalan, Guerrero, *South, Rural*. c-Secondary schooling at the Normal School, Chilpancingo, Guerrero; teaching certificate; preparatory studies at the National Preparatory School, Mexico, D.F.; legal studies, National School of Law, UNAM, on a government scholarship; law degree, 1912; founding member of a group of students who formed the Escuela Libre de Derecho; studies at the Sorbonne, Paris, on a scholarship from the Secretary of Education, 1913–14; advanced studies, Columbia University, New York, 1916; Professor of Constitutional Law, UNAM, 1928. d-Federal Deputy from Coyuca de Catalan, Guerrero, 1922–24, 1924–26; Federal Deputy from the State of Guerrero, 1932–34; *Senator* from the Federal District, 1934–40; *Senator* from the State of Guerrero, 1964–70. e-State Delegate of PRI in Guerrero; candidate for President of Mexico for the Mexican Democratic Party, 1946. f-Minister to Hungary and to Italy, 1930–32; Attorney General of Mexico, 1928; Secretary of Public Education, 1928–30; *Secretary of Foreign Relations*, 1940–45. g-None. h-Author of several books. i-Knew *Francisco Gaxiola* and *Ernesto Enriquez Coyro* in preparatory school and at the Escuela Libre de Derecho; student companion of *Emilio Portes Gil* at the Escuela Libre de Derecho; father, an impoverished lawyer in Coyuca de Catalan; mother was a schoolteacher; married Maria G. Couttolenc. **j-**Joined the Revolution; served under Emiliano Zapata as a common soldier; served as a secretary to several generals fighting under Francisco Villa; fled Mexico in 1916 after Villa's defeat. **k-***Padilla* received government scholarships for all of his professional education, beginning with a scholarship to study at normal school, Chilpancingo, Guerrero; precandidate for the PRI nomination for President, 1945; Brandenburg considers *Padilla* in the Inner Circle of influence in Mexico, 1940–45; self-exile in Cuba and the United States until 1922; *Padilla*'s family accused of controlling excessively large plots of land in Guerrero by the Secretary General of the state CNC, Aug. 1972. **l-**WWM45, 89; DBM68, 474; Morton, 47, 49, 51; EBW46, 14; Scott, 210; HA, 13 Sept. 1971, 21; Brandenburg, 80; letters; Kirk, 205–10; Strode, 381–88; CB, 1942; *Excelsior*, 29 Aug. 1972, 27; Daniels, 108ff; Peral, 607; Enc. Mex., X, 1977, 73; Lopez, 817; HA, 8 Dec. 1944, 5.

Padilla Segura, Jose Antonio

a-Mar. 12, 1922. **b-**San Luis Potosi, San Luis Potosi, *East Central*, *Urban*. **c-**Primary studies in Aguascalientes, Aguascalientes and in Mexico, D.F.; secondary studies at the Higher School of Mechanical and Electrical Engineering, Mexico, D.F.; degree in electrical engineering, National School of Engineering, UNAM, Aug., 1942; Ph.D. in Science, UNAM; professor, School of Engineering, UNAM; professor of electrical engineering, National Polytechnic Institute; Chief of Laboratories, Higher School of Mechanical and Electrical Engineering, IPN; Vice President of the Research Center, National Polytechnic Institute. **d-**None. **e-**None. **f-***Director General of the National Polytechnic Institute*, 1963–64; *Secretary of Communication and Transportation*, 1964–70; *Director General of the National Steel Industry of Mexico*, *S.A.*, 1971–76; *Director General of the National Steel Industry of Mexico*, *S.A.*, 1976–78. **g-**None. **h-**Engineer for the National Irrigation Commission. **i-**Married Maria Elena Longoria; father a white collar worker; mother related to Antonio Diaz Soto y Gama, prominent politician in the 1920s. **j-**None. **k-**Precandidate for Senator from San Luis Potosi, 1976. **l-**DBM68, 476; WWMG, 30; HA, 7 Dec. 1964, 19; DPE65, 103; WNM, 169; HA, 1 Sept. 1975, 13; *Justicia*, Sept., 1971; HA, 23 May 1977, 64; HA, 15 Jan. 1979, 10–11.

Paez, Manuel M.

a-Apr. 5, 1885. **b-**Culiacan, Sinaloa, *West, Urban*. **c-**Early education unknown; teaching certificate. **d-***Governor of Sinaloa*, 1934–35. **e-**None. **f-**Interim

Governor of Sinaloa, 1927–28. **g-**None. **h-**Director of medical laboratories; purveyor for manufacturing companies. **k-**Powers as Governor of Sinaloa were dissolved by the Federal Government because Paez was too friendly with President Calles. **l-**Dulles, 661; D de S, 10 Aug. 1935, 1; Peral, 608.

Paez Urquidi, Alejandro

a-Sept. 25, 1907. **b-**Gomez Palacio, Durango, *West, Rural*. **c-**Early education unknown; secondary studies at the Juarez Institute of Durango; engineering studies at the Mechanical and Engineering Institute of San Antonio, Texas, and at the National School of Engineering, UNAM; electrical engineering degree, UNAM, 1929; studied law and economics, UNAM, 1942–43. **d-***Governor of Durango*, 1968–74. **e-**Representative of the CEN of PRI in Durango. **f-***Director General of the Federal Electric Commission*, 1946–52. **g-**None. **h-**Technical positions in the Compania Impulsora de Empresas Electricas, S.A. **i-**Married Alicia Aragon. **j-**None. **k-**None. **l-**DGF51, II, 345, 355; DGF50, 245; HA, 12 May 1950, 24; WNM, 169.

Palacios, Manuel R.

a-Nov. 1, 1906. **b-**Oaxaca, Oaxaca, *South, Urban*. **c-**Primary studies at the Relacimiento School, Oaxaca; secondary studies at the Institute of Arts and Sciences, Oaxaca, Oaxaca, 1916–19; preparatory studies at the Institute of Arts and Sciences, Oaxaca, 1919–21, and at the National Preparatory School, 1922; law degree from the National School of Law, UNAM, Nov. 8, 1926, with a thesis on the church; Professor of Sociology, School of Commerce and Administration, UNAM, 1933; Professor of Revolutionary Legislation, National Teachers School, 1936–42; Professor of Sociology, Higher Normal School, 1938–46; Professor of Economic Policy, National School of Law, UNAM (31 years); co-founder of the Higher Normal School. **d-***Senator* from the State of Oaxaca, 1946, but did not serve in the Senate. **e-**None. **f-**President of the Technical Commission, Secretariat of Public Education, 1935–37; Director, Department of Legal Affairs, Secretariat of Government, 1938–39; member of the Presidential Study Commission, 1937; Judge, Federal Board of Conciliation and Arbitration, 1938–39; President, Federal Board of Conciliation and Arbitration, 1941–43; adviser, Department of Social Welfare, Secretariat of Government, 1938–46; *Subsecretary of Labor*, 1943–46; *Director General of the National Railroads of Mexico*, 1946–52. **g-**President of the Alumni Association of the Students of the Institute of Arts and Sciences of Oaxaca; Adviser to the National Railroads of Mexico, 1943–46; founder and Director of the Seminar for Social Science for Workers, 1933; practicing lawyer, 1973. **i-**Published the student magazine *Eureka* at the National Preparatory School with *Miguel Aleman*, *Antonio Ortiz Mena*, *Gabriel Ramos Millan*, and *Adolfo Zamora*; father a well-known artisan in tin; his uncle was a justice of the Supreme Court; married Maria del Carmen Sierra. **j**-None. **k**-Supported the candidacy of Gilberto Valenzuela for President, 1924; campaigned as an orator for Jose Vasconcelos, 1929, with *Adolfo Lopez Mateos* and *Salvador Azuela*. **l**-Letter; Peral, 609; DGF51, I, 7; DGF51, II, 127, 529; WWM45, 90; DGF47, 21, 413; Enc. Mex., V, 45; Correa, 37; Lopez, 819.

Palomares (Navarro), Noe

a-Nov. 10, 1913. **b**-Alamos, Sonora, *North*, *Urban*. **c**-Primary studies in Alamos, Sonora; teaching certificate from the Normal School of Hermosillo; preparatory studies from the National Preparatory School, 1934–36; law degree from the National School of Law, UNAM, with a thesis on "Our Federal System and the Dissolution of Local Powers," 1940; primary school teacher; Professor of Law, National School of Law, UNAM. **d**-*Alternate Senator* from the State of Sonora, 1946–49; *Federal Deputy* from the State of Sonora, Dist. 1, 1949–51, member of the Gran Comision, the Second Legislative Studies Committee, the First Government Committee, the Securities Committee, and the First Labor Committee; *Senator* from the State of Sonora, 1952–58. **e**-State committeeman for PRI; coordinator for the presidential campaign of *Adolfo Lopez Mateos*, 1958. **f**-Lawyer, Legal Department, Secretary of Agriculture, 1940–42; Judge of the Superior Court of Justice of Sonora; Director, Legal Department, Secretariat of Government; private secretary to the Secretary of Government, *Hector Perez Martinez*, 1946–48, *Oficial Mayor of the Secretariat of Government* under *Gustavo Diaz Ordaz*, 1958–64; *Oficial Mayor of Agriculture*, 1964–65; *Subsecretary of Agriculture*, 1965–70. **g**-None. **h**-None. **i**-Married Dolores Hilton. **k**-None. **l**-HA, 8 Dec. 1958, 40; DPE61, 11; C de D, 1949–51, 83; *Libro de Oro*, xxxiii; WWMG, 31; DGF56, 7; DGF47, 21, 71; HA, 22 Dec. 1958, 7; Ind. Biog., 113–14.

Pamanes Escobedo, Aurelio

a-Aug. 3, 1903. **b**-Ojo Caliente, Zacatecas, *East Central*, *Urban*. **c**-Engineering degree from the National Military College; professor at the National Military College; professor at the Superior War College. **d**-*Federal Deputy* from the State of Zacatecas, Dist. 1, 1940–43. **e**-None. **f**-None. **g**-None. **h**-Director of many conferences on engineering tactics. **i**-Brother of *Fernando Pamanes Escobedo*, Oficial Mayor of the Secretariat of National Defense, 1958–64. **j**-Graduated as a career army officer. **k**-None. **l**-C de D, 1940–42; Peral, 613.

Pamanes Escobedo, Fernando

a-Feb. 19, 1909. **b**-Ojo Caliente, Zacatecas, *East Central*, *Urban*. **c**-Primary studies in Ojo Caliente; graduated from the National Military College, 1922–25; Captain of Cadets, National Military College, 1931; graduated from the Superior War College, 1932–36; professor of military tactics, National Military College. **d**-*Federal Deputy* from the State of Zacatecas, Dist. 4, 1955–58, member of the Committee on War Materiels, the First Committee on National Defense, the First Budget and Accounts Committee; substitute member of the Foreign Relations Committee; President of the Chamber, 1957; *Alternate Senator* from Zacatecas, 1964–70; *Governor of Zacatecas*, 1974–80. **e**-PRI delegate to Coahuila during the 1958 presidential campaign. **f**-Administrative Subchief of Staff of the Secretariat of National Defense, 1953–54; *Oficial Mayor of the Secretariat of National Defense*, 1958–64; Military Attache to China, 1944–46; *Ambassador to Cuba*, 1964–67; Ambassador to Indonesia, 1967–69. **g**-None. **h**-None. **i**-Brother *Aurelio Pamanes Escobedo* served as a Federal Deputy from Zacatecas, 1940–43; married Rafaela Beristain. **j**-Career army officer; participated in thirty-one battles in the Bajio region, 1925–31; stationed in Guerrero, 1938–40; member of the military staff of President *Avila Camacho*, 1942–43; Director of Civil Defense, Secretariat of National Defense, 1943; Chief of Staff of the Second Infantry Division, Guanajuato, 1947–49; Chief of Staff of the First Volunteer Infantry Division, 1949–53; Commander of the 39th Batallion, Tampico; Commander of the 5th Military Zone, Chihuahua, 1971–73; rank of Divisionary General. **k**-Most commentators did not believe he could capture the gubernatorial nomination in Zacatecas. **l**-McAlister, 224; C de D, 1940–42, 59; DPE61, 32; Peral, 613; DPE65, 25; DGF56, 29, 32, 35, 36; MGF69, 106; *Excelsior*, 26 Dec. 1973, 4; HA, 4 Mar. 1974, 45–46; Enc. Mex., Annual, 1977, 553; HA, 19 Aug. 1974, 36; *Excelsior*, 5 Feb. 1974, 9.

Pape, Harold R.

a-Dec. 12, 1903. **b**-Fort Wayne, Indiana, *Foreign*, *Urban*. **c**-Engineering degree from Purdue University, Lafayette, Indiana, 1925. **d**-None. **e**-None. **f**-Technical representative and Vice President for European Operations, ARMCO, Paris, France, 1926–44; *Gerente General of National Steel Industry*, 1946–70. **g**-None. **h**-Engineer, American Rolling Mills Company (ARMCO), Hamilton, Ohio, 1925–26; adviser to the Mexican government on the construction of a new mint; principal designer of Altos Hornos, 1941–44. **j**-None. **k**-Founder of the *Pape* Foundation which has financed a children's hospital, a grammar school, and a school for mechanical and electrical engineers in Mexico; *Pape* has held the subdirectorship of a major decentralized agency longer than any other person in Mexico from 1935 to 1980. l-Letter; DGF51, II, 231, 327.

Pardo Aspe, Emilio
(Deceased 1963)
a-1889. b-Federal District, *Federal District, Urban*. c-Studies in Belgium and France; law degree, National School of Law, UNAM; Professor of Penal Law, National School of Law, UNAM, 1932–35; Director of the National School of Law, 1935–38. d-None. e-None. f-Agent of the Ministerio Publico of the Office of the Attorney General of Mexico; *Justice of the Supreme Court*, 1941–46, 1947. g-None. h-Author of several legal studies; contributor to the magazine *Criminalia*. i-Son of Emilio Pardo Sabariego, Jr., prominent lawyer, judge and federal deputy. j-None. k-As Director of the Law School, was responsible for revising the curriculum and emphasizing public law. l-Letter; DP70, 1577.

Paredes Ramos, Higinio
a-Nov. 13, 1896. b-San Esteban Tizatlan, Tlaxcala, *East Central, Rural*. c-Primary studies in Tlaxcala, Tlaxcala; rural school teacher. d-*Senator* from the State of Tlaxcala, 1952–58, member of the National Properties and Resources Committee, First Secretary of the Second Navy Committee, Second Secretary of the First Public Works Committee, member of the First Balloting Group and President of the Second Ejido Committee. e-None. f-Adviser to the National Bank of Cooperative Development; Director of the Cooperative Society of Maritime Transportation. g-None. h-Organized the Cooperative Society of Maritime Transportation in Veracruz; member of the Merchant Marine in Veracruz. j-None. k-None. l-Ind. Biog., 115.

Parra (Gutierrez), Manuel German
a-May 7, 1914. b-Federal District, *Federal District, Urban*. c-Primary studies in Mexico, D.F.; preparatory studies at the National Preparatory School, 1931; studied law at the National School of Law, UNAM, 1932–34; degree in economics from the National School of Economics, UNAM, 1935–37; Ph.D. in economics, National School of Economics, UNAM, 1944–48; professor at UNAM. d-*Federal Deputy* from the Federal District, Dist. 11, 1979–82. e-None. f-President of the National Convention for Technical Education, 1940; head of a department, Secretariat of Public Education, 1941; economic adviser to the Presidency, 1943–46; *Subsecretary of Industry and Commerce*, 1946–48, under *Antonio Ruiz Galindo*; investigator under *Aguirre Beltran* for the Indigenous Coordinating Center, Tzeltal-Tzotzil Region, Chiapas, Secretariat of Public Education,

1951; coordinator of the Commission for Urban Development, 1972. g-Adviser to the Latin American Federation of Labor, 1943; leader in the SNTE; Secretary of the National Electoral Committee, SNTE, 1979. h-Author of many books on education and economics. i-Married Emilia Prado Huante. j-None. k-Resigned from the Secretariat of Industry and Commerce, Jan. 7, 1948, when his superior, *Ruiz Galindo* also resigned; precandidate for Secretary General of the FSTSE, 1979. l-HA, 7 Feb. 1972, 21; DGF51, II, 636; HA, 23 Jan. 1948, 35; HA, 27 Dec. 1946, 38; WWM45, 92; DGF47, 155; HA, 29 Oct. 1948, 1; HA, 18 Apr. 1952, 42; Lopez, 829; *Excelsior*, 24 Apr. 1979, 12.

Parres Guerrero, Jose G.
(Deceased July 5, 1949)
a-Dec. 15, 1889. b-Real Mineral del Monte, Hidalgo, *East Central, Urban*. c-Medical degree. d-Governor of Morelos, July 10, 1920 to Dec. 14, 1923. e-None. f-Subsecretary of the Agrarian Department, 1927; Subsecretary in charge of the Agrarian Department, 1927; Subsecretary of Agriculture and Livestock, 1933–34; *Subsecretary of Agriculture and Livestock*, 1934–37; *Secretary of Agriculture and Livestock*, Aug. 16, 1937, to Nov. 30, 1940; Minister to Ecuador, 1930–32; adviser to the National Agrarian Council, 1932; President of the National Irrigation Commission; executive member of the National Irrigation Commission, 1940–46. g-None. h-Practicing physician, 1914. j-Head of an Army Brigade in the Army of the South, 1916; head of Sanitary Services for the Army of the South, 1916–20. k-Removed from the Governorship of Morelos by a leading Zapatista, General De la O; resigned from the Agrarian Department to run for the governorship of Hidalgo, 1928, but not selected as the candidate; investigators from the Secretariat of Government considered *Parres* an honest Governor of Morelos. l-EBW46, 186; Womack, 367–81; Peral, 617; Enc. Mex., V, 44; DP70, 1088; Gruening, 659; Q es Q; Enc. Mex., X, 1977, 148–49.

Pasquel Jimenez Unda, Leonardo
a-Oct. 6, 1910. b-Jalapa, Veracruz, *Gulf, Urban*. c-Early education unknown; law degree, National School of Law, UNAM, 1940; two years of study in literature; secondary school teacher. d-None. e-None. f-Auditor, National Lottery; Assistant Director of the Legal Department, National Lottery; Director of Sales, National Lottery; Director, Federal Highway and Traffic Police; consulting attorney, Governor of Tlaxcala; *Oficial Mayor, Secretariat of Health*, 1945–46; President, National Council of Wheat, 1947; Justice of the Superior Tribunal of Justice of the Federal District and Federal Territories,

1956; Research Historian, Department of the Federal District, 1959. g-None. h-Author of many books. i-Married Alicia Lozano Barrios. j-None. k-None. l-WNM, 170–71; DGF56, 514.

Patino Navarrete, Jesus
(Deceased 1970)

a-1911. b-Tlalpujahua, Michoacan, *West Central*, *Rural*. c-Agricultural engineering degree, National School of Agriculture, Chapingo. d-None. e-None. f-Administrator of the National Bank of Foreign Commerce; Administrator of the National Commission of Maize; Subgerente of the National Bank of Ejido Credit; *Subsecretary of Agriculture and Livestock*, 1958–64; Subdirector of the National Bank of Mexico, 1964–70. g-None. h-The National School of Agriculture twice named *Patino Navarrete* the outstanding agronomist in Mexico. i-Married Elsa Nunez. j-None. k-Considered to have been one of Mexico's experts on forestry problems. l-DP70, 1585; DPE61, 69.

Patino Rodriguez, Julio

a-June 30, 1935. b-Jalapa, Veracruz, *Gulf, Urban*. c-Early education unknown; law degree. d-None. e-None. f-Investigative agent of the Ministerio Publico; Subdirector General of Government, Secretariat of Government, 1964; Director General of Legal Affairs, Secretariat of Government, 1969–70; Director General of Legal Affairs, President of Mexico, 1971–72; Director of Legal Affairs and Legislation, Secretariat of the Presidency, 1973–74; *Oficial Mayor of the Secretariat of the Presidency*, 1974–76. g-None. j-None. k-none. l-DPE65, 15; MGF73, 303; DPE71, 5; HA, 17 June 1974, 9–10; MGF69, 161.

Pawling (Dorantes), Alberto J.
(Deceased 1955)

a-July 25, 1887. b-Campeche, Campeche, *Gulf, Urban*. c-Engineering degree, Naval College, Veracruz, Veracruz. d-None. e-None. f-Director General of the Department of the Navy; Director of Ports, Department of the Navy; *Subsecretary of the Navy*, 1946–49; *Secretary of the Navy*, Oct. 21, 1949, to Feb. 7, 1952. g-Gerente of the Henequeneros de Yucatan. h-Author of various works on the construction of naval ports. i-Son, Alberto Jose Pawling Salazar, was a technician for the Department of Economic Studies, Bank of Mexico, 1961. j-Career navy officer; 1st Captain for twenty-five years. k-Considered an expert on merchant marine problems in Mexico; constructed numerous naval projects to improve Mexico's port system. l-DGF51, I, 379; DP70, 1561; HA, 15 Oct. 1948, 3; STYRBIWW54, 944; *Excelsior*, 20 Oct. 1949.

Pedrajo, Rafael M.

a-July 5, 1896. b-San Luis Potosi, *East Central*. c-Primary and secondary studies in San Luis Potosi; graduated from the National Military College. d-Mayor of Morelia, Michoacan, 1930–32. e-None. f-Private Secretary to General *Lazaro Cardenas* as Secretary of War, 1933; head of Services for the Chief of Police, Department of the Federal District, 1933–34; Director of the Traffic Department, Department of the Federal District, 1934–37; *Governor of Baja California del Sur*, 1937–40. g-None. h-None. i-Close friend of *Abelardo L. Rodriguez*. j-Joined the Revolution, 1919; fought under *Lazaro Cardenas*; career army officer; rank of Brigadier General. k-None. l-Peral, 621; *Hoy*, 21 Dec. 1946, 60–64; Cardenas, 175.

Pellicer, Carlos
(Deceased Feb. 16, 1977)

a-Nov. 23, 1899. b-Tabasco, *Gulf*. c-Primary studies in Mexico City; secondary studies at the Colegio del Rosario, Bogota, Colombia; studies at the IPN and at institutions in Paris and Rome in history and art; Professor of Modern Poetry, School of Philosophy and Letters, UNAM; secondary and preparatory teacher, Mexico City. d-*Senator* from the State of Tabasco, 1976–77. e-Supported Jose Vasconcelos for president, 1929. f-Director of the Department of Fine Arts, Secretariat of Public Education. g-None. h-Renowned poet and author; winner of the 1964 National Prize in Literature; founder of various museums. i-Never married; nephew Juan Pellicer Lopez was Ambassador to Iceland, 1977. j-None. k-Member of the innovative literary group, *Contemporaneos*, which included *Jaime Torres Bodet* and *Jose Gorostiza*. l-HA, 28 Feb. 1977, 12; *Proceso*, 19 Feb. 1977, 28; Enc. Mex., X, 1977, 195; DAPC, 55.

Peniche Bolio, Francisco Jose

a-Apr. 23, 1926. b-Merida, Yucatan, *Gulf, Urban*. c-Primary and secondary studies at the Colegio Montejo, Merida, Yucatan; preparatory studies at the Escuela Libre de Yucatan; law degree from the School of Law, University of Yucatan, Jan. 28, 1948, and law studies at the National School of Law, UNAM; LLD from the National School of Law, UNAM, April 29, 1969; Professor by Competition of Introduction to the Study of Law, National School of Law, UNAM, 1964– . d-*Federal Deputy* from PAN (party deputy), 1970–73, member of the Social Action Committee (1st year), the Tariff and Foreign Commerce Committee, the First Justice Committee, and the Sixth Agrarian Section of the Legislative Studies Committee; *Federal Deputy* from PAN (party deputy), 1976–79. e-Joined PAN, 1942; Secretary of the State Committee of PAN, Yucatan.

f-Secretary of Studies, Circuit Collegiate Courts, Mexico, D.F., 1968; Secretary of Studies, Supreme Court of Justice, 1969. g-None. h-Author of a basic text on law; practicing lawyer. i-Married Marilu Vazquez. j-None. k-Candidate for Federal Deputy from PAN, 1964. l-*Directorio*, 1970–72; C de D, 1970–72, 129–30; HA, 26 Feb. 1979, VI; C de D, 1976–79, 59.

Peraldi Ferrino, Laura

a-July 25, 1917. b-Cuatro Cienegas, Coahuila, *North*, *Rural*. c-Primary studies at La Corregidora, Saltillo, Coahuila (6 years); teaching certificate, Normal School, Saltillo; teacher, Orientation of Family Activities, Mexican Institute of Social Security. d-*Federal Deputy* from PARM (party deputy), 1970–73, member of the Library Committee (1st year) and the Instructive Committee for the Grand Jury (2nd Section). e-Member of PARM. f-None. g-None. h-None. i-Daughter of General Fernando Peraldi. j-None. k-None. l-*Directorio*, 1970–72; C de D, 1970–72, 130.

Perdomo (Garcia), D. Elpidio

a-March 4, 1896. b-Tlaquiltenango, Morelos, *West Central*, *Rural*. c-Early education unknown; no degree. d-*Alternate Senator* from the State of Morelos, 1934–38; *Governor of Morelos*, 1938–42; *Senator* from the State of Morelos, 1946–52, member of the Gran Comision and the Military Health Committee, substitute member of the Public Welfare Committee and the First Credit, Money, and Credit Institutions Committee; *Federal Deputy* from Morelos, Dist. 2, 1967–70, member of the Military Industries Committee; *Senator* from Morelos, 1970–76, member of the Gran Comision, president of the War Materiels Committee, First Secretary of the Second National Defense Committee. e-None. f-Inspector of Police, Monterrey, Nuevo Leon. g-None. h-None. j-Joined the Revolution; Zapatista; career army officer; reached rank of Brigadier General, June 16, 1942. k-His inauguration as governor was marked by violence. l-DGF51, 7, 9, 10, 11, 14; HA, 15 May 1942, 3; Peral, 627–28; MGF69, 93; C de D, 1967–69, 75; NYT, 3 May 1938, 10; C de S, 1970–76.

Perez Abreu Jimenez, Juan

c-Law degree from the National School of Law, UNAM, 1948. d-None. e-None. f-Private secretary to *Hugo Rangel Couto*, Subsecretary of National Patrimony, 1950; Director of Primary Level Planning Studies, City of Campeche, 1951–52; representative of the Secretariat of Government in the Reorganization of Immigration Offices for the Northern Border, 1954; Director of the Division of the Boards of Material, Moral, and Civic Improvements, Secretariat of Government; investigator of Political Affairs, Secretariat of Government, 1958; Director of Publications, Senate of Mexico; Administrative Director of nine Interparliamentary Congresses between Mexico and the United States; *Oficial Mayor of Communication and Transportation*, 1970–73; Director General of the Workers Cooperative Society of Clothing and Equipment, May 7, 1973 to 1976. g-Secretary General of the Student Society of the National Law School, 1945. j-None. k-None. l-HA, 14 Dec. 1970, 22; DGF51, I, 443; DPE71, 73; HA, 14 May 1973, 25; *El Nacional*, 18 Oct. 1945.

Perez Arce, Enrique

a-1888. b-El Rosario, Sinaloa, *West*, *Rural*. c-Secondary studies in Guadalajara; preparatory studies in Guadalajara and Mexico City; law degree. d-Federal Deputy from the State of Sinaloa, Dist. 4, 1932–34; *Governor of Sinaloa*, 1951–53. e-None. f-Provisional Governor of Nayarit; Justice of the Superior Tribunal of Justice of the Federal District, 1940; Judge of the Superior Tribunal of Justice of the State of Sinaloa, 1949; *Justice of the Supreme Court*, 1949–50. g-None. i-Father a lawyer. j-None. k-Forced to resign from governorship because of disputes with the Federal government over municipal elections and administrative incompetence according to Scott and Anderson. l-Scott, 277; DGF51, I, 88; HA, 19 Jan. 1951, 13–16; *Hoy*, 7 Mar. 1943, 6–7; Anderson.

Perez Camara, Carlos

a-1922. b-Campeche, Campeche, *Gulf*, *Urban*. c-Early education unknown; law degree, School of Law, University of Campeche. d-*Federal Deputy* from the State of Campeche, Dist. 1, 1964–67, member of the Gran Comision; *Senator* from the State of Campeche, 1970–76; President of the National Properties Committee, First Secretary of the Second Tariff and Foreign Trade Committee, Second Secretary of the First Treasury Committee, member of the Fifth Section of the Legislative Studies Committee, and member of the Second Balloting Group. e-None. f-Treasurer of the State of Campeche; Secretary General of Government of the State of Campeche; Syndic of the City Council of Campeche; Attorney, Department of Labor, State of Campeche; President of the Board of Conciliation and Arbitration, Campeche; *Interim Governor* of Campeche, 1973. g-Student leader of the Federation of Students of Campeche; President of the Rotary Club; Assistant Director of the Legal Department of the SNTE, Campeche; Delegate of CNOP. j-None. k-Precandidate for the PRI nomination for Mayor of Campeche. l-C de S, 1970–76, 83; C de D, 1964–67.

Perez Duarte, Constantino

(Deceased 1956)
a-Mar. 11, 1886. **b-**Pachuca, Hidalgo, *East Central, Urban.* **c-**Engineering degree from the National School of Engineering, UNAM. **d-**None. **e-**None. **f-**Technical consultant to the Secretariat of the Treasury, 1924–35; member of the Mexican Delegation to the London Economic Conference, 1931; and to the Economic Conference, Montevideo, 1934; adviser to Altos Hornos de Mexico, the National Railroads of Mexico; *Subsecretary of Industry and Commerce,* 1952–56. **g-**None. **h-**Metallurgist, Dos Estrellas Mining Company, 1911–14; Director of the Company Metalurgica Atotonilco El Chico, 1914–19; General Manager of the Golden Girl Mine, 1935–45; organizer of major mining operations; President of the Compania de Fomento Minero, S.A.; author of a book on silver mining. **i-**Son, Jorge Perez Duarte Sellerier, was Subdirector of the Division of Agriculture, Secretariat of Agriculture and Livestock, 1961; married Sara Sellerier. **j-**None. **k-**None. **l-**DP70, 1611; WWM45, 93; DPE61, 77; DGF51, II, 127.

Perez Gallardo, Reynaldo

a-Sept. 16, 1896. **b-**Ciudad Fernandez, San Luis Potosi, *East Central, Rural.* **c-**Early education unknown; no degree. **d-***Governor of San Luis Potosi,* 1939–41. **e-**None. **f-**None. **g-**None. **h-**Author of many works. **i-***Gilberto Flores Munoz* was his campaign manager for Governor; later, they became political enemies. **j-**Joined the Revolution; career army officer; rank of Brigadier General, May 1, 1938; fought against *Cedillo,* 1938. **k-**Removed from the governorship after a disastrous administration characterized by debts and accusations in the press of his being responsible for the murder of a sister of *Saturnino Cedillo,* Aug. 19, 1941. **l-**Letter; Peral47, 254–55; Correa41; Anderson, 332; NYT, 21 Aug. 1941, 8.

Perez Gasca, Alfonso

(Deceased 1964)
a-June 28, 1890. **b-**Pinotepa Nacional, Oaxaca, *South, Rural.* **c-**Primary studies in Oaxaca; secondary studies at the Institute of Arts and Sciences, Oaxaca; law degree from the Institute of Arts and Sciences, Oaxaca; professor at the Institute of Arts and Sciences; Director of the Institute of Arts and Sciences; Professor of Military Justice, National Military College. **d-**Federal Deputy from Oaxaca, 1920–22; *Federal Deputy* from the State of Oaxaca, Dist. 3, 1949–52, Secretary of the Gran Comision, member of the Legislative Studies Committee (1st and 2nd year), the Second Constitutional Affairs Committee, President of the Chamber of Deputies, Oct., 1949; *Senator* from Oaxaca, 1952–56, member

of the Gran Comision, Second Secretary of the Second Government Committee; President of the First Constitutional Affairs Committee and Second Secretary of the Social Security Committee; *Governor of Oaxaca,* 1956–62. **e-**None. **f-**Public defender in Veracruz, 1915–18; Oficial Mayor of the Tribunal Superior of Justice for the Federal District; Secretary of the Auxiliary Claims Commission (War Damages), 1918–23; Judge of the 5th District of the Federal District; Assistant Attorney General of the Federal District; *Justice of the Supreme Court of Mexico,* 1933–38; Secretary of Resolutions for the Military Tribunal of Justice; member of various legislative commissions for the Federal District, the Secretariat of the Treasury, and the Secretariat of Industry and Commerce. **g-**None. **h-**Author of many literary and scientific articles. **i-**Brother Flavio served as a Deputy to the Constitutional Congress, 1916–17, and later as a Federal Deputy from Oaxaca and Secretary General of the State. **j-**Assistant Director of the Department of Military Justice; Director of Military Justice during the Revolution; reached the rank of General in the Army. **k-**None. **l-**DP70, 1612; DGF56, 14; Peral, 632; C de D, 1949–51, 83; DGF51, I, 24, 27, 29, 32, 34; Peral, 633; Hayner, 211; Enc. Mex., X, 1977, 215; Lopez, 845; Ind. Biog., 117–118.

Perez H., Arnulfo

a-July 18, 1902. **b-**Chignahuapan, Alatriste, Puebla, *East Central, Rural.* **c-**Primary and secondary school in Chignahuapan; teaching certificate from the Normal School of Puebla, 1917; teacher in Puebla; MA degree in higher education; two years of law studies. **d-**Federal Deputy from the State of Puebla, Dist. 15, 1922–24, Federal Deputy from Tabasco, Dist. 1, 1932–34, member of the Gran Comision. **e-***Secretary of Labor Action of the CEN of the PNR,* 1936. **f-***Oficial Mayor of the Secretariat of Agriculture,* 1935–38; *Oficial Mayor of Public Education,* 1938–40; *Oficial Mayor of the Department of Agrarian Affairs,* 1940–46; Director of Education, State of Tabasco; Director of Education, State of Puebla; Customs Director, Ciudad Juarez, 1948; Customs Director, Tampico, Nuevo Laredo and Nogales. **h-**Widely published poet in Mexico. **i-**Political collaborator of *Garrido Canabal* in Tabasco. **j-**None. **k-**None. **l-**DBP, 525–26; DGF51, I, 162; CyT, 525–26; PS, 4844.

Perez Jacome, Dionisio

b-Veracruz, *Gulf.* **c-**Early education unknown; CPA degree from the University of Veracruz, Jalapa; law degree, School of Law, University of Veracruz, Jalapa. **d-**None. **e-**None. **f-**Delegate of the Secretariat of the Labor to Veracruz, Veracruz, 1965; Subdirector of Operations, CONASUPO, 1976–77;

Private Secretary to the Director General of CON-ASUPO, *Jorge de la Vega Dominguez*, 1977–79; *Subsecretary of Regulation*, Secretariat of Commerce, 1979– . **g-**None. **h-**Various positions in the state government of Veracruz; various positions in the Secretariat of the Treasury, the Secretariat of Government Properties, and the Secretariat of Labor. **j-**None. **k-**None. **l-***Excelsior*, 24 May 1979, 16; DGF65, 159.

Perez Martinez, Hector

(Deceased Feb. 13, 1948)
a-Mar. 21, 1906. **b-**Campeche, Campeche, *Gulf, Urban.* **c-**Primary and secondary studies at the Instituto Campechano, Campeche; preparatory studies at the National Preparatory School, Mexico, D.F., 1920; dental degree from the National School of Medicine, UNAM, 1928. **d-***Federal Deputy* from the State of Campeche, Dist. 1, 1937–39; *Governor of Campeche*, 1939–44. **e-**None. **f-**Style rewrite man for *El Nacional*, Mexico, D.F., 1929; reporter for *El Nacional*, 1929; Editor, *El Nacional*, 1931; Director of Information, *El Nacional*, 1932; Secretary of the Editorial Staff, *El Nacional*, 1935; Editor-in-Chief of *El Nacional*, 1936; Editor and Assistant Director of *El Nacional*, 1937; *Oficial Mayor of the Secretariat of Government*, 1945; *Subsecretary of Government*, June 18, 1945, to 1946; *Secretary of Government*, 1946–48. **g-**Member of the National Congress of Youth, 1926. **h-**Wrote a column for many years in the paper *El Universal* under the directorship of *Manlio Fabio Altamirano*; author of many books of poetry and biographies of Mexican leaders. **i-***Miguel Aleman* knew *Perez Martinez* as a student at UNAM; he was also a longtime friend of *Salvador Novo*; early political mentor to *Pedro Guerrero Martinez*, Justice of the Supreme Court. **j-**None. **k-**Considered by Brandenburg to be in the Inner Circle from 1939–48; defeated Senator *Gongora Gola* for the governorship of Campeche, 1939. **l-**EBW46, 179; WWM45, 93; DP70, 613; Peral, 634; HA, 20 Feb. 1948, 3; Brandenburg, 80, 102; Correa, 360; Informes, 1941, 1942, 1943; Enc. Mex., X, 1977, 216–17; Lopez, 848; Raby, 235.

Perez Moreno, Jose

a-Jan. 20, 1902. **b-**Jalisco, *West Central.* **c-**Secondary studies at the Padre Guerra Liceo; preparatory studies at the National Preparatory School; studies at the Higher School of Business; pre-med studies at the National School of Medicine, UNAM; no degree; Professor of Human Geography in various schools and institutes; founder of the Technical Police Institute. **d-***Federal Deputy* from the State of Jalisco, Dist. 5, 1958–61, member of the Bellas Artes Committee, the Protocol Committee, the

Editorial Committee (1st year), the First Public Education Committee, and the Third Section of the Legislative Studies Committee. **e-**Oficial Mayor of PRI. **f-**Department head, Secretariat of Hydraulic Resources; Consul General, Milan, Italy; *Oficial Mayor of Hydraulic Resources*, 1956–58. **g-**None. **h-**Became a journalist in 1916; Director of the *Mexico Nuevo*; wrote for *El Democrata*, *Hoy*, *El Sol*, and *El Universal*, *Siempre*, *Manana*, and *La Prensa*. **j-**None. **k-**None. **l-**DGF56, 411; Func., 244; C de D, 1958–60, 88; Enc. Mex., X, 1977, 217.

Perez Rios, Francisco

(Deceased Mar. 27, 1975)
a-Aug. 14, 1908. **b-**Temascaltepec, Mexico, *East Central, Rural.* **c-**Primary studies in Toluca and Mexico City; secondary and preparatory studies at the School of Mechanical and Electrical Engineering, IPN; completed fourth year of his professional studies in electrical engineering at IPN. **d-***Federal Deputy* from the State of Mexico, Dist. 5, 1952–55, member of the Library Committee, the Editorial Committee, the Legislative Studies Committee and the Electric Industry Committee; *Federal Deputy* from the State of Mexico, Dist. 5, 1958–61; member of the Railroad Committee, the Electric Industry Committee, the Budget Committee and the Labor Committee; *Federal Deputy* from the State of Mexico, Dist. 2, 1964–67, member of the Agricultural Development Committee, the Electric Industry Committee and the General Accounting Office Committee; *Senator* from the State of Mexico, 1970–75, member of the Gran Comision, First Secretary of the Second Committee on Credit, Money, and Credit Institutions, President of the Electric Industry Committee, Second Secretary of the First Navy and the Social Security Committees and First Secretary of the General Means of Communication Committee. **e-**None. **f-**Chief of Machinery, National Highway Commission; Chief of Machinery, National Irrigation Commission; Chief of Machinery, Federal Electric Commission; Magistrate of the Federal Board of Conciliation and Arbitration. **g-**Co-founder of the National Union of Government Electricians; Secretary General of the Union of Government Electricians; joined his union with the National Union of Electricians of Mexico, 1944; Secretary of Political Affairs of the CEN of the CTM, 1956–75; Secretary of Relations of the CEN of the CTM, 1950; *Secretary General of the National Union of Electricians*, 1944–72; *Secretary General of the Only Union of Electrical Workers* (SUTERM), 1972–75. **h-**Left IPN to work; one of the founding workers of the Federal Electric Commission, 1937. **i-**Close friend of *Fidel Velazquez*; married Rosa del Castillo. **j-**None. **k-**Participated in several labor movements and strikes in Guerrero, 1930s. **l-**Func.; C de S, 1970–76, 81;

Excelsior, 28 Mar. 1975, 1, 12; HA, 7 Apr. 1975, 12–13; C de D, 1964–67, 85, 89; C de D, 1958–61, 88; C de D, 1952–55, 46, 49, 52, 56.

Perez Vela, Juan

a-Feb. 27, 1916. **b-**Celaya, Guanajuato, *West Central*, *Urban*. **c-**Medical degree, National School of Medicine, UNAM, 1942. **d-**Mayor of Valle de Santiago, 1948–49; *Federal Deputy* from the State of Guanajuato, Dist. 6, 1961–64, member of the Committee on Bellas Artes, the Fifth Section on Labor of the Legislative Studies Committee, the Agricultural Development Committee; *Senator* from the State of Guanajuato, 1964–70. **e-**Many positions in PRI organizations. **f-**Director of the Center of Hygiene of the Regional Hospital, Valle de Santiago, 1944–49; *Oficial Mayor of Agriculture*, 1970–72. **g-**None. **h-**None. **j-**None. **k-**Resigned as Oficial Mayor of Agriculture, Aug. 2, 1972. **l-**HA, 14 Dec. 1970, 22; 14 Aug. 1972, 24; C de S, 1964–70; C de D, 1961–63, 87; DPE71, 63.

Perez (y Perez), Celestino

a-Jan. 21, 1892. **b-**Tlacolula de Matamoros, Oaxaca, *South*, *Rural*. **c-**Primary studies at the Pestalozzi Normal School, Oaxaca; preparatory studies from the Institute of Arts and Sciences of Oaxaca; law degree, Institute of Arts and Sciences of Oaxaca, Aug., 1914; Rector of the Institute of Arts and Sciences of Zacatecas. **d-***Senator* from the State of Oaxaca, 1970–76, President of the Second Constitutional Affairs Committee, Secretary of the Second Section of the Grand Jury, Second Secretary of the Second Treasury Committee, First Secretary of the Third Labor Committee, member of the Second Balloting Group and member of the Third Section of the Legislative Studies Committee. **e-**None. **f-**Syndic of the First Revolutionary Government of Oaxaca, 1916; Agent of the Ministerio Publicio in Istmo, Oaxaca and elsewhere, 1918–30; Attorney General of Zacatecas; President of the Board of Conciliation and Arbitration, Baja California del Norte; Secretary of the Federal Board of Conciliation and Arbitration; General Counsel for the PEMEX employees, 1946–53; Judge of the 1st Mixed Court of Appeals, Baja California del Norte; public defender, Zacatecas. **g-**None. **j-**Supported Madero, 1909. **k-**Precandidate for the PRI nomination for senator from Oaxaca, 1958. **l-**C de S, 1970–76, 83.

Pesqueira de Endara, Manuel E.

a-Dec. 18, 1901. **b-**Hermosillo, Sonora, *North*, *Urban*. **c-**Early education unknown; medical degree from the National School of Medicine, UNAM, 1920–25; Professor of Medicine, National School of Medicine, UNAM, 1931–52. **d-**None. **e-**None. **f-**Physician, General Hospital, Mexico City, 1931–

52; *Subsecretary of Health*, 1952–58. **g-**President of the Mexican Society of Urology, 1948–59. **h-**Author of numerous medical articles. **i-**Son of lawyer Jose de Jesus Pesqueira; married Carmen Olea, 1927. **j-**None. **k-**None. **l-**DGF56, 332; HA, 16 May 1955, 5; letter; WNM, 175.

Petricioli (Iturbide), Gustavo

a-Aug. 19, 1928. **b-**Federal District, *Federal District*, *Urban*. **c-**Degree in economics from the Technological Institute of Mexico, 1952; studies at the English Language Institute, University of Michigan, 1955; Master of Arts in Economics, Yale University, 1955–58; Professor of Monetary Theory, Technological Institute of Mexico, 1959; Professor of Monetary Theory, UNAM. **d-**None. **e-**None. **f-**Assistant economist, Bank of Mexico, 1948; economist, Department of Economic Studies, Bank of Mexico, 1948–51; economist, National Price Commission, 1951–52; economist, Bank of Commerce, 1952–55; economist to the Director of the Bank of Mexico, 1958; Director of the Technical Office, Bank of Mexico; Gerente, Bank of Mexico; Director General of Treasury Studies, Secretariat of the Treasury, 1967–70; *Subsecretary of the Treasury*, 1970 to Oct. 10, 1974; Subdirector of the Bank of Mexico, 1975–76; President of the National Securities Commission, 1976– . **g-**None. **h-**None. **i-**Married Rosa Morales. **j-**None. **k-**None. **l-**B de M, 210; HA, 14 Dec. 1970, 20; DPE71, 27; HA, 21 Oct. 1974, 21.

Pichardo Pagaza, Ignacio

a-Nov. 13, 1935. **b-**Toluca, Mexico, *West Central*, *Urban*. **c-**Primary studies from the Colegio Mexico; secondary and preparatory studies from the Centro Universitario Mexico, Mexico City; economics degree, National School of Economics, UNAM; degree in industrial relations, Latin American University; special studies, Dartmouth College; MA in economics from the School of Economics, University of London. **d-***Federal Deputy* from the State of Mexico, Dist. 4, 1967–70; *Federal Deputy* from the State of Mexico, Dist. 27, 1979–82. **e-**Editor of the newspaper for the PRI Youth Sector, 1958; participated in the 1964 presidential campaign; member of the IEPES of PRI; member of the Technical Council of Economists, CEN of PRI; Secretary of Press and Publicity of the National Youth Sector of PRI, 1959–61. **f-**Director, Department of Publications, National Foreign Trade Bank, 1965–67; Editor, *Comercio Exterior*; Director of the Department of Utilities, Secretariat of the Treasury; Subdirector, Income Tax Department, Secretariat of the Treasury; *Subsecretary of Revenues*, 1976–78. **g-**Member of the Technical Council of the CNC, 1966. **h-**Official in the state government of Mexico under Governor

Hank Gonzalez. **i-**Son of Carlos Pichardo, lawyer and federal deputy from the State of Mexico. **j-**None. **k-**None. **l-***Excelsior*, 18 Jan. 1978, 4; letter.

Pimentel, Rafael S.
(Deceased 1954)
a-1909. **b-**Colima, *West*, *Urban*. **c-**Teaching certificate; taught in Nayarit and Guanajuato. **d-***Federal Deputy* from the Federal District, Dist. 1, 1949–52, member of the First Committee on General Means of Communication, the Committee on Cooperative Development, the Second General Accounting Committee, and the Auto Transportation Committee; *Senator* from the State of Colima, 1952–54. **e-**President of the National Transportation Commission for the campaign of *Adolfo Ruiz Cortines* for President. **f-**None. **g-**Secretary General of the Mexican Alliance of Truckdrivers; Secretary of Interior of the Mexican Alliance of Truckdrivers; President of the Mexican Alliance of Truckdrivers. **h-**None. **j-**None. **k-**None. **l-**DP70, 633; C de S, 1952–58; C de D, 1949–51, 84; DGF51, I, 20, 30, 33, 35, 36; Enc. Mex., X, 1977, 311.

Pineda (Pineda), Salvador
a-Jan. 1, 1916. **b-**Nucupetaro, Michoacan, *West Central*, *Rural*. **c-**Early education unknown; law degree, National School of Law, UNAM; MA in history, School of Philosophy and Letters, UNAM. **d-***Federal Deputy* from the State of Michoacan, Dist. 6, 1949–52, member of the First Public Education Committee, the Legislative Studies Committee, the Second Government Committee, the Foreign Relations Committee, and the Gran Comision; *Federal Deputy* from the State of Michoacan, Dist. 7, 1955–58, member of the Gran Comision and the Committee on Etiquette. **e-***Secretary of Political Action of the CEN of PRI*, 1952; *Oficial Mayor of the CEN of PRI*, 1959–63. **f-**Subdirector of Civic Action, Department of the Federal District; Private Secretary to the Attorney General of Mexico; Subdirector of the National Institute of Fine Arts; Judge of the Federal Tax Court. **g-**None. **i-**Son *Raul Pineda Pineda* elected as a federal deputy from the State of Michoacan, 1979–82. **j-**None. **k-**None. **l-**DGF51, I, 23, 29, 33, 34, 36; C de D, 1949–52, 84; C de D, 1955–58; DGF56; Ind. Biog., 121.

Pintado Borrego, Fausto
a-1921. **b-**Tacotalpa, Tabasco, *Gulf*, *Rural*. **c-**Primary and secondary studies in Villahermosa, Tabasco; preparatory studies at the National Preparatory School; law degree from the National School of Law, UNAM, 1948; teacher of civics in secondary school; Professor of Administrative Law, School of Law, University of Tabasco. **d-***Senator* from the State of Tabasco, 1964–70. **e-**None. **f-**First

Appeals Court Judge, Tenango de Doria, Ciudad Teapa, Ciudad Hidalgo and Frontera, Tabasco; legal adviser to the State Government of Tabasco; Justice of the Superior Tribunal of Justice of the State of Tabasco; President of the Superior Tribunal of Justice of the State of Tabasco; Subdirector of Government of the State of Tabasco, 1962–63. **g-**None. **h-**Co-author of the Legal Code of Tabasco, 1959. **i-**Member of *Carlos Madrazo*'s political group. **j-**None. **k-**None. **l-**C de S, 1964–70; MGF69.

Pizano Saucedo, Roberto
a-Apr. 14, 1923. **b-**Colima, Colima, *West*, *Urban*. **c-**Primary and secondary education at the public schools, Colima; graduated as a private accountant. **d-***Alternate Federal Deputy* from the State of Colima, Dist. 2, 1952–55; *Federal Deputy* from the State of Colima, Dist. 2, 1955–58; President of the Chamber of Deputies, 1957, member of the Gran Comision, the Fourth Ejido Committee; *Alternate Senator* from the State of Colima, 1958–64; *Senator* from the State of Colima, 1970–76; Mayor of Colima, 1978– . **e-**President of the State Regional Committee of PRI, Colima; Secretary General of the IEPES of PRI, Colima, Colima. **f-**Employee, Federal Treasury Office, Colima, 1937–39; Assistant Census Office, 1939–40; Secretary of the First Civil Court District, Colima; Secretary of the First Criminal Appeals Court, Colima; Federal Delegate of the Secretariat of Industry and Commerce; representative of the ISSSTE in Colima. **g-**Member of the National Union of Social Security and Public Welfare Workers; Secretary of Organization of Section 52 of the Union of Workers of the Secretariat of Public Works, 1944–47; representative of the CEN of the CNC to the National Institute of Better Nourishment. **h-**Postal Assistant, 1944–47; Telegrapher, 1947; Director of the weekly newspaper, *La Voz*, and *El Regional*, Colima; Director General of the *Diario de Colima*. **i-**First cousin of *Arturo Noriega Pizano*, Governor of Colima. **j-**None. **k-**None. **l-**DBM68, 493–94; C de D, 1952–54, 17; DGF56, 22, 30, 33; *Excelsior*, 4 Nov. 1978, 17; Ind. Biog., 121–22.

Pizarro Suarez (Mercado), Nicolas
a-Oct. 19, 1907. **b-**Federal District, *Federal District*, *Urban*. **c-**Primary studies at the Colegio Ingles, Mexico, D.F.; secondary studies at the Colegio Mexicano, Mexico, D.F.; preparatory studies at the National Preparatory School; law degree, National School of Law, UNAM, May 31, 1932, with a thesis on judicial value of damages; Professor of Civil and of Labor Law, National School of Law, UNAM. **d-**None. **e-**None. **f-**President of the Local Board of Conciliation and Arbitration, Merida, Yucatan; *Director General of Civil Pensions* (forerunner of ISSSTE), 1953–60; *Director General of the ISSSTE*,

1960–64. **g**-None. **h**-Practicing lawyer, 1964–76; Gerente of the Association of Insurance Institutions; Subgerente of the National Insurance Company, S.A.; author of several books. **i**-Son of a lawyer; student assistant to *Agustin Garcia Lopez*. **j**-None. **k**-None. **l**-HA, 7 Mar. 1960, 9; *Siempre*, 4 Feb. 1959, 6; HA, 10 Dec. 1962, 20–21; WNM, 176.

Portes Gil, Emilio
(Deceased Dec. 10, 1978)
a-Oct. 3, 1890. **b**-Ciudad Victoria, Tamaulipas, *North*, *Urban*. **c**-Primary studies in Ciudad Victoria; secondary studies at the Normal School, Ciudad Victoria, 1906–10; law studies, Escuela Libre de Derecho, 1912–14, degree in 1915; professor of primary schools, Ciudad Victoria, 1910–12; Professor of Agrarian Legislation, School of Law, UNAM, 1930. **d**-Federal Deputy from Tamaulipas, 1916–17, 1921–22, and 1924–25; Governor of Tamaulipas, 1925–28. **e**-President of the CEN of PRI, Apr. 22, 1930, to Oct. 15, 1930; *President of the CEN of PRI*, June 15, 1935, to Aug. 20, 1936; founder of the Partido Socialista Fronterizo, Tamaulipas. **f**-First Official of the Department of War and Navy, 1914; Subchief of the Department of Military Justice, Department of War and Navy, 1915; Judge of the 1st Instance, Civil Section, Hermosillo, Sonora; Judge of the Superior Tribunal of Justice of Sonora, 1916; consulting lawyer to the Secretary of War, 1917; Secretary General of Government of the State of Tamaulipas, 1918–19; Provisional Governor of Tamaulipas, 1920; general lawyer for the National Railroads of Mexico, 1921–22; President of Mexico, Dec. 1, 1928, to Feb. 5, 1930; Secretary of Government, Aug., to Dec., 1928; Secretary of Government, June to Nov., 1930; Minister to France, 1931–32; delegate to the League of Nations, 1931–32; Attorney General of Mexico, 1932–34; Secretary of Foreign Relations, 1934–35; Special Ambassador to the Dominican Republic, 1944; Special Ambassador to Ecuador, 1946; First Ambassador from Mexico to India, 1951; President of the National Securities Committee, 1959; adviser to the Constructora Nacional de Carros de Ferrocarril, S.A., 1966; President of the Advisory Technical Committee, National Banking Commission, 1970. **g**-None. **h**-Author of books on the Church, labor, and politics in Mexico. **i**-Attended the Escuela Libre de Derecho with *Francisco Javier Gaxiola* and *Ezequiel Padilla*; married Carmen Garcia. **j**-Administrative positions during the Revolution. **k**-One of the founders of the Escuela Libre de Derecho. **l**-Letter; DBM68, 495–96; Gaxiola, 12, etc.; letter; Brandenburg, 80, 63; Peral, 648; WWM45, 94; Daniels, 43, 104; IWW40, 912; DP70, 1663–64; Strode, 28, 87; Dulles; Enc. Mex., X, 405–06; *Justicia*, Aug., 1970; HA, 18 Dec. 1978, 17–18.

Posada, Angel
(Deceased 1976)
a-1890. **b**-Parral, Chihuahua, *North*, *Urban*. **c**-Agricultural engineering degree, Agricultural College, Ciudad Juarez. **d**-Federal Deputy from the State of Chihuahua, Dist. 5, 1932–34, member of the Gran Comision; *Senator* from the State of Chihuahua, 1934–38. **e**-Secretary of Agrarian Action of the CEN of the PNR, 1934. **f**-Oficial Mayor of the State Government of Chihuahua; Oficial Mayor of the National Agrarian Commission, 1933–34; Director of the Agrarian Department, 1934. **g**-None. **h**-None. **j**-None. **k**-Assassinated during his campaign for Governor of Chihuahua. **l**-DP70, 1665; Peral, 650; C de S, 1934–40; Enc. Mex., X, 1977, 411.

Pozo, Agapito
(Deceased 1976)
a-Apr. 21, 1899. **b**-Queretaro, Queretaro, *East Central*, *Urban*. **c**-Primary studies with the La Sallists Brothers; preparatory studies at the Colegio Civil of Queretaro; law degree from the Colegio Civil of the State of Queretaro, 1923; Rector of the University of Queretaro, 1970–72. **d**-*Senator* from the State of Queretaro, 1940–43; *Governor of Queretaro*, 1943–49. **e**-State committeeman for PRI. **f**-Agent of the Ministerio Publico in Leon, Guanajuato, 1924–26; Civil Judge; Judge of the Superior Tribunal of Justice of the State of Guanajuato; Justice of the Superior Tribunal of the Federal District and Federal Territories, 1940; Secretary of the City Council of Leon, Guanajuato; Secretary of the City Council of Queretaro; Secretary of Government of the State of Queretaro; Director of the Administrative Office, Chief of Police for the Federal District; private secretary to the Chief of Police of the Federal District; private secretary to the head of the Federal District; agent of the Ministerio Publico of the Office of the Attorney General; *Justice of the Supreme Court of Mexico*, 1950–52, 1952–58, and 1958–64; *President of the Supreme Court*, 1958, 1964–68. **g**-None. **h**-Practicing attorney. **i**-Son of a lawyer. **j**-None. **k**-None. **l**-DBM68, 497; WWMG, 32; HA, 14 Apr. 1958, 8; DGF56, 568; Peral, 651–52; DGF51, I; Enc. Mex., X, 1977, 420; Casasola, V, 2422; *Justicia*, Aug., 1967.

Prado (Proano), Eugenio
(Deceased 1969)
a-Nov. 12, 1897. **b**-San Buenaventura, Chihuahua, *North*, *Rural*. **c**-Primary studies at the public school attached to the State Normal School, Chihuahua; no degree. **d**-Local deputy to the State Legislature of Chihuahua, 1934–35; Mayor of Chihuahua, 1935; *Federal Deputy* from the State of Chihuahua, Dist. 1, 1937–40; *Senator* from the State of Chihuahua,

1940–46, President of the Senate, president of the First Government Committee and the Treasury Committee, member of the Gran Comision; *Federal Deputy* from the State of Chihuahua, Dist. 1, 1946–49, President of the Permanent Committee of Congress, 1949, member of the First Committee on Government, the First Treasury Committee. e-None. f-Director of the Cooperative Sugar Mill of Zacatepec, Morelos; Director of the Cooperative Ejido Mill Emiliano Zapata, 1951; Interim Governor of Chihuahua. h-None. j-None. k-None. l-C de D, 1946–48, 84; DGF51, Ii; WWMG, 94; Peral, 651; DP70, 1669; C de S, 1940–46; C de D, 1937–39, 17; Lopez, 874; *Excelsior*, 8 July 1949; Enc. Mex., X, 1977, 420.

Preciado Hernandez, Rafael

a-Apr. 29, 1908. b-Cucupiapa, El Grullo, Jalisco, *West*, *Rural*. c-Early education unknown; law degree, University of Guadalajara, 1930; Professor, Normal School for Women, Guadalajara, Jalisco, 1930–32; Professor, University of Guadalajara, 1931–33; Professor, Autonomous University of Guadalajara, 1934–35; Professor of Law, Free Law School, Mexico City, 1937–70; Professor of Law, National School of Law, UNAM, 1941–70. d-*Federal Deputy* (Party Deputy for PAN), 1967–70, member of the Department of the Federal District Committee, the Constitutional Affairs Section of the Legislative Studies Committee and the Second Balloting Committee. e-Representative to the Federal Electoral Commission from PAN, 1953–58; founding member of the National Council of PAN, 1939; member of the CEN of PAN, 1939, 1947–70; Director of the Regional Committee of PAN in the Federal District, 1943–46. f-Civil Judge, Guadalajara, 1933. g-None. h-Practicing lawyer. i-Married Carmen Briseno. j-None. k-Responsible for recruiting many prominent members of PAN from his law classes. l-WNM, 178; Mabry; C de D, 1967–70.

Priego Ortiz, Luis

a-Aug. 19, 1929. b-Villahermosa, Tabasco, *Gulf*, *Urban*. c-Early education unknown; law degree, National School of Law, UNAM; certificate in political science from the University of Paris; Professor at UNAM. d-*Federal Deputy* from the Federal District, Dist. 11, 1964–67, member of the Forest Affairs Committee, the Government Committee, the Labor Section of the Legislative Studies Committee, and the Constitutional Affairs Committee; *Federal Deputy* from the State of Tabasco, Dist. 1, 1976–79. e-General Delegate of the CEN of PRI to Hidalgo and Michoacan; Political Adviser to the CEPES of PRI in the Federal District; member of the Editorial Committee to revise the declaration of principles of PRI. f-Delegate of Ixtapalapa, 1966–70; employee

of the Secretariat of Agriculture. g-None. i-None. k-None. l-C de D, 1964–67, 79, 84, 92; C de D, 1976–79; D de C, 1976–79; *Excelsior*, 1 Sept. 1976, 1C.

Prieto Fortun, Guillermo

a-June 10, 1935. b-Federal District, *Federal District*, *Urban*. c-Early education unknown; economics degree, National School of Economics, UNAM, 1953–57, graduating in 1960 with an honorable mention; degree in business administration from the Panamerican Institute. d-None. e-None. f-Economist, Income Tax Division, Secretariat of the Treasury, 1955; Subdirector of the Department of Technical Calculations, Secretariat of the Treasury; Adviser to *Hugo B. Margain*, Oficial Mayor of Industry and Trade, 1960–62; Adviser to *Hugo B. Margain*, Subsecretary of Industry and Trade, 1962–63; Adviser to the First National Committee for the Participation of Workers in the Utilities Industry, 1963–64; economist, Department of Workers Participation in Utilities, Secretariat of Labor, 1964–70; Director General of the Income Tax Division, 1970–76; Director General of Tax Administration, Secretariat of the Treasury, 1976–78; *Subsecretary of Revenues*, Secretariat of the Treasury, January 17, 1978– . g-None. h-None. i-Protege of *Hugo B. Margain*. j-None. k-None. l-Letter; DAPC, 77, 57.

Prieto Laurens, Jorge

a-May 2, 1895. b-San Luis Potosi, San Luis Potosi, *East Central*, *Urban*. c-Primary studies in private Catholic schools, San Luis Potosi; preparatory studies at the National Preparatory School, 1909–13; no degree. d-Council member of the first City Council of the Federal District; Federal Deputy from the Federal District, Dist. 11 (representing the Cooperatist Party), 1922–23, President of the Chamber of Deputies; Mayor of the Federal District, 1923; Governor of San Luis Potosi, 1923. e-President of the Cooperatist Party, 1923–24; political supporter (civilian) of the Adolfo de la Huerta rebellion, 1923; political supporter of Jose Vasconcelos for president, 1928–29; supporter (civilian) of the Escobar rebellion, 1929; President of the National Independent Party, 1938; Secretary General of the National Democratic Party which supported *Ezequiel Padilla* for president, 1945–46. f-Department head, Secretary of Industry and Commerce, 1935. g-Student leader in 1910; led a student movement against Victoriano Huerta, 1913. h-Director of *La Tribuna*, Houston, Texas. i-Son of engineer Antonio Prieto Trillo. j-Fought in the Revolution with Zapata's forces; aide to the General Staff of General *Enrique Estrada*; military commander of Zacatecas; participant in taking the city of

Guadalajara, 1920. **k-**In exile in the United States, 1923–33. **l-**Lopez; C de D, 1922–24, 33; Casasola, V; Enc. Mex., V, 1977, 431.

Puente Leyva, Jesus

a-Sept. 24, 1937. **b-**Federal District, *Federal District*, *Urban*. **c-**Primary and secondary studies in the Federal District; economic studies at the University of Nuevo Leon, 1958–63, economics degree in 1966; Professor of Economic Development and the Sociology of Development at the University of Nuevo Leon, 1966–69; postgraduate work in the field of general economic planning, the Latin American Institute of Planning of ECLA, Mar. to Dec., 1964; studies at Harvard University, summer, 1965; Master of Arts in Economics from Williams College, in the field of economic development, 1965–66, degree, July, 1966; Professor of Economic Development, National School of Economics, UNAM, 1969–72; Subdirector of the Center for Economic Studies, University of Nuevo Leon. **d-***Federal Deputy* from the State of Nuevo Leon, 1976–79, member of the Gran Comision. **e-**None. **f-**Economic investigator for the Center for Economic Investigations, University of Nuevo Leon, 1966–69; research specialist in urban economics, Office of Planning, State of Nuevo Leon, 1966–69; technical adviser to the Secretariat of Public Works, 1971–72; adviser to the Presidency; *Subdirector of the National Finance Bank*, May, 1972, to 1976. **g-**None. **h-**Author of numerous articles and pamphlets on urban problems; winner of the National Prize for Economics, 1968. **i-**Father a businessman; married Doctor Blanca Trevino Garza; student of *Raul Rangel Frias* at the University of Nuevo Leon. **j-**None. **k-**None. **l-**HA, 15 May 1972, 31; letters; *Latin America*, 12 Mar. 1976, 83.

Pulido Islas, Alfonso

a-Aug. 13, 1907. **b-**Ixtlan, Nayarit, *West*, *Urban*. **c-**Primary studies in Ixtlan; secondary studies at the Catholic Seminary of Tepic and in Guadalajara; preparatory studies at the preparatory school of Jalisco at the University of Guadalajara; law studies at the University of Guadalajara; degree in economics from the National School of Economics, UNAM, April 15, 1939, with a thesis on the "Cinematography Industry of Mexico;" professor at the National School of Economics, UNAM; Director of the National School of Economics, UNAM, 1942–44; professor at the National School of Law, UNAM; professor at the School of Philosophy and Letters, UNAM; professor at the National School of Commerce, UNAM; Director, Institute of Social Investigations, UNAM. **d-**None. **e-**Member of the League of Professionals and Intellectuals of PRI; member of the IEPES of PNR, 1933–39; founding member of PNR, 1929.

f-Director, Office of Economic Statistics, Director General of Statistics, 1935–36; Oficial Mayor of PIPSA, 1937–39; Director of the Federal Department of Labor Inspection, 1939–40; Subdirector of the National Council of Economics, 1940–41; Subdirector General of the National Commission of Economic Planning, 1941–42; Director General of the Federal Board of Economic Planning, 1942; organizer and Director of the Small Business Bank, 1943–50; Director, Department of Alcohol, Department of the Federal District, 1950–53; Gerente of Mexican Cinema, S.A., Secretariat of Government, 1953–58; Comptroller General of the Secretariat of National Patrimony, 1961–64; Subdirector of Administration, IMSS, 1964–65; adviser, Secretariat of the Treasury, 1965–74. **g-**Director of the Workers Federation of Jalisco, 1925–29; Secretary General of the Revolutionary Group "Claridad," 1934–44; Director of the League of Revolutionary Professionals, Popular Sector of PNR, 1935; founder and Director of the Front of Revolutionary Economists, 1936; organizer and President of the National Federation of Students for Obregon, 1927–28. **h-**Author of many books. **i-**Father, a campesino and laborer, became a self-educated artisan; attended UNAM with *Sealtiel Alatriste*. **j-**None. **k-**None. **l-**WWM45, 95; DPE61, 56; DGF51; DGF56; letters; Lopez, 887; Enc. Mex., X, 1977, 566.

Quevedo Moreno, Guillermo

a-May 6, 1911. **b-**Casas Grandes, Chihuahua, *North*, *Urban*. **c-**Early education unknown; no degree. **d-**Local Deputy to the State Legislature of Chihuahua; *Federal Deputy* from the State of Chihuahua, Dist. 2, 1937–40; *Federal Deputy* from the State of Chihuahua, Dist. 4, 1943–46; *Federal Deputy* from the State of Chihuahua, Dist. 5, 1955–58, member of the Gran Comision, the Livestock Committee and the Second National Defense Committee. **e-**None. **f-**None. **g-**None. **i-**Father a small businessman; brother of *Rodrigo Quevedo Moreno*, Governor of Chihuahua, 1932–36, and Senator from Chihuahua, 1958–64. **j-**None. **k-**None. **l-**Ind. Biog., 123–24; C de D, 1955–58; DGF56, 22, 30, 32, 33; C de D, 1943–46; C de D, 1937–40.

Quevedo Moreno, Rodrigo M.

(Deceased Jan. 18, 1967)
a-Nov. 29, 1889. **b-**Casas Grandes, Chihuahua, *North*, *Urban*. **c-**Early education unknown; no degree. **d-***Governor of Chihuahua*, 1935; *Senator* from the State of Chihuahua, 1958–64, member of the Gran Comision, the Third Committee on National Defense, and the Agricultural Development Committee; substitute member of the Immigration Committee, the Second Committee on Mines, and the First Balloting Committee. **e-**None. **f-**None. **g-**None.

h-None. i-Relative, *Guillermo Quevedo Moreno*, served as Federal Deputy from Chihuahua, Dist. 2, 1943–46; father, a small businessman. j-Joined the Revolution under Pascual Orozco, 1911; fought with Orozco against Madero, 1912–13; fought under Juan G. Cabral; joined Villa's forces, 1917; fought with *Juan Andreu Almazan* against the Constitutionalists; supported the Obregon movement, 1920; fought against the De la Huerta rebellion, 1923; rank of Divisionary General, Apr. 2, 1929; Commander of the 4th Cavalry Brigade under *Almazan* which fought against the Escobar Rebellion, 1929; Commander of the 25th Military Zone, Puebla, Puebla, 1938; Commander of the 1st Military Zone, Federal District, 1941–45; Commander of the 22nd Military Zone, Toluca, Mexico, 1934; Commander of the 8th Military Zone, Tampico, Tamaulipas, 1951–56. k-Participated in the Flores Magon movement, 1908; *New York Times* reported that he was arrested in 1938 in connection with the killing of a state politician; Meyer reports that there was little local support for his selection as governor in 1935. l-D de Y, 5 Sept. 1935, 1; DGF56, 201; DGF51, I, 183; Peral, 658; C de S, 1961–64, 66; WWM45, 95; NYT, 27 July 1935, 14; NYT, 13 Mar. 1938, 28; Enc. Mex., XI, 1977, 3; Ind. Biog., 123–24.

Quintanilla (Lerdo de Tejada), Luis
(Deceased Mar. 16, 1980)
a-Nov. 22, 1900. b-Paris, France, *Foreign, Urban*. c-Undergraduate and graduate studies in philosophy and letters at the Sorbonne, Paris; Ph.D. in Political Science; professor at the Dr. Mora Secondary School; Professor of English at the National Preparatory School; Professor of International Organizations and Political Parties at UNAM; lecturer at Johns Hopkins University, Williams College, the University of Virginia, and the University of Kansas; Professor of Political Science, George Washington University, 1937–42; professor at the School of Political and Social Sciences, UNAM, 1968. d-None. e-None. f-Joined the Foreign Service, 1922; Second Protocol Assistant, 1922; Third Assistant for Protocol, 1924; Third Secretary, Guatemala, 1926; Second Secretary, Guatemala, 1926; Second Secretary, Brazil, 1927; Second Secretary, Washington, D.C.; General Secretary of the Mexican Delegation to the League of Nations, 1932; First Secretary, United States, 1942; Ambassador to the Soviet Union, 1942–45; Inspector General of Languages for Technical and Elementary Schools, Secretariat of Public Education; Chairman, Fact Finding Committee to Central America, 1948; Chairman, Inter-American Peace Commission, 1948–49; Ambassador to Colombia, 1945; delegate to the United Nations Conference, San Francisco, 1945; *Ambassador to the Organization of American States*, 1945–58; Director

General of the National Housing Institute, 1958–64. g-None. h-Adviser to the Center for Study of Democratic Institutions, Santa Barbara; author of several books. i-From a wealthy family; father was an artist who lived in Paris, supported the denunciation of Victoriano Huerta by Mexican residents in France; married Ruth Stallsmith; good friend of *Antonio Rocha*. j-None. k-None. l-STYRBIWW, 54, 962; *Quien Sera*, 1953–55; Kirk, 12; WWM45, 96; DGF51, I, 110; DGF56, 128; DBM68, 502–03; WWMG, 33; Enc. Mex., XI, 1977, 30; Lopez, 897; *NYT*, 3 Dec. 1942; *Excelsior*, 14 May 1974, 18; *NYT*, 27 July, 1954, 10; *Excelsior*, 17 Mar. 1980, 17.

Quiroga Fernandez, Francisco
a-Dec. 10, 1913. b-Federal District, *Federal District, Urban*. c-Primary studies in a free private school and public school; secondary studies at a public school in the Federal District; preparatory studies at the National Preparatory School; medical degree, National School of Medicine, UNAM, 1940; special studies, Children's Hospital, Mexico City, 1945; professor at the National Teachers College, Mexico City. d-*Federal Deputy* from the Federal District, Dist. 1, 1964–67. e-Joined PAN, 1952; member of the National Committee of PAN, 1954–64; President of the Regional Committee of PAN in the Federal District, 1962–64. f-None. g-Member of the Catholic Association of Mexican Youth, 1929–46; member of the Mexican Catholic Union, 1946–64; President of the National Union of Parents, 1955–59. h-Delegate to the World Congress of Pax Romana, 1946. j-None. k-None. l-C de D, 1964–67; PS, 4999.

Quiroga Trevino, Pablo
a-Jan. 25, 1903. b-Cienega de Flores, Nuevo Leon, *North, Rural*. c-Secondary studies at the Colegio Civil, Monterrey, Nuevo Leon, 1917–22; law degree from the National School of Law, UNAM, June 15, 1928; Professor of Law, University of Nuevo Leon, 1930–32. d-*Federal Deputy* from the State of Nuevo Leon, Dist. 1, 1949–52, member of the First Constitutional Affairs Committee, the Social Welfare Committee, the Consular and Diplomatic Committee, and the Child Welfare Committee. e-None. f-Agent of the Ministerio Publico of the Office of the Attorney General; Judge of the District Court of Nuevo Leon, 1929; Oficial Mayor of the State of Nuevo Leon, 1930; Secretary General of Government of the State of Nuevo Leon, 1930–33; Interim Governor of Nuevo Leon, Dec. 27, 1933, to 1935; Judge of the Superior Tribunal of Justice of Nuevo Leon, 1943–49; Administrator of the Regional Cashier's Office of the IMSS, Monterrey, 1952–58. g-None. h-Scribe for the 3rd District Court, Nuevo

Leon; scribe for the Department of Military Justice, Department of the Navy; scribe for the 7th Judicial District, Federal District; Notary Public No. 24, Monterrey, Nuevo Leon, 1953–74. **i-**Brother Ambrosio was a physician for IMSS. **j-**None. **k-**None. **l-**DBM68, 503–04; WWM45, 96; P de M, 300–01; Peral, 662; C de D, 1949–51, 85; HA, 12 Dec. 1952, 5; DGF51, I, 30, 35, 36; DGF51, Ii, 131; DJBM, 115.

Rabasa, Emilio O.

a-Jan. 23, 1925. **b-**Federal District, *Federal District, Urban*. **c-**Law degree, National School of Law, UNAM; LLD, National School of Law, UNAM; Professor of Law, National School of Law, UNAM (15 years). **d-**None. **e-**None. **f-**Lawyer for the Banking Department, Secretariat of the Treasury; department head, UNAM, 1948; legal adviser to the Secretary of Health, *Ignacio Morones Prieto*, 1956; legal adviser to the head of the Department of Agrarian Affairs; head of the Department of Legal Affairs for the National Bank of Ejido Credit; Director General of Afianzadora Mexicana, S.A.; Director General of the Cinematographic Bank, 1965–70; *Ambassador to the United States*, Sept., 1970, to Dec., 1970; *Secretary of Foreign Relations*, 1970–75. **g-**None. **h-**Author of several books on constitutional law. **i-**From a distinguished Mexican diplomatic family; grandfather, Emilio Rabasa, was a Federal Deputy, 1922–24, and represented the Mexican government at the Niagara Falls Conference, 1914; father, *Oscar Rabasa*, a distinguished writer, professor of constitutional law, and Ambassador in the Mexican Foreign Service, served as special adviser to the President of Mexico; Emilio was a student of *Alfonso Noriega* and *Luis Garrido Diaz* while attending law school at UNAM; son-in-law of *Rafael P. Gamboa*, President of the CEN of PRI, 1946; married Socorro Gamboa. **j-**None. **k-**Fought for the creation of the National School of Political and Social Sciences, UNAM; resigned as Secretary of Foreign Relations, Dec. 29, 1975. **l-**DGF56, 331; DPE70–71, 6; HA, 7 Dec. 1970, 23; *Hoy*, December, 1970.

Rabasa, Oscar

(Deceased Feb. 26, 1978)

a-Feb. 27, 1896. **c-**Preparatory studies at the National Preparatory School; law degree from the University of Pennsylvania, 1917; law degree, National School of Law, UNAM, 1920; professor at the National School of Law, UNAM, 1933–34; professor at the Escuela Libre de Derecho, 1928–29, 1931. **d-**None. **e-**None. **f-**Legal adviser to the Secretary of Communications and Public Works, 1922–25; consulting lawyer to the Assistant Attorney for the Mexican-United States Claims Commission, 1926–35; Director of the Department of Legal Affairs, Sec-

retariat of the Treasury; Director General of Legal Affairs, Secretariat of Foreign Relations, 1946–51; Director General of the Diplomatic Service, 1951–56; Director-in-Chief of the Foreign Service and American Affairs, Secretariat of Foreign Relations, 1961; legal adviser to the Secretary of Foreign Relations, 1964–70; special adviser to the President of Mexico, 1971–76; rank of Ambassador in the Foreign Service. **g-**None. **h-**Author of numerous books on law and history in Mexico. **i-**Son of a distinguished Mexican jurist, Emilio Rabasa, who served as a Mexican representative at the 1914 Niagara Falls Conference, and Federal Deputy, 1922–24; father of *Emilio Rabasa*, Secretary of Foreign Relations, 1970–75. **j-**None. **k-**None. **l-**DGF50, II, 91; HA, 22 Feb. 1971, 31; DPE61, 15; WWM45, 97; DGF56, 124; DGF47, 97; DPE65, 17.

Rafful Miguel, Fernando

a-1935. **b-**Ciudad del Carmen, Campeche, *Gulf, Urban*. **c-**Early education unknown; degree in economics from the National School of Economics, UNAM, 1935; professor, National School of Economics, UNAM. **d-***Senator* from Campeche, 1976. **e-**None. **f-**Adviser to the Department of Control and Inspection of Federal Decentralized Agencies and Businesses, Secretariat of Government Properties, 1965–66; Director, Department of Economic Studies, Secretariat of Government Properties, 1967–70; Director General, Department of Control and Inspection of Federal Decentralized Agencies and Businesses, 1970–73; *Subsecretary of Government Properties*, Apr. 30, 1973, to 1976; *Subsecretary of Fishing*, Secretariat of Commerce, 1976–77; *Director General, Department of Fishing*, 1977– . **g-**None. **i-**Protege of *Horacio Flores de la Pena*. **j-**None. **k-**None. **l-**HA, 7 May 1973, 50; *Excelsior*, 2 May 1973, 5.

Ramirez, Alfonso Francisco

a-Nov. 15, 1896. **b-**Teposcolula, Oaxaca, *South, Rural*. **c-**Primary studies at a parochial school; secondary studies at the Colegio Union, Oaxaca; preparatory studies at the Institute of Arts and Sciences, Oaxaca; law degree from the Institute of Arts and Sciences, Oaxaca, June 20, 1919; Professor of Spanish Language and Literature at the Institute of Arts and Sciences, Oaxaca; professor at the Superior School of Business Administration, Mexico, D.F.; Professor of Logic and Ethics; Professor of World History at the National Preparatory School. **d-**Federal Deputy from Oaxaca, 1924–26, 1926–28, 1928–30, 1930–32; *Federal Deputy* from Oaxaca, Dist. 6, 1937–40. **e-**Founding member, PNR, 1929; orator for *Avila Camacho*. **f-**Judge of the 7th Correctional Court, Federal District, 1924–26; Judge of the 8th Correctional Court, 1926; Subdirector of the

Legal Department for the Department of Federal Pensions; consulting lawyer to the Secretariat of Government, 1933; *Justice of the Supreme Court*, 1941–46, 1946–52, 1952–58. **g-**Student leader in Oaxaca, 1916; president of the Alumni Society of the Institute of Arts and Sciences of Oaxaca. **h-**Author of many works; contributor to *Hoy*, *Excelsior*, *El Universal*; poet. **i-**Father was a lawyer, Supreme Court Justice, and his professor at law school; married Carmen Palacios. **j-**None. **k-**None. **l-**WWM45, 97; DGF56, 567; DGF51, I; C de D, 1937–39, 18; DBM68, 505; EBW46, 72; STYRBIWW54, 965; Peral, 665; HA, 25 Dec. 1972, 15; letters; Lopez, 902.

Ramirez, Margarito
(Deceased Feb. 2, 1979)
a-Feb. 22, 1891. **b-**Atotonilco el Alto, Jalisco, *West*, *Urban*. **c-**Early education unknown; no degree. **d-***Federal Deputy* from the State of Jalisco, Dist. 7, 1937; *Senator* from Jalisco, 1932–36. **e-**Founder and President of the Great Revolutionary Party of Jalisco, 1927. **f-**Chief of Trains, National Railroads of Mexico, 1916–20; Superintendent of Trains, National Railroads of Mexico, 1920–27; Interim Governor of Jalisco, 1927–29; Superintendent of Trains, National Railroads of Mexico, 1929–32, 1936–37; Director of the Federal Penitentiary, Islas Marias, 1937–40; *Director General of the National Railroads of Mexico*, Oct., 1942–45; *Governor of Quintana Roo*, 1945–46, 1946–52, 1952–58, 1958–59. **g-**None. **h-**Started working on the railroad as a laborer, 1908; machinist; train conductor, 1911. **i-**Son *Carlos Ramirez Ladewig*, was a federal deputy from Jalisco, 1955–58, 1964–67; married Ana Ladewig Camarena. **j-**None. **k-**Brandenburg considered him in the Inner Circle from 1942–46; saved the life of General Obregon, 1920. **l-**WWM45, 97; DGF56, 103; Peral, 670; Brandenburg, 102; C de D, 1937–39; DGF51, I, 91; Lopez, 910; *Excelsior*, 13 Feb. 1979, 21; HA, 12 Feb. 1979, 72; *Proceso*, 5 Feb. 1977, 68; Enc. Mex., XI, 1977, 51–52.

Ramirez, Porfirio
a-Feb. 26, 1894. **b-**Santa Rosa del Oro, Mexico, *West Central*, *Rural*. **c-**Early education unknown; no degree. **d-**Mayor of Santiago Estepan, Mexico; *Federal Deputy* from the State of Mexico, Dist. 6, 1940–43; member of the Second Treasury Committee. **e-**None. **f-**None. **g-**None. **h-**Miner by profession. **k-**Proposed legislation as a Federal Deputy for a labor code to cover miners. **l-**Peral, 670; C de D, 1940–42, 19, 52; Lopez, 910.

Ramirez Acosta, Abel
a-June 4, 1915. **b-**Molango, Hidalgo, *East Central*, *Rural*. **c-**Primary studies in Molango; secondary studies in Molango until 1930; law degree, National School of Law, UNAM. **d-***Federal Deputy* from the State of Hidalgo, Dist. 4, 1970–73, member of the Lands and Natural Resources Committee and the First Public Education Committee. **e-***Secretary of Finances of the CEN of PRI*, 1970–72. **f-**Oficial Mayor of the State of Hidalgo. **g-**Member of the SNTE; Secretary of Finances of the SNTE, 1955. **i-**Cousin and political protege of *Manuel Sanchez Vite*; married Natalina Gonzalez. **j-**None. **k-**None. **l-***Directorio*, 1970–72; C de D, 1970–72, 131; HA, 28 Nov. 1955, 13.

Ramirez Ayala, Oscar Mauro
a-1942. **b-**Gomez Palacio, Durango, *West*, *Urban*. **c-**Early education unknown; completed two years of law school. **d-**None. **e-**Joined PARM, 1962; General Delegate of the CEN of PARM to various municipalities; Secretary of Urban Development and Public Housing of the CEN of PARM, 1979. **f-**Official of the National Federation of Tenants and Settlers. **g-**None. **j-**None. **k-**None. **l-**HA, 23 Apr. 1979, III.

Ramirez Cuellar, Hector
a-July 17, 1947. **b-**Ciudad Juarez, Chihuahua, *North*, *Urban*. **c-**Early education unknown; degree from the School of Political and Social Sciences, UNAM; professor at Vocational School No. 1, IPN; professor at the Vicente Lombardo Toledano Workers University, Mexico City. **d-***Federal Deputy* (Party Deputy) from the PPS, 1976–79, member of the Permanent Committee. **e-**Member of the Central Committee of the PPS; Secretary General of the Popular Socialist Youth. **f-**None. **g-**None. **h-**Writer for *El Dia*. **j-**None. **k-**None. **l-**HA, 14 May 1979, IV; C de D, 1976–79.

Ramirez Genel, Marcos
a-Apr. 3, 1923. **b-**Villa Victoria, Michoacan, *West Central*, *Rural*. **c-**Agricultural engineering degree, National School of Agriculture, 1941–45, degree, 1947; Master of Science, Cornell University, 1950–52; Doctorate in Agricultural Science, College of Agriculture, Cornell University (specialty in entomology), 1957; Professor of Graduate Studies at the National School of Agriculture, 1959; founding professor of the Graduate School, National School of Agriculture; Director of the National School of Agriculture. **d-**None. **e-**None. **f-**Investigator of the Office of Special Studies, Secretariat of Agriculture and Livestock, 1947–50, 1952–54; Head of the Department of Entomology, Graduate School, National School of Agriculture; Specialist in Entomology, Office of Special Studies, Secretary of Agriculture and Livestock; Coordinator General of Studies for the

Plan Chapingo; Executive Director of the Plan Chapingo; Agricultural Attache to the United States; *Subsecretary of Livestock*, 1970–72. **g-**None. **h-**Expert in agricultural investigations, International Bank for Reconstruction and Development; author of many scientific works. **i-**Married Maria Refugio Irigoyen. **j-**None. **k-**Studied at Cornell on a scholarship from the National Institute of Agricultural Investigations; resigned as Subsecretary of Livestock, Oct., 1972. **l-**DPE71, 63; B de M, 217–18; HA, 14 Dec. 1970, 21; letter.

Ramirez Guerrero, Carlos

a-Mar. 13, 1909. **b-**Pachuca, Hidalgo, *East Central, Urban.* **c-**Preparatory studies at the Scientific and Literary Institute of Hidalgo; law degree from the National School of Law, UNAM, 1928–32; professor at the Scientific and Literary Institute of Hidalgo; Director of the Scientific and Literary Institute of Hidalgo; Director of the Normal Schools of the State of Hidalgo. **d-***Federal Deputy* from the State of Hidalgo, Dist. 3, 1955–58, member of the Economics and Statistics Committee, the Legislative Studies Committee (1st year), and the Second Justice Committee; *Senator (Alternate)* from Hidalgo, but replaced *Julian Rodriguez Adame*, 1958–63, member of the Gran Comision, the Mail and Telegraph Committee, and the Third Labor Committee; President of the Second Government Committee; substitute member of the Treasury Committee; *Governor of Hidalgo*, 1963–69. **e-**None. **f-**Federal tax attorney; agent of the Ministerio Publico of the Office of the Attorney General; Municipal Judge for Pachuca, Hidalgo; Oficial Mayor of the State of Hidalgo; Assistant Attorney General of the State of Hidalgo; Director of the Department of Economy, State of Hidalgo; Secretary of State for Hidalgo. **g-**None. **h-**None. **i-**Co-student with *Vicente Aguirre*, Governor of Hidalgo, 1946–51. **j-**None. **k-**None. **l-**WWMG, 33; DBM68, 505–06; DGF56, 24, 32, 33, 35; C de S, 1961–64, 66; Ind. Biog., 126–27.

Ramirez Guerrero, Ricardo

a-Feb. 6, 1906. **b-**Morelia Michoacan, *West Central, Urban.* **c-**Early education unknown; no degree. **d-***Federal Deputy* from the State of Michoacan, Dist. 1, 1943–46; *Senator* from the State of Michoacan, 1946–52, member of the Colonization Committee, the Third National Defense Committee, the War Materiels Committee and the Military Health Committee. **e-**None. **f-**Oficial Mayor of Baja California del Norte under Governor *Rodolfo Sanchez Taboada*, 1937–39. **g-**None. **h-**None. **i-**Married *Lazaro Cardenas'* wife's sister. **j-**Military aide to President *Lazaro Cardenas*. **k-**None. **l-**C de D, 1943–46; C de S, 1946–52; DGF51, I, 6, 10, 11, 13, 14.

Ramirez Ladewig, Carlos
(Deceased Sept. 12, 1975)
a-Sept. 20, 1929. **b-**Guadalajara, Jalisco, *West, Urban.* **c-**Primary and secondary studies in Guadalajara; preparatory studies from the University of Guadalajara; law degree, School of Law, University of Guadalajara; Professor of the University of Guadalajara. **d-***Federal Deputy* from the State of Jalisco, Dist. 7, 1955–58, member of the Administration and the Second General Means of Communication Committees; *Federal Deputy* from the State of Jalisco, Dist. 5, 1964–67, member of the Agricultural Committee, the Indigenous Affairs Committee and the Rules Committee. **e-**Member of the PRM; President of the Youth Committee of PRI in Jalisco. **f-**Delegate of the IMSS to the State of Jalisco. **g-**Student leader at the University of Guadalajara; founder and director of the Federation of Students of Guadalajara, 1950. **i-**Son of *Margarito Ramirez*, Governor of Quintana Roo, 1945–59; brother Alvaro Ramirez Ladewig was a candidate of an opposition party for federal deputy, 1979. **j-**None. **k-**Youngest member of the Chamber of Deputies, 1955–58; in an interview he said that *Adolfo Ruiz Cortines* was directly responsible for selecting him as the PRI candidate for federal deputy from Jalisco, 1955; assassinated by his political opponents in Guadalajara. **l-***Proceso*, 5 Feb. 1977, 6, 68; *Proceso*, 12 Feb. 1977, 8; C de D, 1964–67, 77, 79, 93; Ind. Biog., 127–28; DGF56, 25, 30, 33, 37; *Excelsior*, 17 Sept. 1979, 15.

Ramirez (Martinez), Jose Antonio

a-Nov. 6, 1910. **b-**San Felipe de Nombre de Dios, Durango, *West, Rural.* **c-**Primary studies only. **d-**Local Deputy to the State Legislature of Durango; *Federal Deputy* from the State of Durango, Dist. 4, 1961–64; *Federal Deputy* from the State of Durango, Dist. 4, 1967–70. **e-**Secretary of Labor Action of PRI in Durango. **f-**Director of Traffic, State of Durango; Director of the Department of Labor, State of Durango. **g-**None. **j-**None. **k-**None. **l-**C de D, 1961–64; C de D, 1967–70; MGF69.

Ramirez Mijares, Oscar

a-Jan. 12, 1922. **b-**Torreon, Coahuila, *North, Urban.* **c-**Teaching certificate. **d-***Federal Deputy* from the Federal District, Dist. 21, 1961–64; *Federal Deputy* from the Federal District, Dist. 21, 1967–70; *Alternate Senator* from the State of Coahuila, 1976–77, but replaced Senator *Eliseo Mendoza Berrueto*, 1978– . **e-**Secretary of Organization of PRI in the Federal District; *Secretary of Agrarian Action of the CEN of PRI*, 1978. **f-**None. **g-**Secretary General of the League of Agrarian Communities and Peasant Unions, Federal District; *Secretary General of the CNC*, 1977– . **h-**None. **i-**Married Egla Millan de Ramos, a teacher; children Egla and Olga are both teachers. **j**-None. **k**-None. **l**-Letter; LA, 11 Feb 1977, 44; C de D, 1961–64; C de D, 1967–70; C de S, 1976–82.

Ramirez Valadez, Guillermo

a-1909. **b**-Arandas, Jalisco, *West*, *Urban*. **c**-Primary and secondary studies in Guadalajara; preparatory studies at the University of Guadalajara; studies in economics, School of Economics, University of Guadalajara, 1936–41, graduating in 1945 with a thesis on social welfare; law degree, National School of Law, UNAM; Professor of Penal Law, National School of Law, UNAM; Rector of the University of Guadalajara, 1955. **d**-Local Deputy to the State Legislature of Jalisco; *Federal Deputy* from the State of Jalisco, Dist. 6, 1949–52, member of the First Constitutional Affairs Committee and Prosecretary of the Chamber; *Alternate Senator* from the State of Jalisco under Senator *Silvano Barba Gonzalez*, 1952–58; *Senator* from the State of Jalisco, 1958–64, Secretary, 1952, Second Secretary of the Government Committee, President of the Consular Service and Diplomatic Committee and of the Special Legislative Studies Committee. **e**-President of PRI in Jalisco. **f**-Justice of the Peace, Jalisco; Agent of the Ministerio Publico, Jalisco; Representative of the Secretariat of the Treasury, Jalisco; Manager, Agricultural Bank of Guadalajara. **g**-None. **i**-Relative of Antonio Valades Ramirez, governor of Jalisco, 1922–23 and senator, 1926–32; Valades Ramirez was the long-time political boss of Arandas according to *Excelsior*. **j**-None. **k**-None. **l**-*Excelsior*, 27 May 1979, 18; EN de E, 196; DGF56, 6; Func., 239; C de S, 1961–64, 66–67; C de D, 1949–52, 85.

Ramirez Vazquez, Manuel

a-June 4, 1906. **b**-Federal District, *Federal District*, *Urban*. **c**-Primary studies in Guanajuato; preparatory studies at the National Preparatory School; law degree from the National School of Law, UNAM, 1925–29. **d**-None. **e**-None. **f**-President of the Superior Tribunal of the State of Veracruz, Jan., 1937, to Nov., 1937; member of the Federal Board of Conciliation and Arbitration, No. 5; Federal Attorney for the Labor Movement, 1946; *Subsecretary of Labor*, 1946–48; *Secretary of Labor*, January 12, 1948, to 1952. **g**-None. **h**-Practicing lawyer, 1930, 1953–76; author of articles on petroleum legislation. **i**-Studied under *Aquiles Elorduy* at UNAM; friend of and co-student with *Miguel Aleman*, *Antonio Carrillo Flores*, *Eduardo Bustamante*, *Alfonso Noriega*, and *Antonio Martinez Baez*; brother of *Mariano Ramirez Vazquez* and *Pedro Ramirez Vazquez;* father a bookstore owner. **j**-None. **k**-None. **l**-STYRBIWW54, 966; DGF50, II, 280; DGF51, II, 529; HA, 15 Oct. 1948, 3; HA, 23 Jan. 1948; DGF47, 247; DGF51, I, 399.

Ramirez Vazquez, Mariano

a-Dec. 24, 1903. **b**-Federal District, *Federal District*, *Urban*. **c**-Primary studies at a public school, Mexico, D.F.; preparatory studies at the National Preparatory School, 1920; law degree from the National School of Law, UNAM, June 8, 1926; Professor of Law, National School of Law, UNAM. **d**-None. **e**-None. **f**-Defense counsel, Criminal Division, Judicial District, Cuautla, Morelos; Judge, Civil Division, Judicial District, Cuernavaca, Morelos; Secretary of Justice for the Penal Division, Federal District; Director of the Department of Legal Services, Department of Labor; Secretary General of the Federal Board of Conciliation and Arbitration; Secretary General of the Department of Labor; *Assistant Attorney General of Mexico*, June 22, 1937, to 1940; Judge of the 14th Penal District, Federal District, 1941; *Justice of the Supreme Court*, 1947–49, 1954–58, 1958–64, 1964–70, and 1970–73; Director of the National Institute of Youth, 1950–52. **g**-None. **h**-None. **i**-Longtime friend of *Salvador Novo* since preparatory school days; longtime friend of *Antonio Luna Arroyo*; brother of *Manuel Ramirez Vazquez* and *Pedro Ramirez Vazquez*. **j**-None. **k**-Retired from the Supreme Court, Dec. 12, 1973. **l**-D de Y, 22 June 1937, 2; DGF51, I, 568; Novo, 716–17, 746–47; DGF56, 567; STYRBIWW54, 966; Casasola, V; *Excelsior*, 12 Dec. 1973, 1C; *Justicia*, May, 1967.

Ramirez Vazquez, Pedro

a-Apr. 16, 1919. **b**-Federal District, *Federal District*, *Urban*. **c**-Primary studies at the Annex to the National Normal School, Mexico City; secondary studies at Secondary School No. 4, Mexico City; preparatory studies at the National Preparatory School; architectural degree, National School of Architecture, UNAM, 1943, with a thesis on urban planning in Ciudad Guzman, Jalisco; Professor of Architectural Composition and Urbanism, National School of Architecture, 1942–58; first Rector of the Metropolitan University, 1973–75. **d**-None. **e**-Technical adviser to the IEPES of PRI, 1969–70; *Secretary of Press and Publicity of the CEN of PRI*, 1975–76. **f**-First Zone Chief of the Federal Program for School Construction (CAPFCE) in Tabasco, 1944–47; Director of the Department of Building Conservation, Secretariat of Public Education, 1947–58; Director General of CAPFCE, 1958–64; founder and Technical Director of the Regional Center for School Construction for Latin America (UNESCO agency), 1964–66; President of the Mexican Organizing Committee of the Olympic Games, 1966–69, 1971–73; General Coordinator of Public Works, State of Mexico, 1971–73; *Secretary of Public Works and Dwellings*, 1976– . **g**-President of the National College of Architects. **h**-Practicing architect; co-designer of the National School of Medicine with *Carlos Lazo*, 1948; designed *Adolfo Lopez Mateos'* home; architect for numerous public buildings, including the Secretariat of Foreign Relations, the Aztec Stadium, and the National Museum of Anthropology and History. **i-**Brother of *Manuel Ramirez Vazquez*, Secretary of Labor, 1948–52, and *Mariano Ramirez Vazquez*, Justice of the Supreme Court, 1947–73; father a bookseller; protege of Professor *Jose Luis Cuevas* and *Carlos Lazo*. **j-**None. **k-**Considered for Subsecretary of Public Works, 1952, but lost out to *Enrique Bracamontes*; supported *Donato Miranda Fonseca* for president, 1964; recognized world-wide for many of his architectural works. **l-***Excelsior*, 1 Apr. 1977, 6, 8; Enc. Mex., XI, 1977, 57–58; DBM68, 507; *Excelsior*, 1 Dec. 1976; *El Dia*, 1 Dec. 1976; letters.

Ramirez y Ramirez, Enrique

a-Mar. 14, 1915. **b-**Federal District, *Federal District*, *Urban*. **c-**Primary and secondary studies in the Federal District; studies at the School of Plastic Arts, 1930–32, 1934–35, 1936–38; preparatory studies at the National Preparatory School; no degree; professor at the Workers University, 1938; member of the Board of Directors, Workers University, 1945; professor for the Institute for Political Training, PRI, 1971– . **d-***Federal Deputy* from the Federal District, Dist. 3, 1964–67, member of the Protocol Committee, the Legislative Studies Commmittee (9th Section on General Affairs), and the Social Security Committee; *Federal Deputy* from the Federal District, Dist. 4, 1976–79. **e-**Member of the Communist Party of Mexico, 1932–43, expelled in March, 1943; member of the National Directive Committee of the Popular Socialist Party, 1948–52; Treasurer of the PPS, 1948; Secretary of the CEN of the PPS, 1951–52; member of PPS, 1948–58; joined PRI, 1964; adviser to the CEN of PRI, 1967–70; Secretary of the Ideological Committee of the CEN of PRI, 1978. **f-**Private Secretary to *Vicente Lombardo Toledano*, 1938–39, 1951–52. **g-**Student leader of the National Student Congress, San Luis Potosi; student leader at the Second Congress of Socialist Students, 1935; member of the Alliance of Revolutionary Writers and Students, 1930–32; member of CTM and leader of the Union of Graphic Arts Industry Workers; Director of the Unified Socialist Youth of Mexico, 1939; Secretary General of the Federation of Revolutionary Students, 1935. **h-**Author of many articles on social problems; founder and Director General of *El Dia*, 1962– ; editorial writer for *El Popular*, 1938–46; began career in journalism, 1929. **j-**None. **k-**None. **l-**Peral, 671; Novo, 150–51, 214; C de D, 1964–66, 80, 84, 94; Enc. Mex., XI, 1977, 56–57; *Excelsior*, 24 Aug. 1978, 14; *Excelsior*, 31 Aug. 1976, C1.

Ramos, Ramon
(Deceased 1937)
a-1894. **b-**Villa de Chinipas, Chihuahua, *North*, *Rural*. **c-**Agricultural engineering degree, National School of Agriculture. **d-**Federal Deputy from the State of Sonora, 1924–26; Federal Deputy from the State of Chihuahua, 1926–28; Senator from the State of Sonora, 1930–34; *Governor of Sonora*, 1935. **f-**Secretary of Government, 1931–32. **g-**None. **h-**None. **k-**Removed from the Governorship because of loyalties to Calles. **l-**DP70, 1723; Dulles, 661.

Ramos Millan, Gabriel
(Deceased Sept. 26, 1949)
a-Apr. 25, 1903. **b-**Ayapango, Mexico, *West Central*, *Rural*. **c-**Preparatory studies at the National Preparatory School; law degree from the Escuela Libre de Derecho. **d-***Federal Deputy* from the State of Mexico, Dist. 9, 1943–46; *Senator* from the State of Mexico, 1946–47, President of the Treasury Committee. **e-**None. **f-**Vice President of the Administrative Council of Produccion Agricola, S.A.; adviser to Guanos y Fertilizantes de Mexico, S.A.; founder and First President of the National Commission of Maiz, Jan. 6, 1947–49. **g-**Founder of the National Association of the Middle Class, 1945, to support *Miguel Aleman* for president. **h-**Defense lawyers for miners in Pachuca, Hidalgo. **i-**Longtime friend of *Miguel Aleman*, President of Mexico, 1946–52; held positions under *Aleman* as Governor of Veracruz; parents were peasants. **j-**None. **k-**Known in Mexico as the "Apostle of Maiz" because of his campaign to improve the cultivation of corn and the development of new hybrid seeds; responsible for the first surplus production of corn since 1910. **l-**DP70, 1724–25; C de S, 1946–52; DGF51, I, 6; C de D, 1943–45, 19; Wise, 60, 139; Q es Q, 487; HA, 7 Oct. 1949, 6; Lopez, 913; HA, 24 Jan. 1947, 34; Enc. Mex., XI, 1977, 61.

Ramos Santos, Matias
(Deceased Mar. 4, 1962)
a-Feb. 24, 1891. **b-**San Salvador, Zacatecas, *East Central*, *Rural*. **c-**Primary and secondary studies in Concepcion del Oro, Zacatecas; no degree. **d-**Federal Deputy from the State of Zacatecas, Dist. 8, 1918–20; *Governor of Zacatecas*, 1932–34, 1935–36. **e-**President of the CEN of PRI, Dec. 14, 1934, to June 15, 1935. **f-**Inspector of Railroads, Secretariat of Public Works, 1917; Oficial Mayor of the Secretariat of War, 1928–29; *Secretary of National Defense*, 1952–58. **g-**None. **i-**Friend of *Marcelino Garcia Barragan* and *Francisco Urquizo*; son, Ismael Ramos, served as 1st Captain of the Chief of Staff of the Secretary of National Defense, 1952. **j-**Joined the Revolution on March 18, 1911 as a private; rank of

Sergeant in the Cavalry, 1914; fought against Victoriano Huerta, 1913–14; fought against Francisco Villa, 1916, under General *Jacinto B. Trevino*; rank of Brigadier General, May 20, 1915; fought against the De la Huerta revolt, 1923; fought against Escobar, 1929; commander of various military zones including Mexico, Hidalgo, Zacatecas, Oaxaca, Tamaulipas, San Luis Potosi, Guerrero; rank of Divisionary General, May 16, 1929; Commander of the 9th Military Zone, Monterrey, Nuevo Leon, 1951. k-Retired from active service, 1959. l-DGF56, 199; Peral, 673; *Polemica*, 1969, Vol. I, 67; McAlister, 223–24; DGF51, I, 183; D de Y, 3 Dec. 1952, 12; Q es Q, 487–88; Dulles, 635; Lopez, 913–14; Enc. Mex., XI, 1977, 61.

Rangel Couto, Hugo

a-1912. b-Guadalajara, Jalisco, *West, Urban*. c-Preparatory studies at the National Preparatory School, 1925–29; law degree, National School of Law, UNAM, 1929–34; economics degree, National School of Economics, UNAM, 1935–39, graduating June 20, 1939, with a thesis on Democracy and Communism in America; Professor of the History of Economic Doctrines, National School of Law, UNAM; Director, Institute for Economic Research, UNAM, 1943–46. d-None. e-None. f-*Oficial Mayor of the Secretariat of Government Properties*, 1946–47; *Subsecretary of Government Properties*, 1947–49; *Subsecretary in Charge of the Secretariat of Government Properties*, 1949–51; *Subsecretary of Government Properties*, 1951–52. g-Secretary of the National School of Economics, 1936–38; member of the 1933 student strike committee. h-Author of numerous articles and books; economist of the Workers Bank for Industrial Development; adviser to the United Nations. i-Important collaborator of *Alfonso Caso*, 1944–49; married Antonia Abreu. j-None. k-None. l-DGF47, 269; DGF51, I, 443; Enc. Mex., V, 46; HA, 10 Aug. 1951, 14; DGF51, II, 383; DGF50, II, 279; EN de E, 62; DNED, 200.

Rangel Frias, Raul

a-Mar. 15, 1913. b-Monterrey, Nuevo Leon, *North, Urban*. c-Primary and secondary studies in Monterrey; preparatory studies at the Colegio Civil, Monterrey; law degree from the National School of Law, UNAM, 1933–38, with a thesis on Kelsen; member of the University Council of UNAM; Professor of the History of Philosophical Doctrines, National Preparatory School, Mexico, D.F., 1936–38; professor of civics in secondary schools, Mexico, D.F., 1936–38, and at the workers centers; Professor of Law, School of Law, University of Nuevo Leon, 1939–43; Rector of the University of Nuevo Leon, 1949–52, 1952–55. d-*Governor of Nuevo Leon*, 1955–61. e-None. f-Public relations officer, De-

partment of the Federal District; Director of the Social Welfare Program, State of Nuevo Leon; Chief, Department of Social Action, University of Nuevo Leon, 1944; Oficial Mayor of the State of Nuevo Leon under Governor *Salinas Leal*. g-Member of the Alfonso Reyes group, 1929; President of the Student Society at the Colegio Civil of Nuevo Leon; delegate to the 7th National Student Congress, 1930. h-Practicing lawyer, 1970–79. i-Son of a medical doctor; married Elena Hinojosa; attended law school with *Hugo B. Margain* and *Alfonso Corona del Rosal*; student of *Manuel Moreno Sanchez*. j-None. k-Supported Jose Vasconcelos, 1929. l-*Excelsior*, 5 Oct. 1961; DBM68, 508–09; WWM45, 98; DGF56, 97; G of NL, 15; HA, 9 May 1955, 10; *Siempre*, 17 Sept. 1956, 6; PdM, 304; letters; Lopez, 914; Enc. Mex., XI, 1977, 65; HA, 24 Aug. 1960.

Rangel (Hurtado), Rafael
(Deceased Aug. 19, 1955)

a-Oct. 31, 1888. b-San Francisco del Rincon, Guanajuato, *West Central, Rural*. c-Law degree, University of Guanajuato. d-Local deputy to the State Legislature of Guanajuato, 1937–38; *Senator* from the State of Guanajuato, 1940–46, President of the Railroads Committee, Second Secretary of the Second Government Committee, member of the First Balloting Committee and the Gran Comision; President of the Rules Committee and the Second Instructive Section of the Grand Jury. e-None. f-Secretary of the City Council of Leon, Guanajuato; Secretary General of Government of the State of Guanajuato, 1928–31; Private Secretary to the Governor of Guanajuato, 1931–32; Secretary General of Government of the Territory of Baja California del Sur, 1934–37; *Interim Governor of Guanajuato*, 1938–39, during the leave of absence of *Luis I. Rodriguez* as President of the CEN of PRM. g-None. j-None. k-Leader of the "Green" Group in Guanajuato, 1943. l-Peral, 673–74; C de S, 1940–46; Lopez, 914; *Libre de Oro*, 1946, 10; PS, 5086.

Ravize, Manuel A.

a-Sept. 20, 1910. b-Tampico, Tamaulipas, *North, Urban*. c-Primary studies at the San Jose Institute, Tacubaya; secondary and preparatory studies at the Colegio Frances "Centro Union," and the Colegio Puente de Alvarado, Mexico, D.F., in the field of commercial studies; studied engineering at the Atlanta Military Academy, Atlanta, Georgia; studied business administration in San Antonio, Texas; no degree. d-*Alternate Senator* from the State of Tamaulipas, 1958–64, under Senator *Emilio Martinez Manatou*; Mayor of Tampico, Tamaulipas, 1955–57; *Governor of Tamaulipas*, 1969–74. e-State committeeman for PRI in Tamaulipas; PRI delegate to Tampico; representative of precandidate for governor, Manuel Collado, 1943. **f**-Trustee of the City Council of Tampico, 1943–45; Director of the Federal Office of the Treasury, 1958–64; President of the Federal Board of Material and Moral Improvements for Tampico, 1964–69. **g**-None. **h**-Businessman. **i**-Parents were 5th generation Tamaulipecos; father worked as a cashier for Ferrocarril del Golfo, 1897, and founded first petroleum company in the Tampico region, 1918; son Manuel is a businessman; married Teresa Matienzo Zubista. **j**-None. **k**-Precandidate for senator from Tamaulipas, 1976. **l**-Letter; *Excelsior*, 8 Dec. 1975, 17.

Real (Encinas), Carlos

a-Jan. 31, 1922. **b**-Federal District, *Federal District*, *Urban*. **c**-Primary and secondary studies in the Federal District; preparatory studies in the Federal District; law degree, Free School of Law, July 20, 1944, LLD, National School of Law, UNAM. **d**-*Federal Deputy* from the State of Durango, Dist. 2, 1949–52, member of the Legislative Studies Committee, the Second Balloting Committee, the Second Committee on General Means of Communication; Vice President of the Chamber of Deputies, Dec., 1949; *Federal Deputy* from the State of Durango, Dist. 1, 1955–58, member of the External and Domestic Trade Committee, the Budget and Accounts Committee (1st year), and the Constitutional Affairs Committee (1st year); Secretary of the Chamber of Deputies, 1956; *Alternate Senator* from Durango, 1964–70. **e**-President of the Regional Committee of PRI, Durango; President of the Board for Material Improvements, Ciudad Juarez and Nuevo Laredo, for Adolfo Ruiz Cortines' presidential campaign, 1951–52. **f**-Private Secretary to *Ignacio Morones Prieto* as Director General of IMSS, 1966–70; Director General of Inspection of Domestic Taxes, Secretariat of the Treasury, Feb., 1972; Delegate of the Department of the Federal District, 1976–77. **g**-None. **i**-Son of *Carlos Real Felix*, Senator from Durango, 1958–64. **j**-None. **k**-None. **l**-HA, 14 Feb. 1972, 23–24; DGF56, 23, 31; DGF51, I, 21, 32, 34, 35, 36; C de D, 1949–51; C de D, 1955–57; C de S, 1964–70; Ind. Biog., 128–29; DAPC, 1977, 59.

Real (Felix), Carlos

a-Nov. 17, 1887. **b**-Tamazula, Durango, *West*, *Rural*. **c**-Primary studies in Durango, Durango; studies at the National Military College; no degree. **d**-*Governor of Durango*, 1932–35; *Senator* from the State of Durango, 1958–64, President of the Second Committee for National Defense, member of the Committee on the Electric Industry, the War Materiels Committee, the Special Livestock Committee, the Second Balloting Committee, and the Second Instructive Committee for the Grand Jury. **e**-Founding member of the PNR, 1929; *Oficial*

Mayor of the CEN of PRI, 1956. **f**-Oficial Mayor of the Chamber of Deputies, 1946–49; Gerente of National Lottery, 1949–52. **g**-None. **i**-Son, *Carlos Real*, served twice as a Federal Deputy from Durango. **j**-Career army officer; rank of Brigadier General, 1932; Commander of the 7th Military Zone, Monterrey, Nuevo Leon; reached the rank of Divisionary General. **k**-Political boss of Durango during the early 1930s; removed from the governorship because of loyalty to Calles. **l**-DGF47, 13, 409; Dulles; C de S, 1961–64, 67; *Siempre*, 14 Jan. 1959, 6; Johnson, 32; D del S, 3 Dec. 1946, 1; Func., 199; *NYT*, 17 Dec. 1935, 1.

Rebolledo Fernandez, Mario G.

b-Jalapa, Veracruz, *Gulf*, *Urban*. **c**-Early education unknown; law degree from the School of Law, University of Veracruz, July, 1935; Professor of Law, University of Veracruz, 1945–50. **d**-None. **e**-None. **f**-Agent of the Ministerio Publico, Veracruz; Assistant Auxiliary Attorney General of the State of Veracruz; Judge of the First Instance, State of Veracruz; President of the Board of Conciliation and Arbitration of the State of Veracruz; Secretary of the Superior Tribunal of Justice of the State of Veracruz; Director, Department of Government, State of Veracruz; Judge of the Superior Tribunal of Justice of the State of Veracruz; Attorney General of the State of Veracruz; Secretary General of Government of the State of Veracruz; Judge, Fifteenth Penal District, Federal District; Judge of the Superior Tribunal of Justice of the Federal District; *Justice of the Supreme Court of Mexico*, 1955–58, 1963–70, 1970–76; *President of the Supreme Court*, 1976–77. **g**-None. **i**-Professor of *Manlio Fabio Tapia Camacho*. **j**-None. **k**-None. **l**-*Justicia*, Apr., 1968; letter; *Excelsior*, 3 Mar. 1976, 1.

Renteria (Acosta), Daniel T.

(Deceased 1965)

a-1897. **b**-Taretan, Michoacan, *West Central*, *Rural*. **c**-Preparatory studies at the Colegio de San Nicolas, Morelia, Michoacan; law degree, Colegio de San Nicolas. **d**-*Federal Deputy* from Michoacan, Dist. 3, 1958–61, member of the Transportation Committee. **e**-None. **f**-Treasurer of the State of Michoacan; Attorney General of Michoacan; Treasurer General of Mexico, 1934–46; Cashier General of the Rio de las Balsas Commission, 1961–65. **g**-None. **h**-None. **i**-Married Maria Acosta; father of *Hector Renteria Acosta*, Federal Deputy from the State of Michoacan, 1970–73 and member of PARM; parents were of Indian ancestry; long-time collaborator of *Lazaro Cardenas* since his term as governor of Michoacan, 1928–31. **j**-None. **k**-None. **l**-Func., 270; C de D, 1970–73; C de D, 1958–61, 89; *Directorio*, 1970–

72; DP70, 1745; Anderson; *La Voz de Michoacan*, 16 Sept. 1949, 1.

Reta Martinez, Carlos

b-Morelia, Michoacan, *West Central, Urban*. **c**-Studied engineering, political science, and public administration at UNAM; no degree. **d**-None. **e**-Youth Director of PRI in the Federal District; President of National Youth Committee of CNOP of PRI; Subdirector of the National Youth Organization of PRI; President of the Mexican Council of Youth; delegate of CNOP and PRI to various cities and states; Auxiliary Secretary of the CEN of PRI. **f**-Assistant to the Resident Engineer of Estructuras y Cimentacion, S.A.; Investigator for the Fondo de Planeacion Industria Azucarera; *Secretary General (C) of the Department of the Federal District*, 1970–73. **g**-None. **h**-Founder and Director of the magazine *Polemica*, official publication of PRI, 1969–70. **j**-None. **k**-Student leader at UNAM. **l**-HA, 14 Dec. 1970, 24; DPE71.

Reta Petterson, Gustavo Adolfo

a-May 26, 1937. **b**-Federal District, *Federal District, Urban*. **c**-Medical degree in veterinary medicine, UNAM, 1959; Master of Science from the University of Indiana, 1963, with a specialty in livestock; professor at the School of Veterinary Medicine, UNAM. **d**-None. **e**-None. **f**-Director of the Agriculture section of the Experimental Fields of El Horno, Chapingo, Secretariat of Agriculture, 1960–63; Head of the Livestock Department for the Plan Lerma, 1963–67; Director General of Animal Health, Secretariat of Agriculture and Livestock, 1967–72; *Subsecretary of Livestock*, Feb. 23, 1972, to 1975. **g**-None. **i**-Father, Manuel Reta Alducin, was an engineer. **j**-None. **k**-Resigned as Subsecretary of Livestock, June 26, 1975; precandidate for federal deputy, 1975. **l**-HA, 6 Mar. 1972, 19; DPE71, 69; *Novedades*, 24 Feb. 1972, 1; HA, 21 Feb. 1972; MGF69, 264; *Excelsior*, 23 Feb. 1973, 5; *El Universal*, 27 June 1975.

Reyes Esparza, Diamantina

a-June 9, 1941. **b**-Villa Matamoros, Chihuahua, *North, Rural*. **c**-Primary studies in Villa Matamoros; completed secondary studies and normal certificate at night school; normal school teacher; Secretary of the Parralance Institute. **d**-*Federal Deputy* from the State of Chihuahua, Dist. 2, 1970–73, member of the Social Action Committee, the Immigration Committee and the Small Industry Committee. **e**-Youth Director of PRI in Chihuahua; Director of the Feminine Sector of PRI in Chihuahua; Secretary General of PRI in the State of Chihuahua. **f**-None. **g**-Secretary of Labor and Conflicts of the Teachers Union of Chihuahua;

Secretary General of the Teachers Union of Chihuahua. **j**-None. **k**-None. **l**-*Directorio*, 1970–72; C de D, 1970–73, 132.

Reyes Heroles, Jesus

a-Apr. 3, 1921. **b**-Tuxpan, Veracruz, *Gulf, Rural*. **c**-Law degree with honorable mention from the National School of Law, UNAM, 1944; graduate studies at the University of La Plata and the University of Buenos Aires, 1945; Assistant Professor of Law, UNAM, 1944–45; Professor of Economics and General Theory, UNAM, 1946–64; professor at the National Polytechnical Institute. **d**-*Federal Deputy* from the State of Veracruz, Dist. 2, 1961–64, member of the Committee on Tariffs and Foreign Trade, the Legislative Studies Committee (4th Section on Administration), the Permanent Commission, and delegate to the Interparliamentary Conference. **e**-Joined PRM in 1939 and began political career as Auxiliary Private Secretary to *Heriberto Jara*, President of the CEN of PRM; assistant to the Private Secretary of *Antonio L. Villalobos*, President of the CEN of PRM, 1940–44; member of the IEPES of PRI, 1949–51, 1960–61; adviser to the Technical Office for the presidential campaign of *Adolfo Lopez Mateos*, 1958; adviser to the President of the CEN of PRI, *Gabriel Leyva Velazquez*, 1952; *President of the CEN of PRI*, Feb. 21, 1972, to 1975. **f**-Adviser to the Secretary of Labor, *Ignacio Garcia Tellez*, 1944; Alternate President of the Special Group No. 1 of the Federal Board of Conciliation and Arbitration, 1946; Secretary General of the Mexican Institute of Books, 1949–53; adviser to the President of Mexico, *Adolfo Ruiz Cortines*, 1952–58; Director of Economic Studies for National Railroads of Mexico, 1953–58; Technical Subdirector General of IMSS, 1958–61; *Director General of PEMEX*, 1964–70; Director General of the Industrial Complex of Ciudad Sahagun, Hidalgo, Dec. 1, 1970, to 1972; *Director General of the IMSS*, 1975–76; *Secretary of Government*, 1976–79. **g**-None. **h**-Author of six books and dozens of articles on political and economic problems; **i**-Attended the National Preparatory School with *Luis Echeverria*. **j**-None. **k**-None. **l**-*Excelsior*, 22 Feb. 1971; *Novedades*, 21 Feb. 1972, 1; *El Universal*, 1 Dec. 1964; WWMG, 34; HA, 22 Dec. 1958, 8; HA, 7 Dec. 1964, 21; *Excelsior*, 21 Feb. 1972, 18; HA, 28 Feb. 1972, 12; D de Y, 2 Dec. 196, 2; IWW67, 1018; *Analisis Politico*, 3 July 1972, 4; Enc. Mex., XI, 1977, 126.

Reyes Osorio, Sergio

a-Aug. 8, 1934. **b**-Federal District, *Federal District, Urban*. **c**-Agricultural engineering degree, National School of Agriculture; masters degree in agricultural economics, University of Wisconsin; Professor of Credit and Agricultural Economics, Graduate

School, National School of Agriculture. d-None. e-None. f-Economist for the Securities and Development Fund for Agriculture; agricultural economist for the Bank of Mexico; member of the Advisory Board, Agricultural Center of Chapingo; Director of the Center of Agricultural Investigations; *Subsecretary of the Department of Colonization and Agrarian Affairs*, 1970–76. g-None. h-President of the National Institute of Agricultural Economics; editor of various agriculture magazines. i-Married Ofelia Flores. j-None. k-None. l-DPE71, 129; DBM68, 512; HA, 21 Dec. 1970, 24.

Reyes Spindola (y Prieto), Octavio
(Deceased 1967)
a-Aug. 24, 1892. b-Federal District, *Federal District, Urban*. c-Law degree. d-*Federal Deputy* from the State of Oaxaca, 1943–46, Dist. 5. e-None. f-Protocol Attache, Independence Centennial, 1921; Chief Secretary to the Embassy in Brazil, 1922; Second Secretary, Guatemala, 1928; Second Secretary-in-Charge, Guatemala, 1929; Second Secretary to Spain, 1930; Second Secretary-in-Charge, Spain, 1930; First Secretary-in-Charge, Spain, 1931; Ambassador to Chile, 1943; Consul, Miami, Florida, 1956; alternate member of the Advisory Council for the Small Business Bank of the Federal District, 1950; adviser to the President of Mexico. g-None. h-Author of several articles. i-Son of Rafael Reyes Spindola, Oaxacan journalist who founded the Mexico, D.F., newspaper *El Universal*, 1888, and *El Imparcial*, 1896. j-Participated in the European Front during World War I. k-Kirk claims that Reyes Spindola was the foreign service officer who most avidly pushed the Revolution abroad. l-DGF51, II, 377; C de D, 1943–45, 19; Peral, 680–81; DP70, 1758; WWM45, 101; DGF56, 139; DGF50, II, 413; Q es Q, 495.

Reyna Ramos, Maximino
a-May 29, 1903. b-Doctor Arroyo, Nuevo Leon, *North, Rural*. c-No formal education, self-educated; no degree. d-*Federal Deputy* from the State of Nuevo Leon, Dist. 4, 1940–43, member of the Public Welfare Committee, the Second Balloting Committee, and substitute member of the General Means of Communication Committee. e-None. f-None. g-Representative of peasant organizations in Nuevo Leon. k-None. l-Peral, 682; C de D, 1940–42, 44, 54, 63.

Reynoso (Gutierrez), Brigido
b-Juchipila, Zacatecas, *East Central, Rural*. c-No formal education; self-educated. d-*Federal Deputy* from the State of Zacatecas, Dist. 3, 1943–46; *Senator* from the State of Zacatecas, 1952–58, member of the Special Legislative Studies Committee, First Secretary of the Second Government Committee, Second Secretary of the Public Education Committee and First Secretary of the National Property and Resources Committee. e-None. f-None. g-None. h-Owner of La Mezquita Sugar Mill; was a peasant as a young man. i-Brother of *Leobardo Reynoso*, senator from Zacatecas, 1934–40 and governor, 1944–50. j-None. k-None. l-Ind. Biog., 130; C de D, 1943–46; C de S, 1952–58; DGF56.

Reynoso (Gutierrez), Leobardo
a-Jan. 18, 1902. b-Zacatecas, Zacatecas, *East Central, Urban*. c-Primary studies, Zacatecas, self-educated; no degree. d-*Senator* from the State of Zacatecas, 1934–40, President of the Revolutionary Bloc in the Senate; Secretary of the Revolutionary Bloc; President of the Permanent Commission; *Federal Deputy* from the State of Zacatecas, Dist. 3, 1940–43, member of the Gran Comision, President of the First Instructive Section of the Grand Jury; President of the Policy Control Committee (1st and 2nd years), Federal Deputy from Zacatecas, 1932–34; *Governor of Zacatecas*, 1944–50. e-Secretary of the CEN of PNR, 1935. f-Cashier for the Federal Senate, 1924–26; paymaster for the Mexican Senate, 1926–32; Ambassador to Portugal, 1958–61; Ambassador to Denmark, 1964–70. g-None. h-Began career as a federal employee, 1920. i-Brother *Brigido Reynoso* served as Federal Deputy from Zacatecas, Dist. 3, 1943–46. j-None. k-Brandenburg considered him to be in the Inner Circle of influence in the 1940s. l-HA, 24 Sept. 1950, xxiv; HA, 28 Sept. 1945, x; DGF61, 24; C de D, 1940–42; C de S, 1934–40; letter; Brandenburg, 44–46, 80; *Excelsior*, 5 Sept. 1973, 18.

Riba y Rincon (Gallardo), Luis
a-Oct. 20, 1934. b-Federal District, *Federal District, Urban*. c-Law degree, Escuela Libre de Derecho, Oct. 23, 1957. d-None. e-None. f-Private Secretary to the Oficial Mayor of Industry and Commerce, *Hugo B. Margain,* 1959–61; Private Secretary to the Subsecretary of Industry and Commerce, *Hugo B. Margain*, 1961–64; Gerente General of the National Association of Automobile Distributors, A.C., 1965–69; *Oficial Mayor of the Secretariat of the Treasury*, 1970–75. g-None. h-None. i-Married Maria Guadalupe Fernandez del Valle. j-None. k-None. l-HA, 14 Dec. 1970, 21; DPE71, 27.

Ricardo Tirado, Jose
(Deceased)
a-Nov., 1907. b-Cueltzalan, Teziutlan, Puebla, *East Central, Rural*. c-Primary studies in Teziutlan and Puebla, Puebla; no degree. d-*Federal Deputy* from the State of Puebla, Dist. 8, 1946–49, member of the Rules Committee; *Federal Deputy* from the State of

Puebla, Dist. 9, 1952–55, member of the Complaints Committee and the Rules Committee; *Federal Deputy* from the State of Puebla, Dist. 8, 1958–61, member of the Administrative Committee; *Senator* from Baja California del Norte, 1964–70. e-Representative of the CEN of PRI to the State of Puebla during the presidential campaigns of 1946, 1952; General Delegate of the CEN of PRI to Baja California del Norte, 1953; President of the PRI in Baja California del Norte; *Secretary of Organization of the CEN of PRI*, 1968. f-Police Chief of Tijuana, 1931; representative of Baja California del Norte in Mexico City, 1959–64. g-Ejido comisariat. j-None. k-None. l-Func., 325; C de D, 1946–49, 85; C de D, 1952–55, 18, 65, 66; C de D, 1958–61, 89; Aguirre, 513.

Rico Islas, Juan Felipe

a-Feb. 5, 1890. b-Federal District, *Federal District, Urban*. c-Cadet at the National Military College, 1906; graduated from the National Military College as a 2nd Lieutenant, 1907. d-None. e-None. f-*Governor of Baja California del Norte*, Aug., 1944, to Dec., 1946. g-None. h-None. j-Inspector in the Army; fought in the Orozco campaign; fought against Felix Diaz in Veracruz, 1912; member of the Division of the North under the command of General Huerta; retired Colonel, 1914–20; returned to active service, fought against De la Huerta, 1923; fought against Escobar, 1929; Divisionary General, Sept. 1, 1942; Commander of the Military Zone for Baja California del Norte, 1946. k-None. l-Peral, 683; WWM45, 102; Lopez.

Rincon Coutino, Valentin

(Deceased July 6, 1968)
a-Oct. 8, 1901. b-Tuxtla Gutierrez, Chiapas, *South, Urban*. c-Primary studies in Tuxtla Gutierrez; preparatory studies at the National Preparatory School; law degree from the National School of Law, UNAM; Professor of Civil Law, National School of Law, UNAM; professor, School of Law, University of Jalapa. d-*Federal Deputy* from the State of Chiapas, Dist. 1, 1949–52, member of the Second Justice Committee. e-None. f-Judge of the 1st Instance; President of the Superior Tribunal of Justice of the State of Veracruz; President of the Tribunal of Justice of the Federal District and Federal Territories, 1940. g-Founder of the Social Front of Lawyers. h-Co-author of the Civil Code of Procedures for the State of Veracruz; President of the Mexican Society of Geography and Statistics, 1966–67; author of numerous articles on law and history. j-None. k-Mason; Grand Master of the Grand Lodge of the Valley of Mexico. l-DP70, 1763; DGF51, I, 34; C de D, 1949–51; Enc. Mex., XI, 1977, 133; DBC, 209–10.

Rincon Gallardo, Gilberto

a-May 15, 1939. b-Federal District, *Federal District, Urban*. c-Early education unknown; law degree, National School of Law, UNAM, 1962; Professor of the Theory of the State, School of Political and Social Science, UNAM, 1963. d-*Federal Deputy* (Party Deputy from the Mexican Communist Party), 1979–82. e-Joined the Mexican Communist Party, 1963; member of the Central Committee of the Mexican Communist Party, 1972–79; representative of the Central Committee of the PCM to the Federal Electoral Commission, 1979. g-None. j-None. k-Imprisoned in Lecumberri Prison, July, 1968 to December, 1971, because of his participation in the 1968 student strike. l-HA, 26 Feb. 1979, IV.

Rios Elizondo, Roberto

(Deceased Jan. 9, 1978)
a-1912. b-Federal District, *Federal District, Urban*. c-Preparatory studies at the National Preparatory School; law degree, National School of Law, UNAM; LLD from the National School of Law, UNAM; Professor of the first and second courses in Administrative Law, National School of Law, UNAM; Professor of Fiscal Legislation; Higher School of Commerce, National Polytechnical School; Professor of Fiscal Legislation, School of Commerce, UNAM. d-None. e-None. f-Subdirector of the Technical Fiscal Department, Treasury of the Federal District; Director of the Technical Fiscal Department, Treasury of the Federal District, 1947–50; Director of the Legal Department, Treasury of the Federal District, 1950–52; Fiscal Attorney for the Department of the Federal District; Assistant Treasurer, Department of the Federal District, 1952–64; *Oficial Mayor of the Secretariat of Public Works*, 1964–70; *Secretary General of the IMSS*, 1970–71; *Secretary General D of the Department of the Federal District*, 1971–73; *Secretary of Works and Services*, 1973–76; *Justice of the Supreme Court*, 1977–78. g-None. h-Delegate to the Department of the Federal District to the Secretariat of the Presidency; co-author of the fiscal and administrative laws of the Department of the Federal District, 1947; author of many articles and essays on administrative law and fiscal subjects; President of the Mexican Academy of Administrative Law, 1966. i-Married Carmen Ferrer. j-None. k-None. l-*Libro de Oro*, xxiv; DPE65, 116; DGF56, 487; DGF51, I, 509; HA, 21 Dec. 1964, 10; DPE61, 146; DBM68, 516–17; HA, 22 Jan. 1973, 36; *Excelsior*, 10 Jan. 1978, 4; HA, 16 Jan. 1978, 10.

Rios Zertuche, Antonio

a-1894. b-Monclova, Coahuila, *North, Urban*. c-Early education unknown; no degree. d-None. e-None. f-Director of the Department of Cavalry,

Secretariat of War; Inspector of Police in the Federal District; *Ambassador to France*, 1945–46. **g**-None. **h**-Constructed military bases in Tapachula, Chiapas and Puerto Madero, Quintana Roo. **j**-Career Army officer; Constitutionalist during the Revolution. **k**-Helped mechanize the Mexican cavalry. **l**-Lopez, 937; letter.

Rius Facious, Antonio

a-1918. **b**-Federal District, *Federal District*, *Urban*. **c**-Early education unknown; no degree. **d**-None. **e**-Member of the Executive Committee of PAN, 1964. **f**-None. **g**-Director of the Mexican Catholic Action Youth, 1940; founder of the Association of Businesses of the Central District of Mexico City. **h**-Journalist; poet and author of many articles and books. **i**-Parents are Spanish immigrants. **j**-None. **k**-None. **l**-Enc. Mex., XI, 1977, 141.

Riva Palacio Morales, Rafael

a-June 3, 1913. **b**-Texcoco, Mexico, *West Central*, *Urban*. **c**-Secondary studies at the Scientific and Literary Institute of Mexico, Toluca; studies at the School of Business, UNAM, 1927–30; economics degree, National School of Economics, UNAM, 1933. **d**-*Federal Deputy* from the State of Mexico, Dist. 3, 1970–73, member of the Radio Industry Committee, the Second Balloting Committee, and the Tourism Committee. **e**-None. **f**-Adviser for Publicity to President *Adolfo Lopez Mateos*. **g**-President of the National Chamber of Broadcasting Industries. **h**-President of the Mexican Association of Publicity Agents; Gerente General of Publicity Salas, S.A., 1968. **i**-Descendant of Vicente Riva Palacio; son of Carlos Riva Palacio, President of the CEN of PNR, 1933–34, and Secretary of Government under Calles; brother of *Emilio Riva Palacio*, Governor of Morelos, 1964–70. **j**-None. **k**-None. **l**-C de D, 1970–72, 132; DBM68, 519.

Rivas Guillen, Genovevo

(Deceased 1947)
a-Jan. 3, 1886. **b**-Rayon, San Luis Potosi, *East Central*, *Rural*. **c**-Primary studies at the public school No. 1, Tampico, Tamaulipas; no degree. **d**-None. **e**-None. **f**-*Provisional Governor of San Luis Potosi*, 1938–39, replacing *Mateo Hernandez Netro*, who joined the *Cedillo* rebellion. **g**-None. **h**-Worked in a general store; worked in photography; self-employed farmer. **i**-Father was captured and shot by Victoriano Huerta during the Revolution, 1913. **j**-Joined the Constitutional Army as a private, Dec. 8, 1913, as a member of the 4th Squad, 25th Regiment, San Luis Potosi; as a Lt. Colonel, fought the North American troops under General Pershing, Carrizal, Chihuahua, 1916; fought the Cristeros, 1926–28; rank of Brigadier General, Apr. 1, 1928; rank of divisionary general, 1933; Commander of the 15th Military Zone, Guadalajara, Jalisco, 1937; Commander of the 12th Military Zone, San Luis Potosi, 1938; fought against Cedillo, 1938; Commander of the Military Zone of Queretaro, Oaxaca, and Sonora. **k**-None. **l**-DP70, 1770–71; WWM45, 102; D de Y, 27 May 1938, 1; Peral, 690; Q es Q, 500–01; Enc. Mex., XI, 1977, 144; Lopez, 938.

Rivera Crespo, Felipe

a-Oct. 9, 1908. **b**-Ciudad Jojutla, Morelos, *West Central*, *Urban*. **c**-Primary studies in Jojutla and in the Federal District; engineering degree in topography from the Superior School of Construction, Technical Industrial Institute (IPN), 1928. **d**-Trustee Attorney for the City of Cuernavaca, 1935; Mayor of Cuernavaca, 1955–57; *Alternate Senator* from the State of Morelos, 1952–58; Mayor of Cuernavaca, 1967–69; *Governor of Morelos*, 1970 to 1976. **e**-Secretary of Agrarian Action of the State Committee of the PNR, Morelos, 1930; Secretary General of CNOP of PRI for the State of Morelos, 1954. **f**-Subdirector of Public Works for the State of Morelos, 1932; founder and President of the Local Highway Commission, 1935–70. **g**-Member of the Mixed Agrarian Commission of Morelos, 1929; President of the Association of Winegrowers of Morelos, 1966; President of the Lions Club of Morelos, 1955. **h**-President of the Board of Tourism for Morelos, 1960. **i**-Half brother, *Diodoro Rivera Uribe*, was a Senator from Morelos, 1964–70. **j**-None. **k**-None. **l**-DGF56, 6; letter; *Hoy*, 20 May 1972, 62–63.

Rivera Marin, Maria Guadalupe

b-Federal District, *Federal District*, *Urban*. **c**-Early education unknown; law degree, National School of Law, UNAM, 1947; LLD from the National School of Law, UNAM, 1952. **d**-*Federal Deputy* from the Federal District, Dist. 22, 1961–64, member of the Penal Section of the Legislative Studies Committee and the Tax Committee; *Federal Deputy* from Guanajuato, Dist. 9, 1979–82. **e**-None. **f**-Employee of the Secretariat of Government Properties, the Secretariat of the Treasury, the National Finance Bank and the Department of the Federal District; representative of Mexico to the International Labor Conference, Geneva, 1955. **g**-None. **h**-Author. **i**-Daughter of painter Diego Rivera, co-founder of the Mexican Communist Party; grandfather was a school teacher and her grandmother an obstetrician. **j**-None. **k**-First woman to win the National Prize in Economics, 1955. **l**-Enc. Mex., XI, 1977, 151; C de D, 1961–64, 88; Lopez, 946; WWM45, 102.

Rivera Perez Campos, Jose

a-Mar. 19, 1907. **b**-Celaya, Guanajuato, *West Central*, *Urban*. **c**-Primary studies in Celaya; preparatory studies at the National Preparatory School; law degree from the National School of Law, UNAM, 1931, with a thesis on the justification of the state; Professor of General History, National Preparatory School, 1929–35; Professor of the History of Philosophical Doctrines, National Preparatory School, 1932; Professor of the General Theory of the State, National School of Law, UNAM, 1935–48; Professor of Introduction to the Study of Law, National School of Law, UNAM, 1932–35; Professor of the History of Political Thought, UNAM, 1932; LLD, National School of Law, UNAM, 1951; Secretary of the University of Guanajuato, 1936; *Secretary General of UNAM*, 1946. **d**-*Alternate Senator* from Guanajuato, 1946–52; *Senator* from Guanajuato, 1970–76, member of the permanent committee, member of the Gran Comision, President of the Second Justice committee, President of the Second Instructive Section of the Grand Jury, and First Secretary of the Constitutional Affairs Committee. **e**-None. **f**-Judge of the Superior Tribunal of Justice of the State of Guanajuato, 1936; Secretary General of PIPSA, 1937–39; *Oficial Mayor of Labor*, 1940; Judge of the Superior Tribunal of Justice of the State of Guanajuato, 1941–46; General Attorney for the Legal Department, National Railroads of Mexico, 1941–45, 1947; Director of the Department of Legal Affairs, PEMEX, 1948–52; *Justice of the Supreme Court*, 1954–58, 1958–64, 1964–70; Director of Legal Affairs, Secretariat of Government, 1979–80; *Subsecretary of Government (3)*, 1980– . **g**-None. **h**-Author of many works; consulting lawyer to the Secretariat of Agriculture, 1932– 34, and to the Secretariat of the Treasury, 1935. **i**-*Antonio Luna Arroyo,* a close family friend; brother Ricardo, a practicing lawyer and formerly director of the National Preparatory School; began early career under *Enrique Fernandez Martinez* in Guanajuato. **j**-None. **k**-Outspoken critic of issues discussed in the Senate, 1974. **l**-DGF56, 567; DJBM, 120; DGF51, I, 6; DGF50, II, 281, 386; *Justicia;* C de S, 1946–52; C de S, 1970–76; WNM, 192; Lopez, 9443; C de S, 1970–76, 84; Enc. Mex., XI, 1977, 152.

Rivera Silva, Manuel

a-1913. **b**-Federal District, *Federal District, Urban.* **c**-Primary studies at public and private schools in the Federal District; secondary studies at Secondary School No. 1, Federal District; preparatory studies at the National Preparatory School; law degree from the National School of Law, UNAM, 1937 (honorable mention), thesis published; professor of law, National School of Law, UNAM (twenty-three years). **d**-None. **e**-None. **f**-Delegate of the Office of the Attorney General to the Federal District, 1937; Minor Judge, Federal District; Criminal Judge of the 5th Criminal Court; Inspector General of the Office of

the Attorney General; Assistant Fiscal Attorney for the Federal Government; Director General of the Division of Social Welfare, Secretariat of Labor, 1952–58; *Justice of the Supreme Court*, 1958–64, 1964–70, 1970–73. **g**-Student activist at the National Preparatory School; founder of the student intellectual magazine, *Barandal*, 1931. **h**-Practiced law, 1937. **i**-Son of a lawyer; married Maria Elvira Delgado; student of *Luis Chico Goerne* and *Francisco Gonzalez de la Vega*. **j**-None. **k**-None. **l**-*Justicia*, July, 1967; DGF56, 398; WNM, 192; *Excelsior*, 29 Feb., 1960.

Rivera Uribe, Diodoro

a-Dec. 19, 1916. **b**-Amacuzac, Morelos, *West Central, Rural.* **c**-Law degree, National School of Law, UNAM; Professor at the Training Academy for Judicial Police of the Federal District; Founding Professor of Agrarian Law, University of Morelos. **d**-*Federal Deputy* from the State of Morelos, 1961–64, Dist. 1, President of the Sugar Industry Committee, the Editorial Committee, and the Fourth Interparliamentary Committee; *Senator* from the State of Morelos, 1964–70, member of the Agrarian Department Committee, the Indigenous Affairs Committee, the Legislative Studies Committee, the National Waters and Irrigation Committee, and President of the Treasury Committee; Secretary and Vice President of the Gran Comision. **e**-General delegate of PRI to Yucatan, Quintana Roo, Oaxaca, San Luis Potosi, Guanajuato, and Tlaxcala; Director of the IEPES of PRI for Morelos; President of the State Committee of PRI for Morelos. **f**-Investigator for the Institute of Historical Investigations, UNAM; Agent of the Ministerio Publico of the Office of the Attorney General; Chief of Special Services of the National Railroads of Mexico; Chief of the Federal Fiscal Police; Assistant Director of the Federal Judicial Police; Director of the Campaign for the Control of the Drug Traffic in the North West; President of the Superior Tribunal of Justice for the State of Morelos. **g**-None. **h**-Created the Social Service System for fourth and fifth year students in Federal Agencies. **i**-Half brother of *Felipe Rivera Crespo*, Governor of Morelos, 1970–76. **j**-None. **k**-Organized the private schools of the Federal District to support *Cardenas* during the petroleum expropriation, 1938. **l**-C de D, 1961–63; C de S, 1964–70; DBM68, 520–21.

Robledo Santiago, Edgar

a-Sept. 20, 1917. **b**-Motozintla, Chiapas (Colonia Belisario Dominguez), *South, Rural.* **c**-Primary studies at the Rural School of Motozintla, Chiapas, and at the Cuauhtemoc School of Huixtla, Chiapas; rural school teacher, 1934; studied on scholarship at the Rural Normal School, Cerrohueco, Chiapas, 1935; urban teaching certificate from the Normal Urban School, Tuxtla, Gutierrez, Chiapas, 1944–49;

professor at the Institute of Arts and Sciences of Chiapas. **d-***Federal Deputy* from the State of Chiapas, Dist. 3, 1967–70, member of the Cultural Affairs Committee; *Senator* from the State of Chiapas, 1970, 1975–76. **e-**None. **f-**Inspector of Rural Normal Schools, Secretariat of Public Education, 1952; *Director General of the FSTSE*, 1968–70; *Director General of the ISSSTE*, 1970–75. **g-**Secretary General of the National Union of Educational Employees, 1964–67. **h-**None. **i-**From very poor economic circumstances; alternated going to school with work as an agricultural laborer; married Cristina Brindis. **j-**None. **k-**None. **l-**HA, 7 Dec. 1970, 27; HA, 5 April 1971, 14; WWMG, 34; C de D, 1967–69, 58; MGF69; DBC, 212–215; *Justicia*, Apr., 1973; WNM, 193; HA, 29 Sept. 1975, 10.

Robles, Gonzalo

a-1895. **b-**Cartago, Costa Rica, *Foreign*. **c-**Preparatory studies in Costa Rica; agricultural engineering degree, National School of Agriculture, 1909–13; degree in civil engineering, Indiana University, 1917–21. **d-**None. **e-**None. **f-**Special mission to the United States to study agricultural colleges for Venustiano Carranza, 1916; technical adviser to President Calles, 1923; adviser to the Office of Economic Statistics, National Railroads of Mexico, 1932; Director General of the National Mortgage and Public Works Bank, 1933–35; *Director General of the Bank of Mexico*, 1935; founder and Director of the Department of Industrial Research, Bank of Mexico, 1946–52; Director General of the Agricultural Bank, 1935–38; adviser to the Bank of Mexico, 1938–79. **g-**Member of the Agrarian Commission in Veracruz. **h-**Participated in various agrarian congresses in Mexico City, 1921–22; worked for a private firm in Molango, Hidalgo, 1914–15. **i-**Grandfather was a physician; long-time friend of *Jesus Silva Herzog* and *Eduardo Villasenor* since the 1920s; he and *Jesus Silva Herzog* attempted to create a system of ejido banks in 1926. **j-**None. **k-**Came to Mexico in 1909. **l-** Villasenor, E. 92; Zevada, 117–18; Beltran, 310–11; MGF47, 322; DGF51, II, 7, 293; DGF50, II, 11; DP, 2365; Villasenor, II, 196.

Robles Leon Martin del Campo, Jaime

b-Jalisco, *West*. **c-**Early education unknown; law degree; Professor of Constitutional Law, Free School of Law, Mexico City; Professor of Constitutional Law, Free School of Law, Guadalajara; co-founder and supporter of the Autonomous University of Guadalajara. **d-***Federal Deputy* from the State of Jalisco, Dist. 3, 1949–52, alternate member of the Consular Service and Diplomatic Committee. **e-**Member of PAN; co-founder of PAN with *Manuel Gomez Morin*, *Efrain Gonzalez Luna* and others. **f-**None.

g-None. **h-**Political commentator in newspapers and radios of Jalisco; practicing lawyer and notary. **i-**Son of Emiliano Robles Leon, lawyer and notary; from three generations of lawyers; daughter is Martha Robles, well-known novelist. **j-**None. **k-**First candidate of PAN to run for governor of Jalisco; opposed *Agustin Yanez* for the governorship in a hotly contested campaign in 1953; as a federal deputy fought for the revision of Articles 145 and 145bis of the federal Constitution. **l-**Letter; C de D, 1949–52; DGF51, I, 22, 36.

Robles Linares, Luis

a-Sept. 11, 1922. **b-**Ensenada, Baja California del Norte, *North*, *Rural*. **c-**Engineering degree from the National Polytechnical Institute, 1944; OAS scholarship to study agricultural planning and regional development in Tel Aviv, 1966. **d-**None. **e-**None. **f-**Chief of Resident Engineers, Obregon Dam, Sonora; Director of Construction, Cuauhtemoc Dam Irrigation zone; Chief of the Sonora Irrigation Zone, Secretariat of Hydraulic Resources; Chief of Construction, Small Irrigation Works, Sonora; Director of Potable Water, Sonora; Second Chief Engineer of Irrigation and Flood Control, Secretariat of Hydraulic Resources, 1968–70; *Subsecretary (A) of Hydraulic Resources*, 1970–76; *Subsecretary in Charge of Hydraulic Resources*, 1976; *Secretary of Hydraulic Resources*, 1976–77. **g-**None. **h-**None. **i-**Married Maria de Jesus Gandara. **j-**None. **k-**Acquired Sonoran residency, 1946; precandidate for governor of Sonora, 1977. **l-**HA, 14 Dec. 1970, 22; DPE71, 88; *Excelsior*, 1 Dec. 1976; HA, 6 Dec. 1976, 23.

Robles Martinez, Jesus

a-Aug. 2, 1913. **b-**Colima, Colima, *West*, *Urban*. **c-**Engineering degree in electrical communications from the Higher School of Mechanical and Electrical Engineering, National Polytechnical Institute; Professor of Physics and Mathematics, National Polytechnical Institute; Director of Instruction, IPN; Subdirector General of IPN. **d-***Federal Deputy* from the State of Colima, Dist. 2, 1952–55, member of the Public Education Committee, the Credentials Committee, and the Consular and Diplomatic Service Committee, President of the Chamber, Sept., 1952; *Senator* from the State of Colima, 1964–65. **e-**PRI state committeeman from Colima. **f-***Secretary General of the FSTSE*, 1964–65; Director General of the National Bank of Public Works and Services, 1965–76. **g-**Leader of student groups at IPN, 1935; President of the National Federation of Technical Students, 1936; Secretary General of the National Union of Educational Employees, 1949–52. **h-**None. **i-**Brother Roberto was Subdirector of the National Public Works Bank; formed a powerful political clique with *Alfonso Martinez Dominguez* and *Romulo Sanchez Mireles* in the FSTSE. **j**-None. **k**-Accused in the press of being a latifundista and using rich lands in San Luis Potosi for cattle raising; leader of the "Colima Group" in his home state; answered *Miguel Aleman*'s last State of the Union address, 1952. **l**-C de D, 1952–54, 18; MGF69, 516; WWMG, 34; HA, 7 Dec. 1970, 27; *Hoy*, 1 May 1971, 12; *Hoy*, 3 June 1972, 9; *Excelsior*, 26 June 1975, 4; *Excelsior*, 10 Dec. 1978, 18; *Excelsior*, 18 Mar. 1977, 12; HA, 8 Apr. 1974, 25.

Rocha (Cordero), Jr., Antonio

a-Apr. 6, 1912. **b**-San Luis Potosi, San Luis Potosi, *East Central*, *Urban*. **c**-Law degree, University of San Luis Potosi, June 13, 1935; Professor of Penal Law. **d**-*Alternate Federal Deputy* from the State of San Luis Potosi, Dist. 1, 1943–46; *Federal Deputy* from the State of San Luis Potosi, Dist. 1, 1949–52, member of the Library Committee (1st year), the First and Second Legislative Studies Committee, the Gran Comision, and the Second Constitutional Affairs Committee; *Alternate Senator* from San Luis Potosi, 1946–49; *Senator* from the State of San Luis Potosi, 1952–58, member of the Gran Comision, the Protocol Committee, the First Government Committee, President of the Second Constitutional Affairs Committee, member of the Third Labor Committee, and the Special Legislative Studies Committee; substitute member of the First Public Education Committee and the First Ejido Committee; *Governor of San Luis Potosi*, 1967–73; *Federal Deputy* from the State of San Luis Potosi, 1979– . **e**-None. **f**-Attorney, City Council, San Luis Potosi, 1939–41; Attorney for the Department of Government, San Luis Potosi; Attorney General of San Luis Potosi, 1943–45; Secretary General of the State of San Luis Potosi; Attorney General of Tamaulipas, 1947–48; *Attorney General of Mexico*, 1964–67; *Justice of the Supreme Court*, 1973–78. **g**-Delegate to the Seventh National Student Congress, San Luis Potosi, 1930. **h**-Practicing lawyer, 1935–43; founder and director of the *Penal Law Review*, University of San Luis Potosi, 1939–43. **i**-Married Socorro Diaz del Castillo; Professor of *Gustavo Carvajal*. **j**-None. **k**-Praised by *Por Que* for his honesty as Governor of San Luis Potosi. **l**-*El Universal*, 1 Dec. 1964; WWMG, 34; DGF56, 7, 9–14; DGF47, 21; HA, 7 Dec. 1964, 21; DPE65, 209; DGF51, I, 7, 25, 29, 31, 32, 35; C de D, 1949–51, 88; *Por Que*, 11 Dec. 1969; Enc. Mex., XI, 1977, 159; Ind. Biog., 132–33; *Excelsior*, 27 Feb. 1979, 14.

Rodriguez, Damian L.

a-June 6, 1887. **b**-Ramos Arizpe, Coahuila, *North*, *Rural*. **c**-Early education unknown; no degree. **d**-*Federal Deputy* from the State of Coahuila, Dist.

3, 1937–40; *Senator* from the State of Coahuila, 1940–46. **e**-None. **g**-None. **h**-None. **j**-Career army officer; rank of Brigadier General. **k**-Grand Master of the National Mexican Masonic Grand Lodge. **l**-Peral, 698; C de D, 1937–39, 19; C de S, 1940–46.

Rodriguez, Jaime Luis Danton

a-Aug. 28, 1933. **b**-Guanajuato, Guanajuato, *West Central*, *Urban*. **c**-Law degree, National School of Law, UNAM, with a thesis on "State Intervention in the Economy;" Professor of Sociology, School of Banking and Commerce; Director of Economic and Social Studies Seminar, Mexican Military Academy Preparatory School; Professor of Administrative Law, National School of Law, UNAM; Professor of Civics and Political Education, CNC. **d**-*Federal Deputy* from the State of Guanajuato, Dist. 1, 1964–67; President of the Budget Committee and of the Tax Committee, member of the Money, Banking, and Credit Institution Committee; President of the Chamber of Deputies, Nov., 1966; *Federal Deputy* from the State of Guanajuato, Dist. 1, 1973–76; President of the Executive Committee, Sept., 1973. **e**-*Director of the IEPES of the CEN of PRI*, 1976–78. **f**-Law intern for Nacional Financiera; Adviser to the Director of the Department of Economic Studies; Assistant Director of the Department of Technical Studies, Department of Income Taxes; Director of the Federal Treasury Office, No. 6, Federal District, 1961; Director of Government, Secretary of Government, 1979– . **g**-Member of the Technical Council of the CNC. **h**-Writer for many magazines; studied at CEMLA under a scholarship from Nacional Financiera. **i**-Son of *Luis I. Rodriguez*. **j**-None. **k**-Answered President *Echeverria*'s third State of the Union address; precandidate for Governor of Guanajuato, 1978; precandidate for senator from Guanajuato, 1976. **l**-DBM68, 530; DPE61, 43; C de D, 1964–66, 55, 90, 91; *Excelsior*, 28 Aug. 1973; *Excelsior*, 30 Apr. 1978.

Rodriguez, Luis I.

(Deceased Aug. 28, 1973)

a-Oct. 21, 1905. **b**-Silao, Guanajuato, *West Central*, *Urban*. **c**-Primary studies in Guanajuato; secondary and preparatory studies in Guanajuato; law degree from the University of Guanajuato, Apr. 29, 1929; Rector of the University of Guanajuato, 1929; Professor of Constitutional Law for many years. **d**-Federal Deputy from Baja California del Sur, 1934–36; local deputy to the State Legislature of Guanajuato, 1930; *Governor of Guanajuato*, 1937–38, 1939–40; *Senator* from the State of Guanajuato, 1952–58, substitute member of the Protocol Committee, member of the First Justice Committee, the Rules Committee, the Second Balloting Committee, and the Legislative Studies Committee, president of the Foreign Relations Committee. **e-***President of the CEN of PRM*, Apr. 2, 1938, to June 19, 1939; founding member of the PRM. **f-**Director of Popular Culture, State of Guanajuato; Oficial Mayor of Government of the State of Guanajuato; Secretary of Government of the State of Guanajuato; Secretary General of Government and Interim Governor of Baja California del Sur under General *Juan B. Dominguez Cota*, 1932–34; *Ambassador to France*, 1939–40; Ambassador to Chile, 1942–46; Ambassador to Canada; Ambassador to Guatemala, 1951; Ambassador to Venezuela, 1961–65; *Private Secretary to the President of Mexico*, 1934–37, under *Lazaro Cardenas*. **g-**Student leader at the University of Guanajuato; president of the Revolutionary Convention of Ciudad Victoria, Tamaulipas, 1926. **h-**None. **i-**Father of *Jaime Luis Danton Rodriguez*; married Eloisa Jaime. **j-**None. **k-**Supported General Obregon for President, 1928; precandidate for President of Mexico, 1939; opposed *Angel Carvajal*'s candidacy for the President of Mexico in 1952 in an open letter with *Heriberto Jara* and *Silvano Barba Gonzalez*; member of the Inner Circle from 1934–40; first President of the revised PRM. **l-**DP70, 1232; *Polemica*, Vol. I, No. 1, 1969, 69; EBW46, 89; DGF56, 6, 10–14; Peral, 702; Brandenburg, 80; Morton, 74–75, 41, 92; Michaels, 3; HA, 3 Sept. 1973, 29; Lopez, 953.

Rodriguez Adame, Julian

a-July 11, 1904. **b-**Pachuca, Hidalgo, *East Central*, *Urban*. **c-**Primary studies in Pachuca; engineering degree in agriculture from the National School of Agriculture, Chapingo; Director of the Central Agricultural School, Mexico, 1932–34; Professor of Agricultural Economics, National School of Economics, UNAM, 1939–56. **d-***Federal Deputy* from the State of Hidalgo, Dist. 1, 1955–57, member of the Gran Comision, the Tariff and Foreign Trade Committee, and the First Treasury Committee; *Alternate Senator* from the State of Hidalgo, 1952–58, but replaced Senator Cravioto after he died, 1957–58; *Senator* from the State of Hidalgo, 1958–64, but never held office. **e-**Founding member of the PNR, 1929. **f-**Engineer in various technical positions for the National Agrarian Commission; Secretary General of the Agrarian Department; Director of the Department of Credit, National Ejido Credit Bank, 1936; Director of the National Bank of Commerce, 1939; Gerente, National Bank of Ejido Credit; Chief of the Agricultural Department, Secretariat of Agriculture, 1940–46; Director General of Prices, Secretariat of Industry and Commerce, 1946–53; *Director General of CONASUPO*, 1958; *Secretary of Agriculture and Livestock*, 1958–64; Ambassador to Japan, 1965–68; Ambassador to Pakistan, 1968–70. **g-**None. **h-**Adviser to

various decentralized agencies. **i-**Friends with *Mario Sousa* and *Adolfo Lopez Mateos* since 1933; married Mercedes Santana. **j-**None. **k-***Por Que* claims he was involved in a land deal with *Juan Jose Torres Landa* while serving as Secretary of Agriculture. **l-**HA, 28 Dec. 1951, 35; HA, 8 Dec. 1958, 28; DGF51, II, 29; DPE61, 69; DFG51, I, 263; *Por Que*, 11 July 1969, 11; HA, 12 Dec. 1952, 6; *Excelsior*, 10 Nov. 1976.

Rodriguez Alcaine, Leonardo

a-May 1, 1919. **b-**Texcoco, Mexico, *West Central*, *Urban*. **c-**Primary studies in Texcoco at the Colegio Juarez, completing his primary studies at the Jose Vicente Villada School, Mexico City; secondary studies at Secondary No. 7, Mexico City; completed two years at the School of Mechanical and Electrical Engineering, IPN; studies at the Customs Academy of the Secretariat of the Treasury. **d-***Federal Deputy* from the Federal District, Dist. 8, 1955–58, member of the Electric Industry Committee; *Alternate Federal Deputy* from the State of Mexico, Dist. 2, 1964–67; *Federal Deputy* from the State of Mexico, Dist. 7, 1967–70, member of the Communications and Transportation Section of the Legislative Studies Committee; *Federal Deputy* from the State of Mexico, Dist. 7, 1973–76; *Senator* from Mexico, 1976–82. **e-**None. **f-**Subdirector of the General Warehouse, Federal Electric Commission. **g-**Secretary of Labor and Conflicts of Section 1, Union of Workers of the Federal Electric Commission, 1941–42; Secretary of Sports Action of the National Executive Committee of the Union of Workers of the Federal Electric Commission, 1942–45; Secretary of Organization of the CEN of the Union of Workers of the Federal Electric Commission, 1945–51; Secretary of Organization and Publicity of the Union of Workers of the Federal Electric Commission, 1951–59; Secretary of Labor of SUTERM, 1975; *Secretary General of SUTERM*, March 28, 1975– . **h-**First employed as a porter at the National Electric Commission, 1938. **i-**Long-time ally of *Francisco Perez Rios* until his death in 1975. **j-**None. **k-**None. **l-**Ind. Biog., 134–35; *Excelsior*, 26 Mar. 1975, 4; DGF56, 25, 34; C de D, 1955–58; C de D, 1967–70, 70; C de D, 1964–67, 55; C de S, 1976–82.

Rodriguez Barrera, Rafael

a-Feb. 10, 1937. **b-**Guadalupe Barrio, Campeche, Campeche, *Gulf*, *Urban*. **c-**Primary studies at the Justo Sierra Mendez Primary School, Campeche, 1942–48; secondary studies at the Instituto Campechano, 1948–53; studied law at the Instituto Campechano and completed his degree at the University of Campeche, Dec. 20, 1958; Professor of English, Spanish, Ethics and Philosophy, Teachers Literacy

Institute, Campeche; Professor of Constitutional Law, University of Campeche. d-Local Deputy to the State Legislature of Campeche, 1962; Mayor of Campeche, 1963–64; *Federal Deputy* from the State of Campeche, Dist. 1, 1970–73, member of the Gran Comision, the Cooperative Development Committee, the Second Treasury Committee, the Fish and Game Committee, and the Second Constitutional Affairs Committee; *Governor of Campeche*, 1973–79. e-President of PRI in Campeche; *Secretary of Organization of the CEN of PRI*, 1972–73; member of the National Council of PRI; Oficial Mayor of the CEN of PRI, 1980– . f-Public Defender, 1957–58; Secretary of the City Council of Campeche, 1958; Private Secretary to the Mayor of Campeche, *Eugenio Echeverria Castellot*, 1961–62; Director of Public Security and Traffic, Campeche; Secretary General of Government of the State of Campeche under Governor *Carlos Sansores Perez*, 1967–69; Gerente, National Chamber of Fishing Industries. g-None. h-Adviser, National Bank of Agricultural Credit. i-Son of a school teacher; married Professora Socorro Cabrera; his cousin, Sergio Mora Rodriguez, was Oficial Mayor of the State Government of Campeche. j-None. k-Resigned as Mayor of Campeche because of grave differences with Governor *Jose Ortiz Avila*. l-*Directorio*, 1970–72; HA, 8 Jan. 1973, 34; C de D, 1970–72, 133; HA, 17 Sept. 1973, 40–43; Enc. Mex., Annual, 1977, 540–41; *Excelsior*, 6 Aug. 1978, 29.

Rodriguez Cano, Enrique

(Deceased 1956)
a-1912. b-Balcazar, Tuxpan, Veracruz, *Gulf*, *Rural*. c-Early education unknown; no degree. d-Local Deputy to the State Legislature of Veracruz, 1944–45; Mayor of Tuxpan, Veracruz, 1936–38; *Federal Deputy* from the State of Veracruz, Dist. 2, 1949–52, member of the Gran Comision, the National Waters and Irrigation Committee, the Agrarian Department Committee, and Vice President for the Preparatory Committees. e-None. f-Tax collector, Alamo, Veracruz; Director of Printing, State Legislature of Veracruz, 1938–40; Director of the Library for the Federal Congress, 1940–42; Subsecretary of Government of the State of Veracruz, under *Ruiz Cortines*, 1948; *Oficial Mayor of Government*, 1951–52, under Secretary *Adolfo Ruiz Cortines*; *Secretary of the Presidency*, 1952–56. g-Secretary General of the League of Agrarian Communities of the State of Veracruz, 1946, under Governor *Ruiz Cortines*. h-None. i-Personal confidant of *Adolfo Ruiz Cortines*. j-None. k-*Ramon Beteta* has stated that *Ruiz Cortines* was not very much at ease with the college graduates of the *Aleman* administration, which is a reason why he placed so much confidence in *Rodriguez Cano* for many years. l-DGF51, I, 26, 29, 30,

31; C de D, 1949–51, 88; HA, 5 Dec. 1962, 10; DGF56, 53; DP70, 1788.

Rodriguez Claveria, Jose

(Deceased June 7, 1957)
a-1895. b-Veracruz, Veracruz, *Gulf*, *Urban*. c-Primary and secondary studies in Veracruz; no degree. d-*Federal Deputy* from the State of Veracruz, Dist. 9, 1949–52, member of the Second Treasury Committee, the Naval Committee, the Budget and Accounts Committee, the Insurance Committee and the Tourism Committee; *Senator* from the State of Veracruz, 1952–57, President of the Gran Comision, President of the First Committee on Credit, Money and Credit Institutions and of the First Treasury Committee. e-None. f-Director General of Tourism, Secretariat of Government, 1948–49. g-None. h-Founder of Financiera y Fiduciaria Veracruz, S.A.; Managing Director of Finanzas Mexicanas, S.A. i-Co-founded Financiera y Fiduciaria Veracruz with *Cosme Hinojosa*; helped *Adolfo Ruiz Cortines* become Oficial Mayor of the Department of the Federal District in 1935 after recommending him to *Cosme Hinojosa*. j-Joined the Revolution under General Salvador Alvarado; member of the General Staff of General Alvarado. k-None. l-HA, 29 Oct. 1956; Lopez, 970; Ind. Biog., 135–36; C de D, 1949–52, 88; DGF56, 8, 9, 10, 11.

Rodriguez Elias, Jose

a-Dec. 21, 1919. b-San Pedro, Zacatecas, *East Central*, *Rural*. c-Primary studies in Santa Piedra Gorda; secondary and preparatory studies in Zacatecas, Zacatecas; engineering degree in topography, National School of Agriculture, Chapingo. d-*Alternate Federal Deputy* from the State of Zacatecas, Dist. 4, 1949–52; *Federal Deputy* from the State of Zacatecas, Dist. 1, 1952–55, Vice President of the Chamber of Deputies, Nov., 1953, member of the Social Welfare Committee, the Securities Committee, and the Agrarian Department Committee; *Senator* from the State of Zacatecas, 1958–62, member of the National Waters and Irrigation Committee, the First Committee on Mines; President of the General Means of Communication Committee, member of the Second Balloting Committee and substitute member of the Special Committee on Small Agricultural Property; *Governor of Zacatecas*, 1962–67. e-Director of the Regional Committee of PRI for the State of Zacatecas. f-Representative of the Department of Agrarian Affairs, Zacatecas, 1951; Director General of the National Bank of Ejido Credit, 1968–70. g-Chairman of the Mexican Agronomy Society, 1955–58; Official of the CNC. h-None. j-None. k-*Por Que* claims he was involved in a 100 million peso scandal as Director of the National Ejido Bank, 1969. l-*Por Que*, 11

July 1969, 3; DGF51, I; C de D, 1949–51; G of M, 10; WWMG, 35; C de D, 1955–57, 18; C de S, 1961–64, 67; MGF69, 505; Func., 411.

Rodriguez Familiar, Ramon

a-Sept. 27, 1898. b-Queretaro, Queretaro, *East Central, Urban*. c-Early education unknown; no degree. d-*Governor of Queretaro*, 1935–39. e-None. f-Private Secretary to Abelardo Rodriguez, Governor of Baja California del Norte, 1929–30; Subchief of Staff, Secretariat of National Defense, 1932–33; Chief of Staff, Secretariat of National Defense, 1933–34; Director of Personnel, Secretariat of National Defense, 1940–46. g-None. h-None. i-Brother Jose is an author. j-Career army officer; fought under General *Abelardo Rodriguez*; rank of Divisionary General; Intendant General of the Army, 1951; Inspector General of the Army, 1970–72. k-*Gaxiola* states that he was selected for the position of Chief of Staff because of his personal loyalty to *Rodriguez*, even though he was only a colonel. l-Peral, 700; WWM45, 104; DGF51, I, 181; DPE71, 14; Gaxiola, 93.

Rodriguez Gomez, Francisco

a-Feb. 11, 1911. b-San Antonio, Ixtlahuacan del Rio, Jalisco, *West, Rural*. c-Teaching certificate; law degree, School of Law, University of Guadalajara; postgraduate studies, 1942–43; Professor, School of Economics, University of Guadalajara, 1937–46. d-*Federal Deputy* from the State of Jalisco, Dist. 6, 1955–58, member of the Legislative Studies Committee (1st year), the Committee on National Properties and Resources; Secretary of the Committee on Agrarian Law and Assistant Secretary of the Chamber of Deputies; *Federal Deputy* from the Federal District, Dist. 6, 1961–64, member of the Second Government Committee, Secretary of the Second Legislative Studies Committee. e-General Delegate of the CNOP of PRI to Baja California; General Delegate of the CEN of PRI to Hidalgo; General Delegate of the CEN of PRI to the Presidential campaign of *Adolfo Lopez Mateos* in Guanajuato; General Delegate of the CEN of PRI in Guanajuato (3 years); Coordinator General of the Economic and Social Assembly during *Gil Preciado*'s campaign for Governor; Coordinator of Presidential Campaigns in the State of Mexico for *Diaz Ordaz*, 1964. f-Director of the Normal School of Jalisco, 1937–39; Director of Secondary Education, State of Jalisco, 1942–43; Chief of the Education Department of Guadalajara, 1944; Secretary to the City Council of Guadalajara, 1944; President of the State Arbitration Board, Jalisco, 1944–45; Secretary General of the State of Jalisco under Governor *Marcelino Garcia Barragan*, 1945–46; Director of Public Education in Jalisco, 1946–52; Legal adviser, State of Jalisco, 1952;

Chief, Legal Department, National Agricultural Credit Bank, 1953–55; Attorney General of Justice of the State of Jalisco; *Oficial Mayor of Industry and Commerce*, 1964–70. g-None. h-None. j-None. k-None. l-DBM68, 529; DPE65, 88; C de D, 1961–63, 89; MGF69, 252; Ind. Biog., 136.

Rodriguez (Lujan), Abelardo L.

(Deceased Feb. 13, 1967)
a-May 12, 1889. b-San Jose de Guaymas, Sonora, *North, Rural*. c-Primary education in Nogales, Sonora; no degree. d-President of Mexico, 1932–34; *Governor of Sonora*, 1943–48. e-None. f-Governor and Military Commander of Baja California del Norte, 1923–29; Governor of Baja California del Norte, 1929–30; Subsecretary of the Navy, 1931–32; Secretary of War and Navy, Aug. 2, 1932, to Sept. 2, 1932; Secretary of Industry and Commerce, Jan. 20, 1932, to Aug. 2, 1932; President of the Advisory Fishing Council, Secretariat of Industry and Commerce, 1961; General Coordinator of National Production, 1942–43. g-None. h-Wealthy businessman in the State of Sonora and Baja California del Norte; began investments in the 1920s. i-From a very poor economic background; worked in a hardware store with brother Fernando; employed at Cananea Copper Mines; professional baseball player. j-Joined the Revolution, Lieutenant, 1913; rank of 1st Captain, 1914; fought against Huerta; rank of Major, 1914; rank of Lt. Col., 1915; Head of the 53rd Battalion under Obregon in the fighting against Villa; rank of Colonel, 1916; Brigadier General, 1920; Military Commander of Baja California del Norte, 1921; rank of Brigade General, 1924; Divisionary General, June 11, 1928; Commander of the Military Zone of the Gulf, 1942. k-Resigned from the governorship of Sonora, April, 1948, giving health as a reason. l-HA, 11 Dec. 1961, 3; Gaxiola, 57ff; NYT, 14 Feb. 1967, 43; Q es Q, 508; IWW40, 957; WWM45, 103; DP70, 1783; Covarrubias, 156; NYT, 26 Mar. 1943, 2; Anderson; *Justicia*, July, 1970.

Rodriguez Ramirez, Eliseo

a-1926. b-Penjamo, Guanajuato, *West Central, Urban*. c-Attended the Escuela Practica de Agricultura de Roque, Celaya; law degree from the National School of Law, UNAM. d-*Federal Deputy* from the State of Guanajuato, Dist. 5, 1961–64, member of the Second National Defense Committee, the Military Justice Committee, and substitute member of the First Justice Committee; *Alternate Senator* from the State of Guanajuato, 1964–70. e-Active member of the Agrarian Sector of PRI since 1953; joined PRI in 1949. f-Oficial Mayor of the Senate, 1971–72. g-None. h-None. j-Career army officer; rank of

Major. k-None. l-C de D, 1961–63, 89; HA, 13 Sept. 1971, 13.

Rodriguez Solorzano, Angel

a-May 31, 1919. b-Durango, Durango, *West*, *Urban*. c-Secondary and preparatory studies at the Juarez Institute, Durango; law degree from the School of Law, Juarez Institute, 1947; Professor of Biology at the Juarez Institute, 1942–66; Rector of the Juarez University of Durango (formerly Juarez Institute), 1953–64. d-*Federal Deputy* from the State of Durango, Dist. 1, 1964–67, member of the Cultural Affairs Committee, the Balloting Committee, and the First Public Education Committee. e-None. f-Secretary of the City Council of Durango, 1942–44; President of the State Board of Conciliation and Arbitration of Durango, 1944; Second Judge of the Civil Court of Durango; Assistant Attorney General of Durango; Attorney General of Durango; *Provisional Governor of Durango*, Aug. 4, 1966, to 1968. g-None. h-None. j-None. k-None. l-DBM68, 532; C de D, 1964–66, 55.

Rodriguez Triana, Pedro

(Deceased 1960)

a-1891. b-San Pedro, Coahuila, *North*, *Urban*. c-Primary studies only; no degree. d-*Governor of Coahuila*, 1938–41. e-Named delegate from Coahuila to the Mexican Liberal Party; Communist Party candidate for President of Mexico, 1929. g-Became an agrarian leader at age 14; agrarian adviser to the states of Durango, San Luis Potosi, Coahuila, Campeche, 1935; cooperative and ejido organizer, 1923. h-Peasant. j-Joined the Revolution, 1912; Chief of Staff for General Benjamin Argumedo, 1915; fought against Carranza, 1920; fought against Francisco Murguia, 1922. k-Remained in hiding after 1929 election in the mountains of northern Mexico, 1929–34; as Governor of Coahuila accused of mishandling funds; Brandenburg places him in the Inner Circle as Governor; removed two weeks before the end of his term as governor for attempting to impose his own candidate, General Lucas Gonzalez, as governor. l-DP70, 1792; Peral, 704–05; D de Y, 2 Nov. 1940, 1; Correa, 500–01; Brandenburg, 80; Anderson, 82–83; PS, 5363.

Rodriguez y Rodriguez, Jesus

a-1915. b-Morelia, Michoacan, *West Central*, *Urban*. c-Preparatory studies at the Colegio Frances Morelos, Mexico City; agricultural engineering degree, National School of Agriculture, 1939; law degree, National School of Law, UNAM, 1942, with his thesis on the "History and Politics of the Municipality in Mexico;" Professor of Administrative Law, National School of Law, UNAM, 1944–54. d-None.

e-None. f-Employee, Office of Public Debt, Secretariat of the Treasury, 1942; Director, Vegetable Production Section, Department of Rural Economy, Secretariat of Agriculture, 1941–42, Director, Office of Statistics, IMSS, 1943–53; alternate member of the National Price Commission, 1946–49; Vice President of the National Price Commission, 1950–52; Director of Services, Department of the Federal District, 1947–52; *Subsecretary of the Treasury*, 1958–64; *Subsecretary of the Treasury*, 1964–70; Executive Director of the Inter–American Development Bank, 1973–78; President, Inter-American Committee of the Alliance for Progress, Washington, D.C. g-None. i-Married Leonor Montero. j-None. k-None. l-DPE61, 40; DGF50, II, 57; DGF51, II, 65; *Siempre*, 14 Jan. 1959, 6; HA, 22 Oct. 1973; HA, 4 Aug. 1944, 7; letter; HA, 22 Oct. 1973.

Roel (Garcia), Santiago

a-Dec. 4, 1919. b-Monterrey, Nuevo Leon, *North*, *Urban*. c-Primary studies at the Colegio Monterrey, Monterrey and the Colegio Americano, Monterrey; secondary studies at the Laurens Institute; preparatory studies from the University of Nuevo Leon and from the Ateneo Fuente, Saltillo, Coahuila; law degree from the University of Nuevo Leon; Professor of Agrarian and Tax Law, Guarantees and Amparo and Constitutional Law, School of Law, University of Nuevo Leon (twenty years); Professor of the History of Mexican Philosophy, School of Philosophy, University of Nuevo Leon; Director of the University Extension Program, University of Nuevo Leon. d-Alternate Local Deputy to the 46th State Legislature of Nuevo Leon; *Alternate Senator* from the State of Nuevo Leon, 1964–70, under *Armando Arteaga y Santoyo*; *Federal Deputy* from the State of Nuevo Leon, Dist. 1, 1970–73, President of the Foreign Relations Committee, member of the Legislative Studies Committee, President of the Chamber of Deputies. e-National Delegate of the IEPES of PRI; Coordinator of Speakers for the presidential campaign of *Jose Lopez Portillo*, 1975–76; Subdirector of the Legal Department of the CEN of PRI. f-Legal adviser to the 7th Military Zone; Director of the Legal Department of the State of Nuevo Leon; adviser to the Secretary of the Treasury, 1973–75; *Secretary of Foreign Relations*, 1976–79. g-Lawyer for the Union of Workers of the National Railroads of Mexico in the State of Nuevo Leon. h-Practicing lawyer in Mexico City in the firm of Farell; author of various books. i-Son of lawyer Santiago Roel Melo, representative to the Constitutional Convention of 1917 and federal deputy; close personal friend of *Jose Lopez Portillo* and *Octavio Senties*. j-None. k-Early precandidate for Governor of Nuevo Leon, 1977; the press claims he was fired as Secretary of Foreign Relations for his mishandling of the ministry and its policies. l-LA, 25 May 1979, 158; HA, 6 Dec. 1976, 22; *Excelsior*, 11 Mar. 1977, 6; HA, 17 Jan. 1977, 8; NYT, 2 Dec. 1976, 3; *Directorio*, 1970; WNM, 196; *Excelsior*, 1 Dec. 1976; *El Dia*, 1 Dec. 1976.

Rojina Villegas, Rafael

b-Orizaba, Veracruz, *Gulf*, *Urban*. c-Primary studies in Orizaba; secondary and preparatory studies at the National Preparatory School, Mexico, D.F.; studied law at the National School of Law, UNAM, 1926–30, law degree, July 7, 1930, with honorable mention; LLD, National School of Law, UNAM, 1951; Professor of Civil Law and Introduction to the Study of Law, National School of Law, UNAM, 1934–64; Professor of Private Law, Graduate School, National School of Law, UNAM, 1954–64. d-None. e-None. f-Secretary of Studies, Supreme Court of Justice, 1945–51; Judge of the First Circuit Collegiate Court, 1951–58; *Justice of the Supreme Court*, 1962–64, 1965–70, 1971–76, 1976–77. g-None. h-Author of a 13-volume work on Mexican civil law; expert on the civil codes. j-None. k-None. l-*Justicia*; April, 1967; DGF56, 585.

Rojo Gomez, Javier

(Deceased Dec. 31, 1970)
a-June 28, 1896. b-Hacienda de Bondojito, Municipio de Huichapan, Hidalgo, *East Central*, *Rural*. c-Primary studies in Huichapan and in the Federal District; preparatory studies at the National Preparatory School; law degree from the National School of Law, UNAM, 1924. d-Local Deputy to the State Legislature of Hidalgo; Federal Deputy from the State of Hidalgo, 1926–28; *Governor of Hidalgo*, 1937–40. e-Adviser to PRI on farm policies, 1967. f-Secretary General of Government of the State of Hidalgo, 1936; Judge of the First District, Federal District; *Head of the Federal District Department*, 1940–46; Ambassador to Indonesia, 1952–55; Ambassador to Japan, 1956–58; *Governor of Quintana Roo*, 1967–70. g-Lawyer for CROM after graduation; *Secretary General of the CNC*, 1962–66. h-Practiced law in the firm of *Emilio Portes Gil*; as a boy was an agrarian laborer on the Hacienda of Tepeji del Rio; Director General of Asegurador Agricola Nacional, 1958; practiced law, 1958–64. i-Son of agricultural laborers; classmate of *Gilberto Loyo* at UNAM; brother-in-law of *Jose Lugo Guerrero*; father of *Jorge Rojo Lugo*; married Isabel Lugo; uncle of *Humberto Lugo Gil*, Federal Deputy from Hidalgo, 1967–70. j-None. k-One of the founders of the National Farmers Federation; formal complaint was brought against him in Oct., 1947, for illegal land sales as Head of the Federal District Department; ostracized by PRI but made a comeback; precandidate for President of Mexico, 1945; Inner Circle

status from 1940–46; his candidacy for the Secretary General of the CNC was supported by the "Old Guard," including *Francisco Mujica*, *Heriberto Jara*, *Graciano Sanchez*, Luis Cabrera, and *Eduardo Suarez*; involved in a scandal as Secretary General of the CNC, along with *Roberto Barrios* and *Leon Garcia*. l-Peral, 707; DP70, 2439–40; DBM68, 534–35; WWM45, 105; DGF56, 127; Nov. de Yuc., 29 Dec. 1971, 3; Correa, 345–52; Brandenburg, 80; *Por Que*, 4 Oct. 1968, 36; Cline, 158; Gonzalez Navarro, 233; letter; Lopez, 958; *Excelsior*, 2 May 1975, 33; *Excelsior*, 29 June 1974, 17; *Excelsior*, 7 Sept. 1974, 17.

Rojo Lugo, Jorge

a-June 18, 1933. b-Huichapan, Hidalgo, *East Central, Rural*. c-Primary and secondary studies in Mexico City; preparatory studies from the National Preparatory School; law degree from the National School of Law, UNAM, 1958. d-*Federal Deputy* from the State of Hidalgo, Dist. 5, 1961–64, member of the Credit, Money and Credit Institutions Committee, and the Agrarian Section of the Legislative Studies Committee; *Governor of Hidalgo*, 1975–76, 1978– . e-General Delegate of the CEN of PRI to Aguascalientes, Tabasco and Chiapas, 1961–64; Auxiliary Secretary of the President of the CEN of PRI, *Alfonso Corona del Rosal*, 1961–63. f-Lawyer, Legal Section, Secretariat of Hydraulic Resources, 1959–60; assistant to the National Arbitration Commission of the Secretariat of the Treasury, 1960–61; Subdirector General of the National Agricultural Bank, 1965–70; Director General of the National Agricultural Bank, 1970–75; *Secretary of Agrarian Reform*, 1976–78. g-Member of the Advisory Council of the CNC. h-None. i-Married to Garcia de Alba; cousin of *Humberto A. Lugo Gil*, senator from Hidalgo, 1976–82; son of *Javier Rojo Gomez*, governor of Hidalgo, 1937–40; nephew of *Jose Lugo Guerrero*, governor of Hidalgo, 1941–45. j-None. k-*Proceso* considered him a strong candidate for the presidency of the CEN of PRI in October, 1978. l-*Proceso*, 12 June 1978, 25; Enc. Mex., Annual, 1977, 545; *Excelsior*, 2 June 1978, 1; HA, 2 June 1975, 33; HA, 6 Dec. 1976, 24; HA, 28 Nov. 1977, 7.

Rojo Perez, Jesus

a-Jan. 2, 1938. b-Ocoyoacac, Mexico, *West Central, Rural*. c-Primary studies at the Leona Vicario School, Ocoyoacac; secondary studies at the Instituto Garcia de Cisneros, Cholula, Puebla; preparatory studies at the Instituto Garcia de Cisneros; secondary teaching certificate, Higher Normal School, Mexico, D.F.; courses in teaching English, Mexican-North American Institute of Cultural Relations; certified as a teacher of foreign languages, UNAM; secondary teacher at Public School No. 2, Colegio Hernan Cortes, and the Marillac Institute. **d-**_Federal Deputy_ from the PAN (party deputy), 1970–73, member of the Agricultural Development Committee and the Second General Means of Communication Committee. **e-**Member of PAN. **f-**None. **g-**None. **h-**None. **i-**Married Maria Elena Amaya Sedano. **j-**None. **k-**None. **l-**C de D, 1970–72, 134; _Directorio_, 1970–72.

Rolland, Modesto C.
(Deceased 1965)
a-1881. **b-**La Paz, Baja California del Sur, _West_, _Urban_. **c-**Engineering degree. **d-**Federal Deputy to the Constitutional Convention, 1916–17. **e-**None. **f-**Director of many government public works projects, including the Plaza Mexico, Jalapa, Veracruz; _Subsecretary of Public Works,_ 1934–40; _Subsecretary of Industry and Commerce,_ 1940–46; Director General of Free Ports, 1946–52. **g-**None. **h-**Author of many technical works on ports and political tracts. **j-**None. **k-**None. **l-**DP70, 1796; HA, 6 Oct. 1950; DGF50, 474; DGF50, II, 645; NYT, 19 Dec. 1940, 6.

Roman Celis, Carlos
a-Feb. 21, 1922. **b-**Coyuca de Catalan, Guerrero, _South_, _Rural_. **c-**Primary studies in the Jose Maria Morelos School, 1933, Coyuca de Catalan; secondary studies at the Ignacio M. Altamirano School, in Teloloapan, Guerrero, and in the Secondary Night School for Workers, No. 5, Mexico City, 1946; social science studies at the National Preparatory Night School, 1947–48; law degree from the National School of Law, UNAM, 1949–53; professor of Literary Groups, Office of Literature, Department of the Federal District, 1945. **d-**_Alternate Federal Deputy_ from the State of Guerrero, Dist. 3, 1952–55, _Federal Deputy_ from the State of Guerrero, Dist. 3, 1955–58, member of the Radio and Television Industry Committee, the Committee on Credit, Money, and Credit Institutions, the Second Labor Committee, and the Gran Comision; _Senator_ from Guerrero, 1958–64, member of the Gran Comision, the Agriculture and Development Committee, the Third National Defense Committee, the National Lands Committee, the Second Balloting Committee, and the Special Legislative Studies Committee; President of the First Justice Committee; Secretary of the Second Instructive Section of the Grand Jury; substitute member of the First Government Committee and the National Railroads Committee. **e-**Official orator in the _Ruiz Cortines_ presidential campaign, 1952. **f-**Treasurer of the Board of Material Improvement, Coyuca, 1942; President of the Patriotic Board, Coyuca, 1943; Subdirector of Filmoteca Nacional,

Secretariat of Public Education, 1947; Director of Press Relations, IMSS, 1953; Director of Legal Affairs, Secretariat of Health, 1976– . **g-**President of the Student Association of the National Preparatory Night School. **h-**Worked in father's store as a youth; news agent in Coyuca; Editor-in-chief, _Revista Coyuca_, 1944; winner of the prize in physics and chemistry, secondary night school, Federal District, 1946; winner of prize for essay on Louis Pasteur, National Preparatory Night School, 1948; reporter for _Manana_ during the 1952 campaign. **i-**Father an owner of a general store. **j-**None. **k-**None. **l-**Func., 219; C de D, 1952–54, 18; C de S, 1961–64, 68; DGF56, 30, 32, 37m, 34, 24; C de D, 1955–57; Ind. Biog., 139–40.

Roman Lugo, Fernando
a-Jan. 16, 1916. **b-**Chilpancingo, Guerrero, _South_, _Urban_. **c-**Primary and secondary studies in Chilpancingo; preparatory studies in Chilpancingo; law degree; professor, School of Law, University of Veracruz. **d-**None. **e-**Director General of the National Voters Registration, 1952. **f-**Secretary General of Government of the State of Veracruz, 1944–48, under governor _Adolfo Ruiz Cortines_; Judge of the Superior Tribunal of Justice of the State of Veracruz, 1952; _Oficial Mayor of the Secretariat of Government_, 1952–53; _Subsecretary of Government_, 1953–58; _Attorney General of the Federal District and Federal Territories_, 1958–64. **g-**Active in the Second Congress of Socialist Students, 1935. **h-**Practicing lawyer, Mexico City, 1964– . **i-**Married Delia Cortes; taught law school with _Angel Carvajal_, University of Veracruz. **j-**None. **k-**None. **l-**HA, 8 Dec. 1958, 30; DGF56, 83; D de Y, 2 Dec. 1958, 7; HA, 27 Feb. 1953, 8–9; Func., 99.

Romandia Ferreira, Alfonso
a-July 28, 1901. **b-**Hermosillo, Sonora, _North_, _Urban_. **c-**Early education unknown; law degree from the National School of Law, UNAM, 1927. **d-**Federal Deputy from the Federal District, Dist. 7, 1928–30. **e-**Organizer of a student party in support of Calles' presidential campaign, 1923; leader of the pro-Obregon students, 1927. **f-**Oficial Mayor of Agriculture, 1932–33; special envoy to Paris, France; Director General of the Bank of Industry and Trade; Director, Credit Department, National Sugar Producers Organization, 1936–46; Director General of the Financiera Industrial Azucarera, 1946–53; Manager of the La Gloria Sugar Mill, 1953–70. **g-**None. **h-**None. **i-**Friend of _Miguel Aleman_ since law school days; married Carmen Macias. **j-**None. **k-**None. **l-**Villasenor, I, 264; Balboa, 23; DBM68, 535; WNM, 197.

Romero, Antonio

a-Feb. 26, 1893. **b-**Encinillas, Jilotepec, Mexico, *West Central*, *Rural*. **c-**Early education unknown; no degree. **d-***Senator* from the State of Mexico, 1934–40. **e-**None. **f-**None. **g-**None. **h-**None. **j-**Career army officer; reached rank of Brigadier General, June 1, 1941. **k-**None. **l-**C de S, 1934–40.

Romero, Jose Ruben

a-Sept. 25, 1890. **b-**Cotija, Michoacan, *West Central, Rural*. **c-**Primary studies in Mexico City, 1897; studies in diplomacy; no degree. **d-**None. **e-**None. **f-**Private Secretary to Governor Miguel Silva, Michoacan, 1912; Private Secretary to Governor Pascual Ortiz Rubio, Michoacan, 1919; Inspector General of Communications, 1920–21; Director of Press and Information, Secretariat of Foreign Relations, 1921–22; Oficial Mayor of the Secretariat of Foreign Relations, 1924–30; Consul General to Barcelona, Spain, 1930–33; Director of the Civil Registry, Mexico City, 1933–35; Consul General in Spain, 1935–37; Ambassador to Brazil, 1937–39; *Ambassador to Cuba*, 1939–43. **g-**None. **h-**Businessman, Patzcuaro, Michoacan, 1913–15; tax collector, Puruandiro, Michoacan, 1911; well-known novelist. **i-**Parents were peasants. **j-**Supported Madero during the Revolution; Chief of Staff under General Salvador Escalante. **k-**Nearly executed during the Revolution. **l-**WWM45, 106; Peral, 1970, 1798; Lopez, 960; letter.

Romero Castaneda, David

b-Mexico, *West Central*. **c-**Preparatory studies at the National Preparatory School; law degree, National School of Law, UNAM, 1936, with a thesis on arbitration in Mexican civil law. **d-***Federal Deputy* from the State of Mexico, Dist. 4, 1946–49, member of the Gran Comision, the Second Government Committee and the General Accounting Office Committee. **e-**None. **f-**Supernumerary Justice of the Superior Tribunal of Justice of the Federal District and Federal Territories, 1940; Attorney General of the Federal Tax Office, 1958–60; *Subsecretary of Revenues* of the Secretariat of the Treasury, 1961–64. **g-**None. **i-**Co-founder of the student newspaper *Eureka* with *Miguel Aleman*; subsecretary of the treasury under classmate *Antonio Ortiz Mena*; married Elena Apis. **j-**None. **k-**None. **l-**DPE61, 40; C de D, 1946–49, 86; *Libro de Oro*, 1959, xxxiii.

Romero de Velasco, Flavio

a-Dec. 22, 1925. **b-**Ameca, Jalisco, *West*, *Urban*. **c-**Early education unknown; law degree, National School of Law, UNAM; special studies (five years) National School of Philosophy and Letters, UNAM.

d-*Federal Deputy* from the State of Jalisco, Dist. 8, 1955–58, President of the Chamber, September, 1955; answered *Adolfo Ruiz Cortines'* 3rd State of the Union address, member of the Gran Comision, member of the Library Committee, member of the Economy and Statistics Committee and member of the Foreign Relations Committee; *Federal Deputy* from the State of Jalisco, Dist. 3, 1961–64, member of the Credit, Money and Credit Institutions Committee and the Justice Committee; *Governor of Jalisco*, 1977– . **e-**Joined PRI, 1950; orator during the *Adolfo Ruiz Cortines* presidential campaign, 1952; Secretary General of PRI in the Federal District; Director of the Committee for Ideological Dissemination during the *Adolfo Lopez Mateos* campaign, 1958; General Delegate of the CEN of PRI to Tamaulipas, 1957; General Delegate of the CEN of PRI to Nayarit, 1964; General Delegate of the CEN of PRI to Nuevo Leon, 1976. **f-**Director of Social and Educational Action, Secretariat of Public Education; Administrator of Customs, Ciudad Juarez, 1965–71. **g-**Champion of Oratory in the Federal District, 1952. **h-**None. **i-**Initiated his career under the guidance of *Luis Echeverria*, 1946, serving as an assistant to *Rodolfo Sanchez Taboada*. **j-**None. **k-**None. **l-**Ind. Biog., 141; DPE61, 103; DGF56, 25, 30–32, 37; *Excelsior*, 18 Feb. 1977; *Excelsior*, 20 Feb. 1977.

Romero Flores, Jesus

a-Apr. 28, 1885. **b-**La Piedad, Michoacan, *West Central*, *Urban*. **c-**Teaching certificate from the University of Michoacan, Oct. 7, 1905; Director of the Normal School for the State of Michoacan, 1915. **d-**Deputy to the Constitutional Convention, 1916–17; local deputy to the State Legislature of Michoacan, 1922; Federal Deputy from the State of Michoacan, 1922–24; *Senator* from the State of Michoacan, 1964–70. **e-**None. **f-**Director of Primary Schools, Valle de Santiago, Guanajuato; director, private school, Piedad Cabados; director of secondary schools, Piedad, Morelia; director of the School of Tangancicuaro de Artista, Zamora, Michoacan, 1910; Inspector General of Public and Private Schools, 1913–14; Director of El Pensador Mexicano Primary School, Mexico City, 1920; Director of Primary Education, Michoacan, 1930; Director of Public Education for the State of Michoacan, 1915–16; Director of Normal Schools, Morelia, 1925; Section Chief, Department of Primary Education, Department of the Federal District, 1918; Private Secretary to General *Francisco Mujica*, 1918; Director of the Public Library of Morelia, 1928; Historian for the National Museum of Mexico, 1935–45. **g-**None. **h-**Author of many works. **i-**Married Refugio Perez; widowed, married Maria Pureco Rasso. **j-**None. **k-**None. **l-**C de S,

1964–70; MGF69; WWM45, 106; HA, 27 Nov. 1972, 11; Bremauntz, 65.

Romero Flores, Jose C.

a-1911. b-Tamaulipas, *Gulf.* c-No formal education; self-educated. d-*Senator* from the State of Tamaulipas, 1970–76, member of the Gran Comision, President of the Rairoads Committee, First Secretary of the Electric Industry Committee and Second Secretary of the Mail and Telegraph Committee. e-None. f-None. g-Local Secretary of the STFRM; Prosecretary of the Mexican Alliance of Railroad Workers; Secretary General of Organization, Education and Statistics of the STFRM, 1962–65; President of the First World Railroad Workers Congress, Mexico City, 1969. h-Railroad employee. j-None. k-None. l-C de S, 1970–76, PS, 5421.

Romero Kolbeck, Gustavo

a-July 3, 1923. b-Federal District, *Federal District, Urban.* c-Early education unknown; economics degree with an honorable mention from the National School of Economics, UNAM, 1946; graduate work at the University of Chicago and at The George Washington University, 1947–48; Professor of Economics, UNAM, 1949; Professor of Economics, National School of Economics, UNAM, 1966–70; Director of the National School of Economics, 1967–69; member of the University Council of UNAM, 1967–69. d-None. e-None. f-Economist, Bank of Mexico, 1944–46; Researcher, Secretariat of Government Properties, 1948; Head, Department of Economic Studies, National Bank of Mexico, 1949–54; Subdirector of the National Research Committee, 1955–58; Director of Research, Secretariat of the Presidency, 1954–61; Adviser to the presidency; Ambassador to Japan, 1971–73; *Director General of National Finance Bank,* Jan. 11, 1974–76; *Director General of the Bank of Mexico,* 1976– . g-None. h-Founder of the Center for Economic Studies of the Private Sector, 1970. i-Married Leonor Martinez. j-None. k-None. l-HA, 21 Jan. 1974, 16–17; letter; WNM, 198; HA, 18 Aug. 1975, 20.

Romero Perez, Humberto

b-La Piedad, Michoacan, *West Central, Urban.* c-Primary studies in La Piedad; secondary studies in the Federal District; preparatory studies from the National Preparatory School; law degree from the National School of Law, UNAM. d-*Federal Deputy* from the State of Michoacan, Dist. 4, 1979–82. e-None. f-Private Secretary to *Francisco Gonzalez de la Vega,* Attorney General of Mexico, 1946–52; Director of Publicity for the Secretariat of Labor under *Adolfo Lopez Mateos,* 1952; Director of Public Relations for President *Adolfo Ruiz Cortines,* 1956–

58; *Private Secretary to the President of Mexico, Adolfo Lopez Mateos,* 1958–64. g-President of the Student Association, National School of Law, UNAM; active in student politics. h-Journalist; contributed to various newspapers and reviews. i-Student and political protege of *Francisco Gonzalez de la Vega*; married Alicia Gudino. j-None. k-None. l-DGF56, 53; DGF51, I, 535; HA, 8 Dec. 1958, 32; DPE61, 9; Func., 63; Libro de Oro, 1959, xxv.

Rosado de Hernandez, Maria Luisa

a-June 18, 1926. b-Tabasco, *Gulf.* c-Primary studies in Villahermosa, Tabasco; teaching certificate, Normal School, Villahermosa, November 15, 1938; teacher for many years. d-*Federal Deputy* from the State of Tabasco, Dist. 1, 1958–61, member of the Second Public Education Committee, the Second Balloting Committee and the Fine Arts Committee. e-Member of PRI. f-Director of various public schools; consultant to the Secretariat of Public Education; adviser to UNESCO. g-None. h-None. i-Father participated in the Revolution. j-None. k-First female deputy from the State of Tabasco. l-Func., 368; C de D, 1958–61, 90.

Rosas Dominguez, Reynaldo

a-Nov. 6, 1937. b-Chihuahua, *North.* c-Early education unknown; studies in law, University of Chihuahua. d-None. e-Joined the Mexican Communist Party, January, 1961; member of the Central Committee of the PCM, 1973–79; Secretary General of the PCM in the Valle de Mexico, 1979; member of the Executive Committee of the PCM, 1979. f-Employee of the Federal Electric Commission. g-Student leader; union organizer for the PCM. j-None. k-None. l-HA, 19 Feb. 1979, xi.

Rosas Magallon, Salvador

a-Aug. 9, 1916. b-Tepic, Nayarit, *West, Urban.* c-Primary studies in Reynosa, Tamaulipas; secondary studies in Jalisco; preparatory and two years of law at the University of Guadalajara, Guadalajara, Jalisco; law degree, National School of Law, UNAM, May 9, 1941. d-*Federal Deputy* from the State of Baja California del Norte, Dist. 2, 1964–67, member of the Hydraulic Resources Committee. e-Joined PAN, 1946; President of the Regional Council of PAN for Baja California del Norte (twice); adviser to the National Executive Council of PAN, 1969; member of the National Council of PAN, 1975. f-Judge in Tixtla, Guerrero, 1941; Agent of the Ministerio Publico, Tlapa, Guerrero, 1942; Agent of the Ministerio Publico, Los Mochis, Sinaloa, 1942–43. g-None. h-Began law practice, Baja California del Norte, 1945. j-None. k-Candidate for Federal Deputy from PAN, 1958; candidate for Governor of Baja California del Norte,

1959; precandidate for the PAN nomination for President, 1963, 1975; known in Baja California del Norte as the lawyer of the people. l-Letter, *Por Que*, 4 Oct. 1968, 50; C de D, 1964–66, 55, 92.

Rosenzweig Diaz, Alfonso de
(Deceased 1963)

a-Jan. 2, 1886. b-Toluca, Mexico, *West Central*, *Urban*. c-Law degree. d-None. e-None. f-Employee of the Mexican Consulate, St. Louis, 1907; Secretary of the Legation, China, 1910; Secretary of the Legation, Guatemala, 1912; member of the Mexican Legation in Japan, 1910; Secretary in Brazil, 1918; Counselor in Brazil, 1921; Charge d' Affairs, Colombia, 1922, Belgium, 1924, Great Britain, 1925; Counselor in France, 1925–26; Chief of Protocol, Secretariat of Foreign Relations, 1927; Minister to El Salvador, 1931; rank of Ambassador, 1942; *Ambassador to Great Britain*, 1942–45; represented Mexico at the First General Assembly of the United Nations, 1945; *Ambassador to France*, 1946; Ambassador to Nicaragua, 1948–51; *Ambassador to the Soviet Union*, 1953–60. g-None. h-Author of a three-volume work on Mexico. i-Son *Alfonso Jr.* served as personal secretary to *Padilla Nervo*, when the latter was Secretary of Foreign Relations, and became Subsecretary (B) of Foreign Relations, 1976– ; son *Roberto* was appointed Permanent Representative of Mexico to the United Nations, 1976. j-None. k-Retired from the Foreign Service, 1960. l-Peral, 717; DGF51, I, 106; DP70, 1808; MGF69, 179; DGF56, 123, 129; WWM45, 106; NYT, 25 Oct. 1941, 3; Lopez, 965; Enc. Mex., XI, 1977, 193.

Rosenzweig Diaz, Jr., Alfonso

a-May 9, 1921. b-Federal District, *Federal District*, *Urban*. c-Early education unknown; law degree, National School of Law, UNAM, 1940–44. d-None. e-None. f-Private Secretary to *Pablo Campos Ortiz*, Oficial Mayor of the Secretariat of Foreign Relations, 1945–46; joined the Foreign Service with the rank of Vice Consul, April 1, 1946; official of the Political Affairs Office of the Department of Political Affairs, United Nations Security Council, November, 1946 to October, 1951; Interim Director General of the Office of International Organizations, Secretariat of Foreign Relations, 1951–52; Private Secretary to *Manuel Tello*, Secretary of Foreign Relations, 1952–58; Director General of the Office of Legal Affairs, Secretariat of Foreign Relations, December, 1958 to May, 1961; Director General of the Diplomatic Service, May, 1961 to May, 1964; Director in Chief, Attached to the First Subsecretary of Foreign Relations, 1964–70; Director in Chief of Bilateral Political Affairs, Secretariat of Foreign Relations, 1970–75; legal advisor, Secretariat of

Foreign Relations, 1975–76; *Subsecretary "B" of Foreign Relations*, 1976– . g-None. h-None. i-Son of *Alfonso Rosenzweig Diaz*, ambassador to Great Britain, 1942–45; brother of *Roberto Rosenzweig Diaz*, permanent representative of Mexico to the United Nations, 1976. j-None. k-None. l-HA, 20 Jan. 1975, 9; DPE65, 18; DPE71, 6; MGF69; *Libro de Oro*, 1967–68, xxiv.

Rosenzweig Diaz, Roberto

a-1925. b-Amsterdam, Holland, *Foreign*, *Urban*. c-Primary studies in Paris, France; degree in political and economic sciences, Oxford University. d-None. e-None. f-Joined the Foreign Service, 1946; Charge d' Affairs, Brazil; Counselor, Mexican Embassy, Brazil; Secretary to the Mexican Embassy in Switzerland; Secretary to the Mexican Embassy in London, England; Counselor, Mexican Embassy, France; Director, International Treaty Department, Diplomatic Service; Director, United Nations Department, Division of International Organizations, Secretariat of Foreign Relations; Ambassador to El Salvador, 1969–73; Ambassador to Egypt, 1974–75; Ambassador to Syria, 1975–76; Permanent Representative of Mexico to the United Nations, 1976–77, Ambassador to German Federal Republic, 1977–79; Ambassador to Low Countries, 1979– . g-None. h-None. i-Son of *Alfonso Rosenzweig Diaz*, Ambassador to Great Britain, 1942–45; brother of *Alfonso Rosenzweig Diaz*, Jr., Subsecretary "B" for Foreign Relations, 1976– . j-None. k-None. l-*Excelsior*, 9 Jan. 1976, 18; HA, 17 Feb. 1975, 17; *Excelsior*, 17 Aug. 1979, 4.

Rossell de la Lama, Guillermo

a-July 22, 1925. b-Pachuca, Hidalgo, *East Central*, *Urban*. c-Early education unknown; architecture degree from the National School of Architecture, UNAM; professor, National School of Architecture, UNAM. d-*Senator* from the State of Hidalgo, 1976, President of the Chamber, September, 1976. e-Founding member of the IEPES of PRI; director of the Councils of Economic and Social Planning, *Adolfo Lopez Mateos'* 1958 presidential campaign; personal adviser to the President of the CEN of PRI, 1957–63. f-Director of the Department of Tourism, Secretariat of Public Works, 1952; Director of Development and Planning, Secretariat of Public Works; *Oficial Mayor of the Secretariat of Government Properties*, 1958–59; *Subsecretary of Real Property and Urbanization*, 1959–64; adviser to the National Housing Institute; President of the Regulatory Commission on Mexican-North American Border Cities; *Secretary of Tourism*, 1976–80. g-None. h-Practicing architect, 1964–75. i-Protege of *Carlos Lazo*, his professor and mentor in the Secretariat of Public Works; boss of *Jose Lopez Portillo* as Subsecretary of Real Property and Urbanization; married Emilia Avitia; son Fernando was a precandidate for federal deputy from Hidalgo, 1979. **j**-None. **k**-None. **l**-HA, 6 Dec. 1976, 24; *Excelsior*, 4 Mar. 1977, 6; HA, 20 Feb. 1978, 8; *Excelsior*, 28 Feb. 1979, 22.

Rovirosa Perez, Gustavo Adolfo
(Deceased 1970)
a-1908. **b**-San Juan Bautista (Villahermosa), Tabasco, *Gulf*, *Urban*. **c**-Primary studies at the Juarez Institute, Villahermosa; preparatory studies from the National Preparatory School; medical degree, School of Medicine, University of Puebla; Rockefeller Foundation Fellow in Public Health, Johns Hopkins University, 1936. **d**-*Senator* from the State of Tabasco, 1964–70. **e**-None. **f**-Director of Health and Social Welfare for the World Health Organization, Korea, 1950–57. **g**-President of the Association of Friends of Mexico and Korea. **i**-Son of engineer Jose N. Rovirosa, well-known Mexican scientist; related to *Leandro Rovirosa Wade*, Governor of Tabasco, 1977– . **j**-None. **k**-None. **l**-Enc. Mex., XI, 197; PS, 5459; C de S 1964–70.

Rovirosa Wade, Leandro
a-June 11, 1920. **b**-Villahermosa, Tabasco, *Gulf*, *Urban*. **c**-Primary studies in Villahermosa; secondary and preparatory at the Instituto Veracruzano, Veracruz; civil engineering degree, National School of Engineering, UNAM, 1943. **d**-*Governor of Tabasco*, 1977– . **e**-None. **f**-Director of Hydraulic Works and Streets, Department of the Federal District, 1944–46; Director of Planning, Department of the Federal District, 1946–52; Director of the Department of Construction, Division of Maritime Works, Secretariat of the Navy, 1952–55; Director of Port Construction, Secretariat of the Navy; Director of the Malpaso Dam project; *Secretary of Hydraulic Resouces*, 1970–76. **g**-President of the Alumni Society of the School of Engineering, UNAM, 1972; president of the National Chamber of the Construction Industry, 1965–67. **h**-Organized the construction firm of Raudals, S.A. **i**-Student of *Antonio Dovali Jaime* at UNAM; friend of *Rodolfo Sanchez Taboada*; longtime friend of *Luis Echeverria*; compadre of *Hugo Cervantes del Rio*; relative of *Rovirosa Perez*, senator from Tabasco, 1964–70; married Celia Gonzalez. **j**-None. **k**-None. **l**-HA, 7 Dec. 1970, 25; *Hoy*, Dec. 1970; DGF56, 383; HA, 1 Mar. 1971, 20; DGF51, I, 483; DPE71, 88; HA, 10 July 1972, 20; HA, 9 May 1955, 3; LA, 20 Aug. 1976; WNM, 200; Enc. Mex., XI, 1977, 197.

Rubio Felix, Lazaro
a-Jan. 6, 1917. **b**-Culiacan, Sinaloa, *West*, *Urban*. **c**-Early education unknown; no degree. **d**-Member of the City Council of Mazatlan, 1940s; *Federal Deputy* (PPS Party Deputy), 1967–70, member of the Agra-

rian Affairs Committee, the Department of the Federal District Committee, the Second Government Committee, the Small Agrarian Properties Committee and the Hydraulic Resources Committee; *Federal Deputy* (PPS Party Deputy), 1973–76. **e**-Joined the PPS, 1948; Secretary of Publicity of the Central Committee of the PPS. **f**-None. **g**-Secretary General of the Regional Peasant Committee No. 1, South Sinaloa; Secretary of Peasant Affairs of the Mexican Association of Workers and Peasants, 1948. **j**-None. **k**-Candidate for governor of the State of Sinaloa (twice); confessed double agent and infiltrator of the PPS and the CIA. **l**-HA, 2 Apr. 1979, IV; C de D, 1973–76, 30; C de D, 1967–70, 58, 61, 73, 82, 85; *Excelsior*, 19 Aug. 1979, 18; Medina, 20, 145.

Rubio (Ortiz), Noradino
a-Apr. 20, 1896. **b**-Pisaflores, Hidalgo, *East Central, Rural*. **c**-Primary education in own home; attended superior schools; no degree. **d**-Local Deputy to the State Legislature of Queretaro, 1927–29; Federal Deputy from the State of Queretaro, 1932–34; *Federal Deputy* from the State of Queretaro, Dist. 2, 1937–40; *Governor of Queretaro*, 1940–44; Mayor of Queretaro. **e**-None. **f**-None. **g**-Member of the National Farmers Federation; active Mason. **h**-Farmer. **i**-Great-grandson of Independence leader Encarnacion Ortiz; friend of *Saturnillo Cedillo*. **j**-None. **k**-Simpson states that when Rubio was governor he employed an army of pistoleros under Saturnino Osorio to control Queretaro. **l**-Peral, 721; EBW46, 191; C de D, 1937–39, 19; Simpson, 342.

Rubio Ruiz, Marcelo
(Deceased Jan. 6, 1977)
a-1923. **b**-Santa Rosalia, Baja California del Sur, *West*, *Rural*. **c**-Teaching certificate; law degree. **d**-*Senator* from the State of Baja California del Sur, 1976–77, President of the Fishing Committee. **e**-President of PRI in the State of Baja California del Sur. **f**-Director of Normal Schools, La Paz, Baja California del Sur; Delegate of the Secretariat of Public Education to the State of Baja California del Sur; Secretary General of Government of the State of Baja California del Sur. **g**-None. **i**-Father was a miner. **j**-None. **k**-None. **l**-*Excelsior*, 7 Jan. 1977, 13; C de S, 1976–82.

Rueda Villagran, Quintin
a-1905. **b**-Huichipan, Hidalgo, *East Central*, *Rural*. **c**-Early education unknown; economics degree; law degree; secondary school teacher; professor at the National Polytechnic Institute. **d**-*Alternate Federal Deputy* from the State of Hidalgo, Dist. 2, 1946–49; *Federal Deputy* from the State of Hidalgo, Dist. 5, 1949–51, member of the Third Ejido Committee and the First Treasury Committee, president of the organizing committees; *Governor of Hidalgo*, 1951–

57. e-None. f-Director General of Information, Department of Paper Products; Director of Information, Secretariat of Government. g-None. j-None. k-*Villasenor* claims Rueda Villagran bought up lands for a government industry to make a personal profit; *Excelsior* suggests that *Miguel Aleman*'s choice of Rueda Villagran as governor was influenced by *Enrique Parra Hernandez*. l-Villasenor, II, 203; *Excelsior*, 24 Dec. 1978, 16–17; DGF51, I, 22, 32, 33, 90; DGF50, II, 409; DGF51, II, 571; C de D, 1949–52, 89; DGF56, 94; DGF47, 8, 360; HA, 6 Apr. 1951, 16–18.

Ruiseco Avellaneda, Alfredo

a-Oct. 14, 1908. b-Veracruz, Veracruz, *Gulf*, *Urban*. c-Primary studies from the Cantonal School of Veracruz and the Colegio Mexicano, Mexico City; preparatory studies from the National Preparatory School, 1925–29; law degree, National School of Law, UNAM, 1930–35; Professor of World History, National Preparatory School; Professor of Mexican History, National Preparatory School and the School of Plastic Arts, UNAM; Professor of Art History, School of Plastic Arts, UNAM; researcher, Institute for Social Research, UNAM; Professor of the History of Philosophical Doctrines, Normal School of Colima. d-Federal Deputy from the State of Colima, Dist. 2, 1961–64, member of the Gran Comision, President of the Chamber, September, 1962; answered President *Adolfo Lopez Mateos*' 4th State of the Union Address, President of the Permanent Committee; member of the Legislative Studies Committee, the Constitutional Affairs Committee, the Fine Arts Committee and the Editorial Committee; *Senator* from the State of Colima, 1964–70, President of the First Public Education Committee and the Second Instructive Section of the Grand Jury. e-Joined the PNR, 1932; member of the National Revolutionary Federation led by *Mario Souza*, which supported General Obregon for president, 1928; campaigned with *Adolfo Lopez Mateos* during his presidential campaign in Aguascalientes, Durango, Zacatecas and Coahuila, 1958. g-Student leader of the Autonomy Movement at UNAM, 1929. h-Secretary General of Government of the State of Colima under Governor *Jose Gonzalez Lugo*, 1951–56. i-Father Alfredo Ruiseco Carbonell ran a shipping business in Manzanillo, 1920–70; married Concepcion Rivera Silva. j-None. k-Moved to Manzanillo, Colima, 1920. l-Letter; C de S, 1964–70; MGF69; *Excelsior*, 29 Aug. 1979, 14.

Ruiz, Francisco H.

(Deceased 1958)
a-1872. b-Jalisco, *West*. c-Primary and secondary studies in Guadalajara; preparatory studies in Guadalajara; law degree from the University of Guadalajara, 1899. d-None. e-None. f-Notary in Guadalajara; Judge and President of the Superior Tribunal of Jalisco; Judge of the First Instance in Jalisco; Civil Judge in various Mexican states including Colima, Zacatecas, Mexico; Judge of the Superior Tribunal of Colima, Veracruz, and Jalisco; District Judge of the State of Mexico; Secretary of the City Council of Guadalajara, 1918–19; Secretary General of Government of the State of Jalisco; Interim Governor of Jalisco; Justice of the Supreme Court, 1928–34; *Justice of the Supreme Court*, 1934–40. g-None. h-Author of law textbook. j-None. k-None. l-DP70, 1815; letter.

Ruiz Almada, Gilberto Sebastian

b-Sinaloa, *West*. c-Early education unknown; engineering degree, University of Sinaloa. d-*Senator* from the State of Sinaloa, 1976– . e-None. f-Director of Public Works, Culiacan, Sinaloa, 1959; Subdirector of Administration of the Secretariat of Government, 1965; Director of Administration of the Secretariat of Government, 1969; *Oficial Mayor of the Secretariat of the Presidency*, 1970–74; *Subsecretary of Fiscal Investigation*, 1974–76. g-None. i-Supported *Leopoldo Sanchez Celis* as a precandidate for governor of Sonora, 1963; close friend of *Luis Echeverria*. j-None. k-None. l-DPE65, 13; MGF69, 161; C de S, 1976–82; *Excelsior*, 18 June 1974, 9.

Ruiz (Camarillo), Leobardo

(Deceased 1965)
a-Jan. 18, 1892. b-Hacienda de Santiago, Pinos Zacatecas, *East Central*, *Rural*. c-Early education unknown; graduated from the National Military College, 1914; professor of equitation, National Military College, 1914; Assistant Director of the National Military College, 1931; Director of the National Military College, 1953–54. d-None. e-None. f-Member of a military study commission to Europe to study cavalry tactics, 1926; Director of the Department of Aeronautics, Secretary of War; Ambassador to Spain; Ambassador to Japan; Consul to Holland, 1935–37; *Charge d' Affairs*, Mexican Embassy, Paris, France, 1937–38; Counselor of the Mexican Embassy, Paris, France, 1938; Director of Recruitment and Reserves, Secretariat of National Defense, 1941; *Oficial Mayor of the Secretariat of National Defense*, 1945–46; Military Attache to the United States; Military Attache to Canada; Ambassador to Peru, 1952–53; Director of Military Education, Secretariat of National Defense, 1954–58. g-Secretary of the Union of Apprentice Mechanics. h-Worked on the railroad as a young man. j-Career army officer; joined the Revolution, 1914; colonel in the forces of Venustiano Carranza, 1920; accompanied Carranza to Veracruz, 1920; commander of artillery in the Army of the North East; rank of brigadier general, 1940; commander of the Third

Military Region, Merida, Yucatan, 1951. **k-**None. **l-**DP70, 1816; DGF56, 200; DGF51, 182; WWM45, 107.

Ruiz Castaneda, Maximiliano

a-Dec. 5, 1900. **b-**Acambay, Mexico, *West Central*, *Rural*. **c-**Preparatory at the Scientific and Literary Institute of Toluca, Mexico, 1912–16; medical degree from the National School of Medicine, UNAM, 1923; postgraduate work, University of Paris, 1924–25; instructor in Bacteriology and Immunology, 1932–36, and research fellow, Harvard Medical School, 1930–36. **d-***Senator* from the State of Mexico, 1958–64, member of the Gran Comision, the Public Welfare Committee, the Second Petroleum Committee, and the Special Committee for the Belisario Dominguez Medal; President of the Second Foreign Relations Committee. **e-**None. **f-**Organizer and researcher, Department of Medical Research, General Hospital, Mexico, D.F., 1937–70; Director of Central Laboratory, Children's Hospital, Mexico City, 1936–70. **g-**None. **h-**Author of medical works. **i-**Married Luisa Ochoa. **j-**None. **k-**None. **l-**WWM45, 108; C de S, 1961–64, 68; letter; Lopez, 970; MGF47, 198.

Ruiz Cortines, Adolfo
(Deceased Dec. 3, 1973)

a-Dec. 30, 1890. **b-**Veracruz, Veracruz, *Gulf*, *Urban*. **c-**Primary studies at La Pastora, Veracruz; studied at the Instituto Veracruzano for four years; no degree. **d-***Federal Deputy* from the State of Veracruz, Dist. 3, 1937–40; *Governor of Veracruz*, 1944–48; *President of Mexico*, 1952–58. **e-**PRI Committeeman from Veracruz; campaign manager for the presidential campaign of *Miguel Aleman*, 1946; campaign treasurer for the presidential campaign of *Manuel Avila Camacho*, 1940. **f-**Aide to Alfredo Robles Dominguez, Governor of the Federal District, 1914; member of Carranza's Secret Service, 1913; assistant to *Heriberto Jara*, Governor of the Federal District, 1914; private secretary to General *Jacinto B. Trevino*, Secretary of Industry and Commerce, 1920–21; employee, Office of Social Statistics, 1921–26; Director of the Office of Social Statistics, 1926–35; *Oficial Mayor of the Department of the Federal District*, 1935–37, under *Cosme R. Hinojosa*; Secretary General of Government of the State of Veracruz, 1939–40, under Governor *Casas Aleman*; *Oficial Mayor of the Secretariat of Government*, 1940–44; *Secretary of Government*, 1948–52; consulting economist to Nacional Financiera, 1959–67. **g-**None. **h-**Abandoned studies at age 16 to support family; employed in a textile mill; worked as an accountant. **i-**Father, a custom's agent, died when he was two months old; Stepson, Mauricio Locken, was appointed 2nd Captain of the Chief of Staff, Secretariat of National Defense, 1952; helped by Al-

fredo Robles Dominguez, who was his civics teacher in Veracruz and was an important influence on his political career; influenced by Miguel Macias, one of his teachers at the Instituto Veracruzano, who later edited a pamphlet about *Ruiz Cortines* as Governor of Veracruz; friend of *Miguel Aleman* since 1935, when he was Oficial Mayor of the Federal District and *Aleman* was a Judge of the Superior Tribunal of Justice of the Federal District; formed friendship with *Adolfo Lopez Mateos* when *Lopez Mateos* represented Mexico in the Senate and before the Secretariat of Government; married Lucia Carrillo, widowed, and married Maria Izaguirre. **j-**Joined the Army, 1914, in Veracruz; rank of 2nd Captain; Aide to Robles Dominguez as Governor of Guerrero, 1914; administrative posts in the Paymaster General's Staff; served under General *Jara*; recovered the federal treasury abandoned by Carranza, 1920; Paymaster of the Army of the East; administrative posts in the Army, 1924; Paymaster General of the Brigade Mariel, 1915–16. **k-**Scott believes that the early contact and friendship between General *Trevino* and *Ruiz Cortines* was the reason why *Trevino*'s political party, PARM, received government recognition. **l-**Cline, 160; *Heroic Mexico*, 352; Scott, 217–18; Gaxiola, 528; Q es Q, 525–26; *Libro de Oro*, liii; DBM68, 542; Morton, 88–89, 92; Covarrubias, 157; WWMG, 36; DGF56, 45; Brandenburg, 107–13; DP70, 1817; C deD, 1937–39, 19; Enc. Mex., XI, 1977, 206–09.

Ruiz de Chavez, Genaro
(Deceased June 3, 1958)

a-June 12, 1892. **b-**San Cristobal Las Casas, Chiapas, *South*, *Urban*. **c-**Primary and secondary studies in San Cristobal; preparatory studies in San Cristobal; law degree, 1915; professor of law, Graduate School of Business Administration, UNAM. **d-**Federal Deputy from the State of Chiapas, 1918–20. **e-**Co-founder of the Civic Front of Revolutionary Affirmation, 1963. **f-**Agent of the Ministerio Publico; Judge of the Superior Tribunal of Justice, State of Chiapas; Oficial Mayor of the State of Chiapas; Judge of the 7th Penal Division, Federal District, 1940; Judge of the 19th Penal Division, Federal District, 1941; Judge of the Superior Tribunal of the Federal District, 8th Division, 1951–53; *Justice of the Supreme Court*, 1954–58. **g-**None. **h-**Director of *El Hijo del Pueblo*, 1909, in which he attacked Porfirio Diaz; author of various legal articles. **j-**None. **k-**None. **l-**DP70, 1819; DGF56, 567; DGF51, I, 487; Cadena Z., 1970; Casasola, V; DB de C, 224.

Ruiz Galindo, Antonio

a-July 30, 1897. **b-**Cordoba, Veracruz, *Gulf*, *Urban*. **c-**Primary studies in Cordoba; secondary studies at the Internado Nacional (National Preparatory Boarding School); studies at the School of Business and Administration, UNAM; no degree. **d**-None. **e**-None. **f**-*Secretary of Industry and Commerce*, 1946–48. **g**-None. **h**-Sales agent for General Fireproofing; founded DM Nacional, 1929; rebuilt a new plant in 1937 after the original factory was destroyed by fire; organizer of a large-scale industrial city on the outskirts of Mexico, D.F., 1944–46; President of the Board of Directors of National Steel Industry; Director General of DM Nacional, 1971–72. **i**-Son Antonio Jr., was Ambassador to Germany, married Serafina Gomez Sariol. **j**-Joined the Revolution under *Candido Aguilar*. **k**-Resigned from the Secretariat of Industry and Commerce, 1948; DM Nacional was one of the first Mexican firms to institute modern automated facilities and methods of mass production in Mexico. **l**-WWM45, 108; HA, 26 Dec. 1951; DBM68, 542–43; DBM70, 490–91; Brandenburg, 102; STYRBIWW54, 986; HA, 23 July 1956, 13; HA, 28 Dec. 1951, 37.

Ruiz Gonzalez, Pedro

a-May 25, 1928. **b**-Luis Moya, Zacatecas, *East Central*, *Rural*. **c**-Primary studies at the Escobar Brothers School, Ciudad Juarez, Chihuahua; agricultural engineering degree, National School of Agriculture. **d**-*Federal Deputy* from the State of Zacatecas, Dist. 4, 1964–67, member of the Gran Comision and the Fourth Ejido Committee, Vice President of the Chamber, October, 1966; *Governor of Zacatecas*, 1968–74. **e**-Secretary General of PRI in Zacatecas, 1962–63; President of PRI in Zacatecas, 1964. **f**-Brigade Director, Hoof and Mouth Disease Campaign, Secretariat of Agriculture, 1949–51; Delegate of the Agricultural Extension Service, Secretariat of Agriculture; Zone Director, National Agricultural Credit Bank, 1956; Subdirector of the Agricultural Experiment Station, State of Zacatecas; Irrigation administrator, Ejido Bank; General Agent, Secretariat of Agriculture, State of Zacatecas, 1959–64. **g**-None. **j**-None. **k**-None. **l**-C de D, 1964–67, 83.

Ruiz Madero, Ramiro

a-Dec. 14, 1916. **b**-Torreon, Coahuila, *North*, *Urban*. **c**-Early education unknown; no degree. **d**-None. **e**-None. **f**-Employee of the Secretariat of Health and Welfare. **g**-Secretary of Organization of Section 39 of the Union of Workers of the Secretariat of Health and Public Welfare; Secretary General of Section 39 of the Union of Workers of the Secretariat of Health; Secretary of Finances of the CTM in Torreon, Coahuila; Secretary of Organization of the Union of Workers of the Secretariat of Health; Secretary General of the Union of Workers of the Secretariat of Health; Secretary of Budget, CEN of the FSTSE; Secretary of Labor Relations, CEN of the FSTSE; Secretary of Labor and Conflicts, CEN of the FSTSE; Secretary of Finances of the CEN of the FSTSE; founder and director of the Finance Committee of the Congress of Labor; General Coordinator of the Congress of Labor, 1978. **h**-None. **j**-None. **k**-None. **l**-HA, 10 July 1978, 10.

Ruiz Soto, Agustin

a-Feb. 15, 1930. **b**-Canatlan, Durango, *West*, *Rural*. **c**-Early education unknown; law degree, School of Law, University of Durango; studies in English and sociology, University of Louisiana; Professor of World History, University of Durango. **d**-Local Deputy to the State Legislature of Durango; *Federal Deputy* from the State of Durango, Dist. 3, 1961–64; *Federal Deputy* from the State of Durango, Dist. 1, 1967–70; *Senator* from the State of Durango, 1970–76, President of the Forestry Committee, Second Secretary of the Second Credit Committee and the National Lands Committee, and First Secretary of the Second Mines Committee. **e**-None. **f**-Subdirector of the Department of Multi-family Control and Administration, ISSSTE; Private Secretary to the Governor of Durango, *Francisco Gonzalez de la Vega*, 1956–61. **g**-Legal adviser to the National Federation of Apple Growers; Secretary of Organization and Statistics of the CEN of CNOP. **i**-Married Magdalena Torres San Martin. **j**-None. **k**-None. **l**-C de D, 1967–70; C de S, 1970–76, 85; PS, 5512.

Ruiz Vasconcelos, Ramon

a-Sept. 16, 1913. **b**-Oaxaca, Oaxaca, *South*, *Urban*. **c**-Law degree. **d**-*Federal Deputy* from the State of Oaxaca, 1955–58, Dist. 9, Secretary of the Gran Comision, member of the Legislative Studies Committee (1st year), the Livestock Committee, the Second Treasury Committee; *Senator* from the State of Oaxaca, 1958–64, member of the Second Government Committee, the First Mines Committee, the First Foreign Relations Committee, the Special Tourist Affairs Committee, and the Special Legislative Studies Committee; President of the Social Security Committee and substitute member of the Securities Committee. **e**-President of the State Committee of PRI in Oaxaca. **f**-Lawyer, Secretariat of Public Works; Agent of the Ministerio Publico of the Office of the Attorney General; Assistant to the Attorney General of Mexico; Chief of Preparatory Investigations, Attorney General of the Federal District; Ambassador to the Dominican Republic, 1965; Ambassador to Yugoslavia, 1969–70. **g**-None. **h**-Technical adviser to the IMSS. **j**-None. **k**-None. **l**-DPE65, 31; Func., 303; C de S, 1961–64, 69; DGF56, 26, 29, 33, 34, 30; Ind. Biog., 142.

Ruvalcaba Gutierrez, Aurora

a-May 24, 1928. **b**-Colima, Colima, *West*, *Urban*. **c**-Primary studies in Sor Juana Ines de la Cruz, Colima; secondary in Colima, Colima; teaching certificate from the Normal School of Colima; degree in diplomacy from the School of Political and Social Sciences, UNAM. **d-***Senator* from the State of Colima, 1970–76, President of the Second Foreign Relations Committee, Second Secretary of the Department of the Federal District Committee, and member of the First Section of the Legislative Studies Committee. **e-**Delegate of the Feminine Sector of PRI in Puebla. **f-**None. **g-**Secretary General of the SNTE in Colima; President of the Feminine Sector of the SNTE, Colima; President of the Women's Sector of the CEN of SNTE; Feminine Sector Director of the FSTSE; Vice-president of the Congress of Labor; President of the Congress of Labor. **j-**None. **k-**First female senator elected from Colima. **l-**C de S, 1970–76, 85; PS, 5519.

Ruvalcaba Sanchez, Filiberto G.

a-Feb. 4, 1905. **b-**Ixtlahuacan del Rio, Jalisco, *West*, Rural. **c-**Primary studies; no further education. **d-***Federal Deputy* from the State of Jalisco, Dist. 7, 1952–55; *Federal Deputy* from the State of Jalisco, Dist. 8, 1961–64; *Senator* from the State of Jalisco, 1964–70. **e-**Joined the PNR, 1929. **f-**None. **g-**Organized the first agrarian workers in Jalisco; representative of Mexican labor to the International Labor Organization Conference, Geneva, Switzerland, 1954; representative of Mexican labor to the United Nations Labor Meetings, New York City, 1959; Secretary General of the National Miners and Metallurgical Workers Union; President of the Latin American Federation of Miners, 1960. **h-**Worked as a farm laborer. **j-**None. **k-**None. **l-**C de D, 1952–55; C de D, 1961–64; C de S, 1964–70; MGF69.

Sabines Gutierrez, Juan

a-1920. **b-**Tuxtla Gutierrez, Chiapas, *South*, *Urban*. **c-**Primary and secondary studies in Tuxtla Gutierrez; no degree. **d-**Mayor of Tuxtla Gutierrez; *Federal Deputy* from the State of Chiapas, Dist. 3, 1952–55, member of the Second Balloting Committee and the Fourth Section of the Credentials Committee; *Federal Deputy* from the State of Chiapas, Dist. 1, 1958–61, member of the Colonization Committee, the Foreign and Domestic Trade Committee, the Fifth Section of the Legislative Studies Committee, the Inspection Committee for the General Accounting Office (1st year), the Credentials Committee, and substitute member of the Consular and Diplomatic Service Committee; *Senator* from Chiapas, 1970–76, member of the Gran Comision, President of the Industries Committee, First Secretary of the Second Instructive Section of the Grand Jury and First Secretary of the Hydraulic Resources Committee; *Governor of Chiapas*, 1980– . **e-**President of the State Regional Committee of PRI in Chiapas; *Secretary General of the CEN of PRI*, 1976–78. **g-**President of the Chamber of Commerce of Tuxtla Gutierrez.

h-Businessman. **i-**Brother *Jaime Sabines Gutierrez* is a well-known poet and was a Federal Deputy from Chiapas, 1976–79. **j-**None. **k-**None. **l-**Func., 154; C de D, 1958–60, 90; C de D, 1952–54, 58; C de S, 1970–76; DB de C, 229.

Sala, Adelor D.

a-Jan. 28, 1897. **b-**Teapa, Tabasco, *Gulf*, *Rural*. **c-**Primary and secondary studies from the Juarez Institute of Villahermosa; preparatory studies from the National Preparatory School; teaching certificate from the National Normal School, Mexico City, 1926; law degree, National School of Law, UNAM, 1934. **d-***Senator* from the State of Tabasco, 1946–52, member of the Gran Comision, the Legislative Studies Committee, the Second Tariff and Foreign Trade Committee and the First Petroleum Committee; member of the Permanent Committee, 1947. **e-**None. **f-**Judge of the Superior Tribunal of Justice of Tabasco; Judge of the 13th Civil Judicial District, Mexico City; Secretary General of Government of the State of Tabasco. **g-**None. **j-**None. **k-**None. **l-**C de S, 1946–52; DGF51, I, 7, 9–11, 13.

Salas, Ismael

a-May 2, 1897. **b-**San Luis Potosi, *East Central*. **c-**Early education unknown; studied accounting degree. **d-**Federal Deputy from the Federal District, Dist. 4, 1930–32; Federal Deputy from the Federal District, Dist. 5, 1932–34; *Federal Deputy* from the State of San Luis Potosi, Dist. 5, 1943–46; *Governor of San Luis Potosi*, 1949–55. **e-***Treasurer of the CEN of the PRM*, 1941–43. **f-**Director, Federal Tax Office, Rio Verde, San Luis Potosi, 1934–37; Director, Administrative Office, Department of Labor, 1937–40; Director, Federal Tax Office, Iguala, Guerrero, 1940–41; Treasurer General of the State of San Luis Potosi under *Gonzalo N. Santos*, 1946–48. **g-**None. **i-**Protege of *Gonzalo N. Santos*; brother of *Herminio Salas*, Federal Deputy from the State of San Luis Potosi, 1940–43; brother-in-law of *Alberto Bremauntz*; father was a small shoestore owner. **j-**None. **k-**Member of the anti-clerical group of deputies in the 1932–34 legislature. **l-**Bremauntz, 109; C de D, 1943–46, 20; C de D, 1930–32; C de D, 1928–30; DGF51, I, 92; HA, 7 Oct. 1949, xxiii–xxvi.

Salazar Martinez, Florencio

a-Dec. 31, 1931. **b-**San Luis Potosi, San Luis Potosi, *East Central*, *Urban*. **c-**Primary studies at the Colegio Ingles, San Luis Potosi; secondary and preparatory studies, University of San Luis Potosi; law degree, School of law, University of San Luis Potosi; Professor of Tributary Law, University of San Luis Potosi. **d-***Federal Deputy* from the State of San Luis Potosi, Dist. 3, 1967–70; *Senator from the State of*

San Luis Potosi, 1970–76, member of the Gran Comision, President of the Agriculture and Development Committee and the First Ejido Committee; First Secretary of the First Justice Committee and member of the Second Section of the Legislative Studies Committee. e-Joined PRI, 1956; Director of Legal Development, PRI, San Luis Potosi, 1964–67; President of PRI in San Luis Potosi, 1967. f-None. g-President of the Association of Lawyers of San Luis Potosi, 1965–67. h-Founder of the newspaper, *Plan de San Luis*. i-Son of *Florencio Salazar Mendez*, federal deputy from San Luis Potosi, 1940–43, 1946–49; married Maria del Socorro Mendoza. j-None. k-None. l-C de D, 1967–70; C de S, 1970–76, 86.

Salazar (Mendez), Florencio

a-1906. b-El Carmen, Tierra Nueva, San Luis Potosi, *East Central*, *Rural*. c-Teaching certificate, on a government scholarship, from the Normal School of San Luis Potosi, 1925. d-*Federal Deputy* from the State of San Luis Potosi, Dist. 1, 1940–43, member of the Gran Comision; Local Deputy to the State Legislature of San Luis Potosi, 1943–45; *Federal Deputy* from the State of San Luis Potosi, Dist. 1, 1946–49; *Alternate Senator* from the State of San Luis Potosi, 1964–70. e-President of PRI in San Luis Potosi, 1965. f-Director of Public Education in the State of San Luis Potosi. g-Founder of the Workers Federation of the State of San Luis Potosi; Secretary General of the CTM of the State of San Luis Potosi. i-From a humble background; father of *Florencio Salazar Martinez*, federal deputy from San Luis Potosi, 1967–70 and Senator, 1970–76. j-None. k-Accompanied *Manuel Avila Camacho* to Monterrey for his meeting with Franklin D. Roosevelt. l-Lopez, 985; MGF69, 106; C de D, 1940–43; C de D, 1946–49.

Salazar (Salazar), Antonio

a-Nov. 14, 1921. b-Villa de Alvarez, Colima, *West*, *Rural*. c-Enrolled in the National Military College 1939; graduated from the National Military College as a 2nd Lieutenant in the Infantry, July 1, 1942; preparatory studies for law at the National Preparatory Night School, Mexico, D.F.; law degree, National School of Law, UNAM, Jan. 25, 1951, with an honorable mention; professor at the University of San Nicolas de Hidalgo, in military law and general theory of the state, 1951. d-*Federal Deputy* from the State of Colima, Dist. 1, 1955–58, member of the Military Justice Committee and the Second National Defense Committee; *Senator* from Colima, 1958–64, member of the Gran Comision, the Second Tariff and Foreign Trade Committee, the Second Constitutional Affairs Committee, the Special Legislative Studies Committee; President of the Third National

Defense Committee and substitute member of the War Materiels Committee; *Senator* from Colima, 1976– . e-None. f-Agent of the Ministerio Publico attached to the 21st Military Zone, Morelia, Michoacan; legal advisor to the Attorney General of Miliary Justice; Public Defender, First Judicial District, 1st Military Region; legal adviser to the Secretariat of National Defense; Chief of the Census Department, CNC. g-None. h-Worked as a farm laborer, age of 16. j-Joined the 17th Cavalry Regiment, Jan. 19, 1938, as a private; fought against *Saturnino Cedillo* in San Luis Potosi; Adjutant General of the 9th Infantry Regiment; Chief of Resolutions, Third Section, Department of Justice and Pensions, Secretariat of National Defense; career army officer; rank of Lt. Colonel. k-Precandidate for Governor of Colima three times. l-Func., 147; DGF56, 22, 32, 35; C de S, 1961–64, 69.

Salcedo (Monteon), Celestino

a-July 26, 1935. b-Ocotlan, Jalisco, *West*, *Urban*. c-Teaching certificate; studied for agricultural engineering degree at the School of Agriculture, Navojoa, Sonora; agricultural engineering degree from the Antonio Narro School, Saltillo, Coahuila, 1957; rural school teacher. d-*Federal Deputy* from the State of Baja California del Norte, Dist. 3, 1967–70, member of the Hydraulic Resources Committee; *Federal Deputy* from the State of Baja California del Norte, Dist. 3, 1973–76; *Senator* from Baja California del Norte, 1976– . e-*Secretary of Agrarian Action of the CEN of PRI*, 1973. f-Director of Colonies, Department of Agrarian Affairs, 1973; Director of National Lands, Department of Agrarian Affairs; Director of the National Agrarian Program, Department of Agrarian Affairs; Director General of FONAFE, 1977– . g-Student leader in Navojoa and Saltillo; Secretary of the League of Agrarian Communities of Baja California del Norte, 1960–70; Ejido Commissioner, Mexicali, 1963–66; delegate of the CNC to Yucatan, 1970; *Secretary General of the CNC*, Feb. 15, 1973–74. h-Ejidatario in Mexicali. i-Father, Pedro Salcedo Rivera, was a peasant and agrarian leader who co-founded the League of Agrarian Communities in Baja California. j-None. k-None. l-*Excelsior*, 8 Mar. 1973, 14; *Excelsior*, 13 Mar. 1973, 11; C de D, 1967–69, 85; MGF69, 89; *Excelsior*, 15 Feb. 1973, 19; HA, 12 Feb. 1973, 11–13; *Excelsior*, 17 Feb. 1973; HA, 18 Mar. 1974; Loret de Mola, 38; *Excelsior*, 27 Jan. 1975, 16; *Excelsior*, 8 Dec. 1975, 22.

Saldana Villaba, Adalberto

a-Apr. 30, 1908. b-Federal District, *Federal District*, *Urban*. c-Primary and secondary studies in the Federal District; preparatory studies in the Federal District; law degree from the National Law School,

UNAM. d-None. e-None. f-Legal adviser to PEMEX; Assistant to the Director of Nacional Financiera; *Director of National Finance Bank*, 1946–52; Gerente of Legal Affairs, Altos Hornos de Mexico, 1964–70. g-None. h-Adviser to Carlos Trouyet, S.A. i-Son of a lawyer. j-None. k-None. l-DGF50, II, 57, etc.; DGF51, II, 77, etc.; DGF47, 344; MGF69, 443.

Salgado Paez, Vicente

a-July 17, 1893. b-Valle de Santiago, Guanajuato, *West Central*, *Urban*. c-Primary studies in the Valle de Santiago and in the Villa de Uriangato, Guanajuato, 1900–06; engineering degree from the University of Guanajuato. d-*Federal Deputy* from the State of Guanajuato, Dist. 3, 1949–52, member of the Department of Agrarian Affairs and Colonization Committee, the First Balloting Committee and the Social Action Committee (1st year), President of the First Instructive Section of the Grand Jury; *Federal Deputy* from the State of Guanajuato, Dist. 6, 1958–61, member of the Agriculture and Development Committee, the Library Committee (1st year), the Plaints Committee, the Credentials Committee, and the National Lands Committee; *Federal Deputy* from the State of Guanajuato, Dist. 5, 1964–67, member of the First Section of the Agrarian Affairs Committee and the Livestock Committee. e-*Agrarian Secretary of the CEN of PRI*, 1952–53. f-Field agent, National Agrarian Commission, 1918; topographical engineer, National Agrarian Commission; agent of the National Ejido Credit Bank; Director of the New Centers for Agricultural Villages, 1937; Subdirector of Henequeneros de Yucatan, 1937–38; adviser to the Department of Agrarian Affairs and Colonization, 1940–49; Director of the Department of Credit, National Ejido Credit Bank, 1953–54; Director of the Department of Commerce, National Ejido Credit Bank, 1954–58. g-Founding member of the Local Agrarian Committees of Oaxaca and Guanajuato, 1916; topographer for the Agrarian Committee of Guanajuato, 1918; founder of the agrarian delegation of Queretaro. h-Worked in a soap factory, 1906–08; assistant stoker, Municipal Light Plant, Valle de Santiago, 1908; topographer, Guanajuato, Guanajuato. j-None. k-None. l-Func., 213; C de D, 1958–60, 91; C de D, 1964–66, 55, 78, 86; DGF51, 21, 31, 33, 34; C de D, 1949–51.

Salgado Salgado, Alberto

a-Nov. 31, 1931. b-Teloloapan, Guerrero, *South*, *Rural*. c-Early education unknown; law degree, National School of Law, UNAM. d-None. e-Legal advisor to the PST. f-None. g-Legal advisor to various labor groups. j-None. k-Candidate of the PST for federal deputy from Guerrero, Dist. 2, 1979. l-HA, 23 Apr. 1979, I.

Salido Beltran, Roberto

a-Oct. 8, 1912. b-Alamos, Sonora, *North*, *Urban*. c-Early education unknown; enrolled in the National Military College, 1929, graduated as a tactical artillery officer, Jan. 1, 1932; graduate of the Military Aviation School as a Lieutenant of Aeronautics and a Pilot, Mar. 1, 1937; studies in air transport in the United States; diploma as an Air Force staff officer, Higher War College, 1948–53; Professor and founder of the course in air staff subjects, Higher War College; Professor of Aeronautical Tactics, Higher War College, 1941–43; Director of Teaching and Instructor in Air Tactics, Higher War College, 1952; Professor of Aerodynamics, Military School of Aviation Mechanics, 1947; founder of the Air Force College; Director of the Military School of Aviation, 1959–64. d-None. e-None. f-Subdirector of the Mexican Air Force, 1953–55; Military Attache to the Mexican Embassy, Washington, D.C., 1964–69; *Director of the Mexican Air Force*, 1970–76. g-None. h-None. i-Son of Divisionary General Conrado C. Salido, zone commander, 1956. j-Career Air Force officer; fought against *Saturnino Cedillo* in San Luis Potosi, 1939, fought in World War II as a member of the 201 Squadron, 1945; rank of Lt. Colonel, 1947; rank of Colonel, 1950; rank of Brigadier General, 1952; reached rank of Divisionary General, Nov. 20, 1969. k-None. l-Enc. Mex., XI, 1977, 235; DPE71, 17; DGF56, 202; Enc. Mex., Annual, 1977, 596.

Salinas Camina, Gustavo

(Deceased 1964)
a-July 19, 1893. b-Monclova, Coahuila, *North*, *Urban*. c-Primary studies in Monclova, Coahuila; secondary studies at the Moviles Military Academy, New York; graduated from the Moisant Aviation School, New York, as a pilot, September 24, 1912. d-None. e-None. f-Military Attache to the Mexican Embassy, Paris, France; Military Attache to the Mexican Embassy, Brussels, Belgium; Military Attache to the Mexican Embassy, London, England; Director of the National Artillery Foundry; Director, Department of Cavalry, Secretariat of National Defense; *Director*, *Mexican Air Force*, 1940; Director General of Military Aviation, 1940–45. g-None. h-None. i-Son of General Emilio Salinas Salamanca, provisional governor of Coahuila; nephew of Venustiano Carranza. j-Joined the Revolution, 1912, fought against Pascual Orozco; rank of 2nd Lieutenant, July 25, 1912; fought against Victoriano Huerta; Chief of the 21st Artillery Regiment, 1915–20; rank of Brigadier General, 1924; supported General Escobar against the government, 1929; fought in World War II in the 201st Air Squadron, which he organized; reached rank of Divisionary General. k-First Mexican to lead an aerial bombardment of a boat, the

"Guerrero," during the Revolution; tried to save Francisco Madero by bombing rebellious troops in Mexico City, 1913. l-Lopez, 987; DP70, 1840; Enc. Mex., XI, 1971, 235–36.

Salinas Carranza, Alberto

(Deceased 1970)
a-Nov. 11, 1892. b-Cuatro Cienegas, Coahuila, *North*, *Rural*. c-Studied mechanics at the Rensselaer Polytechnic Institute, New York; studied aviation at the School of Aviation of Moisant, Garden City, New York, 1911–12. d-*Senator* from the State of Coahuila, 1934–40. e-None. f-Founder and Director of the First Department of Aviation, Department of War, 1915; Director of the Cartridge Industry, Secretariat of National Defense; Director of Stores and Inventories, Secretariat of Public Works; Director of the Military Industry Department, Secretary of National Defense; Director of Civil Aviation; *Chief of the Mexican Air Force*, 1939–40, 1941–46; Military Attache to Washington, D.C.; Military Attache to Rome; Military Attache to Belgrade; adviser to the President of Mexico. g-President of the Veterans of the Revolution in the Service of the State. h-Author of various books. i-Nephew of President Carranza. j-Joined the first air squadron under Carranza during the Revolution; career army officer; Brigadier General, July 1, 1942; Brigade General, Jan. 1, 1951. k-Founder of the first School for military pilots; promised the official party nomination for governor of Coahuila in 1957 by PRI president *Agustin Olachea Aviles*. l-Peral, 738–39; DP70, 2441; WWM45, 110; C de S, 1934–40; Lopez, 987; *Excelsior*, 23 Dec. 1979, 18.

Salinas Leal, Bonifacio

a-May 14, 1900. b-General Bravo, Nuevo Leon, *North*, *Rural*. c-Graduated from the National Military College. d-*Governor of Nuevo Leon*, 1939–43; *Senator* from the State of Nuevo Leon, 1970–76, member of the Gran Comision, president of the Second National Defense Committee, First Secretary of the Navy Committee, and Second Secretary of the Second Petroleum Committee. e-None. f-Inspector General of Police, Monterrey, Nuevo Leon, 1915; *Governor of Baja California del Sur*, 1959–65. g-None. h-None. j-Career army officer; joined the army, 1913, fought under Carranza; rank of Major, 1918; rank of Brigadier General, 1929; Commander of the 3rd Cavalry Regiment, 1937, Silao, Guanajuato; Brigade General, June 1, 1938; Divisionary General, Sept. 16, 1946; Commander of the 8th Military Zone, Tampico, 1946; Commander of the 5th Military Region, Guadalajara, Jalisco, 1951–56. k-Founder of the Nursery Schools for children of military men; *New York Times* claims he resigned from the governorship of Baja California del Sur be-

cause he lost the support of labor and professional groups. l-DGF51, 183; Brandenburg, 80; Q es Q, 536; DBM68, 562; DBM70, 508; DGF56, 201; Casasola, V; NYT, 12 Apr. 1965, 11.

Salinas Lozano, Raul

a-May 1, 1917. b-Monterrey, Nuevo Leon, *North*, *Urban*. c-Primary and secondary studies in Monterrey; preparatory studies in the Federal District; economics degree from the National School of Economics, UNAM, 1944, with a thesis on state intervention and prices; Master of Arts in Public Administration, American University, 1945; Master of Arts in Economics, Harvard University, 1946, on a fellowship from the government; Professor of Economics, National School of Economics, UNAM, 1947–58; Professor of Economics, Ibero-American University; Professor of Economics, University of San Salvador, 1950–52. d-None. e-None. f-Economist, National Bank of Foreign Commerce; economist, CONASUPO; Chief, Department of Economic Studies, Secretariat of the Treasury, 1948–50; tax consultant to the government of Honduras, 1950–52; economist; Technical Commission, Secretariat of National Patrimony, 1952–54; Director of Treasury Studies, Secretariat of the Treasury, 1952–54; Director of the National Investment Commission, 1954–58; Director of Economic Investigations, Secretariat of the Treasury, 1950–51, Alternate Governor of the International Monetary Fund, 1956–58; *Secretary of Industry and Commerce*, 1958–64; adviser to various public agencies, 1965–76; Technical Director of the National Price Commission, 1977–79; *Ambassador to the Soviet Union*, 1979–80; Director General of the Mexican Institute of Foreign Trade, 1980– . g-None. h-Author of many books and articles. i-Student of *Eduardo Bustamante* at UNAM; attended UNAM with *Flores de la Pena*; married Margarita de Gortari; son Carlos Salinas Gortari was appointed Director of the National Price Commission. j-None. k-None. l-*El Universal*, 2 Dec. 1958, 1; HA, 8 Dec. 1958, 25–26; DGF56, 59; DGF51, I, 149; D de Y, 2 Dec. 1958, 7; Func., 79; Enc. Mex., XI, 1977, 236; *Excelsior*, 1 Nov. 1978, 22; *Excelsior*, 14 Nov. 1977, 9; *Excelsior*, 28 July 1979, 1.

Salinas Ramos, Alberto

a-Apr. 8, 1905. b-Federal District, *Federal District*, *Urban*. c-Secondary studies at the Vocational School of Mechanical Engineers; graduated from the Electrical-Mechanical Institute of San Francisco, California. d-None. e-Secretary of Rural Policy of the CEN of PARM. g-Delegate to the Constitutive Assembly of the CTM, 1936; founder and President of the Mexican Federation of Agricultural Organizations, 1979; Secretary General of the Inter-American

Agrarian Organization, 1979. **i-**Collaborator of *Graciano Sanchez* in the CNC. **j-**None. **k-**None. **l-**HA, 2 Apr. 1979, II.

Salmoran de Tamayo, Maria Cristina

b-Oaxaca, Oaxaca, *South*, *Urban*. **c-**Primary studies in Oaxaca; secondary studies at Public School No. 8, Mexico, D.F.; preparatory studies at the National Preparatory School, Mexico, D.F.; studies at the School of Humanities, UNAM; law degree from the National School of Law, UNAM, with her thesis on "The Condition of Women under Labor Law;" LLD studies at the National School of Law, UNAM, 1951–52; studies in France at the International Labor Organization; founding teacher of Preparatory School No. 5, Coapa; Professor of the second course in Labor Law, National School of Law, UNAM, 1955–61; Professor of Agricultural Law, Superior School of Commerce and Administration, IPN. **d-**None. **e-**None. **f-**Employee for the Federal Board of Conciliation and Arbitration, 1941–42; Secretary of Hearings, Federal Board of Conciliation and Arbitration, 1942; Secretary of Resolutions, Federal Board of Conciliation and Arbitration; Assistant for Groups, under *Mario de la Cueva*, President of the Federal Board of Conciliation and Arbitration; assistant member of the Federal Board of Conciliation and Arbitration, 1949, under *Manuel Ramirez Vazquez*; President of the Federal Board of Conciliation and Arbitration, Jan. 2, 1954, to May 12, 1961; *Justice of the Supreme Court*, 1961–64, 1964–70, 1970–76, 1976– . **g-**None. **h-**Mexican delegate to the International Office of Labor. **i-**Student of *Alfonso Noriega*, Salvador Azuela, and *Mario de la Cueva*; married Alberto Tamayo, a lawyer. **j-**None. **k-**First woman member of the Supreme Court of Mexico. **l-**DGF56, 399; DPE61, 117; WWW70–71, 888; letter; *Justicia*, Mar., 1968.

Salvat Rodriguez, Agustin

a-Oct. 23, 1908. **b-**Veracruz, Veracruz, *Gulf*, *Urban*. **c-**Primary studies at the Escuela Benito Juarez, Salina Cruz, Oaxaca, and in Mexico City; preparatory studies at the Night Preparatory School, No. 5, 1934–35; law degree from the National School of Law, UNAM; Professor of World History, 1942–43. **d-**None. **e-***Secretary of Finances of the CEN of PRI*, 1952–58; *Secretary of Finances of the CEN of PRI*, 1958–64; organized youth groups for the 1940 presidential campaign of *Avila Camacho*; personal representative of *Adolfo Ruiz Cortines* during his campaign for the presidency in the Federal District, 1952. **f-***Head of the Department of Tourism*, 1964–70. **g-**Foreign Secretary of the Mexican Union of Electricians, 1935. **h-**Employed by the Mexican Power and Light Company, 1924–39; author of numerous articles on technical subjects. **i-**Married

Julieta Dorantes; son Agustin Salvat Dorantes is the manager of a public relations firm; father a street car conductor; grandfather a sea captain. **j-**None. **k-**Had to leave school at age 16 to support himself. **l-**HA, 29 Dec. 1958, 8; HA, 7 Dec. 1964, 20–21; letter; WWW70–71, 794; DBM68, 565; *El Universal*, 1 Dec. 1964; DBM70, 509; *Excelsior*, 22 Aug. 1978, 22.

Samayoa (Leon), Mariano

(Deceased Mar. 16, 1960)
a-Apr. 17, 1895. **b-**Chiapa de Corzo, Chiapas, *South*, *Urban*. **c-**Primary and secondary studies in Tuxtla Gutierrez, Chiapas and in Mexico City; normal teaching certificate, Normal School of Mexico, Mexico City, 1914. **d-**Federal Deputy from the State of Chiapas, 1922–24; *Federal Deputy* from the State of Chiapas, Dist. 4, 1940–43, member of the Permanent Commission, the Second Committee on Public Education, the Second Balloting Committee, the Tourism Committee, and the Second Instructive Section of the Grand Jury; Secretary of the Chamber of Deputies, Sept. 1942. **e-**Founding member of the CNOP of PRI; member of the Cooperatist Party. **f-**Director of Public Education, State of Chiapas; Subdirector of Agricultural Education, Secretariat of Public Education; Director of Indigenous Affairs, Secretariat of Public Education, 1946–52; Secretary General of Government of the State of Chiapas under *Efrain Gutierrez*, 1936–37; Interim Governor of Chiapas. **g-**None. **h-**None. **j-**Participated in the Revolution, but in non-military affairs; Major in the Veterans of the Revolution. **k-**None. **l-**DGF51, I, 290; DGF51, II, 635; DGF50, II, 465; C de D, 1940–42, 49, 54, 55; Peral, 740; DP70, 1845; DBdeC, 231–32; Lopez, 989.

San Pedro (Salem), Fernando

a-Feb. 14, 1902. **b-**Tampico, Tamaulipas, *North*, *Urban*. **c-**Primary studies at public school No. 1, Tampico; secondary studies in New York, San Antonio, and Houston; no degree. **d-**Councilman for Tampico, 1928–29, and 1936; local deputy from the Tampico district to the State Legislature of Tamaulipas, 1943–45; Mayor of Tampico, 1946–48, and 1972–75; *Federal Deputy* from the State of Tampico, Dist. 5, 1976–79, member of the Government Properties Committee. **e-**Member of the Partido Socialista Fronterizo of Tamaulipas; member of PRI but elected mayor of Tampico, 1972, as PPS candidate; elected Federal Deputy as a representative of PARM. **f-**Traffic Inspector, Tampico, 1926; Alternate Councilman, Tampico, 1930–31; Director of the 9th Forestry District, 1931; head of the Office of Rents, State of Tamaulipas, 1934–35; adviser to the Board of Water and Drainage, 1959–61; adviser to the Federal Board for Material and Moral Improvement, Tampico (20 years); adviser to the Chamber of Commerce of Tampico, 1962–68; Vice President of the Chamber of Commerce of Tampico. g-None. h-Businessman in automobiles and trucks, 1918–56. j-None. k-None. l-Letter; C de D, 1976–79, 63.

Sanchez, Graciano

(Deceased 1957)
a-1890. b-San Luis Potosi, San Luis Potosi, *East Central*, *Urban*. c-Rural teacher certificate; no degree; rural school teacher. d-Local deputy to the State Legislature of San Luis Potosi; Federal Deputy from the State of Tamaulipas, 1930–32; *Federal Deputy* from the State of Tamaulipas, Dist. 2, 1943–46. e-None. f-Head of the Department of Indigenous Affairs, Secretariat of Public Education. g-Founding member of the League of Agrarian Communities, State of Tamaulipas, during the Governorship of *Emilio Portes Gil*; founder of the Mexican Peasant Federation, which supported *Lazaro Cardenas*, 1933–34, and eventually became the CNC; *Secretary General of the National Farmers Federation*, 1938–42. h-None. i-Longtime friend of *Portes Gil*. j-None. k-Member of the "Old Guard" of the CNC; Brandenburg places him in the Inner Circle of power from 1940–46. l-*Annals*, March, 1940; Brandenburg, 80; Peral, 743; DP70, 1907; C de D, 1943–45, 20; Kirk, 331; Lopez, 992.

Sanchez, Marcos

a-Oct. 7, 1903. b-Acapulco, Guerrero, *South*, *Rural*. c-Primary studies in Acapulco; law degree. d-*Federal Deputy* from the State of Guerrero, Dist. 6, 1940–43, member of the First Ejidal Committee; substitute member of the National Waters and Irrigation Committee. e-None. f-Trustee of the City Government of Acapulco; lower court judge. g-Secretary General of the Peasant League of Acapulco. h-None. j-None. k-Originally elected as an Alternate Deputy. l-Peral, 745; C de D, 1940–42, 43.

Sanchez Celis, Leopoldo

a-Feb. 14, 1916. b-Cosala, Sinaloa, *West*, *Rural*. c-Primary and secondary studies in Cosala; no degree. d-*Federal Deputy* from the State of Sinaloa, Dist. 4, 1955–58, member of the Gran Comision, the Third Ejidal Committee, the Legislative Studies Committee (2nd year), the Instructive Committee for the Grand Jury, and the Balloting Committee; *Senator from the State of Sinaloa, 1958–63*, President of the Second Naval Committee, member of the Social Welfare Committee, and the First Balloting Committee; *Governor of Sinaloa*, 1963–67. e-Member of the peasant sector of the PRM; member of the National Council of the PRM; general delegate of the PRM to Jalisco, Zacatecas, Guanajuato, Tamaulipas; President of the Regional Committee of PRI, Sinaloa, 1955; *Secretary of Political Action of the CEN of PRI*, 1959. f-None. g-Considered as a precandidate for the Secretary Generalship of the National Farmers Federation, 1962. h-None. i-Close personal friend of *Amado Estrada*, senator from Sinaloa, 1964–70; *Alfredo Valdez Montoya* was Treasurer of Sinaloa during his governorship and was his candidate to succeed him; son, Leopoldo Sanchez Duarte, was a delegate of the Federal District Department to Coyoacan. j-None. k-One of the PRI leaders most responsible for the defeat of *Carlos Madrazo's* reform program and the ouster of *Madrazo* from the party leadership; peasants were reported to be invading lands owned illegally by Sanchez Celis in Sinaloa in the summer of 1972. l-DGF56, 28; *El Universal*, 1 July 1972; Gonzalez Navarro, 232; *Por Que*, 25 Sept. 1969, 29; *Excelsior*, 1 Feb. 1974, 10; *Excelsior*, 30 July 1978, 23.

Sanchez Colin, Salvador

a-May 14, 1912. b-Atlacomulco, Mexico, *West Central*, *Rural*. c-Studied at the Industrial Technical Institute; studied at the Central Agricultural School of El Mexe, Hidalgo, under a government scholarship; studied on a scholarship from the Secretariat of Agriculture at the National School of Agriculture, 1930–35, and received an agricultural engineering degree with a specialty in agricultural industry from the same institution in 1939; Professor of Botany and Mathematics at the Industrial Institute of Tijuana, Baja California del Norte; advanced studies in the United States in citrus fruit production. d-*Alternate Senator* from the State of Mexico, 1946–52; local deputy from Texcoco to the State Legislature of Mexico, 1950; *Governor of Mexico*, 1951–57. e-Member of the Technical Advisory Commission on Agricultural Questions during *Aleman's* presidential campaign, 1946; co-founder of the Civic Front for Revolutionary Affirmation, 1963. f-Director of Agricultural Instruction, Department of Prevocational Education, Secretariat of Public Education, 1936–37; Chief of Instruction, Schools for Military Dependents, Secretariat of National Defense, 1937–38; Director of Agricultural Instruction, Industrial Institute of Tijuana, Baja California del Norte, 1939–40; Technical Inspector for the National Bank of Agricultural Credit, 1941–43; Scientific Investigator for the Department of Agriculture, Secretariat of Agriculture, 1944–46; Director General of Agriculture, 1946–51; adviser to the National Ejido Credit Bank, 1948; Technical consultant to the President, 1949; adviser to the Secretary of Agriculture, 1972. g-None. h-Founder of the magazine *Tierra*, 1946, official publication of the Secretariat of Agriculture; founder of the publishing house, Agricola Mexicana; author of numerous technical studies. i-Son of peasants; worked in a printshop as a boy. j-None.

k-Created a special variety of lemon known as the Colin lemon. l-Q es Q, 539–40; DGF51, I, 6, 206; DGF56, 95; DGF47, 20, 123; HA, 11 Sept. 1956, 17–20; DGF51, II, 181; DGF50, II, 139; letter; Colin, 242–51.

Sanchez Cono, Edmundo M.

a-Nov. 20, 1894. b-Oaxaca, Oaxaca, *South*, *Urban*. c-Early education unknown; medical degree from the Free School of Homeopathy of Mexico. d-*Governor of Oaxaca*, 1944–47. e-*Secretary of Social and Military Action*, CEN of the PNR, 1938–40. f-None. g-None. j-Career army officer; returned to active duty, 1948; rank of brigadier general; director of schools for the children of army personnel. k-Precandidate for governor of Oaxaca, 1940; forced to resign as governor, January 19, 1947, because of his financial policies and municipal political impositions. l-Anderson, 86–87; NYT, 20 Jan. 1947, 4; NYT, 26 Jan. 1947, 37; HA, 25 Aug. 1944, 23; Correa, 377.

Sanchez Corral, Rogelio

a-May 18, 1910. b-Chihuahua, Chihuahua, *North*, *Urban*. c-Agricultural engineering degree, National School of Agriculture. d-*Federal Deputy* from the State of Chihuahua, Dist. 1, 1940–43, member of the Agricultural and Livestock Committee and the General Means of Communication Committee. e-None. f-Subdirector of the Forestry Department, Secretary of Agriculture and Livestock. h-Representative to the Agricultural Conference, Washington, D.C. j-None. k-None. l-Peral, 742; C de D, 1940–42, 43.

Sanchez Cuen, Manuel

c-Preparatory studies from the National Preparatory School; law degree from the National School of Law, UNAM, 1925–29; professor at UNAM. d-None. e-None. f-Adviser to the Bank of Mexico; personal adviser to various Secretaries of the Treasury; Subdirector of Income, Secretariat of the Treasury, under *Jesus Silva Herzog*, 1934–39; *Oficial Mayor of Industry and Commerce*, 1939–40, under *Efrain Buenrostro*; Subdirector General of PEMEX, 1940–46, under *Efrain Buenrostro*; *Subsecretary of Industry and Commerce*, October 23, 1948–52; Director General of the National Mortgage Bank, 1952–58. g-None. i-Attended UNAM with *Jose Castro Estrada*, *Antonio Carrillo Flores*, *Miguel Aleman*, and *Alfonso Noriega*; student of *Antonio Martinez Baez* and *Eduardo Suarez*. j-None. k-None. l-D de Y, 23 Oct. 1948, 1; DGF51, I, 95; DGF50, II, 78; *Siempre*, 28 Jan. 1959, 6; letters.

Sanchez de Mendiburu, Fidela

a-May 10, 1909. b-Merida, Yucatan, *Gulf*, *Urban*. c-Primary and secondary studies in Merida; normal teaching certificate, Dec. 30, 1931; certificate as an educator, 1945; special courses in mental hygiene, Superior Normal School, Federal District, 1950; urban normal teacher. d-*Federal Deputy* from the State of Yucatan, Dist. 1, 1964–67, member of the Social Action Committee (1st year), Public Welfare Committee, Second Public Education Committee, and Third Ejido Committee. e-Director of Feminine Action for PRI in Merida; Director of Feminine Action, CNOP of PRI, member of the State Delegation; organizer of the Feminine Congress of CNOP, 1957. f-Director of the Federal School No. 5, Merida, 1970. g-None. h-Director of various children's nurseries. j-None. k-Organized the first Civic Orientation Course for Women in Yucatan. l-C de ·D, 1964–66, 77, 78, 82; Q es QY, 231.

Sanchez de Velasco, Abraham

a-1909. b-Hustla, Jalisco, *West*, *Rural*. c-Primary studies in the Episcopal Boarding School of Chilapa and the Colegio Frances, Mexico City; secondary studies in Mexico City; preparatory studies at the National Preparatory School; economic studies, National School of Economics, 1929–33; economics degree, University of Guadalajara, 1936; professor at the School of Law, the School of Economics, and the Business School, University of Guadalajara, 1935–61. d-None. e-None. f-Chief of Economic Archives, Secretariat of the Treasury, 1934–35; consultant to the General Archives, State Government of Jalisco, 1935–36; representative of the National Workers Industrial Development Bank, Jalisco, 1937–38; Secretary General of Government of the State of Jalisco, 1942–44; Chief of Economic Studies, Costal Planning Commission, Guadalajara, 1954–59; President of the Water Services Board, Guadalajara, 1959–64; Director of Economic Development, State of Jalisco, 1959–61; department head, Treasury Office, State of Guadalajara, 1961–64; President of the Popular Planning Assembly, 1964; *Oficial Mayor of the Secretariat of Agriculture*, 1964–70; Director of the Department of Statistics, IMSS, 1971–74, Subdirector of Personnel, IMSS, 1974–76. g-None. h-Consulting economist, 1942–44; President of the Committee for the Industrial Development of Jalisco, 1942–44; adviser to many private industries, 1940–55; adviser to the Chamber of Commerce and Industries, Guadalajara, 1939–41. j-None. k-None. l-Enc. Mex., XI, 1977, 341–42; EN de E, 228.

Sanchez Diaz, Raul

a-Apr. 15, 1915. b-Guadalajara, Jalisco, *West*, *Urban*. c-Early education unknown; engineering degree from the National School of Engineering, UNAM. d-*Governor of Baja California del Norte*, 1965–71. e-None. f-Division Engineer, Sonora-Baja California Railroad; Director of the Campeche Division of the Southeast Railroad, 1949; Director of the Sonora-

Baja California Railroad, 1965. **g-**None. **i-**Student of *Antonio Dovali Jaime*, Director General of PEMEX, 1970–76. **j-**None. **k-**Moved to Baja California del Norte, 1942. **l-**Aguirre, 515; DPF65, 109.

Sanchez (Garcia), Enrique Wenceslao

a-Sept. 28, 1911. **b-**Canatlan, Durango, *West*, *Rural*. **c-**Primary studies in Canatlan; secondary studies at the Conciliar Seminary of Durango; teaching certificate, Federal Institute of Teacher's Education and the Normal School of Mexico, 1928. **d-**President of the State Legislature of the Durango; *Federal Deputy* from the State of Durango, Dist. 3, 1958–61, member of the Library Committee, the Second Public Education Committee, the 6th Section of the Legislative Studies Committee and the Consular and Diplomatic Service Committee; *Federal Deputy* from the State of Durango, Dist. 3, 1964–67, member of the Library Committee and the First Public Education Committee. **e-**Secretary of Political Action of PRI in Durango, 1950–54. **f-**Director of the Tax Office, Canatlan, Durango, 1944. **g-**Secretary of the Federation of Teachers, 1936; joined the Union of Teachers of Durango, 1940; assistant to the Secretary of Conflicts and Organization, SNTE; Director, Department of Labor and Social Welfare, SNTE, Durango; Secretary of Educational Action, CTM, Durango; Secretary of Section X of the STERM; *Secretary General of the SNTE*, 1955–58. **h-**None. **j-**None. **k-**None. **l-**C de D, 1964–67, 82; Func., 202; C de D, 1958–61, 92.

Sanchez Gavito, Vicente

(Deceased Jan. 20, 1977)
a-May 25, 1910. **b-**Federal District, *Federal District*, *Urban*. **c-**Primary and secondary studies in the Federal District; preparatory studies at the National Preparatory School, Mexico, D.F., 1928; law degree from the Escuela Libre de Derecho, October 27, 1933. **d-**None. **e-**None. **f-**Joined the Foreign Service, 1935; career foreign service officer; consultant to the United States-Mexican Claims Commission; Director, North American Affairs, Secretariat of Foreign Relations, 1939–43; Counselor, Mexican Embassy, Washington, D.C., 1944–47; Director General of the Diplomatic Service, 1947–51; member of the United Nations Tribunal for the Libya and Eritrea Question, 1951–55; Minister to Washington, D.C., 1956–59; *Ambassador to the Organization of American States*, 1959–65; Ambassador to Brazil, 1965–70; *Ambassador to Great Britain*, 1970–73; Ambassador to Germany, 1974–77. **g-**None. **h-**Chairman and member of various international committees. **i-**Student of *Javier Gaxiola* at the Escuela Libre de Derecho; personal adviser to *Manuel Tello*; married Maria Murguia. **j-**None. **k-**None. **l-**DPE61, 25; DPE65, 24; IWW67, 1072; letter; *Excelsior*, 8 May

1972, 2B; HA, 8 Apr. 1974, 13; HA, 31 Jan. 1977, 15; *Excelsior*, 21 Jan. 1977, 4.

Sanchez Hernandez, Tomas

a-Oct. 17, 1894. **b-**Leon, Guanajuato, *West Central*, *Urban*. **c-**Graduated from the National Military College, 1911–14, as a lieutenant in artillery; industrial engineering degree, National Military College, 1920–23; graduated from the Artillery School, Fontainblau, France, 1925–28; General Staff School, Paris, 1931–33; Director of the Superior War College, Secretariat of National Defense, 1934–40; Director of the National Military College, 1950–53. **d-**Federal Deputy from the State of Guanajuato, Dist. 4, 1973–76. **e-**None. **f-**Subsecretary of Public Education, 1943–46; Chief of Staff, Secretariat of National Defense, 1942–43; Chief of Staff, Secretariat of National Defense, 1954–57. **g-**None. **h-**Author of many technical military articles. **i-**Married Jeannette Marle. **j-**Career army officer; rank of Major, 1920; Assistant Director of Technical Schools, Secretariat of National Defense, 1924; rank of Colonel, 1928; commander of a mountain artillery regiment, 1928–30; Director of the National Artillery Foundry, 1933–34; Technical Military Director, 1940–42; rank of Divisionary General, 1950; Inspector General of the Army, June 16, 1953 to June 16, 1954; Director of the Military Industry Department, Secretariat of National Defense, 1958–60; Chief of the Mexican delegation to the United States-Mexican Defense Board during World War II. **k-**None. **l-**WWM45, 111; DGF56, 199; Peral, 744; Kirk, 254; DPE61, 31; DGF51, I, 179; *Excelsior*, 13 Mar. 1973, 13; Lopez, 993.

Sanchez Juarez, Delfin

a-Oct. 6, 1916. **c-**Early education unknown; law degree. **d-**None. **e-**None. **f-**Director of Internal Affairs, IMSS, 1958; Special Ambassador of Mexico to the inaguration of President Romulo Betancourt, Caracas, Venezuela, 1958; *Secretary General of Tourism*, 1959–60; joined the Foreign Service, 1961; Ambassador to the Low Counries, 1964–65; Ambassador to Poland, 1965–66; Ambassador to Guatemala, 1966–70; Delegate of the Department of the Federal District to Cuauhtemoc, 1971–73; Private Secretary to the Secretary of Public Education, *Porfirio Munoz Ledo*, 1976–77. **g-**None. **j-**None. **k-**None. **l-**MGF73, 395; HA, 26 Feb. 1973, 27; DAPC, 66; *Siempre*, 14 Jan. 1959, 6; *Siempre*, 18 Feb. 1959; MGF69, 182.

Sanchez Madariaga, Alfonso

a-Nov. 15, 1904. **b-**Federal District, *Federal District*, *Urban*. **c-**Early education unknown; no degree. **d-**Senator from the Federal District, 1940–46; member of the Gran Comision, president of the Department of the Federal District Committee, president of the First Labor Committee; *Federal Deputy* from the Federal District, Dist. 8, 1949–52, member of the Second Balloting Committee, the General Means of Communication Committee, and the Second Labor Committee; *Federal Deputy* from the Federal District, Dist. 5, 1955–58; president of the Child Welfare and Social Security Committee (1st year) and the First Labor Committee; *Senator* from the Federal District, 1970–76, president of the Senate, September, 1974. **e-**Secretary General of the PRM in the Federal District, 1938; *Secretary of Labor Action of the CEN of the PRM*, 1938–40; *Secretary of Labor Action of the CEN of PRI*, 1949–52. **f-**Member of the Advisory Council of the Department of the Federal District, 1929. **g-**Representative of labor before the Federal Board of Conciliation and Arbitration, 1939; Secretary General of the Inter-American Labor Organization (ORIT); co-organizer of the Union of Workers of the Federal District, 1929; member of the Secretariat of the Federation of Regional Workers and Farmers for the Federal District. **h-**Worked in a milk plant. **j-**None. **k-**Helped *Fidel Velazquez* form the Milkworkers Union, 1920s, which adhered to CROM, 1925; longtime labor leader who split with Luis Morones of CROM, 1929, to help form the CTM, 1936; candidate against *Joaquin Gamboa Pascoe* for Secretary General of the Workers Confederation of the Federal District, 1973. **l-**Brandenburg, 154; Peral, 745; DGF51, I, 21, 34, 36; DGF51, II, 127; DGF56, 23, 31, 33, 36, 37; C de D, 1949–51; C de D, 1955–57; C de S, 1940–46; C de S, 1970–76; Lopez, 994.

Sanchez Meza de Solis (Ogarrio), Guillermina

a-Jan. 22, 1926. **b-**Federal District, *Federal District, Urban*. **c-**Primary studies at the Benito Juarez School, Mexico City; secondary studies at Secondary School No. 11; preparatory studies at the National Preparatory School; economics degree from the National School of Economics, UNAM, with a thesis on an economic interpretation of Latin America, 1942–46; degree in consular law and diplomacy, School of Political and Social Sciences, UNAM; Professor of Economic Geography and Credit Institutions, the Women's University of Mexico. **d-**Federal Deputy from the Federal District, Dist. 22, 1970–73, member of the Tariff and Foreign Trade Committee, the First Tax Committee, the Money and Institutions of Credit Committee and the Budget and Accounts Committee. **e-**Collaborator of the IEPES of PRI. **f-**Mexican representative to the United Nations Conference on Trade Organizations; Director of the Office of Regional Economic Organizations, Secretariat of Industry and Commerce; Director of the Office of Medicines, Secretariat of Industry and Commerce; *Oficial Mayor of the Secretariat of Foreign Rela-*

tions, 1976–78; *Subsecretary of Foreign Relations "D"*, 1978–79. **g-**Member of the Executive Council of the College of Economists; President of the League of Revolutionary Economists. **i-**Co-student with *Jose Lopez Portillo* in elementary and high school; married Jorge Solis Ogarrio, a lawyer. **j-**None. **k-**One of two Mexican women to have held both the position of oficial mayor and subsecretary in a cabinet agency prior to 1980. **l-**Excelsior, 22 June 1979, 18; *Directorio*, 1970–72, 184–85; C de D, 1970–73, 136; EN de E, 239.

Sanchez Mireles, Romulo

a-1914. **b-**Coahuila, *North*. **c-**Preparatory studies at the Ateneo Fuente, Saltillo, Coahuila; law degree, National School of Law, UNAM. **d-**Federal Deputy from the Federal District, Dist. 8, 1952–55, member of the Department of the Federal District Committee, the Legislative Studies Committee, and the First Balloting Committee; *Federal Deputy* from the Federal District, Dist. 14, 1961–64; President of the Gran Comision, member of the First Government Committee and the Constitutional Affairs Committee; President of the Chamber of Deputies, Sept., 1963; member of the Inter-Parliamentary Congress of Mexico and the United States. **e-**Subsecretary of Popular Action of the CEN of PRI, 1952. **f-**Director General of the ISSSTE, 1964–70. **g-**Delegate to the National Convention of Preparatory Schools from the Ateneo Fuente; President of the Society of Law School Students and member of the University Council; longtime leader of the Federal Workers Union; First Oficial Mayor of CNOP, 1943; *Secretary General of the FSTSE*, 1958–64. **h-**Author of an article on bureaucracy. **j-**None. **k-**Formed a political alliance with *Alfonso Martinez Dominguez* and *Jesus Robles Martinez* called the "Three Colonels." **l-**Padgett, 129; Gonzalez Navarro, 118; WWMG, 37; C de D, 1961–63, 90; C de D, 1952–54, 19; *Hoy*, Dec., 1952; *Siempre*, 4 Feb. 1959, 6; *Excelsior*, 10 Dec. 1978, 18; PS, 5665.

Sanchez Navarrete, Federico

a-Mar. 22, 1917. **b-**Federal District, *Federal District, Urban*. **c-**Primary studies in the Colegio Frances de Mixcoac, Mexico City; studies at the National Contractors School; degree in agricultural engineering with a specialty in parasitology, National School of Agriculture, February 6, 1943; studies at the English Language Institute, University of Michigan, 1948; Masters of Science, with a thesis on sugar cane diseases, Louisiana State University, 1949–50, graduating July 19, 1956, on a fellowship from the Bank of Mexico and the Secretariat of Agriculture; Ph.D. in agricultural sciences, Louisiana State University; professor of sugar cane diseases, Veracruz Technological Institute of Sugarcane. **d-**Federal De-

puty from the State of Morelos, Dist. 1, 1955–58. **e-**Member of PAN. **f-**Delegate to the State of Morelos, Secretariat of Agriculture, 1942–48; Zone Director, Secretariat of Agriculture; Technician, Secretariat of Agriculture, 1951–55; Director of the Agricultural Experiment Station, Zacatepec, 1955; Technical Inspector, Institute for the Improvement of Sugar Production, 1956–57; Chief of the Sugar Cane Research Program, Institute of Agricultural Research, 1959. **g-**None. **j-**None. **k-**None. **l-**Ind. Biog., 147; DGF56, 26; C de D, 1955–58; BdM, 236–37.

Sanchez Piedras, Emilio

a-Nov. 1, 1915. **b-**Tlaxcala, Tlaxcala, *East Central*, *Urban*. **c-**Primary and secondary studies in Tlaxcala; preparatory studies in the Federal District; law degree with honorable mention from the National School of Law, UNAM, February 3, 1941. **d-**Local Deputy to the State Legislature of Tlaxcala (ten years); *Federal Deputy* from the State of Tlaxcala, Dist. 2, 1952–55, member of the Legislative Studies Committee, the Second Justice Committee, and the Consular Service Committee; substitute member of the Military Justice and Small Agricultural Property Committees; *Federal Deputy* from the State of Tlaxcala, Dist. 1, 1958–61, President of the Gran Comision, member of the First Government Committee and the Rules Committee; *Governor of Tlaxcala*, 1975– . **e-**Representative of *Adolfo Lopez Mateos* during his presidential campaign in the State of Coahuila; general delegate of the CEN of PRI to Yucatan, Colima, Jalisco, and Coahuila. **f-**Agent of the Ministerio Publico, Attorney General of the Federal District and Federal Territories, 1941–44; Consulting Lawyer, Department of Indigenous Affairs, under *Isidro Candia*, 1941–44; Director of Public Works, State of Tlaxcala, 1944–51; private secretary to Governors *Mauro Angulo* and *Rafael Avila Breton*, 1945–51; president of the Committee for the Industrial Development of Tlaxcala, 1951–52; Director of Legal Affairs, Federal Electric Commission, 1965. **g-**Active in student politics; President of the Student Association at the National School of Law, UNAM. **h-**Practicing lawyer since he received his degree. **j-**None. **k-**Caused the government of *Adolfo Lopez Mateos* diplomatic difficulties with the United States after making a speech favoring Cuba, 1960; supposedly lost presidency of Gran Comision, October, 1960. **l-**Func., 382; C de D, 1958–60, 92; C de D, 1952–54, 19, 52, 60, 69; *Excelsior*, 13 Nov. 1978, 6; *Excelsior*, 15 Nov. 1978, 23.

Sanchez Ponton, Luis
(Deceased June 19, 1969)

a-Aug. 5, 1889. **b-**Puebla, Puebla, *East Central*, *Urban*. **c-**Primary and secondary education in public and private schools in Puebla; preparatory studies at the National Preparatory School; law degree, National School of Law, UNAM, 1912; Professor of Law and Economics, UNAM, 12 years; founder and President of the Council of Primary Education, 1932–40. **d-**Federal Deputy from the State of Puebla, 1914–15; Constitutional Deputy from the State of Puebla, 1916–17; Senator from the State of Puebla. **e-**Member of the Constitutional Liberal Party, 1916, but opposed Venustiano Carranza for President. **f-**Secretary General of Government of the Federal District and of Veracruz, 1914–15; Oficial Mayor of the Secretariat of the Treasury, 1930–31; Interim Governor of Puebla, 1920–21; Director, Budget Department, Secretariat of the Treasury, 1928–29; Minister to Ecuador, 1942; *Ambassador to the Soviet Union*, 1946–47; Ambassador to Canada; Ambassador to Switzerland; *Secretary of Public Education*, 1940 to Sept. 12, 1941. **g-**Member of the First Congress of Students, 1910. **h-**Author of education books; President of the Financiera Hispano-Mexicana, S.A.; member of the National Council of Higher Education; Mexican delegate to the Seventh Pan American Conference. **i-***Carlos Madrazo* and *German Parra* were close collaborators when he served as Secretary of Education; attended school with *Juan Andreu Almazan*; married Ana Maria Garfias. **j-**None. **k-**A distinguished student at law school; asked for the resignation of Porfirio Diaz as a student leader, 1910; one of the first of the radical holdovers from the *Cardenas* period to be forced out of a cabinet position. **l-**D de Y, 3 Dec. 1940, 6; Correa, 41, 96; *Hoy*, Dec. 1940, 3–4; EBW46, 516; Kirk, 137, 148; Strode, 374; DP70, 1914; WWM45, 111; Vazquez de Knauth, 200; Enc. Mex., XI, 1977, 340; Lopez, 996.

Sanchez Taboada, Rodolfo
(Deceased May 2, 1955)

a-1895. **b-**Tepeaca (Hacienda de Macuila), Acatzingo, Puebla, *East Central*, *Rural*. **c-**Primary studies in San Sebastian Villa Nueva, Acatzingo, Puebla; secondary studies at the Colegio de San Jose and the Hospicio de Puebla, Puebla; preparatory studies at the Colegio del Estado de Puebla; completed second year in a pre-medical program at the Colegio del Estado de Puebla, but terminated his studies in 1914; enrolled in the National Military College to become a 2nd lieutenant in the Medical Corp; no degree. **d-**None. **e-**President of the Regional Committee of PRI for the Federal District during the *Aleman* presidential campaign, 1946; *President of the CEN of PRI*, Dec. 5, 1946 to Dec. 1, 1952; one of the national directors of *Ruiz Cortines'* presidential campaign, 1952. **f-**Assistant to President *Cardenas*, 1935; Director of the Budget Office for the Presidency, 1935; *Governor of Baja California del Norte*, Feb. 22, 1937 to 1940; 1940–44; *Secretary of*

the Navy, 1952–55. **g**-None. **h**-None. **i**-Brother
Ruperto was a Federal Deputy from Puebla, 1946–
49; son *Rodolfo Sanchez Cruz* was a Federal Deputy
from Puebla, 1970–73 and a precandidate for governor of Puebla, 1974; close friend of *Teofilo Borunda*.
j-Career army officer; joined the Revolution as a 2nd
lieutenant under General Fortunato Maycotte,
November 10, 1914; fought Zapata in Morelos under
Col. Jesus Guajardo; rank of Brigade General, Nov.
1, 1952; reached rank of Divisionary General.
k-Brandenburg places him in the Inner Circle during
the 1940s; *Lopez Avelar* was his assistant in 1919;
resigned from the Governorship July 31, 1944 because of the supposed discontent with the ineffi-
ciency of his regime and the incompetent men he
appointed; remained at the direct disposal of President *Avila Camacho*, Aug. 1, 1944 to Oct. 15, 1945;
considered a benefactor to the University Pentathlon.
l-Brandenburg, 80; HA, 9 May 1955; HA, 25 Aug.
1944; Morton, 59; HA, 5 Dec. 1952, 9; DP70, 1915;
Peral, 749; *Polemica*, No. 1, 1969, 73; *Excelsior*, 3
Mar. 1974, 16; Lopez, 998; *Excelsior*, 7 Nov. 1978,
13; Anderson; *Excelsior*, 3 Mar. 1974, 16; Enc.
Mex., XI, 1977, 340–41; Loret de Mola, 76.

Sanchez Tapia, Rafael
(Deceased 1946)
a-Sept. 24, 1887. **b**-Aguilillas, Michoacan, *West
Central, Rural*. **c**-Primary and secondary studies at
the Seminary of Zamora, Michoacan; abandoned
studies, 1911; no degree. **d**-Governor of Michoacan,
Dec. 3, 1934 to June 30, 1935. **e**-None. **f**-Prefect of
Jiquilpan, Michoacan; Prefect of Coalcoman,
Michoacan; *Secretary of Industry and Commerce*,
June 18, 1935 to Dec. 31, 1937. **g**-High-level
member of the Cardenas Schismatic Masonic Lodge.
h-None. **i**-Married Dolores Revs. **j**-Joined the Revolution, 1911; Brigadier General, 1915; Divisionary
General, Apr. 1, 1938; Commander of the 1st Military Zone, Federal District, 1937–39; retired from
active duty, 1940. **k**-Appointed governor of
Michoacan by the state legislature after his predecessor was killed in an accident; precandidate for President of Mexico, 1939, but in the opinion of Bermudez, had the least chance of receiving the official
party nomination; ran for President on the Centro
Unificador, 1939; Inner Circle status, 1934–37.
l-Michaels, 3, 50; NYT, 12 Feb. 1939; Bermudez,
88; Brandenburg, 80; Peral, 749; DP70, 1915;
Lieuwen, 130; DP64, 1314; Lopez, 998; Enc. Mex.,
XI, 1977, 341.

Sanchez Vargas, Julio
a-Aug. 17, 1914. **b**-Ojo de Agua, Veracruz, *Gulf,
Rural*. **c**-Law degree from the Escuela Libre de Derecho, May 18, 1936. **d**-None. **e**-None. **f**-Lawyer for
the Legal Department of the Secretariat of Foreign

Relations, 1936–37; Attorney General of the State of
San Luis Potosi under Governor *Reynaldo Perez Gallardo*, 1940–42; Oficial Mayor of Government of the
State of San Luis Potosi, 1942–43; Secretary General
of Government of the State of San Luis Potosi under
General *Ramon Jimenez*, 1943–44; secretary to the
Chief of Police of the Federal District, 1944–46; Justice of the Superior Tribunal of Justice of the Federal
District and Federal Territories, 1947–52; Supernumerary Justice of the Superior Tribunal of Justice
of the Federal District and Federal Territories,
1952–56; Justice and President of the Superior Tribunal of Justice of the Federal District and Federal
Territories; *Assistant Attorney General of Mexico*,
1967; *Attorney General of Mexico*, 1967–70,
1970–71; *Justice of the Supreme Court*, 1977– .
g-None. **h**-Director General of the Mexican Society
of Industrial Credit, 1971–72. **i**-Attended the Escuela Libre de Derecho with *Julio Santos Coy* and
Donato Miranda Fonseca; married Rosa Beristain.
j-None. **k**-Resigned from the Attorney General's office after the student demonstration. **l**-*Excelsior*, 21
Aug. 1971, 1; DGF56, 514; DPE71, 160; HA, 7
Dec. 1970, 26; WNM, 212.

Sanchez Vite, Manuel
a-Mar. 17, 1915. **b**-Molango, Hidalgo, *East Central, Rural*. **c**-Secondary studies at the Escuela Normal Rural, El Mexe, Hidalgo, rural teaching certificate; normal certificate from the National Teachers
School, Mexico City, 1942–44; law degree, National
School of Law, UNAM, 1947–51; teacher in various
rural schools in El Mexe and Actopan, Mexico.
d-*Federal Deputy* from the State of Hidalgo, Dist. 2,
1955–58, member of the Social Action Committee,
the Public Education Committee, the Third Ejido
Committee, and the Committee on the Development
and Promotion of Sports; *Senator* from the State of
Hidalgo, 1964–69, Secretary of the Gran Comision;
Governor of Hidalgo, 1969–70, 1972–75.
e-*President of the CEN of PRI*, 1970–72. **f**-Legal
adviser to the National Teachers Union and to the
ISSSTE; Attorney General of the State of Hidalgo.
g-Secretary of the National Teachers Union of
Hidalgo, 1942–44; Secretary General of Section
Nine, SNTE, 1947; Secretary, National Committee,
SNTE; Secretary General of Section Fourteen,
SNTE; *Secretary General of the SNTE*, Nov. 19,
1952–55. **h**-None. **i**-Married Maria Guadalupe
Jimenez; *Abel Ramirez Acosta* part of his political
group. **j**-None. **k**-As President of PRI, asked for
three six-month leaves from the Governorship of
Hidalgo, making it possible for him to return to the
Governorship in May, 1972, in a rather unusual fashion even by Mexican political standards; imposed his
own successor as governor, 1975, but he remained in
office only one month. **l**-HA, 15 Mar. 1971, 12; *Hoy,*

19 Dec. 1970, 4; MGF69; DBM70, 514; DGF56, 24; HA, 28 Nov. 1955, 10; WNM, 212; *Excelsior*, 24 Jan. 1975, 18.

Sandoval Lopez, Rodolfo

a-1912. **b**-Oaxaca, Oaxaca, *South*, *Urban*. **c**-Secondary studies from the Annex School, Normal School of Oaxaca, 1920–26; preparatory studies from the Institute of Arts and Sciences of Oaxaca; law degree, Institute of Arts and Sciences of Oaxaca, 1934–39; professor at the preparatory and law school Institute of Arts and Sciences of Oaxaca, 1929–42; fellowship student of the Center of Social Studies, Colegio de Mexico, 1943–45. **d**-*Alternate Senator* from the State of Oaxaca, 1964–68, but replaced Senator *Jose Pacheco Iturribarria*, 1969–70. **e**-None. **f**-Employee of the Legal Department of the Petroleum Workers Union, 1946–50; employee of the Legal Department of the Federal Electric Commission, 1951–55; Interim Secretary General of Government of Oaxaca under General *Jose Pacheco Iturribarria*, 1956; Director of Aprovechamientos Forestales of Oaxaca, 1963–65; representative of the Secretariat of Industry and Commerce and the Hydroelectric Company of Oaxaca, 1957–65. **g**-None. **h**-Practicing lawyer in Oaxaca. **j**-None. **k**-None. **l**-C de S, 1964–70; MGF69; PS, 5689.

Sandoval Rodriguez, Eufrasio

a-Apr. 9, 1908. **b**-Ramos Arizpe, Coahuila, *North*, *Rural*. **c**-Engineering studies, National School of Engineering, UNAM, 1930–34, received degree in 1955. **d**-None. **e**-None. **f**-Began career with the National Railroads of Mexico, 1934, worked as a leveler, assistant engineer, engineer, and supervisory engineer, 1934–43, principal engineer, Southern Zone, 1943–44; principal engineer, Northern Zone, 1944; Conservation Engineer, Tracks, 1954–55; Second Assistant of Studies and Projects of the Director General, 1955–58; Department head, Tracks and Structures, 1958–62; Subdirector of Tracks and Structures, 1962–64; *Director General of the National Railroads of Mexico*, 1964–70. **g**-None. **h**-None. **i**-Member of a political clique called "Los Compadres" headed by *Benjamin Mendez Aguilar* as Director General of the National Railroads. **j**-None. **k**-None. **l**-WWMG, 37; DPE65, 109; *Excelsior*, Dec. 1964; PS, 5690.

Sandoval Vallarta, Manuel

(Deceased Apr. 18, 1977)
a-Feb. 11, 1899. **b**-Federal District, *Federal District*, *Urban*. **c**-Preparatory studies at the National Preparatory School, 1912–16; Bachelor of Science, Massachusetts Institute of Technology, 1921; Sc.D. in physics, 1924; Guggenheim Fellow, Berlin, 1927–28; Visiting Professor, University of Louvain,

1935–36; Lecturer, Harvard University, 1937; Lecturer, University of Toronto, 1937; Research Associate, MIT, 1923–26; Assistant Professor of Physics, MIT, 1926–30; Associate Professor of Physics, MIT, 1930–39; Professor, MIT, 1939, Resident Associate of the Carnegie Institute, Washington, D.C., 1939–43. **d**-None. **e**-None. **f**-Director of the Department of Scientific Research, UNAM, 1943–44; *Director General of the National Polytechnical Institute*, 1943–46; *Subsecretary of Public Education*, 1955–58; Director of the Mexican-North American Cultural Institute, 1961–66; member of the National Commission of Nuclear Energy, 1961–67. **g**-None. **h**-Author of many articles in the physical sciences; President of the Commission for the Promotion and Coordination of Scientific Cooperation in Mexico. **i**-Brother-in-law of *Hugo B. Margain*; married Maria Luisa Margain; student of Albert Einstein. **j**-None. **k**-None. **l**-WWM45, 111; DGF56, 299; EBW46, 876; DP70, 1076; *Libro de Oro*, 67–68, xvi; DGF51, I, 629; Peral, 750; DGF50, I, 455; HA, 9 Feb. 1954; HA, 2 May 1977, 56; *Excelsior*, 30 Apr. 1977; letter.

Sandoval Zavala, Inocencio

a-Dec. 28, 1920. **b**-Puruandiro, Michoacan, *West Central*, *Urban*. **c**-Primary studies at the Escuela Maestro Vicente Lombardo Toledano, Mexico, D.F. (6 years); no secondary or preparatory education; no degree. **d**-*Federal Deputy* from the PAN (party deputy), 1970–73, member of the Public Assistance Committee, the Rural Electrification Committee, the Television Industry Committee, and the Second Section of the Instructive Committee of the Grand Jury. **e**-Member and District Director of PAN. **f**-None. **g**-None. **h**-Textile worker. **j**-None. **k**-Candidate for Federal Deputy from PAN (five times). **l**-C de D, 1970–72, 136; *Directorio*, 1970–72.

Sansores Perez, Carlos

a-Dec. 25, 1918. **b**-Champoton, Campeche, *Gulf*, *Rural*. **c**-Secondary studies, Instituto Campechano; law degree, School of Law, University of Campeche. **d**-*Federal Deputy* from the State of Campeche, Dist. 2, 1946–49, member of the Gran Comision, the National Waters and Irrigation Committee, and the Hunting and Fishing Committee; *Federal Deputy* from the State of Campeche, Dist. 2, 1955–58, member of the Committee on Credit, Money, and Credit Institutions, the Legislative Studies Committee, and the Rules Committee; Vice President of the Chamber of Deputies, 1955; Secretary of the Chamber of Deputies, 1956; *Federal Deputy* from the State of Campeche, Dist. 2, 1961–64, Secretary of the Permanent Commission, 1963, member of the Treasury Committee, the Balloting Committee, the Instructive Committee for the Grand Jury, and the

Budget and Accounts Committee; Vice President of
the Chamber of Deputies, Dec., 1962; *Senator* from
the State of Campeche, 1964–67; *Governor of Campeche*, 1967–73; *Federal Deputy* from the Federal
District, Dist. 26, 1973–76, President of the Gran
Comision; *Senator* from the State of Campeche,
1976, President of the Gran Comision, 1976.
e-Founding member of PRI in Campeche; Secretary
General of the Committee to elect *Miguel Aleman* in
Campeche; Auxiliary Secretary to the CEN of PRI,
1966; delegate of PRI to Chihuahua, 1965; *Subsecretary General of the CEN of PRI*, 1973–74; *Presi-
dent of the CEN of PRI*, 1976–79. **f-**Secretary to the
Penal Court, State of Campeche, 1941–43; Justice of
the Penal Courts, State of Campeche; Chief of the
Judicial Police, Campeche, 1943–44; Secretary
General of Government of the State of Campeche,
1949–50, under *Manuel Lopez Hernandez*; agent of
the Ministerio Publico of the Federal District; Federal
Defense Attorney for Labor, 1953–55; *Director
General of the ISSSTE*, 1979– . **g-**Delegate of the
National Farmers Federation; President of the Cam-
peche Student Federation, 1935–37. **h-**None.
i-Supporter of *Carlos Hank Gonzalez*; daughter *Rosa
Maria Martinez Denegri* was a senator, 1976–82.
j-None. **k-**Early supporter of woman suffrage in the
Chamber of Deputies; resigned as Governor of Cam-
peche to become Majority Leader of the Chamber of
Deputies, 1973. **l-***Hoy*, 4 Mar. 1967, 7; WWMG, 37;
DGF56, 21; DGF47, 5; Morton, 55; HA, 1 Jan.
1965, 8; C de D, 1961–63, 91; C de D, 1946–48, 89;
HA, 12 Mar. 1973, 31; *Excelsior*, 18 Dec. 1973, 15;
HA, 27 Aug. 1973, 7; Ind. Biog., 148–49; *Proceso*,
10 Oct. 1977, 6–9; HA, 7 Jan. 1974, 12; *Proceso*,
11 Dec. 1976, 20; *Proceso*, 19 June 1978, 29.

Santa Ana (Garcia), Miguel
(Deceased Aug. 8, 1972)
a-Nov. 5, 1896. **b-**Colima, Colima, *West*, *Urban*.
c-Primary studies, Colegio San Luis Gonzaga; secondary, Liceo de Varones, Guadalajara, 1912.
d-*Governor of Colima*, 1935–39; *Senator* from the
State of Colima, 1940–46, secretary of the Senate,
member of the Gran Comision, the Second Balloting
Committee, First Secretary of the National Defense
Committee, and Second Secretary of the Military
Justice Committee. **e-**None. **f-**None. **g-**None.
h-None. **i-**Son *Cuauhtemoc Santa Ana* served as
Federal Deputy from the Federal District, 1970–73,
and was Secretary of the Gran Comision and President of PRI in the Federal District, 1972. **j-**Joined the
Revolution; fought under General Miguel Dieguez,
1914; career army officer; commander of various
military zones; rank of Brigadier General. **k-**None.
l-Peral, 751; D de Y, 8 Nov. 1935, 1; letter; *Excelsior*, 9 Aug. 1972, 10; Correa41, 76–77; Enc. Mex.,
II, 1977, 588.

Santa Ana (Seuthe), Cuauhtemoc
a-Oct. 10, 1938. **b-**Colima, Colima, *West*, *Urban*.
c-Primary studies, Emiliano Zapata Primary School,
1944–49; secondary studies, Public Secondary
School No. 16, 1950–52; preparatory studies at the
National Preparatory School, 1953–55; law degree,
National School of Law, UNAM, 1956–60; studied
at the University of Geneva, 1963–64. **d-***Federal
Deputy* from the Federal District, Dist. 17, 1970–73,
member of the Department of the Federal District
Committee, the Second Government Committee, and
the First Constitutional Affairs Committee; Secretary
of the Gran Comision. **e-**President of PRI in the Federal District, 1973–75; *Secretary of Political Action
of the CEN of PRI*, 1970–73; Director of Publications for the National Youth sector of PRI.
f-Subdirector General of Government, Secretariat of
Government; private secretary to the Subsecretary of
Government; auxiliary secretary to the Oficial Mayor
of Government, 1968–69; auxiliary secretary to *Luis
Echeverria*, 1969–70; Delegate of the Department of
the Federal District to Cuauhtemoc, 1976–79; *Secretary of Works and Services of the Federal District*,
1979– . **g-**Practicing lawyer for the CNC. **h-**None.
i-Son of Governor *Miguel Santa Ana*. **j-**None.
k-Precandidate in 1973 for Governor of Colima, but
lost the nomination. **l-***Directorio*, 1970–72; C de D,
1970–72, 136; DAPC, 1977, 66.

Santamaria, Francisco J.
(Deceased 1963)
a-Sept. 10, 1889. **b-**Cacaos, Tabasco, *Gulf*, *Rural*.
c-Primary studies in Macuspana, Tabasco; secondary
education, Instituto Juarez, Villahermosa; normal
teaching certificate, Instituto Juarez, Tabasco; law
degree, National School of Law, UNAM; Professor
of Mathematics, Instituto Juarez (University of
Tabasco). **d-***Governor of Tabasco*, 1947–52.
e-Orator for the candidacy of A. R. Gomez for Governor of the Federal District; campaigned for Generals Gomez and Serrano during their 1927 presidential
campaign. **f-**Penal Judge, Third District, Mexico,
D.F.; Secretary General of Government of the State
of Tabasco; consulting lawyer to the Mexican Embassy in Washington. **g-**Member of the National Student League, 1927. **h-**Member of the National Language Academy, 1954; author of numerous geographical, historical, and language dictionaries on
Mexico, especially on the state of Tabasco; poet.
i-Participated with *Miguel Aleman, Braulio
Maldonado Sanchez* and *Efrain Brito Rosado*
in the 1927 campaign; married Isabel Calzada.
j-Constitutionalist; supported the Escobar movement, 1929; represented the movement abroad.
k-The only survivor of a massacre at Huitzilac,
Cuernavaca, 1927. **l-**Peral, 752–53; DP70, 1943;
WWM45, 111–12; DGF51, 92; STYRBIWW54,

994–95; Dulles, 443; Lopez, 1008; Bremauntz, 71; Enc. Mex., XI, 1977, 346–47.

Santillan (Osorno), Manuel

a-Sept. 29, 1894. b-Hacienda de Xalostoc, Tlaxcala, *East Central, Rural.* c-Preparatory studies in Jalapa, Veracruz; engineering degree from the National School of Engineering, UNAM; advanced studies in geology. d-*Governor of Tlaxcala*, 1941–44. e-None. f-Chief of Geologists for Mining and Petroleum, Secretariat of Industry and Commerce, 1929; Consulting Engineer to the Presidency, 1933; Chief Geologist of the Secretariat of Industry and Commerce, 1934; member of the Technical Commission of the Presidency, 1935; Director of the National Institute of Geology, 1929; *Subsecretary of Industry and Commerce*, 1935–36, Director General of the administration of petroleum, 1937–38; *Subsecretary of Public Works*, 1939–40. g-None. h-Began career as a mining engineer, Pachuca, Hidalgo, 1919; author of several geology books. i-Married Luz Gamper. j-None. k-Anderson says he was forced to resign as governor because he tried to oppose the national PRM leadership, 1933. l-WWM45, 112; EBW46, 1090; Peral, 754; Anderson, 86; Lopez, 1010.

Santos, Gonzalo N.

(Deceased Oct. 17, 1978)
a-1895. b-Villa Guerrero, San Luis Potosi, *East Central, Rural.* c-Early education unknown; no degree. d-Federal Deputy from the State of San Luis Potosi, 1924–26, 1926–28, 1928–30, 1930–32, 1932–34, president of the Gran Comision, 1926–28; *Senator* from the State of San Luis Potosi, 1934–40; *Governor of San Luis Potosi*, 1943–49. e-Secretary of Affairs for the Federal District, CEN of the PRM, 1929; Secretary General of the CEN of the PNR, 1931. f-Customs agent, 1917; Minister to Belgium, 1940; Director of Fishing, Secretariat of Industry and Commerce, 1959–61. g-None. h-None. i-Son Gaston Santos involved in San Luis Potosi politics; political enemy of *Federico Medrano*. j-Fought with Venustiano Carranza during the Revolution; rank of general in the army. k-Regional caudillo in San Luis Potosi; Brandenburg places him in the Inner Circle during *Aleman*'s administration; his power in San Luis Potosi declined after the middle 1950s; accused of large-scale illegal land holdings in San Luis Potosi; important Callista congressional leader and member of the "Reds" in congress; answered Calles' State of the Union address, 1926. l-*Por Que*, 4 Oct. 1968, 35; Hoy, 3 June 1972, 9; HA, 7 Oct. 1949, xxii; Peral, 755; Johnson, 32–33; HA, 28 Sept. 1944, VIII; DP70, 1581; Brandenburg, 80, 102; HA, 8 Oct. 1943, 13; HA, 28 Aug. 1978, 20; HA, 23 Oct. 1978, 18; *Excelsior*, 26 June 1975, 4; NYT, 7 Jan. 1959, ll; *Excelsior*, 28 Sept. 1976; *Excelsior*, 2 Sept. 1972, 11; NYT, 18 May 1958, 7; NYT, 4 Dec. 1958, 13; *Excelsior*, 23 Aug. 1978; Campa, 157.

Santos Cervantes, Angel

a-Sept. 1, 1905. b-Villa Aldama, Nuevo Leon, *North, Rural.* c-Primary studies in Villa Aldama; law degree from the University of Nuevo Leon, 1929; Professor of Obligations and Contracts, School of Law, University of Nuevo Leon. d-*Senator* from the State of Nuevo Leon, 1958–64, member of the Gran Comision, President of the Second Tariff and Foreign Trade Committee, First Secretary of the Second Credit, Money and Credit Institutions Committee, President of the Tax Committee, First Secretary of the Insurance Committee, Second Secretary of the Second Mines Committee and member of the First Balloting Group. e-None. f-Secretary General of Government of the State of Nuevo Leon under Governor Pablo Quiroga, 1935; President of the Water and Drainage Services of Monterrey. g-None. j-None. k-None. l-C de S, 1961–64, 70; Func., 293.

Santos Coy Perea, Julio

a-July 18, 1909. b-Piedras Negras, Coahuila, *North, Rural.* c-Law degree from the Escuela Libre de Derecho, June 21, 1922. d-None. e-None. f-Agent of the Ministerio Publico of the Office of the Attorney General in the Isthmus of Tehuantepec, 1934; federal agent of the District Courts; assistant agent of the Attorney General of Mexico; Director of the Department of Preliminary Investigations, Department of the Federal District; legal adviser to *Adolfo Lopez Mateos*, Secretary of Labor, 1952–56; labor conciliator for the Secretariat of Labor, 1956; Director of Conciliators, Secretariat of Labor, 1956–58; *Subsecretary of Labor*, 1958–64; *Subsecretary (A) of Labor*, 1964–70. g-None. h-Private law practice, 1940–52. i-Son of General (and lawyer), Julio Santos Coy, from a longtime Liberal political family in Coahuila; married Angelina Cobo. j-None. k-None. l-DPE65, 154; DGF56, 398; DBM68, 571–72; D de Y, 6 Dec. 1958; DPE61, 115; *Libro de Oro*, xxxvi.

Santos Guajardo, Vicente

(Deceased May 26, 1962)
a-Feb. 9, 1895. b-Villa de Progreso, Coahuila, *North, Rural.* c-Primary studies in Villa Union and Muzquiz, Coahuila; preparatory studies from the Ateneo Fuente, Saltillo; law degree, National School of Law, UNAM, 1921; Professor of Administrative Law, National School of Law, UNAM; Professor of Law, Ateneo Fuente, 1922. d-Local Deputy to the State Legislature of Coahuila, 1922–23; Federal Deputy from Coahuila, 1924–26. e-None. f-Director of the Legal Department, Secretariat of Agriculture and Livestock; Judge of the Superior Tribunal of Justice

of the Federal District, 1928–34; *Assistant Attorney General of Mexico*, 1934–37; *Subsecretary of Government*, 1937–40; *Subsecretary of Labor*, 1940–43; *Director General of the Mexican Institute of Social Security*, 1943–44; *Subsecretary of Foreign Relations*, 1944; *Justice of the Supreme Court*, 1944–52, 1952–57; President of the Supreme Court, 1955–56. g-None. i-Collaborated with *Ignacio Garcia Tellez* in several positions; met him at the National School of Law. j-Student leader during the Revolution. k-None. l-D de Y, 5 Jan. 1938, 2; DGF51, I, 568; DP70, 1342, 1953; Peral, 755; STYRBIWW57, 416; DGF56, 567; Lopez, 1011; NYT, 4 Jan. 1944, 31.

Santoyo, Ramon Victor
(Deceased 1957)
a-Mar. 6, 1901. b-Guanajuato, Guanajuato, *West Central*, *Urban*. c-Law degree from the University of Guanajuato; Professor of Political Science, School of Political and Social Science, UNAM. d-Federal Deputy from the State of Guanajuato, 1928–30, 1930–32; Federal Deputy from the State of Guanajuato, 1935–37, Secretary of the Chamber, September, 1936; *Federal Deputy* from the State of Guanajuato, Dist. 1, 1946–49, member of the Second Credentials Committee, the Budget and Accounts Committee, the Second Constitutional Affairs Committee, and the Inspection Committee of the General Accounting Office (1st year). e-None. f-Lower Court Judge; Judge of the Ministerio Publico; Judge of the Superior Tribunal of Justice; Secretary General of Government of the State of Guanajuato; Oficial Mayor of Government of the State of Jalisco; Secretary General of Government of the State of Jalisco; Secretary General of Government of Baja California del Norte, 1931; head of Lawyers for the Department of the Federal District; *Assistant Attorney General of Mexico (2)*, 1949–52; *Assistant Attorney General of Mexico*, 1952–57. g-None. h-Representative of the Government on the Federal Board of Conciliation and Arbitration, Federal District, 1957. i-Son Ramon a lawyer. j-None. k-None. l-DP70, 1953–54; DGF51, I, 535; DGF51; C de D, 1946–48, 89; Casasola, V; Aguirre.

Santoyo Nunez, Hortensia
a-June 1, 1933. b-Acapulco, Guerrero, *South*, *Urban*. c-Teaching certificate; social work degree; completed studies as a private accountant. d-*Federal Deputy* from the State of Guerrero, Dist. 4, 1976–79. e-Organizer of the Feminine Assemblies for PRI. f-Director of Center of Educational Action No. 36, Secretariat of Public Education. g-President of the Consumer Protection Committee, Acapulco. i-Married Emilio Garcia Velez. j-None. k-None. l-*Excelsior*, 27 Aug. 1976, 1C; C de D, 1976–79.

Sarmiento Sarmiento, Manuel
b-Sinaloa, *West*. c-Primary and secondary studies in Sinaloa; preparatory studies in Sinaloa; graduated as a 2nd Lieutenant, National Military College. d-Local Deputy to the State Legislature of Sinaloa, 1944–46; Mayor of Guasave, Sinaloa, 1948; *Federal Deputy* from the State of Sinaloa, Dist. 2, 1961–64; *Senator* from the State of Sinaloa, 1964–70. e-None. f-None. g-Secretary of Finances of the CEN of the CNC, 1964. j-Career Army officer; rank of Lt. Colonel. k-None. l-C de D, 1961–64; C de S, 1964–70; MGF69.

Sarro (Tresarrieu), Enrique
a-Sept. 14, 1905. b-Federal District, *Federal District*, *Urban*. c-Primary studies, Mexico, D.F.; secondary studies, Colegio Aleman, Mexico, D.F.; professional studies at the National School of Law and Economics, UNAM; no degree; Professor of Economics, National School of Economics, 1934, 1938–39; Professor at the School of Commerce, UNAM; Professor at the National School of Law, UNAM. d-None. e-None. f-Assistant to *Jesus Silva Herzog*, Chief of the Library and Economic Archives, Secretary of the Treasury, 1928; Assistant to *Jesus Silva Herzog*, Department of Economic Studies, National Railroads, 1932–33; Assistant Director of Economic Studies, Secretariat of Industry and Commerce, 1933–34; Director, Department of Special Taxes, Secretariat of the Treasury, 1935–37; Director, Department of Economic Studies, Bank of Mexico, 1937–40; *Director of the National Finance Bank*, Feb. 21, 1941, to Nov. 15, 1945; *Director General of National Steel Industry*, 1946–52. g-None. h-Author of numerous works on economics. i-Co-authored several books with *Jesus Silva Herzog*; married Maria Teresa Perez Pliego. j-None. k-Served as the first Director of Nacional Financiera. l-WWM45, 112; DGF51, II, 231, 327; DGF50, II, 225, 229; letter; Lopez, 1014–15.

Saucedo (Perez), Salvador
(Deceased Mar. 1963)
a-Nov. 9, 1890. b-Colima, Colima, *West*, *Urban*. c-Early education unknown; no degree. d-Constitutional Deputy, 1916–17; Federal Deputy from the State of Colima, 1918–20, 1920–22; *Governor of Colima*, Nov. 20, 1931, to Aug. 21, 1935. e-None. f-Director of Government Printing, 1914, under Governor J. Trinidad Alamillo, State of Colima; Director of the Federal Treasury Office, Tuxtla Gutierrez, Chiapas; Tuxpan, Veracruz, and the Federal District; Director of the Federal Treasury Office, Colima, 1961–63; Director of the Federal Treasury Office, Zacatecas, Zacatecas, 1956. g-None. h-Became a printer in his youth; writer for the newspaper *La Revancha*; published the newspaper, *El*

Popular, 1909; founded the *Colima Libre*, 1917; newspaper editor in Guadalajara. **i-**Brother Miguel was interim governor of Colima, 1935, and a federal deputy. **j-**Maderista during the Revolution. **k-**Removed from the office of Governor through a federal dissolution of powers because of friendship with Calles. **l-**Peral, 759; letter; DP70, 1958; DGF56, 168.

Schaufelberger (Alatorre), Luis F.
(Deceased Feb. 11, 1958)
a-June 21, 1893. **b-**Puebla, Puebla, *East Central, Urban*. **c-**Primary and secondary studies in Puebla; graduated from the Naval College at Veracruz, as a coastguardsman. **d-**None. **e-**None. **f-***Subsecretary-in-charge of the Secretariat of the Navy*, 1946–48. **g-**None. **h-**None. **j-**Career naval officer; Commander of the corvette "Zaragoza;" Commander of the destroyer "Bravo;" Commander of the Pacific Naval Zone; Commander of the Gulf Naval Zone; Inspector General; rank of Vice Admiral; Commander of the Naval Zone, Isla Margarita, Baja California. **k-**None. **l-**DGF47; DBP, 636–37; CyT, 636–37.

Senties de Ballesteros, Yolanda
b-Toluca, Mexico, *West Central, Urban*. **c-**Early education unknown; degree in chemical pharmaceutical biology. **d-**Local Deputy to the State Legislature of Mexico, 1972–75; Mayor of Toluca, Mexico, 1975–78; *Federal Deputy* from the State of Mexico, 1979–82, member of the Gran Comision. **e-**Secretary of Cultural Action of the PRI in Mexico; Assistant Secretary General of the CEN of PRI, 1980– . **f-**None. **g-**Secretary General of the National Revolutionary Feminists Association, 1980– . **h-**Active in social works; founded many children's theaters in Toluca. **i-**Daughter of *Octavio Senties*, head of the Department of the Federal District, 1971–76. **j-**None. **k-**Won over 70 percent of the votes as a candidate for federal deputy. **l-**HA, 21 Aug. 1972, 39; HA, 30 July 1979, 29; C de D, 1979–82.

Senties (Gomez), Octavio
a-Feb. 9, 1915. **b-**Veracruz, Veracruz, *Gulf, Urban*. **c-**Primary, secondary, and preparatory studies in Veracruz; law degree from the National School of Law, UNAM, Nov. 17, 1942, with a thesis on "Constitutional Federalism and Economic Centralism;" Temporary Professor of Commercial Law, National School of Law, UNAM, 1958. **d-***Federal Deputy* from the State of Mexico, Dist. 8, 1943–46; *Federal Deputy* from the Federal District, Dist. 4, 1970–71, president of the Gran Comision, 1970–71, member of the Department of the Federal District

Committee, the First Government Committee, the Gran Comision, and the First Constitutional Affairs Committee; President of the Chamber of Deputies, Sept., 1970. **e-**Member of the PNR. **f-**Private secretary to the Governor of Mexico, *Wenceslao Labra Garcia*, 1937–41; *Head of the Federal District Department*, 1971–76. **g-**Student leader of the Vasconcelos movement in Veracruz, 1929; editor of *El Eco Estudiantil*. **h-**Mexican delegate to international conferences on motor transportation; private law practice with a specialty in transportation law, 1942, 1947–70. **i-**Student of *Alfonso Noriega* at the National Law School, UNAM; daughter Yolanda served as Secretary of Cultural Action of PRI for the State of Mexico and was elected Local Deputy to the State Legislature, 1972 and Mayor of Toluca, 1975; married to Maria del Carmen Echeverria; related to *Roberto Mantilla Molina*; wife related to *Luis Echeverria*. **j-**None. **k-**Precandidate for Governor of Veracruz, 1979. **l-**HA, 21 Aug. 1972, 39; *Hoy*, 16 June 1971, 6; *Hoy*, 27 Feb. 1971, 10; DPE71, 140; HA, 8 Jan. 1973, 29; C de D, 1970–72, 136; Enc. Mex., XI, 1977, 378; WNM, 215.

Septien Garcia, Carlos
(Deceased 1953)
a-1915. **b-**Queretaro, Queretaro, *East Central, Urban*. **c-**Primary studies at the Colegio Civil of Queretaro and at a Catholic school; law degree, National School of Law, UNAM, 1940; Director, School of Journalism, UNAM. **d-**None. **e-**Co-founder of PAN, 1939; member of the CEN of PAN, 1949; founder of *La Nacion* of PAN. **f-**None. **g-**Active leader of the Catholic student organizations, 1930s. **h-**Journalist; founder of *El Chinto*, 1927; founder of *El Escolapia*, 1930; writer for *Excelsior*; founder of the *Revista de la Semana* of *El Universal*; editor of *Provincia*, Queretaro, Queretaro; writer for *Heraldo de Navidad*. **i-**Father, Alfonso Maria Septien Diaz, a prominent lawyer in Queretaro. **j-**None. **k-**Catholic Action journalism school named for him. **l-**Mabry; Lemus, 38; Enc. Mex., XI, 1977, 379; DP70, 1978.

Sepulveda, Cesar
a-1916. **b-**United States, *Foreign*. **c-**Primary and secondary studies at the Colegio Hidalgo, Monterrey; preparatory studies at the University of Nuevo Leon, Monterrey, 1933–34, and at the National Preparatory School, 1934–39; law degree, National School of Law, UNAM, 1940–44; Professor of International Public Law, National School of Law, UNAM; Professor of Law and International Relations, Colegio de Mexico; Visiting Professor, School of Law, University of Michigan; Secretary of the Nation Preparatory School; Director, National School of Law, UNAM, 1962–66; Director, Institute of Comparative

Law, UNAM. **d-**None. **e-**None. **f-**Director General of Scholarly Services, UNAM; adviser, Secretary of Foreign Relations, 1946–50; Director General of Industrial Property, Secretariat of Industry and Commerce, 1950–59; Director of the Diplomatic Studies Institute, 1970–76; Ambassador, 1976; Director of the Diplomatic Studies Institute, 1979– . **g-**Student leader; candidate for president of his law school class. **h-**Director, Inter-American Center for Social Security, 1977–79. **i-**Son of Ricardo A. Sepulveda, self-made businessman, banker and supporter of Madero and Villa during the Revolution; mother a teacher. **j-**None. **k-**None. **l-**DBM68, 578; DGF56, 284; letters.

Serna (Leal), Donaciano

a-1919. **b-**Hidalgo, *East Central*. **c-**Early education unknown; teaching certificate; studies for a Ph.D. in education; Ph.D in pedagogy. **d-**Local deputy to the State Legislature of Hidalgo. **f-**Treasurer General of the State of Hidalgo, 1969–70; *Interim Governor of Hidalgo*, 1970–72. **g-**None. **h-**None. **j-**None. **k-**Precandidate for Mayor of Pachuca, Hidalgo, 1972; precandidate for federal deputy from the State of Hidalgo, Dist. 4, 1973; appointed by the state legislature to replace *Manuel Sanchez Vite* when he took a leave to become President of the CEN of PRI. **l-**Novedades, 21 Feb. 1972, 13; *Excelsior*, 17 Mar. 1973, 13; *Excelsior*, 27 Mar. 1973, 12; HA, 20 Dec. 1971, 44.

Serra Rojas, Andres

a-Oct. 13, 1907. **b-**Pichucalco, Chiapas, *South*, *Urban*. **c-**Primary studies in Veracruz, Veracruz; preparatory studies, Instituto Veracruzano and the National Preparatory School, 1924; law degree, National School of Law, UNAM, 1928; LLD, National School of Law, UNAM; professor in Administrative Law, General Theory of the State, Sociology, Political Economy, and Mexican Economy, National School of Law, UNAM; professor at the National Polytechnic Institute; professor at the National Preparatory School. **d-***Federal Deputy* from the State of Chiapas, Dist. 1, 1943–46; *Senator* from the State of Chiapas, 1964–70. **e-**Assistant Director of the Institute for Social and Political Studies, PNR, 1936; Official Orator in the presidential campaign of *Miguel Aleman*, 1946. **f-**Agent of the Ministerio Publico, Attorney General's Office of the Federal District, 1929–30; Director, Department of the Nationalization of Property, Office of the Attorney General of Mexico, 1930; Assistant Attorney General of Mexico, 1933; Director General of National Properties, Secretariat of the Treasury, 1935; private secretary to the Secretary of Health, *Gustavo Baz*, 1940–42; *Secretary of Labor*, Dec. 1, 1946, to Jan. 12,

1948; Director General of the National Cinematography Bank, 1949–52. **g-**Member of the executive committee of the Fifth National Student Congress, 1928. **h-**Adviser to the Mexican Delegation to the United Nations, 1945; author of numerous works on administration and law. **i-**Personal friend of *Octavio S. Mondragon*, Subsecretary of Health, 1946; friend of *Antonio Carrillo Flores*, *Antonio Armendariz*, *Alfonso Noriega*, *Jose Castro Estrada*, *Miguel Aleman*, and *Eduardo Bustamante* at the National Preparatory School or at the National Law School. **j-**None. **k-**Was fired for not finding *Valentin Campa* guilty on government charges, 1930; according to Valentin Campa, Serra Rojas resigned as Secretary of Labor because of intrigues by his subsecretary. **l-**WWMG, 38; WWM45, 112–13; HA, 6 Feb. 1948, 9; DGF50, 292; DGF50, I, 292; DGF51, I, 83; HA, 29 Oct. 1943, 14; DB de C, 235–37; Campa, 70–71; letter.

Serrano, Gustavo P.
(Deceased Sept. 10, 1979)

a-Nov. 23, 1887. **b-**Altar, Sonora, *North*, *Rural*. **c-**Law degree, National School of Law, UNAM; member of the Board of Trustees, UNAM. **d-**Federal Deputy from Sonora, 1920–22. **e-**None. **f-**Secretary, Mexican Section, International Boundary Commission, 1922; President, International Boundary Commission, 1923; Secretary of Communication and Public Works, 1931–32; Ambassador to Guatemala, 1931–34; member of the Mexico-United States International Water Commission, 1935–38; Commissioner, Mexican-United States Agrarian Claims Commission, 1938–45; Executive Director of the National Irrigation Commission, 1939–44; *Secretary of Industry and Commerce*, 1944–46; adviser to the Administrative Council of the Federal Electric Commission, 1951. **g-**Member of the First Student Congress, UNAM, 1910; President of the National Chamber of Mining Industries, 1940. **h-**None. **i-**Father-in-law of Engineer Jose B. Zozaya. **j-**None. **k-**None. **l-**DGF51, 345; DP70, 1088; WWM45, 113; DGF50, II, 245; EBW46, 132; HA, 7 July 1944, 7; Correa, 319; HA, 21 July 1944, 54; NYT, 2 July, 1944, 11; Lopez, 1021; *Excelsior*, 12 Sept. 1979, 4.

Serrano Castro, Julio

a-Apr. 12, 1907. **b-**Tuxtla Gutierrez, Chiapas, *South*, *Urban*. **c-**Primary studies in Juchitlan, Oaxaca; secondary studies in Tapachula, Chiapas; preparatory studies at the Institute of Arts and Sciences of Chiapas, Tuxtla Gutierrez; law degree from the National School of Law, UNAM, Oct. 31, 1930, with a thesis on agrarian reform. **d-***Senator* from the State of Chiapas, 1949–52; *Senator* from the State of Chiapas, 1952–58, President of the Second Petroleum Committee, member of the Gran Comision, the Third Labor Committee and the Special Legislative Studies Committee. e-None. f-Judge of the First Civil District Court of the Federal District; President of the Federal Board of Conciliation and Arbitration, 1946; Chief of the Office of Strikes and Conflicts, Secretariat of Labor; *Subsecretary of Labor and Social Welfare*, 1946; *Technical Subdirector of PEMEX*, 1946–50. g-President of the Socialist Front of Lawyers of the Federal District; represented workers in petroleum conflicts; President of the Union of Trucks and Buses of the Federal District, 1958. h-Specialist in labor law. i-Attended UNAM with *Miguel Aleman*. j-None. k-Precandidate for Governor of Chiapas, 1948. l-DGF47; DGF56, 5; HA, 5 Jan. 1959, 14; HA, 6 Feb. 1948, 10; DBC, 238; Ind. Biog., 149–51.

Serrano del Castillo, Nicanor

a-Nov. 1, 1918. b-Zacatelco, Tlaxcala, *East Central, Rural*. c-Primary studies in Tlaxcala; secondary studies at the School for Workers Children, Coyoacan, Federal District; preparatory studies from the National Preparatory School; economics degree, National School of Economics, UNAM. d-*Senator* from the State of Tlaxcala, 1970–76, President of the Foreign and Domestic Trade Committee, First Secretary of the Economics and Statistics Committee, and Second Secretary of the Electric Industry Committee. e-None. f-Archivist, Secretariat of the Treasury, 1941–45; General Manager of the Small Business Bank, 1952–55; economist, Federal Electric Commission, 1955–56; General Manager of the Federal Electric Commission, 1965–67; Oficial Mayor of the Federal Electric Commission, 1968–70. g-None. h-Department head, Properties and Services, S.A., 1956–59; General Manager, Laminated Copper, S.A., 1960–64. j-None. k-None. l-C de S, 1970–76, 86; MGF69.

Serrano (Tellechea), Raul

a-May 28, 1908. b-Guaymas, Sonora, *North, Urban*. c-Engineering agronomy degree, Agricultural School of Ciudad Juarez. d-*Federal Deputy* from the State of Mexico, Dist. 2, 1940–43, member of the Administration Committee (2nd year) and the National Waters and Irrigation Committee, substitute member of the Budgets and Accounts Committee; *Federal Deputy* from the State of Mexico, Dist. 8, 1949–52, member of the Foreign and International Trade Committee. e-None. h-None. j-None. k-None. l-Peral, 764; DGF51, I, 23, 31; C de D, 1940–42, 43, 57; C de D, 1949–51, 90.

Sierra Macedo, Manuel

a-Mar. 4, 1919. b-Federal District, *Federal District, Urban*. c-Primary, secondary and preparatory studies at the Colegio Frances (presently the Colegio Mexico), Mexico City; law degree, Free Law School, November 3, 1943, with a thesis on bills of exchange. d-*Federal Deputy* from the Federal District, Dist. 9, 1955–58, member of the Legislative Studies Committee and the Insurance Committee. e-Joined PAN, 1949; member of the National Executive Committee of PAN, 1944; Director of PAN for the Federal District, 1959. f-None. g-President of the Parents Association of the Colegio Franco-Ingles, 1963. h-Practicing lawyer, 1944– . i-Son of lawyer Manuel Sierra; married Margarita Arratia. j-None. k-Candidate of PAN for senator, 1958. l-Ind. Biog., 151–52; WNM, 216; ELD, 96; DGF56, 23, 33, 37; C de D, 1955–58.

Sierra (Mayora), Manuel J.
(Deceased 1970)

a-Jan. 4, 1885. c-Early education unknown; law degree, University of Campeche; LLD, National School of Law, UNAM; Professor of History and International Public Law, National School of Law, UNAM, 1930; Director, Institute of Public International Law, UNAM. d-None. e-None. f-Director, Diplomatic Department, Secretariat of Foreign Relations, 1921; Director, Consular Department, Secretariat of Foreign Relations, 1921; representative on a special mission to the United States, 1924; Director of the Press Department, Secretariat of Foreign Relations; Director of the Diplomatic Department, Secretariat of Foreign Relations, 1927; Director, Department of Political Affairs, Secretariat of Foreign Relations, 1933; President of the Spanish-Mexican Arbitration Commission; Delegate to the Seventh Pan American Conference; *Oficial Mayor of Foreign Relations*, 1935–36; Director of Press and Publications, Secretariat of the Treasury, 1952–58; *Oficial Mayor of the Treasury*, 1959–64. g-None. h-Author of several books. i-Son of Justo J. Sierra, Justice of the Supreme Court and Secretary of Public Education under Diaz; uncle of *Javier Barros Sierra*; married Margarita Casasus; father-in-law Joaquin de Casasus, senator, banker and diplomat; uncle of Miguel Lanz Duret, Jr.; became friends with *Adolfo Lopez Mateos* during a regular breakfast gathering, 1933. j-None. k-None. l-*Libro de Oro*, 1935–36, 258; Enc. Mex., XI, 1977, 387; Beltran, 361; DGF56, 172.

Silva Herzog, Jesus

a-Nov. 14, 1892. b-San Luis Potosi, San Luis Potosi, *East Central, Urban*. c-Primary studies at a seminary in San Luis Potosi, completed, 1905; secondary studies at Paine Uptown Business School, New York City, 1912–14; studies at the Graduate School, UNAM, 1919–23; economics degree from UNAM; founder of the National School of Economics, UNAM; Professor of Economic Policy, General Economic History and History of Economic

Thought, National School of Agriculture, 1923–38; Professor of Literature and English, College for Primary Teachers, 1919–24; Professor of Economic Policy, National Teachers College, 1925–28; Professor Emeritus of UNAM, 1960; Professor of the History of Economic Thought, UNAM, 1931–59; Professor of Economic and Social Problems, School of Philosophy, UNAM, 1928–30; Director of the National School of Economics, UNAM, 1940–42. **d**-None. **e**-Writer during the campaign of *Aurelio Manrique* for Governor of San Luis Potosi, 1923; Secretary of Foreign Affairs, CEN of PNR, 1930. **f**-Employed in the Customs Office, San Luis Potosi, 1910–12; Director of Economic Statistics, National Statistics Department, 1926–27; Oficial Mayor of the Secretariat of Public Education, 1932; Subsecretary of Public Education, 1933–34; Founder and director of Economic Studies, the National Railroads of Mexico, 1931–32; Founder and director of the Department of Libraries and Economic Archives, Secretariat of the Treasury, 1928; Minister to the Soviet Union, 1928–30; economic adviser, petroleum conflict, 1937–38; General Manager of the National Petroleum Company, 1939–40 (before it became PEMEX); founder and Director of the Department of Financial Studies, Secretariat of the Treasury, 1942–45; *Subsecretary of the Treasury*, 1945–46; President of the Technical Council, Secretariat of National Patrimony, 1947–48. **g**-None. **h**-Reporter, 1914–15; businessman, 1916–17; author of major works on political and economic history; founder of the Mexican Institute of Economic Investigations, 1928; founder of several Revolutionary newspapers; adviser to the Secretary of National Patrimony, 1946–47; member of the Board of Governors, UNAM, 1945–62; Director of the magazine *Cuadernos Americanos*, 1948–81. **i**-Father, an English teacher; boyhood friend of *Aurelio Manrique*; studied under *Antonio Caso*, Carlos Lazo, Ezequiel A. Chavez, and Alfonso Goldschmidt; son, *Jesus Silva Herzog Flores*, was Director General of the National Housing Institute, 1972–76. **j**-Accompanied Eulalio Gutierrez during the Revolution as a reporter and supporter, 1914. **k**-Jailed in 1916 for four months. **l**-Wilkie, 634–35; Strode, 336–37; DGF59, II, 129; Peral, 769; DBM68, 582–83; Dulles, 934; WWM45, 113; Lopez, 1029; Enc. Mex., XI, 1977, 394–95; *Excelsior*, 27 Jan. 1973, 9.

Silva Herzog (Flores), Jesus

a-May 8, 1935. **b**-Federal District, *Federal District, Urban*. **c**-Primary, secondary, and preparatory studies in Mexico, D.F.; studied economics at the National School of Economics, UNAM, 1953–57; scholarship to study at CEMLA, 1958; economics degree with honorable mention from UNAM, 1959,

with a thesis on ''Considerations about the Petroleum Industry and the Economic Development on Mexico;'' Masters degree in economics from Yale University, 1960–62; Professor of Theory and Monetary Fiscal Policy at the Center of Economic and Demographic Studies, Colegio de Mexico; Professor of International Economic Cooperation, National School of Economics, UNAM. **d**-None. **e**-None. **f**-Economist, Department of Economic Studies, Bank of Mexico, 1956–60; Economist, Division of Economic Development, Inter-American Development Bank, 1962–63; Director of the Technical Office, Bank of Mexico, 1964–68; Coordinator for the Bank of Mexico, 1969–70; Director General of Credit, Secretariat of the Treasury, 1970–72; Director General of the National Institute of Housing, Apr. 24, 1972–76; Director General of Credit, Secretariat of the Treasury, 1978–79; *Subsecretary of Credit*, May 22, 1979– . **g**-None. **h**-Delegate to Inter-American and International Economic Conferences; author of several articles and a book on economics. **i**-Son of *Jesus Silva Herzog*, Subsecretary of the Treasury, 1945–46; friend of *Carlos Bermudez Limon*, Director General of PIPSA, 1970–72, while both were students at UNAM. **j**-None. **k**-None. **l**-*Excelsior*, 30 Apr. 1972, 418; letter; HA, 7 May 1973, 17.

Siurob Ramirez, Jose
(Deceased Nov. 5, 1965)
a-Nov. 11, 1886. **b**-Queretaro, Queretaro, *East Central, Urban*. **c**-Medical degree, National School of Medicine, UNAM, 1912. **d**-Constitutional Deputy, 1916–17; Federal Deputy from the State of Queretaro, 1918–20, President of the Congress (twice). **e**-None. **f**-Governor of Queretaro, 1914–15; Governor of Guanajuato, 1915–16; Governor of Quintana Roo, 1928–31; Director of Military Health, Secretariat of National Defense, 1934–35; *Secretary of the Department of Public Health*, June 19, 1935, to Jan. 4, 1938; *Head of the Department of the Federal District*, 1938–39; *Secretary of Health*, Aug. 5, 1939, to Nov. 30, 1940. **g**-None. **h**-Author of books on medicine and health in Mexico. **i**-Distant relative of Father Hidalgo. **j**-Joined the Revolution as a medical student in support of Madero, 1910; physician in the Northeast Medical Corps; career army officer; rank of brigadier general, 1915; rank of Divisionary General; Director of Military Health, Secretariat of National Defense, 1945; retired from the Army, 1945; Commander of the 17th Military Zone, Queretaro, Queretaro; Inspector General of the Army, 1932–34. **k**-One of the founders of the Army Bank; Brandenburg puts him in the Inner Circle of influence, 1934–40. **l**-Peral, 771; DP70, 1996, 2022; Brandenburg, 80; D del S, 19 June 1935, 1; Lopez, 1035; Enc. Mex., XI, 1977, 442.

Sobarzo, Horacio

(Deceased 1963)
a-1896. **b-**Magdalena, Sonora, *North, Rural*.
c-Primary studies at the Colegio de Estado, Sonora;
law degree, National School of Law, UNAM, 1925.
d-None. **e-**Founding member of the National Council
of PAN, 1939. **f-**Judge in Nogales, Sonora, 1928;
Judge of the Superior Tribunal of the State of Sonora,
1929–37; Secretary General of Government of the
State of Sonora, 1946–49; *Acting Governor of Sonora*, Apr. 1948, to Aug. 31, 1949, for General
Abelardo Rodriguez. **g-**None. **h-**Author of several
historical biographies. **k-**None. **l-**DP70, 1997; Anderson; Mabry; Enc. Mex., XI, 1977, 443.

Sobarzo Loaiza, Alejandro

b-Hermosillo, Sonora, *North, Urban*. **c-**Early educa-
tion unknown; law degree, National School of Law,
UNAM, April 24, 1965; LLD, National School of
Law, UNAM; Professor of International Law, Na-
tional School of Law, UNAM; Professor of Interna-
tional Law, Political Science Graduate School,
UNAM. **d-***Federal Deputy* from the State of Sonora,
Dist. 2, 1973–76; *Alternate Senator* from the State of
Sonora, 1976–79; *Federal Deputy* from the State of
Sonora, Dist. 2, 1979–82. **e-***Secretary of Organization*, CEN of PRI, 1978; *Secretary of International
Affairs*, CEN of PRI, 1978–79. **f-**None. **g-**None.
h-Author of many articles and monographs.
i-Related to *Horacio Sobarzo*, Interim Governor of
Sonora, 1948–49; married Maria Dolores Morelos.
j-None. **k-**Precandidate for governor of Sonora,
1978. **l-**HA, 19 Mar. 1979, I; *Excelsior*, 10 Sept.
1978, 12; C de D, 1973–76; C de S, 1976–82.

Soberanes Munoz, Manuel

a-Feb. 11, 1911. **b-**La Paz, Baja California del Sur,
West, Urban. **c-**Primary studies at the Melchor
Ocampo School; preparatory studies at the National
Preparatory School; graduated from the National
Military College, 2nd Lieutenant of Infantry, 1929;
law degree, National School of Law, UNAM, 1939;
Professor of Military Ethics, National Military Col-
lege. **d-***Federal Deputy* from the State of Queretaro,
Dist. 2, 1952–55; *Senator* from the State of Queret-
aro, 1964–70. **e-**Advisor to the Military Sector of the
PNR; President of PRI in Queretaro; General Delegate of the CEN of PRI to various states. **f-**Private
Secretary to the Governor of Hidalgo, *Alfonso
Corona del Rosal*, 1957–58; Director of the Office of
Business Revenues, Treasury of the Department of
the Federal District; Director of the Office of Infractions, Department of the Federal District; Diector of
the License Office, Department of the Federal District; Treasurer of the State of Queretaro. **g-**None.
h-Part of *Alfonso Corona del Rosal*'s political group.
j-Career Army officer; reached rank of Colonel.

k-None. **l-**C de D, 1952–55; C de S, 1964–70;
MGF69.

Soberon (Acevedo), Guillermo

a-Dec. 29, 1925. **b-**Iguala, Guerrero, *South, Urban*.
c-Early education unknown; medical degree from the
National School of Medicine, UNAM, 1949, received an honorable mention for his thesis on "Some
Aspects of Paludism in Apatzingan, Michoacan;"
Ph.D. in Chemical Physiology, University of Wisconsin, 1952–56, with a dissertation on the "Study
of the Peroxidatic System of Leucocytes and its Role
in the Formation of Alloxan from Uric Acid;" professor at the School of Chemical Sciences and at the
National School of Medicine, UNAM; professor at
the Graduate School, IPN; visiting professor at various United States universities. **d-**None. **e-**None.
f-Intern at the National Institute of Nutrition, 1949;
Chief of the Department of Biology, National Institute of Nutrition, 1956–65; Director of Research,
National Institute of Nutrition, 1956–65; Director of
Biomedical Research, UNAM, 1965–71; founder
and coordinator of Scientific Research, UNAM,
1971–73; *Rector of UNAM,* Jan. 3, 1973–77, 1977– .
g-Founding President of the Mexican Society of
Bio-Chemistry. **h-**Author of numerous articles on
medical subjects; employed as a medical expert by
the United Nations. **i-**Studied under *Enrique Beltran*
at UNAM; brother of *Jorge Soberon Acevedo*,
senator from Guerrero, 1976–82. **j-**None. **k-**None.
l-HA, 8 Jan, 1973, 18; letter; Enc. Mex., XI, 1977,
443.

Soberon Acevedo, Jorge

a-Oct. 6, 1921. **b-**Iguala, Guerrero, *South, Urban*.
c-Early education unknown; medical degree, with
specialized studies in cardiology, National School of
Medicine, UNAM; Professor, National School of
Medicine, UNAM. **d-***Federal Deputy* from the State
of Guerrero, Dist. 2, 1955–58, member of the Health
Committee, the Budget Committee and the Instructive Section of the Grand Jury; *Senator* from the State
of Guerrero, 1976–82. **e-**Became active in CNOP,
1948. **f-**None. **g-**Founder of the Mexican Association
of Guerrero Residents, Mexico City. **h-**Founder of
the *Voz del Sur* newspaper. **i-**Brother of *Guillermo
Soberon*, Rector of UNAM, 1973– . **j-**None.
k-None. **l-**Ind. Biog., 152–53; DGF56, 24, 34, 35,
37; C de D, 1955–58; C de S, 1976–82.

Solana (Morales), Fernando

a-Feb. 8, 1931. **b-**Federal District, *Federal District*,
Urban. **c-**Early education unknown; studies in civil
engineering, National School of Engineering,
UNAM, 1948–52; studies in philosophy, School of
Philosophy and Letters, UNAM, 1955; degree in
political science and public administration, School of

Political and Social Sciences, UNAM, 1964, with an honorable mention; Professor of Economic Organization and Mexican Public Administration, National School of Economics, UNAM, 1965–66; Professor of World Politics, 1964–65, Government and Politics of Mexico, 1967–70, State of Political Science, 1970, Society and Politics of Contemporary Mexico, 1971–72, Political Science, 1973–74, and Political Analysis of Public Finance, 1976, School of Political and Social Sciences, UNAM; Professor of Theory and Politics, Graduate School, UNAM, 1973– ; Director of the Seminar of Public Administration, UNAM, 1965–68; *Secretary General of UNAM*, 1966–70. **d-**None. **e-**Member of the advisory board of the IEPES of PRI. **f-**Researcher in international economic problems, National Finance Bank, 1961–65; member of the Committee on Public Administration, Secretariat of the Presidency, 1965–66; Subdirector of Planning and Finance, Conasupo, 1970–76; Managing Director of Industries, Conasupo, 1975–76; *Secretary of Industry and Commerce*, 1976–77; *Secretary of Commerce*, 1977; *Secretary of Public Education*, 1977– . **g-**Representative of the faculty of the School of Political Science, UNAM, 1975–79; adviser to the National Sugar Producers Union, 1964–66. **h-**Journalist, 1952–66; editor of *Transformacion*, 1963–64; Director of Informac, S.A., 1965–66; member of the Board of the National Productivity Council, 1966–70; Subdirector of *Manana*; author of many works on public administration. **i-**Collaborator of *Javier Barros Sierra*; student of *Victor Flores Olea*. **j-**None. **k-**None. **l-***Plural*, Dec. 1977, 97–98; *Excelsior*, 13 May 1977, 6; *Excelsior*, 10 Dec. 1977, 13, 1; HA, 31 Jan. 1977, 19; WNM, 217; HA, 6 Dec. 1976, 22; *Excelsior*, 3 Dec. 1976, 15.

Solis Manjarrez, Leopoldo

a-Sept. 2, 1928. **c-**Early education unknown; economics degree, National School of Economics, UNAM, 1948–52; graduate studies in macro–economic models, Yale University, 1957–59; Professor of International Trade, Technological Institute of Mexico, 1960–62; Professor of Macro and Micro Economic Theory, Monetary Theory, Growth Theories and Economic Development, Center for Economic and Demographic Studies, Colegio de Mexico; researcher, Center for Economic and Demographic Studies, Colegio de Mexico, 1976. **d-**None. **e-**None. **f-**Director of the Department of Economic Studies, Bank of Mexico, 1964–70; Director; Joint Commission of Economic and Social Planning, Secretariat of the Presidency, 1970–75; *Subsecretary of Commercial Planning*, Secretary of Commerce, 1977; *Subdirector General of the Bank of Mexico*, 1976– . **g-**None. **h-**Author of various ar-

ticles and books on economics; member of the National College; member of the Executive Board of the Latin American Institute of Economic and Social Planning, Santiago, Chile, 1971–74; President of the Board of Directors, International Bank, 1973–74. **j-**None. **k-**None. **l-**Letters; Enc. Mex., XI, 1977, 451.

Solorzano, Roberto A.

b-Colima, Colima, *West*, *Urban*. **c-**Primary studies in Colima; secondary studies at the Colegio Frances La Salle; preparatory studies from the National Preparatory School; law degree, National School of Law, UNAM, 1930. **d-***Federal Deputy* from the State of Colima, Dist. 1, 1949–52, member of the Tariff and Foreign Trade Committee, the Gran Comision, the General Accounting Office Committee; *Senator* from Colima, 1952–58, member of the Second Tariff and Foreign Trade Committee, the Treasury Committee and the Second Constitutional Affairs Committee. **e-**None. **f-**Attorney for the Workers of the Mexican Light and Power and Streetcar Company, 1930–45; Director of the Trolley Car Company of the Department of the Federal District. **g-**None. **h-**Practicing lawyer. **i-**Co-student of *Miguel Aleman* and *Manuel Ramirez Vazquez* at the National School of Law. **j-**None. **k-**None. **l-**Ind. Biog., 153–54; DGF51, I, 20, 29, 30, 34; C de D, 1949–52, 91; DGF56, 5, 8, 9, 11, 12.

Soto Guevara, Carlos

(Deceased 1957)
a-1897. **b-**Puebla, Puebla, *East Central*, *Urban*. **c-**Early education unknown; law degree, University of Puebla, 1927. **d-**Local Deputy to the State Legislature of Puebla, 1925–26; Federal Deputy from the State of Puebla, 1932–34; *Alternate Senator* from the State of Puebla, 1934–39. **e-**None. **f-**Director of the Department of Economic Statistics, Secretariat of the Economy, 1931–32; Justice of the Superior Tribunal of Justice of the Federal District and Federal Territories, 1939–42; Justice of the Federal Tax Court, 1942–57. **g-**None. **j-**None. **k-**None. **l-**DP70, 2015; C de S, 1934–40; C de D, 1932–34; DGF51, I, 550; DGF56, 552.

Soto Maynes, Oscar

b-Chihuahua, *North*. **c-**Early education unknown; law degree, National School of Law, UNAM. **d-***Federal Deputy* from the State of Chihuahua, Dist. 1, 1949–50, member of the Administration Committee and the First Grand Jury; *Governor of Chihuahua*, 1950–55. **e-**None. **f-**Adviser to the Private Secretary to the President of Mexico, 1946–48. **g-**None. **i-**Member of the "Aleman generation" at UNAM; brother *Roberto Soto Maynez* was a federal deputy from Chihuahua, 1946–49. **j**-None. **k**-Took leave from the governorship after a minor riot and popular campaign against him; accused in the press of graft; precandidate for senator from Chihuahua, 1970. **l**-DGF51, I, 20, 34, 89; HA, 29 Aug. 1955, 16; Anderson; *Excelsior*, 10 Aug. 1955; Scott, 277; C de D, 1949–52, 91; Hoy, 12 Feb. 1955, 23; DGF47; Hoy, 21 Mar. 1970, 4; NYT, 10 Aug. 1955, 13; HA, 25 Oct. 1954, 15; letter.

Soto Izquierdo, Enrique

a-Dec. 13, 1935. **b**-Cusihuiriachi, Chihuahua, *North*, *Rural*. **c**-Primary studies at the Victor Maria Flores School in Cusihuiriachi and in the Miguel de Unamuno School in the Federal District; secondary studies at the Secondary School No. 3, Federal District; preparatory studies at the National Preparatory School No. 1; law degree, National School of Law, UNAM, 1961. **d**-*Federal Deputy* from the Federal District, No. 23, 1976–79, member of the Agrarian Affairs Committee, the Scientific and Technological Development Committee; Physical Education Subcommittee, the Fourth Tourism Development Committee, the Fourth Housing Development Committee, the Second Government Committee, the Credit Section of the Treasury Committee, and the Juvenile Study Committee. **e**-Director of *La Republica* (official magazine of PRI), 1968–70. **f**-Director General of the National Institute of Youth, 1970–76. **g**-Member of the Technical Advisory Council of the CNC, 1967. **h**-Subchampion of oratory at the National Preparatory School, 1952; international oratory champion of the *El Universal* contest, 1957; translated the Mexican Constitution into English and French for the Senate, 1961; published the first trilingual (English, French, and Spanish) edition of the Mexican Constitution, 1962; Director of the Sunday Supplement of Culture for *El Dia* and *El Gallo Illustrado*, 1965–70. **i**-Student leader at the National Preparatory School with *Alfredo Bonfil*, *Pedro Vazquez Colmenares*, and *Pindaro Uriostegui*, 1952–53; father, Engineer Enrique Soto, was a Federal Deputy. **j**-None. **k**-None. **l**-HA, 12 Nov. 1973; Enc. Mex., XI, 1977, 500; HA, 19 Feb. 1979, V–VI; *Excelsior*, 5 Sept. 1976, 1; D de C, 1976–79, 5, 15, 22, 43, 45, 56, 58, 77.

Soto (Martinez), Ignacio

(Deceased 1962)
a-1890. **b**-Bavispe, Sonora, *North*, *Rural*. **c**-Early education unknown; no degree. **d**-*Governor of Sonora*, Sept. 1, 1949, to Sept. 1, 1955. **e**-None. **f**-None. **g**-None. **h**-Businessman in grains; owner of several industries in Sonora; early investor in the cement industry in Hermosillo and Mazatlan. **j**-None. **k**-None. **l**-DP70, 2014; DGF51, I, 92; Alonso, 219.

Soto Resendiz, Enrique

a-Apr. 15, 1927. **b**-Tecosautla, Hidalgo, *East Central*, *Rural*. **c**-Primary studies in Tecosautla; secondary studies at the Military Institute Benjamin N. Velasco, Queretaro; preparatory studies at the Laurents Institute, Monterrey, Nuevo Leon; law degree from the National School of Law, UNAM. **d**-*Federal Deputy* from the State of Hidalgo, Dist. 5, 1970–73, member of the Ninth Section of the Legislative Studies Committee, the Rules Committee, and the First Tax Committee. **e**-Participated in the first and second oratory contests sponsored by PRI, 1949–50, winner of first and second place in the State of Hidalgo and second and fourth for Mexico; Director of Youth Action of PRI in Hidalgo, Mexico, and the Federal District; Official Orator of the *Lopez Mateos* presidential campaign, 1958; delegate to various PRI conventions; General Coordinator of the Popular Program Boards of PRI for Hidalgo; Secretary of Organization of PRI in Hidalgo; Secretary General of the State Committee of PRI in Hidalgo; *Subsecretary of Organization of the CEN of PRI*, 1973–74. **f**-Subdirector of the Offices of Government, Department of the Federal District; Subdirector of the Rules and License Inspection Office, Government Division, Department of the Federal District; Director of the Special Tax Department, State of Hidalgo. **g**-Technical adviser to the CNC. **h**-Practicing lawyer. **j**-None. **k**-None. **l**-*Directorio*, 1970–72; C de D, 1970–72, 137.

Soto Reyes, Ernesto

(Deceased Apr. 29, 1972)
a-Apr. 16, 1899. **b**-Puruandiro, Michoacan, *West Central*, *Urban*. **c**-Secondary studies at the Colegio Primitivo; preparatory studies at the Colegio de San Nicolas, Morelia, Michoacan; professional studies at the Colegio de San Nicolas and at UNAM; no degree. **d**-Mayor of Morelia, Michoacan, 1921; Federal Deputy from the State of Michoacan; *Senator* from the State of Michoacan, 1934–40; president of the Senate, 1935; president of the National Revolutionary Block. **e**-Founding member of the Michoacan Socialist Party, 1917; President of the PNR in Michoacan, 1929–32; Secretary of the CEN of the PNR, 1932–34; member of *Cardenas'* presidential campaign committee, 1933–34; *Secretary of Agrarian Action of the CEN of the PNR*, 1936. **f**-Minister to Paraguay, 1941–43; Ambassador to Venezuela, 1943–46; Ambassador to Uruguay, 1946; Ambassador to Haiti, 1965; member of the Federal Electoral Commission, 1936. **g**-None. **h**-Author of several books. **i**-Close personal friend of *Lazaro Cardenas* and *Francisco Mugica*; member of the *Mugica* political group; nephew of *Alberto Bremauntz*; brother Arturo was active in politics; mother Abigail Reyes ran

the first student boarding house in Morelia. **j**-None. **k**-Leader of the Michoacan radicals in the Senate; led the fight to defeat *Portes Gil's* candidates for the Senate, which eventually caused *Portes Gil* to resign on Aug. 19, 1936, as President of the CEN of the PNR; head of the National Orientation Committee in favor of General *Henriquez Guzman*, 1951–52. **l**-DPE65, 27; Kirk, 141; EBW46, 54; *Excelsior*, 30 April, 1972; Morton, 334, 26, 19–20; Gonzalez Navarro, 122; Lopez, 1044; Casasola, V; Bremauntz, 56, 59, 101.

Sousa (Gordillo), Mario

a-Apr. 7, 1903. **b**-Veracruz, Veracruz, *Gulf*, *Urban*. **c**-Primary studies in Veracruz, preparatory studies at the National School; law degree, National School of Law, UNAM, 1925, economics degree, National School of Economics, UNAM, 1940; LLD, National School of Law, UNAM, 1950; professor, National School of Law, UNAM; Professor of Economics, UNAM, 1925–38; Director, National School of Economics, UNAM, 1938–40. **d**-None. **e**-Secretary of the National Federation for Renovation, in support of General Obregon for president, 1927. **f**-Economic adviser, National Bank of Ejido Credit; Chief, Legal Department, Secretariat of Agriculture; Chief, Legal Department, Secretariat of Labor; Chief, Institute of Rural Economy, Secretariat of Agriculture; Secretary of the National Workers Bank for Industrial Development; private secretary to the Rector of UNAM, *Roberto Medellin*, 1933; *Subsecretary of Industry and Commerce*, 1940–42; Director General of the Government Printing Office, 1942–46; *Head of the Department of Agrarian Affairs and Colonization*, 1946–52. **g**-None. **h**-Writer for the magazine *Hoy*; author of articles on economics. **i**-Knew *Eduardo Bustamante* at UNAM; close friend of Enrique Gonzalez Aparicio. **j**-None. **k**-None. **l**-WWM45, 113; DP70, 2386; *Hoy*, 14 Dec. 1940; DGF51, I, 465; DGF51, II, 165, 181; DGF50, II, 129, 139; Lopez, 1045.

Stephens Garcia, Manuel

a-June 2, 1925. **b**-Bellavista, Nayarit, *West*, *Rural*. **c**-Primary studies at the Benito Juarez School, Bellavista, Nayarit; secondary studies at the Normal School of Jalisco and the Normal Institute of Sciences, Nayarit; teaching certificate from the Higher Normal School of Mexico, Mexico, D.F.; secondary school teacher. **d**-*Federal Deputy* from the State of Nayarit, Dist. 1, 1961–64, member of the Plaints Committee and the General Means of Communication Committee; *Federal Deputy* from the PPS (party deputy), 1970–73, member of the National Lands and Resources Committee, the First Public Education Committee, the Second Tax Committee, and the

Military Health Committee. **e**-Secretary of Press and Publicity of the PPS; Secretary General of the PPS in the Federal District. **f**-Director of Foreign Secondary Schools, Tuxpan, Nayarit. **g**-Secretary of Union Education of the 20th Section of the SNTE, Nayarit. **h**-None. **j**-None. **k**-Candidate of the PPS for Senator; candidate of the PPS for Governor of Nayarit. **l**-C de D, 1961–63, 92; C de D, 1970–72, 137; *Directorio*, 1970–72.

Suarez (Aranzolo), Eduardo
(Deceased Sept. 19, 1976)

a-Jan. 3, 1895. **b**-Texcoco, Mexico, *West Central*, *Rural*. **c**-Primary studies at the Colegio del Estado, Mexico, and at the Colegio Williams, Mexico City; preparatory studies from the National Preparatory School, 1908–12; law degree from the National School of Law, UNAM, 1913–17; Professor of Juridical Sociology, National School of Law, UNAM, 1916; Professor of Civil Procedures, National School of Law, UNAM, 1917; Professor of Mercantile Law, School of Business, UNAM, 1917; Professor of Industrial Law and General Theory of the State, UNAM, 1920–32. **d**-None. **e**-None. **f**-Oficial Mayor in charge of the Secretary General of Government, State of Hidalgo, 1917–19; President of the Board of Conciliation and Arbitration of the Federal District, 1926; Assistant Lawyer, Mexican-United States General Claims Commission, 1926–28; Assistant Agent, Mexican-British Claims Commission, 1928–29; technical adviser, Legal Department, Secretary of Foreign Relations, 1929–30, member of the Mexican-French Claims Commission, 1930; member of the Mexican delegation to the International Monetary Conference, 1934; *Secretary of the Treasury*, 1935–40, 1940–46; *Ambassador to Great Britain*, 1965–70; President of the Federal Board of Conciliation and Arbitration. **g**-None. **h**-Member of the Drafting Commission, General Banking Law, 1932; Member of the Technical Commission, International Waters Commission (Mexican-United States); technical adviser to PEMEX, the National Finance Bank, and the National Railroads of Mexico; Director of the Mexican-North American Institute of Cultural Relations, 1959–61. **i**-Father a notary and lawyer; great uncle Julian Villagran was a general in the insurgent army of Nicolas Bravo; married Leonor Vazquez, widowed, married Luz Maria Davila; mentor to *Antonio Carrillo Flores*. **j**-None. **k**-Ran for local deputy in Hidalgo, 1920, election disputed, and won by his friend *Javier Rojo Gomez*; offered an appointment as Justice of the Supreme Court and Subsecretary of Government by *Emilio Portes Gil*. **l**-Kirk, 168; DGF51, II, 5; Peral, 779; DGF50, II, 10; HA, 30 July 1945; WWM45, 114; DP70, 1076; DPE65, 26; Enc. Mex., XI, 1977, 509; Lopez, 1046; NYT, 26

Oct. 1942, 28; HA, 30 July 1943, 38; HA, 27 Sept. 1976, 7.

Suarez (Ruiz), Marcos Manuel

a-Jan. 5, 1935. **b**-Cuernavaca, Morelos, *West Central, Urban*. **c**-Primary studies at the Colegio Mexico, Mexico City; secondary studies at Secondary School No. 2, Mexico City; studies at Loyola College, Montreal, Canada; engineering degree, MIT, Boston, Massachusetts; completed fourth year of law at the National School of Law, UNAM. **d**-Substitute Mayor of Cuernavaca, 1966–68; Local Deputy to the State Legislature of Morelos, 1968–70; *Federal Deputy* from the State of Morelos, Dist. 1, 1970–73, member of the Artisans Committee, the Public Works Committee, the Public Housing Committee and the Gran Comision; Majority Leader of the Chamber of Deputies, 1973. **e**-Secretary of Housing of the CEN of CNOP, 1975–76. **f**-Executive Director of Tourism Development, State of Morelos; *Oficial Mayor of Labor*, 1976–78. **g**-Founding member of the Platform of Mexican Professionals. **h**-None. **i**-Friend of *Pedro Ojeda Paullada* since the founding of the Platform of Mexican Professionals. **j**-None. **k**-Precandidate for governor of Morelos, 1974. **l**-*Excelsior*, 26 Dec. 1974, 15; *Directorio*, 1970–72, C de D, 1970–73, 138.

Suarez Torres, Gilberto

a-Feb. 5, 1912. **b**-Oaxaca, Oaxaca, *South, Urban*. **c**-Primary studies at the Pestalozzi School, Oaxaca, Oaxaca; secondary studies at the Institute of Arts and Sciences of Oaxaca; law degree, National School of Law, UNAM, 1932–37. **d**-*Senator* from the State of Oaxaca, 1970–76, member of the Gran Comision, president of the Second Government Committee and First Secretary of the Rules Committee. **e**-General Delegate of the CEN of PRI. **f**-Secretary of the Second Judicial District of Oaxaca, 1933–34; local judge, Oaxaca, Oaxaca, 1934–35; Consulting lawyer to the Chief of Police, Oaxaca, 1935–46; agent of the Ministerio Publico, Office of the Attorney General for the Federal District, 1946–52; Subdirector of the Department of Federal Security, Secretariat of Government, 1952–58; *Assistant Attorney General of Mexico (2)*, 1958–64; *Attorney General for the Federal District and Federal Territories*, 1964–70. **g**-None. **h**-Practicing lawyer, 1935–46. **i**-Married Maria de la Luz Herrera. **j**-None. **k**-None. **l**-*Libro de Oro*, xl; DPE65, 211; DGF56, 89; HA, 22 Dec. 1958, 8; D de Y, 2 Dec. 196, 2; D de Y, 9 Dec. 1958, 1; *Por Que*, 4 Dec. 1969, 7; letter.

Talamantes, Gustavo L.

(Deceased 1958)

a-Aug. 10, 1891. **b**-Hacienda de Roncesualles, Matamoros, Chihuahua, *North, Rural*. **c**-Early education unknown; agricultural engineering degree, College of Agriculture of Ciudad Juarez. **d**-Mayor of Ciudad Juarez, Chihuahua, 1916; Senator from the State of Chihuahua, 1930–34; *Governor of Chihuahua*, 1935–40. **e**-*Secretary of Agrarian Action of the CEN of the PNR*, 1935–36. **f**-Delegate of the Secretariat of Agriculture; Gerente of the National Ejido Bank, Durango; Director of the Federal Treasury Office, Aguascalientes, Aguascalientes. **g**-President of the Agrarian Commission of the State of Chihuahua, 1920–24. **k**-Imposed Col. *Alfredo Chavez* as his successor over PRM's choice of *Fernando Foglio Miramontes* by running him on the Independent Revolutionary Party of Chihuahua. **l**-*Siempre*, 3 Dec. 1958, 6; Peral, 783; Anderson, 74–76; C de S, 1930–34.

Tamayo, Jorge

a-July 17, 1937. **b**-Oaxaca, Oaxaca, *South, Urban*. **c**-Early education unknown; economics degree, National School of Economics, UNAM, 1960, with a thesis on integration in the state of Oaxaca; graduate studies at Georgetown University, 1960; graduate studies at the Central School of Planning and Statistics, Warsaw, Poland, 1962–63; Assistant Professor to *Mario Ramon Beteta* in Economic Theory, 1961–63; Professor of Planning, National School of Economics, UNAM, 1964–73; Professor and Director of the Seminar on the Economics of Production, 1968–70. **d**-None. **e**-None. **f**-Subdirector General of the Central Light and Power Company, Mexico City, 1970–76; *Subsecretary of Internal Trade*, Secretariat of Commerce, 1976– . **g**-President of the National College of Economists, 1974. **i**-Son of Martha Lopez Portillo; cousin of *Jose Lopez Portillo*; son of *Jorge L. Tamayo*, a member of the Popular Party, famous geographer and Executive Director of the Papaloapan Commission, 1974–78. **j**-None. **k**-None. **l**-Letter; *Excelsior*, 9 Oct. 1978, 12.

Tamayo, Jorge L.

(Deceased Dec. 17, 1978)

a-Aug. 8, 1912. **b**-Oaxaca, Oaxaca, *South, Urban*. **c**-Primary and secondary studies in Oaxaca and in Mexico City; preparatory studies in mathematics and physical sciences, Mexico City; civil engineering degree, National School of Engineering, UNAM, October, 1936; founder of the School of Irrigation; member of the Governing Board of UNAM; Professor of Regional Geography; Economic Geography; Geological Resources and Necessities of Mexico, Superior Normal School and the Workers University, Mexico City. **d**-None. **e**-Member of the Popular Party; member of the PRM until 1944. **f**-Director of the Water Department of the Lagunera Irrigation District, 1935–37; Director of Technical Water Inspections, Valle de Mexico, 1937–38; engineering, Secretariat of Hydraulic Resources, 1939–43; Comptroller, Mexicano Railroads, 1946–49; Comptroller, National Railroads of Mexico, 1947–49; Technical Consultant to the Economic Commission for Latin America, 1950; Director General of the Tuxtepec Paper Company, 1973–78; Executive Secretary of the Papaloapan Commission, 1974–78. **g-**Student leader at the National School of Engineering, 1935. **h-**Author of dozens of books; Sales Manager, Mechanical Equipment, S.A., 1951–56. **i-**Married Martha Lopez Portillo, cousin of *Jose Lopez Portillo*; father of *Jorge Tamayo*. **j-**None. **k-**Resigned from the PRM after he felt unjustly denied of being elected a federal deputy, 1944; candidate for governor of Oaxaca several times. **l-**HA, 25 Dec. 1978, 16; *Excelsior*, 9 Oct. 1978, 12; Enc. Mex., XII, 1977, 1; *Excelsior*, 19 Dec. 1978, 4.

Tame Shear, Amado

a-1927. **b-**Federal District, *Federal District*, *Urban*. **c-**Early education unknown; no degree. **d-**Alternate Federal Deputy (Party Deputy of the PPS), 1964–67; **e-**Member of the Mexican Communist Party, 1949–60; Joined the PPS, 1960; Secretary of Educational Policy of the Central Committee of the PPS. **f-**None. **g-**None. **j-**None. **k-**Candidate of the PPS for Federal Deputy from Dist. 33, Federal District, 1979. **l-**HA, 16 Apr. 1979, V.

Tamez (Cavazos), Ramiro

a-Jan. 18, 1889. **b-**General Teran, Nuevo Leon, *North*, *Rural*. **c-**Primary studies in General Teran; secondary and preparatory studies at the Colegio Civil, Monterrey; medical degree from the National School of Medicine, UNAM. **d-**Mayor of General Teran, Nuevo Leon; local deputy to the State Legislature of Nuevo Leon; Interim Governor of Nuevo Leon; 1922–23; Director of Coordinating Services, State of Nuevo Leon; *Senator* from the State of Nuevo Leon, 1940–46, President of the Consular and Diplomatic Service Committee, member of the Health Committee, alternate member of the tariff and Second Foreign Trade Committee. **e-**None. **f-**Secretary General of Government of the State of Nuevo Leon, 1936–39, under Governor *Anacleto Guerrero*. **g-**None. **h-**Author of several amendments to the Federal Labor Law concerning strikes dealing with workers employed in public services; practicing physician, 1946–68. **i-**During the Revolution, he became friends with Dr. *Francisco Castillo Najera* and *Aurelio Manrique*; met *Antonio Diaz Soto y Gama* at UNAM; brother Nicandro was a senator and deputy from Nuevo Leon. **j-**Left Medical School in his third year, 1911, to participate in the Revolution with other medical students; Francisco Villa had a great affection for him because he saved a friend's life. **k-**President Obregon forced him from office as Governor of Nuevo Leon in 1923; Tamez went into exile and practiced medicine in San Benito, Texas, 1924–35; he returned to Mexico in 1936; retired from medical practice. **l-**C de S, 1940–46; PdM, 362; Peral, 785; letter; Lopez, 1055.

Tapia Camacho, Manlio Fabio

a-Sept. 18, 1928. **b-** Veracruz, Veracruz, *Gulf*, *Urban*. **c-**Primary studies in the Xicotencatl School; secondary and preparatory studies at the Illustrious Preparatory School of Veracruz, 1941–45; law degree, School of Law, University of Veracruz, May 18, 1951; Professor of Agrarian Law, University of Veracruz, 1951–64; Secretary of the School of Law, University of Veracruz; Professor of Civil Law, University of Veracruz, 1951–64; professor at the secondary school, Vespertina Veracruz, and at the normal and preparatory schools, Veracruz, 1953–64. **d-**Local Deputy to the State Legislature of Veracruz, 1959–62; *Alternate Senator*, 1964–68, but replaced Senator *Murillo Vidal* from 1968 to 1970, as Senator from Veracruz; Mayor of Veracruz, 1964–67. **e-**Member of PRI since 1947; Director of the official PRI newspaper, *El Constitucionalista*; President of PRI in Veracruz, 1960–62. **f-**Director of Publicity, Department of Health, State of Veracruz; assistant in the office of the Secretary General of Government of Veracruz; Group Secretary for the Board of Conciliation and Arbitration of the State of Veracruz; Director of the Legal Department of the State of Veracruz, 1956–59; Judge of the Superior Tribunal of Justice of Veracruz, 1962–64; Private Secretary to the Secretary of Agriculture, *Bernardo Aguirre*, 1970–73; Private Secretary to the Governor of Chihuahua, *Bernardo Aguirre*, 1974–77. **g-**Lawyer for the League of Agrarian Communities of the State of Veracruz. **h-**As a student, worked for the Judicial Police of Veracruz; State of Veracruz oratory champion from the University of Veracruz, 1950; national subchampion of Revolutionary Oratory; founder of several magazines; professional newspaperman since student days. **i-**Son of a professor; studied under *Angel Carvajal* and *Fernando Roman Lugo* at the University of Veracruz. **j-**None. **k-**None. **l-**C de S, 1964–70; DBM68, 594; letter; DAPC, 1977; *Excelsior*, 11 Aug., 1978, 23.

Tapia Freyding, Jose Maria

(Deceased 1969)

a-May 16, 1896. **b-**Nogales, Sonora, *North*, *Rural*. **c-**Early education unknown; no degree. **d-**Federal Deputy from Baja California del Norte, 1932; *Senator* from the State of Baja California del Norte, 1958–64, President of the Mail and Telegraph Committee and of the First National Defense Committee, member of the Committee on Taxes, the Military Justice Committee, and the War Materiels

Committee; Vice President of the Senate, Sept., 1961. e-None. f-Chief of Staff for President *Emilio Portes Gil*, 1929–30; Governor and Military Commander of Baja California del Norte; Director General of Federal Retirement and Pensions; Director General of Public Charities, 1932–35; Consul General, New York City; Director General of the Mails, 1944; Director General of Customs; Director General of the National Army-Navy Bank, 1964–69. g-None. h-None. j-Fought in the Revolution, 1913–20; fought against General Maytorena; fought against Victoriano Huerta, 1913; career army officer; Brigadier General, May 16, 1929; reached rank of Divisionary General; Chief of Staff for Baja California del Norte, Nayarit and Sinaloa; Commander of the 1st Infantry Regiment; Commander of the 6th Military Region, Tijuana, 1956. k-None. l-C de S, 1961–64, 70; Peral, 785; D070, 2045; Func., 122.

Taracena, Antonio

a-Jan. 17, 1901. b-Villahermosa, Tabasco, *Gulf, Urban*. c-Primary studies in a public school, Villahermosa; preparatory studies at the National Preparatory School, 1918–21; law degree, National School of Law, UNAM, May 21, 1926; Professor of Criminal Law, National School of Law, UNAM, 1930–35; Professor of Labor Law, School of Law, University of Guanajuato, 1940–41; Professor of Civics and Ethics, Juarez Institute of Tabasco, 1943–44. d-*Senator* from the State of Tabasco, 1946–52, member of the Legislative Studies Committee, the Electric Industry Committee, the Public Works Committee and the Second Balloting Group. e-None. f-Scribe in a criminal court, 1923–26; Assistant Attorney General of Baja California del Sur, 1926; Agent of the Ministerio Publico in the Federal District, 1926–28; Attorney General of the State of Tabasco under Governor *Noe de la Flor Casanova*, 1943–46; Judge of the Superior Tribunal of Justice of the Federal District and Federal Territories, 1963–70. g-None. h-Practicing lawyer, 1928–43, 1952–63; author of the Penal Code of Tabasco. j-None. k-Involved in the trial of Jose Leon Toral, assassin of General Obregon, 1928. l-Letters; Lopez, 1056; DGF51, I, 7, 11–14.

Tejeda (Olivares), Adalberto

(Deceased Sept. 8, 1960)
a-Mar. 28, 1883. b-Chicontepec, Veracruz, *Gulf, Rural*. c-Primary studies in the Cantonal School, Chicontepec; preparatory studies at the National Preparatory School, Mexico, D.F.; engineering studies, Mexico, D.F.; no degree. d-Deputy to the Constitutional Congress from the State of Veracruz, 1916–17; Senator from the State of Veracruz, 1918–20; Governor of Veracruz, 1920–24; Governor of Veracruz, 1928–32. e-Candidate for President of

Mexico on the Communist Party Ticket, 1934. f-Secretary of Communications and Public Works, Dec. 1, 1924, to Aug. 25, 1925; Secretary of Government, 1925–28; *Ambassador to France*, 1936–37; Ambassador to Spain, 1937–39; Ambassador to Peru, 1942. g-None. h-None. i-Son Luis Tejeda Tejeda served under his father in Spain and became a consul in the Mexican Consulate Service, 1961; mentor to Fabio Manlio Altamirano. j-Maderista during the Revolution; Chief of Staff of the Eastern Division under General *Candido Aguilar*; fought Victoriano Huerta; head of Military Operations for the North; rank of Brigadier General, 1948. k-Did not attend the Constitutional Congress because of military activities and personal affairs; caudillo of the State of Veracruz during the 1920s; Brandenburg considers him an Inner Circle favorite of President Calles, 1924–28. l-DP70, 2064; Scott, 122; Brandenburg, 63; Peral, 787; DBM68, 595; Lopez, 1058; Michaels, 28–29; Enc. Mex., XII, 1977, 34.

Telleache (Merino), Ramon

(Deceased Feb. 22, 1972)
a-May 3, 1914. b-Villahermosa, Tabasco, *Gulf, Urban*. c-Primary studies in Villahermosa; secondary studies in Puebla; preparatory studies at the National Preparatory School; law degree from the National School of Law, UNAM, 1940. d-Mayor of Frontera, Tabasco, 1965–67. e-None. f-Agent of the Ministerio Publico of the Office of the Attorney General of the Federal District, 1940–43; Substitute President of the Federal Board of Conciliation and Arbitration, 1944–47; *Subsecretary of Livestock*, 1970–72. g-President of the Livestock Association of Frontera, Tabasco (3 times); Delegate to the National Federation of Cattlemen; member of the Executive Council, State Cattlemen's Association, Tabasco. h-Involved in cattle ranching in Tabasco since 1947; Secretary and Treasurer of the Tabasco Credit Union. j-None. k-None. l-HA, 14 Dec. 1970, 21; D del S, 23 Feb. 1972, 1.

Tellez Benoit, Maria Emilia

a-Dec. 27, 1921. b-Washington, D.C., *Foreign, Urban*. c-Primary studies in Washington, D.C.; secondary studies in Rome; law degree from the National School of Law, UNAM, 1947, with a thesis on "The Continental Shelf;" Assistant Professor of Public International Law, National School of Law, UNAM, 1946; Assistant Professor, Public International Law and General State Theory Seminar, UNAM, 1946–47, 1958–61; Professor of International Public Law, Women's University of Mexico, 1949–50; Professor of Public International Law, National School of Law, UNAM, 1957–58. d-None. e-None. f-Career Foreign Service officer; joined the Foreign Service, Apr. 1, 1946, with the rank of Vice

Consul; Assistant in the Office of Protocol, Secretariat of Foreign Relations, 1946; lawyer for the Department of Legal Affairs, Secretariat of Foreign Relations, 1946; Director of the Post-War Section, Secretariat of Foreign Relations, 1946–48; Director of the United States and Canada Section, Secretariat of Foreign Relations, 1948–55; Director of the Europe, Asia, and Africa Department, Secretariat of Foreign Relations, 1958–59; Director of the Department of American Affairs, Secretariat of Foreign Relations, 1959; Director of the Department of Information, Secretariat of the Presidency, 1959; Third Secretary, Washington, D.C., 1947–48; Vice Consul, Washington, D.C., 1947–48; Second Secretary, Havana, Cuba, 1955–58; Director General of International Organizations, Secretariat of Foreign Relations, 1964–68; Subdirector General of International Organizations, 1961–64; *Oficial Mayor of the Secretariat of Foreign Relations,* 1970–76; *Subsecretary of Foreign Relations,* 1976–. **g-**None. **h-**None. **i-**Father, Manuel C. Tellez, was Secretary of Government and Secretary of Foreign Relations, 1931–32; attended UNAM with *Luis Echeverria* and *Jose Lopez Portillo*. **j-**None. **k-**She is the first woman Oficial Mayor in a Mexican cabinet. **l-**HA, 14 Dec. 1970, 20; DPE61, 17; *Libro de Oro*, xxv; letter.

Tellez Oropeza, Esperanza

a-1920s. **b-**Zacatlan, Puebla, *East Central, Urban.* **c-**Primary studies in the Benito Juarez School, Zacatlan; completed secretarial studies, Oliver Pestalozzi Academy, Mexico City, 1931; teacher, Oliver Pestalozzi Academy. **d-***Federal Deputy* from the State of Puebla, Dist. 10, 1958–61, member of the Library Committee and the Committee on the Radio and Television Industry. **e-**None. **f-**Personal secretary to *Enrique Rodriguez Cano*, Secretary of the Presidency, 1952–56; employee, Administrative Department, Secretariat of the Presidency, 1956–58. **g-**Employee of the National Teachers Union, 1937. **j-**None. **k-**First female deputy from the state of Puebla. **l-**Func., 327; C de D, 1958–61, 92.

Tello (Baurraud), Manuel J.

(Deceased Nov. 27, 1971)
a-Nov. 1, 1898. **b-**Zacatecas, Zacatecas, *East Central, Urban.* **c-**Primary studies at the Christian Brothers School, Zacatecas; secondary studies at the Instituto Cientifico, Zacatecas; preparatory studies at the National Preparatory School; law studies at the Escuela Libre de Derecho and at the National School of Law, UNAM; law degree; advanced studies at the Graduate School, UNAM. **d-***Senator* from the State of Zacatecas, 1964–70. **e-**None. **f-**Consul, Brownsville, Texas, 1924; Consul, Nuevo Laredo, 1925; Vice Consul, Antwerp, 1925–27; Consul, Geneva, Berlin, and Hamburg, 1927–29; Consul,

Yokohama, 1930–33; joined the Foreign Service, 1935; Mexican delegate to the International Conferences on Labor, 1934–39; Secretary General and Delegate to the United Nations, 1939; Director General of the Diplomatic Service and Political Affairs, Secretariat of Foreign Relations, Jan., 1942, to Feb., 1943; *Oficial Mayor of Foreign Relations*, 1943–44; *Subsecretary of Foreign Relations*, 1944–48; *Subsecretary-in-Charge of the Secretariat*, 1948–51; *Secretary of Foreign Relations*, 1951–52; *Ambassador to the United States*, 1952–58; *Secretary of Foreign Relations*, 1958–64. **g-**None. **h-**None. **i-**Student of *Aquiles Elorduy* at UNAM; married Guadalupe Macias; son, *Manuel Tello Macias*, became Ambassador to Great Britain in 1976; son *Carlos*, was appointed Secretary of the Presidency, 1976; nephew, Xavier Chavez Tello, candidate for federal deputy from Sonora, 1978. **j-**None. **k-**None. **l-**HA, 10 Aug. 1951, 14; DGF56, 126; WWW70–71, 894; EBW46, 128; HA, 6 Dec. 1971, 22; HA, 8 Dec. 1958, 25; WWMG, 38; WWM45, 116; DPE70, 7; STYRBIWW54, 1046; Lopez, 1059; NYT, 29 Nov. 1971, 42; LA, 3 Dec. 1976.

Tello Macias, Carlos

a-Nov. 4, 1938. **b-**Federal District, *Federal District, Urban.* **c-**Early education unknown; BS degree from Georgetown University, 1955–58; MS degree from Columbia University, New York, 1958–59; economics degree, King's College, Cambridge University, 1961–63; Assistant Professor of Modern Economic Systems, National School of Economics, UNAM, 1960–61; Professor of the Seminar on Foreign Trade, School of Political Science, UNAM, 1964; researcher, Colegio de Mexico, 1963–64; Professor of Economic Theory, Colegio de Mexico, 1964–70; Professor of Economic Doctrines, National School of Economics, UNAM, 1966–75; Professor of the Revision of Economic Concepts, CEMLA, Inter-American Development Bank. **d-**None. **e-**None. **f-**Economist, Department of External Savings, National Finance Bank, 1959–60; economist, Governing Board of State Organizations and Enterprises, 1960–61; adviser to *Jose Lopez Portillo*, Subsecretary of the Presidency, 1965–70; *Subsecretary of Revenues*, Secretariat of the Treasury, 1975–76; Subdirector General of Credit, Secretariat of the Treasury, 1970–75; *Secretary of the Presidency*, 1976–77. **g-**None. **h-**Author of many economic works. **i-**Son of *Manuel Tello*, Secretary of Foreign Relations, 1958–63; brother of *Manuel Tello Macias, Ambassador to Great Britain*, 1977–79. **j-**None. **k-**Resigned as Secretary of the Presidency because of policy disagreements with *Julio Moctezuma Cid* and *Jose Lopez Portillo*; not a member of PRI; *Lopez Portillo* personally chose him as his undersecretary when he headed the treasury ministry.

l-*Excelsior*, 4 Jan. 1975, 10; *Excelsior*, 1 Dec. 1976; *El Dia*, 1 Dec. 1976; *Excelsior*, 17 Nov. 1977; LA, Nov. 1977; HA, 13 Jan. 1975, 9; HA, 6 Dec. 1976, 24; DPE71, 32.

Tello Macias, Manuel

a-1935. c-Early education unknown; undergraduate studies in Washington, D.C. and Mexico City; no degree. d-None. e-None. f-Joined the Foreign Service with the rank of Vice Consul, 1957; rank of Third Secretary, 1960; rank of Second Secretary, 1962; rank of First Secretary, 1964; rank of Counselor, September, 1966; rank of Minister, October 15, 1969; Subdirector of the Department of International Organizations, Secretariat of Foreign Relations, 1967–70; Director General of International Organizations, Secretariat of Foreign Relations, 1970–72; Director-in-Chief of International Organizations, 1972–75; Director-in-Chief, Bilateral Political Affairs, Secretariat of Foreign Relations, 1975–76; *Ambassador to Great Britain*, 1976–79; *Subsecretary of Multilateral Relations*, 1979– . g-None. h-None. i-Son of *Manuel J. Tello*, Secretary of Foreign Relations, 1958–63; brother of *Carlos Tello Macias*, Secretary of the Presidency, 1976–77. j-None. k-None. l-HA, 20 Jan. 1975, 9; HA, 11 June 1979, 9.

Tena, Felipe de Jesus

(Deceased 1958)
a-1873. b-Panindicuaro, Puruandiro, Michoacan, *West Central*, *Rural*. c-Secondary studies at the Colegio de San Simon, Zamora, Michoacan; preparatory studies at the Seminario de Morelia; law degree, School of Law, University of Michoacan, July 24, 1899; Professor of Law, University of Michoacan; Director of the School of Law, University of Michoacan; Professor of Mercantile Law, National School of Law, UNAM, 1930. d-Local deputy to the State Legislature of Michoacan, 1911. e-None. f-Secretary General of Government of the State of Michoacan, 1911, under Governor Miguel Silva; Director of the Legal Department, Secretariat of Agriculture; Director of the Legal Department, Secretariat of Government; *Justice of the Supreme Court of Mexico*, 1941–43. g-None. h-Member of the Editorial Committee writing the new Commercial Code; translator of various legal works; author of works on commercial law. i-Father of Supreme Court Justice *Felipe Tena Ramirez*; father a lawyer. j-None. k-One of Mexico's outstanding jurists. l-DP70, 2072; letter; Enc. Mex., XII, 1977, 53.

Tena Ramirez, Felipe

a-Apr. 23, 1905. b-Morelia, Michoacan, *West Central, Urban*. c-Early education unknown; law degree, Escuela Libre de Derecho, May 18, 1929; LLD, National School of Law, UNAM, 1950; Professor of Civil Proceedings, National School of Law, UNAM, 1931–64; Professor of Constitutional Law, National School of Law, UNAM. d-None. e-None. f-*Supernumerary Justice of the Supreme Court*, 1947, 1951–56; *Justice of the Supreme Court*, 1957–69. g-None. h-Author of law books. i-Son of Supreme Court Justice *Felipe de J. Tena*. j-None. k-None. l-*Justicia*, Dec., 1966; WNM, 224.

Teran Mata, Juan Manuel

a-Mar. 2, 1917. b-Tampico, Tamaulipas, *North*, *Urban*. c-Primary studies in Tampico; secondary studies in the Federal District; preparatory studies at the National Preparatory School, Mexico, D.F.; law degree with honorable mention from the National School of Law, UNAM, 1939; MA in philosophy, UNAM, 1941; Ph.D. in philosophy from UNAM, 1954 (magna cum laude); professor at the National Preparatory School since 1937; professor by competition of law and political philosophy, National School of Law, UNAM; professor of the theory of knowledge, Normal School; professor of legal philosophy, School of Philosophy and Liberal Arts, UNAM. d-*Federal Deputy* from the State of Tamaulipas, Dist. 1, 1952–55, member of the Legislative Studies Committee, the Military Justice Committee, the Budget and Accounts Committee (3rd year), the Constitutional Affairs Committee, and the First Section of the Credentials Committee; *Senator* from the State of Tamaulipas, 1958–64, member of the Gran Comision, the Special Legislative Studies Committee, the First Tariff and Foreign Trade Committee, the First Justice Committee, the Second Petroleum Committee, and the Committee on Taxes; President of the Second Constitutional Affairs Committee. e-None. f-Member of the legislative studies committee, Secretariat of Public Education; head of the Department of University Studies, Secretariat of Public Education; private secretary to the Director of the Mexican Delegation to UNESCO, *Jaime Torres Bodet*, 1945; President of the Advisory Council of the Secretariat of the Navy; Director General of the Professions Division, Secretariat of Public Education, 1955–57; President of the Advisory Council of the Secretariat of the Navy, 1965–70. g-None. h-Author and notable legal philosopher. i-Student of Antonio Caso; married Olga Contreras. j-None. k-None. l-Func., 373; DGF56, 302; DPE65, 55; C de D, 1952–54, 51; C de S, 1961–64, 71; WNM, 224; DP70, 775.

Teran Torres, Hector

a-Feb. 4, 1922. b-Zitacuaro, Michoacan, *West Central, Rural*. c-Early education unknown; law degree, National School of Law, UNAM; professor of law, National School of Law, UNAM. d-*Federal Deputy* from the State of Michoacan, Dist. 8, 1976–79. e-None. f-Lawyer, Office of the Attorney General of the Federal District; Judge (criminal division), Federal District; First Assistant Attorney General of the Federal District, 1975–76; Justice of the Superior Tribunal of Justice of the Federal District, 1975. g-None. j-None. k-None. l-*Excelsior*, 1 Sept. 1976, 1C; C de D, 1976–79.

Teran (Zozaya), Horacio
(Deceased 1970)

a-1905. b-Ciudad Victoria, Tamaulipas, *North*, *Urban*. c-Law degree, National School of Law, UNAM. d-*Governor of Tamaulipas*, 1951–57. e-None. f-Agent of the Ministerio Publico; Second Civil Judge, Mexico, D.F.; Penal Judge, Eighteenth Court District, Mexico, D.F.; Civil Judge, Tampico; Director of the Legal Department, Department of the Federal District; *Oficial Mayor of the Secretariat of Government*, 1946–50; Delegate of the National Council of Tourism, San Antonio, Texas, 1970. g-None. i-Law School companion of *Miguel Aleman*. j-None. k-None. l-DGF56, 101; DP70, 2096; *Siempre*, 19 Sept. 1956, 10; DGF47, 71; HA, 25 Oct. 1954, 15; Casasola, V.

Terrazas Lozaya, Samuel

a-Apr. 7, 1924. b-Federal District, *Federal District*, *Urban*. c-Early education unknown; no degree. d-*Senator* from the State of Veracruz, 1970–76, member of the Gran Comision, President of the First Petroleum Committee, First Secretary of the Second Labor Committee and Second Secretary of the Second Tariff and Foreign Trade Committee. e-None. f-None. g-Member of the CTM, 1950; Secretary of Education of the Petroleum Workers Union of the Mexican Republic, 1962; Treasurer of the STPRM, 1964–66; Secretary General of the STPRM, Poza Rica, Veracruz, 1966–68. j-None. k-None. l-C de S, 1970–76, 86; MGF73; PS, 5982.

Terrones Benitez, Alberto

a-June 3, 1887. b-Villa de Nombre de Dios, Durango, *West*, *Rural*. c-Primary studies in Nazas, Topoia and Durango, Durango; preparatory studies at the Juarez Institute, Durango, 1900; preparatory studies in engineering, National Preparatory School; studies toward a degree in mining engineering, National School of Engineering, UNAM; law degree, Juarez Institute, December 10, 1910, with a specialty in mining labor law. d-Deputy to the Constitutional Convention at Queretaro from the State of Durango, Dist. 6, 1916–17; Alternate Federal Deputy from the State of Durango, Dist. 4, 1920–22; Alternate Federal Deputy from the State of Durango, Dist. 4, 1922–24; Federal Deputy from the State of Durango, Dist. 6, 1924; Senator from the State of Durango,

1924–26; Provisional Governor of Durango, 1929–30; *Senator* from the State of Durango, 1952–58, member of the Indigenous Affairs Committee, the Special Legislative Studies Committee; President of the Special Committee on Small Agricultural Property, President of the First Mines Committee and First Secretary of the Military Justice Committee; *Senator* from the State of Durango, 1964–70. e-None. f-Lawyer, Attorney General's Office; official of the Department of Agrarian Affairs. g-Organized the Agrarian Union of Durango, 1917. h-Practicing lawyer, Mexico City. i-Father was a school teacher; brother of General Adolfo Terrones Benitez, Director of the Infantry, Secretariat of National Defense, 1956. j-None. k-Removed as provisional governor of Durango after attempting to implement stronger pro-agrarian reforms. l-C de D, 1922–24, 34; C de D, 1920–22, 34; C de D, 1924–26, 35; C de S, 1924–26; Ind. Biog., 155; DGF56, 6, 8, 9, 11, 12, 14.

Tiburcio Gonzalez, Adrian
(Deceased Sept. 21, 1972)

a-June 22, 1906. b-Alvarado, Veracruz, *Gulf*, *Rural*. c-Primary and secondary studies in Veracruz; preparatory studies in Veracruz; naval studies at the Fernando Siliceo Nautical School; Professor of Algebra, Analytical Mechanics and Physics, School of Engineering, UNAM; Professor at the National Military College. d-*Federal Deputy* from the State of Veracruz, Dist. 11, 1967–70. e-Member of the Authentic Party of the Mexican Revolution; orator for *Lazaro Cardenas*, 1939–40. g-Founder of the General Federation of Labor. h-Seaman by profession. i-Father in the navy and later a successful businessman; personal friend of *Lazaro Cardenas*. j-Captain in the Navy. k-Headed a dissident faction of PARM, 1962; candidate for federal deputy numerous times. l-MGF69, 96; C de D, 1967–69; HA, 2 Oct. 1972, 64; Lopez, 1067; *Excelsior*, 29 Sept. 1974.

Toledo Corro, Antonio

a-Apr. 1, 1919. b-Escuinapa, Sinaloa, *West*, *Rural*. c-Primary and secondary studies in Sinaloa; no degree. d-Local Deputy to the State Legislature of Sinaloa, 1952; Mayor of Mazatlan, Sinaloa, 1957–62; Mayor of Mazatlan, 1970–76; *Federal Deputy* from the State of Sinaloa, Dist. 4, 1976–78, coordinator of the deputies from the CNC sector, 1976; *Governor of Sinaloa*, 1980– . e-Participant in the presidential campaigns of *Adolfo Lopez Mateos*, 1958, *Gustavo Diaz Ordaz*, 1964, and *Luis Echeverria*, 1970. f-Director of the National Grain Promotion Program, Juchitlan Irrigation District; Director of Rural Mechanization, Secretariat of Agrarian Reform; *Secretary of Agrarian Reform*, June 9, 1978–

80. **g-**President of the Chamber of Commerce of Mazatlan, 1957; Delegate of the Livestock Association of Southern Sinaloa; member of the National Livestock Federation. **h-**Rancher; owner of an agricultural machinery business. **i-**Married Estela Ortiz; part of the *Francisco Merino Rabago* camarilla. **j-**None. **k-**Precandidate for governor of Sinaloa against *Leopoldo Sanchez Celis*, 1963, suffered political ostracism; strongest precandidate for governor of Sinaloa against *Alfonso Calderon Velarde*, 1974; *Adolfo Lopez Mateos* praised him as an outstanding mayor of Mazatlan; *Excelsior* accused him of being a large landholder in El Rosario Region. **l-***Excelsior*, 28 Aug. 1976, 1C; *Excelsior*, 10 June 1978, 1, 4, 8, 18; *The News*, 10 June 1978, 2; *Proceso*, 12 June 1978, 7; *Excelsior*, 27 Apr. 1980, 4.

Topete Ibanez, Rosendo

a-1892. **b-**Jicaltepec, Veracruz, *Gulf*, *Rural*. **c-**Primary studies in Martinez de la Torre, Veracruz; secondary studies in Tlapacoyan, Veracruz; studied business and accounting, Tlapacoyan, Veracruz. **d-**Local Deputy to the State Legislature of Veracruz under Governor *Adolfo Ruiz Cortines*, 1947–50; *Federal Deputy* from the State of Veracruz, Dist. 4, 1955–58, President of the Gran Comision, member of the First Government Committee; *Senator* from the State of Veracruz, 1958–64, member of the Gran Comision, the Second National Defense Committee, the Second Petroleum Committee, the Special Livestock Committee, and the Consular and Diplomatic Service Committee; President of the Special Hydraulic Resources Committee. **e-**Assistant to the treasurer of the Pro *Avila Camacho* Political Committee, 1940; official of the *Adolfo Ruiz Cortines* campaign, 1952. **f-**Treasurer General of Veracruz under Governor *Adolfo Ruiz Cortines*, 1944–47; Chief of the Presidential Offices under *Adolfo Ruiz Cortines*, 1952–55. **g-**None. **h-**Businessman, 1929–30, 1946. **i-**Brother of Ricardo Topete, federal deputy under President Calles. **k-**None. **l-**Func., 387; C de S, 1961–64, 71; DGF56, 29, 33, 30; Ind. Biog., 155–57.

Torres Bodet, Jaime

a-Apr. 17, 1902. **b-**Federal District, *Federal District*, *Urban*. **c-**Preparatory studies at the National Preparatory School, graduating, 1917; law degree, National School of Law, UNAM, 1918–22; instructor of free preparatory course in general literature, 1920; Secretary of the National Preparatory School under Ezequiel Chavez, 1920; Professor of Art History, National Preparatory School, 1922–23; Professor of French Literature, School of Philosophy and Letters, UNAM, 1925–29. **d-**None. **e-**None. **f-**Private secretary to Jose Vasconcelos, Rector of UNAM, 1921; Director, Department of Libraries,

Secretariat of Public Education, 1922–24; joined the Foreign Service, 1929; Second Secretary, Spain, 1929–31; First Secretary of the Legation, Paris, 1935–36; Secretary Buenos Aires, 1934–35; Charge d'Affaires, Holland, 1932–34; Director of the Diplomatic Service, Secretariat of Foreign Relations, 1936–37; Charge d'Affaires, Brussels, Belgium, 1938–40; *Subsecretary of Foreign Relations*, 1940–43; *Secretary of Public Education*, 1943–46; *Secretary of Foreign Relations*, 1946–48; Secretary General of UNESCO, 1949–52; *Ambassador to France*, 1953–58; *Secretary of Public Education*, 1958–64; Ambassador-at-large, 1970–71. **g-**None. **h-**National Prize for Literature, 1966; founded and published *Contemporaneos*, 1928–31, which included such authors as Xavier Villaurrutia and *Salvador Novo*; head of the Mexican delegation which formed UNESCO, 1945; head of the Mexican delegation to the Bogota Conference, 1948; writer and poet, published first book at age 16. **i-**Studied under *Alfonso Caso* at UNAM, 1918; founding member of the Ateneo de la Juventud, 1918, which included *Luis Garrido* and *Jose Gorostiza*; studied with *Rafael de la Colina* at preparatory and at UNAM; classmate of *Salvador Novo*; attended UNAM with Daniel Cosio Villegas. **j-**None. **k-**Member of the Revolutionary family, 1940–48. **l-**HA, 8 Dec. 1958, 26; WWMG, 39; Daniels, 108–09, 140–41; Brandenburg, 178, 80; IWW, 1231; WWM5, 117; DGF56, 126; HA, 11 Oct. 1972, 18–21; Peral, 798; HA, 4 Oct. 1971, 18; Novo, 166; STYRBIWW54, 1054; letters; Enc. Mex., XII, 1977, 193–94.

Torres Chavarria, Celia

a-June 3, 1928. **b-**Iztapaluca, Mexico, *West Central*, *Rural*. **c-**Primary and secondary studies in Mexico City; studies in journalism and labor law; five years of special studies at the Conservatory of Music of the National Institute of Fine Arts; no degree. **d-***Federal Deputy* from the Federal District, Dist. 25, 1976–79, member of the Public Foodstuffs Committee, the Agrarian Affairs Committee and the Development of Social Security and Public Health Committees. **e-**Member of PRI. **f-**Representative of the Women of Indigenous Origin to the Secretariat of Agrarian Reform and the Department of the Federal District; Director of the Indigenous Cultural Center, Secretariat of Public Education. **g-**None. **i-**Father a peasant leader in the Valle del Tenango; recruited to PRI by *Rodolfo Gonzalez Guevara*; married to Fernando Sanchez Ramirez. **j-**None. **k-**None. **l-**D de C, 1976–79, 3, 5, 37; HA, 31 May 1976, 10–11; *Excelsior*, 3 Sept. 1976.

Torres Gaitan, Ricardo

a-Dec. 1, 1911. **b-**Calcoman, Michoacan, *West Central*, *Rural*. **c-**Economics degree from the National School of Economics, UNAM, April 12, 1944, with a thesis on Mexican Monetary policy; Assistant Professor of Organization and Financing of Private Enterprise, National School of Economics, UNAM; Assistant Professor of Credit Operations and Institutions, National School of Economics, UNAM; Professor of International Trade Theory, National School of Economics, UNAM; Director of the National School of Economics, UNAM, 1953–59. d-None. e-None. f-Director of the Department of Administration and Development of Enterprises, National Finance Bank, 1950–52; Director of the Institute of Economic Research, UNAM, 1950–53; Chief of the Banking Department, Secretariat of the Treasury; Director of Statistics, Secretariat of Industry and Commerce; *Oficial Mayor of Industry and Commerce*, 1952–53; Director General of the National Ejidal Bank, 1958–64. g-None. i-Professor of *Julio Faesler Carlisle*, Director General of the Mexican Institute of Foreign Trade, 1970–76; relative of *Carlos Torres Manzo*. j-None. k-Supported *Carlos Torres Manzo* for Governor of Michoacan, 1974. l-D de Y, Dec. 1958; HA, 15 Dec. 1958, 5; letter.

Torres Landa, Juan Jose

a-Apr. 16, 1911. b-Cueramaro, Guanajuato, *West Central*, *Rural*. c-Law degree, National School of Law, UNAM, 1935, with a thesis on the regulation of marriage. d-*Federal Deputy* from the State of Guanajuato, Dist. 2, 1949–52, member of the Second Administrative Committee, the First Treasury Committee, and the Consular Service and Diplomatic Committee; *Governor of Guanajuato*, 1961–67. e-Delegate of PRI to Baja California; 1968–70; General Delegate to the CEN of PRI to Michoacan, 1978. f-Director of the Preparatory Schools of Guanajuato, 1943–44; Ambassador to Brazil, 1971. g-Student leader, 1933 strike at UNAM. i-Son, Juan Jose Torres Landa Garcia was a precandidate for Federal Deputy, 1976. j-None. k-*Por Que* claims he left the state of Guanajuato 1500 million pesos in debt after the fiasco of his Plan Guanajuato; *Por Que* also claims he has been involved in several land scandals. l-C de D, 1949–51, 92; *Por Que*, 18 Sept. 1968, 32ff; *Hoy*, 13 Mar. 1971, 10; *Por Que*, 4 Dec. 1969, 20, 22; *Excelsior*, 7 Nov. 1978, 13.

Torres Manzo, Carlos

a-Apr. 25, 1923. b-Coalcoman, Michoacan, *West Central*, *Rural*. c-Primary studies, Ignacio Manuel Altamirano School, Uruapan, Michoacan, 1937–41; secondary studies, Boarding School of Workers' Children, Zamora, Michoacan, 1942–44; preparatory studies, National Preparatory School, Mexico, D.F., 1945–46; economics degree, National School of Economics, UNAM, 1947–52, with a thesis on the pure theory of international trade; thesis received

recognition from the Bank of Mexico; graduate studies, London School of Economics, 1955–57; diploma from the Government of Japan for studies in Tokyo on economic planning and free trade; professor of literature, etymology, history of economic thought, economic theory and international trade, National School of Economics, UNAM, 1958–70. d-*Governor of Michoacan*, 1974–80. e-Joined PRI, 1947; Director of the Foreign Commerce Studies Commission, IEPES of PRI; campaigned for *Luis Echeverria* for President by presenting reports on tourism, the electrical industry, and industrialization. f-Librarian, secondary school of Zamora, 1944–45; employee of the Secretariat of Education, 1946–47; warehouseman, Commerce Bank, 1947; Technician, Secretariat of National Properties, 1947–49; economist, Secretariat of Industry and Commerce, 1958; economist, National Ejido Bank, 1959–61; Director, Department of Commercial Policy, Secretariat of Industry and Commerce, 1961–64; Supervisor, Department of Commercial Policy, Secretariat of Industry and Commerce, 1952–54; Gerente of CONASUPO, 1964–70; *Secretary of Industry and Commerce*, 1970–74. g-President of the Federation of University Students, 1950; Secretary General of the League of Revolutionary Economists of the CNOP of PRI; President of the College of Economists, 1970–71; Director of the Association of Small Business Banks. h-Researcher, Institute of Investigations, National School of Economics, UNAM, 1958–64; author of many articles on economic subjects for *El Nacional* and *Prensa Grafica*. i-Studied under *Eduardo Bustamante* and *Ricardo Torres Gaitan* at UNAM; as a student at UNAM, knew *Jorge de la Vega Dominguez* and *Jesus Silva Herzog Flores*. j-None. l-Letters; HA, 7 Dec. 1970, 24; *Hoy*, 9 Jan. 1971, 4; *Excelsior*, 19 Jan. 1974, 8; Enc. Mex., Annual, 1977, 546; Enc. Mex., XII, 195; HA, 16 Sept. 1974, 36.

Torres Mesias, Luis

a-Mar. 26, 1916. b-Merida, Yucatan, *Gulf*, *Urban*. c-Primary and secondary studies in Merida; teaching certificate; no degree. d-Mayor of Merida, Yucatan, 1959–60; *Federal Deputy* from the State of Yucatan, Dist. 1, 1961–64, member of the Gran Comision, member of the Public Works Committee and the Budget and Accounts Committee; *Governor of Yucatan*, 1964–70. e-President of the Regional Committee of PRI for Yucatan, 1956–58; member of the PRI student political group in Yucatan, Juventudes Sociales. f-Secretary General of Government of the State of Yucatan, Feb. to Oct., 1958, under Governor *Agustin Franco Aguilar*. g-None. h-None. j-None. k-Unpopular gubernatorial candidate; opposed Jose Vallejo Novelo; member of the *Ernesto Novelo Torres* group. l-*Informes*, 1964–70; C de D,

1961–63, 93; D de Y, 24 Nov. 1964, Q es Q, 242–43; Richmond, 395; *Siempre*, 23 Oct. 1963, 93; *Novedades*, 5 Aug. 1963.

Torres Ortiz, Pedro

a-May 13, 1887. b-Colima, Colima, *West*, *Urban*. c-Early education unknown; no degree. d-Mayor of Zamora, Michoacan; *Governor of Colima*, Nov. 1, 1939, to Oct. 31, 1940; *Senator* from the State of Colima, 1934–39. e-None. f-Provisional Governor of Colima, Aug. 6, 1931, to Nov. 20, 1931. g-None. h-None. j-Career army officer; Commander of the 57th Cavalry Regiment; supported Carranza, 1920; supported General Maycotte in Oaxaca against Obregon, 1923; rank of Brigadier General, Oct. 1, 1942. k-Political opponent of *Miguel G. Santa Ana*. l-Letter; Peral, 800–01; Lopez.

Torres Pancardo, Oscar

a-May 20, 1935. b-Poza Rica, Veracruz, *Gulf*, *Rural*. c-Early education unknown; no degree. d-None. e-None. f-None. g-Secretary of Conflicts of Section 30 of the STPRM, 1967–69; Secretary of Bargaining of Section 30 of the STPRM, 1969–70; President of the General Council of Vigilance of the STPRM, 1970–73; Secretary of Interior and Accords of Section 30 of the STPRM, 1973–76; Secretary General of Section 30 of the STPRM, 1976–77; Secretary General of the Union of Petroleum Workers of the Mexican Republic, 1977– ; President of the Congress of Labor, 1978. h-Joined PEMEX as a laborer, 1952; assistant plumber, PEMEX, 1961. i-Married Olivia Plascencia. j-None. k-None. l-HA, 10 July 1978, 9.

Torres Rojas, Juan Manuel

a-Mar. 30, 1903. b-Merida, Yucatan, *Gulf*, *Urban*. c-Normal School, Colima; dental surgeon degree. d-*Federal Deputy* from the State of Yucatan, Dist. 4, 1940–43. e-President of the State Regional Committee of PNR of Yucatan, 1942. f-School Director, Yucatan, 1923–29; Federal Education Inspector in Yucatan, Secretariat of Public Education, 1929–34; Chief of Dental Services, Department of Public Education, State of Yucatan, 1937–40. g-None. h-Author; founder of the magazine *Orion*, Cozumel; editor of the newspaper *El Correo*. j-None. k-Leader of Mexican masonry. l-EBW46, 80; C de D, 1940–42.

Torres Sanchez, Enrique

a-Feb., 1903. b-Nazas, Durango, *West*, *Rural*. c-Primary and secondary studies in Durango, Durango; preparatory studies at the National Preparatory School; law degree from the National School of Law, UNAM, 1927. d-*Governor of Durango*, 1950–56. e-None. f-Judge of the Superior

Tribunal of Justice of Durango, 1932–35. g-None. h-Practicing lawyer. i-Student with *Miguel Aleman*, *Mariano Azuela*, *Eduardo Bustamante*, *Angel Carvajal*, *Manuel Sanchez Cuen*, and *Horacio Teran Z.* at UNAM in the 1920s. j-None. k-None. l-HA, 25 Oct. 1954, 15; DGF56, 92.

Torres Torija, Jose

(Deceased 1952)
a-1885. b-Federal District, *Federal District*, *Urban*. c-Early education unknown; medical degree, School of Medicine, UNAM, 1908; Professor of Clinical Surgery and Legal Medicine, School of Medicine, UNAM; *Secretary General of UNAM*, 1940–42; member of the Governoring Board of UNAM. d-None. e-None. f-Oficial Mayor of the Department of Public Health; Director of the Juarez Hospital, 1921. g-None. h-Physician at the Juarez Hospital, 1908–48; author of many medical books; President of the Mexican Academy of Medicine, 1929. j-None. k-None. l-Enc. Mex., 12, 196; Lopez, 1002; DP70, 2156; Q es Q, 584.

Toxqui Fernandez de Lara, Alfredo

a-Aug. 5, 1913. b-Cholula, Puebla, *East Central*, *Urban*. c-Primary studies at the Jose Maria Lafragua School, Puebla; secondary studies in Puebla; preparatory studies at the University of Puebla; medical degree, University of Puebla, Oct., 1940, with a thesis on autochemotherapy; professor, School of Medicine, University of Puebla, Professor of General Surgery, IMSS Hospital, Puebla. d-Substitute Councilman of Puebla, 1948–51; *Federal Deputy* from the State of Puebla, Dist. 3, 1955–58, member of the Second Public Education Committee, the Second Balloting Committee, and the Military Health Committee; *Senator* from the State of Puebla, 1970–74, member of the Gran Comision, First Secretary of the Immigration Committee and President of the Insurance Committee; *Governor of Puebla*, 1975– . e-Secretary General of PRI in Puebla; Official Orator of PRI, 1948; co-founder of the CEPES in Puebla; President of the Regional Committee of PRI in Puebla. f-Director of Sanitorium No. 1, IMSS Regional Hospital; Director of IMSS Clinics No. 1 and 2; Subdirector of Government for the State of Puebla, 1966–67; Oficial Mayor of Puebla, 1967. g-General delegate of the CNOP of PRI to Puebla, 1957; Secretary General of the CNOP for Puebla, 1957–63; member of the student directorate at preparatory school at the University of Puebla, 1933; Secretary of the University of Puebla Student Federation, 1934. h-Winner of the First Prize in Oratory at the University of Puebla, 1938; Intern, General Hospital, Puebla; Medical Director of the Green Cross, Puebla. j-None. k-None. l-DBP, 679–80; C de D, 1955–57;

DGF56, 27, 32, 35, 37; letter; CyT, 679–80; C de S, 1970–76, 87; Ind. Biog., 157–58.

Trejo Hernandez, Melquiades

a-Dec. 10, 1918. b-Puebla, Puebla, *East Central*, *Urban*. c-Primary studies only; no degree. d-Local Deputy to the State Legislature of Puebla; Councilman from Puebla; *Federal Deputy* from the State of Puebla, Dist. 1, 1964–67, member of the Textile Industry Committee and the First General Means of Communication Committee; *Federal Deputy* from the State of Puebla, Dist. 1, 1970–73, member of the Public Assistance Committee, the Small Industries Committee, and the First General Means of Communication Committee. e-None. f-None. g-Secretary of Labor of the CTM for the State of Puebla. h-None. j-None. k-None. l-C de D, 1970–72, 138; C de D, 1964–66, 87, 95; *Directorio*, 1970–72.

Trevino (Gonzalez), Jacinto B.

(Deceased Nov. 6, 1971)

a-Sept. 11, 1883. b-Ciudad Guerrero, Coahuila, *North*, *Rural*. c-Primary studies in Ciudad Guerrero and in the Colegio Hidalgo and Colegio Bolivar, Monterrey; preparatory studies at the Colegio Civil of Monterrey, enrolled in the National Military College, December 26, 1901, graduated as an industrial engineer with the rank of artillery lieutenant, December 6, 1908. d-Constitutional Deputy, 1916–17; Federal Deputy from Coahuila; *Senator* from the State of Coahuila, 1952–58, member of the Second Foreign Relations Committee, the Public Welfare Committee, and the Gran Comision. e-Supporter and organizer of the pro-*Almazan* Revolutionary Committee for National Reconstruction, 1939–40; founder and *President of PARM*, 1957–65. f-Secretary of Industry, Commerce and Labor, June 6, 1920 to Nov. 30, 1920; Oficial Mayor of the Secretariat of War, 1914; Director of Mexican Free Ports, 1957–66. g-None. h-None. i-Son-in-law of Col. Lauro Carrillo, governor of Chihuahua; father a Colonel in the National Guard. j-Rank of 2nd Captain, 1910; member of Madero's staff, 1911; organized the 25th Irregular Regiment, Saltillo, Coahuila, 1912; fought General Huerta, 1913; rank of major; Chief of Staff for Carranza, 1913; rank of Colonel, June 8, 1913; Brigadier General, June 5, 1914; rank of Brigade General, 1915; rank of divisionary general, December 22, 1915; General in Chief of the forces against Francisco Villa, 1916; Military Commander of Chihuahua, 1916; supported Obregon against Carranza, 1920; supported De la Huerta; supported Escobar, 1929; Commander of the 1st Brigade of the 1st Division of the Army of the Center, 1914. k-First signer of the Plan of Guadalupe, Mar. 26, 1913; supported the De la Huerta movement, 1923; jailed,

1923–25; opposed Obregon's reelection, 1927; supported Escobar rebellion, 1929; in exile, 1929–36; returned to Mexico, rejoined the Army, 1940, at the rank of Divisionary General, 1941; precandidate for Governor of Coahuila, 1957. l-DGF56, 8, 9; HA, 15 Nov. 1971; Peral, 806; Enc. Mex., Annual, 1977, 597–98; Ind. Biog., 159.

Trevino Rios, Oscar

c-Primary, secondary, and preparatory studies in Monterrey, Nuevo Leon; law degree from the National School of Law, UNAM, 1929–34. d-None. e-None. f-Director General of Legal Affairs, Secretariat of Foreign Relations, 1946–52, 1952–58; *Assistant Attorney General of Mexico (1)*, 1958–62; *Attorney General of Mexico*, 1962–64. g-None. h-Practicing lawyer. i-Married Guadalupe Serrato. j-None. k-None. l-Letter; DGF47, 89; HA, 22 Dec. 1958, 8; D de Y, 9 Dec. 1958, 1; DGF56, 150.

Trevino Zapata, Norberto

a-1911. b-Matamoros, Tamaulipas, *North*, *Urban*. c-Early education unknown; medical degree, National School of Medicine, UNAM; Professor of Medicine, National School of Medicine, UNAM. d-*Federal Deputy* from the State of Tamaulipas, Dist. 2, 1952–55, President of the Gran Comision, member of the First Government Committee; *Governor of Tamaulipas*, 1957–63. e-None. f-Director General of the National Institute for the Protection of Infants, 1970–72; Ambassador to Italy, 1972–76. g-Delegate to the 10th National Student Congress, 1933; Delegate to the Student University Federation, 1933–34; President of the Student Association of the National School of Medicine, 1933–34. h-Practicing physician. i-Political mentor of *Emilio Martinez Manatou*, with whom he practiced medicine. j-None. k-None. l-Hayner, 211; Sebastian Mayo, 70; Ind. Biog., 102; HA, 21 June 1976, 20; Morton, 67; HA, 8 Dec. 1958, 42; HA, 23 Oct. 1972, 21.

Trigo (Cortinez), Octavio Marciano

(Deceased Dec. 1, 1973)

a-Nov. 2, 1885. b-Veracruz, Veracruz, *Gulf*, *Urban*. c-Primary and secondary studies in Veracruz, Veracruz; preparatory studies at the School of Law, Jalapa; law degree, School of Law, Jalapa, Veracruz; Professor of Law, National School of Law, UNAM. d-Federal Deputy from the State of Chihuahua, 1915. e-None. f-Agent of the Ministerio Publico of the Attorney General of Mexico, Judge of the Superior Tribunal of Justice, and Public Defender, each in the states of Chihuahua and Coahuila; District Court Judge; Secretary General of Veracruz, 1911; Interim Governor of Chihuahua; *Justice of the Supreme Court*, 1936–40. g-None. h-Author of a federal labor law book, 1937. **i**-Married Angelina Gomez. **j**-Fought in the Revolution, 1913; fought with Francisco Murguia; member of Carranza's staff. **k**-Precandidate for Governor of Veracruz, 1937, but was prevented from campaigning after a grave injury suffered in an automobile accident. **l**-Novo35, 216; HA, 10 Dec. 1973, 16; Lopez, 1095.

Truchuello, Jose Maria
(Deceased 1953)
a-Apr. 29, 1880. **b**-Queretaro, Queretaro, *East Central, Urban.* **c**-Early education unknown; law degree, University of Queretaro; Professor of Constitutional Law, School of Law, University of Queretaro. **d**-Governor of Queretaro; Deputy to the Constitutional Convention of Queretaro, 1916–17 from the State of Queretaro; Secretary of the Constitutional Convention. **e**-None. **f**-Syndic to the City Council of Queretaro, Queretaro; public defender, Queretaro; Secretary of the First Civil Judicial District of Queretaro, Queretaro; consulting lawyer to the government of the State of Queretaro; Secretary General of Public Instruction of the State of Queretaro; Justice of the Supreme Court, 1917–18; President of the Superior Tribunal of Justice of the Federal District and Federal Territories; *Justice of the Supreme Court*, 1935–40. **g**-None. **j**-None. **k**-Initiated the idea of dividing the Supreme Court into four divisions. **l**-DP70, 2176; Lopez, 1096.

Trueba Rodriguez, Salvador
b-Toluca, Mexico, *West Central, Urban.* **c**-Early education unknown; law degree, National School of Law, UNAM, 1948. **d**-None. **e**-None. **f**-Private Secretary to the Director General of the National Finance Bank, *Antonio Carrillo Flores*, 1947–50; Director, Office of Liquidation of Credit Institutions, Secretariat of the Treasury, 1950–54; Director of Legal Affairs, National Finance Bank, 1976–77; *Oficial Mayor of the Secretariat of the Treasury*, 1977–80; *Subsecretary of Tax Investigation*, Secretariat of the Treasury, 1980– . **g**-Director General of the National Union of Sugarcane Producers, 1972–74; Director General of the Coordinating Council of Entrepreneurs, 1975–76. **h**-Private practice as a lawyer, 1954–72. **j**-None. **k**-None. **l**-*Excelsior*, 8 Apr. 1980, 23; *Excelsior*, 9 Apr. 1980, 22; HA, 21 Apr. 1980, 21.

Trueba Urbina, Alberto
a-Sept. 19, 1906. **b**-Campeche, Campeche, *Gulf, Urban.* **c**-Preparatory studies at the Instituto Campechano; law degree from the University of the Southeast; Professor of Law, National School of Law, UNAM, 1937–45. **d**-*Federal Deputy* from the State of Campeche, Dist. 1, 1940–43, member of the

First Constitutional Affairs Committee and the Fourth Labor Committee; *Federal Deputy* from the State of Campeche, Dist. 1, 1949–52, member of the Legislative Studies Committee (1st and 2nd years), and the First Labor Committee; *Senator* from the State of Campeche, 1952–55; *Governor of Campeche*, 1955–61. **e**-None. **f**-Civil and Criminal Judge, Merida, Yucatan, 1928–29; Attorney General for Yucatan, 1930; Lawyer, Office of the Attorney General for the Federal District, 1935; Assistant Director, Department of Social Security, Federal District Department, 1936; President of the Federal Board of Conciliation and Arbitration for the Federal District, 1937; Adviser to the Presidency, 1944–45. **g**-Director of the Legal Department, Mexican Federation of Labor, 1944. **h**-Adviser to the Mexican delegation of the United Nations, San Francisco, 1945; author of widely used texts on law. **i**-Son, Jorge, a Professor of Law at UNAM, and co-author with his father of a 1972 book on labor law. **j**-None. **k**-None. **l**-D del S, 1 Dec. 1940, 1; D de Y, 26 June 1937, 1; C de D, 1949–51, 92; G of M, 10–11; WWM45, 118–19; DGF56, 6, 90; Peral, 808; C de D, 1940–42, 21.

Trujillo Garcia, Mario
a-Jan. 21, 1920. **b**-Villahermosa, Tabasco, *Gulf, Urban.* **c**-Primary and secondary studies in Villahermosa; preparatory studies in social science at the National Preparatory School; law degree, National School of Law, UNAM. **d**-*Federal Deputy* from the State of Tabasco, Dist. 1, 1967–70, member of the Petroleum Committee; *Senator* from the State of Tabasco, 1970–71; *Governor of Tabasco*, 1971–77. **e**-Delegate of the CEN of PRI to the State of Mexico and Guerrero; President of PRI in Guerrero; official of CNOP. **f**-Managing Director of the Santa Rosalia Mill; adviser to the State of Tabasco; Director General of Social Welfare, Secretariat of Labor, 1951; Private Secretary to the Secretary of Labor; Director of the National Sugar Industry Commission, 1978– . **g**-None. **i**-Related to *Francisco Trujillo Gurria*, Governor of Tabasco, 1939–43. **j**-None. **k**-None. **l**-*Excelsior*, 11 Oct. 1978, 22; HA, 6 Sept. 1971; C de D, 1967–70, 82; DGF51, I, 400.

Trujillo Gurria, Francisco
(Deceased)
a-1900. **b**-Villahermosa, Tabasco, *Gulf, Urban.* **c**-Secondary education in Mexico, D.F.; law degree. **d**-Federal Deputy from the State of Tabasco, 1928–30; *Senator* from the State of Tabasco, 1934–39; *Governor of Tabasco*, 1939–43. **e**-None. **f**-Subsecretary of Government of the State of Tabasco; Secretary of Government of the State of Tabasco; *Secretary of Labor*, Mar. 1, 1943 to Nov.

30, 1946. **g-**None. **h-**Special diplomatic mission to Europe for *Lazaro Cardenas*. **i-**Relative of *Ernesto E. Trujillo Gurria*, federal deputy from Tabasco, 1943–46; became friend of *Manuel Avila Camacho* when he was zone commander of Tabasco, 1932–33; cousin of *Alfonso Gutierrez Gurria*, Senator from Tabasco, 1940–46. **j-**Member of the Constitutional Forces. **k-**None. **l-**HA, 12 Mar. 1943, 11; WWM45, 119; letter; Enc. Mex., V, 45; Peral, 808–09; NYT, 3 Mar. 1943, 4; Lopez, 1097.

Ugarte, Gerzayn
(Deceased July 31, 1955)
a-January 13, 1881. **b-**Terrenate, Tlaxcala, *East Central*, *Rural*. **c-**Primary studies in Huamantla, Tlaxcala; preparatory studies at the University of Puebla, Puebla; school teacher. **d-**Federal Deputy from the State of Tlaxcala, Dist. 2, 1914–16; Local Deputy to the State Legislature of Tlaxcala, 1908; Deputy to the Constitutional Convention from the Federal District, Dist. 3, 1916–18; Senator from the State of Tlaxcala, 1918–20; Senator from the State of Tlaxcala, 1920–24; *Senator* from the State of Tlaxcala, 1946–52, member of the Foreign and Domestic Trade Committee, the Gran Comision, the First National Defense Committee, the First Instructive Section of the Grand Jury and the First Balloting Group. **e-**Supported General Bernardo Reyes for Vice President of Mexico; member of the Antireelectionist Party; campaigned for Francisco Madero. **f-**Private Secretary to Prospero Cahuantzi, Governor of Tlaxcala; Minister to Venezuela, Colombia and Ecuador, 1918–20; Subdirector of Inspectors, Traffic Department, Federal Highway Police, 1935–40; Director of the Department of Traffic, Federal Highway Police, 1940–46, 1952–55. **g-**None. **h-**Director of *El Liberal* with Venustiano Carranza. **j-**Member of the Staff of Venustiano Carranza, 1914–15; rank of First Captain, 1915. **k-**Representative of General Arnulfo Gomez in the United States, 1927; representative of General Gonzalo Escobar in the United States, 1929; had to leave school to work in the textile factories of Puebla and Tlaxcala. **l-**DGF51, I, 8–14; C de S, 1946–52; DP70, 320; PS, 6098.

Ulloa Ortiz, Manuel
(Deceased May 30, 1975)
c-Combined secondary and preparatory studies at the National Preparatory School, 1924–28; law degree, National School of Law, UNAM, 1928–32; Professor, National School of Law, UNAM, 1934–69. **d-**None. **e-**Member of the CEN of PAN, 1939–49; author of numerous pamphlets for PAN. **f-**None. **g-**Founder of the National Union of Catholic Students, 1931. **h-**Subdirector General of the Bank of Mexico and London. **i-**Son of lawyer Manuel G. Ulloa; greatly influenced by *Manuel Gomez Morin*, his

law school professor; among his students was *Jose Gonzalez Torres*, President of PAN, 1958–62. **j-**None. **k-**None. **l-**Letter; Mabry.

Urbina y Frias, Salvador
(Deceased Sept. 12, 1961)
a-June 4, 1885. **b-**Federal District, *Federal District*, *Urban*. **c-**Primary studies at a private school and public school No. 5, Mexico City; secondary studies, Colegio de Joaquin Norena; preparatory studies, National Preparatory School; law degree, National School of Law, UNAM, 1902–07, with a thesis on the conflict of administrative laws in international law; Professor of Political Economy, National School of Law, UNAM, 1912; Professor of Civil Proceedings, National School of Law, UNAM. **d-***Senator* from the Federal District, 1952–58. **e-**None. **f-**Agent of the Ministerio Publico of the District Court of Durango, 1909; Oficial Mayor of the Supreme Court of Mexico, 1910–12; First Agent of the Ministerio Publico, 1913; First Agent of the Ministerio Publico, Office of the Attorney General of Mexico, 1914; Presidential negotiator to Carranza, 1914; Director of the Advisory Department, Secretariat of the Treasury, 1915–16; Oficial Mayor of the Secretariat of the Treasury; Attorney General of Mexico; Justice of the Supreme Court of Mexico, 1923–35; President of the Supreme Court, 1929–34; Subsecretary of the Treasury, 1922, Interim Secretary of the Treasury, 1922; *Justice of the Supreme Court*, 1940; *President of the Supreme Court*, 1941–46, 1946–51; Director of the National Lottery, 1958. **g-**None. **h-**Delegate to the Pan American Conference, 1928; private law practice, 1914–15, 1935–40; founder and principal author of *Mexican Petroleum Review*, 1915. **i-**Son of a doctor; married Leticia Bolland. **j-**None. **k-**Gruening considered him completely honest as a public official in the 1920s. **l-**Gruening, 504; WWM45, 119; DGF56, 6; Peral, 811; EBW46, 411; DGF47, 29–30; DP70, 2201; HA, 14 Dec. 1951, 6; Ind. Biog., 160–61; Enc. Mex., XII, 1977, 277.

Urquizo (Benavides), Francisco L.
(Deceased Apr. 6, 1969)
a-Oct. 4, 1891. **b-**San Pedro de las Colonias, Coahuila, *North*, *Urban*. **c-**Primary education in Torreon, Coahuila; secondary education at the Liceo Fournier, Federal District; no degree. **d-**None. **e-**None. **f-**Oficial Mayor of the Secretariat of War; Subsecretary of War (in charge of the ministry), 1920; Director of the Federal Office of the Treasury, Pachuca, Hidalgo; Bureau Director, Secretariat of the Treasury, 1930–34; Chief of Staff, Secretariat of National Defense; *Subsecretary of National Defense*, 1940–45; *Secretary of National Defense*, 1945–46;

Director of the Military Industry Department, 1952–58. **g-**None. **h-**Author of many books and articles on the history of the Revolution. **i-**Parents were campesinos; he was forced into the Federal Army for disobeying the hacendado; friend of *Matias Ramos Santos* and *Marcelino Garcia Barragan*. **j-**2nd Lieutenant in the Federal Army, 1911; joined Madero, 1913; Brigadier General, 1920; Chief of Military Operations in Veracruz, 1918; Military Zone Commander, 1938–40; member of the Presidential Council for National Defense, 1959–69. **k-**Retired from the Army but later rejoined, reaching the rank of Divisionary General. **l-**WWM45, 119; DBM68, 612; DGF56, 529; *Hoy*, 19 Apr. 1969, 8; DP70, 1104–05; STYRBIWW54, 299; Peral, 814; Strode, 261; EBW46, 1148; *Siempre*, 4 Feb. 1959, 6; Enc. Mex., XII, 1977, 279–80.

Uruchurtu, Ernesto Peralta

a-Feb. 28, 1906. **b-**Hermosillo, Sonora, *North, Urban*. **c-**Primary studies in Alamos, and Hermosillo, Sonora; secondary studies at the Escuela Normal, Hermosillo; law studies, National School of Law, UNAM, 1925–29, degree in 1931. **d-**None. **e-**Auxiliary Subsecretary during the *Aleman* presidential campaign; *Secretary General of the CEN of PRI*, 1946; first party position, 1937; State Chairman of the Regional Committee of PRI, Sonora. **f-**Justice of the State Supreme Court of Sonora under Governor Yocupicio; Judge, State Court, Nogales, Sonora; agent of the Ministerio Publico of the State of Sonora; adviser, Department of Legal Affairs, Secretariat of Agriculture and Livestock; legal adviser to the National Bank of Ejido Credit; Director, Department of Legal Affairs, Secretariat of Agriculture; Director of the Legal Department, National Bank of Ejido Credit, 1940–46; *Subsecretary of Government*, 1946–51; *Secretary of Government*, Oct. 14, 1951–52; *Head of the Federal District*, 1952–58, 1958–64, 1964–66. **g-**None. **h-**Practicing lawyer, Ciudad Obregon, 1937; practicing lawyer, 1967–70. **i-**Son of Dr. *Gustavo A. Uruchurtu*, Senator from Sonora, 1946–52; attended UNAM with *Miguel Aleman, Antonio Carrillo Flores, Andres Serra Rojas*, and *Alfonso Noriega*. **j-**None. **k-**Precandidate for the PRI presidential nomination, 1958, but considered too close to the right wing; precandidate for Governor of Sonora, 1972; resigned from Head of the Federal District in the midst of an anti-corruption campaign after the mishandling of a squatter's affair; precandidate for Governor of Sonora, 1978. **l-**D del S, 6 Dec. 1946; HA, 15 Feb. 1952, 3; *Quien Sera*, 136–37; Morton, 63; Q es Q, 592; HA, 7 Dec. 1964, 21; DGF56, 465; HA, 8 Dec. 1958, 30; HA, 2 Nov. 1964, 30; WWMG, 39–40; *Excelsior*, 23 Nov. 1977, 18; HA, 16 Aug. 1946; NYT, 28 July, 1957, 2, Scott, 78.

Uruchurtu, Gustavo A.

b-Hermosillo, Sonora, *Urban, North*. **c-**Medical degree (Surgeon), National School of Medicine, UNAM. **d-**Federal Deputy from the State of Sonora, 1928–30; *Senator* from the State of Sonora, 1946–52. **e-**None. **f-**Director of Hygenic Education, Secretariat of Public Education; Director of the Department of Disinfection; Secretariat of Health and Welfare. **g-**None. **h-**Author of numerous articles on medical subjects; specialist in urology; internship at the General Hospital, Mexico, D.F. **i-**Father of *Ernesto P. Uruchurtu*, Head of the Department of the Federal District, 1952–66. **j-**None. **k-**None. **l-**C de S, 1946–52; Peral, 814; Lopez, 1105.

Urzua Flores, Maria Guadalupe

a-Dec. 12, 1922. **b-**San Martin Hidalgo, Jocotepec, Jalisco, *West, Rural*. **c-**Primary studies at the Josefa Ortiz de Dominguez School, San Martin Hidalgo; secondary studies in Guadalajara, Jalisco; studies at the Pedro J. Vizcarra School of Commerce and Accounting, Guadalajara, Jalisco (3 years). **d-**Councilman of San Martin Hidalgo, 1953–55; *Federal Deputy* from the State of Jalisco, Dist. 11, 1955–58, member of the Second Government Committee and the Second Balloting Committee; *Federal Deputy* from the State of Jalisco, Dist. 10, 1964–67, member of the Public Assistance Committee and the National Lands Committee; *Federal Deputy* from the State of Jalisco, Dist. 9, 1970–73, member of the First Ejido Committee, the Small Agricultural Properties Committee, and the National Lands Committee. **e-**Secretary of Women's Action for PRI, San Martin Hidalgo, 1948–50; *Federal Deputy* from the State of Jalisco, Dist. 9, 1976–79. **f-**Ejido Commissioner for San Martin Hidalgo, Jalisco; Secretary of the Civic and Moral Improvement Board, San Martin Hidalgo, 1949–52; Solicitor for the Department of Plaints, Office of Agrarian Affairs, Secretariat of the Presidency. **g-**Secretary of Women's Action, Peasants Committee, San Martin Hidalgo; Secretary of Women's Action, League of Agrarian Communities and Peasants, Jalisco, 1938, 1953; Secretary of Feminine Action, CEN of the CNC, 1953–56, 1964–67. **h-**None. **j-**None. **l-**Directorio, 1970–72; C de D, 1955–57; C de D, 1970–72, 139; C de D, 1964–66, 78, 94; DGF56, 25, 34, 35; C de D, 1976–79, 80; Ind. Biog., 161–62.

Uscanga Uscanga, Cesar

b-Ignacio de la Llave, Veracruz, *Gulf, Rural*. **c-**Secondary studies at Secondary School No. 3, Mexico City; preparatory studies at the National Preparatory School; chemical engineering degree, National School of Biological Sciences; teacher at the Rafael Donde School; Director of the Rafael Donde School. **d-**None. **e-**None. **f-**Director of Technical,

Industrial, and Commercial Schools, Secretariat of Public Education; Subdirector of Technical, Industrial, and Foreign Schools, Secretariat of Public Education; Director of Technological and Industrial Education, Secretariat of Public Education, 1970–74; *Subsecretary of Intermediate, Technical, and Higher Education*, Mar. 15, 1974 to 1976; *Subsecretary of Technical Education*, 1977; Adviser to the Secretary of Public Education, 1977– . **g-**None. **j-**None. **k-**None. **l-**HA, 25 Mar. 1974, 10; DPE71, 106; DAPC, 1977, 71; *Excelsior*, 16 June 1976, 4.

Valades, Jose C.
(Deceased 1976)
a-Dec. 10, 1902. **b-**Mazatlan, Sinaloa, *West*, *Urban*. **c-**Early education unknown; preparatory studies at the University of Guadalajara and the Free Preparatory School, Mexico City; studies at Saint Vincent College, Los Angeles, California; studies at the National Homeopathic College, Mexico City; no degree; Professor of History, UNAM, 1941–45. **d-**None. **e-**Secretary of the Latin American Bureau of the Third Communist International, 1922; supported Jose Vasconcelos for president, 1929; Secretary General of the Federation of the Peoples Parties, 1946. **f-**Private Secretary to the Secretary of Foreign Relations, *Ezequiel Padilla*, 1940–42; Ambassador to Colombia, 1953–56; Ambassador to Uruguay, 1956–57; Ambassador to Portugal, 1963–66. **g-**Founder and director of the World Youth Organization, 1920; organizer of the Communist Youth Organization; Secretary General of a labor union, 1921. **h-**Author of dozens of books; Director of *El Correo de Occidente*, Mazatlan, 1942–45. **i-**Father a successful pharmacist; grandfather was a weathly businessman; members of his father's family were actively involved in Sinaloan politics. **j-**None. **k-**Skirius, 205; WWM45, 120; Enc. Mex., XII, 1977, 290–91.

Valadez Montoya, Miguel Jose
a-Mar. 22, 1949. **b-**Aguascalientes, Aguascalientes, *West*, *Urban*. **c-**Primary and secondary studies in Aguascalientes; preparatory studies in Aguascalientes; law degree, National School of Law, UNAM, August 1, 1976; Professor of Law, Carlos Septien Garcia School of Journalism. **d-**None. **e-**Secretary of Labor Action of the Mexican Democratic Party, 1979. **f-**Lawyer, Legal Department, Secretary of Communications and Transportation, 1979. **g-**None. **h-**None. **j-**None. **k-**None. **l-**HA, 12 Feb. 1979, 23.

Valdes, Jose Ramon
a-Aug. 31, 1888. **b-**Santiago Pasquiaro, Durango, *West*, *Rural*. **c-**Primary and secondary studies in Durango; no degree. **d-**Federal Deputy from the State of Durango, Dist. 1, 1928–30; Substitute Governor of Durango, 1930–31; Federal Deputy from the State of Durango, Dist. 5, 1930–32, member of the Gran Comision; *Substitute Governor of Durango*, 1947–50. **e-**None. **f-**Inspector of Police, Durango; Oficial Mayor of the Federal Auditor's Office, Secretariat of the Treasury; Oficial Mayor of the Chamber of Deputies. **g-**None. **h-**None. **j-**Commander of military forces in Durango; rank of Colonel. **k-**None. **l-**HA, 6 Feb. 1948, 8; Peral, 820; Lopez, 1109.

Valdez Montoya, Alfredo
a-1921. **b-**Ahome, Sinaloa, *West*, *Rural*. **c-**Early education unknown; studies in economics, National School of Economics, UNAM; economics degree, School of Economics, University of Guadalajara, 1943. **d-***Governor of Sinaloa*, 1969–74. **e-**None. **f-**Employee of the Secretariat of Public Education; employee of the Secretariat of the Treasury; Treasurer of the State of Sinaloa, 1968. **g-**None. **i-**Married Judith Gaxiola; related to *Francisco Gaxiola*. **j-**None. **k-**Accused by *Proceso* of representing large landowners' interests in Sinaloa as governor. **l-***Proceso*, 7 Aug. 1978, 12; DNED, 255.

Valencia Moguel, Orlando
a-Oct. 28, 1928. **b-**Merida, Yucatan, *Gulf*, *Urban*. **c-**Primary studies, Escuela Nicolas Bravo; secondary studies, Colegio Americano; preparatory studies, Escuela Preparatory of the University of Yucatan; medical degree from the University of Yucatan, Feb. 1, 1954; Professor of Technical Operations, School of Odontology, University of Yucatan. **d-***Federal Deputy* from the State of Yucatan, Dist. 1, 1970–73; member of the Auto Transportation Committee, the Naval Committee, and the Second General Means of Communication Commitee. **e-**Secretary General of the State Delegation of the CNOP of PRI, Yucatan. **f-**Director of pre-hospital services, Hospital O'Horan, Merida, 1959–62. **g-**Secretary of Acts and Agreements, IMSS Union, 1961–62; Secretary of Social Welfare of the IMSS Union, 1962–65; representative of the Executive Committee of the IMSS Workers. **h-**Rural Doctor, Hecelchacan, Campeche, 1954–59; Red Cross physician, 1955–57. **j-**None. **k-**None. **l-**Q es QY, 249–50; *Directorio*, 1970–72; C de D, 1970–72, 139.

Valenzuela (Esquerro), Gilberto
a-1922. **b-**Federal District, *Federal District*, *Urban*. **c-**Engineering degree, National University of Mexico, 1947. **d-**None. **e-**None. **f-**Director, Office of Paving, Secretariat of Public Works, 1952–55; Subdirector of the Department of Construction, Secretariat of Public Works, 1955–58; Subdirector General of Public Works, Department of the Federal District, 1958–59; Director General of Public Works,

Department of the Federal District, 1959–64; *Secretary of Public Works,* 1964–70; *Secretary of Works and Services*, Department of the Federal District, 1978–79. g-None. h-Consulting engineer for Ford, Bacon, and Davis; private engineering practice; engineer for National Railroads of Mexico; consulting engineer to the Department of Public Works, 1953. i-Student of *Antonio Dovali Jaime* at the National School of Engineering and later worked with him in several positions; brother of Raul Valenzuela Esquerro, Subdirector General of the Consular Service, Secretariat of Foreign Relations, 1967; son of *Gilberto Valenzuela*, Secretary of Government, 1923–25 and Justice of the Supreme Court, 1953–60. j-None. k-None. l-HA, 7 Dec. 1964, 19; DGF56, 467; *Hoy*, 12 July 1969, 10; DBM68, 615; WWMG, 40; *El Universal*, 1 Dec. 1964; *Libro de Oro*, xxxiv; D de Y, 2 Dec. 1964, 2; HA, 5 Dec. 1977, 31; HA, 9 Jan. 1978, 25; *Excelsior*, 10 Feb. 1978, 5.

Valles Vivar, Tomas

a-Oct. 31, 1900. b-Camargo, Chihuahua, *North, Rural*. c-Primary studies in Camargo; secondary studies in Camargo; no degree. d-*Federal Deputy* from the State of Chihuahua, Dist. 1, 1943–46; *Senator* from the State of Chihuahua, 1958–64, member of the First Credit, Money, and Credit Institutions Committee, the First Tariffs and Foreign Trade Committee, President of the First Mines Committee and the Special Livestock Committee. e-None. f-Treasurer of the National Railroads of Mexico; *Director General of CONASUPO*, 1952–56. g-None. h-Businessman in Camargo; livestock dealer. j-None. k-Resigned from CONASUPO because of internal policy disputes on imports and food prices, March 10, 1956. l-Func. 163; C de S, 1961–64, 71–72; D de Y, 6 Dec. 1952, 1; NYT, 11 Mar. 1956, 24.

Valner Onjas, Gregorio

a-June 26, 1929. b-Toluca, Mexico, *East Central, Urban*. c-Primary studies in Toluca; medical degree, National School of Medicine, UNAM, 1954; postgraduate studies in psychiatry and psychoanalysis, Mexican Psychoanalytical Association; Professor of Psychoanalysis, UNAM; Professor of Psychoanalysis, Mexican Association of Psychotherapy. d-None. e-Joined PRI as a member of the IEPES, 1970; member of the Advisory Council of the CEPES of the State of Mexico; Coordinator of Advisers to the IEPES in public housing; Director of the CEPES of the Federal District during *Jose Lopez Portillo's* presidential campaign, 1975–76. f-President of the Regulatory Commission on Land Tenure, State of Mexico, 1970–75; *Subsecretary of Public Housing*. 1976–. g-Founding Director General of the Institute of Urban Action and Social Inte-

gration, State of Mexico, 1970. h-Practicing physician, Benito Juarez General Hospital, Mexico City; physician, Central Military Hospital; physician, National Institute of Nutrition; intern, National Institute of Cardiology and Michael Reese Hospital, Chicago. j-None. k-None. l-Letter; DAPC, 72.

Varela Mayorga, Juan. J.

a-May 1, 1915. b-Huejucar, Jalisco, *West, Rural*. c-Primary studies at the Zaragoza School, Zacatecas, Zacatecas; secondary studies at the Institute of Sciences, Zacatecas (3 years); preparatory studies at the National Preparatory School, Federal District (2 years); studies at the National School of Law, UNAM; no degree. d-Council member in Leon, Guanajuato, 1952–54; local deputy to the State Legislature of Guanajuato; *Federal Deputy* from the State of Guanajuato, Dist. 4, 1964–67; *Federal Deputy* from the State of Guanajuato, Dist. 6, 1970–73, member of the Second Public Education Committee and the Plaints Committee (1st year); *Federal Deputy* from the State of Guanajuato, Dist. 3, 1976–79, member of the Second Labor Committee, the Complaints Committee, the Pension Subcommittee and the Cooperatives Development Commitee. e-None. f-General Inspector of Alcohol, Industry, and Commerce, State of Guanajuato. g-Secretary General of the CTM in Guanajuato; Secretary General of Section 12 of the Union of Cement Workers; secretary to the Secretary General of the Cement Workers Union. h-Technician for Portland Cement. i-Married Olga Flores. j-None. k-None. l-C de D, 1970–72, 139; C de D, 1964–66; *Directorio*, 1970–72; C de D, 1976–79, 81; *Excelsior*, 31 Aug. 1976, C1.

Vargas Bravo, David

a-Jan. 2, 1913. b-San Luis Potosi, San Luis Potosi, *East Central, Urban*. c-Primary education in Mexico City; secondary studies at the Felipe Carrillo Puerto Night School, Mexico City; preparatory studies at the National Preparatory School in social sciences; law degree, National School of Law, UNAM, 1953. d-*Senator* from the State of San Luis Potosi, 1952–58, President of the Second Labor Committee, member of the First Instructive Section of the Grand Jury; First Secretary of the Electrical Industry Committee and Second Secretary of the Railroad Committee. e-None. f-Director, Electrical Department, National Railroads of Mexico; Director of Real Property, National Railroads of Mexico; Director of the Legal Department, National Railroads of Mexico; Assistant to the Controller General, National Railroads of Mexico; Subdirector and Director of Finances, National Railroads of Mexico; General Attorney for the National Railroads. g-Co-founder of the National Railroad Workers Union (later the STFRM), 1931; Secretary of Local 16 of the

STFRM; general representative of the STFRM, 1938; representative of labor on the Federal Board of Arbitration and Conciliation, 1948; Secretary General of the STFRM, 1951–54. h-Began working for the National Railroads of Mexico as a laborer, 1927; later an electrician. i-Active in the Unified Socialist Action group with *Valentin Campa*. j-None. k-Forced into exile, 1954–58, for union political activities. l-Proceso, 18 Dec. 1976, 18–19; HA, 1 Feb, 1954, 6–7; Ind. Biog., 163; DGF56, 7, 9, 11, 13.

Vargas de Montemayor, Carlota

a-Feb. 8, 1943. b-Nuevo Leon, *North*. c-Early education unknown; economics degree, University of Nuevo Leon; post graduate work in London; Professor of Economics and Macro Economics, University of Veracruz. d-*Federal Deputy* from the State of Nuevo Leon, Dist. 1, 1976–79. e-None. f-Director of the Department of Economic Studies, State of Nuevo Leon; Oficial Mayor of the State Government of Nuevo Leon. g-None. h-Author of various articles on urban planning. j-None. k-None. l-*Excelsior*, 27 Aug. 1976, 1C; C de D, 1976–79.

Vasconcelos, Eduardo

(Deceased Apr. 26, 1953)
a-Oct. 11, 1895. b-Oaxaca, Oaxaca, *South*, *Urban*. c-Primary studies in Oaxaca; secondary and preparatory studies at the Instituto of Arts and Sciences of Oaxaca; law degree from the National School of Law, UNAM, 1910 with a thesis on Article 123; professor at the Preparatory School of Chilpancingo, Guerrero; professor at the Institute of Arts and Sciences of Oaxaca, professor at Institute of Sciences and Letters, Toluca, Mexico. d-Local deputy to the State Legislature of Oaxaca; Federal Deputy from the State of Oaxaca, Dist. 1, 1920–22, 1922–24, President of the Chamber of Deputies, 1921. e-Founder of the Socialist Student Party, 1912. f-Secretary of Government, Baja California del Norte, 1917; Secretary General of Government of the State of Mexico, 1926; Attorney General of Guerrero, 1925–26; Legal Adviser to the cities of Chilpancingo, Cuernavaca and Toluca; *Justice of the Supreme Court,* 1940–46, 1947; Minister to Italy, 1935–36; Oficial Mayor of the Secretariat of Government, 1930–32; Secretary of Government, 1932–34; Secretary of Public Education, May 9, 1934, to Nov. 30, 1934; *Interim Governor of Oaxaca*, 1947–50. g-None. h-None. i-Nephew of Jose Vasconcelos, Secretary of Education, 1920–23. j-Joined the Revolution under General Mosta in Sinaloa, 1915; fought under General Benjamin Hill, 1919. k-None. l-Gaxiola 90, etc.; Hayner, 214; Enc. Mex., 42; STYRBIWW54, 1070; Peral, 832–33; Lopez, 1123.

Vazquez, (Osequerra) Gabino

a-1889. b-Morelia, Michoacan, *West Central*, *Urban*. c-Preparatory studies at the Colegio de San Nicolas, Morelia; law degree, Colegio de San Nicolas, 1924–29; Rector of the Colegio de San Nicolas. d-Federal Deputy from the State of Michoacan, Dist. 1, 1932–34; *Federal Deputy* from Michoacan, Dist. 5, 1964–67. e-Member of the National Committee for *Lazaro Cardenas'* presidential campaign, 1933–34; Secretary General of the PNR, 1934. f-Judge of the Superior Court of the State of Michoacan; Provisional Governor of Michoacan, 1930–31; Secretary General of Government of the State of Michoacan, 1930–32; Attorney General of Michoacan; personal representative of General *Cardenas* to the committee writing the 1934 Agrarian Code; *Head of the Department of Colonization and Agrarian Affairs*, 1934–40. g-None. i-Married Consuelo Alfano; co-student at the Colegio de San Nicolas with *Alberto Bremauntz* and *Jose Maria Mendoza Pardo*. j-None. k-None. l-Peral, 47, 48; Kirk, 3, 118; Gaxiola, 448; Peral, 834; Lopez, 1127; Bremauntz, 93; Meyer, 227.

Vazquez, Genaro V.

(Deceased May 6, 1967)
a-1892. b-Oaxaca, Oaxaca, *South*, *Urban*. c-Secondary studies, Institute of Arts and Sciences of Oaxaca; law degree, National School of Law, UNAM. d-Federal Deputy from the State of Oaxaca, 1920–22; Senator from the State of Oaxaca; Governor of Oaxaca, Dec. 1, 1928 to Nov. 30, 1932. e-Secretary General of the PNR, 1930; General Delegate of the PNR to the State of Oaxaca, 1930. f-Director of the Consultation Department, Secretariat of Government; Secretary General of the Department of the Federal District; *Secretary of Labor*, 1935–37; *Attorney General of Mexico*, 1937–40; *Justice of the Supreme Court*, 1935 and 1952. g-None. h-Author of legislation for Indian groups in Mexico. i-Son, *Pedro Vazquez C*. j-None. k-Precandidate for Governor of Oaxaca, 1939; founder of the Department of Indigenous Affairs; political enemy of Col. *Constatino Chapital*, governor of Oaxaca, 1936–40. l-D del S, 21 June 1937; DP70, 2230; Peral, 835; D de Y, 22 June 1937, 2; Lopez, 1128.

Vazquez Colmenares, Pedro

a-Nov. 2, 1934. b-Tuxtepec, Oaxaca, *South*, *Rural*. c-Law degree, National School of Law, UNAM, 1960; Professor of Sociology, National Preparatory School, Mexico, D.F., 1959–65; Professor by opposition in penal law and sociology, National School of Law, UNAM. d-*Governor of Oaxaca*, 1980– . e-Subdirector of Youth Action, Regional Executive Committee of PRI for the Federal District, 1955;

Oficial Mayor of PRI in the Federal District, 1975–76. f-Private Secretary to the Governor of Baja California del Sur, *Hugo Cervantes del Rio*, 1965–70; Private Secretary to the Secretary of the Presidency, *Hugo Cervantes del Rio*, 1970–71; *Oficial Mayor of the Secretariat of the Presidency*, 1971–73; Director General of Airports, 1973–74; *Subsecretary of New Population Centers*, *Secretariat of Agrarian Reform*, 1976; Director General of Aero Mexico, 1977–80. g-President of the National Federation of University Students, 1956; President of the National Association of Law Students, 1957. h-Member of the National Association of Lawyers since 1964; directed conferences at the Schools of Law in Guatemala and El Salvador. i-Father, *Genaro Vazquez*; brother, *Genaro Vazquez Colmenares*, served as a Federal Deputy from Oaxaca, 1961–63. j-None. k-Lost as a precandidate for Governor of Oaxaca, 1974; lost as a precandidate for senator from Oaxaca, 1976. l-HA, 1 Nov. 1971, 5; *Tiempo Mexicano*, 56; *Excelsior*, 16 Oct. 1975, 12; HA, 5 Dec. 1977, 30; HA, 12 Apr. 1976, 32; *Excelsior*, 29 Jan. 1974, 13; HA, 19 Apr. 1980, 32.

Vazquez del Mercado, Antonio

a-Nov. 2, 1903. b-Federal Disrict, *Federal District*, *Urban*. c-Primary studies in Puebla, Puebla; enrolled in the Naval Academy, Apr. 8, 1917; Director of the Naval College, 1941. d-None. e-Vice President of PARM, 1977–79. f-Gerente of the Navy Department, Petroleos Mexicanos, S.A.; Secretary General of the Department of the Navy, 1940–41; Naval Attache to Washington, D.C. 1948; Director General of Fishing and Related Industries, Secretariat of Industry and Commerce, 1960–64; *Secretary of the Navy*, 1964–70. g-None. h-None. j-Career naval officer; rank of navy lieutenant, 1928; commander of the coastguard ship Guaymas, 1928; commander of the naval garrison, Islas Marias, 1929; Director General of the Merchant Marine, 1947–48; Commander of the 4th Naval Zone; rank of admiral, 1956; Commander of the Fleet, 1956; rank of Rear Admiral. k-Precandidate of PARM for federal deputy, 1978. l-WWMG, 40; DGF56, 386; HA, 7 Dec. 1964, 18; D de Y, 2 Dec. 1964, 2; DPE61, 65; *Excelsior*, 2 July 1977, 15; HA, 16 Apr. 1979, I.

Vazquez Pallares, Natalio

a-Jan. 5, 1913. b-Coalcoman, Michoacan, *West Central*, *Rural*. c-Preparatory studies at the Colegio de San Nicolas de Hidalgo, Morelia, Michoacan; studies in law, University of Guadalajara; law degree from the School of Law, University of Michoacan; Rector of the University of Michoacan, 1939. d-*Federal Deputy* from the State of Michoacan, Dist. 8, 1949–52, member of the Editorial Committee, the Legislative Studies Committee, the Petroleum Com-

mittee, and the Second Constitutional Affairs Committee; Secretary of the Second Constitutional Affairs Committee (2nd year); *Senator* from the State of Michoacan, 1958–64, member of the Gran Comision, the National Lands Committee, the Special Legislative Studies Committee, and the Lands and Natural Resources Committee; substitute member of the First Labor Committee; President of the Agriculture and Development Committee and the Second Ejido Committee. e-None. f-Various judgeships in the state of Michoacan; private secretary to the Governor of Michoacan; Attorney General of Michoacan; Ambassador to Yugoslavia, 1965; agrarian adviser No. 4, Department of Agrarian Affairs and Colonization, 1970–72; Subdirector General of the National Fund for Ejido Development, 1973–75. g-Leader of the Federation of Socialist Students of the West; director of Unified Socialist Youth of Mexico. i-None. k-Supported *Cuauhtemoc Cardenas* for Governor of Michoacan, 1973; precandidate for Governor of Michoacan, 1962. l-Func., 267; C de S, 1961–64, 72; C de D, 1949–51, 93; DGF51, 23, 32, 35; DPE65, 32; DPE71, 130; NYT, 20 May 1962, 30; DBM68, 618; *Excelsior*, 30 Oct. 1973, 12; Enc. Mex., XII, 310.

Vazquez Perez, Francisco

a-Apr. 25, 1904. b-Chilpancingo, Guerrero, *South*, *Urban*. c-Early education unknown; law degree, Free School of Law, 1922, with an honorable mention. d-None. e-None. f-President of the Committee to Revise the Health Code, 1933; Director, Legal Services Department, Department of Health, 1931–34; *Oficial Mayor of the Department of Agrarian Affairs*, 1935; Oficial Mayor of the Department of Indigenous Assistance, 1937; President of the Committee on the Organization of Territorial Properties, 1935–39; Secretary, Federal Electoral Commission, 1960. g-None. i-Son of General Francisco Vazquez de Hurtado; married Magdalena Fernandez Diaz. j-None. k-None. l-WNM, 232–33.

Vazquez Ramirez, Celso

a-July 28, 1913. b-Tlacotalpan, Veracruz, *Gulf*, *Rural*. c-Primary studies in Tlacotalpan; secondary studies in Alvarado, Veracruz; preparatory studies in Veracruz; graduated from the National Military College. d-*Federal Deputy* from the State of Veracruz, Dist. 11, 1958–61, member of the Forest Affairs Committee, the First National Defense Committee, the War Materiels Committee, the Social Welfare Committee and the Complaints Committee; *Federal Deputy* from the State of Veracruz, Dist. 13, 1967–70, member of the Internal Trade Committee, the First National Defense Committee, the Military Industry Committee, the Foreign Relations Committee and the Military Justice Committee. e-None.

f-Officer, Presidential Staff, 1946–52. g-President of the student society at his preparatory school. h-None. i-Married Carmen Enrique. j-Career army officer; rank of Colonel. k-None. l-Func., 398; PS; C de D, 1958–61, 94; C de D, 1967–70, 61, 75, 80, 86.

Vazquez Rojas, Genaro
(Deceased Feb. 2, 1972)
a-June 10, 1931. b-San Luis Acatlan, Guerrero, *South*, *Rural*. c-Primary studies in Guerrero; primary teaching certificate from the National Teachers School, 1950; preparatory studies in law at the National Preparatory School. d-None. e-Organizer of the political organization known as the Comite Civico Guerrerense, which rallied support in opposition to the government of General *Caballero Aburto* in Guerrero, 1960–61; head of various guerrilla groups in the State of Guerrero, 1968–72. f-School teacher at School No. 5, Federal District, 1957; left teaching because of political activities, 1960. g-Student leader at the National Teachers School; delegate of the Independent Peasant Federation (CCI) to Guerrero, 1961. h-None. i-Son of peasants; married to Consuelo Solis, a teacher. j-None. k-The Comite Civico Guerrerense helped students to organize strikes against the state government in Guerrero, 1961, which eventually forced the Federal Government to remove *Caballero Aburto* as Governor; captured at MLN headquarters in Mexico, D.F., 1967, and imprisoned in Iguala until 1968, when he escaped in April after his group attacked the prison; responsible for the much publicized kidnapping of the Rector of the University of Guerrero, *Jaime Castrejon Diaz*; died in the Public Hospital of Morelia from head fractures as a result of an automobile accident; his supporters and some critics of the Mexican government maintain he was killed by the army. l-HA, 14 Feb. 1972, 14–15.

Vazquez Torres, Ignacio
a-Aug. 13, 1939. b-Penjamo, Guanajuato, *West Central*, *Urban*. c-Early education unknown; law degree, National School of Law, UNAM, August 12, 1961. d-*Federal Deputy* from the State of Guanajuato, Dist. 15, 1967–70, member of the National Properties and Resources Committee, the Budget and Accounts Committee and the General Means of Communication Committee; *Federal Deputy* from the State of Guanajuato, Dist. 8, 1973–76; *Federal Deputy* from the State of Guanajuato, Dist. 7, 1979–82. e-General Delegate of the CEN of PRI to the State of Veracruz, Mexico, Yucatan, Jalisco, Zacatecas, Hidalgo, Nayarit and Puebla. f-Director General of Political and Social Research, Secretariat of Government, 1976–78; *Oficial Mayor of Government*, 1978–79. g-None. j-None. k-None. l-DAPC,

73; C de D, 1973–76; C de D, 1967–70, 60, 83, 90; PS, 6250; *Excelsior*, 8 June 1979, 4, 12.

Vazquez Vela, Gonzalo
(Deceased Sept. 28, 1963)
a-Nov. 7, 1894. b-Jalapa, Veracruz, *Gulf*, *Urban*. c-Primary studies in Veracruz; Preparatory studies at the University of Veracruz, law degree, National School of Law, UNAM. d-*Governor of Veracruz*, 1932–35. e-Member of the League of Professionals and Intellectuals of the PRM. f-Secretary General of Government of the State of Veracruz, 1920–24, under *Adalberto Tejeda*; Oficial Mayor of the Secretariat of Government, 1925–28; *Secretary of Public Education*, June 17, 1935, to Nov. 30, 1940. g-None. h-Advisor to various businesses, the President of Mexico, and the National Mortgage Bank; manager of Aseguradora Mexicana. i-Protege of *Adalberto Tejeda*. j-None. k-None. l-DP64, 1537; DP70, 2234; *Excelsior*, 18 June 1935; Dulles, 629; Gaxiola, 167–68; *Hoy*, 4 Nov. 1939, 18; Michaels, 128; Meyer, 13, 280; Heldt, 226.

Vega Alvarado, Renato
a-Jan. 19, 1937. b-San Miguel de Allende, Guanajuato, *West Central*, *Urban*. c-Primary studies, Alvaro School, Culiacan, Sinaloa; secondary and preparatory studies, University of Sinaloa; agricultural engineering degree, Higher School of Agriculture, Ciudad Juarez, Chihuahua, with a thesis on the cultivation of tomatoes in the Culiacan Valley, 1960. d-*Federal Deputy* from the State of Sinaloa, Dist. 3, 1970 to Sept. 28, 1972, member of the Administrative Committee (2nd year), the Agricultural Committee, the Fourth Ejido Committee, and the Agricultural Development Committee; President of the Chamber of Deputies, 1972. e-Technical adviser in public administration to the CEPES of PRI in Sinaloa; Secretary General of PRI in the Federal District, 1975–76. f-Agent of the National Ejido Credit Bank, Sinaloa; agent of the Agricultural Credit Bank, Jalisco; *Oficial Mayor of the Department of Federal District*, Aug. 9, 1972–75; Director General of Population, Secretariat of Government, 1976–79; Director of Immigration, Secretariat of Government, 1979– . g-Subsecretary of Workers Action of the Central Executive Committee of the Mexican Agronomy Society; President of the Mexican Agronomy Society in Martinez de la Torre, Veracruz, and in Los Mochis, Sinaloa; Secretary General of the Mexican Agronomy Society, Jalisco; member of the CNC. h-Agricultural extension agent, States of Mexico and Jalisco. i-Son of General Renato Vega Amador, former Chief of Police of the Federal District and Director General of Traffic. j-None. k-Precandidate for Governor of Sinaloa, 1974. l-*Directorio*, 1970–

72; HA, 13 Sept. 1971, 10; C de D, 1970–72, 139–40; HA, 21 Aug. 1972, 13; *Excelsior*, 10 Aug. 1972, 10; HA, 9 Oct. 1972, 12; *Excelsior*, 20 Feb. 1974; DAPC, 1977.

Vega Garcia, Antonio

a-Jan. 4, 1909. **b-**Santa Inez Zacatelo, Tlaxcala, *East Central*, *Rural*. **c-**Early education unknown; no degree. **d-***Federal Deputy* from the Federal District, Dist. 3, 1946–49; *Federal Deputy* from the State of Tlaxcala, Dist. 2, 1976–79. **e-**Campaigned in various elections for federal deputy and for senator; delegate from Tlaxcala to the PRI Basic Plan of Government, 1976–82; founder and president of the National Railroads Political Committee of PRI. **f-**None. **g-**Director of the Statistics, STFRM. **j-**None. **k-**None. **l-**C de D, 1946–49; MGF49, 6; *Excelsior,* 3 Sept. 1976, 1C; C de D, 1976–79.

Vejar Vazquez, Octavio

(Deceased Nov. 10, 1974)

a-Apr. 20, 1900. **b-**Jalapa, Veracruz, *Gulf, Urban*. **c-**Primary and secondary studies in Jalapa; preparatory studies at the National Preparatory School; law degree, National School of Law, UNAM, Dec. 6, 1923; LLD, National School of Law, UNAM; Professor of Aeronautic Law, School of Military Aviation; Professor of Military Law, National School of Law, UNAM; professor, National War College; professor, National Military College. **d-**None. **e-**Founder of the National Independent Democratic Party, 1944; member of the National Coordinating Committee of the Popular Party, 1947–48; Vice President of the Popular Party (PPS), 1951; Interim President of the Popular Party, 1949, 1952. **f-**Public defender; agent of the Ministerio Publico; Justice, Superior Tribunal of Military Justice; Prosecuting Attorney of Military Justice; *Attorney General of the Federal District and Federal Territories*, 1940–41; *Secretary of Public Education*, Sept. 12, 1941, to Dec. 22, 1943. **g-**None. **h-**Practicing attorney, 1923; President of the Post War Studies Commission, 1943; member of the committee in charge of writing the second Six Year Plan, 1940. **i-**Close friend of Jose Vasconcelos. **j-**None. **k-**Detained in the military prison of Tlatelolco, 1952, for ostensibly disobeying a superior's military order, raising the issue of whether or not career officers were really free to participate in politics. **l-***Hoy*, 20 Sept. 1941; WWM45, 123; Millon, 156; EBW46, 568; Peral, 841–42; Correa, 2; Kirk, 335, 148–55; Strode, 374–75; D del S, 2 Dec. 1940, 1–6; Gonzalez Navarro, 161; Lopez, 1134; NYT, 12 Sept. 1941, 8; Raby, 63; *Excelsior*, 12 Nov. 1949; HA, 18 Nov. 1974, 10; NYT, 15 Apr. 1952; NYT, 18 Apr. 1952, 5; *Excelsior*, 11 Nov. 1974, 20.

Velasco Curiel, Francisco

a-Sept. 15, 1917. **b-**Cuauhtemoc, Colima, *West, Rural*. **c-**Primary studies, Gertrudis Bocanegra School, Colima, Colima; preparatory studies, National Preparatory School; law degree, National School of Law, UNAM, April 28, 1944, with a thesis on cooperatism in Mexico and other countries. **d-***Senator* from the State of Colima, 1958–61, member of the Economics and Statistics Committee, the First Ejido Committee, and the Agricultural Development Committee; substitute member of the Agriculture and Development Committee; *Governor of Colima*, 1961–67. **e-**Delegate of PRI to Jalisco, Guanajuato, Colima, and Queretaro. **f-**Director, Federal Automobile Registration Department, Secretariat of Industry and Commerce; Director, Department of Special Studies and Administrative Affairs, Secretariat of the Treasury, 1952–58. **g-**None. **i-**Student of *Eduardo Bustamante* at UNAM; school companion of *Antonio Salazar Salazar*, Senator from Colima, 1958–64. **j-**None. **k-**None. **l-**WWMG, 40; DBM70, 558; DGF56, 164; letter; Func., 146.

Velasco Ibarra, Enrique

a-June 28, 1927. **b-**Acambaro, Guanajuato, *West Central, Urban*. **c-**Primary studies at a public school and at the Franco-Spanish School, 1933–36; secondary and preparatory studies, Colegio Frances; law degree, National School of Law, UNAM, 1944–48 with an honorary mention; highest grades of his generation at the National School of Law, 1947; Professor of Political Philosophy, School of Political and Social Sciences, UNAM, 1962–65; professor, Graduate School of Business Administration, UNAM, 1958; member of the Governing Board of UNAM, 1974; Professor of General Theory of the State, National School of Law, UNAM, 1958–66. **d-***Governor of Guanajuato*, 1979– . **e-**None. **f-**Director of the Banking Section, Secretariat of the Treasury, 1956; General Attorney for the Mexican Tobacco Company, 1960–61; Private Secretary to the Rector of UNAM, *Ignacio Chavez*, 1962–66; Subdirector General of Planning of the Secretariat of the Presidency, 1966–70; Auxiliary Secretary General of UNAM, 1970–73; Coordinator of Planning and Development, UNAM, 1973; Director General of Administration, Secretariat of the Treasury, 1974–75; *Oficial Mayor of the Secretariat of the Treasury*, 1975–76; *Private Secretary to President Jose Lopez Portillo*, 1976–78. **g-**Executive Secretary of the Industrial Center for Productivity, 1956–60. **h-**Author of many works; researcher, Institute of Comparative Law, UNAM, 1959–62; practicing lawyer, 1949–55. **i-**Long-time collaborator of *Jose Lopez Portillo*. **j-**None. **k-**Reportedly handled *Lopez Portillo*'s personal finances as his secretary. **l-***El*

Dia, 1 Dec. 1976; *Proceso*, 4 Dec. 1976, 27; LA, 15 Dec. 1978, 388; HA, 25 Dec. 1978, 39; *Excelsior*, 1 Dec. 1976.

Velasco Lafarga, Ernesto

a-Nov. 14, 1911. **b**-Tampico, Tamaulipas, *North, Urban*. **c**-Primary studies, Colegio San Borja, Colonia del Valle, Federal District; preparatory, Colegio "La Salle" and the Colegio Morelos, Federal District; engineering degree from the School of Mining and from the School of Engineering, UNAM, May 9, 1935. **d**-*Federal Deputy* from PAN (party deputy), 1970–73, member of the Sugar Industry Committee, the Department of the Federal District Committee, and the Second Section of the Agrarian Affairs Committee. **e**-Active member of PAN since 1939; head of PAN in Mazatlan, Sinaloa; Director of PAN for the 17th District, Federal District. **f**-Head of the Board of Civic and Moral Improvement, Mazatlan, Sinaloa; adviser to the City of Mazatlan; engineer for the National Mortgage Bank, 1935; engineer for the National Irrigation Commission, 1936–37; Superintendent and resident engineer, Irrigation Works, Ixmiquilpan, Hidalgo, 1938–47. **g**-Adviser to the National Chamber of Construction Industries. **h**-Civil engineer. **j**-None. **k**-Candidate for Federal Deputy from the Federal District, Dist. 17, 1967. **l**-*Directorio*, 1970–72; C de D, 1970–72, 139.

Velasco, Miguel Angel

a-1903. **b**-Jalapa, Veracruz, *Gulf, Urban*. **c**-Early education unknown; no degree. **d**-None. **e**-Joined the PCM, 1926; member of the CEN of the PCM, 1928–43; member of the Unified Socialist Action, 1948–50; member of the Mexican Workers and Peasants Party, 1955; member of the PPS, 1963–68; Secretary General of the Socialist Action and Unity Movement, 1977– . **f**-None. **g**-Began union activity, 1919; founder of the Federation of Workers and Peasants Union in Cordoba, Veracruz, 1925; organizer of the Only Chamber of Labor of Nuevo Leon, 1932; organized peasants on the Lombardia and New Italy haciendas, 1933; representative of the Only Union Federation, 1935; member of the CEN of the CTM, 1936. **h**-Author of many books; Director of *La Voz de Mexico*, 1942. **j**-Fought against Adolfo de la Huerta in Jilotepec, Veracruz, 1923; member of the staff of *Heriberto Jara*. **k**-Imprisoned in Islas Marias penal colony, 1932. **l**-Enc. Mex., 12, 314–15.

Velasco Suarez, Manuel

a-Dec. 18, 1915. **b**-San Cristobal de las Casas, Chiapas, *South, Urban*. **c**-Primary, secondary and preparatory studies in San Cristobal de las Casas; medical degree, National School of Medicine,

UNAM, 1933–39; studies in Orthopedic Surgery, University of Iowa, 1940; studies in neurology and neurosurgery, Harvard University and at Massachusetts General Hospital, 1941–42; studies in neuropathology, Washington, D.C., 1942–43; Professor, National School of Medicine, UNAM, 1944–70; Professor of Neurosurgery, National School of Medicine, UNAM, 1959–70; Professor of Clinical Surgery, National School of Medicine, UNAM, 1950–59. **d**-*Governor of Chiapas*, 1970–76. **e**-None. **f**-Neurosurgeon, Juarez Hospital, Mexico City, 1947–58; Director, Neuropsychiatric Assistance, Secretariat of Health, 1953–59; Director, Neuro and Neurosurgery Services, Juarez Hospital, 1958–70; founder and Director of the National Neurology Institute; Director General of the Neurological, Mental Health and Rehabilitation Division, Secretariat of Health, 1959–70. **g**-None. **h**-Author of numerous works in his specialty. **i**-Physician and close friend to *Luis Echeverria*; son of lawyer Jose Manuel Velasco Balboa; married Elvira Siles. **j**-None. **k**-Founder of numerous hospitals in Mexico City. **l**-DPE65, 151; DPE61, 111; letter; WNM, 234–35; DBC, 261–63.

Velazquez de Alba, Elpidio G.
(Deceased Nov. 14, 1977)

a-May 12, 1892. **b**-San Juan de Guadalupe, Durango, *West, Rural*. **c**-Primary and secondary studies in the state rural schools of Durango; studied at the Military Academy of Mexico. **d**-*Governor of Durango*, 1941–44. **e**-None. **f**-Assistant Director, Administrative Department, Secretariat of National Defense; Director of the War Materiels Department, Secretariat of National Defense, 1935. **g**-Member of the Durango Chamber of Commerce. **h**-General merchant in Durango; first employment as a factory laborer before 1910. **j**-Joined the Revolution in 1910 under Aguirre Benavides, with the rank of 2nd Lieutenant; Assistant Chief of Staff for General *Lazaro Cardenas*, 1933; Chief of Staff for various Revolutionary Generals; Commander of the 55th Regiment; Commander of the 64th Regiment; rank of Brigadier General, 1939. **k**-None. **l**-WWM45, 123; Peral, 847–48; EBW46, 1135; *Hoy*, 4 May 1940, 13; Lopez, 1138; Casasola, V.

Velazquez Jaaks, Luis

a-June 21, 1936. **b**-Federal District, *Federal District, Urban*. **c**-Primary studies at the Orozco y Berra and Damian Carmon Schools, Mexico City; secondary studies in Mexico City; preparatory studies from the National Preparatory School No. 1; law degree, National School of Law, UNAM; Professor of the Sociology of Education and Economic Policy, Pasteur Institute. **d**-*Federal Deputy* from the Federal

District, Dist. 14, 1970–73, member of the Department of the Federal District Committee, the Labor Section of the Legislative Studies Committee and the Promotion and Development of Sports Committee; *Federal Deputy* from the Federal District, Dist. 37, 1979– . **e-**Assistant Director of the National Youth Sector of PRI. **f-**None. **g-**President of the Subcommittee on Youth of the Congress of Labor; adviser, International Labor Organization; Secretary of Social Action of the CTM; Director, National Youth Sector of the CTM. **i-**Nephew of long-time CTM leader, *Fidel Velazquez*; son of *Gregorio Velazquez*, four-time federal deputy from Mexico. **j-**None. **k-**None. **l-***Directorio*, 1970–72, 140; C de D, 1970–73, 140.

Velazquez Sanchez, Fidel

a-Apr. 2, 1900. **b-**Villa Nicolas Romero, Mexico, *West Central*, *Rural*. **c-**Primary studies in Villa Nicolas Romero, completed, 1914; no degree. **d-***Senator* from the Federal District, 1946–52; *Senator* from the Federal District, 1958–64, member of the Department of the Federal District Committee, the Social Welfare Committee, the First Labor Committee, the First Balloting Committee, the First Instructive Section of the Grand Jury. **e-**Representative of labor to PRI. **f-**None. **g-**Secretary of Interior of the Union of Milk Industry Workers, 1921; Secretary General of the Union of Milk Industry Workers for the Federal District, 1929; member of the Executive Committee of the Federation of Mexican Labor, 1936–40; Secretary of Organization and Propaganda, CEN of the CTM, 1936; founding member of the General Federation of Mexican Workers and Farmers, 1933; *Secretary General of the Mexican Federation of Labor*, 1940–46; *Secretary General of the CTM*, 1946–52, 1952–58, 1958–64, 1964–70, 1970–76, 1976– . **h-**Worked as a field laborer, in a lumberyard, and on a hacienda; employed as a milkman. **i-**Close personal friend of *Lauro Ortega* and *Jesus Yuren*; parents were farmers; married Nora Quintana Perera; brother *Gregorio* was Secretary General of the CTM for Mexico and a federal deputy, 1955–58; nephew *Luis Velazquez Jaaks*, was a federal deputy, 1970–73. **j-**None. **k-**Brandenburg puts him in the Inner Circle of influence, 1940–46; one of the most powerful labor leaders in Mexico; founded the Milk Industry Workers Union with *Alfonso Sanchez Madariaga*; co-founder of the General Federation of Mexican Workers and Farmers (CGOCM) with *Vicente Lombardo Toledano*. **l-**WWW70–71; HA, 7 Feb. 1972, 12–14; Brandenburg, 80, 93; Johnson, 68; Morton, 47, 90; C de S, 1946–52; Padgett, 170–72; C de S, 1961–64, 72–73; Strode, 373; Kirk, 90–93; Enc. Mex., XII, 1977, 318; Lopez, 1138; HA, 20 Oct. 1950; *Excelsior*, 22 May 1973, 19; *Excelsior*, 16 Mar. 1973, 22.

Velazquez Sanchez, Gregorio

a-Mar. 5, 1910. **b-**Villa Nicolas Romero, Mexico, *West Central*, *Rural*. **c-**Primary studies in a public school, Mexico City; secondary studies at Night Secondary School No. 5, Mexico City; no degree. **d-**Local Deputy to the State Legislature of Mexico, 1940–42; *Federal Deputy* from the State of Mexico, Dist, 1, 1943–46; *Federal Deputy* from the State of Mexico, Dist. 5, 1949–52, member of the Administration Committee and the Budgets and Accounts Committee; *Federal Deputy* from the State of Mexico, Dist. 5, 1955–58, member of the Economics and Statistics Committee, the Second Balloting Committee and the General Accounting Office Committee; *Federal Deputy* from the State of Mexico, Dist. 2, 1967–70, member of the Tenth Section of the Legislative Studies Committee, the General Accounting Office Committee and the Social Welfare Committee. **e-**Secretary of Labor Organizations of PRI in the State of Mexico, 1946. **f-**Supervisor of Theaters, Department of the Federal District, 1938–40. **g-**Founder of the Regional Organization of the CTM in Tlalnepantla; representative of the CTM to the International Labor Organization Meeting on Social Security, Rio de Janeiro, 1952; Delegate of the CTM in Mexico, 1946. **h-**Began working at the La Sirena Iron Works, 1924; milk industry employee, 1925; employee of the National Railroads of Mexico, 1932–38. **i-**Brother of *Fidel Velazquez Sanchez*, Secretary General of the CTM; father of *Luis Velazquez Jaaks*, federal deputy from the Federal District, 1970–73, 1979–82; parents were peasants. **j-**None. **k-**Federal deputy from the State of Mexico more times between 1934 to 1979 than any other Mexican. **l-**Ind. Biog., 164–65; C de D, 1949–42, 94; C de D, 1955–58; DGF56, 25, 32, 34–35; C de D, 1967–70, 68, 78, 83.

Verdugo Quiroz, Leopoldo

a-Mar. 1, 1898. **b-**Alamos, Sonora, *North*, *Urban*. **c-**Primary studies in Alamos; no degree. **d-***Senator* from the State of Baja California del Norte, 1952–58, President of the Public Health Committee, First Secretary of the Social Security Committee and the Agricultural and Development Committee and Second Secretary of the Administration Committee. **e-**None. **f-**Director of Customs, Mexicali; Director of the Customs Officers, Mexicali, Matamoros and Veracruz. **g-**None. **j-**Fought in the Revolution as an enlisted man. **k-**None. **l-**Ind. Biog., 166–67; DGF56, 5, 9, 13; C de S, 1952–58.

Verduzco Rios, Leobardo

a-1945. **b-**Zamora, Michoacan, *West Central*, *Urban*. **c-**Primary studies in Morelia; secondary studies in Mexico City; law degree, National School of Law, UNAM; professor at the National Polytechnic Institute. **d-**None. **e-**Joined PARM, 1970; Secretary of Information and Publicity of the Executive Committee of PARM; Secretary of Information, Press and Publicity of the Regional Committee of PARM for the Federal District, 1979. **f-**None. **g-**None. **h-**Administrator, National Center of Industrial Technical Instruction. **j-**None. **k-**Candidate for federal deputy from PARM. **l-**HA, 7 May 1979, I.

Verges (Xochihua), Juan Victor

a-1913. **b-**Federal District, *Federal District, Urban.* **c-**Preparatory studies at the National Preparatory School; economics degree, National School of Economics, UNAM, 1939–42, graduating in 1944 with a thesis on military insurance. **d-**None. **e-**None. **f-**Director of Technical Administrative Organizations, Secretariat of Government Properties; Director General of Administration, Secretariat of Government Properties, 1951–55; Subdirector General of Administration, Secretariat of Government, 1956–61; Director General of Administration, Secretariat of Government, 1965–68; *Oficial Mayor of Government Properties,* 1968–70. **g-**None. **j-**None. **k-**None. **l-**EN de E, 265; DGF51, I, 445; DPE61, 11; DGF56, 83; DPE65, 13.

Vicencio Tovar, Abel

b-Mexico, *East Central.* **c-**Early education unknown; law degree, National School of Law, UNAM, 1952, with a thesis on the citizen and public rights. **d-***Federal Deputy* from the Federal District, Dist. 17, 1964–67, member of the Labor Section of the Legislative Studies Committee; *Federal Deputy* from PAN (Party Deputy), 1973–76. **e-**Joined PAN, October, 1958; *Secretary General of the CEN of PAN,* 1960–61; member of the CEN of PAN, 1969; *President of the CEN of PAN,* 1978– . **f-**None. **g-**None. **h-**Practicing lawyer. **i-**Brother of *Astolfo Vicencio Tovar,* Secretary General of PAN, 1961–66; son of Gustavo A. Vicencio, Justice of the Supreme Court, 1926–28. **j-**None. **k-**None. **l-**C de D, 1973–76, 29; C de D, 1964–67, 84; Mabry; letter.

Vicencio Tovar, Astolfo

a-Mar. 20, 1927. **b-**Federal District, *Federal District, Urban.* **c-**Primary studies; completed secondary and preparatory studies; completed four years of a CPA program. **d-***Federal Deputy* (PAN Party Deputy), 1967–70. **e-**President of the Regional Committee of PAN in the Federal District, 1960; member of the CEN of PAN, 1961–70; member of the regional council of PAN and delegate of the CEN of PAN to the State of Mexico, 1964–70; National Director of Electoral Campaigns for PAN, 1966–68; *Secretary General of the CEN of PAN,* 1961–66; director of the 1970 PAN presidential campaign. **f-**None. **g-**None. **h-**Industrialist. **i-**Son of Gustavo A.

Vicencio, Justice of the Supreme Court, 1926–28 and former Rector of the Institute of Arts and Sciences of Mexico, Toluca; brother of *Abel Vicencio Tovar,* President of PAN, 1978; good friend of *Jose Gonzalez Torres,* president of PAN, 1959–62; married Maria del Carmen Acevedo. **j-**None. **k-**Candidate of PAN for federal deputy, 1958; candidate of PAN for senator from the State of Mexico, 1964; candidate for Mayor of Naucalpan, Mexico, 1969. **l-**Mabry; C de D, 1967–70; letter; PS, 6336.

Vildosola Almada, Gustavo

a-Sept. 15, 1905. **b-**Alamos, Sonora, *North, Urban.* **c-**Primary studies in Mexicali; secondary and preparatory studies in Hermosillo, Sonora; no degree. **d-***Senator* from the State of Baja California del Norte, 1958–64, member of the Gran Comision, First Secretary of the National Properties Committee, Second Secretary of the Economy and Statistics Committee, and member of the Second Balloting Group. **e-**None. **f-**None. **g-**President of the Chamber of Industries, Baja California del Norte; President of the Regional Agricultural Union, Baja California del Norte; President of the Highway Association of Baja California del Norte. **h-**Businessman. **j-**None. **k-**None. **l-**Func., 123; C de S, 1961–64, 73.

Villa Michel, Primo

(Deceased Aug. 22, 1970)

a-Nov. 7, 1893. **b-**Ciudad Carranza, Jalisco, *West, Rural.* **c-**Primary and secondary studies at the Colegio de la Inmaculada, Zapopan, Jalisco; preparatory studies at the Instituto San Jose, Guadalajara, Jalisco; law studies, School of Law, University of Guadalajara; law degree, National School of Law, UNAM. **d-**None. **e-**None. **f-**Judge of the lower court of Sonora, 1915; Public Defender, Nogales, Sonora, 1917; Federal Public Defender for the State of Sonora, 1920; Director of Records, Secretariat of Government, 1923; Oficial Mayor, Secretariat of Industry and Commerce, 1923–24; Subsecretary of Government, 1925; Secretary General of the Department of the Federal District, 1925–26; Head of the Department of the Federal District, 1927–28; Ambassador to Germany, 1929; Subsecretary of Industry and Commerce, 1930–32; Secretary of Industry and Commerce, 1932–34; Ambassador to Uruguay, 1935; *Ambassador to Great Britain,* 1937–38; Ambassador to Japan, 1939–41; First Secretary of the Mexican Embassy, Washington, D.C., 1941–43; *Oficial Mayor of the Secretariat of Government,* 1944–45; *Secretary of Government,* 1945–46; Ambassador to Canada, 1947–51; Ambassador to Guatemala, 1952–53; Ambassador to Belgium, 1958–64. **g-**Secretary, National Chamber of Commerce. **h-**Delegate to many international conferences; manager, Petroleos Mexicanos; Director, National Institute of Housing; Director of the Bulletin of Federal Statutes, Secretariat of Government, 1923. i-Son, Primo Jr., was Director of the Department of Primary Statistics, Investment Commission, 1956; married Maria Davila. j-None. k-None. l-WWM45, 125; DP64, 1968; DP70, 2266; D de Y, 23 Aug. 1970; Correa, 360; STYRBIWW54, 1074; EBW46, 128; DPE61, 20; Peral, 859; Lopez, 1162; NYT, 15 May 1938, 36; NYT, 27 July 1954, 10; NYT, 24 Dec. 1941, 3; NYT, 3 Dec. 1942; HA, 5 July 1946, 4; Enc. Mex., XII, 1977, 404–05.

Villa Trevino, Jorge

a-1930. b-Federal District, *Federal District*, *Urban*. c-Law degree, National School of Law, UNAM, with a thesis on gambling and the law, 1963. d-None. e-*Secretary of Press and Publicity of the CEN of PRI*, Aug. 3, 1972–75; member of various commissions for the IEPES and the CNOP; active in the presidential campaign of *Luis Echeverria*; joined PRI, 1957. f-Member, Department of Publicity, Secretariat of Public Works, 1955–56; adviser to the administration of the Federal Post Office, 1968; Subdirector (A) of PIPSA. g-None. h-Co-founder of the magazine *Voz* with *Mario Moya Palencia*; editor of the magazine *Ferronales*, official publication of the National Railroads of Mexico. j-None. k-None. l-HA, 14 Aug. 1972, 11–12; *Hoy*, 19 Aug. 1972, 65; *Excelsior*, 4 Aug. 1972, 4–5.

Villalobos (Mayar), Antonio

(Deceased Dec. 27, 1965)
a-Dec. 16, 1894. b-Federal District, *Federal District*, *Urban*. c-Preparatory studies at the National Preparatory School, Mexico, D.F.; law degree, National School of Law, UNAM. d-Federal Deputy from the State of Oaxaca, 1918–20; Federal Deputy from the Federal District, Dist. 4, 1934–35; *Senator* from the Federal District, 1940–46, First Secretary of the Department of the Federal District Committee, and president of the First Constitutional Affairs Committee. e-Private secretary to the President of the PNR, *Lazaro Cardenas*, 1930–31; Secretary General of the CEN of the PNR, 1934–35; *President of the CEN of the PRM*, 1940–46. f-Agent of the Ministerio Publico; Judge of the District Court of San Luis Potosi, La Paz, Aguascalientes, Zacatecas, Pachuca, and Tijuana, 1927–30; Secretary General of Government to Governor *Jesus Agustin Castro*, State of Oaxaca, 1915–16; Secretary General of the State of Durango, under Governor *Jesus Agustin Castro*, 1921–24; Attorney for Military Justice; Oficial Mayor of the Secretariat of Government; *Secretary General of the Department of the Federal District*, 1935–37; Secretary General of Government of Baja California del Norte, 1933–34, under General *Agustin Olachea Aviles*; *Secretary of Labor and Social*

Welfare, 1937–40; Ambassador to Brazil, 1946–52; President of the Federal Board of Conciliation and Arbitration for the Federal District, 1952–58. g-None. h-Member of the Commission for the Adjustment of the Public Debt, Secretariat of the Treasury. j-Joined the Revolution under General *Jesus Agustin Castro* in Veracruz, 1914. k-Brandenburg places him in the Inner Circle from 1940–46. l-WWM45, 126; *Polemica*, 1969, 71; DGF56, 559; DP70, 2269; letter; Peral, 861; HA, 5 Nov. 1943, 35; Brandenburg, 80; STYRBIWW54, 1074; Lopez, 1160; NYT, 3 Dec. 1940, 12.

Villarreal, Antonio I.

(Deceased Dec. 16, 1944)
a-July 3, 1879. b-Lampazos, Nuevo Leon, *North*, *Rural*. c-Secondary education at the Normal School of San Luis Potosi and Monterrey; teacher in Monterrey normal schools. d-None. e-Three-time candidate for the President of Mexico, the last time in 1934; Secretary of the Organization Committee for the Mexican Liberal Party, Saint Louis, Mo., 1906. f-Consul General for President Madero in Barcelona, Spain, 1912–13; Secretary of Agriculture, June 1, 1920 to November 26, 1921. g-Reopened the Casa del Obrero Mundial, 1914. h-Writer for the Liberal newspaper *Regeneration*, published by Juan Sarabia and Ricardo Flores Magon, 1904. i-Relative of General Zuazua, Commander of the Northern Armies during the War of the Reform; good friend of Jose Vasconcelos during the Revolution. j-Joined the Revolution, 1910; rank of Brigade General, 1913, supported the Plan of Guadalupe; Governor and Military Commander of the State of Nuevo Leon; First President of the Convention of Aguascalientes, 1914; supported Carranza until 1920; supported De la Huerta, 1923; supported General Serrano and Gomez, 1927; supported General Escobar, 1929; rank of Divisionary General, Nov. 16, 1940. k-Went into exile, 1920; imprisoned several times. l-DP70, 2274; Peral, 863; Womack, 202–03; Lopez, 1163; Enc. Mex., XII, 1977, 407.

Villarreal Caravantes, Guillermo

a-Jan. 10, 1921. b-Durango, Durango, *West*, *Urban*. c-Economics degree, Superior School of Economics, National Polytechnic School, 1943; Professor of Economics, Superior School of Economics, IPN; member of the Advisory Commission of the Superior School of Economics. d-None. e-None. f-Economist, Secretary of the Treasury, 1938–45; economist, Secretariat of Agriculture; economist, CONASUPO; economist, Department (Regulatory) of Acquisitions, Secretariat of National Patrimony; economist, Bank of Mexico, 1954–70; Oficial Mayor of the Federal Electric Commission, 1970–

71; *Director General of the Federal Electric Commission*, 1971 to Aug. 8, 1972. **g-**None. **h-**Author of numerous economic studies. **i-**Married Doctor Alicia Chavez. **j-**None. **k-**None. **l-**HA, 7 Dec. 1970, 27; HA, 12 April, 1971; WNM, 237.

Villasenor, Victor Manuel

a-Dec. 23, 1904. **b-**Federal District, *Federal District, Urban*. **c-**Professional studies at the University of Southern California, 1921–24; studies at Cornell University; specialized studies, University of Michigan, 1924–26; law degree, University of Michigan, 1926; law degree, National School of Law, UNAM, 1929; founder with *Lombardo Toledano* of the Worker's University, 1936; Director of the Karl Marx Workers University, 1936–40. **d-**None. **e-**Founder and President of the Socialist League, 1944; Secretary General of the Partido Popular, 1948–49. **f-**Lawyer, Mexico-United States Claims Commission, 1929–33; delegate, Seventh Pan American Conference, 1933; legal adviser, Mexican Ambassador, Washington, D.C., 1934; Director of Archives, Secretariat of the Treasury, 1934; member, National Council of Higher Education, 1935–38; Director, Department of the Six-Year Plan, Secretariat of Government, 1939–40; Director of the Siderurgica Nacional, 1949–52; Director General of the Constructora Nacional de Carros de Ferrocarril, 1952–58; Director General of Diesel Nacional, 1959–70; *Director General of National Railroads of Mexico*, 1971 to May 7, 1973. **g-**Founding member of the CTM; representative of the CTM in Zurich, 1939. **h-**Member of the National Council of Scientific Investigation; Director of *Futuro*, 1936–40; Director General of Siderurgica Nacional, 1964–70. **i-**Long-time friend of *Narciso Bassols* and in his youth, of *Vicente Lombardo Toledano*; practiced law with Luis Cabrera, 1927–28; father, Manuel F. Villaseñor, was an engineer and federal deputy under Madero; grandfather was a senator and supreme court justice under Porfirio Diaz; married Martha de la Portilla. **j-**None. **k-**Attended the IX Olympic Games, Amsterdam, 1928; champion in the 400 meters; candidate for Federal Deputy, 1943. **l-**Millon, 156; HA, 7 Dec. 1970, 26–27; WWM45, 126; *Hoy*, 13 Mar. 1971, 10; HA, 19 April 1971, 16; letters; Enc. Mex., XII, 1977, 408.

Villasenor (Angeles), Eduardo

(Deceased Oct. 15, 1978)
a-Sept. 13, 1896. **b-**Angamacutiro, Villa Union, Michoacan, *West Central, Rural*. **c-**Primary studies in Angamacutiro; preparatory studies at the Colegio de San Nicolas de Hidalgo, Morelia, Michoacan; studies at the University of London; two years of study in engineering; three years of study in law;

graduate studies in philosophy; never formally received a degree; Professor of Economics, National School of Agriculture, 1921–25; Professor of International Trade, National School of Economics, UNAM, 1932; Secretary of UNAM, 1921. **d-**None. **e-**None. **f-**Director, Department of Cooperative Societies, National Agricultural Bank, 1926–28; Director of Economic Statistics, British-Mexican Claims Commission, 1928–29; Secretary, British-Mexican Claims Commission, 1928–29; Commercial Attache, Mexican Delegation, London, 1929–31; Director of the Consular Department, Secretariat of Foreign Relations, 1931–32; Director, Department of Printing and Publicity, Secretariat of Finance, 1932; member, National Banking Commission, 1932–33; Secretary, National Council of Economics, 1932–34; Secretary, Board of Directors, National Mortgage Bank of Urban and Public Works, 1932–34; Consul General, New York City, 1935; Director of the National Bank of Agricultural Credit, 1936–37; *Subsecretary of the Treasury*, Jan. 17, 1938, to 1940; *Director General of the Bank of Mexico*, 1940–46. **g-**Leader of the student movement at the Colegio de San Nicolas de Hidalgo, Morelia; Alternate Delegate to the International Congress of Students, Mexico City, 1921. **h-**Author of many books on economic questions in Mexico; co-founder of the Fondo de Cultura Economica, 1934; President of the Banco del Atlantico, 1949–65; President of the Bank of Mexico City, 1966–70. **i-**Brother, Roberto, was Director General of the National Institute of Forestry Research; married Margarita Urueta; friends since the 1920s with *Eduardo Suarez*, *Manuel Gomez Morin*, and *Daniel Cosio Villegas*; father a small store keeper. **j-**None. **k-**None. **l-**Letter; EBW46, 311; Peral, 865; Kirk, 174–76; Strode, 394; D de Y, 18 Jan. 1938, 1; WWM45, 126; Simpson, 368; Novo35, 196; Lopez; HA, 23 Oct. 1978, 13; NYT, 16 May 1945, 11; HA, 16 Apr. 1945, 34.

Virues del Castillo, Rodolfo

a-Oct. 28, 1931. **b-**Misantla, Veracruz, *Gulf, Rural*. **c-**Primary studies, Veracruz; secondary and preparatory studies, Mexico, D.F.; law degree, National School of Law, UNAM, 1953. **d-***Federal Deputy from the State of Veracruz, Dist. 5, 1967–70*, member of the Colonization Committee, the Agrarian Section of the Legislative Studies Committee (2nd year). **e-**Joined PRI, 1951; youth delegate for PRI from Veracruz, 1955. **f-**None. **g-**President of the National Student Association of Secondary Boarding School Students; private secretary to the Secretary General of the National Farmers Federation; Auxiliary Secretary of the National Executive Committee of the CNC. **h-**Author of a book on the CNC. **j-**None. **k-**None. **l-***Hoy*, 11 Oct. 1969, 62; C de D, 1967–70, 61, 69; MGF69.

Vista Altamirano, Flavio

a-Mar. 7, 1922. b-Jalapa, Veracruz, *Gulf, Urban*. c-Law degree, University of Veracruz, Jalapa, 1943. d-*Federal Deputy* from the State of Veracruz, Dist. 5, 1964–67, Vice President of the Gran Comision, Vice President of the Chamber, Dec., 1964; member of the Legislative Studies Committee, Third Section on Criminal Affairs; the First Government Committee; the Budget and Accounts Committee (1st year); the Foreign Relations Committee. e-Secretary General of the CNOP of the PRI of Veracruz; Secretary of Interior for the CNOP; *Secretary of Political Action for the CEN of PRI*, 1964–65; *Oficial Mayor of PRI*, 1968–70. f-Agent of the Ministerio Publico attached to the State Supreme Court of Veracruz; agent of the Ministerio Publico of the Criminal Courts for the Federal District; President of the Board of Conciliation and Arbitration, Orizaba, Veracruz; Judge of the Superior Court of Justice of the State of Veracruz; Oficial Mayor of the State Legislature of Veracruz; *Oficial Mayor of the Department of the Federal District*, 1970. g-None. h-None. j-None. k-None. l-HA, 14 Dec. 1970, 25; DBM70, 570; C de D, 1964–66, 57.

Vivanco (Lozano), Jose S.

a-Mar. 29, 1899. b-Linares, Nuevo Leon, *North, Rural*. c-Primary and secondary studies in Monterrey, Nuevo Leon; studies in business administration; no degree. d-*Senator* from the State of Nuevo Leon, 1946–52. e-None. f-Treasurer of the State of Nuevo Leon, 1939–46; Secretary General of Government of the State of Nuevo Leon, 1952; *Substitute Governor of Nuevo Leon*, 1952–55; *Director General of CONASUPO*, 1956–58; Director General of the National Border Program, 1966–69. g-None. h-Sales agent in Monterrey, 1939. j-None. k-None. l-DGF47, 21; HA, 28 Sept. 1945, xvi; DBM68, 629; PdM, 395–96; letter; NYT, 14 Mar. 1956, 27.

Vizcaino Murray, Francisco

a-Oct. 31, 1935. b-Guaymas, Sonora, *North, Urban*. c-Accounting degree, Certified Public Accountant; Master of Arts from the National Polytechnic Institute; Ph.D. in administrative sciences, National Polytechnic School. d-None. e-None. f-Fiscal adviser to the Secretary of Industry and Commerce, 1967; Auditor General of the Department of Agrarian Affairs, 1965–70; financial adviser to the State of Durango, 1968–70; Subdirector General of Accounting for IMSS; *Secretary General of the IMSS*, 1970; *Subsecretary of the Environment, Secretariat of Health*, 1972–76; Director of the Institute of Nuclear Energy, 1977– . g-None. h-Vice president of his own accounting firm; representative of Mexico to various international conferences on the environment. i-Protege of *Manuel B. Aguirre*. j-None.

k-Precandidate for Governor of Sonora, 1973, 1978. l-Letter; HA, 14 Aug. 1972, 14; *Excelsior*, 6 Jan. 1973; *Excelsior*, 23 Nov. 1977, 18; *Excelsior*, 10 Sept. 1978, 12; *Excelsior*, 11 Aug. 1978, 1, 11.

Yanez Ruiz, Manuel

a-1903. b-Huehuetoca, Hidalgo, *East Central, Rural*. c-Primary studies in Tulancingo; secondary studies in Tulancingo; preparatory studies at the National Preparatory School; law degree from the National School of Law, UNAM, June 2, 1926, with a specialty in fiscal legislation. d-*Federal Deputy* from the State of Hidalgo, Dist. 2, 1958–61, member of the Legislative Studies Committee (4th Section), the Tax Committee, and the Budget and Accounts Committee; substitute member of the Foreign Relations Committee. e-None. f-Judge of the First Instance, Mextitlan, Hidalgo, 1926–27; judicial conciliator, Pachuca, Hidalgo, 1927–28; Judge of the Second Penal Court, Pachuca, 1927–28; Judge of the Second Penal Court, Pachuca, 1928–29; Judge of the First *Instance, Tulancingo, Hidalgo, 1929*–30; Judge of the Civil Court, Pachuca, 1930–31; Judge of the Superior Tribunal of Justice of the State of Hidalgo, 1931; President of the Conciliation and Arbitration Board of Hidalgo, 1933; Secretary General of Government of the State of Hidalgo under Governor *Rojo Gomez*, 1937–40; Treasurer of the Federal District, Representative of the Central Zone before the National Arbitration Commission, Secretariat of the Treasury, 1946–53; Director General of Domestic Taxes, Secretariat of the Treasury, 1953–58; *Justice of the Supreme Court*, 1961–64, 1965–70, 1971–73. g-President of the National Student Federation, 1925. i-Political protege of *Javier Rojo Gomez*; descendant of Mariano Yanez, Secretary of the Treasury in the 19th century; married Maria Teresa Crespo. j-None. k-None. l-Func., 231; C de D, 1958–60, 9; DGF56, 165; letter; *Justicia*, June, 1968; WNM, 245; HA, 26 Nov. 1973, 10.

Yanez (Santos Delgadillo), Agustin

(Deceased Jan. 17, 1980)

a-May 4, 1904. b-Guadalajara, Jalisco, *West, Urban*. c-Primary and secondary studies in Guadalajara; preparatory studies in Guadalajara; law degree, University of Guadalajara, Oct. 15, 1929, with a thesis on "Towards an American International Law;" professor, Preparatory School Jose Paz Camacho, Guadalajara, 1926–29; professor, Preparatory School, University of Guadalajara, 1931–32; normal school teacher, Guadalajara, 1923–29; professor at UNAM, 1932–42; professor, Women's University of Mexico, 1946–50; professor of Spanish and Literature, National Preparatory School, 1932–76 (with leaves); founder and Director of the Institute of the State of Nayarit, 1930–31; Professor of Literary

Theory, School of Philosophy and Letters, UNAM, 1942–53, 1959–62. **d-***Governor of Jalisco*, 1953–58. **e-**Member of the Political Education Section of the IEPES of PRI, 1972. **f-**Director of Radio Educational Extension Programs, Secretariat of Public Education, 1932–34; Director of Primary Education for the State of Nayarit, 1930–31; Assistant Director and Director of the Library and Economic Archives, Secretariat of the Treasury, 1934–52; President of the Editorial Committee of UNAM, 1944–47; President of the Technical Council of Humanistic Research, UNAM, 1945–52; adviser to the Secretariat of the Presidency, 1959–62; Special Ambassador to Argentina, 1960; *Subsecretary of the Presidency*, 1962–64; *Secretary of Public Education*, 1964–70; President of the Free Textbook Commission, 1978–79. **g-**Member of the Mexican Catholic Youth Association with *Efrain Gonzalez Luna* in the 1920s. **h-**Member of the Education Committee of UNAM, 1945–52; major Mexican novelist and author of many literary studies. **i-**Parents were peasants; married Olivia Ramirez Ramos. **j-**None. **k-**Sympathetic to the Cristero movement in Jalisco, 1928–29; supported Jose Vasconcelos, 1929; candidate for Director of the National Preparatory School, Aug. 1944, but did not win. **l-**DBM68, 633–34; WWMG, 41; Johnson, 183; HA, 10 July, 1972, 10; DGF56, 94; IWW67–68, 1341; Correa, 255; Peral, 873; DEM, 13–14; Enc. Mex., XII, 1977, 433–34; letter; Lopez, 1172–73; HA, 17 Dec. 1973, 30; *Excelsior*, 19 Jan. 1980, B1, 3.

Yocupicio, Roman

(Deceased 1950)

a-Feb. 28, 1890. **b-**Masiaca, Alamos, Sonora, *North*, *Rural*. **c-**Primary education in Masiaca; no degree. **d-**Mayor of Navojoa, Sonora, 1921–23. **e-**None. **f-***Substitute Governor of Sonora*, Jan. 4, 1937, to Aug. 31, 1939. **g-**None. **j-**Joined the Revolution, 1909; joined the Constitutional Army, 1913; fought Francisco Villa; rank of Major, 1915; opposed the Convention of Aguascalientes, 1914–15; fought against De la Huerta, 1923; supported General Escobar against the Federal Government, 1929; reached rank of Divisionary General. **k-**Unsympathetic to the *Cardenas'* agrarian reform program in his state, supported the interests of industrialists and large landowners; the CTM accused him of being a fascist. **l-**DP70, 2312; Millon, 134; *Annals*, Mar., 1940, 18; Peral, 874–75; NYT, 17 July 1938; NYT, 20 Aug. 1938, 4.

Yuren Aguilar, Jesus

(Deceased Sept. 22, 1973)

a-Jan. 1, 1901. **b-**Federal District, *Federal District*, *Urban*. **c-**Primary studies in the Federal District; studies in business administration in the Federal Dis-

trict; left school in 1915; no degree. **d-***Federal Deputy* from the Federal District, Dist. 9, 1937–40; *Federal Deputy* from the Federal District, Dist. 8, 1943–46; *Senator* from the Federal District, 1952–58, member of the Gran Comision, the Second Navy Committee, the Securities Committee, and the Legal Studies Committee; *Senator* from the Federal District, 1964–70. **e-***Secretary of Labor Action of the CEN of PRI*, 1958–64. **f-**Driver for the Department of the Federal District; head of the Chauffeurs Department of the Department of the Federal District. **g-**Began union activity, 1922; head of the Sanitation Workers of the Department of the Federal District; organized the workers central in the Federal District, 1928; leader of the Street Cleaners and Transportation Workers Union, 1929; chief of the Mexican delegation to the International Labor Conference, Geneva, 1938; First Secretary of the Federation of Workers of the Federal District, 1941–43; member of the executive committee of the CTM, 1952; Secretary General of the Federation of Workers of the Federal District, 1949–73. **h-**Worked for El Aguila Petroleum Company. **i-**Married Blanca Guerrero; early labor ally of *Vicente Lombardo Toledano*; political supporter of *Fidel Velazquez* since 1941; founded the CTM with *Fidel Velazquez, Fernando Amilpa*, and *Alfonso Sanchez Madariaga* in 1936; co-founder with *Fidel Velazquez* of the Federation of Workers of the Federal District, 1941. **j-**Fought in the Constitutionalist Army under Carranza, 1920. **k-**None. **l-**C de S, 1952–58; C de D, 1937–39; C de S, 1964–70; C de D, 1943–45; DGF56, 6, 8, 11, 13, 14; HA, 30 Sept. 1973, 18; Ind. Biog., 168.

Zamora, Adolfo

b-Nicaragua, *Foreign*. **c-**Preparatory studies at the National Preparatory School, Mexico, D.F., 1921–24; irregular studies at the School of Liberal Arts and the Law School, Sorbonne, Paris, 1926–30; completed legal studies at the National School of Law, UNAM, 1931; law degree, Jan., 1932; professor at the Higher School of Commerce and Administration, National Polytechnic Institute, 1931–40; Professor of Social Welfare at UNAM. **d-**None. **e-**None. **f-**Technician, Department of Social Welfare, Secretariat of Labor, 1932; President of the Editorial Committee of the Social Security Law, 1932–40; lawyer for the National Urban Mortgage Bank of Public Works, 1933; founder and Director of the Office of Municipal Studies, National Urban Mortgage Bank of Public Works; Director of the Legal Department, National Urban Mortgage Bank of Public Works; founder and Director General of the Housing Development Bank, 1946; Subdirector of the National Urban Mortgage Bank of Public Works, 1947; Director General of the National Urban Mortgage Bank of Public Works, 1947–53. **g-**None. **h-**Author of the 1941 Social Security Law approved by Congress; author of several articles on social security; wrote for Jose Vasconcelos' magazine, *Antorcha*; lawyer for the Federal Comptroller General, 1932; investigator for the Institute of Social Investigations, UNAM, 1930. **i**-Friend of *Antonio Ortiz Mena* in preparatory school. **j**-None. **k**-None. **l**-Letter; DGF47.

Zapata Loredo, Fausto

a-Dec. 18, 1940. **b**-San Luis Potosi, San Luis Potosi, *East Central*, *Urban*. **c**-Degree from the University of San Luis Potosi; studies at the World Press Institute, Macalester College, Minnesota; Professor of the Informational Sciences, School of Political and Social Sciences, UNAM. **d**-*Alternate Federal Deputy* from the State of San Luis Potosi, Dist. 4, 1967–70; *Senator* from the State of San Luis Potosi, 1976– . **e**-Member of the National Council of the PRI; campaigned for *Antonio Rocha* during his gubernatorial campaign, 1967; National Press Coordinator for the presidential campaign of *Luis Echeverria*, 1970. **f**-*Subsecretary of the Presidency*, 1970–76; Ambassador to Italy, 1977. **g**-Secretary of Press and Publicity for the National Farmers Federation, 1968, under *Gomez Villanueva*. **h**-Reporter for *La Prensa*, Mexico, D.F.; Assistant Director of Information, *La Prensa*; Director of Information, *La Prensa*. **j**-None. **k**-The first Subsecretary of Information for the Secretariat of the Presidency; elected as an Alternate Deputy but replaced *Guillermo Fonseca Alvarez*, 1968–70. *Hoy*, 19 Dec. 1970, 4; HA, 14 Dec. 1970, 23; MGF69, 95; LA, 3 Dec. 1976, 3.

Zapata Portillo de Manrique, Ana Maria

a-June 22, 1915. **b**-Cuautla, Morelos, *West Central*, *Urban*. **c**-Completed primary studies. **d**-*Federal Deputy* from the State of Morelos, Dist. 2, 1958–61, member of the Library Committee and the Agrarian Committee. **e**-Began political activities, 1934; Secretary of Feminine Action of PRI for the State of Morelos. **f**-Syndic for the City Council of Cuautla, Morelos. **g**-President of the National Union of Revolutionary Women; Secretary of Feminine Action of the League of Agrarian Communities. **i**-Related to Emiliano Zapata. **j**-None. **k**-First female deputy elected from the state of Morelos. **l**-Func., 283; C de D, 95.

Zapata Vela, Carlos

c-Preparatory studies at the National Preparatory School; law degree, National School of Law, UNAM, with a thesis on the "Socialization of Land," 1931. **d**-*Federal Deputy* from the Federal District, Dist. 10, 1940–43, Secretary of the Preparatory Groups, member of the Second Constitutional Affairs Committee, the First Government

Committee and the Political Control Committee; *Federal Deputy* from the Federal District, Dist. 11, 64, member of the Credit, Money and Institutions of Credit Committee and the Second Balloting Committee. **e**-Member of the Legal Section of the Advisory Body to the National Revolutionary Bloc of the Senate, 1937. **f**-Subdirector of the National Agricultural Credit Bank, 1946–50; *Ambassador to the USSR*, 1967–69. **g**-None. **h**-Director of the Institute of Friendship and Inter-Cultural Exchanges, USSR—Mexico, 1974. **i**-Assistant to General *Jara*. **j**-None. **k**-Leader of the 1929 Strike Movement at UNAM; editor of the National Preparatory School newspaper, *Avalancha;* Marxist. **l**-NYT, 24 May 1964, 3; DGF47, 354; DGF49, 468; C de D, 1961–63, 95; C de D, 1940–42, 22, 46, 51; DGF49, 468; Novo35, 570.

Zarate Albarran, Alfredo

(Deceased March 8, 1942)

b-Mexico, *West Central*. **c**-Early education unknown; no degree. **d**-*Federal Deputy* from the State of Mexico, Dist. 9, 1937–40; *Senator* from the State of Mexico, 1940–41; *Governor of Mexico*, 1941–42. **e**-None. **g**-None. **i**-Parents were peasants. **j**-None. **k**-Assassinated by Fernando Ortiz Rubio, police inspector and president of the State Legislature of Mexico; his assassination reopened the political career of *Isidro Fabela* who replaced him as governor. **l**-Correa, 134; NYT, 7 Mar. 1942, 5; *Hoy*, Dec., 1940, 64–65; HA, 8 Jan. 1943; HA, 5 Mar. 1942.

Zarate Aquino, Manuel

a-Dec. 25, 1911. **b**-Yanhuitlan, Nochixtlan, Oaxaca, *South*, *Rural*. **c**-Early education unknown; normal teaching certificate, 1933; certificate in primary education, Normal Urban School, March 27, 1946; law degree, University of Oaxaca (Benito Juarez), 1955, with a thesis on the anticonstitutionality of the civil administrative boards; professor at the Institute of Arts and Sciences of Oaxaca, 1948– ; professor at the Normal Urban School, Oaxaca. **d**-Councilman, Oaxaca, Oaxaca, 1933, 1936–38; *Federal Deputy* from the State of Oaxaca, Dist. 6, 1964–67, President of the Chamber, Nov., 1964, secretary of the Gran Comision, member of the First General Means of Communication Committee, the Second Constitutional Affairs Committee, the Editorial Committee, and Secretary of the Legislative Studies Committee; *Governor of Oaxaca*, 1974 to March 3, 1977. **e**-Member of the Oaxacan Socialist Party, 1929; President of the Economic, Social, and Planning Council of PRI for the *Lopez Mateos* presidential campaign, 1958; former member of the PPS. **f**-Penal judge, Oaxaca, Oaxaca, 1958–60; President of the Superior Tribunal of Justice of Oaxaca, 1960–64, 1969–74. **g**-Secretary General of the Section

Twenty-Two of the SNTE, 1951; Secretary General of the FSTSE, State of Oaxaca, 1949–52. **i**-Personal friend of *Victor Bravo Ahuja*, Secretary of Public Education, 1970–74. **j**-None. **k**-PRI candidate for Governor of Oaxaca, 1974; his candidacy surprised most political observers; political enemy of *Jesus Robles Martinez* during his union activities in the SNTE in the 1950s; resigned from the governorship. **l**-*Excelsior*, 14 Mar. 1974, 11; *Excelsior*, 15 Mar. 1974, 17; C de D, 1964–67, 81, 83, 92, 95; *Excelsior*, 4 Mar. 1977; HA, 14 Mar. 1977, 20; *Excelsior*, 11 Aug. 1978, 4.

Zarur Saab, Juan

a-1950. **f**-Federal District, *Federal District*, *Urban*. **c**-Early education unknown; economics degree, National School of Economics, UNAM. **d**-None. **e**-Joined the Popular Socialist Youth, 1969; Secretary of Press and Publicity of the National Executive Committee of the PPS; member of the National Committee of Political, Economic and Social Studies of the PPS, 1979. **f**-None. **g**-None. **j**-None. **k**-Candidate for Federal Deputy, 1973; candidate for Party Deputy from the PPS, 1979. **l**-HA, 7 May 1979, III.

Zavala, Silvio

a-Feb. 7, 1909. **b**-Merida, Yucatan, *Gulf*, *Urban*. **c**-Preparatory studies at the University of the Southeast, Merida, Yucatan; law degree, National School of Law, UNAM, 1931; LLD from the Central University of Madrid, 1933, on a fellowship; Professor, History of Social Institutions of America, School of Philosophy and Letters, UNAM, 1945; founder, Director and Professor, Center of Historical Studies, Colegio de Mexico, 1940–56; lectured at Columbia University, Princeton University and the University of Pennsylvania under a grant from the Carnegie Endowment for International Peace; Guggenheim Fellow, Library of Congress, 1938–40; Rockefeller Foundation Fellow, 1944. **d**-None. **e**-None. **f**-Researcher, Hispanic American Section, Center of Historical Studies, Madrid, Spain, 1933–36; Secretary, National Museum, Mexico City, 1937–38; Director, Mexican Historical Series of Unedited Works, 1938–40; Director, National Museum of History of Mexico, 1946–54; Director, Educational and Cultural Section, United Nations, 1947; Cultural Adviser, Mexican Embassy, Paris, France, 1954–58; Permanent Delegate of Mexico to UNESCO, 1956–62; President of the Colegio de Mexico, 1963–66; *Ambassador to France*, 1970–75. **g**-Member of the Colegio Nacional. **h**-Director of the *Revista de Historia de America*, 1938. **i**-Married Maria Castelo Biedma; studied under *Daniel Cosio Villegas*. **j**-None. **k**-None. **l**-Letters; Enc. Mex., XII, 1977,

569–70; Lopez, 1188; WNM, 247–48; B de M, 267–68; WWM45, 129.

Zebadua (Lievano), Jose Humberto

a-Mar. 14, 1921. **b**-San Cristobal Las Casas, Chiapas, *South*, *Urban*. **c**-Primary studies in San Cristobal; secondary studies in Mexico City; BA degree from Holy Cross College, Worcester, Massachusetts. **d**-*Federal Deputy* from the State of Chiapas, Dist. 2, 1958–61, member of the Legislative Studies Committee, the Fourth Ejido Committee and the First General Means of Communication Committee. **e**-Joined PAN, 1957. **f**-None. **g**-None. **h**-Businessman. **j**-None. **k**-Elected as Alternate Federal Deputy from the Federal District, Dist. 6, but replaced *Antonio Zoreda Cebada* as the deputy from Chiapas. **l**-Func., 155; C de D, 1958–61, 95.

Zermeno Araico, Manuel

a-Oct. 26, 1901. **b**-Guadalajara, Jalisco, *West*, *Urban*. **c**-Primary and secondary studies in Guadalajara; graduated from the Naval Academy of Veracruz; professor at the Higher War College; Director of the Naval School of Mazatlan. **d**-None. **e**-Vice President of PARM, 1977– . **f**-Adviser to the Chief of Staff under President *Cardenas*, 1935–39; Chief of Staff for the Navy, 1946–47; Naval Attache to the Mexican Embassy, Washington, D.C., 1941–45; Director General of the Fleet, Secretariat of the Navy, 1951–55; Ambassador to Norway, 1955–58; *Secretary of the Navy*, 1958–64. **g**-None. **h**-Author of various works on naval subjects. **i**-Married Maria Antonia del Peon. **j**-Career naval officer; joined the Navy, 1917; put down a revolt in Frontera, Tabasco, April 22, 1924; fought against the De la Huerta Rebellion, 1923; rank of frigate captain, 1940; rank of navy captain, 1943; rank of commodore, 1946; Commander of the 3rd Naval Zone, Veracruz (3 times); Commander of the Anahuac Unit; served on the corvette "Zaragoza"; rank of Rear Admiral, 1950; rank of Vice Admiral, 1952; rank of Admiral, 1952; Adjutant General of the Naval College at Veracruz; retired from active duty, 1967. **k**-None. **l**-D de Y, 2 Dec. 1958, 7; HA, 8 Dec. 1958, 30; DGF56, 128; DGF47, 234; D de S, 3 Dec. 1952, 1; Func.; HA, 19 Mar. 1979, VI; *Excelsior*, 2 July 1977, 15.

Zertuche Munoz, Fernando

a-Feb. 3, 1936. **b**-Federal District, *Federal District*, *Urban*. **c**-Early education unknown; law degree, National School of Law, UNAM, 1961; developed a course in methodology and historical research, Colegio de Mexico; Professor of Sociology and Constitutional Law, Women's University of Mexico, 1957–58; researcher for the Seminar of History, Colegio de Mexico, 1959–60; Professor of History of the Mexican Revolution, 1968–70; Professor of Labor Law, School of Accounting and Administration, UNAM, 1962–64. **d-**None. **e-**None. **f-**Director of the Department of Labor Relations, Telefonos de Mexico, S.A., 1961–66; Assistant Secretary of the Technical Council of the IMSS, 1966–70; *Oficial Mayor of Labor*, 1970–74; President of the Federal Board of Conciliation and Arbitration, 1974–76; *Secretary General of the IMSS*, 1976– . **g-**None. **h-**Executive Secretary of *Medio Siglo,* 1956–58, founded by *Porfirio Munoz Ledo.* **i-**Married to Martha Sanchez; father an engineer. **j-**None. **k-**None. **l-**HA, 14 Dec. 1970, 23; DPE71; letters; *Excelsior,* 14 June 1974, 19.

Zevada, Ricardo Jose
(Deceased Oct. 25, 1979)
a-July 5, 1904. **b-**Federal District, *Federal District, Urban.* **c-**Primary studies in Colima and in Mexico City; law degree, National School of Law, UNAM, 1925; professor of Administrative Law, UNAM, 1927–34. **d-**None. **e-**None. **f-**Chief of Lawyers, Committee to Liquidate Old Banks, 1930–32; chief lawyer, National Mortgage Bank of Urban and Public Works, 1932–34; Director General of Credit, Secretariat of the Treasury, 1934–36; financial adviser to Ambassador *Narciso Bassols,* London, 1936–37; Director, Department of Credit, National Bank of Ejido Credit, 1937–38; Executive Director of the Commodities Market Regulatory Commission, 1938–40; member of the Editorial Committee for the Second Six-Year Plan, 1940; Founder and Director General of the National Savings Bank, 1941–52; *Director General of the National Bank of Foreign Trade,* 1952–58, 1958–64, 1965; President of the Board of Directors, National Savings Bank, 1965–76. **g-**None. **h-**Book clerk at UNAM; author of many works on Mexico; founder of the National Bank of Ejido Credit, 1936; practicing lawyer with *Narciso Bassols,* 1925–34. **i-**Friend of *Antonio Martinez Baez* at UNAM; close personal friend of *Narciso Bassols;* son of a mining engineer; married Guadalupe Moreno Garcini. **j-**None. **k-**None. **l-**Letter; Gonzalez Navarro, 161; WWM45, 129; Enc. Mex., XII, 1977, 572–73.

Zierold Reyes, Pablo
b-Federal District, *Federal District, Urban.* **c-**Early education unknown; degree in veterinary medicine, UNAM, 1938; Professor, School of Veterinary Medicine, UNAM, 1957–65; Director of the School of Veterinary Medicine, UNAM, 1965. **d-**None. **e-**None. **f-**Veterinarian, Secretariat of Agriculture and Livestock (fourteen years); *Subsecretary of Livestock,* Secretariat of Agriculture, 1975–76. **g-**None. **h-**President of the Third and Fourth Pan American

Veterinary Congresses. **j-**None. **k-**None. **l-***El Universal,* 27 June 1975, 2; *The News;* HA, 7 July 1975, 20.

Zincunegui Tercero, Leopoldo
a-Feb. 23, 1895. **b-**Zinapecuaro, Michoacan, *West Central, Rural.* **c-**Secondary studies at the Scientific and Literary Institute of Toluca, Mexico; preparatory studies at the National Preparatory School, Mexico, D.F.; law degree, Mexico, D.F. **d-**Federal Deputy from the State of Michoacan, 1918–20, 1920–22, 1924–26, 1926–28, 1928–30; *Alternate Federal Deputy* from the State of Michoacan, Dist. 11, 1937–40; *Federal Deputy* from the State of Michoacan, Dist. 11, 1940–43, member of the Permanent Commission, 1940, member of the Protocol Committee, the First Balloting Committee, the Rules Committee, and the First Instructive Section of the Grand Jury. **e-**None. **f-**Judge of the Civil Registry, Mexico, D.F.; Federal Inspector for the Secretariat of the Treasury; Subdirector of the Technical Industrial Department, Secretariat of Public Education. **g-**None. **h-**Author of several works. **i-**Descendant of General Miguel Zincunegui, Governor of Michoacan in the 1850s. **j-**None. **k-**None. **l-**Peral, 886–87; DP70, 2345; C de D, 1937–39; C de D, 1940–42, 47, 53, 55, 59; Lopez, 1190–91.

Zorrilla (Carcano), Manuel
a-1921. **c-**Early education unknown; engineering degree; Director of the Graduate School of Mechanical and Electrical Engineering, IPN, 1968; Director of the Electronics and Communication Engineering Curriculum, IPN, 1970. **d-**None. **e-**None. **f-***Director General of the National Polytechnic Institute,* 1970–76. **g-**President of the Mexican Association of Engineers. **h-**None. **j-**None. **k-**Remained on good terms with the students during the 1968 strike. **l-**HA, 6 Sept. 1971, 21; HA, 21 Dec. 1970, 72; Glade and Ross, 178.

Zorrilla Martinez, Pedro Gregorio
a-July 30, 1933. **b-**Monterrey, Nuevo Leon, *North, Urban.* **c-**Primary, secondary, and preparatory studies in Monterrey; first year of law studies, Law School, University of Nuevo Leon; legal studies at the National School of Law, 1950–54, law degree, Oct. 27, 1955; LLD from the School of Law and Economic Sciences, University of Paris, 1956–58; Ph.D., Dec. 2, 1958; post-graduate work in economic planning and public finance, University of London and at the International Academy at the Hague, 1958; Professor of Public Administration and Economic Development, National Preparatory School; Professor in the Ph.D. program of the School of Political and Social Sciences, UNAM, 1967–73;

Professor of Administrative Law, Ibero American University, 1966–67; Professor of Labor Law, School of Social Workers, 1959–60; guest professor, CEMLA, 1967–70; visiting professor, St. Mary's University, San Antonio, Texas; Professor of Administrative Theory, National School of Law, UNAM, 1959–74. **d-***Governor of Nuevo Leon*, 1973–79. **e-**Professor at the Institute of Political Training, PRI. **f-**Legal adviser to the Federal Board for Decentralized Agencies; Secretary to the Third Division, Superior Tribunal of Justice of the Federal District, 1952–53; Director General of Population, Secretariat of Government, 1970–71; Secretary General of the State of Tamaulipas, 1968–70; adviser to the Secretariat of the Presidency; Subdirector of Legal Counsel, Secretariat of the Presidency, 1966–68; General Attorney for the National Border Program, 1961–65; legal adviser, Secretariat of National Patrimony, 1961; Commissioner of the Public Administration Commission, Secretariat of the Presidency, 1964–70; *Oficial Mayor of the Department of the Federal District*, 1971–72; *Attorney General of the Federal District and Federal Territories*, Aug. 9, 1972–73. **g-**None. **h-**Considered an expert on administrative theory. **i-**Brother, Rodrigo, an architect; assistant to *Horacio Flores de la Pena*, impressed *Octavio Senties* as an adviser to the 11th Interparliamentary Reunion between Mexico and the United States. **j-**None. **k-**As Secretary General of Government under governor *Ravize*, *Zorrilla Martinez* actually served as governor for a year when *Ravize* was ill, giving him the opportunity to meet *Luis Echeverria* in 1969. **l-**B de M, 269–70; HA, 13 Sept. 1971; HA, 21 Aug. 1972, 13; *Excelsior*, 10 Aug. 1972, 10; *Excelsior*, 8 Mar. 1973, 14; HA, 13 Aug. 1973, 33; letter; Q es Q, 77, 243–44; Enc. Mex., Annual, 1977, 547–48.

Zubiran (Anchondo), Salvador

a-Dec. 23, 1898. **b-**Federal District, *Federal District*, *Urban*. **c-**Preparatory studies at the National Preparatory School, Mexico, D.F., 1913–16; medical degree, National School of Medicine, UNAM, 1923; advanced studies at Harvard University and Brigham Hospital, 1924–25; Professor of Medicine, Graduate School, UNAM, 1946–66; Professor of Therapeutics, National School of Medicine, UNAM, 1925–27; Professor of Clinical Medicine, National School of Medicine, UNAM, 1934–67; Professor Emeritus, School of Medicine, UNAM, 1967– . **d-**None. **e-**None. **f-**Director, Office of Food and Drink, Secretariat of Health, 1931–35; member of the presidential study commission, 1935–37; First Director of the Department of Child Welfare, 1937–38; *Subsecretary of Health*, 1938–40 (in charge of the secretaryship, 1938–39); *Subsecretary of Health*, 1940–43; *Rector of UNAM*, 1946–48; Director General of the National Industry of Pharmaceutical Chemicals, 1949–52; Director, Dietetics Service, General Hospital, 1943–45; Director of the Hospital for Nutritional Diseases, 1949–64; Director of the Institute of Nutrition, Secretariat of Health, 1964–70. **g-**None. **h-**Author of various medical studies. **i-**Personal friend of *Gustavo Baz* since preparatory school days; personal physician to Presidents Calles, *Cardenas*, and *Avila Camacho*; Married Ana Maria Villarreal. **j-**None. **k-**Resigned from the Rectorship of UNAM after students rioted and held him prisoner in his own office. **l-**Novo, 173; D de Y, 25 June 1937, 1; DGF50, 348; DPE61, 114; D de S, 2 Dec. 1940, 1, 6; letter; DPE65, 153; Simpson, 354–55; Hayner, 247; letter; Enc. Mex., XII, 1977, 595; Lopez, 1194.

Zuckermann Duarte, Conrado

a-Nov. 7, 1900. **b-**Merida, Yucatan, *Gulf, Urban*. **c-**Preparatory studies at the National Preparatory School, Mexico, D.F., 1913–16; medical degree, National School of Medicine, UNAM, Aug. 22, 1924; professor, National School of Medicine, UNAM, 1928–37; graduate studies in various hospitals. **d-**None. **e-**None. **f-**Intern, General Hospital, Mexico, D.F., 1924–36; Director of Interns, General Hospital, 1936; Clinical Assistant, National School of Medicine, UNAM, 1924–27; Clinical Investigator, Cancer Section, Department of Health, 1925–27; Surgeon and Director, Mexican Clinic of Surgery and Radiotherapy; Director of the National Campaign Against Cancer, 1941–43, 1970–76; *Subsecretary of Welfare*, Mar. 1 1960, to 1964. **g-**None. **h-**Book clerk as a student at UNAM; author of various articles on surgery and medicine; received many awards for his work on cancer. **i-**Married Carmen Quintero. **j-**None. **k-**None. **l-**Letter; DPE61, 109; Peral, 889; WWM45, 130; DBM70, 580; Lopez, 1195.

Appendixes

Italicized names in appendixes have biographical entries in the text.

Supreme Court Justices
1935–1980

1935

President:*
Daniel V. Valencia

Presidents:†
Jose Ortiz Tirado
Francisco H. Ruiz
Alonso Aznar Mendoza
Xavier Icaza y Lopez Negrete

Members:
Rodolfo Asiain
Abenamar Eboli Paniagua
Hermilo Lopez Sanchez
Sabino M. Olea
Rodolfo Chavez S.
Luis Basdresch
Daniel Galindo
Alfonso Perez Gasca
Genaro V. Vazquez
Alfredo Inarritu
Agustin Aguirre Garza
Octavio M. Trigo
Jose Maria Truchuelo
Vicente Santos Guajardo
Jesus Garza Cabello
Salomon Gonzalez Blanco

1936

President:
Daniel V. Valencia

Presidents:
Francisco H. Ruiz
Luis Basdresch
Alonso Aznar Mendoza
Daniel Galindo

Members:
Abenamar Eboli Paniagua
Xavier Icaza y Lopez Negrete
Rodolfo Chavez S.
Alfredo Inarritu
Vicente Santos Guajardo
Jesus Garza Cabello
Salomon Gonzalez Blanco
Jose Ortiz Tirado
Sabino M. Olea
Hermilo Lopez Sanchez
Jose Maria Truchuelo
Rodolfo Asiain
Octavio M. Trigo
Agustin Gomez Campos
Alfonso Perez Gasca
Agustin Aguirre Garza

1937

President:
Daniel V. Valencia

Presidents:
Francisco H. Ruiz
Luis Basdresch
Alonso Aznar Mendoza
Daniel Galindo

Members:
Abenamar Eboli Paniagua
Xavier Icaza y Lopez Negrete
Rodolfo Chavez S.
Alfredo Inarritu
Vicente Santos Guajardo
Jesus Garza Cabello
Salomon Gonzalez Blanco

Jose Ortiz Tirado
Sabino M. Olea
Hermilo Lopez Sanchez
Jose Maria Truchuelo
Rodolfo Asiain
Octavio M. Trigo
Agustin Gomez Campos
Alfonso Perez Gasca
Agustin Aguirre Garza

1938

President:
Daniel V. Valencia

Presidents:
Francisco H. Ruiz
Luis Basdresch
Fernando Lopez Cardenas
Alonso Aznar Mendoza

Members:
Abenamar Eboli Paniagua
Xavier Icaza y Lopez Negrete
Rodolfo Chavez S.
Alfredo Inarritu
Vicente Santos Guajardo
Jesus Garza Cabello
Salomon Gonzalez Blanco
Jose Ortiz Tirado
Sabino M. Olea
Hermilo Lopez Sanchez
Jose Maria Truchuelo
Rodolfo Asiain
Octavio M. Trigo
Agustin Gomez Campos
Alfonso Perez Gasca
Agustin Aguirre Garza

---

*The President serves as the chief justice of the Supreme Court.

†The Mexican Supreme Court is divided into four divisions—criminal, administrative, civil, and labor—with a president presiding over each.

[325]

1939

President:
Daniel V. Valencia

Presidents:
Francisco H. Ruiz
Alonso Aznar Mendoza
Fernando Lopez Cardenas
Rodolfo Chavez S.

Members:
Abenamar Eboli Paniagua
Jesus Garza Cabello
Jose Maria Truchuelo
Jose Ortiz Tirado
Luis G. Caballero
Hermilo Lopez Sanchez
Agustin Gomez Campos
Rodolfo Asiain
Sabino M. Olea
Agustin Aguirre Garza
Octavio M. Trigo
Luis Basdresch
Salomon Gonzalez Blanco
Xavier Icaza y Lopez Negrete
Alfonso Perez Gasca

1940

President:
Daniel V. Valencia

Presidents:
Francisco H. Ruiz
Alonso Aznar Mendoza
Fernando Lopez Cardenas
Rodolfo Chavez S.

Members:
Abenamar Eboli Paniagua
Jesus Garza Cabello
Jose Maria Truchuelo
Jose Ortiz Tirado
Luis G. Caballero
Hermilo Lopez Sanchez
Agustin Gomez Campos
Rodolfo Asiain
Sabino M. Olea
Agustin Aguirre Garza
Octavio M. Trigo
Luis Basdresch
Salomon Gonzalez Blanco
Xavier Icaza y Lopez Negrete
Alfonso Perez Gasca

1941

President:
Salvador Urbina

Presidents:
Jose Ortiz Tirado
Hilario Medina
Gabino Fraga Magana
Roque Estrada

Members:
Antonio Islas Bravo
Hermilo Lopez Sanchez
Fernando de la Fuente
Carlos L. Angeles
Niceforo Guerrero Mendoza
Jose Rebolledo
Eduardo Vasconcelos
Emilio Pardo Aspe
Alfonso Francisco Ramirez
Manuel Bartlett Bautista
Tirso Sanchez Taboada
Teofilo Olea y Leyva
Jose Maria Mendoza Pardo
Felipe de J. Tena
Franco Carreno
Octavio Mendoza Gonzalez

1942

President:
Salvador Urbina

Presidents:
Carlos L. Angeles
Emilio Pardo Aspe
Gabino Fraga Magana
Eduardo Vasconcelos

Members:
Antonio Islas Bravo
Jose Rebolledo
Fernando de la Fuente
Manuel Bartlett Bautista
Niceforo Guerrero Mendoza
Teofilo Olea y Leyva
Alfonso Francisco Ramirez
Felipe de J. Tena
Carlos I. Melendez
Octavio Mendoza Gonzalez
Jose Maria Mendoza Pardo
Jose Ortiz Tirado
Franco Carreno
Hilario Medina
Hermilo Lopez Sanchez
Roque Estrada

1943

President:
Salvador Urbina

Presidents:
Jose Rebolledo
Felipe de J. Tena
Franco Carreno
Hermilo Lopez Sanchez

Members:
Antonio Islas Bravo
Octavio Mendoza Gonzalez
Fernando de la Fuente
Jose Ortiz Tirado
Niceforo Guerrero Mendoza
Hilario Medina
Alfonso Francisco Ramirez
Roque Estrada
Carlos I. Melendez
Carlos L. Angeles
Jose Maria Mendoza Pardo
Gabino Fraga Magana
Manuel Bartlett Bautista
Emilio Pardo Aspe
Teofilo Olea y Leyva
Eduardo Vasconcelos

1944

President:
Salvador Urbina

Presidents:
Fernando de la Fuente
Hilario Medina
Alfonso Francisco Ramirez
Antonio Islas Bravo

Members:
Niceforo Guerrero Mendoza
Eduardo Vasconcelos
Carlos I. Melendez
Angel Carvajal*
Manuel Bartlett Bautista
Agustin Mercado Alarcon
Teofilo Olea y Leyva
Vicente Santos Guajardo
Octavio Mendoza Gonzalez
Luis G. Corona
Jose Ortiz Tirado
Jose Rebolledo
Roque Estrada
Franco Carreno
Carlos L. Angeles
Hermilo Lopez Sanchez
Emilio Pardo Aspe

---

*Angel Carvajal was nominated in 1944, and resigned the same year. This accounts for the listing of 17 members, instead of the usual 16.

1945

President:
Salvador Urbina

Presidents:
Teofilo Olea y Leyva
Carlos I. Melendez
Octavio Mendoza Gonzalez
Eduardo Vasconcelos

Members:
Niceforo Guerrero Mendoza
Luis G. Corona
Manuel Bartlett Bautista
Jose Rebolledo
Jose Ortiz Tirado
Franco Carreno
Roque Estrada
Hermilo Lopez Sanchez
Carlos L. Angeles
Fernando de la Fuente
Emilio Pardo Aspe
Alfonso Francisco Ramirez
Agustin Mercado Alarcon
Hilario Medina
Vicente Santos Guajardo
Antonio Islas Bravo

1946

President:
Salvador Urbina

Presidents:
Jose Ortiz Tirado
Vicente Santos Guajardo
Manuel Bartlett Bautista
Luis G. Corona

Members:
Niceforo Guerrero Mendoza
Fernando de la Fuente
Roque Estrada
Alfonso Francisco Ramirez
Carlos L. Angeles
Hilario Medina
Emilio Pardo Aspe
Antonio Islas Bravo
Agustin Mercado Alarcon
Teofilo Olea y Leyva
Jose Rebolledo
Octavio Mendoza Gonzalez
Franco Carreno
Carlos I. Melendez
Hermilo Lopez Sanchez
Eduardo Vasconcelos

1947

President:
Salvador Urbina

Presidents:
Carlos L. Angeles
Agustin Mercado Alarcon
Franco Carreno
Antonio Islas Bravo

Members:
Niceforo Guerrero Mendoza
Teofilo Olea y Leyva
Roque Estrada
Octavio Mendoza Gonzalez
Emilio Pardo Aspe
Carlos I. Melendez
Jose Rebolledo
Eduardo Vasconcelos
Hermilo Lopez Sanchez
Jose Ortiz Tirado
Fernando de la Fuente
Manuel Bartlett Bautista
Alfonso Francisco Ramirez
Vicente Santos Guajardo
Hilario Medina
Luis G. Corona

Supernumerary:*
Felipe Tena Ramirez

1948

President:
Salvador Urbina

Presidents:
Luis Chico Goerne
Roque Estrada
Alfonso Francisco Ramirez
Mariano Ramirez Vazquez

Members:
Niceforo Guerrero Mendoza
Carlos I. Melendez
Carlos L. Angeles
Jose Ortiz Tirado
Emilio Pardo Aspe
Manuel Bartlett Bautista
Jose Rebolledo
Vicente Santos Guajardo
Fernando de la Fuente
Luis G. Corona
Hilario Medina
Agustin Mercado Alarcon
Teofilo Olea y Leyva
Franco Carreno
Octavio Mendoza Gonzalez
Hermilo Lopez Sanchez

1949

President:
Salvador Urbina

Presidents:
Jose Rebolledo
Vicente Santos Guajardo
Niceforo Guerrero Mendoza
Hermilo Lopez Sanchez

Members:
Emilio Pardo Aspe
Luis G. Corona
Jose Ortiz Tirado
Agustin Mercado Alarcon
Fernando de la Fuente
Franco Carreno
Hilario Medina
Luis Chico Goerne
Teofilo Olea y Leyva
Alfonso Francisco Ramirez
Octavio Mendoza Gonzalez
Roque Estrada
Carlos I. Melendez
Enrique Perez Arce
Manuel Bartlett Bautista
Mariano Ramirez Vazquez

1950

President:
Salvador Urbina

Presidents:
Luis G. Corona
Roque Estrada
Octavio Mendoza Gonzalez
Agapito Pozo

Members:
Jose Ortiz Tirado
Luis Chico Goerne
Fernando de la Fuente
Alfonso Francisco Ramirez
Hilario Medina
Armando Z. Ostos
Teofilo Olea y Leyva
Luis Diaz Infante
Carlos I. Melendez
Jose Rebolledo
Manuel Bartlett Bautista
Niceforo Guerrero Mendoza
Agustin Mercado Alarcon
Vicente Santos Guajardo
Franco Carreno
Hermilo Lopez Sanchez

---

*A supernumerary is not assigned to any of the four divisions of the Court, but is called upon to sit on a case when another minister is ill or on leave of absence. Often the supernumeraries may be the source of new ministers of the Court when one dies or resigns. A list of supernumeraries does not appear regularly throughout the appendix, because they are not always listed in official records and their names are not available on a consistent year-by-year basis.

1951

President:
Salvador Urbina

Presidents:
Teofilo Olea y Leyva
Carlos I. Melendez
Manuel Bartlett Bautista
Armando Z. Ostos

Members:
Jose Ortiz Tirado
Jose Rebolledo
Fernando de la Fuente
Vicente Santos Guajardo
Hilario Medina
Hermilo Lopez Sanchez
Agustin Mercado Alarcon
Luis G. Corona
Franco Carreno
Octavio Mendoza Gonzalez
Luis Chico Goerne
Agapito Pozo
Alfonso Francisco Ramirez
Roque Estrada
Luis Diaz Infante
Arturo Martinez Adame

Supernumeraries:
Felipe Tena Ramirez
Gabriel Garcia Rojas
Angel Gonzalez de la Vega
Mariano Azuela
Rafael Matos Escobedo

1952

President:
Roque Estrada

Presidents:
Luis Chico Goerne
Agustin Mercado Alarcon
Octavio Mendoza Gonzalez
Luis Diaz Infante

Members:
Jose Castro Estrada
Vicente Santos Guajardo
Gabriel Garcia Rojas
Hilario Medina
Arturo Martinez Adame
Alfonso Francisco Ramirez
Alfonso Guzman Neyra
Rafael Rojina Villegas
Jose Rivera Perez Campos
Genaro V. Vazquez
Luis G. Corona

Edmundo Elorduy
Agapito Pozo
Ernesto Aguilar Alvarez
Franco Carreno
Teofilo Olea y Leyva

Supernumeraries:
Angel Gonzalez de la Vega
Felipe Tena Ramirez
Juan Jose Gonzalez Bustamante

1953

President:
Hilario Medina

Presidents:
Jose Ortiz Tirado
Gabriel Garcia Rojas
Alfonso Francisco Ramirez
Arturo Martinez Adame

Members:
Luis G. Corona
Vicente Santos Guajardo
Luis Chico Goerne
Jose Castro Estrada
Teofilo Olea y Leyva
Rafael Rojina Villegas
Franco Carreno
Alfonso Guzman Neyra
Niceforo Guerrero Mendoza
Gilberto Valenzuela
Octavio Mendoza Gonzalez
Luis Diaz Infante
Jose Rivera Perez Campos
Agapito Pozo
Agustin Mercado Alarcon
Vacancy

Supernumeraries:
Angel Gonzalez de la Vega
Mariano Azuela
Juan Jose Gonzalez Bustamante
Rafael Matos Escobedo
Felipe Tena Ramirez

1954

President:
Jose Ortiz Tirado

Presidents:
Luis Chico Goerne
Jose Castro Estrada
Jose Rivera Perez Campos
Alfonso Guzman Neyra

Members:
Luis G. Corona

Luis Diaz Infante
Teofilo Olea y Leyva
Agapito Pozo
Franco Carreno
Genaro Ruiz de Chavez
Niceforo Guerrero Mendoza
Mariano Ramirez Vazquez
Octavio Mendoza Gonzalez
Hilario Medina
Agustin Mercado Alarcon
Alfonso Francisco Ramirez
Vicente Santos Guajardo
Gabriel Garcia Rojas
Gilberto Valenzuela
Arturo Martinez Adame

Supernumeraries:
Felipe Tena Ramirez
Mariano Azuela
Angel Gonzalez de la Vega
Rafael Matos Escobedo
Juan Jose Gonzalez Bustamante

1955

President:
Vicente Santos Guajardo

Presidents:
Genaro Ruiz de Chavez
Mariano Ramirez Vazquez
Jose Rivera Perez Campos
Agapito Pozo

Members:
Teofilo Olea y Leyva
Alfonso Francisco Ramirez
Franco Carreno
Gabriel Garcia Rojas
Niceforo Guerrero Mendoza
Arturo Martinez Adame
Octavio Mendoza Gonzalez
Luis Chico Goerne
Agustin Mercado Alarcon
Jose Castro Estrada
Gilberto Valenzuela
Alfonso Guzman Neyra
Luis Diaz Infante
Rodolfo Chavez S.
Hilario Medina
Mario G. Rebolledo Fernandez

Supernumeraries:
Mariano Azuela
Juan Jose Gonzalez Bustamante
Felipe Tena Ramirez
Rafael Matos Escobedo
Angel Gonzalez de la Vega

1956

President:
Vicente Santos Guajardo

Presidents:
Agustin Mercado Alarcon
Gilberto Valenzuela
Octavio Mendoza Gonzalez
Mario G. Rebolledo Fernandez

Members:
Franco Carreno
Jose Castro Estrada
Niceforo Guerrero Mendoza
Alfonso Guzman Neyra
Luis Diaz Infante
Rodolfo Chavez S.
Hilario Medina
Agapito Pozo
Alfonso Francisco Ramirez
Mariano Ramirez Vazquez
Gabriel Garcia Rojas
Jose Rivera Perez Campos
Arturo Martinez Adame
Genaro Ruiz de Chavez
Luis Chico Goerne
Carlos Franco Sodi

Supernumeraries:
Mariano Azuela
Juan Jose Gonzalez Bustamante
Felipe Tena Ramirez
Rafael Matos Escobedo
Angel Gonzalez de la Vega

1957

President:
Hilario Medina

Presidents:
Rodolfo Chavez S.
Vicente Santos Guajardo
Franco Carreno
Luis Diaz Infante

Members:
Luis Chico Goerne
Jose Rivera Perez Campos
Alfonso Francisco Ramirez
Genaro Ruiz de Chavez
Gabriel Garcia Rojas
Carlos Franco Sodi
Arturo Martinez Adame
Felipe Tena Ramirez
Jose Castro Estrada
Agustin Mercado Alarcon
Alfonso Guzman Neyra

Octavio Mendoza Gonzalez
Agapito Pozo
Gilberto Valenzuela
Mariano Ramirez Vazquez
Mario G. Rebolledo Fernandez

Supernumeraries:
Mariano Azuela
Juan Jose Gonzalez Bustamante
Angel Gonzalez de la Vega
Rafael Matos Escobedo

1958

President:
Agapito Pozo

Presidents:
Luis Chico Goerne
Alfonso Guzman Neyra
Alfonso Francisco Ramirez
Arturo Martinez Adame

Members:
Gabriel Garcia Rojas
Octavio Mendoza Gonzalez
Jose Castro Estrada
Gilberto Valenzuela
Mariano Ramirez Vazquez
Juan Jose Gonzalez Bustamante
Jose Rivera Perez Campos
Rodolfo Chavez S.
Angel Gonzalez de la Vega
Franco Carreno
Carlos Franco Sodi
Jose Lopez Lira
Felipe Tena Ramirez
Angel Carvajal
Agustin Mercado Alarcon
Manuel Rivera Silva

Supernumerary:
Rafael Matos Escobedo

1959

President:
Alfonso Guzman Neyra

Presidents:
Juan Jose Gonzalez Bustamante
Gabriel Garcia Rojas
Felipe Tena Ramirez
Angel Gonzalez de la Vega

Members:
Agapito Pozo
Agustin Mercado Alarcon
Luis Chico Goerne
Octavio Mendoza Gonzalez

Arturo Martinez Adame
Gilberto Valenzuela
Rafael Matos Escobedo
Rodolfo Chavez S.
Jose Castro Estrada
Franco Carreno
Mariano Ramirez Vazquez
Jose Lopez Lira
Jose Rivera Perez Campos
Angel Carvajal
Carlos Franco Sodi
Manuel Rivera Silva

1960

President:
Alfonso Guzman Neyra

Presidents:
Juan Jose Gonzalez Bustamante
Jose Castro Estrada
Felipe Tena Ramirez
Angel Carvajal

Members:
Gabriel Garcia Rojas
Jose Rivera Perez Campos
Alberto R. Vela
Carlos Franco Sodi
Mariano Azuela
Agustin Mercado Alarcon
Agapito Pozo
Octavio Mendoza Gonzalez
Luis Chico Goerne
Gilberto Valenzuela
Arturo Martinez Adame
Franco Carreno
Rafael Matos Escobedo
Jose Lopez Lira
Mariano Ramirez Vazquez
Manuel Rivera Silva

1961

President:
Alfonso Guzman Neyra

Presidents:
Juan Jose Gonzalez Bustamante
Jose Lopez Lira
Jose Rivera Perez Campos
Agapito Pozo

Members:
Agustin Mercado Alarcon
Mariano Ramirez Vazquez
Alberto R. Vela
Gabriel Garcia Rojas
Manuel Rivera Silva

1961 (cont.)

Mariano Azuela
Angel Gonzalez de la Vega
Maria Cristina Salmoran de
    Tamayo*
Rafael Matos Escobedo
Jose Castro Estrada
Felipe Tena Ramirez
Adalberto Padilla Ascencio
Octavio Mendoza Gonzalez
Angel Carvajal
Franco Carreno
Manuel Yanez Ruiz
Jose Castro Estrada

1962

President:
    Alfonso Guzman Neyra
Presidents:
    Juan Jose Gonzalez Bustamante
    Mariano Ramirez Vazquez
    Octavio Mendoza Gonzalez
    Agapito Pozo
Members:
    Jose Rivera Perez Campos
    Mariano Azuela
    Agustin Mercado Alarcon
    Maria Cristina Salmoran de
        Tamayo
    Alberto R. Vela
    Jose Castro Estrada
    Manuel Rivera Silva
    Adalberto Padilla Ascencio
    Angel Gonzalez de la Vega
    Angel Carvajal
    Rafael Matos Escobedo
    Manuel Yanez Ruiz
    Felipe Tena Ramirez
    Rafael Rojina Villegas
    Franco Carreno
    Vacancy
    Jose Castro Estrada

1963

President:
    Alfonso Guzman Neyra
Presidents:
    Juan Jose Gonzalez Bustamante
    Mariano Azuela
    Franco Carreno
    Agapito Pozo

Members:
    Octavio Mendoza Gonzalez
    Jose Castro Estrada
    Mariano Ramirez Vazquez
    Pedro Guerrero Martinez
    Jose Rivera Perez Campos
    Maria Cristina Salmoran de
        Tamayo
    Agustin Mercado Alarcon
    Adalberto Padilla Ascencio
    Alberto R. Vela
    Angel Carvajal
    Manuel Rivera Silva
    Manuel Yanez Ruiz
    Angel Gonzalez de la Vega
    Rafael Rojina Villegas
    Felipe Tena Ramirez
    Mario G. Rebolledo Fernandez
Supernumeraries:
    Alberto Gonzalez Blanco
    Raul Castellano Jimenez

1964

President:
    Alfonso Guzman Neyra
Presidents:
    Angel Gonzalez de la Vega
    Rafael Rojina Villegas
    Pedro Guerrero Martinez
    Agapito Pozo
Members:
    Mariano Azuela
    Maria Cristina Salmoran de
        Tamayo
    Octavio Mendoza Gonzalez
    Adalberto Padilla Ascencio
    Mariano Ramirez Vazquez
    Angel Carvajal
    Jose Rivera Perez Campos
    Manuel Yanez Ruiz
    Agustin Mercado Alarcon
    Enrique Martinez Ulloa
    Manuel Rivera Silva
    Abel Huitron y Aguado
    Felipe Tena Ramirez
    Jorge Inarritu
    Mario G. Rebolledo Fernandez
    Jose Castro Estrada
Supernumeraries:
    Alberto Gonzalez Blanco
    Ramon Canedo Aldrete
    Raul Castellano Jimenez
    Jose Luis Gutierrez Gutierrez

1965

President:
    Agapito Pozo
Presidents:
    Manuel Rivera Silva
    Enrique Martinez Ulloa
    Jorge Inarritu
    Manuel Yanez Ruiz
Members:
    Angel Gonzalez de la Vega
    Mariano Azuela
    Agustin Mercado Alarcon
    Jose Castro Estrada
    Mario G. Rebolledo Fernandez
    Rafael Rojina Villegas
    Abel Huitron y Aguado
    Angel Carvajal
    Octavio Mendoza Gonzalez
    Alfonso Guzman Neyra
    Jose Rivera Perez Campos
    Maria Cristina Salmoran de
        Tamayo
    Felipe Tena Ramirez
    Adalberto Padilla Ascencio
    Pedro Guerrero Martinez
    Mariano Ramirez Vazquez
Supernumeraries:
    Raul Castellano Jimenez
    Jose Luis Gutierrez Gutierrez
    Alberto Gonzalez Blanco
    Ramon Canedo Aldrete

1966

President:
    Agapito Pozo
Presidents:
    Abel Huitron y Aguado
    Jose Castro Estrada
    Felipe Tena Ramirez
    Manuel Yanez Ruiz
Members:
    Manuel Rivera Silva
    Mariano Azuela
    Jorge Inarritu
    Rafael Rojina Villegas
    Enrique Martinez Ulloa
    Angel Carvajal
    Agustin Mercado Alarcon
    Alfonso Guzman Neyra
    Mario G. Rebolledo Fernandez
    Maria Cristina Salmoran de
        Tamayo

---

*First woman member of the Supreme Court.

Jose Rivera Perez Campos
Adalberto Padilla Ascencio
Pedro Guerrero Martinez
Jose Luis Gutierrez Gutierrez
Mariano Ramirez Vazquez
Octavio Mendoza Gonzalez

Supernumeraries:
Raul Castellano Jimenez
Ezequiel Burguete Farrera
Alberto Gonzalez Blanco
Ernesto Solis Lopez
Ramon Canedo Aldrete

1967

President:
Agapito Pozo

Presidents:
Mario G. Rebolledo Fernandez
Mariano Ramirez Vazquez
Jose Rivera Perez Campos
Manuel Yanez Ruiz

Members:
Abel Huitron y Aguado
Rafael Rojina Villegas
Felipe Tena Ramirez
Angel Carvajal
Jose Castro Estrada
Alfonso Guzman Neyra
Manuel Rivera Silva
Maria Cristina Salmoran de
  Tamayo
Jorge Inarritu
Ezequiel Burguete Farrera
Enrique Martinez Ulloa
Ramon Canedo Aldrete
Octavio Mendoza Gonzalez
Pedro Guerrero Martinez
Mariano Azuela
Vacancy

Supernumeraries:
Raul Castellano Jimenez
Ernesto Solis Lopez
Alberto Gonzalez Blanco

1968

President:
Agapito Pozo

Presidents:
Ezequiel Burguete Farrera
Mariano Ramirez Vazquez
Octavio Mendoza Gonzalez
Ramon Canedo Aldrete

Members:
Mario G. Rebolledo Fernandez
Mariano Azuela
Jose Rivera Perez Campos
Rafael Rojina Villegas
Manuel Yanez Ruiz
Angel Carvajal
Abel Huitron y Aguado
Alfonso Guzman Neyra
Felipe Tena Ramirez
Maria Cristina Salmoran de
  Tamayo
Manuel Rivera Silva
Ernesto Aguilar Alvarez
Jorge Inarritu
Ernesto Solis Lopez
Enrique Martinez Ulloa
Pedro Guerrero Martinez

Supernumeraries:
Raul Castellano Jimenez
Salvador Mondragon Guerra
Alberto Orozco Romero
Luis Felipe Canudas Orezza

1969

President:
Alfonso Guzman Neyra

Presidents:
Ernesto Aguilar Alvarez
Ernesto Solis Lopez
Pedro Guerrero Martinez
Angel Carvajal

Members:
Ezequiel Burguete Farrera
Jorge Inarritu
Mariano Ramirez Vazquez
Enrique Martinez Ulloa
Ramon Canedo Aldrete
Alberto Orozco Romero
Mario G. Rebolledo Fernandez
Mariano Azuela
Jose Rivera Perez Campos
Rafael Rojina Villegas
Manuel Yanez Ruiz
Maria Cristina Salmoran de
  Tamayo
Abel Huitron y Aguado
Carlos del Rio Rodriguez
Felipe Tena Ramirez
Manuel Rivera Silva

Supernumeraries:
Raul Castellano Jimenez
Alberto Jimenez Castro
Salvador Mondragon Guerra

Antonio Capponi Guerrero
Luis Felipe Canudas Orezza

1970

President:
Alfonso Guzman Neyra

Presidents:
Manuel Rivera Silva
Maria Cristina Salmoran de
  Tamayo
Carlos del Rio Rodriguez
Mariano Azuela

Members:
Ezequiel Burguete Farrera
Mariano Ramirez Vazquez
Mario G. Rebolledo Fernandez
Rafael Rojina Villegas
Abel Huitron y Aguado
Enrique Martinez Ulloa
Ernesto Aguilar Alvarez
Ernesto Solis Lopez
Alberto Jimenez Castro
Ramon Canedo Aldrete
Jorge Inarritu
Manuel Yanez Ruiz
Jorge Saracho Alvarez
Salvador Mondragon Guerra
Pedro Guerrero Martinez
Angel Carvajal

Supernumeraries:
Antonio Capponi Guerrero
Raul Castellano Jimenez
Ramon Palacios Vargas
Alfonso Lopez Aparicio
Luis Felipe Canudas Orezza
Euquerio Guerrero Lopez

1971

President:
Alfonso Guzman Neyra

Presidents:
Ezequiel Burguete Farrera
Mariano Ramirez Vazquez
Alberto Jimenez Castro
Ramon Canedo Aldrete

Members:
Mario G. Rebolledo Fernandez
Rafael Rojina Villegas
Abel Huitron y Aguado
Enrique Martinez Ulloa
Ernesto Aguilar Alvarez
Ernesto Solis Lopez
Manuel Rivera Silva

1971 *(cont.)*

Manuel Yanez Ruiz
Carlos del Rio Rodriguez
Salvador Mondragon Guerra
Jorge Inarritu
Angel Carvajal
Jorge Saracho Alvarez
Maria Cristina Salmoran de Tamayo
Pedro Guerrero Martinez
Mariano Azuela

Supernumeraries:
Euquerio Guerrero Lopez
Raul Castellano Jimenez

1972

President:
Alfonso Guzman Neyra

Presidents:
Ezequiel Burguete Farrera
Mariano Ramirez Vazquez
Alberto Jimenez Castro
Ramon Canedo Aldrete

Members:
Mario G. Rebolledo Fernandez
Rafael Rojina Villegas
Abel Huitron y Aguado
Enrique Martinez Ulloa
Ernesto Aguilar Alvarez
Ernesto Solis Lopez
Manuel Rivera Silva
Manuel Yanez Ruiz
Carlos del Rio Rodriguez
Salvador Mondragon Guerra
Jorge Inarritu
Angel Carvajal
Jorge Saracho Alvarez
Maria Cristina Salmoran de Tamayo
Pedro Guerrero Martinez
Mariano Azuela

Supernumeraries:
Euquerio Guerrero Lopez
Raul Castellano Jimenez

1973

President:
Alfonso Guzman Neyra

Presidents:
Ezequiel Burguete Farrera
Maria Cristina Salmoran de Tamayo
Jorge Inarritu
J. Ramon Palacios Vargas

Members:
Mario G. Rebolledo Fernandez
Mariano Ramirez Vazquez
Manuel Rivera Silva
Rafael Rojina Villegas
Abel Huitron y Aguado
Enrique Martinez Ulloa
Ernesto Aguilar Alvarez
Ernesto Solis Lopez
Pedro Guerrero Martinez
Ramon Canedo Aldrete
Carlos del Rio Rodriguez
Salvador Mondragon Guerra
Alberto Jimenez Castro
Euquerio Guerrero Lopez
Jorge Saracho Alvarez

Supernumeraries:
Antonio Capponi Guerrero
David Franco Rodriguez
Alfonso Lopez Aparicio
Raul Cuevas Mantecon
Arturo Serrano Robles

1974

President:
Euquerio Guerrero Lopez

Presidents:
Ernesto Aguilar Alvarez
Enrique Martinez Ulloa
Antonio Rocha Cordero
Ramon Canedo Aldrete

Members:
Mario G. Rebolledo Fernandez
Ernesto Solis Lopez
Manuel Rivera Silva
J. Ramon Palacios Vargas
Abel Huitron y Aguado
David Franco Rodriguez
Ezequiel Burguete Farrera
Maria Cristina Salmoran de Tamayo
Pedro Guerrero Martinez
Jorge Saracho Alvarez
Jorge Inarritu
Salvador Mondragon Guerra
Carlos del Rio Rodriguez
Alfonso Lopez Aparicio
Alberto Jimenez Castro
Rafael Rojina Villegas

Supernumeraries:
Antonio Capponi Guerrero
Agustin Tellez Cruz
Arturo Serrano Robles
Fernando Castellanos Tena
Raul Cuevas Mantecon

1975

President:
Euquerio Guerrero Lopez

Presidents:
Manuel Rivera Silva
David Franco Rodriguez
Carlos del Rio Rodriguez
Ramon Canedo Aldrete

Members:
Ernesto Aguilar Alvarez
Agustin Tellez Cruz
Eduardo Langle Martinez
Juan Moises Calleja Garcia
Abel Huitron y Aguado
Alfonso Lopez Aparicio
Mario G. Rebolledo Fernandez
Maria Cristina Salmoran de Tamayo
Antonio Rocha Cordero
Jorge Saracho Alvarez
Jorge Inarritu
Salvador Mondragon Guerra
Alberto Jimenez Castro
J. Ramon Palacios Vargas
Arturo Serrano Robles
Rafael Rojina Villegas

Supernumeraries:
Raul Cuevas Mantecon
Fernando Castellanos Tena
Raul Lozano Ramirez
Livier Ayala Manzo

1976

President:
Mario G. Rebolledo Fernandez

Presidents:
Ernesto Aguilar Alvarez
Maria Cristina Salmoran de Tamayo
Salvador Mondragon Guerra
Arturo Serrano Robles

Members:
Raul Cuevas Mantecon
David Franco Rodriguez
Manuel Rivera Silva
J. Ramon Palacios Vargas
Fernando Castellanos Tena
Ramon Canedo Aldrete
Antonio Rocha Cordero
Alfonso Lopez Aparicio
Eduardo Langle Martinez
Juan Moises Calleja Garcia
Jorge Inarritu
Raul Lozano Ramirez
Carlos del Rio Rodrigue

Jorge Saracho Alvarez
Agustin Tellez Cruz
Alfonso Abitia Arzapalo

Supernumeraries:
Atanasio Gonzalez Martinez
Jorge Olivera Toro
Francisco H. Pavon
Vasconcelos
Luis Felipe Canudas Orezza
Gloria Leon Orantes

1977

President:
Agustin Tellez Cruz

Presidents:
Mario G. Rebolledo Fernandez
Alfonso Lopez Aparicio
Eduardo Langle Martinez
Raul Lozano Ramirez

Members:
Ernesto Aguilar Alvarez
Manuel Rivera Silva
Fernando Castellanos Tena
Antonio Rocha Cordero
Jorge Inarritu
Carlos del Rio Rodriguez
Arturo Serrano Robles
Atanasio Gonzalez Martinez
Salvador Mondragon Guerra
Raul Cuevas Mantecon
J. Ramon Palacios Vargas
Jose Alfonso Abitia Arzapalo
Maria Cristina Salmoran de
Tamayo
Julio Sanchez Vargas
Juan Moises Calleja Garcia
David Franco Rodriguez

Supernumeraries:
Gloria Leon Orantes
Jorge Olivera Toro
Francisco H. Pavon
Vasconcelos
Luis Felipe Canudas Orezza
Roberto Rios Elizondo

1978

President:
Agustin Tellez Cruz

Presidents:
Mario G. Rebolledo Fernandez
Alfonso Lopez Aparicio
Eduardo Langle Martinez
Raul Lozano Ramirez

Members:
Fernando Castellanos Tena
Manuel Rivera Silva
Jorge Inarritu
Antonio Rocha Cordero
Arturo Serrano Robles
Carlos del Rio Rodriguez
J. Ramon Palacios Vargas
Atanasio Gonzalez Martinez
Maria Cristina Salmoran de
Tamayo
Raul Cuevas Mantecon
Jose Alfonso Abitia Arzapalo
Juan Moises Calleja Garcia
David Franco Rodriguez
Julio Sanchez Vargas
Gloria Leon Orantes
Francisco H. Pavon
Vasconcelos

1979

President:
Agustin Tellez Cruz

Presidents:
Mario G. Rebolledo Fernandez
Alfonso Lopez Aparicio
Eduardo Langle Martinez
Raul Lozano Ramirez

Members:
Fernando Castellanos Tena
Manuel Rivera Silva
Jorge Inarritu
Carlos del Rio Rodriguez
Arturo Serrano Robles
Atanasio Gonzalez Martinez

J. Ramon Palacios Vargas
Raul Cuevas Mantecon
Maria Cristina Salmoran de
Tamayo
Jose Alfonso Abitia Arzapalo
Juan Moises Calleja Garcia
Julio Sanchez Vargas
David Franco Rodriguez
Gloria Leon Orantes
Francisco Pavon Vasconcelos
Jorge Olivera Toro

1980

President:
Agustin Tellez Cruz

Presidents:
Mario G. Rebolledo Fernandez
Juan Moises Calleja Garcia
Eduardo Langle Martinez
Gloria Leon Orantes

Members:
Manuel Rivera Silva
Raul Lozano Ramirez
Francisco Pavon Vasconcelos
Jorge Olivera Toro
J. Ramon Palacios Vargas
Fernando Castellanos Tena
Jose Alfonso Abitia Arzapalo
Raul Cuevas Mantecon
Jorge Inarritu
David Franco Rodriguez
Arturo Serrano Robles
Julio Sanchez Vargas
Carlos del Rio Rodriguez
Alfonso Lopez Aparicio
Atanasio Gonzalez Martinez
Maria Cristina Salmoran de
Tamayo

Supernumeraries:
Manuel Gutierrez de Velasco
Tarsicio Marquez Padilla
Santiago Rodriguez Roldan
Ernesto Diaz Infante
Enrique Alvarez del Castillo

Senators
1934–1982

1934–40 (36th and 37th Legislatures)

State	Senator	Alternate
Aguascalientes	*Vicente L. Benitez*	
	J. Jesus Marmolejo	
Campeche	Carlos Gongora Gala	
	Angel Castillo Lanz	
Chiapas	*Juan M. Esponda*	
	Gustavo R. Marin	
Chihuahua	Julian Aguilar G.	
	Angel Posada	
Coahuila	*Alberto Salinas Carranza*	Francisco Rivera
	Nazario S. Ortiz Garza	
Colima	*Manuel Gudino*	
	Pedro Torres Ortiz	
Distrito Federal	*Jose Maria Davila*	Jose Torres Ch.
	Ezequiel Padilla	
Durango	*Domingo Arrieta*	
	Alejandro Antuna Lopez	
Guanajuato	*Ignacio Garcia Tellez*	*Niceforo Guerrero*
	David Ayala	
Guerrero	Miguel F. Ortega	
	Roman Campos Viveros	
Hidalgo	Polioptro F. Martinez	
	Antonio Cadena	
Jalisco	Fernando Basulto Limon	
	J. Jesus Gonzalez Gallo	
Mexico	Manuel Riva Palacio	Armando P. Arroyo
	Antonio Romero	
Michoacan	*Ernesto Soto Reyes*	
	Luis Mora Tovar	
Morelos	Elias Perez Gomez	*Elpidio Perdomo*
	Benigno Abundez	Alfonso R. Samano
Nayarit	Jose Alejandro Anaya	
	Guillermo Flores Munoz	
Nuevo Leon	Federico Idar	Manuel Perez Mendoza
	Julian Garza Tijerina	
Oaxaca	*Wilfrido C. Cruz*	
	Francisco Lopez Cortes	

Puebla	Bernardo L. Bandala	Carlos Soto Guevara
	Gonzalo Bautista	
Queretaro	Gilberto Garcia	Fidencio Osornio
	Ignacio L. Figueroa	
San Luis Potosi	Gonzalo N. Santos	
	Eugenio B. Jimenez	
Sinaloa	Cristobal Bon Bustamante	Agustin G. del Castillo
	Rodolfo T. Loaiza	
Sonora	Camilo Gastelum Jr.	Andres H. Peralta
	Francisco L. Terminel	
Tabasco	Augusto Hernandez Olive	Bartolome Flores
	Francisco Trujillo Gurria	Salomon Gonzalez Blanco
Tamaulipas	Francisco Castellanos Jr.	
	Manuel Garza Zamora	
Tlaxcala	Felix C. Rodriguez	Joaquin Ballina Vela
	Mauro Angulo	
Veracruz	Miguel Aleman Valdes	Jose Murillo
	Candido Aguilar	
Yucatan	Bartolome Garcia Correa	Laureano Cardos Ruz
	Gualberto Carrillo Puerto	
Zacatecas	Leobardo Reynoso	
	Luis R. Reyes	

1940–46 (38th and 39th Legislatures)

State	Senator	Alternate
Aguascalientes	Ramon B. Aldana	Abelardo Reyes S.
	Enrique Osornio Camarena	
Campeche	Eduardo R. Mena Cordova	
	Pedro Tello Andueza	
Chiapas	F. Gustavo Gutierrez R.	
	Emilio Araujo	
Chihuahua	Eugenio Prado Proano	
	Benjamin Almeida Jr.	
Coahuila	Joaquin Martinez Chavarria	
	Damian L. Rodriguez	Jose Maria Hernandez
Colima	Miguel G. Santana	
	Conrado Torres Ortiz	
Distrito Federal	Alfonso Sanchez Madariaga	
	Antonio Villalobos Mayar	
Durango	Salvador Franco Urias	
	Maximo Garcia	
Guanajuato	Celestino Gasca	
	Rafael Rangel Hurtado	
Guerrero	Nabor A. Ojeda	
	Arturo Martinez Adame	
Hidalgo	Vicente Aguirre	Fernando Cruz Chavez
	Jose Lugo Guerrero	
Jalisco	Esteban Garcia de Alba	
	Abraham Gonzalez	
Mexico	Alfonso Flores M.	Augusto Hinojosa
	Alfredo Zarate Albarran	
Michoacan	Antonio Mayes Navarro	
	J. Trinidad Garcia	
Morelos	Fernando Amilpa	
	Jesus Castillo Lopez	

State	Senator	Alternate
Nayarit	*Luis Aranda del Toro*	
	Evaristo Jimenez Valdez	
Nuevo Leon	*Dionisio Garcia Leal*	
	Ramiro Tamez	
Oaxaca	Eleodoro Charis Castro	
	Fernando Magro Soto	
Puebla	*Noe Lecona*	Narciso Guarneros
	Rosendo Cortes	
Queretaro	Carlos Ortega Zavaley	Isidro Zuniga Solorzano
	Jose Perez Tejeda	
San Luis Potosi	*Gilberto Flores Munoz*	
	Leon Garcia Pujou	
Sinaloa	*Gabriel Leyva Velazquez*	Arturo Arcaraz
	Alejandro Pena	
Sonora	Alejo Bay	
	Francisco Martinez Peralta	
Tabasco	Huberto Sala Rueda	*Tito Livio Calcaneo*
	Alfonso Gutierrez Gurria	
Tamaulipas	Genovevo Martinez P.	
	Abel Oseguera Alvarez	
Tlaxcala	Samuel Hoyo Castro	Gerardo Juarez
	Rafael Avila Breton	
Veracruz	*Vidal Diaz Munoz*	
	Adolfo E. Ortega	
Yucatan	*Jose Castillo Torre*	
	Florencio Palomo Valencia	
Zacatecas	*Enrique Estrado*	Lamberto Elias
	Adrian Morales Salas	

1946–52 (40th and 41st Legislatures)

State	Senator	Alternate
Aguascalientes	*Edmundo Gamez Orozco*	Salvador Gallardo Davalos
	Jose Gonzalez Flores	Gonzalo Padilla Diaz
Campeche	*Pedro Guerrero Martinez*	Jose Maria Guerrero Lopez
	Fernando Berron Ramos	Mauro Perez
Chiapas	*Efrain Aranda Osorio*	Rafael Gomez
	Efrain Lazos	Manuel Borges
Chihuahua	*Alfredo Chavez*	*Teofilo R. Borunda*
	Antonio J. Bermudez	*Manuel Lopez Davila*
Coahuila	*Raul Lopez Sanchez*	*Ricardo Ainslie R.*
	Manuel Lopez Guitron	Manuel de Leon Lodoza
Colima	Ruben Vizcarra	Antonio Tirado Mayagoitia
	Meliton de la Mora	Carlos Alcaraz Ahumada
Distrito Federal	Carlos I. Serrano	Juan Jose Rivera Rojas
	Fidel Velazquez S.	Emiliano Barrera Esqueda
Durango	*Marino Castillo Najera*	Fernando Alvarez Lozoya
	Atanasio Arrieta Garcia	Juan Manuel Tinoco
Guanajuato	*Federico Medrano Valdivia*	*Jose Rivera Perez C.*
	Roberto Guzman Araujo	Jose Lanuza Araujo
Guerrero	*Donato Miranda Fonseca*	Andres Jaimes
	Ruffo Figueroa Figueroa	Francisco Diaz y Diaz
Hidalgo	Alfonso Corona del Rosal	Gregorio Hernandez
	Jose Gomez Esparza	Joel Perez
Jalisco	Miguel Moreno Padilla	Justo Gonzalez
	J. Jesus Cisneros Gomez	Manuel Romero Rojo
Mexico	*Gabriel Ramos Millan*	Malaquias Huitron
	Adolfo Lopez Mateos	*Salvador Sanchez Colin*

State	Senator	Alternate
Michoacan	*Felix Ireta Viveros*	Jose Torres Caballero
	Ricardo Ramirez Guerrero	Roberto E. Rodriguez
Morelos	*Elpidio Perdomo Garcia*	Manuel Aranda
	Carlos Lopez Uriza	Jose Balbuena
Nayarit	*Candelario Miramontes*	Ricardo Marin Ramos
	Jose Limon Guzman	Jesus Mora Yanez
Nuevo Leon	*Juan Manuel Elizondo*	Francisco Vela Gonzalez
	Jose S. Vivanco	Rodolfo Gaitan
Oaxaca	*Manuel R. Palacios*	Demetrio Flores Fagoaga
	Armando Rodriguez Mujica	*Manuel Mayoral Heredia*
Puebla	Alfonso Moreyra Carrasco	Agustin Hernandez Duperrain
	Gustavo Diaz Ordaz	Mariano Rayon Aguilar
Queretaro	Gilberto Garcia Navarro	Jose E. Calzada
	Eduardo Luque Loyola	Antonio Perez Alcocer
San Luis Potosi	*Fernando Moctezuma*	*Antonio Rocha Jr.*
	Manuel Alvarez Lopez	*Pablo Aldrett*
Sinaloa	Fausto A. Marin	Guillermo Osuna y Osuna
	Vacant	Vacant
Sonora	Antonio Canale	Manuel Gandara Jr.
	Gustavo A. Uruchurtu	*Noe Palomares Navarro*
Tabasco	*Antonio Taracena*	Luis Leon Olivos
	Adelor D. Sala	Jesus Lombardini
Tamaulipas	Eutimio Rodriguez	Jose Cardenas Vazquez
	Magdaleno Aguilar	Ladislao Cardenas Jr.
Tlaxcala	*Mauro Angulo*	Ezequiel M. Garcia
	Gersayn Ugarte	Baltasar Maldonado
Veracruz	*Fernando Lopez Arias*	Jose Fernando Villegas
	Fernando Casas Aleman	Alfonso Palacios L.
Yucatan	*Gonzalo Lopez Manzanero*	Adalberto Aguilar Osorio
	Ernesto Novelo Torres	Felix Rosado Iturralde
Zacatecas	*Jesus B. Gonzalez*	J. Jesus Maria Garcia Martinez
	Salvador Castanedo R.	Valente Lozano

1952–58 (42nd and 43rd Legislatures)

State	Senator	Alternate
Aguascalientes	*Pedro de Alba*	*Roberto Diaz*
	Aquiles Elorduy	Joaquin Cruz Ramirez
Baja California del Norte	*Leopoldo Verdugo Quiroz*	Jesus Montano Monge
	Esteban Cantu Jimenez	Manuel Quiroz Labastida
Campeche	*Rigoberto Otal Briseno*	Raul Loyo y Loyo
	Alberto Trueba Urbina	Manuel Pavon Bahaine
Chiapas	Rodolfo Suarez Coello	Hector Yanez
	Julio Serrano Castro	Alejandro Rea Moguel
Chihuahua	*Teofilo R. Borunda*	Salvador Gonzalez Regalado
	Oscar Flores	Luis de la Garza O.
Coahuila	*Jacinto B. Trevino*	Domingo Ortiz Garza
	Gustavo Cardenas Huerta	Rafael Duarte Nunez
Colima	*Rafael S. Pimentel*	Salvador G. Govea
	Roberto A. Solorzano	Jorge Alvarez Gutierrez
Distrito Federal	*Jesus Yuren Aguilar*	Jose Lopez Peral
	Salvador Urbina	Jesus Lozoya Solis
Durango	*Francisco Gonzalez de la V.*	Alfonso Perez Gavilan
	Alberto Terrones Benitez	Francisco Celis M.
Guanajuato	*Luis I. Rodriguez*	*Rafael Corrales Ayala*
	Francisco Garcia Carranza	
Guerrero	*Alfonso G. Alarcon*	*Alfonso L. Nava*
	Emigdio Martinez Adame	*Caritino Maldonado Perez*

State	Senator	Alternate
Hidalgo	*Raul Fernandez Robert*	Eduardo Manzano
	Alfonso Cravioto	*Julian Rodriguez Adame*
Jalisco	*Silvano Barba Gonzalez*	Guillermo Ramirez Valadez
	Saturnino Coronado O.	Luis Ramirez Meza
Mexico	*Alfredo del Mazo Velez*	Hermilo Arcos Perez
	Juan Fernandez Albarran	Eulalio Nunez Alonso
Michoacan	*David Franco Rodriguez*	Ignacio Ochoa Reyes
	Enrique Bravo Valencia	Jose Garibay Romero
Morelos	*Norberto Lopez Avelar*	*Felipe Rivera Crespo*
	Fausto Galvan Campos	Nicolas Zapata
Nayarit	*Emilio M. Gonzalez*	Manuel Villegas Arellano
	Esteban B. Calderon	Francisco Garcia Monteros
Nuevo Leon	*Anacleto Guerrero Guajardo*	Felix Gonzalez Salinas
	Rodrigo Gomez Gomez	*Roberto A. Cortes Muniz*
Oaxaca	*Alfonso Perez Gasca*	Ernesto Meixueiro
	Rafael E. Melgar	Dario L. Vasconcelos
Puebla	*Luis C. Manjarrez*	Alfonso Castillo Borsani
	Guillermo Castillo F.	Felix Guerrero Mejia
Queretaro	*Jose Figueroa Balvanera*	Enrique Montes Dorantes
	Manuel Gonzalez Cosio	Francisco Rodriguez Aguillon
San Luis Potosi	*Antonio Rocha*	*Jesus Noyola*
	David Vargas Bravo	Benito Noyola
Sinaloa	*Macario Gaxiola Urias*	Jesus Gil Ryathga
	Jesus Celis Campos	Humberto Batiz Ramos
Sonora	*Fausto Acosta Romo*	Antonio Quiroga Rivera
	Noe Palomares Navarro	Francisco Enciso Mezquita
Tabasco	Marcelino Inurreta	Salvador Camelo Soler
	Agustin Beltran Bastar	Felipe Ferrer Trujeque
Tamaulipas	*Raul Garate L.*	Jose Lopez Cardenas
	Manuel Guzman Willis	Crisoforo Barragan Albino
Tlaxcala	*Higinio Paredes Ramos*	*Anselmo Cervantes Hernandez*
	Miguel Osorio Ramirez	Maximiliano Cervantes Perez
Veracruz	*Roberto Amoros Guiot*	*Isauro Acosta Garcia*
	Jose Rodriguez Claveria	Hermenegildo J. Aldana
Yucatan	*Efrain Brito Rosado*	*Victor Mena Palomo*
	Antonio Mediz Bolio	Armando Medina Alonso
Zacatecas	*Brigido Reynoso*	Roberto del Real
	Lauro G. Caloca	Gonzalo Castanedo

1958–64 (44th and 45th Legislatures)

State	Senator	Alternate
Aguascalientes	*Manuel Moreno Sanchez*	J. Guadalupe Lopez Velarde
	Alfredo de Lara Isaacs	Maria del Carmen Araiza Lopez
Baja California del Norte	*Jose Maria Tapia Freyding*	Jorge Riva Palacio
	Gustavo Vildosola Almada	Francisco Duenas Montes
Campeche	*Fernando Lanz Duret*	Luis Felipe Martinez Mezquida
	Nicolas Canto Carrillo	Jose Dolores Garcia Aguilar
Chiapas	*Jose Castillo Tielemans*	J. Guadalupe Hernandez de Leon
	Abelardo de la Torre G.	Marcelina Galindo Arce
Chihuahua	*Rodrigo M. Quevedo Moreno*	Valente Chacon Vaca
	Tomas Valles V.	Jaime Canales Lira
Coahuila	*Vicente Davila Aguirre*	*Rafael Carranza H.*
	Federico Berrueto Ramon	*Salvador Hernandez Vela*

Colima	*Antonio Salazar Salazar*	*Roberto Pizano Saucedo*
	Francisco Velasco Curiel	Raymundo Anzar Nava
Distrito Federal	*Hilario Medina Gaona*	Raoul Fournier Villada
	Fidel Velazquez Sanchez	*Joaquin Gamboa Pascoe*
Durango	*Carlos Real*	Pablo Avila de la Torre
	Enrique Dupre Ceniceros	Abdon Alanis Ramirez
Guanajuato	*Jesus Lopez Lira*	*Jose Lopez Bermudez*
	Vicente Garcia Gonzalez	Efren Alcocer Herrera
Guerrero	*Caritino Maldonado*	Francisco Vazquez Anorve
	Carlos Roman Celis	*Jorge Soberon Acevedo*
Hidalgo	*Julian Rodriguez Adame*	*Carlos Ramirez Guerrero*
	Leonardo M. Hernandez M.	Agustin Mariel Anaya
Jalisco	*Mariano Azuela*	Elias Mendoza Gonzalez
	Guillermo Ramirez Valadez	Marcos Montero Ruiz
Mexico	*Abel Huitron y Aguado*	Felipe J. Sanchez
	Maximiliano Ruiz Castaneda	*Mario Colin Sanchez*
Michoacan	*Manuel Hinojosa Ortiz*	Lauro Pallares Carrasquedo
	Natalio Vazquez Pallares	Norberto Vega Villagomez
Morelos	*Porfirio Neri Arizmendi*	Antonio Flores Mazari
	Eliseo Aragon Rebolledo	Gonzalo Pastrana Castro
Nayarit	*Alberto Medina Munoz*	Ricardo Gomez Garcia
	Enrique Ledon Alcaraz	Amador Cortes Estrada
Nuevo Leon	*Angel Santos Cervantes*	*Napoleon Gomez Sada*
	Eduardo Livas	*Margarita R. Garcia Flores*
Oaxaca	*Rodolfo Brena Torres*	Manuel Rivera Toro
	Ramon Ruiz Vasconcelos	Nicolas Grijalva Miron
Puebla	*Donato Bravo Izquierdo*	Carlos Vergara Soto
	Rafael Moreno Valle	*Jose Ignacio Morales Cruz*
Queretaro	*Rafael Altamirano Herrera*	Avertano Mondragon Ochoa
	Domingo Olvera Gamez	Realino Frias Rodriguez
San Luis Potosi	*Juan Enrique Azuara*	Agustin Olivo Monsivais
	Pablo Aldrett Cuellar	Jacinto Maldonado Villaverde
Sinaloa	*Teofilo Alvarez Borboa*	Enrique Riveros Castro
	Leopoldo Sanches Celis	Hector Manuel Lopez Castro
Sonora	*Guillermo Ibarra*	Ernesto Salazar Giron
	Carlos B. Maldonado	Manuel Torres Escobosa
Tabasco	Cesar A. Rojas	Diogenes Zurita Suarez
	Julian A. Manzur O.	Joaquin Bates Caparroso
Tamaulipas	*Emilio Martinez Manautou*	Rafael Sierra de la Garza
	Juan Manuel Teran Mata	*Manuel A. Ravize*
Tlaxcala	*Francisco Hernandez y H.*	Raul Juarez Carro
	Samuel Ortega Hernandez	Ricardo Velazquez Vazquez
Veracruz	*Roberto Gomez Maqueo*	*Ferrer Galvan Bourel*
	Rosendo Topete Ibanez	Manuel Meza Hernandez
Yucatan	*Edgardo Medina Alonso*	J. Enrique Millet Espinosa
	Antonio Mena Brito	Artemio Alpizar Pacheco
Zacatecas	*Mauricio Magdaleno*	Bernardo del Real de Leon
	Jose Rodriguez Elias	Salvador Esparza Gutierrz

1964–70 (46th and 47th Legislatures)

State	Senator	Alternate
Aguascalientes	*Alberto Alcala de Lira*	Jose Ramirez Gamez
	Luis Gomez Zepeda	Roberto Diaz Rodriguez
Baja California del Norte	*Hermenegildo Cuenca Diaz*	*Milton Castellanos Everado*
	Jose Ricardi Tirado	Eduardo Tonella Escamilla

Campeche	*Maria Lavalle Urbina*	Carlos Cano Ruiz
	Carlos Sansores Perez	Ramon Marrero Ortiz
Chiapas	*Andres Serra Rojas*	Gustavo Lescieur Lopez
	Arturo Moguel Esponda	Amadeo Narcia Ruiz
Chihuahua	*Luis L. Leon Uranga*	*Ricardo Carrillo Duran*
	Manuel Bernardo Aguirre S.	Mariano Valenzuela Ceballos
Coahuila	*Eulalio Gutierrez Trevino*	Raymundo Cordoba Zuniga
	Florencio Barrera Fuentes	Ramiro Pena Guerra
Colima	*Jesus Robles Martinez*	Alberto Larios Gaytan
	Alfredo Ruiseco Avellaneda	Crescencio Flores Diaz
Distrito Federal	*Luis Gonzalez Aparicio*	*Renaldo Guzman Orozco*
	Jesus Yuren Aguilar	*Rodolfo Echeverria Alvarez*
Durango	*Alberto Terrones Benitez*	*Carlos Real Encinas*
	Cristobal Guzman Cardenas	*Ignacio Castillo Mena*
Guanajuato	*Juan Perez Vela*	Virginia Soto Rodriguez
	Manuel Moreno Moreno	Eliseo Rodriguez Ramirez
Guerrero	*Baltasar R. Leyva Mancilla*	*Jeronimo Gomar Suastegui*
	Ezequiel Padilla Penaloza	*Moises Ochoa Campos*
Hidalgo	*Oswaldo Cravioto Cisneros*	Carlos Raul Guadarrama M.
	Manuel Sanchez Vite	Federico Ocampo Noble
Jalisco	*Salvador Corona Bandin*	Luis Ramirez Meza
	Filiberto Rubalcaba Sanchez	Jose G. Mata Lopez
Mexico	*Fernando Ordorica Inclan*	Alejandro Arzate Sanchez
	Mario C. Olivera Gomez T.	Eduardo Arias Nuville
Michoacan	*J. Jesus Romero Flores*	Manuel Lopez Perez
	Rafael Galvan Maldonado	J. Jesus Arreola Belman
Morelos	*Diodoro Rivera Uribe*	Ramon Hernandez Navarro
	Antonio Flores Mazari	Luis Flores Sobral
Nayarit	*Alfonso Guerra Olivares*	Raul Llanos Lerma
	J. Ricardo Marin Ramos	*Rogelio Flores Curiel*
Nuevo Leon	*Armando Artega Santoyo*	*Santiago Roel Garcia*
	Napoleon Gomez Sada	Jose Ovalle Morales
Oaxaca	*Jose Pacheco Iturribarria*	*Rodolfo Sandoval Lopez*
	Raul Bolanos Cacho	Manuel Martinez Soto
Puebla	*Gonzalo Bautista O' Farrill*	Eduardo Naude Anaya
	Eduardo Cue Merlo	Jorge Vergara Jimenez
Queretaro	*Eduardo Luque Loyola*	Alfonso Alexander Hernandez
	Manuel Soberanes Munoz	*Fernando Espinosa Gutierrez*
San Luis Potosi	*Juan Jose Gonzalez B.*	*Florencio Salazar Mendez*
	Jesus N. Noyola Zepeda	Adalberto Tamayo Lopez
Sinaloa	*Manuel Sarmiento Sarmiento*	Canuto Ibarra Guerrero
	Amado Estrada Rodriguez	Hector Gonzalez Guevara
Sonora	*Juan de Dios Bojorquez Leon*	Mario Morua Johnson
	Alicia Arellano Tapia	Fernando Pesqueira Juvera
Tabasco	*Gustavo A. Rovirosa Perez*	Jose Leonides Gallegos A.
	Fausto Pintado Borrego	Fernando Hernandez Lorono
Tamaulipas	*Magdaleno Aguilar Castillo*	Manuel Guerra Hinojosa
	Antonio Garcia Rojas	Alfonso Barnetche Gonzalez
Tlaxcala	*Ignacio Bonilla Vazquez*	Rafael Minor Franco
	Luciano Huerta Sanchez	Jose Hernandez Diaz
Veracruz	*Rafael Murillo Vidal*	*Manlio Fabio Tapia Camacho*
	Arturo Llorente Gonzalez	Martin Diaz Montero
Yucatan	*Rafael Matos Escobedo*	*Ramon Osorio Carbajal*
	Carlos Loret de Mola	Ruben Marin y Kall
Zacatecas	*Manuel Tello Baurrand*	*Fernando Pamanes Escobedo*
	Jose Gonzalez Varela	Aurelio Lopez de la Torre

1970–76 (48th and 49th Legislatures)

State	Senator	Alternate
Aguascalientes	*Miguel Angel Barberena Vega*	*Augusto Gomez Villanueva*
	Enrique Olivares Santana	Roberto Diaz Rodriguez
Baja California del Norte	Ramon Alvarez Cisneros	Pablo Villarino
	Gustavo Aubanel Vallejo	Adolfo Ramirez Mendez
Campeche	*Ramon Alcala Ferrera*	Ruben Selem Salum
	Carlos Perez Camara	Enrique Escalante Escalante
Chiapas	Ramiro Yanez Cordova	*Edgar Robledo Santiago*
	Juan Sabines Gutierrez	Maria Celorio Vda. de Rovelo
Chihuahua	Jose I. Aguilar Irungaray	Jose Pacheco Loya
	Arnaldo Gutierrez Hernandez	Samuel I. Valenzuela
Coahuila	*Braulio Fernandez Aguirre*	Mauro Berrueto Ramon
	Oscar Flores Tapia	Pedro Gonzalez Rivera
Colima	*Roberto Pizano Saucedo*	Alfonso Garcia Franco
	Aurora Ruvalcaba Gutierrez	Miguel Trejo Ochoa
Distrito Federal	*Martin Luis Guzman*	Alfonso Sanchez Silva
	Alfonso Sanchez Madariaga	Luis Diaz Vazquez
Durango	*Salvador Gamiz Fernandez*	Salvador Nava Rodriguez
	Agustin Ruiz Soto	Hortensia Flores Varela
Guanajuato	*Jose Rivera Perez Campos*	Ramon Lopez Diaz
	Jose Castillo Hernandez	Alfonso Sanchez Lopez
Guerrero	*Ruben Figueroa Figueroa*	Ismael Andraca Navarrete
	Vicente Fuentes Diaz	Jose Guadalupe Solis Galeana
Hidalgo	*Raul Lozano Ramirez*	Rafael Anaya Ramirez
	German Corona del Rosal	Vicente Trejo Callejas
Jalisco	*Javier Garcia Paniagua*	Vicente Palencia Murillo
	Ignacio Maciel Salcedo	*Renaldo Guzman Orozco*
Mexico	Felix Vallejo Martinez	Manuel Huitron y Aquado
	Francisco Perez Rios	Sixto Noguez Estrada
Michoacan	*J. Jesus Garcia Santacruz*	Gerardo Jimenez Escamilla
	Norberto Mora Plancarte	Maria Teresa Calderon C.
Morelos	*Elpidio Perdomo Garcia*	Ignacio Guerra Tejeda
	Francisco Aguilar Hernandez	Marcos Figueroa Ocampo
Nayarit	*Rogelio Flores Curiel*	Santos Ramos Contreras
	Emilio M. Gonzalez Parra	Pedro Lopez Diaz
Nuevo Leon	*Luis M. Farias*	Arnulfo Guerra Guajardo
	Bonifacio Salinas Leal	Hilario Contreras Molina
Oaxaca	*Celestino Perez Perez*	Mario Melgar Pacchiano
	Gilberto Suarez Torres	Diodoro Carrasco Palacios
Puebla	*Guillermo Morales B.*	*Guadalupe Lopez Breton*
	Alfredo Toxqui F. de Lara	Enrique Martinez Marquez
Queretaro	*Arturo Guerrero Ortiz*	Ricardo Rangel Andrade
	Salvador Jimenez del Prado	Jose Gonzalez Olvera
San Luis Potosi	*Florencio Salazar Martinez*	Juan Antonio Ledesma
	Guillermo Fonseca Alvarez	Carlos Manuel Castillo Varela
Sinaloa	*Alfonso G. Calderon Velarde*	*Ramon F. Iturbe*
	Gabriel Leyva Velazquez	Mateo Camacho Ontiveros
Sonora	*Benito Bernal Miranda*	Ramon Angel Amante E.
	Alejandro Carrillo Marcor	Benjamin Villaescusa R.
Tabasco	*Pascual Bellizzia Castaneda*	Hernan Rabelo Wade
	Enrique Gonzalez Pedrero	Maximo Evia Ramon
Tamaulipas	*Enrique Cardenas Gonzalez*	Jose Bruno del Rio Cruz
	Jose C. Romero Flores	Jose Maria Vargas Perez

Tlaxcala	*Vicente Juarez Carro*	Guillermo Villeda Hernandez
	Nicanor Serrano del C.	Esteban Minor Quiroz
Veracruz	*Samuel Terrazas Zozaya*	Daniel Sierra Rivera
	undecided	undecided
Yucatan	*Victor Manzanilla Schaffer*	Francisco Repetto Milan
	Francisco Luna Kan	Hernan Morales Medina
Zacatecas	*Calixto Medina Medina*	Manuel Ibarguengoitia Llaguno
	Aurora Navia Millan	Abundio Monsivais Garcia

1976–82 (50th and 51st Legislatures)

State	Senator	Alternate
Aguascalientes	Rodolfo Landeros Gallegos	Roberto Diaz Rodriguez
	Hector Hugo Olivares V.	Jose de Jesus Medellin M.
Baja California del Norte	*Celestino Salcedo Monteon*	Rafael Garcia Vazquez
	Roberto de la Madrid R.	Oscar Baylon Chacon
Baja California del Sur	*Alberto A. Alvarado A.*	Prisca Melgar de Tuchmann
	Marcelo Rubio Ruiz	Victor Manuel Liceaga Ruiba
Campeche	*Carlos Sansores Perez*	Rosa Maria Martinez Denegri
	Fernando Rafful Miguel	Joaquin E. Repetto Ocampo
Chiapas	*Salomon Gonzalez Blanco*	Roberto Corzo Gay
	Horacio Castellanos Coutino	Maria Guadalupe Cruz Aranda
Chihuahua	*Oscar Ornelas Kuckle*	Santiago Nieto Sandoval
	Mario Carballo Pasos	Federico Estrada Meraz
Coahuila	*Eliseo F. Mendoza Berrueto*	*Oscar Ramirez Mijares*
	Gustavo Guerra Castanos	Ramiro Ruiz Madero
Colima	*Griselda Alvarez P. de Leon*	Aquileo Diaz Virgen
	Antonio Salazar Salazar	Roberto Anzar Martinez
Distrito Federal	*Hugo Cervantes del Rio*	Luis del Toro Calero
	Joaquin Gamboa Pascoe	Rodolfo Martinez Moreno
Durango	*Ignacio Castillo Mena*	Antonio Calzada Guillen
	Tomas Rangel Perales	Felipe Ibarra Barbosa
Guanajuato	*Euquerio Guerrero Lopez*	Ignacio Vazquez Torres
	Jesus Cabrera Munoz Ledo	Adolfo Gonzalez Aguado
Guerrero	*Jorge Soberon Acevedo*	Luis Leon Aponte
	Alejandro Cervantes Delgado	Ruben Uriza Castro
Hidalgo	*Humberto A. Lugo Gil*	Juan Sanchez Roldan
	Guillermo Rossell de la L.	Jose Luis Suarez Molina
Jalisco	*Jose Maria Martinez R.*	*Maria Guadalupe Martinez de H.*
	Arnulfo Villasenor Saavedra Reyes	Rodolfo Flores Zara
Mexico	*Leonardo Rodriguez Alcaine*	Ignacio Guzman Garduno
	Gustavo Baz Prada	Humberto Lira Mora
Michoacan	*Cuauhtemoc Cardenas S.*	Jose Luis Escobar Herrer
	Guillermo Morfin Garcia	Jose Berber Sanchez
Morelos	Angel Ventura Valle	Bernardo Heredia Valle
	Javier Rondero Zubieta	Roque Gonzalez Urriza
Nayarit	Leobardo Ramos Martinez	Felix Torres Haro
	Daniel Espinosa Galindo	Jose Manuel Rivas Allende
Nuevo Leon	*Napoleon Gomez Sada*	Jose Diaz Delgado
	Federico Amaya Rodriguez	Adrian Yanez Martinez
Oaxaca	*Eliseo Jimenez Ruiz*	*Rodolfo Alavez Flores*
	Jorge Cruickshank Garcia	Mario Vazquez Martinez
Puebla	*Horacio Labastida Munoz*	Ignacio Cuauhtemoc Paleta
	Blas Chumacero Sanchez	Marco Antonio Rojas Flores
Queretaro	*Rafael Camacho Guzman*	Cesar Ruben Hernandez E.
	Manuel Gonzalez Cosio	Telesforo Trejo Uribe

Quintana Roo	Vicente Coral Martinez	Jose Enrique Azueta Orlaynet
	Jose Blanco Peyrefitte	Hernan Pastrana Pastrana
San Luis Potosi	*Carlos Jongitud Barrios*	Rafael A. Tristan Lopez
	Fausto Zapata Loredo	Francisco Padron Puyou
Sinaloa	*Hilda J. Anderson Nevares*	Silvestre Perez Lorens
	Gilberto Sebastian Ruiz A.	Cesar Alfredo Lopez Garcia
Sonora	*Juan Jose Gastelum Salcido*	*Alejandro Sobarzo Loaiza*
	Adolfo de la Huerta Oriol	Juan Antonio Ruibal Corella
Tabasco	*David Gustavo Gutierrez R.*	Antonio Ocampo Ramirez
	Carlos Pellicer Camara	Nicolas Reynes Berezaluce
Tamaulipas	*Morelos Jaime Canseco G.*	Fernando Garcia Arellano
	Martha Chavez Padron	Enrique Fernandez Perez
Tlaxcala	Jesus Hernandez Rojas	Joaquin Cisneros Fernandez
	Rafael Minor Franco	Alvaro Salazar Lozano
Veracruz	*Silverio R. Alvarado A.*	Angel Gomez Calderon
	Sergio Martinez Mendoza	Delia de la Paz Rebolledo
Yucatan	*Victor Manuel Cervera P.*	Efrain Zumarraga Ramirez
	Graciliano Alpuche Pinzon	Martin Garcia Lizaman
Zacatecas	Jorge Gabriel Garcia Rojas	Jose Bonilla Robles
	Jose Guadalupe Cervantes C.	Arturo Romo Gutierrez

Federal Deputies
1937–1982

1937–40 (37th Legislature)

State	Deputy	Alternate
Aguascalientes		
1.	Ramon B. Aldana	J. Concepcion Rodriguez
2.	Pedro Quevedo	Carlos R. Ramos
Baja California del Norte (Territory)		
1.	Hipolito Renteria	Ramon M. Hernandez
Baja California del Sur (Territory)		
1.	Adan Velarde	Manuel Gomez
Campeche		
1.	*Hector Perez Martinez*	*Pedro Guerrero Martinez*
2.	Ignacio Reyes Ortega	Emilio M. Perez Arroyo
Chiapas		
1.	Gil Salgado Palacio	Gustavo Lopez Gutierrez
2.	*Rafael P. Gamboa*	Adolfo C. Corzo
3.	*Emilio Araujo*	Armando Guerra A.
4.	*Efrain Aranda Osorio*	Carlos Albores C.
5.	Agustin Fuentevilla, Jr.	Jose Orantes
Chihuahua		
1.	*Eugenio Prado*	Leobardo Chavez
2.	*Guillermo Quevedo Moreno*	Tito Herrera Rojas
3.	Francisco Garcia Carranza	Enrique Acosta E.
4.	Ismael C. Falcon	Ignacio Leon
5.	Carlos Terrazas	Justino Loya
Coahuila		
1.	Tomas Garza Felan	Apolonio Martinez
2.	Juan Perez	Fernando Rivera
3.	*Damian L. Rodriguez*	Manuel Rodriguez F.
4.	Emilio N. Acosta	Arturo V. Ibarra M.
Colima		
1.	*Jose Campero*	Rafael C. Ceballos
2.	Pablo Silva	Julio Santa Ana
Distrito Federal		
1.	Jose Munoz Cota	Juventino Aguilar
2.	Salvador Ochoa Renteria	Roberto Aguilera C.

3.	J. Maximino Molina	Juan de Dios Flores
4.	Jose Escudero Andrade	Rafael Cardenas R.
5.	Francisco Sotomayor Ruiz	Fernando Carrillo
6.	Francisco Martinez V.	Manuel Ramos Z.
7.	*Fernando Amilpa y Rivera*	Sebastian Pavia Gonzalez
8.	Luis S. Campa	Erasmo Resendis
9.	*Jesus Yuren Aguilar*	Miguel Fraire
10.	Miguel Flores Villar	Rodolfo Morales Alamilla
11.	J. Jesus Rico	Francisco Vargas Rivera
12.	*Leon Garcia*	*Aaron Camacho Lopez*

Durango

1.	Alfredo Mena	Rafael R. Torres
2.	Tomas Palomino Rojas	Jose Garcia Gutierrez
3.	Ernesto Calderon R.	Emilio Bueno
4.	Manasio Arrieta	Jesus M. Rosales

Guanajuato

1.	Benigno Arredonde Rivera	Tomas Soria
2.	*Celestino Gasca*	Baltazar Villalpando
3.	*Jose Hernandez Delgado*	Adelaido Gomez
4.	J. Jesus Guzman Vaca	Sebastian Ortiz Hernandez
5.	Francisco Vallejo	Luis Chabolla
6.	Manuel L. Farias	J. Jesus Franco
7.	*Jose Aguilar y Maya*	Adolfo Martinez Guerrero
8.	Antolin Pina Soria	Antonio Bucio
9.	Pascual Alcala	Victorio Flores Paz
10.	Federico Hernandez A.	Jose T. Arvide

Guerrero

1.	Francisco S. Carreto	Moises H. Villegas
2.	Galo Soberon y Parra	Job R. Gutierrez
3.	Bolivar Sierra	Pedro Popoca
4.	Miguel Andreu Almazan	Alberto Mendez
5.	*Nabor A. Ojeda*	Jesus Rodriguez Maldonado
6.	Feliciano Radilla	Julio Diego

Hidalgo

1.	Daniel C. Santillan	*Eleazar Canale*
2.	Honorado Austria	Napoleon Perez Chavez
3.	Agustin Olvera	Nicolas Solis
4.	*Vicente Aguirre*	Marciano Viveros
5.	*Jose Lugo Guerrero*	Felipe Estrada
6.	Leopoldo Badillo	Luis F. Flores
7.	Eduardo B. Jimenez	Felipe Castillo

Jalisco

1.	J. Jesus Ocampo	Anacleto Tortolero
2.	Guillermo Ponce de Leon	Juan I. Godinez
3.	Marcelino Barba Gonzalez	Antonio Gonzalez Alatorre
4.	Miguel Moreno	Jesus L. Perez
5.	Luis Alvarez del Castillo	Jose Romero Gomez
6.	Rodolfo Delgado	Jose Aguilera
7.	*Margarito Ramirez*	Manuel Basulto Limon
8.	David Perez Ruflo	Vicente P. Fajardo
9.	*Cesar Martino*	Fructuoso Arreola
10.	Alfredo Cuellar Castillo	Ladislao Velasco
11.	Manuel Palomera Calleja	Arturo B. Gomez
12.	J. Rosalio Ahedo	Pedro G. Narvaez
13.	J. Teobaldo Perez	Juan Manuel Sanchez Robles

Mexico

1.	Gonzalo Peralta A.	Sidronio Choperena
2.	Alfredo Sanchez Flores	Javier Salgado
3.	Carlos Aguirre	Miguel Espejel Villagran
4.	Jose L. Rosas	Estanislao Mejia
5.	Antonio S. Sanchez	Jose Jimenez
6.	Efren Pena Aguirre	Angel Aguilar
7.	*Alfonso Flores M.*	Leopoldo Quiroga
8.	Joaquin Mondragon	Dario Nava
9.	*Alfredo Zarate Albarran*	Felipe Estrada
10.	Jesus Mondragon Ramirez	Juan Albarran

Michoacan

1.	Elias Miranda G.	Jose Montejano
2.	Aurelio Munguia H.	Pedro S. Talavera
3.	Alfonso Garcia Gonzalez	Felipe Anguiano
4.	Jose M. Cano	Antonio Soto Aldaz
5.	Ernesto Prado	Conrado Magana
6.	*Baltazar Gudino*	Francisco Zepeda Maciel
7.	Rafael Vaca Solorio	J. Guadalupe Rojas
8.	Leopoldo O. Arias	Matilde Pimentel
9.	Juan Guajardo H.	Arturo Pineda H.
10.	Jose Zavala Ruiz	Luiz Mora Gomez
11.	Jaime Chaparro	*Leopoldo Zincunegui Tercero*

Morelos

1.	Andres Duarte Ortiz	Zeferino Ortega
2.	Gregorio Carrillo	Juan Lima

Nayarit

1.	*Luis Aranda del Toro*	*Candelario Miramontes*
2.	Jose Angulo Araico	Marcos Jimenez

Nuevo Leon

1.	Manuel Flores	Jose Ojeda
2.	*Miguel Z. Martinez*	Julian V. Dominguez
3.	*Dionisio Garcia Leal*	Eliseo B. Sanchez
4.	Hilario Contreras Molina	Margarito Osorio

Oaxaca

1.	Heliodora Charis Castro	Cuberto Chagoya
2.	Arturo Vado	Heriberto Jimenez
3.	Carlos Santibanez	Ildefonso Zorrilla
4.	Jorge Meixueiro	Antonio Sumano
5.	Maximino Gonzalez Fernandez	Luis Mora Rojas
6.	*Alfonso Francisco Ramirez*	Jacobo Ramirez Gomez
7.	*Antolin Jimenez*	Enrique E. Sumano
8.	Adan Ramirez Lopez	Ignacio Gamboa Zebadua
9.	Ranulfo Calderon Sanchez	Adelaido Ojeda
10.	Benito Zaragoza	*Dagoberto Flores Betancourt*
11.	Felix de la Lanza	Delfino Cruz

Puebla

1.	Juan Salamanca V.	Carlos M. Mora
2.	Mauricio Ayala L.	Porfirio Martinez
3.	Froylan C. Manjarrez	Luciano M. Sanchez
4.	Miguel Hidalgo Salazar	Pedro L. Romero
5.	Francisco Hernandez	Marcos Fuentes
6.	Agustin Huerta	Jesus Guerrero
7.	Julian Cacho	Rafael Herrera A.
8.	Rosendo Cortes	*Sacramento Joffre Vazquez*
9.	Luis Vinals Leon	*Fausto M. Ortega*

10.	*Rafael Molina Betancourt*	Adan M. Vazquez
11.	Luis Lombardo Toledano	Benigno Campos
12.	Lindoro Hernandez A.	Alberto Jimenez

Queretaro

1.	Emiliano Siurob	Jose D. Luque
2.	*Noradino Rubio Ortiz*	Genaro Canto

Quintana Roo (Territory)

1.	Diodoro Tejero	Pedro Perez Garrido

San Luis Potosi

1.	Victor Alfonso Maldonado	Valentin Narvaez
2.	Epifanio Castillo	Florencio Galvan T.
3.	Francisco Arellano B.	Julio Munoz Ontanon
4.	Josue Escobedo	Ignacio Cuellar
5.	Arnulfo Hernandez Z.	Pedro Izaguirre
6.	Jose Santos Alonso	Tomas Oliva B.
7.	Alfonso R. Salazar	Andres Zarate Sanchez

Sinaloa

1.	Raul Simaneas	Miguel Sandoval A.
2.	*Gabriel Leyva Velazquez*	Eligio Samaniego
3.	*Roman F. Iturbe*	Jesus P. Cota
4.	J. Ignacio Lizarraga	Antonio Topete

Sonora

1.	Humberto Obregon	Ramon M. Real
2.	*Francisco Martinez P.*	Elias A. Salazar
3.	Ricardo G. Hill	Antonio C. Ramos

Tabasco

1.	*Alfonso Gutierrez Gurria*	Enrique Becerra Martinez
2.	Carlos Dominquez Lopez	Felipe Trejo

Tamaulipas

1.	*Jose Cantu Estrada*	Alberto Cardenas
2.	Juan Rincon	Bernardo Turrubiates
3.	Ignacio Alcala	Gonzalo Zaragoza

Tlaxcala

1.	Alberto Rios Conde	Andres C. Jimenez
2.	Francisco Mora Plancarte	Juan Rodriguez

Veracruz

1.	*Manuel E. Miravete*	Aureliano Azuara
2.	Manuel Jasso	Vicente Gutierrez
3.	*Adolfo Ruiz Cortines*	Antonio Pulido
4.	Odilon Montero	Leandro Garcia
5.	Jesus M. Rodriguez	Geronimo Garcia
6.	Demetrio Gutierrez	Efren Aburto
7.	Alfonso Perez Redondo	Juan Alarcon Garcia
8.	Adolfo E. Ortega	Crispin Vargas
9.	Silvestre Aguilar	Jose Zuniga
10.	Santos Perez Abascal	Bonifacio Seyde Molina
11.	Manuel Ayala	
12.	Rodolfo T. Marquez	Sebastian Fabian
13.	Joaquin Jara Diaz	Rafael Escobar Perez
14.	Luis R. Torres	Benjamin E. Lule

Yucatan

1.	Miguel A. Menendez Reyes	Manuel Lopez Amabilis
2.	*Victor Mena Palomo*	Rene Almeida
3.	Alvaro Perez Alpuche	Tomas Briceno
4.	Agustin Franco V.	German Pech

Zacatecas
1.	Luis Flores G.	Tomas Hernandez
2.	Daniel Z. Duarte	Tomas Zapata
3.	*Enrique Estrada*	Heraclio Rodriguez
4.	Mariano Vazquez del Mercado	Onesimo Ramirez

1940–43 (38th Legislature)

State	Deputy	Alternate
Aguascalientes		
1.	Benjamin Resendiz	Andres M. Esquivel
2.	Vicente Madrigal Guzman	Carlos M. Ramos
Baja California del Norte (Territory)		
1.	Blas Valdivia	Simon Flores
Baja California del Sur (Territory)		
1.	Isidro Dominguez Cota	Jesus Adarga
Campeche		
1.	*Alberto Trueba Urbina*	Jose del Carmen Gonzalez
2.	Ramon Berzunza Pinto	Barbaciano Chuc
Chihuahua		
1.	Rogelio Sanchez Corral	Epifanio de Anda
2.	Valento Chacon Baea	Lorenzo Oropeza
3.	Jesus U. Melina	J. Trinidad Saenz
4.	*Manuel Bernardo Aguirre*	Carlos Enriquez Ch.
5.	Rafael F. Lazo	Anselmo Ramos
Coahuila		
1.	Pedro Cerda	Enrique Guzman
2.	Genaro S. Cervantes	Manuel Arenas
3.	Arturo Carranza	Manuel Perez Bernea
4.	Carlos Samaniego G.	Domingo Marquez
Colima		
1.	*Manuel Gudino*	Jose C. Fuentes
2.	*Jesus Michel Espinosa J.*	Ruben Vizearra
Distrito Federal		
1.	Lamberto Zuniga	Clemente S. Suarez
2.		
3.	Rafael Cardenas	Luis Yuren
4.	Alfonso Pena Palafaz	Felix Cortes
5.	Carlos M. Orloineta	Fidel Guerrero
6.	Cesar M. Cervantes	Salvador Lopez Abitia
7.	*Alejandro Carrillo*	Ramon Castilleja
8.		
9.	Luis Quintero Gutierrez	Rafael Gaona
10.	*Carlos Zapata Vela*	Estanislao Martinez
11.	Jesus de la Garza	Gonzalo Elizalde
12.	*Aaron Camacho Lopez*	Octaviano Nunez
Durango		
1.	Enrique Carrola Antura	Severo Reyes
2.	Mariano Padilla	Mariano Borrego
3.	*Braulio Meraz Nevarez*	Alberto Perez E.
4.	Manuel Solorzano Soto	Margarito Gonzalez
Guanajuato		
1.	J. Buenaventura Lara	Amado Arenas
2.	Rafael Rionda	Juan H. Diaz

3.	*Ricardo Acosta V.*	J. Cruz Sanchez
4.	Joaquin Madrazo	Ignacio Castro
5.	Ernesto Gallardo S.	Alberto Gonzalez B.
6.	Rafael Otero y Gama	Abundio Toral
7.	Arnulfo Rosas	Arnulfo Lopez Orozco
8.	Adolfo Martinez G.	Dionisio Castilla
9.	Reynaldo Lecona Soto	Alfredo Guerrero Tarquin
10.	Fausto Villagomez	Emilio Garcia

Guerrero

1.	Mario Lasso	Francisco Amigon
2.	*Ruben Figueroa*	Mucio Cardenas
3.	Amadeo Melendez	Ramiro Cruz Manjarrez
4.	Alfredo Cordoba Lara	Rafael Mendoza G.
5.	J. Jesus Munoz Vergara	Roberto Arzate Olea
6.	Antonio Molina Jimenez	Marcos Sanchez

Hidalgo

1.	Jose Perez, Jr.	Ignacio Hidalgo Quesada
2.	*Leonardo M. Hernandez*	Casimiro Benitez
3.	Gumersindo Gomez	*Jose Gomez Esparza*
4.	Gregorio Hernandez	Felipe Contrera
5.	*Alfonso Corona de Rosal*	Jesus Martinez
6.	Otilio Villegas	Erasto Olguin
7.	Juvencio Nochebuena	Pedro Velez

Jalisco

1.	Juan I. Godinez	Emilio Gutierrez Duran
2.	Catarino Issac	J. Jesus Silva Romero
3.	Manuel Martinez Sicilia	Emilio Gonzalez Gutierrez
4.	Ismael M. Lozano	Jose Ana Castaneda
5.	Lucio Gonzalez Padilla	Pablo Esqueda
6.	Felipe R. Diaz Rodriguez	Jose I. Chavez Nuno
7.	Fernando Basulto Limon	Moises Chavez Hernandez
8.	J. Jesus Cisneros Gomez	Jose Maria Chavez
9.	J. Jesus Landeros	Ramon Urzua
10.	Jaime Llamas	Jose Ramirez
11.	Martiniano Sendis	Candelario Loreto
12.	Alfonso G. Cebalius	Miguel Rosales
13.	*Juan Gil Preciado*	Eliseo Navarro

Mexico

1.	Adolfo Manero	Joaquin Gonzalez Aragon
2.	Raul Serrano T.	Luis Martinez
3.	Ignacio Gomez Arroyo	Jose Enriquez Infante
4.	Juan N. Garcia	Pedro Posada
5.	Tomas Perez R.	Justo Martinez
6.	*Porfirio Ramirez*	Amador Mora
7.	Jose Hernandez Mota	Martin Velazquez
8.	Antonio Mancilla Bauza	Gabriel Maldonado
9.	Daniel Tenorio	Felipe Estrada
10.	Armando P. Arroyo	Ignacio Bustamante

Michoacan

1.	Jose Molina	Luis G. Zumaya
2.	Pablo Rangel Reyes	Sabino Cruz
3.	Pascual Abarea Perez	J. Encarnacion Castillo
4.	Jose Alfaro Perez	Ignacio Torres Espinosa
5.	Ignacio Urbina Mercado	Jose Torres
6.	Juan S. Picazo	Genaro Guerrero
7.	Ramon Medina	Manuel Magana

8.	Luis Ordorica Cerda	Dunstano Morfin Perez
9.	Ignacio Ramirez Palacios	Silviano Diaz Barriga
10.	Heli M. Lopez	David Soto
11.	*Leopoldo Zincunegui Tercero*	Tiburcio Correa Medina

Morelos

1.	*Porfirio Neri Arizmendi*	Jose Cuevas
2.	Ignacio Acevedo	Matias Polanco

Nayarit

1.	*Candelario Miramontes*	Luis Rivera
2.	*Emilio M. Gonzalez*	Jose C. Villasenor

Nuevo Leon

1.	J. Refugio F. Rodriguez	Ramon Villarreal
2.	Leandro Martinez L.	Gregorio Lecca
3.		
4.	Maximino Reyna	Marcos Quintanilla

Oaxaca

1.	Fernando de Gyves Pineda	Jose B. Calvo
2.	Manuel Rueda Magro	Francisco Jimenez
3.	Hermenegildo Luis	Rosendo Perez
4.	*Demetrio Bolanos Espinosa*	Zeferino Canseco
5.	Manuel Chavez	Genaro Ramos
6.	Adalberto Lagunas Calvo	Flavio Perez Gasca
7.	Adelaido Ojeda Caballero	Benigno Cisneros
8.	Luis E. Velasco	Cupertino Zarate
9.	Carlos R. Balleza, Jr.	Vicente Castillo Ramirez
10.	Ignacio Gamboa Zebadua	Rosendo Mendoza
11.	Narciso Medina Estrada	Javier R. Villar

Puebla

1.	Martin Torres	Eustasio Mozo
2.	*Blas Chumacero*	Juan F. Rojas
3.	Bernardo Chavez V.	Jacinto Natario
4.	Tomas Covarrubias	Agustin Bayon
5.	Fernando S. Romero	Jose Solis
6.	*Aaron Merino Fernandez*	Eustolio Tapia
7.	Gabriel Cuevas Victoria	Rafael Rodriguez Meza
8.	Antonio Portas	Rafael Arguelles
9.	*Luis Vazquez Lapuente*	Manuel Gonzalez Aguirre
10.	Julio Lobato M.	Abelardo Bonilla
11.	*Emilio Gutierrez Roldan*	Gabriel Herrera G.
12.	*Antonio Nava Castillo*	Roberto M. L. Castelan

Queretaro

1.	Alfredo Felix Diaz Escobar	Medardo Trejo
2.	Enrique Montes	Felix Mendez

Quintana Roo (Territory)

1.	Raymundo Sanchez Corral	Ricardo Villanueva

San Luis Potosi

1.	*Florencio Salazar*	Fidel Cortes
2.	J. Delfino Moreno	J. Felix Reyes
3.	Benjamin Gutierrez R.	Jose Maria P. Pelaez
4.	Luis Aguilera	Alfredo Garfias
5.		
6.	Luis Marquez Ricano	Domingo Candelario
7.	Herminio Salas	J. Guadalupe Espinosa

Sinaloa

1.	Jose Jimenez Acevedo	Jesus Garcia
2.	Rafael Granja Lizarraga	Jose Medina Velazquez

| 3. | Cuauhtemoc Rios Martinez | Jesus Osuna P. |
| 4. | Modesto Antimo | Zeferino Urias |

Sonora
1.	Jacinto Lopez	Antonio M. Cano
2.	Ramon M. Duron	Rafael A. Moraga
3.	Miguel A. Salazar	Antonio C. Encinas

Tabasco
| 1. | Rogelio Castanares Jamet | Juan Mendoza Valles |
| 2. | Ulises Gonzalez Blengio | Jaime Cancino Tadeo |

Tamaulipas
1.	*Hugo Pedro Gonzalez*	Jose H. Hernandez
2.	*Silverio Meza P.*	Florentino Guevara
3.	Benjamin Zapata	Salvador Ortiz Silva

Tlaxcala
| 1. | Miguel Moctezuma | Abraham Rojas |
| 2. | Ezequiel Selley | Armando Flores Cardenas |

Veracruz
1.	Alfredo S. Sarrelangne L.	Zenon Gonzalez Ortiz
2.	Salvador Gonzalez	Onofre Morales
3.	*Cesar Garizurieta*	Ricardo D. Gonzalez
4.	Leandro Garcia	Vicente Calderon M.
5.	Eduardo S. Arellano	Rosalino Jimenez
6.	Josafat Melgarejo	Ignacio R. Ojeda
7.	*Fernando Lopez Arias*	Jose Garcia
8.	Julio Lopez Silva	Ascension Vazquez Arenzano
9.	Gonzalo Casas Aleman	Andres Ceron H.
10.	Ramon Camarena Medina	Ricardo Rodal
11.	Jesus Arizmendi	Jose C. Gonzalez
12.	*Eduardo Hernandez Chazaro*	Rafael Arriola Molina
13.	Jose Ch. Ramirez	Ramon B. Prieto
14.	Bernardino F. Simeneen	Jose Pera

Yucatan
1.	Jose M. Bolio Mendez	Humberto Lara y Lara
2.	Carlos Jordan Arjona	Emilio Pacheco
3.	*Antonio Betancourt Perez*	Hernan Morales Medina
4.	Juan Manuel Torres	Ernesto Alcocer Osorno

Zacatecas
1.	*Aurelio Pamanes Escobedo*	Mauricio Castillo
2.	Carlos Ponzio M.	Jose Fernandez Cortes
3.	*Leobardo Reynoso*	Salvador Castanedo
4.	Paulino Perez	J. Jesus Valencia
5.	Antonio Ramirez	Salvador Mora

1943–46 (39th Legislature)

State	*Deputy*	*Alternate*
Aguascalientes		
1.	Voided	Voided
2.	*Manuel Moreno Sanchez*	Felipe Hernandez
Baja California del Norte (Territory)		
1.	Eduardo Garza Senande	Jose Ines Oviedo
Baja California del Sur (Territory)		
1.	Adan Velarde	Benito Beltran Beltran

Campeche
1.   *Pedro Guerrero Martinez*   Alfredo Ferraez
2.   Arcadio Che Cunche   Francisco Alvarez Barrett

Chiapas
1.   *Andres Serra Rojas*   Tomas Martinez
2.   *Juan M. Esponda*   Filberto Santiago Flores
3.   Jose Pantaleon Dominguez   Humberto Pascacio Gamboa
4.   Francisco Jose Burelo   David Perez N.
5.   Rafael Jimenez Bolan   Julio Munoz Castillo

Chihuahua
1.   *Tomas Valles V.*   Carlos Sanchez Rubio
2.   Gustavo Chavez   Felipe Gonzalez N.
3.   *Teofilo Borunda*   Alberto C. Castillo
4.   *Guillermo Quevedo Moreno*   Francisco Millan Millan

Coahuila
1.   Francisco Lopez Serrano   Alejandro V. Soberon
2.   Ubaldo Veloz A.   Eduardo B. Alvarado
3.   *Raul Lopez Sanchez*   Andres Montoya
4.   Victor M. Bosque   Secundino Ramos y Ramos

Colima
1.   Ruben Vizcarra   Jose S. Benitez
2.   Carlos Alcaraz Ahumada   Miguel S. Fuentes

Distrito Federal
1.   Francisco Linares T.   Fortunato Reyes II
2.   *Carlos A. Madrazo*   *Marcelino Inureta*
3.   Filemon Manrique   Antioco Ramirez
4.   *Ruffo Figueroa Figueroa*   Manuel E. Trejo
5.   J.Leonardo Flores Vazquez   Carlos L. Diaz y Diaz
6.   Juan Best Gareta   Luis Martinez Mezquida
7.   Pedro Tellez Vargas   Francisco Mayorga
8.   *Jesus Yuren Aguilar*   Rafael Gaona
9.   Roberto Aguilera Carbajal   Nemesio Fuentes Fuentes
10.   Antonio Ulibarri   Eugenio de la Torre Gomez
11.   *Sacramento Joffre Vazquez*   Emiliano Aguilar
12.   Leopoldo Hernandez   Bonifacio Moreno Jr.

Durango
1.   Jose Donaciano Sosa   Juan B. Najera
2.   Miguel Breceda   Domingo Garibaldi
3.   *Marino Castillo Najera*   Miguel Arrieta
4.   Juan Manuel Tinoco   Marcelo Chairez

Guanajuato
1.   Fernando Mora   Luis Carreon
2.   Luis Madrazo Basuri   Justo Pedroza
3.   *Federico Medrano Valdivia*   Ciro Aree
4.   *Fernando Diaz Duran*   J. Jesus L. Vargas
5.   Jose R. Velazquez Nuno   Antonio Bucio
6.   Francisco Garcia Carranza   Antonio E. Perez
7.   *Guillermo Aguilar y Maya*   Miguel Hernandez Garibay

Guerrero
1.   Jose Maria Suarez Tellez   Angel Tapia Alarcon
2.   Carlos F. Carranco Cardoso   Alberto Salgado Cuevas
3.   Isauro Lopez Salgado   Odilon C. Flores
4.   Ramon Mata y Rodriguez   Ignacio Victoria
5.   *Donato Miranda Fonseca*   Arquimides Catalan Guevara

Hidalgo
1. Daniel Olguin Diaz   Panfilo Hernandez
2. *Ramon G. Bonfil*   Gorgonio Rodriguez
3. *Victor M. Aguirre*   Felipe Contreras Ruiz
4. *Raul Lozano Ramirez*   Manuel Lara Salguero
5. Adolfo Lugo Guerrero   Luis de la Concha

Jalisco
1. Alberto Velazquez   J. Jesus Macias Perez
2. Miguel Moreno Padilla   J. Martin del Campo
3. Heliodoro Hernandez Loza   Manuel Ayala Perez
4. Fidencio Vazquez Cerda   Guillermo Lara Mendoza
5. Adalberto Oriega Huizar   Procopio Dominguez
6. Ignacio Luis Velazquez   Aurelio Arrayo
7. Jorge Contreras Bobadilla   Narciso Martinez
8. Jose de Jesus Lima   Cosme Moran
9. Wenceslao Partida Hernandez   J. Ascension Andrade Berumen

Mexico
1. *Gregorio Velazquez Sanchez*   Antonio Galvan Albarran
2. *Antonio Manero*   Agustin Gonzalez Arguelles
3. Juan Jose Rivera Rojas   Arturo Chavez Vazquez
4. Jose D. Izquierdo   Agustin Albarran
5.
6. Federico S. Sanchez   Ernesto Dominquez
7. *Juan Fernandez Albarran*   Fernando Pruneda Batres
8. *Octavio Senties G.*   Felipe Estrada
9. *Gabriel Ramos Millan*   Bartolome Requena Gonzalez

Michoacan
1. *Ricardo Ramirez Guerrero*   Melesio Aguilar Ferrera
2. Salvador Ochoa Renteria   Homero Areiniega
3. Agustin Otero Gutierrez   Antonio Licca Luna
4. Francisco de P. Jimenez   Silverio Ceja
5. Jose Zavala Ruiz   Alfredo Ayala
6. Diego Hernandez Topete   Jose Concepcion Padilla
7. Jesus Torres Caballuo   J. Jesus Bantista
8. Gabriel Chavez Tejeda   Salvador Mendez

Morelos
1. Manuel Aranda   Mayolo Alcazar
2. Eliseo Aragon Rebolledo   Arturo M. Cortina

Nayarit
1. Alberto Tapia Carrillo   Alfonso Llanos Ramirez
2. Gabriel Castaneda Landozuri   Jose Maria Narvaez

Nuevo Leon
1. Rodolfo Gaytan   Zacarias Villarreal
2. *Julian Garza Tijerina*   J. Cruz Acevedo
3. Delfino Garcia Saenz   Carlos F. Osuna
4. Hilario Contreras Molina   Isaac Medina

Oaxaca
1. Alberto Ramos Sesma   Julio Gomez Lopez
2.
3. Demetrio Flores Fagoaga   Rogelio Jimenez
4. Melquiades Ramirez   Rafael Pineda Leon
5. *Octavio Reyes Spindola*   Fernando Leon Diaz
6. *Francisco Lopez Cortes*   Manuel Castellanos
7. *Norberto Aguirre*   Salvador Velazquez
8. Jose Larrazabal Gonzalez   Ricardo Vazquez Echeverria

Puebla
1.   *Gustavo Diaz Ordaz*   Agustin Huerta
2.   Mariano Rayon   Gustavo Romero Aldaz
3.   *Antonio J. Hernandez*   Rigoberto Gonzalez
4.   Cosme Aguilera Alvarez   Jacobo Ojeda
5.   Andres Robago Castellanes   Enrique Pacheco G.
6.   Alfonso M. Moreyra   Miguel Barcena
7.   Jose Manuel Galvez   Jorge W. Sanchez
8.   Luis Huidobro   Javier N. Luna
9.   Carlos I. Betancourt   Alvaro Lechuga

Queretaro
1.   *Eduardo Luque Loyola*   Antonio Martinez Montes
2.   Gilberto Garcia   *Domingo Olvera Gamez*

Quintana Roo (Territory)
1.   Arturo Gonzalez Villarreal   Francisco Cordero Nunez

San Luis Potosi
1.   Luis Jimenez Delgado   *Antonio Rocha*
2.   *Pablo Aldrett*   Manuel Chavez
3.   Victor Alfonso Maldonado   *Enrique Parra Hernandez*
4.   *Fernando Moctezuma*   Manuel Garcia
5.   *Ismael Salas*   Ignacio Moralea
6.   Manuel Alvarez   Emilio Lopez R.

Sinaloa
1.   Rosendo G. Castro   Conrado Ochoa
2.   Fausto A. Marin   Enrique Pera G.
3.   *Bernardo Norzagaray*   Miguel Navarro Franco

Sonora
1.   Jesus M. Figueroa   Carlos Escardante
2.   Herminio Ahumada, Jr.   Jesus Maria Suarez, Jr.
3.   Saturnino Saldivar   Edmundo Olachea

Tabasco
1.   Nicolas Quintana Valenzuela   Bertino Madrigal Camelo
2.   Ernesto E. Trujillo Gurria   Rafael Leon Caceres

Tamaulipas
1.   Felix Cabanas Hernandez   Antonio de Leon
2.   *Graciano Sanchez*   Martin Martinez
3.   Saul Cantu Balderas   Francisco Romero Cortes

Tlaxcala
1.   *Mauro Angulo*   Ricardo Altamirano
2.   Adalberto Santillan   Agustin Lopez

Veracruz
1.   Manuel Jasso   Meliton T. Polito
2.   *Rafael Murillo Vidal*   *Silverio R. Alvarado*
3.   Jose Fernandez Gomez   Nieves Martinez
4.   Gorgonio Quesnel Acosta   Fulgencio Arellano
5.   *Juan Cerdan*   Fernando Campos
6.   *Silvestre Aguilar*   Fernando de la Garza
7.   Genaro Lapa   Arnulfo Sanchez
8.   *Candido Aguilar*   Vicente Romero
9.   Rodolfo Tiburcio Marquez   Jose A. Lemus
10.   Carlos I. Serrano   Jose Luis Tejeda
11.   *Benito Coquet*   Delfino Beltran
12.   Manuel Martinez Ch.   Pablo S. Pina

Yucatan
1.   Mauricio Escobedo Granados   Esteban Duran Rosado

2.	*Efrain Brito Rosado*	Alfonso Baquerio Canton
3.	Laureano Cardos Ruz	Pedro Perez Chavez
4.	Alvaro Vivas Marfil	Adalberto Aguilar

Zacatecas

1.	Rafael Lopez W.	Jose Fernandez Cortes
2.	Panfilo Natera, Jr.	Manuel Zamudio
3.	*Brigido Reynoso*	Jose Garcia Ortega
4.	Jesus Maria Garcia Martinez	Abraham R. Frias

1946–49 (40th Legislature)

State	*Deputy*	*Alternate*
Aguascalientes		
1.	*Aquiles Elorduy*	Salvador Hernandez Duque
2.	Roberto J. Rangel	Reynaldo Negrete
Baja California del Norte (Territory)		
1.	*Braulio Maldonado*	Ignacio Gutierrez Argil
Baja California del Sur (Territory)		
1.	*Antonio Navarro Encinas*	
Campeche		
1.	Manuel J. Lopez Hernandez	Eduardo Negrin B.
2.	*Carlos Sansores Perez*	Pedro Balan
Chiapas		
1.	Antonio Cachon Ponce	Eduardo Sanchez Chanona
2.	Ramon Franco Esponda	Manuel Castellanos Cancino
3.	Gil Salgado Palacios	Ciceron Trujillo Fernandez
4.	Jose Castanon	Conrado de la Cruz Albores
5.	Gonzalo Lopez Lopez	Salvador Duran Perez
Chihuahua		
1.	*Eugenio Prado*	Benito E. Romero
2.	Undecided	Undecided
3.	Luis R. Legarreta	Estanislao Apodaca
4.	*Jose Lopez Bermudez*	Jose Ramon Garcia
Coahuila		
1.	*Frederico Berrueto Ramon*	Antonio Zamora
2.	Leon V. Paredes	Juan M. Borjon
3.	Jose de Jesus Urquizo	Santiago Aguirre
4.	Federico Meza Zuniga	Francisco Moreno
Colima		
1.	Jose S. Benitez	Francisco J. Yanez
2.	*J. Jesus Espinosa Michel*	Jose Serratos
Distrito Federal		
1.	Manuel Pena Vera	Juan Reyes Ch.
2.	*Lauro Ortega Martinez*	Bartolo G. Sanabria
3.	*Antonio Vega Garcia*	Trinidad Morales Davila
4.	*Alfonso Martinez D.*	Luis R. Velasco
5.		
6.	Leobardo Wolstano Pineda	Alonso Echanove Acereto
7.	Cesar M. Cervantes	Leonilo Salgado Figueroa
8.	*Juan Gutierrez Lascurain*	Francisco Garcia Sainz
9.	*Fernando Amilpa Rivera*	Fernando Jimenez C.
10.	*Manuel Orijel Salazar*	Adan Montano
11.	Victor Herrera Gonzalez	Jose Villanueva Aguilera
12.	Trinidad Rosales Rojas	Enrique Yanez D.

Durango
1.   J. Guadalupe Bernal   Armando Gomez Navarrete
2.   J. Encarnacion Chavez   Francisco Landeros
3.   Ramiro Rodriguez Palafox   Fernando Arenas Esquivel
4.   Eulogio V. Salazar   Jesus Garcia Escobar

Guanajuato
1.   Ramon V. Santoyo   Luciano Landeros
2.   Luis Diaz Infante   Enrique Gomez Guerra
3.   Pascual Aceves Barajas   J. Jesus Rotunno Soto
4.   Ernesto Gallardo S.   Daniel Hernandez
5.   Manuel Aleman Perez   Alfonso Sanchez Castaneda
6.
7.   Manuel Rocha Lasseaul Z.   Jose Antonio de la Vega

Guerrero
1.   Angel Tapia Alarcon   Margarito S. Ortiz
2.   Nabor A. Ojeda   Francisco Uriostegui
3.   Alberto Jaimes Miranda   Adolfo Arce
4.   Alejandro Gomez Maganda   Antonio Rosas Abarca
5.   Alejandro Sanchez Castro   Jesus Rodriguez Maldonado

Hidalgo
1.   David Cabrera Villagran   Francisco Soto G.
2.   Galileo Bustos Valle   *Quintin Rueda Villagran*
3.   Felipe Contreras Ruiz   Camilo Serrano Angeles
4.   Juvencio Nochebuena   Jesus Perez
5.   Fernando Cruz Chavez   Vicente Trejo

Jalisco
1.   Rodolfo Gonzalez Gonzalez   Jose Montes de Oca
2.   Roberto Soto Maynez   Angel Davalos Rodriguez
3.   J. Ramon Hidalgo Jaramillos   Avelino Castellon Lara
4.   Ramon Castellanos Camacho   Ignacio Nava
5.   Francisco Torres Rojas   Aureliano Navarro R.
6.   Arturo Guzman Mayagoitia   Ramon Gonzalez
7.   Jose Maria Ibarra G.   Amado Madrigal
8.   Jaime Llamas Garcia   Pomposo Preciado
9.   Abraham Gonzalez Rivera   Alfredo Trejo Romero

Mexico
1.   Esteban Marin Chaparro   Antonio Garcia Lobera
2.   *Gustavo Castrejon y Chavez*   Alfonso Garcia Ortega
3.   Francisco Sanchez Garnica   Roberto Cornejo Cruz
4.   *David Romero Castaneda*   Domingo Rivas Chavez
5.   Fernando Guerrero Esquivel   Ernesto Lopez Soriano
6.   Mucio Cardoso Jr.   Hermilo Arcos Perez
7.   Santiago Velasco   Anselmo Davila Gamez
8.   Fernando Riva Palacio   Antonio Pena Navarrete
9.   Salvador Mena Rosales

Michoacan
1.   Francisco Nunez Chavez   David Gutierrez H.
2.   Francisco Mora Plancarte   Eleuterio Paramo
3.
4.   *Enrique Bravo Valencia*   Francisco Vega Ramirez
5.   *Victoriano Anguiano*   Luis Martinez
6.   Miguel Ramirez Munguia   Primitivo Gomez
7.   Horacio Tenorio   Antonio Guijosa Mercado
8.   Luis Ordorica Cerda   Carlos Loreto Martinez

Morelos
1.   Porfirio Palacios   Manuel Ocampo
2.   Nicolas Zapata   Leobardo Alanis

Nayarit
1.   Antonio Perez Cisneros   Jose Stephens
2.   Angel Mesa Lopez   Federico Gonzalez Gallo

Nuevo Leon
1.   Antonio L. Rodriguez   Francisco Morales
2.   *Armando Arteaga y Santoyo*   Rodolfo Jimenez
3.   Santos Cantu Salinas   Ismael Leal Galan
4.   Simon Sepulveda   Enedino Martinez

Oaxaca
1.   Efren Ortiz Bartolo   Agustin Carballo
2.   Francisco Eli Siguenza   Rafael Diaz Hernandez
3.   Martino Rojas Villavicencio   Jacinto Reyes
4.   Nemesio Roman Guzman   Manuel Oseguera Sarmiento
5.   Alfonso Patino Cruz   Artemio Guzman Garfias
6.   Manuel Sodi del Valle   Jorge O. Acevedo
7.   Fernando Magro Soto   Wulfrano Estevez
8.   Vicente J. Villanueva   Jenaro Ramos

Puebla
1.   *Blas Chumacero Sanchez*   Francisco Marquez
2.   Ricardo Luna Morales   Luis C. Manjarrez
3.   Agustin Perez Caballero   Nemesio Viveros R.
4.   Ruperto Sanchez Taboada   Raymundo Ramirez
5.   Miguel Barbosa Martinez   Erasto Enriquez
6.   Bernardo Chavez Velazquez   Andres Hernandez Mendez
7.   Fausto M. Ortega   Salvador Vega Bernal
8.   *Jose Ricardi Tirado*   Benjamin Mendez Luna
9.   Luis Marquez Ricano   Samuel Lechuga Mendez

Queretaro
1.   Pablo Munoz Gutierrez   *Manuel Gonzalez Cosio*
2.   Enrique Montes Dorantes   Romulo Vega M.

Quintana Roo (Territory)
1.   Manuel Perez Avila   Antonio Erales Abdelnur

San Luis Potosi
1.   *Florencio Salazar*   Manuel Vazquez Cerda
2.   Ignacio Gomez del Campo   Aurelio Guerrero
3.   Agustin Olivo Monsivais   Eugenio Quintero
4.   Jesus Medina Romero
5.   Francisco Purata Herrera   Felipe Raga Gonzalez
6.   Miguel Moreno Ibarra   Erasto Roque

Sinaloa
1.   *Alfonso G. Calderon*   Francisco R. Verduzco
2.   Armando Molina Trujillo   Jesus Ledon Ruiz
3.   Miguel Gaxiola y V.   Cuauhtemoc Rios M.

Sonora
1.   *Francisco Martinez Peralta*   Antonio Vazquez Corzo
2.   Jesus Maria Suarez, Jr.   Jesus Maria Preciado
3.   Rafael Contreras Monteon   Alejo Gastelum

Tabasco
1.   Manuel Antonio Romero   Rafael Barjau Diaz
2.   Manuel Flores Castro, Jr.   Candelario Rosada Munoz

Tamaulipas

1.	Antonio Yanez Salazar	Basilio Ramos
2.	Bernardo Turrubiates	Pablo Villanueva
3.	Antonio Salmon Ortiz	Zenaido Romero

Tlaxcala

1.	Moises Rosalio Garcia	Fidel Camacho Era
2.	Jose Estrada Romero	Luis Granillo A.

Veracruz

1.	Rafael Herrera Angeles	Jose Osorio Cruz
2.	Josue Benignos Hideroa	Pedro L. Menendez
3.	Rafael Gomez	Jose Abraham Rubio
4.	Ernesto Nunez Velarde	Gustavo Lavalle G.
5.	Fernando Campos Montes	Ezequiel Dominguez
6.	Ramon Camarena Medina	Angel Luis Archer
7.	Daniel Sierra R.	Luis Fernandez Olarzabal
8.	Francisco Sarquis Carriedo	Alfonso Colina
9.	Ricardo Rodal Jimenez	Gustavo Huerta
10.	Rafael Arriola Molina	Raul Zamorano Marquez
11.	*Vidal Diaz Munoz*	Abelardo Maldonado
12.	Bulmaro A. Rueda	Fermin Leon Tello

Yucatan

1.	Humberto Carrillo Gil	Francisco Acosta
2.	Carlos Villamil Castillo	Eustaquio Blanco
3.	Rafael Cebada Teneiro	Javier Magana Zapata
4.	Gaudencio Peraza Esquiliano	Gaspar Garcia Rodriguez

Zacatecas

1.	Jesus Aguirre D.	Francisco E. Garcia
2.	Lorenzo Hinojosa Rodriguez	Ramon Meza R.
3.	Joel Pozos Leon	Alfredo U. Marquez
4.	Alfonso Hernandez Torres	Luis de la Fuente

1949–52 (41st Legislature)

State	Deputy	Alternate
Aguascalientes		
1.	Jesus Avila Vazquez	Luis Garcia Cortes
2.	Salvador Luevano Romo	Jose Santos Reyna Martinez
Baja California del Norte (Territory)		
1.	*Ricardo Alzalde Arellano*	Mariano Cordova de la Torre
Baja California del Sur (Territory)	Vacant	
Campeche		
1.	*Alberto Trueba Urbina*	Fernando Turriza Pena
2.	Alberto Perera Castillo	Antonio Chable Caamal
Chiapas		
1.	*Valentin Rincon Coutino*	Manuel Orduna
2.	J. Rodolfo Suarez Coello	Carmen M. Morales
3.	Emilio Zebadua Robles	Roberto Castanon de la Vega
4.	*Milton Castellanos Everardo*	Alfonso Macias Zebadua
5.	Felipe Pagola Reyes	Roman Reyes Velazquez
Chihuahua		
1.	*Oscar Soto Maynez*	Oscar Ornelas Armendariz
2.	Jose Aguilar Irungaray	Jesus Alvirez Mendoza
3.	*Teofilo R. Borunda*	Guillermo Salas Najera
4.	Esteban Uranga	Armando Esquivel

Coahuila
1. Evelio H. Gonzalez Trevino — *Florencio Barrera Fuentes*
2. Juan Magos Borjon — *Braulio Fernandez Aguirre*
3. Fernando Vargas Meza — Adan A. Rocha Sanchez
4. Ramon Quintana Espinosa — Felix Zavala Lopez

Colima
1. *Roberto A. Solorzano* — Jorge Ochoa Gutierrez
2. Salvador Gonzalez Ventura — Antonio Morentin Rocha

Distrito Federal
1. *Rafael S. Pimentel* — Fortunato Reyes H.
2. Jose Tovar Miranda — Francisco Hernandez Navarro
3. Adolfo Omana Avelar — J. Jesus Jimenez Torres
4. *Francisco Fonseca Garcia* — Mario Guerrero
5. J. Leonardo Flores — J. Jesus Bautista
6. *Gabriel Garcia Rojas* — Efren Franco Lugo
7.
8. *Alfonso Sanchez Madariaga* — J. Jesus Palacios
9. Uriel Herrera Estua — Javier Rodriguez Ascorve
10. Eduardo Facha Gutierrez — Jose Cortina Goribar
11. *Aaron Camacho Lopez* — Gregorio Flores Torres
12. Enrique Rangel Melendez — Angel Velazquez Gomez

Durango
1. Enrique Campos Luna — Jesus Lopez de la Cruz
2. *Carlos Real Encinas* — Felipe Gutierrez
3. Gustavo Duron Gonzalez — Epifanio Alanis Navar
4. Armando del Castillo Franco — Efrain Acosta Garcia

Guanajuato
1. *Rafael Corrales Ayala* — Rodrigo Vazquez
2. *Juan Jose Torres Landa* — Enrique Mendoza Ortiz
3. *Vicente Salgado Paez* — J. Refugio Acosta
4. Francisco Garcia Carranza — Martin Zuloaga Vargas
5. *Benjamin Mendez Aguilar* — Fernando Lizardi
6. J. Jesus Yanez Maya — Pedro Espinosa Martinez
7. Meliton Cardenas V. — Moises Rangel Huerta

Guerrero
1. Lamberto Alarcon Catalan — Domingo Adame Vega
2. *Alfonso L. Nava* — Heberto Aburto Palacios
3. Nicolas Wences Garcia — Rogelio Aranda Gonzalez
4. Mario Romero Lopetegui — Rafael Jaime Silva
5. *Caritino Maldonado Perez* — Gonzalo A. Carranza

Hidalgo
1. Jorge Viesca y Palma — Roberto Quezada
2. Miguel Angel Cortes — Manuel Castelan
3. *Victor M. Aguirre C.* — Cesar Tovar Angeles
4. Domitilo Austria Garcia — Carlos Manuel Andrade
5. *Quintin Rueda Villagran* — Luis de la Concha Paulin

Jalisco
1. *Saturnino Coronado O.* — Salvador Sanchez Sigala
2. Manuel Ayala Perez — Genaro Salazar Vega
3. *Jaime Robles Martin C.* — Angel Oyarzabal
4. Angel Ruiz Vazquez — Daniel Celso Zacarias
5. Luis F. Ibarra Plascencia — Isidro Camacho Contreras
6. *Guillermo Ramirez Valadez* — Felipe Torres Polanco
7. *Francisco Galindo Ochoa* — Pedro Rodriguez Gonzalez
8. Edmundo Sanchez Gutierrez — Fidencio Cobian Regalado
9. Jorge Saracho Alvarez — Jose Maria Guillen

Mexico

1.	Rafael Suarez Ocana	Antero Gonzalez Torrescano
2.	Tito Ortega Sanchez	David Martinez Garcia
3.	Roberto Ocampo Gonzalez	Apolonio Rojas Guereque
4.	Enrique Gonzalez Mercado	Luis Millan Boisson
5.	*Gregorio Velazquez Sanchez*	J. Guadalupe Angeles Barrios
6.	Eulalio Nunez Alonso	Salvador Maldonado Rodea
7.	*Abel Huitron y Aguado*	Luis Berrueta Valencia
8.	*Raul Serrano Tellechea*	Felipe Avila Sil
9.	Daniel Moreno Castelan	Luis Pozos Quiroz

Michoacan

1.	Norberto Vega Villagomez	Leopoldo Carrasco Sandoval
2.	Gonzalo Chapela	Manuel Garcia Padilla
3.	Alfonso Reyes Hernandez	Jose Solorio Zaragoza
4.	*David Franco Rodriguez*	Maximino Padilla Hernandez
5.	Martin Rivera Godinez	J. Trinidad Hernandez Herrera
6.	*Salvador Pineda Pineda*	Roberto Antunez Vazquez
7.	Matias Rebollo Telles	Andres Rojas Herrera
8.	*Natalio Vazquez Pallares*	Fernando Urena Mendez

Morelos

1.	Julian Gonzalez Guadarrama	Celestino Alvear Munoz
2.	*Norberto Lopez Avelar*	Nabor Galicia Gonzalez

Nayarit

1.	Francisco Garcia Montero	Otilio Diaz Quintero
2.	*Emilio M. Gonzalez*	Nazario Meza Pena

Nuevo Leon

1.	*Pablo Quiroga Trevino*	Pedro Escamilla Flores
2.	Antonio Coello Elizondo	Felipe Flores Mancilla
3.	*Juan Jose Hinojosa*	Juventino Garcia Villagomez
4.	Alfredo Garza Rios	Mauro Reyes

Oaxaca

1.	Graciano Pineda Carrasco	Julio Gomez Lopez
2.	Ernesto Meixueiro	Alfredo D. Altamirano M.
3.	*Alfonso Perez Gasca*	Raul Bolanos Cacho
4.	Carlos R. Balleza, Jr.	Daniel Carbajal Rodriguez
5.	Leopoldo Flores Zavala	Benjamin Bolanos Jimenez
6.	Efren Davila Sanchez	Cirilo R. Luna
7.	*Norberto Aguirre*	Cirino Perez Aguirre
8.	Alberto Mayoral Pardo	*Rodolfo Alavez Flores*

Puebla

1.	Francisco Marquez Ramos	Jose A. Centeno Rodriguez
2.	Luis Cruz Manjarrez	Salvador Diaz Valdivia
3.	Nemesio Viveros Rodriguez	Miguel Munive Alvarado
4.	Undecided	Undecided
5.	Alfredo Reguero Gutierrez	Alvaro Lechuga Cabrera
6.	Salvador Martinez Aguirre	Edumundo Meza Zayas
7.	Luis Nunez Velarde	Alejandro Macip Alcantara
8.	Francisco Landero Alamo	Armando Cortes Bonilla
9.	Eduardo Vargas Diaz	Evencio Cabrera Tello

Queretaro

1.	*Manuel Gonzalez Cosio*	Ricardo Rivas Maldonado
2.	David Rodriguez Jauregui	Rosalio Herrera Maldonado

Quintana Roo (Territory)
1.   Abel Pavia Gonzalez   Antonio Erales Abdelnur

San Luis Potosi
1.   *Antonio Rocha, Jr.*   Jose de la Luz Cerda
2.   Pedro Pablo Gonzalez   Agapito Beltran Perez
3.   Fidel Cortes Carranco   Francisco Gonzalez Arellano
4.   Nicolas Perez Cerrillo   J. Guadalupe Martinez Sanchez
5.   Ignacio Morales Altamirano   Macario Balderas
6.   *J. Jesus N. Noyola*   Manuel Toledano Zugasti

Sinaloa
1.   Samuel Cabrera Castro   Jose I. Liera Lopez
2.   Teodulo Gutierrez Laura   Abraham Hernandez Ochoa
3.   Othon Herrera y Cairo   Manuel Sanchez Guerra

Sonora
1.   *Noe Palomares Navarro*   Felipe Arriola Gandara
2.   Ignacio Pesqueira F.   Teodoro O. Paz
3.   Leobardo Limon Marquez   Juan Francisco Olguin

Tabasco
1.   Agustin Beltran Bastar   Salomon Quintero Carrillo
2.   Mario S. Colorado Iris   Andres Salagurria

Tamaulipas
1.   Lauro Villalon de la Garza   Indalecio Esquivel
2.   Agustin Aguirre Garza   Manuel Flores Montalvo
3.   Manuel Jimenez San Pedro   Tomas Lopez Rico

Tlaxcala
1.   *Joaquin Cisneros*   Juan F. Perez Amador
2.   *Francisco Hernandez y H.*   J. Caridad Martinez

Veracruz
1.   Meliton T. Polito   Roberto Robles Nava
2.   *Enrique Rodriguez Cano*   Vitelio Ruiz Gomez
3.   *Cesar Garizurieta E.*   Roberto Nunez y Dominguez
4.   *Rafael Murillo Vidal*   Antonio Islas Morin
5.   Rafael Ortega Cruz   Encarnacion Contreras Fuentes
6.   *Silvestre Aguilar*   Jesus Castelan
7.   Vicente Luna Campos   Ernesto Bravo Pozos
8.   *Hermenegildo J. Aldana*   Juan Herrera Soriano
9.   *Jose Rodriguez Claveria*   Raul Barcelata Aldama
10.   Jose Fernandez Villegas   Octaviano Corro R.
11.   Francisco Turrent Artigas   Armando Pavon Moscoso
12.   Carlos Real   Gabriel E. Morales

Yucatan
1.   Humberto Esquivel Medina   Miguel F. Vidal Rivero
2.   *Jose Castillo Torre*   Gabriel Ferrer Mendiolea
3.   *Efrain Brito Rosado*   Aurelio Velazquez
4.   Samuel Espadas Centeno   Antonio Fernandez Vivas

Zacatecas
1.   Blas Bocardo   Arnulfo Torres Gonzalez
2.   David Valle Camacho   Jose Rosso Martinez
3.   *Jose Minero Roque*   *Mauricio Magdaleno*
4.   Roberto T. Amezaga   *Jose E. Rodriguez Elias*

1952–55 (42nd Legislature)

State	Deputy	Alternate
Aguascalientes		
1.	Luis T. Diaz	Francisco Gonzalez Sanchez
2.	Benito Palomino Dena	Fernando Ramos Jauregui
Baja California del Norte (Territory)		
1.	*Braulio Maldonado Sanchez*	Francisco Benitez Mendez
2.	Aurora Jimenez de Palacios	Onesimo Lopez Alvarez
Baja California del Sur (Territory)		
1.	Guillermo Corssen Luna	Lamberto Verdugo Lopez
Campeche		
1.	*Fernando Lanz Duret*	Hermilo Sandoval Campos
2.	Leopoldo Sales Rovira	Emilio Ceh Gamboa
Chiapas		
1.	Roque Vidal Rojas	Omelino Villator
2.	*Abelardo de la Torre G.*	Adolfo Celerino Lopez Carpio
3.	*Juan Sabines Gutierrez*	Eduardo Tovar Armendariz
4.	Nephtali Nucamendi Serrano	Francisco Fernandez Aguilar
5.	Salvador Duran Perez	Pablo Coeto Rosales
Chihuahua		
1.	Genaro R. Martinez	Miguel R. Esquivel
2.	Mariano Valenzuela Ceballos	Raul Soto Reyes
3.	Pedro Diaz Gonzalez	David M. Chavez Guerra
4.	Luis Gonzalez Herrera	Justino Loya Chavez
5.	Hipolito Villa Renteria	Lorenzo Torres H.
Coahuila		
1.	*Rafael Carranza H.*	Jesus Santos Cepeda
2.	Jose Villarreal Corona	Antonio Alonso Hernandez
3.	Antonio Marmolejo Barrera	Jose Ma. Rangel Abundiz
4.	Feliciano Morales Ramos	Jorge Frias Ruiz
Colima		
1.	Jorge Huarte Osorio	Emiliano Ramirez Suarez
2.	*Jesus Robles Martinez*	*Roberto Pizano Saucedo*
Distrito Federal		
1.	Pedro Julio Pedrero Gomez	Ignacio Capistran Lazcano
2.	*Juan Jose Osorio Palacios*	Leopoldo Lopez Munoz
3.	*Felipe Gomez Mont*	Patricio Aguirre Andrade
4.	Alberto Hernandez Campos	Jorge Riva Palacio
5.	Jose Maria L. A. Ruiz Z.	Francisco Hernandez Mavarro
6.	Narciso Contreras Contreras	Manuel Barroso Petris
7.	Mariano Ordorica Burgos	Antonio Aguilar Sandoval
8.	*Romulo Sanchez Mireles*	Margarito Curiel Sosa
9.	Javier de la Riva	Adolfo Guevara Pren.
10.	Antonio Rivas Ramirez	Victor Manuel Avila Romero
11.	*Eugenio Ibarrola Santoyo*	Ignacio Limon Maurer
12.	Heriberto Garrido Ordonez	Carlos Couto Alba
13.	Fidel Ruiz Moreno	Alfonso Hermoso Najera
14.	Juventino Aguilar Moreno	Juan Ramirez
15.	Luis Quintero Gutierrez	Alfonso Trejo Chavez
16.	Ramon Cabrera C.	Angel Ortega Acosta
17.	*Alfonso Martinez Dominguez*	Ramon Romero Gomez
18.	*Rodolfo Echeverria Alvarez*	Mario Cordova Curtis
19.	Enrique Marcue Pardinas	Juan Negrete Lopez

Durango
1. Maximo Gamiz Fernandez — Jesus Cisneros Roldan
2. *Enrique Dupre Ceniceros* — Jesus Maria Romo Romo
3. Ramiro Rodriguez Palafox — Edilberto Aguirre Medina
4. *Braulio Meraz Nevarez* — Pedro Davila de la O.

Guanajuato
1. J. Jesus Lomelin M. — Ignacio Vazquez Sanchez
2. Herculano Hernandez Delgado — Antonio Castro
3. Cayetano Andrade Lopez — Antonio Ramirez Maldonado
4. Ezequiel Gomez Hernandez — Maximiano Villafana Ibarra
5. Ernesto Gallardo Sanchez — Salvador Alvarado Vargas
6. Vicente Munoz Castro — Luis Solis Mugica
7. Oliverio Ortega — Ocatavio Lizardi Gil
8. Rodrigo Moreno Zermeno — Juan Anselmo Serrano D.

Guerrero
1. Pedro Ayala Fajardo — Heliodoro Salgado Valencia
2. Jesus Mastache Roman — Alberto Salgado Cuevas
3. Heberto Aburto Palacios — *Carlos Roman Celis*
4. Jose Gomez Velasco — Mario de la O. Tellez
5. Damaso Lanche Guillen — Jose Ventura Neri

Hidalgo
1. Librado Gutierrez — Eduardo Vergara
2. Jose Luis Suarez Molina — Gorgonio de la Concha Moreno
3. *Jose Maria de los Reyes* — Leonardo Ramirez
4. Juvencio Nochebuena — Juan Ramirez Reyes
5. Antonio Ponce Lagos — Pedro Caravantes

Jalisco
1. *Rodolfo Gonzalez Guevara* — Miguel de Alva Arroya
2. Ramon Garcilita Partida — Martin Coronado Ramon
3. J. Jesus Ibarra Navarro — Flavio Gutierrez Casillas
4. *Ramon Garcia Ruiz* — Elias Gomez Rodriguez
5. Abraham Gonzalez Rivera — Jose Gutierrez Zermeno
6. J. Jesus Cordero Mendoza — Jesus Navarro Gonzalez
7. *Filiberto G. Rubalcaba S.* — Salvador Hernandez Mata
8. Fidencio Vazquez Cerda — Manuel Zamora Negrete
9. Alfredo Medina Guerra — Francisco Torres Flores
10. J. Jesus Landeros Amezola — Sergio Corona Blake
11. Angel F. Martinez Gutierrez — Salvador Chavez Magana

Mexico
1. *Roberto Barrios Castro* — Jesus Alarcon Moreno
2. Manuel Martinez Orta — Francisco Moguel Martinez
3. Fernando Guerrero Esquivel — Adolfo Ramirez Fragoso
4. Hilario Carrillo Gasca — Jesus Sanchez Lara
5. *Francisco Perez Rios* — Jesus Garcia Lovera
6. Carlos Garduno Gonzalez — Eduardo Betancourt Aguilar

Michoacan
1. Fernando Ochoa Ponce de L. — Cayetano Vivanco Reyes
2. Aquiles de la Pena Ortega — Francisco Nunez Chavez
3. *Agustin Arriaga Rivera* — Cresencio Cruz Morales
4. *Daniel P. Mora Ramos* — J. Jesus Magana Ortiz
5. Miguel Pinedo Gil — Angel Ayala Alfaro
6. *Manuel Hinojosa Ortiz* — Alberto Perez Villanueva
7. Raul de la Puente Diaz — Abelardo Sierra Sanchez
8. Francisco Chavez Gonzalez — Roberto Lopez Maya
9. Juan Figueroa Torres — Jacinto Hernandez Gonzalez

Morelos
1.	Lorenzo R. Jimenez	Manuel Diaz Leal
2.	Porfirio Palacios	Vicente Lahera

Nayarit
1.	Jose Angulo Araico	Juventino Espinosa Jr.
2.	Bernardo M. de Leon	Ricardo Gomez Garcia

Nuevo Leon
1.	Caleb Sierra Ramos	Donato Gonzalez Castillo
2.	Jose Carrera Franco	Gil Paez Cardona
3.	Eugenio Morales Nunez	Ernesto Serna Villarreal
4.	Jesus Garza Cantu	Isauro S. Santos
5.	*Arturo Luna Lugo*	J. Refugio Solis

Oaxaca
1.	Heliodoro Charis Castro	Mariano Escobar Barrientos
2.	Eustorgio Cruz Aguilar	Hermenegildo Luis Perez
3.	*Manuel Aguilar y Salazar*	Victor Diaz Hernandez
4.	Jacobo Aragon Aguillon	Angel Galindo N.
5.	Gilberto Alamirano H.	Emilio Morales Angulo
6.	Cirilo R. Luna	Agustin Solano
7.	*Miguel Garcia Cruz*	Manuel Martell Gomez
8.	Manuel Sodi del Valle	Jose A. Salinas Narvaez
9.	Crisanto Aguilar Perez	Antonio J. Perez Cordoba

Puebla
1.	*Blas Chumacero Sanchez*	Jesus Ramos Rodriguez
2.	Angel Pacheco Huerta	Jesus H. Ramirez
3.	*Antonio Montes Garcia*	Esau Torres Pastrana
4.	Luis H. Jimenez	Virginio Ayaquica Nava
5.	Leopoldo Rivera Gonzalez	Miguel Angel Godinez
6.	Mario Andrade Balseca Lara	Benito Guzman Cid
7.	Arnulfo Valdes Rodriguez	Ernesto Rodriguez Orea
8.	Carlos Diaz Pumarino	Benjamin Guzman
9.	*Jose Ricardi Tirado*	Jose Maria Arroyo
10.	Alberto Jimenez V.	Elias Cortes Gonzalez

Queretaro
1.	Eduardo Ruiz Gutierrez	Ricardo Rivas Maldonado
2.	*Manuel Soberanes Munoz*	Samuel Palacios Borja

Quintana Roo (Territory)
1.	Antonio Erales Abdelnur	Alfonso Godoy Castillo

San Luis Potosi
1.	Agustin Olivo Monsivais	J. Jesus Blanco Vega
2.	*Pablo Aldrett Cuellar*	Hector Mendoza de la Rosa
3.	Alfonso R. Garcia	Adalberto Torres Rodriguez
4.	Jorge Ferretis	Jacinto Maldonado Villaverde
5.	Alfonso Viramontes Gonzalez	Primitivo Contreras Ugalde

Sinaloa
1.	Miguel Leon Lopez	Tomas Romanillo Rodrigo
2.	Felix Lopez Montoya	Porfirio Lopez Mejia
3.	Amado Ibarra Corral	Andrea Mariscal Vda. de V.
4.	*Bernardo Norzagaray Angulo*	Alberto Tripp Flores

Sonora
1.	Jesus Lizarraga Gastelum	Jesus Siqueiros Moreno
2.	Jesus Maria Suarez Arvizu	Benito de la Ree
3.	Rafael Contreras Monteon	Manuel V. Quintana

Tabasco
1.   Ernesto Brown Peralta   Jose Maria Valenzuela O.
2.   Federico Jimenez Paoli   Aristides Pratts Salazar

Tamaulipas
1.   *Juan Manuel Teran Mata*   Francisco Morales Nunez
2.   *Norberto Trevino Zapata*   Aureliano Caballero Gonzalez
3.   Juan Baez Guerra   Jose Jesus Betancourt
4.   Antonio H. Abrego   Eligio Contreras Maldonado

Tlaxcala
1.   Ezequiel Selley Hernandez   Agustin Garcia Quintos
2.   *Emilio Sanchez Piedras*   Cenobio Perez Romero

Veracruz
1.   Jose Polito Morales
2.   Leonardo Silva Espinosa   Lazaro Vargas Segura
3.   Pedro Vivanco Garcia   Alberto Bache Herrera
4.   Manuel Zorrilla Rivera   Agustin G. Alvarado
5.   Manuel Gonzalez Montes   David de la Medina
6.   Lorenzo Azua Torres   Miguel Dominguez
7.   Agustin Ramirez Romero   Manuel Abascal Sherwell
8.   Manuel Meza Hernandez   Aurelio Moreno Serna
9.   *Roberto Gomez Maqueo*   Donaciano Caballero
10.   Juan Chiunti Rico   Angel Estrada Loyo
11.   Jose Ch. Ramirez   Rafael Barreiro Gutierrez
12.   Felipe L. Mortera Prieto   Francisco Rocha Ruiseco

Yucatan
1.   *Ramon Osorio y Carvajal*   Ruben Frias Bobadilla
2.   Antonio Bustillos Carrillo   Jorge Martinez Rios
3.   Fernando Vargas Ocampo   Mauricio Escobedo Granados

Zacatecas
1.   Alfredo Lozano Salazar   Carlos Zorrilla Enciso
2.   Cornelio Sanchez Hernandez   J. Jesus Vela Ruiz
3.   *Jose Rodriguez Elias*   Fidel B. Serrano
4.   Alfredo Munoz Cervantes   Francisco Olvera Peralta

1955–58 (43rd Legislature)

Alternate   *State*   *Deputy*

Aguascalientes
1.   Edmundo L. Bernal Alonso   Maria del Carmen Martin
2.   *Alberto Alcala de Lira*   *Alfredo de Lara Isaacs*

Baja California del Norte
(Territory)
1.   Emilio Hernandez Armenta   Roberto Cannet Gonzalez
2.   Guilebaldo Silva Cota   Abelardo Rodriguez Ortega

Baja California del Sur
(Territory)   Vacant

Campeche
1.   Tomas Aznar Alvarez   Felipe Rubio Ortiz
2.   *Carlos Sansores Perez*   Porfirio Reyna Salazar

Chiapas
1.   Guadalupe Fernandez de Leon   Fernan Pavia Farrera
2.   Jesus Argueta Lopez   Francisco S. Becerra Perez
3.   Octavio Esponda Rovelo   Esteban Jimenez Miranda
4.   *Marcelina Galindo Arce*   Martiniano Jacob M.
5.   Gamaliel Becerra Ochoa   Roberto Mandujano Herrera

Chihuahua

1.	Leonardo Revilla Romero	Andres Quezada Pallares
2.	Manuel Villa Atayde	Feliciano Morales Garcia
3.	Jesus Sanz Cerrada Lopez	Raul Garcia Baca
4.		
5.	*Guillermo Quevedo Moreno*	Adolfo Baca Garcia

Coahuila

1.	Carlos Valdes Villarreal	Tomas Algaba Gomez
2.	Amador Robles Santibanez	Salvador Hernandez Rodriguez
3.	Jesus Rodriguez Silva	Eduardo Davila Garza
4.	Antonio Hernandez Mendez	Juan F. Villarreal

Colima

1.	*Antonio Salazar Salazar*	J. Jesus Plascencia Ortiz
2.	*Roberto Pizano Saucedo*	Crispin Casian Zepeda

Distrito Federal

1.	Cesar Velazquez Sanchez	Arturo Esponda Gallegos
2.	Roberto Herrera Leon	Jacinto Gonzalez Mejia
3.	Patricio Aguirre Andrade	Guillermo Martinez Estape
4.	Salvador Carrillo Echeveste	*Joaquin del Olmo Martinez*
5.	*Alfonso Sanchez Madariaga*	Francisco Robles Rodriguez
6.	*Baltazar Dromundo Chorne*	Javier Salgado Estrada
7.	Ricardo Velazquez Vazquez	Guillermina Garcia Cruz M.
8.	Jose Gutierrez Diaz	Miguel Conde Rodriguez
9.	*Manuel Sierra Macedo*	Julian Aguilar Fernandez
10.	Jose Rodriguez Granada	Francisco Iturbe Madero
11.	Francisco Aguirre Alegria	Feliciano Montero Abasolo
12.	Juan Gomez Salas	Evaristo Orozco Lopez
13.		
14.	Ramon Castilleja Zarate	Salvador Padilla Flores
15.	Jorge Ayala Ramirez	Aristeo Ponce Huerta
16.	*Luis M. Farias*	Tomas Gonzalez Arias
17.	*Alfonso Ituarte Servin*	Ubaldo Vargas Martinez
18.	Julio Ramirez Colozzi	Eulalio Cabanas Gonzalez
19.	Marcelino Murrieta Carreto	Emiliano Aguilar Garces

Durango

1.	*Carlos Real Encinas*	Macedonio Rodda Cordoba
2.	Manuel Garcia Santibanez	Francisco Galindo Chavez
3.	Juan Pescador Polanco	Ismael Mora
4.	Pablo Picharra Esparza	Ismael Mora Hernandez

Guanajuato

1.	*Rafael Corrales Ayala E.*	Bernardino Aguilar Montano
2.	Enrique Mendoza Ortiz	Jose Hidalgo Quiroz
3.	Gonzalo Maldonado Cervantes	Francisco Granados Gonzalez
4.	Manuel Padilla Villa	Aurelio Garcia Sierra
5.	Alfonso Fernandez Monreal	Florencio Orozco Quiroz
6.	*Jose Lopez Bermudez*	Manuel Rosillo Morales
7.	Jesus Madrigal Yanez	Miguel Roncal Gener
8.	*Agustin Arroyo Damian*	Juan Flores Echeverria

Guerrero

1.	*Jose Inocente Lugo Lagunas*	Augusto Lozano Hernandez
2.	*Jorge Soberon Acevedo*	Faustino Rivera Diaz
3.	*Carlos Roman Celis*	Alvaro Negrete Perez
4.	Gustavo Rueda Medina	Florencio Encarnacion Urzua
5.	Aaron Pelaez Salazar	Rodolfo Rodriguez Ramos

Hidalgo
1. *Julian Rodriguez Adame* — Andres Manning Valenzuela
2. *Manuel Sanchez Vite* — Angela Barrientos Montiel
3. *Carlos Ramirez Guerrero* — Ignacio Mora Pina
4. Agustin Mariel Anaya — Florentino Gomez Estrella
5. Miguel Gomez Mendoza — Gabriel Parrodi Casaux

Jalisco
1.
2. Aurelio Altamirano Gonzalez — Jose Montes de Oca Avalos
3. Marcos Montero Ruiz — Luis Escobar Reyes
4. Diego Huizar Martinez — J. Jesus Toledo Villegas
5. Agustin Pineda Flores — Isidro Alferez Espinosa
6. *Francisco Rodriguez Gomez* — Flavio Ramirez Alvarez
7. *Carlos Ramirez Ladewig* — Jose Bracamontes Ortega
8. *Flavio Romero de Velasco* — Pedro Parra Centeno
9. David Perez Rulfo — *Luis Javier Luna B.*
10. *Maria Guadalupe Urzua F.* — Alfredo Trejo Romero
11. *Francisco Galindo Ochoa* — Jose Ramos Gomez

Mexico
1. Jose Guadalupe Cisneros — Hermenegildo Castro Padilla
2. Luis Berroeta Valencia — Benito Monroy Ortega
3. Leopoldo Trejo Aguilar — Abel Gonzalez Marino
4. *Mario Colin Sanchez* — Alfonso Valencia Medrano
5. *Gregorio Velazquez Sanchez* — Juan Gomez Mondragon
6. Remedios Albertina Ezeta — Margarita Colin Mondragon
7. Ruben Osuna Perez — Arcadio Escalante Cortes
8. *Leonardo Rodriguez Alcaine* — Santiago Montes Cerros

Michoacan
1. Enrique Aguilar Gonzalez — Maria Dolores Pacheco G.
2. Agustin Carreon Florian — Maria Dolores Tregoni de R.
3. Antonio Arriaga Ochoa — Victoriano Cazares Sanchez
4. Conrado Magana Cerda — Jose Maria Cano Ramos
5. Alfonso Sanchez Flores — Luis Patino Carrillo
6. Roberto Gonzalez Zamudio — Cornelio Mendez Gomez
7. *Salvador Pineda Pineda* — Adolfo Arias Ochoa
8. Jose Campuzano Ramirez — Emilio Padilla Garcia
9. Jose Garibay Romero — David Perez Zepeda

Morelos
1. *Federico Sanchez Navarrete* — Cristobal Rojas Romero
2. *Benigno Abundez Chavez* — Antonio A. Pliego Noyola

Nayarit
1. Felipe Ibarra Partida — Jose Maria Zamorano Aguirre
2. Manuel Villegas Arellano — Joaquin Hernandez Curiel

Nuevo Leon
1. Angel Lozano Elizondo — Luis Diaz de Leon Arrieta
2. Leopoldo Banda Romero — Jesus Malacara Garcia
3. Rafael Gonzalez Montemayor — Heliodoro Lozano Gonzalez
4. *Margarita Garcia Flores* — Roberto M. Gonzalez Gutierrez
5. J. Ascension Charles Luna — Dustano Muniz Leija

Oaxaca
1. Adolfo Gurrion Gurrion — Bulmaro Antonio Rueda
2. Graciano Federico Hernandez — Zeferino Gonzalez Diego
3. *Raul Bolanos Cacho G.* — *Fernando Gomez Sandoval*
4. Marcos Carrillo Cardenas — Rufino Lopez Gonzalez

5.	Melquiades Ramirez Santiago	Federico Ramirez Juarez
6.	Manuel Cantu Mendez	Antonio Lopez y Lopez
7.	Fidel Lopez Sanchez	Manuel Hernandez Hernandez
8.	Angel G. Arreola Martinez	Leopoldo Jimenez Cordova
9.	*Ramon Ruiz Vasconcelos*	Guillermo Meixueiro Salgado

Puebla

1.	Salvador Lobato Jimenez	Rodolfo Arriaga Martinez
2.	Manuel Rivera Anaya	Carlos Rosas Mendoza
3.	*Alfredo Toxqui Fernandez*	Heriberto Genis Solis
4.	*Antonio J. Hernandez J.*	Salvador Serrano Ramirez
5.	Eduardo Rodriguez Mendez	Irene Ramirez Benavides
6.	*Amador Hernandez Gonzalez*	Alberto Victoria Arenas
7.	*Fernando Cueto Fernandez*	Alfonso Valderrama Gonzalez
8.	Jesus Lopez Avila	Jose Cid Sanchez
9.	Javier Ruperto Bonilla C.	Francisco Albarran Cortes
10.	*Jose Ignacio Morales Cruz*	Bernardo Gonzalez Munoz

Queretaro

1.	Roman Esquivel Pimentel	Domingo Olvera Gamez
2.	Rosalio Herrera Maldonado	Palemon Ledesma Ledesma

Quintana Roo (Territory)

1.	Gaston Perez Rosado	Tiburcio May Uh

San Luis Potosi

1.	Jesus Medina Romero	Miguel Angel Alvarez Sanchez
2.	Felix Dauajare Torres	Santiago Lara Jara
3.	Rodolfo Rico Diaz	Perfecto Dominguez Hernandez
4.	Jose de la Luz Blanco Govea	Narciso Garcia Tovar
5.	Jacinto Maldonado V.	Domingo Luis Rocha Rangel

Sinaloa

1.	Eliseo Galaviz Bernal	Ramon Lopez Gutierre
2.	Manuel Luna Quintero	Luis Gutierrez Figueroa
3.	Joaquin Duarte Lopez	Alejandra Retamoza Reynaga
4.	*Leopoldo Sanchez Celis*	Mateo Camacho Ontiveros

Sonora

1.	Luis Mendoza Lopez	Santos Sanchez Ochoa
2.	*Emiliano Corella Molina*	Francisca Cordoba Macalpin
3.	Saturnino Saldivar Alcala	Eulalio Vazquez Cota

Tabasco

1.	Joaquin Bates Caparroso	Roberto Nunez Martinez
2.	*Agapito Dominguez*	Jose del Carmen Palma

Tamaulipas

1.	Jose Cruz Contreras Gamboa	Cipriano Montemayor Gonzalez
2.	*Emilio Martinez Manautou*	Bernardo Reyes Flores
3.	Jesus Betancourt Vergara	Florentino Lopez Mireles
4.	Ignacio Pacheco Leon	Rafael Salinas Medina

Tlaxcala

1.	Raul Juarez Carro	Ricardo Altamirano Flores
2.	*Samuel Ortega Hernandez*	Antonio de la Lanza M.

Veracruz

1.	*Raymundo Flores Fuentes*	Raul Lince Medellin
2.	Antonio Pulido Cobos	Alvaro Lorenzo Fernandez
3.	Telesforo Reyes Chargoy	Luis Salas Garcia
4.	*Rosendo Topete Ibanez*	Prisciliano Nava Vay
5.	Raul Navarro Chanes	Mario de la Garza Castro
6.	Telesforo Contreras Solano	Jose de Jesus Solis Tapia

7.	Antonio Garcia Molina	Carlos Hernandez Fabela
8.	Hesiquio Aguilar Maranon	Jose Zuniga Acevedo
9.	Juan Malpica Mimendi	Juan Mendez Martinez
10.	*Hermenegildo J. Aldana*	Auxilio M. Tejeda
11.	Ruben B. Dominguez	Agustin Ortega Santos
12.	Francisco Rocha Ruiseco	Armando Velazquez Vazquez

Yucatan
1.	Carlos R. Castillo C.	Alfredo Canto Lopez
2.	Aurelio Carrillo Puerto	Alberto Peniche Barrera
3.	Jose Manuel Lopez Lliteras	Gustavo Flota Rosas

Zacatecas
1.	Roberto del Real Carranza	Alfonso Jose Cardona Pena
2.	Gonzalo Bretado Sanchez	Rafael Yanez Sosa
3.	Fidel B. Serrano	Francisco Rodriguez Haro
4.	*Fernando Pamanes Escobedo*	Abundio Monsivais Garcia

1958–61 (44th Legislature)

State	Deputy	Alternate
Aguascalientes		
1.	Heriberto Bejar Jauregui	Manuel Jimenez Hernandez
2.	*Enrique Olivares Santana*	Rafael Reyes Rangel
Baja California del Norte (Territory)		
1.	*Ricardo Alzalde Arellano*	Rafael Gomez Garcia
2.	German Brambila Gomez	Jose Carmen Moreno Ramirez
Baja California del Sur (Territory)		
1.	Alejandro D. Martinez R.	Bartolo Geraldo Camacho
Campeche		
1.	*Jose Ortiz Avila*	Eduardo Negrin Baeza
2.	Carlos Cano Cruz	Maria Reyes Ortiz
Chiapas		
1.	*Juan Sabines Gutierrez*	*Maximo Contreras Camacho*
2.	Antonio Zoreda Cebada	Jorge Octavio Cepeda Ramos
3.	Francisco Arguello C.	Francisco Quinones Leon
4.	Esteban Corzo Blanco	Augusto Castellanos Hernandez
5.	Juan Trinidad Lopez	Jorge Chamlati Trinidad
Chihuahua		
1.	Miguel A. Olea Enriquez	J. Bonifacio Fernandez F.
2.	Jose R. Munoz Espinosa	Raul Soto Reyes
3.	Marcos Flores Monsivais	J. Ascension Tarelo Garcia
4.	*Arnaldo Gutierrez Hernandez*	Jose Pena Flores
5.	*Alfredo Chavez Vazquez, Jr.*	Jesus Sagarnaga Alarcon
Coahuila		
1.	*Florencio Barrera Fuentes*	Raul Malacara Flores
2.	Manuel Calderon Salas	Julio Vega Arreola
3.	Pablo Orozco Escobar	Octavio Villa Coss
4.	Daniel Hernandez Medrano	Jaime Borjon Valdes
Colima		
1.	Othon Bustos Solorzano	Hector Duenas Aguilar
2.	Tomas Bejarano Figueroa	*Jorge Lang Islas*

Distrito Federal

1.	Antonio Aguilar Sandoval	Juan Antonio Samano Olaez
2.	*Joaquin de Olmo Martinez*	Juan Federico Villalpando C.
3.	*Felipe Gomez Mont*	Jose Bayon Arciniega
4.	Ramon Villarreal Vazquez	Luis Diaz Vazquez
5.	Jose Maria Leoncio A. Ruiz	Victor Manuel Avila Romero
6.	*Marta Andrade del Rosal*	*Jose Humberto Zebadua Lieuano*
7.	Manuel Moreno Cardenas	Jose Alvarez Garduno
8.	*Emilio Gandarilla Aviles*	Rosa Gomez de Davila
9.	*Arturo Lopez Portillo*	Manuel Zenteno Cuevas
10.	Roberto Gavaldon Leyva	Alfonso Acevedo Belbouis
11.	J. Jesus Lopez Gonzalez	Rafael Montano Montes de Oca
12.	Adan Hernandez Rojas	Alberto Martinez Carrero
13.	Gaston Novelo Von Glumer	Luisa Martinez de Castelazo
14.	Rafael Buitron Maldonado	Salvador Lecona Santos
15.	*Juan Jose Osorio Palacios*	Manuel Nunez Villegas
16.	Ruben Marin y Kall	Filemon Tapia Hernandez
17.	Gonzalo Pena Manterola	Mariano Chavez Lopez
18.	*Antonio Castro Leal*	Justo Olmedo Martinez
19.	Emiliano Aguilar Garces	*Oscar Ramirez Mijares*

Durango

1.	Jose Guillermo Salas A.	Guadalupe Camacho
2.	Ricardo Thompson Rivas	Francisco Torres Garcia
3.	*Enrique W. Sanchez Garcia*	Fernando Barraza Aguilar
4.	Ezequiel Nevarez Ramirez	Ramon Ortiz Serrato

Guanajuato

1.	Manuel Tinajero Orosio	Pablo Arenas Sanchez
2.	Pompeyo Gomez Lerma	Pedro Lona Quezada
3.	Antonio Lomeli Garduno	Daniel Bravo Hernandez
4.	*Aurelio Garcia Sierra*	J. Jesus Aguirre Reynoso
5.	*Fernando Diaz Duran*	Juan Perez Vela Rosa
6.	*Vicente Salgado Paez*	Rosa Gonzalez de Carmona
7.	Javier Guerrero Rico	Salvador Montes Redondo
8.	Luis Ferro Medina	Juan Pons Pons

Guerrero

1.	*Moises Ochoa Campos*	Andres Alarcon Rojas
2.	Macrina Rabadan Santana	Elodia Salgado Figueroa
3.	Enrique Salgado Samano	Antonio Sanchez Molina
4.	Mario Castillo Carmona	Guillermo Leyva Ventura
5.	Heron Varela Alvarado	Efrain Guillen de la Barrera

Hidalgo

1.	Andres Manning Valenzuela	Adalberto Cravioto Meneses
2.	*Manuel Yanez Ruiz*	Antonio Hernandez Garcia
3.	Federico Ocampo Noble Perez	Heberto Malo Paulin
4.	Francisco Rivera Caretta	Norberto Hernandez Arenas
5.	Martiniano Martin Alvarez	Guillermo Barcena B.

Jalisco

1.	Luis Ramirez Meza	Primitivo Tolentino Mancilla
2.	*Maria Guadalupe Martinez*	Juan Ramirez Garcia
3.	*Porfirio Cortes Silva*	Felipe Lopez Prado
4.	*Carlos Guzman y Guzman*	Rodrigo Ortega Anzures
5.	*Jose Perez Moreno*	Salvador Quezada Ramirez
6.	Tito Padilla Lozano	Jesus Navarro Gonzalez
7.	Vacancy	Vacancy
8.	Jose Luis Martinez R.	David Alvarez Miramontes

9.	*Jose Maria Martinez R.*	Jose Mendoza Cortes
10.	*Sebastian Garcia Barragan*	Alejandro Soltero Vidrio
11.	Jose de Jesus Castro R.	Raul Rojas Ruiz

Mexico

1.	Enrique Tapia Aranda	Raul Mancera Alfaro
2.	Manuel Martinez Orta	Eduardo Soberanes Romero
3.	Sidronio Choperena Ocariz	Pedro B. Noguez Becerril
4.	Fernando Guerrero Esquivel	Filiberto Cortes Ponce
5.	*Francisco Perez Rios*	Angel Celorio Lujambjo
6.	*Carlos Hank Gonzalez*	Francisco Garcia Rubio
7.	Benito Contreras Garcia	Silvano Ortega Sanchez
8.	Graciana Becerril Bernal	Guillermo Garcia Alcantara

Michoacan

1.	Jesus Ortega Calderon	Ignacio Tapia Fernandez
2.	Adolfo Gandara Baron	Manuel Garcia Mendoza
3.	*Daniel T. Renteria Acosta*	Carlos Grajeda Rodriguez
4.	Jose Garcia Castillo	Jose Luis Villegas Magana
5.	*Baltazar Gudino Canela*	Salvador Valdez Ayala
6.	Jose R. Castaneda Zarragoza	Antonio Iniguez Canela
7.	Silvestre Garcia Suazo	Maria Perez Rios
8.	Horacio Tenorio Carmena	Indalecio Pena Reyes
9.	Ruben Vargas Garibay	Salvador Mendez Solorzano

Morelos

1.	Manuel Castillo Solter	Jesus Galindo Pichardo
2.	*Ana Maria Zapata Portillo*	Francisco Sanchez Benitez

Nayarit

1.	Salvador Arambul Ibarra	Genoveva Suarez Vda. de T.
2.	Pedro Luna Mercado	Jose Ramirez Rodriguez

Nuevo Leon

1.	*Leopoldo Gonzalez Saenz*	Alfonso Garza y Garza
2.	Rosalio Delgado Elizondo	Jose Ovalle Morales
3.	Aaron S. Villarreal V.	Jocobo Dominguez Lacea
4.	Antonio Garza Pena	*Carolina Morales Farias*
5.	Ramon Berzosa Cortes	Pedro Hernandez Tovar

Oaxaca

1.	*Andres Henestrosa Morales*	Francisco Luis Castillo
2.	Jenaro Maldonado Matias	Eufrosino Sanchez Moreno
3.	*Federico Ortiz Armengol*	Jose Morales Paz
4.	Antonio Acevedo Gutierrez	Agustin Dominguez Herrera
5.	Bulmaro A. Rueda	Samuel Lopez Martinez
6.	Enrique Sada Baigts	Carlos Merino Camarillo
7.	*Manuel Hernandez Hernandez*	Antonio Velasco Ortiz
8.	Adan Cuellar Layseca	Jesus Guzman Rubio
9.	Jacobo Aragon Aguillon	Carlos Innes Acevedo

Puebla

1.	*Blas Chumacero Sanchez*	Juan Galindo Quintero
2.	Porfirio Rodriguez Flores	Norberto Espinosa Ceron
3.	*Miguel Garcia Sela*	Sebastian Cordero Jimenez
4.	Salvador Serrano Ramirez	Miguel Munive Alvarado
5.	Antonio Lopez y Lopez	Jesus Benavides Bazan
6.	Joaquin Paredes Roman	Perfecto de los Santos Valerio
7.	Carlos Trujillo Perez	Alfonso Valderrama Gonzalez
8.	*Jose Ricardi Tirado*	Carlos Viveros Castillo
9.	Amando Cortes Bonilla	Jose de la Llave Arroyo
10.	*Esperanza Tellez Oropeza*	Alfonso Sosa Dominguez

Queretaro
1.   Luis Escobar Santeliees   Rafael Ayala Echavarri
2.   Palemon Ledesma Ledesma   Vacancy
Quintana Roo (Territory)
1.   Felix Morel Peyefitte   Julio Mac H.
San Luis Potosi
1.   *Francisco Martinez de la V.*   Pedro Pablo Gonzalez
2.   *Manuel Moreno Torres*   Jose Rodriguez Alvarez N
3.   Juan Diaz Macias   Galdino Martinez Rodriguez
4.   Ignacio Aguinaga Castaneda   Roberto Iglesias Garcia
5.   Joaquin Guzman Martinez   Simitrio Sagahon Dominguez
Sinaloa
1.   *Samuel Castro Cabrera*   Nicolas Mariscal Mariscal
2.   Arcadio Camacho Luque   Pablo Rubio Espinosa
3.   Jose Concepcion Carrillo C.   Alejandro Gaxiola Ramos
4.   *Aurora Arrayales de Morales*   Modesto Antimo Rivas
Sonora
1.   Jose A. Montano Torres   *Alicia Arellano Tapia*
2.   Benito Bernal Dominguez   Ciro Arce Fonseca
3.   Aurelio Garcia Valdes   Matias Mendez Limon
Tabasco
1.   *Maria Luisa Rosado de H.*   Jose Luis Gallegos Avendano
2.   Hilario Garcia Canul   Candido Rivera Cortazar
Tamaulipas
1.   Tiburcio Garza Zamora   Ruperto Villarreal Montemayor
2.   Pompeyo Gomez Lerma   Silvestre Mata Carrizales
3.   Aureliano Caballero G.   Leopoldo de la Fuente Nunez
4.   Carlos Parga Gonzalez   Pedro Castaneda Zuniga
Tlaxcala
1.   *Emilio Sanchez Piedras*   Nicolas Lopez Galindo
2.   Crisanto Cuellar Abaroa   Maria Guadalupe Juarez C.
Veracruz
1.   Manuel Herrera Angeles   Maria Lucia Molina de Lince
2.   German Granda Garcia   Florencio T. Cobos Ovando
3.   Raul Lara Mendoza   Manuel Salas Castelan
4.   Antonio Marroquin Carlon   Diego Arrazola Becerra
5.   *Salvador Olmos Hernandez*   Luis E. Murillo
6.   Humberto Celis Ochoa   Aristeo Rivas Andrade
7.   Samuel Vargas Reyes   Angel Contreras Cerrilla
8.   Rafael Espinosa Flores   Ruben Calatayud Balaguero
9.   *Arturo Llorente Gonzalez*   Ismael Lagunes Lastra
10.   Octaviano Coro Ramos   Jose Antonio Tejeda Panama
11.   *Celso Vazquez Ramirez*   Manuel Malpica Mortera
12.   Felipe L. Mortera Prieto   Delfino Santos Fernandez
Yucatan
1.   *Eduardo Jose Molina C.*   Humberto Lizcano Rios
2.   Gustavo Flota Rosas   Mario Ceballos Novelo
3.   Jose Vallejo Novelo   Bruno Mezquita Cisneros
Zacatecas
1.   Jaime Haro Rodriguez   Ana Maria Segura Dorantes
2.   Antonio Ledesma Gonzalez   Jose Acevedo Solis
3.   Hugo Romero Macias   Valentin Rivero Azearraga
4.   Leandro Castillo Venegas   Antonio Betancourt Hernandez

1961–1964 (45th Legislature)

State	Deputy	Alternate
Aguascalientes		
1.	Manuel Trujillo Miranda	Joaquin Diaz de Leon Gil
2.	Carmen Maria Araiza Lopez	Camilo Lopez Gomez
Baja California del Norte (Territory)		
1.	Gustavo Arevalo Gardoqui	*Alfonso Garzon Santibanez*
2.	*Gustavo Aubanel Vallejo*	Alfonso Siordia Davales
3.	Luis Gonzalez Ocampo	Quintin Hurtado Olivares
Baja California del Sur (Territory)		
1. La Paz	*Antonio Navarro Encinas*	*Alberto Alvarado Aramburo*
Campeche		
1.	Manuel Pavon Bahaine	Armida del Carmen Reyes Ruiz
2.	*Carlos Sansores Perez*	Genaro Espadas Barrera
Chiapas		
1.	Rafael P. Gamboa Cano	Oscar Rueda Escobar
2.	Amadeo Narcia Ruiz	Abraham Aguilar Paniagua
3.	Romeo Rincon Serrano	Pedro J. Cancino Gordillo
4.	*Maximo Contreras Camacho*	Enrique Cruz Vals
5.	Gustavo Lescieur Lopez	Jose Oscar Castellanos Jimenez
6.	*Arturo Moguel Esponda*	Maria Celorio Rovelo
Chihuahua		
1.	*Manuel Bernardo Aguirre*	Francisco Romo Ortiz
2.	Jose I. Aguilar Irungaray	Manuel Primo Corral
3.	*Ricardo Carrillo Duran*	Roberto Delgado Urias
4.	Esteban Guzman Vazquez	Armando B. Chavez M.
5.	Fernando Figueroa Tarango	Enrique Miramontes Maldonado
6.	Carlos Chavira Becerra	Manuel Pazos Cano
Coahuila		
1.	Salvador Gonzalez Lobo	Nemesio Lopez Ramos
2.	*Braulio Fernandez Aguirre*	Rodolfo Siller Rodriguez
3.	Felix de la Rosa Sanchez	Pedro Tijerina Ortegon
4.	Esteban Guzman Vazquez	Oscar Brown Gutierrez
Colima		
1.	Carlos Gariby Sanchez	Juan Hernandez Pizano
2.	*Alfredo Ruiseco Avellaneda*	Herminio Malaga Rojas
Distrito Federal		
1.	Jorge Abarea Calderon	Haide Espinosa Segura
2.	Francisco Garcia Silva	Dario Garcia Gonzalez
3.	Javier Blanco Sanchez	Jose Luis Aristi Garay
4.	Neftali Mena Mena	Alfonso Ortiz Martinez
5.	Agustin Vivanco Miranda	Alberto Morales Jimenez
6.	*Rodolfo Echeverria Alvarez*	Tomas Covarrubias Blancas
7.	Guillermo Solorzano G.	Miguel Cubian Perez
8.	Javier Gonzalez Gomez	Gustavo Reyes Cruz
9.	Mercedes Fernandez Austri	Luis del Moral Flores
10.	Manuel Alvarez Gonzalez	Miguel Rendon Blanco
11.	*Carlos Zapata Vela*	Maria Guadalupe Santoyo
12.	Rodolfo Garcia Perez	Juan Aguilar Castro
13.	Carlos L. Diaz	Humberto Antunez Barrera
14.	*Romulo Sanchez Mireles*	*Norberto Mora Plancarte*

15.	Francisco Aguirre Alegria	Ramiro Ruiz Madero
16.	Salvador Lopez Avitia	Juan Jose Castillo Mota
17.	*Gonzalo Castellot Madrazo*	Jose Maria Hernandez
18.	*Joaquin Gamboa Pascoe*	Pedro Guerrero Manriquez
19.	Salvador Carrillo Echeveste	Alejandro Arzate Sanchez
20.	*Renaldo Guzman Orozco*	Juan Gomez Salas
21.	*Oscar Ramirez Mijares*	Santiago Mar Zuniga
22.	*Maria Guadalupe Rivera M.*	Jorge Aurelio Rocha Cordero
23.	Antonio Vargas MacDonald	Fernando Gonzalez Pinon
24.	Humberto Santiago Lopez	Margarita Rodriguez Meza

Durango

1.	*Oscar Valdes Flores*	Maria Zatarain del Valle
2.	Gonzalo Salas Rodriguez	Amador Perez Ramirez
3.	*Agustin Ruiz Soto*	Antonio Martinez Rivas
4.	*Jose Antonio Ramirez M.*	Jesus Samaniego Nevarez

Guanajuato

1.	Virginia Soto Rodriguez	Luis Macias Luna
2.	Enrique Aranda Guedea	J. Guadalupe Carreno Rangel
3.	Rodrigo Moreno Zermeno	Romeo Rincon Serrano
4.	Manuel B. Marquez Escobedo	Jose E. Bravo Aranjo
5.	Eliseo Rodriguez Ramirez	Margarito Juarez Rizo
6.	*Juan Perez Vela*	Cirilo Bravo Bravo
7.	*Manuel Moreno Moreno*	Isauro Zuniga Flores
8.	*Jose Lopez Bermudez*	Carlos Lira Leyva
9.	Enrique Rangel Melendez	Roberto Arteaga Saavedra

Guerrero

1.	Salvador Castro Villalpando	*Vicente Fuentes Diaz*
2.	Maria Lopez Diaz	Ismael Pineda Flores
3.	Leopoldo Ortega Lozano	Humberto Najera Gomez Cana
4.	Gabriel Lagos Beltran	Martin Sanchez Rodriguez
5.	Simon Guevara Ramirez	Abel Garcia Garnelo
6.	Luis Vazquez Campos	Ruben Maurilio Vazquez

Hidalgo

1.	Jorge Quiroz Sanchez	Samuel Zenteno Ramirez
2.	Jose Luis Suarez Molina	Antonio Ramirez Perez
3.	Daniel Campuzano Barajas	Rodrigo Ordonez Mejia
4.	Contran Noble Perez R.	Joaquin Calva Olguin
5.	*Jorge Rojo Lugo*	Anatolio Romero Trejo

Jalisco

1.	*Jose Luis Lamadrid Sauza*	Roberto S. Weeks Lopez
2.	Miguel de Alon Arroyo	Amalia Mendoza Trujillo
3.	*Flavio Romero de Vlasco*	Jose G. Armas Gonzalez
4.	Jose Felix Zermeno Venegas	J. Concepcion Guzman Guzman
5.	Guillermo Mayoral Espinosa	Salvador Guerrero Gomez
6.	Francisco Rodriguez Gomez	Carlos Anaya Gomez
7.	*J. Jesus Gonzalez Cortazar*	Alfredo Gutierrez Rivera
8.	*Filiberto Ruvalcaba Sanchez*	Salvador Avalos Alvarado
9.	*Salvador Corona Bandin*	Clemente Nuno Guerrero
10.	Jose Guadalupe Mata Lopez	Guillermo Preciado Gomez
11.	Florentino Robles Flores	Salvador Ruesga Garcia
12.	Agustin Coronado Gutierrez	Gustavo de la Torre Arias

Mexico

1.	Abraham Saavedra Albiter	Fernando Macedo Estrada
2.	David Lopez Sencion	Wenceslao Rangel
3.	Heliodoro Diaz Lopez	Clara del Moral Ramirez

4.	Benito Sanchez Henkel	Victor Javier Guadarrama
5.	Eduardo Arias Huville	Faustino Sanchez Pinto
6.	Daniel Benitez Villalpando	Leonel Dominguez Rivero
7.	Federico Nieto Garcia	Armando Becerril Estrada
8.	Silverio Perez Gutierrez	Marciano Trueba Ruiz
9.	Froylan Barrios Villalobos	Jesus Arana Morales

Michoacan

1.	Daniel Franco Lopez	Antonio Chavez Samano
2.	Agustin Carreon Florian	Guillermo Chavez Cordoba
3.	Rafael Morelos Valdes	Antonio Lara Lopez
4.	Luis Aguilar Garibay	Nabor Servin Orozco
5.	*Enrique Bravo Valencia*	Jorge Hernandez Miranda
6.	Juan Velasco Vargas	Enrique Bautista Adame
7.	Eligio Aguilar Ortiz	Salvador Rosales Angeles
8.	Melchor Diaz Rubio	Lazaro Correa Osornio
9.	Elias Perez Avalos	David Perez Zepeda

Morelos

1.	*Diodoro Rivera Uribe*	Susana Peralta Colin
2.	Alfonso Munoz	Joel Hernandez Ramos

Nayarit

1.	*Manuel Stephens Garcia*	Genaro Navarro Rivera
2.	Leopoldo T. Garcia Esteves	Flavio Gomez Hernandez

Nuevo Leon

1.	Noe G. Elizondo Martinez	Francisco Morales Morales
2.	Jose Carmen Rodriguez Perez	Ramiro Gonzalez Moya
3.	Virgilio Cardenas Garcia	Filiberto Villarreal Ayala
4.	*Armando Arteaga Santoyo*	Leonides Cueva Cantu
5.	Dustano Muniz Leija	Jose Antonio Garza Garza

Oaxaca

1.	Pio Ortega Grapain	Jose Julio Hernandez Casanova
2.	Manuel Orozco Mendoza	Antonio Figueroa Jimenez
3.	*Norberto Aguirre*	Ernesto Miranda Barriguete
4.	Jenaro Vazquez Cruz	*Rodrigo Bravo Ahuja*
5.	Meliton Vargas Martinez	Emilio Alvarez Moguel
6.	Heriberto Camacho Ambrosio	Miguel Moran Ramirez
7.	Enrique Pacheco Alvarez	Gilberto Cruz Pantoja
8.	Manuel Sodi del Valle	Manuel Iglesias Meza
9.	Everardo Gustavo Varela S.	Fernando Castillo Castillo

Puebla

1.	Francisco Marquez Ramos	Andres Rojas Romero
2.	*Juan Figueroa Velasco*	Andres Funes Mendez
3.	Ciriaco Tista Montiel	Enrique Zamora Palafox
4.	*Antonio J. Hernandez*	Eleazar Camarillo Ochoa
5.	*Gonzalo Bautista O'Farrill*	Irene Godinez Orta
6.	*Amador Hernandez Gonzalez*	Gabriel Dominguez y Dominguez
7.	Ezequiel Meza Zayas	Guillermo Martinez Anaya
8.	Luis Vinals Carsi	Rodolfo Garces Mauardon
9.	Benjamin Mendez Luna	Luis Rivera Leon
10.	Jorge Vergara Jimenez	Israel Gomez Diaz

Queretaro

1.	*Eduardo Luque Loyola*	Alfonso Alexander Hernandez
2.	Teofilo Gomez Centeno	Arturo Dominguez Paulin

Quintana Roo (Territory)

1.	Delio Paz Angeles	Pedro Salazar Gonzalez

San Luis Potosi
1. Alfonso Guerrero Briones — Nicolas Vazquez Cruz
2. Aurelio Guerrero Carreon — Rafael Yrizar Ruiz
3. Baltasar Ruiz Jimenez — Avelino de Leon Guevara
4. Fidel Nieto Flores — Gregorio Martinez Narvaez
5. Sixto Garcia Pacheco — Hugo Arnoldo Gomez Rivas

Sinaloa
1. *Ernesto Alvarez Nolasco* — Jose Maria Robles Quintero
2. *Manuel Sarmiento Sarmiento* — Manuel de Jesus Garcia Castro
3. Maria del Refugio Baez S. — Alejandra Retamoza Reynaga
4. Joaquin Noris Saldana — J. Bartolo Gonzalez Zuniga

Sonora
1. Jesus Ortiz Ruiz — Maria Cruz Serrano Covarrubias
2. *Alicia Arellano Tapia* — Jorge Flores Valdes
3. Gilberto Borrego Zamudio — Raymundo Lopez Lerma
4. Gerardo Campoy Campoy — Roman Arguelles Obregon

Tabasco
1. Manuel Rafael Mora Martinez — Jose del Carmen Mendez Almeida
2. Voltaire Merino Pintado — Roberto Rosado Sastre

Tamaulipas
1. Advento Guerra Barrera — Oscar Herrera Flores
2. *Antonio Garcia Rojas* — Marciano Aguilar Mendoza
3. Juan Jose Domene Flor — Pantaleon de los Santos C.
4. Manuel Guerra Hinojosa — Isidro Gomez Reyes
5. Ricardo Camero Cardiel — J. Guadalupe Silva Ochoa

Tlaxcala
1. *Anselmo Cervantes Hernandez* — Filemon Sanchez Hernandez
2. Bernardo Ceballos Gomez — Salvador Espejel Espejel

Veracruz
1. Rafael Santibanez Fernandez — Gilberto Valenzuela Vera
2. *Jesus Reyes Heroles* — Lazaro Vargas Segura
3. Jose Vinas Zunzunegui — Raymundo Villegas Sanchez
4. Carlos V. Torres Torija — Amado Ceja Galindo
5. Eduardo S. Arellano Sandria — Gonzalo Anaya Jimenez
6. Martin Diaz Montero — Daniel Parra Garcia
7. Irene Bourell Galvan — Abraham D. Contreras Garcia
8. Miguel Angel Rodriguez R. — Nicolas Garcia Hernandez
9. Ruben Hernandez y Hernandez — Gilberto Tenorio Cortes
10. Joaquin Calatayud Gonzalez — Pascual Gonzalez Rojas
11. Vicente Ortiz Lagunes — Emilio Aguirre Campos
12. *Gonzalo Aguirre Beltran* — Humberto M. Fentanes Cunco
13. Amadeo Gonzalez Caballero — Arturo M. Vargas Sanchez
14. Jose Vasconcelos Morales — Guillermo Rodriguez Morfin

Yucatan
1. *Luis Torres Mesias* — Juan de Dios Ancona Fierros
2. Manuel Pasos Peniche — Joaquin Reyes Andrade
3. *Carlos Loret de Mola* — Melchor Sozaya Raz

Zacatecas
1. Alfonso Mendez Barraza — Benito Lopez Mauricio
2. J. Jesus Saucedo Melendez — Juan Manuel Carrillo Berumen
3. Guadalupe Cervantes Corona — Aurelio Lopez de la Torre
4. Antonio Betancourt H. — Jose Leal Langoria

1964–67 (46th Legislature)

State	Deputy	Alternate
Aguascalientes		
1.	Antonio Femat Esparza	Jorge Diaz de Leon
2.	*Augusto Gomez Villanueva*	Enrique Torres Calderon
Baja California del Norte (Territory)		
1.	Jose Luis Noriega Magana	Dionisio Hirales Corral
2.	*Salvador Rosas Magallon*	Fausto Cedillo Lopez
3.	Luis Mario Santana Cobian	Rogelio Zepeda Villasenor
Baja California del Sur (Territory)		
1.	*Alberto Aramburo Alvarado*	Crisoforo Salido Almado
Campeche		
1.	*Carlos Perez Camara*	Rodolfo Dorantes Salazar
2.	Jose Dolores Garcia Aguilar	Felipe Ehuan Yeh
Chiapas		
1.	Jesus Cancino Casahonda	Martha Luz Rincon Castillejos
2.	Abraham Aguilar Paniague	Hector Salinas Gomez
3.	*Jorge de la Vega Dominguez*	Jorge Guillen Ortiz
4.	Gilberto Balboa Escobar	Ignacio Lara Penagos
5.	Jose Leon Cruz	Oscar Chapa Castanon
	Alberto Orduna Culebro	Ovidio de la Rosa Lopez
6.	Alfonso Gonzalez Blanco	Mario Balboa Robles
Chihuahua		
1.	Saul Gonzalez Herrera	Amador Campoya Almazan
2.	Florentina Villalobos C.	Roman Pineda Casas
3.	Raul H. Lezama Gil	Salvador de la Torre Grajales
4.	Pedro N. Garcia Martinez	Armando Gonzalez Soto
5.	*Arnaldo Gutierrez Hernandez*	Carlos Enriquez Chavez
6.	Jose Martinez Alvidrez	Esperanza Dominguez de Marrufo
Coahuila		
1.	Tomas Algaba Gomez	Jose Dimas Galindo Villarreal
2.	Alfonso Reyes Aguilera	Francisco Perez Gutierrez
3.	Francisco Padilla Rodriguez	Gonzalo Navarro Chavez
4.	Mauro Berrueto Ramon	Amado Flores Pena
5.	Argentina Blanco Fuentes	Juan Jose Elguezabal Perches
Colima		
1.	Mario Llerenas Ochoa	Juan Eusebio Mejia
2.	Rafael Paredes	Antonio Suarez Orijel
Distrito Federal		
1.	*Arturo Lopez Portillo*	Magdaleno Gutierrez Herrera
	Francisco Quiroga Fernandez	Agustin Velazquez Uribe
2.	*Felipe Gomez Mont*	*Hiram Escudero Alvarez*
	Arnulfo Vazquez Trujillo	Macario Gutierrez Navarro
3.	*Enrique Ramirez y Ramirez*	Alfonso Gutierrez Gutierrez
4.	Salvador Rodriguez Leija	Consuelo Grajales Caracas
5.	Everardo Gamiz Fernandez	Raul Macias Guevara
6.	Luis Ignacio Santibanez P.	Eduardo Field Romero
7.	Francisco Ortiz Mendoza	Leonides Guadarrama Jimenez
	Jesus Hernandez Diaz	Hector Guillermo Gonzalez G.
8.	*Juan Landerreche Obregon*	Rene Ostos Mora
	Manuel Orijel Salazar	Francisco Prieto Herrera

9.	Federico Estrada Valera	*Jose Blas Briseno Rodriguez*
	Emilio Gandarilla Aviles	Blas Nieto Valdez
10.	*Juan Moises Calleja*	Jose C. Salinas Vazquez
11.	Jorge Avila Blancas	Hector Federico Ling A.
	Luis Priego Ortiz	Tito Pequeno Pedroza
12.	*Marta Andrade del Rosal*	Miguel Barrera Fernandez
13.	*Hilda Anderson Nevarez*	Leopoldo Arias Ochoa
14.	Manuel Contreras Carrillo	Manuel Morales Vargas
15.	Rodolfo Rivera Rueda	Pedro Luis Bartilotti Perea
16.	*Jorge Garabito Martinez*	Carlos Oropeza Gomez
	Ramon Zentella Asencio	Guillermo Prieto Sanchez
17.	*Alejandro Carrillo Marcor*	Gabriel Sanchez Gomez
	Abel Carlos Vicencio Tovar	Nicolas Gonzalez Rodriguez
18.	Enrique Torres Calderon	Jose Oropeza Ceron
19.	Rafael Estrada Villa	Ruben Alvarez del Castillo
	Marciano Gonzalez V.	Guillermo Marquez Panteon
	Salvador Padilla Flores	Jose Gamboa Paredes
20.	Roberto Guajardo Tamez	Nehemias Gonzalez Chimal
	Antonio Martinez Manatou	Manuel Esquivel Cisneros
21.	*Miguel Covian Perez*	Dimas Martinez Ramos
22.	*Gonzalo Martinez Corbala*	Miguel Hernandez Labastida
	Jacinto G. Silva Flores	Arturo Tinajero Contreras
23.	*Adolfo Christlieb Ibarrola*	Ascension Almaraz Espinosa
	Fernando Gonzalez Pinon	Tomas Ordaz Padilla
24.	Bonifacio Moreno Tenorio	J. Felix Gonzalez Organo

Durango

1.	*Angel Rodriguez Solorzano*	Josefina Lugo de Rueda Leon
2.	Jesus Jose Reyes Acevedo	Jesus Ibarra Rayas
3.	*Enrique Wenceslao Sanchez*	Rodolfo Reyes Soto
4.	*Braulio Meraz Nevarez*	J. Ines Rodriguez Diaz

Guanajuato

1.	J. Jesus Orta Guerrero	Matilde Rangel Lopez
	Jaime Luis Danton Rodriguez	Antonio Arellano Gonzalez
2.	Luis Manuel Aranda Torres	Jose Ayala Frausto
3.	Domingo Camarena Lopez	Efren Perez Guajardo
4.	*Juan J. Varela Mayorga*	Vicente Lopez Diaz
5.	*Vicente Salgado Paez*	Enrique Fernandez Martinez A.
6.	*Luis H. Ducoing Gamba*	J. Jesus Arroyo Celedon
7.	Enrique Gomez Guerra	Jose Jimenez Diaz
8.	Ricardo Chaurand Concha	Manuel Hernandez Tamayo
	Agustin Arroyo Damian	Luis Martinez Aguado
9.	Antonio Vazquez Perez	Alfredo Guerrero Tarquin

Guerrero

1.	*Vicente Fuentes Diaz*	Maria Teresa Bernal Castanon
2.	*Ruben Figueroa Figueroa*	Daniel Molina Miranda
3.	*Miguel Osorio Marban*	Antonio Sanchez Molina
4.	Rafael Camacho Salgado	Dario Esteves Legua
5.	Arquimedes Catalan Guevara	Crisoforo Alvarez Iriarte
6.	Juan Francisco Andraca M.	Faustino Garcia Silverio

Hidalgo

1.	Humberto Velasco Aviles	Hilario Ortega Portillo
2.	Domingo Franco Sanchez	Raul Vargas Ortiz
3.	Herberto J. Malo Paulin	Leornardo Vega Perez
4.	*Raul Lozano Ramirez*	Gustavo Castillo Diaz
5.	Jaime Lopez Peimbert	Jesus Hernandez Trejo

Jalisco

1.	Raul Padilla Gutierrez	Jose Vicente Palencia Murillo
2.	*Guillermo Ruiz Vazquez*	Jose Guadalupe Rodriguez P.
	Heliodoro Hernandez Loza	J. Ventura Flores Navarro
3.	*Ruben Moheno Velasco*	Abel Galvan Chavez
4.	Francisco Silva Romero	Rafael Madrigal Vazquez
5.	*Carlos Ramirez Ladewig*	Victor Manuel Marquez Huizar
6.	Raul Alvarez Gutierrez	Guillermo Munoz Hernandez
7.	Gregorio Contreras Miranda	Jose Martin Barba
8.	Constancio Hernandez A.	Juan Valdivia Gomez
9.	Vicente Madrigal Guzman	Jose de Jesus Rubio Neri
10.	Jose Maria Martinez R.	*Salvador Aguilar Vazquez*
11.	*Francisco Villafana C.*	*Maria Guadalupe Urzua Flores*
12.	Jose de Jesus Limon Munoz	Javier Michel Vega

Mexico

1.	Juan de Dios Osuna Perez	Ernesto Gomez Gomez
2.	*Francisco Perez Rios*	*Leonardo Rodriguez Alcaine*
3.	Enrique Gonzalez Vargas	Gildardo Herrera Gomez Tagle
4.	Guillermo Molina Reyes	Enrique Castaneda Ornelas
5.	*Mario Colin Sanchez*	Maximino Perez Camara
6.	Jesus Moreno Jimenez	Ernestina Gonzalez Cano
7.	Jose Chiquillo Juarez	Rodolfo Ruiz Perez
8.	Raul Legaspi Donis	Enrique Chavez Montes de Oca
9.	Enedino Ramon Macedo	Bernardo Aragon Sanchez

Michoacan

1.	Celia Gallardo Gonzalez	Jose Alvarado Vega
2.	Enrique Lopez Narango	Jose Rodriguez Espinosa
3.	Roberto Chavez Silva	J. Jesus Sanchez Ortiz
	Ernesto Reyes Rodriguez	Alfredo Pimentel Ramos
4.	Domingo Garcia Lopez	Jose Arroyo Dominguez
5.	*Gabino Vazquez Oseguera*	Hector Pantoja Vazquez
	Miguel Estrada Iturbide	Alfonso Arias Sanchez
6.	Enrique Bautista Adame	Guillermo Navarro Quiroz
7.	*Jose Servando Chavez H.*	Wilfrido Ruiz Balderas
8.	Raul Reyes Hernandez	Pedro Rubio Sataray
9.	*J. Jesus Garcia Santacruz*	Lorenzo Escobar Bejar

Morelos

1.	Gonzalo Pastrana Castro	Esther Galvan Figueroa
2.	Antonio Pliego Noyola	Adalberto Samano Salgado

Nayarit

1.	Eugenio Cardenas Andrade	Luis Romero Castillo
2.	Marina Nunez Guzman	Saturnino Gonzalez Ismerio

Nuevo Leon

1.	*Leopoldo Gonzalez Saenz*	Fulberto Chavarria Trevino
2.	Arnulfo Trevino Garza	Hilario Salazar Tamez
	Pedro Reyes Velazquez	Felix Lazcano Elizondo
3.	Guillermo Ochoa Rodriguez	Jose Gonzalez Alvarado
4.	*Alfonso Martinez Dominguez*	Antonio Garza Ayala
5.	Ricardo Covarrubias	Anastasio Santana Martinez

Oaxaca

1.	*Jorge Cruickshank Garcia*	Crisoforo Chinas Mendoza
	Andres Henestrosa Morales	Jose Maria Luna Martinez
2.	*Eliseo Jimenez Ruiz*	Wilfrido Sanchez Contreras
3.	Juan I. Bustamante V.	Maria Toledo de Ramirez
4.	Aurelio Fernandez Enriquez	Pedro Castillo Estrada

5.	Justina Vasconcelos de B.	Diodoro Carrasco Palacios
6.	*Manuel Zarate Aquino*	Jose Manuel Alvarez Martin
7.	*Rodolfo Alavez Flores*	Ignacio Montes Martinez
8.	Gustavo Martinez Trejo	Heriberto Perez Aguirre
9.	Jesus Torres Marquez	Fernando Moncada Diaz

Puebla

1.	Melquiades Trejo Hernandez	Jose Gomez Salinas
2.	Manuel Rivera Anaya	Dionisio del Razo Espinosa
3.	*Pablo Solis Carrillo*	Filemon Perez Cazares
4.	Rigoberto Gonzalez Flores	Salvador Serrano Ramirez
5.	Enrique Marin Retif	Ruperto Zafra Hernandez
6.	Rodolfo Rossano Fraga	Felipe Balderrama Garcia
7.	Eloy Linares Zambrano	Federico Hernandez Cortes
8.	Alfonso Castillo Borzani	Gloria Rodriguez de Campos
	Vicente Lombardo Toledano	Luis Martinez Aguado
9.	Jorge Ruben Herta Perez	Jose Guevara Minor
10.	*Guillermo Morales B.*	Ramon Herrera Cravioto

Queretaro

1.	*Arturo Guerrero Ortiz*	Antonio Pesa Pena
2.	Arturo Dominguez Paulin	J. Concepcion Vega Perez

Quintana Roo (Territory)

1.	Luz Maria Zaletade Elsner	Jose Antonio Ascencio N.

San Luis Potosi

1.	*Juan Barragan Rodriguez*	Jose Martinez Castro
	Diana Torres Ariceaga	Alvaro Salguero Franco
2.	Jose Rodriguez Alvarez	Pedro Delgado Calzada
3.	Miguel Gascon Hernandez	J. Guadalupe Martinez Sanchez
4.	Luis Tudon Hurtado	Mauro Gutierrez Compean
5.	Librado Bicavar Garcia	Julian Pozos Caro

Sinaloa

1.	Samuel Castro Cabrera	Carlos Beltran Flores
2.	Humberto Morales Corrales	Pedro Mondaca Robles
3.	Joaquin Salgado Medrano	Rigoberto Arriaga Ruiz
4.	Francisco Alarcon Fregoso	Jorge Luis Osuna y Osuna

Sonora

1.	Manuel Duarte Jimenez	Luis Mendoza Lopez
2.	*Faustino Felix Serna*	Alfonso Reyna Celaya
3.	*Manuel Bobadilla Romero*	Mario Moraga Borquez
	Jacinto Lopez Moreno	Florentino Rios Barragan
4.	Rodolfo Velazquez Grijalva	Ofelia Arredondo Corral

Tabasco

1.	*Manuel Gurria Ordonez*	Manuel Ramon Ramon
2.	Rosendo Taracena Alpuin	Luis Antonio Zurita Zurita

Tamaulipas

1.	Luis G. Olloqui Guerra	Julia Garcia Soto
	Mariano Gonzalez Gutierrez	Virgilio Barrera Fuentes
2.	Angel J. Lagarda Palomares	Victor Vargas Cuellar
3.	Ladislao Cardenas Martinez	Gregorio Soto Guerrero
4.	Lauro Rendon Valdez	Dario Manuel Hernandez C.
5.	Salvador Barragan Camacho	Jose Bruno del Rio Cruz

Tlaxcala

1.	*Tulio Hernandez Gomez*	Faustino Zempoaltecatl T.
2.	Luis Granillo Astorga	Cenobio Perez Romero

State	Deputy	Alternate
Veracruz		
1.	Raul Lince Medellin	Andres Tovar Gonzalez
2.	Francisco Rodriguez Cano	Jose Fernandez Gomez
3.	Pedro Vivanco Garcia	Eleazar Pulido Valdez
4.	Cesar del Angel Fuentes	Julio Cesar Gutierrez Calderon
5.	*Fluvio Vista Altamirano*	Bricio Rincon Hernandez
6.	Mario Hernandez Posadas	Juan H. Sanchez Hernandez
7.	Serafin Iglesias Hernandez	Abraham Contreras Garcia
8.	Agustin Gonzalez Alvarado	Candido G. Rojas Cruz
9.	Miguel Castro Elias	Agustin de Jesus Valerio
	Ramon Rocha Garfias	Hermenegildo Lobato Ceron
10.	Pastro Murguia Gonzalez	Victor Manuel Ocampo M.
11.	Mario Vargas Saldana	Manuel Hernandez Delgado
12.	Jose Antonio Cobos Panama	Cipriano Villasana Jimenez
13.	Ramiro Leal Dominguez	Lucio Martinez Salas
14.	Pablo Pavon Rosado	Brigida Rodriguez Fuster
Yucatan		
1.	Eduardo Trueba Barrera	Miguel F. Vidal Rivero
	Fidelia Sanchez de M.	Bibiano Segura Leon
2.	Fabio Espinosa Granados	Magda Bauza Romero
3.	*Francisco Luna Kan*	Pablo Caamal
Zacatecas		
1.	Aurora Navia Millan	J. Cruz Guerrero Encinas
2.	Adolfo Rodriguez Ortiz	Arturo Ortiz Arechar
3.	Jose Muro Saldivar	Angel Estrada Gonzalez
4.	*Pedro Ruiz Gonzalez*	Antonio Cortes Hurtado

1967–70 (47th Legislature)

State	Deputy	Alternate
Aguascalientes		
1.	*Francisco Guel Jimenez*	Juan Romo Hernandez
2.	*J. Refugio Esparza Reyes*	J. Guadalupe Delgado de Lira
Baja California del Norte (Territory)		
1.	Francisco Munoz Franco	Guillermo Cannet Gonzalez
2.	*Gustavo Aubanel Vallejo*	Josefina Vazquez Calderon
3.	*Celestino Salcedo Monteon*	Nicolas Bojorquez Ayala
Baja California del Sur (Territory)		
1.	*Angel Cesar Mendoza A.*	Fortunato Garcia Yuen
Campeche		
1.	*Ramon Alcala Ferrera*	Sixto Sosa Almeida
2.	Manuel Pavon Bahaine	Pascual Hernandez
Chiapas		
1.	Martha Luz Rincon C.	Romeo Noriega Chamlati
2.	Roberto Coello Lescieur	Augusto Castellanos Hernandez
3.	*Edgar Robledo Santiago*	Armando Chacon Antonio
4.	Daniel Robles Sasso	Adrian Contreras Romero
5.		
6.	*Jose Patrocinio Gonzalez*	Jose Oscar Moscoso Moscoso
Chihuahua		
1.	Mariano Valenzuela Ceballos	Ofelia Baez Duarte
2.	Pablo Picharra Esparza	Juan Antonio Sanchez Monge

3.	Guillermo Quijas Cruz	Rafael Veloz Alatorre
4.	Armando B. Chavez Montanez	Alfredo Caraveo Martinez
5.	Everardo Escarcega Lopez	Ruben Montano Camarena
6.	Armando Bejarano Pedroza	Alfredo Rohana Estrada

Coahuila

1.	*Jose de las Fuentes R.*	Carlos Gutierrez Salazar
2.	Heriberto Ramos Gonzalez	Daniel Martinez Peral
3.	Juan Manuel Berlanga	Eladio Perales Herrera
4.	Feliciano Morales Ramos	Maria del Pueblito Villarreal

Colima

1.	Ricardo Guzman Nava	Agustin Gonzalez Villalobos
2.	Ramiro Santa Ana Ugarte	Inocencio Palomares Sanchez

Distrito Federal

1.	Pedro Luis Bartilotti Perea	Andres Diaz Vadia
2.	Jose del Valle de la Cajiga	Miguel Angel Celis Ponce
3.	Ernesto Quinones Lopez	Ramiro Rodriguez Gutierrez
4.	*Octavio Andres Hernandez G.*	Cesar Velazquez Sanchez
5.	*Gilberto Aceves Alcocer*	Graciela Valles Griego
6.	*Ignacio Castillo Mena*	Tomas Covarrubias Blanca
7.	*Jorge Duran Chavez*	Jose Luis Sanchez Diaz
8.	*Eleuterio Macedo Valdez*	Hernan Estrada Unda
9.	Javier Blanco Sanchez	Aurora Fernandez Fernandez
10.	Manuel Alvarez Gonzalez	Luis Mayen Ruiz
11.	Pedro Rosas Rodriguez	Leonor Ferron de Madera
12.	Martin Guaida Lara	J. Jesus Jimenez Torres
13.	*Joaquin Gamboa Pascoe*	Enrique Melgarejo Phario
14.	Alberto Briceno Ruiz	*Carlos Jongitud Barrios*
15.	Enrique Bermudez Olvera	Eduardo Gutierrez Evia
16.	Fernando Cordoba Lobo	Arturo Marin Oropeza
17.	*Raul Noriega Ondovilla*	Alberto Perez Azpeitia
18.	*Joaquin del Olmo Martinez*	Rodolfo Martinez Moreno
19.	Adolfo Ruiz Sosa	Roberto Gonzalez Torres
20.	Ignacio Guzman Garduno	Sebastian Gonzalez Galvan
21.	*Oscar Ramirez Mijares*	Jose Luis Preciado Gutierrez
22.	Maria Guadalupe Aguirre S.	Francisco Javier Ogarrio P.
23.	*Hilario Galguera Torres*	Joaquin Ventura Mosso
24.	Maria Elena Jimenez Lozano	Ernesto Aguilar Cordero

Durango

1.	*Agustin Ruiz Soto*	Carlos Leonardo Ruiz Pina
2.	J. Natividad Ibarra Rayas	Francisco Navarro Veloz
3.	Juan Antonio Orozco Fierro	Andres Calvo Ramirez
4.	*Jose Antonio Ramirez M.*	J. Bernabe Silvestre Federico

Guanajuato

1.	Daniel Chowell Cazares	Gabriel Perez Saavedra
2.	*Jose Castillo Hernandez*	Heron Aiza Torres
3.	Andres Sojo Anaya	Rafael Garcia Meza
4.	*Fernando Diaz Duran*	Roberto Rodriguez Ramirez
5.	*Ignacio Vazquez Torres*	Maria de la Luz Bravo G.
6.	Adolfo Meza Arredondo	Gilberto Munoz Mosqueda
7.	Maria Contreras Martinez	Pedro Mandujano Mendoza
8.	Manuel Orozco Yrigoyen	Ezequiel Nieto Gonzalez
9.	Enrique Rangel Melendez	Raymundo Patlan Amador

Guerrero

1.	Juan Pablo Leyva Cordoba	Altagracia Alarcon Sanchez
2.	Humberto Acevedo Astudillo	Rafael Reyes Ramirez

3.	Alberto Diaz Rodriguez	Filiberto Vigueras Lazaro
4.	*Israel Nogueda Otero*	Alfonso Argudin Alcaraz
5.	Eusebio Mendoza Avila	Leandro Alvarado Vazquez

Hidalgo

1.	Adalberto Cravioto Meneses	Abundio Rodriguez Resendiz
2.	Raul Vargas Ortiz	Luis Barrios Saldierna
3.	Sergio Butron Casas	Daniel Campuzano Barajas
4.	Jose Gonzalo Badillo	Rene Espinosa Sagaon
5.	*Humberto A. Lugo Gil*	Aurelio Gomez Membrillo

Jalisco

1.	Adalberto Padilla Quiroz	David Alvarez Viramontes
2.	Miguel de Alba Arroyo	Miguel Arroyo Garcia
3.	Jose Maria Garcia P.	Adalberto Gomez Rodriguez
4.	Felipe Lopez Prado	Roberto Neri Rodriguez
5.	*Leopoldo Hernandez Partida*	Jose Santos Salas Aparicio
6.	Alfonso de Alba Martin	Elias Munoz S. Alba
7.	*Renaldo Guzman Orozco*	J. Jesus Gonzalez Martin
8.	*Jose de Jesus Bueno Amezcua*	Guillermo Jimenez Gonzalez
9.	Ignacio Gonzalez Rubio	Clemente Nuno Guerrero
10.	*Luis Javier Luna B.*	Alfredo Gonzalez Vargas
11.	*Sebastian Garcia Barragan*	Esquivel Paz Espinosa
12.	*Guillermo Cosio Vidaurri*	Enrique Salgado Vega

Mexico

1.	Arturo Flores Mercado	Jose Santaolaya Consuelo
2.	*Gregorio Velazquez Sanchez*	Guillermo Choussal V.
3.	Fernando Suarez del Solar	Javier Hinojosa Trigos
4.	*Ignacio Pichardo Pagaza*	Jose Gil Valdez
5.	Faustino Sanchez Pinto	David Maldonado Rodea
6.	Leonel Dominguez Rivero	Juan Monroy Ortega
7.	*Leonardo Rodriguez Alcaine*	Agustin Chavez Magallon
8.	*Antonio Bernal Tenorio*	Guillermo Perez Calva
9.	Angel Bonifaz Ezeta	Gonzalo Barquin Diaz

Michoacan

1.	*Maria Guadalupe Calderon*	Marco Antonio Aguilar Cortes
2.	Pedro Rubio Zataray	J. Jesus Garcia Bucio
3.	Jose Encarnacion Tellitud	Victor Cazares Sanchez
4.	Jose Valdovinos Garza	Jose Rodriguez Lopez
5.	Carlos Grajeda Rodriguez	Jesus Alcazar Quiroz
6.	Roberto Reyes Perez O.	Santiago Vargas Reyes
7.	*Norberto Mora Plancarte*	Aureliano Martinez B.
8.		
9.	Guillermo Morfin Garcia	Mario Cortes Garcia

Morelos

1.	Javier Bello Yllanes	Jose Nares Alvarez
2.	*Elpidio Perdomo Garcia*	Abel Sanchez Aguilar

Nayarit

1.	*Roberto Gomez Reyes*	Pedro Lopez Diaz
2.	*Emilio M. Gonzalez Parra*	Simon Pintado Carrillo

Nuevo Leon

1.	Pedro Francisco Quintanilla Mario	Jasso Grimaldo
2.	*Luis M. Farias*	Julio Camelo Martinez
3.	Virgilio Cardenas Garcia	Saturnino Torres Sena
4.	Graciano Bortoni Urteaga	Mario Canales Saenz
5.	Eloy Trevino Rodriguez	Juan Saldana Muniz

Oaxaca

1.	Macedonio Benitez Fuentes	Fortino Paulo Hernandez
2.	Juvencio Molina Valera	Wilfrido Luis Perez M.
3.	Jorge Fernando Iturribarria	Ernesto Miranda Barriguete
4.	*Rodrigo Bravo Ahuja*	Saturnino Mendoza Garcia
5.	Diodoro Carrasco Palacios	Federico Ramirez Juarez
6.	*Dagoberto Flores Betancourt*	David Moran Maceda
7.	*Manuel Hernandez y H.*	Virginia Cisneros Reyna
8.	Manuel Iglesias Meza	Leon Oloarte Espinosa
9.	Fernando Moncada Diaz	Fernando Castillo Castillo

Puebla

1.	*Blas Chumacero Sanchez*	Juan Hernandez Cardel
2.	Atilano Pacheco Huerta	Agustin Castillo Flores
3.	Alfonso Meneses Gonzalez	Elias Rivera Sanchez
4.	*Antonio J. Hernandez J.*	Miguel Munive Alvarado
5.	Cosme Aguilera Alvarez	Jose Guadalupe Ramirez Vargas
6.		
7.	Esteban Rangel Alvarado	Gonzalo Pacheco Navarro
8.	Rene Tirado Fuentes	Porfirio Camarena Sanchez
9.	Humberto Diaz de Leon	Gonzalo Cruz Perez
10.	Horacio Hidalgo Mendoza	Abraham Fosado Gutierrez

Queretaro

1.	Jose Arana Moran	Alberto Fernandez Riveroll
2.	Enrique Redentor Albarran	Enrique Rabell Trejo

Quintana Roo (Territory)

1.	Eliezer Castro Souza	Alejandro Tamay Ancona

San Luis Potosi

1.	Jorge Marquez Borjas	Gabriel Echenique Portillo
2.	Francisco Padron Puyou	Adalberto Lara Nunez
3.	*Florencio Salazar Martinez*	Rodolfo Ortiz Reyes
4.	*Guillermo Fonseca Alvarez*	*Fausto Zapata Loredo*
5.	Jose de Jesus Gonzalez L.	J. Refugio Zavala Rodriguez

Sinaloa

1.	*Alfonso G. Calderon Velarde*	Froylan Rodriguez Cota
2.	Mateo Camacho Ontiveros	Jesus Maria Cervantes Atondo
3.	Miguel Leyson Perez	Jose Herrera Mares
4.	*Ernesto Alvarez Nolasco*	Juan Tirado Osuna

Sonora

1.	Ignacio Guzman Gomez	Fernando Pena Benitez
2.	*Guillermo Nunez Keith*	Jesus Reyes Lamas
3.	Francisco Villanueva C.	Francisco Arispuro Calderon
4.	*Carlos Armando Biebrich T.*	Juan Pedro Camou Cubillas

Tabasco

1.	*Mario Trujillo Garcia*	Cecilio Antonio Pedrero G.
2.	*Agapito Dominguez Canabal*	Luz Zalaya de Garcia

Tamaulipas

1.	Antonio Guerra Diaz	Luis Rocha Acosta
2.	Cristobal Guevara Delmas	Juan Mendoza Lopez
3.	Jesus Elias Elias	Antonio Caballero Gonzalez
4.	Elvia Rangel de la Fuente	Isaias Rodriguez Onate
5.	Candelario Perez Malibran	Miguel Hernandez Lemus

Tlaxcala

1.	Nicolas Lopez Galindo	Angel Mendez Cano
2.	German Cervon del Razo	Hector Vazquez Paredes

Veracruz
1.	Hector Cequera Rivera	Julio Contreras Sains
2.	*Silverio Ricardo Alvarado*	Miguel Lopez Lince
3.	Heriberto Keohoe Vincent	Miguel Rivadeneyra Herrera
4.	Julio Cesar Gutierrez C.	Leocadio Azua Torres
5.	*Rodolfo Virues del Castillo*	Simitrio Amador Ballinas
6.	Raul Olivares Vionet	Reyna Oyarzabal de Caraza
7.	Acela Servin Murrieta	Crispino Ruiz Contreras
8.	Helio Garcia Alfaro	Delfino Rosas Nolasco
9.	Daniel Sierra Rivera	Gustavo Mayorga Daza
10.	Hesiquio Aguilar Maranon	Pascual Gonzalez Rojas
11.	Roman Garzon Arcos	Adolfo Sanchez Guzman
12.	Mariano Ramos Zarrabal	Julio Castillo Pitalua
13.	*Celso Vazquez Ramirez*	Jonas Bibiano Landero
14.	Rafael Cardenas Lomeli	Gabino Reyes Alafita

Yucatan
1.	*Ruben Encalada Alonzo*	Maria Luisa Loza Rivas
2.	*Julio Bobadilla Pena*	Jorge Gasque Gomez
3.	*Victor Manzanilla Schaffer*	Pablo Medina Acosta

Zacatecas
1.	*Calixto Medina Medina*	Enrique Mendoza Figueroa
2.	Rosa Maria Ortiz de C.	Nicolas Marquez Acosta
3.	Antonio Ruelas Cuevas	J. Jesus de Leon Luna
4.	Juan Martinez Tobias	Gabino Diaz Diaz

1970–73 (48th Legislature)

State	Deputy	Alternate
Aguascalientes		
1.	Luciano Arenas Ochoa	Luis Gilberto de Leon Pedroza
2.	Baudelio Lariz Lariz	J. Refugio Jimenez Luevano
Baja California del Norte (Territory)		
1.	Francisco Zarate Vidal	Carlos Rubio Parra
2.	Marco Antonio Bolanos C.	Hector Lutteroth Camou
3.	*Alfonso Garzon Santibanez*	Luis Ayala Garcia
Baja California del Sur (Territory)		
1.	Rafael Castillo Castro	Antonio Verdugo Verduzco
Campeche		
1.	*Rafael Rodriguez Barrera*	Jorge Munoz Icthe
2.	Abelardo Carrillo Z.	Lilia Gonzalez Vda. de Ayala
Chiapas		
1.	Jose Casahonda Castillo	Ariosto Oliva Ruiz
2.	Angel Pola Berttolini	Hermilo Flores Gomez
3.	*Maximo Contreras Camacho*	Rogerio Roman Armendariz
4.	Eloy Morales Espinosa	Hugo Calderon Vidal
5.	Antonio Melgar Aranda	Pantaleon Orella Machique
6.	*Octavio Cal y Mayor Sauz*	Daniel Gonzalez Damas
Chihuahua		
1.	Ramiro Salas Granado	Humberto Martinez Delgado
2.	*Diamantina Reyes E.*	Manuel Garfio Chaparro
3.	Mario Jaquez Provencio	Fernando Pacheco Parra
4.	Armando Gonzalez Soto	Antonio Barrio Mendoza
5.	Abelardo Perez Campos	Homero Corral Pinon
6.	*J. Refugio Mar de la Rosa*	J. Refugio Rodriguez Ramirez

Coahuila
1.   Gustavo Guerra Castanos   Jose Cruz Salazar
2.   Luis Horacio Salinas A.   Horacio Gutierrez Crespo
3.   Aureliano Cruz Juarez   Jesus Barraza Renteria
4.   *Salvador Hernandez Vela*   Conrado Marines Ortiz

Colima
1.   Jose F. Rivas Guzman   Jorge Arellano Amezcua
2.   Jose Ernesto Diaz Lopez   Fidel Nando Vazquez

Distrito Federal
1.   Leon Michel Vega   Antonio Cueto Citalan
2.   Mauricio Martinez Solano   Francisco Perez Turlay
3.   *Jose Luis Alonzo Sandoval*   Eleazar T. Cruz R.
4.   *Octavio Senties Gomez*   Carlos Hernandez Marquez
5.   Raul Gomez Pedroso Suzan   Marina Masso Soto
6.   Jorge Baeza Rodriguez   Ignacio Colunga Mones
7.   Jaime Fernandez Reyes   Jesus Araujo Hernandez
8.   *Manuel Orijel Salazar*   Francisco Rivera Munoz
9.   *Aurora Fernandez F.*   Arturo Romo Gutierrez
10.   *Juan Moises Calleja G.*   Ofelia Castillas Ontiveros
11.   Juan Rodriguez Salazar   Jose Luis Lobato Campos
12.   Ignacio Sologuren Martinez   Jose Servien Bolanos
13.   Leopoldo Ceron Sanchez   Isaac Diaz Ramirez
14.   *Luis Velazquez Jaacks*   Carlos Onofre Hernandez R.
15.   Roberto Duenas Ramos   Alvaro Roldan Olvera
16.   Rafael Arguelles Sanchez   Marie Edith Arroniz de F.
17.   *Cuauhtemoc Santa Ana S.*   Joaquin Ortiz Lombardini
18.   Rodolfo Martinez Moreno   Jesus Anlen Lopez
19.   *Hilda Anderson Nevarez*   Samuel Mora Zamudio
20.   Oscar Hammeken Martinez   Juan Canales Perez
21.   J. Hector Ayala Guerrero   Teofilo Aguilar Riojas
22.   *Guillermina Sanchez Meza*   Juan Villarreal Lopez
23.   Ignacio F. Herrerias M.   Ruffo Perez Pleigo
24.   Tarsicio Gonzalez Gutierrez   Raul Garcia Olvera

Durango
1.   Manuel Aguilera Tavizon   Pedro Avila Nevarez
2.   Manuel Esquivel Gamez   Leobardo Martinez Amador
3.   Francisco Navarro Veloz   Rodolfo Reyes Soto
4.   Jacinto Moreno Villalba   Zacarias Luna Antuna

Guanajuato
1.   Vicente Martinez Santibanez   Manuel Barajas Morales
2.   Antonio Hernandez Ornelas   Rafael Avila Perez
3.   Jose Arturo Lozano Madrazo   Taurino Murillo Navarro
4.   Roberto Sanchez Davalos   Francisco Robles Acosta
5.   Bonifacio Ibarra Morales   Juan Flores Aguilar
6.   *Juan J. Varela Mayorga*   J. Guadalupe Enriquez M.
7.   J. Jesus Arroyo Garcia   Luis Martinez Aguado
8.   Roberto Suarez Nieto   Constantino Olalde Moreno
9.   *Luis H. Ducoing Gamba*   Manuel Martinez Maldonado

Guerrero
1.   *Moises Ochoa Campos*   Elias Cuauhtemoc Tabares J.
2.   Jaime Pineda Salgado   Lorenzo Roman Adan
3.   Ramiro Gonzalez Casales   Albino Macedo Rivera
4.   Rogelio de la O Almazan   Franco Nunez Ramirez

5.	Ramon Uribe Urzua	Primitivo Solano R.
6.	Jose Ma. Serna Maciel	Jose Ma. Robles de la Cruz

Hidalgo

1.	Dario Perez Gonzalez	Ma. Cristina Alvarez de S.
2.	Antonio Hernandez Garcia	Ricardo Avila Yanez
3.	Humberto Cuevas Villegas	Fernando Leon Hernandez
4.	*Abel Ramirez Acosta*	Maria Isabel Fayad
5.	*Enrique Soto Resendiz*	Adolfo Langenschet

Jalisco

1.	Jose Carlos Osorio Aguilar	Enrigue Rosales Shamon
2.	*Maria Guadalupe Martinez*	Juan Ramirez Garcia
3.	Genaro Cornejo Cornejo	Raul Bracamontes Gutierrez
4.	*Porfirio Cortes Silva*	Miguel Nuno Casillas
5.	*Humberto Hiriart Urdanivia*	Alfonso Lozano Gonzalez
6.	*Ruben Moheno Velasco*	Ernesto Rios Gonzalez
7.	Jose Martin Barba	Rigoberto Gonzalez Quezada
8.	Arnulfo Villasenor Saavedra J.	Guadalupe Covarrubias Iba
9.	*Oscar de la Torre Padilla*	Oscar Navarro Franco
10.	*Jose Ma. Martinez Rodriguez*	Adolfo Medrano Rebolledo
11.	*Maria Guadalupe Urzua F.*	Manuel Robles Moran
12.	Abel Salgado Velasco	Francisco Marquez Hernandez

Mexico

1.	Alberto Hernandez Curiel	Marciana Valdespino S.
2.	*Jose Delgado Valle*	Ma. de Carmen Colin Pouche
3.	Rafael Riva Palacio	Florentino Rebollo Velazquez
4.	Alfonso Solleiro Landa	Alfredo Ramos Zuniga
5.	Enrique Diaz Nava	Maria Martinez Rivera
6.	Guillermo Olguin Ruiz	Habacuc Acosta Ayala
7.	Jesus Martinez Cabrera	Cuauhtemoc Sanchez Barrales
8.	*Mario Colin Sanchez*	Alfonso Funes Tiarado
9.	Roman Ferrat Sola	Juan Ortiz Montoya

Michoacan

1.	Salvador Resendiz Arreola	Angel Bolanos Guzman
2.	J. de Jesus Arroyo Alanis	Moises Martinez Munoz
3.	*Esvelia Calderon Corona*	Amador Reyes Tinajero
4.	*Daniel Mora Ramos*	Antonio Perez Zavala
5.	Ignacio Galvez Rocha	Miguel Garcia Vega
6.	Agapito Hernandez Hernandez	J. Jesus Rangel Aguilar
7.	Julio Antonio Gallardo O.	Delia Velez Romero
8.	Roberto Estrada Salgado	Martha Arana Penaloza
9.	Ildefonso Estrada Jacobo	Rafael Martinez Infante

Morelos

1.	*Marcos Manuel Suarez Ruiz*	Raul Arana Pineda
2.	*Filomeno Lopez Rea*	Otilio Rivera Almada

Nayarit

1.	Salvador Diaz Coria	Jose Felix Torres Haro
2.	Celso H. Delgado Ramirez	Eugenio Plantillas Grajeda

Nuevo Leon

1.	*Santiago Roel Garcia*	Carlos Canseco Gonzalez
2.	Francisco Cerda Munoz	Flavio Perales Galvan
3.	Pedro Beceira Chavez	Manuel Flores Varela
4.	*Arturo de la Garza Gonzalez*	Fortunato Zuazua Zertuche
5.	*Carolina Morales Farias*	Gorgonio Garcia Bernal

Oaxaca

#		
1.	Jose Estefan Acar	Gudelia Pineda Luna
2.	*Rodolfo Alavez Flores*	Aurelio Ramirez Garcia
3.	Alberto Canseco Ruiz	Genoveva Medina de Marquez
4.	Mario Prieto Sanchez	Juan Bueno Lazaro
5.	Francisco Rosado Lobo	Magdaleno Villegas Dominguez
6.	Ramon Mendoza Cortes	Mauro Gomez Ruiz
7.	Fernando Castillo Castillo	Reynaldo Daza de Jimenez
8.	Abdon Ortiz Cruz	Ma. Guadalupe Perez B.
9.	Jesus Rojas Villavicencio	Eloisa Ortiz de Contreras

Puebla

#		
1.	Melquiades Trejo Hernandez	Adolfo Garcia Camacho
2.	*Juan Figueroa Velasco*	Manuel Perez Hernandez
3.	Francisco Vazquez O'Farrill	Antonio Montes Garcia
4.	Eleazar Camarillo Ochoa	Agustin Perez Caballero
5.	Rodolfo Sanchez Cruz	Jesus Salmoran Malpica
6.	*Fernando Cueto Fernandez*	Conrado Tapia Cardoso
7.	Carlos Trujillo Perez	Federico Hernandez Cortes
8.	Alberto Guerrero C.	Armando Gonzalez Sanchez
9.	Sixto Uribe Maltos	Octavio Manzano Diaz
10.	Julio Abrego Estrada	Isidro Herrera Maldonado

Queretaro

#		
1.	*Consuelo Garcia Escamilla*	Pedro Jesus Montiel Cardenas
2.	*Alfredo V. Bonfil Pinto*	Manuel Garcia Mancebo

Quintana Roo (Territory)

#		
1.	Hernan Pastrana Pastrana	Delio Paz Angeles

San Luis Potosi

#		
1.	Ramiro Robledo Trevino	Ruth Arvides Sanchez
2.	Juan Pablo Cortes Cruz	Eduardo Rocha Perez
3.	Salvador Diaz Macias	Jose Victor Garcia Villar
4.	Luis Tudon Hurtado	Raymundo Escobar Nieto
5.	Tomas Medina Ponce	Angel Martinez Manzanares

Sinaloa

#		
1.	Salvador Esquer Apodaca	Efrain Robles Robles
2.	Marco Antonio Espinosa P.	Emeterio Carlon Lopez
3.	*Renato Vega Alvarado*	Victor Manuel Gandarilla C.
4.	Alejandro Rios Espinosa	Angel Villalpando Brizuela

Sonora

#		
1.	Jesus Gamez Soto	Jose Luis Aguilar
2.	Enrique Fox Romero	Jesus Enriquez Burgos
3.	*Manuel R. Bobadilla Romero*	Heraclio Sotelo Leal
4.	Javier R. Bours Almada	Enrique Rubio Canedo

Tabasco

#		
1.	Manuel Pinera Morales	Cirilo Rodriguez Torres
2.	Ruben Dario Vidal R.	Justo Priego Alipi

Tamaulipas

#		
1.	Donaciano Munoz Martinez	Jose Perez Cardona
2.	Gerardo Balli Gonzalez	Gregorio Perales de la Garza
3.	*Agapito Gonzalez Cavazos*	Francisco de la Fuente
4.	Marciano Aguilar Mendoza	Esperanza Quijano Herrera
5.	Cirilo Rodriguez Guerrero	Martin Aguirre Marquez

Tlaxcala

#		
1.	J. Dolores Diaz Flores	Hector Cano Cano
2.	*Ma. de los Angeles Grant*	Wilulfo Candia Monter

Veracruz

1.	Raymundo Flores Bernal	Sofia Maza de De Leon
2.	Noe Ortega Martinez	Antonio San Juan Rodriguez
3.	Salvador Veronica Sanchez	Luis de la Tejera Pina
4.	Mario V. Malpica Bernabe	Luis Salas Garcia
5.	Agustin Alvarado Gonzalez	Marco Antonio Ramirez Luzuria
6.	Ignacio Gonzalez Rebolledo	Frida Pabello de Mazzott
7.	Jose Roman Mortera Cuevas	Angel Gomez Calderon
8.	Juan Zurita Lagunes	Pascual Cuacua Mendoza
9.	Santiago Villalvazo Marquez	Angel Castro Ruiz
10.	Marco Antonio Ros Martinez	Ulpiano Gomez Vargas
11.	Roberto Avila Gonzalez	Gervasio Triana Arano
12.	Ignacio Altamirano Marin	Onesimo Senties Cue
13.	Hilario Gutierrez Rosas	Ernestina Gutierrez Reyes
14.	Sergio Martinez Mendoza	Rafael Cordoba Garcia

Yucatan

1.	*Orlando Valencia Moguel*	Pedro Silveira Rodriguez
2.	Alejandro Peraza Uribe	Rita Maria Medina de Catin
3.	Jorge Carlos Gonzalez R.	Bartolome Moo Dzib

Zacatecas

1.	Raul Rodriguez Santoyo	Jose Ma. Pino Mendez
2.	Nicolas Marquez Acosta	Francisco Arellano Macias
3.	J. Jesus Yanez Castro	Salvador Lopez Olmos
4.	J. Jesus Barcenas Gallegos	Patricio Garcia Perez

Party Deputies (PAN)

Guillermo Baeza Somellera
Alfonso Orozco Rosales
Miguel Hernandez Labastida
Mayo Arturo Bravo Hernandez
Jesus Rojo Perez
Juan Landerreche Obregon
Hiram Escudero Alvarez
Inocencio Sandoval Zavala
Juan Manuel Lopez Sanabria
Jorge Garabito Martinez

Magdaleno Gutierrez Herrera
Bernardo Batiz Vazquez
Francisco Jose Peniche Bolio
Guillermo Islas Olguin
Jose Blas Briseno Rodriguez
Guillermo Ruiz Vazquez
Miguel Lopez Gonzalez
Roberto Flores Granados
Ernesto Velasco Lafarga
Jose Melgarejo Gomez

Party Deputies (PPS)

Felipe Cerecedo Lopez
Jesus Lujan Gutierrez
Simon Jimenez Cardenas
Emilia Dorado Baltazar
Manuel Stephens Garcia

Francisco Hernandez Juarez
Jorge Cruickshank Garcia
Francisco Ortiz Mendoza
Maximiliano Leon Murillo
Alejandro Gascon Mercado

Party Deputies (PARM)

Juan Barragan Rodriguez
Hector Renteria Acosta
Laura Peraldi Ferrino

Roberto Herrera Giovanini
Fortino Alejandro Garza Cardenas

1973–76 (49th Legislature)

State	Deputy	Alternate
Aguascalientes		
1.	Jose de Jesus Medellin M.	Adelina Hernandez de V.
2.	Higinio Chavez Marmolejo	Gilberto Calderon Romo
Baja California del Norte (Territory)		
1.	Federico Martinez Manatou	Margarita Ortega Villa
2.	Rafael Garcia Vazquez	Manuel Trasvina Perez
3.	*Celestino Salcedo Monteon*	Jorge Moreno Bonet
Baja California del Sur (Territory)		
1.	Antonio Carrillo Huacuja	Agapito Duarte Hernandez
Campeche		
1.	Rosa Maria Martinez Denegri	Mario Boeta Blanco
2.	Luis Fernando Solis Patron	Ismael Estrada Cuevas
Chiapas		
1.	Carlos Moguel Sarmiento	Enrique Enciso Solis
2.	Rafael Moreno Ballinas	Jorge Paniagua Herrera
3.	Fedro Guillen Castanon	Roberto Bonifaz Caballero
4.	Nereo Gonzalez Camacho	Miguel Hernandez Gomez
5.	Jaime Jesus Coutino Esquina	Norberto de Gives Goches
6.	Maria Guadalupe Cruz Aranda	Darvelio Macosay Luna
Chihuahua		
1.	Julio Cortazar Terrazas	Normando Perales Ramirez
2.	Luis Parra Orozco	Juan Heredia Arteaga
3.	Francisco Rodriguez Perez	Roberto Delgado Urias
4.	Luis Fuentes Molinar	Fernando Martinez Tafoya
5.	Angel Gonzalez	Alfredo Gonzalez Brondo
6.	Ernesto Villalobos Payan	Artemio Iglesias Miramontes
Coahuila		
1.	Jesus Roberto Davila Narro	Gasper Valdez Valdez
2.	Francisco Rodriguez Ortiz	Ma. del Carmen Arreola Robles
3.	Arnoldo Villarreal Zertuche	Jose Alvarez Alfaro
4.	Jesus Lopez Gonzalez	Oswaldo Villarreal Valdez
Colima		
1.	Daniel A. Moreno Diaz	Crispin Casian Zepeda
2.	Jorge Armando Gaitan Gudino	Hilario Contreras Lopez
Distrito Federal		
1.	Guillermo G. Vazquez Alfaro	Alfonso del Rosal Andrade
2.	*Angel Olivio Solis*	Victor Manuel Avila Romero
3.	Ofelia Casillas Ontiveros	Gilberto Villegas Ralda
4.	Efrain H. Garza Flores	Leopoldo Nunez Flores
5.	Hilario Punzo Morales	Carlos Molina Osorio
6.	Concepcion Rivera Centeno	Graciano Morales Ortiz
7.	Jorge Duran Chavez	Maria Elena Marquez Rangel
8.	Carlos Dufoo Lopez	Silvia Hernandez Enriquez
9.	Daniel Mejia Colin	Leonardo Ochoa Merida
10.	Simon Garcia Rodriguez	Gloria Carrillo Salinas
11.	*Juan Jose Hinojosa Hinojosa*	Rene Martinez Tinajero
12.	Alberto Juarez Blancas	Rafael Meneses Narvaez
13.	Javier Blanco Sanchez	Reyes Roldan Moreno
14.	Onofre Hernandez Rivera	Roberto Valdez Amezquita
15.	Luis Gonzalez Escobar	Mario Berumen Ramirez

16.	Luis del Toro Calero	Graciela Valles de Moctezuma
17.	Jose Humberto Mateos Gomez	Carlos Hidalgo Cortes
18.	*Joaquin del Olmo Martinez*	Salustio Salgado Guzman
19.	Jose Maria Ruiz Zavala	Jesus Ibarra Tenorio
20.	Ricardo Castaneda Gutierrez	Aurora Larrazolo Flores
21.	Mariano Araiza Zayas	Janitzio Mujica Rodriguez Cabo
22.	*Arturo Gonzalez Cosio Diaz*	Jose N. Iturriaga de la F.
23.	*Carlos Madrazo Pintado*	Rosalinda Nunez Perea
24.	*Rodolfo Echeverria Ruiz*	Marcelo Bolanos Martinez
25.	Luis Adolfo Santibanez B.	

Durango

1	Maria Aurelia de la Cruz	Jose Ramon Hernandez Meraz
2.	Jesus Jose Gamero Gamero	Francisco Javier Morales F.
3.	Victor Rocha Marin	Francisco Javier Cueto Arreola
4.	Jose Maria Rivas Escalante	Maria Cristina Arreola Rocha

Guanajuato

1.	*Jaime Luis Danton Rodriguez*	Aurora Guerrero Olivares
2.	Carlos Machiavelo Martin	Salvador Munoz Padilla
3.	Antonio Torres Gomez	Guillermo Liceaga Diaz
4.	*Tomas Sanchez Hernandez*	Jose Luis Vazquez Camarena
5.	Jose Luis Estrada D.	J. Jesus Gomez Leon
6.	Gilberto Munoz Mosqueda	Alfredo Carrillo Juarez
7.	Francisco Gonzalez Martinez	Humberto Soto Morales
8.	*Ignacio Vazquez Torres*	Sergio Tovar Alvarado
9.	Jose Mendoza Lugo	Silvestre Bautiste Lopez

Guerrero

1.	Luis Leon Aponte	Florencio Salazar Adame
2.	Pindaro Uriostegui Miranda	Efigenia Marquez Rodriguez
3.	*Alejandro Cervantes Delgado*	Alicia Buitron Brugada
4.	Graciano Astudillo Alarcon	Vicente Rueda Saucedo
5.	Ismael Andraca Navarrete	Angelina Morlet Leyva
6.	Gustavo Nabor Ojeda Delgado	Constantino Flores Pena

Hidalgo

1.	Rafael Cravioto Munoz	Augusto Ponce Coronado
2.	Oscar Bravo Santos	Enrique Gutierrez Escobedo
3.	Maria Estela Rojas de Soto	Daniel Campuzano Barajas
4.	Javier Hernandez Lara	Antonio Flores Roldan
5.	Ismael Villegas Rosas	Francisco Escamilla Velazquez

Jalisco

1.	Reyes Rodolfo Flores Z.	Genaro Muniz Padilla
2.	Gilberto Acosta Bernal	Reynaldo Duenas Villasenor
3.	Guillermo A. Gomez Reyes	Javier Antonio Chavez Anaya
4.	Marcos Montero Ruiz	Pedro Martinez Lopez
5.	Amelia Villasenor y V.	Jose Luis Leal Sanabria
6.	Hector Castellanos Torres	Jose Luis Pena Loza
7.	*Gilberto Aceves Alcocer*	J. Merced Valle Navarro
8.	Rafael Gomez Garcia	Enrique Chavero Ocampo
9.	*Flavio Romero de Velasco*	Luis Albino Reyes Robles
10.	Ramon Diaz Carrillo	Jose Munguia Rodriguez
11.	*Jose Luis Lamadrid Sauza*	Jose Ramirez Ruelas
12.	Francisco Marquez Hernandez	Jesus Octavio Urquides Verdugo
13.	Carlos Rivera Aceves	Daniel Aguirre Cortines

Mexico

1.	Sergio L. Benhumea Munguia	Juan Ugarte Cortes
2.	Jesus Garcia Lovera	Hiram Garcia Garces

3.	Jorge Hernandez Garcia	Bricio Escalante Quiroz
4.	Alfonso Gomez de Orozco	Jose Luis Garcia Garcia
5.	Javier Barrios Gonzalez	Oscar Gonzalez Cesar
6.	Jesus Moreno Jimenez	Juan Monroy Ortega
7.	*Leonardo Rodriguez Alcaine*	Jose Antonio Rivas Roa
8.	Humberto Lira Mora	Fernando Rivapalacio
9.	Cuauhtemoc Sanchez Barrales	Angel Garcia Bravo
10.	Sixto Noguez Estrada	Miguel Perez Guadarrama
11.	Maria de la Paz Becerril	Angel Otero Rivero
12.	Abraham Talavera Lopez	Javier Perez Olagaray
13.	Mario Ruiz de Chavez Garcia	Luis Manuel Valle Caro
14.	Pedro Garcia Gonzalez	Abel Dominguez Rivero
15.	Maria Martinez Rivera	Rogelio Torres Galicia

Michoacan

1.	Gustavo Garibay Ochoa	Salvador Ruiz Garcia
2.	Jorge Canedo Vargas	Macario Castro Apastillado
3.	*Antonio Martinez Baez*	Miguel Garcia Flores
4.	Jose Alvarez Cisneros	Rodolfo Ramirez Trillo
5.	Jose Luis Escobar Herrera	Roberto Garibay Ochoa
6.	Octavio Pena Torres	Manuel Cruz Diaz
7.	Maria Villasenor Diaz	Jose Octavio Leon Infante
8.	Francisco Valdes Zaragoza	Antonio Chavez Samano
9.	Rafael Ruiz Bejar	Vicente Sanchez Cervantes

Morelos

1.	Jose Castillo Pombo	Ubaldo Palacios Betancourt
2.	Roque Gonzalez Urriza	David Pacheco Saucedo

Nayarit

1.	Joaquin Canovas Puchades	Jose Angel Ceron Alba
2.	Anselmo Ibarra Beas	Jose Luis Bejar Fonseca

Nuevo Leon

1.	*Margarita Garcia Flores*	Ramiro Martinez Lozano
2.	Raul Gomez Danes	Ricardo Ayala Villarreal
3.	Gerardo Cavazos Cortes	Gilberto Montero Rodriguez
4.	*Leopoldo Gonzalez Saenz*	Rosendo Gonzalez Quintanilla
5.	Ramiro Rodriguez Cabello	Eleazar Bazaldua Bazaldua
6.	Francisco Javier Gutierrez	Rogelio Emilio Gonzalez
7.	Julio Camelo Martinez	Laura Hinojosa de Domeno

Oaxaca

1.	Cecilio de la Cruz Pineda	Josafat Espinosa Rodriguez
2.	Jorge Reyna Toledo	Wilfrido Luis Perez Mendez
3.	Hugo Manuel Felix Garcia	Ricardo Hernandez Casanova
4.	Antonio Jimenez Puya	Guadalupe Castro Moreno
5.	Diodoro Carrasco Palacios	Maclovio Rodriguez Perez
6.	Jaime Esteva Silva	Victor Espindola Loyola
7.	Jose Murat Casas	Fernando Mimiaga Sosa
8.	Jose Rivera Arreola	Moises Cabrera Tellez
9.	Efren Ricardez Carrion	Genoveva Medina de Marquez

Puebla

1.	Miguel Fernandez del Campo	Rosalia Ramirez de Ortega
2.	Alejandro Canedo Benitez	Maria del Rosario Huerta L.
3.	Matilde del Mar Hidalgo	Marcelino Naranjo Santillan
4.	Lino Garcia Gutierrez	Moises Alonso Amador
5.	Jose Octavio Ferrer Guzman	Armando Garcia Mendoza
6.	Rafael Pedro Cano Merino	Silvino Jimenez Perez
7.	Nefthali Lopez Paez	Venustiano Andrade del C.

8.	Enrique Zamora Palafox	Samuel Herrera Alvarado
9.	*Horacio Labastida Munoz*	Arturo Alonso Hidalgo
10.	Guillermo Jimenez Morales	Angel Esquitin Lechuga

Queretaro

1.	Jose Ortiz Aranda	Jose Borbolla Patino
2.	Telesforo Trejo Uribe	Severiano Perez Enriquez

Quintana Roo (Territory)

1.	*Jesus Martinez Ross*	Sebastian Uc Yam

San Luis Potosi

1.	Ernesto Baez Lozano	Maria de Jesus Mena de Zavala
2.	Adalberto Lara Nunez	Claudio Diaz Diaz
3.	Angel Rubio Huerta	Jorge Amaya Verastegui
4.	Vicente Ruiz Chiapetto	Roberto Guerrero Guerrero
5.	Rafael Tristan Lopez	Leonardo Zuniga Azuara

Sinaloa

1.	Silvestre Perez Lorenz	Raul Miguel Otondo Sanchez
2.	Maria Edwigis Vega Padilla	Pablo Moreno Cota
3.	Fernando Uriarte Hernandez	Rafael Cesar Borbon Ramos
4.	Salvador Robels Quintero	Jesus Arnoldo Millan
5.	Ignacio Carrillo Carrillo	Juan Manuel Inzunza Lara

Sonora

1.	Ramiro Oquita y Melendrez	Pedro Zamora Lopez
2.	*Alejandro Sobarzo Loaiza*	Rita Silvina Agramont
3.	Jesus Enriquez Burgos	Fernando Elias Calles Alvarez
4.	Gilberto Gutierrez Quiroz	Jose Rosario Ruelas

Tabasco

1.	Feliciano Calzada Padron	Armando Leon Franyutti
2.	Humberto Hernandez Haddad	Alfredo Dominguez Hernandez
3.	Julian Montejo Velazquez	Elvira Gutierrez de Alvarez

Tamaulipas

1.	Carlos Enrique Cantu Rosas	Gilberto Ortiz Medina
2.	Gilberto Bernal Mares	Silvestre Mata Carrizales
3.	Juan Baez Guerra	Lorenzo Mendez Soto
4.	Jesus Elias Pina	Eustolia Turrubiates Guzman
5.	Gabriel Legorreta V.	Manuel Mendez Villagrana
6.	Jorge Antonio Torres Zarate	Diego Vidal Balboa

Tlaxcala

1.	Esteban Minor Quiroz	Ernesto Garcia Sarmiento
2.	Aurelio Zamora Garcia	Hector Vazquez Paredes

Veracruz

1.	*Silverio R. Alvarado A.*	Francisco Romero Azuara
2.	Demetrio Ruiz Malerva	Olga Ruiz de Oviedo
3.	Ignacio Mendoza Aguirre	Jose Lima Cobos
4.	Patricio Chirinos Calero	Antonio Martinez Garcia
5.	*Rafael Hernandez Ochoa*	Juan Pablo Prom Lavoignet
6.	Jose Luis Melgarejo Vivanco	Carlos Dominguez Millan
7.	Delia de la Paz Rebolledo	Rene Leon Marquez
8.	Lilia Berthely Jimenez	Marco Vinicio Mendez C.
9.	Rogelio Garcia Gonzalez	Carlos Hernandez Fabela
10.	*Modesto A. Guinart Lopez*	Eustaquio Sosa Barba
11.	Mario Vargas Saldana	Juan Zomoano Aragon
12.	Fidel Herrera Beltran	Cesar Fentanes Mendez
13.	Serafin Dominguez Ferman	Alfredo Vielma Villanueva
14.	David Ramirez Cruz	Pablo Martin Cruz Hernandez
15.	Manuel Ramos Gurrion	Manuel Perez Escalante

Yucatan
1.	Victor Cervera Pacheco	Horacio Herve Rodriguez
2.	Hernan Morales	Nelly Guadalupe Valencia B.
3.	Efrain Ceballos Gutierrez	Augusto Briseno Contreras

Zacatecas
1.	Luis Arturo Contreras S.	Consuelo Garibaldi Castillo
2.	Arturo Romo Gutierrez	Jose Haro Avila
3.	Filiberto Soto Solis	Salvador Enriquez Cid
4.	Alfredo Rodriguez Ruiz	Abel Chaires Baez

Party Deputies (PAN)

Graciela Aceves de Romero	Carlos Gomez Alvarez
Alfredo Oropeza Garcia	Jorge Baeza Somellera
Hector G. Gonzalez Garcia	*Eugenio Ortiz Walls*
Javier Blanco Sanchez	*Manuel Gonzalez Hinojosa*
Margarita Prida de Yarza	Armando R. Calzada Ramos
Jose Eduardo Limon Leon	Lorenzo Reynoso Ramirez
Jose Angel Conchello Davila	Alberto A. Loyola Perez
Federico Ruiz Lopez	Alejandro Coronel Oropeza
Jose de Jesus Martinez Gil	Jose de Jesus Sanchez Ochoa
Fernando Estrada Samano	Gerardo Medina Valdez
Abel Carlos Vicencio Tovar	Alvaro Fernandez de Cevallos Ramos

Party Deputies (PPS)

Belisario Aguilar Olvera	Miguel Hernandez Gonzalez
Ruben Rodriguez Lozano	Pedro Bonilla Diaz de la Vega
Alicia Mata Galarza	*Lazaro Rubio Felix*
Salvador Castaneda O'Connor	Alejandro Mujica Montoya
Hector Guillermo Valencia M.	Jesus Guzman Rubio
Juan C. Pena Ochoa	Mario Vazquez Martinez
Javier Heredia Talavera	Ezequiel Rodriguez Arcos

1976–79 (50th Legislature)

State	Deputy	Alternate
Aguascalientes		
1.	*Jesus Martinez Gotari*	Rosa Guerrero de Reyes
2.	Camilo Lopez Gomez	Camilo Lopez Gomez
Baja California del Sur		
1.	Victor M. Peralta Osuna	Antonio Flores Mendoza
2.	Agapito Duarte Hernandez	Gloria Davis de Benzinger
Baja California del Norte		
1.	Ricardo Eguia Valderrama	Guadalupe Trejo de Conteras
2.	Alfonso Ballesteros Pelayo	Mario Mayans Concha
3.	*Alfonso Garzon Santibanez*	Ma. de la Luz Mangas Gonzalez
Campeche		
1.	Abelardo Carrillo Zavala	Ruben Uribe Aviles
2.	Jorge Munoz Icthe	Nery Granados Martinez

Chiapas

1.	*Jaime Sabines Gutierrez*	Luis Manuel Zuarth Moreno
2.	J. Fernando Correa Suarez	Antonio Perez Perez
3.	Homero Tovilla Cristiani	Javier Pinto y Pinto
4.	Manuel Villafuerte Mijangos	Adrian Contreras Romero
5.	Gonzalo A. Esponda Zebadua	Salvador Duran Perez
6.	Leonardo Leon Cerpa	Adan Lara Beltran

Chihuahua

1.	Alberto Ramirez Gutierrez	Tomas Garcia Garcia
2.	Oswaldo Rodriguez Gonzalez	Silverio Garcia Bustillos
3.	Jose Estrada Aguirre	Luis J. Vidal Quinones
4.	Juan E. Madera Prieto	Jose Moran Cruz
5.	Artemio Iglesias Miramontes	German Hernandez Dominguez
6.	*Jose R. Mar de la Rosa*	Irma Aceves de Galindo

Coahuila

1.	*Jose de las Fuentes Rodriguez*	Guadalupe Gonzalez Ortiz
2.	Carlos Oritz Tejeda	Fernando Roque Villanueva
3.	Fernando Cabrera Rodriguez	Enrique Meave Muniz
4.	Julian Munoz Uresti	Ariel Cueto Rodriguez

Colima

1.	Ramon Serrano Garcia	Guillermina Cedano Castillo
2.	Fernando Moreno Pena	Isidro Estrada Diaz

Distrito Federal

1.	Eduardo Andrade Sanchez	Luis Rendon de Lara
2.	Jose Salvador Lima Zuno	Manuel Gutierrez Montoya
3.	Carlos Riva Palacio V.	Leonardo Salas Valenci
4.	*Enrique Ramirez y Ramirez*	Fernando Crocker Solorzano
5.	Miguel Molina Herrera	Ma. Gpe. Geniz Paredes
6.	Alfonso Rodriguez Rivera	Isabel Vivanco Montalvo
7.	Ma. Elena Marques de T.	Rosa Lilia Rosas Pons
8.	Julio C. Mena Brito Andrade	Francisco Pena Avila
9.	Venustiano Reyes Lopez	Consuelo Marques de Vallejo
10.	Gloria Carrillo Salinas	Antonio Fuentes Aguilar
11.	Jaime Aguilar Alvarez	Noe Marcos Lazcano Rivero
12.	Miguel Lopez Riveroll	Salvador Villasenor Franco
13.	*Rodolfo Gonzalez Guevara*	Raquel Ocharan de Sanchez
14.	Jorge Mendicutti Negrete	Rosa Ma. de la Pena Garcia
15.	*Juan J. Osorio Palacios*	Fernando Zamora Lopez
16.	Silvia Hernandez	Alfonso Argudin Laria
17.	Hector Hernandez Casanova	Hector Gutierrez de Alba
18.	Hugo Diaz Velazquez	Jose Herra Arango
19.	Abraham Martinez Rivero	Raimundo Baldamis Pelaez
20.	Jesus Gonzalez Balandrano	Jose Sanchez Miranda
21.	*Marta Andrade de Del Rosal*	Manuel Granados Chirino
22.	*Ifigenia Martinez Hernandez*	Ernesto Garcia Herrera
23.	*Enrique Soto Izquierdo*	Guadalupe Salazar de Zamora
24.	*Enrique Alvarez del Castillo*	Juan Balanzario Diaz
25.	*Celia Torres de Sanchez*	Humberto Casillas Padilla
26.	Humberto Serrano Perez	Pablo Leon Orta
27.	Hugo R. Castro Aranda	Xochil Elena Llarena de G.

Durango

1.	Angel S. Guerrero Mier	Zina Ruiz de Leon
2.	Maximiliano Silerio Esparza	Carlos Cruz Molina
3.	Salvador Reyes Nevares	Rodolfo Reyes Soto
4.	Jose Ramirez Gamero	Vicente Soria Barbosa

Guanajuato

1.	Esteban M. Garaiz	Lucio Loyola Gonzalez
2.	Enrique Gomez Guerra	Felix Vilchis Rios
3.	*Juan J. Varela Mayorga*	J. Dolores Urbieta Hernandez
4.	*Miguel Montes Garcia*	Cirilo Soto Barajas
5.	Aurelio Garcia Sierra	Ruben Garcia Farias
6.	Alfredo Carrillo Juarez	Luis Rosiles Flores
7.	Enrique Leon Hernandez	Isidro Hernandez Gomez
8.	Graciela Meave Torrescano	Carlos Chaurand Arzate
9.	Donaciano Luna Hernandez	Alfredo Zavala Ramirez

Guerrero

1.	Isaias Gomez Salgado	Isidro Mastache Suarez
2.	Isaias Duarte Martinez	Gustavo Martinez Martinez
3.	Miguel Bello Pineda	Rafael Garcia Vergara
4.	*Hortensia Santoyo de Garcia*	Efren Diaz Castellanos
5.	Reveriano Garcia Castrejon	Javier Jimenez Vazquez
6.	Salustio Salado Guzman	Eloy Polanco Salinas

Hidalgo

1.	Ladislao Castillo Feregrino	Elvia Fernandez Sogovia
2.	Luis J. Dorantes Segovia	Ruben Vargas Torres
3.	Efrian Mera Arias	Alvaro Cortes Azpeitia
4.	Jose Antonio Zorrilla Perez	Nicandro Castillo Gomez
5.	Vicente J. Trejo Callejas	Jose Guadarrama Marquez

Jalisco

1.	*Guillermo Cosio Vidaurri*	Jamie Alberto Ramirez
2.	Reynaldo Duenas Villasenor	Agapito Isaac Lopez
3.	Felix Flores Gomez	Antonio Brambila Meda
4.	*Porfirio Cortes Silva*	Ricardo Moreno Delgado
5.	Jose Mendoza Padilla	Gabriel Ponce Miranda
6.	Rigoberto Gonzalez Quezada	Salvador Huerta Herrera
7.	Ma. Refugio Castillon C.	Jose Luis Gonzalez Sanchez
8.	Ricardo P. Chavez Perez	Juan Valdivia Gomez
9.	*Maria G. Urzua Flores*	Raul Juarez Valencia
10.	Francisco J. Santillan O.	Lorenzo Zepeda Uribe
11.	Hector F. Castaneda Jimenez	Gregorio Velez Montes
12.	Rafael Gonzalez Pimienta	Antonio Zepeda Pacheco
13.	Jesus A. Mora Lopez	Miguel Armando Naranjo

Mexico

1.	Gildardo Herrera Gomez T.	Filemon Salazar Buenc
2.	*Josefina Esquivel de Quintana*	Federico Osorio Hernandez
3.	*Jose Delgado Valle*	Bricio Escalante Quiroz
4.	Arturo Martinez Legorreta	Miguel Portilla Saldana
5.	Jose Martinez Martinez	Julio Garduno Cervantes
6.	Rosendo Franco Escamilla	Antonio Solanes Oviedo
7.	Julio Zamora Batiz	Francisco Meixhueiro Soto
8.	Armando Labra Manjarrez	Martha Elena Reyes de Campos
9.	Juan Ortiz Montoya	Albino Pazos Tellez
10.	Jose Luis Garcia Garcia	Carlos Cortes Ocana
11.	Guillermo Choussal Valladares	Fernando de Moral Bermudez
12.	Ceclio Salas Galvez	Ignacio Legaria Ramirez
13.	Pedro Avila Hernandez	J. Concepcion Silva German
14.	Armando Hurtado Navarro	Rodolfo Gonzalez Martinez
15.	Hector Ximenez Gonzalez	Saul Rayon Vazquez

Michoacan

1.	Nicanor Gomez Reyes	Maria de la Luz Vera
2.	Antonio Jaimes Aguilar	Abel Perez Guzman

3.	Raul Lemus Garcia	Natalio Flores Lazaro
4.	Roberto Garibay Ochoa	J. Tariacuri Cano Soria
5.	Jaime Bravo Ramirez	Jose Maria Montejano Delgao
6.	Eduardo Estrada Perez	Salvador Castillo Nunez
7.	Juan Rodriguez Gonzalez	Adimanto Vladimir Hernandez V.
8.	*Hector Teran Torres*	Luis Yarza Solorzano
9.	Roberto Ruiz del Rio	Valente Genel Manzo

Morelos

1.	Antonio Riva Palacio Lopez	Simona Rico de Urueta
2.	*Filomeno Lopez Rea*	Leopoldo Rivas Pizano

Nayarit

1.	Ignacio Langarica Quintana	Fausto Ramos Cervantes
2.	Ma. Hilaria Dominguez A.	Simon Pintado Carrillo

Nuevo Leon

1.	*Carlota Vargas de Montemayor*	Roberto Garza Gonzalez
2.	Heriberto D. Santos Lozano	Guillermo Guzman
3.	Raul Caballero Escamilla	Alfonso Trevino Gonzalez
4.	Eleazar Ruiz Cerda	Zenen Ramirez Villalba
5.	*Arturo Luna Lugo*	Salvador Capistran Alvarado
6.	*Jesus Puente Leyva*	Alfonso Ayala Villarreal
7.	Roberto Olivares Vera	Felipe Zambrano Paez

Oaxaca

1.	Lucia Betanzos de Bay	Tomas Vicente Martinez
2.	Gustavo Santaella Cortes	Tadeo Cruz Lopez
3.	Ericel Gomez Nucamendi	Fortino Perez Medina
4.	Ernesto Aguilar Flores	Serafin Aguilar Franco
5.	Luis C. Jimenez Sosa	Magdaleno Villegas Dominguez
6.	Heladio Ramirez Lopez	Fidel Herrera Salbuena
7.	*Zoraida Bernal de Badillo*	Irma Pineiro Arias
8.	Julio Esponda Solana	Honorina Betanzos de Chunga
9.	Raul Bolanos Cacho Guzman	Benjamin Juana Fernandez Pieja

Puebla

1.	Nicolas Perez Pavon	Hilda Luisa Valdemar
2.	Jorge E. Dominguez Ramirez	Melquiades Morales Flore
3.	Antonio Montes Garcia	Adoracion Youshimatz Morales
4.	*Antonio J. Hernandez Jimenez*	Salvador Zavala Villafuerte
5.	*Sacramento Jofre Vazquez*	Jesus Reyes Nieto
6.	Antonio Tenorio Adame	Felipe Valderrama Garcia
7.	*Guadalupe Lopez Breton*	Jose Isabel Alonso Carrio
8.	Jesus Sarabia y Ordonez	Amando Gonzalez Sanchez
9.	Manuel Rivera Anaya	Jorge Murat Macluf
10.	Adolfo Rodriguez Juarez	Marcos Gutierrez Garrido

Queretaro

1.	Eduardo D. Ugalde Vargas	Maria Luisa Medina
2.	Vicente Montes Velazquez	Severiano Orduna Ocana

Quintana Roo

1.	Carlos Gomez Barrera	Faride Cheluja de Aguilar
2.	Emilio Oxte Tah	Salvador Ramos Bustamante

San Luis Potosi

1.	Roberto Leyva Torres	Juan Manuel Fortuna Trujillo
2.	J. Guadalupe Vega Macias	J. Refugio Guerrero Alvarado
3.	Victor A. Maldonado Moreleon	J. Guadalupe Martinez Samche
4.	Hector Gonzalez Larraga	Petronilo Lara Nunez
5.	Eusebio Lopez Sainz	Saul Azua Jacob

Sinaloa

1. Tolentino Rodriguez Felix — Tolentino Rodriquez Felix
2. Felipe Armenta Gallardo — Miguel Ahumada Cortes
3. Gil Rafael Oceguerra Ramos — Jose Carlos Loaiza
4. *Antonio Toledo Corro* — Leonardo Peraza Zamudio
5. Patricio Robles Robles — Gustavo Felix Beltran

Sonora

1. Ricardo Castillo Peralta — Raul Corella Ruiz
2. Augusto C. Tapia Quijada — Alfonso Garcia Gallegos
3. Jose Luis Vargas Gonzalez — Jose Antonio Ruiz Gonzalez
4. Bernabe Arana Leon — Ruben Duarte Corral

Tabasco

1. Luis Priego Ortiz — Elvira Gutierrez de Alvarez
2. Roberto Madrazo Pintado — Edgar Mendez Garrido
3. Francisco Rabelo Cupido — Manuel de Jesus Martinez

Tamaulipas

1. Abdon Rodriguez Sanchez — Francisco Martinez Cortes
2. Oscar Mario Santos Gomez — Diodora Guerra Rodriguez
3. *Agapito Gonzalez Cavazos* — Moises Lozano Padilla
4. *Aurora Cruz de Mora* — Luis Quintero Guzman
5. *Fernando San Pedro Salem* — Rogelio Carlos Caballero
6. Julio D. Martinez Rodriguez — Armando Garcia Pena

Tlaxcala

1. Nazario Romero Diaz — Raymundo Perez Amador
2. Antonio Vega Garcia — Salvador Dominguez Sanchez

Veracruz

1. Guilebaldo Flores Fuentes — Roberto Mendoza Medina
2. Pericles Namorado Urrutia — Toribio Garcia Lorenzo
3. Emilio Salgado Zubiaga — Vanancio Caro Benavides
4. Manuel Gutierrez Zamora — Guadalupe Solares de Martinez
5. Seth Cardena Luna — Lucia Mendez Hernandez
6. Carlos M. Vargas Sanchez — Sara Luz Quiros Ruiz
7. Daniel Nogueira Huerta — Benjamin Dominguez Rivera
8. Celeste Castillo Moreno — Miguel Angel Yunes Linares
9. Mario Martinez Dector — Rosa Maria Martinez Najera
10. Pastor Murguia Gonzalez — Armando Garcia Lebres
11. Miguel Portela Cruz — Raul Ramos Vicarte
12. Mario Hernandez Posadas — Miguel Aguirre Lavalle
13. Francisco Cinta Guzman — Victor White Fonseca
14. Juan Melendez Pacheco — Simeon Chinas Valdiviesco
15. Eduardo Thomae Dominguez — Plinio Priego Gutierrez

Yucatan

1. *Mirna E. Hoyos de Navarrete* — Carlos Velazquez Franco
2. Carlos R. Calderon Cecilio — Alvaro Hernando Brito Alonso
3. *Victor Manzanilla Schaffer* — Noe Antonio Peniche Patron

Zacatecas

1. Gustavo Salinas Iniguez — Albino Tizcareno Hernandez
2. Crescencio Herrera Herrera — Lorenzo Ruvalcaba Carillo
3. Jose Leal Longoria — Juvenal Rivas Zacarias
4. Julian Macias Perez — Honorio Perez Marin

Party Deputies (PAN)

Gonzalo Altamirano Dimas
Fausto Alarcon Escalona
Miguel Campos Martinez
Jorge Garabito Martinez
Sergio Lujambio Rafols
Jose L. Martinez Galicia
Francisco Pedraza Villarreal
Ramon Garcilita Partida
Carlos G. De Carcer Ballesca
Miguel Hernandez Labastida

Guillermo Islas Olguin
Rosalba Magallon Camacho
Teodoro Ortega Garcia
Francisco J. Peniche Bolio
Jose Ortega Mendoza
Ma. E. Alvarez Vicencio
Adrian Pena Soto
Jacinto G. Silva Flores
Juan Torres Cipres

Party Deputies (PPS)

Rafael Campos Lopez
Victor Manuel Carrasco
Felipe Cerecedo Lopez
Roman Ramirez Contreras
Alberto Contreras Valencia
Francisco Hernandez Juarez

Marcela Lombardo de Gutierrez
Ildefonso Reyes Soto
Jesus Lujan Gutierrez
Francisco Ortiz Mendoza
Hector Ramirez Cuellar

Party Deputies (PARM)

Saul Castorena Monterrubio
Manuel Hernandez Alvarado
Raul Guillen Perez Vargas
Fortino A. Garza Cardenas
Edilio Hinojosa Lopez

Arcelia Sanchez de Guzman
Pedro Gonzalez Azcuaga
Apolinar Ramirez Meneses
Eugenio Soto Sanchez

1979–82 (51st Legislature)

State	Deputy	Alternate
Aguascalientes		
1.	Roberto Diaz Rodriguez	
2.	Gilberto Romo Najera	
Baja California del Norte		
1.	*Jose Luis Andrade*	
2.	Juan Villalpando Cuevas	
3.	Luis Ayala Garcia	
4.	Rodolfo Fierro Marquez	
5.	Maria del Carmen Marquez	
6.	Rafael Garcia Vazquez	
Baja California del Sur		
1.	Armando Trasvina Taylor	
2.	Ramon Ojeda Suarez	
Campeche		
1.	Rafael Armando Herrera Morales	
2.	Jose Edilberto Vazquez Rios	
Chiapas		
1.	Rafael Pascacio Gamboa Cano	
2.	Pedro Pablo Zepeda Bermudez	
3.	Leyver Martinez Gonzalez	
4.	Salvador de la Torre Grajales	

5.	Jaime J. Coutino Esquinca
6.	Alberto Ramon Cerdio Bado
7.	Antonio Cueto Citalan
8.	Juan Alberto Iran Cuesy
9.	Cesar Augusto Santiago Ramirez

Chihuahua

1.	Margarita Moreno Mena
2.	Jesus Chavez Baeza
3.	Rene Franco Barreno
4.	Miguel Lerma Candelario
5.	Enrique Perez Gonzalez
6.	Enrique Sanchez Silva
7.	Demetrio Bernardo Franco Derma
8.	Mario Legarreta Hernandez
9.	Rebeca Anchondo Vda. de Rodriguez
10.	Alfonso Jesus Armendariz Duran

Coahuila

1.	*Rafael Carranza Hernandez*
2.	Juan Antonio Garcia Villa
3.	Rafael Ibarra Chacon
4.	Angel Lopez Padilla
5.	Conrado Martinez Ortiz
6.	Alonso Hernandez Hernandez
7.	Lorenzo Garcia Zarate

Colima

1.	Agustin Gonzalez Villalobos
2.	Arnaldo Ochoa Gonzalez

Distrito Federal

1.	Carlos Dufoo Lopez
2.	Angel Olivo Solis
3.	Hugo Domenzain Guzman
4.	Rodolfo Siller Rodriguez
5.	Juan Araiza Cabrales
6.	Daniel Mejia Colin
7.	David Reynoso Flores
8.	Lidia Camarena Adame
9.	*Gonzalo Castellot Madrazo*
10.	Ignacio Zuniga Gonzalez
11.	*Manuel German Parra y Prado*
12.	Roberto Castellanos Tovar
13.	Joel Ayala Almeida
14.	Eduardo Anselmo Rosas
15.	Jose Herrera Arango
16.	Jorge Flores Vizcarra
17.	Ruben Figueroa Alcocer
18.	Leobardo Salgado Arroyo
19.	Francisco Simeano y Chavez
20.	Ricardo Ignacio Castaneda G.
21.	Enrique Gomez Corchado
22.	Enrique Gonzalez Flores
23.	Cuauhtemoc Anda Gutierrez
24.	Carlos Robles Loustaunau
25.	Maria Eugenia Moreno Gomez
26.	Marcos Medina Rios
27.	Humberto Olguin y Hermida
28.	Carlos Romero Deschamps

29.	Isabel Vivanco Montalvo
30.	Roberto Blanco Moheno
31.	Ofelia Casillas Ontiveros
32.	Joaquin Alvarez Ordonez
33.	Miguel Angel Camposeco C.
34.	Carlos Hidalgo Cortes
35.	Arturo Robles Aparicio
36.	Consuelo Velazquez Torres
37.	*Luis Velazquez Jaacks*
38.	Tristan M. Canales Najjar
39.	*Antonio Carrillo Flores*
40.	Mario Alfonso Berumen Ramirez

Durango
1.	Luis Angel Tejada Espino
2.	*Eduardo Lopez Faudoa*
3.	Armando del Castillo Franco
4.	Miguel Angel Fragoso Alvarez
5.	Gonzalo Salas Rodrigues
6.	Praxedis Nevarez Cepeda

Guanajuato
1.	*Rafael Corrales Ayala*
2.	Rafael Hernandez Ortiz
3.	Juan Rojas Moreno
4.	Martin Montano Arteaga
5.	Jorge Martinez Dominguez
6.	Gilberto Munoz Mozqueda
7.	*Ignacio Vazquez Torres*
8.	Ofelia Ruiz Vega
9.	*Guadalupe Rivera Marin*
10.	Guillermo Gonzalez Aguado
11.	Andres Sojo Anaya
12.	Raul Moreno Mujica
13.	Enrique Betanzos Hernandez

Guerrero
1.	Heron Varela Alvarado
2.	Porfirio Camarena Castro
3.	Aristeo Roque Jaimes Nunez
4.	Guadalupe Gomez Maganda
5.	Ulpiano Gomez Rodriguez
6.	H. Israel Martinez Galeana
7.	Jorge Montufar Araujo
8.	Filiberto Vigueras Lazaro
9.	Jose Maria Serna Maciel
10.	Damasco Lanche Guillen

Hidalgo
1.	Adolfo Castelan Flores
2.	Jose Ernesto Gil Elorduy
3.	Maria Amelia Olguin Vargas
4.	Jesus Murillo Karan
5.	Jose Guadarrama Marquez
6.	Manual Rangel Escamilla

Jalisco
1.	Eduardo Avina Batiz
2.	Agapito Isaac Lopez
3.	Adalberto Gomez Rodriguez

4.	Octavio Rafael Bueno Trujillo
5.	Manuel Ojeda Orozco
6.	Juan Diego Castaneda Ceballos
7.	Ignacio Gonzalez Rubio V.
8.	Gabriel Gonzalez Acero
9.	Jose Maria Sotelo Amaya
10.	Javier Michel Vega
11.	Ismael Orozco Loreto
12.	Luis Rey Casillas Rodriguez
13.	Juan Delgado Navarro
14.	Francisco Rodriguez Gomez
15.	Enrique Chavero Ocampo
16.	Carlos Rivera Aceves
17.	Margarita Gomez Juarez
18.	Felipe Lopez Prado
19.	Carlos Martinez Rodriguez
20.	Antonio Ruiz Rosas

Mexico

1.	Juan Ugarte Cortes
2.	Armando Neyra Chavez
3.	Alberto Rabago Camacho
4.	Jose Merino Manon
5.	Antonio Huitron Huitron
6.	Guillermo Olguin Ruiz
7.	Jorge Antonio Diaz de Leon V.
8.	Mauricio Valdes Rodriguez
9.	Eugenio Rosales Gutierrez
10.	Antonio Mercado Guzman
11.	Hector Jarquin Hernandez
12.	Lorenzo Valdepenas Machuca
13.	Fernando Leyva Medina
14.	Juan Martinez Fuentes
15.	Graciela Santana Benhumea
16.	*Yolanda Senties de Ballesteros*
17.	Herberto Barrera Velazquez
18.	Enrique Jacob Soriano
19.	Humberto Lira Mora
20.	Jose Antonio Rivas Roa
21.	Flor Elena Pastrana Villa
22.	Maria Elena Prado Mercado
23.	Juan Alvarado Jacco
24.	Francisco Javier Gaxiola Ochoa
25.	Leonel Dominguez Rivero
26.	Elba Esther Gordillo Morales
27.	*Ignacio Pichardo Pagaza*
28.	Odon Madariaga Cruz
29.	Fernando Riva Palacio I.
30.	Vicente Coss Ramirez
31.	Hector Moreno Toscano
32.	Jesus Alcantara Miranda
33.	Jose Luis Garcia Montiel
34.	Jose Maria Tellez Rincon

Michoacan

1.	Marco Antonio Aguilar Cortez
2.	Jose Luis Lemus Solis
3.	*Norberto Mora Plancarte*

4.	*Humberto Romero Perez*
5.	Javier Zepeda Romero
6.	Rafael Ruiz Vejar
7.	Raul Pineda Pineda
8.	Artemio Yanez
9.	Alfonso Quintero Larios
10.	Jaime Genovevo Figueroa
11.	Leticia Amezcua de Sanchez
12.	Abimael Lopez Castillo
13.	Jose Luis Gonzalez Aguilera

Morelos

1.	David Jimenez Gonzalez
2.	Francisco Pliego Nava
3.	Gonzalo Pastrana Castro
4.	*Lauro Ortega Martinez*

Nayarit

1.	Alberto Tapia Carrillo
2.	*Emilio M. Gonzalez Parra*
3.	Carlos Serafin Ramirez

Nuevo Leon

1.	Fernando de Jesus Canales Clariond
2.	Juan Carlos Camacho Salinas
3.	Luis Medina Pena
4.	Filiberto Villarreal Ayala
5.	Jose Faud Gonzalez Amille
6.	*Luis M. Farias*
7.	Andres Montemayor Hernandez
8.	Francisco Valero Sanchez
9.	Maria Amparo Aguirre Hernandez
10.	Armando Thomae Cerna

Oaxaca

1.	Jose Murat Casas
2.	Leandro Martinez Machuca
3.	Elezar Santiago Cruz
4.	Rosalino Porfirio Lopez Ortiz
5.	Genoveva Medina de Marquez
6.	Alicio Rafael Ordono Gonzalez
7.	Aurelio Mora Contreras
8.	*Norberto Aguirre Palancares*
9.	Ruben Dario Somuano Lopez
10.	Ignacio Villanueva Vazquez

Puebla

1.	Angel Aceves Saucedo
2.	David Bravo y Cid de Leon
3.	Meliton Morales Sanchez
4.	Eleazar Camarillo Ochoa
5.	Juan Bonilla Luna
6.	*Amador Hernandez Gonzalez*
7.	Elizabeth Rodriguez de Casas
8.	Guillermo Melgarejo Palafox
9.	Constantino Sanchez Romano
10.	Alfonso Zegbe Sanen
11.	Guillermo Jimenez Morales
12.	Francisco Sanchez Diaz de Rivera
13.	Rodolfo Alvarado Hernandez
14.	Melquiades Morales Flores

Queretaro
1.   Fernando Ortiz Arana
2.   Federico Flores Tavares
3.   Rodolfo Luis Monroy Sandoval

Quintana Roo
1.   Pedro Joaquin Coldwell
2.   Primitivo Alonso Alcocer

San Luis Potosi
1.   *Antonio Rocha Cordero*
2.   Antonio Sandoval Gonzalez
3.   Jose Refugio Araujo del Angel
4.   Angel Martinez Manzanares
5.   Bonifacio Fernandez Padilla
6.   Guillermo Medina de los Santos
7.   Jose Ramon Martel Lopez

Sinaloa
1.   Salvador Esquer Apodaca
2.   Francisco Alarcon Fregoso
3.   Jesus Enrique Hernandez Chavez
4.   Hector Enrique Gonzalez Guevara
5.   Palemon Bojorquez Atondo
6.   Fortino Gomez Mac Hatton
7.   Baldomero Lopez Arias
8.   Maria del Rosario Hernandez B.
9.   Jose Carlos de Saracho C.

Sonora
1.   Luis Antonio Bojorquez Serrano
2.   Alejandro Sobarzo Loaiza
3.   Hugo Romero Ojeda
4.   Ruben Duarte Corral
5.   Salomon Faz Sanchez
6.   Fernando Mendoza Contreras
7.   Carlos Amaya Rivera

Tabasco
1.   Angel Augusto Buendia Tirado
2.   Angel Mario Martinez Zentella
3.   Carlos Mario Pinera y Rueda
4.   Humberto Hernandez Haddad
5.   Hernan Rabelo Wade

Tamaulipas
1.   Pedro Perez Ibarra
2.   Ernesto Donato Cerda Ramirez
3.   Miguel Trevino Emparan
4.   Jaime Baez Rodriguez
5.   Javier Gonzalez Alonso
6.   Hugo Eduardo Barba Islas
7.   Jose Bruno del Rio Cruz
8.   Pedro Reyes Martinez
9.   Enrique Fernandez Perez

Tlaxcala
1.   Salvador Dominguez Sanchez
2.   Beatriz Elena Paredes Rangel

Veracruz
1.   Gustavo Gamez Perez
2.   Demetrio Ruiz Malerva

3.	*Oscar Torres Pancardo*
4.	Gonzalo Anaya Jimenez
5.	Lucia Mendez Hernandez
6.	Luis Porte Petit
7.	Carlos Roberto Smith Veliz
8.	Hesiquio Aguilar de la Para
9.	Miguel Castro Elias
10.	Silvio Lagos Martinez
11.	Juan Maldonado Pereda
12.	Gonzalo Vazquez Bravo
13.	Marco Antonio Munoz Turnball
14.	Sebastian Guzman Cabrera
15.	Francisco Mata Aguilar
16.	Fidel Herrera Beltran
17.	Manuel Ramos Gurrion
18.	Noe Ricardo Ortega Martinez
19.	Gonzalo Morgado Huesca
20.	Gonzalo Sedas Rodriguez
21.	Carolina Hernandez Pinzo
22.	Rosa Maria Campos Gutierrez
23.	Enrique Carrion Solana

Yucatan

1.	Federico Granja Ricalde
2.	Gonzalo Navarro Baez
3.	Jorge Jure Cejin
4.	Roger Milton Rubio Madera

Zacatecas

1.	Arturo Romo Gutierrez
2.	Hermenegildo Fernandez Arroyo
3.	Rafael Cervantes Acuna
4.	Gonzalo Garcia Garcia
5.	Aurora Navia Millan

Plurinominal Deputies (PAN)

Graciela Aceves de Romero
Esteban Aguilar Jaquez
David Alarcon Zaragoza
Rafael Alonso y Preito
Avila Sotomayor
Luis Calderon Vega
Luis Castaneda Guzman
Juan de Dios Castro Lozano
Alvaro Elias Loredo
Hiram Escudero Alvarez
Jesus Gonzalez Schmal
Edmundo Gurza Villarreal
Maria del Carmen Jimenez
Juan Landerreche Obregon
Hector Federico Ling
Juan Manuel Lopez Sanabria
Pablo Emilio Madero Belden
Miguel Martinez Martinez

Jose Gregorio Minondo
Salvador Morales Munoz
Rafael Morales Valdes
Gilberto Rafael Morgan
Antonio Padilla Obregon
Eugenio Ortiz Walls
Delfino Parra Banderas
Alberto Pettersen Biester
Carlos Pineda Flores
Marta Cecilia Pinon Reyna
Manuel Rivera del Campo
Augusto Sanchez Losada
Carlos Stephano Sierra
Francisco Ugalde Alvarez
Raul Velasco Zimbron
Abel C. Vicencio Tovar
Esteban Zamora Camacho

Plurinominal Deputies (PCM)

Valentin Campa Salazar
Antonio Becerra Gaytan
Ramon Danzoa Palomino
Santiago Fierro Fierro
Pablo Gomez Alvarez
Roberto Jaramillo Flores

Evaristo Perez Arreola
Gilberto Rincon Gallardo
Othon Salazar Ramirez
Carlos Sanchez Cardenas
Gerardo Unzueta Lorenzana

Plurinominal Deputies (PPS)

Belisario Aguilar Jaquez
Ernesto Rivera Herrera
Martin Tavira Uriostegui
Juan Manuel Elizondo
Ezequiel Rodriguez Arcos
Lazaro Rubio Felix

Manuel Stephens Garcia
Humberto Pliego Arenas
Amado Tame Shear
Gilberto Velazquez Sanchez
Alejandro Gascon Mercado

Plurinominal Deputies (PST)

America Abaroa Zamora
Jesus Ortega Martinez
Pedro Rene Etienne Llano
Juan Manuel Rodriguez G.

Manuel Terrazas Guerrero
Aldofo Mejia Gonzalez
Abreu Graco Ramirez G.

Plurinominal Deputies (PDM)

Jose Valencia Gonzalez
Roberto Picon Robledo
Jose E. Guzman Gomez
Jose M. Valadez Montoya
Adelaida Marquez Ortiz

Luis Cardenas Murillo
Felipe Perez Gutierrez
Gumersindo Magana Negrete
Juan Aguilera Azpeitia

Plurinominal Deputies (PPM)

Luis Fernando Pedraza M.

Sabino Hernandez Tellez

Plurinominal Deputies (PARM)

Antonio Vazquez del Mercado

Juan Manuel Lucia Escalera

APPENDIX D

Directors of Federal Departments, Agencies and Banks, 1935–1980

Attorney General of Justice for the Federal District

Attorney General of Justice

Castellano Jimenez, Jr., Raul
18 June 1935–31 Dec. 1937
Coutino, Amador
4 Jan. 1938–11 Jan. 1940
Ornelas Villarreal, Antonio
12 Jan. 1940–14 June 1940
Garcia, Luis G.
15 June 1940–30 Nov. 1940
Vejar Vazquez, Octavio
1 Dec. 1940–12 Sept. 1941

Castellanos, Francisco
12 Sept. 1941–30 Nov. 1946
Franco Sodi, Carlos
1 Dec. 1946–30 Nov. 1952
Aguilar y Maya, Guillermo
1 Dec. 1952–15 Oct. 1956
Acosta Fuentes, Ignacio
25 Oct. 1956–30 Nov. 1958
Roman Lugo, Fernando
1 Dec. 1958–30 Nov. 1964
Suarez Torres, Gilberto
1 Dec. 1964–30 Nov. 1970

Garcia Ramirez, Sergio
1 Dec. 1970–9 Aug. 1972
Zorilla Martinez, Pedro
9 Aug. 1972–14 Dec. 1972
Castellanos Coutino, Horacio
15 Dec. 1972–3 Mar. 1976
Narvaez Angulo, Fernando
4 Mar. 1976–30 Nov. 1976
Alanis Fuentes, Agustin
1 Dec. 1976–

Attorney General of the Republic

Attorney General

Guerrero, Silvestre
18 June 1935–25 Aug. 1936
Vazquez, Genaro V.
21 June 1937–30 Nov. 1940
Aguilar y Maya, Jose
1 Dec. 1940–30 Nov. 1946
Gonzalez de la Vega, Francisco
1 Dec. 1946–30 Nov. 1952
Franco Sodi, Carlos
1 Dec. 1952–1955
Gutierrez, Jose Luis
1955
Aguilar y Maya, Jose
29 Oct. 1955–30 Nov. 1958
Lopez Arias, Fernando
1 Dec. 1958–1962
Trevino Rios, Oscar
1962–30 Nov. 1964
Rocha, Antonio
1 Dec. 1964–1967
Sanchez Vargas, Julio
1967–Aug. 1971

Ojeda Paullada, Pedro
Aug. 1971–30 Nov. 1976
Flores Sanchez, Oscar
1 Dec. 1976–

Assistant Attorney General

Santos Guajardo, Vicente
1934–21 June 1937
Ramirez Vazquez, Mariano
22 June 1937–30 Nov. 1940
Matos Escobedo, Rafael
Dec. 1946–1950
Canudas Orezza, Luis Felipe
1951–1952
Gutierrez y Gutierrez, Jose L.
Dec. 1952–30 Nov. 1958
Trevino Rios, Oscar
1 Dec. 1958–1962
Vacant
1962–1964
Franco Rodriguez, David
1 Dec. 1964–1973
Rosales Miranda, Manuel
1973–

Assistant Attorney General (2)

Carvajal, Angel
Aug. 1936–24 Feb. 1944
Corrales Ayala, Rafael
Dec. 1946–1949
Canudas Orezza, Luis F.
1949–1951
Santoyo, Victor Ramon
Dec. 1952–1957
Acosta, Jose Luis
1957–30 Nov. 1958
Suarez Torres, Gilberto
Dec. 1958–30 Nov. 1964
Acosta Romo, Fausto
Dec. 1964–1967
Sanchez Vargas, Julio
1967
Rosales Miranda, Manuel
1967–1973
Alba Leyva, Samuel
1 Jan. 1974–

[407]

Bank of Mexico

Director General

Robles, Gonzalo
  1935–30 Dec. 1935
Montes de Oca, Luis
  31 Dec. 1935–6 Sept. 1940
Villasenor Angeles, Eduardo
  7 Sept. 1940–30 Nov. 1946

Novoa, Carlos
  1 Dec. 1946–30 Nov. 1952
Gomez, Rodrigo
  1 Dec. 1952–14 Aug. 1970
Fernandez Hurtado, Ernesto
  18 Sept. 1970–30 Nov. 1976
Romero Kolbeck, Gustavo
  1 Dec. 1976–

Subdirector General (1)

Espinosa Porset, Ernesto
  1938–1970
Bello, Daniel J.
  1971–1976
Solis, Leopoldo
  1976–

Department of the Air Force

Chief

Fierro, Roberto
  1935–36
Rojas Razo, Samuel C.
  1937–38
Salinas Carranza, Alberto
  1939–40

  1940–41
  1941–46

Cardenas Rodriguez, Antonio
  1946–52
Vietiz y V., Alberto
  1952–54
Cruz Rivera, Alfonso
  1954–59
Fierro, Roberto
  1959–64
Vergara, Jose C.
  1964–70

Berthier Aguiluz, Hector
  1970–76
  1976–

Secretariat of Agrarian Reform
(Department of Agrarian Affairs and Colonization, 1959–75; Agrarian Department, 1934–58)

Secretary

Vazquez, Gabino
  18 June 1935–30 Nov. 1940
Foglio Miramontes, Fernando
  1 Dec. 1940–19 Jan. 1944
Barba Gonzalez, Silvano
  20 Jan. 1944–30 Nov. 1946
Sousa, Mario
  1 Dec. 1946–30 Nov. 1952
Villasenor Luquin, Castulo
  1 Dec. 1952–30 Nov. 1958
Barrios, Roberto
  1 Dec. 1958–30 Nov. 1964
Aguirre Palancares, Norberto
  1 Dec. 1964–30 Nov. 1970
Gomez Villanueva, Augusto
  1 Dec. 1970–26 Sept. 1975
Barra Garcia, Felix
  27 Sept. 1975–30 Nov. 1976
Rojo Lugo, Jorge
  1 Dec. 1976–8 June 1978
Toledo Corro, Antonio
  9 June 1978–28 Apr. 1980
Garcia Paniagua, Javier
  29 Apr. 1980–

Secretary General (1935–75)

Villafuerte, Clicerio
  1935–40
Teusser, Salvador
  1940–46
Gandara Machorro, Manuel J.
  Dec. 1946–1950
Villasenor Luquin, Castulo
  1950–30 Nov. 1952
Lopez Bermudez, Jose
  1 Dec. 1952–1955
Carranza Hernandez, Rafael
  1955–30 Nov. 1958
Noguera Vergara, Arcadio
  1 Dec. 1958–30 Nov. 1964
Alcerreca Garcia Pena, Luis G.
  1 Dec. 1964–30 Nov. 1970
Torres Ramirez, Victor M.
  1 Dec. 1970–30 Nov. 1976

Secretary General of Colonization (1958–64)

Lopez Serrano, Francisco
  1958–30 Nov. 1964

Secretary General of the New Ejido Population Centers (1964)

Franco Bencomo, Joaquin
  1 Dec. 1964–30 Nov. 1970
Chavez Padron de Velazquez, Marta
  1 Dec. 1970–Apr. 1976
Vazquez Colmenares, Pedro
  Apr. 1976–30 Nov. 1976
Mora, Prudencio
  1 Dec. 1976–18 June 1978
Armienta Calderon, Gonzalo
  19 June 1978–

Secretary General of Legal Affairs (1971–75)

Canudas Orezza, Luis Felipe
  1971–75

Secretary General of Organization and Ejido Development (1971–76)

Reyes Osorio, Sergio
  1971–30 Nov. 1976

Secretary General of Agrarian Development (1975)

Garza Gonzalez, Manuel
1 Dec. 1976–31 July 1978

Subsecretary of Agrarian Action (1975)

Osorio Marban, Miguel
1 Dec. 1976–18 June 1978
Galvan Bouver, Ferrer
19 June 1978–

Oficial Mayor

Vazquez Perez, Francisco
1935
Teusser, Salvador
1936–40
Valero, Pedro S.
1940–46
Mendieta y Nunez, Lucio
1946–48
Fernandez Albarran, Juan
1948–52

Garizurieta, Cesar
1952–58
Badillo Garcia, Roman
1958–64
Varela, Everardo G.
1964–70
Esparza Reyes, Jose R.
1970–74
del Campo, Gustavo Martin
1976–

Department of the Federal District

Head

Hinojosa, Cosme
18 June 1935–3 Jan. 1938
Siurob, Jose
4 Jan. 1938–23 Jan. 1939
Castellano, Raul
24 Jan. 1939–30 Nov. 1940
Rojo Gomez, Javier
1 Dec. 1940–30 Nov. 1946
Casas Aleman, Fernando
1 Dec. 1946–30 Nov. 1952
Uruchurtu, Ernesto P.
1 Dec. 1952–14 Sept. 1966
Corona del Rosal, Alfonso
21 Sept. 1966–30 Nov. 1970
Martinez Dominguez, Alfonso
1 Dec. 1970–14 June 1971
Senties, Octavio
15 June 1971–30 Nov. 1976
Hank Gonzalez, Carlos
1 Dec. 1976–

Secretary of Government (Secretary General 1935–73)

Villalobos Mayar, Antonio
1935–19 June 1937
Priani, Alfonso
1937–39
Garcia Garcia, Luis
1939–30 Nov. 1940
Sanchez, Antonio
1 Dec. 1940–30 Nov. 1946
Carrillo Marcos, Alejandro
1 Dec. 1946–30 Nov. 1952

Candano y Garcia de la Mata, Jose
1 Dec. 1952–54
Quirasco, Antonio M.
4 June 1954–2 June 1956
Garcia Torres, Arturo
16 Oct. 1956–23 Sept. 1966
Gonzalez Guevara, Rodolfo
24 Sept. 1966–30 Nov. 1970
Hernandez, Octavio A.
1 Dec. 1970–17 May 1979
Gurria Ordonez, Manuel
30 May 1979–

Secretary of Works and Services (Secretary General "C," 1970–73)

Reta Martinez, Carlos
1 Dec. 1970–Jan. 1973
Rios Elizondo, Roberto
Jan. 1973–30 Nov. 1976
Gomez de Orozco, Alfonso
1 Dec. 1976–2 Jan. 1978
Valenzuela, Gilberto
2 Jan. 1978–27 Mar. 1979
Santa Ana, Cuauhtemoc
28 Mar. 1979–

Secretary General (B) 1970–73; 1978

Gonzalez Blanco Garrido, Jose P.
1 Dec. 1970–73
Gurria Ordonez, Manuel
1978–29 May 1979
Mondragon Hidalgo, Gustavo
30 May 1979–

Secretary General (D) 1970–73

Rios Elizondo, Roberto
1 Dec. 1970–73

Oficial Mayor

Ruiz Cortines, Adolfo
1935–37
Gonzalez Villarreal, Marciano
1937–38
Gonzalez Herrejon, Carlos
1940–46
Gonzalez Cardenas, Antonio
1946–52
Lopez Arias, Fernando
1952
Garcia Torres, Arturo
1952–55
Aguilar Velasco, Fernando
1958–64
Coudurier, Luis
1964–66
Lerdo de Tejada, Guillermo
1966–70
Vista Altamirano, Fluvio
1970–71
Zorilla Martinez, Pedro
1971–72
Vega Alvarado, Renato
1972–75
Jimenez San Pedro, Manuel
1975–76
Garduno Villavicencio, Jesus
1976–

Department of Fishing (1977)

Head

Rafful Miguel, Fernando
1 Jan. 1977–

Department of Health (1930–43)

Head

Siurob, Jose
19 June 1935–4 Jan. 1938

Andreu Almazan, Leonides
17 Jan. 1938– 4 Aug. 1939
Siurob, Jose
5 Aug. 1939–30 Nov. 1940

Fernandez Manero, Victor
1 Dec. 1940–15 Oct. 1943

Secretariat of Tourism
(Department of Tourism, 1959–75)

Secretary

Garcia Gonzalez, Alfonso
1 Jan. 1959–2 Dec. 1961
Aguilar, Manuel
2 Dec. 1961–6 July 1962
Gonzalez de la Vega, Francisco
7 July 1962–30 Nov. 1964
Salvat Rodriguez, Agustin
1 Dec. 1964–30 Nov. 1970
Olachea Borbon, Agustin
1 Dec. 1970–2 Nov. 1973
Hirschfield Almada, Julio
3 Nov. 1973–30 Nov. 1976
Rossell de la Lama, Guillermo
1 Dec. 1976–13 Aug. 1980

Alegria Escamilla, Rosa*
14 Aug. 1980–

**Secretary General
(1959–76)**

Sanchez Juarez, Delfin
1959–60
Aguilar, Manuel
1961
Corrales Ayala, Rafael
1962–64
De la Huerta Oriol, Adolfo
Dec. 1964–74
De la Torre Padilla, Oscar
1974–30 Nov. 1976

**Subsecretary of Tourism
and Planning (1976)**

Enriquez Savignac, Antonio
1 Dec. 1976–Nov. 1977
Ortiz Salinas, Antonio
Nov. 1977–

**Subsecretary of Operations
(1976)**

Herrerias, Armando
1 Dec. 1976–

**Subsecretary of Development
(1979)**

de Santiago, Manuel
4 Apr. 1979–

Federal Electric Commission

Director General

Paez Urquidi, Alejandro
1946–52
Ramirez Ulloa, Carlos
1952–58

Moreno Torres, Manuel
1958–64
Martinez Dominguez, Guillermo
1 Dec. 1964–30 Nov. 1970
Villarreal Caravantes, Guillermo
1 Dec. 1970–8 Aug. 1972

Lopez Portillo, Jose
9 Aug. 1972–29 May 1973
Farrell, Arsenio
29 May 1973–30 Nov. 1976
Cervantes del Rio, Hugo
1 Dec. 1976–12 July 1980

Federal Highways and Bridges and Adjacent Entrances
and Exits (Federal Entry Roads)

Director General

Pedrero, Andres
1958–July 1959
Cervantes del Rio, Hugo
July 1959–May 1965

Patino, Ernesto
May 1965–Oct. 1965
Sanchez Teruel, Jorge
Oct. 1965–Dec. 1970

Bernal, Antonio
Dec. 1970–30 Nov. 1976
Calderon, Hector M.
1 Dec. 1976–

---

*First woman to reach cabinet rank in Mexico.

Institute of Insurance and Social Services for Federal Employees (1959) (Director General of Pensions and Retirement, 1925–58)

Director

Liekens, Enrique
1935–40
Manrique de Lara Hernandez, A.
1940–45
Gamboa, Rafael P.
1945–46

Garcia de Alba, Esteban
1946–52
Pizarro Suarez, Nicolas
1952–64
Sanchez Mireles, Romulo
1964–70
Robledo Santiago, Edgar
1970–75

Sanchez Vazquez, Salvador
1975–76
Jongitud Barrios, Carlos
1976–79
Sansores Perez, Carlos
1979–

Mexican Institute of Social Security (1943)

Director General

Santos Guajardo, Vicente
19 Jan. 1943–1 Jan. 1944
Garcia Tellez, Ignacio
1 Jan. 1944–30 Nov. 1946
Diaz Lombardo, Antonio
1 Dec. 1946–30 Nov. 1952
Ortiz Mena, Antonio
1 Dec. 1952–30 Nov. 1958
Coquet Laguna, Benito
1 Dec. 1958–30 Nov. 1964
Alatriste, Sealtiel
1 Dec. 1964–25 Jan. 1966

Morones Prieto, Ignacio
26 Jan. 1966–30 Nov. 1970
Galvez Betancourt, Carlos
1 Dec. 1970–26 Sept. 1975
Reyes Heroles, Jesus
27 Sept. 1975–30 Nov. 1976
Farrell, Arsenio
1 Dec. 1976–

Secretary General

Garcia Cruz, Miguel
22 Jan. 1943–21 Dec. 1958
Orozco Uruchurtu, Jose Manuel
22 Dec. 1958–4 Jan. 1965

Alvarez del Castillo, Enrique
5 Jan. 1965–25 Apr. 1966
Munoz Ledo, Porfirio
26 Apr. 1966–1 Dec. 1970
Vizcaino Murray, Francisco
2 Dec. 1970–13 Dec. 1970
Rios Elizondo, Roberto
14 Dec. 1970–26 Sept. 1971
Lopez Faudoa, Eduardo
27 Sept. 1971–7 Dec. 1976
Zertuche Munoz, Fernando
8 Dec. 1976–

Mexican Petroleum Company (Petroleos Mexicanos) (1938)

Director General

Cortes Herrera, Vicente
1938–40
Buenrostro Ochoa, Efrain
Dec. 1940–Nov. 1946
Bermudez, Antonio J.
Dec. 1946–Nov. 1958
Gutierrez Roldan, Pascual
Dec. 1958–Nov. 1964
Reyes Heroles, Jesus
Dec. 1964–Nov. 1970
Dovali Jaime, Antonio
Dec. 1970–Nov. 1976
Diaz Serrano, Jorge
Dec. 1976–

Subdirector of Production

Amor, Antonio M.
1940–48

Colomo Corral, Jose
1950–69
Iguanzo–Suarez, Francisco
1970–76
Lastra Andrade, Adolfo
1976–

Subdirector of Administration

Sanchez Cuen, Manuel
1940–46
Serrano Castro, Julio
1946–50
Gray, Juan
1950–52
Balboa, Praxedis
1952–62
Diaz de Leon, Octavio
1963–65

Benhumea, Sergio L.
1966–70
Carrillo Duran, Ricardo
1970–76
Orozco Sosa, Carlos
1976–

Subdirector of Finances

Padilla, Fernando
1955–65
Barros Sierra, Manuel
1965–67
Zorrilla de la Garza, Carlos
1968–70
De la Madrid, Miguel
1970–72
Navarrete, Alfredo
4 May 1972–1976
Ruiz de la Pena, Francisco
1976–

National Bank of Foreign Commerce (1937)

Director General

Lopez, Roberto
16 May 1937–20 Jan. 1950
Parra Hernandez, Enrique
21 Jan. 1950–8 Dec. 1952
Zevada, Ricardo Jose
9 Dec. 1952–1 Feb. 1965
Armendariz, Antonio
2 Feb. 1965–11 Dec. 1970

Alcala Quintero, Francisco
12 Dec. 1970–26 Apr. 1979
Lajou- Martinez, Adrian
1979–

Subdirector General

Flores, Enrique J.
1 June 1937–30 Sept. 1939
Mendiola Miranda, Carlos C.
1 July 1940–15 May 1942

Mendiola Miranda, Mario
27 July 1942–15 Aug. 1953
Alcala Quintero, Francisco
16 Aug. 1953–15 Jan. 1964
Calderon Martinez, Antonio
21 July 1964–11 Dec. 1970
Bravo Silva, Jose
11 Dec. 1970–

National Company of Public Commodities CONASUPO
(National Distributor and Regulator, 1941;
Mexican Export–Import Company, 1949)

Director General

Trejo, Amado J.
1941–Aug. 1943
Ortiz Garza, Nazario S.
1943–46
Cinta, Carlos M.
1947
Ampudia, Eduardo
1950–52

Valles Vivar, Tomas
Dec. 1952–10 Mar. 1956
Vivanco, Jose S.
13 Mar. 1956–1958
Rodriguez Adame, Julian
1958
Amoros Guiot, Roberto
1 Dec. 1958–30 Nov. 1964
Hank Gonzalez, Carlos
1 Dec. 1964–1969

Mondragon Hidalgo, Gustavo
1969–30 Nov. 1970
De la Vega Dominguez, Jorge
1970–11 Feb. 1976
Diaz Ballesteros, Enrique
12 Feb. 1976–30 Nov. 1976
Gonzalez Cosio, Manuel
1 Dec. 1976–3 May 1979
Diaz Ballesteros, Enrique
4 May 1979–

National Finance Bank (Nacional Financiera)

Director General

Mesa Andraca, Manuel
1935–36
Espinosa de los Monteros, Antonio
1936–45
Carrillo Flores, Antonio
1945–52
Hernandez Delgado, Jose
1 Dec. 1952–30 Nov. 1970
Martinez Dominguez, Guillermo
Dec. 1970–11 Jan. 1974

Romero Kolbeck, Gustavo
11 Jan. 1974–30 Nov. 1976
Ibarra, David
1 Dec. 1976–17 Nov. 1977
Espinosa de los Reyes, Jorge
23 Nov. 1977–

Subdirector 1

Sarro, Enrique
25 Feb. 1941–15 Nov. 1945
Martinez Ostos, Raul
16 Nov. 1945–1 May 1946

Saldana Villalba, Adalberto
1 May 1946–52
Martinez Ostos, Raul
1952–8 Feb. 1965
Diaz Arias, Julian
8 Feb. 1965–May 1972
Puente Leyva, Jesus
May 1972–1976
Ibarra, David
1976–30 Nov. 1976

National Railroads of Mexico (1941)

General Manager

Hernandez, Pablo Mario
1941–2 Jan. 1941
Estrada, Enrique
3 Jan. 1941–3 Nov. 1942
Ramirez, Margarito
4 Nov. 1942–16 Feb. 1944

Ortiz, Andres
17 Feb. 1944–18 Jan. 1945
Hernandez, Pablo M.
6 Feb. 1945–30 Nov. 1946
Palacios, Manuel R.
1 Dec. 1946–30 Nov. 1952
Amoros, Roberto
1 Dec. 1952–30 Nov. 1958

Mendez Aguilar, Benjamin
1 Dec. 1958–30 Nov. 1964
Sandoval Rodriguez, Eufrasio
1 Dec. 1964–30 Nov. 1970
Villasenor, Victor Manuel
1 Dec. 1970–7 May 1973
Gomez Zepeda, Luis
7 May 1973–

National Steel Industry (Altos Hornos de Mexico, 1946–78)

Director General

Sarro Tresarrieu, Enrique
1 Dec. 1946–30 Nov. 1952
Gutierrez Roldan, Pascual
1 Dec. 1952–30 Nov. 1958

Bay Salido, Tomas
1 Dec. 1958–30 Nov. 1970
Padilla Segura, Antonio
1 Dec. 1970–29 Jan. 1978

General Manager

Pape, Harold R.
1944–70

Private Secretary to the President

Private Secretary

Rodriguez, Luis I.
1935–37
Garcia Tellez, Ignacio
1937–38
Castellano Jimenez, Raul
3 Jan. 1938–24 Jan. 1939
Lenero, Agustin
1939–40

Gonzalez Gallo, J. Jesus
1940–46
Viesca y Palma, Jorge
1946–52
Olmos, Salvador
1952–58
Romero Perez, Humberto
1958–64
Cisneros, Joaquin
1964–70

Ovalle Fernandez, Ignacio
1970–13 Nov. 1972
Bremer Martino, Juan Jose
14 Nov. 1972–4 Oct. 1975
Gil Elorduy, Ernesto
4 Oct. 1975–30 Nov. 1976
Velasco Ibarra, Enrique
30 Nov. 1976–1978
Casillas, Roberto
1978–

Secretariat of Agriculture and Hydraulic Resources (Secretariat of Agriculture and Livestock, 1946–76; Agriculture and Development, 1917–46)

Secretary

Cedillo, Saturnino
11 June 1935–16 Aug. 1937
Parres, Jose A.
16 Aug. 1937–30 Nov. 1940
Gomez, Marte R.
1 Dec. 1940–30 Nov. 1946
Ortiz Garza, Nazario
1 Dec. 1946–30 Nov. 1952
Flores Munoz, Gilberto
1 Dec. 1952–30 Nov. 1958
Rodriguez Adame, Julian
1 Dec. 1958–30 Nov. 1964
Gil Preciado, Juan
1 Dec. 1964–30 Nov. 1970
Aguirre, Manuel Bernardo
1 Dec. 1970–2 Jan. 1974
Brauer Herrera, Oscar
2 Jan. 1974–30 Nov. 1976
Merino Rabago, Francisco
1 Dec. 1976–

Subsecretary of Agriculture

Parres, Jose A.
1 Dec. 1934*–16 Aug. 1937
Foglio Miramontes, Fernando
16 Aug. 1934–1940
Vazquez del Mercado, Francisco
30 Jan. 1940–30 Nov. 1940
Gonzalez Gallardo, Alfonso
1 Dec. 1940–30 Nov. 1946
Merino Fernandez, Jesus
1 Dec. 1946–1954
Patino Navarrete, Jesus
1 Dec. 1958–30 Nov. 1964
Acosta Velasco, Ricardo
1 Dec. 1964–30 Nov. 1970
Ramirez Genel, Marcos
1 Dec. 1970–Oct. 1972
Brauer Herrera, Oscar
Oct. 1972–2 Jan. 1974
Martinez Medina, Lorenzo
2 Jan. 1974–30 Nov. 1976
Ortega, Benjamin
1 Dec. 1976–

Subsecretary of Livestock

Liera B., Guillermo
1 Dec. 1940–30 Nov. 1946
Flores Sanchez, Oscar
1 Dec. 1946–30 Nov. 1952
Ortega Martinez, Lauro
1 Dec. 1952–30 Nov. 1958
Mercado Garcia, Daniel
1 Dec. 1958–30 Nov. 1964
Valdes Ornelas, Oscar
1 Dec. 1964–14 Sept. 1965
Guzman Willis, Manuel
14 Sept. 1965–30 Nov. 1970
Telleache Merino, Ramon
1 Dec. 1970–22 Feb. 1972
Reta Petterson, Gustavo A.
23 Feb. 1972–26 June 1975
Zierold Reyes, Pablo
27 June 1975–30 Nov. 1976
Fernandez Gomez, Ruben
1 Dec. 1976–

---

*Most subsecretaries joining a new presidential administration are appointed in the middle of December, although the government often uses the December 1 date as the official point of tenure.

Subsecretary of Forest Resources and Fauna

Castro Estrada, Jose
  1951–31 Nov. 1951
Hinojosa Ortiz, Manuel
  1 Dec. 1952–30 Nov. 1958
Beltran Castillo, Enrique
  1 Dec. 1958–30 Nov. 1964
Palomares Navarro, Noe
  1 Dec. 1964–30 Nov. 1970
De la Garza Ollervides, Eulogio
  1 Dec. 1970–8 June 1972
Vazquez Soto, Jesus
  9 June 1972–30 Nov. 1976
Cardenas, Cuauhtemoc
  1 Dec. 1976–1 Mar. 1980
Villa Salas, Avelino B.
  10 Mar. 1980–

Subsecretary of Hydraulic Infrastructure (1977)

Villarreal Guerra, Americo
  1977–

Subsecretary of Hydraulic Planning (1977)

Cruickshank Garcia, Gerardo
  1977–9 Mar. 1980
Highland Gomez, Mario
  10 Mar. 1980–

Oficial Mayor

Castillo, Epifano
  1935–37
Florencio, Antonio
  1937–39
Liera, Guillermo
  1940

Gomez, Andres E.
  1946–51
Barrera Fuentes, Florencio
  1951–52
Gomez, Andres E.
  1952–58
Uranga Prado, Esteban
  1958–64
Palomares, Noe
  1964
Sanchez de Velasco, Abraham
  1964–70
Perez Vela, Juan
  1970–72
Barraza Allende, Luciano
  1972
Bucio Alanis, Lauro
  1972–76
Highland Gomez, Mario
  1976–80
Rocha Bandala, Juan F.
  1980–

Secretariat of Communications and Transportation (1959)

Secretary

Buchanan, Walter Cross
  1 Jan. 1959–30 Nov. 1964
Padilla Segura, Jose A.
  1 Dec. 1964–30 Nov. 1970
Mendez Docurro, Eugenio
  1 Dec. 1970–30 Nov. 1976
Mujica Montoya, Emilio
  1 Dec. 1976–

Subsecretary

Ramirez Caraza, Juan Manuel
  1 Jan. 1959–30 Nov. 1964

Mendez Docurro, Eugenio
  Dec. 1964–30 Nov. 1970
Barrientos, Javier A.
  1 Dec. 1970–30 Nov. 1976
Barbarena, Miguel A.
  1 Dec. 1976–

Subsecretary of Broadcasting (1970)

Herrera, Enrique
  1 Dec. 1970–Oct. 1972
Alvarez Acosta, Miguel
  Oct. 1972–30 Nov. 1976

Velarde Bonnin, Jose Juan
  1 Dec. 1976–

Oficial Mayor

Medina Urbizo, Eduardo
  1959–64
Fabela, Ramon
  1964–70
Perez Abreu Jimenez, Juan
  1970–73
Bobadilla Pena, Julio
  1973–76
Altamirano Calderon, Carlos
  1976–

Secretariat of Foreign Relations

Secretary

Gonzalez Roa, Fernando
  17 June 1935–18 June 1935
Ceniceros, Jose Angel
  18 June 1935–30 Nov. 1935
Hay, Eduardo
  30 Nov. 1935–30 Nov. 1940
Padilla, Ezequiel
  1 Dec. 1940–10 July 1945
Tello, Manuel
  10 July 1945–31 Aug. 1945

Castillo Najera, Francisco
  1 Sept. 1945–30 Nov. 1946
Torres Bodet, Jaime
  1 Dec. 1946–24 Nov. 1948
Tello, Manuel
  24 Nov. 1948–30 Nov. 1952
Padilla Nervo, Luis
  1 Dec. 1952–30 Nov. 1958
Tello, Manuel
  1 Dec. 1958–30 Mar. 1964
Gorostiza, Jose
  30 Mar. 1964–30 Nov. 1964

Carrillo Flores, Antonio
  1 Dec. 1964–30 Nov. 1970
Rabasa, Emilio O.
  1 Dec. 1970–28 Dec. 1975
Garcia Robles, Alfonso
  29 Dec. 1975–30 Nov. 1976
Roel, Santiago
  1 Dec. 1976–16 May 1979
Castaneda, Jorge
  16 May 1979–

Subsecretary (Bilateral Affairs) (A)

Ceniceros, Jose
16 June 1935–30 Apr. 1936
Beteta, Ramon
12 May 1936–30 Nov. 1940
Torres Bodet, Jaime
1 Dec. 1940–31 Dec. 1943
Santos Guajardo, Vicente
3 Jan. 1944–June 1944
Tello, Manuel
1 July 1944–30 Nov. 1951
Guerra, Alfonso
30 Nov. 1951–1 July 1953
Gorostiza, Jose
1 July 1953–30 Nov. 1964
Fraga Magana, Gabino
1 Dec. 1964–30 Nov. 1970
Gonzalez Sosa, Ruben
1 Dec. 1970–30 Nov. 1976
de Olloqui, Jose Juan
1 Dec. 1976–June 1979
Tello Macias, Manuel
22 June 1979–

Secretary

Barba Gonzalez, Silvano
8 June 1935–24 Aug. 1936
Guerrero, Silvestre
25 Aug. 1936–31 Dec. 1937
Garcia Tellez, Ignacio
4 Jan. 1938–30 Nov. 1940
Aleman, Miguel
1 Dec. 1940–17 June 1945
Villa Michel, Primo
18 June 1945– 30 Nov. 1946
Perez Martinez, Hector
1 Dec. 1946–13 Feb. 1948
Uruchurtu, Ernesto P.
13 Feb. 1948–29 June 1948
Ruiz Cortines, Adolfo
30 June 1948–12 Oct. 1951
Uruchurtu, Ernesto P.
13 Oct. 1951–30 Nov. 1952
Carvajal, Angel
1 Dec. 1952–30 Nov. 1958
Diaz Ordaz, Gustavo
1 Dec. 1958–18 Nov. 1963
Echeverria Alvarez, Luis
19 Nov. 1963–10 Nov. 1969
Moya Palencia, Mario
11 Nov. 1969–30 Nov. 1976

Subsecretary of Multilateral and Cultural Affairs (B)

Campos Ortiz, Pablo
1 June 1960–1 Apr. 1964
Garcia Robles, Alfonso
1 Apr. 1964–30 Nov. 1970
Gallastegui, Jose S.
1 Dec. 1970–30 Nov. 1976
de Rosenzweig, Alfonso de
1 Dec. 1976–

Subsecretary of Special Studies and International Affairs (C) (1976)

Castaneda, Jorge
12 Jan. 1976–30 Nov. 1976
Tellez Benoit, Maria
1 Dec. 1976–

Subsecretary (D) (1978)

Sanchez Meza de Solis, Guillermina
1978–June, 1979
Navarrete, Jorge Eduardo
June, 1979–

Secretariat of Government

Reyes Heroles, Jesus
1 Dec. 1976–16 May 1979
Olivares Santana, Enrique
17 May 1979–

Subsecretary

Arroyo Ch., Agustin
12 Sept. 1935–4 Jan. 1938
Santos Guajardo, Vicente
4 Jan. 1938–30 Nov. 1940
Casas Aleman, Fernando
1 Dec. 1940–17 June 1945
Perez Martinez, Hector
18 June 1945–30 Nov. 1946
Uruchurtu, Ernesto P.
1 Dec. 1946–30 Nov. 1952
Ortiz Tirado, Jose Maria
1 Dec. 1952–5 Feb. 1953
Roman Lugo, Fernando
6 Feb. 1953–30 Nov. 1958
Echeverria Alvarez, Luis
1 Dec. 1958–15 Nov. 1963
Hernandez Ochoa, Rafael
1 Dec. 1964–30 Nov. 1970
Gutierrez Barrios, Fernando
1 Dec. 1970–

Oficial Mayor

Sierra, Manuel J.
1935–36
Hidalgo, Ernesto
1936–42
Campos Ortiz, Pablo
1944–46
Guerra, Alfonso
1946–51
Lelo de Larrea, Jose
1951–52
Campos Ortiz, Pablo
1952–57
Dario Ojeda, Carlos
1957–64
Gallastegui, Jose
1965–70
Tellez Benoit, Maria
1970–76
Sanchez Meza de Solis, Guillermina
1976–78
Garza Plaza, Adrian
1978–79
Gonzalez Martinez, Aida
1979–

Subsecretary 2 (1958)

Galvez Betancourt, Carlos
30 Nov. 1964–68
Moya Palencia, Mario
1 July 1969–10 Nov. 1969
Biebrich Torres, Carlos
1 Dec. 1970–22 Dec. 1972
Garcia Ramirez, Sergio
30 Apr. 1973–30 Nov. 1976
Echeverria, Rodolfo
1 Dec. 1976–14 Aug. 1978
Lamadrid, Jose Luis
15 Aug. 1978–21 May 1979
Gonzalez Guevara, Rodolfo
22 May 1979–

Subsecretary 3 (1978)

Garcia Paniagua, Javier
15 Aug. 1978–29 Apr. 1980

Oficial Mayor

Barba Gonzalez, Silvano
1934–35
Garcia de Alba, Esteban
1935–40
Ruiz Cortines, Adolfo
1940–44

Secretariat of Government—Oficial Mayor (cont.)

Villa Michel, Primo
1944–45
Guzman Araujo, Roberto
1945–46
Coquet Laguna, Benito
1946
Teran Zozaya, Horacio
1946–51
Rodriguez Cano, Enrique
1951–52

Roman Lugo, Fernando
1952–53
Diaz Ordaz, Gustavo
1953–58
Palomares Navarro, Noe
1958–64
Galvez Betancourt, Carlos
1964–65
Murillo Vidal, Rafael
1965–68

Heredia Ferraez, Jorge
1968–70
Ibarra Herrera, Manuel
1970–76
Lamadrid, Jose Luis
1976–78
Vazquez Torres, Ignacio
1978–79
Hernandez Gomez, Tulio
1979–80

Secretariat of Property and Industrial Development
(Secretariat of Government Properties, 1947–77)

Secretary

Caso, Alfonso
1 Jan. 1947–9 Jan. 1949
Rangel Couto, Hugo
9 Jan. 1949–1 Aug. 1951
Carvajal, Angel
1 Aug. 1951–30 Nov. 1952
Lopez Lira, Jose
1 Dec. 1952–30 Nov. 1958
Bustamante, Eduardo
1 Dec. 1958–30 Nov. 1964
Corona del Rosal, Alfonso
1 Dec. 1964–15 Sept. 1966
Franco Lopez, Manuel
21 Sept. 1966–30 Nov. 1970
Flores de la Pena, Horacio
1 Dec. 1970–2 Jan. 1975
Alejo, Javier
3 Jan. 1975–30 Nov. 1976
Oteyza, Jose Andres
1 Dec. 1976–

Subsecretary of State Industry
(Subsecretary, 1947–77)

Carvajal, Angel
1947
Rangel Couto, Hugo
1947–30 Nov. 1952
Lopez Arias, Fernando
Dec. 1952–53
Barocio Barrios, Alberto
1953–30 Nov. 1958
Alatriste, Sealtiel
1 Dec. 1958–30 Nov. 1964

Gonzalez Guevara, Rodolfo
1 Dec. 1964–23 Sept. 1966
Langle Martinez, Eduardo
1966–68
De la Torre Grajales, Abelardo
1968–30 Nov. 1970
Lopez Portillo, Jose
1 Dec. 1970–9 Aug. 1972
Garcia Ramirez, Sergio
9 Aug. 1972–30 Apr. 1973
Rafful Miguel, Fernando
30 Apr. 1973–Mar. 1976
Cebreros, Alfonso
Mar. 1976–30 Nov. 1976
Garcia Sainz, Ricardo
1 Dec. 1976–16 Nov. 1977
Hiriart Balderrama, Fernando
23 Nov. 1977–28 Jan. 1978
Garcia Ramirez, Sergio
29 Jan. 1978–

Subsecretary of Nonrenewable Resources (1958–78)

Franco Lopez, Manuel
1 Dec. 1964–21 Sept. 1966
De la Pena Porth, Luis
1 Dec. 1970–2 Mar. 1973
Leipen Garay, Jorge
5 Mar. 1973–29 Jan. 1978

Subsecretary of Real Property and Urbanization (1958–76)

Rossell de la Lama, Guillermo
1959–30 Nov. 1964

Medellin, Jorge L.
1 Dec. 1964–30 Nov. 1970
Moctezuma Diaz Infante, Pedro
1 Dec. 1970–30 Nov. 1976

Subsecretary of Mines and Energy (1978)

Balderrama, Hiriart
30 Jan. 1978–

Oficial Mayor

Lazo, Carlos
1947–49
Silva, Leonardo
1949–52
Lopez Arias, Fernando
1952–53
Gomez Esparza, Jose
1953–58
Rossell de la Lama, Guillermo
1958–59
Orozco Gonzalez, Juan
1959–64
de la Torre Grajales, Abelardo
1964–68
Verges X., Juan Victor
1968–70
Guzman Bracho, Roberto
1970–75
Sordi Sodi, Antonio
1976–

Secretariat of Health and Welfare (1938)

Secretary

Hernandez Alvarez, Enrique
3 Jan. 1938–2 Nov. 1938
Guerrero, Silvestre
24 Jan. 1939–30 Nov. 1940
Baz, Gustavo
1 Dec. 1940–30 Nov. 1946
Gamboa, Rafael P.
1 Dec. 1946–30 Nov. 1952
Morones Prieto, Ignacio
1 Dec. 1952–30 Nov. 1958
Alvarez Amezquita, Jose
1 Dec. 1958–30 Nov. 1964
Moreno Valle, Rafael
1 Dec. 1964–15 Aug. 1968
Aceves Parra, Salvador
17 Aug. 1968–30 Nov. 1970
Jimenez Cantu, Jorge
1 Dec. 1970–2 Mar. 1975
Navarro Diaz de Leon, Gines
2 Mar. 1975–30 Nov. 1976
Martinez Manatou, Emilio
1 Dec. 1976–4 June 1980
Calles, Mario
5 June 1980–

Subsecretary (1938–58)

Zubiran, Salvador
1938–43 (in charge 1938–39)
Martinez Baez, Manuel
18 Oct. 1943–1 Mar. 1946
Mondragon Guerra, Salvador
Mar. 1946–30 Nov. 1946
Morones Prieto, Ignacio
1 Dec. 1946–31 Dec. 1947

Argil Camacho, Gustavo
1 Jan. 1948–30 Nov. 1952
Pesqueira y D'endara, Manuel E.
1 Dec. 1952–30 Nov. 1958

Subsecretary of Assistance (1958)

Castro Villagrana, Jose
1 Dec. 1958–27 Jan.1960
Zuckermann, Conrado
1 Mar. 1960–30 Nov. 1964
Aceves Parra, Salvador
1 Dec. 1964–21 Oct. 1968
Loyo Diaz, Mauro
21 Nov. 1968–30 Nov. 1970
Campillo Sainz, Carlos
1 Dec. 1970–30 Nov. 1976
Gual Castro, Carlos
1 Dec. 1976–3 July 1980

Subsecretary of Health (1959)

Bustamante, Miguel
1959–30 Nov. 1964
Martinez Garcia, Pedro D.
1 Dec. 1964–30 Nov. 1970
Guzman Orozco, Renaldo
1 Dec. 1970–30 Nov. 1976
Calles, Mario
1 Dec. 1976–4 June 1980

Subsecretary of the Environment (1972)

Torres H., Marco Aurelio
20 Jan. 1972–25 Jan. 1972

Vizcaino Murray, Francisco
26 Jan. 1972–30 Nov. 1976
Romero Alvarez, Humberto
1 Dec. 1976–3 July 1980
Lopez Portillo, Manuel
4 July 1980–

Oficial Mayor

Trevino, Julio Cesar
1935–37
Lopez Lira, Jose
1937–39
Mondragon, Octavio S.
1940–45
Pasquel Jimenez Unda, Leonardo
1945–46
Morones Prieto, Ignacio
1946
Argil Camacho, Gustavo
1946–48
Guzman, Jr., Saturnino
1949–52
Mayoral Pardo, Demetrio
1952–58
de la Riva Rodriguez, Javier
1958–64
Maldonado Perez, Caritino
1965–69
Lopez Faudoa, Eduardo
1970–71
Soto Prieto, Roberto
1971–76
Hernandez Rizo, Jose
1976–

Secretariat of Hydraulic Resources (1947–77)

Secretary

Orive Alba, Adolfo
1 Jan. 1947–30 Nov. 1952
Chavez, Eduardo
1 Dec. 1952–25 Apr. 1958
Echegaray Bablot, Luis
25 Apr. 1958–30 Nov. 1958
Del Mazo Velez, Alfredo
1 Dec. 1958–30 Nov. 1964
Hernandez Teran, Jose
1 Dec. 1964–30 Nov. 1970
Rovirosa Wade, Leandro
1 Dec. 1970–21 Aug. 1976

Robles Linares, Luis
22 Aug. 1976–31 Dec. 1976

Subsecretary (A) of Construction

Riquelme, Eugenio
1 Jan. 1947–30 Nov. 1952
Ehegaray Bablot, Luis
Dec. 1952–30 Nov. 1958
Colin Varela, Alfredo E.
Dec. 1958–30 Nov. 1964
Aguilar Chavez, Salvador
Dec. 1964–30 Nov. 1970

Robles Linares, Luis
Dec. 1970–31 Dec. 1976

Subsecretary (B) of Operations (1964–76)

Barnetche Gonzalez, Alberto
Dec. 1964–30 Nov. 1970
Amaya Brondo, Abelardo
Dec. 1970–30 Nov. 1976

Subsecretary of Planning (1970–76)

Cruickshank, Gerardo
Dec. 1970–30 Nov. 1976

Oficial Mayor

Cardenas Huerta, Gustavo
1947–52

Perez Moreno, Jose
1952–58
Castrejon y Chavez, Gustavo
1958–64

Ibarra, Guillermo
1964–70
Castanos Patoni, Fernando
1970–76

Secretariat of Commerce
(Secretariat of Industry and Commerce, 1958–76; National Economy, 1936–46; Economy, 1947–58)

Secretary

Sanchez Tapia, Rafael
18 June 1935–31 Dec. 1937
Buenrostro, Efrain
3 Jan. 1938–30 Nov. 1940
Gaxiola, Francisco
1 Dec. 1940–30 June 1944
Serrano, Gustavo
1 July 1944–30 Nov. 1946
Ruiz Galindo, Antonio
1 Dec. 1946–20 Oct. 1948
Martinez Baez, Antonio
21 Oct.1948–30 Nov. 1952
Loyo, Gilberto
1 Dec. 1952–30 Nov. 1958
Salinas Lozano, Raul
1 Dec. 1958–30 Nov. 1964
Campos Salas, Octaviano
1 Dec. 1964–30 Nov. 1970
Torres Manzo, Carlos
1 Dec. 1970–18 Jan. 1974
Campillo Sainz, Jose
18 Jan. 1974–30 Nov. 1976
Solana, Fernando
1 Dec. 1976–8 Dec. 1977
de la Vega Dominguez, Jorge
9 Dec. 1977–

Subsecretary (1935–76)

Santillan, Manuel
1935–36
Moctezuma, Mariano
1936–38
Sousa, Mario
1940–42
Rolland, Modesto C.
1942–30 Nov. 1946
Parra, Manuel German
1 Dec. 1946–7 June 1948
Sanchez Cuen, Manuel
23 Oct. 1948–30 Nov. 1952
Perez Duarte, Constantino
1 Dec. 1952–56

Segura y Gama, David
1956–30 Nov. 1958
Garcia Reynoso, Placido
1 Dec. 1958–30 Nov. 1970
Campillo Sainz, Jose
1 Dec. 1970–18 Jan. 1974
Becker Arreola, Juan G.
18 Jan. 1974–30 Nov. 1976

Subsecretary of Foreign Trade (Trade, 1959–76)

Diaz Arias, Julian
1959–Sept. 1961
Margain, Hugo B.
Sept. 1961–30 Nov. 1964
Cano Luebbert, Sergio
1 Dec. 1964–30 Nov. 1970
Mendoza Berrueto, Eliseo
1 Dec. 1970–23 Feb. 1976
Hernandez Cervantes, Hector
24 Feb. 1976–

Subsecretary of Fishing (1971–77)

Medina Neri, Hector
1971–30 Nov. 1976
Rafful Miguel, Fernando
1 Dec. 1976–77

Subsecretary of Commercial Planning (1976–78)

Solis, Leopoldo
1 Dec. 1976–1977
Diaz Ballesteros, Enrique
1 Jan. 1978–1 Dec. 1978

Subsecretary of Regulation and Foodstuffs (1978)

Diaz Ballesteros, Enrique
1 Dec. 1978–3 May 1979

Perez Jacome, Dionisio E.
23 May 1979–

Subsecretary of Internal Trade (1976)

Tamayo, Jorge
1 Dec. 1976–

Oficial Mayor

Padilla, Guillermo C.
1935–36
Sanchez Cuen, Miguel
1936–37
Bernard, Miguel
1937–38
Sanchez Cuen, Manuel
1939–40
Cebada, Manuel J.
1940–41
Avila Camacho, Rafael
1942–46
Munoz Turnball, Marco
1946–49
Marquez Padilla, Tarciscio
1949–52
Torres Gaitan, Ricardo
1952–58
Diaz Arias, Julian
1958–59
Margain, Hugo B.
1959–61
Rodriguez Gomez, Francisco
1964–70
Fabre del Rivero, Carlos
1970–76
Duahlt Kraus, Miguel
1976–

Secretariat of Labor and Social Welfare

Secretary

Vazquez, Genaro
8 June 1935–18 June 1937
Villalobos, Antonio
19 June 1937–21 Jan. 194
Arroyo Ch., Agustin
21 Jan. 1940–30 Nov. 1940
Garcia Tellez, Ignacio
1 Dec. 1940–16 Jan. 1943
Palacios, Manuel R.
16 Jan. 1943–28 Feb. 1943
Trujillo Gurria, Francisco
1 Mar. 1943–30 Nov. 1946
Serra Rojas, Andres
1 Dec. 1946–30 Nov. 1952
Lopez Mateos, Adolfo
1 Dec. 1952–18 Nov. 1957
Gonzalez Blanco, Salomon
18 Nov. 1957–30 Nov. 1970
Hernandez Ochoa, Rafael
1 Dec. 1970–11 Sept. 1972
Munoz Ledo, Porfirio
12 Sept. 1972–26 Sept. 1975
Galvez Betancourt, Carlos
27 Sept. 1975–30 Nov. 1976
Ojeda Paullada, Pedro
1 Dec. 1976–

Subsecretary (1940)

Cantu Estrada, Jose
1935–37

Padilla, Florencio
1937–40
Santos Guajardo, Vicente
1940–Jan. 1943
Palacios, Manuel R.
1943–Apr. 1946
Serrano Castro, Julio
Apr. 1946–30 Nov. 1946
Ramirez Vazquez, Manuel
1 Dec. 1946–48
Canale Munoz, Eleazar
Oct. 1948–30 Nov. 1952
Gonzalez Blanco, Salomon
1 Dec. 1952–30 Nov. 1958
Santos Coy Perea, Julio
1 Dec. 1958–30 Nov. 1970
Llorente Gonzalez, Arturo
1 Dec. 1970–30 Nov. 1976
Carvajal, Gustavo
1 Dec. 1976–10 Aug. 1978
Echeverria, Rodolfo
15 Aug. 1978–

Subsecretary of Social Welfare

Canales Valverde, Tristan
Dec. 1964–30 Nov. 1970
Alanis Fuentes, Agustin
1 Dec. 1970–30 Nov. 1976
Gonzalez Lopez, Guillermo
1 Dec. 1976–

Oficial Mayor

Ortiz Armengol, Federico
1935–36
Olive, Issac
1937–39
Rivera Perez Campos, Jose
1940
Lanuza Araujo, Agustin
1940–46
Gonzalez Blanco, Salomon
1946–52
Quirasco, Antonio M.
1952–53
Aguirre Zertuche, Santiago
1953–58
Candiani, Guillermo
1958–61
Canales Valverde, Tristan
1961–64
Hori Robaina, Guillermo
1965–70
Zertuche Munoz, Fernando
1970–74
Uribe Castaneda, Manuel
1974–76
Suarez, Marcos Manuel
1976–78
Brastifer Hernandez, Gloria
1978–

Secretariat of National Defense

Secretary

Figueroa, Andres
18 June 1935–17 Oct. 1935
Avila Camacho, Manuel
17 Oct. 1935–17 Jan. 1939
Castro, Jesus Agustin
23 Jan. 1939–30 Nov. 1940
Macias Valenzuela, Pablo E.
1 Dec. 1940–11 Sept. 1942
Cardenas, Lazaro
11 Sept. 1942–27 Aug. 1945
Urquizo, Francisco
1 Sept. 1945–30 Nov. 1946
Limon, Gilberto R.
1 Dec. 1946–30 Nov. 1952
Ramos Santos, Matias
1 Dec. 1952–30 Nov. 1958
Olachea Aviles, Agustin
1 Dec. 1958–30 Nov. 1964

Garcia Barragan, Marcelino
1 Dec. 1964–30 Nov. 1970
Cuenca Diaz, Hermenegildo
1 Dec. 1970–30 Nov. 1976
Galvan Lopez, Felix
1 Dec. 1976–

Subsecretary

Avila Camacho, Manuel
1935–1 Nov. 1937
Corral, Blas
1 Jan. 1938–40
Urquizo, Francisco
1940–31 Aug. 1945
Limon, Gilberto R.
1 Sept. 1945–30 Nov. 1946
Gonzalez Lugo, Jesus
1 Dec. 1946–49

Calles Pordo, Aureo L.
1949–52
Guinart Lopez, Modesto A.
1 Dec. 1952–30 Nov. 1958
Flores Torres, Juan
1 Dec. 1958–30 Nov. 1964
Gastelum Salcido, Juan Jose
1 Dec. 1964–30 Nov. 1970
Gomar Suastegui, Jeronimo
1 Dec. 1970–21 Jan. 1972
Sandoval Castarrica, Enrique
1972–30 Nov. 1976
de la Fuente Rodriguez, Juan
1 Dec. 1976–1979
Portillo Jurado, Hector
1979–

Oficial Mayor

Avila Camacho, Manuel
1934–35
Corral Martinez, Blas
1936–37
Orozco Camacho, Miguel
1937–39
Gonzalez Villarreal, Marciano
1939–40
Montes Alanis, Federico
1940–40
Sanchez, J. Salvador
1940–41

Corral Martinez, Blas
1941–44
Ruiz Camarillo, Leobardo
1945–46
Cabrera Carrasquedo, Manuel
1946–48
Leyva Velazquez, Gabriel
1948–50
Lopez Sanchez, Arturo
1951–52
Corsen Leon, Adolfo E.
1952–53
Leyva Mancilla, Baltasar
1953–58

Pamanes Escobedo, Fernando
1958–64
Gurza Falfan, Alfonso
1965–65
Perez Ortiz, Basilio
1965–70
Corona Mendioroz, Arturo
1970–76
Ochoa Palencia, Arturo
1976–

Secretariat of the Navy (1940)

Secretary

Gomez Maqueo, Roberto
1 Jan. 1940–31 Dec. 1940
Jara, Heriberto
1 Jan. 1941–30 Nov. 1946
Schaufelberger, Luis F.
1 Dec. 1946–8 Oct. 1948
Coello, David
8 Oct. 1948–20 Oct. 1949
Pawling, Alberto J.
21 Oct. 1949–6 Feb. 1952
Lopez Sanchez, Raul
7 Feb. 1952–30 Nov. 1952
Sanchez Taboada, Rodolfo
1 Dec. 1952–1 May 1955
Poire Ruelas, Alfonso
2 May 1955–22 Dec. 1955
Gomez Maqueo, Roberto
23 Dec. 1955–2 Apr. 1958
Meixueiro Alexandre, Hector
7 Apr. 1958–30 Nov. 1958
Zermeno Araico, Manuel
1 Dec. 1958–30 Nov. 1964
Vazquez del Mercado, Antonio
1 Dec. 1964–30 Nov. 1970

Bravo Carrera, Luis
1 Dec. 1970–30 Nov. 1976
Chazaro Lara, Ricardo
1 Dec. 1976–

Subsecretary

Vazquez del Mercado, Antonio
1 Jan. 1940–30 Nov. 1940
Blanco, Othon P.
5 Dec. 1940–30 Nov. 1946
Schaufelberger, Luis F.
1 Dec. 1946–8 Oct. 1948
Pawling, Alberto J.
9 Oct. 1948–30 Nov. 1952
Poire Ruelas, Alfonso
1 Dec. 1952–30 Nov. 1958
Orozco Vela, Oliverio F.
1 Dec. 1958–30 Nov. 1964
Fritsche Anda, Oscar
1 Dec. 1964–2 July 1965
Aznar Zetina, Antonio J.
13 July 1965–30 Nov. 1970
Chazaro Lara, Ricardo
1 Dec. 1970–30 Nov. 1976
Montejo Sierra, Jose M.
1 Dec. 1976–

Oficial Mayor

Munoz Medina, Lorenzo
1935–40
Valencia, Roberto Laurencio
1940–46
Perez Zavala, Cuauhtemoc
1946
Coello Ochoa, David
1946–47
Lagos Beltran, Gabriel
1948–52
Montalvo Salazar, Gonzalo
1952–54
Meixueiro, Alexandre
1955–58
Luque Salanieva, Victor
1958
Otal Briseno, Rigoberto
1958–64
Castro y Castro, Fernando
1964–70
Cubria Palma, Jose Luis
1970–76
Artigas Fernandez, Mario
1976–

Secretariat of Programming and Budget
(Secretariat of the Presidencey, 1958–76; Confidential Secretary, 1946–58)

Secretary

Amoros, Roberto
July 1946–30 Nov. 1946
De la Selva, Rogerio
Dec. 1946–30 Nov. 1952
Rodriguez Cano, Enrique
1 Dec. 1952–55

Coquet Laguna, Benito
1956–30 Nov. 1958
Miranda Fonseca, Donato
1 Dec. 1958–30 Nov. 1964
Martinez Manautou, Emilio
1 Dec. 1964–30 Nov. 1970
Cervantes del Rio, Hugo
1 Dec. 1970–3 Oct. 1975

Ovalle Fernandez, Ignacio
4 Oct. 1975–30 Nov. 1976
Tello Macias, Carlos
1 Dec. 1976–16 Nov. 1977
Garcia Sainz, Ricardo
17 Nov. 1977–16 May 1979
De la Madrid, Miguel
17 May 1979–

Subsecretary of Evaluation (Subsecretary, 1948–76)

Amoros, Roberto
  1 Jan. 1948–13 Nov. 1951
Coquet, Benito
  1 Dec. 1952–56
Ortiz Mena, Raul
  1 Dec. 1958–61
Yanez, Agustin
  1961–64
Ortiz Mena, Raul
  15 Dec. 1964–6 Nov. 1968

Lopez Portillo, Jose
  Nov. 1968–30 Nov. 1970
Munoz Ledo, Porfirio
  1 Dec. 1970–14 Nov. 1972
Ovalle Fernandez, Ignacio
  14 Nov. 1972–4 Oct. 1975
Bremer, Juan J.
  4 Oct. 1975–30 Nov. 1976
Alegria Escamilla, Rosa
  1 Dec. 1976–13 Aug. 1980
Lopez Portillo, Jose Ramon
  18 Aug. 1980–

Subsecretary of Programming (Information, 1970–76)

Zapata Loredo, Fausto
  1970–25 Feb. 1976
Jimenez Lazcano, Mauro
  26 Feb. 1976–30 Nov. 1976
Pasquel Moncayo, Eduardo
  1 Dec. 1976–26 Jan. 1978
Cebreros Murillo, Alfonso
  26 Jan. 1978–

Secretariat of Public Education

Secretary

Vazquez Vela, Gonzalo
  18 June 1935–30 Nov. 1940
Sanchez Ponton, Luis
  1 Dec. 1940–11 Sept. 1941
Vejar Vazquez, Octavio
  12 Sept. 1941–20 Sept. 1943
Torres Bodet, Jaime
  22 Dec. 1943–30 Nov. 1946
Gual Vidal, Manuel
  1 Dec. 1946–30 Nov. 1952
Ceniceros, Jose A.
  1 Dec. 1952–30 Nov. 1958
Torres Bodet, Jaime
  1 Dec. 1958–30 Nov. 1964
Yanez, Agustin
  1 Dec. 1964–30 Nov. 1970
Bravo Ahuja, Victor
  1 Dec. 1970–30 Nov. 1976
Munoz Ledo, Porfirio
  1 Dec. 1976–8 Dec. 1977
Solana, Eduardo
  9 Dec. 1977–

Subsecretary General (1921–76)

Moctezuma, Mariano
  1934–35
Lucio Arguelles, Gabriel
  1935–36
Chavez Orozco, Luis
  1936–38
Nicodemo, Francisco
  1938–40
Arreguin, Enrique
  1 Dec. 1940–11 Sept. 1941
Bonilla Cortes, Roberto T.
  12 Sept. 1941–30 Dec. 1943

Sanchez Hernandez, Tomas
  31 Dec. 1943–30 Nov. 1946
Chavez, Leopoldo
  1 Dec. 1946–47
Merino Fernandez, Aaron
  7 Jan. 1948–30 Nov. 1952
Gomez Robleda, Jose
  1 Dec. 1952–54
Sandoval Vallarta, Manuel
  1954–30 Nov. 1958
Enriquez Coyro, Ernesto
  1 Dec. 1958–30 Nov. 1964
Berrueto Ramon, Federico
  1 Dec. 1964–30 Nov. 1970
Bonfil, Ramon G.
  1 Dec. 1970–30 Nov. 1976

Subsecretary of Education and Technical Investigation (Subsecretary of Intermediate, Technical and Higher Education, 1958–76)

Bravo Ahuja, Victor
  1958–68
Ortiz Macedo, Luis
  Feb. 1969–30 Nov. 1970
Mayagoitia Dominguez, Hector
  1 Dec. 1970–15 Mar. 1974
Uscanga Uscanga, Cesar
  15 Mar. 1974–28 Dec. 1977
Mendoza Berrueto, Eliseo
  2 Jan. 1978–Apr. 1978
Massieu Helguera, Guillermo
  Apr. 1978–June 1979
Carranza, Jose Antonio
  June 1979–

Subsecretary of Culture and Recreation (Subsecretary of Popular Culture and Educational Extension, 1976–78)

Flores Olea, Victor
  1 Dec. 1976–14 Nov. 1978
Diaz de Cossio, Roger
  15 Nov. 1978–

Subsecretary of Youth and Sports (1976–78)

Garcia Ramirez, Sergio
  1 Dec. 1976–11 Jan. 1978

Subsecretary of Cultural Affairs (1958–76)

Castillo Ledon, Amalia
  1958–30 Nov. 1964
Magdaleno, Mauricio
  1 Dec. 1964–30 Nov. 1970
Aguirre Beltran, Gonzalo
  1 Dec. 1970–30 Nov. 1976

Subsecretary of Educational Planning (Planning, 1971–76)

Diaz de Cossio, Roger
  1971–30 Nov. 1976
Bonilla Garcia, Javier
  1 Dec. 1976–28 Dec. 1977
Rosenblueth, Emilio
  29 Dec. 1977–

Oficial Mayor

Molina Betancourt, Rafael
1934–36
Nicomedo, Francisco
1937–38
Perez H., Arnulfo
1938–40
Enriquez Coyro, Enrique
1944–46

Merino Fernandez, Aaron
1946–48
Fraga Magana, Santiago
1948–52
Miranda Basurto, Angel
1952–53
Echeverria, Luis
1954–57
Lopez Davila, Manuel
1958–61

Aguilera Dorantes, Mario
1961–70
Barbosa Heldt, Antonio
1970–73
Hedding Garcia, Marcelo
1973–76
Lopez Mestre, Severo
1976–

Secretariat of Public Works and Dwellings
(Communication and Public Works, 1891–1958; Public Works, 1958–76)

Secretary

Mugica, Francisco J.
18 June 1935–22 Jan. 1939
Angulo, Melquiades
23 Jan. 1939–30 Nov. 1940
De la Garza Gutierrez, Jesus B.
1 Dec. 1940–28 Sept. 1941
Avila Camacho, Maximino
29 Sept. 1941–17 Feb. 1945
Martinez Tornel, Pedro
28 Feb. 1945–30 Nov. 1946
Garcia Lopez, Agustin
1 Dec. 1946–30 Nov. 1952
Lazo, Carlos
1 Dec. 1952–5 Nov. 1955
Buchanan, Walter Cross
8 Nov. 1955–30 Nov. 1958
Barros Sierra, Javier
1 Dec. 1958–30 Nov. 1964
Valenzuela Jr., Gilberto
1 Dec. 1964–30 Nov. 1970
Bracamontes, Luis Enrique
1 Dec. 1970–30 Nov. 1976
Ramirez Vazquez, Pedro
1 Dec. 1976–

Subsecretary of Public Works
(Subsecretary, 1935–76)

Cortes Herrera, Vicente
1935–6 Apr. 1938
Angulo, Melquiades
1938–23 Jan. 1939

Santillan, Manuel
1939–30 Nov. 1940
Cortes Herrera, Vicente
Dec. 1940–41
Betancourt, Carlos I.
1941–43
Martinez Tornel, Pedro
1943–46
Dovali Jaime, Antonio
1 Dec. 1946–30 Nov. 1952
Buchanan, Walter C.
1 Dec. 1952–30 Nov. 1958
Bracamontes, Luis E.
1 Dec. 1958–30 Nov. 1964
Espinosa Gutierrez, Fernando
23 Dec. 1964–3 Apr. 1966
Felix Valdes, Rodolfo
1966–

Subsecretary of Public Works
(1946–58)

Mayoral Heredia, Manuel
1946–50
Gonzalez, Enrique M.
1950–52
Bracamontes, Luis E.
1952–58

Subsecretary of Real Property
and Public Works
Subsecretary B (1972–76)

Etcharren Gutierrez, Rene
26 Jan. 1972–30 Nov. 1976

Gonzalez Saenz, Leopoldo
1 Dec. 1976–

Subsecretary of Human
Dwellings (1977)

Valner, Gregorio
1977–

Subsecretary of National
Territories (1976–77)

Martinez Corbala, Gonzalo
1 Dec. 1976–3 Feb. 1977

Oficial Mayor

Anglie L., J. Enrique
1935–40
Betancourt, Carlos I.
1940–41
Ortega, Fausto M.
1942–45
Ostos, Guillermo
1946–52
Rocha Sagaon, Gustavo
1953–64
Rios Elizondo, Roberto
1964–70
Caso Lombardo, Andres
1970–76
Madrazo Pintado, Carlos
1976–

Secretariat of the Treasury and Public Credit

Secretary

Suarez, Eduardo
18 June 1935–30 Nov. 1946

Beteta, Ramon
1 Dec. 1946–30 Nov. 1952
Carrillo Flores, Antonio
1 Dec. 1952–30 Nov. 1958

Ortiz Mena, Antonio
1 Dec. 1958–16 Aug. 1970
Margain, Hugo B.
17 Aug. 1970–29 May 1973

Lopez Portillo, Jose
29 May 1973–26 Sept. 1975
Beteta, Mario Ramon
27 Sept. 1975–30 Nov. 1976
Moctezuma Cid, Julio Rodolfo
1 Dec. 1976–16 Nov. 1977
Ibarra, David
17 Nov. 1977–

Subsecretary (1934–58)
Buenrostro Ochoa, Efrain
1934–16 Jan. 1938
Villasenor, Eduardo
17 Jan. 1938–8 Sept. 1940
Espinosa de los Monteros, Antonio
9 Sept. 1940–30 Nov. 1940
Beteta, Ramon
1 Dec. 1940–2 Oct. 1945
Silva Herzog, Jesus
3 Oct. 1945–30 Nov. 1946
Bustamante, Eduardo
1 Dec. 1946–30 Mar. 1949
Gonzalez de la Vega, Angel
1949–50
Iturriaga Alarcon, Bernardo
1950–30 Nov. 1952
Armendariz, Antonio
1 Dec. 1952–30 Nov. 1958

Subsecretary of Credit (1946)
Mancera Ortiz, Rafael
1946–30 Nov. 1958

Rodriguez y Rodriguez, Jesus
1 Dec. 1958–30 Nov. 1970
Beteta M., Mario Ramon
1 Dec. 1970–26 Sept. 1975
De la Madrid, Miguel
29 Sept. 1975–17 May 1979
Silva Herzog F., Jesus
22 May 1979–

Subsecretary of Expenditures (1958–76)
Caamano Munoz, Enrique
1958–30 Nov. 1970
Isoard, Carlos A.
1 Dec. 1970–30 Nov. 1976

Subsecretary of Revenues
Garduno, Eduardo
1958–61
Romero Castaneda, David
1961–64
Alcala Quintero, Francisco
1 Dec. 1964–30 Nov. 1970
Petricioli, Gustavo
1 Dec. 1970–10 Oct. 1974
Alejo, Javier
10 Oct. 1974–3 Jan. 1975
Pichardo Pagaza, Ignacio
1 Dec. 1976–16 Jan. 1978
Prieto Fortun, Guillermo
17 Jan. 1978–

Subsecretary of Tax Investigation
Cardenas Gonzalez, Enrique
19 Jan. 1972–29 May 1974
Ruiz Almada, Gilberto
29 May 1974–25 Feb. 1976
Carrillo Olea, Jorge
26 Feb. 1976–30 Nov. 1976
Reyes Retena, Oscar
1 Dec. 1976–6 June 1979
Acosta Lagunes, Agustin
6 June 1979–

Oficial Mayor
Cardenas, J. Raymundo
1935–40
Martinez Sicilia, Manuel
1946–49
Iturriaga Alarcon, Bernardo
1950
Noriega, Raul
1951–58
Sierra, Manuel J.
1958–64
Cordera Pastor, Mario
1964–70
Riba Ricon, Luis
1970–75
Velasco Ibarra, Enrique
1975–76
Azuara Salas, Enrique
1976–77
Trueba Rodriguez, Salvador
1977–

Ambassadors to the United Kingdom, the United States, France, Soviet Union, OAS, Cuba and the United Nations 1935–1980

The United Kingdom

Andreu Almazan, Leonides
1 Jan. 1935–3 Dec. 1935
Bassols, Narciso
4 Jan. 1936–4 Jan. 1937
Villa Michel, Primo
1937–38
No Relations
1938–42
Rosenzweig Diaz, Alfonso de
21 Jan. 1942–14 Feb. 1945
Jimenez O' Farrell, Federico
15 Feb. 1945–10 Mar. 1952
de Icaza, Francisco A.
11 Mar. 1952–55
Vacant
1955–57
Campos Ortiz, Pablo
4 July 1957–17 Jan. 1961
Armendariz, Antonio
18 Jan. 1961–3 May 1965
Suarez, Eduardo
4 May 1965–70
Sanchez Gavito, Vicente
1970–73
Margain, Hugo B.
1973–76
Tello Macias, Manuel
1976–25 June 1979
De Olloqui, Jose Juan
1979–

The United States

Castillo Najera, Francisco
1935–45
Espinosa de los Monteros, Antonio
1945–49
De la Colina, Rafael
1949–52
Tello, Manuel
1952–58
Carrillo Flores, Antonio
1958–64
Margain, Hugo B.
31 Dec. 1964–Aug. 1970
Rabasa, Emilio O.
Sept. 1970–Dec. 1970
De Olloqui y Labastida, Jose Juan
1971–76
Margain, Hugo B.
1976

France

Gomez, Marte R.
1935–36
Tejeda, Adalberto
1936–37
Ruiz C., Leobardo
1937–38
Bassols, Narciso
1938–39

Rodriguez, Luis I.
1939–40
Aguilar, Francisco J.
1940–41
Bosquez, Gilberto
1941–45
Rios Zertuche, Antonio
1945–46
Rosenzweig Diaz, Alfonso
1946
Fernandez Manero, Victor
1946–51
Jimenez O' Farrill, Federico
1951–53
Torres Bodet, Jaime
1953–58
Morones Prieto, Ignacio
1958–65
Apodaca Osuna, Francisco
1965–70
Zavala, Silvio
1970–75
Fuentes, Carlos
1975–77
Flores de la Pena, Horacio
1977–78
Flores Olea, Victor
1978–

Soviet Union (1942)

Quintanilla, Luis
1942–45
Bassols, Narciso
1945–46
Sanchez Ponton, Luis
1946
Joublanc Rivas, Luciano
1946–48
Rennou Hay, German L.
1948–51
Alemanza Gordoa, Ricardo
1952–53
Rosenzweig Diaz, Alfonso de
1953–60
Iturriaga Suaco, Jose
1961–66
Zapata Vela, Carlos
1967–69
Gonzalez Salazar, Roque

Martinez Aguilar, Rogelio
1977–79
Salinas Lozano, Raul
1979–

OAS (1945)

Quintanilla, Luis
1945–58
Sanchez Gavito, Vicente
1959–65
de la Colina, Rafael
1965–

Cuba

Cravioto, Alfonso
1934–38
Reyes Spindola, Octavio
1938–39
Romero, Jose Ruben
1939–43
Ceniceros, Jose Angel
1944–47
Coquet, Benito
1947–52
Bosquez, Gilberto
1953–64
Pamanes Escobedo, Fernando
1964–67

Covian Perez, Miguel
1967–70
Maldonado, Victor Alfonso
1970–
Madero Vazquez, Ernesto
1976–80
Martinez Corbala, Gonzalo
1980–

United Nations (1946)

Padilla Nervo, Luis
1946–52
de la Colina, Rafael
1952–58
Padilla Nervo, Luis
1958–64
Cuevas Canciano, Francisco
1965–71
Garcia Robles, Alfonso
1971–75
Cuevas Canciano, Francisco
1976–79
Munoz Ledo, Porfirio
1979–

Governors, 1935–1980

Aguascalientes

Osornio Camarena, Enrique
1 Dec. 1932–30 Nov. 1936
Alvarado, Juan G.
29 June 1937–30 Nov. 1940
Del Valle, Alberto
1 Dec. 1940–30 Nov. 1944
Rodriguez Flores, Jesus M.
1 Dec. 1944–30 Nov. 1950
Games Orozco, Edmundo
1 Dec. 1950–July 1953
(died in office)
Palomino Dena, Benito
9 Sept. 1953–30 Nov. 1956
Ortega Douglas, Luis
1 Dec. 1956–30 Nov. 1962
Olivares Santana, Enrique
1 Dec. 1962–30 Nov. 1968
Guel Jimenez, Francisco
1 Dec. 1968–30 Nov. 1974
Esparza Reyes, J. Refugio
1 Dec. 1974–30 Nov. 1980
Landeros Gallegos, Rodolfo
1 Dec. 1980–

Baja California del Norte

Magana, Gildardo (Lt.Col.)
21 Aug. 1935–18 Feb. 1936
Gavira, Gabriel
19 Feb. 1936–15 Aug. 1936
Navarro Cortina, Rafael (Gen.)
16 Aug. 1936–22 Feb. 1937
(resigned)
Sanchez Taboada, Rodolfo (Lt.Col.)
23 Feb. 1937–31 July 1944
(leave*)

Rico Islas, Juan Felipe (Gen.)
2 Aug. 1944–20 Dec. 1946
Aldrete, Alberto V.
20 Dec. 1946–Oct. 1947
(resigned)
Garcia Gonzalez, Alfonso
1947–30 Nov. 1953
Maldonado, Braulio
1 Dec. 1953–30 Nov. 1959
Esquivel Mendez, Eligio
1 Dec. 1959–64 (died in office)
Aubanel Vallejo, Gustavo
18 Dec. 1964–31 Oct. 1965
Sanchez Diaz, Raul
1 Nov. 1965–31 Oct. 1971
Castellanos, Milton Everardo
1 Nov. 1971–31 Oct. 1977
De la Madrid, Roberto
1 Nov. 1977–

Baja California del Sur (Territory until 1975)

Dominguez, Juan (Gen.)
1932–Oct. 1937
Pedrajo, Rafael M. (Lt. Col.)
1937–40
Mugica, Francisco J. (Gen.)
1940–45
Olachea Aviles, Agustin (Gen.)
1945–56 (resigned)
Flores Castellanos, Petronilo (Gen.)
14 Apr. 1956–4 Apr. 1957
(died in office)
Rebolledo, Luciano M. (Lt. Col.)
1957–Dec. 1958 (resigned)
Salinas Leal, Bonifacio (Gen.)
1958–11 Apr. 1965 (resigned)

Cervantes del Rio, Hugo
20 Apr. 1965–70
Agramont Cota, Felix
1970–75
Mendoza Aramburo, Angel Cesar
1975–

Campeche

Mena Cordova, Eduardo
16 Sept. 1935–15 Sept. 1939
Perez Martinez, Hector
16 Sept. 1939–15 Sept. 1943
Lavalle Urbina, Eduardo J.
16 Sept. 1943–15 Sept. 1949
Lopez Hernandez, Manuel J.
16 Sept. 1949–15 Sept. 1955
Trueba Urbina, Alberto
16 Sept. 1955–15 Sept. 1961
Ortiz Avila, Jose (Col.)
16 Sept. 1961–15 Sept. 1967
Sansores Perez, Carlos
16 Sept. 1967–3 Mar. 1973
(leave)
Perez Camara, Carlos
3 Mar. 1973–15 Sept. 1973
Rodriguez Barrera, Rafael
16 Sept. 1973–15 Sept. 1979
Echeverria Castellot, Eugenio
16 Sept. 1979–

Chiapas

Grajales, Victorio R. (Col.)
1932–22 Sept. 1936
(dissolution of powers)
Coutino, Amador
23 Sept. 1936–15 Dec. 1936

---

*The term *leave* indicates that a governor has been granted permission by the state legislature to leave his office, usually for a period of six months, either for personal or political reasons. In rare cases, a governor may be granted successive six–month leaves and later return to office. See Manuel Sanchez Vite, Governor of Hidalgo for such a case.

Gutierrez Rincon, Efrain A.
15 Dec. 1936–30 Nov. 1940
Gamboa, Rafael P.
1 Dec. 1940–30 Nov. 1944
Esponda, Juan (Gen.)
1 Dec. 1944–Jan. 1947
(resigned)
Lara, Cesar (Gen.)
1947–30 Nov. 1948
Grajales, Francisco J. (Gen.)
1 Dec. 1948–30 Nov. 1952
Aranda Osorio, Efrain
1 Dec. 1952–30 Nov. 1958
Leon Brindis, Samuel
1 Dec. 1958–30 Nov. 1964
Castillo Tielemans, Jose
1 Dec. 1964–30 Nov. 1970
Velasco Suarez, Manuel
1 Dec. 1970–30 Nov. 1976
De la Vega Dominguez, Jorge
1 Dec. 1976–8 Dec. 1977
Gonzalez Blanco, Salomon
9 Dec. 1977–Jan. 1980
Sabines Gutierrez, Juan
Jan. 1980–

Chihuahua

Quevedo, Rodrigo M. (Gen.)
1932–3 Oct. 1936
Talamantes, Gustavo L.
4 Oct. 1936–39
Prado Proano, Eugenio
1939–3 Oct. 1940
Chavez, Alfredo (Col.)
4 Oct. 1940–3 Oct. 1944
Folgio Miramontes, Fernando
4 Oct. 1944–3 Oct. 1950
Soto Maynes, Oscar
4 Oct. 1950–Aug. 1955 (leave)
Lozoya Solis, Jesus
10 Aug. 1955–3 Oct. 1955
Borunda, Teofilo R.
4 Oct. 1955–3 Oct. 1962
Giner Duran, Praxedes
4 Oct. 1962–3 Oct. 1968
Flores Sanchez, Oscar
4 Oct. 1968–3 Oct. 1974
Aguirre Samaniego, Manuel
Bernardo
4 Oct. 1974–3 Oct. 1980
Ornelas Kuckle, Oscar
4 Oct. 1980–

Coahuila

Valdez Sanchez, Jesus
1 Dec. 1933–30 Nov. 1937

Rodriguez Triana, Pedro V.
1 Dec. 1937–1 Nov. 1941
Cevera, Gabriel R.
15 Nov. 1941–30 Nov. 1941
Lopez Padilla, Benecio (Gen.)
1 Dec. 1941–30 Nov. 1945
Cepeda Davila, Ignacio
1 Dec. 1945–47
(committed suicide)
Ainslie, Ricardo
1947–Mar. 1948 (resigned)
Faz Riza, Paz (Gen.)
Mar. 1948–5 June 1948
Lopez Sanchez, Raul
1948–30 Nov. 1951
Cepeda Flores, Ramon
1 Dec. 1951–30 Nov. 1957
Madero Gonzalez, Raul (Gen.)
1 Dec. 1957–30 Nov. 1963
Fernandez Aguirre, Braulio
1 Dec. 1963–30 Nov. 1969
Gutierrez Trevino, Eulalio
1 Dec. 1969–30 Nov. 1975
Flores Tapia, Oscar
1 Dec. 1975–

Colima

Saucedo, Salvador
1935–21 Aug. 1935
(dissolution of powers)
Santa Ana, Miguel (Gen.)
10 Nov. 1935–31 Oct. 1939
Torres Ortiz, Pedro (Col.)
1 Nov. 1939–31 Oct. 1943
Gudino Diaz, Manuel
1 Nov. 1943–31 Oct. 1949
Gonzalez Lugo, J. Jesus (Gen.)
1 Nov. 1949–31 Oct. 1955
Chavez Carrillo, Rodolfo
1 Nov. 1955–31 Oct. 1961
Velasco Curiel, Francisco
1 Nov. 1961–3 Oct. 1967
Silva Garcia, Pablo
1 Nov. 1967–31 Oct. 1973
Ramirez Garcia, Leonel
1 Nov. 1973–31 Dec. 1973
Noriega Pizano, Arturo
1 Jan. 1974–31 Dec. 1979
Alvarez, Griselda
1 Jan. 1980–

Durango

Real, Carlos
1932–31 Dec. 1935
(dissolution of powers)

Ceniceros, Severino (Gen.)
1 Jan. 1936–Aug. 1936
(resigned)
Calderon Rodriguez, Enrique
Aug. 1936–40
Velazquez, Elpidio G. (Gen.)
1940–44
Corral Martinez, Blas (Gen.)
15 Sept. 1944–30 Apr. 1947
(died in office)
Celis M., Francisco
30 Apr. 1947–18 Sept. 1947
Valdes, Jose Ramon
19 Sept. 1947–14 Sept. 1950
Torres Sanchez, Enrique
15 Sept. 1950–14 Sept. 1956
Gonzalez de la Vega, Francisco
15 Sept. 1956–3 July 1962
Dupre Ceniceros, Enrique
15 Sept. 1962–4 Aug. 1966
(dissolution of powers)
Rodriguez Solorzano, Angel
1966–14 Sept. 1968
Paez Urquidi, Alejandro
15 Sept. 1968–14 Sept. 1974
Mayagoitia Dominguez, Hector
15 Sept. 1974–14 Dec. 1979
Gamiz Fernandez, Salvador
15 Dec. 1979–14 Sept. 1980
Del Castillo Franco, Armando
15 Sept. 1980–

Guanajuato

Yanez Maya, Jesus
16 Dec. 1935
(dissolution of powers)
Fernandez Martinez, Enrique
18 Dec. 1935–20 Apr. 1937
Rodriguez, Luis I.
21 Apr. 1937–27 Apr. 1938
(leave)
Rangel Hurtado, Rafael
27 Apr. 1938–39
Rodriguez, Luis I.
1939–25 Sept. 1939
Fernandez Martinez, Enrique
26 Sept. 1939–25 Sept. 1943
Hidalgo, Ernesto
26 Sept. 1943–8 Jan. 1946
(dissolution of powers)
Guerrero Mendoza, Niceforo
10 Jan. 1946–22 Sept. 1947
(resigned)
Castorena, J. Jesus
22 Sept. 1947–29 Oct. 1948

Guanajuato (cont.)

Diaz Infante, Luis
    30 Oct. 1948–25 Sept. 1949
Aguilar y Maya, Jose
    26 Sept. 1949–25 Sept. 1955
Rodriguez Gaona, J. Jesus
    26 Sept. 1955–25 Sept. 1961
Torres Landa, Juan Jose
    26 Sept. 1961–25 Sept. 1967
Moreno, Manuel M.
    26 Sept. 1967–25 Sept. 1973
Ducoing Gamba, Luis Humberto
    26 Sept. 1973–25 Sept. 1979
Velasco Ibarra, Enrique
    26 Sept. 1979–

Guerrero

Guevara, Gabriel R. (Gen.)
    25 Mar. 1933–5 Nov. 1935
    (dissolution of powers)
Lugo, Jose (Gen.)
    5 Nov. 1935–31 Mar. 1937
Berber, Alberto F. (Gen.)
    1 Apr. 1937–18 Feb. 1941
Carraco Cardoso, Carlos
    19 Feb. 1941–30 June 1941
Catalan Calvo, Rafael
    30 June 1941–31 Mar. 1945
Leyva Mancilla, Gabriel (Gen.)
    1 Apr. 1945–31 Mar. 1951
Gomez Maganda, Alejandro
    1 Apr. 1951–21 May 1954
    (dissolution of powers)
Arrieta M., Dario L.
    21 May 1954–31 Mar. 1957
Caballero Aburto, Raul (Gen.)
    1 Apr. 1957–3 Jan. 1961
    (dissolution of powers)
Martinez Adame, Arturo
    Jan. 1961–31 Mar. 1963
Abarca Alarcon, Raimundo
    1 Apr. 1963–31 Mar. 1969
Maldonado Perez, Caritino
    1 Apr. 1969–17 Apr. 1971 (died)
Nogueda Otero, Israel
    Apr. 1971–31 Jan. 1975
    (dissolution of powers)
Olea Munoz, Javier
    Feb. 1975–1 Apr. 1975
Figueroa, Ruben
    1 Apr. 1975–

Hidalgo

Viveros, Ernesto
    1933–37

Rojo Gomez, Javier
    1937–40
Villegas, Ofilio (Gen.)
    1940–41
Lugo Guerrero, Jose
    1941–45
Aguirre, Vicente
    1945–31 Mar. 1951
Rueda Villagran, Quintin
    1 Apr. 1951–31 Mar. 1957
Corona del Rosal, Alfonso (Gen.)
    1 Apr. 1957–4 Dec. 1958
    (resigned)
Cravioto, Oswaldo
    6 Dec. 1958–31 Mar. 1963
Ramirez Guerrero, Carlos
    1 Apr. 1963–31 Mar. 1969
Sanchez Vite, Manuel
    1 Apr. 1969–Dec. 1970
    (leave)
Serna, Donaciano
    Dec. 1970–May 1972
Sanchez Vite, Manuel
    May 1972–31 Mar. 1975
Miranda Andrade, Otoniel
    1 Apr. 1975–29 Apr. 1975
    (dissolution of powers)*
Lozano Ramirez, Raul
    May 1975–Aug. 1975
Rojo Lugo, Jorge
    Aug. 1975–1 Dec. 1976 (leave)
Suarez Molina, Jose Luis
    3 Dec. 1976–1 June 1978
Rojo Lugo, Jorge
    2 June 1978–

Jalisco

Topete, Everardo
    1 Mar. 1935–39
Barba Gonzalez, Silvano
    1939–43
Garcia Barragan, Marcelino
    1943–17 Feb. 1947 (removed)
Gonzalez Gallo, Jesus
    1 Mar. 1947–28 Feb. 1953
Yanez, Agustin
    1 Mar. 1953–28 Feb. 1959
Gil Preciado, Juan
    1 Mar. 1959–4 Dec. 1964
    (resigned)
De Jesus Leiman, Jose
    Dec. 1964–28 Feb. 1965
Medina Asencio, Francisco
    1 Mar. 1965–28 Feb. 1971

Orozco Romero, Alberto
    1 Mar. 1971–28 Feb. 1977
Romero de Velasco, Flavio
    1 Mar. 1977–

Mexico

Solorzano, Jose Luis
    1933–27 June 1936 (resigned)
Lopez, Eucario
    3 July 1936–15 Sept. 1937
Labra Garcia, Wenceslao (Col.)
    16 Sept. 1937–15 Sept. 1941
Zarate Albarran, Alfredo
    16 Sept. 1941–5 Mar. 1942
    (assassinated)
Gutierrez, Jose L.
    8 Mar. 1942–15 Mar. 1942
Fabela, Isidro
    16 Mar. 1942–15 Sept. 1945
Del Mazo Velez, Alfredo
    16 Sept. 1945–15 Sept. 1951
Sanchez Colin, Salvador
    16 Sept. 1951–15 Sept. 1957
Baz, Gustavo
    16 Sept. 1957–15 Sept. 1963
Fernandez Albarran, Juan
    16 Sept. 1963–15 Sept. 1969
Hank Gonzalez, Carlos
    16 Sept. 1969–15 Sept. 1975
Jimenez Cantu, Jorge
    16 Sept. 1975–

Michoacan

Ordorico Villamar, Rafael (Gen.)
    18 June 1935–15 Sept. 1936
    (provisional)
Magana, Gildardo (Gen.)
    16 Sept. 1936–13 Dec. 1939
    (died in office)
Ireta Viveros, Felix (Gen.)
    16 Sept. 1940–15 Sept. 1944
Mendoza Pardo, Jose Maria
    16 Sept. 1944–26 Aug. 1949
Renteria, Daniel T.
    1949–15 Sept. 1950
Cardenas del Rio, Damaso
    16 Sept. 1950–15 Sept. 1956
Franco Rodriguez, David
    16 Sept. 1956–15 Sept. 1962
Arriaga Rivera, Agustin
    16 Sept. 1962–15 Sept. 1968
Galvez Betancourt, Carlos
    16 Sept. 1968–15 Sept. 1971

---

*Shortest term ever served by a constitutionally elected governor in Mexico since 1935.

Chavez Hernandez, Jose
16 Sept. 1971–15 Sept. 1974
Torres Manzo, Carlos
16 Sept. 1974–15 Sept. 1980
Cardenas Solorzano, Cuauhtemoc
16 Sept. 1980–

Morelos

Bustamante, Jose Refugio
1934–6 May 1938
(dissolution of powers)
Samano, Alfonso (Col.)
6 May 1938–16 May 1938
Perdomo, D. Elpidio (Gen.)
17 May 1938–16 May 1942
Castillo Lopez, Jesus
17 May 1942–17 May 1946
Escobar Munoz, Ernesto
18 May 1946–17 May 1952
Lopez de Nava, Rodolfo (Gen.)
18 May 1952–17 May 1958
Lopez Avelar, Norberto (Col.)
18 May 1958–17 May 1964
Riva Palacio, Emilio
18 May 1964–17 May 1970
Rivera Crespo, Felipe
18 May 1970–17 May 1976
Leon Bejarano, Armando
18 May 1976–

Nayarit

Parra, Francisco
1 Jan. 1934–31 Dec. 1937
Espinosa Sanchez, Juventino (Gen.)
1 Jan. 1938–31 Dec. 1941
Miramontes, Candelario
1 Jan. 1942–31 Dec. 1945
Flores Munoz, Gilberto
1 Jan. 1946–31 Dec. 1951
Limon Guzman, Jose
1 Jan. 1952–31 Dec. 1957
Garcia Montero, Francisco
1 Jan. 1958–31 Dec. 1963
Gascon Mercado, Julian
1 Jan. 1964–31 Dec. 1969
Gomez Reyes, Roberto
1 Jan. 1970–31 Dec. 1975
Flores Curiel, Rogelio
1 Jan. 1976–

Nuevo Leon

Quiroga, Pablo
1933–27 Sept. 1935
Morales Sanchez, Gregorio (Gen.)
28 Sept. 1935–36

Guerrero, Anacleto (Gen.)
1936–39
Salinas Leal, Bonifacio
1939–43
Arteaga y Santoyo, Armando
1943–44
De la Garza, Arturo B.
1944–49
Morones Prieto, Ignacio
4 Oct. 1949–Dec. 1952
Vivanco, Jose S.
Dec. 1952–3 Oct. 1955
Rangel Frias, Raul
4 Oct. 1955–3 Oct. 1961
Livas Villarreal, Eduardo
4 Oct. 1961–3 Oct. 1967
Elizondo, Eduardo A.
4 Oct. 1967–June 1971 (resigned)
Farias, Luis M.
June 1970–3 Oct. 1973
Zorrilla, Pedro
4 Oct. 1973–3 Oct. 1979
Martinez Dominguez, Alfonso
4 Oct. 1979–

Oaxaca

Garcia Toledo, Anastasio
1 Dec. 1932–30 Nov. 1936
Chapital, Constatino (Col.)
1 Dec. 1936–30 Nov. 1940
Gonzalez Fernandez, Vicente (Col.)
1 Dec. 1940–30 Nov. 1944
Sanchez Cono, Edmundo (Gen.)
1 Dec. 1944–19 Jan. 1947
Vasconcelos, Eduardo
20 Jan. 1947–30 Nov. 1950
Mayoral Heredia, Manuel
1 Dec. 1950–31 July 1952
(dissolution of powers)
Cabrera Carrasquedo, Manuel
(Gen.)
1 Aug. 1952–1 Oct. 1955
Pacheco Iturribarria, Jose (Gen.)
11 Oct. 1955–30 Nov. 1956
Perez Gasca, Alfonso
1 Dec. 1956–30 Nov. 1962
Brena Torres, Rodolfo
1 Dec. 1962–30 Nov. 1968
Bravo Ahuja, Victor
1 Dec. 1968–30 Nov. 1970
(resigned)
Gomez Sandoval, Fernando
1 Dec. 1970–30 Nov. 1974
Zarate Aquino, Manuel
1 Dec. 1974–3 Mar. 1977
(resigned)

Jimenez Ruiz, Eliseo (Gen.)
4 Mar. 1977–30 Nov. 1980
Vazquez Colmenares, Pedro
1 Dec. 1980–

Puebla

Mijares Palencia, Jose (Gen.)
1933–31 Jan. 1937
Avila Camacho, Maximino (Gen.)
1 Feb. 1937–3 Jan. 1941
Bautista, Gonzalo
1 Feb. 1941–31 Jan. 1945
Betancourt, Carlos I.
1 Feb. 1945–31 Jan. 1951
Avila Camacho, Rafael
1 Feb. 1951–31 Jan. 1957
Ortega, Fausto M.
1 Feb. 1957–31 Jan. 1963
Nava Castillo, Antonio (Gen.)
1 Feb. 1963–30 Oct. 1964
(resigned)
Merino Fernandez, Aaron
1 Nov. 1964–31 Jan. 1969
Moreno Valle, Rafael
1 Feb. 1969–Apr. 1972 (leave)
Bautista O'Farrill, Gonzalo
14 Apr. 1972–8 Mar. 1972
(resigned)
Morales Blumenkron, Guillermo
9 Mar. 1973–31 Jan. 1975
Toxqui Fernandez, Alfredo
1 Feb. 1975–

Queretaro

Rodriguez Familiar, Ramon (Gen.)
1 Oct. 1935–30 Sept. 1939
Rubio Ortiz, Noradino
1 Oct. 1939–30 Sept. 1943
Pozo, Agapito
1 Oct. 1943–17 Apr. 1949
Luque Loyola, Eduardo
18 Apr. 1949–30 Sept. 1949
Mondragon, Octavio S.
1 Oct. 1949–30 Sept. 1955
Gorraez, Juan C.
1 Oct. 1955–30 Sept. 1961
Gonzalez Cosio, Manuel
1 Oct. 1961–30 Sept. 1967
Castro Sanchez, Juventino
1 Oct. 1967–30 Sept. 1973
Calzada, Antonio
1 Oct. 1973–30 Sept. 1979
Camacho Guzman, Rafael
1 Oct. 1979–

Quintana Roo
(Territory until 1975)

Melgar, Rafael E.
  1935–40
Guevara, Gabriel R. (Gen.)
  Dec. 1940–44
Ramirez, Margarito
  30 Mar. 1944–Feb. 1959
  (resigned)
Merino Fernandez, Aaron
  16 Jan. 1959–Nov. 1964
Mendoza Becerra, Eligio
  Nov. 1964–19 Mar. 1965
Figueroa, Ruffo
  20 Mar. 1965–67 (resigned)
Rojo Gomez, Javier
  2 June 1967–31 Dec. 1970
  (died in office)
Gutierrez Ruiz, David Gustavo
  7 Jan. 1971–4 Apr. 1975
Martinez Ross, Jesus
  4 Apr. 1975–

San Luis Potosi

Anaya, Aurelio G.
  1935–36
Hernandez Netro, Mateo (Col.)
  26 Sept. 1936–22 May 1938
Rivas Guillen, Genovevo (Gen.)
  26 May 1938–39
Perez Gallardo, Reynaldo (Gen.)
  1939–19 Aug. 1941
  (dissolution of powers)
Jimenez Delgado, Ramon (Gen.)
  20 Aug. 1941–25 Sept. 1943
Santos, Gonzalo N.
  26 Sept. 1943–25 Sept. 1949
Salas, Ismael
  26 Sept. 1949–25 Sept. 1955
Alvarez Lopez, Manuel
  26 Sept. 1955–Jan. 1959
  (resigned)
Martinez de la Vega, Francisco
  2 Apr. 1959–25 Sept. 1961
Lopez Davila, Manuel
  26 Sept. 1961–25 Sept. 1967
Rocha, Antonio
  26 Sept. 1967–25 Sept. 1973
Fonseca Alvarez, Guillermo
  26 Sept. 1973–25 Sept. 1979
Jongitud Barrios, Carlos
  26 Sept. 1979–

Sinaloa

Paez, Manuel
  1933–16 Dec. 1935
  (dissolution of powers)

Leyva Velazquez, Gabriel (Gen.)
  17 Dec. 1935–15 Sept. 1936
Delgado, Alfredo (Gen.)
  16 Sept. 1936–15 Sept. 1940
Loaiza, Rodolfo (Col.)
  16 Sept. 1940–20 Feb. 1944
  (assassinated)
Cruz, Ricardo Teodoro
  1944–31 Dec. 1944
Macias Valenzuela, Pablo E.
(Gen.)
  1 Jan. 1945–31 Dec. 1950
Perez Arce, Enrique
  1 Jan. 1951–Feb. 1953 (resigned)
Aguilar Pico, Rigoberto
  19 Aug. 1953–31 Dec. 1956
Leyva Velazquez, Gabriel (Gen.)
  1 Jan. 1957–31 Dec. 1962
Sanchez Celis, Leopoldo
  1 Jan. 1963–31 Dec. 1968
Valdez Montoya, Alfredo
  1 Jan. 1969–31 Dec. 1974
Calderon Velarde, Alfonso
  1 Jan. 1975–31 Dec. 1980
Toledo Corro, Antonio
  1 Jan. 1980–

Sonora

Ramos, Ramon
  1 Sept. 1935–16 Dec. 1935
  (dissolution of powers)
Gutierrez Cazares, Jesus (Gen.)
  17 Dec. 1935–3 Jan. 1937
Yocupicio, Roman
  4 Jan. 1937–31 Aug. 1939
Macias Valenzuela, Anselmo (Gen.)
  1 Sept. 1939–31 Aug. 1943
Rodriguez, Abelardo L.
  1 Sept. 1943–Apr. 1948 (leave)
Sobarzo, Horacio
  Apr. 1948–31 Aug. 1949
Soto, Ignacio
  1 Sept. 1949–31 Aug. 1955
Obregon, Alvaro
  1 Sept. 1955–31 Aug. 1961
Encinas Johnson, Luis
  1 Sept. 1961–31 Aug. 1967
Felix Serna, Faustino
  1 Sept. 1967–31 Aug. 1973
Biebrich Torres, Carlos A.
  1 Sept. 1973–25 Oct. 1975
  (resigned)
Carrillo Marcor, Alejandro
  25 Oct. 1975–31 Aug. 1979
Ocana Garcia, Samuel
  1 Sept. 1979–

Tabasco

Lastra Ortiz, Manuel
  1935–23 July 1935
  (dissolution of powers)
Calles, Aureo (Gen.)
  24 July 1935–36
Fernandez Manero, Victor
  1936–31 Dec. 1938
Trujillo Gurria, Francisco
  1 Jan. 1939–31 Dec. 1943
De la Flor Casanova, Noe
  1 Jan. 1944–31 Dec. 1947
Santamaria, Francisco J.
  1 Jan. 1948–31 Dec. 1952
Bartlett Bautista, Manuel
  1 Jan. 1953–22 Mar. 1955
  (leave)
Orrico de los Llanos, Miguel (Gen)
  23 Mar. 1955–31 Dec. 1958
Madrazo, Carlos
  1 Jan. 1959–31 Dec. 1964
Mora, Manuel R.
  1 Jan. 1965–31 Dec. 1970
Trujillo Garcia, Mario
  1 Jan. 1971–31 Dec. 1976
Rovirosa Wade, Leandro
  1 Jan. 1977–

Tamaulipas

Villarreal, Rafael
  5 Feb. 1935–20 Nov. 1935
  (resigned)
Canseco, Enrique
  16 Aug. 1935–4 Feb. 1937
Gomez, Marte R.
  5 Feb. 1937–4 Feb. 1941
Aguilar Castillo, Magdaleno
  5 Feb. 1941–4 Feb. 1945
Gonzalez, Hugo P.
  5 Feb. 1945–10 Apr. 1947
  (dissolution of powers)
Garate Legleu, Raul
  17 Apr. 1947–4 Feb. 1951
Teran Z., Horacio
  5 Feb. 1951–4 Feb. 1957
Trevino Zapata, Norberto
  5 Feb. 1957–4 Feb. 1963
Balboa Gojon, Praxedis
  5 Feb. 1963–4 Feb. 1969
Ravize, Manuel A.
  5 Feb. 1969–4 Feb. 1975
Cardenas Gonzalez, Enrique
  5 Feb. 1975–

Tlaxcala

Bonilla, Adolfo
  1933–37

Candia, Isidro (Col.)
1937–41
Santillan, Manuel
1941–Aug. 1944 (resigned)
Angulo, Mauro
1944–14 Jan. 1945
Avila Breton, Rafael
15 Jan. 1945–14 Jan. 1951
Mazarrasa, Felipe
15 Jan. 1951–14 Jan. 1957
Cisneros Molina, Joaquin
15 Jan. 1957–14 Jan. 1963
Cervantes Hernandez, Anselmo
15 Jan. 1963–14 Jan. 1969
Bonilla Vazquez, Ignacio (Gen.)
15 Jan. 1969–19 Jan. 1970
(died in office)
Huerta Sanchez, Luciano
Apr. 1970–14 Jan. 1975
Sanchez Piedras, Emilio
15 Jan. 1975–14 Jan. 1981
Hernandez Gomez, Tulio
15 Jan. 1981–

Veracruz

Vazquez Vela, Gonzalo
1 Dec. 1932–1935 (leave)
Rebolledo, Guillermo
3 July 1935–30 Nov. 1936
Aleman V., Miguel
1 Dec. 1936–39 (resigned)
Casas Aleman, Francisco
1939–30 Nov. 1940
Cerdan, Jorge
1 Dec. 1940–30 Nov. 1944

Ruiz Cortines, Adolfo
1 Dec. 1944–48
Carvajal, Angel
1948–30 Nov. 1950
Munoz T., Marco A.
1 Dec. 1950–30 Nov. 1956
Quirasco, Antonio M.
1 Dec. 1956–30 Nov. 1962
Lopez Arias, Fernando
1 Dec. 1962–30 Nov. 1968
Murillo Vidal, Rafael
1 Dec. 1968–30 Nov. 1974
Hernandez Ochoa, Rafael
1 Dec. 1974–30 Nov. 1980
Acosta Lagunes, Agustin
1 Dec. 1980–

Yucatan

Alayola Barrera, Cesar
2 Feb. 1934–5 Oct. 1935
(resigned)
Lopez Cardenas, Fernando
5 Oct. 1935–30 June 1936
Palomo Valencia, Florencio
1 July 1936–31 Jan. 1938
Canto Echeverria, Humberto
1 Feb. 1938–31 Jan. 1942
Novelo Torres, Ernesto
1 Feb. 1942–31 Jan. 1946
Gonzalez Beytia, Jose
1 Feb. 1946–Sept. 1952
(resigned)
Marentes Miranda, Tomas
1 Feb. 1952–15 June 1953
(resigned)

Mena Palomo, Victor
18 June 1953–31 Jan. 1958
Franco Aguilar, Agustin
1 Feb. 1958–31 Jan. 1964
Torres Mesias, Luis
1 Feb. 1964–31 Jan. 1970
Loret de Mola, Carlos
1 Feb. 1970–31 Jan. 1976
Luna Kan, Francisco
1 Feb. 1976–

Zacatecas

Ramos Santos, Matias
28 Nov. 1932–15 Sept. 1936
Banuelos, J. Felix
16 Sept. 1936–15 Sept. 1940
Natera, Panfilo
16 Sept. 1940–15 Sept. 1944
Reynoso, Leobardo
16 Sept. 1944–15 Sept. 1950
Minero Roque, Jose
16 Sept. 1950–15 Sept. 1956
Garcia, Francisco E.
16 Sept. 1956–15 Sept. 1962
Rodriguez Elias, Jose
16 Sept. 1962–15 Sept. 1968
Ruiz Gonzalez, Pedro
16 Sept. 1968–15 Sept. 1974
Pamanes Escobedo, Fernando
16 Sept. 1974–15 Sept. 1980
Cervantes Corona, Jose
16 Sept. 1980–

APPENDIX G

Rectors and Directors General
of the National Universities 1935–1980

National Autonomous University of Mexico
Universidad Nacional Autonoma de Mexico (UNAM)
(founded 1551)

Rector

Ocaranza Carmona, Fernando
26 Nov. 1934–17 Sept. 1935
Chico Goerne, Luis
24 Sept. 1935–21 June 1939
Baz, Gustavo
21 June 1939–3 Dec. 1940
De la Cueva y de la Rosa, Mario
3 Dec. 1940–17 June 1942
Brito Foucher, Rodulfo
18 June 1942–27 July 1944
Caso y Andrade, Alfonso
15 Aug. 1944–24 Mar. 1945
Fernandez Macgregor, Genaro
24 Mar. 1945–4 Mar. 1946
Zubiran Anchondo, Salvador
4 Mar. 1946–23 Apr. 1948
Garrido Diaz, Luis
23 Apr. 1948–14 Feb. 1952
Carrillo Flores, Nabor
14 Feb. 1952–13 Feb. 1961

Chavez Sanchez, Ignacio
13 Feb. 1961–5 May 1966
Barros Sierra, Javier
5 May 1966–5 May 1970
Gonzalez Casanova, Pablo
5 May 1970–8 Dec. 1972
Soberon, Guillermo
3 Jan. 1973–

Secretaries General

Gual Vidal, Manuel
1935–38
De la Cueva, Mario
1938–40
Torres Torrija, Jose
1940–42
Noriega, Alfonso
1942
Ramirez Moreno, Samuel
1942–44

Jimenez Rueda, Julio
1944
Garcia Maynez, Eduardo
1944–46
Gonzalez Castro, Francisco
1946–47
Rivera Perez Campos, Jose
1947–48
Gonzalez Bustamante, Juan Jose
1948–52
Carranca y Trujillo, Raul
1952–53
Del Pozo, Efren C.
1953–61
Mantilla Molina, Roberto
1961–66
Solana Morales, Fernando
1966–70
Madrazo Garamendi, Manuel
1970–72
Perez Correa, Fernando
1972–

National Polytechnic Institute — Instituto Politecnico Nacional
(founded 1937)

Director General

Medellin Ostos, Roberto
1937
Bernard, Miguel
1938–39
Cerrillo Valdivia, Manuel
1940
Massieu, Wilfrido
1940–42
Laguardia, Jose
1942–43
Sandoval Vallarta, Manuel
1943–46

Alvarado Pies, Gustavo
1946–48
Guillot Schiaffino, Alejandro
1948–50
Ramirez Caraza, Juan Manuel
1950–53
Hernandez Corzo, Rodolfo
1953–56
Peralta Diaz, Alejo
1956–59
Mendez Docurro, Eugenio
1959–63

Padilla Segura, Jose Antonio
1963–64
Massieu Helguera, Guillermo
1964–70
Zorrilla, Manuel
1970–12 Dec. 1973
Gerstl Valenzuela, Jose
13 Dec. 1973–14 Dec. 1976
Vinals, Sergio
15 Dec. 1976–13 Dec. 1979
Mayagoitia Dominguez, Hector
14 Dec. 1979–

[432]

National Executive Committees
of PNR, PRM, and PRI 1935–1980

National Revolutionary Party
(Partido Nacional Revolucionario, PNR)

18 June 1935

President
Emilio Portes Gil
Secretary General
Ignacio Garcia Tellez
Labor Secretary
Gustavo Talamantes
Agrarian Secretary
Ernesto Soto Reyes
Press Secretary
Roque Estrada
Economic Secretary
Rodolfo T. Loaiza
Education Secretary
David Ayala
Organization Secretary
Juan Ignacio Garcia
IEPES Secretary
Julian Garza Tijerina

27 Aug. 1936

President
Silvano Barba Gonzalez
Secretary General
Esteban Garcia de Alba
Labor Secretary
Arnulfo Perez H.
Agrarian Secretary
Antonio Mayes Navarro
Press Secretary
Gilberto Bosquez S.
Organization Secretary
Wenceslao Labra
Economic Secretary
Julian Aguilar G.
Education Secretary
Gilberto Flores Munoz
IEPES Secretary
Enrique Calderon

1937

President
Silvano Barba Gonzalez
Secretary General
Gilberto Flores Munoz
Labor Secretary
Arnulfo Perez H.
Agrarian Secretary
Antonio Mayes Navarro
Education Secretary
Gilberto Bosquez S.
Press Secretary
Rafael Molina Betancourt
Organization Secretary
Wenceslao Labra
Economic Secretary
Julian Aguilar G.
IEPES Secretary
Enrique Calderon

Party of the Mexican Revolution
(Partido Revolucionario Mexicano, PRM)

2 Apr. 1938

President
Luis I. Rodriguez
Secretary General
Esteban Garcia de Alba
Labor Secretary
Alfonso Sanchez Madariaga
Agrarian Secretary
Leon Garcia
Popular Secretary
Leopoldo Hernandez Partida
Military Secretary
Edmundo Sanchez Cano

Press Secretary
Gilberto Bosquez S.
Finance Secretary
Elias Miranda

19 June 1939

President
Heriberto Jara
Secretary General
Gustavo Cardenas Huerta
Finance Secretary
Carlos Serrano

Popular Secretary
Leopoldo Hernandez Partida
Agrarian Secretary
Leon Garcia
Military Secretary
Edmundo Sanchez Cano
Labor Secretary
Alfonso Sanchez Madariaga
IEPES Secretary
Alejandro Carrillo

[433]

Party of the Mexican Revolution (cont.)

2 Dec. 1940

President
Antonio I. Villalobos
Secretary General
Gustavo Cardenas Huerta
Labor Secretary
Fernando Amilpa
Agrarian Secretary
Sacramento Jofre Vazquez

Popular Secretary
Antonio Nava Castillo
Military Secretary
Alfonso Corona del Rosal

1943

President
Antonio Villalobos
Secretary General
Florencio Padilla

Agrarian Secretary
Francisco Cruz Chavez
Labor Secretary
Fernando Amilpa
Popular Secretary
Antonio Nava Castillo
Finance Secretary
Ismael Salas

Institutional Revolutionary Party
(Partido Revolucionario Institucional, PRI)

19 Jan. 1946

President
Rafael P. Gamboa
Secretary General
Ernesto P. Uruchurtu
Labor Secretary
Fernando Amilpa
Agrarian Secretary
Francisco Martinez Peralta
Popular Secretary
Rafael Murillo Vidal
Political Secretary
Jesus Lima
Political Secretary
Augusto Hinojosa
Finance Secretary
Sealtiel Alatriste

5 Dec. 1946

President
Rodolfo Sanchez Taboada
Secretary General
Teofilo R. Borunda
Agrarian Secretary
Jesus Molina Urquidi
Labor Secretary
Blas Chumacero Sanchez
Popular Secretary
Ernesto Gallardo
Political Secretary
Fernando Lopez Arias
Political Secretary
Norberto Lopez Avelar
Finance Secretary
Guillermo M. Canales
Press Secretary
Luis Echeverria Alvarez
IEPES Secretary
Armando Arteaga y Santoyo

Women's Secretary
Margarita Garcia Flores
Youth Secretary
Antonio Mena Brito

1 Mar. 1949

President
Rodolfo Sanchez Taboada
Secretary General
Jose Lopez Bermudez
Agrarian Secretary
Jesus Molina Urquidi
Labor Secretary
Blas Chumacero
Popular Secretary
Ernesto Gallardo
Political Secretary
Fernando Lopez Arias
Political Secretary
Rafael Arriola Molina
Finance Secretary
Guillermo M. Canales
Press Secretary
Luis Echeverria
Oficial Mayor
Manuel Jasso

1 July 1951

President
Rodolfo Sanchez Taboada
Secretary General
Jose Lopez Bermudez
Agrarian Secretary
Vicente Salgado Paez
Labor Secretary
Blas Chumacero
Popular Secretary
Ernesto Gallardo
Political Secretary
Fernando Lopez Arias

Political Secretary
Norberto Lopez Avelar
Oficial Mayor
Manuel Jasso
Finance Secretary
Francisco Galindo Ochoa
Press Secretary
Luis Echeverria
Youth Secretary
Agustin Arriaga Rivera
IEPES Secretary
Armando Arteaga Santoyo
Feminine Secretary
Margarita Garcia Flores

3 June 1952

President
Rodolfo Sanchez Taboada
Secretary General
Adolfo Lopez Mateos
Agrarian Secretary
Vicente Salgado Paez
Labor Secretary
Alfonso Sanchez Madariaga
Popular Secretary
Angel Luis Archer
Political Secretary
Fernando Lopez Arias
Political Secretary
Salvador Pineda
IEPES Secretary
Armando Arteaga Santoyo
Press Secretary
Luis Echeverria
Youth Secretary
Antonio Mena Brito
Feminine Secretary
Margarita Garcia Flores
Oficial Mayor
Manuel Jasso

July 1952

President
  Rodolfo Sanchez Taboada
Secretary General
  Jose Gomez Esparza
Labor Secretary
  Alfonso Sanchez Madariaga
Agrarian Secretary
  Vicente Salgado Paez
Popular Secretary
  Angel Luis Archer
Political Secretary
  Fernando Lopez Arias
Political Secretary
  Norberto Lopez Avelar
IEPES Secretary
  Armando Arteaga y Santoyo
Youth Secretary
  Antonio Mena Brito
Feminine Secretary
  Margarita Garcia Flores
Finance Secretary
  Agustin Salvat
Press Secretary
  Moises Ochoa Campos

4 Dec. 1952

President
  Gabriel Leyva Velazquez
Secretary General
  Gilberto Garcia Navarro
Agrarian Secretary
  Magdaleno Aguilar
Labor Secretary
  Fidel Velazquez
Popular Secretary
  Caritino Maldonado
Political Secretary
  Emigdio Martinez Adame
Political Secretary
  Rodolfo Gonzalez Guevara
Finance Secretary
  Agustin Salvat
Press Secretary
  Moises Ochoa Campos
IEPES Secretary
  Armando Arteaga y Santoyo
Women's Secretary
  Margarita Garcia Flores
Youth Secretary
  Antonio Mena Brito

5 Jan. 1953

President
  Gabriel Leyva Velazquez
Secretary General
  Jose Gomez Esparza

Agrarian Secretary
  Vicente Salgado Paez
Labor Secretary
  Alfonso Sanchez Madariaga
Popular Secretary
  Jorge Saracho
Political Secretary
  Emigdio Martinez Adame
Political Secretary
  Rodolfo Gonzalez Guevara
Women's Secretary
  Margarita Garcia Flores
IEPES Secretary
  Armando Arteaga Santoyo
Press Secretary
  Moises Ochoa Campos
Youth Secretary
  Antonio Mena Brito
Finance Secretary
  Agustin Salvat

1 Apr. 1953

President
  Gabriel Leyva Velazquez
Secretary General
  Gilberto Garcia Navarro Aguilar
Agrarian Secretary
  Magdaleno Castillo
Labor Secretary
  Fidel Velazquez
Popular Secretary
  Caritino Maldonado
Political Secretary
  Emigdio Martinez Adame
Political Secretary
  Rodolfo Gonzalez Guevara
Finance Secretary
  Agustin Salvat
Oficial Mayor
  Carlos Real F.
IEPES Secretary
  Armando Arteaga Santoyo
Youth Secretary
  Antonio Mena Brito
Press Secretary
  Moises Ochoa Campos
Feminine Secretary
  Margarita Garcia Flores

26 Apr. 1956

President
  Agustin Olachea Aviles
Secretary General
  Rafael Corrales Ayala
Agrarian Secretary
  Magdaleno Aguilar

Labor Secretary
  Fidel Velazquez
Popular Secretary
  Caritino Maldonado
Political Secretary
  Francisco Galindo Ochoa
Finance Secretary
  Agustin Salvat
Press Secretary
  Moises Ochoa Campos
Women's Secretary
  Margarita Garcia Flores
Oficial Mayor
  Carlos Real F.

15 May 1956

President
  Agustin Olachea Aviles
Secretary General
  Gilberto Garcia Navarro
Popular Secretary
  Caritino Maldonado
Agrarian Secretary
  Magdaleno Aguilar Castillo
Labor Secretary
  Fidel Velazquez
Political Secretary
  Emigdio Martinez Adame
Political Secretary
  Francisco Galindo Ochoa
Finance Secretary
  Agustin Salvat
Press Secretary
  Moises Ochoa Campos
Oficial Mayor
  Carlos Real F.

4 Dec. 1958

President
  Alfonso Corona del Rosal
Secretary General
  Juan Fernandez Albarran
Agrarian Secretary
  Magdaleno Aguilar Castillo
Labor Secretary
  Jesus Yuren
Popular Secretary
  Antonio Mena Brito
Political Secretary
  Luis Vazquez Campos
Political Secretary
  Fernando Diaz Duran
Finance Secretary
  Agustin Salvat
Press Secretary
  Francisco Galindo Ochoa

4 Dec. 1958 (cont.)

Women's Secretary
  Margarita Garcia Flores
Oficial Mayor
  Salvador Pineda
Organization Secretary
  Abelardo de la Torre Grajales

1962

President
  Alfonso Corona del Rosal
Secretary General
  Juan Fernandez Albarran
Agrarian Secretary
  Magdaleno Aguilar Castillo
Labor Secretary
  Jesus Yuren
Popular Secretary
  Alfonso Martinez Dominguez
Political Secretary
  Antonio Salazar Salazar
Political Secretary
  Manuel M. Moreno
Organization Secretary
  Abelardo de la Torre Grajales
Finance Secretary
  Agustin Salvat
Oficial Mayor
  Salvador Pineda

Jan. 1964

President
  Alfonso Corona del Rosal
Secretary General
  Manuel M. Moreno
Agrarian Secretary
  Magdaleno Aguilar
Labor Secretary
  Jesus Yuren
Popular Secretary
  Alfonso Martinez Dominguez
Political Secretary
  Rafael Moreno Valle
Political Secretary
  Manuel Bernardo Aguirre
Organization Secretary
  Abelardo de la Torre Grajales
Press Secretary
  Francisco Galindo Ochoa
Finance Secretary
  Agustin Salvat
Oficial Mayor
  Salvador Pineda

4 Dec. 1964

President
  Carlos A. Madrazo

Secretary General
  Lauro Ortega Martinez
Agrarian Secretary
  Leopoldo Hernandez Partida
Labor Secretary
  Blas Chumacero Sanchez
Popular Secretary
  Renaldo Guzman Orozco
Political Secretary
  Armando Arteaga y Santoyo
Political Secretary
  Fluvio Vista Altamirano
Organization Secretary
  Fernando Diaz Duran
Finance Secretary
  Jose Espinosa Rivera
Press Secretary
  Jose Luis Lamadrid
IEPES Secretary
  Octaviano Campos Salas

April 1965

President
  Carlos A. Madrazo
Secretary General
  Lauro Ortega
Agrarian Secretary
  Leopoldo Hernandez Partida
Popular Secretary
  Renaldo Guzman Orozco
Labor Secretary
  Blas Chumacero
Political Secretary
  Armando Arteaga Santoyo
Political Secretary
  Fluvio Vista Altamirano
Organization Secretary
  Fernando Diaz Duran
Press Secretary
  Jose Luis Lamadrid
Finance Secretary
  Jose Espinosa Rivera
Youth Director
  Rodolfo Echeverria Ruiz
IEPES Secretary
  Carlos Andrade Munoz

22 Nov. 1965

President
  Lauro Ortega Martinez
Secretary General
  Fernando Diaz Duran
Agrarian Secretary
  Amador Hernandez Gonzalez
Labor Secretary
  Blas Chumacero Sanchez
Popular Secretary
  Renaldo Guzman Orozco

Political Secretary
  Cristobal Guzman Orozco
Political Secretary
  Ruben Moheno Velasco
Organization Secretary
  Oswaldo Cravioto Cisneros
IEPES Secretary
  Carlos Andrade Munoz
Press Secretary
  Noe G. Elizondo
Finance Secretary
  Juan Antonio Orozco

July 1966

President
  Lauro Ortega
Secretary General
  Fernando Diaz Duran
Organization Secretary
  Oswaldo Cravioto Cisneros
Agrarian Secretary
  Amador Hernandez
Popular Secretary
  Renaldo Guzman Orozco
Labor Secretary
  Blas Chumacero
Political Secretary
  Cristobal Guzman Cardenas
Political Secretary
  Ruben Moheno Velasco
Press Secretary
  Noe G. Elizondo
IEPES Secretary
  Ignacio Machorro

27 Feb. 1968

President
  Alfonso Martinez Dominguez
Secretary General
  Enrique Olivares Santana
Agrarian Secretary
  Augusto Gomez Villanueva
Labor Secretary
  Blas Chumacero Sanchez
Popular Secretary
  Renaldo Guzman Orozco
Political Secretary
  Cristobal Guzman Cardenas
Political Secretary
  Victor Manzanilla Schaffer
Organization Secretary
  Jose Ricardo Tirado
Finance Secretary
  Pedro Luis Bartilotti
Press Secretary
  Humberto Lugo Gil
IEPES Secretary
  Jorge de la Vega Dominguez

Oficial Mayor
  Flavio Vista Altamirano
Feminine Action
  Maria Lavalle Urbina

4 Dec. 1970

President
  Manuel Sanchez Vite
Secretary General
  Vicente Fuentes Diaz
Agrarian Secretary
  Alfredo V. Bonfil
Labor Secretary
  Blas Chumacero Sanchez
Popular Secretary
  Julio Bobadilla Pena
Political Secretary
  Salvador Gamiz Fernandez
Political Secretary
  Cuauhtemoc Santa Ana
Organization Secretary
  Carlos Jongitud Barrios
Finance Secretary
  Abel Ramirez Acosta
Press Secretary
  Rene Vinet Lopez
IEPES Secretary
  Jorge de la Vega Dominguez
Oficial Mayor
  Rodolfo Echeverria Ruiz
Political Education Secretary
  Enrique Gonzalez Pedrero
Social Action Secretary
  Enrique Cardenas Gonzalez

21 Feb. 1972

President
  Jesus Reyes Heroles
Secretary General
  Enrique Gonzalez Pedrero
Agrarian Secretary
  Alfredo V. Bonfil
Labor Secretary
  Blas Chumacero Sanchez
Popular Secretary
  Julio Bobadilla Pena
Political Secretary
  Enrique Olivares Santana
Political Secretary
  Luis H. Ducoing Gamba
Organization Secretary
  Rafael Rodriguez Barrera
Finance Secretary
  Sergio L. Benhumea
Press Secretary
  Victor Manzanilla Schaffer
IEPES Secretary
  Santiago Roel

Oficial Mayor
  Rodolfo Echeverria Ruiz
Political Education Secretary
  Arturo Gonzalez Cosio
Social Action Secretary
  Alejandro Peraza Uribe

16 Mar. 1973

President
  Jesus Reyes Heroles
Secretary General
  Enrique Gonzalez Pedrero
Subsecretary General
  Carlos Sansores Perez
Oficial Mayor
  Rodolfo Echeverria Ruiz
Agrarian Secretary
  Celestino Salcedo Monteon
Labor Secretary
  Blas Chumacero Sanchez
Popular Secretary
  Oscar Flores Tapia
Political Secretary
  Enrique Olivares Santana
Political Secretary
  Luis H. Ducoing Gamba
Organization Secretary
  Miguel Angel Barberena
Political Education Secretary
  Arturo Gonzalez Cosio
Press Secretary
  Jorge Villa Trevino
Social Action Secretary
  Jose Luis Lamadrid
Finance Secretary
  Sergio L. Benhumea
Political Subsecretary
  Salvador Gamiz Fernandez
Political Subsecretary
  Humberto Hiriart Urdanivia
Organization Subsecretary
  Enrique Soto Resendiz
Press Subsecretary
  Ernesto Alvarez Nolasco
IEPES Secretary
  Horacio Labastida

Apr. 1975

President
  Jesus Reyes Heroles
Secretary General
  Miguel Angel Barberena
Oficial Mayor
  Rodolfo Echeverria Ruiz
Agrarian Secretary
  Celestino Salcedo Monteon
Labor Secretary
  Blas Chumacero Sanchez

Popular Secretary
  David Gustavo Gutierrez Ruiz
Political Secretary
  Enrique Olivares Santana
Political Secretary
  Carlos Sansores Perez
Organization Secretary
  Fidel Herrera Beltran
Political Education Secretary
  Arturo Gonzalez Cosio
Press Secretary
  Ernesto Alvarez Nolasco
Finance Secretary
  Sergio L. Benhumea
Social Action Secretary
  Jose Luis Lamadrid
IEPES Secretary
  Julio Rodolfo Moctezuma Cid

4 Mar. 1976

President
  Porfiro Munoz Ledo
Secretary General
  Augusto Gomez Villanueva
Oficial Mayor
  Rodolfo Echeverria Ruiz
Agrarian Secretary
  Celestino Salcedo Monteon
Labor Secretary
  Blas Chumacero Sanchez
Popular Secretary
  David Gustavo Gutierrez Ruiz
Political Secretary
  Carlos Sansores Perez
Political Secretary
  Enrique Olivares Santana
Organization Secretary
  Leopoldo Gonzalez Saenz
Political Education Secretary
  Arturo Gonzalez Cosio
Press Secretary
  Pedro Ramirez Vazquez
Finance Secretary
  Severo Lopez Mestre
Social Action Secretary
  Carlos Jongitud Barrios
IEPES Secretary
  Julio Rodolfo Moctezuma Cid

9 Dec. 1976

President
  Carlos Sansores Perez
Secretary General
  Juan Sabines Gutierrez
Oficial Mayor
  Miguel Covian Perez
Agrarian Secretary
  Celestino Salcedo Monteon

9 Dec. 1976 (cont.)

Labor Secretary
Blas Chumacero Sanchez
Popular Secretary
Jose de las Fuentes Rodriguez
Political Secretary
Joaquin Gamboa Pascoe
Political Secretary
Augusto Gomez Villanueva
Organization Secretary
Alberto Alvarado Aramburo
Political Education Secretary
Jose Murat
Press Secretary
Humberto Lugo Gil
Finance Secretary
Tristan Canales
Social Action Secretary
Onofre Hernandez Rivera
IEPES Secretary
Luis Danton Rodriguez

28 July 1978

President
Carlos Sansores Perez
Secretary General
Gustavo Carvajal Moreno
Subsecretary General
Enrique Alvarez del Castillo
Oficial Mayor
Miguel Covian Perez

Agrarian Secretary
Oscar Ramirez Mijares
Agrarian Subsecretary
Alfonso Garzon Santibanez
Popular Secretary
Jose de las Fuentes Rodriguez
Political Secretary
Joaquin Gamboa Pascoe
Political Secretary
Rodolfo Gonzalez Guevara
Organization Secretary
Humberto Lugo Gil
Labor Secretary
Blas Chumacero Sanchez
Labor Subsecretary
Antonio J. Hernandez Jimenez
Press Secretary
Rodolfo Landeros Gallegos
International Relations Secretary
Alejandro Sobarzo
IEPES Secretary
Alejandro Cervantes Delgado

27 Oct. 1979

President
Gustavo Carvajal
Secretary General
Jose de las Fuentes Rodriguez
Secretary of Political Action
Joaquin Gamboa Pascoe

Secretary of Political Action
Lauro Ortega
Oficial Mayor
Humberto Lugo Gil
Secretary of Agrarian Action
Oscar Ramirez Mijares
Secretary of International Affairs
Rafael Rodriguez Barrera
Secretary of Ideological
Divulgation
Sergio Guerrero Mier
Secretary of Labor Action
Blas Chumacero
Secretary of Popular Action
Carlos Riva Palacio
Secretary of Press
Rodolfo Landeros
Secretary of Organization
Victor Cervera Pacheco
Secretary of Political Education
Victor Manuel Barcelo
Secretary of Social Action
Jose Luis Andrade Ibarra
Secretary of Finances
Eduardo Guerrero del Castillo
IEPES Secretary
Guillermo Fonseca Alvarez

Presidents of the National Action Party, the Authentic Party of the Mexican Revolution, and the Popular Socialist Party. 1939–1980

National Action Party

Presidents		Secretaries General	
1939–49	*Manuel Gomez Morin*	1939–51	*Roberto Cossio y Cossio*
1949–56	*Juan Gutierrez Lascurain*	1954–57	Raul Velasco Zimbron
1956–59	*Alfonso Ituarte Servin*	1957–58	*Jose Gonzalez Torres*
1959–62	*Jose Gonzalez Torres*	1960–61	*Abel Vicencio Tovar*
1962–68	*Adolfo Christlieb Ibarrola*	1961–66	*Astolfo Vicencio Tovar*
1968–69	Ignacio Limon Maurer	1966–68	Ignacio Limon Maurer
1969–72	*Manuel Gonzalez Hinojosa*	1969–72	*Juan Manuel Gomez Morin*
1972–75	*Jose Angel Conchello Davila*	1972–75	*Bernardo Batiz Vazquez*
1975	*Efrain Gonzalez Morfin*	1975–78	*Raul J. Gonzalez Schmal*
1975–78	*Manuel Gonzalez Hinojosa*	1978–	Alfonso Arronte Dominguez
1978–	*Abel Vicencio Tovar*		

Authentic Party of the Mexican Revolution

Presidents			
1954–64	*Jacinto B. Trevino*	1975–79	*Antonio Gomez Velasco*
1964–74	*Juan Barragan Rodriguez*	1980–	Jesus Guzman Rubio
1974–75	*Pedro Gonzalez Azcuaga*		

Popular Socialist Party
(Popular Party, 1948–60)

Presidents			
1948–68	*Vicente Lombardo Toledano*	1968–81	*Jorge Cruickshank Garcia*

Secretaries General of CTM, CNC, CNOP, FSTSE and SUTERM 1935–1980

Mexican Federation of Laborers (Confederacion de Trabajadores de Mexico, 1936)

Lombardo Toledano, Vicente
  Feb. 1936–24 Feb. 1941
Velazquez, Fidel
  25 Feb. 1941–46
Amilpa, Fernando
  1946–49
Velazquez, Fidel
  1949–

National Farmers Confederation (Confederacion Nacional Campesina, 1938)

Sanchez, Graciano
  15 July 1938–30 Dec. 1942
Leyva Velazquez, Gabriel
  31 Dec. 1942–28 May 1947
Barrios, Roberto
  29 May 1947–May 1950
Gandara, Manuel J.
  May 1950–21 Jan. 1952
Galvan, Ferrer
  22 Jan. 1952–53
Azua Torres, Lorenzo
  1953–20 July 1954
Luna Lugo, Arturo
  21 July 1954–18 Jan. 1957
Flores Fuentes, Raymundo
  19 Jan. 1957–26 Aug. 1959
Hernandez y Hernandez, Francisco
  27 Aug. 1959–26 Aug. 1962
Rojo Gomez, Javier
  27 Aug. 1962–25 Aug. 1965

Hernandez, Amador
  26 Aug. 1965–21 Sept. 1967
Gomez Villanueva, Augusto
  Oct. 1967–Dec. 1970
Bonfil, Alfredo V.
  Dec. 1970–25 Jan. 1973
Salcedo, Celestino
  Feb. 1973–1977
Ramirez Mijares, Oscar
  27 Aug. 1977–

National Federation of Popular Organizations (Confederacion Nacional de Organizaciones Populares, 1943)

Nava Castillo, Antonio
  1943–46
Murillo Vidal,Rafael
  1946
Gallardo, Ernesto
  1946–49
Archer, Angel Luis
  1949–52
Maldonado Perez, Caritino
  1952–58
Vazquez Campos, Luis
  1958–61
Martinez Dominguez, Alfonso
  1961–65
Guzman Orozco, Renaldo
  1965–71
Bobadilla Pena, Julio
  1971–72
Flores Tapia, Oscar
  1972–75

Gutierrez Ruiz, David G.
  1975–76
De la Fuentes Rodriguez, Jose
  1976–79
Riva Palacio, Carlos
  1979–

Federation of Government Employees' Unions (Federacion de Sindicatos de Trabajadores al Servicio del Estado, 1938)

Patino Cruz, Francisco
  1938–40
Jaramillo, Candido
  1940–42
Villanueva, Ignacio
  1942
Galaviz, Gabriel
  1942
Herrera Angeles, Rafael
  1943–44
Figueroa Figueroa, Ruffo
  1944–47
Soto Ruiz, Armando
  1947–50
Martinez Dominguez, Alfonso
  1950–53
Aguirre Alegria, Francisco
  1953–56
De la Torre Grajales, Abelardo
  1956–59
Sanchez Mireles, Romulo
  1959–64

Robles Martinez, Jesus
    1965
Bernal, Antonio
    1965–67
Robledo Santiago, Edgar
    1967–70
Aceves Alcocer, Gilberto
    1970–75

Sanchez Vargas, Salvador
    1975–76
Espinosa Galindo, Daniel
    1976–77
Riva Palacio, Carlos
    1977–

The Union of Electrical Workers (Sindicato Unico de Trabajadores Electristas de la Republica Mexicana, 1944)

Perez Rios, Francisco
    1944–27 Mar. 1975
Rodriguez Alcaine, Leonardo
    28 Mar. 1975–

A Selected Bibliographical Essay

Earlier bibliographical sources on public figures in Mexico have been characterized by their unavailability, inaccuracy, and lack of information. In general, the sources used for this work can be divided into four types: privately published directories, government directories, magazines and newspapers, and monographs and biographies, which are not discussed individually because they are of value only for information about a single person. The following essay attempts to describe the strengths and shortcomings of a selective list of works which have proved most useful as sources for this book.

Privately Published Directories

The English language sources of privately published directories which are useful in gathering biographical information on Mexican public men are limited to a small number. The two most important publications of this type were both published in 1946, which limits their usefulness to persons prominent enough to have been included before that date. These two works are the *Who's Who in Latin America* (Stanford: Stanford University Press) and the *Biographical Encyclopedia of the World* (New York: Institute for Research in Biography). The first of the two works has been published in three editions (1935, 1940, 1945–50), with the first two editions covering Latin American personalities in one volume, and the last edition devoting a single volume to Mexico in 1945. Even though the first two editions assist the reader interested in Mexico by including an index of names by country, the third and final edition is by far the most useful because of the larger number of Mexicans included. (An indication of the state of scholarship on biography of Latin American leaders is illustrated by the fact that Blaine Ethridge Press recently reprinted this edition just as it appeared from 1945 to 1950.) The 1946 volume on Mexico, under the editorship of Ronald Hilton, is the most accurate English language source published since 1935. *The Biographical Encyclopedia of the World* went

through five editions, changing its title at mid-point to *World Biography* in 1948. The three most valuable editions are the third, fourth, and fifth, 1946, 1948, and 1954 respectively, because they contain more Mexican and Latin American personalities. Like the *Who's Who in Latin America*, the *Biographical Encyclopedia of the World* is quite accurate and contains political personages at all levels. However, its great disadvantage is that the Mexicans are dispersed among other nationalities and the 1946 edition is not in alphabetical order.

A newer source, however, and useful because of its breadth and accuracy, is Lucien Lajoie's *Who's Notable in Mexico* (Mexico, 1972). Although not widely available, it contains many political leaders from recent decades who were living at the time of publication. Unfortunately, no further volumes were published.

The only attempt which has been made since 1946 to provide a guide to Mexican public men has been the work of Marvin Alisky. The most important of a series of small pamphlets put out by the Arizona State University Center for Latin American Studies is his *Who's Who in Mexican Government* (Tempe, 1969), which contains only about a dozen biographies of any length. The listings for the rest of the individuals give only the most recent or present position held, sometimes the state of birth, and the type of university education. Most of this information is duplicated much more completely in the various Mexican government organizational manuals (excepting state of birth). Other publications by Alisky, notably the *Guide to the Government of the Mexican State of Sonora* (Tempe: Arizona State University, 1971) and the *Guide to the Government of the Mexican State of Nuevo Leon* (Tempe: Arizona State University, 1971), do contain some relevant biographical information on recent governors, incomplete though they may be.

Of the standard world *Who's Who* sources, the most useful is the *International Year Book and Statemen's Who's Who*. All editions of this work are helpful because they normally list the cabinet members, supreme court justices, and governors holding office at the time of publication. The earlier editions also include diplomatic posts, information which is helpful in tracing Mexicans with foreign service careers. The 1954 edition is particularly generous with the amount of biographical data on prominent Mexicans, but the coverage is quite limited and superficial. *The Who's Who in the World*, 1971–72 (Marquis) contains short, outdated, and very brief Mexican biographies, a characteristic continued in subsequent editions.

The two most readily available Spanish language sources and the most useful are the *Diccionario Porrua* (Mexico: Editorial Porrua) and the *Diccionario Biografico de Mexico* (Monterrey: Editorial Revesa). The first is a standard reference work of Mexican biography, geography, and history, published in four editions, the most recent in 1976. The limitations of the *Diccionario Porrua* are that it contains only persons who have died, and many of the biographies, while generally accurate, are incomplete and lack dates for the positions held by the individual. However, the *Diccionario Porrua* does contain one of the few published sources of the cabinet positions with the names of the men who held them and their tenure in office. It also contains a considerable amount of historical information describing political affairs and the men who took part in them, making it one of the best sources for tracing Mexican political families.

The second work, the *Diccionario Biografico de Mexico*, is the most complete up-to-date general *Who's Who* published in Mexico, and it has been issued in two editions, 1968 and 1970. The 1968 edition is far more useful for public men since the 1970 volume tends to be padded with duplicates of the biographies in the first volume. It is more complete than the *Diccionario Porrua* for individual biographies, but tends to be very uneven in coverage, including losing candidates for federal deputy but omiting many cabinet members and governors.

The only other general Mexican source published in the last thirty years is the *Diccionario Biografico Mexicano* by Miguel Angel Peral. Peral's dictionary could have been excellent, but it must be used with some care because of the numerous inaccuracies about birth dates and legislative sessions. If the researcher keeps these limitations in mind, however, Peral provides the most complete coverage of the officeholders available from 1935 to 1945, and his 1947 supplemental volume brings old biographies up-to-date and adds many new ones.

A more specific and unusual source is the *Quien es quien en la nomenclatura de la ciudad de Mexico* (Mexico, 1962), by Carlos Morales Diaz, which has gone through two editions, the most recent being 1971. This is a fascinating book, and as the title indicates, it includes persons whose names have been used somewhere in Mexico City to name streets, parks, or public places. Although the persons included usually have died, this is not always the case. The biographies are generally quite complete and very accurate.

One of the best single sources, but one limited to a certain group of public figures, is the book by Sergio Serra Dominguez and Roberto Martinez Barreda entitled *Mexico y sus funcionarios* (Mexico: Litografico Cardenas, 1959). Available at the University of Texas Library, it contains biographies of nearly all cabinet members, senators, and federal deputies serving under President Adolfo Lopez Mateos in 1958. While many of the biographies contain laudatory rhetoric by the authors, many include difficult to obtain information on political friendships and educational background. A more specific work of this type is Arturo R. Blancas and Tomas L. Vidrio's *Indice biografico de la xliii legislatura federal* (Mexico, 1956), which contains biographical information about members of the 1955–58 federal legislature, but is not readily available.

Encyclopedias provided another source of biographical information. The standard *Diccionario Enciclopedia UTEHA* (Mexico: UTEHA, 1950) contains many biographical sketches, but these are rather short. The newer *Enciclopedia de Mexico* (Mexico: Enciclopedia de Mexico,S.A., 1976) has been revised and expanded by Jose Rogelio Alvarez, and now includes numerous, excellent biographies in its twelve volumes. The *1977 Yearbook* also includes detailed biographies of all governors currently in office. The *Enciclopedia de Mexico* contains a complete list of cabinet members and their tenure in office from independence to 1977. It is extremely accurate. The other important reference work is that by Juan B. Iguiniz, Mexico's leading bibliographer on biography. The work, entitled *Bibliografia biografica mexicana* (Mexico: UNAM, 1969) is a detailed, annotated work of biographical source material on thousands of prominent figures in Mexican history. The book is extremely useful as a starting point for biographical research because it is cross-indexed, with a complete alphabetical list of the names of Mexican personalities followed by the page on which a biographical source appears for that individual.

Other works in Spanish are limited either by geography, such as state directories, or by subject, such as directories of writers. A great deal of searching can produce state dictionaries (usually published early in the century, such as Eduardo Bolio Ontiveros, *Diccionario historico, geografico y biografico de Yucatan* [Mexico, 1945]), or more recent social and business directories (such as Raul Vazquez Galindo, *Quien es quien en Durango*, 1966–67). Such works vary considerably in quality and coverage, and their availability is generally limited to Mexican libraries. The most useful of all social directories is the *Libro de oro de Mexico*, which was published annually from 1924 to 1973, when it ceased publication. It is valuable because it lists higher-level officeholders by position, with their wives, and gives the latest official and home addresses of each person. It was one of the best sources for locating prominent individuals of former administrations who continue to maintain a residence in Mexico City.

Public Directories

Public directories are confined to Spanish language sources. The most readily available sources are the various government organization manuals published over the years. The first serious attempt of the government to publish such a manual was the one-volume *Directorio del gobierno federal*, published by the federal government in 1947. In 1948, it was republished in two volumes, the first contained judicial, legislative, and executive branch positions, and the second, decentralized agencies, companies, and banks. This *Directorio* was published in a similar fashion each year until 1951. Extremely well indexed, these manuals contain a position as well as name index and contain a complete listing of most positions in the federal government from bureau chief on up. In 1956, the manual was published in a larger, one-volume version which again contained the names and positions of officeholders in all three branches of government, indexed in the same fashion. The most complete collection of these manuals in the United States are in the Department of State Library, Washington, D.C., and the Columbus Memorial Library, Pan American Union.

In 1961, the government issued a new manual entitled the *Directorio del poder ejecutivo federal*, published under the Secretariat of the National Patrimony and available at the University of Florida Library. Unfortunately, while very complete for the cabinet agencies, the manual did not include the judicial, legislative, or decentralized agency positions. Further, it did not include an administrative history of each agency or department, nor a description of the legal powers of the administrative units as was true of the manuals issued from 1947 to 1956. The 1961 manual, did, however, contain the dual person and position index, which made it easy to use. In 1965, the government produced another manual under the same title which followed the format of the 1961 edition. In 1969, the Secretary of the Presidency published the *Manual de organizacion del gobierno federal, 1969–70*, which followed the format of the 1956 guide, containing all branches of government

and administrative descriptions. Unfortunately, however, the number of officeholders listed under each agency was limited to only the highest levels, and there was no index of names. In 1971, the government issued a manual under the title, *Directorio del poder ejecutivo federal*, and it went back to the 1961 and 1965 editions in format and content. But in 1972, this was followed with a loose-leaf version, and in 1973, replacement pages for the original. Lopez Portillo's administration published a cross-indexed directory of cabinet agency directors in 1977, but it is very limited in the depth of the positions covered.

Some state governments have published imitations of the federal manuals, but these are not readily available in Mexico or the United States. Individual agencies have also published small directories, but the only agency directory with valuable biographical data which the author has encountered is the *Programas de becas y datos profesionales de los becarios*, published by the Bank of Mexico in 1961 to describe the educational backgrounds and careers of most of its scholarship holders up to the publishing date (available at the Columbus Memorial Library). Many of these individuals have since become prominent public figures. The data are quite accurate, but vary in completeness from one individual to the next, partly due to the fact that most individuals had only just begun their careers at the date of publication.

The other major government source has been the official directories for individual legislatures of both houses of Congress. For the most part, these must be obtained through private sources or from the Congressional Library in Mexico City. The Library of Congress in Washington, D.C., and the library at the University of Texas each hold only two individual legislative directories published in this century. They list the legislator by state, district, name, and committee assignments. Since the 1930s these directories have been published under the title of *Directorio de la camara de diputados* or *senadores* followed by the name of the legislature. In addition to these published directories, the lower chamber has occasionally put together an unpublished directory with biographical information filled in by the deputies or their assistants. Unfortunately, these are not readily available even to the researcher in Mexico, and the author cannot determine if these exist for any past legislatures other than the 1955–58 and 1970–73 legislatures. These would be extremely useful if available, since they are very detailed and accurate.

Magazines and Newspapers

Among the periodical sources of biographical data, credit must be given to *Tiempo* (*Hispano Americano* in the United States) as the most useful. It has the best coverage of lower-level officials and governors, and it regularly takes note of resignations and appointments. At one time or another it will devote a cover story to each cabinet officer. During the beginning months of the last four administrations, it provided some biographical information on subsecretaries and oficiales mayores. The main limitation of *Tiempo* is its lack of an index and the fact that it is not published during the first ten years of this study.

In terms of usefulness, *Hoy*, *Siempre*, and other Mexican weeklies follow far behind *Tiempo*. While *Hoy* has a regular weekly feature covering events of the past week, including anecdotes about public figures, biographical notes are not very frequent. *Siempre*, like *Hoy*, usually limits biographical notes to occasional stories about individuals. For consistently critical views about the behavior of many government officials, *Por que* was the best source, although it did not contain any biographical notes per se. More recently, *Proceso* has played this role, and is the most widely read political magazine critical of the government. The most accurate newspaper source is *Excelsior*, which attempts to cover resignations and appointments with the same regularity as *Tiempo*. The "Frentes Politicos" section is a source of fascinating information, especially at election time, about the political careers of many people. *Uno mas uno*, Mexico City's newest important daily, has proved to be equally valuable for career anecdotes. The obituaries placed at the end of the first section of *Excelsior* are about the only means of determining recent deaths of public officials, unless the person is notable enough to receive attention by the press. While there is no obituary index for Mexican newspapers, *The New York Times Obituary Index* occasionally does include a Mexican, usually a person involved in foreign affairs. Anyone receiving coverage in *The New York Times* would also receive attention in the Mexican papers at approximately the same date. As is true of Mexican periodicals, there are no Mexican newspaper indexes of any type, a fact which limits the usefulness of these publications.

A new source which provides discussion of political activities as well as some information about public leaders is the *Analisis Politico*, a survey of major newspapers which is published by the Mexican Institute of Political Studies in Mexico. *Polemica*, an official publication of PRI, has had some biographies of former PRI party presidents, but it contains mostly articles and speeches by party members. Lastly, publications by individual institutions often have biographical data on their more distinguished members. Probably the most notable of such publications is *La Justicia*, which since 1962 has published a detailed biography each month of a well-known Mexican from one of a variety of fields.

Monographs and Biographies

Monographs on Mexico would, of course, provide an endless list of sources. The bibliography of sources cited includes neither individual biographies nor monographs which may have had relevent information for two or three persons whose biographies appear in this work. Most monographs are readily available, well known by students and scholars, and are indexed for easy use. The reason so few have been cited is that they usually deal with a person's notable political activities, not with career data appropriate for this directory. Five works deserve to be mentioned because they have dealt with men's careers in greater detail than do standard works. Two are in English: John W. F. Dulles, *Yesterday in Mexico* (Austin: University of Texas Press, 1961) and Ernest Gruening, *Mexico and Its Heritage* (New York: D.Appleton-Century, 1928). Both books, unfortunately, deal only with Mexico before the late 1930s. Gruening, who had access to frank reports of government agents, has some career comments unequaled in any other source. Furthermore, he deals with state governments and political activities in those states in more detail than any other writer since 1928, and does an excellent job of tracing personal political ties. Dulles' account is full of anecdotes, often provided by persons who were still living at the time Dulles researched the book. His work is useful from a biographical standpoint because it contains some unusual information about selected individuals.

The other three books are in Spanish: James Wilkie and Edna Wilkie, *Mexico Visto en el siglo xx* (Mexico: Instituto Mexicano de Investigaciones Economicas, 1969) and Salvador Novo, *La Vida en Mexico en el periodo presidencial de Lazaro Cardenas* (Mexico: Empresas Editoriales, 1964) and his *La Vida en Mexico en el periodo presidencial de Miguel Aleman* (Mexico: Empresas Editoriales, 1967). The Wilkie volume is a frequently cited but, the author fears, not a frequently used collection of taped and edited interviews with a number of distinguished public men in Mexico. Not only is the biographical data of the interviewees in great abundance, but comments about their careers and friendships with other well known Mexicans contributes to understanding their personal development and later participation in Mexican public life in this century. The Novo works, basically a collection of articles he wrote for newspapers during the regimes of Cardenas and Aleman, contain a great deal of anecdotal information which completes some biographies and determines contacts and friendships among the men and women in the directory.

Probably the greatest source of information has been correspondence to the author and interviews by the author. These sources deserve some comment. During the last eight years, the author wrote to more than four hundred individuals who themselves qualified for inclusion in this book, or who had information about others who should be included. During that time, over two hundred replies provided a substantial amount of information contained in the biographical section, as well as in the appendices. Many governmental and non-governmental agencies assisted the author with detailed lists of officeholders and their dates in office. PAN headquarters, for example, sent the author a number of biographies of various party leaders. Correspondents have ranged from the Dean of Notre Dame University, where one of the biographees graduated, to a living ex-president of Mexico. Much of the information contained in this directory comes from unpublished sources, and therefore remains uncited except for the word *letters* in the source section.

Also by Roderic Camp

Mexico's Leaders
Their Education and Recruitment

"Roderic Camp's study of Mexico's top-level political leadership provides fresh perspectives on key dimensions of Mexican politics, such as personalism, trust, political cliques (*camarillas*), family loyalties, continuism and cooptation....essential reading for the Mexicanists and Latin Americanists in the social sciences. It is also useful for comparative political analysis in its treatment of education in the recruitment process. It is, moreover, a major contribution which can substantially serve policy makers in the 1980s."

—*American Political Science Review*

"*Mexico's Leaders* focuses on a useful aspect of elite careers in what is now generally regarded as a 'successful' authoritarian regime. Camp is to be commended for compiling such extensive data."

—*Hispanic American Historical Review*

Published by
The University of Arizona Press
Tucson, Arizona